THE
CATALOG
OF
CATALOGS

By Edward L. Palder

CATALOGS IV

The Complete Mail-Order Directory

WOODBINE HOUSE • 1995

Published by Woodbine House, 6510 Bells Mill Road, Bethesda, MD 20817. 800/843–7323.

Library of Congress Cataloging-in-Publication Data

Palder, Edward L.
    The catalog of catalogs IV : the complete mail-order directory / by Edward L. Palder.
      p.   cm.
    Rev. and updated ed. of : The catalog of catalogs III.
    Includes index.
    ISBN 0–933149–75–1 (pbk.)
    1. Commercial catalogs—United States—Directories. 2. Mail-order business—United States—Directories.
I. Palder Edward L. Catalog of catalogs III. II. Title.
HF5466.P35 1995
381'.142'029473—dc20   95–6645
                                              CIP

Manufactured in the United States of America

10 9 8 7 6 5 4 3 2

Dedicated to everyone who makes
catalog shopping fun.

Dear Reader:

I am planning to periodically update **The Catalog of Catalogs.** To do this, I need your help.

If you know of a company that you think should be included in the next edition, or if you are dissatisfied, for any reason, with the response you receive from a company, please let me know. I will closely evaluate all your recommendations for the next edition of **The Catalog of Catalogs.**

I would also like to invite merchants or manufacturers who would like to be considered for a listing in the next edition, or whose address or telephone number has changed, to send their mailing address and telephone number, along with a copy of their latest catalog(s) to:

> The Catalog of Catalogs
> P.O. Box 6590
> Silver Spring, MD 20916–6590

To those readers of the previous editions who took the time to write me suggesting subjects and companies to be added or deleted—thanks a million. And I thank all of you in advance for your help in making future editions of **The Catalog of Catalogs** as complete as possible.

Happy catalog shopping!

> Sincerely,
> *Edward L. Palder*

❖ TABLE OF CONTENTS ❖

If you're holding this book in your hands, you probably don't need to be sold on the convenience of catalog shopping.

You already know that catalog shopping can help you avoid the hassles of going to a store in person. You don't have to hunt for a parking space, wait in endless lines, or leave your home in inclement weather. You also know that you can often shop at hours when the stores at the mall are closed. You know that if you need to have something right away, you can almost always get it the very next day. You know that you can comparison shop without anyone pressuring you to buy. You know that there is often a larger selection of colors, sizes, models, and styles in stock to choose from, and that you can purchase products that just may not be for sale in your neighborhood stores. . . . But you also know that you can only reap these benefits *if* you have catalogs that carry the products you are looking for.

The **Catalog of Catalogs IV** is designed to help consumers track down exactly the catalogs they need. This new edition of **The Catalog of Catalogs** contains listings for over 12,000 different retailers, wholesalers, and manufacturers, grouped into over 650 subject areas. There is a larger selection of catalogs than ever to choose from; many of the categories have been expanded and new ones have been added. As in previous editions, companies that offer a diverse line of products are sometimes listed in more than one category. The number of double listings, however, has been kept to a minimum, so that as many different catalog suppliers as possible could be included. As before, the **Catalog of Catalogs IV** also includes companies that will send free or low-cost information about particular brands of merchandise, or lists of nearby dealers who carry those brands.

The **Catalog of Catalogs IV** will enable you to choose merchandise from some of the largest possible selections. Retail stores order their inventories from many of the same companies whose catalogs are listed in this book, but stores only have room to display a few items. When you browse through a catalog, you get to see all the possibilities. What's more, you can often save yourself a bundle in the process. First, if you don't live in the state where the mail-order company is based, you might not have to pay sales tax. (A few states have entered into reciprocal arrangements with other states and require that sales tax be paid even on catalog orders.) Second, since mail-order houses don't have to pay for fancy window displays or expensive floor space, they often pass their savings on to you, the catalog shopper.

Making *The Catalog of Catalogs IV* Work for You

The **Catalog of Catalogs IV** is a directory for obtaining catalogs and information, not an order catalog. The information given in each listing is intended to help you decide whether you'd like to order a particular catalog and to tell you how to do so if the answer is "yes."

Many of the catalogs, brochures, price lists, and information packets in **The Catalog of Catalogs IV** are free. You can request free information simply by calling the phone number in the catalog description or by sending in a postcard. Some mail-order companies ask that a business-size, self-addressed, stamped envelope (SASE) accompany requests for catalogs or other information. When this is the case, you'll find the notation immediately following the address in the catalog listing. If there's a charge for a catalog, you'll also find this information right after the address—with information about how much of the charge, if any, is refundable after you place an order.

No matter how little the charge for a catalog is, *never send cash through the mail.* Pay by money order or personal check. That way, if you don't receive the information you requested, you'll have proof of your payment. Not that this is likely to happen. In compiling this new edition of **The Catalog of Catalogs,** I reviewed all of the listings in the third edition to verify they were still in business, and that their addresses hadn't changed. I sent at least one letter to each company—whether a repeat or new listing—and requested that they verify the information I had on file. However, merchants do go out of business, change their names, combine with other companies, or move to new addresses without notifying the Post Office. I therefore apologize in advance should any of your requests for information go unanswered.

I'm continually updating the information in **The Catalog of Catalogs IV,** so if any of your catalog requests are returned as undeliverable, I invite you to send me the returned correspondence and any other information available. If I have a more recent address, I'll send it to you. Your requests for this information should be sent to: Edward L. Palder, The Catalog of Catalogs, P.O. Box 6590, Silver Spring, MD 20906–6590.

One final note about ordering catalogs: try to be patient. Catalogs are usually mailed fourth class, and delivery can take from two to three weeks. Possible delays can occur when companies are revising or reprinting their catalogs, and some companies process catalog requests only once or twice a month. Remember, too, that some companies *will not send the information requested unless a SASE is enclosed.*

Finding the Catalogs You Need

Catalogs in **The Catalog of Catalogs IV** are grouped according to subject matter. For example, all computer catalogs are listed in the *Computer* section, and all food catalogs appear in the *Foods* section. Long sections are further divided into subsections. In the *Computer* section, for example, catalog listings for manufacturers; retailers; dust covers & cases; software (public domain, shareware & CD-ROMS); software publishers; Software & CD-ROM retailers; and supplies are grouped together. In the *Foods* section, catalogs featuring cakes & cookies; maple syrup; meats; and other types of food are grouped together.

Within **The Catalog of Catalogs IV,** subjects are listed alphabetically, from *Air Compressors* to *Yoga.* Within each subject area, I've listed catalogs alphabetically by company name. *Narco Avionics* comes before *Northstar Avionics,* and so on. Please note that when a company name begins with a personal name, it's alphabetized by last name, instead of first name. For example, *Earl May Seeds & Nursery Company,* is alphabetized as though it began with an "M" instead of an "E"; *Fred Struthers Books* is alphabetized as if it began with an "S." Also, names that include numerals are alphabetized as though the numerals were spelled out.

You can find catalogs within **The Catalog of Catalogs IV** one of two ways—either by a company's name or by the type of product it sells. To locate the catalog of a company whose name you already know, simply turn to the Corporate Index near the end of the book. This index lists the names of every source of product information described in **The Catalog of Catalogs IV,** alphabetized according to the rules outlined above. Sometimes a company is listed more than once because it carries several different types of products. To locate catalogs that offer a specific type of product, check the Table of Contents first. Like the book as a whole, the Table of Contents is arranged alphabetically by subject. So if you were looking for catalogs of pet supplies, you'd turn to the "P's" in the Table of Contents to find the page number you needed.

If you can't find exactly what you're looking for in the Table of Contents, turn to the Subject Index at the very back of the book. Here I've listed topics under as many alternate names as I could think of—for example, the words "dishes" and "plates" will refer you to the pages listing suppliers of china. Through cross references ("See also's") the Subject Index can also direct you to related topics you might otherwise overlook. For instance, the listing for *Greeting Cards* instructs you to see also *Birth Announcements* and *Wedding Invitations.*

Your Mail-Order Rights

Although shopping by mail can be fun and adventuresome, it's not entirely without its hassles. Although I made every effort to ensure that **The Catalog of Catalogs IV** includes only reputable merchants, sometimes your catalog orders may be damaged in transit, fail to live up to your expectations, take too long to be delivered, or never arrive. Fortunately, in each of these instances, you can take steps to get a refund, repairs, or replacement.

Packages Damaged in Transit

Let's start with the simplest situation. If something you've ordered arrives with obvious damage to the package, write "refused" on the wrapper and return it unopened. Don't sign for it if it arrives insured, registered, certified, or C.O.D., or you'll have to pay the return postage. If you don't discover that your merchandise is damaged until you've opened the package, repackage it with a note describing the problem. Then mail it back by certified or insured mail and wait for the company to send you a free replacement.

Unsatisfactory Merchandise

If something you ordered breaks soon *after* it arrives, or is unsatisfactory for other reasons (it's the wrong size, shoddily made, or completely different from the description in the catalog), your next step depends on the exchange policy of the company you ordered from. Many companies allow you to return unsatisfactory merchandise within thirty days after purchase; others offer unconditional money-back guarantees for the lifetime of their products. Check a company's warranty policies *before you buy:* a bargain is no bargain if it comes without a guarantee. Consult the catalog for the company's return policies and for any special procedures to be followed when returning merchandise for a replacement or refund.

If the company has no stated returns policy, don't give up. Noted consumer activist David Horowitz recommends that you send back the unsatisfactory item with a letter explaining why you're disappointed, a copy of your proof of purchase (cancelled check, money order, or credit card statement), and a copy of the original ad. If you don't receive a reply within two weeks, place a collect call to the president of the company to ask what action he or she intends to take. (Horowitz notes that you may not get through to the president, but should at least find out his or her name.) If your phone call doesn't resolve your problem, write a letter to the president informing him that you'll contact the deputy chief postal inspector in his region if you don't get a refund or replacement in seven days. Then do what you said you would. Bring copies of your letters and proof of purchase to the local post office and fill out a Consumer Service form. Your postmaster will turn the matter over to the postal inspectors and the Post Office Consumer Advocate for investigation of possible fraud.

Delayed or Missing Orders

What if your order never arrives? What if you wait days or weeks longer than the delivery time promised in the catalog and still no package? Under the Mail-Order Rule of the Federal Trade Commission, you can take immediate recourse. The Mail-Order Rule requires a company to ship your order within the time promised in its ad or within thirty days of receiving your order and payment. In case of delay, the merchant must notify you of the new shipment date. If the new date is more than thirty days later than the original date, you can cancel your order (in writing) for a full refund. If the new date is less than thirty days later, you can still cancel for a refund, but if you don't respond, it means that you accept the new date. In either case, it is advisable to send your reply by registered or certified mail so you have a return receipt to show that your letter was delivered.

The merchant must refund your money within ten days of receiving your cancellation (or notify your credit card company within one billing cycle to credit your account). If the merchant does not give you a refund, credit, or the merchandise, take or send a copy of your letter and proof of payment to the: Direct Marketing Association, 1101 17th St. NW, Suite 705, Washington, DC 20036. If the merchant is a member of the DMA, the Association can pressure the merchant to refund your money.

Preventing and Reducing Problems

I hope you don't run into any of the problems described above, but on the off chance that you might, there are several precautions that can make resolution of problems easier. When in doubt about a product, contact the merchant *before you buy* for information about warranties, exchange policies, missing facts, or unbelievable claims. Second, make sure you fill out the order form accurately and completely, and enclose all shipping and handling charges requested by the company. And finally, always pay by check, money order, or credit card so you have proof of payment. Keep a record of the name and address of the company, the merchandise ordered, the date you placed the order, the name of the publication in which the merchandise was described, and the number of your money order or check.

Let the World Come to You

Now that you know the ground rules of mail-order shopping **The Catalog of Catalogs** way, why not take a moment to glance through the Table of Contents and Subject Index? I hope you will not only find what you are looking for, but also hundreds of other teasers you'll want to send away for. Don't resist the urge!

Ordering by mail is by far the easiest, most convenient, and most cost-effective way I know of to shop. It can also be highly addictive, as the long-suffering civil servant who delivers all my catalogs and packages can attest. But don't worry. In the unlikely event you ever want to break the habit of catalog shopping, you can have your name removed from many merchants' mailing lists by contacting the Mail Preference Service, Direct Marketing Association, P.O. Box 9008, Farmingdale, NY 11735–9008. So, sit back and take advantage of all **The Catalog of Catalogs IV** has to offer you. Send away for what you want, and let the world come to you.

AIR COMPRESSORS

Campbell Hausfeld, 100 Production Dr., Harrison, OH 45030: Free information ❖ Air compressors. 800–543–8622.

DeVilbiss, 213 Industrial Dr., Jackson, TN 38301: Free brochure ❖ Air compressors and air-operated tools. 800–888–2468; 901–423–7000 (in TN).

Sanborn Manufacturing Company, 118 W. Rock St., P.O. Box 206, Springfield, MN 56087: Free information ❖ Air compressors. 800–533–0365.

Stanley-Bostitch Inc., One Feltloc Ln., East Greenwich, RI 02818: Free information ❖ Air compressors. 800–556–6696.

AIR CONDITIONERS & CONTROLS

Carrier Corporation, P.O. Box 4808, Syracuse, NY 13221: Free information ❖ Furnaces, heat pumps, and air conditioners. 800–CARRIER.

Friedrich Air Conditioning & Refrigeration Company, P.O. Box 1540, San Antonio, TX 78295: Free brochure ❖ Room air conditioners, air cleaners, heat pumps, and electric heaters. 512–225–2000.

G.E. Appliances, General Electric Company, Appliance Park, Louisville, KY 40225: Free information ❖ Air conditioners and heat pumps. 800–626–2000.

Hunter Fan Company, 2500 Fisco Ave., Memphis, TN 38114: Brochure $1 ❖ Programmable thermostats. 901–745–9222.

Jameson Home Products, 2820 Thatcher Rd., Downers Grove, IL 60515: Free information ❖ Programmable thermostats. 708–963–2850.

Thomas Industries Inc., 1419 Illinois Ave., Sheboygan, WI 53082: Free information ❖ Air conditioners. 414–457–4891.

AIRCRAFT
Aircraft Kits

Adventure Air, P.O. Box 368, Berryville, AR 72616: Information $25 ❖ Two- or four-place amphibian and two-place high-wing kitplane with optional tailwheel or retractable amphibian landing gear. 501–423–5366.

Aero Designs Inc., 11910 Radium St., San Antonio, TX 78216: Information $8 ❖ Two-place low-wing kitplane. 210–308–9332.

Avid Aircraft, P.O. Box 728, Caldwell, ID 83606: Information $13 ❖ Four-place seaplane and two-place high-wing kitplane with optional jump seat. 208–454–2600.

Bushby Aircraft Inc., 674 Rt. 52, Minooka, IL 60447: Information $5 (specify model) ❖ One- and two-place low-wing kitplanes. 815–467–2346.

Co-Z Development Corporation, 2046 N. 63rd Pl., Mesa, AZ 85205: Information $10 ❖ Four-place pusher-type airplane. 602–981–6401.

Falconar Aviation Ltd., 19 Airport Rd., Edmonton, Alberta, Canada T5G 0W7: Information $8 (specify model) ❖ High-wing airplane with wheels and floats and one- and two-place low-wing kitplanes. 403–454–7272.

Fisher Aero Visions, 7118 St. Road 335, Portsmouth, OH 45662: Information $8 ❖ Two-place high-wing kitplane. 614–820–2219.

Fisher Flying Products Inc., P.O. Box 468, Edgeley, ND 58433: Information $5 (specify model) ❖ Two-place biplane and one- and two-place high-wing kitplanes. 701–493–2286.

Flightworks Corporation, 4211 Todd Ln., Austin, TX 78744: Information $5 (specify model) ❖ One- and two-place high-wing kitplanes. 512–441–8844.

Full Lotus Manufacturing Inc., 111–7400 Wilson Ave., Delta, British Columbia, Canada V4G 1E5: Information $8 ❖ High-wing pontoon airplane. 604–940–9378.

Hipp's Superbird's Inc., P.O. Box 266, Saluda, NC 28773: Information $4 ❖ One-place high-wing kitplanes. 704–749–9134.

I.S.A.E., 1850 N. 600 West, Logan, UT 84321: Information $10 ❖ Two-place low-wing kitplane. 801–753–2224.

Innovation Engineering Inc., Davenport Municipal Airport, 8970 Harrison, Davenport, IA 52804: Information $5 ❖ Pusher-type, high-wing kitplane. 319–386–6966.

Keuthan Aircraft Corporation, 910 Airport Rd., Merritt Island, FL 32952: Free information ❖ One- and two-place side-by-side amphibian, tandem, land, and canard aircraft. 407–452–2000.

Kolb Company Inc., RD 3, Box 38, Phoenixville, PA 19460: Information $5 ❖ One- and two-place high-wing kitplane. 215–948–4136.

Leading Edge Airfoils Inc., 331 S. 14th St., Colorado Springs, CO 80904: Catalog $6 ❖ Open cockpit biplanes. 719–632–4959.

Light Miniature Aircraft, Opa Locka Airport, Bldg. 411, Opa Locka, FL 33054: Information $5 (specify model) ❖ One- and two-place high-wing kitplanes. 305–681–4068.

The Lightning Bug Aircraft Corporation, P.O. Drawer 40, Sheldon, SC 29941: Free information ❖ One-place low-wing kitplane. 803–549–1800.

Loehle Aviation Inc., 380 Shipmans Creek Rd., Wartrace, TN 37183: Information $10 ❖ One-place low-wing kitplane. 615–857–3419.

Merlin Aircraft Inc., 509 Airport Rd., Muskegon, MI 49441: Information $10 ❖ One-place high-wing kitplane. 616–798–1622.

Mosler Motors Inc., 140 Ashwood Rd., Hendersonville, NC 28739: Information $15 (specify model) ❖ One- and two-place high-wing kitplanes. 704–692–7713.

Murphy Aircraft Manufacturing Ltd., 8880 Young Rd. South, Chilliwack, British Columbia, Canada V2P 4P5: Information $15 ❖ Two-place biplanes. 604–792–5855.

Neico Aviation Inc., 2244 Airport Way, Redmond, OR 97756: Information $15 (specify model) ❖ Two- and four-place low-wing kitplanes. 503–923–2244.

Barney Oldfield Aircraft Company, P.O. Box 228, Needham, MA 02192: Information $10 (specify model) ❖ One- and two-place biplanes. 617–444–5480.

Osprey Aircraft, 3741 El Ricon Way, Sacramento, CA 95825: Information $12 ❖ High-wing seaplane and two-place kitplanes. 916–483–3004.

Phantom Sport Airplane Corporation, P.O. Box 1209, Carthage, NC 28327: Brochure $2 ❖ One-place, easy-to-build ultralight aircraft. 919–947–4744.

Preceptor Aircraft, 1230 Shepard St., Hendersonville, NC 28792: Information $5 ❖ Two-place high-wing airplane with folding wings. 704–697–8284.

Progressive Aerodyne, 400 E. Pine St., Orlando, FL 32824: Free information ❖ Two-place amphibian. 407–859–8340.

Quad City Ultralight Aircraft Corporation, 3610 Coaltown Rd., Moline, IL 61265: Information $5 (specify model) ❖ One- and two-place high-wing kitplanes. 309–764–3515.

Quesstair, 3800 McAree Rd., Waukegan, IL 60087: Information $30 ❖ Two-place low-wing kitplane. 708–244–0005.

Quickkit, 9002 Summer Glen, Dallas, TX 75243: Information and video $21.95 ❖ Two-place amphibian. 214–349–0462.

Quicksilver Enterprises, P.O. Box 1572, Temecula, CA 92390: Information $3 (specify model) ❖ One- and two-place high-wing kitplanes. 714–676–6886.

Rand Robinson Engineering Inc., 15641 Product Ln., Huntington Beach, CA 92649: Information $8 (specify model) ❖ One- and two-place low-wing kitplanes. 714–898–3811.

RANS Company, 4600 Hwy., 183 Alternate, Hays, KS 67601: Catalog $15 ❖ One- and two-place high-wing kitplanes. 913–625–6346.

W.W. Redfern, 211 S. Spencer St., Post Falls, ID 83854: Information $6 ❖ One-place biplanes. 208–683–2264.

Skystar Aircraft Corporation, 100 N. Kings Rd., Nampa, ID 83687: Information $15 ❖ Two-place high-wing kitplane. 208–466–1711.

Stoddard-Hamilton Aircraft Inc., 18701 58th Ave. NE, Arlington, WA 98223: Information $20 ❖ Two-place low-wing kitplanes. 206–435–8533.

Stolp Starduster Corporation, 4301 Twining St., Riverside, CA 95209: Information $5 (specify model) ❖ One- and two-place biplanes. 714–686–7943.

TEAM Inc., 10790 Ivy Bluff Rd., Bradyville, TN 37026: Information $5 ❖ One-place mid-wing kitplane. 615–765–5397.

Titan Aircraft, 2730 Walter Main Rd., Geneva, OH 44041: Free information ❖ One- and two-place high-wing sport/trainer airplane. 216–466–0602.

Tri-R Technologies, 1114 E. 5th St., Oxnard, CA 93030: Information $10 ❖ Two-place low-wing sport airplane. 805–385–3680.

Ultravia Aero International Inc., 300–D Airport Rd., Mascouche, Quebec, Canada J7K 3C1: Brochure $10 ❖ Two-place high-wing monoplane. 514–953–1491.

Van's Aircraft Inc., P.O. Box 160, North Plains, OR 97133: Information $8 ❖ One- and two-place low-wing kitplanes. 503–647–5117.

Velocity Aircraft, 200 W. Airport Rd., Sebastian, FL 32958: Information $29.50 ❖ Easy-to-fly four-place airplane. 407–589–1860.

Zenith Aircraft Company, Mexico Memorial Airport, Mexico, MO 65265: Information $15 (specify model) ❖ One- and two-place low-wing kitplanes. 314–581–9000.

Aircraft Recovery Systems

Aircraft Recovery Systems Inc., 4910 Aircenter Circle, Reno, NV 89502: Free information ❖ Custom built rocket, motor, or A.I.R. parachute recovery systems. 702–829–2077.

Avionics Equipment

Aircraft Spruce & Specialty, 201 W. Truslow Ave., Box 424, Fullerton, CA 92632: Catalog $5 ❖ Avionics equipment. 800–824–1930; 714–870–7551 (in CA).

AirStar Sales, 11353 Pyrites, Rancho Cordova, CA 95670: Catalog $5 ❖ Instruments, avionics equipment, and radio equipment. 800–247–7827.

Airwich Avionics Inc., 1611 S. Eisenhower, Wichita, KS 67209: Free brochure ❖ Used and repaired avionics equipment. 316–942–8721.

AlliedSignal General Aviation Avionics, Bendix/King, 400 N. Rogers Rd., Olathe, KS 66062: Free information ❖ Instrument displays, flight controls, and communications, navigation, and identification systems. 913–768–3000.

American Avionics Inc., 7675 Perimeter Rd. South, Seattle, WA 98108: Free brochure ❖ New and used avionics equipment. 206–767–9781.

Century Instrument Corporation, 4440 Southeast Blvd., Wichita, KS 67210: Free catalog ❖ Rebuilt avionics equipment. 800–733–0116; 316–683–7571 (in KS).

Chief Aircraft Inc., 1301 Brookside Blvd., Grants Pass Airport, Grants Pass, OR 97526: Free information ❖ Avionics, communication, and other equipment. 800–447–3408.

David Clark Company Inc., 360 Franklin St., Box 15054, Worcester, MA 01615: Free information ❖ Aircraft intercom and communications equipment. 508–751–5800.

Eventide Avionics, One Alsan Way, Little Ferry, NJ 07643: Free information ❖ Avionics equipment. 800–446–7878.

Flightcom, 7340 SW Durham Rd., Portland, OR 97224: Free information ❖ Communications equipment. 800–432–4342.

Gulf-Coast Avionics Corporation, 4243 N. Westshore Blvd., Tampa, FL 33614: Free information ❖ Avionics and communications equipment. 813–879–9714.

ICOM America, 2380 116th Ave. NE, Bellevue, WA 98004: Free information ❖ Avionics equipment. 800–999–9877.

IIMorrow, 2345 Turner Rd. South, Salem, OR 97302: Free information ❖ Avionics equipment. 800–742–0077.

Microflight Products Inc., 16141–6 Pine Ridge Rd., Fort Myers, FL 33980: Catalog $3 ❖ Communications, instrumentation, and avionics equipment. 800–247–6955.

Narco Avionics, 2825 Laguna Canyon Rd., Laguna Beach, CA 92652: Free information ❖ Avionics equipment. 800–223–3636.

Northstar Avionics, 30 Sudbury Rd., Acton, MA 01720: Free information ❖ Avionics equipment. 800–628–4487.

SkySports, Hangar 1, Linden-Price Airport, Linden, MI 48451: Free catalog ❖ Avionics and communications equipment. 313–735–9433.

Vista Aviation Inc., 12653 Osborne St., Pacoima, CA 91331: Free brochure ❖ New and used radios. 800–328–8442; 818–896–6442 (in CA).

Gliders

Schweizer Aircraft Corporation, P.O. Box 147, Elmira, NY 14902: Free list ❖ Glider pilot equipment and books. 607–739–3821.

Gyro Aircraft Kits

Aerostar, 25060 Hancock Ave., Murrieta, CA 92562: Catalog $10 ❖ Ultralight one- and two-place gyrocopters.

B.W. Rotor Company Inc., P.O. Box 391, Tonowanda, KS 67144: Information $5 ❖ One- and two-place jet-powered gyroplanes.

Barnett Rotorcraft, 4307 Olivehurst Ave., Olivehurst, CA 95961: Information $15 (specify model) ❖ One- and two-place gyroplanes. 916–742–7416.

Ken Brock Manufacturing, 11852 Western Ave., Stanton, CA 90680: Catalog $5 ❖ One-place gyroplane and parts. 714–898–4366.

Froen Brothers Aviation Inc., 1784 W. 500 South, Salt Lake City, UT 84104: Information

$15 ❖ One-, two-, and five-place gyroplanes. 801–973–0177.

Helicraft Inc., P.O. Box 50, Riderwood, MD 21139: Catalog $10 ❖ Helicopter kits. 410–583–6366.

Revolution Helicopter Corporation, 1905 W. Jesse James Rd., Excelsior Springs, MO 64024: Information $15 ❖ One-place easy-to-assemble helicopter. 800–637–6867.

Robinson Helicopter Company, 24747 Crenshaw Blvd., Torrance, CA 90505: Free information ❖ One-place helicopter. 310–539–0508.

Rotary-Air Force Inc., Box 1236, Kindersley, Saskatchewan, Canada S0L 1S0: Information $12 ❖ Cross-country gyroplane. 306–463–6030.

RotorWay International, 300 S. 25th Ave., Phoenix, AZ 85009: Brochure $15 ❖ Two-place helicopter. 602–278–8899.

SnoBird Aircraft Inc., 13007 122nd Ave. NW, Gig Harbor, WA 98335: Information $10 (specify model) ❖ One- and two-place gyroplanes. 206–961–1001.

Sport Copter, 7246 N. Mohawk, Portland, OR 97203: Information $10 ❖ Two-place tandem seating gyroplane. 503–286–5462.

Star Aviation Inc., 821 Lone Star Dr., New Braunfels, TX 78130: Information $15 ❖ Easy-to-build helicopter kit.

Hang Gliding

Flytec, P.O. Box 561732, Miami, FL 33156: Free information ❖ Flight instruments. 800–662–2449.

Hall Brothers, P.O. Box 1010, Morgan, UT 84050: Free information ❖ Airspeed indicator. 801–829–3232.

High Energy Sports, 2236 W. 2nd St., Santa Ana, CA 92703: Free information ❖ Harness and parachute systems. 714–972–8186.

Miami Hang Gliding, 2640 S. Bayshore Dr., Coconut Grove, FL 33133: Free information ❖ Hang gliding tow chute. 305–285–8978.

Mountain High Equipment & Supply Company, 516 12th Ave., Salt Lake City, UT 84103: Free information ❖ Electronic-on-demand oxygen system. 800–468–8185.

North American Sports Distributing Inc., 18301 W. Colfax Ave., Golden, CO 80401: Free information ❖ Communications equipment. 303–278–9566.

Parts & Tools

The Aeroplane Store, Kampel Airport, 8930 Carlisle Rd., Wellsville, PA 17365: Free catalog ❖ Aircraft building supplies. 717–432–9688.

Aircraft Components Inc., P.O. Drawer W, Edwardsburg, MI 49112: Information $5 ❖ Aircraft parts and pilot supplies. 800–253–0800.

Aircraft Spruce & Specialty, 201 W. Truslow Ave., Box 424, Fullerton, CA 92632: Catalog $5 ❖ Tools, construction materials, instruments, engines, pilot supplies, and books. 800–824–1930; 714–870–7551 (in CA).

Alexander Aeroplane Company Inc., P.O. Box 909, Griffin, GA 30224: Free catalog ❖ Aircraft building supplies. 800–358–5228.

Avery Enterprises, Hicks Airfield, 2290 W. Hicks Rd., Hanger 54–1, Fort Worth, TX 76131: Free catalog ❖ Aircraft sheet metal tools. 817–439–8400.

B & F Aircraft Supply Inc., 9524 W. Gulfstream Rd., Frankfort, IL 60423: Catalog $4 ❖ Supplies for building and maintaining aircraft. 800–345–2558; 815–469–2473 (in IL).

California Power Systems Inc., 790 139th Ave., San Leandro, CA 94578: Catalog $6.95 ❖ Ultralight aircraft parts. 800–AIRWOLF; 510–357–2403 (in CA).

Eastside Ultralight Aircraft Inc., 4700 188th St. NE, Arlington, WA 98223: Catalog $7 ❖ Aircraft supplies. 206–435–3737.

Leading Edge Airfoils Inc., 331 S. 14th St., Colorado Springs, CO 80904: Catalog $6 ❖ Aircraft building materials, hardware, tools, engines and propellers, and books. 719–632–4959.

Wil Neubert Aircraft Supply, 403 3rd Ave., Watervliet, NY 12189: Catalog $5 (refundable) ❖ Avionics equipment, engines, radios and antennas, aircraft components, engine mounts, hardware, and batteries. 800–831–7527; 518–273–2327 (in NY).

Poly Fiber Aircraft Coatings, P.O. Box 3129, Riverside, CA 92519: Free information ❖ Fabric for covering aircraft. 800–362–3490.

Stits Poly-Fiber Aircraft Coatings, P.O. Box 3084, Riverside, CA 92519: Free information ❖ Aircraft covering materials. 714–684–4280.

Superflite Aircraft Supplies, 2149 E. Pratt Blvd., Elk Grove Village, IL 60007: Catalog $5 ❖ Aircraft building supplies. 800–323–0611.

U.S. Industrial Tool & Supply Company, 15119 Cleat St., Plymouth, MI 48170: Catalog $3 (refundable) ❖ Aircraft building tools. 800–521–4800.

Wag-Aero Group of Aircraft Services, 1216 North Rd., P.O. Box 181, Lyons, WI 53148: Free information ❖ Avionics equipment, engines, and tools. 800–558–6868.

Watkins Aviation Inc., 15770 Midway Rd., Hanger #6, Dallas, TX 75244: Free catalog ❖ Pilot's clothing, emblems and insignia, parachutes, communications equipment, and survival gear. 214–934–0033.

White Industries Inc., P.O. Box 198, Bates City, MO 64011: Free information ❖ Used aircraft parts. 800–821–7733.

Wicks Aircraft Supply, 410 Pine St., Highland, IL 62249: Catalog $5 ❖ Tools, construction materials, instruments, fabric, engines, and propellers. 800–221–9425; 618–654–7447 (in IL).

Pilot Supplies & Equipment

Aircraft Components Inc., P.O. Drawer W, Edwardsburg, MI 49112: Information $5 ❖ Aircraft parts and pilot supplies. 800–253–0800.

Aircraft Spruce & Specialty, 201 W. Truslow Ave., Box 424, Fullerton, CA 92632: Catalog $5 ❖ Tools, construction materials, instruments, engines, fabrics, flight equipment, and books. 800–824–1930; 714–870–7551 (in CA).

BRS Inc., Fleming Field, 1845 Henry Ave., South St. Paul, MN 55075: Free information ❖ Emergency parachute systems. 612–457–7491.

Butler Parachute Systems Inc., 6399 Lindbergh Blvd., California City, CA 93505: Catalog $2 ❖ Parachute systems. 619–373–4991.

Flight Products International Inc., P.O. Box 1558, Kalispell, MT 59901: Free information ❖ Cockpit equipment. 800–526–1231.

M. Golden Discount Sales, 8690 Aero Dr., San Diego, CA 92123: Free information ❖ Pilot equipment. 619–569–5220.

Chris Murphy, Occidental Western Marketing Company, 136 E. 7th Dr., Mesa, AZ 85210: Catalog $5 ❖ Flight jackets and clothing, helmets, oxygen masks, and other equipment. 602–964–0794.

National Parachute Industries, 47 E. Main St., Box 1000, Flemington, NJ 08822: Free brochure ❖ Parachute systems. 908–782–1646.

PCR Systems, 6851 Hwy. 73, Evergreen, CO 80439: Free information ❖ Personal cockpit voice recorder. 800–321–2359; 303–674–2379 (in CO).

Schweizer Aircraft Corporation, P.O. Box 147, Elmira, NY 14902: Free list ❖ Glider flight equipment and books. 607–739–3821.

Sporty's Pilot Shop, Clermont Airport, Batavia, OH 45103: Free catalog ❖ Flight equipment. 800–543–8633.

Strong Enterprises, 11236 Satellite Blvd., Orlando, FL 32837: Free catalog ❖ Emergency parachutes. 407–859–9317.

Watkins Aviation Inc., 15770 Midway Rd., Hanger #6, Dallas, TX 75244: Free catalog ❖ Clothing, emblems and insignia, helmets, parachutes, communications equipment, and survival gear. 214–934–0033.

AIR PURIFIERS

AirXchange Inc., 401 V.F.W. Dr., Rockland, MA 02370: Free information ❖ Energy recovery ventilators. 617–871–4816.

Altech Energy Corporation, 7009 Raywood Rd., Madison, WI 53713: Free information ❖ Air-to-heat exchange ventilators. 608–221–4499.

Carrier Corporation, P.O. Box 4808, Syracuse, NY 13221: Free information ❖ Electronic air cleaners. 800–CARRIER.

Enviracaire, 747 Bowman Ave., Hagerstown, MD 21740: Free brochure ❖ Air cleaners.

Friedrich Air Conditioning & Refrigeration Company, P.O. Box 1540, San Antonio, TX 78295: Free brochure ❖ Room air conditioners, air cleaners, heat pumps, and electric heaters. 512–225–2000.

Honeywell Inc., Residential Division, 1985 Douglas Dr. North, Golden Valley, MN 55422: Free information ❖ Electronic air cleaners. 800–328–5111.

Nortec Industries, Box 698, Ogdensburg, NY 13669: Free information ❖ Home air filters. 315–425–1255.

Sanyo, 21350 Lassen St., Chatsworth, CA 91311: Free information ❖ Electrostatic air cleaner/ionizer with an automatic smoke sensor. 818–998–7322.

ALARM SYSTEMS & REMOTE CONTROL EQUIPMENT

ADT Security Systems, 7399 Boston Blvd., Springfield, VA 22153: Free information ❖ Burglar alarm systems. 800–238–4636.

Advanced Security, 2964 Peachtree St., Atlanta, GA 30305: Catalog $1 ❖ Burglar and fire alarm systems. 800–241–0267.

Aqualarm, 1151 Bay Blvd., Chula Vista, CA 91911: Free information ❖ Multipurpose alarm systems. 619–575–4011.

ARK Systems Inc., 22125 17th Ave. SE, Ste. 101, Bothell, WA 98021: Free information ❖ Wireless security alarm systems. 800–877–4275; 206–487–3105 (in WA).

ATV Research Inc., 1301 Broadway, Dakota City, NE 68731: Catalog $3 ❖ Closed circuit surveillance TV systems. 402–987–3771.

Berk International, Box 5294, Garden Grove, CA 92645: Free information ❖ Self-contained sensor-operated alarm systems. 714–898–8648.

CCTV Corporation, 315 Hudson St., New York, NY 10013: Free information ❖ Closed circuit cameras for TV sets. 800–221–2240; 212–989–4433 (in NY).

Complete Home Automation, Box 2175, Goldenrod, FL 32733: Free information ❖ Home automation security systems. 407–830–5535.

Dakota Alert Inc., Box 130, Elk Point, SD 57025: Free information ❖ Wireless driveway alarms. 605–356–2772.

Direct Sales Center, P.O. Box 1074, Moorhead, MN 56561: Catalog $5 (refundable) ❖ Security, alarm, and surveillance/counter-surveillance systems. 701–232–5107.

Doorking, 120 Glasgow Ave., Inglewood, CA 90301: Free information ❖ Telephone entry and other access control systems. 800–826–7493.

Electronic Security Systems, 5275 Forest Glen, Salem, OR 97306: Catalog $5 ❖ Electronic security systems.

Fyrnetics Inc., 1055 Stevenson Ct., Roselle, IL 60172: Free information ❖ Burglar and smoke alarm systems with selective control options. 800–654–7665.

Heath Company, 455 Riverview Dr., Benton Harbor, MI 49022: Free catalog ❖ Easy-to-install home security, entertainment, and automation equipment. 616–925–6000.

Home Automation Inc., 2709 Ridgelake Dr., Metairie, LA 70052: Free information ❖ Home automation control and security systems.

Home Control Concepts, 9520 Padgett St., Ste. 108, San Diego, CA 92126: Free information ❖ Security and home automation equipment. 619–693–8887.

Home Systems Network, P.O. Box 3006, Edmond, OK 73083: Free catalog ❖ Do-it-yourself home and industrial automation control equipment and video camera kits. 405–330–0718.

Interactive Technologies Inc., 2266 N. 2nd St., St. Paul, MN 55109: Free information ❖ Telephone-based home security systems. 612–777–2690.

Ja Mar Distributing/Su-Mar Enterprises, 1292 Montclair Dr., Pasadena, CA 91104: Free catalog ❖ Remote control equipment, personal assistance systems, alarms, motion detectors, and telephone systems. 410–437–4181.

JDS Technologies, 16750 W. Bernardo Dr., San Diego, CA 92127: Free information ❖ Telephone-based home security systems and remote controls for computers, lights, and other devices. 619–487–8787.

Lutron Lighting Controls, Coopersburg, PA 18036: Free information ❖ Button-operated door jamb and lighting controls. 800–523–9466.

Makita USA Inc., Drapery Opener Division, 14930 Northam St., La Mirada, CA 90638: Free information ❖ Automatic drapery opener. 800–4–MAKITA.

Mountain West Alarm Supply Company, Alpha Omega Security Group Inc., 9420 E. Doubletree Ranch Rd., Scottsdale, AZ 85258: Catalog $1 ❖ Burglar and fire-protection security systems. 800–528–6169; 602–971–1200 (in AZ).

New Century, 1422 Boswell, Crete, NE 68333: Free brochure with long SASE ❖ Automatic/remote control house monitoring systems. 800–728–4155.

NuTone Inc., P.O. Box 1580, Cincinnati, OH 45201: Catalog $3 ❖ Video door-answering system with voice transmission over telephones and a wireless security system that can be zone programmed. 800–543–8687.

Oxford Chime Works, P.O. Box 665, Ridgecrest, CA 93555: Catalog $3 ❖ Handcrafted door bells, chimes, and annunciators. 619–384–4385.

Paladin Electronics, 19425 Soledad Cyn Rd., Ste. 333, Canyon Country, CA 91351: Free information ❖ Talking security systems. 805–251–8725.

Radio Shack, Division Tandy Corporation, 1500 One Tandy Center, Fort Worth, TX 76102: Free information ❖ Easy-to-install burglar and fire alarm system for homes. Will work with an automatic message dialer. 817–390–3700.

Sea Sentry Inc., 3030 Bern Dr., Laguna Beach, CA 92651: Free information ❖ Wireless alarm systems. 800–832–8344.

Sentry Devices, 33 Rustic Gate Ln., Dix Hills, NY 11746: Free information ❖ Burglar alarms. 516–491–3191.

Siemens Solar, P.O. Box 6032, Camarillo, CA 93011: Free information ❖ Solar-powered motion sensor light. 800–233–1106.

Spectre Security Systems, 843 Dumont Pl., #22, Rochester Hills, MI 48307: Free information ❖ Home and automotive security systems. 810–652–8117.

Video Surveillance Corporation, 1050 E. 14th St., Brooklyn, NY 11230: Free information ❖ Surveillance TV cameras. 718–258–1310.

ANTIQUES & REPRODUCTIONS

Antiques & Reproductions

Akins & Aylesworth Ltd., Hinsdale, IL 60521: Free information ❖ Antiques and collectibles. 708–325–3355.

The Antique Centre, 6644 Barrington Rd., Hanover Park, IL 60103: Free information ❖ Antiques and collectibles. 708–483–1100.

Antique Imports Unlimited, P.O. Box 2978, Covington, LA 70434: Catalog $3 ❖ Imported antiques and jewelry. 504–892–0014.

Baker's International Antiques & Collectibles, P.O. Box 558, Oakdale, NY 11769: Catalog $12 ❖ Antique and collectible toys. 516–567–9295.

Bargain John's Antiques, 700 S. Washington, Lexington, NE 68850: Free information ❖ Antique Victorian furniture, from 1840 to 1900. 303–324–4576.

Benedikt & Salmon Record Rarities, 3020 Meade Ave., San Diego, CA 92116: Free catalogs, indicate choice of (1) autographs and rare books; (2) classical; (3) jazz, big bands and blues; and (4) personalities, soundtracks and country music ❖ Early phonographs and cylinders, autographed memorabilia and rare books in music and the performing arts, and hard-to-find phonograph recordings from 1890 to date. 619–281–3345.

Warren Blake, Old Science Books, 308 Hadley Dr., Trumbull, CT 06611: Free catalog ❖ Hard-to-find astronomy books and prints. 203–459–0820.

The Brass Lion, 5935 S. Broadway, Tyler, TX 75703: Catalog $5 ❖ English antiques, reproduction 17th- and 18th-century light fixtures and sconces, and other gifts. 903–561–1111.

Chinese Porcelain Company, 822 Madison Ave., New York, NY 10021: Free information ❖ Chinese porcelain antiques. 212–628–4101.

Civil War Antiques, P.O. Box 87, Sylvania, OH 43560: Catalog subscription $8 ❖ Civil War collectibles. 419–882–5547.

Doll Emporium, P.O. Box 1000, Studio City, CA 91604: Free information ❖ Antique dolls. 818–763–5937.

Dovetail Antiques, 474 White Pine Rd., Columbus, NJ 08022: Catalog $5 ❖ Antique wicker furniture. 609–298–5245.

Dubrow Antiques, P.O. Box 128, Bayside, NY 11361: Free information ❖ 19th-century American-style furniture. 718–767–9758.

Dunbar's Gallery, 76 Haven St., Milford, MA 01757: Free brochure ❖ Advertising nostalgia, Americana, folk art, pottery, comic character toys, mechanical and still banks, and other antiques. 508–634–TOYS.

Bill Egleston Inc., 509 Brentwood Rd., Marshalltown, IA 50158: Free price list ❖ Cloisonne, ivory, netsuke, stone, and Oriental collectibles. 800–798–4579.

Charles Faudree, 2042 Utica Square, Tulsa, OK 74114: Free information ❖ Antiques and collectibles. 918–747–9706.

The Federalist Antiques, 515 Park Dr., Kenilworth, IL 60043: Free information ❖ Antiques and collectibles. 708–256–1791.

N. Flayderman & Company Inc., P.O. Box 2446, Fort Lauderdale, FL 33303: Catalog $10 ❖ Antique guns, swords, knives, and other western, nautical, and military antiques. 305–761–8855.

Games People Played, P.O. Box 1540, Pinedale, WY 82941: Catalog $3 ❖ Antique replica game boards. 307–367–2502.

Gasoline Alley, 6501 20th NE, Seattle, WA 98115: Free information with long SASE ❖ Baseball and football collectibles and toys, from 1875 to 1975. 206–524–1606.

The Gemmary, P.O. Box 816, Redondo Beach, CA 90277: Free catalog ❖ Rare books and antique scientific instruments. 213–372–5969.

Hake's Americana, P.O. Box 1444, York, PA 17405: Catalog $5 ❖ Americana and other collectibles. 717–848–1333.

Heirlooms Inc., 219 S. 33rd St., West Des Moines, IA 50265: Free information ❖ Antiques and collectibles. 515–255–1821.

Hillman-Gemini Antiques, 927 Madison Ave., New York, NY 10021: Free information with long SASE ❖ Antique toys and banks, folk art, and Americana. 212–734–3262.

Historical Technology Inc., 6 E. Mugford St., Marblehead, MA 01945: Annual catalog subscription $12 ❖ Rare books and antique scientific instruments. 617–631–2275.

Hoosier-Peddler, Dave Harris, 5400 S. Webster St., Kokomo, IN 46902: Price list $2 ❖ Banks, Walt Disney collectibles, and wind-up, character, and other toys. 317–453–6172.

Huzza Antiques, 136 Main St. East, Harbor Springs, MI 49740: Free information ❖ Antiques and collectibles. 616–526–2128.

Jacques Noel Jacobsen, 60 Manor Rd., Ste. 300, Staten Island, NY 10310: Catalog $10 ❖ Military insignia, weapons, photos and paintings, band instruments, and Native American and western collectibles. 718–981–0973.

Jukebox Junction, P.O. Box 1081, Des Moines, IA 50311: Catalog $2.50 ❖ Antique jukeboxes. 515–981–4019.

Lake Forest Antiquarians, P.O. Box 841, Lake Forest, IL 60045: Free catalog ❖ English and Continental silver and other antiques. 708–234–1990.

Leonard's Reproductions & Antiques, 600 Taunton Creek, Seekonk, MA 02771: Catalog $4 ❖ Original and reproduction antique beds. 508–336–8585.

Melton's Antiques, 4201 Indian River Rd., Chesapeake, VA 23325: Free information with long SASE ❖ Antique dolls. 804–420–9226.

MidAtlantic Antiques, P.O. Box 691, Mt. Laurel, NJ 08054: Free catalog ❖ Antiques and collectible memorabilia. 609–234–2651.

Gerald Murphy Antiques Ltd., 60 Main St. South, Woodbury, CT 06798: Free brochure ❖ Furniture, desks, clocks, watercolors, pottery, glass, and other antiques. 203–266–4211.

Neon Etc., Robert Newman, 10809 Charnock Rd., Los Angeles, CA 90034: Free information ❖ Neon signs, gas pumps, coke, machines, neon clocks, wood telephone booths, and restored antique mechanical memorabilia. 213–559–0539.

Old Friends Antiques, P.O. Box 754, Sparks, MD 21152: Annual subscription of monthly lists $10 ❖ Steiff bears and other stuffed animals in mint condition. 410–472–4632.

Philadelphia Print Shop Ltd., 8441 Germantown Ave., Philadelphia, PA 19118: Catalog $4 ❖ Antique maps, prints, and books. 215–242–4750.

Elax Putting Antiques, 226 E. 51st St., New York, NY 10022: Free information ❖ Antiques and collectibles. 212–838–3850.

Quester Gallery, On the Green, P.O. Box 446, Stonington, CT 06378: Catalog $10 ❖ Marine art and antiques. 203–535–3860.

Eugene & Ellen Reno, Box 191, Lawrence, MA 01842: Free information ❖ Cut and depression glass, other glassware, dolls and toys, miniatures, jewelry, sterling silver, china, and other collectibles. 603–898–7426.

John F. Rinaldi Nautical Antiques, P.O. Box 785, Kennebunkport, ME 04046: Catalog $3 ❖ American paintings, scrimshaw, and nautical antiquities. 207–967–3218.

Samurai Antiques, 229 Santa Ynez Ct., Santa Barbara, CA 93103: Price list $1 with long SASE ❖ Japanese antique Samurai, Emperor, and Empress dolls. 805–965–9688.

S.J. Shrubsole, 104 E. 57th St., New York, NY 10022: Free information ❖ American and English antique silver, jewelry, art, gold boxes, and other collectibles. 212–753–8920.

Southampton Antiques, 172 College Hwy., Rt. 10, Southampton, MA 01073: Video catalog $25 ❖ Antique American oak and Victorian furniture. 413–527–1022.

Spivack's Antiques, 54 Washington St., Wellesley, MA 02181: Free information ❖ Antiques and collectibles. 617–235–1700.

Tesseract Early Scientific Instruments, Box 151, Hastings-On-Hudson, NY 10706: Free information ❖ Antique scientific and medical instruments and books. 914–478–2594.

Edith Weber & Company, 994 Madison Ave., New York, NY 10021: Free information ❖ Antique jewelry. 212–688–4331.

Worldwide Treasure Bureau, 2230 W. Sunnyside Ave., Ste. 2, P.O. Box 5012, Visalia, CA 93278: Free catalog ❖ Antique coins and other collectibles. 209–732–2252.

Antique & Art Restoration

Antique & Art Restoration by Wiebold, 413 Terrace Pl., Cincinnati, OH 45174: Free brochure ❖ Restoration services for antiques and art objects. 513–831–2541.

Antique Restoring Studio Inc., 99 Cabot St., Needham, MA 02194: Free information ❖ Restoration services for art objects. 617–444–2685.

Fine Art Restoration, RFD 2, Box 1440, Brooks, ME 04921: Free information ❖ Restoration services for paintings. 207–722–3464.

A. Ludwig Klein & Son Inc., 683 Sumneytown Pike, P.O. Box 145, Harleysville, PA 19438: Free information ❖ Conservation and restoration services for Neolithic antiquities and other 20th-century collectibles. 215–256–9004.

Poster Restoration Studio, 7466 Beverly Blvd., Ste. 205, Los Angeles, CA 90036: Free information ❖ Restoration services for posters. 213–934–4219.

VanDyke's, Box 278, Woonsocket, SD 57385: Catalog $1 ❖ Hardware, hardwoods, curved glass, trim, and other supplies for restoring antiques. 800–843–3320; 605–796–4425 (in SD).

Diana Wight, 30 Lafayette St., Randolph, MA 02368: Free information ❖ Restoration and repair services for porcelain collectibles. 617–961–1028.

APPLIANCES
Manufacturers

Amana Refrigeration, Ruppman Marketing Services, Inquiry Fulfillment Center, 8800 N. Allen Rd., Peoria, IL 61615: Free information ❖ Refrigerators. 800–843–0304.

Andi Company Appliances, 65 Campus Plaza, Edison, NJ 08837: Free information ❖ Electric and gas cooktop stoves, dishwashers, and ranges. 800–344–0043.

Black & Decker, 6 Armstrong Rd., Shelton, CT 06484: Free information ❖ Small appliances. 203–926–3000.

Braun Appliances, 66 Broadway, Rt. 1, Lynnefield, MA 01940: Free information ❖ Small appliances. 800–272–8622.

Frigidaire Company, 6000 Perimeter Rd., Dublin, OH 43017: Free information ❖ Refrigerators, freezers, dishwashers, and other appliances. 800–451–7007.

G.E. Appliances, General Electric Company, Appliance Park, Louisville, KY 40225: Free information ❖ Electric cooktop stoves, microwave ovens, dishwashers, refrigerators, freezers, washers and dryers, and small appliances. 800–626–2000.

Hotpoint, 9500 Williamsburg Plaza, Louisville, KY 40222: Free information ❖ Dishwashers, microwave ovens, refrigerators, freezers, and other appliances. 800–626–2000.

In-Sink-Erator, Emerson Electric Company, 4700 21st St., Racine, WI 53406: Free information ❖ Dishwashers and other appliances. 800–558–5712.

Jenn-Air Company, 3035 Shadeland Ave., Indianapolis, IN 46226: Free information ❖ Cooktop stoves, dishwashers, ranges, and range hoods. 800–536–6247.

Kelvinator, Ruppman Marketing Services, Inquiry Fulfillment Center, 8800 N. Allen Rd., Peoria, IL 61615: Free information ❖ Appliances. 800–843–0304.

KitchenAid Inc., 701 Main St., St. Joseph, MI 49805: Free information ❖ Cooktop stoves, dishwashers, range hoods, small appliances, wall ovens, washing machines and dryers, and refrigerators. 800–422–1230.

Magic Chef, 740 King Edward Ave., Cleveland, TN 37311: Free information ❖ Electric cooktop stoves, wall ovens, refrigerators, and dishwashers. 800–332–4432.

Miele Appliance Inc., 525 Pleasant St., Worcester, MA 01602: Free information ❖ Electric and gas cooktop stoves, dishwashers, ranges, washers and dryers, and wall ovens. 800–962–6458.

Panasonic, Panasonic Way, Secaucus, NJ 07094: Free information ❖ Microwave ovens. 201–348–7000.

Sanyo, 21350 Lassen St., Chatsworth, CA 91311: Free information ❖ Under-the-counter refrigerators, microwave ovens, portable laundry washers and dryers, and electronics. 818–998–7322.

Sharp Electronics, Sharp Plaza, Mahwah, NJ 07430: Free information ❖ Microwave ovens. 800–BE-SHARP.

Tappan, 6000 Perimeter Dr., Dublin, OH 43017: Free information ❖ Electric cooktop stoves, ranges, and dishwashers. 800–451–7007.

Thermador/Waste King, 5119 District Blvd., Los Angeles, CA 90040: Free information ❖ Electric and gas cooktop stoves, ranges, wall ovens, and other appliances. 213–562–1133.

Vent-A-Hood Company, P.O. Box 830426, Richardson, TX 75080: Free information ❖ Range hoods. 214–235–5201.

Viking Range Corporation, 111 Front St., Greenwood, MS 38930: Free brochure ❖ Gas ranges, range hoods, and cooktops. 601–455–1200.

Waring Products, 283 Main St., New Hartford, CT 06057: Free information ❖ Small appliances. 203–379–0731.

West Bend, 400 Washington St., West Bend, WI 53095: Free information ❖ Small appliances. 414–334–2311.

Whirlpool Corporation, 2000 M63 North, Benton Harbor, MI 49022: Free information ❖ Electric cooktop stoves, wall ovens, dishwashers, refrigerators, and freezers. 800–253–1301.

Retailers

Bernie's Discount Center Inc., 821 6th Ave., New York, NY 10001: Catalog $1 (refundable) ❖ Video equipment, telephones and answering machines, and large and small appliances. 212–564–8758.

Bondy Export Corporation, 40 Canal St., New York, NY 10002: Free information ❖ Large and small appliances, cameras, video and TV equipment, office machines and typewriters, and luggage. 212–925–7785.

Cole's Appliance & Furniture Company, 4026 Lincoln Ave., Chicago, IL 60618: Free information with long SASE ❖ Furniture, audio and video equipment, TV sets, and large and small appliances. 312–525–1797.

Dial-A-Brand Inc., 57 S. Main St., Freeport, NY 11520: Free information with long SASE

❖ TVs, large and small appliances, and video equipment. 516–378–9694.

Focus Electronics, 4523 13th Ave., Brooklyn, NY 11219: Free catalog ❖ Appliances, computers, audio and video equipment, and TV sets. 718–436–4646.

Foto Electric Supply Company, 31 Essex St., New York, NY 10002: Free information ❖ Appliances. 212–673–5222.

Harry's Discounts & Appliances Corporation, 8701 18th Ave., Brooklyn, NY 11214: Free information with long SASE ❖ Electronics and appliances. 718–236–3507.

Percy's Inc., 19 Glennie St., Worcester, MA 01605: Free information ❖ Appliances and electronics. 508–755–5334.

Richlund Sales, 75695 Hwy. 1053, Kentwood, LA 70444: Free information ❖ Ice-maker, central vacuum system, trash compactor, rear vision camera, electric heat equipment, combination washer-dryer, and other appliances for recreational vehicles. 504–229–4922.

APPLIQUES

Badhir Trading Inc., 8429 Sisson Hwy., Eden, NY 14057: Catalog $2.50 (refundable) ❖ Beaded, sequined, and jeweled appliques, and trims and fringes for dresses, costumes, and bridal fashions. 800–654–9418.

Laube's Stretch & Sew Fabrics, 609 W. 98th St., Bloomington, MN 55420: Catalog $1 with long SASE ❖ Applique kits with designs for adults and children. 612–884–7321.

Sequin Imports, 3265 E. Tropicana, Las Vegas, NV 89121: Catalog $2 ❖ Sequined appliques.

Winslow Stitchery, 908 Winslow, West St. Paul, MN 55118: Catalog $1 (refundable) ❖ Stitchery patterns for appliques. 612–457–8624.

ARCHERY & BOW HUNTING

Advanced Bowsights, P.O. Box 279, Dunlap, TN 37327: Free information ❖ Bow sights. 615–949–4812.

AFC, Division of MMFG, 1610 Hwy. 52 South, Chatfield, MN 55923: Free information ❖ Carbon shaft arrows. 507–867–3479.

Aimpoint, 580 Herndon Pkwy., Herndon, VA 22070: Free brochure ❖ Archery equipment. 703–471–6828.

Alpine Archery Inc., P.O. Box 319, Lewiston, ID 83501: Free information ❖ Archery equipment. 208–746–4717.

American Archery, P.O. Box 320, Florence, WI 54121: Free information ❖ Bows and equipment. 800–255–4939; 715–528–3000 (in WI).

Anderson Archery, P.O. Box 130, Grand Ledge, MI 48837: Free catalog ❖ Archery equipment. 517–627–3251.

Archery Corporation, P.O. Box 537, Saddle Brook, NJ 07662: Free information ❖ Portable treestand safety harness and other equipment. 201–843–0159.

Barnett International, P.O. Box 934, Odessa, FL 33556: Free information ❖ Arrow holders, bow cases, quivers, bows, and sights. 800–237–4507; 813–920–2241 (in FL).

Bay Archery Sales, 1001 N. Johnson St., Bay City, MI 48708: Free catalog ❖ Archery equipment. 517–894–0777.

Bear Archery Inc., 4600 SW 41st Blvd., Gainesville, FL 32608: Free information ❖ Arrows, arrow-making components, bows, sights, and targets. 800–874–4603; 904–376–2327 (in FL).

Bingham Projects Inc., 5739 Monte Verde Dr., Mountain Green, UT 84050: Catalog $2 ❖ Bow- and arrow-making supplies. 801–876–2639.

Bohning Company Ltd., 7361 N. Seven Mile Rd., Lake City, MI 49651: Free information ❖ Archery equipment, arrows, and arrow-making components. 616–229–4247.

Bonnie Bowman Inc., 2511 W. Winton Ave., Hayward, CA 94545: Free information ❖ Bows, arrows, arrow-making components, arm guards, arrow holders, gloves, quivers, tabs, tools, and sights. 800–289–2117; 510–785–2500 (in CA).

Bowhunter Supply Inc., 1158 46th St., P.O. Box 5010, Vienna, WV 26105: Free information ❖ Arrows, arrow-making components, bows, sights, targets, game calls, targets, camouflage clothing, and camping equipment. 800–289–2211; 304–295–8511 (in WV).

Bowhunter's Discount Warehouse Inc., 1045 Ziegler Rd., Wellsville, PA 17365: Free catalog ❖ Rifles, game calls, targets, camouflage clothing, and equipment for hunting, bow hunting, archery, and camping. 717–432–8611.

Broward Shooter's Exchange, 250 S. 60th Ave., Hollywood, FL 33023: Catalog $8 ❖ Shooting, reloading, muzzleloading, hunting, and archery equipment. 800–554–9002.

Browning Company, Dept. C006, One Browning Pl., Morgan, UT 84050: Catalog $2 ❖ Arm guards, arrow holders, gloves, point sharpeners, scents and lures, quivers, tabs, wax, bows, arrows, arrow-making components, and sights. 800–333–3288.

BSI Sporting Goods, P.O. Box 5010, Vienna, WV 26105: Free catalog ❖ Firearm and muzzleloading supplies, optics, clothing, and archery, fishing, and hunting equipment. 304–295–8511.

Buckeye Sports Supply, John's Sporting Goods, 2655 Harrison Ave. SW, Canton, OH 44706: Free information ❖ Archery equipment. 800–533–8691.

Cascade Archery, 12930 228th St. NE, Arlington, WA 98223: Brochure $1 ❖ Archery equipment and supplies.

Darton Archery, 3540 Darton Dr., Hale, MI 48739: Free catalog ❖ Bow hunting equipment. 517–728–4231.

Delta Industries, 117 E. Kenwood St., Reinbeck, IA 50669: Free information ❖ Life-size 3–dimensional archery targets. 319–345–6476.

Easton, 5040 W. Harold Gatty Dr., Salt Lake City, UT 84116: Free information and list of retailers ❖ Arrow shafts. 801–539–1400.

Fine-Line Inc., Sales/Catalog Department, 11220 164th St., East Puyallup, WA 98374: Free information ❖ Bow quiver for arrows. 206–848–4222.

Gander Mountain Inc., P.O. Box 248, Gander Mountain, Wilmot, WI 53192: Free catalog ❖ Archery equipment. 414–862–2331.

Golden Eagle Archery, 1111 Corporate Dr., Farmington, NY 14425: Free information ❖ Bows, quivers, scents and lures, slings, and sights. 716–924–1880.

Great Northern Longbow Company, 201 N. Main St., Nashville, MI 49073: Brochure $1 ❖ Archery equipment.

High Country Archery, P.O. Box 1269, 312 Industrial Park Rd., Dunlap, TN 37327: Free information ❖ Archery equipment. 615–949–5000.

Hoyt USA, 475 N. Neil Armstrong Rd., Salt Lake City, UT 84116: Free information ❖ Bows, cases, stabilizers, strings, quivers, slings, sights, arrows, and arrow-making supplies. 801–363–2990.

Kolpin Manufacturing Inc., P.O. Box 107, Fox Lake, WI 53933: Free information ❖ Arm guards, arrow holders, bow cases, gloves, tabs, and arrow-making components. 414–928–3118.

Kustom King Arrows, 1200 E. 86th Pl., Merrillville, IN 46410: Free catalog ❖ Archery supplies. 219–769–6640.

Martin Archery Inc., Rt. 5, Box 127, Walla Walla, WA 99362: Free information ❖ Arrows, arrow-making components, bows, sights, and targets. 306–757–1221.

Modern Camouflage, P.O. Box 224785, Dallas, TX 75222: Free catalog ❖ Bowhunting clothing, winterwear, and rainwear. 800–929–0987.

Morrell Manufacturing Inc., Rt. 2, Box 699, Alma, AR 72921: Free information ❖ Solid-foam targets with replaceable covers. 501–632–5920.

Mountaineer Archery Inc., 1312 7th Ave., P.O. Box 2208, Huntington, WV 25722: Free information ❖ Archery equipment. 304–525–9222.

O.H. Mullen Sales Inc., RR 2, Oakwood, OH 45873: Free information ❖ Bows and strings, arm guards, arrow holders, cases, strings, stabilizers, gloves, nock locks, point sharpeners, quivers, racks, scents and lures, slings, tabs, arrows, arrow-making components, sights, and targets. 800–258–6625; 800–248–6625 (in OH).

Oneida Labs Inc., P.O. Box 68, Phoenix, NY 13135: Brochure $2 ❖ Bow hunting equipment.

Petersen Sales, 3712 N. 2900 East, Liberty, UT 84310: Free information ❖ Archery targets with replaceable covers. 801–745–1517.

PGS Archery Corporation, 825 S. Chelsea Dr., Rt. 47, Vineland, NJ 08360: Catalog $1 ❖ Archery supplies. 800–257–7040.

Pro Line Company, 1675 West Gun Lake Rd., Hastings, MI 49058: Free information ❖ Arrows, arrow-making components, bows, and sights.

Rattlesnake Archery Inc., P.O. Box 936, Peoria, AZ 85380: Free information and list of retailers ❖ Archery equipment. 602–486–5317.

Saunders Archery Company, P.O. Box 476, Columbus, NE 68601: Free information ❖ Arm guards, arrow holders, cases, strings, stabilizers, gloves, nock locks, point sharpeners, quivers, scents and lures, slings, tools, arrows, arrow-making components, sights, and targets. 800–228–1408; 402–564–7176 (in NE).

Screaming Eagle, P.O. Box 4507, Missoula, MT 59806: Free catalog ❖ Bowhunting equipment. 800–458–2017.

Spence's Targets, 947 Jonathan, Crete, IL 60417: Free information ❖ Multi-layered foam animal targets. 708–672–0977.

Sport Shop, Rt. 3, Box 187, Auden, NC 28530: Free catalog ❖ Archery and bow hunting equipment. 919–746–8288.

Springer Archery Supply Inc., 12731 Huron River Dr., P.O. Box 338, Romulus, MI 48174: Free information ❖ Arrows, arrow-making components, bows, sights, and targets. 800–521–7766; 313–941–6010 (in MI).

Three Rivers Archery Supply, P.O. Box 517, Ashley, IN 46705: Catalog $2 (refundable) ❖ Archery equipment and supplies. 219–587–9501.

Timberline Archery Products, P.O. Box 333, Lewiston, ID 83501: Free catalog ❖ Archery equipment. 208–746–2708.

Xi Compound Bows & Accessories, P.O. Box 889, Evansville, IN 47706: Free catalog ❖ Archery equipment. 812–467–1200.

York Archery, P.O. Box 11804, Fort Smith, AR 72917: Free information ❖ Bows, arm guards, cases, strings, gloves, point sharpeners, quivers, arrows, arrow-making components, sights, and targets. 800–526–5040; 918–436–2432 (in MO).

ART SUPPLIES & EQUIPMENT
Graphic Art Supplies

Accent Products Division, Borden Inc., 300 E. Main St., Lake Zurich, IL 60047: Free information ❖ Acrylic paints. 708–540–1604.

Aiko's Art Materials Import, 3347 N. Clark St., Chicago, IL 60657: Catalog $1.50 ❖ Japanese handmade paper, Oriental art supplies, and fabric dyes. 312–404–5600.

William Alexander Art Supplies, P.O. Box 20250, Salem, OR 97305: Catalog $1 ❖ Painting kits, art supplies, and books. 800–547–8747.

Alvin & Company Inc., P.O. Box 188, Windsor, CT 06095: Catalog $6 ❖ Art supplies for artists, drafters, engineers, and surveyors. 203–243–8991.

American Tomorrow Inc., 4467–C Park Dr., Norcross, GA 30093: Free information ❖ Dual brush- and sketching-point colored pens. 800–835–3232; 404–381–6800 (in GA).

Anco Wood Specialties Inc., 71–08 80th St., Glendale, NY 11385: Free information ❖ Easels. 800–262–6963; 718–326–2023 (in NY).

Art Essential of New York Ltd., 3 Cross St., Suffern, NY 10901: Free catalog ❖ Tools, how-to videos, and gold, silver, and other metal leaf in sheets and rolls. 800–283–5323.

Art Express, P.O. Box 21662, Columbia, SC 29221: Catalog $3.50 ❖ Art supplies. 800–535–5908.

Art Mart, 533 Seabright Ave., Santa Cruz, CA 95062: Free catalog ❖ Art supplies. 800–688–5798.

The Art Store, 935 Erie Blvd. East, Syracuse, NY 13210: Price list $3 ❖ Fabric dyeing, screen printing, and marbling supplies. 800–669–2787.

Art Supply Warehouse Inc., 360 Main Ave., Norwalk, CT 06851: Free catalog ❖ Art supplies. 800–243–5038; 203–846–2279 (in CT).

Artisan/Santa Fe Inc., 717 Canyon Rd., Santa Fe, NM 87501: Free catalog ❖ Art supplies. 800–331–6375.

Artograph Inc., 13205 16th Ave. North, Minneapolis, MN 55441: Free information ❖ Projector that enlarges and reduces opaque compositions, photographs, drawings, and other illustrations. 800–328–4653; 612–553–1112 (in MN).

Badger Air-Brush Company, 9128 W. Belmont Ave., Franklin Park, IL 60131: Brochure $1 ❖ Air brushes. 708–678–3104.

Binney & Smith/Liquitex, Box 431, Easton, PA 18044: Free information ❖ Acrylic paints.

Dick Blick Company, P.O. Box 1267, Galesburg, IL 61401: Catalog $1 ❖ Books, videos, airbrushes, and printing, drafting, and commercial art supplies. 800–447–8192.

Arthur Brown & Bros. Inc., P.O. Box 7820, Maspeth, NY 11378: Catalog $3 ❖ Art supplies. 800–772–7367; 718–628–0600 (in NY).

Stan Brown's Arts & Crafts Inc., 13435 NE Whitaker Way, Portland, OR 97230: Catalog $3.50 ❖ Art supplies and books. 800–547–5531.

Caran d'Ache of Switzerland Inc., 19 W. 24th St., New York, NY 10010: Free information ❖ Gouache colors. 212–689–3590.

Chaselle Inc., 9645 Gerwig Ln., Columbia, MD 21046: Catalog $4 ❖ Books, ceramic molds and kilns, sculpture equipment, and art, silk-screen painting, and other craft supplies. 800–242–7355.

Chatham Art Distributors, 11 Brookside Ave., Chatham, NY 12037: Free information ❖ Art supplies and books. 800–822–4747.

Cheap Joe's Art Stuff, 300 Industrial Park Rd., Boone, NC 28607: Free catalog ❖ Art supplies. 800–227–2788.

Co-Op Artists' Materials, P.O. Box 53097, Atlanta, GA 30355: Free catalog ❖ Art supplies. 800–877–3242.

Conrad Machine Company, 1525 S. Warner, Whitehall, MI 49461: Free catalog ❖ Etching and lithography presses. 616–893–7455.

Createx Colors, 14 Airport Park Rd., East Granby, CT 06026: Free information ❖ Liquid permanent dyes, pure pigments, and pearlescent, iridescent, acrylic, and other fabric colors. 800–243–2712.

Crown Art Products, 90 Dayton Ave., Passaic, NJ 07055: Free catalog ❖ Silk-screening supplies. 201–777–6010.

Decart Inc., P.O. Box 309, Morrisville, VT 05661: Free information ❖ Fabric paints and dyes for use with air brushes, water-based enamels and paints for transfer techniques, and glass crafting, silk-screening, and other art and craft supplies. 802–888–4217.

Deco Art Americana, Box 360, Stanford, KY 40484: Free information ❖ Acrylic paints.

Delta Technical Coatings, 2550 Pellissier Pl., Whittier, CA 90601: Free catalog ❖ Acrylics, oils, casein paints, and paint sticks. 800–423–4135; 213–686–0678 (in CA).

Dickerson Press Company, P.O. Box 8, South Haven, MI 49090: Free information ❖ Etching and lithography presses in manual and electric models, and a press that prints intaglio, relief, lithographs, stone, plate, and other medias. 616–637–4251.

Dixie Art Supplies, 2612 Jefferson Hwy., New Orleans, LA 70121: Free catalog ❖ Airbrush equipment. 800–783–2612.

Dove Brushes, 280 Terrace Rd., Tarpon Springs, FL 34689: Catalog $2.50 ❖ Art supplies. 800–334–3683; 813–934–5283 (in FL).

Duncan, 5673 E. Shields Ave., Fresno, CA 93727: Free information ❖ Fabric paints, outline writers, and glitter dispensers. 800–438–6226; 209–291–4444 (in CA).

Dutch Door Inc., P.O. Box 21662, Columbia, SC 29221: Free catalog ❖ Art supplies. 803–798–8441.

Ebersole Lapidary Supply, 11417 West Hwy. 54, Wichita, KS 67209: Catalog $2 *Shells, lapidary equipment, and supplies for art, calligraphy, and jewelry- and clock-making. 316–722–4771.

Fairgate Rule Company Inc., 22 Adams Ave., P.O. Box 278, Cold Spring, NY 10516: Free catalog ❖ Rulers, other measuring devices, stencils, and drawing aids. 800–431–2180; 914–265–3677 (in NY).

The Fine Gold Leaf People, Art Essentials, Three Cross St., Suffern, NY 10901: Free information ❖ Genuine, imitation, and variegated sheets and rolls of metallic foil, brushes, other supplies, and books. 800–283–5323.

Flax Artist Materials, P.O. Box 7216, San Francisco, CA 94120: Catalog $6 ❖ Supplies for artists, architects, drafters, and sign painters. 800–547–7778.

Fletcher-Lee & Company, P.O. Box 626, Elk Grove Village, IL 60009: Free information ❖ Acrylic paints and other art supplies. 800–468–2897; 708–766–8888 (in IL).

Foster Manufacturing Company, 414 N. 13th St., Philadelphia, PA 19108: Free catalog ❖ Equipment and storage cabinets for graphic artists. 800–523–4855; 215–625–0500 (in PA).

A.I. Friedman Art Supplies, 44 W. 18th St., New York, NY 10011: Catalog $5 ❖ Art supplies. 212–243–9000.

Frisk Products USA Inc., 5240 Snapfinger Park Dr., Decatur, GA 30035: Free information ❖ Art supplies. 404–593–0031.

Gamblin, P.O. Box 625, Portland, OR 97207: Free brochure ❖ Oil paints, oil painting mediums, and etching inks. 503–228–9763.

Gill Mechanical Company, P.O. Box 7247, Eugene, OR 97401: Free information ❖ Tube wringers. 503–686–1606.

Gold Leaf & Metallic Powders, 74 Trinity Pl., Ste. 1807, New York, NY 10006: Free information ❖ Genuine and composition leaf in rolls, sheets, and books, and other supplies and tools. 800–322–0323; 212–267–4900 (in NY).

Graphic Chemical & Ink Company, P.O. Box 27, Villa Park, IL 60181: Free catalog ❖ Print-making supplies for etching, block prints, lithography, and other reproduction processes. 708–832–6004.

Graphics for Industry Inc., Box 332, Piermont, NY 10968: Free price list ❖ Art supplies. 800–342–5434.

J.L. Hammett Company, Hammett Pl., P.O. Box 9057, Braintree, MA 02184: Free catalog ❖ Art supplies. 800–225–5467; 617–848–1000 (in MA).

Hearlihy & Company, 714 W. Columbia St., Springfield, OH 45504: Free catalog ❖ Art supplies and drafting furniture. 800–622–1000.

Hobby Game Distributors Inc., 3710 W. Tuohy, Skokie, IL 60076: Free information ❖ Art supplies. 800–621–6419.

Hofcraft, P.O. Box 72, Grand Haven, MI 49417: Catalog $4 ❖ How-to art books, brushes, dyes, paints, and handcrafted wood items. 800–828–0359.

HK Holbein Inc., Box 555, Williston, VT 05495: Catalog $5 ❖ Art supplies.

Christian J. Hummul Company, 11001 York Rd., Hunt Valley, MD 21030: Free catalog ❖ Carving tools, art supplies, and how-to-books. 800–762–0235.

International Distribution, 434 DeAnza St., San Carlos, CA 94070: Free catalog ❖ Instant multi-color printers and supplies. 800–392–7476.

The Italian Art Store, 84 Maple Ave., Morristown, NJ 07960: Free catalog ❖ Art supplies.

Jerry's Artarama Inc., P.O. Box 1105, New Hyde Park, NY 11040: Catalog $2.50 ❖ Art supplies. 800–221–2323.

Kaufman Supply, Rt. 1, Centertown, MO 65023: Free catalog ❖ Supplies for sign painters. 314–893–2124.

Krylon, 31500 Solon Rd., Solon, OH 44139: Free information ❖ Textured paints that make wood, metal, plastic, ceramic, and painted surfaces look like stone. 800–247–3270.

Loew-Cornell Inc., 563 Chestnut Ave., Teaneck, NJ 07666: Free brochure ❖ Brushes for all mediums and surfaces.

Maggie's Inc., 1053 Carlisle St., Hanover, PA 17331: Catalog $3 ❖ Art, tole decorating, craft, and needlework supplies and books.

Marx Brush Manufacturing Company Inc., 130 Beckwith Ave., Paterson, NJ 07503: Catalog $2 ❖ Brushes. 800–654–6279.

Medea Airbrush, P.O. Box 14397, Portland, OR 97214: Free information ❖ Airbrush textile colors.

Michael's Artist Supplies, 314 Sutter St., San Francisco, CA 94108: Catalog $3 ❖ Equipment for graphic artists. 415–421–1576.

Multimedia Artboard, 15727 NE 61st Ct., Redmond, WA 98052: Free information ❖ Archival artboard for all mediums. 800–701–ART1; 206–881–5304 (in WA).

The Napa Valley Art Store, 1041 Lincoln Ave., Napa, CA 94558: Free catalog ❖ Art supplies. 800–648–6696.

Nasco, 901 Janesville Ave., Fort Atkinson, WI 53538: Free catalog ❖ Paints, brushes, airbrushes, pastels and crayons, drawing and drafting equipment, and other craft supplies. 800–558–9595.

Naz-Dar Company, 1087 Branch St., Chicago, IL 60622: Free catalog ❖ Graphic art and silk-screening equipment. 312–943–8338.

New York Central Art Supply Company, 62 3rd Ave., New York, NY 10003: Free information ❖ Art supplies.

Nova Color, 5894 Blackwelder St., Culver City, CA 90232: Free price list ❖ Pearls, metallics, and other acrylic paints. 213–870–6000.

OAS Art Supplies, P.O. Box 6596, Huntington Beach, CA 92615: Free information ❖ Brushes, rice paper, ink, Chinese colors, books, and other supplies for Chinese brush painting. 800–969–4471.

Paasche Airbrush Company, 7440 W. Lawrence Ave., Harwood Heights, IL 60656: Free information ❖ Airbrushing and spraying equipment. 708–867–9191.

Pearl Paint, 308 Canal St., New York, NY 10013: Catalog $1 ❖ Art supplies. 800–221–6845; 212–431–7932 (in NY).

Plaid Enterprises, P.O. Box 7600, Norcross, GA 30091: Free information ❖ Acrylic paints and other art supplies. 404–923–8200.

Professional's Source Inc., 14707 SE Rive Rd., Milwaukee, OR 97267: Free information ❖ Airbrushes and supplies. 503–629–4865.

Pyramid of Urbana, 2107 N. High Cross Rd., Urbana, IL 61801: Catalog $5 ❖ Art and craft supplies, and office and school equipment. 217–328–3099.

Salis International Inc., 4093 N. 28th Way, Hollywood, FL 33020: Free information ❖ Airbrush acrylic and fluorescent colors. 800–843–8293; 305–921–6971 (in FL).

Sargent Art Inc., 100 E. Diamond Ave., Hazleton, PA 18201: Free information ❖ Crayons, powdered tempera, liquid tempera, water colors, and finger paints. 717–454–3596.

Savoir-Faire, P.O. Box 2021, Sausalito, CA 94966: Catalog $1 ❖ Handcrafted brushes.

Heinz Scharff Brushes, P.O. Box 746, Fayetteville, GA 30214: Free catalog ❖ Brushes for tole, chinaware, and decorative painting. 404–461–2200.

Sepp Leaf Products Inc., 381 Park Ave. South, New York, NY 10016: Free information ❖ Gold and palladium leaf, rolled gold, tools, and kits. 212–683–2840.

Daniel Smith Art Supplies Inc., 4150 1st Ave. South, Seattle, WA 98134: Free catalog ❖ Art and framing supplies, books, studio equipment, and furniture. 800–426–6740.

M. Swift & Sons Inc., 10 Love Ln., Hartford, CT 06141: Free information ❖ Silver, palladium, aluminum, and composite gold leaf for decorating and restoring art and other surfaces. 800–628–0380.

Symphony Fine Art Instruments, 130 Beckwith Ave., Paterson, NJ 07503: Free catalog ❖ Brushes for artists, muralists, sign painters, and crafters.

Technical Papers Corporation, P.O. Box 546, Dedham, MA 02027: Free catalog ❖ Sheets and rolls of handmade rice paper in prints, solid colors, and multi-colors. 617–461–1111.

Testrite Instrument Company Inc., 133 Monroe St., Newark, NJ 07105: Free catalog ❖ Lightweight aluminum and chrome steel easels, portable light boxes, lighting and photography equipment, and opaque projectors. 201–589–6767.

Texas Art Supply Company, 2001 Montrose Blvd., Houston, TX 77006: Catalog $5 ❖ Furniture for the artist. 800–888–9278.

Thayer & Chandler, 28835 N. Herky Dr., Lake Bluff, IL 60044: Free brochure ❖ Air brushes. 800–548–9307; 708–816–1611 (in IL).

Think Ink, 7526 Olympic View Dr., Edmonds, WA 98026: Free information ❖ Easy-to-use multiple color machine for printing greeting cards, stationery, ribbons, and T-shirts. 800–778–1935; 206–778–1935 (in WA).

Tole Americana Inc., 5750 NE Hassalo, Portland, OR 97213: Free information ❖ Brushes, oils, acrylics, fabric paints, sealers, mediums, varnishes, tole supplies, unfinished wood products, and decorative art and tole painting how-to books. 800–547–8854; 800–452–8663 (in OR).

Tulip, 24 Prime Pkwy., Netick, MA 01760: Free information ❖ Paints and transfer art books.

United Art Supply Company, Box 9219, Fort Wayne, IN 46899: Free catalog ❖ Art supplies. 800–322–3247.

Utrecht Art & Drafting Supply, 33 35th St., Brooklyn, NY 11232: Free catalog ❖ Art, sculpture, and print-making supplies. 718–768–2525.

Visual Systems Company Inc., 1596 Rockville Pike, Rockville, MD 20852: Free catalog ❖ Art and drawing supplies. 800–368–2803; 301–770–0500 (in MD).

Wild West Supply, P.O. Box 5678, Borgel, TX 79008: Free price list ❖ Canvasses, art supplies, and picture frames. 806–274–4455.

Windsor & Newton, 1100 Constitution, Piscataway, NJ 08855: Free catalog ❖ Paints, brushes, and other supplies.

Modeling & Casting Supplies

American Art Clay Company Inc., 4717 W. 16th St., Indianapolis, IN 46222: Free catalog ❖ Modeling clay, self-hardening clay, paper mache, casting compounds, mold-making materials, acrylics, fabric dyes, fillers and patching compounds, wood stains, and metallic finishes. 800–374–1600; 317–244–6871 (in IN).

Chaselle, 9645 Gerwig Ln., Columbia, MD 21046: Catalog $4 ❖ Books, ceramic molds and kilns, sculpture equipment, and art, silk-screen painting, and other craft supplies. 800–242–7355.

The Clay Factory of Escondido, P.O. Box 460598, Escondido, CA 92046: Free information ❖ Modeling materials. 619–741–3242.

Concrete Machinery Company, P.O. Box H99, Hickory, NC 28603: Information $10 ❖ Supplies and aluminum molds for making ornamental concrete items. 704–322–7710.

Craft Time Catalog, 211 S. State College Blvd., Ste. 341, Anaheim, CA 92806: Catalog $2 ❖ Ready-to-paint figurines. 714–671–1639.

Creative Paperclay Company, 1800 S. Robertson Blvd., Ste. 907, Los Angeles, CA 90035: Free information ❖ Soft, fine-textured modeling material that air dries light-weight. 310–839–0466.

DMK Enterprises, 333 Orchard Ave., Hillside, IL 60162: Catalog $3 (refundable) ❖ Molds, ready-to-paint figurines, and kits.

Edelcrafts, 4271 N. 1st St., San Jose, CA 95134: Catalog $4 ❖ Plastercraft kits.

Margaret's Place, P.O. Box 3, Perris, CA 92572: Information $1.50 ❖ Dough art, tool kits, and books.

Frank Mittermeir Inc., 3577 E. Tremont Ave., P.O Box 2, Bronx, NY 10465: Free information ❖ Tools for sculptors, ceramists, potters, woodcarvers, and engravers. 212–828–3843.

Montoya/MAS International Inc., 435 Southern Blvd., West Palm Beach, FL 33405: Catalog $3 ❖ Bronze casting (lost wax process), mold-making, polishing and stone finishing, and alabaster, steatite, soapstone, marble, and onyx carving stones. 800–682–8665.

Nasco, 901 Janesville Ave., Fort Atkinson, WI 53538: Free catalog ❖ Modeling materials, non-firing and firing clays, tools, molds, and other craft supplies. 800–558–9595.

Plycrete Mold Company Inc., 121 Ames St., Elk Rapids, MI 49629: Catalog $2 ❖ Fiberglass molds and supplies for casting with concrete. 616–264–8093.

Polyform Products Company, P.O. Box 2119, Schiller Park, IL 60176: Free information ❖ Shatter- and chip-proof ceramic-like sculpting compound, paints, glazes, tools, and modeling sets. 708–678–4836.

Polytek Development Corporation, P.O. Box 384, Lebanon, NJ 08833: Free catalog ❖ Mold rubbers, resins, and accessories. 908–534–5990.

Sculpture House, 38 E. 30th St., New York, NY 10016: Catalog $2 ❖ Sculpting tools, materials, books, and wax, clay, wood, stone, and plaster modeling mediums. 212–679–7474.

Smooth-On, 1000 Valley Rd., Gillette, NJ 07933: Free information ❖ Liquid plastic compounds. 800–766–6841; 908–647–5800 (in NJ).

Terrific Little Crafts, 4140 Oceanside Blvd., Oceanside, CA 92056: Catalog $1 ❖ Jewelry findings and paper clay, quilling, and other craft supplies.

ARTHRITIS AIDS

Danmar Products Inc., 221 Jackson Industrial Dr., Ann Arbor, MI 48103: Free brochure ❖ Easy-to-hold utensil handles and other arthritis aids. 800–783–1998; 313–761–1990 (in MI).

Fashion Ease, Division M & M Health Care, 1541 60th St., Brooklyn, NY 11219: Free catalog ❖ Clothing with velcro closures, wheelchair attachments, and incontinence supplies. 800–221–8929; 718–871–8188 (in NY).

Miles Kimball Company, 41 W. 8th Ave., Oshkosh, WI 54906: Free catalog ❖ Assistive devices and aids for people with arthritis and other physical disabilities. 800–546–2255.

Prime Time Fashions, P.O. Box 10510, Rochester, NY 14610: Free catalog ❖ Clothing for older women with arthritis. Some styles feature velcro fasteners.

ARTWORK
Posters, Paintings & Prints

Alcala Gallery, 950 Silverado St., La Jolla, CA 92037: Free catalog ❖ Fine art. 619–454–6610.

American Arts & Graphics Inc., P.O. Box 888, Mukilteo, WA 98275: Catalog $1 ❖ All-star pinup, sports, art, photo, and fun posters for kids, and humorous, animal, art, photo, and scenic calendars. 800–524–3900.

American Print Gallery, P.O. Box 4477, Gettysburg, PA 17325: Information $1 ❖ Military art prints and note cards. 800–448–1863.

Animation Celection, 1002 Prospect St., La Jolla, CA 92037: Free catalog ❖ Animation art collectibles. 800–223–5328.

Animators, 65 Pondfield Rd., Bronxville, NY 10708: Free catalog ❖ Production cels, drawings, backgrounds, and limited edition cartoon art. 800–972–6688.

Around the Corner Art, 5135 Pheasant Ridge Rd., Fairfax, VA 22030: Catalog $5 ❖ American, European, Victorian, and traditional posters, prints, and canvas art replicas. 703–631–3227.

Artrock Posters, 1153 Mission St., San Francisco, CA 94103: Catalog $3 ❖ Original rock concert posters.

Barnstable Originals, 50 Harden Ave., Camden, ME 04843: Free information with long SASE ❖ Original New England scenes, animal and flower art, and other renditions. 207–236–8162.

Best Rockart Gallery, 2801 Leavenworth St., San Francisco, CA 94133: Free information ❖ Comics, original rock art, toys, rock posters, and handbills. 800–775–1966.

Breedlove Enterprises, P.O. Box 436, Zoar, OH 44697: Free information ❖ Limited edition, numbered, and signed Civil War lithographs. 800–221–1863.

Brush Strokes, 19312 Haviland Dr., South Bend, IN 46637: Brochure $3 ❖ Signed and numbered, limited editions of reproduction prints of oil paintings, with optional framing. 219–277–5414.

Buchanan Aviation Art, 56 S. Broad St., Milford, CT 06460: Free catalog ❖ Aviation art. 800–659–4174; 203–876–0560 (in CT).

Buck Hill Associates, Box 501, North Creek, NY 12857: Free catalog ❖ Reproduction posters, prints, and handbills. 518–251–2349.

CA Animation Galleries, 69 Middle Neck Rd., Great Neck, NY 11021: Catalog $3 ❖ Vintage and modern animation art. 800–541–2278; 516–487–3556 (in NY).

Cartoon Art Unlimited, 379 Belmont Ave., Haledon, NJ 07508: Free catalog ❖ Animation art. 800–966–TOON; 201–942–1003 (in NJ).

Cel-ebration, P.O. Box 123, Little Silver, NJ 07739: Free catalog ❖ Animation art. 908–842–8489.

Cherokee National Museum Gift Shop, P.O. Box 515, TSA-LA-GI, Tahlequah, OK 74464: Free price list with long SASE ❖ Original paintings, prints, sculptures, and Native American crafts and art. 918–456–6007.

Cheshire Fine Art Inc., 265 Sorghum Mill Dr., Cheshire, CT 06410: Free information ❖ Fine art. 203–272–0114.

Cincinnati Art Museum, Eden Park, Cincinnati, OH 45202: Free catalog ❖ Reproductions of posters, postcards, and other museum collectibles. 513–721–5204.

The Cooley Gallery, 25 Lyme St., P.O. Box 447, Old Lyme, CT 06371: Free price list ❖ Fine art. 203–434–8807.

Covington Fine Arts Gallery, 4951 E. Grant Rd., Tucson, AZ 85712: Free catalog ❖ 19th- and 20th-century American art. 602–326–6111.

Creative Brush Studio, 9257 Lee Ave., Ste. 205, Manassas, VA 22110: Free information ❖ Oil paintings and limited edition prints of people, pets, and wildlife. 703–335– 8005.

The Cricket Gallery, 5525 Glen Errol Rd., Atlanta, GA 30327: Free catalog ❖ Vintage and contemporary animation cels, drawings, and Disney backgrounds. 800–289–2357.

Dance Mart, Box 994, Teaneck, NJ 07666: Free catalog with long SASE ❖ Books, prints, music, autographs, and other dance collectibles. 201–833–4176.

The Decoy, P.O. Box 3652, Carmel, CA 93921: Free brochure ❖ Hand-carved wood birds, antique decoys, limited edition prints, and original art. 800–332–6988.

DeRus Fine Art, 9100 Artesia Blvd., Bellflower, CA 90706: Free list ❖ 19th- and early 20th-century fine art. 310–920–1312.

Editions Limited Inc., 625 2nd St., Ste. 400, San Francisco, CA 94107: Free catalog ❖ Fine art posters and prints. 800–228–0928.

Film Prints Inc., 3101 N. Rack Rd., Ste. 120, Wichita, KS 67226: Free information with long SASE ❖ Limited edition film posters. 316–636–5340.

Filmart Galleries, P.O. Box 128, Old Bethpage, NY 11804: Free catalog ❖ Vintage and contemporary animation art. 516–935–8493.

Wally Findlay Gallery, 814 N. Michigan Ave., Chicago, IL 60602: Free information ❖ Original paintings. 312–649–1500.

Fine Art Impressions, 4002 Lynn Ave., Minneapolis, MN 55416: Free catalog ❖ Framed and unframed impressionist art reproductions.

Folio One, 635 C St., Ste. 403, San Diego, CA 92101: Free catalog ❖ Signed, limited edition lithographs by theatrical designers. 800–597–2710.

Fortress Editions, 326 W. Kalamazoo Ave., Ste. 303, Kalamazoo, MI 49007: Free information ❖ Limited edition aviation art prints and original oil paintings. 800–682–4781; 616–345–6265 (in MI).

Framing Fox Art Gallery, P.O. Box 679, Lebanon, NJ 08833: Free information with long SASE ❖ Civil War prints. 800–237–6077.

Gallerie Robin, 345 Harpeth Ridge Rd., Nashville, TN 37221: Free information ❖ Limited edition art prints. 800–635–8279.

Gallery Graphics Inc., 227 Main St., P.O. Box 502, Noel, MO 64854: Catalog $5 (refundable) ❖ Antique prints, note and Christmas cards, and other art reproductions. 417–475–6116.

Gallery Lainzberg, 200 Guaranty Bldg., Cedar Rapids, IA 52401: Catalog $4.95 ❖ Limited edition, classic, and modern production cels, serigraphs, and other animation art from most major studios. 800–678–4608.

Gallery 247, 814 Merrick Rd., Baldwin, NY 11510: Free brochure ❖ Collectible plates and prints. 516–868–4800.

Gifted Images Gallery, P.O. Box 34, Baldwin, NY 11510: Free catalog ❖ Animation art. 800–726–6708; 516–536–6886 (in NY).

Godel & Company Fine Art Inc., 969 Madison Ave., New York, NY 10021: Catalog $10 ❖ Folk art, Hudson River School art, marine scenes, American impressionism, still lifes, and other art. 212–288–7272.

Graphic Encountering Inc., 15236 Burbank Blvd., Ste. 201, Sherman Oaks, CA 91411: Free information ❖ Hand-cast paper sculptures, hand-painted acrylics, and mixed media serigraphs. 800–472–7445; 818–988–9623 (in CA).

The Greenwich Workshop Inc., 30 Liondeman Dr., Trumbull, CT 06611: Free information ❖ Fantasy, wilderness, western, exotic lands, aviation themes. and other limited edition prints. 800–243–4246; 203–371–6568 (in CT).

Grunewald Folk Art, P.O. Box 721, Wauconda, IL 60084: Catalog $2 ❖ Signed and numbered, limited edition lithographs of animals and people in rural American settings. 708–526–1417.

Guarisco Gallery, 2828 Pennsylvania Ave. NW, Washington, DC 20007: Catalog $10 ❖ European, British, and American 19th-century paintings. 202–333–8533.

Harvest Gallery Inc., 1527 Beverly Dr., Wichita Falls, TX 76309: Free brochure ❖ Limited edition prints. 800–545–8231.

Heirloom Editions, Box 520–B, Rt. 4, Carthage, MO 64836: Catalog $4 ❖ Lithographs, greeting cards, stickers, miniatures, stationery, framed prints, and other turn-of-the-century art and paper collectibles. 800–725–0725.

Heritage Art, 125 Kemp Ln., P.O. Box 1587, Easton, MD 21601: Free information ❖ Limited edition, signed prints and boxed note card assortments. 800–727–6006.

Homespun Country, 10132 N. Memorial Pkwy., Huntsville, AL 35810: Brochure $3 ❖ Framed folk art prints. 205–859–1460.

F.B. Horowitz Fine Art Ltd., 830 Edgemoor Dr., Hopkins, MN 55305: Free list ❖ Fine art. 612–935–2120.

I.P.C.'s Animation Company, 19806 N. 4th St., Ste. 63, Phoenix, AZ 85024: Free catalog ❖ Limited edition Disney, Warner Brothers, Hanna-Barbera, and other production art and sericels. 602–581–0125.

Incredible Arts, P.O. Box 342, Carmel, CA 93921: Catalog $4 ❖ Reprints of 19th-century lithographs and drawings. 408–372–0873.

Kennedy Galleries, 40 W. 57th St., New York, NY 10019: Catalog $5 ❖ Prints and other art. 212–541–9600.

Leslie Levy Fine Art, 7135 Main St., Scottsdale, AZ 85262: Free information ❖ Contemporary American paintings, drawings, and sculptures. 800–283–ARTS; 602–947–2925 (in AZ).

Liros Gallery Inc., P.O. Box 946, Blue Hill, ME 04614: Free catalog ❖ Art prints and paintings. 207–374–5370; 800–287–5370 (in ME).

Lublin Graphics, 124 W. Putnam, Greenwich, CT 06830: Catalog $2 ❖ Original graphics by contemporary American and European artists. 800–243–4004; 203–622–8777 (in CT).

The Masters' Collection, Drawer D-701, Somersville, CT 06072: Catalog $5 ❖ Canvas replicas of art masterpieces. 800–222–6827.

The Masters Gallery, Box 5601, Middletown, CA 95461: Catalog $7.50 (refundable) ❖ Original art in handcrafted period frames. 800–642–5537.

Nedra Matteucci's Fenn Galleries, 1075 Paseo de Peralta, Santa Fe, NM 87501: Free information ❖ Historical American art and contemporary Southwestern paintings and sculpture. 505–982–4631.

Meehan Military Posters, P.O. Box 477, New York, NY 10028: Catalog $10 ❖ Original, authentic World War I and II posters. 212–734–5683.

Merril Chase Art Galleries, 835 N. Michigan Ave., Chicago, IL 60602: Free catalog ❖ Prints, paintings, and other 19th-century art.

Metropolitan Museum of Art, 255 Gracie Station, New York, NY 10028: Catalog $1 ❖ Porcelain, ceramics and glass, scarves, shawls, neckties, books, jewelry, and original lithographs, prints, and graphics from around the world. 800–468–7386.

The Moss Portfolio, 2878 Hartland Rd., Falls Church, VA 22043: Catalog $10 ❖ Collectible prints. 703–849–0845.

Motorhead, 1300 SW Campus Dr., Federal Way, WA 98023: Catalog $4 ❖ Automotive art prints and collectibles. Also scale model cars and kits. 800–859–0164.

C.W. Mundy Studio/Gallery, 8609 Manderley Dr., Indianapolis, IN 46240: Free information ❖ American impressionistic paintings. 317–848–1330.

Museum Editions of New York Ltd., 12 Harrison St., 3rd Floor, New York, NY 10013: Catalog $5 ❖ Reproductions of contemporary to modern posters. 212–431–1913.

Mystic Seaport Museum Stores, Greemanville Ave., Mystic, CT 06355: Free catalog ❖ Marine paintings and sculptures. 800–248–1066.

Jeannie Nash, Artist, 974 Marlin Dr., Jupiter, FL 33458: Free information ❖ Watercolors, embossings, and limited edition prints. 407–575–2030.

National Archives & Records Administration, National Archives Books, Washington, DC 20408: Free brochure ❖ Historic patriotic posters and postcards. 202–523–3164.

NDP, Nature Discovery Catalog, P.O. Box 200, Hull, MA 02045: Free catalog ❖ Wildlife art prints. 800–777–4703.

The Old Print Gallery, 1220 31st St. NW, Washington, DC 20007: Catalog $3 ❖ Prints and maps from the 18th- and 19th-century. 202–965–1818.

Original Print Collectors Group Ltd., 88 Astor Sq., Rhinebeck, NY 12572: Free catalog ❖ Numbered, signed, and framed original limited-edition prints, serigraphs, etchings, and lithographs. 800–556–6200.

Poster Originals, 330 Hudson St., New York, NY 10021: Catalog $10 ❖ Art posters and billboards, with optional framing. 212–861–0422.

Posters of Santa Fe, 111 E. Palace Ave., Santa Fe, NM 87501: Free catalog ❖ Art posters. 800–827–6745.

Steven S. Raab, 2033 Walnut St., Philadelphia, PA 19103: Free catalog ❖ Autographs, signed books and photos, old newspapers, World War I posters, and other historic memorabilia. 215–446–6193.

Red Fox Fine Art, 7 N. Liberty St., P.O. Box 385, Middleburg, VA 22117: Free catalog ❖ 19th-century animal and sports paintings and sculptures. 703–687–5780.

Red Lancer, P.O. Box 8056, Mesa, AZ 85214: Catalog $6 ❖ Original 19th-century military art, rare books, Victorian campaign medals and helmets, toy soldiers, and other collectibles. 602–964–9667.

Alexander Reeves Fine Art,$IAlexander Reeves Fine Art [Reeves] P.O. Box 17936, Richmond, VA 23226: Free information ❖ 19th- and early 20th-century American paintings. 804–355–7298.

Ronin Gallery, 605 Madison Ave., New York, NY 10022: Catalog $6 ❖ Japanese woodblock prints. 212–688–0188.

Rosenbaum Fine Art, 5181 NE 12th Ave., Fort Lauderdale, FL 33334: Free information ❖ Limited edition paintings, sculptures, and water colors. 800–344–2787; 305–772–1386 (in FL).

Salzer's, 5801 Valentine Rd., Ventura, CA 93003: Free information ❖ Vintage concert posters.

Scheele Fine Arts, P.O. Box 18869, Cleveland Heights, OH 44118: Free information ❖ Original paintings and drawings of prehistoric and contemporary animals. 216–421–0600.

Connie Seaborn Studio, P.O. Box 23795, Oklahoma City, OK 73132: Free information with long SASE ❖ Original paintings, drawings, and hand-pulled prints. 405–728–3903.

Philip Sears Disney Collectibles, 1457 Avon Terr., Los Angeles, CA 90026: Free catalog ❖ Walt Disney autographs, animation art, and other memorabilia. 213–666–3740.

Sentimental Times Inc., 234 5th Ave., New York, NY 10001: Catalog $1 (refundable) ❖ Full-color enlarged reproductions of rare 1893 to 1918 American postcards.

Silver Image Gallery, 92 S. Washington St., Seattle, WA 98104: Catalog $4 (refundable) ❖ Posters made with different mediums, used alone or in combination with graphic design, offset lithography, photography, or typography. 206–623–8119.

Starland Collector's Gallery, P.O. Box 622, Los Olivos, CA 93441: Catalog $2.50 ❖ Sports cards, movie posters, original comic art, and hard-to-find movies. 805–686–5122.

Taggart Galleries, 3233 P St. NW, Washington, DC 20007: Free information ❖ American paintings from the 19th- and 20th-century and contemporary realism art. 202–298–7676.

Vestal Press Ltd., P.O. Box 97, Vestal, NY 13851: Catalog $2 ❖ Posters, books, and recordings that relate to museum antiquities and the theater. Includes carrousels, music boxes, player pianos and other music machines, antique radios and phonographs, theater pipe and reed organs, early movie theater and film stars, and radio personalities. 607–797–4872.

Vintage Animation, 1404 3rd Street Promenade, Santa Monica, CA 90404: Free information ❖ Original animation art, from the 1940s, 1950s, and 1960s. 310–393–8666.

Vladimir Arts U.S.A. Inc., 5401 Portage Rd., Kalamazoo, MI 49002: Free information ❖ Original oils, acrylics, watercolors, and graphics.

Sidney Wolff Art, P.O. Box 21, Perry, NY 14530: Free list ❖ Paintings, drawings, and prints. 716–237–3092.

Sculptures & Carvings

Kurt S. Adler Inc., 1107 Broadway, New York, NY 10010: Free information ❖ Woodcarvings. 800–243–9627; 212–924–0900 (in NY).

Arrow Gems & Minerals Inc., P.O. Box 9068, Phoenix, AZ 85068: Free catalog ❖ Pewter figurines. 602–997–6373.

Ballard Designs, 1670 DeFoor Ave. NW, Atlanta, GA 30318: Catalog $3 ❖ Sculptured castings, furniture, lamps, decor and fireplace accessories, garden and landscaping items, frames, and pictures. 404–351–5099.

Henry Bonnard Bronze Company, 4305 S. Hwy. 17–92, Casselberry, FL 32707: Free catalog ❖ Bronze statuary with optional marble bases. 800–521–3179; 407–339–9103 (in FL).

Boone Trading Company, 562 Coyote Rd., Brinnon, WA 98320: Catalog $3 ❖ Oriental and Eskimo carvings. 206–796–4330.

Heirlooms: Bridal Collector's Hearts of Holly, P.O. Box 105, Amherst, NH 03031: Free information with long SASE ❖ Vintage figurines and other holiday gifts. 603–673–1885.

Cherokee National Museum Gift Shop, P.O. Box 515, TSA-LA-GI, Tahlequah, OK 74464: Free price list with long SASE ❖ Original paintings, prints, sculptures, baskets, and other Native American arts and crafts. 918–456–6007.

Churchills, Twelve Oaks Mall, Novi, MI 48377: Free information ❖ Art collectibles and plates. 800–388–1141.

Duncan Royale, 1141 S. Acacia Ave., Fullerton, CA 92631: Free information ❖ Sculptured figurines. 800–366–4646.

Eleganza Ltd., Magnolia Village, 3217 W. Smith, Seattle, WA 98199: Catalog $6 ❖ Sculptures made from oxolyte that resembles Carrara marble. 206–283–0609.

Enesco Corporation, 1 Enesco Plaza, Elk Grove Village, IL 60007: Free information and list of retailers ❖ Figurines, sculptures, and ornaments. 708–640–3566.

European Imports & Gifts, 7900 N. Milwaukee Ave., Niles, IL 60648: Free information ❖ Art, porcelains, Christmas ornaments, and pewter. 708–967–5253.

Excalibur Bronze Sculpture Foundry, 85 Adams St., Brooklyn, NY 11201: Catalog $10 (refundable) ❖ Bronze sculptures. 718–522–3330.

FMI Bronzes, 401 E. Cypress, Visalia, CA 93277: Free catalog ❖ Fine art bronze sculptures. 800–777–8126.

Bill Glass Studio, Star Route South, Box 39B, Locust Grove, OK 74352: Free

information with long SASE ❖ Original stone sculptures, carvings, bronzes, and pottery. 918–479–8884.

Goebel Inc., Goebel Plaza, P.O. Box 10, Pennington, NJ 08534: Free information ❖ Miniature sculptures of characters from Walt Disney's animated film classics. 800–366–4632.

Kelley Haney Art Gallery, P.O. Box 103, Seminole, OK 74868: Free brochure with long SASE ❖ Original Native American paintings, sculptures, jewelry, baskets, and pottery. 405–382–3915.

Heath Studio, 224 Heatherton Way, Winston-Salem, NC 27104: Free information ❖ Bird carvings. 910–768–3049.

The Huntington Bronze Collection, 401 E. Cypress, Visalia, CA 93277: Free catalog ❖ Art bronze sculpture. 800–777–8126.

Imagine That, 5903 Queens Chapel, Hyattsville, MD 20782: Free information ❖ Sculptures, figurines, and other art objects. 800–223–5903.

Imperial Manufacturing, 14502 Resort Ln., Lakewood, WI 54138: Free catalog ❖ Pewter figurines. 715–276–7865.

Judaic Folk Art, Lois Kramer, 8101 Timber Valley Ct., Dunn Loring, VA 22027: Free brochure ❖ Judaic folk art. 703–560–2914.

Last Eras Figurines, 1511 W. Howard St., Chicago, IL 60626: Free information ❖ Vintage figurines. 312–764–7400.

Leslie Levy Fine Art, 7142 Main St., Scottsdale, AZ 85262: Free information ❖ Contemporary American paintings, drawings, and sculptures. 800–283–ARTS; 602–947–2925 (in AZ).

Munyon & Sons, 1119 Waverly Hills Dr., Thousand Oaks, CA 91360: Free catalog ❖ Reproductions of Remington bronzes. 800–289–2850.

Mystic Seaport Museum Stores, 39 Greemanville Ave., Mystic, CT 06355: Free catalog ❖ Marine paintings and sculptures. 800–248–1066.

Bob Parker's Sports Collectibles, 500 Adamas Ln., Apt 18–F, North Brunswick, NJ 08902: Free information ❖ Sports statuary and plates. 800–543–7794.

Red Fox Fine Art, 7 N. Liberty St., P.O. Box 385, Middleburg, VA 22117: Free catalog ❖ 19th-century animal and sports paintings and sculptures. 703–687–5780.

Rostand Fine Jewelers, 8349 Foothill Blvd., Sunland, CA 91040: Free information ❖ Lladro porcelain. 800–222–9208; 818–352–7814 (in CA).

Shorebird Decoys Inc., 124 Forest Ave., Hudson, MA 01749: Catalog $2 ❖ Authentic reproductions of works by early carvers. 508–562–7841.

SUKUSA Company, 369 S. Doheny Dr., Ste. 186, Beverly Hills, CA 90211: Free list ❖ Handcrafted tin receptacles and ornaments, wood items, papier mache, and miscellaneous media. 310–785–7957.

Treasure Chest Art Collectibles, 1221 E. Powell, Gresham, OR 97030: Free information ❖ Art collectibles. 800–228–1297; 503–667–2999 (in OR).

Wolf Chief Graphics, 907 C Ave. NW, Great Falls, MT 59404: Free price list with long SASE ❖ Original watercolor paintings, alabaster and bronze sculptures, hand pulled serigraphs, bone chokers, and other art. 406–452–4449.

Wood Carvings by Ted Nichols, P.O. Box 1050, Salisbury, MD 21802: Catalog $1 ❖ Handcarved and painted woodcarvings. 301–546–9522.

ASTRONOMY
Astrophotography

Electrim Corporation, P.O. Box 2074, Princeton, NJ 08543: Free information ❖ Electronic imaging equipment. 609–683–5546.

Santa Anita Camera & Optical Company, 1031 S. Baldwin Ave., Arcadia, CA 91007: Free catalog ❖ Astrophotography equipment and binoculars. 818–447–1854.

SIG Astronomical Instruments, Santa Barbara Instrument Group, 1482 E. Valley Rd., Santa Barbara, CA 93108: Free catalog ❖ Color imaging equipment. 805–969–1851.

Sky Scientific, 28578 Hwy. 18, P.O. Box 184, Skyforest, CA 92385: Catalog $1 ❖ Astrophotography equipment and telescopes. 909–337–3440.

Spectra Astronomy, 6631 Wilbur Ave., Ste. 30, Reseda, CA 91335: Free catalog ❖ Astrophotography and other telescopes and equipment for beginning and advanced astronomers. 800–735–1352.

Observatories & Planetariums

Ace Dome, 3186 Juanita, Las Vegas, NV 89102: Free brochure ❖ Ready-to-use and easy-to-assemble portable domes. 702–873–5790.

Ash Manufacturing Company Inc., Box 312, Plainfield, IL 60544: Free catalog ❖ Mechanical- and electrical-operated observatory domes from 10 to 36 feet in diameter. 815–436–9403.

Learning Technologies Inc., 59 Walden St., Cambridge, MA 02140: Free catalog ❖ Portable planetarium system. 800–537–8703.

Minolta, 101 Williams Dr., Ramsey, NJ 07446: Free brochure ❖ Planetariums. 201–825–4000.

Observa-Dome Laboratories Inc., 371 Commerce Park Dr., Jackson, MS 39213: Free information ❖ Domes for amateur astronomers, professional tracking, research, communications, and defense systems. 800–647–5364; 601–982–3333 (in MS).

Stewart Research Enterprises, 1658 Belvoir Dr., Los Altos, CA 94022: Free information ❖ Lightweight fiberglass observatory domes. 415–941–6699.

Technical Innovations Inc., 22500 Old Hundred Rd., Barnesville, MD 20838: Free brochure ❖ Easy-to-assemble observatories for amateur astronomers. 301–972–8040.

Radio Astronomy

Bob's Electronic Service, 7605 Deland Ave., Fort Pierce, FL 34951: Catalog $3 ❖ Radio astronomy equipment. 407–464–2118.

Noctilume, P.O. Box 7800, Fox Hills, CA 90233: Free brochure ❖ Radio astronomy equipment.

Software

Andromeda Software Inc., P.O. Box 605–G, Amherst, NY 14226: Free catalog ❖ Astronomy software for IBM compatibles. 716–6691–4510.

ARC Software, P.O. Box 1955S, Loveland, CO 80539: Free information ❖ Astronomy simulation software for IBM compatibles. 303–667–1168.

The Arizona Database Project Inc., P.O. Box 86909, Phoenix, AZ 85080: Free information ❖ Astronomy software. 602–992–2813.

Astronomical Research Network, 206 Bellwood Ave., Maplewood, MN 55117: Free information ❖ Astronomy software. 612–488–5178.

Axiom Research, 1304 E. 8th St., Tucson, AZ 85719: Free information ❖ Astronomy software. 602–791–2864.

Carina Software, 830 Williams St., San Leandro, CA 94577: Free information ❖ Astronomy software for Macintosh computers. 510–352–7328.

CEB Metasystems, 1200 Lawrence Dr., Ste. 175, Newbury Park, CA 91320: Free brochure ❖ Astronomy software. 800–232–7830; 805–499–0958 (in CA).

CompuScope, 3463 State St., Ste. 431, Santa Barbara, CA 93105: Free catalog ❖ Astronomy software. 805–687–7879.

E.L.B. Software, 8910 Willow Meadow, Houston, TX 77031: Information $2 ❖ Astronomy software. 713–541–9723.

Etion Software, 1936 Quail Cir., Louisville, CO 80027: Free information ❖ Astronomy software. 303–665–3444.

Lewis-Michaels Engineering, 48 Delemere Blvd., Fairport, NY 14450: Free catalog ❖ Astronomy software and telescope-making supplies. 716–425–3470.

Maxis Software, 2 Theatre Square, Orinda, CA 94563: Free information ❖ Astronomy software. 800–556–2947.

Nova Astronomics, P.O. Box 31013, Halifax, Nova Scotia, Canada B3K 5T9: Free information ❖ Astronomy software. 902–443–5989.

picoScience, 41512 Chadbourne Dr., Fremont, CA 94539: Free information with long SASE ❖ Astronomy software for IBM compatibles. 510–498–1095.

Planet Mac, P.O. Box 186, Stillwater, ME 04489: Catalog $1 ❖ Astronomy software for Macintosh computers.

Science Lab Software, 93 Albemarle Rd., Norwood, MA 02062: Free information ❖ Astronomy software. 617–769–5153.

Software Bisque, 912 12th St., Golden, CO 80401: Free information ❖ Astronomy software. 800–843–7599.

Stellar Software, P.O. Box 10183, Berkeley, CA 94709: Free information ❖ Astronomy software. 510–845–8405.

Virtual Reality Labs Inc., 2341 Ganador Ct., San Luis Obispo, CA 93401: Free catalog ❖ Astronomy software for Macintosh, Amiga, and IBM compatible computers. 800–829–8754; 805–545–8515 (in CA).

Willmann-Bell Inc., P.O. Box 35025, Richmond, VA 23235: Catalog $1 ❖ Astronomy software. 804–320–7016.

Zephyr Services, 1900 Murray Ave., Pittsburgh, PA 15217: Free catalog ❖ Astronomy software for IBM compatible, Apple, and Commodore computers. 412–422–6600.

Telescopes & Accessories

Adorama, 42 W. 18th St., New York, NY 10011: Catalog $3 ❖ Telescopes, telescope-making supplies, photographic equipment, audiovisual aids, mounts, charts and star maps, books, and binoculars. 212–741–0052.

Advance Camera Corporation, 15 W. 46th St., New York, NY 10036: Free information ❖ Telescopes, telescope-making supplies, audiovisual aids, photographic equipment, charts and star maps, and binoculars. 212–944–1410.

Analytical Scientific, 11049 Bandera Rd., San Antonio, TX 78250: Catalog $3 (refundable) ❖ Telescopes. 512–684–7373.

Aries Optics, Rt. 1, Box 143G, Palouse, WA 99161: Catalog $3 ❖ Telescopes. 509–878–1713.

Astro-Tech, 222 W. Main, P.O. Box 2001, Ardmore, OK 73402: Catalog $1 ❖ Telescopes, binoculars, books, electron-optical equipment, science equipment, star maps, and atlases. 405–226–3074.

Astro-Track Engineering, 9811 Brentwood Dr., Santa Ana, CA 92704: Free information ❖ Equatorial mounts that will hold up to 20–inch telescopes. 714–289–0402.

Astro World, 5126 Belair Rd., Baltimore, MD 21206: Free price list with long SASE ❖ Telescopes, telescope-making supplies, audiovisual aids, photographic equipment, charts and star maps, domes, books, binoculars, used equipment, and coating and repair services. 410–483–5100.

Astronomical Enterprise, 5920 Roswell Rd., Atlanta, GA 30328: Free catalog: Free information ❖ Telescopes. 404–843–3838.

Astronomics, 2401 Tee Cir., Ste. 106, Norman, OK 73069: Free information ❖ Astronomy equipment. 405–364–0858.

The Astronomy Shoppe, 15836 N. Cave Creek Rd., Phoenix, AZ 85032: Free information with long SASE ❖ Telescopes,

maps and star charts, and books. 602–971–3170.

AstroSystems Inc., 5348 Ocotillo Ct., Johnstown, CO 80534: Free catalog ❖ Truss tube components. 303–587–5838.

Bausch & Lomb, 9200 Cody, Overland Park, KS 66214: Free information ❖ Telescopes. 800–423–3537.

Berger Brothers Camera Exchange, 209 Broadway, Amityville, NY 11701: Free information ❖ Telescopes, telescope-making supplies, audiovisual aids, photographic equipment, mounts, charts and star maps, books, and binoculars. 800–262–4160.

Black Forest Observatory, 12815 Porcupine Ln., Colorado Springs, CO 80908: Free information with long SASE ❖ Telescopes, binoculars, books, cameras, computers and software, star maps and atlases, and science equipment. 719–495–3828.

Brite Sky, 454 Central Ave., Dover, NH 03820: Free information ❖ Cleaning fluid for telescopes, binoculars, and other lenses. 603–743–4083.

Byers Company, 29001 W. Hwy. 58, Barstow, CA 92311: Information $2 ❖ Telescope drives. 619–256–2377.

California Telescope Company, P.O. Box 1338, Burbank, CA 91507: Catalog $5 ❖ Telescopes, telescope-making supplies, audiovisual aids, photographic equipment, computer software, charts and star maps, books, and binoculars. 818–505–8424.

Celestron International, 2385 Columbia St., Torrance, CA 90503: Catalog $2 ❖ Telescopes. 310–328–9560.

Ceravolo Optical Systems, Box 1427, Ogdensburg, NY 13669: Brochure $2 ❖ Astronomy optical systems. 613–258–4480.

Chicago Optical & Supply Company, Box 1361, Morton Grove, IL 60053: Free catalog ❖ Telescopes, view finders, and photographic equipment. 708–827–4846.

City Camera, 15336 W. Warren, Dearborn, MI 48126: Free information ❖ Telescopes. 800–359–5085.

Cosmic Connection, 32 Ashgrove Blvd., Brandon, Manitoba, Canada R7B 1C2: Free information ❖ Telescopes. 204–727–3111.

Cosmic Connections Inc., P.O. Box 7, Aurora, IL 60505: Catalog $2 ❖ Telescopes, telescope-making supplies, photographic equipment, charts and star maps, domes, books, and binoculars. 800–634–7702.

Cosmos Ltd., 9215 Waukegan Rd., Morton Grove, IL 60053: Free catalog ❖ Ultra wide-field telescopes. 800–643–2351.

Coulter Optical Company, P.O. Box K, Idyllwild, CA 92349: Free information ❖ Telescopes, mirrors, and mounts. 714–659–4621.

D & G Optical, 6490 Lemon St., East Petersburg, PA 17520: Catalog $2 ❖ Ready-to-use tube assemblies with objective lens, 2–inch focusing lens, 50mm finderscope, dewcap, and dustcover. 717–560–1519.

Davilyn Corporation, 13406 Saticoy St., North Hollywood, CA 91605: Free information ❖ Star drives and declination motors. 800–235–6222; 818–787–3334 (in CA).

Daystar Filter Corporation, P.O. Box 5110, Diamond Bar, CA 91765: Free catalog ❖ Filters. 909–591–4673.

DFM Engineering Inc., 1035 Delaware Ave., Unit D, Longmont, CO 80501: Brochure $4 ❖ Computer-controlled telescopes. 303–678–8143.

Dino Productions, P.O. Box 3004, Englewood, CO 80155: Catalog $2 (refundable) ❖ Fossils, rocks and minerals, ecology and oceanography equipment, and supplies for chemistry, general science, astronomy, biology, and other supplies. 303–741–1587.

Dobbins Instrument Company, 5168 Lynd Ave., Lyndhurst, OH 44124: Catalog $2 ❖ Telescope mounts and refractors.

Eagle Optics, 716 S. Whitney Way, Madison, WI 53711: Free catalog ❖ Telescopes, photographic equipment, books, and binoculars. 608–271–4751.

Edmund Scientific Company, Edscorp Building, Barrington, NJ 08007: Free catalog ❖ Telescopes, telescope-making supplies, audiovisual aids, photographic equipment, charts and star maps, domes, books, and binoculars. 609–573–6260.

Efstonscience Inc., 3350 Dufferin St., Toronto, Ontario, Canada M6A 3A4: Catalog $6 ❖ Telescopes, telescope-making supplies, audiovisual aids, books, cameras, computers and software, and planetariums. 416–787–4581.

Epoch Instruments, 1689 Abram Ct., San Leandro, CA 94577: Free catalog ❖ Telescope mounts, clock drives, setting circles, telescopes, and other optical instruments. 510–351–1288.

Equatorial Platforms, 11065 Peaceful Valley Rd., Nevada City, CA 95969: Brochure $2 ❖ Direct roller-drive equatorial platforms with computer controls. 916–265–3183.

Focus Camera, 4419 13th Ave., Brooklyn, NY 11219: Free information ❖ Telescopes, audiovisual aids, photographic equipment, and binoculars. 718–436–6262.

Fort Davis Astronomical Supply, P.O. Box 922, Fort Davis, TX 79734: Free information ❖ Telescopes. 915–426–3794.

Galaxy Optics, P.O. Box 2045, Buena Vista, CO 81211: Catalog $2 ❖ Telescope-making supplies and Newtonian optics. 719–395–8242.

Gemini, 8930 Blue Smoke Dr., Gaithersburg, MD 20879: Free catalog ❖ Astronomical clocks. 301–921–0157.

Edwin Hirsch, 29 Lakeview Dr., Tomkins Cove, NY 10986: Free brochure ❖ Telescopes. 914–786–3738.

A. Jaegers Optical Supply Company, 11 Roosevelt Ave., Spring Valley, NY 11581: Free catalog ❖ Telescopes, telescope-making supplies, photographic equipment, and binoculars. 516–599–3167.

Jim's Mobile Inc., 810 Quail St., Unit E, Lakewood, CO 80215: Catalog $3 ❖ Dedicated computers with object databases, telescope-to-PC links, focusing motors, push- and snap-on declination motors, drive controls, locking easels, telescopes, software, and other astronomy equipment. 303–233–5353.

Jupiter Telescope Company, 810 Saturn St., Ste. 16, Jupiter, FL 33477: Brochure $2 ❖ Portable equatorial telescopes. 407–694–1154.

Khan Scope Center, 3243 Dufferin St., Toronto, Ontario, Canada M6A 2T2: Free price list ❖ Telescopes, telescope-making supplies, binoculars, audiovisual aids, books, photographic equipment, computers and software, and planetariums. 416–783–4140.

La Maison de l'Astronomie P.L. Inc., 8056 St. Hubert, Montreal, Quebec, Canada H2H 2P3: Free catalog ❖ Telescopes. 514–279–0063.

Lewis-Michaels Engineering, 48 Delemere Blvd., Fairport, NY 14450: Free catalog ❖ Astronomy software and telescope-making supplies. 716–425–3470.

Lire La Nature Inc., 1699 Chemin Chandly, Longueuil, Quebec, Canada J4J 3X7: Free price list ❖ Telescopes, microscopes, and other equipment. 514–463–5072.

Los Angeles Optical Company, P.O. Box 4868, North Hollywood, CA 91617: Free information ❖ Telescopes, books, maps and charts, filters, and photographic equipment. 818–762–2206.

Lumicon, 2111 Research Dr., Livermore, CA 94550: Free catalog ❖ Telescopes, binoculars, eye pieces and filters, mirrors and lenses, mounts, star maps and atlases, computers and software, and photographic equipment. 510–447–9570.

Mardiron Optics, 4 Spartan Cir., Stoneham, MA 02180: Free brochure with two 1st class stamps ❖ Telescopes and binoculars. 617–938–8339.

Meade Instruments Corporation, 16542 Millikan Ave., Irvine, CA 92714: Catalog $3 ❖ Telescopes, spotting scopes, and telephoto lenses. 714–556–2291.

F.C. Meichsner Company, 182 Lincoln St., Boston, MA 02111: Free information ❖ Telescopes, antique instruments, photographic equipment, charts and star maps, books, and binoculars. 800–321–VIEW.

MMI Corporation, P.O. Box 19907, Baltimore, MD 21211: Catalog $2 ❖ Portable planetariums, 35mm slides, videos, celestial globes, computer software, laser disks, teaching manuals, and telescopes. 410–366–1222.

National Camera Exchange, 9300 Olson Memorial Hwy., Golden Valley, MN 55427: Free information ❖ Telescopes, audiovisual aids, photographic equipment, charts and star maps, books, and binoculars. 800–624–8107; 612–546–6831 (in MN).

New England Astro-Optics Inc., P.O. Box 834, Simsbury, CT 06070: Catalog $2 ❖ Telescopes, photographic equipment, and books. 203–658–0701.

New Mexico Astronomical, 834 N. Gabaldon Rd., Belen, NM 87002: Free information ❖ Telescopes. 505–864–2953.

Kenneth F. Novak & Company, Box 69, Ladysmith, WI 54848: Free catalog ❖ Telescopes, mounts, and books. 715–532–5102.

Nurnberg Scientific, 6310 SW Virginia Ave., Portland, OR 97201: Free information ❖ Telescopes. 503–246–8297.

Optica b/c Company, 4100 MacArthur Blvd., Oakland, CA 94619: Catalog $5 ❖ Telescopes, telescope-making supplies, mounts, binoculars, audiovisual aids, books, photographic equipment, computers and software, and planetariums. 510–530–1234.

Optico Glass Fabrication Inc., 3164 El Camino Real, Atascadero, CA 93422: Free information ❖ Optical components. 805–461–9402.

Optron Systems, 15840 E. Alta Vista Way, San Jose, CA 95127: Free information ❖ Telescopes, binoculars, and other optical equipment. 408–923–6800.

Orion Telescope Center, P.O. Box 1158, Santa Cruz, CA 95062: Free catalog ❖ Telescopes, photographic equipment, charts and star maps, books, other science equipment, and binoculars. 800–447–1001.

Palomar Optical Supply, P.O. Box 1310, Wildomar, CA 92595: Catalog $2 ❖ Mirror-making kits, pyrex blanks, grinding and polishing compounds, primary and elliptical mirrors, and other supplies. 619–631–2835.

Parks Optical Company, 270 Easy St., Simi Valley, CA 93065: Catalog $3 ❖ Telescopes and other optical equipment. 805–522–6722.

Pauli's Wholesale Optics, 29 Kingswood Rd., Danbury, CT 06811: Catalog $10 (refundable) ❖ Telescopes, telescope-making supplies, photographic equipment, computer software, other science equipment, books, and binoculars. 203–746–3579.

Perceptor, Brownsville Junction Plaza, Box 38, Ste. 201, Schomberg, Ontario, Canada L0G 1T0: Free information ❖ Telescopes, telescope-making supplies, mounts, audiovisual aids, books, cameras, computers and software, planetariums, and binoculars. 905–939–2313.

Pocono Mountain Optics, RR 6, Box 6329, Moscow, PA 18444: Catalog $6 ❖ Astronomy equipment, binoculars, sighting scopes, telescope-making supplies, charts and star maps, photographic equipment, and books. 800–569–4323; 717–842–1500 (in PA).

Precision City Camera Optics, 15336 W. Warren, Dearborn, MI 48126: Free information ❖ Telescopes. 313–846–3922.

Royal Optics, 20 Glassco Ave. South, Hamilton, Ontario, Canada L8H 1B3: Free brochure ❖ Eyepieces and binoculars.

Quasar Optics, 3715 51st St. SW, Calgary, Alberta, Canada T3E 6V2: Catalog $4 ❖ Telescopes, telescope-making supplies, photographic equipment, eyepieces, other science equipment, books, and binoculars. 403–240–0680.

Questar, P.O. Box 59, New Hope, PA 18938: Catalog $5 ❖ Telescopes. 215–862–5277.

R.V.R. Optical, P.O. Box 62, Eastchester, NY 10709: Catalog $5 ❖ Telescopes. 914–337–4085.

Redlich Optical, 711 W. Broad St., Falls Church, VA 22046: Free information with long SASE ❖ Telescopes, telescope-making equipment, binoculars, books, cameras, photographic equipment, computers and software, star maps, and atlases. 703–241–4077.

S & S Optika, 5174 S. Broadway, Englewood, CO 80110: Free information ❖ Telescopes, binoculars, and other optical equipment. 303–789–1089.

Safari Telescopes, 110 Pascack Rd., Pearl River, NY 10965: Catalog $1 ❖ Dobsonian telescopes and binocular mounts. 914–735–4163.

Santa Anita Camera & Optical Company, 1031 S. Baldwin Ave., Arcadia, CA 91007: Free catalog ❖ Telescopes. 818–447–1854.

Sarasota Camera Exchange & Video Center, 1055 S. Tamiami Trail, Sarasota, FL 34236: Free information ❖ New and used telescopes. 813–366–7484.

Scope City, P.O. Box 440, Simi Valley, CA 93065: Catalog $7 (refundable) ❖ Telescopes, telescope-making supplies, photographic equipment, books, and binoculars. 805–522–6646.

Shutan Camera & Video, 312 W. Randolph, Chicago, IL 60606: Free catalog ❖ Telescopes, telescope-making supplies, photographic equipment, charts and star maps, binoculars, video equipment, and other electronics. 800–621–2248; 312–332–2000 (in IL).

Sky Designs, 4100 Felps, Ste. C, Colleyville, TX 76034: Free catalog ❖ Portable telescopes. 817–581–9878.

Sky Scientific, 28578 Hwy. 18, P.O. Box 184, Skyforest, CA 92385: Catalog $1 ❖

Telescopes and astrophotography equipment. 909–337–3440.

Spectra Astronomy, 6631 Wilbur Ave., Ste. 30, Reseda, CA 91335: Free catalog ❖ Astrophotography and other telescopes and equipment for beginning and advanced astronomers. 800–735–1352.

Stano Components, P.O. Box 2048, Carson City, NV 89702: Catalog $4 ❖ Night-vision optical equipment. 702–246–5281.

Star-Liner Company, 1106 S. Columbus Blvd., Tucson, AZ 85711: Catalog $6 ❖ Telescopes, from 6–inch amateur units to observatory research equipment. 602–795–3361.

Sunwest Space Systems, P.O. Box 20500, St. Petersburg, FL 33742: Free information ❖ Telescopes. 813–577–0629.

Swift Instruments Inc., 952 Dorchester Ave., Boston, MA 02125: Free information ❖ Telescopes, weather instruments, binoculars, and other optics. 800–446–1115; 617–436–2960 (in MA).

Tele Vue Optics, 100 Rt. 59, Suffern, NY 10901: Catalog $3 ❖ Telescopes and other optical equipment. 914–357–9522.

Texas Nautical Repair Company, Land, Sea & Sky, 3110 S. Shepherd, Houston, TX 77098: Free catalog ❖ Portable camera mounting and tracking systems, telescopes, other science equipment, star maps, and atlases. 713–529–3551.

Thousand Oaks Optical, Box 4813, Thousand Oaks, CA 91359: Free brochure ❖ Solar filters and astronomy equipment. 805–491–3642.

Roger W. Tuthill Inc., Box 1086, Mountainside, NJ 07092: Free catalog with 9x12 self-addressed envelope and four 1st class stamps ❖ Telescopes, audiovisual aids, telescope-making supplies, photographic equipment, books, and binoculars. 800–223–1063.

Unitron Inc., 170 Wilbur Pl., P.O. Box 469, Bohemia, NY 11716: Free catalog ❖ Telescopes, spotting scopes, binoculars, and other optical instruments. 516–589–6666.

University Optics, P.O. Box 1205, Ann Arbor, MI 48106: Free catalog ❖ Telescopes. 800–521–2828.

VERNONscope & Company, Box 105, Candor, NY 13743: Catalog $3 ❖ Portable telescopes. 607–659–7000.

Vista Instrument Company, P.O. Box 1919, Santa Maria, CA 93454: Catalog $2 ❖ Precision camera tracker with optional accessories. 800–552–9170.

Vogel Enterprises Inc., 38W150 Hickory Ct., Batavia, IL 60510: Free information ❖ Quartz-controlled drive correctors. 800–457–8725; 708–879–8725 (in IL).

Ward's Natural Science, P.O. Box 92912, Rochester, NY 14692: Free information with long SASE ❖ Telescopes, telescope-making supplies, binoculars, audiovisual aids, books, computers and software, planetariums, and meteorites. 716–359–2502.

Wholesale Optics Division, Professional Building #401, 57 North St., Danbury, CT 06810: Catalog $10 (refundable) ❖ Telescopes. 203–746–3579.

Willmann-Bell Inc., P.O. Box 35025, Richmond, VA 23235: Catalog $1 ❖ Telescopes and books. 804–320–7016.

Wonder Works, 280 W. Coleman, Mt. Pleasant, SC 29464: Free information ❖ Telescopes. 800–352–2316.

AUTOGRAPHS

Bruce Allen, 40347 US Hwy. 19 North, Ste. 231, Tarpon Springs, FL 34689: Free information ❖ Autographed memorabilia and unsigned photographs of sports figures. 813–937–0026.

American Historical Guild, 130 Circle Dr., Ste. 200, Roslyn Heights, NY 11577: Catalog $2 ❖ Original letters and documents by famous Americans, world leaders, scientists, authors, composers, artists, and others. 800–944–1947.

Ray Anthony Autograph Company, 505 S. Beverly Dr., Ste. 1265, Beverly Hills, CA 90212: Catalog $8 ❖ Autographed letters, albums, books, photographs, and other documents. 800–626–3393.

Authentic Cinema Collectibles, 7726 Girard St., La Jolla, CA 92037: Free information ❖ Autographs, posters, lobby cards, and other memorabilia. 619–551–9886.

B & J Collectibles, 999 Airport Rd., Unit 2, Lakewood, NJ 08701: Free information with long SASE ❖ Autographed sports cards, balls, photos, and other memorabilia. 908–905–5000.

Catherine Barnes Autographs, P.O. Box 30117, Philadelphia, PA 19103: Free information ❖ Letters, documents, manuscripts, and signed books and photographs. 215–854–0175.

Benedikt & Salmon Record Rarities, 3020 Meade Ave., San Diego, CA 92116: Free catalogs, indicate choice of (1) autographs and rare books, (2) classical, (3) jazz, big bands and blues and (4) personalities, soundtracks and country music ❖ Autographed memorabilia and rare books in music and the performing arts, hard-to-find rare phonograph recordings, from 1890 to date, and antique phonographs and cylinders for collectors. 619–281–3345.

Walter R. Benjamin, Autographs, P.O. Box 255, Hunter, NY 12442: Catalog subscription $10 ❖ Letters and documents from historical, literature, musical, and scientific areas. 518–263–4133.

Book City Collectibles, 6631 Hollywood Blvd., Hollywood, CA 90028: Free information ❖ Autographs from the early days of Hollywood to the present and signed photographs, letters, contracts, and other collectibles by movie and music stars, writers, directors, producers, and other theatrical personalities. 800–4–CINEMA; 213–466–0120 (in CA).

Broadway Rick's Strike Zone, 1840 N. Federal Hwy., Boynton Beach, FL 33435: Free information with long SASE ❖ Autographed sports memorabilia, sports cards, and other collectibles. 800–344–9103; 407–364–0453 (in FL).

Kevin G. Browning, P.O. Box 360486, Melbourne, FL 32936: Free information ❖ Autographs by sports greats, cartoonists, movie stars, and television performers. 407–258–9796.

Champion Sports Collectables Inc., 150 E. Santa Clara, Arcadia, CA 91006: Free information ❖ Autographed sports memorabilia, sports and non-sports cards, and collecting supplies. 818–574–5500.

Colonnade of History, P.O. Box 4255, Irvine, CA 92716: Free catalog ❖ Autographs by historical figures. 714–551–2040.

Dance Mart, Box 994, Teaneck, NJ 07666: Free catalog with long SASE ❖ Books, prints, music, autographs, and other dance collectibles. 201–833–4176.

Eileen Delaney Autographs, 1593 Monrovia, Newport Beach, CA 92663: Catalog $10 (refundable) ❖ Autographed rarities by Hollywood stars, presidents, scientists and inventors, and other personalities. 800–966–7448.

Documents of Distinction, 751 Laurel St., Ste. 330, San Carlos, CA 94070: Free information ❖ Autographs and historical documents. 415–365–2356.

A. Lovell Elliott, 940 Crescent Beach Rd., Vero Beach, FL 32963: Free information ❖ Autographed letters, photos, and other documents. 407–234–1034.

Elmer's Nostalgia Inc., 3 Putnam St., Sanford, ME 04073: Free catalog ❖ Entertainment, political, historical, literary, and pop culture autographs and memorabilia. 207–324–2166.

Empire State Sports Memorabilia & Collectibles Inc., 331 Cochran Pl., Valley Stream, NY 11581: Free information ❖ Baseball and other sports cards, autographs, and other memorabilia. 516–791–9091.

Golden Age Autographs, P.O. Box 20408, Park West Finance Station, New York, NY 10025: Free catalog with two 1st class stamps ❖ Autographs and signed photographs, by entertainers and other personalities. 212–866–5626.

Golden State Autographs, P.O. Box 24066, Los Angeles, CA 90024: Free information with long SASE ❖ Autographs from all fields. 310–273–1068.

Jerry Granat/Manuscripts, P.O. Box 92, Woodmere, NY 11596: Free information with long SASE ❖ Letters and autographs from famous people. 516–374–7809.

Roger Gross Ltd., 15 W. 81st St., New York, NY 10024: Free list ❖ Autographs, books, memorabilia, and unsigned photographs of opera stars. 212–759–2892.

Jim Hayes, Box 12560, James Island, SC 29422: Catalog subscription $6 ❖ Autographs from the Civil and Revolutionary war periods. 803–795–0732.

Historical Documents International Inc., P.O. Box 10488, Bedford, NH 03110: Free information ❖ Historical documents, autographs, and manuscripts. 800–225–6233.

Hollywood Legends, The Autograph Store, 6631 Hollywood Blvd., Hollywood, CA 90028: Free information ❖ Celebrity autographs from the early days of Hollywood to the present. 213–466–0120.

Houle Rare Books & Autographs, 7260 Beverly Blvd., Los Angeles, CA 90036: Catalog $5 ❖ Autographs in all fields. 213–937–5858.

Jeanne Hoyt Autographs, P.O. Box 1517, Rohnert Park, CA 94927: Free catalog ❖ Autographs from all areas. 707–584–4077.

Jefferson Rarities, 2400 Jefferson Hwy., 6th Floor, Jefferson, LA 70121: Free catalog ❖ Rare autographs, manuscripts, newspapers, and books. 800–877–8847.

Michael E. Johnson, Autographs, 862 Thomas Ave., San Diego, CA 92109: Free information ❖ Autographs of theatrical performers and other famous persons. 619–483–8632.

Mark R. Jordan Inc., 1600 Airport Freeway, Ste. 508, Bedford, TX 76022: Free information ❖ Autographs by college and pro football players and entertainment personalities. 800–888–3784.

Kaller Historical Documents Inc., P.O. Box 173, Allenhurst, NJ 07711: Free information ❖ Autographs and historical documents. 908–774–0222.

Robert A. LeGresley, P.O. Box 1199, Lawrence, KS 66044: Free catalog with long SASE ❖ Autographs, signed letters, photographs, and original comic art. 913–749–5458.

Abraham Lincoln Book Shop, 357 W. Chicago Ave., Chicago, IL 60610: Catalog $10 (2–year subscription) ❖ New and used books, autographed letters, prints, oils, photographs, and other Lincolniana, U.S. Civil War, and U.S. Presidential documents. 312–944–3085.

William Linehan Autographs, Box 1203, Concord, NH 03301: Catalog $3 ❖ Autographs and costumes of movie stars. 800–346–9827.

Lone Star Autographs, P.O. Box 500, Kaufman, TX 75142: Free catalog ❖ Books signed or owned by Presidents and First Ladies and autographed letters, documents, and photographs, from the Civil War, movie stars, scientific community, authors, musicians, astronauts and space, military greats, and politicians. 214–932–6050.

Joseph M. Maddalena, 345 N. Maple Dr., Ste. 202, Beverly Hills, CA 90210: Free information ❖ Letters, photos, other documents, signed books, and memorabilia from presidents, statesmen, movie stars, scientists, authors, inventors, and others. 800–942–8856.

Main Street Fine Books & Manuscripts, 301 S. Main St., Galena, IL 61036: Free information ❖ American literature and Civil

War and U.S. Grant, Lincolniana, Illinoisana, and other autographed memorabilia. 815–777–3749.

Menig's Memorabilia, 517 Manor, Peotone, IL 60468: Free catalog ❖ Civil War autographs, newspapers, and other documents. 708–258–9487.

J.B. Muns, Bookseller, 1162 Shattuck Ave., Berkeley, CA 94707: Price list $1 ❖ Autographs by classical singers, musicians, and composers. 510–525–2420.

Nate's Autographs, 1015 Gayley Ave., Los Angeles, CA 90024: Catalog subscription (4 issues) $24 ❖ Autographs and memorabilia by entertainers, presidents, other historic personalities, air space and science figures, and sports greats. 310–575–3851.

North Shore Manuscript Company Inc., P.O. Box 458, Roslyn Heights, NY 11577: Free information ❖ Autographed memorabilia. 516–484–6826.

Odyssey Auctions Inc., 510–A S. Corona Mall, Corona, CA 91719: Catalog $20 ❖ Autographed letters, manuscripts, photographs, and documents, from the arts and sciences to politics and entertainment, and other movie memorabilia. 800–395–1359.

Olde Soldier Books Inc., 18779 N. Frederick Ave., Gaithersburg, MD 20879: Free information ❖ Civil War books, documents, autographs, prints, and other Americana. 301–963–2929.

Tom Peper, 32 Shelter Cove Lane, #109, Hilton Head Island, SC 29928: Price list $1 ❖ Autographs, lobby cards and posters, and original comic and animation art. 800–628–7497.

R & R Enterprises, P.O. Box 2000, Amherst, NH 03031: Free catalog ❖ Autographs of movie, television, sport, music, and history personalities. 603–672–6611.

Steven S. Raab, 2033 Walnut St., Philadelphia, PA 19103: Free catalog ❖ Autographs, signed books and photos, historic newspapers, World War I posters, and other memorabilia. 215–446–6193.

Kenneth W. Rendell Inc., 989 Madison Ave., New York, NY 10021: Catalog $5 ❖ Autographs and documents by famous persons, from early American history to the present. 212–717–1776.

Paul C. Richards, Autographs, High Acres, Templeton, MA 01468: Catalog $5 ❖ Letters, manuscripts, documents, and signed photographs. 800–637–7711.

Safka & Bareis, Autographs, P.O. Box 886, Forest Hills, NY 11375: Free catalog ❖ Signed photos, letters, and other autographs by opera, music, and movie entertainers. 718–263–2276.

St. Louis Baseball Cards, 5456 Chatfield, St. Louis, MO 63129: Free information ❖ Sports cards and memorabilia, autographs, uniforms, press pins, and advertising collectibles. 314–892–4737.

H. Drew Sanchez, P.O. Box 2618, Apple Valley, CA 92307: Free catalog ❖ Cartoon art and autographs by entertainers and other personalities. 619–242–9092.

The Score Board Inc., 1951 Old Cuthbert Rd., Cherry Hill, NJ 08034: Free information ❖ Autographed sports memorabilia. 800–327–4145; 609–354–8011 (in NJ).

Seaport Autographs, 6 Brandon Ln., Mystic, CT 06355: Free catalog ❖ Autographed letters, manuscripts, and documents. 203–572–8441.

Philip Sears Disney Collectibles, 1457 Avon Terr., Los Angeles, CA 90026: Free catalog ❖ Walt Disney autographs, animation art, and other memorabilia. 213–666–3740.

R.M. Smythe, 26 Broadway, New York, NY 10004: Price list $2 ❖ Obsolete stocks and bonds, bank notes, and autographs. 800–622–1880; 212–943–1880 (in NY).

SportsCards Plus, 28221 Crown Valley Pkwy., Laguna Niguel, CA 92677: Free information ❖ Sports cards, autographs, and other sports memorabilia. 800–350–2273.

Stampede Investments, P.O. Box 1772E, North Riverside, IL 60546: Free catalog ❖ Fine books and autographs for historical enthusiasts. 708–788–9022.

Star Shots, 5389 Bearup St., Port Charlotte, FL 33981: Free catalog ❖ Celebrity autographs. 813–697–6935

Starr Autographs, P.O. Box 1392, Clackamas, OR 97015: Free catalog ❖ Entertainment and sports celebrity autographs. 503–698–2711.

Jim Stinson Sports Collectibles, P.O. Box 756, St. George, UT 84771: Free information ❖ Autographed sports cards, photos, and other sports memorabilia. 801–574–3355.

Swann Galleries, 104 E. 25th St., New York, NY 10010: Free information (specify interest, catalog price varies) ❖ Autographs, rare books, manuscripts, photographs, Americana, and other memorabilia. 212–254–4710.

Georgia Terry, Autographs, 840 NE Cochran Ave., Gresham, OR 97030: Free catalog ❖ Autographs by entertainment personalities. 503–667–0950.

Mark Vardakis Autographs, Box 1430, Coventry, RI 02816: Catalog $2 ❖ Autographs, paper Americana, pre-1900 stocks, bonds and checks, and other collectibles. 401–823–8440.

Wex Rex Records & Collectibles, P.O. Box 702, Hudson, MA 01749: Catalog $3 ❖ Autographs, movie and TV show character toys, and other collectibles. 508–229–2662.

AUTOMOTIVE PARTS & ACCESSORIES
Automotive Art & Gifts

American Classic Three, 110 Hickory Ln., Kingman, KS 67068: Catalog $2 ❖ 1955 to 1957 Chevrolet-decorated coffee mugs, hat pins, sweat shirts, jackets, belt buckles, T-shirts, metal signs, telephones, and other gifts.

Atlanta Gallery of Automotive Art, P.O. Box 420024, Atlanta, GA 30342: Free information ❖ Automotive lithographs. 404–351–9100.

Auto Dimensions, P.O. Box 133, Mountain Lakes, NJ 07046: Free information with long SASE ❖ T-shirts, posters, and other gifts for automobile buffs. 201–625–4388.

Auto Motif Inc., 2968 Atlanta Rd., Smyrna, GA 30080: Catalog $3 ❖ Books, prints, puzzles, models, candy, office accessories, lamps, original art, posters, and other gifts with an automotive theme. 800–367–1161.

Automobilia, 44 Glendale Rd., Park Ridge, NJ 07656: Catalog $3 ❖ Die-cast and pewter automotive miniatures, car badges, cruise ship models, and toy cars of the 1950s. 201–573–0173.

Automotive Emporium, Preston Forest Village, Dallas, TX 75230: Free information with long SASE ❖ Automotive books and original literature, art and other memorabilia, miniatures, and bronze sculptures. 214–361–1969.

Benkin & Company, 14 E. Main St., Tipp City, OH 45371: Free information ❖ Automotive automobilia. 513–667–5975.

Car Collectables, 32 White Birch Rd., Madison, CT 06443: Free brochure ❖ Christmas cards, note cards, and gifts with an automotive theme. 203–245–2242.

Carswell's Creations, 3476 Alward Rd., Pataskala, OH 43062: Catalog $1 ❖ Buttons, magnets, mirrors, bumper stickers, rubber stamps, note cards, award certificates, and other automotive gifts. 614–927–5224.

Cobweb Collectibles, 9 Walnut Ave., Cranford, NJ 07016: Free information with long SASE ❖ Books, postcards, toys, pins, factory badges, and other collectible automotive memorabilia. 201–272–5777.

Collectors Glassware, 24666 W. River Rd., Perrysburg, OH 43551: Catalog $2 (refundable) ❖ Old-fashioned glasses and ceramic coffee mugs with silk-screened automotive art. 419–878–5556.

Gee Gee Studios Inc., 6636 S. Apache Dr., Littleton, CO 80120: Catalog $2 (refundable) ❖ Original pen and ink drawings and numbered lithographs of famous cars. 303–794–2788.

Motorhead, 1300 SW Campus Dr., Federal Way, WA 98023: Catalog $4 ❖ Art prints and collectibles. Also scale model cars and kits. 800–859–0164.

Pelham Prints, 2819 N. 3rd St., Clinton, IA 52732: Free information ❖ Note cards, antique and classic automotive art, and pen and ink drawings. 319–242–0280.

Universal Tire Company, 987 Stony Battery Rd., Lancaster, PA 17601: Free catalog ❖ Lucas electric parts, wheel hardware, moldings, and antique and classic tires, and other automotive memorabilia. 800–233–3827.

Weber's Nostalgia Supermarket, 6611 Anglin Dr., Fort Worth, TX 76119: Catalog $4 (refundable) ❖ Gas globes, gas pump restoration supplies, car models, photographs, posters, and other automotive gifts. 817–335–3833.

Body Repair Parts

Auto Body Specialties Inc., Rt. 66, P.O. Box 455, Middlefield, CT 06455: Catalog $5 ❖ Reproduction and original quarter panels, fenders, repair panels, grilles, bumpers, and carpets for 1950 to 1986 American and foreign cars, pickups, and vans. 203–346–4989.

Bill's Speed Shop, 13951 Millersburg Rd. SW, Navarre, OH 44662: Free information ❖ Hard-to-find panels for older cars and current models. 216–832–9403.

Made-Rite Auto Body Products Inc., 869 E. 140th St., Cleveland, OH 44110: Free information ❖ Steel replacement panels for cars, pickups, and vans. 216–681–2535.

Mill Supply, 3241 Superior Ave., Cleveland, OH 44114: Catalog $4 ❖ Steel replacement panels, tools, and body shop equipment for most United States cars, vans, pickups, and foreign cars. 800–888–5072; 216–241–5072 (in OH).

Rootlieb Inc., P.O. Box 1829, Turlock, CA 95381: Free catalog ❖ Hoods, fenders, running boards, splash aprons, and other parts for older Ford and Chevrolet cars. 209–632–2203.

Scarborough Faire, 1151 Main St., Pawtucket, RI 02860: Catalog $3 (specify year and car) ❖ Body repair panels for most cars. 401–724–4200.

Books & Miscellaneous Publications

ADP Hollander Inc., 14800 28th Ave. North, Ste. 190, Plymouth, MN 55447: Free information ❖ Reference parts interchange manuals, from the 1920s and later. 800–825–0644.

Applegate & Applegate, Box 1, Annville, PA 17003: Free information ❖ Sales literature, owner manuals, tune-up charts, and photographs. 717–964–2350.

Auto Literature Shoppe, Box 328, Fort Littleton, PA 17223: Catalog $2 ❖ Shop and owner's manuals, showroom literature, and memorabilia. 717–987–3702.

The Auto Review, P.O. Box 510, Florissant, MO 63032: Free information ❖ Books and other information on antique and classic car history and restoration. 314–355–3609.

Auto World Books, P.O. Box 562, Camarillo, CA 93011: Free information with long SASE ❖ Automobile, truck, and motorcycle books, service manuals, and back issues of magazines. 805–987–5570.

Automotive Information Clearinghouse, P.O. Box 1746, La Mesa, CA 92041: Free information with long SASE ❖ Original automobile service manuals. 619–447–7200.

Aztex Corporation, P.O. Box 50046, Tucson, AZ 85703: Free list with long SASE ❖ Books on transportation and how-to automotive subjects. 602–882–4656.

Francis Burley, Rt. 7, P.O. Box 1281, Moultrie, GA 31768: Free information with long SASE ❖ Automobile shop manuals, parts catalogs, and owner manuals. 912–985–6860.

Car Books, 1660 93rd Ln. NE, Minneapolis, MN 55449: Free information ❖ Automotive books and manuals. 800–642–3289.

Chewning's Auto Literature Ltd., 123 Main St., P.O. Box 727, Broadway, VA 22815: Free information (specify year and car) ❖ Shop and owner automotive manuals, parts, and sales catalogs. 703–896–6838.

Chilton Book Company, One Chilton Way, Radnor, PA 19089: Free catalog ❖ Books on automotive mechanics and repair. 215–964–4000.

Classic Motorbooks, P.O. Box 1, Osceola, WI 54020: Free catalog ❖ Driving manuals, technical information resource books, other books and manuals on cars, repairs, and buying guides. 800–826–6600.

Crank'en Hope Publications, 461 Sloan Alley, Blairsville, PA 15717: Free information with long SASE ❖ Original and reprinted shop and owner manuals, parts books, and sales literature. 412–459–8853.

Dragich Auto Literature, 1660 93rd Ln. NE, Minneapolis, MN 55434: Free catalog ❖ Original and reproduction automotive books and manuals. 800–348–BOOK; 612–786–3925 (in MN).

European Automotive Literature Inc., 1 Cambria, Pawtucket, RI 02860: Free information ❖ European and Japanese sales literature. 401–722–7367.

The Evergreen Press, Box 306, Avalon, CA 90704: Free information with long SASA ❖ Reference books on Fords (Model A, T, and pre-war V-8), Chevrolet, Volkswagen, Thunderbird, Mustang, Falcon, Corvette, Camaro, and others. 213–510–1700.

Faxon Auto Literature, 1655 E. 6th St., Corona, CA 91719: Free information ❖ Automobile factory manuals and literature. 800–458–2734.

Haynes Publications Inc., 861 Lawrence Dr., Newbury Park, CA 91320: Free catalog ❖ Automotive and motorcycle repair manuals. 818–889–5400.

Ernie Hemmings, Bookseller, P.O. Box 3906, Quincy, IL 62305: Price list 25¢ ❖ Hard-to-find Ford Model T and A books. 217–224–1670.

Bob Johnson's Auto Literature, 21 Blandin Ave., Framingham, MA 01701: Free information ❖ Automotive shop manuals, interchange manuals, and other literature. 800–334–0688.

Lloyd's Literature, P.O. Box 491, Newbury, OH 44065: Free information with long SASE ❖ Shop manuals, parts books, owner manuals, data books, and other literature. 216–338–1527.

Walter Miller, 6710 Brooklawn Pkwy., Syracuse, NY 13211: Free information ❖ Original repair manuals, owner manuals, sales brochures, and parts books for domestic and foreign cars. 315–432–8282.

Motorbooks International, 729 Prospect Ave., P.O. Box 1, Osceola, WI 54020: Free catalog ❖ Automotive books. 800–458–0454.

Portrayal Press, P.O. Box 1190, Andover, NJ 07821: Catalog $3 ❖ Books and manuals for early Jeeps, military vehicles, and trucks. 201–579–5781.

Schiff European Automotive Literature Inc., 1 Cambria Ct., Pawtucket, RI 02860: Free information with long SASE ❖ European automotive publications. 401–722–7367.

Clothing

Donovan Uniform Company, 171 Parkhouse, Dallas, TX 75207: Free information ❖ Caps, goggles, and dusters for men and women. 214–741–3971.

Exhaust Systems & Mufflers

Kanter Auto Parts, 76 Monroe St., Boonton, NJ 07005: Free catalog ❖ Heavy-duty replacement exhaust systems for most cars, from 1909 to 1970. 201–334–9575.

John Kepich, 17370 Alico Center Rd., Fort Myers, FL 33912: Free information ❖ Heavy-duty stainless steel exhaust systems. 813–267–2550.

King & Queen Mufflers, Box 423, Plumsteadville, PA 18949: Free information ❖ N.O.S. exhaust system parts for cars and trucks, 1926 and later. 215–766–8699.

Never Rust Exhaust Systems, 4279 Ohio River Blvd., Pittsburgh, PA 15202: Free information ❖ Stainless steel exhaust systems. 412–766–7775.

Glass

Buchingers, P.O. Box 66114, Chicago, IL 60666: Free information ❖ Windshields and side and back windows, for 1940 to 1970 cars. 800–892–8636; 815–246–7221 (in IL).

Diamond Auto Glass Corporation, 105 Emjay Blvd., Brentwood, NY 11717: Free information with long SASE ❖ Automotive glass for domestic and foreign cars and trucks. 800–888–3241.

Iowa Glass Depot, P.O. Box 122, Cedar Rapids, IA 52406: Free information ❖ Hard-to-find windshields for most pre-1960 cars. 800–553–8134; 800–332–5402 (in IA).

Lo-Can Glass International, 693 McGrath Hwy., P.O. Box 45248, Somerville, MA 02145: Free information ❖ Hard-to-find glass for old and new cars. 800–345–9595; 617–396–9595 (in MA).

Headlights & Headlight Covers

Extang Corporation, 2298 S. Industrial Hwy., Ann Arbor, MI 48104: Free brochure ❖ Headlight covers for most American cars, from 1980 and later. 313–665–5270.

Headlight Headquarters, 35 Timson St., Lynn, MA 01902: Catalog $2 ❖ Headlight units, lenses, and parts for 1914 to 1939 American cars, except Fords. 617–598–0523.

License Plates

A.V. Polio License Plate Restorations, 746 N. Greenbrier Dr., Orange, CT 06477: Free information with long SASE ❖ Restores antique license and city plates and political tags. 203–795–6434.

Eurosign Metalwerke Inc., P.O. Box 636331, Margate, FL 33063: Free information ❖ Antique license plate replicas. 305–979–1448.

Bob Lint Motor Shop, P.O. Box 87, Danville, KS 67036: Free information ❖ Old license plates. 316–962–5247.

Locks & Keys

Aero Locksmith Inc., P.O. Box 16434, Memphis, TN 38186: Free information with long SASE ❖ Replacement and original keys and locks for domestic and foreign automobiles. 901–398–8708.

Key Shop-Locksmiths, 144 Crescent Dr., Akron, OH 44301: Free information with long SASE ❖ N.O.S. keys and locks for antique, classic, and modern cars. 216–724–3822.

Paint & Touch-Up Supplies

Bill Hirsch, 396 Littleton Ave., Newark, NJ 07103: Free information ❖ High-temperature engine enamels for spray or brush application. 800–828–2061; 201–642–2404 (in NJ).

Seelig's Custom Finishes, 10456 Santa Monica Blvd., Los Angeles, CA 90025: Catalog $2 ❖ Gold leaf and pin-striping supplies. 213–475–1111.

Parts for All Makes & Models

A & S Auto Supply, P.O. Box 95, Braxton, MS 39044: Free information ❖ Parts for cars and pickups, from late 1940 to 1970. 601–847–4414.

A-1 Auto Wrecking, 13818 Pacific Ave., Tacoma, WA 98444: Free information ❖ Brake drums, axles, transmission parts, wheels, and other parts for old cars. 206–537–3445.

Aero Enhancements Ltd., 18511 E. Gate Ave., La Puente, CA 91748: Free brochure ❖ Enhanced aerodynamic accessories for most cars, trucks, and sport utility vehicles. 800–523–7388.

Alley Auto Parts, Rt. 2, Box 551, Immokalee, FL 33934: Free information ❖ Parts for cars and trucks, from 1948 to 1975. 813–657–3541.

Antique Auto Parts Cellar, P.O. Box 3, South Weymouth, MA 02190: Free information with long SASE ❖ N.O.S. and reproduction mechanical parts for most cars, from 1909 to 1965. 617–335–1579.

Arnold's Auto Parts, 1484 Crandall Rd., Tiverton, RI 02878: Free information ❖ Parts for American cars and trucks, from 1930 to 1970. 401–624–6936.

Auto Body Specialties Inc., Rt. 66, P.O. Box 455, Middlefield, CT 06455: Catalog $5 ❖ Reproduction and original quarter panels, fenders, repair panels, grilles, bumpers, and carpets for 1950 to 1986 American and foreign cars, pickups, and vans. 203–346–4989.

Auto World Motorsports, 701 N. Keyser Ave., Scranton, PA 18508: Catalog $3 ❖ Performance parts and racing equipment for vintage and current sports cars. 717–344–7258.

B.C. Automotive Inc., 2809 Damascus, Zion, IL 60099: Free information ❖ Parts for 1960 to 1982 domestic cars, and 1970 to 1984 foreign cars. 708–746–8056.

Bartnik Sales & Service, 6524 Van Dyke, Cass City, MI 48726: Free information ❖ Parts for cars and trucks, from 1960 to 1970. 517–872–3541.

Becker's Auto Salvage, Hwy. 30 West, Atkins, IA 52206: Free information ❖ Parts for AMC, Ford, Studebaker, Edsel, Chevrolet, and other cars. 319–446–7141.

Big Ben's Used Cars & Salvage, Hwy. 79 East, Fordyce, AR 71742: Free information ❖ Used parts for 1975 and older cars. 501–352–7423.

Bob & Art's Auto Parts, 2641 Reno Rd., Schodack Center, Castleton, NY 12033: Free information ❖ Parts for the Rambler, Hudson, Studebaker, Ford, and other cars, from late 1940 to 1980. 518–477–9183.

Bob's Auto Parts, 6390 N. Lapeer Rd., Fostoria, MI 48435: Free information with long SASE ❖ Parts for most 1930 to 1970 cars. 313–793–7500.

Bradley Auto Inc., 2026 Hwy. A, West Bend, WI 53095: Free information ❖ Parts for American cars, imports, and light duty trucks, 1975 and later. 414–334–4653.

Bryant's Auto Parts, RR 1, Westville, IL 61883: Free information with long SASE ❖ Parts for most 1939 to 1988 cars. 217–267–2124.

Burlington Foreign Car Parts Inc., 863 Shelburne Rd., Shelburne, VT 05482: Free information ❖ Parts for imported and domestic cars. 800–343–3033.

California Discount Warehouse, 2320 E. Artesia Blvd., Long Beach, CA 92805: Catalog $5 ❖ High-performance automobile parts. 310–423–4346.

Canfield Motors, 22–24 Main, New Waverly, IN 46961: Free information ❖ Parts for American cars, 1940 and later. 219–722–3230.

Cedar Auto Parts, 1100 Syndicate St., Jordan, MN 55352: Free information ❖ Parts for cars, from 1949 to current models. 800–755–3266.

Cherry Auto Parts, 5650 N. Detroit Ave., Toledo, OH 43612: Free brochure ❖ Used and rebuilt parts for foreign cars. 419–476–7222.

Chuck's Used Auto Parts, 4722 St. Barnabas Rd., Marlow Heights, MD 20748: Free information ❖ Parts for General Motors early and late model cars and trucks. 301–423–0007.

Jim Cook Racing, 5450 Katella Ave., Los Alamitos, CA 90720: Catalog $6 ❖ Performance accessories for the Nissan, Honda, Toyota, and Mazda. 714–828–9122.

Del-Car Auto Wrecking, 6650 Harlem Rd., Westerville, OH 43081: Free information ❖ Parts for cars and trucks, from 1965 to 1992.

Doc's Auto Parts, 38708 Fisk Lake Rd., Paw Paw, MI 49079: Free information ❖ Parts for most cars, from 1930 to 1970. 616–657–5268.

Don-A-Vee Motorsports, 17308 Bellflower Blvd., Bellflower, CA 90706: Free catalog ❖ Specialty parts and accessories for Wranglers, CJs, Cherokees, and Grand Chereokees. 800–59–PARTS.

E & J Used Auto & Truck Parts, 315 31st Ave., P.O. Box 6007, Rock Island, IL 61201: Free information ❖ Parts for 1940 to 1987 American and foreign cars and trucks. 800–728–7686; 309–788–7686 (in IL).

East End Auto Parts, 75 10th Ave. East, Box 183, Dickinson, ND 58601: Free information ❖ Parts for 1940 to 1980 Chevrolets, Fords, Dodges, and foreign cars. 701–225–4206.

Eastern Nebraska Auto Recyclers, Mile Marker 351 on Hwy. 34, P.O. Box 266, Elmwood, NE 68349: Free information ❖ Parts for cars, from late 1940 to 1980. 402–994–4555.

Easy Jack Welsh Antique Auto Parts, 2725 S. Milford Lake Rd., Junction City, KS 66441: Free information ❖ Used parts, from 1912 to 1982. 913–238–7541.

Egge Machine Company, 8403 Allport, Santa Fe Springs, CA 90670: Catalog $2 ❖ Parts for older American cars. 800–866–EGGE; 310–945–3419 (in CA).

Ellington Auto Parts, 5840 Contest Rd., Paducah, KY 42001: Free information ❖ Parts and glass for cars, from 1970 and up. 502–554–2685.

Faggelli's Auto Parts, 5850 Oakland Rd., Sykesville, MD 21784: Free information ❖ Parts for domestic cars and trucks, from late 1940 to the present. 410–795–3007.

Fast Freddy's, 2604 S. Harbor Blvd., Santa Ana, CA 92704: Free information ❖ High-performance automobile parts. 714–540–3801.

Ferrill's Auto Parts Inc., 18306 Hwy. 99, Lynwood, WA 98037: Free information ❖ Parts for American cars, from 1970 to 1985. 206–778–3147.

Fitz Auto Parts, 24000 Hwy. 9, Woodinville, WA 98072: Free information ❖ Parts for Ford, General Motors, Chrysler, AMC, and

some European and Japanese cars. 206–483–1212.

Fleetline Automotive, P.O. Box 291, Highland, NY 12528: Free information ❖ Parts for Chevrolet cars and trucks, Corvairs, Novas, Camaros, Chevelles, Buicks, Pontiacs, Cadillacs, and Oldsmobiles. 914–895–2381.

Fort Auto Parts, P.O. Box 4528, Huachuca City, AZ 85616: Free information ❖ Parts for most cars, from 1923 to 1973. 602–456–9082.

Hidden Valley Auto Parts, 21046 N. Rio Bravo Rd., Maricopa, AZ 85239: Free information with long SASE ❖ Used antique and classic parts for older American and foreign cars. 602–568–2945.

Hoctor's Hidden Valley Auto Parts, 21046 N. Rio Bravo, Maricopa, AZ 85239: Free information with long SASE ❖ Parts for new, foreign, and vintage cars. 602–568–2945.

J & B Auto Parts Inc., 17105 E. Hwy. 50, Orlando, FL 32820: Free information with long SASE ❖ Parts for most makes and models of American and foreign cars and trucks. 305–568–2131.

J & M Vintage Auto, P.O. Box 297, Goodman, MO 64843: Free information ❖ Parts for 1930 to 1968 cars. 417–364–7203.

Kalend's Auto Wrecking, 8237 East Hwy. 26, Stockton, CA 95205: Free information with long SASE ❖ Parts for 1978 to 1988 foreign and domestic cars. 209–931–0929.

Kanter Auto Parts, 76 Monroe St., Boonton, NJ 07005: Free catalog ❖ Automotive parts. 201–334–9575.

Kelsey Auto Salvage, Rt. 2, Iowa Falls, IA 50126: Free information ❖ Parts for 1948 to 1981 American cars. 515–648–3066.

Meier Auto Salvage, RR 1, Box 6L, Sioux City, IA 51108: Free information ❖ Automotive parts, from 1935 to 1988. 712–239–1344.

Memory Lane Car Parts, 1131 Pendleton, Sun Valley, CA 91352: Free information ❖ Pre-1974 American-made used car parts. 818–504–3341; 800–AT–1–YARD (in CA).

Steve Millen Racing, 3176 Airway Ave., Costa Mesa, CA 96626: Catalog $5 ❖ Parts for sports cars.

Gus Miller, Box 634, Heyworth, IL 61745: Free information with long SASE ❖ Parts for 1940 to 1950 cars. 309–473–2979.

Minot Wrecking & Salvage Company, P.O. Box 566, Minot, ND 58701: Free information

❖ Parts for most domestic and foreign cars, from 1925 to the present. 800–533–5904.

Morgan Auto Parts, 722 Kennie Rd., Pueblo, CO 81001: Free information ❖ Parts for most cars. 303–545–1702.

Nash Auto Parts, Pump Rd., Weedsport, NY 13166: Free information ❖ N.O.S. and other 1920 to 1975 parts. 800–526–6334.

North End Wrecking Inc., 55 W. 32nd St., Dubuque, IA 52001: Free information with long SASE ❖ Parts for late-model cars. 319–556–0044.

Northern Auto Parts Warehouse Inc., P.O. Box 3147, Sioux City, IA 51102: Free catalog ❖ Electrical components, tools, repair manuals, and engine, chassis, and brake parts. 800–831–0084.

Northern Tire & Auto Sales, N. 8219 Hwy. 51, Irma, WI 54442: Free information with long SASE ❖ Parts for most cars, from the 1920s to the 1970s. 715–453–5050.

Old Car City USA, P.O. Box 480, White, GA 30184: Video catalog $19.95 ❖ Parts for cars 1969 and later. 404–382–6141.

Old Gold Cars & Parts, Rt. 2, Box 1133, Old Town, FL 32680: Free information ❖ Parts for American cars, from 1948 to 1978. 904–542–8085.

Over the Hill Parts, Rt. 2, Box 357, Micanopy, FL 32667: Free information with long SASE ❖ Antique auto parts from 1936 to 1978 for GM and Mopar automobiles. 904–335–1848.

Pacific Auto Accessories, 5882 Machine Dr., Huntington Beach, CA 92649: Brochure $3 ❖ Easy-to-install ground effect styling parts for most cars, trucks, and sport utility vehicles. 800–854–7685; 714–891–3669 (in CA).

Pearson's Auto Dismantling & Used Cars, 2343 Hwy. 49, Mariposa, CA 95338: Free information ❖ Parts for 1940 to 1960 cars. 209–742–7442.

Performance Automotive Warehouse, 8966 Mason Ave., Chatsworth, CA 91311: Catalog $5 ❖ Stock, performance, and racing engine parts. 818–998–6000.

Petry's Junk Yard Inc., 800 Gorsuch Rd., Westminster, MD 21157: Free information with long SASE ❖ Parts for most cars, from 1940 to 1970. 410–876–3233.

Philbates Auto Wrecking Inc., Rt. 1, P.O. Box 28, New Kent, VA 23124: Free information ❖ Parts for most cars, from 1940 to 1982. 804–843–9787.

Pine River Salvage, Hwy. 371 North, Pine River, MN 56474: Free information with long SASE ❖ Parts for cars, from 1940 and 1980. 218–587–2700.

Porter Auto Repair & Salvage, Rt. 1, Park River, ND 58270: Free information ❖ Parts for Ford, Chevrolet, Dodge, Oldsmobile, Buick, Pontiac cars, and pickups and trucks, from 1950 and 1975. 701–284–6517.

Reliable Motoring Accessories, 1751 Spruce St., Riverside, CA 92505: Catalog $3 ❖ Parts for most automotive repairs. 800–854–4770; 714–781–0261 (in CA).

Richard's Auto Sales & Salvage, Rt. 3, Box 140, Denton, NC 27239: Free information with long SASE ❖ Parts for 1950 to 1970 cars. 919–857–2222.

Rick's Auto Wrecking, 14315 Aurora North, Seattle, WA 98133: Free information with long SASE ❖ Parts for cars, from the 1950s, 1960s, 1970s, and 1980s. 206–363–6800.

Ron's Auto Salvage, RR 2, Box 54, Allison, IA 50602: Free information ❖ Parts for most cars, from 1949 to 1977. 319–267–2871.

Seward Auto Salvage Inc., Rt. 2, Milton, WI 53563: Free information with long SASE ❖ Parts for American and foreign cars, from 1946 to 1986. 608–752–5166.

Bill Shank Auto Parts, 14648 Promise Rd., Noblesville, IN 46060: Free information with long SASE ❖ Parts for 1948 to 1988 cars. 317–776–0080.

Sil's Foreign Auto Parts Inc., 1498 Spur Dr. South, Islip, NY 11751: Free information with long SASE ❖ Parts for late model European and Japanese cars. 516–581–7624.

Sleepy Eye Salvage Company, RR 4, Box 60, Sleepy Eye, MN 56085: Free information ❖ Parts for 1937 to 1977 cars. 507–794–6673.

Gale Smyth Antique Auto, 8316 East A.J. Hwy., Whitesburg, TN 37891: Free information ❖ Parts for 1935 to 1972 American cars. 615–235–5221.

Lynn H. Steele Rubber Products, 1601 Hwy. 150 East, Denver, NC 28037: Catalog $2 (specify car) ❖ Reproduction rubber parts for Cadillacs, Pontiacs, Buicks, Chevrolets, Chryslers, Oldsmobiles, Packards, and GM trucks. 800–544–8665; 704–483–9343 (in NC).

Stevens Auto Wrecking, 160 Freeman Rd., Charlton, MA 01507: Free information with long SASE ❖ Parts for early and late model cars and trucks. 508–347–9650.

Summit Racing Equipment, P.O. Box 909, Akron, OH 44309: Catalog $3 ❖ Performance automobile parts. 216–630–0230.

Sunrise Auto Sales & Salvage, Rt. 3, Box 6, Lake City, FL 32055: Free information ❖ Parts for most cars, from the 1950s through early 1970s. 904–755–1810.

Van's Auto Salvage, Rt. 2, Box 164, Waupun, WI 53963: Free information with long SASE ❖ Parts for most cars, from 1947 to 1976. 414–324–2481.

West 29th Auto Inc., 3200 W. 29th St., Pueblo, CO 81003: Free information ❖ Old and new parts for most cars. 719–543–4247.

J.C. Whitney & Company, 1917–19 Archer Ave., P.O. Box 8410, Chicago, IL 60680: Free catalog ❖ Automotive parts, tools, and specialized equipment. 312–431–6102.

Leo Winakor & Sons Inc., 470 Forsyth Rd., Salem, CT 06420: Free information ❖ Parts for most cars, from 1930 through 1981. 203–859–0471.

Windy Hill Auto Parts, 9200 240th Ave. NE, New London, MN 56273: Free information ❖ Parts for American cars and trucks, from 1915 to 1990, with most parts pre-1968. 612–354–2201.

Winnicks Auto Sales & Parts, Rt. 61, P.O. Box 476, Shamokin, PA 17872: Free information with long SASE ❖ Parts for American and imported cars and trucks, and Ford and Chevrolet engines. 717–648–6857.

Wiseman's Auto Salvage, 900 W. Cottonwood Ln., Casa Grande, AZ 85222: Free information with long SASE ❖ Parts for 1930 to 1970 cars. 602–836–7960.

Woller Auto Parts Inc., 8227 Rd. South, Lamar, CO 81052: Free information ❖ Parts for 1955 to 1984 domestic cars and pickups. 719–336–2108.

Parts for Specific Makes & Models

ACURA

A & H Motorsport, 660 Easton Rd., Easton, PA 19044: Free catalog ❖ Performance parts. 215–657–0775.

Alpharetta Auto Parts Inc., 5770 Hwy. 10 North, Alpharetta, GA 30201: Free information ❖ BMW, Honda, and Acura parts. 404–475–1929.

HKS USA Inc., 20312 Gramercy Pl., Torrance, CA 90501: Catalog $8 ❖ Performance parts. 310–328–8100.

Jackson Racing, 16291 Gothard St., Huntington Beach, CA 92647: Catalog $5 ❖ High-performance and styling accessories. 714–841–3001.

MSO Parts, 1543 Easton Rd., Roslyn, PA 19001: Free information ❖ Acura factory parts. 800–628–0817; 215–657–8423 (in PA).

ALFA-ROMEO

Alfa Ricambi, 6644 San Fernando Rd., Glendale, CA 91201: Free information ❖ Alfa-Romeo high-performance and competition parts. 818–956–7933.

Algar Enterprises Inc., 1234 Lancaster Ave., P.O. Box 167, Rosemont, PA 19010: Free information ❖ Alfa-Romeo parts. 800–441–9824; 215–527–1100 (in PA).

Beach Imports, 30 Auto Center Dr., Tustin, CA 92680: Free information ❖ Alfa-Romeo parts. 800–777–4895.

Bobcor Motors, 243 W. Passaic St., Maywood, NJ 07607: Catalog $6 ❖ Alfa-Romeo performance parts. 800–526–0337.

Ereminas Imports Inc., P.O. Box 1214, Torrington, CT 06790: Catalog $3 ❖ Alfa-Romeo parts. 203–496–9800.

International Autosport, Catalog Sales, Rt. 29 North, P.O. Box 9036, Charlottesville, VA 22906: Free catalog ❖ Replacement, restoration, and performance parts for the Alfa-Romeo. 800–726–1199.

Prestige Imports, 14800 Biscayne Blvd., North Miami Beach, FL 33181: Free information ❖ Alfa-Romeo parts. 305–944–1800.

AMX

American Parts Depot, 409 N. Main St., West Manchester, OH 45382: Free information ❖ New, used, reproduction, and N.O.S. parts. 513–678–7249.

Byers Jeep-Eagle, 390 E. Broad St., P.O. Box 16513, Columbus, OH 43216: Free catalog ❖ Original factory parts. 614–221–9181.

Year One Inc., P.O. Box 129, Tucker, GA 30085: Catalog $5 ❖ New, used, and reproduction AMX restoration parts. 800–950–9503.

ANTIQUE & CLASSIC CARS

A-1 Auto Wrecking, 13818 Pacific Ave., Tacoma, WA 98444: Free information ❖ Parts for old cars. 206–537–3445.

B & W Antique Auto, 4653 Guide Meridian Rd., Bellingham, WA 98226: Catalog $3 (specify year and model) ❖ Antique Ford automotive parts. 604–743–3274.

Burchill Antique Auto Parts, P.O. Box 610637, Port Huron, MI 48061: Catalog $5 ❖ Parts for early vintage passenger and commercial vehicles. 313–385–3838.

Egge Machine Company, 8403 Allport, Santa Fe Springs, CA 90670: Catalog $2 ❖ Parts for old cars. 800–866–EGGE; 213–945–3419 (in CA).

Bob Lint Motor Shop, P.O. Box 87, Danville, KS 67036: Free information ❖ Collectible license plates and parts for early Fords, Chevrolets, Pontiacs, Plymouths, Dodges, and Buicks. 316–962–5247.

OlCar Bearing Company, 455 Lakes Edge Dr., Oxford, MI 48371: Free information ❖ Bearings and seals for antique, classic, and special interest cars, trucks, and tractors. 313–969–2628.

PRO Antique Auto Parts, 50 King Spring Rd., Windsor Locks, CT 06096: Catalog $2 ❖ Restoration parts for antique cars. 203–623–0070.

Zimp's Enterprises, 2800 S. Montana, Butte, MT 59701: Free list ❖ Antique car parts. 406–782–5674.

AUBURN

W.H. Lucarelli, 14 Hawthorne Ct., Wheeling, WV 26003: Free information ❖ Parts for 1931 to 1933 and 1935 to 1936 Auburns. 304–232–8906.

AUDI

Discount Auto Parts, 4703 Broadway SE, Albuquerque, NM 87105: Free information with long SASE ❖ Audi parts. 505–877–6782.

Europarts, 2048 Aldergrove, Escondido, CA 92025: Free information with long SASE ❖ Audi parts. 619–743–3377.

O.E.M. Parts Distributor, P.O. Box 25312, San Mateo, CA 94402: Free information ❖ Audi parts. 415–342–1343.

Parts Hotline, 10325 Central Ave., Montclair, CA 91763: Free information with long SASE ❖ Audi parts. 800–637–4662; 714–625–4888 (in CA).

AUSTIN HEALEY

British Auto, 703 Penfield Rd., Macedon, NY 14502: Free information ❖ Austin Healey parts, from 1950 to 1982. 315–986–3097.

British Miles, 222 Grove, Morrisville, PA 19067: Free information ❖ Austin Healy parts. 215–736–9300.

English Car Spares Ltd., 345 Branch Rd SW, Alpharetta, GA 30201: Free information ❖ Austin Healey parts. 800–241–1916; 404–475–2662 (in GA).

Moss Motors Ltd., 7200 Hollister Rd., P.O. Box 847, Goleta, CA 93116: Free catalog (specify model) ❖ Hard-to-find Austin Healey parts. 800–235–6954.

Scotland Yard British Cars Ltd., 3101 E. 52nd Ave., Denver, CO 80216: Free information with long SASE ❖ New, used, and remanufactured Austin Healey parts. 800–222–1415; 800–328–8716 (in CO).

Sports & Classics, 512 Boston Post Rd., Darien, CT 06820: Catalog $5 ❖ Restoration, engine, electrical, body parts for the Austin Healey. 203–655–8731.

AVANTI

Expressly Avanti, 1542 Main St., Box 115, Rt. 23, Goodville, PA 17528: Catalog $3 ❖ Avanti parts. 215–445–9364.

Newman & Altman Inc., P.O. Box 4276, South Bend, IN 46634: Catalog $5 ❖ Avanti parts. 800–722–4295.

Southwest Avanti, 21824 N. 19th Ave., Phoenix, AZ 85027: Free information with long SASE ❖ Avanti parts, from 1963 to 1989. 602–943–6970.

BARRACUDA

Jim's Auto Parts, 40 Lowell Rd., Rt. 38, P.O. Box 908, Salem, NH 03079: Catalog $7 ❖ Barracuda and Challenger parts. 603–898–0535.

BENTLEY

Carriage House Motor Cars Ltd., 407 E. 61st St., New York, NY 10021: Free information ❖ Rolls Royce and Bentley parts. 800–883–2462.

George Haug Company Inc., 517 E. 73rd St., New York, NY 10021: Free information ❖ Bentley parts. 212–288–0176.

Rolls-Royce Obsolete Parts Inc., P.O. Box 796, Ann Maria, FL 34216: Free information with long SASE ❖ Bentley and Rolls-Royce parts and literature. 813–778–7270.

Alpharetta Auto Parts Inc., 5770 Hwy. 10 North, Alpharetta, GA 30201: Free information ❖ BMW, Honda, and Acura parts. 404–475–1929.

The Auto Works, 1130 NE 6th Ave., Fort Lauderdale, FL 33304: Free information ❖ Used BMW parts. 800–377–2520.

Bavarian Auto Service Inc., 44 Exeter St., Newmarket, NH 03857: Catalog $3 ❖ BMW parts. 800–535–2002.

Bavarian Motor Wrecking, 3688 Omcc Circle, Rancho Cordova, CA 95742: Free information ❖ New, rebuilt, and used BMW parts. 800–726–4269.

BMP Design, 5100 Old Bullard, Tyler, TX 75703: Catalog $5 ❖ BMW parts. 800–648–7278.

Campbell/Nelson Volkswagon, P.O. Box 220, Edmonds, WA 98020: Free information ❖ Used BMW parts. 206–771–4931.

Dinan Performance Engineering, 150 S. Whisman, Mountain View, CA 84041: Free catalog ❖ Performance accessories for the BMW. 415–962–9417.

Electrodyne Inc., 4750 Eisenhower Ave., P.O. Box 9670, Alexandria, VA 22304: Catalog $3 ❖ BMW parts. 800–658–8850; 703–823–0202 (in VA).

Europarts, 2048 Aldergrove, Escondido, CA 92025: Free information with long SASE ❖ BMW parts. 619–743–3377.

Express Automotive Industries, P.O. Box 756, Moorpark, CA 93020: Free information ❖ BMW interior trim. 800–525–9080.

Greenfield Imported Car Parts, 335 High St., Greenfield, MA 01301: Free information ❖ BMW parts. 413–774–2819.

Hoffman BMW Parts, 425 Bloomfield Ave., Bloomfield, NJ 07003: Free information ❖ BMW parts. 800–238–8373.

MSO Parts, 1543 Easton Rd., Roslyn, PA 19001: Free information ❖ BMW factory parts. 800–628–0817; 215–657–8423 (in PA).

Noble Foreign Auto Parts, 355 Federal Rd., Brookfield, CT 06804: Catalog $5 ❖ BMW parts. 203–740–7868.

O.E.M. Parts Distributor, P.O. Box 25312, San Mateo, CA 94402: Free information ❖ BMW parts. 415–342–1343.

Perfect Plastics Industries Inc., 14th St., New Kensington, PA 15068: Free information ❖ BMW body parts. 800–245–6520; 412–339–3568 (in PA).

The Ultimate Source, 94 W. Woodhull Rd., Huntington, NY 11743: Catalog $3 ❖ BMW parts. 800–537–8248.

Zygmunt Motors, 70 Green St., Doylestown, PA 18901: Catalog $5 ❖ BMW parts. 215–348–3121.

BRITISH SPORTS CARS

Atlanta Imported British Auto Parts, 5383 Buford Hwy., Doraville, GA 30340: Catalog $1 (refundable) ❖ New and used Leyland parts. 404–451–4411.

British Auto, 703 Penfield Rd., Macedon, NY 14502: Free information ❖ Parts for the Austin Healey, MG, Triumph, Jensen, Lotus, Sunbeam, English Ford, and Jaguar, 1950 to the present. 315–986–3097.

British Car Specialists, 2060 N. Wilson Way, Stockton, CA 95205: Catalog $2 ❖ MG, Jaguar, Triumph, and Austin Healey parts. 209–948–8754.

British Miles, 222 Grove, Morrisville, PA 19067: Free information ❖ British Leyland parts. 215–736–9300.

FASPEC British Parts, 1036 SE Stark St., Portland, OR 97214: Free catalog (specify MGA/MGB, Sprite-Midget, or Austin Healey) ❖ New and used parts. 800–547–8788; 503–232–1232 (in OR).

Mini Mania, 31 Winsor St., Milpitas, CA 95035: Free catalog ❖ Parts for the Morris Minor, Mini Cooper, Austin Sprite, and MG Midget. 408–9421–5595.

Moss Motors Ltd., 7200 Hollister Rd., P.O. Box 847, Goleta, CA 93116: Free catalog (specify model) ❖ Hard-to-find parts for British sports cars. 800–235–6954.

Perfect Plastics Industries Inc., 14th St., New Kensington, PA 15068: Free information ❖ Body parts for MGA, MGB, Midget, Austin Healey, and Triumph TR-4 and TR-6. 800–245–6520; 412–339–3568 (in PA).

Scarborough Faire, 1151 Main St., Pawtucket, RI 02860: Catalog $3 (specify year and car) ❖ Parts for the MGB, MGA, Austin Healey, and Sprite. 401–724–4200.

Sports & Classics, 512 Boston Post Rd., Darien, CT 06820: Catalog $5 ❖ Restoration, engine and electrical, and body parts. 203–655–8731.

TS Imported Automotive, Pandora, OH 45877: Catalog $2 (refundable) ❖ New, used, and N.O.S. parts for British cars. 800–543–6648.

Victoria British Ltd., P.O. Box 14991, Lenexa, KS 66215: Free catalog ❖ Original and reproduction Austin Healey and other British sports car parts. 800–255–0088.

BRONCO

Bill Alprin, 184 Rivervale Rd., Rivervale, NJ 07675: Free information ❖ N.O.S. parts for the Bronco. 201–666–3975.

BUICK

B & B Used Auto Parts, Rt. 1, Box 691, Big Pine Key, FL 33043: Free information ❖ Parts for Buicks, 1950 and later. 305–872–9761.

Bob's Automobilia, Box 2119, Atascadero, CA 93423: Catalog $3 ❖ Parts, rubber, literature, upholstery fabrics, and hardware for 1919 to 1953 Buicks. 805–434–2963.

Buick Farm, 4143 W. Hwy. 166, Carrollton, GA 30117: Catalog $2 ❖ Parts for postwar Buicks, 1950 to 1975.

Cars Inc., Pearl St., Neshanic, NJ 08853: Catalog $3 (specify year) ❖ New, used, and reproduction parts for 1935 to 1975 Buicks. 201–369–3666.

Classic Buicks Inc., 4632 Riverside Dr., Chino, CA 91710: Catalog $5 ❖ New, used, and reproduction parts for 1946 to 1975 Buicks. 909–591–0283.

Fannaly's Auto Exchange, 701 Range Rd., P.O. Box 23, Ponchatoula, LA 70454: Free information ❖ Parts for 1939 to 1975 Buicks. 504–386–3714.

GM Muscle Car Parts Inc., 10345 75th Ave., Palos Hills, IL 60465: Free information ❖ Buick parts, from 1964 to 1987. 708–599–2277.

PRO Antique Auto Parts, 50 King Spring Rd., Windsor Locks, CT 06096: Catalog $2 ❖ New parts for 1929 to 1964 Buicks. 203–623–0070.

Speedway Automotive, 2300 Broadway, Phoenix, AZ 85041: Free information with long SASE ❖ Buick parts, from 1961 to 1987. 602–276–0090.

Swanson's, 3574 Western Ave., Sacramento, CA 95838: Free information ❖ Vintage parts, from 1938 to 1948. 916–646–0430.

Terrill Machine Inc., Rt. 2, Box 61, DeLeon, TX 76444: Free information with long SASE ❖ Engine overhaul parts for Buicks, from 1937 to 1958. 817–893–2610.

Terry's Auto Parts, Box 131, Granville, IA 51022: Free information with long SASE ❖

Parts for 1940 to 1984 Buicks and 1963 to 1984 Rivieras. 712–727–3273.

Year One Inc., P.O. Box 129, Tucker, GA 30085: Catalog $5 ❖ New, used, and reproduction Skylark restoration parts. 800–950–9503.

CADILLAC

Aabar's Cadillac & Lincoln Salvage, 9700 NE 23rd, Oklahoma City, OK 73141: Free information with long SASE ❖ Cadillac and Lincoln parts, from 1939 and later. 405–769–3318.

Akerman Old Cadillac Parts, Box 7363 Village West, Laconia, NH 03247: Free information with long SASE ❖ N.O.S. and used Cadillac parts, from 1930 to 1960. 603–524–8115.

All Cadillacs of the 40's, 12811 Foothill Blvd., Sylmar, CA 91342: Catalog $2 ❖ Used and reproduction parts, from 1940 to 1950. 818–361–1147.

Automotive Obsolete, 1023 E. 4th St., Santa Ana, CA 92701: Catalog $3 ❖ New parts for Cadillacs, from 1926 to 1970. 714–541–5167.

B & B Used Auto Parts, Rt. 1, Box 691, Big Pine Key, FL 33043: Free information ❖ Cadillac parts, from 1950 and later. 305–872–9761.

Caddy Shack Cadillac, 2410 Harvard St., Sacramento, CA 95815: Catalog $3 ❖ New, rebuilt, and used mechanical and auto body parts. 916–921–2575.

Cadillac King Inc., 9840 San Fernando Rd., Pacoima, CA 91331: Free information with long SASE ❖ New, used, and rebuilt Cadillac parts. 818–890–0621.

Classic Auto Parts, 550 Industrial Dr., Carmel, IN 46032: Free information ❖ Genuine classic Cadillac parts, from 1928 to 1941. 317–844–8154.

Continental Enterprises, 1673 Cary Rd., Kelowna, British Columbia, Canada V1X 2C1: Information $12 ❖ Cadillac dress-up accessory kits, from 1949 to 1993. 604–763–7727.

CR Auto, P.O. Box 237, Hay Lakes, Alberta, Canada T0B 1W0: Free information ❖ Original owner and shop manuals and N.O.S. Cadillac parts, from 1947 to 1978. 403–878–3263.

F.E.N. Enterprises, P.O. Box 1559, Wappingers Falls, NY 12590: Free catalog (specify year and model) ❖ New, used, and reproduction parts. 914–462–5094.

Fannaly's Auto Exchange, 701 Range Rd., P.O. Box 23, Ponchatoula, LA 70454: Free information ❖ Parts for 1939 to 1974 Cadillacs. 504–386–3714.

Global Auto Parts Connection, P.O. Box 15548, Phoenix, AZ 86060: Parts list $3 ❖ Parts for most Cadillacs. 602–376–1561.

Ted M. Holcombe Cadillac Parts, 2933 Century Ln., Bensalem, PA 19020: Free information ❖ Cadillac parts. 215–245–4560.

PRO Antique Auto Parts, 50 King Spring Rd., Windsor Locks, CT 06096: Catalog $2 ❖ New parts for 1929 to 1964 Cadillacs. 203–623–0070.

Robinson's Auto Sales, 200 New York Ave., New Castle, IN 47362: Free information ❖ Parts for 1960 to 1970 models. 317–529–7603.

Silverstate Cadillac Parts, P.O. Box 2161, Sparks, NV 89432: Free information ❖ N.O.S. Cadillac parts, from 1932 to 1982. 702–331–7252.

Lynn H. Steele Rubber Products, 1601 Hwy. 150 East, Denver, NC 28037: Catalog $2 (specify car) ❖ Reproduction rubber parts for Cadillacs and LaSalles. 800–544–8665; 704–483–9343 (in NC).

Terrill Machine Inc., Rt. 2, Box 61, DeLeon, TX 76444: Free information with long SASE ❖ Engine overhaul parts for Cadillacs, from 1936 to 1962. 817–893–2610.

Vintage Tin Auto Parts, 4550 Scotty Ln., Hutchinson, KS 67502: Free information with long SASE ❖ Cadillac parts, from 1940 to 1970. 316–669–8449.

CAMARO

Auto Heaven, 103 W. Allen St., Bloomington, IN 47401: Free information ❖ Parts for 1967 to 1969 models. 800–777–0297; 812–332–9401 (in IN).

California Classic Chevy Parts, 13545 Sycamore Ave., San Martin, CA 95046: Free information ❖ New, used, and reproduction parts for 1967 to 1969 Camaros. 408–683–2438.

Camaro Connection, 139 Cortland St., Lindenhurst, NY 11757: Free information with long SASE ❖ N.O.S. and reproduction parts for 1967 to 1988 Camaros, and sheet metal, interiors, electrical items, and decals. 800–835–8301.

Camaro Country Inc., 18591 Centennial Rd., Marshall, MI 49068: Catalog $3 ❖ New, used, and reproduction parts. 616–781–2906.

Camaro Specialties, 900 E. Fillmore Ave., East Aurora, NY 14052: Catalog $1 ❖ New, used, N.O.S., and reproduction parts for 1967 to 1972 Camaros. 716–652–7086.

Chicago Muscle Car Parts, 912 E. Burnett Rd., Island Lake, IL 60042: Catalog $5 (refundable) ❖ New and used Camaro parts, from 1967 to 1981. 708–526–2200.

Classic Camaro, 17832 Gothard St., Huntington Beach, CA 92647: Catalog $4 ❖ Camaro parts. 714–847–6887.

Classic Industries, 17832 Gothard St., Huntington Beach, CA 92647: Catalog $4 ❖ Camaro parts and accessories. 800–854–1280.

Dick's Chevy Parts, 1821 Columbus Ave., Springfield, OH 45503: Catalog $3 ❖ Rubber, chrome, moldings, interiors, emblems, and other parts, from 1928 to 1972. 513–325–7861.

Harmon's Inc., P.O. Box 6, Hwy. 27 North, Geneva, IN 46740: Free catalog ❖ Camaro restoration parts, from 1967 to 1980. 219–368–7221.

J & M Auto Parts, 10 Spaulding Mill Rd., Pelham, NH 03076: Price list $1 ❖ N.O.S. and reproduction 1967 to 1973 Camaro parts. 302–734–4177.

Luttys Chevys, RD 2, Box 61, Cheswick, PA 15024: Catalog $3 ❖ Carpets, interiors, weatherstripping, moldings, sheet metal, replacement panels, and other new, used, and reproduction parts, from 1955 to 1967. 412–265–2988.

Martz Classic Chevy Parts, RD 1, Box 199, Thomasville, PA 17364: Free catalog (specify year) ❖ N.O.S. and reproduction parts, from 1955 to 1975. 717–225–1655.

Musclecar Specialties, 1 Coach Lantern Dr., Hopewell, NY 12533: Free information with long SASE ❖ New, N.O.S., and used parts for 1962 to 1972 Camaros. 914–227–6837.

National Parts Depot, 3101 SW 40th Blvd., Gainsville, FL 32608: Free catalog ❖ Camaro parts and accessories, from 1967 to 1981. 904–378–9000.

The Paddock Inc., 221 W. Main, Knightstown, IN 46148: Catalog $1 ❖ Camaro parts. 317–345–2131.

Rick's Camaros, 120 Commerce Blvd., Bogart, GA 30622: Catalog $3 ❖ New, used, and reproduction parts for 1967 to 1969 Camaros. 706–546–9217.

Show Cars Automotive Inc., 409 Super Sport Ln., Rt. 3, Box 9, New Ulm, MN

56073: Free catalog ❖ Camaro parts. 507–354–1958.

Super Sport Restoration Parts Inc., 7138 Maddox Rd., P.O. Box 7, Lithonia, GA 30058: Free information ❖ Camaro, Chevy II, Nova, and Chevelle parts. 404–482–9219.

Tamraz's Parts Discount Warehouse, 10 South 123 Normantown Rd., Naperville, IL 60564: Free information ❖ Camaro parts. 708–851–4500.

Tom's Obsolete Chevy Parts, 14 Delta Dr., Pawtucket, RI 02860: Catalog $1 ❖ Camaro parts, from 1955 to 1972. 401–723–7580.

Year One Inc., P.O. Box 129, Tucker, GA 30085: Catalog $5 ❖ New, used, and reproduction Camaro restoration parts. 800–950–9503.

CAPRI

Bill Alprin, 184 Rivervale Rd., Rivervale, NJ 07675: Free information ❖ N.O.S. parts for the Capri. 201–666–3975.

Dobi Capri Catalog, 320 Thor Pl., Brea, CA 92621: Catalog $2 ❖ Capri parts. 714–529–1977.

Racer Walsh Company, 5906 Macy, Jacksonville, FL 32211: Catalog $3 ❖ Engines, suspensions, and other parts for the Capri. 800–334–0151; 904–743–8253 (in FL).

CAPRICE

Old Car Parts, 109 N. 15th St., Box 184, Clear Lake, IA 50428: Catalog $3.75 (specify year) ❖ N.O.S., new, and reproduction Caprice parts, from 1965 to 1970. 515–357–5510.

CHALLENGER

Jim's Auto Parts, 40 Lowell Rd., Rt. 38, P.O. Box 908, Salem, NH 03079: Catalog $7 ❖ Barracuda and Challenger parts. 603–898–0535.

CHEVELLE

Ausley's Chevelle Parts, 300 S. Main St., Graham, NC 27253: Catalog $2 (specify year) ❖ Parts for 1964 to 1972 Chevelles. 910–228–6701.

Chevelle Classics, 17832 Gothard St., Huntington Beach, CA 92647: Catalog $4 ❖ Chevelle parts. 800–CHEVELLE; 714–841–5363 (in CA).

Chevy Craft, 3414 Quirt, Lubbock, TX 79404: Catalog $5 ❖ New and used parts, for 1955 and later Chevelles. 806–747–4848.

Chicago Muscle Car Parts, 912 E. Burnett Rd., Island Lake, IL 60042: Catalog $5

(refundable) ❖ New and used Chevelle parts, from 1964 to 1967. 708–526–2200.

D & R Classic Automotive, 31 W. 280 Diehly Rd., Naperville, IL 60563: Free price list ❖ Chevelle parts. 800–472–6952.

Danchuk Manufacturing Inc., 3201 S. Standard Ave., Santa Ana, CA 92705: Catalog $4 ❖ Parts for 1964 to 1972 Chevelles. 800–854–6911; 714–751–1957 (in CA).

Dick's Chevy Parts, 1821 Columbus Ave., Springfield, OH 45503: Catalog $3 ❖ Rubber, chrome, moldings, interiors, emblems, and other Chevelle parts, from 1928 to 1972. 513–325–7861.

Harmon's Inc., P.O. Box 6, Hwy. 27 North, Geneva, IN 46740: Free catalog ❖ Chevelle restoration parts, from 1964 to 1972. 219–368–7221.

J & M Auto Parts, 10 Spaulding Mill Rd., Pelham, NH 03076: Price list $1 ❖ N.O.S. and reproduction 1964 to 1972 Chevelle parts. 302–734–4177.

John's N.O.S. Chevelle Parts, Box 1445, Salem, NH 03079: Price list $1 (specify year) ❖ Chevelle N.O.S. and reproduction parts, chrome, emblems, grilles, and rubber. 603–898–4452.

Luttys Chevys, RD 2, Box 61, Cheswick, PA 15024: Catalog $3 ❖ Carpets, interiors, weatherstripping, moldings, sheet metal, replacement panels, and other new, used, and reproduction parts, from 1955 to 1957. 412–265–2988.

Martz Classic Chevy Parts, RD 1, Box 199, Thomasville, PA 17364: Free catalog (specify year) ❖ Chevelle N.O.S. and reproduction parts, from 1955 to 1975. 717–225–1655.

Musclecar Specialties, 1 Coach Lantern Dr., Hopewell, NY 12533: Free information with long SASE ❖ New, N.O.S., and used parts for 1962 to 1972 Chevelles. 914–227–6837.

National Parts Depot, 3101 SW 40th Blvd., Gainsville, FL 32608: Free catalog ❖ Chevelle parts and accessories, from 1964 to 1972. 904–378–9000.

Original Parts Group Inc., 17892 Gothard St., Huntington Beach, CA 92647: Catalog $4 ❖ Chevelle parts. 800–243–8355.

The Paddock Inc., 221 W. Main, Knightstown, IN 46148: Catalog $1 ❖ Chevelle parts. 317–345–2131.

Show Cars Automotive Inc., 409 Super Sport Ln., Rt. 3, Box 9, New Ulm, MN

56073: Free catalog ❖ Chevelle parts. 507–354–1958.

Super Sport Restoration Parts Inc., 7138 Maddox Rd., P.O. Box 7, Lithonia, GA 30058: Free information ❖ Parts for the Chevelle, Chevy II, Nova, and Camaro. 404–482–9219.

Tamraz's Parts Discount Warehouse, 10 South 123 Normantown Rd., Naperville, IL 60564: Free information ❖ Chevelle parts. 708–851–4500

Tom's Obsolete Chevy Parts, 14 Delta Dr., Pawtucket, RI 02860: Catalog $1 ❖ Chevelle parts, from 1955 to 1972. 401–723–7580.

Tri County Auto Parts, 7625 Marsh Rd., Marine City, MI 48039: Free list ❖ Parts for 1966 to 1967 Chevelles. 313–765–3114.

Year One Inc., P.O. Box 129, Tucker, GA 30085: Catalog $5 ❖ New, used, and reproduction Chevelle restoration parts. 800–950–9503.

CHEVETTE

Year One Inc., P.O. Box 129, Tucker, GA 30085: Catalog $5 ❖ New, used, and reproduction Chevette restoration parts. 800–950–9503.

CHEVROLET

Adler's Antique Autos Inc., 562 Main St., Stephentown, NY 12168: Free information ❖ Parts for Chevrolet cars and trucks, from 1940 to 1970. 518–733–5749.

All Chevy Auto Parts, 4999 Vanden Rd., Vacaville, CA 95668: Free information ❖ Parts for 1955 to 1988 Chevrolet cars and trucks. 707–437–5466.

American Classic Automotive, P.O. Box 50286, Denton, TX 76206: Free catalog (specify year) ❖ Chevrolet car and GMC truck parts, from 1936 to 1959 and 1960 to 1972. 817–497–2456.

Antique Cars-Trucks & Parts, 526 E. 2nd, Blue Springs, NE 68318: Free information ❖ Chevrolet parts, from 1925 to 1948. 402–645–3546.

Automotive Obsolete, 1023 E. 4th St., Santa Ana, CA 92701: Catalog $3 ❖ Parts for Chevrolet cars and trucks, from 1914 to 1964. 714–541–5167.

B & B Used Auto Parts, Rt. 1, Box 691, Big Pine Key, FL 33043: Free information ❖ Parts for the Chevrolet, from 1950 and on. 305–872–9761.

C & P Chevy Parts, Box 348, Kulpsville, PA 19443: Catalog $2 ❖ New and restoration parts for 1955 to 1957 Chevrolet cars. 215–721–4300.

C.A.R.S. Inc., 1964 W. 11 Mile Rd., P.O. Box 721187, Berkley, MI 48072: Catalog $4 ❖ Parts for the 1955 to 1972 Bel-Air, Impala, Camaro, Nova, and Chevelle. 800–521–2194; 800–451–1955 (in CA & AZ).

California Classic Chevy Parts, 13545 Sycamore Ave., San Martin, CA 95046: Free information ❖ New, used, and reproduction parts for 1955 to 1957 Chevrolets. 408–683–2438.

Can Am Restoration Supply, 1964 W. Eleven Mil Rd., Berkley, MI 48072: Free information ❖ Original Chevrolet parts and interiors, from 1955 to 1964.

Chev's of the 40's, 18409 NE 28th St., Vancouver, WA 98682: Catalog $3.75 ❖ Chevrolet parts, from 1937 to 1954. 206–835–9799.

Chicago Muscle Car Parts, 912 E. Burnett Rd., Island Lake, IL 60042: Catalog $5 (refundable) ❖ New and used Chevy II parts, from 1962 to 1974. 708–526–2200.

Ciadella Ent., 3757 E. Broadway, Phoenix, AZ 85040: Free information ❖ Reproduction Chevrolet interiors. 800–528–1342.

Continental Enterprises, 1673 Cary Rd., Kelowna, British Columbia, Canada V1X 2C1: Information $12 ❖ Chevrolet dress-up accessory kits, from 1949 to 1993. 604–763–7727.

Danchuk Manufacturing Inc., 3201 S. Standard Ave., Santa Ana, CA 92705: Catalog $4 ❖ Parts for 1955 to 1957 Chevrolets. 800–854–6911; 714–751–1957 (in CA).

Howard Dobuck Chevrolet Parts, 3841 S. Ridgeland Ave., Berwyn, IL 60402: Free information ❖ New, used, and reproduction parts for 1955 to 1957 Chevrolets. 708–788–1955.

Doug's Auto Parts, Hwy. 59 North, Box 811, Marshall, MN 56258: Free information ❖ Chevrolet parts, from 1955 to 1961. 507–537–1487.

Mike Drago Chevrolet Parts, 141 E. Saint Joseph St., Easton, PA 18042: Catalog $3 ❖ N.O.S., reproduction, and used Chevrolet parts, from 1955 to 1957. 215–252–5701.

Drake Restoration, 4504 Del Amo Blvd., Torrance, CA 90503: Catalog $1 ❖

Reproduction and rubber parts, manuals, emblems, weatherstrips, and interiors, for 1955 to 1957 Chevrolets. 310–370–0080.

Edmonds Old Car Parts, 307 E. Pearl, P.O. Box 303, McLouth, KS 66054: Free information ❖ Chevrolet parts, from 1928 to 1957. 913–796–6415.

Fiberglass & Wood Company, Rt. 3, Box 900, Nashville, GA 31639: Catalog $3 ❖ Chevrolet parts, from 1927 to 1957. 912–686–3838.

The Filling Station, 990 S. 2nd St., Lebanon, OR 97355: Catalog $5 ❖ Reproduction parts for the 1929 to 1954 Chevrolet, and 1929 to 1972 trucks. 800–841–6622.

Fleetline Automotive, P.O. Box 291, Highland, NY 12529: Free information ❖ Parts for 1935 to 1975 Chevrolet cars and trucks. 914–895–2381.

GM Muscle Car Parts Inc., 10345 75th Ave., Palos Hills, IL 60465: Free information ❖ Chevrolet parts, from 1964 to 1987. 708–599–2277.

Harmon's Inc., P.O. Box 6, Hwy. 27 North, Geneva, IN 46740: Free catalog ❖ Chevrolet restoration parts, from 1955 to 1972. 219–368–7221.

J & M Auto Parts, 10 Spaulding Mill Rd., Pelham, NH 03076: Price list $1 ❖ N.O.S. and reproduction 1955 to 1976 Chevrolet parts. 302–734–4177.

Jim's Chevrolet Parts, 112567 Coloma Rd., Rancho Cordova, CA 95670: Catalog $2 ❖ Chevrolet parts for 1955 to 1957 Chevrolets. 916–635–8790.

Lange's Classics, P.O. Box 2039, Scotia, NY 12302: Catalog $5 ❖ Parts for 1955, 1956, and 1957 Chevrolet cars. 518–372–5024.

Martz Classic Chevy Parts, RD 1, Box 199, Thomasville, PA 17364: Free catalog (specify year) ❖ N.O.S. and reproduction 1955 to 1975 Chevrolet parts. 717–225–1655.

Modern Performance Classics, 1127 W. Collins, Orange, CA 92667: Free information ❖ N.O.S., reproduction, and used Nova and Chevy II parts. 800–457–NOVA.

Musclecar Specialties, 1 Coach Lantern Dr., Hopewell, NY 12533: Free information with long SASE ❖ New, N.O.S., and used parts for 1929 to 1961 Chevrolets. 914–227–6837.

New England Old Car Barn, US Rt. 1, Box 608, North Hampton, NH 03862: Free information with long SASE ❖ Chevrolet

parts, books, and memorabilia. 603–964–7100.

Norm's Antique Auto Supply, 1921 Hickory Grove Rd., Davenport, IA 52804: Free information ❖ Parts for 1923 to 1953 Chevrolets. 319–322–8388.

North Yale Auto Parts, Rt. 1, Box 707, Sperry, OK 74073: Free information ❖ Chevrolet parts, from the 1960s to 1980s. 800–256–6927; 918–288–7218 (in OK).

Obsolete Chevrolet Parts Company, P.O. Box 68, Nashville, GA 31639: Catalog $2.50 (specify year) ❖ Reproduction Chevrolet parts. 912–686–7230.

Ol' 55 Chevy Parts, 4154–A Skyron Dr., Doylestown, PA 18901: Catalog $4 ❖ Chevrolet parts, from 1955, 1956, and 1957. 215–348–5568.

Old Car Parts, 109 N. 15th St., Box 184, Clear Lake, IA 50428: Catalog $3.75 (specify year) ❖ N.O.S., new, and reproduction Chevrolet parts, from 1950 to 1954 and 1965 to 1970. 515–357–5510.

Out of the Past Parts, 3720 SW 23rd St., Gainesville, FL 32601: Free information ❖ Chevrolet parts, 1935 and later. 904–377–4079.

PRO Antique Auto Parts, 50 King Spring Rd., Windsor Locks, CT 06096: Catalog $2 ❖ New parts for 1923 to 1964 Chevrolets. 203–623–0070.

R & B Classics Chevy Parts, 10014 Old Lincoln Trail, Fairview Heights, IL 62208: Free catalog ❖ Chevrolet parts, from 1955 to 1957. 618–398–3477.

Schuster Auto Wrecking, 406 Benton, Box 31, Wathena, KS 66090: Free information with long SASE ❖ Chevrolet parts, from 1938 to 1982. 913–989–4719.

Show Cars Automotive Inc., 409 Super Sport Ln., Rt. 3, Box 9, New Ulm, MN 56073: Free catalog ❖ Chevrolet parts, from 1955 to 1972. 507–354–1958.

Southwestern Classic Chevrolet, 1230 Dan Groul Dr., Arlington. TX 76017: Catalog $4.95 ❖ Reproduction, and original GM parts for the Camaro, Chevelle, El Camino, Nova, and 1961 to 1968 Chevrolet. 817–473–6061.

Specialized Auto Parts, 7130 Capitol, P.O. Box 9405, Houston, TX 77011: Catalog $5 ❖ Chevrolet parts for 1934 to 1948 models. 713–928–3707.

Super Sport Restoration Parts Inc., 7138 Maddox Rd., P.O. Box 7, Lithonia, GA

30058: Free information ❖ Parts for the Chevy II, Nova, Chevelle, and Camaro. 404–482–9219.

Terrill Machine Inc., Rt. 2, Box 61, DeLeon, TX 76444: Free information with long SASE ❖ Engine overhaul parts for Chevrolets, from 1929 to 1951. 817–893–2610.

Volunteer State Obsolete Chevy Parts, P.O. Drawer D, Greenbrier, TN 37073: Catalog $3 (specify year) ❖ Obsolete Chevrolet parts for cars and trucks, from 1934 to 1972. 615–643–4583.

Winnicks Auto Sales & Parts, Rt. 61, P.O. Box 476, Shamokin, PA 17872: Free information with long SASE ❖ Ford and Chevrolet engines and parts for American and imported cars and trucks. 717–648–6857.

Year One Inc., P.O. Box 129, Tucker, GA 30085: Catalog $5 ❖ New, used, and reproduction Nova and Chevy II restoration parts. 800–950–9503.

CHRYSLER

B & B Used Auto Parts, Rt. 1, Box 691, Big Pine Key, FL 33043: Free information ❖ Parts for Chrysler cars, 1950 and up. 305–872–9761.

Andy Bernbaum Auto Parts, 315 Franklin St., Newton, MA 02158: Catalog $4 ❖ Chrysler parts. 617–244–1118.

Find-A-Part, Box 358, Ridgeland, MS 39158: Free information with long SASE ❖ Chrysler N.O.S. parts, automotive literature, signs, and calendars. 601–856–7214.

Hardens Muscle Car World, P.O. Box 306, Lexington, MO 64067: Catalog $4 ❖ N.O.S., reproduction, and used Chrysler parts. 800–633–4690.

Ken's Auto Wrecking, 5051 Coppersage St., Las Vegas, NV 89115: Free information ❖ Chrysler parts, 1956 to 1980. 702–643–1516.

Lasiter's Cars & Parts, Rt. 2, Box 39, Wilmar, AR 71675: Free information ❖ Parts for 1949 to 1976 models. 501–469–5453.

Mike's Auto Parts, Box 358, Ridgeland, MS 39157: Free information with long SASE ❖ Chrysler parts. 601–856–7214.

Mitchell Motor Parts Inc., 2467 Jackson Pike, Columbia, OH 43223: Free information with long SASE ❖ Chrysler parts, from 1928 to the present. 614–875–4919.

Norm's Antique Auto Supply, 1921 Hickory Grove Rd., Davenport, IA 52804: Free information ❖ Chrysler parts, from 1929 to 1955. 319–322–8388.

North Yale Auto Parts, Rt. 1, Box 707, Sperry, OK 74073: Free information ❖ Parts for Chrysler cars, 1977 and later. 800–256–6927; 918–288–7218 (in OK).

PRO Antique Auto Parts, 50 King Spring Rd., Windsor Locks, CT 06096: Catalog $2 ❖ New parts for 1929 to 1964 Chrysler cars. 203–623–0070.

Roberts Motor Parts, 17 Prospect St., West Newbury, MA 01985: Catalog $4 ❖ Parts for Chrysler cars. 508–363–5407.

Terrill Machine Inc., Rt. 2, Box 61, DeLeon, TX 76444: Free information with long SASE ❖ Engine overhaul parts for Chryslers, from 1937 to 1954. 817–893–2610.

Vintage Tin Auto Parts, 4550 Scotty Ln., Hutchinson, KS 67502: Free information with long SASE ❖ Chrysler parts, from 1940 to 1970. 316–669–8449.

CITROEN

B & B Used Auto Parts, Rt. 1, Box 691, Big Pine Key, FL 33043: Free information ❖ Parts for Citroens, 1968 and later. 305–872–9761.

COBRA

Cobra Restorers, 3099 Carter, Kenesaw, GA 30144: Catalog $5 ❖ Parts for Cobra cars. 404–427–0020.

Contemporary Classic Motor Car Company Inc., 115 Hoyt Ave., Mamaroneck, NY 10543: Catalog $5 ❖ Cobra parts. 914–381–5678.

COMET

Bill Alprin, 184 Rivervale Rd., Rivervale, NJ 07675: Free information ❖ N.O.S. parts for the Comet. 201–666–3975.

City Motor Company, P.O. Box 526, Clarkston, WA 99403: Catalog $2 ❖ Original and reproduction parts for the 1964 to 1967 Comet. 509–758–6262.

Bob Cook Classic Auto Parts, North 3rd St., Hazel, KY 42049: Catalog $6 (specify year) ❖ Reproduction parts for the 1956 to 1972 Comet. 502–492–8166.

King & Wesley Obsolete Parts Inc., Courthouse Square, Liberty, KY 42539: Free information ❖ Sheet metal, moldings, hubcaps, grilles, suspension parts, and other Comet N.O.S. and reproduction parts. 606–787–5031.

New Ford Goodies, 18008 St. Clair Ave., Cleveland, OH 44110: Free information with long SASE ❖ Genuine and reproduction

Comet parts, from 1949 and later. 216–531–8685.

Northwest Classic Falcons, 1964 NW Pettygrove, Portland, OR 97209: Parts list $2 ❖ Used, new, reproduction, and N.O.S. Comet parts, from 1960 to 1970. 503–241–9454.

CORD

J.K. Howell, 455 N. Grace St., Lombard, IL 60148: Catalog $1 ❖ Cord parts. 708–495–1949.

CORVAIR

Clark's Corvair Parts Inc., Rt. 2, Shelburne Falls, MA 01370: Catalog $5 ❖ Corvair parts. 510–625–9776.

Corvair Underground, P.O. Box 404, Hillsboro, OR 97123: Catalog $4 ❖ New, used, reproduction, and rebuilt Corvair parts. 800–825–VAIR.

Robinson's Auto Sales, 200 New York Ave., New Castle, IN 47362: Free information ❖ Parts for 1960 to 1970 models. 317–529–7603.

CORVETTE

Blue Ribbon Products Ltd., 4965 Old House Trail NE, Atlanta, GA 30342: Free catalog ❖ Corvette parts, from 1956 to 1967. 404–843–8414.

Central Corvette, 5865 Sawyer Rd., Sawyer, MI 49125: Catalog $4 ❖ Corvette parts, from 1953 to 1982. 616–426–3342.

Chevy Craft, 3414 Quirt, Lubbock, TX 79404: Catalog $5 ❖ New and used parts for the Corvette, 1955 and later. 806–747–4848.

Chicago Corvette Supply, 7322 S. Archer Ave., Justice, IL 60458: Catalog $3 ❖ New and reproduction parts for 1953 to 1982 Corvettes. 800–872–2446; 708–458–2500 (in IL).

Corvette Central, 16 Sawyer Rd., Sawyer, MI 49125: Free information with long SASE ❖ New, used, and reproduction parts for 1953 to 1982 Corvettes. 616–426–3342.

Corvette Rubber Company, 10640 W. Cadillac Rd., Cadillac, MI 49601: Free catalog (specify year) ❖ Rubber parts for Corvettes. 616–779–2888.

Corvette Specialties of MD, 1912 Liberty St., Eldersburg, MD 21784: Free information ❖ New, used, and reproduction Corvette parts. 410–795–3180.

Howard's Corvettes, RR 3, Box 162, Sioux Falls, SD 57106: Free inventory list ❖ Parts for 1968 to 1986 Corvettes. 605–743–5233.

J.B.'s Corvette Supplies, 1992 White Plains Rd., Bronx, NY 10462: Catalog $5 ❖ Corvette parts. 800–874–6019; 718–823–3100 (in NY).

Legendary Corvette Inc., P.O. Box 660, Warrington, PA 18976: Free catalog ❖ Corvette parts and body panels. 800–346–2426; 215–343–2424 (in PA).

Long Island Corvette Supply Inc., 1445 Strong Ave., Copiague, NY 11726: Catalog $3 ❖ Corvette parts, from 1963 to 1967. 516–225–3000.

Mid America Designs Inc., P.O. Box 1368, Effingham, IL 62401: Catalog $5 ❖ Corvette replacement and performance parts. 800–500–8388.

Stoudt Auto Sales, 1350 Carbon St., Reading, PA 19601: Free catalog ❖ Corvette parts, from 1953 to 1987. 800–523–8485.

Vette Products of Michigan, 2330 W. Clarkston, Lake Orion, MI 48035: Free list (specify year) ❖ Corvette parts. 313–693–1907.

Zip Products, 1250 Commercial Centre, Mechanicsville, VA 23111: Catalog $2 (refundable) ❖ Parts for restoring and maintaining Corvettes. 804–746–2290.

COUGAR

Bill Alprin, 184 Rivervale Rd., Rivervale, NJ 07675: Free information ❖ N.O.S. parts for the Cougar. 201–666–3975.

Auto Krafters Inc., P.O. Box 8, Broadway, VA 22815: Catalog $1 (specify year) ❖ New, used, and reproduction parts. 703–896–FORD.

City Motor Company, P.O. Box 526, Clarkston, WA 99403: Catalog $2 ❖ Original and reproduction parts for the 1967 to 1973 Cougar. 509–758–6262.

Bob Cook Classic Auto Parts, North 3rd St., Hazel, KY 42049: Catalog $6 (specify year) ❖ Reproduction parts for 1965 to 1973 Cougars. 502–492–8166.

King & Wesley Obsolete Parts Inc., Courthouse Square, Liberty, KY 42539: Free information ❖ Sheet metal, moldings, hubcaps, grilles, suspension parts, and other N.O.S. and reproduction parts. 606–787–5031.

Mustangs Unlimited, 185 Adams St., Manchester, CT 06040: Catalog $3 (specify year) ❖ Cougar parts. 800–978–2647.

New Ford Goodies, 18008 St. Clair Ave., Cleveland, OH 44110: Free information with long SASE ❖ Genuine and reproduction Cougar parts, from 1949 and later. 216–531–8685.

CUTLASS

Mid-Atlantic Performance, P.O. Box 333, Simpsonville, MD 21150: Catalog $2 ❖ Cutlass 4–4–2 parts. 914–735–7203.

Tamraz's Parts Discount Warehouse, 10 South 123 Normantown Rd., Naperville, IL 60564: Free information ❖ Cutlass parts. 708–851–4500

Year One Inc., P.O. Box 129, Tucker, GA 30085: Catalog $5 ❖ New, used and reproduction Cutlass restoration parts. 800–950–9503.

DATSUN

Autoshow, 8148 Woodland Dr., Indianapolis, IN 46278: Catalog $3 (refundable) ❖ Parts for the Datsun Z and other models. 800–428–2200; 317–875–0076 (in IN).

Dobi Datsun Catalog, 320 Thor Pl., Brea, CA 92621: Catalog $2 ❖ Replacement parts for the Datsun Z, 200SX, and 510. 714–529–1977.

HKS USA Inc., 20312 Gramercy Pl., Torrance, CA 90501: Catalog $8 ❖ Performance accessories for the Datsun. 310–328–8100.

Motorsport, 1139 W. Collins Ave., Orange, CA 92667: Free catalog ❖ Parts for the Datsun Z and ZX. 800–633–6331.

Perfect Plastics Industries Inc., 14th St., New Kensington, PA 15068: Free information ❖ Body parts for the Datsun Z. 800–245–6520; 412–339–3568 (in PA).

Bob Sharp Racing/Accessories, Danbury Rd., Rt. 7, Wilton, CT 06897: Catalog $1 ❖ Styling and racing accessories for the Datsun. 203–544–8386.

DE SOTO

Andy Bernbaum Auto Parts, 315 Franklin St., Newton, MA 02158: Catalog $4 ❖ Parts for the De Soto. 617–244–1118.

Mike's Auto Parts, Box 358, Ridgeland, MS 39157: Free information with long SASE ❖ De Soto parts. 601–856–7214.

PRO Antique Auto Parts, 50 King Spring Rd., Windsor Locks, CT 06096: Catalog $2 ❖ New parts for 1929 to 1964 De Sotos. 203–623–0070.

Roberts Motor Parts, 17 Prospect St., West Newbury, MA 01985: Catalog $4 ❖ Parts for De Sotos. 508–363–5407.

Terrill Machine Inc., Rt. 2, Box 61, DeLeon, TX 76444: Free information with long SASE ❖ Engine overhaul parts for De Sotos, from 1937 to 1954. 817–893–2610.

Vintage Tin Auto Parts, 4550 Scotty Ln., Hutchinson, KS 67502: Free information with long SASE ❖ De Soto parts. 316–669–8449.

DELOREAN

Delorean One, 9006 Owensmouth Ave., Canoga Park, CA 91304: Free information ❖ Delorean parts. 818–341–1796.

Delorean Service & Parts, 10728 N. 96th Ave., Peoria, AZ 85345: Free information with long SASE ❖ Delorean parts and service. 602–979–2673.

DODGE

Antique Cars-Trucks & Parts, 526 E. 2nd, Blue Springs, NE 68318: Free information ❖ Dodge parts, from 1920 to 1926. 402–645–3546.

Andy Bernbaum Auto Parts, 315 Franklin St., Newton, MA 02158: Catalog $4 ❖ Parts for Dodge cars. 617–244–1118.

Hardens Muscle Car World, P.O. Box 306, Lexington, MO 64067: Catalog $4 ❖ N.O.S., reproduction, and used Dodge parts. 800–633–4690.

Koller Dodge, 1565 W. Ogden Ave., Naperville, IL 60540: Catalog $7 ❖ Dodge restoration parts. 800–275–5655.

Mike's Auto Parts, Box 358, Ridgeland, MS 39157: Free information with long SASE ❖ Dodge parts. 601–856–7214.

Out of the Past Parts, 3720 SW 23rd St., Gainesville, FL 32601: Free information ❖ Dodge parts, 1935 and later. 904–377–4079.

PRO Antique Auto Parts, 50 King Spring Rd., Windsor Locks, CT 06096: Catalog $2 ❖ New parts for 1929 to 1964 Dodge cars. 203–623–0070.

Roberts Motor Parts, 17 Prospect St., West Newbury, MA 01985: Catalog $4 ❖ Dodge parts. 508–363–5407.

Terrill Machine Inc., Rt. 2, Box 61, DeLeon, TX 76444: Free information with long SASE ❖ Engine overhaul parts for Dodges, from 1937 to 1954. 817–893–2610.

Vintage Tin Auto Parts, 4550 Scotty Ln., Hutchinson, KS 67502: Free information with long SASE ❖ Dodge parts, from 1940 to 1970. 316–669–8449.

Year One Inc., P.O. Box 129, Tucker, GA 30085: Catalog $5 ❖ New, used, and reproduction Dodge restoration parts. 800–950–9503.

EDSEL

Beckers Auto Salvage, Hwy. 30 West, Atkins, IA 52206: Free information ❖ Parts for Edsel cars. 319–446–7141.

Bob Cook Classic Auto Parts, North 3rd St., Hazel, KY 42049: Catalog $6 (specify year) ❖ Reproduction parts for 1958 to 1960 Edsels. 502–492–8166.

Dunville Garage-Restaurant, P.O. Box 68, Dunville, KY 41528: Free information ❖ Edsel parts. 606–787–7542.

EL CAMINO

Ausley's Chevelle Parts, 300 S. Main St., Graham, NC 27253: Catalog $2 (specify year) ❖ El Camino parts for 1964 to 1972 models. 910–228–6701.

Chevelle Classics, 17892 Gothard St., Huntington Beach, CA 92647: Catalog $4 ❖ El Camino parts. 800–CHEVELLE; 714–841–5363 (in CA).

Danchuk Manufacturing Inc., 3201 S. Standard Ave., Santa Ana, CA 92705: Catalog $4 ❖ Parts for the 1964 to 1972 El Camino. 800–854–6911; 714–751–1957 (in CA).

John's N.O.S. Chevelle Parts, Box 1445, Salem, NH 03079: Price list $1 (specify year) ❖ El Camino N.O.S. and reproduction parts, chrome, emblems, grilles, and rubber. 603–898–4452.

Original Parts Group Inc., 17892 Gothard St., Huntington Beach, CA 92647: Catalog $4 ❖ El Camino parts. 800–243–8355.

Year One Inc., P.O. box 129, Tucker, GA 30085: Catalog $5 ❖ New, used, and reproduction El Camino restoration parts. 800–950–9503.

ENGLISH FORD

Dave Bean Engineering Inc., 636 E. Saint Charles St., San Andreas, CA 95249: Catalog $6 ❖ Parts for the English Ford. 209–754–5802.

ESCORT

Racer Walsh Company, 5906 Macy, Jacksonville, FL 32211: Catalog $3 ❖ Engines, suspensions, and other parts for Escorts. 800–334–0151; 904–743–8253 (in FL).

FAIRLANE

Bill Alprin, 184 Rivervale Rd., Rivervale, NJ 07675: Free information ❖ N.O.S. parts for the Fairlane. 201–666–3975.

Auto Krafters Inc., P.O. Box 8, Broadway, VA 22815: Catalog $1 (specify year) ❖ New, used, and reproduction parts for 1962 to 1971 Fairlanes. 703–896–FORD.

City Motor Company, P.O. Box 526, Clarkston, WA 99403: Catalog $2 ❖ Original and reproduction parts for the 1962 to 1971 Fairlane. 509–758–6262.

Bob Cook Classic Auto Parts, North 3rd St., Hazel, KY 42049: Catalog $6 (specify year) ❖ Reproduction parts for 1960 to 1972 Fairlanes. 502–492–8166.

Ford Parts Specialists, 98–11 211th St., Queens Village, NY 11429: Catalog $2 (specify year) ❖ Parts for the Fairlane. 212–468–8585.

Ford Parts Store, P.O. Box 226, Bryan, OH 43506: Catalog $2 ❖ Fairlane parts. 419–636–2475.

King & Wesley Obsolete Parts Inc., Courthouse Square, Liberty, KY 42539: Free information ❖ Sheet metal, moldings, hubcaps, grilles, suspension parts, and other N.O.S. and reproduction parts. 606–787–5031.

New Ford Goodies, 18008 St. Clair Ave., Cleveland, OH 44110: Free information with long SASE ❖ Genuine and reproduction Fairlane parts, from 1949 and later. 216–531–8685.

Obsolete Ford Parts Inc., 6601 S. Shields, Oklahoma City, OK 73149: Catalog $3 (specify year and car) ❖ Parts for 1960 to 1972 Fairlanes. 405–631–3933.

Ranchero Classics, P.O. Box 1248, Sunset Beach, CA 90742: Catalog $3 ❖ Fairlane parts. 714–847–7107.

Sixties Ford Parts, 639 Glanker St., Memphis, TN 38112: Catalog $4 ❖ Fairlane parts, from 1960 to 1968.

FALCON

Bill Alprin, 184 Rivervale Rd., Rivervale, NJ 07675: Free information ❖ N.O.S. parts for the Falcon. 201–666–3975.

Auto Krafters Inc., P.O. Box 8, Broadway, VA 22815: Catalog $1 (specify year) ❖ New, used, and reproduction parts for 1960 to 1965 Falcons. 703–896–FORD.

Dennis Carpenter Ford Reproductions, P.O. Box 26398, Charlotte, NC 28221: Catalog $3 ❖ Rubber parts for 1960 to 1965 Falcons. 704–786–8139.

City Motor Company, P.O. Box 526, Clarkston, WA 99403: Catalog $2 ❖ Original and reproduction parts for the 1960 to 1966 Falcon. 509–758–6262.

Bob Cook Classic Auto Parts, North 3rd St., Hazel, KY 42049: Catalog $6 (specify year) ❖ Reproduction parts for 1960 to 1972 Falcons. 502–492–8166.

Ford Parts Specialists, 98–11 211th St., Queens Village, NY 11429: Catalog $2 (specify year) ❖ Falcon parts. 212–468–8585.

King & Wesley Obsolete Parts Inc., Courthouse Square, Liberty, KY 42539: Free information ❖ Sheet metal, moldings, hubcaps, grilles, suspension parts, and other N.O.S. and reproduction parts. 606–787–5031.

New Ford Goodies, 18008 St. Clair Ave., Cleveland, OH 44110: Free information with long SASE ❖ Genuine and reproduction Falcon parts, from 1949 and later. 216–531–8685.

Northwest Classic Falcons, 1964 NW Pettygrove, Portland, OR 97209: Parts list $2 ❖ Hard-to-find new, used, and reproduction 1960 to 1970 Falcon parts. 503–241–9454.

Obsolete Ford Parts Company, 311 E. Washington Ave., Nashville, GA 31639: Catalog $2.50 (specify year) ❖ N.O.S. and reproduction parts for 1960 to 1970 Falcons. 912–686–2470.

Obsolete Ford Parts Inc., 6601 S. Shields, Oklahoma City, OK 73149: Catalog $3 (specify year and car) ❖ Parts for 1960 to 1972 Falcons. 405–631–3933.

Ranchero Classics, P.O. Box 1248, Sunset Beach, CA 90742: Catalog $3 ❖ Falcon parts. 714–847–7107.

Sixties Ford Parts, 639 Glanker St., Memphis, TN 38112: Catalog $4 ❖ Falcon parts, from 1960 to 1968.

Thunderbird & Falcon Connection, 728 E. Dunlap, Phoenix, AZ 85020: Catalog $2 (specify year) ❖ New and used Falcon parts. 602–997–9285.

FERRARI

Alfa Ricambi, 6644 San Fernando Rd., Glendale, CA 91201: Free information ❖ Parts for the Ferrari. 818–956–7933.

Algar Enterprises Inc., 1234 Lancaster Ave., P.O. Box 167, Rosemont, PA 19010: Free information ❖ Ferrari parts. 800–441–9824; 215–527–1100 (in PA).

International Auto Parts Inc., Rt. 29 North, P.O. Box 9036, Charlottesville, VA 22906: Free catalog ❖ Ferrari parts. 804–973–0555.

FIAT

Asian Italian Auto Parts, 3736 Buford Hwy., Duluth, GA 30136: Free information ❖ New and used Fiat parts. 404–476–2279.

Bayless Inc., 1111 Via Bayless, Marietta, GA 30066: Catalog $4 ❖ High performance replacement parts. 404–928–1446.

Celiberti Motors, 615 Oak St., Santa Rosa, CA 95404: Free information ❖ Fiat parts. 800–USA-FIAT.

International Auto Parts Inc., Rt. 29 North, P.O. Box 9036, Charlottesville, VA 22906: Free catalog ❖ Replacement and restoration parts and performance accessories. 804–973–0555.

Perfect Plastics Industries Inc., 14th St., New Kensington, PA 15068: Free information ❖ Body parts for the FIAT. 800–245–6520; 412–339–3568 (in PA).

FIERO

The Fiero Store, 219 Buff Cap Rd., Tolland, CT 06084: Catalog $4 ❖ Fiero parts. 203–870–7167.

FIREBIRD

Ames Performance Engineering, Bonney Rd., Marlborough, NH 03455: Free catalog ❖ Firebird parts. 800–421–2637.

Auto Heaven, 103 W. Allen St., Bloomington, IN 47401: Free information ❖ Parts for 1967 to 1969 Firebirds. 800–777–0297; 812–332–9401 (in IN).

Camaro Specialties, 900 E. Fillmore Ave., East Aurora, NY 14052: Catalog $1 ❖ New, used, N.O.S., and reproduction parts for 1967 to 1972 Firebirds. 716–652–7086.

Chicago Muscle Car Parts, 912 E. Burnett Rd., Island Lake, IL 60042: Catalog $5 (refundable) ❖ New and used Firebird parts, from 1967 to 1981. 708–526–2200.

Classic Industries, 17832 Gothard St., Huntington Beach, CA 92647: Catalog $4 ❖ Firebird parts and accessories. 800–854–1280.

D & R Classic Automotive, 31 W. 280 Diehly Rd., Naperville, IL 60563: Free price list ❖ Firebird parts. 800–472–6952.

Firebird/Trans Am America, Rt. 322, Box 427, Boalsburg, PA 16827: Free information

with long SASE ❖ Parts for 1967 to 1987 Firebirds. 800–458–3475.

The Paddock Inc., 221 W. Main, Knightstown, IN 46148: Catalog $1 ❖ Firebird parts. 317–345–2131.

Year One Inc., P.O. Box 129, Tucker, GA 30085: Catalog $5 ❖ New, used, and reproduction Firebird restoration parts. 800–950–9503.

FORD

Bill Alprin, 184 Rivervale Rd., Rivervale, NJ 07675: Catalog $5 (specify year) ❖ Trim, sheet metal, mechanical, steering, and transmission parts for 1932 to 1979 Fords. 201–666–3975.

B & B Used Auto Parts, Rt. 1, Box 691, Big Pine Key, FL 33043: Free information ❖ Ford parts, from 1950 and later. 305–872–9761.

B & W Antique Auto, 4653 Guide Meridian Rd., Bellingham, WA 98226: Catalog $3 (specify year and model) ❖ Antique Ford automotive parts. 604–743–3274.

Russ Blanton Ford Parts, 2011 Ford Ln., P.O. Box 165, Nacy, KY 42544: Free information with long SASE (specify year and model) ❖ Genuine and reproduction parts for 1960 to 1970 Falcon, 1949 to 1972 Ford, 1962 to 1971 Fairlane and Torino, 1960 to 1969 Comet, 1967 to 1971 Cougar, 1966 to 1977 Bronco, and 1948 to 1972 Ford pickups. 606–636–6878.

C & G Early Ford Parts, Commercial St., Escondido, CA 92029: Catalog $6 ❖ Reproduction parts for 1932 to 1956 Ford cars and trucks. 800–266–0470.

Dennis Carpenter Ford Reproductions, P.O. Box 26398, Charlotte, NC 28221: Catalog $3 ❖ Rubber parts for 1932 to 1964 Fords. 704–786–8139.

Concours Parts & Accessories, 3563 Numancia St., P.O. Box 1210, Santa Ynez, CA 93460: Catalog $4 ❖ Ford parts, from 1949 to 1966. 805–688–7795.

Continental Enterprises, 1673 Cary Rd., Kelowna, British Columbia, Canada V1X 2C1: Information $12 ❖ Ford dress-up accessory kits, from 1949 to 1993. 604–763–7727.

Bob Cook Classic Auto Parts, North 3rd St., Hazel, KY 42049: Catalog $6 ❖ Carpet, sheet metal, and new, obsolete, and reproduction parts for 1960 to 1972 Fords. 502–492–8166.

Doug's Auto Parts, Hwy. 59 North, Box 811, Marshall, MN 56258: Free information

❖ Ford parts, from 1932 to 1948. 507–537–1487.

Bob Drake Reproductions Inc., 1819 NW Washington Blvd., Grants Pass, OR 97526: Catalog $5 (specify model) ❖ Reproduction Ford and Ford pickup parts. 800–221–3673.

Early Ford Parts, 2948 Summer Ave., Memphis, TN 38112: Catalog $4 ❖ New parts for 1928 to 1969 Ford cars and 1928 to 1972 Ford pickup trucks. 901–323–2179.

Find-A-Part, Box 358, Ridgeland, MS 39158: Free information with long SASE ❖ Ford N.O.S. parts, automotive literature, signs, and collectible calendars. 601–856–7214.

Ford Parts Store, P.O. Box 226, Bryan, OH 43506: Catalog $2 ❖ Ford parts. 419–636–2475.

Garton's Auto Ford Parts & Accessories, 5th & Vine, Millville, NJ 08332: Free information with long SASE (specify car) ❖ Fenders, grilles, trim, ornaments, and mechanical, chassis, and other 1932 to 1960 Ford parts. 609–825–3618.

King & Wesley Obsolete Parts Inc., Courthouse Square, Liberty, KY 42539: Free information ❖ Sheet metal, moldings, hubcaps, grilles, suspension parts, and other N.O.S. and reproduction parts. 606–787–5031.

Lakeview Vintage Distributing, 1410 E. Genesee, Skaneateles, NY 13152: Free information ❖ Reproduction parts for 1928 to 1948 Ford cars. 315–685–7414.

Lasiter's Cars & Parts, Rt. 2, Box 39, Wilmar, AR 71675: Free information ❖ Parts for 1949 to 1979 Fords and trucks. 501–469–5453.

McDonald Ford Parts Company, RR 3, Box 94, Rockport, IN 47635: Catalog $5 ❖ Parts for 1932 to 1982 Fords. 812–359–4965.

Medicine Bow Motors Inc., 5120 Hwy. 93 South, Missoula, MT 59801: Free information ❖ Parts for 1928 to 1948 Fords. 406–251–2244.

Mustangs Unlimited, 185 Adams St., Manchester, CT 06040: Catalog $3 (specify year) ❖ Ford performance parts, from 1965 to 1973. 800–978–2647.

New England Old Car Barn, US Rt. 1, Box 608, North Hampton, NH 03862: Free information with long SASE ❖ Ford V-8 parts, books, and memorabilia. 603–964–7100.

New Ford Goodies, 18008 St. Clair Ave., Cleveland, OH 44110: Free information with long SASE ❖ Genuine and reproduction Ford parts, from 1949 and later. 216–531–8685.

Norm's Antique Auto Supply, 1921 Hickory Grove Rd., Davenport, IA 52804: Free information ❖ Ford parts, from 1917 to 1969. 319–322–8388.

North Yale Auto Parts, Rt. 1, Box 707, Sperry, OK 74073: Free information ❖ Parts for 1977 and later Fords. 800–256–6927; 918–288–7218 (in OK).

Obsolete Ford Parts Company, 311 E. Washington Ave., Nashville, GA 31639: Catalog $2.50 (specify year) ❖ N.O.S. and reproduction parts for 1949 to 1964 Fords. 912–686–2470.

Obsolete Ford Parts Inc., 6601 S. Shields, Oklahoma City, OK 73149: Catalog $3 (specify year and car) ❖ Ford parts, from 1928 to 1932. 405–631–3933.

Out of the Past Parts, 3720 SW 23rd St., Gainesville, FL 32601: Free information ❖ Ford parts, 1935 and later. 904–377–4079.

Papke Enterprises, 17202 Gothard St., Huntington Beach, CA 92647: Catalog $4 ❖ Parts for 1949 to 1951 Fords. Some 1952 to 1953 parts available. 714–843–6969.

PRO Antique Auto Parts, 50 King Spring Rd., Windsor Locks, CT 06096: Catalog $2 ❖ New parts for 1928 to 1964 Fords. 203–623–0070.

Schuster Auto Wrecking, 406 Benton, Box 31, Wathena, KS 66090: Free information with long SASE ❖ Ford parts, from 1938 to 1982. 913–989–4719.

Sixties Ford Parts, 639 Glanker St., Memphis, TN 38112: Catalog $4 ❖ Ford parts, from 1960 to 1968.

Dick Spadaro Early Ford Reproductions, 124 Maple Ave., Altamont, NY 12009: Catalog $4 ❖ Ford parts, from 1932 to 1948. 518–861–5367.

Specialized Auto Parts, 7130 Capitol, P.O. Box 9405, Houston, TX 77011: Catalog $5 ❖ Parts for 1909 to 1948 Fords. 713–928–3707.

T-Bird Nest, P.O. Box 1012, Grapevine, TX 76051: Free information ❖ New parts for 1928 to 1959 Fords. 817–481–1776.

Tee-Bird Products Inc., Box 153, Exton, PA 19341: Catalog $2 ❖ Ford passenger car parts, from 1955 and 1956. 215–363–1725.

Valley Ford Parts, 11610 Van Owen St., North Hollywood, CA 91605: Free information ❖ New and used parts for 1928 to 1970 Fords. 818–982–5303.

Vintage Tin Auto Parts, 4550 Scotty Ln., Hutchinson, KS 67502: Free information with long SASE ❖ Ford parts, from 1940 to 1970. 316–669–8449.

Winnicks Auto Sales & Parts, Rt. 61, P.O. Box 476, Shamokin, PA 17872: Free information with long SASE ❖ Ford and Chevrolet engines, and parts for American and imported cars and trucks. 717–648–6857.

FRAZER

Wayne's Auto Salvage, RR 3, Box 41, Winner, SD 57580: Free information ❖ Frazer parts. 605–842–2054.

GALAXIE

Bill Alprin, 184 Rivervale Rd., Rivervale, NJ 07675: Free information ❖ N.O.S. parts for the Galaxie. 201–666–3975.

City Motor Company, P.O. Box 526, Clarkston, WA 99403: Catalog $2 ❖ Original and reproduction parts for the 1960 to 1966 Galaxie. 509–758–6262.

Bob Cook Classic Auto Parts, North 3rd St., Hazel, KY 42049: Catalog $6 (specify year) ❖ Reproduction parts for 1960 to 1972 Galaxies. 502–492–8166.

GRAHAM

Graham Factory Service, 1919 S. Wayne, Auburn, IN 46706: Free catalog ❖ Original engines, chassis, body parts, and instruments. 219–925–2210.

GRANADA

Bill Alprin, 184 Rivervale Rd., Rivervale, NJ 07675: Free information ❖ N.O.S. parts for the Granada. 201–666–3975.

GTO

Ames Performance Engineering, Bonney Rd., Marlborough, NH 03455: Free catalog ❖ GTO parts. 800–421–2637.

Chicago Muscle Car Parts, 912 E. Burnett Rd., Island Lake, IL 60042: Catalog $5 (refundable) ❖ New and used GTO parts, from 1964 to 1972. 708–526–2200.

Obsolete Ford Parts Inc., 6601 S. Shields, Oklahoma City, OK 73149: Catalog $3 (specify year and car) ❖ Ford parts, from 1928 to 1932. 405–631–3933.

The Paddock Inc., 221 W. Main, Knightstown IN 46148: Catalog $1 ❖ GTO parts. 317–345–2131.

HONDA

A & H Motorsport, 660 Easton Rd., Easton, PA 19044: Free catalog ❖ Honda parts. 215–657–0775.

A-T Engineering, 115 S. Main St., Newton, CT 06470: Catalog $4 ❖ Honda parts. 203–270–9914.

Alpharetta Auto Parts Inc., 5770 Hwy. 10 North, Alpharetta, GA 30201: Free information ❖ BMW, Honda, and Acura parts. 404–475–1929.

Dobi Honda Catalog, 320 Thor Pl., Brea, CA 92621: Catalog $2 ❖ Honda parts. 714–529–1977.

HKS USA Inc., 20312 Gramercy Pl., Torrance, CA 90501: Catalog $8 ❖ Performance parts for the Honda. 310–328–8100.

Ide Honda, 875 Panoma, Rochester, NY 14625: Free information ❖ Factory parts. 800–362–9012.

Jackson Racing, 16291 Gothard St., Huntington Beach, CA 92647: Catalog $5 ❖ High performance and styling accessories for the Honda. 714–841–3001.

MSO Parts, 1543 Easton Rd., Roslyn, PA 19001: Free information ❖ Genuine factory parts for the Honda. 800–628–0817; 215–657–8423 (in PA).

HUDSON

American Motor Haven, 1107 Campbell Ave., San Jose, CA 95126: Free information with long SASE ❖ Obsolete and hard-to-find Hudson parts. 408–246–0957.

Dunville Garage-Restaurant, P.O. Box 68, Dunnville, KY 41528: Free information ❖ Hudson parts. 606–787–7542.

Vintage Tin Auto Parts, 4550 Scotty Ln., Hutchinson, KS 67502: Free information with long SASE ❖ Hudson parts. 316–669–8449.

Wayne's Auto Salvage, RR 3, Box 41, Winner, SD 57580: Free information ❖ Hudson parts. 605–842–2054.

IMPALA

Chevy Craft, 3414 Quirt, Lubbock, TX 79404: Catalog $5 ❖ New and used parts for the Impala, 1955 and later. 806–747–4848.

Luttys Chevys, RD 2, Box 61, Cheswick, PA 15024: Catalog $3 ❖ Carpets, interiors, weatherstripping, moldings, sheet metal, replacement panels, and other new, used, and reproduction parts, from 1955 to 1957. 412–265–2988.

Musclecar Specialties, 1 Coach Lantern Dr., Hopewell, NY 12533: Free information with long SASE ❖ New, N.O.S., and used parts for the 1962 to 1972 Impala. 914–227–6837.

Old Car Parts, 109 N. 15th St., Box 184, Clear Lake, IA 50428: Catalog $3.75 (specify year) ❖ N.O.S., new, and reproduction Impala parts, from 1965 to 1970. 515–357–5510.

Sinclair's Impala Parts, 3324 Westover Dr., Danville, VA 24541: Catalog $2 ❖ Impala parts. 804–685–2337.

Tom's Obsolete Chevy Parts, 14 Delta Dr., Pawtucket, RI 02860: Catalog $1 ❖ Impala parts, from 1955 to 1972. 401–723–7580.

JAGUAR

G.W. Bartlett Company, 1912 Granville Ave., P.O. Box 1673, Muncie, IN 47308: Free catalog ❖ Interior restoration parts. 800–338–8034.

Bassett's Jaguar Inc., P.O. Box 245, Wyoming, RI 02898: Free catalog ❖ Jaguar parts. 401–539–3010.

Bluff City British Cars, 1810 Getwell, Memphis, TN 38111: Free information ❖ Parts for Jaguars. 800–621–0227; 901–743–4422 (in TN).

British Auto, 703 Penfield Rd., Macedon, NY 14502: Free information ❖ Jaguar parts, from 1950 to 1982. 315–986–3097.

British Auto/USA, 92 Londonberry Tnpk., Manchester, NH 03104: Catalog $4 ❖ Jaguar upholstery and hard-to-find chrome, electrical, mechanical, and brake system parts. 603–622–1050.

British Motorsports Inc., 1143 Dell Ave., Campbell, CA 95008: Free information with long SASE ❖ New, used, and rebuilt Jaguar parts. 408–370–7174.

British Parts Northwest, 4105 SE Lafayette Hwy., Dayton, OR 97114: Catalog $2.50 ❖ Jaguar parts. 503–864–2001.

British Vintages Inc., 645 Tank Farm Rd., San Luis Obispo, CA 93401: Catalog $3 ❖ New, used, and reproduction Jaguar parts, from 1948 and later. 800–350–JAGS.

Classic Automobiles, 1974 Charles St., Costa Mesa, CA 92627: Catalog $5 ❖ Jaguar parts, maintenance aids, books, and owner's manuals. 714–646–6293.

Engel Imports Inc., 5850 Stadium Dr., Kalamazoo, MI 49009: Free information with long SASE ❖ Discontinued, obsolete, and "dealer only" parts for cars, 1953 to the present. 800–253–4080; 616–375–1000 (in MI).

English Car Spares Ltd., 345 Branch Rd SW, Alpharetta, GA 30201: Free information ❖ Jaguar parts. 800–241–1916; 404–475–2662 (in GA).

Exotic Car Parts, 923 N. Central Ave., Upland, CA 91786: Free information ❖ Parts for Jaguar XK120 and MKVII to XXJ6 and XJS. 800–231–3588.

Greystone Automotive, 1733 Victory Blvd., Glendale, CA 91201: Free information ❖ New and used Jaguar parts. 818–246–7385.

George Haug Company Inc., 517 E. 73rd St., New York, NY 10021: Free information ❖ Jaguar parts. 212–288–0176.

Jaguar & SAAB of Troy, 1815 Maplelawn, Troy, MI 48084: Free catalog ❖ Parts for the Jaguar. 800–832–5839; 313–643–7894 (in MI).

Jaguar Heaven, 1433 Tillie Lewis Dr., Stockton, CA 95206: Free information ❖ Used Jaguar parts. 209–942–4524.

Jaguar Motor Works, 3701 Longview Dr., Atlanta, GA 30341: Free information ❖ New, used, and rebuilt parts for XJ6 and XJS Jaguars. 800–331–2193; 404–451–3839 (in GA).

Moore Jaguar, 14116 Manchester, St. Louis, MO 63011: Free information ❖ Jaguar parts. 800–JAG-PART; 314–394–0900 (in MO).

Moss Motors Ltd., 7200 Hollister Rd., P.O. Box 847, Goleta, CA 93116: Free catalog (specify model) ❖ Hard-to-find parts for Jaguars. 800–235–6954.

Peninsula Imports, 3749 Harlem, Buffalo, NY 14215: Free catalog ❖ Jaguar parts. 800–999–1209.

Regency Motors, Bloomfield Ave. & Valley Rd., Montclair, NJ 07042: Free information with long SASE ❖ Jaguar parts. 201–746–4500.

Scotland Yard British Cars Ltd., 3101 E. 52nd Ave., Denver, CO 80216: Free information with long SASE ❖ New, used, and remanufactured parts for the Jaguar. 800–222–1415; 800–328–8716 (in CO).

Special Interest Car Parts, 1340 Hartford Ave., Johnston, RI 02919: Free catalog ❖ Parts for 1948 to 1988 Jaguars. 800–556–7496.

Terry's Jaguar Parts, 117 E. Smith St., Benton, IL 62812: Free catalog ❖

High-performance Jaguar parts. 800–851–9438.

XK's Unlimited, 850 Fiero Ln., San Luis Obispo, CA 93401: Catalog $6 ❖ Parts for Jaguars, from 1948 and later. 800–445–JAGS.

JAVELIN

American Parts Depot, 409 N. Main St., West Manchester, OH 45382: Free information ❖ New, used, reproduction, and N.O.S. parts. 513–678–7249.

Byers Jeep-Eagle, 390 E. Broad St., P.O. Box 16513, Columbus, OH 43216: Free catalog ❖ Original parts. 614–221–9181.

JEEP

American Motor Haven, 1107 Campbell Ave., San Jose, CA 95126: Free information with long SASE ❖ Obsolete and hard-to-find parts for the Jeep. 408–246–0957.

Byers Jeep-Eagle, 390 E. Broad St., P.O. Box 16513, Columbus, OH 43216: Free catalog ❖ Original parts. 614–221–9181.

Find-A-Part, Box 358, Ridgeland, MS 39158: Free information with long SASE ❖ N.O.S. parts and automotive literature. 601–856–7214.

Kennedy American Inc., 7100 State Rt. 142 SE, West Jefferson, OH 43162: Free catalog ❖ Jeep, Rambler, and American Motors reproduction, used, and performance parts. 614–879–7283.

Obsolete Jeep & Willys Parts, 6110 17th St. East, Bradenton, FL 34203: Free information ❖ New, used, rebuilt, and N.O.S. parts. 813–756–7844.

Quadratec, 5133 Westchester Pike, Newtown Square, PA 19073: Free information ❖ Mechanical and performance parts for Jeep Wranglers. 800–745–5337.

Sports & Classics, 512 Boston Post Rd., Darien, CT 06820: Catalog $5 ❖ Restoration, engine, electrical, and body parts. 203–655–8731.

Willys & Jeep Parts, 572 Ramtown Rd., Howell, NJ 07731: Free information ❖ Hard-to-find mechanical and body parts, convertible tops, hubcaps, and books. 908–458–3966.

JENSEN

Dave Bean Engineering Inc., 636 E. Saint Charles St., San Andreas, CA 95249: Catalog $6 ❖ Jensen parts. 209–754–5802.

British Auto, 703 Penfield Rd., Macedon, NY 14502: Free information ❖ Jensen parts, from 1950 to 1982. 315–986–3097.

Delta Motorsports Inc., 2724 E. Bell Rd., Phoenix, AZ 85032: Free catalog ❖ Jensen factory parts. 602–265–8026.

KAISER-FRAZER

Fannaly's Auto Exchange, 701 Range Rd., P.O. Box 23, Ponchatoula, LA 70454: Free information ❖ A limited selection of Kaiser-Fraser parts. 504–386–3714.

Wayne's Auto Salvage, RR 3, Box 41, Winner, SD 57580: Free information ❖ Kaiser parts. 605–842–2054.

Zeug's K-F Parts, 1449 E. Uppingham Dr., Thousand Oaks, CA 91360: Parts list $2 ❖ N.O.S. and used Kaiser-Frazer, Henry J, and Kaiser-Darrin parts. 805–492–5895.

LANCIA

Alfa Ricambi, 6644 San Fernando Rd., Glendale, CA 91201: Free information ❖ Parts for the Lancia. 818–956–7933.

Bayless Inc., 1111 Via Bayless, Marietta, GA 30066: Catalog $4 ❖ Replacement parts. 404–928–1446.

Celiberti Motors, 615 Oak St., Santa Rosa, CA 95404: Free information ❖ Lancia parts. 800–USA-FIAT.

International Autosport, Catalog Sales, Rt. 29 North, P.O. Box 9036, Charlottesville, VA 22906: Free catalog ❖ Replacement, restoration, and performance parts for the Lancia. 800–726–1199.

LASALLE

Automotive Obsolete, 1023 E. 4th St., Santa Ana, CA 92701: Catalog $3 ❖ New parts for 1926 to 1970 Lasalle cars. 714–541–5167.

Classic Auto Parts, 550 Industrial Dr., Carmel, IN 46032: Free information ❖ Genuine classic LaSalle parts, from 1928 to 1941. 317–844–8154.

Out of the Past Parts, 3720 SW 23rd St., Gainesville, FL 32601: Free information ❖ Parts for 1935 and later LaSalles. 904–377–4079.

LE MANS

Chicago Muscle Car Parts, 912 E. Burnett Rd., Island Lake, IL 60042: Catalog $5 (refundable) ❖ New and used Le Mans parts, from 1964 to 1972. 708–526–2200.

LEYLAND

Atlanta Imported British Auto Parts, 5383 Buford Hwy., Doraville, GA 30340: Catalog $1 (refundable) ❖ New, used, and imported Leyland parts. 404–451–4411.

LINCOLN

Aabar's Cadillac & Lincoln Salvage, 9700 NE 23rd, Oklahoma City, OK 73141: Free information with long SASE ❖ Lincoln and Cadillac parts, from 1939 and later. 405–769–3318.

Bill Alprin, 184 Rivervale Rd., Rivervale, NJ 07675: Free information ❖ N.O.S. parts for the Lincoln Mark II to Mark VII, and for the Continental. 201–666–3975.

Classic Cars Unlimited, P.O. Box 249, Lakeshore, MS 39558: Catalog $3 (specify year) ❖ Lincoln parts, from 1960 to 1976. 800–543–8691; 601–467–9633 (in MS).

Classique Cars Unlimited, P.O. Box 249, Lakeshore, MS 39558: Parts list $4 ❖ Lincoln parts, from 1958 to 1988. 601–467–9633.

Continental Enterprises, 1673 Cary Rd., Kelowna, British Columbia, Canada V1X 2C1: Information $12 ❖ Lincoln dress-up accessory kits, from 1949 to 1993. 604–763–7727.

Bob Cook Classic Auto Parts, North 3rd St., Hazel, KY 42049: Catalog $6 (specify year) ❖ Reproduction parts for 1960 to 1972 Lincolns. 502–492–8166.

Fannaly's Auto Exchange, 701 Range Rd., P.O. Box 23, Ponchatoula, LA 70454: Free information ❖ Parts for 1946 to 1956 Lincolns. 504–386–3714.

Narragansett Reproductions, Woodville Rd., P.O. Box 51, Wood River Junction, RI 02894: Catalog $2 (specify car) ❖ Parts for 1936 to 1948 Lincolns, 1956 to 1957 Lincoln Continentals, and the Lincoln Zephyr. 401–364–3839.

New Ford Goodies, 18008 St. Clair Ave., Cleveland, OH 44110: Free information with long SASE ❖ Genuine and reproduction Lincoln parts, from 1949 and later. 216–531–8685.

Reliable Motoring Accessories, 1751 Spruce St., Riverside, CA 92505: Catalog $3 ❖ New and reproduction Continental Mark II parts. 800–854–4770; 714–781–0261 (in CA).

LOTUS

Dave Bean Engineering Inc., 636 E. Saint Charles St., San Andreas, CA 95249: Catalog $6 ❖ Lotus parts. 209–754–5802.

British Auto, 703 Penfield Rd., Macedon, NY 14502: Free information ❖ Lotus parts, from 1950 to 1982. 315–986–3097.

British Motorsports Inc., 1143 Dell Ave., Campbell, CA 95008: Free information with long SASE ❖ New, used, and rebuilt parts. 408–370–7174.

Kampena Motors, 140 S. Linden Ave., South San Francisco, CA 94080: Free information ❖ Lotus parts. 415–583–5480.

MASERATI

Algar Enterprises Inc., 1234 Lancaster Ave., P.O. Box 167, Rosemont, PA 19010: Free information ❖ Maserati parts. 800–441–9824; 215–527–1100 (in PA).

Beach Imports, 30 Auto Center Dr., Tustin, CA 92680: Free information ❖ Maserati parts. 800–777–4895.

International Autosport, Catalog Sales, Rt. 29 North, P.O. Box 9036, Charlottsville, VA 22906: Free catalog ❖ Replacement, restoration, and performance parts for the Maserati. 800–726–1199.

Maserati Automobiles Inc., 1501 Caton Ave., Baltimore, MD 21227: Free information ❖ Maserati parts. 301–646–6400.

MAVERICK

Bill Alprin, 184 Rivervale Rd., Rivervale, NJ 07675: Free information ❖ N.O.S. parts for the Maverick. 201–666–3975.

MAZDA

Autoshow, 8148 Woodland Dr., Indianapolis, IN 46278: Catalog $3 (refundable) ❖ Parts for the Mazda Rx-7. 800–428–2200; 317–875–0076 (in IN).

Dobi Mazda Catalog, 320 Thor Pl., Brea, CA 92621: Catalog $2 ❖ Parts for the Mazda Rx7 and GLC. 714–529–1977.

HKS USA Inc., 20312 Gramercy Pl., Torrance, CA 90501: Catalog $8 ❖ Performance parts for the Mazda. 310–328–8100.

MSO Parts, 1543 Easton Rd., Roslyn, PA 19001: Free information ❖ Genuine factory parts for the Mazda. 800–628–0817; 215–657–8423 (in PA).

Bob Sharp Racing/Accessories, Danbury Rd., Rt. 7, Wilton, CT 06897: Catalog $1 ❖ Mazda racing and styling components. 203–544–8386.

MERCEDES-BENZ

Aase Brothers Inc., 701 E. Cypress St., Anaheim, CA 92805: Free information ❖

Mercedes-Benz parts. 800–444–7444; 714–956–2419 (in CA).

Adsit MB Supply, 12440 S. Old Rd., Muncie, IN 47303: Free information ❖ New parts for the Mercedes-Benz. 800–521–7650; 317–282–1593 (in IN).

ATVM Automotive Parts, 97 Mount Royal Ave., Aberdeen, MD 21001: Free information with long SASE ❖ Mercedes-Benz parts, from 1934 to 1972. 410–272–2252.

C.A.R.S. Inc., 1964 W. 11 Mile Rd., P.O. Box 721187, Berkley, MI 48072: Catalog $4 ❖ Parts for 1976 to 1985 Mercedes-Benz cars. 800–521–2194; 800–451–1955 (in CA & AZ).

Embee Parts, 4000 Lee Rd., Smyrna, GA 30080: Free information ❖ Parts for 1934 to 1988 Mercedes-Benz. 404–434–5686.

Express Automotive Industries, P.O. Box 756, Moorpark, CA 93020: Free information ❖ Mercedes-Benz parts. 800–525–9080.

Europarts, 2048 Aldergrove, Escondido, CA 92025: Free information with long SASE ❖ Mercedes-Benz parts. 619–743–3377.

IMPCO Inc., 5300 Glenmont Dr., Houston, TX 77081: Free catalog ❖ Original 1977 to 1985 diesel Mercedes-Benz parts. 800–243–1220; 713–868–1638 (in TX).

Miller's Incorporated, 7391 Prince Dr., Huntington Beach, CA 92647: Free catalog ❖ Replacement parts. 800–338–7787; 714–375–6565 (in CA).

MERCURY

Bill Alprin, 184 Rivervale Rd., Rivervale, NJ 07675: Catalog $5 (specify year) ❖ Trim, sheet metal, mechanical, steering, and transmission parts for 1939 to 1979 Mercury cars. 201–666–3975.

Continental Enterprises, 1673 Cary Rd., Kelowna, British Columbia, Canada V1X 2C1: Information $12 ❖ Mercury dress-up accessory kits, from 1949 to 1993. 604–763–7727.

Bob Cook Classic Auto Parts, North 34th St., Hazel, KY 42049: Catalog $6 (specify year) ❖ Reproduction parts for the 1956 to 1972 Mercury. 502–492–8166.

McDonald Ford Parts Company, RR 3, Box 94, Rockport, IN 47635: Catalog $5 ❖ Parts for 1932 to 1982 Mercury cars. 812–359–4965.

Mercury Research Company, 639 Glankler St., Memphis, TN 38112: Catalog $4 ❖ New parts for 1949 to 1959 Mercury cars.

Mustangs Unlimited, 185 Adams St., Manchester, CT 06040: Catalog $3 (specify year) ❖ Cougar reproduction and original restoration parts, from 1965 to 1973. 800–243–7278.

New Ford Goodies, 18008 St. Clair Ave., Cleveland, OH 44110: Free information with long SASE ❖ Genuine and reproduction Mercury parts, from 1949 and later. 216–531–8685.

Papke Enterprises, 17202 Gothard St., Huntington Beach, CA 92647: Catalog $4 ❖ Parts for 1949 to 1951 Mercury cars. 714–843–6969.

PRO Antique Auto Parts, 50 King Spring Rd., Windsor Locks, CT 06096: Catalog $2 ❖ New parts for the 1928 to 1964 Mercury. 203–623–0070.

METEOR

Bob Cook Classic Auto Parts, North 3rd St., Hazel, KY 42049: Catalog $6 (specify year) ❖ Reproduction parts for the 1956 to 1964 Meteor. 502–492–8166.

MG

Abingdon Spares Ltd., South St., P.O. Box 37, Walpole, NH 03608: Catalog $6 ❖ MG parts. 800–225–0251.

Aurora Auto Wrecking Inc., 9217 Aurora Avenue North, Seattle, WA 98103: Free information ❖ New, used, and rebuilt MG parts. 800–426–6464.

British Auto, 703 Penfield Rd., Macedon, NY 14502: Free information ❖ MG parts, from 1950 to 1982. 315–986–3097.

British Miles, 222 Grove, Morrisville, PA 19067: Free information ❖ Reconditioned and new MG parts. 215–736–9300.

Burnett's Garage Inc., 60 Maple St., Wenham, MA 01984: Free information ❖ MG parts. 508–468–4011.

Dobi MGB Catalog, 320 Thor Pl., Brea, CA 92621: Catalog $2 ❖ Parts for MGB cars. 714–529–1977.

Engel Imports Inc., 5850 Stadium Dr., Kalamazoo, MI 49009: Free information with long SASE ❖ Discontinued, obsolete, and "dealer only" parts for MG cars, 1953 to the present. 800–253–4080; 616–375–1000 (in MI).

English Car Spares Ltd., 345 Branch Rd SW, Alpharetta, GA 30201: Free information ❖ MG parts. 800–241–1916; 404–475–2662 (in GA).

Greystone Automotive, 1733 Victory Blvd., Glendale, CA 91201: Free information ❖ New and used MG parts. 818–246–7385.

George Haug Company Inc., 517 E. 73rd St., New York, NY 10021: Free information ❖ MG parts. 212–288–0176.

M & G Vintage Auto, 265 Rt. 17, Box 226, Tuxedo Park, NY 10987: Free information ❖ Parts for the MGA, MGB, and MGT. 914–753–5900.

MG Bits & Spares, 105 Azalea Ln., P.O. Box 864, Jonesboro, AR 72401: Free information ❖ Parts for the MGB and MGB-GT. 501–932–7150.

Moss Motors Ltd., 7200 Hollister Rd., P.O. Box 847, Goleta, CA 93116: Free catalog (specify model) ❖ MG parts. 800–235–6954.

New England Old Car Barn, US Rt. 1, Box 608, North Hampton, NH 03862: Free information with long SASE ❖ MG parts and books. 603–964–7100.

Northwest Import Parts, 10915 SW 64th Ave., Portland, OR 97219: Information $1 ❖ Parts for the MGB, MGA, and Midget. 503–245–3806.

Peninsula Imports, 3749 Harlem, Buffalo, NY 14215: Free catalog ❖ MG parts. 800–999–1209.

Scarborough Faire, 1151 Main St., Pawtucket, RI 02860: Catalog $3 (specify year and car) ❖ MGB body repair parts and panels. 401–724–4200.

Scotland Yard British Cars Ltd., 3101 E. 52nd Ave., Denver, CO 80216: Free information with long SASE ❖ New, used, and remanufactured parts. 800–222–1415; 800–328–8716 (in CO).

Sports & Classics, 512 Boston Post Rd., Darien, CT 06820: Catalog $5 ❖ Restoration, engine, electrical, and body parts. 203–655–8731.

Victoria British Ltd., P.O. Box 14991, Lenexa, KS 66215: Free catalog ❖ Original, replacement, and reproduction parts for the MG and other British sports cars. 800–255–0088.

Vintage Specialists, P.O. Box 772, Hobe Sound, FL 33475: Catalog $2 ❖ New and used MG parts. 407–546–3177.

MITSUBISHI

HKS USA Inc., 20312 Gramercy Pl., Torrance, CA 90501: Catalog $8 ❖ Performance parts for the Mitsubishi. 310–328–8100.

MODEL A & MODEL T FORDS

Antique Cars-Trucks & Parts, 526 E. 2nd, Blue Springs, NE 68318: Free information ❖ Ford Model A and T parts, from 1917 to 1931. 402–645–3546.

Bob's Antique Auto Parts, 7826 Forest Hills Rd., P.O. Box 2523, Rockford, IL 61132: Catalog $2 ❖ Ford Model T parts. 815–633–7244.

Bratton's Antique Ford Parts, 9410 Watkins Rd., Gaithersburg, MD 20879: Free catalog ❖ Parts for the Model A Ford. 301–253–1929.

BSIA Mustang Supply, 278 S. 700 East, Mill Creek, IN 46365: Free information ❖ Parts from 1928 to 1931. 219–326–1300.

C.A.R. Distributors, 12375 New Holland St., Holland, MI 48072: Free information with long SASE ❖ Ford Model A parts. 616–399–6783.

Carlin Manufacturing & Distributor Inc., 1250 Gulf St., Beaumont, TX 77701: Catalog $2 ❖ Wood, sheet metal, seat springs, engine and chassis parts for Ford Model T, A, and V8 cars. 409–833–9757.

Cars & Parts, Rt. 1, Dyer, TN 38330: Free information ❖ Parts for Ford Model A and T cars. 901–643–6448.

Connecticut Antique Ford Parts, 985 Middlesex Tnpk., Old Saybrook, CT 06475: Free information ❖ Model A Ford parts. 203–388–5872.

Dunville Garage-Restaurant, P.O. Box 68, Dunnville, KY 41528: Free information ❖ Model A parts. 606–787–7542.

Ford Parts Specialists, 98–11 211th St., Queens Village, NY 11419: Free catalog (specify year) ❖ Ford Model A and T parts. 718–468–8585.

Gaslight Auto Parts Inc., P.O. Box 291, Urbana, OH 43078: Catalog $2 ❖ Replacement parts for the Ford Model A and T. 513–652–2145.

LeBaron Bonney Company, P.O. Box 6, Chestnut St., Amesbury, MA 01913: Catalog $1 ❖ Interiors and tops, seat upholstery, panels and headlining, top kits, and top assemblies for 1928 to 1931 Fords. 508–388–3811.

Mac's Antique Auto Parts, P.O. Box 337, Lockport, NY 14094: Free catalog ❖ Parts for 1928 to 1931 Model A; 1909 to 1927 Model T; and early Ford V-8s, from 1932 to 1948. 800–828–7948; 800–777–0948 (in NY).

Mal's A Sales, 4966 Pacheco Blvd., Martinez, CA 94553: Catalog $2 ❖ New parts for 1909 to 1931 Fords. 510–228–8180.

Masonville Garage, Box 57, Masonville, IA 50654: Catalog $2 (refundable) ❖ Model A parts. 319–927–4290.

New England Old Car Barn, US Rt. 1, Box 608, North Hampton, NH 03862: Free information with long SASE ❖ Ford Model A and T parts, books, and memorabilia. 603–964–7100.

Obsolete Ford Parts Inc., 6601 S. Shields, Oklahoma City, OK 73149: Catalog $3 (specify year and car) ❖ Model A and T parts. 405–631–3933.

Rootlieb Inc., P.O. Box 1829, Turlock, CA 95381: Free catalog ❖ Sheet metal parts for early vintage Ford cars. 209–632–2203.

Sacramento Vintage Ford Parts Inc., 4675 Aldona Ln., Sacramento, CA 95841: Catalog $5 ❖ Model T parts, from 1909 to 1927; Model A parts, from 1928 to 1931. 916–489–3444.

Smith & Jones Antique Parts, 1 Biloxi Square, Columbia Airport, West Columbia, SC 29170: Catalog $2.50 ❖ Reproduction Model A and T Ford parts. 803–822–4141.

Snyder's Antique Auto Parts, New Springfield, OH 44443: Catalog $1 ❖ Model T parts, 1909 to 1927 and Model A parts, 1928 to 1931. 216–519–5313.

Tin Lizzie Antique Auto Parts, 1549 Ellinwood, Des Plaines, IL 60016: Catalog $3 ❖ Antique Ford parts, from 1928 to 1931. 708–298–7889.

Vintage Auto Parts, 11318 Beach Blvd., Stanton, CA 90680: Free information with long SASE ❖ New parts for Ford Model A and T. 714–894–5464.

MONTE CARLO

Chevrolet Specialties, 4335 S. Highland Ave., Butler, PA 16001: Catalog $3 ❖ Monte Carlo parts, from 1970 to 1977. 412–482–2670.

Chicago Muscle Car Parts, 912 E. Burnett Rd., Island Lake, IL 60042: Catalog $5 (refundable) ❖ New and used Monte Carlo parts, from 1970 to 1972. 708–526–2200.

Harmon's Inc., P.O. Box 6, Hwy. 27 North, Geneva, IN 46740: Free catalog ❖ Monte Carlo restoration parts, from 1970 to 1977. 219–368–7221.

Original Parts Group Inc., 17892 Gothard St., Huntington Beach, CA 92647: Catalog $4 ❖ Monte Carlo parts. 800–243–8355.

Tamraz's Parts Discount Warehouse, 10 South 123 Normantown Rd., Naperville, IL 60564: Free information ❖ Monte Carlo parts. 708–851–4500

Year One Inc., P.O. Box 129, Tucker, GA 30085: Catalog $5 ❖ New, used, and reproduction Monte Carlo restoration parts. 800–950–9503.

MONTEGO

Bill Alprin, 184 Rivervale Rd., Rivervale, NJ 07675: Free information ❖ N.O.S. parts for the Montego. 201–666–3975.

Bob Cook Classic Auto Parts, North 3rd St., Hazel, KY 42049: Catalog $6 (specify year) ❖ Reproduction parts for the 1965 to 1972 Montego. 502–492–8166.

Monte Carlo Exclusive, P.O. Box 1368, Huntington Beach, CA 92647: Free catalog ❖ Interiors, moldings, body parts, body panels, and other 1962 to 1970 parts. 800–72–CARLO.

MORRIS MINOR

Greystone Automotive, 1733 Victory Blvd., Glendale, CA 91201: Free information ❖ New and used Morris Minor parts. 818–246–7385.

MUSTANG

Bill Alprin, 184 Rivervale Rd., Rivervale, NJ 07675: Free information ❖ N.O.S. parts for the Mustang. 201–666–3975.

American Mustang Parts, 8345 Sunrise Blvd., Rancho Cordova, CA 95670: Free information ❖ Interiors, exterior sheet metal, rust repair panels, chrome interior and exterior accessories, and other restoration parts. 916–635–7271.

American Pony Parts, 18121 Alderwood Mall Blvd., Lynnwood, WA 98037: Catalog $3 ❖ Mustang parts, from 1965 to 1973. 206–771–4447.

Arizona Mustang Parts, 9153 W. Utopia Rd., Phoenix, AZ 85382: Free brochure ❖ Mustang parts. 602–566–8777.

Auto Krafters Inc., P.O. Box 8, Broadway, VA 22815: Catalog $1 (specify year) ❖ New, used, and reproduction parts for 1965 to 1973 Mustangs. 703–896–FORD.

Branda Shelby & Mustang Parts, 1434 E. Pleasant Valley Blvd., Altoona, PA 16602: Catalog $3 ❖ Mustang parts. 800–458–3477.

BSIA Mustang Supply, 278 S. 700 East, Mill Creek, IN 46365: Free information ❖ Mustang parts, from mid-1964 to 1973. 219–326–1300.

C.A.R. Distributors, 12375 New Holland St., Holland, MI 48072: Free information with long SASE ❖ Mustang parts. 616–399–6783.

California Mustang Parts & Accessories, 18435 Valley Blvd., La Puenta, CA 91744: Catalog $3 ❖ Upholstery, body panels, and engine and transmission, electrical, and other parts for Mustangs. 818–964–0911.

Canadian Mustang, 73311 Oak St., Victoria, British Columbia, Canada V8X 1P9: Catalog $3 ❖ Mustang parts, from 1965 to 1973. 604–385–7161.

Circle City Mustang, Rt. 1, Box 27, Midland City, AL 36350: Free information with long SASE ❖ Mustang parts and literature. 205–983–5450.

City Motor Company, P.O. Box 526, Clarkston, WA 99403: Catalog $2 ❖ Original and reproduction parts for the 1965 to 1973 Mustang. 509–758–6262.

Classic Auto Air Mfg. Company, 2020 W. Kennedy Blvd., Tampa, FL 33606: Free catalog ❖ Air-conditioning systems and parts for mid-1964 to 1966 Mustangs. 813–251–4994.

Classic Mustang, 24 Robert Porter Rd., Southington, CT 06489: Catalog $3 ❖ Mustang parts, from 1965 to 1973. 203–276–9704.

Bob Cook Classic Auto Parts, North 3rd St., Hazel, KY 42049: Catalog $6 (specify year) ❖ Reproduction parts for 1964 to 1973 Mustangs. 502–492–8166.

Crossroads Classic Mustang, 12421 Riverside Ave., Mira Loma, CA 91752: Free catalog ❖ Parts for mid-1964 and later Mustangs. 800–GIODY-UP.

Dallas Mustang Parts, 10720 Sandhill Rd., Dallas, TX 75238: Free catalog ❖ Mustang parts. 800–527–1223.

King & Wesley Obsolete Parts Inc., Courthouse Square, Liberty, KY 42539: Free information ❖ Sheet metal, moldings, hubcaps, grilles, suspensions, and other

N.O.S. and reproduction Mustang parts. 606–787–5031.

Larry's Thunderbird & Mustang Parts, 511 S. Raymond Ave., Fullerton, CA 92631: Catalog $2 ❖ New and used parts for 1965 to 1973 Mustangs and replacement upholstery. 714–871–6432.

Mid County Mustang, Rt. 100, P.O. Box 189, Eagle, PA 19480: Free information with long SASE ❖ Mustang parts, from 1964 to 1973. 215–458–8083.

Mr. Mustang Inc., 5088 Wolf Creek Pike, Dayton, OH 45426: Free information with long SASE ❖ Mustang parts, from mid-1964 to 1972. 513–275–7439.

Mostly Mustang's Inc., 55 Alling St., Hamden, CT 06517: Free catalog ❖ New, used, and reproduction Mustang parts. 203–562–8804.

Muscle Car Corral, RR 3, Box 218, Paris, IL 61944: Catalog $2 ❖ Parts for 1965 to 1968 Mustangs. 217–465–8386.

Mustang Corral, Rt. 6, Box 242, Edwardsville, IL 62065: Free information with long SASE ❖ New and used parts for 1965 to 1973 Mustangs. 800–327–2897.

Mustang Headquarters, 1080 Detroit Ave., Concord, CA 94518: Free catalog ❖ Parts, upholstery, and interior fittings for 1965 to 1969 Mustangs. 800–227–2174.

Mustang Mart Inc., 655 McGlincey Ln., Campbell, CA 95008: Catalog $3 ❖ New, used, and reproduction parts. 408–371–5771.

Mustang of Chicago, 1321 W. Irving Park Rd., Bensenville, IL 60106: Catalog $3 ❖ New and used Mustang parts, from 1965 to 1991. 708–860–7077.

Mustang Parts Corral of Texas, 2100 E. Main, #4A, Grand Prairie, TX 75050: Free catalog ❖ Mustang parts. 800–888–1672.

Mustang Parts of Oklahoma, 6505 S. Shields, Oklahoma City, OK 73149: Catalog $3 (specify year) ❖ Mustang parts. 405–631–1400.

Mustang Specialties, 308 Washington Ave., Nutley, NJ 07110: Free information ❖ Reproduction and Ford factory replacement parts for mid-1964 to 1973 Mustangs. 201–661–3001.

Mustangs & More, 2065 Sperry Ave., Ventura, CA 93003: Free catalog ❖ New and reproduction parts, from mid-year 1964 to 1973. 800–356–6573.

Mustangs Unlimited, 185 Adams St., Manchester, CT 06040: Catalog $3 (specify year} ❖ Performance parts for Mustang and Shelby, 1965 to 1973; Mustang, 1974 to present. 800–243–7278.

National Parts Depot, 3101 SW 40th Blvd., Gainesville, FL 32608: Free catalog ❖ Mustang parts and accessories, from 1965 to 1973. 904–378–9000.

New Ford Goodies, 18008 St. Clair Ave., Cleveland, OH 44110: Free information with long SASE ❖ Genuine and reproduction Mustang parts, from 1949 and later. 216–531–8685.

Obsolete Ford Parts Company, 311 E. Washington Ave., Nashville, GA 31639: Catalog $2.50 (specify year) ❖ N.O.S. and reproduction parts for 1960 to 1970 Mustangs. 912–686–2470.

The Paddock Inc., 221 W. Main, Knightstown, IN 46148: Catalog $1 ❖ Mustang parts. 317–345–2131.

Pennsylvania Mustang, P.O. Box 660, Riegelsville, PA 18077: Catalog $2 ❖ Mustang parts, from 1969 to 1970. 215–749–0411.

Racer Walsh Company, 5906 Macy, Jacksonville, FL 32211: Catalog $3 ❖ Engines, suspensions, and other Mustang parts. 800–334–0151; 904–743–8253 (in FL).

Stilwell's Obsolete Car Parts, 1617 Wedeking Ave., Evansville, IN 47711: Catalog $3 ❖ New and reproduction Mustang parts. 812–425–4794.

Texas Mustang Parts, Rt. 6, Box 996, Waco, TX 76706: Free catalog ❖ New and reproduction parts for 1965 to 1973 Mustangs. 817–662–2793.

Valley Ford Parts, 11610 Van Owen St., North Hollywood, CA 91605: Free information ❖ New and used parts for 1965 to 1973 Mustangs. 818–982–5303.

Virginia Classic Mustang Inc., P.O. Box 487, Broadway, VA 22815: Catalog $3 ❖ Mustang parts, from mid-1964 to 1973. 703–896–2695.

NASH

American Motor Haven, 1107 Campbell Ave., San Jose, CA 95126: Free information with long SASE ❖ Nash parts. 408–246–0957.

Blaser's Auto, 3200 48th Ave., Moline, IL 61265: Free information ❖ Nash parts. 309–764–3571.

Vintage Tin Auto Parts, 4550 Scotty Ln., Hutchinson, KS 67502: Free information with long SASE ❖ Nash parts. 316–669–8449.

Wayne's Auto Salvage, RR 3, Box 41, Winner, SD 57580: Free information ❖ Nash parts. 605–842–2054.

NOVA

Chevrolet Specialties, 4335 S. Highland Ave., Butler, PA 16001: Catalog $3 ❖ Nova parts, from 1962 to 1974. 412–482–2670.

Chicago Muscle Car Parts, 912 E. Burnett Rd., Island Lake, IL 60042: Catalog $5 (refundable) ❖ New and used Nova parts, from 1962 to 1974. 708–526–2200.

Classic Industries, 17832 Gothard St., Huntington Beach, CA 92647: Catalog $4 ❖ Nova parts and accessories. 800–854–1280.

D & R Classic Automotive, 31 W. 280 Diehly Rd., Naperville, IL 60563: Free price list ❖ Nova parts. 800–472–6952.

Dick's Chevy Parts, 1821 Columbus Ave., Springfield, OH 45503: Catalog $3 ❖ Rubber, chrome, moldings, interiors, emblems, and other Nova parts, from 1938 to 1972. 513–325–7861.

Harmon's Inc., P.O. Box 6, Hwy. 27 North, Geneva, IN 46740: Free catalog ❖ Nova restoration parts, from 1962 to 1972. 219–368–7221.

Luttys Chevys, RD 2, Box 61, Cheswick, PA 15024: Catalog $3 ❖ New, used, and reproduction parts, from 1955 to 1957. 412–265–2988.

Martz Classic Chevy Parts, RD 1, Box 199, Thomasville, PA 17364: Free catalog (specify year) ❖ N.O.S. and reproduction parts, from 1955 to 1975. 717–225–1655.

Modern Performance Classics, 1127 W. Collins, Orange, CA 92667: Free information ❖ N.O.S., reproduction, and used Nova and Chevy II parts. 800–457–NOVA.

Musclecar Specialties, 1 Coach Lantern Dr., Hopewell Junction, NY 12533: Free information with long SASE ❖ New, N.O.S., and used parts for 1962 to 1972 Novas. 914–227–6837.

SC Automotive, 409 Super Sport Ln., Rt. 3, Box 9, New Ulm, MN 56073: Free catalog ❖ Nova parts. 507–354–1958.

Super Sport Restoration Parts Inc., 7138 Maddox Rd., P.O. Box 7, Lithonia, GA 30058: Free information ❖ Parts for the Nova, Chevy II, Chevelle, and Camaro. 404–482–9219.

Tom's Obsolete Chevy Parts, 14 Delta Dr., Pawtucket, RI 02860: Catalog $1 ❖ Nova parts, from 1955 to 1972. 401–723–7580.

Year One Inc., P.O. Box 129, Tucker, GA 30085: Catalog $5 ❖ New, used, and reproduction Nova and Chevy II restoration parts. 800–950–9503.

OLDSMOBILE

Automotive Obsolete, 1023 E. 4th St., Santa Ana, CA 92701: Catalog $3 ❖ New parts for 1926 to 1970 Oldsmobiles. 714–541–5167.

Fusick Automotive Products, P.O. Box 655, East Windsor, CT 06088: Catalog $3 (specify car) ❖ Parts for Oldsmobiles, 1937 to 1960, 1961–1972; Cutlass, 1961 to 1972; and Toronados, 1988 and later. 203–623–1589.

GM Muscle Car Parts Inc., 10345 75th Ave., Palos Hills, IL 60465: Free information ❖ Oldsmobile parts, from 1964 to 1987. 708–599–2277.

Musclecar Specialties, 1 Coach Lantern Dr., Hopewell Junction, NY 12533: Free information with long SASE ❖ New, N.O.S., and used parts for the 1958 to 1969 Oldsmobile. 914–227–6837.

Out of the Past Parts, 3720 SW 23rd St., Gainesville, FL 32601: Free information ❖ Oldsmobile parts, 1935 and later. 904–377–4079.

PRO Antique Auto Parts, 50 King Spring Rd., Windsor Locks, CT 06096: Catalog $2 ❖ New parts for 1929 to 1964 Oldsmobiles. 203–623–0070.

Terrill Machine Inc., Rt. 2, Box 61, DeLeon, TX 76444: Free information with long SASE ❖ Engine overhaul parts for Oldsmobiles, from 1937 to 1960. 817–893–2610.

Vintage Tin Auto Parts, 4550 Scotty Ln., Hutchinson, KS 67502: Free information with long SASE ❖ Oldsmobile parts, from 1940 to 1970. 316–669–8449.

OPEL

Opel GT Source, 8030 Remmet Ave., Canoga Park, CA 91304: Catalog $4 ❖ Opel parts. 818–992–7776.

Opeleo Automotive Parts, 15822 11th Ave. NE, Seattle, WA 98155: Free information with long SASE ❖ Parts for 1957 to 1975 Opel cars. 206–367–6360.

PACKARD

Classic Auto Parts, 550 Industrial Dr., Carmel, IN 46032: Free information ❖ Genuine classic Packard parts, from 1928 to 1941. 317–844–8154.

Fannaly's Auto Exchange, 701 Range Rd., P.O. Box 23, Ponchatoula, LA 70454: Free information ❖ Parts for 1946 to 1956 Packards. 504–386–3714.

Kanter Auto Parts, 76 Monroe St., Boonton, NJ 07005: Free catalog ❖ Used and reproduction parts for rebuilding Packards. 201–334–9575.

Norm's Antique Auto Supply, 1921 Hickory Grove Rd., Davenport, IA 52804: Free information ❖ Packard parts, from 1935 to 1952. 319–322–8388.

Packard Farm, 97 N. 150 West, Greenfield, IN 46140: Free information ❖ Engine and transmission parts and exhaust systems. 317–462–3124.

Steve's Studebaker-Packard, 2287 2nd St., Napa, CA 94559: Free information with long SASE ❖ Packard parts, from 1951 to 1956. 707–255–8945.

Terrill Machine Inc., Rt. 2, Box 61, DeLeon, TX 76444: Free information with long SASE ❖ Engine overhaul parts for 1935 to 1956 Packards. 817–893–2610.

Vintage Tin Auto Parts, 4550 Scotty Ln., Hutchinson, KS 67502: Free information with long SASE ❖ Packard parts, from 1940 to 1970. 316–669–8449.

PANTERA

Mostly Mustang's Inc., 55 Alling St., Hamden, CT 06517: Free catalog ❖ New, used, and reproduction Pantera parts. 203–562–8804.

PIERCE ARROW

Classic Auto Parts, 550 Industrial Dr., Carmel, IN 46032: Free information ❖ Genuine classic Pierce Arrow parts, from 1928 to 1941. 317–844–8154.

PINTO

Bill Alprin, 184 Rivervale Rd., Rivervale, NJ 07675: Free information ❖ N.O.S. parts for the Pinto. 201–666–3975.

Racer Walsh Company, 5906 Macy, Jacksonville, FL 32211: Catalog $3 ❖ Engines, suspensions, and other parts. 800–334–0151; 904–743–8253 (in FL).

PLYMOUTH

Andy Bernbaum Auto Parts, 315 Franklin St., Newton, MA 02158: Catalog $4 ❖ Parts for Plymouth cars. 617–244–1118.

Hardens Muscle Car World, P.O. Box 306, Lexington, MO 64067: Catalog $4 ❖ N.O.S., reproduction, and used Plymouth parts. 800–633–4690.

Mike's Auto Parts, Box 358, Ridgeland, MS 39157: Free information with long SASE ❖ Plymouth parts. 601–856–7214.

Mr. Plymouth, 452 Newton, Seattle, WA 98109: Catalog $1 ❖ Parts for Plymouth cars, 1946 to 1954. 206–285–6534.

Out of the Past Parts, 3720 SW 23rd St., Gainesville, FL 32601: Free information ❖ Plymouth parts, 1935 and later. 904–377–4079.

PRO Antique Auto Parts, 50 King Spring Rd., Windsor Locks, CT 06906: Catalog $2 ❖ New parts for 1929 to 1934 Plymouths. 203–623–0070.

Roberts Motor Parts, 17 Prospect St., West Newbury, MA 01985: Catalog $4 ❖ Parts for Plymouth cars. 508–363–5407.

Terrill Machine Inc., Rt. 2, Box 61, DeLeon, TX 76444: Free information with long SASE ❖ Engine overhaul parts for Plymouths, from 1933 to 1952. 817–893–2610.

Vintage Tin Auto Parts, 4550 Scotty Ln., Hutchinson, KS 67502: Free information with long SASE ❖ Parts for 1940 to 1970 Plymouths. 316–669–8449.

Year One Inc., P.O. Box 129, Tucker, GA 30085: Catalog $5 ❖ New, used, and reproduction Plymouth restoration parts. 800–950–9503.

PONTIAC

Ames Performance Engineering, Bonney Rd., Marlborough, NH 03455: Free catalog ❖ Pontiac parts. 800–421–2637.

Continental Enterprises, 1673 Cary Rd., Kelowna, British Columbia, Canada V1X 2C1: Information $12 ❖ Dress-up accessory kits for Pontiacs, from 1949 to 1993. 604–763–7727.

GM Muscle Car Parts Inc., 10345 75th Ave., Palos Hills, IL 60465: Free information ❖ Pontiac parts, from 1964 to 1987. 708–599–2277.

Musclecar Specialties, 1 Coach Lantern Dr., Hopewell Junction, NY 12533: Free information with long SASE ❖ New, N.O.S., and used parts for the 1929 to 1961 Pontiac. 914–227–6837.

Original Parts Group Inc., 17892 Gothard St., Huntington Beach, CA 92647: Catalog $4 ❖ Parts for the LeMans and Tempest. 800–243–8355.

Out of the Past Parts, 3720 SW 23rd St., Gainesville, FL 32601: Free information ❖ Parts for 1935 and later Pontiacs. 904–377–4079.

PRO Antique Auto Parts, 50 King Spring Rd., Windsor Locks, CT 06096: Catalog $2 ❖ New parts for 1929 to 1964 Pontiacs. 203–623–0070.

Terrill Machine Inc., Rt. 2, Box 61, DeLeon, TX 76444: Free information with long SASE ❖ Engine overhaul parts for Pontiacs, from 1937 to 1956. 817–893–2610.

Vintage Tin Auto Parts, 4550 Scotty Ln., Hutchinson, KS 67502: Free information with long SASE ❖ Pontiac parts, from 1940 to 1970. 316–669–8449.

PORSCHE

Aase Brothers Inc., 701 E. Cypress St., Anaheim, CA 92805: Free information ❖ Porsche parts. 800–444–7444; 714–956–2419 (in CA).

Allchevy Auto Parts, 4999 Vanden Rd., Vacaville, CA 95688: Free information ❖ New and reproduction parts for 1953 to 1986 Porsches. 707–437–5466.

Automotion, 3535 Kifer Rd., Santa Clara, CA 95051: Catalog $4 (refundable) ❖ Porsche parts. 800–777–8881.

Best Deal Porsche, 8171 Monroe, Stanton, CA 90680: Free information ❖ New, used, and reproduction parts for 1953 to 1986 models. 714–995–0081.

Campbell/Nelson Volkswagon, P.O. Box 220, Edmonds, WA 98020: Free information ❖ Used Porsche parts. 206–771–4931.

Europarts, 2048 Aldergrove, Escondido, CA 92025: Free information with long SASE ❖ Porsche parts. 619–743–3377.

O.E.M. Parts Distributor, P.O. Box 25312, San Mateo, CA 94402: Free information ❖ Porsche parts. 415–342–1343.

Par-Porsche Specialists, 206 S. Broadway, Yonkers, NY 10705: Free information ❖ New and used Porsche parts. 914–476–6700.

Parts Hotline, 10325 Central Ave., Montclair, CA 91763: Free information with long SASE ❖ Porsche parts. 800–637–4662; 714–625–4888 (in CA).

Performance Products, 16129 Leadwell, Van Nuys, CA 91406: Catalog $4 ❖ Parts and tools for Porsche cars. 800–423–3173; 818–787–7500 (in CA).

Stoddard Imported Cars Inc., 38845 Mentor Ave., Willoughby, OH 44094: Catalog $5 ❖ Restoration parts for the Porsche. 800–342–1414; 216–951–1040 (in OH).

Troutman Porsche, 38725 Avenida Bonita, Murrieta, CA 92362: Catalog $3 ❖ Porsche parts. 714–979–3295.

RAMBLER

Blaser's Auto, 3200 48th Ave., Moline, IL 61265: Free information ❖ Rambler parts. 309–764–3571.

Bob & Art's Auto Parts, 2641 Reno Rd., Schodack Center, Castleton, NY 12033: Free information ❖ Rambler parts. 518–477–9183.

Byers Jeep-Eagle, 390 E. Broad St., P.O. Box 16513, Columbus, OH 43216: Free catalog ❖ New, factory original parts. 614–221–9181.

Kennedy American Inc., 7100 State Rt. 142 SE, West Jefferson, OH 43162: Free catalog ❖ Jeep, Rambler, and American Motors reproduction, used, and performance parts. 614–879–7283.

Vintage Tin Auto Parts, 4550 Scotty Ln., Hutchinson, KS 67502: Free information with long SASE ❖ Rambler parts. 316–669–8449.

Webb's Classic Cars, 5084 W. State Rd. 114, Huntington, IN 46750: Free information with long SASE ❖ Parts for Rambler and AMC cars, 1950 and later. 219–344–1714.

RENAULT

French Car Connection, 1885 Clairmont Rd., Decatur, GA 10033: Free information ❖ Parts for the Renault. 800–255–9870; 404–321–6661 (in GA).

ROLLS-ROYCE

Albers Rolls-Royce, 360 S. 1st St., Zionsville, IN 46077: Free information ❖ Rolls-Royce parts. 317–873–2360.

Carriage House Motor Cars Ltd., 407 E. 61st St., New York, NY 10021: Free information ❖ Rolls Royce and Bentley parts. 800–883–2462.

George Haug Company Inc., 517 E. 73rd St., New York, NY 10021: Free information ❖ Rolls-Royce parts. 212–288–0176.

Rolls-Royce Obsolete Parts Inc., P.O. Box 796, Anna Maria, FL 34216: Free information with long SASE ❖ Rolls-Royce and Bentley parts and literature. 813–778–7270.

The Vintage Garage, North Brookfield, MA 01535: Free information ❖ Hard-to-find parts for the Rolls-Royce. 508–867–2892.

ROVER

Atlantic British Parts, P.O. Box 110, Mechanicsville, NY 12118: Free catalog ❖ Parts for the Rover. 800–533–2210.

Bluff City British Cars, 1810 Getwell, Memphis, TN 38111: Free information ❖ Parts for the Range Rover. 800–621–0227; 901–743–4422 (in TN).

British Motorsports Inc., 1143 Dell Ave., Campbell, CA 95008: Free information with long SASE ❖ New, used, and rebuilt parts. 408–370–7174.

The British Northwest Land-Rover Company, 1043 Kaiser Rd. SW, Olympia, WA 98512: Free information ❖ New, rebuilt, and used parts for Land-Rovers. 206–866–2254.

Engel Imports Inc., 5850 Stadium Dr., Kalamazoo, MI 49009: Free information with long SASE ❖ Discontinued, obsolete, and "dealer only" parts for 1953 to present cars. 800–253–4080; 616–375–1000 (in MI).

Rovers West, 4060 E. Michigan, Tucson, AZ 85714: Free information ❖ Parts for the Rover Sedan, Range Rover, and Land Rover. 602–748–8115.

SAAB

Jaguar & SAAB of Troy, 1815 Maplelawn, Troy, MI 48084: Free catalog ❖ Parts for the SAAB. 800–832–5839; 313–643–7894 (in MI).

O.E.M. Parts Distributor, P.O. Box 25312, San Mateo, CA 94402: Free information ❖ Saab parts. 415–342–1343.

SHELBY

Branda Shelby & Mustang Parts, 1434 E. Pleasant Valley Blvd., Altoona, PA 16602: Catalog $3 ❖ Shelby parts. 800–458–3477.

Cobra Restorers, 3099 Carter, Kenesaw, GA 30144: Catalog $5 ❖ Parts for the Shelby. 404–427–0020.

Mostly Mustang's Inc., 55 Alling St., Hamden, CT 06517: Free catalog ❖ New, used, and reproduction Shelby parts. 203–562–8804.

Mustangs Unlimited, 185 Adams St., Manchester, CT 06040: Catalog $3 (specify year) ❖ Shelby parts. 800–243–7278.

Valley Ford Parts, 11610 Van Owen St., North Hollywood, CA 91605: Free information ❖ New and used parts for the 1965 to 1973 Shelby. 818–982–5303.

SPITFIRE

British Parts Northwest, 4105 SE Lafayette Hwy., Dayton, OR 97114: Catalog $2.50 ❖ Spitfire parts. 503–864–2001.

STERLING

Bluff City British Cars, 1810 Getwell, Memphis, TN 38111: Free information ❖ Parts for the Sterling. 800–621–0227; 901–743–4422 (in TN).

Jaguar & SAAB of Troy, 1815 Maplelawn, Troy, MI 48084: Free catalog ❖ Parts for the Sterling. 800–832–5839; 313–643–7894 (in MI).

STUDEBAKER

Beckers Auto Salvage, Hwy. 30 West, Atkins, IA 52206: Free information ❖ Parts for Studebakers. 319–446–7141.

Jim's Auto Sales, Rt. 2, Inman, KS 67546: Free information ❖ Studebaker parts, from 1935 to 1966. 316–585–6648.

Newman & Altman Inc., P.O. Box 4276, South Bend, IN 46634: Catalog $5 ❖ Studebaker parts and accessories, for 1947 to 1966 cars and trucks. 800–722–4295.

Packard Farm, 97N 150 West, Greenfield, IN 46140: Free information ❖ Studebaker engine and transmission parts, and exhaust systems. 317–462–3124.

Parmer Studebaker Sales, 408 S. Lincoln, Van Wert, IA 50262: Free information ❖ Parts for Studebakers, from 1947 to 1966. 515–445–5692.

Steve's Studebaker-Packard, 2287 2nd St., Napa, CA 94559: Free information with long SASE ❖ Studebaker parts, from 1953 to 1966. 707–255–8945.

Tucker's Auto Salvage, RD 1, Box 170, Burke, NY 12917: Free information ❖ Studebaker N.O.S. and used parts. 518–483–5478.

Wayne's Auto Salvage, RR 3, Box 41, Winner, SD 57580: Free information ❖ Studebaker parts. 605–842–2054.

SUBARU

Parts Hotline, 10325 Central Ave., Montclair, CA 91763: Free information with long SASE ❖ Subaru parts. 800–637–4662; 714–625–4888 (in CA).

SUNBEAM

Moss Motors Ltd., 7200 Hollister Rd., P.O. Box 847, Goleta, CA 93116: Free catalog (specify model) ❖ Parts for the Sunbeam. 800–235–6954.

Sunbeam Specialties, P.O. Box 771, Los Gatos, CA 95031: Free catalog ❖ Parts for 1959 to 1968 Tigers and Alpines. 408–371–1642.

THUNDERBIRD

Bill Alprin, 184 Rivervale Rd., Rivervale, NJ 07675: Free information ❖ Thunderbird N.O.S. parts. 201–666–3975.

Bob's Bird House, 124 Watkins Ave., Chadds Ford, PA 19317: Catalog $3 ❖ New and used parts for 1958 to 1978 Thunderbird cars. 215–358–3420.

Dennis Carpenter Ford Reproductions, P.O. Box 26398, Charlotte, NC 28221: Catalog $3 ❖ Rubber parts for 1958 to 1966 Thunderbirds. 704–786–8139.

Classic Auto Supply Company Inc., 795 High St., P.O. Box 810, Coshocton, OH 43812: Free catalog ❖ Parts for 1955 to 1957 Thunderbird cars. 614–622–8561.

Classique Cars Unlimited, P.O. Box 249, Lakeshore, MS 39558: Parts list $4 ❖ Thunderbird parts, from 1958 to 1988. 601–467–9633.

Concours Parts & Accessories, 3563 Numancia St., P.O. Box 1210, Santa Ynez, CA 93460: Catalog $4 ❖ Thunderbird 1955 to 1957 parts. 805–688–7795.

Continental Enterprises, 1673 Cary Rd., Kelowna, British Columbia, Canada V1X 2C1: Information $12 ❖ Thunderbird dress-up accessory kits, from 1949 to 1993. 604–763–7727.

Bob Cook Classic Auto Parts, North 3rd St., Hazel, KY 42049: Catalog $6 (specify year) ❖ Reproduction parts for 1958 to 1960, 1961 to 1964, 1965 to 1966, and 1967 to 1972 Thunderbirds. 502–492–8166.

Ford Parts Specialists, 98–11 211th St., Queens Village, NY 11429: Free catalog (specify year) ❖ Thunderbird parts. 718–468–8585.

Larry's Thunderbird & Mustang Parts, 511 S. Raymond Ave., Fullerton, CA 92631: Catalog $2 ❖ New and used parts and upholstery, for 1955 to 1957 cars. 714–871–6432.

LeBaron Bonney Company, P.O. Box 6, Chestnut St., Amesbury, MA 01913: Catalog $1 ❖ Thunderbird parts. 508–388–3811.

New Ford Goodies, 18008 St. Clair Ave., Cleveland, OH 44110: Free information with long SASE ❖ Genuine and reproduction Thunderbird parts, from 1949 and later. 216–531–8685.

Obsolete Ford Parts Inc., 6601 S. Shields, Oklahoma City, OK 73149: Catalog $3 (specify year and car) ❖ Parts for 1949 to 1959 and 1960 to 1972 Thunderbirds. 405–631–3933.

Prestige Thunderbird Inc., 10215 Greenleaf Ave., Santa Fe Springs, CA 90670: Catalog $1 ❖ Parts and upholstery. 310–944–6237.

Sixties Ford Parts, 639 Glanker St., Memphis, TN 38112: Catalog $4 ❖ Thunderbird parts, from 1960 to 1968.

T-Bird Nest, P.O. Box 1012, Grapevine, TX 76051: Free information ❖ Thunderbird parts, from 1958 to 1966. 817–481–1776.

The T-Bird Sanctuary, 9997 SW Avery, Tualatin, OR 97062: Catalog $5 ❖ Parts for 1958 to 1972 Thunderbirds. 503–641–0556.

Tee-Bird Products Inc., Box 153, Exton, PA 19341: Catalog $2 ❖ Parts for 1955 to 1957 Thunderbirds. 215–363–1725.

Thunderbird & Falcon Connection, 728 E. Dunlap, Phoenix, AZ 85020: Catalog $2 (specify year) ❖ New and used parts for 1958 to 1971 Thunderbirds. 602–997–9285.

Thunderbird Center, 23610 John R., Hazel Park, MI 48030: Free catalog ❖ Upholstery, sheet metal, weatherstripping, and new, used, N.O.S., and reproduction parts for 1956 to 1957 Thunderbirds. 800–562–1955.

Thunderbird Headquarters, 1080 Detroit Ave., Concord, CA 94518: Free catalog ❖ Thunderbird parts, from 1955 to 1957. 800–227–2174; 800–642–2405 (in CA).

Thunderbird Parts & Restoration, 5844 Goodrich Rd., Clarence Center, NY 14032: Free information ❖ N.O.S., reproduction, used, and remanufactured parts. 800–289–2473; 716–741–2866 (in NY).

Thunderbirds USA Parts Supply, 3621 Resource Dr., Tuscaloosa, AL 35401: Free catalog ❖ 1955 to 1957 Thunderbird upholstery, decals, radios, books, and N.O.S., used, and reproduction parts. 800–842–5557; 205–758–5557 (in AL).

TORINO

Bill Alprin, 184 Rivervale Rd., Rivervale, NJ 07675: Free information ❖ N.O.S. parts for the Torino. 201–666–3975.

Auto Krafters Inc., P.O. Box 8, Broadway, VA 22815: Catalog $1 (specify year) ❖ New, used, and reproduction parts for 1962 to 1971 Torinos. 703–896–FORD.

Bob Cook Classic Auto Parts, North 3rd St., Hazel, KY 42049: Catalog $6 (specify year) ❖ Reproduction parts for 1960 to 1972 Torino cars. 502–492–8166.

Ford Parts Store, P.O. Box 226, Bryan, OH 43506: Catalog $2 ❖ Torino parts. 419–636–2475.

New Ford Goodies, 18008 St. Clair Ave., Cleveland, OH 44110: Free information with long SASE ❖ Genuine and reproduction Torino parts, from 1949 and later. 216–531–8685.

Obsolete Ford Parts Company, 311 E. Washington Ave., Nashville, GA 31639: Catalog $2.50 (specify year) ❖ N.O.S. and reproduction parts for 1949 to 1964 Torino cars. 912–686–2470.

Ranchero Classics, P.O. Box 1248, Sunset Beach, CA 90742: Catalog $3 ❖ Torino parts. 714–847–7107.

TOYOTA

Dobi Toyota Catalog, 320 Thor Pl., Brea, CA 92621: Catalog $2 ❖ Replacement parts for the Toyota Celica and Corolla. 714–529–1977.

HKS USA Inc., 20312 Gramercy Pl., Torrance, CA 90501: Catalog $8 ❖ Toyota performance parts. 310–328–8100.

Impact Parts, Glen Wild Rd., Glen Wild, NY 12738: Catalog $1 ❖ Parts for the Toyota. 800–431–3400.

Jaguar & SAAB of Troy, 1815 Maplelawn, Troy, MI 48084: Free catalog ❖ Parts for the Toyota. 800–832–5839; 313–643–7894 (in MI).

Price Toyota Newark, 1344 Marrows Rd., Newark, DE 19711: Free information ❖ Toyota parts. 800–537–4510.

Russel Toyota, 6700 Baltimore National Tnpk., Baltimore, MD 21208: Free information ❖ Toyota parts. 800–638–8401.

Bob Sharp Racing/Accessories, Danbury Rd., Rt. 7, Wilton, CT 06897: Catalog $1 ❖ Racing, styling components, and other Toyota parts. 203–544–8386.

TRANS AM

Firebird/Trans Am America, Rt. 322, Box 427, Boalsburg, PA 16827: Free information with long SASE ❖ Trans Am parts, from 1967 to 1987. 800–458–3475.

TRIUMPH

Aurora Auto Wrecking Inc., 9217 Aurora Avenue North, Seattle, WA 98103: Free information ❖ New, used, and rebuilt Triumph parts. 800–426–6464.

British Auto, 703 Penfield Rd., Macedon, NY 14502: Free information ❖ Triumph parts, from 1950 to 1982. 315–986–3097.

British Miles, 222 Grove, Morrisville, PA 19067: Free information ❖ Reconditioned and new Triumph parts. 215–736–9300.

British Motorsports Inc., 1143 Dell Ave., Campbell, CA 95008: Free information with long SASE ❖ New, used, and rebuilt parts. 408–370–7174.

British Parts Northwest, 4105 SE Lafayette Hwy., Dayton, OR 97114: Catalog $2.50 ❖ Triumph parts. 503–864–2001.

EightParts, 4060 E. Michigan, Tucson, AZ 85714: Free information ❖ Parts for 8–cylinder Triumphs. 602–748–8115.

Engel Imports Inc., 5850 Stadium Dr., Kalamazoo, MI 49009: Free information with long SASE ❖ Discontinued, obsolete, and "dealer only" parts for 1953 to present models. 800–253–4080; 616–375–1000 (in MI).

English Car Spares Ltd., 345 Branch Rd SW, Alpharetta, GA 30201: Free information ❖ Triumph parts. 800–241–1916; 404–475–2662 (in GA).

George Haug Company Inc., 517 E. 73rd St., New York, NY 10021: Free information ❖ Triumph parts. 212–288–0176.

Moss Motors Ltd., 7200 Hollister Rd., P.O. Box 847, Goleta, CA 93116: Free catalog (specify model) ❖ Triumph parts. 800–235–6954.

New England Old Car Barn, US Rt. 1, Box 608, North Hampton, NH 03862: Free information with long SASE ❖ Triumph parts, books, and memorabilia. 603–964–7100.

Peninsula Imports, 3749 Harlem, Buffalo, NY 14215: Free catalog ❖ Triumph parts. 800–999–1209.

Roadster Factory, P.O. Box 332, Armagh, PA 15920: Free catalog ❖ Parts for the Triumph, TR2 through TR8, Spitfire, and GT6. 800–678–8764.

Scotland Yard British Cars Ltd., 3101 E. 52nd Ave., Denver, CO 80216: Free information with long SASE ❖ New, used, and remanufactured parts for the Triumph. 800–222–1415; 800–328–8716 (in CO).

Sports & Classics, 512 Boston Post Rd., Darien, CT 06820: Catalog $5 ❖ Restoration, engine, electrical, and body parts. 203–655–8731.

Victoria British Ltd., P.O. Box 14991, Lenexa, KS 66215: Free catalog ❖ Original, replacement, and reproduction parts for the Triumph and other British sports cars. 800–255–0088.

VOLKSWAGEN

Discount Auto Parts, 4703 Broadway SE, Albuquerque, NM 87105: Free information with long SASE ❖ Volkswagen parts. 505–877–6782.

Electro Automotive, P.O. Box 1113, Felton, CA 95018: Catalog $5 ❖ Bolt-in kit for converting a gas or diesel Rabbit to electricity. 408–429–1989.

Europarts, 2048 Aldergrove, Escondido, CA 92025: Free information with long SASE ❖ Volkswagen parts. 619–743–3377.

Johnny's Speed Chrome, 6411 Beach Blvd., Buena Park, CA 90620: Catalog $3 ❖ Parts for the Volkswagen. 800–854–3411.

Rocky Mountain Motorworks, 901 Rampart Range Rd., Woodland Park, CO 80863: Free catalog ❖ Restoration parts. 800–258–1996.

West Coast Metric Inc., 24002 Frampton Ave., Harbor City, CA 91320: Free catalog ❖ Parts and body replacement accessories for the Bug, Bus, Type 3, and Ghia. 805–247–3202.

VOLVO

B & B Used Auto Parts, Rt. 1, Box 691, Big Pine Key, FL 33043: Free information ❖ Parts for the Volvo, 1968 and later. 305–872–9761.

Beechmont Volvo, 8639 Beechmont Ave., Cincinnati, OH 45255: Free catalog ❖ Volvo parts. 800–255–3601.

Brentwood Volvo, 7700 Manchester Rd., St. Louis, MO 63143: Free information ❖ Volvo parts. 800–844–9502.

Frank's Foreign Auto, 595 Valley St., Orange, NJ 07050: Free information ❖ New and used Volvo parts. 201–674–2254.

Impact Parts, Glen Wild Rd., Glen Wild, NY 12738: Catalog $1 ❖ Parts for the Volvo. 800–431–3400.

Import Motors Volvo Inc., 6375 Hwy. 290 East, Austin, TX 78723: Free information ❖ Volvo parts. 800–880–2101.

Swedish Classics, P.O. Box 557, Oxford, MD 21654: Free information ❖ Volvo parts. 410–226–5183.

Voluparts, 751 Trabert Ave., Atlanta, GA 30318: Free information ❖ New and used Volvo parts. 404–352–3402.

WILLYS

American Motor Haven, 1107 Campbell Ave., San Jose, CA 95126: Free information with long SASE ❖ Parts for the Willys. 408–246–0957.

Obsolete Jeep & Willys Parts, 6110 17th St. East, Bradenton, FL 34203: Free information ❖ New, used, rebuilt, and N.O.S. parts. 813–756–7844.

Plating

A-1 Plating, 2170 Acoma St., Sacramento, CA 95815: Free information ❖ Chrome plating. 916–927–5071.

Custom Chrome Plating, 963 Mechanic St., P.O. Box 125, Grafton, OH 44044: Free information ❖ Chrome, nickel, and copper plating. 216–926–3116.

Custom Plating, 3030 Alta Ridge Way, Snellville, GA 30278: Free information ❖ Chrome plating.

Gary's Plastic Chrome Plating Inc., 39312 Dillingham, Westland, MI 48185: Free brochure with long SASE ❖ Plating of car parts using the original vacuum metalizing process. 313–326–1858.

Graves Plating Company, Industrial Park, P.O. Box 1052, Florence, AL 35631: Free information ❖ Chrome, nickel, brass, and gold plating. 205–764–9487.

J.P. Custom Plating, 1750 N. Campbell Ave., Chicago, IL 60647: Free information ❖ Chrome plating. 312–486–0466.

Martin's of Philadelphia, 7327 State Rd., Philadelphia, PA 19136: Free information ❖ Metal finishing and plating. 215–331–5565.

Paul's Chrome Plating Inc., 341 Mars-Valencia Rd., Mars, PA 16046: Free information ❖ Plating and pot metal restoration. 800–245–8679; 412–625–3135 (in PA).

Pot Metal Restorations, 4794 Woodlane Cir., Tallahassee, FL 32303: Free brochure ❖ Pot metal chrome plating with a smooth "show chrome" finish. 904–562–3847.

Radar Detectors Manufacturers

Audiovox, 150 Marcus Blvd., Hauppage, NY 11788: Free information ❖ Mini and standard-size radar detectors. 516–436–6200.

Cincinnati Microwave, One Microwave Plaza, Cincinnati, OH 45296: Free information ❖ Micro and standard-size radar detectors. 800–543–1608.

Cobra, 6500 W. Cortland St., Chicago, IL 60635: Free information ❖ Micro, remote, and standard-size radar detectors. 800–COBRA-22.

Craig, 13845 Artesia Blvd., Cerritos, CA 90701: Free information ❖ Standard-size radar detectors. 310–537–1233.

Escort Detectors, 5200 Fields-Ertel Rd., Cincinnati, OH 45249: Free information ❖ Radar and laser detectors. 800–433–3487.

Fultron, P.O. Box 177, Memphis, TN 38101: Free information ❖ Pocket-size and standard-size radar detectors. 901–525–5711.

K-40 Electronics, 1500 Executive Dr., Elgin, IL 60123: Free brochure ❖ Radar detectors. 800–323–5608.

Kraco, 505 E. Euclid Ave., Compton, CA 90224: Free information ❖ Standard-size and micro radar detectors. 310–639–0666.

Maxon Electronics, 10828 NW Airworld Dr., Kansas City, MO 64153: Free information ❖ Micro and standard-size radar detectors. 816–891–6320.

Radar U.S.A., 1749 Golf Rd., Mt. Prospect, IL 60056: Free information ❖ Radar units and accessories. 800–777–6570; 708–350–0201 (in IL).

Radio Shack, Division Tandy Corporation, One Tandy Center, Fort Worth, TX 76102: Free information ❖ Mini, remote, and standard-size radar detectors. 817–390–3011.

Uniden, 4700 Amon Carter Blvd., Fort Worth, TX 76155: Free information ❖ Standard-size radar detectors. 817–858–3300.

Whistler, 5 Liberty Way, Westford, MA 01886: Free information ❖ Remote and standard-size radar detectors. 508–692–3000.

Radar Detectors
Retailers

ComputAbility Consumer Electronics, P.O. Box 17882, Milwaukee, WI 53217: Free catalog ❖ Radar detectors. 800–558–0003.

Executive Photo & Electronics, 120 W. 31st St., New York, NY 10001: Free information ❖ Radar detectors and other electronics. 212–947–5290.

MHz Enterprise Corporation, 264 161st St., Belle Harbor, NY 11694: Free information ❖ Radar detectors and other electronics. 800–572–5349; 718–634–2220 (in NY).

Pandora's Box Mail Order, 1820 S. West Ave., Ste. 150A, Freeport, IL 61032: Catalog $5 (refundable) ❖ Radar and laser detectors, and other items for the home office, and car. 815–369–4047.

Radar U.S.A., 1749 Golf Rd., Mt. Prospect, IL 60056: Free information ❖ Radar detectors. 800–777–6570; 708–350–0201 (in IL).

S.B.H. Enterprises, 1678 53rd St., Brooklyn, NY 11204: Free information ❖ Radar detectors. 800–451–5851; 718–438–1027 (in NY).

Replica & Conversion Kits
ALLARD

Hardy Motors, 156 N. Broad St., Mooresville, NC 28115: Brochure $5 ❖ Reproduction car kits. 704–663–3930.

AUBURN

The Classic Factory, 1454 E. 9th St., Pomona, CA 91766: Information $3 ❖ Replica car kits. 714–629–5968.

Elegant Motors Inc., P.O. Box 30188, Indianapolis, IN 46230: Free information ❖ Reproduction car kits. 317–253–9898.

BRADLEY GT

Sun Ray Products Corporation, 8017 Ranchers Rd., Fridley, MN 55432: Free brochure ❖ Replica car kits. 612–780–0774.

BUGATTI

Ironsmith Company, 434 E. Cypress Ave., Redding, CA 96002: Free information ❖ Replica car kits. 916–221–2436.

CAMARO

Exotic Specialty Car Emporium, P.O. Box 23837, Fort Lauderdale, FL 33307: Information $5 ❖ Replica car kits. 305–565–0800.

Knudsen Automotive, P.O. Box 540698, Omaha, NE 68154: Free information with long SASE ❖ Replica car conversion kits. 402–896–3221.

CHEETAH

Elegant Motors Inc., P.O. Box 30188, Indianapolis, IN 46230: Free information ❖ Reproduction car kits. 317–253–9898.

COBRA

Ace Auto Services Ltd., 21422 Parthenia, Canoga Park, CA 91304: Brochure $5 ❖ Reproduction car kits. 818–885–5097.

Advanced Chassis, 2435 Blanding Ave., Alameda, CA 94501: Information $10 ❖ Replica car kits. 510–769–8019.

American Roadsters, 937 E. Weber, Tempe, AZ 85281: Free information ❖ Reproduction car kits. 602–968–9284.

Antique & Collectible Autos Inc., 35 Dole St., Buffalo, NY 14210: Free brochure ❖ Replica car kits. 716–825–3990.

Auto Sport Performance Products Inc., 1930 E. 3rd, Tempe, AZ 85281: Free brochure ❖ Replica car kits. 602–966–9906.

Bennett Automotive, 3385 Enterprise, Hayward, CA 94545: Free brochure ❖ Replica car kits. 510–782–0705.

Butler Racing Inc., 103 Santa Felicia Dr., Goleta, CA 93117: Free brochure ❖ Replica car kits. 805–685–3535.

Contemporary Classic Motor Car Company, 115 Hoyt Ave., Mamaroneck, NY 10543: Catalog $5 ❖ Replica car kits. 914–381–5678.

Elegant Motors Inc., P.O. Box 30188, Indianapolis, IN 46230: Free information ❖ Reproduction car kits. 317–253–9898.

ERA Replica Automobiles, 608 E. Main St., New Britain, CT 06051: Brochure $10 ❖ Replica car kits. 203–229–7968.

Everett-Morrison Motorcars, 5137 W. Clifton St., Tampa, FL 33634: Brochure $5 ❖ Replica car kits. 813–887–5885.

Frank's Classic Autos Inc., 3700 Dundee Rd., Winter Haven, FL 33884: Information $5 ❖ Replica car kits. 813–324–8485.

John's Custom Fabrication, 1515 Newmark, Coos Bay, OR 97420: Information $5 ❖ Reproduction car kits. 503–888–9313.

L.A. Exotics, 6900 Knott Ave., Buena Park, CA 90621: Information $10 ❖ Replica car kits.

Lone Star Classics Inc., 715 Katy Rd., Ste. 2306, Keller, TX 76248: Brochure $5 ❖ Replica car kits.

MidStates Classic Cars, 835 W. Grant, P.O. Box 427, Hooper, NE 68031: Catalog $5 ❖ Replica car kits. 402–654–2772.

S.C. Motorcar Company, P.O. Box 9, Eucha, OK 74342: Free information ❖ Replica car kits. 918–253–4175.

Shell Valley Motors, Rt. 1, Box 69, Platte Center, NE 68653: Free information ❖ Replica car kits. 402–246–2355.

Southern Roadcraft USA, 102 New Haven Ave., Milford, CT 06460: Free information ❖ Reproduction car kits. 203–878–7352.

Unique Motorcars Inc., 230 E. Broad St., Gadsden, AL 35903: Brochure $5 ❖ Reproduction car kits. 205–546–3708.

West Coast Cobra, 6785 16 Mile Rd., Sterling Heights, MI 48077: Information $5 ❖ Replica car kits. 519–736–7274.

CORD

Elegant Motors Inc., P.O. Box 30188, Indianapolis, IN 46230: Free information ❖ Reproduction car kits. 317–253–9898.

CORVETTE

Beck Development, 1531 W. 13th St., Upland, CA 91786: Free information ❖ Replica car kits. 909–981–3840.

D & D Corvette, 1985 Manchester Rd., Akron, OH 44314: Information $5 ❖ Replica car kits. 216–745–2544.

Lone Star Classics Inc., 715 Katy Rd., Ste. 2306, Keller, TX 76248: Brochure $5 ❖ Replica car kits.

Memory Motors Inc., 110 W. Avenue G, Conroe, TX 77301: Information $3 ❖ Replica car kits. 409–760–3500.

ESCORT

AutoTek Unlimited, 2476 S. Stone Mountain/Lithonia Rd., Lithonia, GA 30058: Information $2 with long SASE ❖ Replica car parts. 404–482–8327.

FERRARI

Corson Motorcars Ltd., P.O. Box 41396, Phoenix, AZ 85080: Brochure $5 ❖ Replica car kits. 602–375–2544.

FIERO

AutoTek Unlimited, 2476 S. Stone Mountain/Lithonia Rd., Lithonia, GA 30058:

Information $2 with long SASE ❖ Replica car parts. 404–482–8327.

Custom Coachcraft, 500 Briarwood, Aledo, TX 76008: Information $5 ❖ Replica body kits. 817–441–9109.

Fiero Conversions Inc., 3410 Walker Rd., Windsor, Ontario, Canada N8W 3S3: Information $5 ❖ Body and aerodynamic conversion accessories. 519–972–4989.

Fiero Plus, 12 Banner Rd., Nepean, Ontario, Canada K2H 5T2: Catalog $7 ❖ Body conversion kits. 613–596–6269.

Mac's Auto Body, 4427 Maygog Rd., Sarasota, FL 34233: Information $2 ❖ Body kits. 813–921–4420.

PISA Corporation, P.O. Box 15088, Phoenix, AZ 85060: Free information ❖ Bolt-on body kit for the Fiero. 602–894–1775.

V-8 Archie Inc., 1307 Lykins Ln., Niles, MI 49120: Information $10 ❖ Conversion car kits. 219–259–1876.

FIREBIRD

AutoTek Unlimited, 2476 S. Stone Mountain/Lithonia Rd., Lithonia, GA 30058: Information $2 with long SASE ❖ Replica car parts. 404–482–8327.

Exotic Specialty Car Emporium, P.O. Box 23837, Fort Lauderdale, FL 33307: Information $5 ❖ Replica car kits. 305–565–0800.

Knudsen Automotive, P.O. Box 540698, Omaha, NE 68154: Free information with long SASE ❖ Replica car conversion kits. 402–896–3221.

FORD

Classic Motor Carriages, 16650 NW 27th Ave., P.O. Box 10, Miami, FL 33054: Information $2 ❖ Replica car kits. 800–252–7742.

GT-40

Lone Star Classics Inc., 715 Katy Rd., Ste. 2306, Keller, TX 76248: Brochure $5 ❖ Replica car kits.

JAGUAR

Antique & Collectible Autos Inc., 35 Dole St., Buffalo, NY 14210: Free brochure ❖ Replica car kits. 716–825–3990.

California Convertible Company Inc., 587 N. Ventu Park Rd., Newbury Park, CA 91320: Free information ❖ Conversion car kits. 805–375–2595.

Eagle Coach Works Inc., 760 Northland Ave., Buffalo, NY 14211: Brochure $3 ❖ Replica car kits. 716–897–4292.

G-T Motorsports, 6893 Root Rd., North Ridgeville, OH 44039: Free brochure ❖ Reproduction car kits. 216–327–6451.

Predator Performance Inc., 12280 7th St. North, Largo, FL 34643: Free information ❖ Replica car kits. 813–539–0218.

MAZDA

Design Energy Inc., 414 N. Salsipuedes, Santa Barbara, CA 93103: Information $5 ❖ Body conversion kits. 805–965–5115.

MERCEDES-BENZ

Classic Motor Carriages, 16650 NW 27th Ave., P.O. Box 10, Miami, FL 33054: Information $2 ❖ Replica car kits. 800–252–7742.

Classics International Ltd., P.O. Box 651, Oakland, FL 34760: Brochure $5 ❖ Replica car kits.

Fiberfab International Inc., 7601 N. Federal Hwy., Boca Raton, FL 33487: Free brochure ❖ Replica car kits. 800–328–5671; 407–241–7702 (in FL).

Lone Star Classics Inc., 715 Katy Rd., Ste. 2306, Keller, TX 76248: Brochure $5 ❖ Replica car kits.

MG

British Coach Works Ltd., Arnold, PA 15068: Information $3 ❖ Replica car kits. 800–245–1369; 412–339–3541 (in PA).

Classic Motor Carriages, 16650 NW 27th St., P.O. Box 10, Miami, FL 33054: Information $2 ❖ Reproduction car kits. 800–252–7742.

Fiberfab International Inc., 7601 N. Federal Hwy., Boca Raton, FL 33487: Free brochure ❖ Replica car kits. 800–328–5671; 407–241–7702 (in FL).

PACKARD

Gibbon Fiberglass Reproductions Inc., P.O. Box 490, Gibbon, NE 68840: Catalog $4 ❖ Replica car kits. 308–468–6178.

PORSCHE

Beck Development, 1531 W. 13th St., Upland, CA 91786: Free information ❖ Reproduction car kits. 909–981–3840.

Classic Motor Carriages, 16650 NW 27th St., P.O. Box 10, Miami, FL 33054: Information $2 ❖ Reproduction car kits. 800–252–7742.

Fiberfab International Inc., 7601 N. Federal Hwy., Boca Raton, FL 33487: Free brochure ❖ Replica car kits. 800–328–5671; 407–241–7702 (in FL).

Premier Marketing, P.O. Box 96, Lake Oswego, OR 97034: Information $2 with long SASE ❖ Restyling kits. 503–636–9245.

Rayco Inc., 1710 Delmar, St. Louis, MO 63103: Free information ❖ Reproduction car kits. 314–621–1321.

Vintage Speedsters, 12112 Centralia Rd., Hawaiian Gardens, CA 90716: Information $5 ❖ Replica car kits. 310–402–4334.

SPECIALTY CARS

Arizona Z Car, 2043 E. Quartz, Mesa, AZ 85213: Free catalog ❖ Conversion car kits. 602–844–9677.

Autospeed Motorcars, 100 S. Lake St., Burbank, CA 91502: Brochure $5 ❖ Replica kits and turnkeys. 800–792–2627; 818–842–0028 (in CA).

Exotic Automotive Designs, 1460 S. Vineyard, Ontario, CA 91761: Information $5 with long SASE ❖ Coupe and convertible body and accessory packages. 909–923–6727.

Exotic Illusions, Rear 347 Main St., Dickson City, PA 18519: Information $5 ❖ Replica car kits. 717–383–1206.

Fiberfab International Inc., 7601 N. Federal Hwy., Boca Raton, FL 33487: Free brochure ❖ Replica car kits. 800–328–5671; 407–241–7702 (in FL).

I.C.M. Industries, 901 S. Greenwood, Montebello, CA 90640: Information $5 ❖ High-performance sports car kits. 213–728–4441.

Innovations in Fiberglass, P.O. Box 60642, Phoenix, AZ 85082: Brochure $4 ❖ Conversion car kits. 602–377–0104.

Legendary Motorworks, 4 Arch St., Canonsburg, PA 15312: Free brochure ❖ Replica classic American sports cars. 800–858–0436; 412–745–7785 (in PA).

Marauder & Company, RR 2, Potomac, IL 61865: Information $12 ❖ Replica car kits.

PISA Corporation, P.O. Box 15088, Phoenix, AZ 85060: Free information ❖ Conversion car kits for the Fiero chassis. 602–894–1775.

ZMC Inc., 11530 Firestone Blvd., Norwalk, CA 90650: Free information ❖ Specialty conversion car kits. 213–929–8484.

TOYOTA

Aeroform, 6300 St. John Ave., Kansas City, MO 64123: Information $5 ❖ Reproduction car kits. 800–345–2376.

TRANS AM

AutoTek Unlimited, 2476 S. Stone Mountain/Lithonia Rd., Lithonia, GA 30058: Information $2 with long SASE ❖ Replica car parts. 404–482–8327.

VOLKSWAGEN

Archway Import Auto Parts Inc., 1900 Telegraph Rd., St. Louis, MO 63125: Catalog $3.95 ❖ Parts for Volkswagen-based kit cars. 314–638–7700.

BGW Spectre, 2534 Woodland Park Dr., Delafield, WI 53018: Free information with long SASE ❖ Conversion car kits. 414–646–4884.

Rubber Parts

Dennis Carpenter Ford Reproductions, P.O. Box 26398, Charlotte, NC 28221: Catalog $3 ❖ Rubber parts for 1932 to 1964 Fords, 1958 to 1966 Thunderbirds, and 1960 to 1965 Falcons. 704–786–8139.

Karr Rubber Manufacturing, 133 Lomita St., El Segundo, CA 90245: Catalog $5 ❖ Reproduction rubber extrusions. 310–322–1993.

Metro Moulded Parts Inc., 11610 Jay St., P.O. Box 33130, Minneapolis, MN 55433: Catalog $3 ❖ Rubber reproduction parts for most American and foreign cars and trucks, from 1929 to 1970. 800–878–2237.

Lynn H. Steele Rubber Products, 1601 Hwy. 150 East, Denver, NC 28037: Catalog $2 (specify car) ❖ Reproduction rubber parts for Cadillac, Packard, Chrysler, Chevrolet, Buick, Oldsmobile, and Pontiac cars and Chevrolet trucks. 800–544–8665; 704–483–9343 (in NC).

Seat & Body Covers

Anything Car Covers Ltd., 11431 Santa Monica, West Los Angeles, CA 90025: Free information ❖ Car covers for small, medium, and large cars, and most vans and trucks. 800–445–4048.

Auto Stand Fine Motoring Gifts & Accessories, 281 S. Beverly Dr., Beverly Hills, CA 90212: Free information ❖

Ready-fit and custom car covers with cable and lock options. 800–334–4196.

Beverly Hills Motoring Accessories, 200 S. Robertson Blvd., Beverly Hills, CA 90211: Catalog $3 (refundable) ❖ Covers for most cars. 800–421–0911; 213–657–4800 (in CA).

Boulevard Motoring Accessories, 7033 Topanga Canyon Blvd., Canoga Park, CA 91303: Catalog $3 ❖ Sheepskin seat covers car covers, and automotive accessories. 818–883–9696.

California Car Cover Company, 21125 Superior St., Chatsworth, CA 91311: Free information ❖ Car covers. 800–423–5525; 818–998–2100 (in CA).

Canvas Shoppe Inc., 3198 S. Dye Rd., Flint, MI 48507: Free catalog ❖ Lined, water-resistant car covers. 800–345–3670.

CarCovers USA, 1015 Galey Ave., Building 1208, Los Angeles, CA 90024: Free information ❖ Car covers. 800–872–6837.

Classic Motoring Accessories, 146 W. Pomona Ave., Monrovia, CA 91016: Catalog $3 ❖ Car covers. 800–327–3045.

Fleetfoot Industries, 2680 Blake St., Denver, CO 80205: Catalog $3.50 (refundable) ❖ Front end covers for cars and trucks. 800–503–2727, ext. 24.

Jean Seat International, P.O. Box 7798, Hollywood, FL 33021: Free information ❖ Seat covers. 800–881–0509.

Kanter Auto Parts, 76 Monroe St., Boonton, NJ 07005: Free catalog ❖ Fitted seat cover and upholstery kits for most United States cars, from 1932 to 1980. 201–334–9575.

MacNeil Automotive Products Ltd., 5161 Thatcher Rd., Downers Grove, IL 60515: Free information ❖ Seat covers and floor mats. 800–441–6287.

Multisheep, 646 S. Hauser Blvd., Los Angeles, CA 90036: Free information ❖ Sheepskin seat covers for most cars. 800–532–1222.

New England Auto Accessories Inc., 2984 E. Main St., Waterbury, CT 06705: Catalog $3 ❖ Car and sheepskin seat covers and other accessories. 800–732–2761; 203–573–1504 (in CT).

928 International, 2900 E. Miralona Ave., Anaheim, CA 92806: Free brochure ❖ Car covers. 714–632–9288.

Quality Sheepskin, 5643 Sale Ave., Woodland Hills, CA 91367: Free brochure ❖

Sheepskin seat covers, floor mats, and car covers. 800–852–4293.

Reliable Motoring Accessories, 1751 Spruce St., Riverside, CA 92505: Catalog $3 ❖ Car and seat covers. 800–854–4770; 714–781–0261 (in CA).

Sickafus Sheepskins, Rt. 78, Exit 7, Strausstown, PA 19559: Free catalog ❖ Sheepskin seat covers. 215–488–1782.

Superior Seat Covers, 2954 NW 72nd Ave., Miami, FL 33122: Free information ❖ Easy-to-install seat covers. 800–635–7617.

J.C. Whitney & Company, 1917–19 Archer Ave., P.O. Box 8410, Chicago, IL 60680: Free catalog ❖ Car covers for American and imported models. 312–431–6102.

Seats

Keiper-Recaro Inc., 905 W. Maple Rd., Clawson, MI 48017: Free information ❖ Orthopaedically-designed car seats. 800–873–2276.

PAR Seating Specialists, 310 Main St., New Rochelle, NY 10802: Free catalog ❖ Office chairs and automotive seats. 800–367–7270.

ProAm, The Seat Warehouse, 6125 Richmond, Houston, TX 77057: Free catalog ❖ Car seats. 800–847–5712.

Relaxo-Back Inc., 319 E. California, P.O. Box 812, Gainesville, TX 76240: Free information ❖ Form-fitting auxiliary seat that can be used to relieve lower back pain. 800–527–5496.

Security Systems Manufacturers

Alpine Electronics of America, 19145 Gramercy Pl., Torrance, CA 90505: Free information ❖ Automotive security systems. 213–326–8000.

Audiovox, 150 Marcus Blvd., Hauppage, NY 11788: Free information ❖ Automotive security systems. 516–436–6200.

Auto Page, 1815 W. 205th St., Ste. 101, Torrance, CA 90501: Free information ❖ Automotive security systems. 800–423–6687.

Chapman Security Industries, 227 James St., Ste. 7, Bensenville, IL 60106: Free information ❖ Automotive security systems. 708–766–4060.

Coustic Company, 4260 Charter St., Vernon, CA 90058: Free information ❖ Automotive security systems. 213–582–2832.

Excalibur of America, P.O. Box 508, Douglasville, GA 30133: Free information ❖ Automotive security systems. 404–942–9876.

Fultron, P.O. Box 177, Memphis, TN 38101: Free information ❖ Automotive security systems. 901–525–5711.

Kenwood, P.O. Box 22745, Long Beach, CA 90801: Free information ❖ Automotive security systems. 800–536–9663.

Radio Shack, Division Tandy Corporation, One Tandy Center, Fort Worth, TX 76102: Free information ❖ Automotive security systems. 817–390–3011.

Sansui Electronics, 1290 Wall St. West, Lyndhurst, NJ 07071: Free information ❖ Automotive security systems. 201–460–9710.

Seco-Larm, 17811 Sky Park Cir., Irvine, CA 92714: Free information ❖ Automotive security systems. 714–261–2999.

Security Systems Retailers

Dometic/A & E Systems Inc., 3100 W. Segerstrom, Santa Ana, CA 92704: Free information ❖ Wireless recreational vehicle alarm system. 714–540–6444.

Spectre Security Systems, 843 Dumont Pl., #22, Rochester Hills, MI 48307: Free information ❖ Home and automotive security systems. 810–652–8117.

Stereo Equipment Manufacturers

Aiwa America Inc., 800 Corporate Dr., Mahwah, NJ 07430: Free information ❖ Stereo receivers. 800–289–2492.

Alpine Electronics of America, 19145 Gramercy Pl., Torrance, CA 90501: Free information ❖ Sound systems. 213–326–8000.

Audiovox, 150 Marcus Blvd., Hauppage, NY 11788: Free information ❖ Stereo receivers. 516–436–6200.

Blaupunkt, 2800 S. 25th Ave., Broadview, IL 60153: Free information ❖ Stereo receivers. 708–865–5200.

Clarion Corporation of America, 661 W. Redondo Beach Blvd., Gardena, CA 90247: Free information ❖ Sound systems. 800–487–9007.

Coustic Company, 4260 Charter St., Vernon, CA 90058: Free information ❖ Stereo receivers and cassette tuners. 213–582–2832.

Craig, 13845 Artesia Blvd., Cerritos, CA 90701: Free information ❖ Stereo receivers. 310–537–1233.

Denon America, 222 New Rd., Parsippany, NJ 07054: Free information ❖ Stereo receivers. 201–575–7810.

Fujitsu America, 2801 Telecom Pkwy., Richardson, TX 75082: Free information ❖ Stereo receivers. 214–690–9660.

Harmon Kardon, 8380 Balboa Blvd., Northridge, CA 91325: Free information ❖ Audio and stereo in-dash receivers and cassette tuners, amplifiers, and other equipment. 818–893–9992.

Hitachi Sales Corporation, 401 W. Artesia Blvd., Compton, CA 90220: Free information ❖ Stereo receivers. 310–537–8383.

Jensen, 4136 N. United Pkwy., Schiller Park, IL 60176: Free information ❖ Stereo receivers. 800–323–0707.

JVC, 41 Slater Dr., Elmwood Park, NJ 07407: Free information ❖ Stereo receivers. 201–794–3900.

Kenwood, P.O. Box 22745, Long Beach, CA 90801: Free information ❖ Audio and stereo sound systems. 800–536–9663.

Marantz, 1150 Feehanville Dr., Mt. Prospect, IL 60056: Free information ❖ Stereo receivers. 708–299–4000.

Mitsubishi Electronics, 5665 Plaza Dr., Cypress, CA 90630: Free information ❖ Stereo receivers. 800–843–2515.

Panasonic, Panasonic Way, Secaucus, NJ 07094: Free information ❖ Stereo receivers. 201–348–7000.

Pioneer Electronics, 1925 E. Dominguez St., Long Beach, CA 90810: Free information ❖ Stereo receivers. 800–421–1404.

Proton Corporation, 16826 Edwards Rd., Cerritos, CA 90701: Free information ❖ Stereo and cassette receivers that play the sound from television shows. 714–952–6900.

Radio Shack, Division Tandy Corporation, One Tandy Center, Fort Worth, TX 76102: Free information ❖ Stereo receivers. 817–390–3011.

Sansui Electronics, 1290 Wall St. West, Lyndhurst, NJ 07071: Free information ❖ Audio and stereo sound systems and removable cassette receivers. 201–460–9710.

Sanyo, 21350 Lassen St., Chatsworth, CA 91311: Free information ❖ Stereo receivers. 818–998–7322.

Sharp Electronics, Sharp Plaza, Mahwah, NJ 07430: Free information ❖ Stereo receivers. 800–BE-SHARP.

Sherwood, 14830 Alondra Blvd., La Mirada, CA 90638: Free information ❖ Stereo receivers. 800–962–3203.

Sony Consumer Products, 1 Sony Dr., Park Ridge, NJ 07656: Free information ❖ Stereo receivers. 201–930–1000.

Technics, One Panasonic Way, Secaucus, NJ 07094: Free information ❖ Stereo receivers. 201–348–9090.

Toshiba, 82 Totowa Rd., Wayne, NJ 07470: Free information ❖ Stereo receivers. 201–628–8000.

Vector Research, 1230 Calle Suerte, Camarillo, CA 93010: Free information ❖ Stereo receivers. 805–987–1312.

Yamaha, P.O. Box 6660, Buena Park, CA 90620: Free information ❖ Audio and stereo receivers. 800–492–6242.

Stereo Equipment Retailers

Crutchfield, 1 Crutchfield Park, Charlottesville, VA 22906: Free catalog ❖ Stereo equipment. 800–955–9009.

Crystal Sonics, 1638 S. Central Ave., Glendale, CA 91204: Catalog $2 ❖ Stereo equipment. 800–545–7310; 818–240–7310 (in CA).

Tires

Belle Tire Industries Inc., 3500 Enterprise Dr., Allen Park, MI 48101: Free catalog ❖ Tires. 313–271–9200.

Coker Tires, P.O. Box 72554, Chattanooga, TN 37402: Free information ❖ Tires for antique cars. 800–251–6336; 615–265–6368 (in TN).

Euro-Tire Inc., 567 Rt. 46, Fairfield, NJ 07006: Free catalog ❖ European tires, light alloy wheels, and shock absorbers. 800–631–0080; 201–575–0080 (in NJ).

Kelsey Tire Inc., Box 564, Camdenton, MO 65020: Free information ❖ Tires and tubes for vintage automobiles. 800–325–0091.

Lucas Automotive, 2850 Temple Ave., Long Beach, CA 90806: Free catalog ❖ Antique and classic tires. 800–952–4333; 800–735–0166 (in CA).

Teletire, 17622 Armstrong Ave., Irvine, CA 92714: Free catalog ❖ Performance-rated steel-belted and other tires. 800–835–8473; 714–250–9141 (in CA).

Tire America, One Bryan Dr., Wheeling, WV 26003: Catalog $2 ❖ RV and high-performance tires and wheels. 800–624–6932.

Tire Rack, 771 W. Chippewa Ave., South Bend, IN 46614: Brochure $3 (specify car) ❖ Tires and wheels for most domestic and imported cars. 800–428–8355; 219–287–2316 (in IN).

Universal Tire Company, 987 Stony Battery Rd., Lancaster, PA 17601: Free catalog ❖ Antique and classic car tires and wheel hardware. 800–233–3827.

Wallace W. Wade Wholesale Tires, 4303 Irving Blvd., Dallas, TX 75247: Free information ❖ Antique and classic automobile tires. 800–666–TYRE; 214–688–0091 (in TX).

Willies Antique Tires, 5257 W. Diversey Ave., Chicago, IL 60639: Free price list ❖ Tires for antique cars. 312–622–4037.

Tools

A & I Supply, 2125 Court St., Pekin, IL 61554: Free information ❖ Electric- and air-operated tools, special-purpose tools, welders, and compressors. 309–353–3002.

Eastwood Company, 580 Lancaster Ave., Box 3014, Malvern, PA 19355: Free catalog ❖ Welding equipment, rust removers, sand blasting equipment, body repair tools, pin striping equipment, and buffing supplies. 800–345–1178.

Griot's Garage, 3500–A 20th St. East, Tacoma, WA 98424: Free catalog ❖ Automotive tools, storage cabinets, workbenches, and diagnostic equipment. 800–345–5789.

RhinoRamps, 99 S. Cameron St., Harrisburg, PA 17101: Free information ❖ Easy-to-use ramps. 800–400–6642.

Tip Sandblast Equipment, P.O. Box 649, Canfield, OH 44406: Free catalog ❖ Sandblasting equipment. 800–321–9260.

Trailers & Recreational Vehicles

Atwood Mobile Products, 4750 Hiawatha Dr., Rockford, IL 61103: Free information ❖ Trailers, appliances, engineered components, and systems for recreational vehicles and boats. 815–877–5700.

Calkins Manufacturing Company, Spokane Industrial Park, P.O. Box 14527, Spokane, WA 99214: Free information ❖ Boat trailers. 509–928–7420.

Camper's Choice, 502 4th St. NW, P.O. Box 1546, Red Bay, AL 35582: Free catalog ❖ Trailer accessories. 800–833–6713; 205–356–2810 (in AL).

Casita Travel Trailers, Box 309, Kerens, TX 75144: Free brochure ❖ Lightweight, all-fiberglass self-contained trailers. 800–442–9986.

Coachmen Recreational Vehicle Company, P.O. Box 350, Elkhart, IN 46515: Free information ❖ Fifth wheels and travel trailers. 219–262–3474.

Correct Craft, 6100 S. Orange Ave., Orlando, FL 32809: Free information ❖ Boat trailers. 800–346–2092; 407–855–4141 (in FL).

Eastern Marine, Rt. 2, P.O. Box 6255, Rochester, NH 03867: Free catalog ❖ Boat trailers, electronic equipment for boats, bimini tops, boat covers, other equipment, and dragger, lobster, skiff, sport fishing, and dive boats. 603–332–9706.

Ezee Tow Trailers Ltd., Hwy. 59 North, P.O. Box 3, Marshall, MN 56258: Free information ❖ Stainless steel tandem boat trailers. 507–537–1431.

Fleetwood Enterprises Inc., P.O. Box 7638, Riverside, CA 92513: Free information ❖ Travel trailers and fifth wheels. 800–444–4905.

Grove Boat-Lift, P.O. Box 8095, Fresno, CA 93727: Free information ❖ Easy-to-use boat lift for cars. 800–447–5115; 209–251–5115 (in CA).

Hi-Lo Trailer Company, 145 Elm St., Butler, OH 44822: Free information ❖ Folding travel trailers. 800–321–6402; 419–883–3000 (in OH).

Holiday Rambler Corporation, P.O. Box 465, Wakarusa, IN 46573: Free information ❖ RV motorhomes. 800–245–4778.

Isley's RV Center, 2225 W. Main St., Mesa, AZ 85201: Free catalog ❖ RV parts. 800–962–5547.

Jensen Enterprises Ltd., 1301 9th Ave. North, Humboldt, IA 50548: Free information ❖ Enclosed and open car and utility trailers. 515–332–5963.

Karry Industries Inc., P.O. Box 5810, Jacksonville, FL 32247: Free information ❖ Automatic, one-step load and unload boat carrier for automotive vehicles. 904–739–1461.

Lance Camper Manufacturing Corporation, 10234 Glenoaks Blvd., Pacoima, CA 91331: Free information ❖ Campers and fifth wheelers.

Owens Classic Trailers, P.O. Box 628, Sturgis, MI 49091: Free information ❖ Open car trailers. 616–651–9319.

Pierce Sales, Expressway 287, Henrietta, TX 76365: Catalog $1 ❖ Cargo carriers, runabouts, horse and stock trailers, and truck beds. 817–538–5646.

QQ's Trailers Inc., Rt. 15, P.O. Box 166, Lafayette, NJ 07848: Free information ❖ Open and enclosed trailers. 201–579–1223.

Richlund Sales, 75695 Hwy. 1053, Kentwood, LA 70444: Free information ❖ Icemaker, central vacuum system, trash compactor, rear vision camera, electric heat equipment, combination washer-dryer, and other RV appliances. 504–229–4922.

S & H Trailer Manufacturing Company, 800 Industrial Dr., Madill, OK 73446: Free information ❖ RVs and horse, cargo, utility, and carryall trailers with optional features. 405–795–5577.

Scamp Eveland's Inc., Box 2, Backus, MN 56435: Free brochure ❖ Trailers. 800–346–4962; 800–432–3749 (in MN).

Sooner Trailers, P.O. Box 1323, Duncan, OK 73534: Free information ❖ Horse trailers. 405–255–6979.

Tommy's Trailers Inc., 1828 Latta Rd., Ada, OK 74820: Free brochure ❖ Single car haulers. 405–332–7785.

Trail-Rite Boat Trailers, 3100 W. Central, Santa Ana, CA 92704: Free information ❖ Boat trailers. 714–556–4540.

Trailer Parts International Inc., P.O. Box 520963, Miami, FL 33152: Catalog $4 ❖ Boat trailers and trailer parts and accessories. 305–592–1879.

Trailer World, P.O. Box 1687, Bowling Green, KY 42102: Free catalog ❖ Enclosed and open car trailers, vendor trailers, and parts. 502–843–4587.

Trailex, 60 Industrial Park Dr., P.O. Box 553, Canfield, OH 44406: Free brochure ❖ Boat trailers. 800–282–5042.

VM Boat Trailers, 5200 S. Peach, Fresno, CA 93725: Free information ❖ Jet ski trailers. 209–486–0410.

Truck Parts

All Chevy Auto Parts, 4999 Vanden Rd., Vacaville, CA 95687: Free information ❖ Parts for Chevrolet cars and trucks, from 1955 to 1990. 707–437–5466.

Alley Auto Parts, Rt. 2, Box 551, Immokalee, FL 33934: Free information ❖ Parts for cars and trucks, from 1948 to 1975. 813–657–3541.

American Classic Automotive, P.O. Box 50286, Denton, TX 76206: Free catalog (specify year) ❖ GMC truck parts, from 1936 to 1959 and 1960 to 1972. 817–497–2456.

Arnold's Auto Parts, 1484 Crandall Rd., Tiverton, RI 02878: Free information ❖ Parts for American cars and trucks, from 1930 to 1970. 401–624–6936.

Auto Body Specialties Inc., Rt. 66, P.O. Box 455, Middlefield, CT 06455: Catalog $5 ❖ Ford, Chevrolet, and Dodge truck body parts, from 1949 to 1992. 203–346–4989.

B & T Truck Parts, P.O. Box 799, Siloam Springs, AR 72761: Catalog $3 ❖ Chevrolet and GMC truck parts, from 1960 to 1966. 501–524–5959.

Bartnik Sales & Service, 6524 Van Dyke, Cass City, MI 48726: Free information ❖ Parts for trucks and cars, from 1960 to 1970. 517–872–3541.

C & P Chevy Parts, Box 348, Kulpsville, PA 19443: Catalog $2 ❖ Restoration supplies for 1955 to 1959 Chevrolet trucks. 215–721–4300.

Carolina Classics, 624 E. Geer St., Durham, NC 27701: Catalog $3 ❖ Ford truck parts, from 1948 to 1966. 919–682–4211.

Dennis Carpenter Ford Reproductions, P.O. Box 26398, Charlotte, NC 28221: Catalog $3 ❖ Parts for Ford pickups. 704–786–8139.

Jim Carter Antique Truck Parts, 1500 E. Alton, Independence, MO 64055: Catalog $1.50 ❖ Chevrolet and GMC truck parts, from mid-1930 to early 1970. 816–833–1937.

Chev's of the 40's, 18409 NE 28th St., Vancouver, WA 98682: Catalog $3.75 ❖ Parts for Chevrolet trucks, from 1937 to 1954. 206–835–9799.

Chevy Duty Pickup Parts, 4319 NW Gateway, Kansas City, MO 64150: Catalog $3 ❖ Restoration supplies for 1947 to 1972 Chevy and GMC pickups. 816–741–8029.

Concours Parts & Accessories, 3563 Numancia St., P.O. Box 1210, Santa Ynez, CA 93460: Catalog $4 ❖ Parts for 1948 to 1966 Ford trucks. 805–688–7795.

E & J Used Auto & Truck Parts, 315 31st Ave., P.O. Box 6007, Rock Island, IL 61201: Free information ❖ Parts for most American and foreign cars and trucks, from 1940 to 1987. 800–728–7686; 309–788–7686 (in IL).

Fiberglass & Wood Company, Rt. 3, Box 900, Nashville, GA 31639: Catalog $3 ❖ Chevrolet and GMC truck parts, from 1931 to 1973. 912–686–3838.

Gilbert's Truck Parts, 470 RD 1 North, P.O. Box 1316, Chino Valley, AZ 86323: Catalog $2 (specify year) ❖ Chevrolet pickup truck parts, from 1947 to 1966. 602–636–5337.

Golden State Pickup Parts, P.O. Box 1019, Santa Ynez, CA 93460: Catalog $3 (specify car) ❖ Chevy and GMC parts for pickup trucks. 805–564–2020.

Heavy Chevy Pickup Parts, P.O. Box 650, Siloam Springs, AR 72761: Catalog $2 ❖ Parts for 1948 to 1959 GMC and Chevrolet trucks. 501–524–4873.

Bruce Horkey Cabinetry, Rt. 4, Box 188, Windom, MN 56101: Catalog $2 ❖ Wood and other parts for 1934 to 1992 Chevrolet, 1939 to 1985 Dodge, and 1928 to 1992 Ford pickups. 507–831–5625.

Mark Jansen, 4319 NW Gateway, Kansas City, MO 64150: Catalog $3 (specify year)* Chevrolet and GMC pickup truck parts, from 1947 to 1972. 816–741–8029.

Lawrence Auto Body, 306 W. Grand River, Brighton, MI 48116: Free price list ❖ Fiberglass fenders and running boards for Chevrolet pickups. 810–227–9444.

North East Ford Truck Parts, 206 N. Main St., Naugatuck, CT 06770: Catalog $4.50 (specify year) ❖ Reproduction and N.O.S. parts, from 1948 to 1972. 800–4–TRUCKS; 1–283–1202 (in CT).

Obsolete Chevrolet Parts Company, P.O. Box 68, Nashville, GA 31639: Catalog $2.50 (specify year) ❖ Reproduction Chevrolet truck parts, from 1929 to 1972. 912–686–7230.

Obsolete Ford Parts Company, P.O. Box 787, Nashville, GA 31639: Catalog for 1948 to 1956 parts $2.50; 1957 to 1972 parts $2.50 ❖ Ford truck parts. 912–686–2470.

Ranchero Classics, P.O. Box 1248, Sunset Beach, CA 90742: Catalog $3 ❖ Ford Ranchero parts. 714–847–7107.

Roberts Motor Parts, 17 Prospect St., West Newbury, MA 01985: Catalog $4 ❖ Chevrolet and GMC truck parts. 508–363–5407.

Don Sumner - The Truck Shop, P.O. Box 5035, Nashville, GA 31639: Catalog $4 (refundable) ❖ Chevrolet and GMC truck parts, from 1927 to 1972. 800–245–0556.

The Truck Shop, 102 W. Marion Ave., P.O. Box 5035, Nashville, GA 31639: Catalog $4 ❖ Parts for 1927 to 1972 Chevrolet and GMC trucks. 912–686–3833.

Vander Haag's Inc., Box 550, Sanborn, IA 51248: Free information ❖ Truck parts. 712–262–7000.

Upholstery & Carpets

ABC Auto Upholstery, 1634 Church St., Philadelphia, PA 19124: Free information ❖ N.O.S. upholstery for 1951 to 1966 Fords. 215–289–0555.

AFTCO Upholstery, P.O. Box 278, Isanti, MN 55040: Catalog $5 ❖ Upholstery for older cars. 612–742–4025.

Auto Custom Carpets Inc., P.O. Box 1167, Anniston, AL 36202: Free information ❖ Original-style carpets for General Motors, Chrysler, and Ford cars and trucks. 800–633–2358.

Automotive Parts, 100 West Hwy 36, Mankato, KS 66956: Free information with long SASE ❖ Easy-to-install upholstery kits for American cars, from 1928 to 1959. 800–255–4100; 913–378–3145 (in KS).

Bob's T-Birds's, 5397 NE 14th Ave., Fort Lauderdale, FL 33334: Free information with long SASE ❖ Upholstery for T-Birds, from 1955 to 1957. 305–491–6652.

Chevelle World, Box 38, Washington, OK 73093: Free information ❖ Interior kits, carpets, and trim. 405–364–0379.

Hampton Coach, 70 High St., P.O. Box 665, Hampton, NH 03842: Free information ❖ Top and interior kits for 1922 to 1954 Chevrolet cars. 603–926–6341.

LeBaron Bonney Company, P.O. Box 6, Chestnut St., Amesbury, MA 01913: Catalog $1 ❖ Upholstery materials for antique, classic, and special-interest cars. 508–388–3811.

Midland Automotive Products, 33 Woolfolk Ave., Midland City, AL 36350: Free information ❖ Chevrolet carpeting, truck mats, landau tops, and convertible top pads. 205–983–1212.

World Upholstery & Trim, P.O. Box 283, Camarillo, CA 93011: Free information (specify model and year) ❖ Headliners, seat upholstery, and carpets for European cars. 805–482–4682.

Wheels & Hubcaps

Agape Auto, 2825 Selzer, Evansville, IN 47712: Free information ❖ Wheel covers from 1949 to 1980 and fender skirts from 1935 to 1972. 812–423–7332.

Calimers Wheel Shop, 30 E. North St., Waynesboro, PA 17268: Free information ❖ Hickory-spoke wheels for antique cars. 717–762–5056.

Dayton Wheel Products, 1147 Broadway St., Dayton, OH 45408: Free information ❖ Wire wheels. 513–461–1707.

Fittipaldi/Motoring Accessories Inc., 1425 NW 82nd Ave., Miami, FL 33126: Free information ❖ Fittipaldi sport wheels. 305–592–8177.

Freedom Design Wheels, 4750 Eisenhower Ave., Alexandria, VA 22034: Brochure $1 ❖ Special-designed wheels. 800–296–1792; 703–823–5606 (in VA).

Hub Cap Annie, 3917 S. Side Blvd., Jacksonville, FL 32216: Free information ❖ New and used hubcaps. 800–624–7179.

Hubcap Capital, P.O. Box 21949, Carson City, NV 89721: Free information ❖ Hubcaps. 702–246–0220.

Tire Rack, 771 W. Chippewa Ave., South Bend, IN 46614: Brochures $3 (specify car) ❖ Tires and wheels for most domestic and imported cars. 800–428–8355; 219–287–2316 (in IN).

Wheel Repair Service Inc., 317 Southbridge St., Auburn, MA 01501: Free information ❖ Hubcaps and wheel covers for most cars, street rods, and replicas; and wire spoke, alloy, and steel disc wheels. 508–832–4949.

Wheelcovers - Robinson's Auto Sales, 200 New York Ave., New Castle, IN 47362: Free information ❖ Hubcaps, wheel covers, hub cap sets, and N.O.S. and used parts. 317–529–7603.

AWARDS & TROPHIES

AA World Class Corporation, 65 Railroad Ave., Ridgefield, NJ 07657: Free information ❖ Letters, ribbons, cups, emblems, pins, plaques, and other awards. 800–526–0411; 201–313–0022 (in NJ).

Ames & Rollinson Studio, 20 W. 22nd St., New York, NY 10010: Free catalog ❖ Hand-lettered award scrolls and certificates. 212–473–7000.

Award Company of America, 2200 Rice Mine Rd. NE, Tuscaloosa, AL 35403: Free brochure ❖ Walnut-finished plaques. 205–349–2990.

Captain's Emporium, 6600 N. Lincoln Ave., Lincolnwood, IL 60645: Free information ❖ Trophies and gifts. 708–675–5411.

Chicago Trophy & Award Company, 3255 N. Milwaukee Ave., Chicago, IL 60618: Free catalog ❖ Trophies and plaques. 312–685–8200.

Classic Medallics, 1–15 Borden Ave., Long Island City, NY 11101: Free information ❖ Letters, ribbons, cups, medals, emblems, pins, plaques, and other awards. 800–221–1348; 718–392–5410 (in NY).

Cornette Ribbon & Trophy Company, 850 Dunbar Ave., Oldsmar, FL 34677: Free catalog ❖ Ribbons, awards, and trophies. 800–869–0234; 813–855–5520 (in FL).

Crown Trophy, 1 Odell Plaza, Yonkers, NY 10701: Free information ❖ Letters, ribbons, cups, emblems, pins, plaques, and other awards. 914–963–0005.

Dinn Brothers Inc., 68 Winter St., P.O. Box 111, Holyoke, MA 01040: Free catalog ❖ Trophies, plaques, ribbons, silverware, medals, and desk sets. 800–628–9657.

Emblem & Badge Inc., P.O. Box 6226, Providence, RI 02940: Free information ❖ Trophies, trophy cases, plaques, medals, pins, and ribbons. 800–875–5444; 401–331–5444 (in RI).

Hodges Badge Company Inc., 42 Valley Rd., Middletown, RI 02840: Free catalog ❖ Brass medals with gold, silver and copper/bronze finish, and award certificates. 800–556–2440; 401–847–2000 (in RI).

Music Stand, 1 Rockdale Plaza, Lebanon, OH 03766: Free catalog ❖ Trophies, plaques, and certificates. 800–515–5010.

Taylor Graphics, P.O. Box 492, Greencastle, IN 46135: Free catalog ❖ Award and recognition plaques, deskplates and doorplates, paperweights, brass identification plates, photo charm products, nameplates, card cases, and luggage tags. 317–653–8481.

Trophy Supply, 1 Odell Plaza, Yonkers, NY 10701: Free information ❖ Trophies, plaques, medals, club awards, around-the-neck medals, pins, and badges. 800–227–1557; 914–237–9500 (in NY).

Trophyland USA Inc., 7001 W. 20th Ave., P.O. Box 4606, Hialeah, FL 33014: Free catalog ❖ Awards for incentive programs, athletic events, and other competitions. 800–327–5820.

Volk Corporation, 23936 Industrial Park Dr., Farmington Hills, MI 48024: Free information ❖ Award ribbons. 800–521–6799; 810–477–6700 (in MI).

AWNINGS & PATIO COVERS

Inter Trade Inc., 3175 Fujita St., Torrance, CA 90505: Free information ❖ Indoor-operated patio covers and awnings for protection from heat, sun, cold, rain, and noise. 310–515–7177.

International E-Z UP Inc., 5525 E. Gibraltar, Ontario, CA 91764: Free information ❖ Easy-to-set-up, spring-loaded center pole instant shelter/canopy. 800–457–4233; 909–466–8333 (in CA).

JIL Industries Inc., 21 Green St., Malden, MA 02148: Free brochure ❖ Retractable deck and patio awnings. 800–876–2340.

Pease Industries Inc., P.O. Box 14–8001, Fairfield, OH 45014: Information $1 ❖ Retractable-arm awning with optional wind sensor for automatic closing and sun sensor that opens the awning. 800–543–1180.

BABY CARE

After the Stork, 1501 12th St. NW, Albuquerque, NM 87104: Free catalog ❖ Natural fiber clothing, records, tapes, books, and toys for children, from birth to age 7. 800–333–5437.

Baby Biz Products Inc., 8102 E. Bucknell Pl., Denver, CO 80231: Free brochure ❖ Diaper covers and diapers. 800–697–BABY.

Baby Bunz & Company, P.O. Box 1717, Sebastopol, CA 95473: Catalog $1 ❖ Diapering and layette supplies. 707–829–5347.

A Baby Carriage, 5617 W. Belmont, Chicago, IL 60634: Free catalog ❖ Strollers for twins and triplets, stroller parts, and cribs. 800–228–8946; 312–237–4300 (in IL).

Biobottoms, P.O. Box 6009, Petaluma, CA 04953: Free catalog ❖ Cotton diapers and wool covers. 800–766–1254; 707–778–7152 (in CA).

Diaperaps, Owensmouth Ave., Chatsworth, CA 91311: Free brochure ❖ Cotton outer layer, polyfoam-protected diaper covers. 800–477–3424.

Hand in Hand, Rt. 26, RR 1, Box 1425, Oxford, ME 04270: Free catalog ❖ Books, toys and games, car seat time occupiers, furniture, bathroom accessories, car seats, housewares and hardware, health aids, and other products that help nurture, teach, and protect children. 800–872–9745.

Lullaby Cribwear Collection, 1939 Michigan Rd., Madison, IN 47250: Free brochure ❖ Crib wear for cradles, porta-cribs, bassinets, and toddler beds. 812–273–2709.

MacNeil Babycare Limited, 5161 Thatcher Rd., Downers Grove, IL 60515: Free catalog ❖ Bottle and breast-feeding products. 708–769–1798.

McGill's, 9007 F St., Omaha, NE 68127: Free brochure ❖ Gifts and novelties for twins. 402–592–0000.

Mother's Wear Diapers, P.O. Box 114, Northampton, MA 01061: Free brochure ❖ Contour-shaped diapers and covers. 800–633–0303; 413–586–3488 (in MA).

The Natural Baby Company Inc., 114 W. Franklin, Pennington, NJ 08534: Free information ❖ Diapering and medical products, wood toys, cotton clothes, and alternative products. 800–388–BABY.

O.T.B.M., P.O. Box 83934, Milwaukee, WI 53223: Free brochure with long SASE ❖ Original items for twins and their families.

One Step Ahead, P.O. 517, Lake Bluff, IL 60044: Free catalog ❖ Baby items for use when travelling, feeding, at bath time, and for security. 800–950–5120.

J.C. Penney Company Inc., Catalog Division, Milwaukee, WI 53263: Free information ❖ Nursery furniture, bedding, strollers, car seats, and other baby care items. 800–222–6161.

Peg Perego U.S.A. Inc., 3625 Independence Dr., Fort Wayne, IN 46818: Free information ❖ Perego Quattro strollers with

easy-to-handle maneuverability. 219–484–3093.

Perfectly Safe, 7245 Whipple Ave. NW, North Canton, OH 44720: Free catalog ❖ Safety items for children age 3 to 6. 216–494–2323.

Pleasant Company, P.O. Box 620190, Middleton, WI 53562: Free catalog ❖ Bassinets, diaper bags, bunting, and knits for newborns and infants. 800–845–0005.

Right Start Catalog, Right Start Plaza, 5334 Sterling Center Dr., Westlake Village, CA 91361: Catalog $2 ❖ Car seats, clothing, educational toys, and shopping carts that convert into strollers. 800–548–8531.

Rubens & Marble Inc., P.O. Box 14900, Chicago, IL 60614: Free brochure with long SASE ❖ Stretch stay-up diapers with elastic ends. 312–348–6200.

Tot Tenders Inc., 9030 Kenamar Dr., Ste. 309, San Diego, CA 92121: Free information ❖ Baby carrier for twins. 800–634–6870.

Tuesday's Twins, P.O. Box 645, Mequon, WI 53092: Free brochure with long SASE ❖ Original specialty items for twins.

Twincerely Yours, 748 Lake Ave., Clermont, FL 34711: Free catalog with long SASE ❖ Gifts, novelties, and T-shirts for twins and their families. 904–394–5493.

BADGES & BUTTONS

AABCO Printing, 628 W. Mitchell St., Milwaukee, WI 53204: Free information ❖ Custom buttons. 414–643–1894.

B & K Buttons, 16 S. Detroit St., Xenia, OH 45385: Free information ❖ Custom buttons. 800–223–4392.

Badge-A-Minit Ltd., Box 800, LaSalle, IL 61301: Free catalog ❖ Badge-making machine, supplies, or beginner's starter kit for making badges and pin-back buttons. 800–223–4103.

Fawcett's Square Dance Shop, 412 W. Sam Houston, Pharr, TX 78577: Free information ❖ Engraved and hot-stamped badges. 512–787–1116.

H & R Badge & Stamp Company, 2585 Mock Rd., Columbus, OH 43219: Free catalog ❖ In-stock and custom badges and rubber stamps. 614–471–3735.

KA-MO Engravers, P.O. Box 30337, Albuquerque, NM 87190: Free catalog ❖ Badges for square and round dancers. 800–352–5266; 505–883–4963 (in NM).

J.R. Kush & Company, 7623 Hesperia St., Reseda, CA 91335: Free information ❖ Handcrafted belt buckles for round and square dancers. 818–344–9671.

Bernie Lasky Inc., 6232 Pembroke Rd., Hollywood, FL 33023: Free information ❖ Custom buttons. 305–966–8236.

C. Lifton's Buckles & More, 121 S. 6th St., Stillwater, MN 55082: Catalog $5 ❖ Authentic reproduction Old West badges and other nickel-plated badges from America's history. 612–439–7208.

Micro Plastics, P.O. Box 847, Rifle, CO 81650: Free information ❖ Custom club badges. 303–625–1718.

Nasco, 901 Janesville Ave., Fort Atkinson, WI 53538: Free catalog ❖ Badge-makers and supplies. 800–558–9595.

Pauly's, P.O. Box 72, Wausau, WI 54402: Free information ❖ Engraved and jeweled badges. 715–845–3979.

N.G. Slater Corporation, 220 W. 19th St., New York, NY 10011: Free catalog ❖ Equipment for making buttons. 212–924–3133.

Super Star, 2338 W. Burnhat, Milwaukee, WI 53204: Free information ❖ Custom buttons. 414–383–2212.

BADMINTON

Alpha Sports Inc., 7208 McNeil Dr., Austin, TX 78729: Free information ❖ Nets, posts, shuttlecocks, racquets, and sets. 800–523–4585; 215–291–0300 (in TX).

Buckeye Sports Supply, John's Sporting Goods, 2655 Harrison Ave. SW, Canton, OH 44706: Free information ❖ Nets, posts, presses, racquets, sets, shuttlecocks, and strings. 800–533–8691.

Cannon Sports Inc., P.O. Box 11179, Burbank, CA 91510: Free information with list of retailers ❖ Nets, posts, racquets, strings, shuttlecocks, and sets. 800–362–3146; 818–753–5940 (in CA).

Century Sports Inc., Lakewood Industrial Park, 1995 Rutgers University Blvd., Box 2035, Lakewood, NJ 08701: Free information ❖ Nets, posts, shuttlecocks, and racquets. 800–526–7548; 908–905–4422 (in NJ).

Douglas Sport Nets & Equipment Company, 3441 S. 11th Ave., P.O. Box 393, Eldridge, IA 52748: Free information ❖ Nets, posts, and sets. 800–553–8907; 319–285–4162 (in IA).

Edwards Sports Products, 429 E. Haddam-Moodus Rd., Moodus, CT 06469: Free information ❖ Nets, posts, and sets. 800–243–2512; 203–873–8625 (in CT).

Fischer Tennis, 2412 Logan Rd., Owings Mills, MD 21117: Free information ❖ Racquets and shuttlecocks. 410–356–0196.

Franklin Sports Industries Inc., 17 Campanelli Pkwy., P.O. Box 508, Stoughton, MA 02072: Free information ❖ Nets, posts, racquets, strings, shuttlecocks, and sets. 617–344–1111.

General Sportcraft Company Ltd., 140 Woodbine Rd., Bergenfield, NJ 07621: Free information ❖ Nets, posts, sets, racquets, strings, and shuttlecocks. 201–384–4242.

Indian Industries Inc., P.O. Box 889, Evansville, IN 47706: Free catalog ❖ Nets, posts, racquets, strings, shuttlecocks, and sets. 800–457–3373; 812–467–1200 (in IN).

Dick Martin Sports Inc., 181 E. Union Ave., P.O. Box 7381, East Rutherford, NJ 07073: Free information ❖ Nets, posts, racquets, strings, and sets. 800–221–1993; 201–438–5255 (in NJ).

Olympia Sports, 745 State Cir., Ann Arbor, MI 48106: Free information ❖ Shuttlecocks, racquets, and sets. 800–521–2832; 313–761–5173 (in MI).

Park & Sun Inc., 2825 S. Tejon St., Englewood, CO 80110: Free information ❖ Nets, posts, and sets. 800–776–7275.

Porter Athletic Equipment Company, 2500 S. 25th Ave., Broadview, IL 60153: Free information ❖ Nets, posts, racquets, sets, and shuttlecocks. 708–338–2000.

Rackets International, 24572 La Cienega St., Laguna Hills, CA 92653: Free information ❖ Badminton rackets. 800–726–8913.

Regent Sports Corporation, 45 Ranick Rd., Hauppage, NY 11788: Free information ❖ Nets, posts, racquets. strings, shuttlecocks, cases, covers, grips, presses, and sets. 516–234–2800.

Saroy Inc., 1125 Carolina Dr., West Chicago, IL 60185: Free information ❖ Shuttlecocks and racquets. 708–293–9831.

Spalding Sports Worldwide, 425 Meadow St., P.O. Box 901, Chicopee, MA 01201: Free information with list of retailers ❖ Nets, posts, racquets, strings, shuttlecocks, cases, covers, grips, presses, and sets. 800–225–6601.

Sport Fun Inc., 4621 Sperry St., Los Angeles, CA 90039: Free information ❖ Nets, posts, racquets, strings, shuttlecocks, and sets. 800–423–2597; 818–240–6700 (in CA).

Sportime, 1 Sportime Way, Atlanta, GA 30340: Free information ❖ Nets, posts, shuttlecocks, racquets, and sets. 800–444–5700; 404–449–5700 (in GA).

Yonex Corporation, 350 Challenger St., Torrance, CA 90503: Free information ❖ Racquets, strings, and shuttlecocks. 800–449–6639.

BALLOONS

Anagram International Inc., 7700 Anagram Dr., Minneapolis, MN 55344: Free information ❖ Balloons with birthday messages and one-of-a-kind designs. Call for names of local distributors. 800–554–4711; 612–949–5600 (in MN).

Balloon Printing Company, P.O. Box 150, Rankin, PA 15104: Free information ❖ Imprinted balloons. 800–533–5221.

Balloon Wholesalers International, 1735 E St., Ste. 104, Fresno, CA 93706: Free catalog ❖ Balloons. 800–444–9840.

Balloons For You, 2152 Chennault, Carrollton, TX 75006: Free information ❖ Balloons. 800–636–4887.

Clown City, 1 Inchcliffe Dr., Gales Ferry, CT 06335: Free information ❖ Balloons and clown supplies. 203–464–7116.

Clown Heaven, 4792 Old State Rd. 37 South, Martinsville, IN 46152: Catalog $3 ❖ Balloons, make-up, puppets, wigs, ministry and gospel items, novelties, magic, clown props, and books. 317–342–6888.

Clowning Around, P.O. Box 691181, San Antonio, TX 78269: Free information ❖ Balloons. 210–696–0064.

Dewey's Good News Balloons, 1202 Wildwood, Deer Park, TX 77536: Free catalog ❖ Gospel clown supplies and balloon books.

The Entertainers Supermarket, 21 Carol Pl., Staten Island, NY 10303: Free brochure ❖ Supplies for balloon sculpturists, clowns, magicians, jugglers, face painters, stilt walkers, and other entertainers. 718–494–6232.

Flowers & Balloons Inc., 325 Cleveland Rd., Bogart, GA 30622: Free catalog ❖ Balloons and gifts. 800–241–2094; 706–548–1588 (in GA).

Gayla Balloons, P.O. Box 920800, Houston, TX 77292: Free catalog ❖ Balloons for the balloon artist. 800–327–9513.

K & K Balloons, 3332 Mather Field Rd., Rancho Cordova, CA 95670: Free information ❖ Twister balloons. 800–655–1764.

La Rock's Fun & Magic Outlet, 3847 Rosehaven Dr., Charlotte, NC 28205: Catalog $3 ❖ Clown and balloon how-to books, balloons, balloon sculpture kits, and magic equipment. 704–563–9300.

Mecca Magic Inc., 49 Dodd St., Bloomfield, NJ 07003: Catalog $10 ❖ Balloons, theatrical make-up, clown equipment, magic, costumes and wigs, puppets, ventriloquism equipment, props, and juggling supplies. 201–429–7597.

More Than Balloons Inc., 2409 Ravendale Ct., Kissimmee, FL 34758: Free information ❖ Regular balloons, balloons for making sculptures, how-to books, balloon accessories, and magic. 800–BALUNES.

Morris Costumes, 3108 Monroe Rd., Charlotte, NC 28205: Catalog $20 ❖ Balloons, costumes, clown props, masks, joke items, magic tricks, special effects, novelties, and books. 704–332–3304.

T. Myers Magic Inc., 1509 Parker Bend, Austin, TX 78734: Free catalog ❖ Balloons and balloon-sculpting supplies. 800–648–6221; 512–263–2313 (in TX).

Novelties Unlimited, 410 W. 21st St., Norfolk, VA 23517: Catalog $5 ❖ Balloons, magic tricks, party decorations, make-up, and clown supplies, props, and gags. 804–622–0344.

Pioneer Balloon Company, 555 N. Woodlawn Ave., Wichita, KS 67208: Free information ❖ Balloons and accessories. Call for names of local distributors. 316–685–2266.

Sally Distributors Inc., 4100 Quebec Ave. North, Minneapolis, MN 55427: Free catalog ❖ Balloons, toys, greeting cards, gifts, and carnival supplies. 612–533–7100.

Suburban Balloon & Helium, 31535 Vine St., Willowick, OH 44094: Free information ❖ Remote and stationary helium or nitrogen filling stations, with hose, connectors, and crimping tool. 800–572–0100.

Toy Balloon Corporation, 204 E. 38th St., New York, NY 10016: Free price list with long SASE ❖ Balloons with optional printing and pumps, seal-off clips, string, and ribbons. 212–682–3803.

BANKS

Apple Patch Toys, 7 Hyatt Rd., Branchville, NJ 07826: Free price list ❖ Banks. 201–702–0008.

Brownies Banks, Michael D. Brown, 834 W. Deerfield, Springfield, MO 65807: Free list with long SASE ❖ ERTL die-cast banks. 417–887–8469.

Carlisle Productions Fulfillment Center, P.O. Box 2149, Sinking Spring, PA 19608: Free information ❖ Automobile banks. 215–779–5552.

Classic Collectibles, 525 W. Lake St., Addison, IL 60101: Free information ❖ Banks and replicas. 708–543–4454.

Domino Ent. Co., P.O. Box 847, Wheatley Heights, NY 11798: Free information ❖ Reproduction Wizard of OZ banks. 516–467–5043.

G & J Toys & Clocks, 28780 Front St., Temecula, CA 92590: Free information with long SASE ❖ Ertl coin banks. 714–676–5508.

Gateway Toys, Ron & Nancy Russell, 2133 Blossom Ln., Arnold, MO 63010: Free price list with long SASE ❖ ERTL banks.

Homestead Collectibles, P.O. Box 173, Mill Hall, PA 17751: Information $1 ❖ Die-cast metal and airplane banks. 717–726–3597.

Karl's Collectibles, 49 Fulton St., Auburn, ME 04210: Free information ❖ Motorcycle banks. 207–784–0098.

R & B Collectibles, P.O. Box 406, Frenchtown, NJ 08825: Free list with long SASE ❖ Airplane, automobile, and other banks. 908–996–2141.

R.P. & Company, P.O. Box 3020, Boscawen, NH 03303: Brochure $2 ❖ Museum-quality, historical coin banks. 603–796–2200.

Toys Plus, 2353 N. Wilson Way, Stockton, CA 95205: Free price list with long SASE ❖ Automobile, airplane, and oil company banks. 209–478–2441.

BARBECUE GRILLS

Bradley's, P.O. Box 1300, Columbus, GA 31993: Free catalog ❖ Gas and charcoal barbecue grills. 800–241–8981.

Char-Broil, P.O. Box 1300, Columbus, GA 31902: Free information ❖ Grills, outdoor furniture, barbecue cookers, and seasonings, spices, and condiments. 800–241–8981.

Charmglow Outdoor Grills, Sunshine Products, P.O. Box J, Neosho, MO 64850: Free information ❖ Gas-operated barbecue grills and motor driven spits. 800–558–5502; 417–451–4550 (in MO).

Contempra Industries, 651 New Hampshire Ave., Lakewood, NJ 08701: Free information ❖ Almost smokeless, electric barbecue grill for indoor use. 908–363–9400.

Hart-Bake Charcoal Ovens, 7656 E. 46th St., Tulsa, OK 74145: Free brochure ❖ Multipurpose outdoor charcoal ovens. 800–426–6836; 918–665–8220 (in OK).

Hasty-Bake, P.O. Box 471285, Tulsa, OK 74147: Free catalog ❖ Gourmet foods, charcoal ovens, and grill accessories. 800–426–6836.

Morrone Company, 465 Albert St., Macon, GA 31206: Free information ❖ Portable cooker with cast-iron gas burner. 800–826–8863.

Pachinko House, 3410 Clairmont Rd., Atlanta, GA 30319: Free brochure ❖ Kamado firebrick smoker and barbecue grill. 404–321–4568.

Weber-Stephen Products, 200 E. Daniels Rd., Palatine, IL 60067: Free information ❖ Permanent-mounted gas barbecues, with cooking chambers, side burners, and warmers. 708–934–5700.

BASEBALL & SOFTBALL
Clothing

Don Alleson Athletic, 2921 Brighton-Henrietta Town Line Rd., Rochester, NY 14623: Free information ❖ Uniforms. 800–641–0041; 716–272–0606 (in NY).

Alpha Shirt Company, $1Alpha Shirt Company 401 E. Hunting Park Ave., Philadelphia, PA 19124: Free information ❖ Caps, jackets, and shorts. 800–523–4585; 215–291–0300 (in PA).

Apsco Inc., 1st Ave. & 50th St., Building 57, Brooklyn, NY 11232: Free information ❖ Caps, uniforms, and socks. 718–965–9500.

Austin Sportsgear Inc., 621 Liberty St., Jackson, MI 49203: Free information ❖ Caps, pants, shorts, and uniforms. 800–999–7543; 517–784–1120 (in MI).

Betlin Manufacturing, 1445 Marion Rd., Columbus, OH 43207: Free information ❖ Uniforms and undershirts. 614–443–0248.

Bike Athletic Company, P.O. Box 666, Knoxville, TN 37901: Free information ❖ Uniforms and undershirts. 615–546–4703.

Body Slide by Ross Athletic, 8417 Santa Fe, Ste. 200, Overland Park, KS 66212: Free information ❖ Uniforms. 800–365–7677; 913–341–2288 (in KS).

Bomark Sportswear, P.O. Box 2068, Belair, TX 77402: Free information ❖ Caps and uniforms. 800–231–3351.

Capco Sportswear Inc., 252 Beinoris Dr., Wood Dale, IL 60191: Free information ❖ Caps. 800–833–5856; 708–766–6000 (in IL).

Champion Products Inc., 475 Corporate Square Dr., Winston Salem, NC 27105: Free information ❖ Uniforms, undershirts, and footwear.

DeLong, 733 Broad St., P.O. Box 189, Grinnell, IA 50112: Free information ❖ Uniforms, caps, and undershirts. 800–733–5664; 515–236–3106 (in IA).

Diamond Sports Company, P.O. Box 637, Los Alamitos, CA 90720: Free information ❖ Baseballs and softballs, bats, gloves and mitts, and bags for balls, bats, and uniforms. 800–366–2999; 310–598–9717 (in CA).

Embroidery Supply Warehouse, 140 Remington Blvd., Ronkonkoma, NY 11779: Free information ❖ Caps and jackets. 516–737–0910.

Empire Sporting Goods Manufacturing Company, 443 Broadway, New York, NY 10013: Free information ❖ Uniforms, undershirts, caps, and socks. 800–221–3455; 212–966–0880 (in NY).

Everett Knitting Company, 234 W. Florida St., Milwaukee, WI 53204: Free information ❖ Caps. 414–276–4647.

Fab Knit Manufacturing, Division Anderson Industries, 1415 N. 4th St., Waco, TX 76707: Free information ❖ Caps, uniforms, and undershirts. 800–333–4111; 817–752–2511 (in TX).

Foremost Midwest, 1307 E. Maple Rd., Troy, MI 48083: Free information ❖ Socks, caps, and undershirts. 313–689–3850.

Georgia Tees Inc., 4200 McEver Industrial Dr., Box Tee, Achworth, GA 30101: Free information ❖ Caps. 800–553–0021; 404–974–0040 (in GA).

Golf & Tennis Headwear, 8315 W. 20th Ave., Hialeah, FL 33014: Free information ❖ Caps. 305–558–4310.

Jewel & Company Inc., 9601 Apollo Dr., Landover, MD 20705: Free information ❖ Caps and jackets. 800–638–8583; 301–925–6200 (in MD).

Majestic Athletic Wear Ltd., 636 Pen Argyl St., Pen Argyl, PA 18072: Free information ❖ Uniforms, caps, and undershirts. 800–955–8555; 215–863–6161 (in PA).

Markwort Sporting Goods, 4300 Forest Park Ave., St. Louis, MO 63108: Catalog $8 with list of retailers ❖ Clothing and equipment. 314–652–3757.

Matrix Group Ltd., 15 Derby Square, Salem, MA 01970: Free information ❖ Caps. 800–370–9300; 508–740–9300 (in MA).

Mitchell & Ness Nostalgia Company, 1229 Walnut St., Philadelphia, PA 19107: Free information ❖ Uniforms. 215–592–6512.

Movin USA, 1733 E. McKellips, Tempe, AZ 85281: Free information ❖ Caps and shorts. 800–445–6684; 602–994–4088 (in AZ).

New South Athletic Company Inc., 301 E. Main, P.O. Box 604, Dallas, NC 28034: Free information ❖ Shoes, uniforms, caps, undershirts, and socks. 800–438–9934; 704–922–1557 (in NC).

Nike Footwear Inc., One Bowerman Dr., Beaverton, OR 97005: Free information ❖ Shoes. 800–344–6453.

One Stop, 2935 Walkent Ct. NW, Grand Rapids, MI 49504: Free information ❖ Caps. 616–784–0404.

Puma USA Inc., 147 Centre St., Brockton, MA 02403: Free information with long SASE ❖ Shoes and other athletic clothing. 508–583–9100.

Ranger Athletic Manufacturing Company, P.O. Box 28405, Dallas, TX 75228: Free information ❖ Uniforms, socks, and undershirts. 800–433–5518; 800–492–9125 (in TX).

Saucony/Hyde, 13 Centennial Dr., Peabody, MA 01961: Free information ❖ Shoes. 800–365–7282.

Sportsprint Inc., 252 S. Florisant Rd., St. Louis, MO 63135: Free information ❖ Uniforms, caps, and socks. 800–325–4858.

Venus Knitting Mills Inc., 140 Spring St., Murray Hill, NJ 07974: Free information ❖ Uniforms, caps, socks, and undershirts. 800–955–4200; 908–464–2400 (in NJ).

Wilson Sporting Goods, 8700 Bryn Mawr, Chicago, IL 60631: Free information ❖ Caps and socks. 800–272–6060; 312–714–6400 (in IL).

Equipment

Apsco Inc., 1st Ave. & 50th St., Building 57, Brooklyn, NY 11232: Free information ❖ Uniform bags, baseballs and softballs, gloves and mitts, and bats. 718–965–9500.

ATEC, 10 Greg St., Sparks, NV 89431: Free information ❖ Baseballs and softballs, field equipment, pitching machines, training aids, and ball, bat, and uniform bags. 800–755–5100; 702–352–2800 (in NV).

The Athletic Connection, 1901 Diplomat, Dallas, TX 75234: Free information ❖ Bat and ball bags, bats, baseballs and softballs, field equipment, protective gear, helmets, and pitching machines. 800–527–0871; 214–243–1446 (in TX).

Bolco Athletic Company, P.O. Box 489, Cooksville, TN 38501: Free information ❖ Bases, home plates, pitchers plates, and other field equipment. 800–423–4321; 615–526–2109 (in TN).

Cannon Sports, P.O. Box 11179, Burbank, CA 91510: Free information with list of retailers ❖ Softballs and baseballs, bats, field equipment, mitts and gloves, protective gear, and bags for bats, balls, and uniforms. 800–362–3146; 818–503–9570 (in CA).

Champion Sports Products Company, P.O. Box 138, Sayreville, NJ 08872: Free information ❖ Ball and bat bags, softballs and baseballs, bats, field equipment, mitts and gloves, and protective gear. 908–238–0330.

Continental Sports Supply, P.O. Box 1251, Englewood, CO 80150: Free information ❖ Bats. 303–934–5657.

Dalco Athletic, P.O. Box 550220, Dallas, TX 75355: Free information ❖ Baseballs and softballs, bats, batting gloves and helmets, catcher masks, chest protectors, and gloves and mitts. 800–288–3252; 214–494–1455 (in TX).

Douglas Sport Nets & Equipment, 3441 S. 11th Ave., P.O. Box 393, Eldridge, IA 52748: Free information ❖ Baseball equipment and supplies. 800–553–8907; 319–285–4162 (in IA).

Dudley Sports Company, 521 Meadow St., Chicopee, MA 01021: Free information ❖ Baseballs and softballs. 800–523–5387; 413–536–1200 (in MA).

Easton Sports Inc., 577 Airport Blvd., Burlingame, CA 94010: Free information ❖ Baseballs and softballs, bats, gloves, and mitts. 800–347–3901; 415–347–4727 (in CA).

Hillerich & Bradsby Company Inc., P.O. Box 35700, Louisville, KY 40232: Free information ❖ Baseball and softball bats, gloves, and other equipment. 502–585–5226.

Jayfro Corporation Inc., Unified Sports Inc., 976 Hartford Tnpk., P.O. Box 400, Waterford, CT 06385: Free catalog ❖ Safety protectors, batting tees, mats, baseball and softball practice cages, batting cubicles, and backstops. 203–447–3001.

Markwort Sporting Goods, 4300 Forest Park Ave., St. Louis, MO 63108: Catalog $8 with list of retailers ❖ Baseballs and softballs, bats, batting gloves and helmets, catcher masks, chest protectors, and gloves and mitts. 314–652–3757.

Dick Martin Sports Inc., 181 E. Union Ave., P.O. Box 7381, East Rutherford, NJ 07073: Free information ❖ Bat bags, baseballs and softballs, gloves, and protective gear. 800–221–1993; 201–438–5255 (in NJ).

Pennsylvania Sporting Goods, 1360 Industrial Hwy., P.O. Box 451, Southampton, PA 18966: Free information ❖ Baseballs and softballs, aluminum bats, field equipment, batting gloves, protective gear, and bags for balls, bats, and uniforms. 800–535–1122.

Rawlings Sporting Goods Company, P.O. Box 22000, St. Louis, MO 63126: Free information ❖ Baseballs, bats, mitts and gloves, protective gear, and bags for balls, bats and uniforms. 314–349–3500.

Riddell Inc., 3670 N. Milwaukee Ave., Chicago, IL 60641: Free information ❖ Baseballs and softballs, gloves and mitts, and protective gear. 800–445–7344; 312–794–1994 (in IL).

Sportime, 1 Sporting Way, Atlanta, GA 30340: Free information ❖ Bats and bags for balls and bats, protective gear, and helmets. 800–444–5700; 404–449–5700 (in GA).

Sports Equipment Inc., Curvemaster Division, P.O. Box 280777, Dallas, TX 75228: Free information ❖ Baseball pitching machines. 800–727–2444; 214–412–4031 (in TX).

SSK Sports, SSK Corporation Japan, 21136 S. Wilmington Ave., Ste. 220, Long Beach, CA 90810: Free information ❖ Bats, gloves, and score books. 800–421–2674; 310–549–2762 (in CA).

Steele's Sports Company, 5223 W. 137th, Brook Park, OH 44142: Free information ❖

Softball and baseball equipment. 800–367–7114; 216–267–5300 (in OH).

Wolvering Sports, 745 State Circle, Box 1941, Ann Arbor, MI 48106: Catalog $1 ❖ Baseball, basketball, field hockey, soccer, football, and other athletic and recreation equipment. 313–761–5691.

BASKETBALL
Clothing

Above the Rim International, 620 C St., Ste. 600, San Diego, CA 92101: Free information ❖ Uniforms, warm-up jackets, and pants. 619–238–8540.

Don Alleson Athletic, 2921 Brighton-Henrietta Town Line Rd., Rochester, NY 14623: Free information ❖ Uniforms and warm-up clothing. 800–641–0041; 716–272–0606 (in NY).

Austin Sportsgear Inc., 621 Liberty St., Jackson, MI 49203: Free information ❖ Uniforms. 800–999–7543; 517–784–1120 (in MI).

AVIA Group International Inc., Box 4710, Beaverton, OR 97076: Free information ❖ Shoes. 800–345–2842; 503–520–1500 (in OR).

Betlin Manufacturing, 1445 Marion Rd., Columbus, OH 43207: Free information ❖ Uniforms, warm-up jackets, and pants. 614–443–0248.

Boast Inc., Box 10176, Riviera Beach, FL 33419: Free information ❖ Uniforms and warm-up clothing. 800–327–7666; 407–848–1096 (in FL).

Champion Products Inc., 475 Corporate Square Dr., Winston Salem, NC 27105: Free information ❖ Uniforms, warm-up jackets, pants, socks, and shoes.

Empire Sporting Goods Manufacturing Company, 443 Broadway, New York, NY 10013: Free information ❖ Uniforms, warm-up jackets, pants, socks, and wristbands. 800–221–3455; 212–966–0880 (in NY).

GeorGI-Sports, P.O. Box 1107, Lancaster, PA 17603: Free information ❖ Uniforms, warm-up jackets, pants, and socks. 800–338–2527; 717–291–8924 (in PA).

Letrell Sports, 3004 Industrial Pkwy. West, Knoxville, TN 37921: Free information ❖ Uniforms and warm-up clothing. 800–325–3975; 615–546–8070 (in TN).

Lotto Sports, 1900 Surveyor Blvd., Carrollton, TX 75006: Free information ❖ Shoes. 800–527–5126; 214–416–4003 (in TX).

Majestic Athletic Wear Ltd., 636 Pen Argyl St., Pen Argyl, PA 18072: Free information ❖ Uniforms and warm-up clothing. 800–955–8555; 215–863–6161 (in PA).

Midwest Sport Sales Inc., 162 S. Platt, Milan, MI 48160: Free information ❖ Uniforms. 313–439–0888.

Pony USA Inc., 676 Elm St., Concord, MA 01742: Free information ❖ Shoes, socks, and wristbands. 800–654–7669; 508–287–0053 (in MA).

Puma USA Inc., 147 Centre St., Brockton, MA 02403: Free information with long SASE ❖ Warm-up jackets, pants, wristbands, shoes, and socks. 508–583–9100.

Purcells Activewear, 5733 San Leandro St., Oakland, CA 94621: Free information ❖ Uniforms and warm-up clothing. 800–641–6868; 510–536–7770 (in CA).

Shaffer Sportswear, 224 N. Washington, Neosho, MO 64850: Free information ❖ Uniforms and warm-up clothing. 417–451–9444.

Southland Athletic Manufacturing Company, P.O. Box 280, Terrell, TX 75160: Free information ❖ Uniforms, warm-up jackets, and pants. 214–563–3321.

Spalding Sports Worldwide, 425 Meadow St., P.O. Box 901, Chicopee, MA 01021: Free information with list of retailers ❖ Uniforms, warm-up jackets, pants, wristbands, socks, shoes, and equipment. 800–225–6601.

Speedline Athletic Wear, 1804 N. Habana, Tampa, FL 33607: Free information ❖ Uniforms and warm-up clothing. 813–876–1375.

Tennessee Sports Company, Box 310, William Northern Field, Tullahoma, TN 37388: Free information ❖ Bat and ball bags. 615–455–7765.

Equipment

Alchester Mills Company Inc., 314 S. 11th St., Camden, NJ 08103: Free information ❖ Pads and guards, supporters, and knee braces. 609–964–9700.

Amko Inc., P.O. Box 5809, Huntsville, AL 35814: Free information ❖ Basketballs. 800–289–2656; 205–851–7080 (in AL).

The Athletic Connection, 1901 Diplomat, Dallas, TX 75234: Free information ❖ Backboards, basketballs, and nets. 800–527–0871; 214–243–1446 (in TX).

Bike Athletic Company, P.O. Box 666, Knoxville, TN 37901: Free information ❖ Pads and guards, supporters, and knee braces. 615–546–4703.

Cannon Sports Inc., P.O. Box 11179, Burbank, CA 91510: Free information with list of retailers ❖ Basketballs, ball carriers, goals, nets, knee braces, pads and guards, supporters, and whistles. 800–223–0064; 818–503–9570 (in CA).

Carron Net Company, 1623 17th St., P.O. Box 177, Two Rivers, WI 54241: Free information ❖ Portable and stationary backboards, ball carriers, goals and nets, and whistles. 800–558–7768; 414–793–2217 (in WI).

Cramer Products Inc., P.O. Box 1001, Gardner, KS 66030: Free information ❖ Knee braces, pads, and guards. 800–345–2231; 913–884–7511 (in KS).

Escalade Sports, P.O. Box 889, Evansville, IN 47706: Free catalog ❖ Backboards and nets. 800–457–3373; 812–467–1200 (in IN).

Franklin Sports Industries Inc., 17 Campanelli Pkwy., P.O. Box 508, Stoughton, MA 02072: Free information ❖ Pads, guards, miscellaneous equipment, and basketballs. 617–344–1111.

Grid Inc., NDL Products, 2313 NW 30th Pl., Pompano Beach, FL 33069: Free information ❖ Supporters, knee braces, pads, and guards. 800–843–3021; 305–942–4560 (in FL).

Holabird Sports Discounters, 9008 Yellow Brick Rd., Rossville Industrial Park, Baltimore, MD 21237: Free catalog ❖ Equipment and clothing for basketball, tennis, running and jogging, golf, exercising, and racquetball. 410–687–6400.

Huffy Sports, 2021 MacArthur Rd., Waukesha, WI 53188: Free information ❖ Portable and stationary backboards, goals and nets, whistles, and other equipment. 800–558–5234; 414–548–0440 (in WI).

Hutch Sports USA, 1835 Airport Exchange Blvd., Erlanger, KY 41018: Free information ❖ Backboards, basketballs, and nets. 800–727–4511; 606–282–9000 (in KY).

Indian Industries Inc., P.O. Box 889, Evansville, IN 47706: Free catalog ❖ Backboards, nets, and poles. 800–457–3373; 812–467–1200 (in IN).

Jayfro Corporation Inc., Unified Sports Inc., 976 Hartford Tnpk., P.O. Box 400, Waterford, CT 06385: Free catalog ❖ Backboards, post standards, portable standards, and goals. 203–447–3001.

M.W. Kasch Company, 5401 W. Donges Bay Rd., Mequon, WI 53092: Free information ❖ Basketballs, backboards, goals, nets, and basketball sets. 414–242–5000.

Pennsylvania Sporting Goods, 1360 Industrial Hwy., P.O. Box 451, Southampton, PA 18966: Free information ❖ Basketballs, basketball sets, goals, nets, protective gear, and score books. 800–535–1122.

Porter Athletic Equipment Company, 2500 S. 25th Ave., Broadview, IL 60153: Free information ❖ Backboards, basketballs, goals, and nets. 708–338–2000.

Rawlings Sporting Goods Company, P.O. Box 22000, St. Louis, MO 63126: Free information ❖ Basketballs, nets, and score books. 314–349–3500.

Riddell Inc., 3670 N. Milwaukee Ave., Chicago, IL 60641: Free information ❖ Basketballs and nets. 800–445–7344; 312–794–1994 (in IL).

Spalding Sports Worldwide, 425 Meadow St., P.O. Box 901, Chicopee, MA 01021: Free information with list of retailers ❖ Basketballs, other equipment, uniforms, warm-up jackets and pants, wristbands, socks, and shoes. 800–225–6601.

Sportime, 1 Sporting Way, Atlanta, GA 30340: Free information ❖ Backboards, basketballs, and nets. 800–444–5700; 404–449–5700 (in GA).

TC Sports, 7251 Ford Hwy., Tecumseh, MI 49286: Free information ❖ Backboards and nets. 800–523–1498; 517–451–5221 (in MI).

Toss Back Inc., Old US 40, P.O. Box 189, Dorrance, KS 67634: Free information ❖ Basketballs, backboards, rims, training equipment, and supports. 800–255–2990; 913–666–4242 (in KS).

Venus Knitting Mills Inc., 140 Spring St., Murray Hill, NJ 07974: Free information ❖ Basketballs, nets, and score books. 800–955–4200; 908–464–2400 (in NJ).

Wolvering Sports, 745 State Circle, Box 1941, Ann Arbor, MI 48106: Catalog $1 ❖ Baseball, basketball, field hockey, soccer, football, and other athletic and recreation equipment. 313–761–5691.

BASKETS

ACP Baskets, P.O. Box 1426, Salisbury, NC 28144: Catalog $1 ❖ Basket-making materials, books, and kits. 704–636–3034.

Allen's Basketworks, 8624 SE 13th, Portland, OR 97202: Catalog $2 ❖ Basket-making supplies. 503–238–6384.

Alvin & Trevie Wood Baskets, 2415 E. Main St., Murfreesboro, TN 37130: Brochure $1 ❖ Handmade and pounded traditional and original white oak Appalachia-style baskets. 615–895–0391.

Karen & Darryl Arawjo, P.O. Box 477, Bushkill, PA 18324: Brochure $1 ❖ White oak Shaker, Nantucket, and Appalachian baskets. 717–588–6957.

Ashwood Basket Corporation, Hadley Rd., Jaffrey, NH 03452: Catalog $1 ❖ Handcrafted baskets. 603–532–4497.

Back Door Country Baskets, 10 Batchellor Dr., North Brookfield, MA 01535: Brochure 50¢ with long SASE ❖ Basket-making kits. 508–867–3079.

Bamboo & Rattan Works Inc., 470 Oberlin Ave. South, Lakewood, NJ 08701: Free information ❖ Rattan, cords, chair canes, matting, and bamboo, flat, and round reeds. 908–370–0220.

Basket Hollow, 1641 Etta Kable Dr., Beavercreek, OH 45432: Free brochure with long SASE ❖ Handwoven round and flat reed baskets, with an optional black walnut finish. 513–429–3937.

The Basket Works, 77 Mellor Ave., Baltimore, MD 21228: Catalog $1 ❖ Basket-making supplies. 410–747–8300.

Baskets & Bears, 398 S. Main St., Geneva, NY 14456: Free brochure with long SASE ❖ Black ash splint baskets in Shaker, Yankee, and Nantucket styles. 315–781–1251.

Basquetrie, 810 Rangeline, Columbia, MO 65201: Catalog $3 ❖ Victorian picnic baskets and accessories, bed trays, and cameos and keepsakes for bridesmaids. 800–342–7278.

Berlin Fruit Box Company, 51 Mechanic St., Berlin Heights, OH 44814: Free information ❖ Baskets for all uses. 800–877–7721.

Braid-Aid, 466 Washington St., Pembroke, MA 02359: Catalog $4 ❖ Braided rug kits and braiding accessories, wool by the pound or yard, and hooking, basket-making, shirret,

and spinning and weaving supplies. 617–826–2560.

Cane & Basket Supply Company, 1283 S. Cochran, Los Angeles, CA 90019: Catalog $2 ❖ Fiber and genuine rush, Danish seat cord, raffia, rattan, seagrass, hoops and handles, other supplies, and flat, oval, and round reeds. 213–939–9644.

Caning Shop, 926 Gilman St., Berkeley, CA 94710: Catalog $1 (refundable) ❖ Supplies and how-to books for basket-making and chair-weaving. 510–527–5010.

Connecticut Cane & Reed Company, 134 Pine St., Manchester, CT 06040: Catalog 50¢ ❖ Caning and basket-making supplies. 203–646–6586.

Country Companions, 35 Chittenden Rd., Hebron, CT 06231: Brochure $2 ❖ Handmade traditional Nantucket Lightship baskets. 203–228–3625.

Country Seat, RD 2, Box 24A, Kempton, PA 19529: Price list $1 ❖ How-to books and basket-making and chair-caning supplies. 215–756–6124.

English Basketry Willows, RFD 1, Box 124A, South New Berlin, NY 13843: Brochure $1 ❖ Imported basket-making willows, tools, and books. 607–847–8264.

Frank's Cane & Rush Supply, 7252 Heil Ave., Huntington Beach, CA 92647: Free information ❖ Wood parts, tools, and cane, rush and other basket-making and seat-weaving supplies. 714–847–0707.

Jeffrey E. Gale, Basketmaker, RFD 1, Box 124A, South New Berlin, NY 13843: Brochure $1 with long SASE ❖ Handmade white ash baskets. 607–847–8264.

GH Productions, 521 E. Walnut St., Scottsville, KY 42164: Catalog $1 (refundable) ❖ Basket-making supplies.

Jack's Upholstery & Caning Supplies, 5498 Rt. 34, Oswego, IL 60543: Catalog $2 (refundable) ❖ Upholstery, basket, and chair-caning supplies and equipment. 708–554–1045.

Jonathan Kline Black Ash Baskets, 5066 Mott Evans Rd., Trumansburg, NY 14886: Brochure $2 ❖ Traditional handmade black ash baskets. 607–387–5718.

Dave Lewis Basketry, RD 2, Box 684, Bedford, PA 15522: Free information with long SASE ❖ Handwoven traditional splint baskets and antique basket restoration services. 814–623–2805.

John E. McGuire Baskets, 398 S. Main St., Geneva, NY 14456: Free price list with two 1st class stamps ❖ Basket-making supplies and tools. 315–781–1251.

Michigan Cane Supply, 5348 N. Riverview Dr., Kalamazoo, MI 49004: List $1 ❖ Chair cane, rush, and basket-weaving supplies. 616–282–5461.

Nasco, 901 Janesville Ave., Fort Atkinson, WI 53538: Free catalog ❖ Basket-making supplies. 800–558–9595.

New England Basket Company, P.O. Box 1335, North Falmouth, MA 02556: Catalog $3 ❖ Bamboo trays, picnic hampers, and rustic rattan, country-style, and willow baskets. 508–759–2000.

Susi Nuss, Basketmaker, 5 Steele Crossing Rd., Bolton, CT 06043: Brochure $2 ❖ Handmade reproduction 19th-century baskets. 203–646–3876.

Gary O'Brien Baskets, Meadow Farm, Ruggles Hill Rd., Hardwick, MA 01037: Catalog $3.50 ❖ Shaker, Yankee, and Indian-style baskets made from New England hardwoods. 413–477–8711.

Ozark Basketry Supply, P.O. Box 599, Fayettville, AR 72702: Catalog $1 ❖ Books, basket-making kits, chair cane, dyes, hoops, and handles. 501–442–9292.

J. Page Basketry, 820 Albee Rd. West, Nokomis, FL 34275: Catalog $2 (refundable) ❖ Basket-making supplies, tools, books, wheat-weaving and pine needlecrafting supplies, and dried and preserved flowers and herbs. 813–485–6730.

Peerless Rattan & Reed, 222 Lake Ave., Yonkers, NY 10701: Catalog 50¢ ❖ Basket-making and chair-caning supplies. 914–968–4046.

H.H. Perkins Company, 10 S. Bradley Rd., Woodbridge, CT 06525: Free catalog ❖ Basket-making and seat-weaving supplies, macrame supplies, books, and how-to instructions. 800–462–6660.

Plymouth Reed & Cane, 1200 W. Ann Arbor Rd., Plymouth, MI 48170: Brochure $1 ❖ Reed, cane, fiber rush, handles, hoops, kits, dyes, tools, books, and other basket-making and chair-caning materials. 313–455–2150.

Royalwood Ltd., 517 Woodville Rd., Mansfield, OH 44907: Catalog $1 ❖ Basket-weaving and caning supplies. 419–526–1630.

Snapvent Company, 147 W. Baxter Ave., Knoxville, TN 37917: Free price list with long SASE ❖ Basket-making and chair caning supplies. 615–523–6784.

Splintworks, P.O. Box 858, Cave Junction, OR 97523: Brochure $1 ❖ Handwoven baskets. 503–592–2311.

Stannard Mountain Basketry, RD 1, Box 1385, East Hardwick, VT 05386: Brochure $1 with long SASE ❖ Sweetgrass and Vermont brown ash traditional baskets. 802–533–7760.

V.I. Reed & Cane, Rt. 5, Box 632, Rogers, AR 72756: Free catalog ❖ Flat and round reeds, smoked reed, cane, hoops, handles, raffia, dyes, and basket-weaving kits. 800–852–0025.

Weaving Works, 4717 Brooklyn Ave. NE, Seattle, WA 98105: Catalog $4.50 ❖ Basket-making supplies, looms, spinning wheels, yarns and fibers, hand- and machine-knitting supplies, dyes, and how-to books. 206–524–1221.

Martha Wetherbee Basket Shop, H.C.R. 69, Box 116, Sanbornton, NH 03269: Catalog $3 ❖ Handwoven and pounded brown ash Shaker basket reproductions. 603–286–8927.

White Oak Basketmakings, Alvin & Trevle Wood, 2415 E. Main St., Murfreesboro, TN 37130: Catalog $2 ❖ Original and traditional white oak Appalachian-style baskets. 615–895–0391.

Stephen Zeh Basketmaker, P.O. Box 381, Temple, ME 04984: Catalog $2 ❖ Hand-split and woven traditional brown ash baskets in Native American, Shaker, and other styles. 207–778–2351.

BATHROOM FIXTURES & ACCESSORIES

A-Ball Plumbing Supply, 12210 SE 21st Ave., Milwaukee, OR 97222: Free catalog ❖ Modern, European, and Victorian plumbing fixtures. 503–228–0026.

Alumax, P.O. Box 40, Magnolia, AR 71753: Free information ❖ Bathroom fixtures and shower enclosures. 800–643–1514.

American China, 3618 E. LaSalle St., Phoenix, AZ 85040: Free brochure ❖ China and marble drop-in and pedestal bathroom lavatories. 800–470–1005.

American Standard Inc., P.O. Box 6820, Piscataway, NJ 08854: Free information ❖ Whirlpool tubs with molded headrest and grab bars, toilets, and other fixtures. 800–821–7700.

Antique Baths & Kitchens, 2220 Carlton Way, Santa Barbara, CA 93109: Catalog $2 ❖ Reproduction sinks, toilets, tank toilets, pedestal basins, marble vanity tops, faucets, medicine chests, and cast-iron tubs. 805–962–8598.

Antique Hardware Store, Easton Rd., Kintnersville, PA 18930: Catalog $3 ❖ Antique pedestal sinks, faucets, high-tank toilets, and cabinet hardware. 800–422–9982.

AquaGlass Corporation, P.O. Box 412, Industrial Park, Adamsville, TN 38310: Free information ❖ Whirlpool baths, combination steam showers, lavatories, wall surrounds, and shower floors. 800–238–3940; 901–632–0911 (in TN).

Baldwin Hardware Corporation, P.O. Box 15048, Reading, PA 19612: Bathroom accessories brochure 75¢; light fixtures brochure $3; door hardware brochure 75¢; decor hardware brochure 75¢ ❖ Brass dead bolts and door hardware, bathroom accessories, and light fixtures. 800–346–5128.

Bathlines, 571 Waukegan Rd., Northbrook, IL 60062: Free information ❖ Bathroom fixtures and shower systems for addition to old-style bathtubs. 708–564–4040.

Bathroom Machineries, 495 Main St., P.O. Box 1020, Murphys, CA 95247: Catalog $3 ❖ Early American and Victorian-style antique and reproduction bathroom fixtures. 209–728–2031.

Baths from the Past, 83 E. Water St., Rockland, MA 02370: Catalog $5 (refundable) ❖ Designer Victorian and traditional bathroom fixtures and plumbing accessories. 800–697–3871; 617–331–2445 (in MA).

Bona Decorative Hardware, 3073 Madison Rd., Cincinnati, OH 45209: Price list $2 ❖ English and French-style bathroom fittings and accessories, cabinet and door hardware, and fireplace tools. 513–321–7877.

Brass Menagerie, 524 St. Louis St., New Orleans, LA 70130: Free information ❖ Plumbing, light fixtures, and hardware. 504–524–0921.

Briggs Industries, 4350 W. Cypress, Ste. 800, Tampa, FL 33607: Free information ❖ Acrylic one-piece tub-shower combination units and multi-jet whirlpool tubs. 813–878–0178.

Country Plumbing, 5042 7th St., Carpinteria, CA 93013: Free information ❖

Antique and new plumbing supplies. 805–684–8685.

D.E.A. Bathroom Machineries, 495 Main St., Box 1020, Murphys, CA 95247: Catalog $3 ❖ Early American bathroom fixtures and hard-to-find parts. 209–728–2031.

Decorum, 235 Commercial St., Portland, ME 04101: Free information ❖ Plumbing and bathroom fixtures in styles from yesteryear. 800–288–3346.

DeWeese Woodworking Company, Hwy. 492, P.O. Box 576, Philadelphia, MS 39350: Free brochure ❖ Oak commode seats, tissue roll holders, toothbrush and glass holders, and towel bars. 601–656–4951.

Dimestore Cowboys, 4500 Hawkins NE, Albuquerque, NM 87109: Catalog $7 ❖ Door sets, cabinet pulls, shutters, bathroom accessories, curtain rods and rings, and other hardware. 505–345–3933.

DuraGlaze Service Corporation, 2825 Bransford Ave., Nashville, TN 37204: Free brochure ❖ Antique bathtubs, sinks, and other plumbing. 615–298–1787.

Eljer Plumbingware, 17120 Dallas Pkwy., Ste. 205, Dallas, TX 75248: Free information ❖ Bathroom accessories in chrome and polished brass, frameless shower doors, and designer tubs with multi jets. 800–435–5372.

Equiparts, 817 Main St., Pittsburgh, PA 15215: Free information ❖ Vintage plumbing, heating, and electrical parts. 800–442–6622.

Granite Lake Pottery Inc., Rt. 9, Munsonville, NH 03457: Free catalog ❖ Handcrafted stoneware sinks, accessories, and tile. 800–443–9908.

Hafele America Company, 3901 Cheyenne Dr., Archdale, NC 27263: Free information ❖ Folding shower seat and textured grab bars. 919–889–2322.

Home Decorators Collection, 2025 Concourse Dr., St. Louis, MO 63146: Free catalog ❖ Oak, high-glazed porcelain, chrome and brass, and wicker bathroom accessories. 800–245–2217; 314–993–6045 (in MO).

Kohler Company, 444 Highland Dr., Kohler, WI 53044: Free information ❖ Functional and decorative bathroom tubs and toilets. 800–456–4537.

MAC the Antique Plumber, 6325 Elvas Ave, Sacramento, CA 95819: Catalog $6 (refundable) ❖ Antique plumbing fixtures. 916–454–4507.

Nexton Industries Inc., 51 S. 1st St., Brooklyn, NY 11211: Free information ❖ Brass decorative hardware and bathroom accessories. 718–599–3837.

Ole Fashion Things, 402 SW Evangeline, Lafayette, LA 70501: Catalog $5 ❖ Clawfoot bathtubs, pedestal lavatories, china bowls, high-tank commodes, faucets, and traditional plumbing supplies. 800–228–4967.

Remodelers & Renovators Supplies, P.O. Box 45478, Boise, ID 83711: Catalog $3 ❖ Vintage hardware and plumbing fixtures. 800–456–2135.

Reon Shower, 5010 Shoreham Pl., Ste. 300, San Diego, CA 92122: Free brochure ❖ Kitchen and bath products from around the world. 800–776–7366.

Research Products, 2639 Andjon, Dallas, TX 75220: Free information ❖ Self-contained INCINOLET electric non-polluting and waterless toilet that incinerates waste to clean ash.

The Restoration Place, 305 20th St., Rock Island, IL 61201: Free brochure ❖ Plumbing, hardware, architectural and decorative accessories, and light fixtures. 309–786–0004.

Restoration Works Inc., 810 Main St., Buffalo, NY 14205: Catalog $3 ❖ Plumbing fixtures and bathroom accessories, ceiling medallions and trims, furniture, and hardware. 800–735–3535.

Roy Electric Company Inc., 1054 Coney Island Ave., Brooklyn, NY 11230: Catalog $6 ❖ Antique plumbing fixtures. 800–366–3347; 718–434–7002 (in NY).

Sancor, 140–30 Milner Ave., Scarborough, Ontario, Canada M1S 3R3: Free information ❖ Composting toilet systems. 800–387–5126.

Showerlux, P.O. Box 20202, Atlanta, GA 30325: Free information ❖ Shower enclosures. 404–355–3550.

The Sink Factory, 2140 San Pablo Ave., Berkeley, CA 94702: Catalog $3 ❖ Traditional oval and round porcelain basins, from the classic styles of 1880 to the 1930s. 800–653–4926.

Sonoma Woodworks Inc., 1285 S. Cloverdale Blvd., Cloverdale, CA 95425: Brochure $1 ❖ High tank pull-chain toilets, solid oak cabinets, and medicine and vanity cabinets. 800–659–9003.

Sterling Plumbing Group, 2900 W. Golf Rd., Rolling Meadows, IL 60008: Free information ❖ Faucets in fired-on epoxy colors, chrome, and polished brass. 708–734–1777.

Studio Workshop, 2808 Tucker St., Omaha, NE 68112: Catalog $2 ❖ Solid oak bathroom accessories. 800–383–7072.

Sunrise Specialty Company, 5540 Doyle St., Emeryville, CA 94608: Catalog $2 ❖ Reproduction Victorian-style bathroom fixtures. 510–654–1794.

Swan Corporation, 1 City Centre, St. Louis, MO 63101: Free information ❖ Shower enclosures. 314–231–8148.

Touch of Class, 1905 N. Van Buren St., Huntingburg, IN 47542: Free catalog ❖ Bathroom accessories, comforters, pillows and shams, window treatments, towels and rugs, and nightwear and robes for men, women, and children. 800–457–7456.

BEAD CRAFTING

Abeada Corporation, 1205 N. Main St., Royal Oak, MI 48067: Free information ❖ Beads, bead-stringing kits, and findings. 800–521–6326; 313–399–6642 (in MI).

Alpha Supply, P.O. Box 2133, Bremerton, WA 98310: Catalog $3 ❖ Beads, engraving and jewelry-making tools, and supplies. 206–373–3302.

ARA Imports, P.O. Box 41054, Brecksville, OH 44141: Catalog $1 ❖ Semi-precious beads, fresh water pearls, precious metal beads, and findings. 216–838–1372.

Arizona Gems & Minerals Inc., 6370 East Hwy. 69, Prescott Valley, AZ 86314: Catalog $2 ❖ Chip and other beads, findings, geodes, silversmithing and lapidary tools, and jewelry-making supplies. 602–772–6443.

Art to Wear, 5 Crescent Pl., St. Petersburg, FL 33711: Catalog $1 ❖ Beads, bead-stringing supplies, findings, and tools.

B & J Rock Shop, 14744 Manchester Rd., Ballwin, MO 63011: Catalog $3 ❖ Rockhounding equipment, beads, quartz crystals, imported and domestic gemstones, and jewelry-making and bead-stringing supplies. 314–394–4567.

Bally Bead Company, P.O. Box 934, Rockwall TX 75087: Catalog $4.95 (refundable) ❖ Beads and findings. 214–771–4515.

Banasch, 2810 Highland Ave., Cincinnati, OH 45212: Free catalog ❖ Beads, pearls, sewing notions, and buttons. 800–543–0355; 513–731–2040 (in OH).

Baubanbea Enterprises, P.O. Box 1205, Smithtown, NY 11117: Catalog $1 ❖ Rhinestones, sequins, beads, semi-precious and precious gemstones, and other craft supplies. 516–724–4661.

Bead Depot, Box 673, Novato, CA 94947: Catalog $3 ❖ Beads from worldwide locations, findings, and earring kits. 415–892–6965.

Bead It, P.O. Box 3505, Prescott, AZ 86302: Catalog $4 ❖ Czechoslovakian beads, other beads, gemstones, charms, findings, and books. 602–445–9234

The Bead Shop, 2263 Old Middlefield Way, Mountain View, CA 94043: Catalog $3 ❖ Beads and bead-stringing supplies.

Bead Source, 7047 Reseda Blvd., Reseda, CA 91335: Catalog $11 ❖ Beads, Austrian crystals, Peruvian beads, findings, and appliques. 818–708–0972.

Bead World, 4931 Prospect NE, Albuquerque, NM 87110: Free catalog ❖ Beads, findings and supplies, and leather cord. 505–884–3133.

Beada Beada, 4262 N. Woodward Ave., Royal Oak, MI 48073: Free catalog ❖ Beads, bead-stringing supplies, and findings. 313–549–1005.

Beadbox Inc., 10135 E. Via Linda, Scottsdale, AZ 85258: Catalog $5 ❖ Beads from worldwide sources and jewelry kits. 800–232–3269.

Beads Galore International Inc., 2123 S. Priest, Tempe, AZ 85282: Free information ❖ Beads and bead-stringing supplies. 800–424–9577.

Beads-By-The-Bay, P.O. Box 5488, Novato, CA 94947: Catalog $4.25 ❖ Czechoslovakian and other beads, findings, and jewelry-making supplies. 415–883–1098.

Beadworks, 139 Washington St., South Norwalk, CT 06854: Catalog $10 ❖ Wood, metal, porcelain, ceramic, bone, plastic, mother of pearl, Swarovski crystal, glass, and other beads from around the world. 203–852–9194.

Beyond Beadery, 54 Tinker St., Woodstock, NY 12498: Catalog $1 ❖ Looms, findings, needles and thread, and Czechoslovakian, Japanese, and Austrian crystal beads. 800–840–5548.

Bourget Bros., 1636 11th St., Santa Monica, CA 90404: Catalog $5 ❖ Beads,

bead-stringing and jewelry-making supplies, and tools. 310–450–6556.

Brahm Limited, P.O. Box 1, Lake Charles, LA 70602: Catalog $2 ❖ Precious and semi-precious costume and designer beads, findings, jewelry-making supplies, and rhinestones.

Bucks County Classic, 73 Coventry Lane, Langhorne, PA 19047: Catalog $2 ❖ Cabochons, fresh water pearls, findings, and gemstone, Chinese cloisonne, Austrian crystal, stone accent, and metal beads. 800–942–GEMS.

Charlie's Rock Shop, 620 J St., Penrose, CO 81240: Free catalog ❖ Beads, bead-stringing and jewelry-making supplies, jewelry boxes, and faceted gemstones. 800–336–6923.

The Cracker Box, Solebury, PA 18963: Catalog $4.50 ❖ Bead crafting kits. 215–862–2100.

Creative Castle, 2373 Michael Dr., Newbury Park, CA 91320: Free catalog ❖ Bead-making jewelry kits. 805–499–1377.

Dawn's Hide & Bead Away, 203 N. Linn, Iowa City, IA 52240: Free catalog ❖ Bead crafting supplies. 319–338–1566.

Discount Bead House, P.O. Box 186, The Plains, OH 45780: Catalog $5 ❖ Seed beads, findings, and tools. 800–793–7592.

E & W Imports Inc., P.O. Box 157032, Tampa, FL 33684: Price list $1 ❖ Gemstone, cloisonne, and Austrian crystal beads and 14k findings. 813–885–1138.

Ebersole Lapidary Supply Inc., 11417 West Hwy. 54, Wichita, KS 67209: Catalog $2 ❖ Beads, bead-stringing supplies, carving materials, tools, findings, mountings, cabochons and rocks, and jewelry kits. 316–722–4771.

Firemountain Gems, 28195 Redwood Hwy., Cave Junction, OR 97523: Catalog $3 ❖ Beads, findings, tools, and bead-stringing and jewelry-making supplies. 800–423–2319.

Frantz Bead Company, E. 1222 Sunset Hill Rd., Shelton, WA 98584: Catalog $5 ❖ Handmade glass beads from India and Thailand. 206–426–6712.

Garden of Beadin', P.O. Box 1535, Redway, CA 95560: Catalog $2 ❖ Seed beads, crystals, semi-precious gemstones, books, and bead-stringing supplies. 800–232–3588; 707–943–9120 (in CA).

Gem-O-Rama Inc., 150 Recreation Park Dr., Hingham, MA 02043: Free catalog ❖ Beads and bead-stringing supplies. 617–749–8250.

The Great Wall Trading Company, 196 Spring St., West Roxbury, MA 02132: Free price list ❖ Imported cloisonne beads from China.

Hansa, 4315 Upton Ave. South, Minneapolis, MN 55410: Catalog $2 ❖ Venetian glass beads. 800–325–2930.

Hedgehog Handworks, P.O. Box 45384, Westchester, CA 90045: Catalog $1 ❖ Semi-precious beads, sewing notions, gold and silver threads, needlecraft and embroidery supplies, and other craft materials. 310–670–6040.

International Bead & Jewelry Supply, 2368 Kettner St., San Diego, CA 92101: Catalog $2 ❖ Exotic hand-fashioned beads from around the world. 619–233–6822.

International Manufacturing Company, 1130 Live Oak St., Lillian Springs, FL 32351: Catalog $1 ❖ Beads, pine cones, potpourri materials, other craft items, silk plants and trees, and flower arranging supplies. 904–875–2918.

Jackson Hole Lapidary, Box 2704, Jackson, WY 83001: Free catalog ❖ Beads, bead-stringing supplies, and gem trees. 307–733–7672.

Jeanne's Rock & Jewelry, 5420 Bissonet, Bellaire, TX 77401: Price list $1 ❖ Beads, bead-stringing and lapidary supplies, seashells, and petrified wood products. 713–664–2988.

Kikico Beads, P.O. Box 8353, Scottsdale, AZ 85252: Catalog $2 ❖ Beads for jewelry designing. 602–953–2728.

KUMA Beads, Box 25049, Glenville, NY 12325: Catalog $2 (refundable) ❖ Beads, bead-stringing supplies, semiprecious gemstones, tools, findings, and craft kits. 518–384–0110.

Victor H. Levy Inc., 1355 S. Flower St., Los Angeles, CA 90015: Catalog $5 ❖ Rocailles, shells, jewelry-making supplies, and seed, bone, fancy, and other beads. 800–421–8021; 213–749–8247 (in CA).

Natureworks Bead Company, Four Jonquill Ln., Kings Park, NY 11754: Catalog $2.50 ❖ Exotic beads from worldwide sources and sterling, 14k gold, gold-filled, and natural stone jewelry.

Necklines, P.O. Box 1042, Paso Robles, CA 93447: Free catalog ❖ Beads, bead-stringing supplies, and kits. 805–239–3965.

New England International Gems, 188 Pollard St., Billerica, MA 01862: Free catalog ❖ Beads and beading supplies. 508–667–7394.

Optional Extras, 55 San Remo Dr., Burlington, VT 05403: Catalog $2 ❖ Jewelry findings and beads from worldwide sources. 802–608–0013.

Pearl International, 24 Case Ave., Patchogue, NY 11772: Catalog $5 ❖ Bead-working, jewelry-making, and lapidary tools. 516–277–6788.

The Peruvian Bead Company, 1601 Callens Rd., Ventura, CA 93003: Catalog $2 ❖ Hand-painted ceramic and porcelain beads. 805–642–0952.

Promenade Le Bead Shop, 1970 13th St., Boulder, CO 80306: Catalog $2.50 (refundable) ❖ Beads, bead crafting kits, and books. 303–440–4807.

Red & Green Minerals Inc., 7595 W. Florida Ave., Lakewood, CO 80226: Free information ❖ Beads, bead-stringing supplies, petrified wood products, clocks, clock movements and parts, and rock and mineral specimens. 303–985–5559.

Ribbons & Lace, Box 30070, Mesa, AZ 85272: Catalog $3 (refundable) ❖ Laces, ribbons, craft supplies, and beads.

River Gems & Findings, 6901 Washington NE, Albuquerque, NM 87109: Free catalog ❖ Beads, beading supplies, sewing notions, and other craft accessories. 800–396–9895.

Riviera Lapidary Supply, 30393 Mesquite, Riviera, TX 78379: Catalog $3 ❖ Beads, bead-stringing supplies and kits, shells, petrified wood products, cabochons, slabs, cabbing rough, gemstones, and crystals. 512–296–3958.

Marvin Schwab, 2313 Distribution Cir., Silver Spring, MD 20910: Catalog $3 ❖ Beads, bead crafting supplies, and findings. 301–652–2588.

Shipwreck Beads Inc., 2727 Westmoor Ct., Olympia, WA 98502: Catalog $3 ❖ Beads, bead-stringing supplies, and findings. 206–754–BEAD.

Soho South, P.O. Box 1324, Cullman, AL 35056: Catalog $2.50 (refundable) ❖ Beads and findings, fabric dyes and paints, silk scarves and fabrics, and marbling supplies. 205–739–6114.

Unicorn Beading Supply Company, 4326 SE Woodstock, Portland, OR 97206: Information $2 ❖ Bead-crafting tools. 503–299–0184.

Warehouse Bead Company, Box 801081, Houston, TX 77280: Free catalog ❖ Beads, findings, conchos, suede lacing, and other supplies.

Westbrook Bead Company, 16641 Spring Gulch Dr., Anderson, CA 96007: Catalog $2 ❖ Bead-stringing supplies and gemstone, faceted glass, cobalt blue, old trade, other beads, and other jewelry components for designers and craftspeople. 916–357–3143.

Western Trading Post, P.O. Box 9070, Denver, CO 80209: Catalog $3 ❖ Beads, how-to books, and Native American crafts. 303–777–7750.

BEAR MAKING

Animal Crackers Patterns, 5824 Isleta SW, Albuquerque, NM 87105: Catalog $2.50 ❖ Bear-making supplies. 800–274–BEAR.

Bear Clawset, 27 Palermo Walk, Long Beach, CA 90803: Catalog $2 ❖ Bear-making supplies. 310–434–8077.

Carver's Eye Company, P.O. Box 16692, Portland, OR 97216: Catalog $1 ❖ Glass and plastic eyes, noses, joints, growlers, and eye glasses for bears and dolls. 503–666–5680.

Casey's Bear Factory, 110 Village Landing Mall, Fairport, NY 14450: Catalog $7 ❖ Manufactured and artist bears and bear-making supplies. 716–223–6280.

CR's Crafts, Box 8, Leland, IA 50453: Catalog $2 ❖ Doll- and bear-making supplies, new jointed bears, electronic melody units, kits, patterns, and other craft items. 515–567–3652.

Edinburgh Imports Inc., P.O. Box 722, Woodland Hills, CA 91365: Free catalog with two 1st class stamps ❖ Bear-making supplies. 800–EDINBRG; 818–591–3800 (in CA).

The Fantasy Den, 25 Morehouse Ave., Stratford, CT 06497: Catalog $2 ❖ Bears, bear-making supplies, bearaphenalia, and artwork. 203–377–2968.

Gaillorraine Originals, P.O. Box 137, Tehachapi, CA 93561: Catalog $2 ❖ Jointed bears, antique replica bear patterns, and bear-making supplies. 805–822–1857.

North Star Bear Country Store, 1126 W. Jefferson St., Brooksville, FL 34601: Free catalog with long SASE ❖ Bears, bear-making supplies, and kits. 904–796–8970.

Patterns by Diane, 1126 Ivon Ave., Endicott, NY 13760: Catalog $2 ❖ Stands, patterns, kits, and bear-making supplies. 607–754–0391.

A. Roosevelt Bear Company, 1016 Nandina Way, Sunnyvale, CA 94086: Brochure $3 ❖ Bear-making patterns and clothing. 408–739–4659.

Spare Bear Parts, P.O. Box 56, Interlochen, MI 49643: Catalog $1 ❖ Bear-making supplies, patterns, and kits. 616–275–6993.

Tailormaid Togs for Teddybears, 4037 161st St. SE, Bellevue, WA 98006: Catalog $4 ❖ Clothing for bears. 206–644–4469.

Teddy Works, 8000 Cooper Ave., Bldg. 28, Glendale, NY 11385: Free catalog ❖ Bear-making parts, patterns, books, and clothing. 718–326–4587.

Unicorn Studios, Box 370, Seymour, TN 37865: Catalog $1 ❖ Wind-up and electronic music box movements, voices for talking dolls and bears, winking light units, and other craft supplies. 615–984–0145.

BEARS

Animal Haus Ltd., 7784 Montgomery Rd., Cincinnati, OH 45236: Free catalog with four 1st class stamps ❖ Bears. 513–984–9955.

Annette's Antique Dolls, P.O. Box 5227, Bellingham, WA 98227: Free information ❖ Antique dolls, teddy bears, and toys. 206–758–2476.

Bear Den Hollow, Rt. 1, Box 48, Muscoda, WI 53573: Information $2 ❖ Artist bears. 608–739–3410.

Bear Hugs, 7 Cooper Ave., Marlton, NJ 08053: Free information ❖ Bears and bear clothing. 609–596–2050.

Bear Hugs & Baby Dolls, 1184 Lexington Ave., New York, NY 10028: Free information ❖ Artist bears. 212–717–1513.

Bear-In-Mind Inc., 53 Bradford St., Concord, MA 01742: Catalog $1 ❖ Exclusive handcrafted bears and other collectibles. 508–369–1167.

Bear Pawse, 502 S. Montezuma, Prescott, AZ 86303: Catalog $6 ❖ Bears. 520–445–3800.

Bearly Ours, 120 N. Leroux St., Ste. 101, Flagstaff, AZ 86001: Catalog $2 ❖ Bears.

Bearly Yours, 12643 State Rd., North Royalton, OH 44133: Free price list ❖ Bears. 216–582–3254.

Bears in the Attic, 227 Main St., Reistertown, MD 21136: Free information ❖ Manufactured and artist bears. 800–232–8842.

The Bears of Bruton Street, 107 S. Bruton St., Wilson, NC 27893: Free information with long SASE ❖ Bears. 800–488–BEAR.

Bears 'N Things, 1491 Bacon Rd., Albion, NY 14411: Monthly list (annual subscription) $10 ❖ Artist bears. 716–589–4066.

Bears 'n Wares, 312 Bridge St., New Cumberland, PA 17070: Brochure $2 ❖ Bears. 717–774–1261.

Casey's Bear Factory, 110 Village Landing Mall, Fairport, NY 14450: Catalog $7 ❖ Manufactured and artist bears and bear-making supplies. 716–223–6280.

Christy's Bears, P.O. Box 509, Buckingham, PA 18912: Free information with long SASE ❖ Bears. 215–794–5840.

Collector's Corner Bears, 13672 Lakeshore, Grand Haven, MI 49417: Catalog $1 ❖ New and retired bears. 616–846–0876.

CR's Crafts, Box 8, Leland, IA 50453: Catalog $2 ❖ Doll- and bear-making supplies, new jointed bears, electronic melody units, kits, patterns, and other craft items. 515–567–3652.

Cynthia's Country Store, 11496 Pierson Rd., Commerce Park-Wellington, West Palm Beach, FL 33414: Catalog $15 ❖ Bears. 407–793–0554.

Doll Den, 231 W. Douglas, El Cajon, CA 92020: Free information with long SASE ❖ Dolls, bears, and other stuffed animals. 619–444–2198.

The Doll House, 5022 N. May, Oklahoma City, OK 73112: Free information ❖ Limited edition bears. 405–943–1498.

dolls 'n bearland, 15001 N. Hayden Rd., Ste. 104, Scottsdale, AZ 85260: Free catalog ❖ Bears.

Dollsville Dolls & Bearsville Bears, 461 N. Palm Canyon Dr., Palm Springs, CA 92262: Catalog $2 ❖ Bears. 619–325–2241.

Enchanted Doll House, Rt. 7A, Manchester Center, VT 05255: Catalog $2 ❖ Bears, toys, and dolls. 802–362–1327.

Ernie's Toyland, 671 Colusa Ave., Yuba City, CA 95991: Free information ❖ Manufactured, limited edition, and discontinued bears. 800–367–1233.

Fairytales Inc., 3 S. Park Ave., Lombard, IL 60148: Catalog $2 ❖ Artist and other bears and plush toys. 708–495–6909.

The Fantasy Den, 25 Morehouse Ave., Stratford, CT 06497: Catalog $2 ❖ Bears, bear-making supplies, bearaphenalia, and art prints. 203–377–2968.

GiGi's Dolls & Sherry's Teddy Bears Inc., 6029 N. Northwest Hwy., Chicago, IL 60631: Free catalog ❖ Bears, dolls, plush toys, and miniatures.

Golden Rule Bears, 1103 Main St., Sumner, WA 98390: Free price list with long SASE ❖ Collectible artist bears. 800–932–BEAR.

Groves Quality Collectibles, 349 S. Jameson Ave., Lima, OH 45805: Catalog $4 (refundable) ❖ Bears from the United States and international sources. 419–229–7177.

Harper General Store, RD 2, Box 512, Annville, PA 17003: Free newsletter ❖ Antique bears. 717–865–3456.

The Honey Bee Bear Shoppe, 494 West St., East Bridgewater, MA 02333: Free price list ❖ Artist bears. 508–378–4558.

House of Bears, P.O. Box 384, Hudson, MA 01749: Free brochure ❖ New and retired Raikes bears and current designs by selected bear artists. 508–562–4849.

Hug A Bear, Seaport Village, 849 W. Harbor Dr., Ste. A, San Diego, CA 92101: Free information ❖ Handmade bears. 619–230–1362.

K.C.'s Collectables-Dolls & Bears Inc., 3263 S. Shore Dr., Delavan, WI 53115: Free information ❖ Bears.

Littlethings, 129 Main St., Irvington, NY 10533: Free list with long SASE ❖ Bears, dollhouses, miniatures, furniture, miniature paintings, and other collectibles. 914–591–9150.

Marj's Doll Sanctuary, 5238 Plainfield Ave. NE, Grand Rapids, MI 49505: Free catalog with three 1st class stamps ❖ Bears and dolls.

McB Bears, 380 N. Andreasen, Escondido, CA 92029: Free information with long SASE ❖ Bears. 619–480–1936.

Lee Middleton Original Dolls Inc., 1301 Washington Blvd., Belpre, OH 45714:

Catalog $3 ❖ Original bears and dolls. 800–843–9572.

Moore Bears, Rt. 896, P.O. Box 232, Strasburg, PA 17579: Catalog $4 ❖ Bears and other collectibles. 717–687–6954.

Jean Nordquist's Collectible Doll & Bear Company, 1421 N. 34th St., Seattle, WA 98103: Free information with long SASE ❖ Bears. 800–468–DOLL; 206–634–3131 (in WA).

North American Bear Company, 401 N. Wabash, Ste. 500, Chicago, IL 60610: Free information with long SASE ❖ Bears. 312–329–0020.

North Star Bear Country Store, 1126 W. Jefferson St., Brooksville, FL 34601: Free catalog with long SASE ❖ Bears, bear-making supplies, and kits. 904–796–8970.

Old Friends Antiques, P.O. Box 754, Sparks, MD 21152: Annual subscription of monthly lists $10 ❖ Steiff bears and other plush animals. 410–472–4632.

Playhouse, Zane Plaza Mall, 1080 N. Bridge St., Chiliccothe, OH 45601: Free list with long SASE ❖ Original artist dolls and bears. 614–774–3655.

R & L Collectibles, 3000 26th St., Metarie, LA 70002: Catalog $5 ❖ Artist bears. 504–242–3091.

The Rare Bear, 21 Mill Rd., Woodstock, NY 12498: Catalog $2 ❖ Collectible, artist, and antique bears from England, Germany, and other sources. 914–679–4201.

Romerhaus Creations, 951 S. Alvord Blvd., Evansville, IN 47714: Catalog $10 ❖ Miniature bears. 812–473–7277.

Rose's Doll House Store, 5826 W. Bluemound, Milwaukee, WI 53213: Free catalog ❖ Bears, dolls, and dollhouse furnishings. 414–259–9965.

Shirley's Doll House, 20509 North Hwy. 21, P.O. Box 99A, Wheeling, IL 60090: Free information with long SASE ❖ Bears and dolls, other collectibles, doll-making supplies, and dollhouse furniture. 708–537–1632.

Stuff'd 'N Stuff, 10001 Westheimer, Houston, TX 77042: Catalog $1 (refundable) ❖ Bears and other plush animals. 713–266–4352.

Swan's Nest, RR 1, Box 21, East Lebanon, ME 04027: Catalog $5 (refundable) ❖ Imported handmade bears from Scotland,

England, Wales, Australia, and New Zealand. 207–457–1845.

T-BRRRs, West 3227 Enoch, Deer Park, WA 99006: Price list $2 ❖ Artist bears. 800–368–5227.

Ted E. Bear's Shoppe, 2120 N. 9th St., Naples, FL 33940: Free information ❖ Handcrafted bears, original bear art, bear clothing, books, miniatures, and novelties. 813–261–2225.

The Teddy Bear Emporium LTD, 51 N. Broad St., Lititz, PA 17543: Free information with long SASE ❖ Bears. 800–598–6853.

Teddytown U.S.A., 76 White Bridge Rd., Nashville, TN 37205: Free information ❖ Bears. 800–874–8648; 615–356–AHUG (in TN).

Tide-Rider Inc., P.O. Box 429, Oakdale, CA 95361: Free information ❖ Handmade bears and stuffed animals from Merrythought Iron Bridge in Great Britain. 209–848–4420.

Timbears, Mary Timme, 2870 N. Range Ave., Colby, KS 67701: Catalog $6 ❖ Handmade original bears. 913–462–2782.

Pamela Wooley Bears, 5021 Stringtown Rd., Evansville, IN 47711: Catalog $7.50 ❖ Bears. 800–359–3305.

BEDDING
Comforters & Bed Coverings

Alden Comfort Mills, P.O. Box 55, Plano, TX 75086: Catalog $2 (refundable) ❖ Down-filled comforters. 800–822–5336; 214–423–4000 (in TX).

Antique Quilt Source, 385 Springview Rd., Carlisle, PA 17013: Catalog $7 ❖ Antique quilts. 717–245–2054.

Arkansas Quilts, 2609 Shay Cove, Little Rock, AR 72204: Free price list ❖ Hand- and machine-made quilts. 501–227–9248.

Betsy Bourdon, Weaver, Scribner Hill, Wolcott, VT 05680: Catalog $3 ❖ Handwoven blankets, rugs, and linens. 802–472–6508.

Carter Canopies, P.O. Box 808, Troutman, NC 28166: Free brochure ❖ Hand-tied cotton fishnet canopies, dust ruffles, coverlets, and other country-style bedroom furnishings. 800–538–4071.

Chambers, Mail Order Department, P.O. Box 7841, San Francisco, CA 94120: Free catalog ❖ Bed and bath furnishings. 800–334–1254.

Cindy's Corner, RD 2, 585 Goode St., Ballston Spa, NY 12020: Brochure $1 (refundable) ❖ Twin, double/queen, and king-size country-style patchwork quilts with matching curtains, dust ruffles, pillows, and shams. 518–885–8182.

The Company Store, 500 Company Store Rd., LaCrosse, WI 54601: Free catalog ❖ Linens, mattress pads, and down-filled pillows, comforters, and outerwear. 800–289–8508.

Laura Copenhaver Industries Inc., P.O. Box 149, Marion, VA 24354: Free brochure ❖ Handmade quilts, coverlets, hand-tied canopies, and curtains. 800–227–6797.

The Coverlet Company, 7135 SE 32nd Ave., Portland, OR 97202: Brochure $2.50 ❖ Reproductions of historical coverlets for beds and tables. 503–771–5946.

Cuddledown of Maine, 312 Canco Rd., Portland, ME 04103: Free catalog ❖ Down and feather/down comforters, sheets, sleepwear, mattress pads, throw pillows, flannel bedding, and nursery items. 800–323–6793.

Domestications, P.O. Box 40, Hanover, PA 17333: Free catalog ❖ Comforters, sheets, pillows, blankets, bedspreads, throws, solid and lace tablecloths, mini blinds, shower curtains, and bathroom accessories. 717–633–3313.

Dona Designs, 825 Northlake Dr., Richardson, TX 75080: Free information ❖ Cotton bedding. 214–235–0485.

Donna's Custom Canopies, 255 Chapel Hills Rd., Boone, NC 28607: Brochure $1 with long SASE ❖ Cotton hand-tied canopies, throw pillows, and down-filled comforters. 704–262–1631.

Down Home Comforts, P.O. Box 2281, West Brattleboro, VT 05303: Brochure $1 ❖ New and re-made down comforters, pillows, and featherbeds. 203–688–3780.

Down Home Factory Outlet, 85 Rt. 46 West, Totowa, NJ 07512: Free catalog ❖ Comforters, pillows, and other bedding. 800–ALL–DOWN.

Dutch Country Designs, 2404 Bellevue Rd., Harrisburg, PA 17104: Catalog $3 ❖ Amish quilts, wall hangings, and pillows. 717–238–9043.

Eldridge Textile Company, 277 Grand St., New York, NY 10002: Catalog $3 (refundable) ❖ Blankets, sheets, towels,

comforters, bedspreads, rugs, and pillows. 212–925–1523.

Family Heir-Loom Weavers, RD 3, Box 59, Red Lion, PA 17356: Catalog $3 ❖ Coverlets woven in the tradition of Pennsylvania German weavers in the early 1800s. 717–246–2431.

Feathered Friends Mail Order, 2013 4th Ave., Seattle, WA 98121: Free information ❖ Down comforters and robes, slip covers, pillows, shams, dust ruffles, and flannel sheets. 206–443–9549.

Freedom Quilting Bee, Rt. 1, P.O. Box 72, Alberta, AL 36720: Free information ❖ Handmade quilts. 205–573–2225.

Garnet Hill, 262 Main St., Franconia, NH 03580: Free catalog ❖ Natural fiber linens and sheets, blankets, comforters, and clothing. 800–622–6216.

Gazebo of New York, 127 E. 57th St., New York, NY 10022: Catalog $6 ❖ Patchwork quilts and hand-woven rag, hooked, and braided rugs. 212–832–7077.

Home Etc, Palo Verde at 34th St., P.O. Box 28806, Tucson, AZ 85726: Free catalog ❖ Bedding ensembles, curtains, bedspreads and comforters, rugs, linens and pillows, and towels. 800–362–8415.

Homecraft Services, 340 W. 5th St., Kansas City, MO 64105: Catalog $3 ❖ Pre-cut quilt kits.

The Horchow Collection, P.O. Box 620048, Dallas, TX 75262: Free catalog ❖ Linens, bed coverings, and home decor accessories. 800–395–5397.

JANICE Corporation, 198 Rt. 46, Budd Lake, NJ 07828: Free catalog ❖ Allergy-free women and men's clothing, towels, bathroom accessories, quilts, linens, personal grooming aids, hats, gloves, and scarves. 800–JANICES.

Kelly & Company, 3080 Coolidge, Conklin, MI 49403: Free information ❖ Machine-washable quilts for cribs up to king-size beds. 616–899–2694.

Kountry Quilts & Kits, P.O. Box 282, Union, MO 63084: Brochure $3 ❖ Ready-made quilts and kits. 800–821–1937; 314–583–0843 (in MO).

Lakota Collection, St. Joseph Lakota Development Council, St. Joseph Indian School, Chamberlain, SD 57326: Free catalog ❖ Sioux Indian Star quilts and other Native American crafts and gifts. 605–734–6021.

Landau Woolens, 114 Nassau St., Princeton, NJ 08542: Free catalog ❖ Machine washable wool blankets. 800–257–9445.

Leron, 750 Madison Ave., New York, NY 10021: Free catalog ❖ Linens, towels, pillows and covers, and imported handkerchiefs for men and women, with optional monogramming. 212–753–6700.

Linen & Lace, 4 Lafayette, Washington, MO 63090: Catalog $2 ❖ Bed ruffles, canopies, and curtains. 800–332–5223.

The Linen Source, 5401 Hangar Ct., P.O. Box 31151, Tampa, FL 33631: Free catalog ❖ Bedroom ensembles, linens, pillows, and curtains. 800–431–2620.

Deborah Mallow Designs Inc., 276 5th Ave., Rm. 303, New York, NY 10001: Free information with long SASE ❖ Quilted bedspreads, pillows, valances, curtains, and draperies. 212–779–0540.

Midwest Quilt Exchange, 495 S. 3rd St., Columbus, OH 43215: Free information ❖ Antique quilts. 614–221–8400.

Missouri Breaks Industries Inc., Quilt Brochure, P.O. Box 262, Timber Lake, SD 57656: Free brochure ❖ Original Sioux Indian Star quilts. 605–865–3418.

Mother Hart's Natural Products, P.O. Box 4229, Boynton Beach, FL 33424: Free information ❖ Natural fiber flannel sheets, blankets, water bed sheets, pillows, quilt covers, shams, down comforters, wool mattress pads, and cotton mattress pads and covers. 407–738–5866.

Ozark Weaving Studio, P.O. Box 286, Cane Hill, AR 72717: Brochure $2.50 ❖ Handwoven wool and cotton coverlets and throws. 501–824–3920.

Quilted Treasures, Judy & Michelle Parcell, P.O. Box 96, Indore, WV 25111: Free information ❖ Handmade quilts and other patchwork items. 304–587–8313.

Quilts Unlimited, 440A Duke of Gloucester St., Williamsburg, VA 23185: Catalog $6 ❖ Antique quilts. 804–253–8700.

Rocky Mountain Tanners Inc., P.O. Box 27918, Lakewood, CO 80227: Brochure $2 ❖ Elk and deer leather throws for beds, couches, and chairs. 303–761–1049.

J. Schachter Corporation, 5 Cook St., Brooklyn, NY 11206: Catalog $1 (refundable) ❖ Shams, ruffles, table covers, and draperies. 800–INTO–BED; 718–384–2100 (in NY).

Warm Things, 180 Paul Dr., San Rafael, CA 94903: Free catalog ❖ Down quilts, covers, and pillows. 415–472–2154.

Western Trading Post, P.O. Box 9070, Denver, CO 80209: Catalog $3 ❖ Blankets, Navajo wool rugs, and Eagle-design bed throws. 303–777–7750.

Yankee Pride, 29 Parkside Cir., Braintree, MA 02184: Catalog $3 (refundable) ❖ Handcrafted quilts, comforters, and bedspreads, and hand-braided, hooked wool, and rag rugs. 617–848–7610.

Pillows & Sheets

Bedroom Secrets, P.O. Box 529, Fremont, NE 68025: Catalog $2 ❖ Linens for the bath and bed. 800–955–2559; 402–727–4004 (in NE).

Betsy Bourdon, Weaver, Scribner Hill, Wolcott, VT 05680: Brochure $3 ❖ Linens, handwoven blankets, and rugs. 802–472–6508.

Celestial Silks, P.O. Box 824, Fairfield, IA 52556: Free information ❖ Silk sheets, pillowcases, and silk-filled comforters. 515–472–9062.

Chrisalem by Malerich, 2158 Charlton Rd., Sunfish Lake, MN 55119: Catalog $1 ❖ Comforters, pillows and sheets, tablecloths, and other linens. 612–451–6690.

Cindy's Corner, RD 2, 585 Goode St., Ballston Spa, NY 12020: Brochure $1 (refundable) ❖ Twin, double/queen, and king-size country-style patchwork quilts with matching curtains, dust ruffles, pillows, and shams. 518–885–8182.

The Company Store, 500 Company Store Rd., LaCrosse, WI 54601: Free catalog ❖ Down-filled pillows and comforters, linens, mattress pads, and down-filled outerwear. 800–289–8508.

Cuddledown of Maine, 312 Canco Rd., Portland, ME 04103: Free catalog ❖ Down and feather/down comforters, sheets, sleepwear, mattress pads, throw pillows, flannel bedding, and nursery items. 800–323–6793.

Domestications, P.O. Box 40, Hanover, PA 17333: Free catalog ❖ Comforters, sheets, pillows, blankets, bedspreads, throws, solid and lace tablecloths, mini blinds, shower curtains, and bathroom accessories. 717–633–3313.

Dona Designs, 825 Northlake Dr., Richardson, TX 75080: Free information ❖ Cotton bedding. 214–235–0485.

Down Home Comforts, P.O. Box 2281, West Brattleboro, VT 05303: Brochure $1 ❖ Down comforters and pillows. 203–688–3780.

Down Home Factory Outlet, 85 Rt. 46 West, Totowa, NJ 07512: Free catalog ❖ Comforters, pillows, and other bedding. 800–ALL–DOWN.

Downtown Design Supply, 4860 Olive St., Commerce City, CO 80022: Free information ❖ Down throw pillows, wicker and rattan furniture cushions, and comforters. 303–287–2863.

Eldridge Textile Company, 277 Grand St., New York, NY 10002: Catalog $3 (refundable) ❖ Blankets, sheets, towels, comforters, bedspreads, rugs, and pillows. 212–925–1523.

Feathered Friends Mail Order, 2013 4th Ave., Seattle, WA 98121: Free information ❖ Down comforters and robes, slip covers, pillows, shams, dust ruffles, and flannel sheets. 206–443–9549.

Garnet Hill, 262 Main St., Franconia, NH 03580: Free catalog ❖ Natural fiber linens and sheets, blankets, and comforters. 800–622–6216.

The Horchow Collection, P.O. Box 620048, Dallas, TX 75262: Free catalog ❖ Linens, bed coverings, and decor accessories. 800–395–5397.

JANICE Corporation, 198 Rt. 46, Budd Lake, NJ 07828: Free catalog ❖ Allergy-free women and men's clothing, towels, bathroom accessories, quilts, linens, personal grooming aids, hats, gloves, and scarves. 800–JANICES.

Leron, 750 Madison Ave., New York, NY 10021: Free catalog ❖ Linens, towels, pillows and covers, and imported handkerchiefs for men and women, with optional monogramming. 212–753–6700.

Harris Levy, 278 Grand St., New York, NY 10002: Free catalog ❖ Linens for tables, beds, and bathrooms. 800–221–7750; 212–226–3102 (in NY).

The Linen Source, 5401 Hangar Ct., P.O. Box 31151, Tampa, FL 33631: Free catalog ❖ Linens, pillows, curtains, and bedroom ensembles. 800–431–2620.

Lullaby Cribwear Collection, 1939 Michigan Rd., Madison, IN 47250: Free brochure ❖ Crib wear for cradles, porta-cribs, bassinets, and toddler beds. 812–273–2709.

M.C. Ltd., P.O. Box 17696, Whitefish Bay, WI 53217: Free information: ❖ Pillows and steerhide rugs. 800–236–5224; 414–263–5422 (in WI).

Deborah Mallow Designs Inc., 276 5th Ave., Rm. 303, New York, NY 10001: Free information with long SASE ❖ Quilted bedspreads for Victorian and country-style beds, pillows, valances, curtains, and draperies. 212–779–0540.

Mother Hart's Natural Products, P.O. Box 4229, Boynton Beach, FL 33424: Free information ❖ Natural fiber flannel sheets, blankets, water bed sheets, pillows, quilt covers, shams, down comforters, wool mattress pads, and cotton mattress pads and covers. 407–738–5866.

The Natural Bedroom, Jantz Design, P.O. Box 3071, Santa Rosa, CA 95402: Free information ❖ Natural bedding. 800–365–6563.

Olde Mill House Shoppe, 105 Strasburg Pike, Lancaster, PA 17602: Catalog $1 ❖ Country-style homespun table linens, handcrafted furniture, braided rugs, and bathroom accessories. 717–299–0678.

Palmetto Linen Company, 145 Shoppes on the Pkwy., Hilton Head, SC 29928: Free information ❖ Sheets and matching dust ruffles, bath towels, blankets, comforters, pillows, tablecloths, place mats, and shower curtains. 800–972–7442.

Rafael, 291 Grand St., New York, NY 10002: Free information with long SASE ❖ Pillowcases, sheets, towels, table linens, and comforters. 212–966–1928.

Rubin & Green, 290 Grand St., New York, NY 10002: Free information with long SASE ❖ Bed, bathroom, and table linens. 212–226–0313.

Rue de France, 78 Thames St., Newport, RI 02840: Catalog $3 ❖ Pillows, tablecloths and runners, and lace curtains. 800–777–0998.

Shaxted of Beverly Hills, 350 N. Camden Dr., Beverly Hills, CA 90210: Free information ❖ Linens for the table, bed, and bath. 310–273–4320.

Warm Things, 180 Paul Dr., San Rafael, CA 94903: Free catalog ❖ Down quilts, pillows, and quilt covers. 415–472–2154.

BEEKEEPING

Archia's Seed Store, 106 E. Main St., Sedalia, MO 65301: Free catalog ❖ Beekeeping equipment, vegetable and flower seeds, and gardening supplies. 816–826–1330.

B & B Honey Farm, Rt. 2, Box 245, Houston, MN 55943: Free catalog ❖ Beekeeping and candle-making supplies. 507–896–3955.

Bee Bob's Apiaries, 7461 Porter Rd., Dixon, CA 95620: Free brochure ❖ Queen bees. 916–678–2495.

Betterbee-Meadery Inc., RR 4, Box 4070, Greenwich, NY 12834: Free information ❖ Beekeeping supplies. 518–692–9669.

Bob Brandi Honey, 1518 Paradise Ln., Los Banos, CA 93635: Free information ❖ Package bees, queens, bulk bees, and nucs. 209–826–0921.

Brushy Mountain Bee Farm, Rt. 1, P.O. Box 135, Moravian Falls, NC 28654: Free catalog ❖ Gloves and protective clothing, equipment for processing honey, books, video tapes, and other beekeeping supplies. 800–BEESWAX.

Calvert Apiaries, P.O. Box 4, Calvert, AL 36513: Free information ❖ Italian package bees and queens. 800–233–7989; 205–829–6183 (in AL).

Dadant & Sons Inc., 51 S. 2nd St., Hamilton, IL 62341: Free catalog ❖ Honey extracting equipment, honey containers, beeswax foundation and plasticell, woodenware, and queen and package bees. 217–847–3324.

Friesen Honey Farms Inc., Rt. 1, Box 283, Glenn, CA 95943: Free information ❖ Italian package bees and queens. 916–934–4944.

Genesis Bee Company, Rt. 4, Box 508, Greenville, TN 37743: Free information ❖ Italian queen bees. 800–864–7577.

Glenn Apiaries, P.O. Box 2737, Fallbrook, CA 92088: Free information ❖ Italian and Carnolian queen bees. 619–728–3731.

Glorybee Honey & Supplies, P.O. Box 2744, Eugene, OR 97402: Catalog 50¢ ❖ Beekeeping and honey processing supplies, honey, honey-prepared foods, and gift assortments. 800–456–7923; 503–689–0913 (in OR).

Hardeman Apiaries, P.O. Box 214, Mt. Vernon, GA 30445: Free price list ❖ Italian packages and queen bees. 912–583–2710.

Harrell & Sons Inc., P.O. Box 215, Haynesville, AL 36040: Free information ❖ Italian package bees and queens. 205–548–2313.

Wayne Harrison, Los Banos, CA 93635: Free information ❖ Italian package bees, nucs, and queens. 209–826–2995.

Heitkam's Honey Bees, Rt. 2, Box 2542, Orland, CA 95963: Free price list ❖ Queen bees. 916–865–9562.

Homan Honey Farm, P.O. Box 365, Shannon, MS 38868: Free price list ❖ Queen and package bees. 601–767–3960.

Walter T. Kelley Company Inc., 3107 Elizabeth Rd., Clarkson, KY 42726: Free catalog ❖ Beekeeping supplies. 502–242–2012.

C.F. Koehnen & Sons Inc., 3131 Hwy. 45, Glenn, CA 95943: Free brochure ❖ Italian packages and queen bees. 916–891–5216.

Kona Queen Company, P.O. Box 768, Captain Cook, HI 96704: Free information ❖ Italian queen bees. 808–328–9016.

Lapp's Bee Supply Center, 500 S. Main St., Reeseville, WI 53579: Free information ❖ Package bees, fructose, beeswax, glass accessories, honey, and woodenware. 414–927–3848.

Mann Lake Supply, County Rd. 40 & 1st St., Hackensack, MN 56452: Free catalog ❖ Beekeeping and honey production equipment, protective clothing, and candle molds. 800–233–6663.

Maxant Industries Inc., P.O. Box 454, Ayer, MA 01432: Catalog $1 ❖ Honey processing equipment. 508–772–0576.

Norman Bee Farms, P.O. Box 727, Ramer, AL 36069: Free information ❖ Italian queen bees. 205–562–3357.

Homer E. Park, P.O. Box 38, Palo Cedro, CA 96073: Free price list ❖ Italian queen bees. 916–547–3391.

Powell Apiaries, Rt. 5, Box 5246, Orland, CA 95963: Free information ❖ Italian package bees and queens, hives, and beekeeping supplies. 916–865–3346.

A.I. Root Company, P.O. Box 706, Medina, OH 44258: Free catalog ❖ Hives, protective clothing and gloves, tools, honey-processing equipment, books, video tapes, smokers, and beekeeping supplies. 800–289–7668.

Rossman Apiaries Inc., P.O. Box 905, Moultrie, GA 31776: Free catalog ❖ Package bees and queens, beekeeping supplies, and starter kit for beginners. 800–333–7677; 912–985–7200 (in GA).

Jerry Shumans Apiaries, Rt. 4, Box 1710, Baxley, GA 31513: Free information ❖ Italian queen and package bees. 800–368–7195; 912–367–2243 (in GA).

Southwestern Ohio Hive Parts Company, 52 Marco Ln., Centerville, OH 45458: Free information ❖ Beekeeping supplies. 800–765–5112; 513–435–5112 (in OH).

Strachan Apiaries Inc., 2522 Tierra Buena Rd., Yuba City, CA 95993: Free information ❖ Queen bees. 916–674–3881.

Tollett Apiaries, 8700 Honey Lane, Millville, CA 96062: Free information ❖ Italian package bees and queens. 916–547–3387.

Howard Weaver & Sons Inc., Rt. 4, Box 24, Navasota, TX 77868: Free information ❖ Caucasian, midnight, starline, double hybrid, and queen bees. 800–247–5520.

The Wilbanks Apiaries, P.O. Box 12, Claxton, GA 30417: Free information ❖ Package bees and queens. 912–739–4820.

York Bee Company, P.O. Box 307, Jesup, GA 31545: Free information ❖ Starline, midnight, Italian, package, and queen bees. 912–427–7311.

BEER CANS & STEINS

Classic Carolina Collection, 1502 N. 23rd St., Wilmington, NC 28405: Free catalog ❖ Limited edition steins with history, sports, entertainment, notable individuals, and significant anniversary themes. 800–457–9700.

D & A Investments, Darrell Bowman, 2055–E Burnside Cir., Salt Lake City, UT 84109: Free price list ❖ Mugs, steins, and other brewery collectibles. 800–336–2055.

Ron Fox Auctions, 416 Throop St., North Babylon, NY 11704: Free catalog ❖ Beer steins. 516–669–7232.

Gene's Can Shop, RD 1, Box 72, Martville, NY 13111: Catalog $1 with long SASE ❖ Hard-to-find beer cans.

Charlie Golden Jr., 345 S. Sterley St., Shillington, PA 19607: United States list, five 1st class stamps; foreign list, five 1st class stamps ❖ Beer cans from over 70 countries. 610–777–7078.

Kansgalore, 505 Bosworth Rd., Knoxville, TN 37919: Free list with long SASE ❖ Beer cans, labels, and coasters.

Chet Kilanowicz, 5446 Rockwood Rd., Columbus, OH 43229: List $1 ❖ Beer cans. 614–888–0917.

Lager Sales, Box 612164, Dallas, TX 75261: Free information ❖ Brewery collectibles. 817–354–0232.

Museum of Beverage Containers, 1055 Ridgecrest Dr., Goodlettsville, TN 37072: Free catalog ❖ Beer and soda cans, signs, trays, caps, openers, and glasses.

Rolf's Steinwerke, 9420 Reseda Blvd., #800, Northridge, CA 91324: Catalog $10 (refundable) ❖ Traditional, limited edition, and retired Thewalt, Girmscheid, Sitzendorfer, Gertz, King, Unterweissbach, Mettlach, and Ceramarte beer steins. 818–368–2786.

Steffen Enterprises, 14 N 679, Rt. 25, Ste. A, Elgin, IL 60120: Free catalog ❖ Beer cans, mugs, and steins. 708–428–3150.

Steins-N-Stuff Unlimited, 2231 Sunset Ave., Wasco, CA 93280: Free price list ❖ Beer mugs, steins, and other collectibles. 805–758–8210.

BICYCLES & ACCESSORIES
Bicycles

Albe's Action Sports, 5759 E. 13 Mile Rd., Warren, MI 48092: Catalog $1 ❖ Bicycles. 800–635–0845; 313–264–1150 (in MI).

Keith Anderson, 1555 Bellefontaine St., Indianapolis, IN 46202: Free information ❖ Racing, touring, sport touring, hybrid, track, and mountain bicycle frames. 317–262–8418.

Anderson Cycles, 350 Fay Way, Mountain View, CA 94043: Free information ❖ Racing, touring, sport touring, track, mountain, and tandem bicycle frames. 415–961–4371.

Angle Lake Cyclery, 20840 Pacific Hwy. South, Seattle, WA 98188: Catalog $2 ❖ Racing bicycles. 800–793–3038.

Matthew Assenmacher Bikes, 8053 Miller Rd., Swartz Creek, MI 48473: Free information ❖ Mountain and tandem bicycles. 313–635–7844.

Avon Seagull Marine, 1851 McGaw Ave., Irvine, CA 92714: Free catalog ❖ Folding bicycles. 714–250–0880.

Bianchi USA, 2371 Cabot Blvd., Hayward, CA 94545: Free information ❖ Racing, mountain, and city bicycles. 800–431–0006; 510–264–1001 (in CA).

Bicycle Corporation of America, 2811 Brodhead Rd., Bethlehem, PA 18017: Free information ❖ Mountain bicycles. 800–225–2453.

Bike Nashbar, 4111 Simon Rd., P.O. Box 3449, Youngstown OH 44512: Free catalog ❖ Racing, sport touring, touring, and mountain bicycles. 800–627–4227.

Bike Rack Inc., 11 Constance Ct., Hauppauge, NY 11788: Free information ❖ Racing and mountain bicycles. 800–645–5477.

Bilenky Cycle Works, 5319 N. 2nd St., Philadelphia, PA 19120: Free catalog ❖ Tandem bicycles. 215–329–4744.

Jeffrey Bock, 929 N. 4th, Ames, IA 50010: Free information ❖ Racing, touring, sport touring, hybrid, track, and tandem bicycle frames. 515–232–9593.

Boulder Bicycles Inc., P.O. Box 1400, Lyons, CO 80540: Free information ❖ Frames and bicycles. 303–532–0133.

Bridgestone Cycle USA Inc., 15021 Wicks Blvd., San Leandro, CA 94577: Free information ❖ Racing, sport touring, and mountain bicycles. 800–328–2453; 510–895–5480 (in CA).

Burley Design Cooperative, 4080 Stewart Rd., Eugene, OR 97402: Free brochure ❖ Tandem bicycles. 503–687–1644.

Cannondale Corporation, P.O. Box 122, Georgetown, CT 06829: Free information ❖ Racing, sport touring, and touring bicycles. 800–245–3872; 203–544–9800 (in CT).

Clark-Kent Innovations, 2200 W. Alemeda, Denver, CO 80223: Free information ❖ Mountain bicycles. 303–935–8289.

Columbia Manufacturing Company, P.O. Box 1230, Westfield, MA 01085: Free information ❖ Racing bicycles. 413–562–3664.

Columbine Cycle Works, 2609 Riverbend Ct., Ste. A, Fort Collins, CO 80525: Free information ❖ Mountain, tandem, and track bicycles. 303–224–1168.

Corso Bicycle Distributors, 349 W. 14th St., New York, NY 10014: Free information ❖ Racing, sport touring, and mountain bicycles. 212–675–2161.

Charlie Cunningham Bicycles, P.O. Box 757, Fairfax, CA 94930: Free information ❖ Mountain bicycle frames. 415–457–1779.

Curtio Cycles, P.O. Box 896, Santa Clarita, CA 91322: Free information ❖ Frames and bicycles. 805–251–9582.

Cycle Composites, 265 Westridge Dr., Watsonville, CA 95076: Free information ❖ Racing and sport touring bicycles. 408–724–9079.

Cycles LaMoure, 416 1st St., Cheney, WA 99004: Free information ❖ Mountain, track, and women's bicycles. 509–235–2297.

Dahon California, 5741 Buckingham Pkwy., Unit B, Culver City, CA 90230: Free information ❖ Folding bicycles. 310–417–3456.

Davidson Cycle, 2116 Western Ave., Seattle, WA 98121: Free information ❖ Mountain, tandem, and women's bicycles. 800–292–5374.

Diamond Back Western States Imports, 4030 Via Pescador, Camarillo, CA 93012: Free information ❖ Off-road and mountain bicycles. 800–776–7641.

Albert Eisentraut Bicycles, 543 E. 11th St., Oakland, CA 94606: Free information ❖ Racing, touring, sport touring, hybrid, track, mountain, and tandem bicycle frames. 510–452–4485.

Erickson Cycles, 6119 Brooklyn NE, Seattle, WA 98115: Free information ❖ Mountain, tandem, women's, track, and touring bicycles. 206–527–5259.

Fat City Cycles, P.O. Box 218, Somerville, MA 02143: Free information ❖ Mountain and racing bicycles. 617–625–4922.

Fuji America, 118 Bauer Dr., Oakland, NJ 07436: Free information ❖ Racing, sport touring, touring, mountain, and city bicycles. 800–631–8474; 201–337–1700 (in NJ).

Steve Garn, Rt. 1, Box 270, Creston, NC 28615: Free information ❖ Racing, touring, sport touring, hybrid, track, and mountain bicycle frames. 910–385–6847.

Giant Bicycle Company, 475 Apra St., Rancho Dominguez, CA 90220: Free information ❖ Racing, mountain, and city bicycles. 800–874–4268; 310–609–3340 (in CA).

Gita Sporting Goods, 12600 Steele Creek Rd., Charlotte, NC 28273: Free information ❖ Racing and track bicycles. 800–366–4482; 704–588–7550 (in NC).

Gitane of America, 2 Union Dr., Olney, IL 62450: Free information ❖ Racing and tandem bicycles. 618–392–3777.

Bruce Gordon Cycles, 613 2nd St., Petaluma, CA 94952: Free information ❖ Frames and bicycles. 707–762–5601.

GT Bicycles, 3100 W. Segerstrom Ave., Santa Ana, CA 92704: Free information ❖ Mountain bicycles. 800–RID-EAGT; 714–513–7100 (in CA).

C. Hansen Classic, 8060 Hwy. 8, Culver, MN 55779: Free information ❖ Frames and bicycles. 218–545–6280.

Haro Designs Inc., 2225 Faraday Ave., Ste. A, Carlsbad, CA 92009: Free information ❖ Mountain bicycles. 619–438–4812.

HH Racing Group, 1901 S. 13th St., Philadelphia, PA 19148: Free information ❖ Racing, touring, tandem, and track bicycles. 215–334–8500.

Bill Holland, 3735 Kenora Dr., Spring Valley, CA 91977: Free information ❖ Racing, track, tandem, triathlon, and time-trial bicycle frames. 619–469–1772.

Ibis Cycles, P.O. Box 275, Sebastopol, CA 95473: Free information ❖ Mountain and tandem bicycles. 707–829–5615.

Jamis Bicycles, 151 Ludlow Ave., Northvale, NJ 07647: Free information ❖ Off-road and mountain bicycles.

KHS Bicycles, 1264 E. Walnut St., Carson, CA 90746: Free information ❖ Mountain and hybrid bicycles. 310–632–7173.

Klein Bicycle Corporation, 118 Klein Rd., Chehalis, WA 98532: Free information ❖ Mountain, road, sport touring, and women's bicycles. 206–262–3305.

Kona Mountain Bikes, 1122 Fir Ave., Blaine, WA 98230: Free information ❖ Mountain bicycles. 206–332–5384.

Lawee Cycles Inc., 3030 Walnut Ave., Long Beach, CA 90807: Free information ❖ Racing, sport touring, touring, mountain, and city bicycles. 310–426–0474.

Lighthouse Cycles, 3498 Willow St., Santa Ynez, CA 95060: Free information ❖ Mountain, hybrid, women's, and track bicycles. 805–688–6385.

Lippy Bikes, 60265 Fuagarwee Cir., Bend, OR 97702: Free information ❖ Tandem bicycles. 503–389–2503.

Maplewood Bicycle, 7534 Manchester, St. Louis, MO 63143: Free information ❖ Bicycles. 314–781–9566.

Marin Mountain Bikes, 16 Mary St., San Rafael, CA 94901: Free information ❖ Mountain bicycles. 800–222–7557; 415–485–5100 (in CA).

Marinoni USA Inc., P.O. Box 374, Montgomery Center, VT 05471: Free information ❖ Racing bicycles. 802–326–4321.

McMahon Racing Cycles, P.O. Box 579, Carpinteria, CA 93013: Free information ❖ Bicycle frames. 805–684–7398.

Miyata Bicycle of America Inc., 2526 W. Pratt Blvd., Elk Grove, IL 60007: Free information ❖ Racing, sport touring, touring, and mountain bicycles. 708–228–5450.

Mongoose Bicycles, 3400 Kashiwa St., Torrance, CA 90505: Free information ❖ Lightweight fitness bicycles. 310–539–8860.

Montague Bicycle Company, P.O. Box 1118, Cambridge, MA 02238: Free information ❖ Mountain, hybrid, and tandem folding bicycles. 800–736–5348.

Morgan's Cycle & Fitness, 2513 Sunset Ave., Rocky Mount, NC 27804: Free information ❖ Recumbent bicycles. 919–443–4480.

Mountain Bike Specialists, 340 S. Camino Del Rio, Durango, CO 81301: Catalog $3 ❖ Mountain bicycles and parts. 800–255–8377; 800–538–9500 (in CO).

Mountain Goat Cycles, 2145 Park Ave., Chico, CA 95927: Free information ❖ Mountain, hybrid, and tandem bicycles. 916–342–4628.

Nobilette Cycles, 1616 S. Horseshoe Cir., Longmont, CO 80501: Free information ❖ Racing, touring, sport touring, mountain, and tandem bicycles. 303–682–9146.

Norco Products USA Inc., 7950 Enterprise St., Burnaby, British Columbia, Canada V5A 1V7: Free information ❖ Racing, sport touring, mountain, and city bicycles. 604–420–6616.

Ochsner International, 4341 W. Peterson Ave., Chicago, IL 60646: Free information ❖ Racing, mountain, and trail bicycles. 312–286–3111.

One-off Titanium, 221 Pine St., Florence, MA 01060: Free information ❖ Racing, touring, sport touring, hybrid, track, mountain, tandem, and recumbent bicycle frames. 413–585–5913.

Palo Alto Bicycles, 171 University Ave., Palo Alto, CA 94301: Free catalog ❖ Bicycles and parts. 800–227–8900.

Panasonic Bicycle Division, Panasonic Way, Secaucus, NJ 07094: Free information ❖ Racing, sport touring, touring, and mountain bicycles. 201–348–5375.

R & A Cycles Inc., 105 5th Ave., Brooklyn, NY 11217: Free information with long SASE ❖ Bicycles and frames. 718–636–5242.

Raleigh Cycle Company of America, 22710 72nd Ave. South, Kent, WA 98032: Free information ❖ Racing, sport touring, and mountain bicycles. 800–222–5527; 206–395–1100 (in WA).

Reflex Bikes, P.O. Box 535037, Salt Lake City, UT 84127: Free information ❖ Mountain bicycles. 801–539–8001.

Tom Ritchey Bicycles, 1326 Hancock Ave., Redwood City, CA 94061: Free information ❖ Mountain, racing, and tandem bicycles.

Rock Lobster Cycles, 219 Trescony St., Santa Cruz, CA 95060: Free information ❖ Mountain, track, and hybrid bicycles. 408–429–1356.

Rock N' Roll Marketing Inc., P.O. Box 1558, Levelland, TX 79336: Free information ❖ Single riders, tandems, and hand and foot-powered cycles with optional seat configurations and custom fitting for individual needs. 800–654–9664.

Rocky Mountain Bicycle Company, 414–5940 No. 6 Rd., Richmond, British Columbia, Canada V6V 1Z1: Free information ❖ Mountain bicycles. 604–270–2710.

Romic Cycle Company, 4434 Steffani Ln., Houston, TX 77041: Free information ❖ Racing, touring, and sport touring bicycles. 713–466–7806.

Ross Bicycles USA, 51 Executive Blvd., Farmingdale, NY 11735: Free information ❖ Mountain and hybrid bicycles. 800–338–7677; 516–249–6000 (in NY).

Rumme Cycles, 10680 NW 44th St., Polk City, IA 50226: Free information ❖ Frames and bicycles. 515–984–6591.

Ryan Recumbent Cycles, One Chestnut St., Nashua, NH 03060: Free information ❖ Recumbent bicycles and tandems. 603–598–1711.

Richard Sachs Cycles, 1 Main St., Chester, CT 06412: Free information ❖ Road and racing bicycles. 203–526–2059.

Salsa Bicycles, 611 2nd St., Petaluma, CA 94952: Free information ❖ Bicycle frames. 707–762–8191.

Schwinn Bicycle Company, 1690 38th St., Boulder, CO 80301: Free information with long SASE ❖ Racing, mountain, tandem, and city bicycles. 303–939–0100.

Scott USA, P.O. Box 2030, Sun Valley, ID 83353: Free information ❖ Mountain bicycles. 208–622–1000.

Specialized Bicycle Components, 15130 Concord Cir., Morgan Hill, CA 95037: Free information ❖ Racing and mountain bicycles. 800–245–3462; 408–779–6229 (in CA).

Spectrum Cycles, 1190 Donney Rd., Breinigsville, PA 18031: Free information ❖ Frames and bicycles. 215–398–1986.

Stuyvesant Bicycles, 349 W. 14th St., New York, NY 10014: Catalog $2.50 ❖ Domestic and imported bicycles, lightweight folding bicycles, unicycles, bicycles built for two, and children's bicycles. 212–254–5200.

Tandems East, RR 8, Box 319–E, Gwynwood Dr., Bridgeton, NJ 08302: Catalog $2 ❖ Tandem bicycles, parts kits, and separate parts. 609–451–5104.

Tandems Limited, 220 Vanessa Dr., Birmingham, AL 35242: Free information ❖ American and English tandems and parts. 205–991–5519.

Terry Precision Bicycles, 1704 Wayneport Rd., Macedon, NY 14502: Free information ❖ Racing, sport touring, touring, and mountain bicycles. 800–289–8379; 315–986–2103 (in NY).

Torelli Imports, 1181 Calle Suerte, Camarillo, CA 93012: Free information ❖ Racing bicycles. 805–484–8705.

Trek Bicycle Corporation, 801 W. Madison St., P.O. Box 183, Waterloo, WI 53594: Free information ❖ Racing, sport touring, touring, mountain, and city bicycles. 800–879–8735; 414–478–2191 (in WI).

Veltec-Boyer, 1793 Catalina St., Sand City, CA 93955: Free information ❖ Racing bicycles. 408–394–7114.

Williams American Cycles, Gurney Ln., Box 244, Queensbury, NY 12804: Free information ❖ Racing, touring, sport touring, hybrid, and mountain bicycle frames. 518–793–6446.

Ted Wojcik, 4 Poplar St., Amesbury, MA 01913: Free information ❖ Mountain, road, sport, hybrid, tandem, and track bicycles. 508–388–4150.

Zinn Bicycles, 4715 N. Broadway, Boulder, CO 80302: Free information ❖ Racing, touring, sport touring, mountain, tandem, and track bicycles. 303–786–7442.

Parts & Accessories

Antique Cycle Supply, Rt. 1, Cedar Springs, MI 49319: Catalog $5 ❖ Bicycle parts, books and literature, and antique, classic, and balloon tires. 616–636–8200.

Avocet Inc., P.O. Box 120, Palo Alto, CA 94302: Free information with long SASE ❖ Bike computer that measures speed, distance, and time. 800–227–8346; 415–321–8501 (in CA).

Bell Helmets, 13875 Cerritos Corporate Dr., Ste. A, Cerritos, Ca 90701: Free information ❖ Lightweight helmet in compliance with ANSI and Snell standards. 310–921–9451.

Bike Nashbar, 4111 Simon Rd., P.O. Box 3449, Youngstown OH 44512: Free catalog ❖ Bicycles, components, and saddlebags. 800–627–4227.

Bikecentennial, P.O. Box 8308, Missoula, MT 59807: Free catalog ❖ Bike touring maps and books. 800–933–1116.

Blue Sky Cycle Carts, P.O. Box 704, Redmond, OR 97756: Brochure $1 ❖ Children's trailers/carts with seats, safety harnesses, and optional canopy. 503–548–7753.

Burley Design Cooperative, 4080 Stewart Rd., Eugene, OR 97402: Free brochure ❖ Bike trailers for children, with chest harness, seat belt, and roll bar. 503–687–1644.

Conrad's Bikeshop, 25 Tudor City Pl., New York, NY 10017: Free information ❖ Bicycles, frames, parts, clothing, and safety gear. 212–697–6966.

Cosmopolitan Motors Inc., 301 Jacksonville Rd., Hatboro, PA 19040: Free information ❖ Bicycle locks, packs and bags, and tires. 800–523–2522; 215–672–9100 (in PA).

Cycle Goods, 2801 Hennepin Ave. South, Minneapolis, MN 55408: Catalog $4 (refundable) ❖ Parts, tools, bicycles, clothing, books, carriers, and safety gear. 612–872–7600.

Cycle Products Company, 2900 Rightview Dr., Memphis, TN 38116: Free information ❖ Car-mounted bicycle carriers, horns, lamps, locks, packs and bags, reflectors, speedometers, tires and tubes, and helmets. 800–842–2472; 901–345–5090 (in TN).

CyclePro, Derbie Cycle, 22710 72nd Ave. South, Kent, WA 98032: Free information ❖ Frame and saddle bags. 800–222–5527.

D & R Industries, 7111 Capitol Dr., Lincolnwood, IL 60645: Free information ❖ Car-mounted bicycle carriers and child carriers, horns, lamps, locks, packs and bags, racks, reflectors and speedometers, tires and tubes, and helmets. 800–323–2852; 708–677–3200 (in IL).

Eastpak, 50 Rogers Rd., P.O. Box 8232, Ward Hill, MA 01835: Free information ❖ Frame and saddle bags. 508–373–1581.

Eldon Group America Inc., 175 Clearbrook Rd., Elmsford, NY 10523: Free catalog ❖ Car-mounted bicycle carriers. 914–592–4812.

Excel Sports International, 3275 Prairie Ave., Boulder, CO 80301: Free catalog ❖ Bicycle computers, off-road equipment, bicycle frame sets, tires, and tubes. 302–444–6737.

Fairfield Processing Corporation, P.O. Box 1130, Danbury, CT 06813: Free information ❖ Lightweight folding bicycle fairing. 800–442–2271; 203–371–1901 (in CT).

Giro Sport Designs, 2880 Research Park Dr., Soquel, CA 90573: Free information ❖ Lightweight foam helmets. 800–969–4476.

Hike-A-Bike Inc., 2706 S. Willow Ave., Fresno, CA 93725: Free information ❖ Easy-to-install automobile carrier for up to four bicycles. 800–541–4453.

Kangaroo, Division Alpenlite, 3891 N. Ventura Ave., Ventura, CA 93001: Free information ❖ Frame and saddle bags. 805–653–0431.

Lone Peak, 3474 S. 2300 East, Salt Lake City, UT 84109: Free information ❖ Frame and saddle bags. 800–777–7679.

Madden USA, 2400 Central Ave., Boulder, CO 80301: Free information ❖ Frame and saddle bags. 303–442–5828.

Overland Equipment, 2145 Park Ave., Ste. 4, Chico, CA 95928: Free information ❖ Frame and saddle bags. 916–894–5605.

Pedal Pusher Ski & Sport, 658 Easton Rd., Rt. 611, Horsham, PA 19044: Free catalog ❖ Bicycles, frames, components, tools, clothing, and car carry-all racks. 215–672–0202.

Pedal Pusher-Top Gear, 1599 Cleveland Ave., Santa Rosa, CA 95401: Free information ❖ Bicycles, frame sets, other components, safety equipment, tools, locks, and pumps. 215–672–0202.

Performance Bicycle Shop, 1 Performance Way, Chapel Hill, NC 27514: Free catalog ❖ Clothing, frames, bicycles and parts, and frame and saddle bags. 919–933–9113.

REI Recreational Equipment Company, Sumner, WA 98352: Free catalog ❖ Frame and saddle bags. 800–426–4840.

Schwinn Bicycle Company, 1690 38th St., Boulder, CO 80301: Free information with long SASE ❖ Bicycle computer that measures current and maximum speeds, trip distance, odometer readings, and cadence. 303–939–0100.

Malcom Smith Products, 252 Granite St., Corona, CA 91719: Free information ❖ Ultralight bicycle helmet that meets ANSI standards. 800–854–4742; 909–340–3301 (in CA).

Specialized Bicycle Components, 15130 Concord Cir., Morgan Hill, CA 95037: Free information ❖ Frame and saddle bags. 800–245–3462; 408–779–6229 (in CA).

Spoke A.R.T., 1715 E. Evans, Denver, CO 80210: Catalog $1 (refundable) ❖ Bicycle parts. 800–327–8532; 800–327–8358 (in CO).

Third Hand, P.O. Box 212, Mt. Shasta, CA 96067: Free catalog ❖ Bicycle repair tools, repair stands, parts, and how-to books. 916–926–2600.

Ultimate Support Systems, 2506 Zurich Dr., Fort Collins, CO 80522: Free information ❖ Bicycle repair stands. 303–493–4488.

Vetta/Orleander USA, 14553 Delano St., Van Nuys, CA 91411: Free information with a long SASE ❖ Bicycle computers. 818–780–8808.

ZZIP Designs, Box 14, Davenport, CA 95017: Catalog $1 ❖ Bicycle fairings. 408–425–8650.

Clothing

Canari Cycle Wear, 10025 Huennekens St., San Diego, CA 92121: Free information ❖ Winter apparel for bikers. 800–929–2925; 619–455–8245 (in CA).

Cannondale Corporation, P.O. Box 122, Georgetown, CT 06821: Free information ❖ Jackets and tights for women and frame and saddle bags. 800–245–3872; 203–544–9800 (in CT).

The Finals, 21 Minisink Ave., Port Jervis, NY 12771: Free catalog ❖ Bicycling, aerobic, swimming, running, and exercise clothing. 914–856–5291.

Pearl Izumi, 2300 Central Ave., Boulder, CO 80301: Free information ❖ Wind-resistant tights and jerseys with zippers for easy removal of the front panel. 303–938–1700.

Lite Speed, 3918 W. 1st Ave., Eugene, OR 97402: Catalog $2 ❖ Clothing and rainwear for men, women, and children. 503–345–6665.

Puma USA Inc., 147 Centre St., Brockton, MA 02403: Free information with long SASE ❖ Clothing, shoes, and gloves. 508–583–9100.

Schnaubelt Shorts Inc., 1128 4th Ave., Coraopolis, PA 15108: Free information ❖ Clothing and T-shirts with silk-screening. 800–782–TEAM.

BILLIARDS

Adam Custom Cues, 25 Hutcheson Pl., Lynbrook, NY 11563: Free information ❖ Pool cues. 800–645–2162; 516–593–5050 (in NY).

Ajay Leisure Products Inc., 1501 E. Wisconsin St., Delavan, WI 53115: Free information with list of retailers ❖ Billiard balls, bridges, chalk, cues and cases, and racks. 800–558–3276; 414–728–5521 (in WI).

Amerola Sports Inc., 4719 Hatfield St., Pittsburgh, PA 15201: Free information ❖ Billiard balls, bridges, chalk, cues and cases, and racks. 800–426–3765.

Beach Manufacturing, 624 Poinsettia, Santa Ana, CA 92701: Free information ❖ Billiard tables. 800–443–5570.

Billiard Pro Shop, 3673 Mendenhall South, Memphis, TN 38115: Free information ❖ Cues, cases, and billiard tables. 800–365–4776; 901–366–1124 (in TN).

Black Boar, 5110 College Ave., College Park, MD 20740: Free information ❖ Handcrafted pool cues. 301–277–3236.

Blatt Billiards, 809 Broadway, New York, NY 10003: Catalog $10 ❖ Custom and antique pool tables. 212–674–8855.

Connelly Billiard Manufacturing, 2540 E. Grant Rd., Tucson, AZ 85716: Free information ❖ Billiard tables. 602–881–5503.

Creative Inventions, 7741 Alabama, Unit 11, Canoga Park, CA 91303: Free information ❖

Cues and cases. 800–388–5132; 818–883–5131 (in CA).

D & R Industries, 7111 Capitol Dr., Lincolnwood, IL 60645: Free information ❖ Billiard balls, bridges, chalk, cues and cases, and racks. 800–323–2852; 708–677–3200 (in IL).

Dufferin Inc., 4240 Grove Ave., Gurnee, IL 60031: Free information ❖ Pool cues. 708–244–4762.

Elite Custom Cues Inc., P.O. Box 4224, Lincoln, NE 68504: Free information ❖ Cues. 402–464–8401.

Escalade Sports, P.O. Box 889, Evansville, IN 47706: Free catalog ❖ Pool tables. 800–457–3373; 812–467–1200 (in IN).

Huebler Industries Inc., P.O. Box 644, Linn, MO 65051: Free information ❖ Pool cues. 314–897–3692.

Indian Industries Inc., P.O. Box 889, Evansville, IN 47706: Free catalog ❖ Racks and cues. 800–457–3373; 812–467–1200 (in IN).

International Billiards Inc., 2311 Washington Ave., Houston, TX 77007: Free information ❖ Billiard balls, bridges, chalk, cues and cases, and racks. 800–255–6386; 713–869–3237 (in TX).

It's George, 360 Gloria St., Shreveport, LA 71105: Free information ❖ Pool cue cases. 800–343–6743.

J-S Sales Company Inc., 5 S. Fulton Ave., Mt. Vernon, NY 10550: Free information ❖ Billiard balls, bridges, chalk, cues and cases, non-slate and slate tables, and racks. 800–431–2944; 914–668–8051 (in NY).

Kasson Game Tables, 11 Commerce Rd., Babbitt, MN 55706: Free information ❖ Billiard tables. 218–827–3701.

Mueller Sporting Goods Inc., 4825 S. 16th, Lincoln, NE 68512: Free catalog ❖ Billiard and dart supplies. 800–925–7665; 402–423–8888 (in NE).

National Merchandise of Virginia, 758 Westover Dr., Danville, VA 24541: Free catalog ❖ Cues and cases. 800–843–3483.

Palmer Billiard Corporation, 307 Morris Ave., Elizabeth, NJ 07208: Free information ❖ Billiard balls, bridges, chalk, cues and cases, and racks. 909–289–4778.

Pennray Billiard & Recreational Products, 6400 W. Gross Point Rd., Niles, IL 60714:

Free catalog ❖ Dart, billiard, and soccer equipment. 800–523–8934.

Schmelke Manufacturing Company, 1879 28th Ave., Rice Lake, WI 54868: Free information ❖ Pool cue cases. 715–234–6553.

Sporty's Preferred Living Catalog, Clermont Airport, Batavia, OH 45103: Free catalog ❖ Billiard tables complete with balls, rack, bridge, and cues. 800–543–8633.

Trusty Enterprises Inc., 4212 Baldwin Ave., El Monte, CA 91731: Free catalog ❖ Cues and cases. 800–222–2174; 818–447–8636 (in CA).

Universal Bowling, Golf & Billiard Supplies, 619 S. Wabash Ave., Chicago, IL 60605: Free catalog ❖ Billiard supplies. 800–523–3037.

Valley Recreation Products Inc., P.O. Box 656, Bay City, MI 48707: Free information ❖ Cues. 800–248–2837; 517–892–4536 (in MI).

Voit Sports, 1451 Pittstand-Victor Rd., 100 Willowbrook Office Park, Fairport, NY 14450: Free information ❖ Billiard balls, bridges, chalk, cues and cases, and racks. 800–444–VOIT.

Wa-Mac Inc., Highskore Products, P.O. Box 128, Carlstadt, NJ 07410: Free information ❖ Billiard balls, bridges, chalk, cues and cases, and racks. 800–447–5673; 201–438–7200 (in NJ).

World of Leisure Manufacturing Company, 9779 Yucca Rd., Adelanto, CA 92301: Free information ❖ Billiard balls, bridges, chalk, cues and cases, and racks. 619–246–3790.

BINOCULARS

Adorama, 42 W. 18th St., New York, NY 10011: Catalog $3 ❖ Binoculars and telescope equipment. 212–741–0052.

Advance Camera Corporation, 15 W. 46th St., New York, NY 10036: Free information ❖ Binoculars. 212–944–1410.

AGS Company, 2750 Clement St., San Francisco, CA 94121: Free information ❖ Night-vision binoculars.

Armchair Sailor Bookstore, 543 Thames St., Newport, RI 02840: Free information ❖ Binoculars. 401–847–4252.

Astro-Tech, 222 W. Main, P.O. Box 2001, Ardmore, OK 73402: Catalog $1 ❖ Binoculars, telescopes, and electro-optical and science equipment. 405–226–3074.

Astro World, 5126 Belair Rd., Baltimore, MD 21206: Free price list with long SASE ❖ Binoculars. 410–483–5100.

Astronomics, 2401 Tee Cir., Ste. 106, Norman, OK 73069: Free information ❖ Binoculars. 405–364–0858.

Beckson Marine, 165 Holland Ave., Bridgeport, CT 06605: Catalog $3.25 ❖ Binoculars. 203–333–1412.

Berger Brothers Camera Exchange, 209 Broadway, Amityville, NY 11701: Free information ❖ Binoculars. 800–262–4160.

Black Forest Observatory, 12815 Porcupine Ln., Colorado Springs, CO 80908: Free information with long SASE ❖ Binoculars. 719–495–3828.

California Telescope Company, P.O. Box 1338, Burbank, CA 91507: Catalog $5 ❖ Binoculars. 818–505–8424.

Celestron International, 2835 Columbia St., Torrance, CA 90503: Catalog $2 ❖ Binoculars. 310–328–9560.

Chinon America Inc., 1065 Bristol Rd., Mountainside, NJ 07092: Free information ❖ Binoculars. 908–654–0404.

Christophers Ltd., 2401 Tee Cir., Ste. 106, Norman, OK 73069: Free information ❖ Binoculars. 405–364–4898.

City Camera, 15336 W. Warren, Dearborn, MI 46126: Free information ❖ Binoculars and spotting scopes. 800–359–5085.

Compass Industries, 104 E. 25th St., New York, NY 10010: Free information ❖ Binoculars. 212–473–2614.

Cosmic Connections Inc., P.O. Box 7, Aurora, IL 60505: Catalog $2 ❖ Binoculars. 800–634–7702.

Cosmos Ltd., 9215 Waukegan Rd., Morton Grove, IL 60053: Free information ❖ Binoculars. 800–643–2351.

Danley's, P.O. Box 4401, Half Moon, NY 12065: Catalog $2 (refundable) ❖ Binoculars and cases. 518–664–2014.

Eagle Optics, 716 S. Whitney Way, Madison, WI 53711: Free catalog ❖ Binoculars. 608–271–4751.

Edmund Scientific Company, Edscorp Building, Barrington, NJ 08007: Free catalog ❖ Binoculars, telescopes, and other educational and science equipment. 609–573–6260.

Europtik Ltd., P.O. Box 319, Dunmore, PA 18509: Free information ❖ Binoculars and riflescopes. 717–347–6049.

Eye-1 Optics, 1525 Xenia Ave., Yellow Springs, OH 45387: Free information ❖ Binoculars and spotting scopes. 800–800–EYE-1.

Focus Camera, 4419 13th Ave., Brooklyn, NY 11219: Free information ❖ Binoculars. 718–436–6262.

Fujinon, 10 High Point Dr., Wayne, NJ 07470: Free information ❖ Binoculars. 201–633–5600.

G & S Photo & Electronics, 2119 Utica Ave., Brooklyn, NY 11234: Free information ❖ Binoculars, photographic equipment, camcorders, and video and audio accessories. 800–879–9438; 215–527–5261 (in PA).

Garden State Camera, 101 Kuller Rd., Clifton, NJ 07015: Free information ❖ Binoculars, photographic equipment, camcorders, and video and audio accessories. 201–742–5777.

Helix, 310 S. Racine, Chicago, IL 60607: Free catalog ❖ Binoculars. 800–33–HELIX; 312–CAMERAS (in IL).

HP Marketing Group, 16 Chapin Rd., Pine Brook, NJ 07058: Free information ❖ Binoculars. 201–808–9010.

ITT Night Vision, 7635 Plantation Rd., Roanoke, VA 24019: Free information and list of retailers ❖ Night vision optical viewer. 800–448–8678.

A. Jaegers Optical Supply Company, 11 Roosevelt Ave., Spring Valley, NY 11581: Free catalog ❖ Surplus binoculars, telescopes, lenses, and prisms. 516–599–3167.

Jason Empire, 9200 Cody, Box 14930, Overland Park, KS 66214: Free information ❖ Binoculars. 913–888–0220.

Kalimar, 622 Goddard Ave., Chesterfield, MO 63017: Free information ❖ Binoculars. 314–532–4511.

Khan Scope Center, 3243 Dufferin St., Toronto, Ontario, Canada M6A 2T2: Free price list ❖ Binoculars. 416–783–4140.

Leica USA Inc., 156 Ludlow St., Northvale, NJ 07647: Free information ❖ Binoculars and camera equipment. 201–767–7500.

Leupold & Stevens Inc., P.O. Box 688, Beaverton, OR 97075: Free catalog ❖ Binoculars. 503–526–5196.

Lumicon, 2111 Research Dr., Livermore, CA 94550: Free catalog ❖ Binoculars. 510–447–9570.

Mardiron Optics, 4 Spartan Cir., Stoneham, MA 02180: Free brochure with two 1st class stamps ❖ Binoculars and astronomy equipment. 617–938–8339.

Meade Instruments Corporation, 16542 Millikan Ave., Irvine, CA 92714: Catalog $3 ❖ Binoculars. 714–556–2291.

F.C. Meichsner Company, 182 Lincoln St., Boston, MA 02111: Free information ❖ Binoculars. 800–321–VIEW.

Minolta, 101 Williams Dr., Ramsey, NJ 07446: Free information ❖ Binoculars. 201–825–4000.

Mirador Optical, P.O. Box 11614, Marina Del Rey, CA 90295: Free information ❖ Binoculars. 213–821–5587.

National Camera Exchange, 9300 Olson Memorial Hwy., Golden Valley, MN 55427: Free information ❖ Binoculars and spotting scopes. 800–624–8107; 612–546–6831 (in MN).

New England Astro-Optics Inc., P.O. Box 834, Simsbury, CT 06070: Catalog $2 ❖ Binoculars. 203–658–0701.

Nikon Photo, Customer Relations, 19601 Hamilton Ave., Torrance, CA 90502: Free information ❖ Binoculars. 800–645–6687.

Optica b/c Company, 4100 MacArthur Blvd., Oakland, CA 94619: Catalog $5 ❖ Binoculars. 510–530–1234.

Optron Systems, 15840 E. Alta Vista Way, San Jose, CA 95127: Free information ❖ Binoculars. 408–923–6800.

Parks Optical Company, 270 Easy St., Simi Valley, CA 93065: Catalog $3 ❖ Binoculars. 805–522–6722.

Pauli's Wholesale Optics, 29 Kingswood Rd., Danbury, CT 06811: Catalog $10 (refundable) ❖ Binoculars. 203–748–3579.

Pentax Corporation, 35 Inverness Dr. East, Englewood, CO 80112: Free information ❖ Binoculars, cameras, lenses, and other optical equipment. 303–799–8000.

Perceptor, Brownsville Junction Plaza, Box 38, Ste. 201, Schomberg, Ontario, Canada L0G 1T0: Free information ❖ Binoculars. 905–939–2313.

Pioneer Research, 216 Haddon Ave., Westmont, NJ 08108: Free information ❖ Binoculars. 800–257–7742; 609–854–2424 (in NJ).

Pocono Mountain Optics, RR 6, Box 6329, Moscow, PA 18444: Catalog $6 ❖ Binoculars, spotting scopes, and astronomy equipment. 800–569–4323; 717–842–1500 (in PA).

Quasar Optics, 3715 51st St. SW, Calgary, Alberta, Canada T3E 6V2: Catalog $4 ❖ Binoculars. 403–240–0680.

Ranging Binoculars, Rt. 5 & 20, East Bloomfield, NY 14443: Free information ❖ Binoculars. 800–828–1495; 716–657–6161 (in NY).

Redlich Optical, 711 W. Broad St., Falls Church, VA 22046: Free information with long SASE ❖ Binoculars, spotting scopes, and telescopes. 703–241–4077.

Ricoh Consumer Products Group, 180 Passaic Ave., Fairfield, NJ 07004: Free brochure ❖ Binoculars. 201–882–7762.

Royal Optics, 20 Glassco Ave. South, Hamilton, Ontario, Canada L8H 1B3: Free brochure ❖ Eyepieces and binoculars.

S & S Optika, 5174 S. Broadway, Englewood, CO 80110: Free information ❖ Binoculars. 303–789–1089.

Santa Anita Camera & Optical Company, 1031 S. Baldwin Ave., Arcadia, CA 91007: Free catalog ❖ Binoculars. 818–447–1854.

Scope City, P.O. Box 440, Simi Valley, CA 93065: Catalog $7 (refundable) ❖ Binoculars. 805–522–6646.

Selsi Binoculars, 40 Veterans Blvd., Carlstadt, NJ 07072: Free information ❖ Binoculars. 201–935–0388.

Shutan Camera & Video, 312 W. Randolph, Chicago, IL 60606: Free catalog ❖ Binoculars. 800–621–2248; 312–332–2000 (in IL).

Simmons Outdoor Company, 201 Plantation Oak Dr., Thomasville, GA 31792: Catalog $2 ❖ Binoculars. 904–878–5100.

Stano Components, P.O. Box 2048, Carson City, NV 89702: Catalog $4 ❖ Night-vision optical equipment. 702–246–5281.

Steiner Binoculars, c/o Pioneer Marketing & Research, 216 Haddon Ave., Westmont, NJ 08108: Free information ❖ Binoculars. 609–854–2424.

Swarovski Optik, One Wholesale Way, Cranston, RI 02920: Free information ❖ Binoculars. 800–426–3089.

Swift Instruments Inc., 952 Dorchester Ave., Boston, MA 02125: Free information ❖ Binoculars and cases, and spotting scopes that can be used on cameras. 800–446–1115; 617–436–2960 (in MA).

Tamron Industries Inc., P.O. Box 388, Port Washington, NY 11050: Free brochure ❖ Binoculars and spotting scopes that can be adapted for camera use as an ultra-telescopic zoom lens. 516–484–8880.

Tasco Sales Inc., P.O. Box 520080, Miami, FL 33152: Free information ❖ Binoculars and other optical equipment. 305–591–3670.

Tokina Optical Corporation, 1512 Kona Dr., Compton, CA 90220: Free information ❖ Binoculars. 310–537–9380.

Roger W. Tuthill Inc., 11 Tanglewood Ln., Mountainside, NJ 07092: Free catalog with 9x12 self-addressed envelope and four 1st class stamps ❖ Binoculars. 800–223–1063.

Unitron Inc., 170 Wilbur Pl., P.O. Box 469, Bohemia,, NY 11716: Free catalog ❖ Binoculars. 516–589–6666.

University Optics, P.O. Box 1205, Ann Arbor, MI 48106: Free catalog ❖ Binoculars. 800–521–2828.

Vivitar Corporation, 1280 Rancho Conejo Blvd., P.O. Box 2559, Newbury Park, CA 91319: Free brochure ❖ Binoculars. 805–498–7009.

Ward's Natural Science, P.O. Box 92912, Rochester, NY 14692: Free information with long SASE ❖ Binoculars. 716–359–2502.

Zeiss Optical Inc., 1015 Commerce St., Petersburg, VA 23803: Free brochure ❖ Binoculars. 800–338–2984.

BIRD FEEDERS & HOUSES

American Pie Company, RD 1, Box 1431, Lake George, NY 12845: Free information ❖ Weatherproof bird feeders. 518–668–3963.

Anyone Can Whistle, P.O. Box 4407, Kingston, NY 12401: Free catalog ❖ Bird feeders, wind chimes, and other musical gifts. 800–435–8863.

Aspects, 245 Child St., Warren, RI 02885: Free information ❖ Wild bird feeders.

The Backyard Sanctuary Company, 550 Warren St., P.O. Box 307, Hudson, NY 12534: Free information ❖ Handcrafted copper feeders. 800–247–3735.

Beck's Feeders, P.O. Box 1030, Williamsburg, IN 47393: Free information ❖

Feeder for chickadees, titmice, nuthatches, and goldfinches.

Bird Bungalows, 620 Ivywood Ln., Simi Valley, CA 93065: Brochure $2 ❖ Handcrafted birdhouses. 805–527–4583.

Bird 'N Hand, 40 Pearl St., Framingham, MA 01701: Free information ❖ Birdseed and feeders. 508–879–1552.

Bluebirds Across America, 293 Piney Bluff Rd., Rembert, SC 29128: Free information ❖ Bluebird houses. 800–524–0291.

Brushy Mountain Bee Farm Inc., Rt. 1, P.O. Box 135, Moravian Falls, NC 28654: Free catalog ❖ Birdhouses, feeders, and beekeeping supplies. 800–BEESWAX.

C & S Products Company Inc., Box 848, Fort Dodge, IA 50501: Free catalog ❖ Wild bird suet products and suet feeders. 515–955–5605.

The Clarion Martin House, RR 1, Box 130, Winfield, MO 63389: Free information ❖ Purple martin house with telescoping pole. 800–845–9178.

Custom Designed Birdhouses, 660 S. Loomis St., Naperville, IL 60540: Brochure $2 (refundable) ❖ Handcrafted birdhouses. 708–961–0417.

Droll Yankees Inc., 27 Mill Rd., Foster, RI 02825: Free catalog ❖ Bird feeders. 401–647–2727.

Duncraft, Penacook, NH 03303: Free catalog ❖ Wild bird supplies, squirrel-proof feeders, birdhouses, bird baths, and books. 603–224–0200.

Erickson Birdhouses, 218 E. Grant St., Lancaster, PA 17602: Free catalog ❖ Wood birdhouses. 800–382–2473.

The Gathering Place, 868 15th St., P.O. Box 163, Otsrego, MI 49078: Free information ❖ Hiking and walking sticks, bamboo and cedar birdhouses, and feeders. 616–694–4477.

Hammer's Wire & Wood, P.O. Box 205, Judson, TX 75660: Free information ❖ Handcrafted birdhouses. 800–227–8841; 903–663–1145 (in TX).

Hyde Bird Feeder Company, 56 Felton St., P.O. Box 168, Waltham, MA 02254: Free catalog ❖ Bird feeders and wild bird food. 617–893–6780.

The Kinsman Company, River Rd., Point Pleasant, PA 18950: Free catalog ❖ Thatched English bird houses. 800–733–4146.

Lady Slipper Designs Inc., Rt. 3, Box 556, Bemidji, MN 56601: Free information with long SASE ❖ Bird houses. 800–950–5903.

Lazy Hill Farm Designs, P.O. Box 235, Colerain, NC 27924: Free information ❖ Bird houses. 919–356–2828.

Lexacon Pet Products, P.O. Box 1091, Kent, OH 44240: Free information ❖ Cage-top play gyms. 800–752–4589.

Los Angeles Audubon Society Bookstore, 7377 Santa Monica Blvd., West Hollywood, CA 90046: Free catalog ❖ Bird and nature books, bookmarks, and feeders. 213–876–0202.

Mac Industries, 8125 South I-35, Oklahoma City, OK 73149: Brochure $1 ❖ Traditional and colonial-style Martin houses, with galvanized steel telescoping and perch pole, stops, and weather vane. 800–654–4970.

Meadowlark Manufacturing Ltd., P.O. Box 689, Liberty, MO 64068: Free information ❖ Bird and bluebird houses, winter roosting boxes, and bird, bluebird, squirrel, and bat feeders. 800–227–9334.

Molly's on Mockingbird Hill, HCR 31, Box 62, Jasper, AR 72641: Catalog $2 ❖ Handmade pine or weathered wood birdhouses. 501–446–2652.

Peters Feeders, Division Peter's Products, P.O. Box 337, Chetek, WI 54728: Free catalog ❖ Hummingbird and oriole feeders and supplies. 800–775–0124.

Plow & Hearth, 301 Madison Rd., P.O. Box 830, Orange, VA 22960: Free catalog ❖ Outdoor furniture, bird houses and feeders, bird baths, and gardening tools. 800–627–1712.

Safeguard Bird Cages, 114–116 Earland Dr., New Holland, PA 17557: Free catalog ❖ Exotic bird and parrot breeding and flight cages. 800–433–1819; 717–354–4586 (in PA).

Studtman's Stuff, P.O. Drawer C, Allegan, MI 49010: Free information ❖ Decorative-style birdhouses.

UPCO, P.O. Box 969, St. Joseph, MO 64502: Free catalog ❖ Cages, birdseed, books, toys, and remedies for birds. 816–233–8800.

Wild Bird Supplies, 4815 Oak St., Crystal Lake, IL 60012: Free catalog ❖ Feeders, bird houses and baths, birdseed mixes, and books on bird care. 815–455–4020.

Zachariasen Studio, N659 Drumm Rd., Denmark, WI 54208: Free brochure ❖

Handmade ceramic birdbaths, fountains, and other garden ornaments. 414–776–1778.

BIRTH ANNOUNCEMENTS

Baby Ink, 11464 Lowell Ave., Overland Park, KS 66210: Free brochure ❖ Birth announcements. 800–467–2696.

Baby Name-A-Grams, P.O. Box 8465, St. Louis, MO 63132: Free brochure ❖ Hand-drawn calligraphy birth announcements. 314–JOY-BABY.

Babygram Service Center, 301 Commerce, Ste. 1010, Fort Worth, TX 76102: Free brochure ❖ Photographic birth announcements. 817–334–0069.

Birth-O-Gram Company, P.O. Box 140398, Miami, FL 33114: Catalog $1 (refundable) ❖ Birth announcements with work-related, sport, and hobby themes. 305–267–1479.

BirthWrites, P.O. Box 684, Owings Mills, MD 21117: Free brochure ❖ Birth announcements with formal, religious, humorous, ethnic, and artistic themes. 410–363–0872.

Contemporary Statements, 9844 S. Hamlin, Evergreen Park, IL 60642: Free brochure ❖ Personalized birth announcements. 800–578–4711.

Custom Cards, RD 2, Box 127, Montgomery, NY 12549: Catalog $3.50 ❖ Birth announcements, gift enclosures, and thank-you cards.

Designs by Denise, P.O. Box 1060, Drexel Hill, PA 19026: Brochure $1 ❖ Birth announcements, thank-you notes, invitations, and greeting cards for twins and multiples. 610–259–1347.

Family News Birth Announcements, 6381 Balmoral Dr., Huntington Beach, CA 92647: Free information ❖ Mini-newspaper style birth announcements.

First Impressions, 3404 W. Wendover Ave., Greensboro, NC 27407: Free brochure with long SASE ❖ Photo baby announcements. 910–292–7088.

Grapevine Graphics, 4231 Knollview Dr., Danville, CA 94506: Free brochure ❖ Birth announcements. 510–736–3871.

H & F Announcements, 3734 W. 95th, Leawood, KS 66206: Free catalog ❖ Birth announcements and invitations. 800–964–4002.

Heart Thoughts Cards, 6200 E. Central, Ste. 100, Wichita, KS 67208: Free brochure ❖ Birth announcements and thank-you notes. 316–688–5781.

MugShot Birth Announcements, P.O. Box 12410, Portland, OR 97212: Free brochure ❖ Birth announcements.

The Personal Touch Birth Announcements, 285 Belvidere Ave., Oxford, NJ 07863: Free information ❖ Personalized birth announcements. 800–453–3882.

Pride & Joy Announcements, 5495 Kendall St., Boise, ID 83706: Free catalog ❖ Birth announcements. 800–657–6404.

Printed Personals, 138 Magnolia St., Westbury, NY 11590: Free brochure ❖ Personalized birth announcements.

BLACKSMITHING

Anchor Tool & Supply Company Inc., P.O. Box 265, Chatham, NJ 07928: Catalog $3 (refundable with $10 order) ❖ Tools and supplies for gold and silversmithing, casting, and blacksmithing. 201–587–8888.

Centaur Forge Ltd., 117 N. Spring St., P.O. Box 340, Burlington, WI 53105: Catalog $5 (refundable) ❖ Blacksmithing equipment. 414–763–9175.

Cumberland General Store, Rt. 3, Box 81, Crossville, TN 38555: Catalog $3 ❖ Blacksmithing equipment, hand pumps, windmills, wood cooking ranges, gardening tools, cast-iron wares, farm bells, buggies, harnesses, and other equipment. 800–334–4640.

Mankel Blacksmith Shop, P.O. Box 29, Cannonsburg, MI 49317: Free information ❖ Forging equipment. 616–874–6955.

NC Tool Company, 6568 Hunt Dr., Pleasant Garden, NC 27313: Free information ❖ Equipment for blacksmiths and farriers. 800–446–6498.

BOATS & BOATING

Boating Apparel & Safety Gear

ACR Electronics, 5757 Ravenswood Rd., Fort Lauderdale, FL 33312: Free information ❖ Marine safety, survival, and security equipment. 305–981–3333.

Atlantis, 30 Barnet Blvd., New Bedford, MA 02745: Free catalog ❖ Foul weather gear and clothing for yachtsmen and fishermen. 508–995–7000.

L.L. Bean, Freeport, ME 04033: Free catalog ❖ Safety apparel, foul weather gear, and deck shoes. 800–221–4221.

Cal-June, 5238 Vineland Ave., North Hollywood, CA 91601: Free information ❖ Safety apparel. 818–761–3516.

Colorado Kayak, P.O. Box 3059, Buena Vista, CO 81211: Free catalog ❖ Men and women's clothing. 800–535–3565.

Commodore Uniform & Nautical Supplies, 335 Lower County Rd., Harwichport, MA 02646: Free information ❖ Boating uniforms, insignia, and flags. 800–438–8643; 508–430–7877 (in MA).

Datrex, P.O. Box 1150, Kinder, LA 70648: Free information ❖ Safety and survival gear. 800–828–1131.

Fireboy Halon Systems, P.O. Box 152, Grand Rapids, MI 49502: Free information ❖ Fire extinguishers for boats. 616–454–8337.

Fletcher-Barnhardt & White, 1211 S. Tyron St., Charlotte, NC 28203: Free catalog ❖ Sportswear. 800–543–5453.

Givens Ocean Survival Systems, I-A Lagoon Rd., Portsmouth, RI 02871: Free information ❖ Safety and survival gear. 800–328–8050; 401–683–7400 (in RI).

Hellamarine, 201 Kelly Dr., Peachtree City, GA 30269: Free information ❖ Hand-held searchlights. 404–631–7500.

Kokatat, 5350 Ericson Way, Arcata, CA 95521: Free information ❖ Waterproof and breathable water sportswear. 800–225–9749; 707–822–7621 (in CA).

Lifesling, Port Supply, 500 Westridge Dr., Watsonville, CA 95076: Free information ❖ Overboard flotation rescue system. 408–728–4417.

Maximum Whitewater Performance, 6211 Ridge Dr., Bethesda, MD 20816: Free catalog ❖ Racing and other boats, paddles, clothing, and safety gear. 301–229–4304.

MRC (Mariner Resource), 86 Orchard Beach Blvd., Port Washington, NY 11050: Free information ❖ Safety harnesses and flotation coats. 800–645–6516.

Mustang Engineered Technical Apparel, 3870 Mustang Way, Bellingham, WA 98226: Free information ❖ Survival flotation clothing for protection against hypothermia and overboard accidents. 800–526–0532; 206–676–1782 (in WA).

Northwest Outdoor Center, 2100 Westlake Ave. North, Seattle, WA 98109: Free catalog ❖ Kayak equipment, safety and rescue equipment, clothing, and books. 800–683–0637.

Patagonia Mail Order, P.O. Box 8900, Bozeman, MT 59715: Free catalog ❖ Sportswear and foul weather clothing. 800–336–9090.

Peconic Paddler, 89 Peconic Ave., Riverhead, NY 11901: Free information ❖ Canoes and kayaks, paddles, life jackets, and dry suits. 516–727–9895.

Port Supply/Lifesling, 500 Westridge Dr., Watsonville, CA 95076: Free information ❖ Overboard rescue system. 800–621–6885; 408–728–4417 (in CA).

Safety Flag Company of America, P.O. Box 1088, Pawtucket, RI 02862: Free catalog ❖ Flags, vests, belts, and other marine safety equipment. 401–722–0900.

Seda Products, 926 Coolidge Ave., National City CA 91950: Free catalog ❖ Kayaks and canoes, life vests, and paddles. 619–336–2444.

Smallwoods Yachtwear, 1001 SE 17th St., Fort Lauderdale, FL 33316: Free catalog ❖ Uniforms and casual boating attire. 800–771–2283.

Survival Products Inc., 5614 SW 25th St., Hollywood, FL 33023: Free information ❖ Emergency life rafts. 305–966–7329.

Survival Technologies Group, 6418 US Hwy. 41 North, Ste. 266, Apollo Beach, FL 33572: Free information ❖ Safety and survival gear. 800–525–2747; 813–645–5586 (in FL).

Switlik Parachute, 1325 E. State St., Trenton, NJ 08607: Free information ❖ Safety and survival gear. 609–587–3300.

Boat-Building Kits & Plans

Benford Design Group, P.O. Box 447, St. Michaels, MD 21663: Catalog $10 ❖ Catboats, yachts, other boat kits, and plans. 410–745–3235.

Boat Plans International, P.O. Box 18000, Boulder, CO 80308: Catalog $24.95 ❖ Boat plans. 604–932–6874.

Boucher Kayak Company, 1907 Ludington Ave., Wauwatosa, WI 53226: Brochure $2 with long SASE ❖ Kayak kits. 414–476–3787.

Bridges Point Boat Yard, Box 342, Brooklin, ME 04616: Free information ❖ Boat kits. 207–359–2713.

Chesapeake Light Craft, 34 S. Pershing Dr., Arlington, VA 22204: Free brochure ❖ Easy-to-build round-bottom kayak kit. 703–271–8787.

Clark Craft Boat Company, 16 Aqualane, Tonawanda, NY 14150: Catalog $3 ❖ Power and sailboat kits, plans, and hardware. 716–873–2640.

Norman Cross Boat Plans, 4326 Ashton, San Diego, CA 92110: Free information ❖ Boat plans. 619–276–0910.

Bruce Farr & Associates, 613 3rd St., P.O. Box 4964, Annapolis, MD 21403: Free information ❖ Boat plans. 410–267–0780.

Farrier Marine, P.O. Box 40675, Bellevue, WA 98015: Free information ❖ Boat plans. 206–957–1903.

Feather Canoes Inc., 3080 N. Washington Blvd., Sarasota, FL 34234: Free information ❖ Boat kits. 813–953–7660.

Glen-L Marine Designs, 9152 Rosecrans, Box 1084, Bellflower, CA 90706: Catalog $5 ❖ Marine hardware, boat-building supplies, and kits for canoes, kayaks and dinghies, plywood and fiberglass boats, and power boats. 310–630–6258.

Great Lakes Boat Building Company, Rt. 5, Box 120, South Haven, MI 49090: Free information ❖ Boat kits. 616–637–6805.

Ken Hankinson Associates, P.O. Box 2551 SE, La Habra, CA 90631: Free information ❖ Boat plans. 310–947–1241.

Monfort Associates, Division Aladdin Products, RFD 2, Wiscasset, ME 04878: Catalog $5.95 ❖ Boat plans and kits. 207–882–5504.

Old Wooden Boatworks, 106 8th St. East, Bradenton, FL 33508: Free information ❖ Dinghy kit. 813–747–8898.

Bruce Roberts International, P.O. Box 10865, Severna Park, MD 21146: Free information ❖ Boat plans. 410–544–4311.

South Shore Boatworks, P.O. Box 29, Hanson, MA 02341: Brochure $2 ❖ Easy-to-build kayak kits and assembled boats. 617–293–9044.

Tri-Star Trimarans, P.O. Box 286, Venice, CA 90291: Free information ❖ Boat plans. 310–396–6154.

Charles W. Wittholz Plans, 100 Williamsburg Dr., Silver Spring, MD 20901: Free information ❖ Boat plans. 301–593–7711.

WoodenBoat Books, Naskeag Rd., P.O. Box 78, Brooklin, ME 04616: Free information ❖ Wood racing shell kit. 800–225–5205; 207–359–4647 (in ME).

Canoes, Kayaks & Paddles

Aire, P.O. Box 3412, Boise, ID 83703: Free catalog ❖ Self-bailing, inflatable touring kayaks. 208–344–7506.

American Traders Classic Canoes, 627 Barton Rd., Greenfield, MA 01301: Free catalog ❖ Wood canoes. 800–782–7816.

Aqua-Bound Technology Ltd., 8938 192nd St., Surrey, British Columbia, Canada V4N 3W8: Free information ❖ Sea cruising and touring kayak paddles. 604–882–2052.

Aquaterra, 11190 Powdersville Rd., Easley, SC 29640: Free information ❖ Kayaks. 803–859–7518.

Baer's River Workshop Inc., P.O. Box 443, Yawgoo Valley Ski Area, Exeter, RI 02822: Free brochure ❖ Canoes, kayaks, and other equipment. 401–295–0855.

Baidarka Boats, Box 6001, Sitka, AK 99835: Free catalog ❖ Folding kayaks. 907–747–8996.

Baldwin Boat Company, RFD 2, Box 268, Orrington, ME 04474: Free information ❖ Kayaks. 207–825–4439.

Balogh Sail Designs, 679 Lola Rd., Cedar Island, NC 28520: Catalog $2 ❖ Folding kayaks and sail rigs and outriggers for hard shell kayaks and canoes. 919–225–6631.

Barton Paddle Company, 402 NW 9th St., Grand Rapids, MI 55744: Free information ❖ Lightweight carbon-fiber canoe paddles. 218–326–8757.

Betsie Bay Kayak, P.O. Box 1706, Frankfort, MI 49635: Free information ❖ Fiberglass and wood/epoxy kayaks. 616–352–7774.

L.L. Bean Inc., Freeport, ME 04033: Free catalog ❖ Canoes and boating and outdoor equipment. 800–221–4221.

Bell Canoe Works, 15355 Hwy. 169, Zimmerman, MN 55398: Information $1 ❖ Kevlar, fiberglass, and graphite canoes. 612–856–2231.

Bending Branches Paddles, 1101 Stinson Blvd. NE, Minneapolis, MN 55413: Free information ❖ Wood cruising paddles with resin-reinforced tips. 612–378–1825.

Berkshire Outfitters, Rt. 8, Cheshire Harbor, Adams, MA 01220: Free information with long SASE ❖ Sea and whitewater kayaks, canoes, paddles, clothing, and other equipment. 413–743–5900.

Black Bart Paddles, 5830 US 45 South, Bruce Crossing, MI 49912: Free information ❖ Ultralight graphite paddles for racing, cruising, and whitewater. 906–927–3405.

Camp Paddle Manufacturing, 9 Averill St., Otego, NY 13825: Free information ❖ Kayak and canoe paddles. 607–988–6842.

Carlisle Paddles, P.O. Box 488, Grayling, MI 49738: Free information ❖ Kayak paddles. 800–258–0290.

Caviness Woodworking Company, P.O. Box 710, Calhoun City, MS 38916: Free information ❖ Paddles and oars. 601–628–5195.

Chesapeake Light Craft, 34 S. Pershing Dr., Arlington, VA 22204: Free brochure ❖ Kits, plans, and finished wood kayaks. 703–271–8787.

William Clements, Boat Builder, 18 Mt. Pleasant St., P.O. Box 87, North Billerica, MA 01862: Catalog $3 ❖ Classic cruising boats, double-paddle and decked sailing canoes, and canoe yawls. 508–663–3103.

Cricket Paddles, 7196 Apen Meadow Dr., Evergreen, CO 80439: Free information ❖ Kayak and canoe paddles. 303–670–1149.

Current Designs, 10124 McDonald Park Rd., Sidney, British Columbia, Canada V8L 5X9: Free catalog ❖ Touring kayaks. 604–655–1822.

Dagger Canoe Company, P.O. Box 1500, Harriman, TN 37748: Free catalog ❖ Canoes and kayaks. 615–882–0404.

Destiny Kayak Company, 1111 S. Pine St., Tacoma, WA 98405: Free information ❖ Touring kayaks. 206–847–7998.

Down River Equipment Company, 12100 W. 52nd Ave., Wheat Ridge, CO 80033: Free catalog ❖ Canoes and inflatable boats. 303–467–9489.

Easy Rider Canoe & Kayak Company, P.O. Box 88108, Seattle, WA 98138: Catalog $5 ❖ Single- and double-seating sea kayaks and canoes, rowing trainers, and paddles. 206–228–3633.

Ecomarine Ocean Kayak Center, 1668 Duranleau St., Vancouver, British Columbia, Canada V6H 3S4: Free brochure ❖ Folding kayaks and kits. 604–689–7575.

Eddyline Kayak Works, 1344 Ashten Rd., Burlington, WA 98223: Free catalog ❖ Kayaks and paddles. 800–788–3634.

Essex Industries, Pelfisher Rd., Mineville, NY 12956: Free catalog ❖ Portable, easy-to-store canoe seat backrest and other accessories. 518–942–6671.

Feathercraft Kayaks, 1244 Cartwright St., Granville Island, Vancouver, British Columbia, Canada V6H 3R8: Free brochure ❖ Lightweight folding kayaks. 604–681–8437.

Bob Foote Products, 4606 E. 11th St., Tulsa, OK 74112: Free information ❖ Whitewater paddles and other canoe equipment. 800–444–1177.

Gillespie Paddles, 1283 Harris Rd., Webster, NY 14580: Free information ❖ Kayak and canoe paddles. 716–872–1723.

Gillies Canoes & Kayaks, Margaretville, Nova Scotia, Canada B0S 1N0: Free information ❖ High-performance canoes and kayaks. 902–825–3725.

Great Canadian Canoe Company, 240 Washington St., Auburn, MA 01501: Free catalog ❖ Handmade canoes. 508–832–4595.

Great River Outfitters, 3721 Shallow Brook, Bloomfield Hills, MI 48302: Catalog $1 ❖ Sea and white water kayaks. 810–683–4770.

Grey Owl Paddle Company, 62 Cowansview Rd., Cambridge, Ontario, Canada N1R 7N3: Free catalog ❖ Paddles. 519–622–0001.

Headwaters, P.O. Box 1356, Harriman, TN 37748: Free information ❖ Kayak and canoe equipment for flat or whitewater. 615–882–8757.

Hydra Tuf-Lite Kayaks, 5061 S. National Dr., Knoxville, TN 37914: Catalog $5 ❖ Touring kayaks for lakes, rivers, or the open sea. 800–537–8888.

Hyside Inflatables, P.O. Box Z, Kernville, CA 93238: Free information ❖ Kayaks, catarafts, and rafts. 619–376–3723.

Impex International Inc., 2979 Montauk Hwy., Ste. 1, Brookhaven, Long Island, New York 11719: Free information ❖ Kayaks. 516–286–1988.

Jersey Paddler, Rt. 88 West, Brick, NJ 08724: Free information ❖ Canoes and kayaks. 908–458–5777.

Keel Haulers Outfitters, 30940 Lorain Rd., North Olmsted, OH 44070: Free catalog ❖ Canoes and kayaks. 216–779–4545.

Ketter Canoeing, 101 79th Ave. North, Minneapolis, MN 55444: Free information ❖ Canoes and paddles. 612–561–2208.

Kiwi Kayak Company, P.O. Box 1140, Windsor, CA 95492: Free information ❖ Two-seat kayaks and other models. 800–K-4–KAYAK.

Klepper America, 168 Kinderkamack Rd., Park Ridge, NJ 07656: Free information and list of retailers ❖ Folding boats and kayaks. 201–476–0700.

Lee's Value Right Inc., P.O. Box 19346, Minneapolis, MN 55419: Free information ❖ Touring kayak paddles. 800–758–1720.

Lightning Paddles, 22800 S. Unger Rd., Colton, OR 97017: Free information ❖ Ultralight paddles. 503–824–2938.

Mad River Canoe Inc., P.O. Box 610, Waitsfield, VT 05673: Free catalog ❖ Canoes for navigating rivers, rapids, or pleasure boating. 802–496–3127.

Mariner Kayaks, 2134 Westlake North, Seattle, WA 98109: Free information ❖ Kayaks. 206–284–8404.

Maximum Whitewater Performance, 6211 Ridge Dr., Bethesda, MD 20816: Free catalog ❖ Racing and other boats, paddles, clothing, and safety gear. 301–229–4304.

Merrimack Canoe Company, 202 Harper Ave., Crossville, TN 38555: Free information ❖ Fiberglass canoes. 615–484–4556.

Mitchell Paddles Inc., RD 2, P.O. Box 922, Canaan, NH 03741: Free information ❖ Canoe and kayak paddles and dry suits. 603–523–7004.

Mohawk Canoes, 963 North Hwy. 427, Longwood, FL 32750: Free information ❖ Solo and tandem canoes. 407–834–3233.

Navarro Canoe Company, 17901 Van Arsdale, Potter Valley, CA 95469: Free information ❖ Lightweight canoes. 707–743–1255.

Necky Kayaks Ltd., 1100 Riverside Rd., Abbotsford, British Columbia, Canada V25 4N2: Free information ❖ Touring kayaks. 604–850–1206.

New Wave Kayak Products, 2535 Roundtop Rd., Middletown, PA 17057: Free catalog ❖ Cruising and racing kayaks, paddles, and helmets. 717–944–6320.

Nimbus Paddles, 2330 Tyner St., Unit 6, Port Coquilam, British Columbia, Canada V3C 2Z1: Free information ❖ Touring, whitewater kayak, and recreational canoe paddles. 604–941–8138.

Northwest Design Works Inc., 12322 Hwy. 99 South, #100, Everett, WA 98204: Free information ❖ Handcrafted kayak and canoe paddles. 800–275–3311.

Northwest Kayaks, 15145 NE 90th, Redmond, WA 98052: Free information ❖ Handcrafted kayaks. 800–648–8908; 206–869–1107 (in WA).

Northwest Outdoor Center, 2100 Westlake Ave. North, Seattle, WA 98109: Free catalog ❖ Kayak equipment, safety and rescue equipment, clothing, and books. 800–683–0637.

Nova Craft Canoe, 4389 Exeter Rd., London, Ontario, Canada N6L 1A4: Free catalog ❖ Whitewater kayaks. 519–652–3649.

Ocean Kayak Inc., 1920 Main St., Ferndale, WA 98248: Free information ❖ Ocean kayaks and clothing. 800–8–KAYAKS.

Old Town Canoe Company, 58 Middle St., Old Town, ME 04468: Free catalog ❖ Canoes. 800–595–4400.

Outdoor Sports Headquarters Inc., 967 Watertower Ln., Dayton, OH 45449: Free information ❖ Inflatable boats, canoes, and paddle boats. 513–865–5855.

Pacific Water Sports, 16055 Pacific Hwy. South, Seattle, WA 98188: Free brochure ❖ Kayaks and paddles. 206–246–9385.

Paddle & Pack Outfitters Inc., P.O. Box 50299, Nashville, TN 37205: Free catalog ❖ Canoeing, kayaking, and backpacking equipment. 800–786–5565.

Pakboats, P.O. Box 700, Enfield, NH 03748: Free information ❖ Folding canoes. 603–632–7654.

Peconic Paddler, 89 Peconic Ave., Riverhead, NY 11901: Free information ❖ Canoes and kayaks, paddles, life jackets, and dry suits. 516–727–9895.

Perception, 111 Kayaker Way, Easley, SC 29642: Free information ❖ Kayaks for river running. 803–859–7518.

Piragis Northwoods Company, 105 N. Central Ave., Ely, MN 55731: Catalog $2 ❖ Canoes, boating gear, boats, videos and tapes, and trail foods. 800–223–6565.

Primex of California, P.O. Box 505, Benicia, CA 94510: Free information ❖ Kayak and canoe carrier, helmets, gloves, face-savers, sailing rigs, and repair supplies. 707–746–6855.

Pro Canoe, 5710 Capital Blvd., Raleigh, NC 27604: Free information ❖ Canoes and kayaks. 919–872–6999.

Pygmy Boat Company, P.O. Box 1529, Port Townsend, WA 98368: Catalog $3 ❖ Kayak and rowing skiff kits. 206–385–6143.

Quimby's Paddle Designs, P.O. Box 677, Mellen, WI 54546: Free information ❖ Recreational and tripping canoes and touring kayak paddles. 715–274–3416.

RGP Composites, 9628 153rd Ave. NE, Redmond, WA 98052: Free information ❖ Whitewater, slalom, touring, canoe, racing, and recreational paddles. 800–899–2610; 206–969–7272 (in WA).

Rutabaga, 220 W. Broadway, Madison, WI 53716: Free information ❖ Canoes and kayaks. 800–I–PADDLE.

Sawbill Canoe Outfitters, Box 2127, Tofte, MN 55615: Free information ❖ Ultralite canoes. 218–387–1360.

Sawyer Paddles & Oars, P.O. Box 624, Rogue River, OR 97537: Free information ❖ Wood paddles and oars with fiberglass tips. 503–535–3606.

Seavivor, 576 Arlington Ave., Des Plaines, IL 60016: Free catalog ❖ Folding kayaks. 708–297–5953.

Seda Products, 926 Coolidge Ave., National City CA 91950: Free catalog ❖ Kayaks and canoes, life vests, and paddles. 619–336–2444.

Sevylor USA, 6651 E. 26th St., Los Angeles, CA 90040: Free information ❖ Inflatable boats, canoes, kayaks, dinghies, paddles, and oars. 213–727–6013.

Shaw & Tenney, P.O. Box 213, Orono, ME 04473: Free catalog ❖ Oars and paddles. 207–866–4867.

SOAR Inflatables, 507 N. 13th St., Ste. 409, St. Louis, MO 63103: Free information ❖ Solo and tandem inflatable canoes. 314–436–0016.

South Shore Boatworks, P.O. Box 29, Hanson, MA 02341: Brochure $2 ❖ Sea kayak kits. 617–293–9044.

Southern Exposure Sea Kayaks, P.O. Box 4530, Tequesta, FL 33469: Free information ❖ Sea kayaks. 407–575–4530.

Spartina Kayak Company, 105 Jordan Rd., South Dartmouth, MA 02748: Free information ❖ Lightweight wood/glass hybrid kayaks. 508–998–5121.

Spring Harbor Kayak Company, 5156 Spring Ct., Madison, WI 63705: Free information ❖ Single and tandem seating kayak kits.

Stowe Canoe & Snowshoe Company, River Rd., Box 207, Stowe, VT 05672: Free information ❖ Lightweight fiberglass canoes. 802–253–7398.

Timberwolf Outdoors, 4606 E. 11th, Tulsa, OK 74112: Free catalog ❖ Canoeing and camping equipment. 800–444–1177.

Venture Sails, 230 Wilkes Cir., Santa Creuz, CA 95060: Free information ❖ Easy-to-use sails for kayaks. 408–427–2267.

We-No-Nah Canoes, Box 247, Winona, MN 55987: Free catalog ❖ Canoes for whitewater and flatwater boating and racing. 507–454–5430.

West Side Boat Shop, 7661 Tonawanda Creek Rd., Lockport, NY 14094: Catalog $1 ❖ Lightweight ocean kayaks.

Western Canoeing Inc., Box 115, Abbotsford, British Columbia, Canada V2S 4N8: Information $1 ❖ Kayaking and canoeing equipment. 604–853–9320.

Wilderness House, 1048 Commonwealth Ave., Boston, MA 02215: Free information ❖ Small boats, sea kayaks, canoes, lightweight sleeping bags, tents, packs, shoes and boots, and clothing. 617–277–5858.

Wildwasser Sport USA Inc., P.O. Box 4617, Boulder, CO 80306: Free information ❖ Racing and touring kayaks. 303–444–2336.

Wildwater Designs, 230 Penllyn Pike, Penllyn, PA 19422: Free catalog ❖ Canoes, paddles, clothing, and accessories. 800–426–2027.

Windspeed Designs, Giant Slide, Mt. Desert, ME 04660: Free information ❖ Single and double-quick reefing spinnakers for kayaks. 207–276–5612.

Wonder Boats, 465 Hamilton Rd., Bossier City, LA 71111: Free brochure ❖ Canoes and dinghy workboats. 318–742–1100.

Inflatable Boats

Academy Broadway Corporation, 5 Plant Ave., Vanderbilt Industrial Park, Smithtown, NY 11787: Free information ❖ Inflatable boats and dinghies. 516–231–7000.

Achilles Inflatable Craft, 355 Murray Hill Pkwy., East Rutherford. NJ 07073: Free information ❖ Inflatable boats. 201–438–6400.

Aire, P.O. Box 3412, Boise, ID 83703: Free catalog ❖ Self-bailing, inflatable touring kayaks. 208–344–7506.

Altco Trading International, 6 Macaulay St. East, Hamilton, Ontario, Canada L8L 8B1: Free information ❖ Soft and rigid bottom inflatable dinghies. 416–521–1061.

Alvimar Manufacturing Company Inc., 51–02 21st St., Long Island City, NY 11101: Free information ❖ Inflatable boats. 718–937–0404.

Avon Seagull Marine, 1851 McGaw Ave., Irvine, CA 92714: Free catalog ❖ Inflatable boats. 714–250–0880.

Berry Scuba Company, 6674 Northwest Hwy., Chicago, IL 60631: Free catalog ❖ Inflatable boats, watches, clothing, skin diving and scuba equipment, diving lights, and underwater cameras. 800–621–6019; 312–763–1626 (in IL).

Bombard, P.O. Box 400, Thompson Creek Rd., Stevensville, MD 21666: Free information ❖ Inflatable boats. 410–643–4141.

Caribe Inflatables USA, 4444 SW 71st Ave., Miami, FL 33155: Free information ❖ Inflatable boats. 305–667–2997.

Coleman Outdoor Products Inc., 250 N. Saint Francis, Wichita, KS 67202: Free information ❖ Inflatable boats, canoes, and dinghies. 800–835–3278.

Down River Equipment Company, 12100 W. 52nd Ave., Wheat Ridge, CO 80033: Free catalog ❖ Canoes and inflatable boats. 303–467–9489.

High Seas Foul Weather Gear, 880 Corporate Woods Pkwy., Vernon Hills, IL 60061: Free information ❖ Inflatable dinghies. 708–913–1100.

Intercoastal Inc., 919 A. Bay Ridge Rd., Annapolis, MD 21403: Free catalog ❖ Inflatable boats. 410–267–0850.

Kirby Kraft, Box 582, Seachelt, British Columbia, Canada V0N 3A0: Free information ❖ Folding fiberglass, rigid bottom inflatable. 614–885–2695.

Nautica International, 6135 NW 167th St., Miami, FL 33015: Free information ❖ Inflatable dinghies. 305–556–5554.

Northwest River Supplies Inc., 2009 S. Maine, Moscow, ID 83843: Free catalog ❖ Inflatable boats. 800–635–5202.

Novurania Inflatable Boats, 4775 NW 132nd St., Miami, FL 33054: Free information ❖ Inflatable boats. 305–685–2464.

Outdoor Sports Headquarters Inc., 967 Watertower Ln., Dayton, OH 45449: Free information ❖ Inflatable boats, canoes, and paddle boats. 513–865–5855.

Quicksilver Inflatables, W6250 W. Pioneer Rd., P.O. Box 1939, Fond du Lac, WI 54936: Free catalog ❖ Easy-to-tow and stow inflatable boats. 414–929–5000.

Sea Eagle, 200 Wilson St., Port Jefferson Station, NY 11776: Free brochure ❖ Inflatable boats that can be used as fishing platforms, motor runabouts, or yacht tenders. 800–852–0925.

Sevylor USA, 6651 E. 26th St., Los Angeles, CA 90040: Free information ❖ Inflatable boats, canoes, kayaks, dinghies, paddles, and oars. 213–727–6013.

SOAR Inflatables, 507 N. 13th St., Ste. 409, St. Louis, MO 63103: Free information ❖ Solo and tandem inflatable canoes. 314–436–0016.

West Marine Products, 500 W. Ridge Rd., P.O. Box 1020, Watsonville, CA 95077: Free catalog ❖ Inflatable boats. 800–463–0775.

Zodiac of North America Inflatable Boats, P.O. Box 400, Stevensville, MD 21666: Free information ❖ Inflatable boats. 410–643–4141.

Miscellaneous Boats

The Anchorage, 57 Miller St., Warren, RI 02885: Free information ❖ Rigid dinghies. 410–245–3300.

Brooklin Boat Yard, Brooklin, ME 04616: Free information ❖ Custom boats. 207–359–2236.

William Clements, Boat Builder, 18 Mt. Pleasant St., P.O. Box 87, North Billerica, MA 01862: Catalog $3 ❖ Classic cruising boats, double-paddle and decked sailing canoes, and canoe yawls. 508–663–3103.

Dayton Marine Products, 2101 N. Lapeer Rd., Lapeer, MI 48446: Free information ❖ Rigid dinghies. 313–664–0850.

Eastern Marine, Rt. 2, P.O. Box 6255, Rochester, NH 03867: Free catalog ❖ Boat trailers, electronic equipment, bimini tops, boat covers, and dragger, lobster, skiff, sport fishing, and dive boats. 603–332–9706.

Ellis Boat Company Inc., Seawall Rd., Manset, ME 04656: Free information ❖ Fiberglass boats with different interiors and options. 207–244–9221.

Folbot Inc., P.O. Box 70877, Charleston, SC 29415: Free catalog ❖ Boat kits and sail, power, paddle wheel, and folding boats. 800–533–5099.

Futura Surf Skis, 730 W. 19th St., National City, CA 92050: Free brochure ❖ Surfing skis. 619–474–8382.

Lowell's Boat Shop, 459 Main St., Amesbury, MA 01913: Brochure $2 ❖ Shoal draft, beachable, trailerable, and other wood boats. 508–388–0162.

Marshall Catboats, Box 266, South Dartmouth, MA 02748: Free information ❖ Rugged shoal boats. 508–994–0414.

Maximum Whitewater Performance, 6211 Ridge Dr., Bethesda, MD 20816: Free catalog ❖ Racing and other boats, paddles, clothing, and safety gear. 301–229–4304.

North River Boatworks, 6 Elm St., Albany, NY 12202: Brochure $4 ❖ River skiffs and other boats for sails, oars, or engines. 518–434–4414.

Norton Boat Works, 535 Commercial, P.O. Box 464, Green Lake, WI 54941: Free information ❖ Ready-to-use ice boats, parts, kits, and plans. 414–294–6813.

Outdoor Sports Headquarters Inc., 967 Watertower Ln., Dayton, OH 45449: Free information ❖ Inflatable boats, canoes, and paddle boats. 513–865–5855.

Pakboats, P.O. Box 700, Enfield, NH 03748: Free information ❖ General boating and whitewater boats that fold and can be carried in one bag. 603–632–7654.

Porta-Bote International, 1074 Independence Ave., Mountain View, CA

94043: Free information ❖ Folding dinghies. 800–227–8882; 415–961–5334 (in CA).

Chris White Designs Inc., 48 Bush St., Dartmouth, MA 02748: Design Portfolio $10 ❖ Cruising catamarans. 508–997–0059.

Rowing Boats & Shells

F.M. Barretta Rowing Boats, P.O. Box 57, Cold Spring Harbor, NY 11742: Free brochure ❖ Long-cockpit, open water rowing shell with extra storage space and oars. 516–421–1103.

Durham Boat Company, 220 Newmarket Rd., Durham, NH 03824: Free information ❖ Rowing equipment and hardware, wood and composite shells, oars, clothes, books, and videos. 603–659–2548.

Johannsen Boat Works, P.O. Box 570097, Miami, FL 33257: Free information ❖ Rowing and sailing dinghies that can be used as cruising tenders. 305–445–7534.

Little River Marine, P.O. Box 986, Gainesville, FL 32602: Free information ❖ Rowing shells. 904–378–5025.

MAAS Rowing Shells, 1453 Harbour Way South, Richmond, CA 94804: Free brochure ❖ Open water rowing shells. 510–232–1612.

Martin Marine Company, 141 Rt. 236, Eliot, ME 03903: Free catalog ❖ Rowing boats, single hull ocean shells, and a sliding seat rowing skiff kit. 800–477–1507.

Pygmy Boat Company, P.O. Box 1529, Port Townsend, WA 98368: Catalog $3 ❖ Kayak and rowing skiff kits. 206–385–6143.

Sailboats & Supplies

Bacon & Associates, 116 Legion Ave., P.O. Box 3150, Annapolis, MD 21403: Free information ❖ Sailboat hardware and equipment. 410–263–4880.

Bainbridge/Aquabatten, 252 Revere St., Canton, MA 02021: Free information ❖ Sail cloth. 800–422–5684; 617–821–2600 (in MA).

James Bliss Marine Company, 201 Meadow Rd., Edison, NJ 08818: Free catalog ❖ Sail and power boat equipment. 908–819–7400.

Bohndell Sails, Commercial St., Rockport, ME 04856: Free information ❖ Sails, rigging, life lines, and canvas. 207–236–3549.

Canvas Crafts, 501 N. Fort Harrison Ave., Clearwater, FL 34615: Free information ❖ Sail fabrics for the do-it-yourselfer. 813–447–0189.

Cut & Stitch Sailkits, 12306 48th St. East, Sumner, WA 98390: Free information ❖ Sail-making kits. 206–863–4381.

Dwyer Aluminum Mast Company Inc., 21 Commerce Dr., North Branford, CT 06471: Free information ❖ Sailboat masts, booms, rigging, and hardware. 203–484–0419.

E & B Marine Supply Inc., 201 Meadow Rd., Edison, NJ 08818: Free catalog ❖ Sail and power boat equipment. 800–533–5007.

Forespar, 22322 Gilberto, Rancho Santa Margarita, CA 92688: Free catalog ❖ Rigging and hardware. 714–858–8820.

Goldbergs' Marine, 201 Meadow Rd., Edison, NJ 08818: Free catalog ❖ Power and sail boating equipment. 800–BOA-TING.

Johannsen Boat Works, P.O. Box 570097, Miami, FL 33257: Free information ❖ Rowing and sailing dinghies that can be used as cruising tenders. 305–445–7534.

M & E Marine Supply Company, P.O. Box 601, Camden, NJ 08101: Catalog $2 ❖ Power and sailboat equipment. 800–541–6501.

The Rigging Company, 1 Maritime Dr., Portsmouth, RI 02871: Catalog $2 ❖ Sailboat rigging and tools. 800–322–1525; 401–683–1525 (in RI).

Sailrite Kits, 305 W. Van Buren, P.O. Box 987, Columbia City, IN 46725: Free catalog ❖ Sail-making supplies.

Sumner Boat, 334 S. Bayview Ave., Amityville, NY 11701: Free information ❖ Sailing and rowing dinghies. 516–264–1830.

West Marine Products, 500 W. Ridge Rd., P.O. Box 50050, Watsonville, CA 95077: Free catalog ❖ Power and sail boat accessories. 800–463–0775.

Whitehall Reproductions, 1908 Store St., Victoria, British Columbia, Canada V8T 4R4: Free brochure ❖ Handcrafted classic rowing and sailing boats. 604–384–6574.

Nathaniel S. Wilson Sailmaker, Lincoln St., P.O. Box 71, East Boothbay, ME 04544: Free information ❖ Hand-finished sails. 207–633–5071.

General Supplies & Equipment

A & B Industries Inc., 1160 Industrial Ave., Petaluma, CA 94952: Free catalog ❖ Marine hardware for power and sailboats.

Aamstrand Corporation, 629 Grove, Manteno, IL 60950: Free information ❖

Anchor, winch, and general rigging ropes. 800–338–0557; 312–458–8550 (in IL).

Adventure 16 Inc., 4620 Alvarado Canyon Rd., San Diego, CA 92120: Free information ❖ Compasses, boat bags, water purifiers, and rigging ropes. 800–854–2672; 800–854–0222 (in CA).

Atwood Mobile Products, 4750 Hiawatha Dr., Rockford, IL 61103: Free information ❖ Appliances and engineered components and systems for recreational vehicles and boats. 815–877–5700.

Avon Seagull Marine, 1851 McGaw Ave., Irvine, CA 92714: Free catalog ❖ Anchors, barometers, bilge pumps, ropes, and other equipment. 714–250–0880.

Barley Sound Marine, 3073 Vanhorne Rd., Qualicum Beach, British Columbia, Canada V9K 1X3: Free information ❖ Solid and laminated sitka spruce oars. 604–752–5115.

Basic Designs, 355 O'Hair Ct., Santa Rosa, CA 95407: Free information ❖ Plastic collapsible boarding ladders. 707–575–1220.

Beckson Marine, 165 Holland Ave., Bridgeport, CT 06605: Catalog $3.25 ❖ OEM marine products and accessories. 203–333–1412.

Berkeley Inc., One Berkeley Dr., Spirit Lake, IA 51360: Free catalog ❖ Bilge pumps, compasses, boating cables, and rigging, anchor, winch, and other ropes. 800–237–5539; 712–336–1520 (in IA).

James Bliss Marine Company, 201 Meadow Rd., Edison, NJ 08818: Free catalog ❖ Sail and power boat equipment. 908–819–7400.

Boat Owners Association of the United States, Washington National Headquarters, 880 S. Pickett St., Alexandria, VA 22304: Free catalog ❖ Boating equipment. 800–937–9307; 703–823–9550 (in VA).

Boulter Plywood Corporation, 24 Broadway, Somerville, MA 02145: Free catalog ❖ Plywood and hardwood lumber for building boats. 617–666–1340.

L.S. Brown Company, Pawley Industries Corporation, 3610 Atlanta Industrial Dr. NW, Atlanta, GA 30331: Free information ❖ Anchors, bumpers, cables, deck chairs, compasses, paddles, ropes, and other equipment. 404–691–8200.

Canor Plarex, P.O. Box 33765, Seattle, WA 98133: Free information ❖ Folding anchors. 206–621–9209.

Classic Canoes, 627 Baron Rd., Greenfield, MA 01301: Free information ❖ Easy-to-use folding boat walker. 800–782–7816; 413–773–9631 (in MA).

Maurice L. Condon Company, 252 Ferris Ave., White Plains, NY 10603: Catalog $2 ❖ Boat-building lumber. 914–946–4111.

Crook & Crook, 2795 SW 27th Ave., P.O. Box 109, Miami, FL 33133: Free catalog ❖ Boating gear. 305–854–0005.

Cruising Equipment, 6315 Seaview Ave. NW, Seattle, WA 98107: Free information ❖ Marine electrical systems. 206–782–8100.

Durham Boat Company, RFD 2, Newmarket Rd., Durham, NH 03824: Free information ❖ Rowing equipment, marine hardware, wood and composite shells, oars, clothes, books, and videos. 603–659–2548.

E & B Marine Supply Inc., 201 Meadow Rd., Edison, NJ 08818: Free catalog ❖ Sail and power boat equipment. 800–533–5007.

Eastern Marine, Rt. 2, P.O. Box 6255, Rochester, NH 03867: Free catalog ❖ Boat trailers, electronic equipment, bimini tops, boat covers, and dragger, lobster, skiff, sport fishing, and dive boats. 603–332–9706.

Edson International, 476 Industrial Park Rd., New Bedford, MA 02745: Free catalog ❖ Marine hardware. 508–995–9711.

Electra Marine, 610 Merrick Rd., Lynnbrook, NY 11563: Catalog $2 ❖ Marine equipment. 516–599–3003.

Essex Industries, Pelfisher Rd., Mineville, NY 12956: Free catalog ❖ Portable, easy-to-store canoe seat backrest, and other accessories. 518–942–6671.

Flounder Bay Boatbuilding, 1019 3rd St., Anacortes, WA 98221: Free information ❖ Imported hardwood, marine plywood, epoxies, fasteners, paint, and varnish for boat-building and repairs. 800–228–4691.

Frabill Inc., 536 Main St., P.O. Box 499, Allentown, WI 53002: Free information ❖ Anchors, bilge pumps, convenience and comfort aids, lighting equipment, and ropes. 414–629–5506.

Gander Mountain Inc., P.O. Box 248, Gander Mountain, Wilmot, WI 53192: Free catalog ❖ Boating equipment. 414–862–2331.

Glenwood Marine, 1627 W. El Segundo Blvd., Gardena, CA 90249: Catalog $3 ❖ Marine hardware. 213–757–3141.

Goldbergs' Marine, 201 Meadow Rd., Edison, NJ 08818: Free catalog ❖ Equipment for power and sail boating. 800–BOA-TING.

Grove Boat-Lift, P.O. Box 8095, Fresno, CA 93727: Free information ❖ Easy-to-use boat lift. 800–447–5115; 209–251–5115 (in CA).

Happy Bumper Buddy, Idea Development Company, P.O. Box 1290, Issaquah, WA 98027: Free information ❖ Easy-on, easy-off, and easy-to-adjust bumpers. 206–222–6441.

The Harbor Sales Company Inc., 1401 Russell St., Baltimore, MD 21230: Information $1 ❖ Boat-building lumber. 800–345–1712.

Hudson Marine Plywoods, P.O. Box 1184, Elkhart, IN 46515: Free information ❖ Flooring, decking boards, marine plywood, and other lumber. 219–262–3666.

Imtra, 30 Barnet Blvd., New Bedford, MA 02745: Free information ❖ Anchors. 508–990–2700.

Jamestown Distributors, 28 Narragansett Ave., P.O. Box 348, Jamestown, R.I. 02835: Free catalog ❖ Boat-building supplies, marine fasteners, and tools. 800–423–0030.

Jukova Ladders, 828 High Ridge Rd., Stamford, CT 06905: Free information ❖ Hinged, folding boarding ladders. 203–322–9310.

Karry Industries Inc., P.O. Box 5810, Jacksonville, FL 32247: Free information ❖ Automatic, one-step load and unload boat-loader for automotive vehicles. 904–739–1461.

M & E Marine Supply Company, P.O. Box 601, Camden, NJ 08101: Catalog $2 ❖ Power and sailboat equipment. 800–541–6501.

Marinetics Corporation, 1638 Placentia Ave., Costa Mesa, CA 92627: Free information ❖ Electrical power systems, distribution panels, alert and alarm systems, and other equipment. 800–762–1414; 714–646–8889 (in CA).

Maritime Lumber Supply, The Teak Connection, 2391 SE Dixie Hwy., Stuart, FL 34996: Free catalog ❖ Teak furnishings and boat building supplies. 800–274–TEAK; 404–287–0463 (in FL).

Matrix Desalination Inc., 3295 SW 11th Ave., Fort Lauderdale, FL 33315: Free information ❖ Desalinization equipment. 305–524–5120.

Nautica International, 6135 NW 167th St., Miami, FL 33015: Free information ❖ Safety and survival gear. 305–556–5554.

New England Ropes, 23 Popes Island, New Bedford, MA 02740: Free information ❖ High-strength and easy-to-splice polyester ropes. 508–999–2351.

New Found Metals Inc., 240 Airport Rd., Port Townsend, WA 98368: Catalog $3 ❖ Silicon and manganese-bronze marine hardware. 206–385–3315.

Offshore Marine Products Inc., 510 Long Meadow Dr., Salisbury, NC 28144: Free brochure ❖ Davits for inflatable boats and dinghies. 704–636–6558.

Peconic Paddler, 89 Peconic Ave., Riverhead, NY 11901: Free information ❖ Canoes and kayaks, paddles, life jackets, and dry suits. 516–727–9895.

Piragis Northwoods Company, 105 N. Central Ave., Ely, MN 55731: Catalog $2 ❖ Canoes, boating gear, boats, videos and tapes, and trail foods. 800–223–6565.

Roloff Manufacturing, P.O. Box 7002, Kaukauna, WI 54130: Free information ❖ Anchors. 414–766–3501.

Rope Store, 615 Tarklin Hill Rd., New Bedford, MA 02745: Free information ❖ Dock and anchor lines, sheets and guys in twisted nylon, spun dacron, hardware, and filament dacron, and braided parallel filament dacron cordage. 800–634–ROPE.

Rule Industries Inc., 70 Blanchard Rd., Burlington, MA 01803: Free information ❖ Compasses, anchors, pumps, and other marine equipment. 617–272–7400.

Sawyer Paddles & Oars, P.O. Box 624, Rogue River, OR 97537: Free information ❖ Wood paddles and oars with fiberglass tips. 503–535–3606.

Shaw & Tenney, P.O. Box 213, Orono, ME 04473: Free catalog ❖ Oars and paddles. 207–866–4867.

Solo Loader, 3260 W. Highview Dr., Appleton, WI 54914: Free information ❖ Easy-to-use canoe and kayak loader for automobiles. 800–394–1744.

Spring Creek Outfitters Inc., P.O. Box 246, Mt. Iron, MN 55768: Free catalog ❖ Canoe accessories. 218–735–8719.

SSI Boating Accessories, P.O. Box 99, Hollywood, MD 20636: Free catalog ❖ Boating and sport fishing equipment. 301–373–2372.

Suncor Marine & Industrial, 440 Corporate Park., Pembroke, MA 02359: Free information ❖ Anchors. 617–829–8899.

Fred Tebb & Sons Inc., 1906 Marc St., Tacoma, WA 98401: Free information ❖ Sitka spruce for masts and spars, canoes, and oars. 206–272–4107.

Travaco Laboratories, 345 Eastern Ave., P.O. Box 297, Chelsea, MA 02150: Free catalog ❖ Boat repair supplies. 617–884–7740.

Value Carpets Inc., Marine Division, 1802 Murray Ave., Dalton, GA 30721: Free information ❖ Do-it-yourself replacement carpet kits for boats. 800–634–3702.

Voyageur, P.O. Box 207, Waitsfield, VT 05673: Free catalog ❖ Waterproof bags, packs, camera bags, storage and flotation systems, and other performance canoe and kayak gear. 800–843–8985.

West Marine Products, 500 W. Ridge Rd., P.O. Box 50050, Watsonville, CA 95077: Free catalog ❖ Power and sail boat equipment. 800–463–0775.

Instruments & Electronics

Alpha Marine Systems, 1235 Columbia Hill Rd., Reno, NV 89506: Free information ❖ Autopilots and compasses. 800–ALPHA-25.

Apelco Marine Electronics, 46 River Rd., Hudson, NH 03051: Free information ❖ Communication equipment, navigation gear, marine instruments, and other electronics. 603–881–9605.

Aqua Meter Instrument Corporation, Rule industries, Cape Ann Industrial Park, Gloucester, MA 01930: Free catalog ❖ Navigation gear and other electronics. 508–281–0440.

Armchair Sailor Bookstore, 543 Thames St., Newport, RI 02840: Free information ❖ Navigation aids. 401–847–4252.

Autohelm, 46 River Rd., Hudson, NH 03051: Free information ❖ Weather and other marine instruments, compasses and autopilots, and navigation and electronic gear. 603–881–5838.

Baker, Lyman & Company, 3220 South I-10 Service Rd., Metairie, LA 70001: Free information ❖ Navigation aids. 800–535–6956; 504–831–3685 (in LA).

Brookes & Gatehouse, New Whitfield St., P.O. Box 308, Guilford, CT, 06437: Free information ❖ Weather and other marine instruments, communications equipment, compasses and autopilots, and navigation and electronic gear. 203–453–6109.

Celestaire, 416 S. Pershing, Wichita, KS 67218: Free information ❖ Navigation instruments and books. 316–686–9785.

Datamarine International Inc., 53 Portside Dr., Pocasset, MA 02559: Free information ❖ Weather and other marine instruments, compasses, communications equipment, and navigation and electronic gear. 617–563–7151.

Davis Instruments, 3465 Diablo Ave., Hayward, CA 94545: Free information ❖ Weather and other marine instruments, compasses, and navigation and electronic gear. 800–678–3669.

Eagle Electronics, 12000 E. Skelly Dr., Tulsa, OK 74128: Free information ❖ Navigation gear and other marine instruments. 918–437–6881.

Euro Marine Trading Inc., 64 Halsey St., Building 27, Newport, RI 02840: Free information ❖ Weather and other marine instruments, compasses and autopilots, and navigation and electronic gear. 401–222–7712.

Furuno USA, P.O. Box 2343, South San Francisco, CA 94083: Free information ❖ Marine instruments, communications equipment, navigation and electronic gear, compasses, and alarm systems. 415–873–9393.

Garmin, 9875 Widmer Rd., Lenexa, KS 66215: Free information ❖ Communications, navigation equipment, and other electronics. 800–800–1020; 913–599–1515 (in KS).

ICOM America, 2380 116th Ave. NE, Bellevue, WA 98004: Free information ❖ Marine instruments, compasses, navigation and electronic gear, and communications equipment. 800–999–9877.

Ray Jefferson, 4200 Mitchell St., Philadelphia, PA 19128: Free information ❖ Weather and other marine instruments, navigation and electronic gear, and communications equipment.

Kleid Navigation, 443 Ruane St., Fairfield, CT 06430: Free information ❖ Navigation equipment and other electronics. 203–259–7161.

KVH Industries Inc., 110 Enterprise Center, Middletown, RI 02842: Brochure $1 ❖ Hand-held pocket-size compasses, weather and other marine instruments, navigation equipment, and electronics gear. 401–847–3327.

Lowrance Electronics, 12000 E. Skelly Dr., Tulsa, OK 74070: Free information ❖ Marine instruments and electronics. 800–324–4737.

Magellan Systems Corporation, 960 Overland Ct., San Dimas, CA 91773: Free information ❖ Navigation equipment, compasses, communications equipment, and other electronics. 909–394–5000.

Marinetek, 2076 Zanker Rd., San Jose, CA 95141: Free information ❖ Marine electronics and communications equipment. 408–441–1661.

Maximum Inc., 30 Barnet Blvd., New Bedford, MA 02745: Free information ❖ Weather and other marine instruments. 508–995–2200.

Micrologic, 9610 DeSoto Ave., Chatsworth, CA 91311: Free information ❖ Navigation, electronics, and communications equipment. 818–998–1216.

Morad Electronics, 1125 NW 46th St., Seattle, WA 98107: Free information ❖ Antennas. 206–789–2525.

Navico Inc., 7411 114th Ave. North, Ste. 310, Largo, FL 34643: Free information ❖ Weather and other marine instruments, compasses and autopilots, and communications equipment. 813–546–4300.

Netcraft Company, Box 5151, Toledo, OH 43613: Free catalog ❖ Marine electronics, fishing rods, reels, rod and lure building components, and fly-tying supplies. 419–472–9826.

Ockam Instruments, 26 Higgins Dr., Milford, CT 06460: Free information ❖ Weather and other marine instruments and navigation gear. 203–877–7453.

Plastimo USA Inc., Airguide Instruments, 1110 Lake Cook Rd., Ste. 220, Buffalo Grove, IL 60089: Free information ❖ Weather and other marine instruments, autopilots, and navigation and electronic gear. 708–215–7888.

C. Plath, 222 Severn Ave., Annapolis, MD 21403: Free information ❖ Marine instruments, other electronics, and navigation gear. 410–263–6700.

Radio-Holland Group, 8943 Gulf Freeway, Houston, TX 77017: Free information ❖ Alarm systems, other electronics, marine instruments, and communications equipment. 713–943–3325.

Raytheon Marine Company, 46 River Rd., Hudson, NH 03051: Free information ❖ Navigation and electronic gear, communications equipment, and alarm systems. 603–881–5200.

Ritchie Compasses, 243 Oak St., Pembroke, MA 02359: Free catalog ❖ Compasses. 617–826–5131.

Robertson-Shipmate Marine Electronics, 400 Oser Ave., Hauppauge, NY 11788: Free information ❖ Marine instruments, compasses and autopilots, navigation gear, and other electronics. 516–273–3737.

Signet Marine, 505 Van Ness Ave., Torrance, CA 90501: Free information ❖ Weather and other marine instruments, compasses, and navigation and electronic gear.

R.A. Simerl Instruments, 528 Epping Forest Rd., Annapolis, MD 21401: Free information ❖ Weather instruments. 410–849–8667.

Si-Tex Marine Electronics, P.O. Box 6700, Clearwater, FL 34618: Free information ❖ Autopilots, navigation and electronic gear, communications equipment, and alarm systems. 813–535–4681.

Skipper Marine Electronics Inc., 3170 Commercial Ave., Northbrook, IL 60062: Free information ❖ Marine electronics. 800–SKIPPER; 708–272–4700 (in IL).

Sperry Marine, 1070 Seminole Trail, Charlottsville, VA 22901: Free information ❖ Weather and other marine instruments, compasses and autopilots, and navigation and electronic gear. 804–974–2000.

Sport Fishing Video Store, P.O. Box 536, Mt. Morris, IL 61054: Free catalog ❖ Navigation equipment, operation guides, and videos for fishermen. 800–827–0837.

SR Instruments, 600 Young St., Tonawanda, NY 14150: Free information ❖ Weather and other marine instruments. 800–654–6360; 716–693–5977 (in NY).

Trimble Navigation, Marine Division, P.O. Box 3642, Sunnyvale, CA 94088: Free information ❖ Navigation and communications equipment and other electronics. 800–TRIMBLE; 800–221–3001 (in CA).

VDO Instruments, 188 Brooke Rd., Winchester, VA 22603: Free information ❖ Weather, other marine instruments, compasses, and electronics gear. 703–665–0100.

W-H Autopilots, 7586 NE Hidden Cove Rd., Bainbridge Island, WA 98110: Free information ❖ Autopilots for power and sail boats.

Yazaki-VDO, 980 Brooke Rd., P.O. Box 2897, Winchester, VA 22601: Free information ❖ Weather and other marine instruments, compasses, and navigation and electronic gear. 703–665–0100.

Nautical Books, Videos & Gifts

Bennett Video Group, 730 Washington St., Marina del Rey, CA 90292: Catalog $2.50 ❖ Boating, sailing, fishing, scuba diving, water spouts, travel, and other videos. 310–821–3329.

Captain's Emporium, 6600 N. Lincoln Ave., Lincolnwood, IL 60645: Free information ❖ Trophies and gifts. 708–675–5411.

International Marine Publishing Company, Tab Books, Division McGraw Hill, 13311 Montrey Ln., Blue Ridge Summit, PA 17294: Free catalog ❖ Nautical books. 800–233–1128.

Moby Dick Marine Specialties, 27 William St., New Bedford, MA 02740: Catalog $5 ❖ Nautical gifts, decor accessories, and scrimshaw. 800–343–8044.

Mystic Seaport Museum Stores, 39 Greemanville Ave., Mystic, CT 06355: Free catalog ❖ Gifts with a nautical and historical theme. 800–248–1066.

Naval Institute Press, Customer Service, 2062 Generals Hwy., Annapolis, MD 21401: Free catalog ❖ Books on navigation, seamanship, naval history, ships, and aircraft. 800–233–8764.

Preston's, Main Street Wharf, Greenport, NY 11944: Free catalog ❖ Ship's wheels, clocks and bells, tavern signs, harpoons, binoculars, nautical lamps, caps and sweaters, antique maps, glassware, and marine paintings. 800–836–1165.

John F. Rinaldi Nautical Antiques, P.O. Box 785, Kennebunkport, ME 04046: Catalog $3 ❖ American paintings, scrimshaw, and nautical antiquities. 207–967–3218.

Ship's Hatch, 10376 Main St., Fairfax, VA 22030: Brochure $1 ❖ Military patches, pins and insignia, official USN ship ball caps, ship's clocks, military and hatchcover tables, nautical and military gifts, jewelry, lamps, lanterns, ship's wheels, jewelry boxes, and plaques. 703–691–1670.

Sport Fishing Video Store, P.O. Box 536, Mt. Morris, IL 61054: Free catalog ❖ Navigation equipment, operation guides, and videos for fishermen. 800–827–0837.

WoodenBoat Books, Naskeag Rd., P.O. Box 78, Brooklin, ME 04616: Free catalog ❖ Books about boats. 800–225–5205; 207–359–4647 (in ME).

BOCCIE

Pennsylvania Sporting Goods, 1360 Industrial Hwy., P.O. Box 451, Southampton, PA 18966: Free information ❖ Boccie sets. 800–535–1122.

Regent Sports Corporation, 45 Ranick Rd., Hauppage, NY 11788: Free information ❖ Boccie balls and sets. 516–234–2800.

Sport Fun Inc., 4621 Sperry St., Los Angeles, CA 90039: Free information ❖ Boccie sets. 800–423–2597; 818–240–6700 (in CA).

Venus Knitting Mills Inc., 140 Spring St., Murray Hill, NJ 07974: Free information ❖ Boccie sets. 800–955–4200; 908–464–2400 (in NJ).

BOOKKEEPING & ACCOUNTING SUPPLIES

Accountants Supply House, 965 Walt Whitman Rd., Melville, NY 11747: Free catalog ❖ Forms, labels, adding machines, shipping materials, disk storage cabinets, office supplies, furniture, and attache cases. 800–342–5274; 516–561–7700 (in NY).

HG Professional Forms Company, 2020 California St., Omaha, NE 68102: Free catalog ❖ Pre-printed forms, accounting and office supplies, record-keeping systems, and computer paper. 800–228–1493.

Medical Arts Press, 8500 Wyoming Ave. North, Minneapolis, MN 55445: Free catalog ❖ Forms for medical and dental professions.

BOOKPLATES & BOOKMARKS

David Howell & Company, 405 Adams St., Bedford Hills, NY 10507: Free catalog ❖ Bookmarks inspired by museum collections. 914–666–4080.

Lixx Labelsz, 2619 14th St. SW, P.O. Box 32055CC4, Calgary, Alberta, Canada T2T 5X0: Catalog $4 ❖ Labels and bookmarks that combine wildlife designs, calligraphy, eco-action, and recycling. 403–245–2331.

Los Angeles Audubon Society Bookstore, 7377 Santa Monica Blvd., West Hollywood,

CA 90046: Free catalog ❖ Bird and nature books, bookmarks, and feeders. 213–876–0202.

My Own Bookplate, P.O. Box 558, Yellow Springs, OH 45387: Free information ❖ Personalized bookplates. 513–767–2042.

BOOK REPAIR & BINDING

Associated Bindery Inc., 405 E. 70th St., New York, NY 10021: Free information ❖ Book repair and binding services. 212–879–5080.

The Book & Documentation Restoration Company, M. Clyde Murray, 154 Plum St., Oil City, PA 16301: Free information ❖ Bookbinding and rare book restoration services. 814–676–5377.

Colophon Book Arts Supply, 3046 Hogum Bay Rd. NE, Olympia, WA 98506: Free information ❖ Bookbinding and marbling supplies. 206–459–2940.

Imperial Fine Books, 790 Madison Ave., Room 200, New York, NY 10021: Catalog $3 ❖ Bookbinding and restoration services. 212–861–6620.

Library Binding Company, 2900 Franklin Ave., Waco, TX 76710: Free price list ❖ Bookbinding and rare book restoration services. 800–792–3352.

John Neal, Bookseller, 1833 Spring Garden St., Greensboro, NC 27403: Free information ❖ Calligraphy and marbling supplies, books, and bookbinding. 800–369–9598.

Sky Meadow Bindery, P.O. Box 936, Suffern, NY 10901: Free information ❖ Book repair and binding services.

TALAS, 213 W. 35th St., New York, NY 10001: Catalog $5 ❖ Bookbinding supplies. 212–736–7744.

BOOKS

Bargain Books

Barnes & Noble, 126 5th Ave., New York, NY 10011: Free catalog ❖ Books, records, and tapes. 800–242–6657.

Critics' Choice Video, P.O. Box 749, Itasca, IL 60143: Free catalog ❖ Books, records, and video cassettes. 800–544–9852.

Daedalus Books Inc., 4601 Decatur St., Hyattsville, MD 20781: Free information ❖ Publisher overstocks and remainders. 301–779–4102.

Edward R. Hamilton, Bookseller, Box 15, Falls Village, CT 06031: Free catalog ❖ Books selected from publishers overstocks.

Children's Books

Advocacy Press, P.O. Box 236, Santa Barbara, CA 93102: Free information ❖ Books for children and young adults on gender equality, career planning, self-esteem, and self-awareness. 805–962–2728.

Aladdin/Collier Books, MacMillan Children's Book Group, 15 Columbus Circle, New York, NY 10023: Free information ❖ Board books, pop-ups, and paperbacks for children age 3 to 16.

Astor Books, 62 Cooper Square, New York, NY 10003: Free catalog ❖ Children's books. 212–777–3700.

Boyds Mill Press, 815 Church St., Homedale, PA 18431: Free information ❖ Children's books. 717–253–1164.

Charington House, P.O. Box 9661, Bradenton, FL 34206: Free catalog ❖ General non-fiction, multi-cultural, poetry, special, art, and books for early and middle readers and young adults. 813–746–3326.

Cheshire Cat Children's Books, 5512 Connecticut Ave. NW, Washington, DC 20015: Free information ❖ Books, records, and tapes. 202–244–3956.

Children's Book Press, 6400 Hollis St., Ste. 4, Emeryville, CA 94608: Free information ❖ Multicultural and bilingual picture books and audio cassettes for children. 510–655–3395.

Children's Press, 5440 N. Cumberland Ave., Chicago, IL 60656: Free catalog ❖ Books for children. 800–621–1115; 312–693–0800 (in IL).

Chinaberry Book Service, 2780 Via Orange Way, Ste. B, Spring Valley, CA 91978: Free catalog ❖ Books and music for children and adults. 800–776–2242.

Collier/Macmillan Publishing Company, 866 3rd Ave., New York, NY 10022: Free catalog ❖ Novelty books, board books, and pop-ups for children age 3 to 16. 212–702–9026.

Disney Press, 114 5th Ave., New York, NY 10011: Free information ❖ Books based on Disney storylines, characters, and movies. 212–633–4400.

Dover Publications Inc., 31 East 2nd St., Mineola, NY 11501: Free catalog ❖ Children's classics, cut-and-assemble books, coloring books, paper dolls and stickers, and

other educational activity books. 516–294–7000.

EDC Publishing, 10302 E. 55th Pl., Tulsa, OK 74146: Catalog $2 (refundable) ❖ Children's educational books. 800–475–4522.

The Evergreen Press, Box 306, Avalon, CA 94523: Free information with long SASE ❖ Adult and children's books, greeting cards, book marks and bookplates, wedding certificates, calendars, ornaments, paper dolls, postcards, and other 19th- and early 20th-century paper memorabilia. 213–510–1700.

Free Spirit Publishing Inc., 400 1st Ave. North, Ste. 616, Minneapolis, MN 55401: Free information ❖ Nonfiction, psychology and self-help materials for and about gifted, talented, and creative young people, their parents, and teachers. 800–735–7323.

W.H. Freeman & Company, 41 Madison Ave., New York, NY 10010: Free information ❖ Adult and children's books on science and computers. 212–576–9400.

Holiday House Inc., 425 Madison Ave., New York, NY 10017: Free catalog ❖ Books for children, from kindergarten and up. 212–688–0085.

Intervisual Books Inc., 2850 Ocean Park Blvd., Ste. 225, Santa Monica, CA 90405: Free information ❖ Pop-up, novelty, three-dimensional, and puppet books. 310–396–8708.

Kar-Ben Copies Inc., 6800 Tildenwood Ln., Rockville, MD 20852: Free catalog ❖ Judaic books and cassettes. 800–452–7236.

Klutz Press, 2121 Staunton Ct., Palo Alto, CA 94306: Free information ❖ How-to, fun, and song books for children. 415–857–0888.

Koenisha Publications, 3196 53rd St., Hamilton, MI 49419: Free catalog ❖ How-to books for children and adults on specialty hobbies and interests.

The Learning Works, P.O. Box 6187, Santa Barbara, CA 93160: Free information ❖ Children's books for the home and school. 800–235–5767.

Metacom Inc., 5353 Nathan Ln., Plymouth, MN 55442: Free catalog ❖ Golden Age Radio programs, comedy super stars of past years, famous radio plays, foreign language cassettes, coloring books with stories, and read-along books and cassettes for teaching children to read. 800–328–0108.

The Mind's Eye, 37 Commercial Blvd., Novato, CA 94949: Free catalog ❖ Children's favorites and classics, military intrigue, mystery, horror, science fiction, adventure, drama, history, comedy, poetry, and self-improvement, and audio cassettes and compact disks. 415–882–7701.

Music for Little People, Box 1460, Redway, CA 95560: Free catalog ❖ Music books, musical instruments, cassettes, and videos. 707–923–3991.

School Zone Publishing Company, 1819 Industrial Dr., P.O. Box 777, Grand Haven, MI 49417: Free information ❖ Educational workbooks, flashcards, games, audio and video items, and books. 800–253–0564.

Silver Burdett Press, 250 James St., Morristown, NJ 07960: Free information ❖ Beginning-to-read books, and books about nature and animals, science, holiday fun, teen issues, and other subjects. 201–285–7937.

General Books

A.R.C. Books, P.O. Box 2, Carlisle, MA 01741: Free information ❖ Books for collectors of antique radios. 508–371–0512.

Harry N. Abrams Inc., 100 5th Ave., New York, NY 10011: Free information ❖ Art books and pictorial non-fiction. 212–206–7715.

Academic Press Inc., 528 B St., Ste. 1900, San Diego, CA 92101: Free information ❖ Scientific and technical books. 619–231–0926.

Academy Group Limited, 220 E. 23rd St., Ste. 909, New York, NY 10010: Free information ❖ Historical and contemporary books on the arts and architecture. 212–683–8333.

ACS Publications Inc., 408 Nutmeg St., San Diego, CA 92103: Free information ❖ Books on astrology, Tarot reading, psychic understanding, nutrition, healing, and channeling. 619–297–9203.

Bob Adams Inc., 260 Center St., Holbrook, MA 02343: Free information ❖ Books on careers, parenting, self-help, job hunting, and business. 617–767–8100.

Addison-Wesley Publishing Company, One Jacob Way, Reading, MA 01867: Free catalog ❖ Books about computers, child care and health, biographies, children's activities, psychology, current affairs, and business. 617–944–3700.

Advanced Vivarium Systems, P.O. Box 408, Lakeside, CA 92040: Free information ❖ Books on reptiles. 619–561–5103.

Always Jukin', 221 Yesler Way, Seattle, WA 98104: Catalog $2 ❖ Jukebox service manuals, books about jukeboxes, and books and manuals about old phonographs and radios. 206–233–9460.

American Diabetes Association, 1660 Duke St., Alexandria, VA 22314: Free catalog ❖ Books for professionals and people with diabetes. 800–232–3472; 703–549–1500 (in VA).

The American Institute of Architects Press, 1735 New York Ave. NW, Washington, DC 20006: Free information ❖ Books on architecture and design. 202–626–7498.

American Map Corporation Inc., 46–35 54th Rd., Maspeth, NY 11378: Free information ❖ Bilingual dictionaries, travel guides and atlases, travel language products, maps, and other educational publications. 718–784–0055.

American Psychiatric Press Inc., 1400 K St. NW, Washington, DC 20005: Free information ❖ Books on psychiatry and mental illness. 202–682–6262.

American Radio Relay League, 225 Main St., Newington, CT 06111: Free information ❖ Books on how to become a HAM radio operator, get a license, learn Morse code, organize equipment, and operate and set up equipment. 203–666–1541.

The Anglers Art, P.O. Box 148, Plainfield, PA 17081: Free catalog ❖ Books on fishing. 800–848–1020; 717–243–9721 (in PA).

Antheil Booksellers, 2177 Isabelle Ct., North Bellmore, NY 11710: Catalog $1.50 ❖ Books about the navy, maritime, aviation, and military. 516–826–2094.

Antique Collectors Club, Market Street Industrial Park, Wappingers Falls, NY 12590: Free brochure ❖ Books on fine and decorative art, architecture, and gardening. 800–252–5231.

Aperture, 20 E. 23rd St., New York, NY 10010: Free information ❖ Fine art photography books. 800–929–2323.

Appalachian Mountain Club Books, 5 Joy Street, Boston, MA 02108: Free catalog ❖ Maps and hiking, river, and recreation guides. 617–523–0636.

Applause Theatre & Cinema Books, 211 W. 71st St., New York, NY 10023: Free catalog ❖ Books on the theater and cinema. 212–496–7511.

Asian World of Martial Arts Inc., 917 Arch St., Philadelphia, PA 19107: Free catalog ❖ Martial arts books. 800–345–2962; 215–925–1161 (in PA).

The Astronomer's Book Center, 2441 St. John Extnd., Dyersburg, TN 38024: Free catalog ❖ Books on astronomy. 901–285–0228.

Audel Library, MacMillan Publishing Company, 15 Columbus Circle, New York, NY 10023: Free catalog ❖ Books about vocational trades and crafts.

Audio-Forum, 96 Broad St., Guilford, CT 06437: Free catalog ❖ Self-instruction foreign language courses. 800–345–8501; 203–453–9794 (in CT).

August House Publishers Inc., P.O. Box 3223, Little Rock, AR 72203: Free information ❖ Story-teller books. 501–372–5450.

B & B Honey Farm, Rt. 2, Box 245, Houston, MN 55943: Free catalog ❖ Beekeeping books. 507–896–3955.

Backcountry Bookstore, P.O. Box 6235, Lynnwood, WA 98036: Catalog $1 ❖ Books, maps, and videos on backpacking, skiing, biking, paddle sports, trekking, and climbing. 206–290–7652.

Bantam Doubleday Dell Publishing Group Inc., 1540 Broadway, New York, NY 10036: Free catalog ❖ Fiction and non-fiction books. 212–354–6500.

Bantam Doubleday Dell Travel Books, 1540 Broadway, New York, NY 10036: Free information ❖ Travel guidebooks, atlases, and other books. 212–354–6500.

Bantam Electronic Publishing, 1540 Broadway, New York, NY 10036: Free information ❖ Computer books. 212–354–6500.

Barron's Educational Series, 250 Wireless Blvd., Hauppage, NY 11788: Free catalog ❖ Test preparatory books, cookbooks, and child care, pet, craft, and children's books. 516–434–3311.

Basic Books Inc., Division HarperCollins, 10 E. 53rd St., New York, NY 10022: Free catalog ❖ Books on psychology, business, history, science, political science, women's studies, and other subjects. 212–207–7057.

Mel Bay Publications Inc., 4 Industrial Dr., Pacific, MO 63069: Free information ❖

How-to books on musical instruments. 314–257–3970.

Berkshire House Publishers, P.O. Box 297, Stockbridge, MA 01262: Free information ❖ Travel, recreation, self-help, crafts, psychology, and cooking books. 800–321–8526.

Berlitz Publishing Inc., 257 Park Avenue South, New York, NY 10010: Free information ❖ Travel guides and self-instruction foreign language courses. 212–930–2499.

Better Homes & Gardens Books, 1716 Locust St., Des Moines, IA 50336: Free information with long SASE ❖ Books on cooking, gardening, how-to, crafts, and other subjects. 800–678–8091.

Betterway Books, 1507 Dana Ave., Cincinnati, OH 45207: Free catalog ❖ Woodworking books.

Bicycle Books Inc., 32 Glen Dr., P.O. Box 2038, Mill Valley, CA 94942: Free information ❖ Books about bicycles. 415–665–8214.

Black Moon Company, Mail Order Specialty Books, P.O. Box 12510, Baltimore, MD 21217: Free catalog ❖ Hard-to-find books. 410–728–6938.

Warren Blake, Old Science Books, 308 Hadley Dr., Trumbull, CT 06611: Free catalog ❖ Hard-to-find, old-to-early astronomy books and prints. 203–459–0820.

Boerum Street Press, 131 Boerum St., Brooklyn, NY 11206: Free information ❖ Travel guides. 718–599–1393.

Bohemian Brigade Book Shop, 7347 Middlebrook Pike, Knoxville, TN 37909: Catalog $1 ❖ Civil War books and militaria. 615–694–8227.

Book Publishing Company, P.O. Box 99, Summertown, TN 38483: Free brochure ❖ Books on cooking, pest control, natural birth control, midwifery, fertility, and spiritual teachings. 615–964–3571.

Book Sales Inc., 114 Northfield Ave., P.O. Box 7100, Edison, NJ 08818: Free catalog ❖ Books on Americana, Civil War, fine arts, militaria, photography, religion, travel, humor, health, cooking, and crafts. 908–225–0530.

Books By Mail, P.O. Box 1444, Corona, CA 91718: Free catalog with two 1st class stamps ❖ Books on clowning. 909–273–0900.

Books on Cloth, P.O. Box 2706, Fort Bragg, CA 95437: Catalog $2.50 ❖ Books on costumes, textiles, needle arts, and fabrics. 707–964–8662.

Boonton Bookshop, 121 Hawkins Pl., Boonton, NJ 07005: Free catalog ❖ Civil War books. 800–234–1862.

Bowling's Bookstore, Tech-Ed Publishing Company, P.O. Box 4, Deerfield, IL 60015: Free information ❖ Books and videos on bowling. 800–521–BOWL.

Brandy Station Bookshelf, P.O. Box 1863, Harrah, OK 73045: Free catalog ❖ New, rare, and out-of-print Civil War books. 405–964–5730.

Broadfoot Publishing Company, 1907 Buena Vista Cir., Wilmington, NC 28405: Free catalog ❖ Books about the Civil War. 910–686–4816.

Broadway Press, P.O. Box 1037, Shelter Island, NY 11964: Free catalog ❖ Books on theatrical production, scenery construction, and backstage direction. 800–869–6372.

Butterworth-Heinemann, 313 Washington St., Newton, MA 02158: Free catalog ❖ Technical, medical, and professional books. 800–366–2665.

T. Cadman, 2029 Meadow Valley Terrace, Los Angeles, CA 90039: Free catalog ❖ World War II and other military history books.

Calibre Press Inc., 666 Dundee Rd., Ste. 1607, Northbrook, IL 60062: Free catalog ❖ Law enforcement videos, books, and survival products. 800–323–0037; 708–498–5680 (in IL).

Cambridge University Press, 40 W. 20th St., New York, NY 10011: Free catalog ❖ Reference and academic books. 212–924–3900.

Capability's Books, 2379 Hwy. 46, Deer Park, WI 54007: Catalog $1 ❖ Books for gardeners. 800–247–8154.

Carousel Press, P.O. Box 6061, Albany, CA 94706: Free catalog with long SASE ❖ Family travel guides. 510–527–5849.

S. Carwin & Sons Ltd., P.O. Box 2145, Winnetka, CA 91306: Free information ❖ Books on aircraft, the military, and adventure. 800–562–9182.

Chessler Books, P.O. Box 399–89, Kittredge, CO 80457: Free catalog ❖ New, used, and rare books on mountaineering. 800–654–8502; 303–670–0093 (in CO).

Chicago Review Press Inc., 814 N. Franklin St., Chicago, IL 60610: Free catalog ❖ Adult non-fiction and young adult books. 312–337–0747.

Chilton Book Company, One Chilton Way, Radnor, PA 19089: Free catalog ❖ Books about automobiles, crafts, antiques, technical, and business books. 610–964–4000.

Chronicle Books, 275 5th St., San Francisco, CA 94103: Free information ❖ Books about cooking and food, art and photography, architecture, nature, travel, and history. 415–777–7240.

Chronimed Publishing, 13911 Ridgedale Dr., Ste. 250, Minneapolis, MN 55305: Free information ❖ Health, nutrition, wellness, fitness, psychology, and cooking books. 800–848–2793.

Stan Clark Military Books, 915 Fairview Ave., Gettysburg, PA 17325: Catalog $2 ❖ Civil War books. 717–337–1728.

Cliff's Notes Inc., P.O. Box 80728, Lincoln, NE 68501: Free information ❖ Study aids, test preparation guides, and complete study editions. 800–228–4078; 402–421–8324 (in NE).

Collector Books, P.O. Box 3009, Paducah, KY 42002: Free catalog ❖ Books on antiques, depression glassware, pottery, toys, dolls, teddy bears, thimbles, and other collectibles. 502–898–6211.

The Collector's Book Source, 900 Frederick St., Cumberland, MD 21502: Free catalog ❖ Books on dolls and teddy bears. 800–554–1447.

Collectors Clearinghouse, P.O. Box 135, North Syracuse, NY 13212: Free catalog ❖ Price guides and other books for record collectors. 315–458–8214.

The College Board, 45 Columbus Ave., New York, NY 10023: Free information ❖ Books that help students and their families in the transition from high school to college and college to work. 212–713–8166.

Columbia University Press, 562 W. 113th St., New York, NY 10025: Free catalog ❖ Scholarly and general interest books. 212–666–1000.

Compass American Guide, 201 E. 50th St., New York, NY 10022: Free information ❖ United States city and state cultural and historical guides. 212–572–8756.

Complete Traveler Bookstore, 199 Madison Ave., New York, NY 10016: Catalog $1 ❖

Travel guides, books, and maps. 212–685–9007.

Computer Publishing Enterprises, 3655 Ruffin Rd., Ste. 110, San Diego, CA 92123: Free information ❖ Easy-to-read books for the novice and intermediate computer user. 619–576–0353.

Congressional Quarterly Inc., 1414 22nd St. NW, Washington, DC 20037: Free information ❖ Books on government, political science, current affairs, and the Congress. 202–887–8501.

Consumer Guide/Publications International, 7373 N. Cicero Ave., Lincolnwood, IL 60646: Free catalog ❖ Books about automobiles, fitness and exercise, health and medicine, entertainment, and other consumer issues. 708–676–3470.

Consumer Information Center, Pueblo, CO 81003: Free catalog ❖ United States Government books and pamphlets for consumers. 719–948–4000.

Consumer Reports Books, 101 Truman Ave., Yonkers, NY 10703: Free catalog ❖ Books on consumer information. 914–378–2627.

The Cotton Patch, 1025 Brown Ave., Lafayette, CA 94549: Catalog $5 ❖ Quilting books. 800–835–4418.

John S. Craig, 111 Edward Ave., P.O. Box 1637, Torrington, CT 06790: Free information ❖ Hard-to-find instruction manuals for photography equipment. 203–496–9791.

Creative Homeowner Press, 24 Park Way, Upper Saddle River, NJ 07458: Free information ❖ How-to books on home improvement and repair. 800–631–7795.

The Creative Woman's Library, 405 River Hills Business Park, Birmingham, AL 35242: Free information ❖ Craft and sewing books. 800–768–5878.

Crown Publishing Group, 201 E. 50th St., New York, NY 10022: Free catalog ❖ Natural history, military, art, language courses, and other fiction and nonfiction books. 212–572–2600.

Cygnus-Quasar Books, P.O. Box 85, Powell, OH 43065: Free information ❖ Radio astronomy and engineering books. 614–548–7895.

Q.M. Dabney & Company, P.O. Box 42026, Washington, DC 20015: Catalog $1 ❖ Old

and rare aviation, World War II, and other military history books.

Dance Mart, Box 994, Teaneck, NJ 07666: Free catalog with long SASE ❖ Books, prints, music, autographs, and dance collectibles. 201–833–4176.

Daw Books Inc., 375 Hudson St., 3rd Floor, New York, NY 10014: Free information ❖ Science fiction, fantasy, and horror books. 212–366–2096.

Cy Decosse Incorporated, 5900 Green Oak Dr., Minnetonka, MN 55343: Free information ❖ How-to books on cooking, sewing, hunting, and fishing. 612–936–4700.

Deltiologists of America, P.O. Box 8, Norwoods, PA 19074: Price list $1 ❖ Postcard reference books.

Demos Publications, 386 Park Ave. South, New York, NY 10016: Free catalog ❖ Health resources for people with disabilities and chronic disease. 800–532–8663; 212–683–0072 (in NY).

Direct Book Service, 701 B Poplar, Wenatchee, WA 98801: Free catalog ❖ Dog and cat books and videos. 509–663–9115.

David Doremus Books, 100 Hillside Ave., Arlington, MA 02174: Catalog subscription $2 ❖ Used and rare Civil War books. 617–646–0892.

Dover Publications Inc., 31 E. 2nd St., Mineola, NY 11501: Free catalog ❖ Books on arts and crafts, business, hobbies, architecture, science, juvenile interests, health, fiction, and other subjects. 516–294–7000.

Drama Book Publishers, 260 5th Ave., New York, NY 10001: Free catalog ❖ Books on theatrical production, direction, make-up, costumes, and scenery design. 212–725–5377.

Durham's Antiques, 909 26th St. NW, Washington, DC 20037: Catalog $2 ❖ Jukebox service manuals and other books on coin-operated machines. 202–338–1342.

Eastman Kodak Company, Information Center, 343 State St., Rochester, NY 14650: Free information ❖ Photography books. 800–462–6495.

Electronic Technology Today Inc., P.O. Box 240, Massapequa Park, NY 11762: Free information ❖ Books on electronics.

Empire Publishing Service, P.O. Box 1344, Studio City, CA 91614: Catalog $1 ❖ Books about the entertainment industry and performing arts, plays and musicals, musical

scores, and film and theatrical personalities. 818–784–8918.

Eureka! Daylily Reference Guide, Ken Gregory, Editor, 5586 Quail Creek Dr., Granite Falls, NC 28630: Free information ❖ Annual (published in February) reference guide and other books on daylilies. 704–396–6107.

The Evergreen Press, Box 306, Avalon, CA 90704: Free information with long SASE ❖ Adult and children's books, greeting cards, book marks and bookplates, wedding certificates, calendars, ornaments, paper dolls, postcards, and other 19th- and early 20th-century paper memorabilia. 213–510–1700.

Exceptional Parent, P.O. Box 8045, Brick, NJ 08723: Free information ❖ Books for parents with exceptional children. 800–535–1910.

Facts on File Inc., 460 Park Ave. South, New York, NY 10016: Free information ❖ Reference and information books. 212–683–2244.

Families International, 11700 W. Lake Park Dr., Milwaukee, WI 53224: Free catalog ❖ Books, videos, and games for human service professionals and their clients. 800–852–1944.

Farnsworth Military Gallery, 401 Baltimore St., Gettysburg, PA 17325: Free information ❖ Art prints and new, used, and rare Civil War books. 717–334–8838.

The Feminist Press, The City University of New York, 311 E. 94th St., New York, NY 10128: Free information ❖ Books by and about women. 212–360–5790.

Fielding Worldwide Inc., 308 S. Catalina Ave., Redondo Beach, CA 90277: Free information ❖ Travel guides. 310–372–4474.

Firefighters Bookstore, 18281 Gothard St., #105, Huntington Beach, CA 92648: Free catalog ❖ Books, software, and videos for firefighters. 714–375–4888.

Focal Press, 313 Washington St., Newton, MA 02158: Free catalog ❖ Books on photography, cinematography, broadcasting, and the theater. 617–928–2500.

Fodor's Travel Publications Inc., 201 E. 50th St., New York, NY 10022: Free information ❖ Travel books. 212–572–8756.

Forsythe Travel Library Inc., P.O. Box 2975, Shawnee Mission, KS 66201: Free brochure ❖ Travel books, maps, and other publications. 800–367–7984; 913–384–3440 (in KS).

W.H. Freeman & Company, 41 Madison Ave., New York, NY 10010: Free information ❖ Adult and children's books on science and computers. 212–576–9400.

Samuel French Catalog, 45 W. 25th St., New York, NY 10010: Catalog $4.50 ❖ Scripts for plays and other theatrical productions. 212–206–8990.

Samuel French Trade, 7623 Sunset Blvd., Hollywood CA 90046: Free catalog ❖ Books about the film industry. 213–876–0570.

Fulcrum Publishing, 350 Indiana St., Ste. 350, Golden, CO 80401: Free catalog ❖ Books on a variety of subjects. 800–992–2908.

Fun Publishing Company, 2121 Alpine Pl., Cincinnati, OH 45206: Free information ❖ Portable keyboard, piano, xylophone, and other teach-yourself-to-play books. 513–533–3636.

Gallaudet University Press, 800 Florida Ave. NE, Washington, DC 20002: Free catalog ❖ Books for children and adults about deafness, hard-of-hearing, and sign language. 800–451–1073.

Gambler's Book Shop, 630 S. 11th St., Las Vegas, NV 89101: Free catalog ❖ Books and computer software on gambling. 800–522–1777; 702–382–7555 (in NV).

GardenWay Publishing, Schoolhouse Rd., Pownal, VT 05261: Free information ❖ How to books on crafts, building, gardening, cooking, nature, beer and wine, and animals. 802–823–5811.

Paul Gaudette Books, 2050 E. 17th St., Tucson, AZ 85719: Catalog $1 ❖ Military aircraft books. 800–874–3097.

The Gemmary, P.O. Box 816, Redondo Beach, CA 90277: Free catalog ❖ Rare books and antique scientific instruments. 213–372–5969.

Gemstone Press, Rt. 4, Sunset Farm Offices, P.O. Box 237, Woodstock, VT 05091: Free catalog ❖ Books for the consumer, hobbyist, investor, and retail trade on buying, identifying, selling, and enjoying jewelry and gems. 802–457–4000.

Genealogical Publishing Company, 1001 N. Calvert St., Baltimore, MD 21202: Free catalog ❖ Books on genealogy. 800–296–6687.

Genealogy Unlimited Inc., P.O. Box 537, Orem, UT 84059: Free catalog ❖ Genealogical books, forms, archival supplies, and historical, topographic, and modern European maps. 800–666–4363.

David Ginn Magic, 4387 St. Michaels Dr., Lilburn, GA 30247: Catalog $10 ❖ Books, props, and how-to magic on video tapes for magicians and clowns.

Glentiques Publishing Inc., P.O. Box 8807, Coral Springs, FL 33075: Catalog $30 a year ❖ Books on exercise and physical fitness. 305–493–6888.

Globe Pequot Press, P.O. Box 833, Old Saybrook, CT 06475: Free catalog ❖ Travel guides, cookbooks, outdoor recreation, how-to, and nature books. 800–243–0495.

Government Printing Office, New Catalog, P.O. Box 37000, Washington, DC 20013: Free catalog ❖ Best-selling Federal government publications.

Graywolf Press, 2402 University Ave., Ste. 203, St. Paul, MN 55114: Free information ❖ New books and poetry, fiction, and nonfiction reprints. 612–641–0077.

Great Chefs Publishing, 421 Frenchmen St., New Orleans, LA 70116: Free information ❖ Cookbooks and videos on the Great Chefs television shows. 504–943–4343.

Green Horizons, 218 Quinlan, Ste. 571, Kerrville, TX 78028: Free brochure ❖ Books on wildflowers, herbs, grasses, fruits and vegetables, trees, shrubs, and woody vines. 210–257–5141.

Gryphon House Books, 3706 Otis St., Mt. Rainier, MD 20712: Free catalog ❖ Books for parents, children, and teachers. 301–779–6200.

Gulf Publishing Company, P.O. Box 2608, Houston, TX 77252: Free information ❖ Camping guides, cookbooks, and books on recreational travel, snorkeling, gardening, and other subjects. 713–520–4444.

Hammond Incorporated, 515 Valley St., Maplewood, NJ 07040: Free information ❖ Maps and prints, travel guides, road atlases, adult and juvenile references, and books on business. 201–763–6000.

Harmonica Music Publishing, P.O. Box 671, Hermosa Beach, CA 90254: Free information ❖ Books, videos, audio cassettes, and instructional tapes on the harmonica. 310–320–0599.

HarperCollins Publishers, 10 E. 53rd St., New York, NY 10022: Free catalog ❖ Books for preschool children through young adult, fiction and nonfiction for adults, cookbooks, business titles, religion, and other subjects. 212–207–7000.

Harrowsmith, Camden House Books, Ferry Rd., P.O. Box 1004, Charlotte, VT 05445: Free catalog ❖ Books and magazines on country living, gardening, food, health, crafts, building, and the environment. 800–827–3333.

Haynes Publications Inc., 861 Lawrence Dr., Newbury Park, CA 91320: Free catalog ❖ Automotive and motorcycle repair manuals and history, travel, and adventure books. 818–889–5400.

Hazelden Publishing Group, P.O. Box 176, Center City, MN 55012: Free catalog ❖ Psychology, self-help. and spirituality books. 612–257–4010.

Health Communications Inc., 3201 SW 15th St., Deerfield Beach, FL 33442: Free information ❖ Self-help recovery books on drug addiction. 305–360–0909.

Heimburger House Publishing Company, 7236 W. Madison St., Forest Park, IL 60130: Free information ❖ Books on model and prototype railroads, cooking, history, humor, and Walt Disney. 708–366–1973.

Claude Held, P.O. Box 515, Buffalo, NY 14225: Price list $1 (specify interest) ❖ Newspaper movie advertisements from the 1940s, pulp magazines, and fantasy and mystery books.

High-Grade Publications, Box 995, Aptos, CA 95001: Catalog $1 ❖ Books and maps on treasure hunting, gold locations and lost mines, ghost towns, gems and minerals, and geology.

High-Lonesome Books, Box 878, Silver City, NM 88062: Free catalog ❖ Books on the outdoors, homesteading, hunting, fishing, and other subjects.

Highsmith Multicultural Bookstore, P.O. Box 800, Fort Atkinson, WI 53538: Free information ❖ Books about African- and Native Americans. 414–563–9571.

Highwood Bookshop, P.O. Box 1246, Traverse City, MI 49685: Free catalog with two 1st class stamps ❖ Books on decoy carving and collecting, fishing tackle collecting, and fish decoys. 616–271–3898.

Dan Hill Books, P.O. Box 49, Dixmont, ME 04932: Free book list with two 1st class stamps ❖ Old books and magazines on farming, hunting, camping, homesteading, woodworking, metalworking, and other subjects.

Himalayan Institute, RR 1, Box 405, Homesdale, PA 18431: Free information ❖ Holistic health, yoga, preventive medicine, meditation, diet and health, and self-development books. 717–253–5551.

Historic Aviation, 1401 Kings Wood Rd., Eagan, MN 55122: Free catalog ❖ History, biography, classic, humor, and aviation books and videos. 800–225–5575.

Hobby House Press Inc., 1 Corporate Dr., Grantsville, MD 21536: Free information ❖ Books on dolls, teddy bears, postcards, costumes, and crafts. 800–554–1447.

Hollywood Creative Directory, 3000 Olympic Blvd., Ste. 2413, Santa Monica, CA 90404: Free information ❖ Entertainment industry directories. 800–815–0503; 310–315–4815 (in CA).

Home Planners Inc., 3275 W. Ina Rd., Ste. 110, Tucson, AZ 85741: Catalog $2 ❖ Books on home planning, architectural design, landscaping, and remodeling. 800–531–2555.

Johns Hopkins University Press, 2715 N. Charles St., Baltimore, MD 21218: Free catalog ❖ Books on a variety of subjects. 410–516–6936.

Hot Off the Press, 1250 NW 3rd, Canby, OR 97013: Catalog $2 ❖ Craft books. 503–266–9102.

Howell Book House Inc., MacMillan Publishing Company, 15 Columbus Circle, New York, NY 10023: Free information ❖ Books about dogs, cats, birds, horses, and other animals.

HR Bookstore, P.O. Box 209, Rindge, NH 03461: Free catalog ❖ Books on amateur radio. 800–457–7373.

Hudson Hills Press, 230 5th Ave., Ste. 1308, New York, NY 10001: Free information ❖ Books on photography and fine art. 212–889–3090.

Human Kinetics, 1607 N. Market St., Champaigne, IL 61820: Free information ❖ Sport and physical fitness books. 217–351–5076.

Humana Press, 999 Riverview Dr., Totowa, NJ 07512: Free information ❖ Books for the general public and professional community on health issues. 201–256–1699.

Humanities Press, 165 1st Ave., Atlantic Highlands, NJ 07716: Free information ❖ Books on philosophy, religion, political science, economics, literature, history, art theory and criticism, women's studies, archeology, and current affairs. 908–872–1441.

Hunter Publishing Inc., 300 Raritan Center Pkwy., Edison, NJ 08818: Free information ❖ Travel guides, language cassette courses, and maps. 908–225–1900.

ICS Books Inc., P.O. Box 10767, Merrillville, IN 46411: Free list ❖ Books on outdoor activities. 219–769–0585.

IDG Books Worldwide, 155 Bovet Rd., San Mateo, CA 94402: Free information ❖ Computer books and magazines. 415–312–0650.

In One Ear Publications, 29481 Manzanita Dr., Campo, CA 91906: Free catalog ❖ Books and audio tapes for easy foreign language learning. 619–478–5619.

Intel Corporation, 2200 Mission College Blvd., Santa Clara, CA 95052: Free catalog ❖ Computer books. 408–765–1709.

International Fabric Collection, 3445 W. Lake Rd., Erie, PA 16505: Catalog $3 ❖ Quilting and embroidery books and fabrics from Italy, India, Japan, Holland, Africa, and other worldwide sources. 800–462–3891; 814–838–0740 (in PA).

International Linguistics Corporation, 3505 E. Red Bridge, Kansas City, MO 64137: Free catalog ❖ Audio tapes for teaching French, German, Russian, Japanese, and foreigners to understand English. 800–765–8855.

International Marine Publishing Company, Tab Books, Division McGraw Hill, 13311 Montrey Ln., Blue Ridge Summit, PA 17294: Free catalog ❖ Nautical books. 800–233–1128.

International Press Publication Inc., 90 Nolan Ct., Ste. 23, Markham, Ontario, Canada L3R 4L9: Free information ❖ Business-trade directories, serials, dictionaries, and other books. 416–946–9588.

Interweave Press, 201 E. 4th St., Loveland, CO 80537: Free catalog ❖ Books on basket-making, weaving and spinning, sweater designing, hand and machine knitting, rug weaving, tapestry-making, fabric designing and sewing, and spinning wheels. 800–645–3675.

Invisible Ink, 1811 Stonewood Dr., Beavercreek, OH 45432: Free catalog ❖ Books on ghosts and haunting. 800–31–GHOST.

Iranbooks Inc., 6831 Wisconsin Ave., Bethesda, MD 20814: Catalog $3 ❖ Books about Iran in Persian and English. 301–986–0079.

Island Press, 1718 Connecticut Ave. NW, Ste. 300, Washington, DC 20009: Free information ❖ Environmental and conservation books for professionals. 800–828–1302.

Israel Book Export Institute, 3 Station Plaza, P.O. Box 101, Woodmere, NY 11598: Free information ❖ History, political, and religion books for adults and children, in Hebrew and English. 516–569–0830.

Japan Publications, 114 5th Ave., New York, NY 10011: Free information ❖ Books on health and macrobiotics, needle- and papercrafts, and other books in English and Japanese. 212–727–6460.

Jerboa-Redcap Books, P.O. Box 1058, Highstown, NJ 08520: Catalog $2 ❖ British military books. 609–443–3817.

Johnson Publishing Company Inc., 820 S. Michigan Ave., Chicago, IL 60605: Free information ❖ Books by and about Afro-Americans. 312–322–9248.

JTG of Nashville, 1024C 18th Ave. South, Nashville, TN 37212: Free information ❖ Professional and educational books and music products. 615–329–3036.

Keats Publishing Inc., P.O. Box 876, New Canaan, CT 06840: Free information ❖ Books on health, nutrition, fitness, alternative medicine, and preventive health care. 800–858–7014; 203–966–8721 (in CT).

Keepsake Quilting, P.O. Box 1459, Meredith, NH 03253: Free catalog ❖ Quilting books, patterns, notions, fabric medlets, quilting aids, scrap bags, cotton fabrics, and batting.

Paul E. Kisselburg, 105 S. Union Alley, Stillwater, MN 55082: Free catalog ❖ World War II books.

Knife World Books, P.O. Box 3395, Knoxville, TN 37927: Free information ❖ Books on knives. 800–828–7751.

Knollwood Books, P.O. Box 197, Oregon, WI 53575: Free catalog ❖ Rare and out-of-print books on astronomy, space exploration, and related fields. 608–835–8861.

Krause Publications, 700 E. State St., Iola, WI 54990: Free information ❖ Books on hobbies, collectibles, and the outdoors. 800–258–0929.

Krieger Publishing Company, P.O. Box 9542, Melbourne, FL 32902: Free information ❖ Books on reptiles and other exotic pets. 407–724–9542.

La Rock's Fun & Magic Outlet, 3847 Rosehaven Dr., Charlotte, NC 28205: Catalog $3 ❖ Clown and balloon how-to books, balloons, balloon sculpture kits, and magic equipment. 704–563–9300.

Lacis, 3163 Adeline St., Berkeley, CA 94703: Catalog $4 ❖ Books on fabrics, costumes, needlecrafts, and beading. 510–843–7178.

Larry's Book Store, 1219 W. Devon Ave., Chicago, IL 60660: Catalog $1 ❖ Movie books and magazines. 312–274–1832.

Leisure Arts/Oxmoor House, P.O. Box 5595, Little Rock, AR 72215: Free information ❖ Cookbooks. 501–868–8800.

Hal Leonard Publishing, P.O. Box 13819, Milwaukee, WI 53213: Free information ❖ Music and music-related books for music-lovers and musicians. 612–332–3344.

Alan Levine Movie & Book Collectibles, P.O. Box 1577, Bloomfield, NJ 07003: Catalog $5 ❖ Books on old-time movie posters, lobby cards, and old radio, television, and movie magazines. 201–743–5288.

Liberty Belle Books, 4250 S. Virginia St., Reno, NV 89502: Catalog $2 ❖ Books on slot and coin-operated machines. 702–826–2607.

Library Corner, P.O. Box 3332, Quartz Hill, CA 93586: Free information with long SASE ❖ Books on ceramics, pottery, porcelain, and doll-making. 805–943–3028.

Light Impressions, 439 Monroe Ave., Rochester, NY 14607: Free catalog ❖ Books on photography. 800–828–6216.

Linden Publishing Company Inc., 3845 N. Blackstone, Fresno, CA 93726: Catalog $1 ❖ New and out-of-print books and videos on woodworking.

Lindsay's Electrical Books, P.O. Box 538, Bradley, IL 60915: Catalog $1 ❖ Electrical books.

Lion House Distributors, Box 91283, Pittsburgh, PA 15221: Free catalog ❖ American regional cookbooks. 412–243–6235.

Lonely Planet Publications, 155 Filbert St., Ste. 251, Oakland, CA 94607: Free information ❖ Guide and phrase books for travelers. 510–893–8555.

Los Angeles Audubon Society Bookstore, 7377 Santa Monica Blvd., West Hollywood, CA 90046: Free catalog ❖ Bird and nature books, bookmarks, and bird feeders. 213–876–0202.

Louisiana State University Press, 102 French House, Baton Rouge, LA 70893: Free catalog ❖ Books about the Civil War and scholarly subjects. 504–388–6666.

Lucidity Institute, 2555 Park Blvd., Ste 2, Palo Alto, CA 94306: Free catalog ❖ Yoga books, tapes, and biofeedback devices. 415–321–9969.

Herbert A. Luft, 46 Woodcrest Dr., Scotia, NY 12302: Free list ❖ Rare and current astronomy books.

J.K. Lutherie Guitars, 11115 Sand Run, Harrison, OH 45030: Free catalog ❖ Vintage guitar parts, new and vintage accessories, catalogs and other literature, guitar magazines, and out-of-print guitar books. 800–344–8880; 513–353–3320 (in OH).

MacMillan Computer Publishing, MacMillan Publishing Company, 201 W. 103rd St., Indianapolis, IN 46290: Free catalog ❖ Computer books. 317–581–3500.

MacMillan Publishing Company, 15 Columbus Circle, New York, NY 10023: Free catalog ❖ Fiction and nonfiction books for children and adults.

Magna Books Inc., 95 Madison Ave., Ste. 1303, New York, NY 10016: Free information ❖ Postcard books. 212–686–8000.

The Mail Order Catalog, P.O. Box 180, Summertown, TN 38483: Free catalog ❖ Books on vegetarian cooking, other health food cookbooks, nutrition, health care, Native American traditions, animal issues, and odds and ends. 800–695–2241.

Bill Mason Books, 104 N. 7th St., Morehead City, NC 28557: Free catalog ❖ Rare, new, and used books, prints, and ephemera on the Civil War, Western Americana, and military and nautical subjects. 919–247–6161.

Suzanne McNeil, 2425 Cullen St., Fort Worth, TX 76107: Catalog $2 ❖ How-to craft books.

Merriam-Webster Inc., 47 Federal St., Springfield, MA 01102: Free brochure ❖ Dictionaries and reference books. 413–734–3134.

Meyerbooks Publisher, P.O. Box 427, Glenwood, IL 60425: Free catalog ❖ Books on stage magic history, herbs, health, cooking, and Americana. 708–757–4950.

Micro Publishing Press, 21150 Hawthorne Blvd., Torrance, CA 90503: Free information ❖ Computer books. 310–371–5787.

Microsoft Press, One Microsoft Way, Redmond, WA 98052: Free information ❖ Books on computers. 800–227–4679.

The Mind's Eye, 4 Commercial Blvd., Ste. 9, Novato, CA 94949: Free catalog ❖ Children's favorites and classics, military intrigue, mystery, horror, science fiction, adventure, drama, history, comedy, poetry, and self-improvement, and audio cassettes and compact disks. 206–882–8080.

The MIT Press, 55 Hayward St., Cambridge, MA 02142: Free catalog ❖ Books on a variety of subjects. 617–253–5641.

Morningside Bookshop, P.O. Box 1087, Dayton, OH 45401: Catalog $3 ❖ Reprints and original Civil War books and other memorabilia. 800–648–0710.

William Morrow & Company, 1350 Avenue of Americas, New York, NY 10019: Free information ❖ Fiction and nonfiction books for adults and children. 212–261–6705.

Motorbooks International, 729 Prospect Ave., P.O. Box 1, Osceola, WI 54020: Free catalog ❖ Automotive, motorcycle, aviation, and other books. 800–458–0454.

Mountain Press Publishing Company, P.O. Box 2399, Missoula, MT 59806: Free catalog ❖ Geology books, outdoor guides, and history titles. 406–728–1900.

The Mountaineers Books, 1011 SW Klickitat Way, Ste. 107, Seattle, WA 98134: Free information ❖ Books about the outdoors, hiking, bicycling, skiing, mountaineering, nature, and conservation. 206–223–6303.

John Muir Publications, P.O. Box 613, Santa Fe, NM 87504: Free information ❖ Books on travel, cultural and environmental topics, and automotive repair. 800–888–7504.

Mystic Seaport Museum Stores, 39 Greenmanville Ave., Mystic, CT 06355: Free catalog ❖ Books about American maritime history and Mystic Seaport Museum collections. 800–248–1066.

National Geographic Society, 1145 17th St. NW, Washington, DC 20036: Free catalog ❖

Books on geography, history, archeology, science, and industry. 800–447–0647.

National Rifle Association, Sales Department, P.O. Box 5000, Kearneysville, WV 25430: Free information ❖ Books on guns and shooting.

National Wildlife Federation,$INational Wildlife Federation 1400 16th St. NW, Washington, DC 20036: Free catalog ❖ Holiday cards and gifts. 800–432–6564.

Naval Institute Press, Customer Service, 2062 Generals Hwy., Annapolis, MD 21401: Free catalog ❖ Books on navigation, seamanship, naval history, ships, and aircraft. 800–233–8764.

John Neal, Bookseller, 1833 Spring Garden St., Greensboro, NC 27403: Free information ❖ Calligraphy and marbling supplies, books, and bookbinding. 800–369–9598.

The New Careers Center Inc., 1515 23rd St., P.O. Box 297, Boulder, CO 80306: Free catalog ❖ Books on alternative careers, new work options, home business opportunities, self-employment, and job hunting. 303–447–1087.

New Harbinger Publications, 5674 Shattuck Ave., Oakland, CA 94609: Free catalog ❖ Self-help books on psychology. 510–652–0215.

New Wireless Pioneers, Jim & Felicia Kreuzer, P.O. Box 398, Elma, NY 14059: Free information ❖ Books, magazines, and other literature on antique radios. 716–681–3186.

Nolo Press, 950 Parker St., Berkeley, CA 94710: Free catalog ❖ Self-help law books and computer software. 800–992–6656; 510–549–1976 (in CA).

O'Reilly & Associates, 103A Morris St., Sebastopol, CA 95472: Free catalog ❖ Computer books. 800–998–9938.

Ohara Publications Inc., P.O. Box 918, Santa Clarita, CA 91380: Free information ❖ Books on martial arts. 805–257–4066.

Olde Soldier Books Inc., 18779 N. Frederick Ave., Gaithersburg, MD 20879: Free information ❖ Civil War books, documents, autographs, prints, and Americana. 301–963–2929.

Olsson's Books & Records, 1239 Wisconsin Ave. NW, Washington, DC 20007: Free catalog ❖ Compact disks, cassettes, and books on fiction, poetry, history, biography, the classics, philosophy, children's stories,

humor, travel, mystery, art, photography, cooking, interior design, antiques, and collecting. 202–337–8084.

Online Press Inc., Quick Course Books, 14320 NE 21st St., Bellevue, WA 98007: Free information ❖ Computer training books. 206–641–3434.

Ortho Information Services, 6001 Bollinger Canyon Rd., Bldg. T, Room 1334, San Ramon, CA 94583: Free information ❖ Books about gardening, cooking, and home improvement. 510–842–1969.

The Overlook Connection, P.O. Box 526, Woodstock, GA 30188: Catalog $1 ❖ Books, audio cassettes, and magazines on horror, science fiction, fantasy, and mystery. 404–926–1762.

Ozark Vintage Radio, 3923 E. Lakota St., Springfield, MO 65809: Free list with long SASE ❖ Books on antique radios.

Pachart Publishing House, 1130 San Lucas Cir., P.O. Box 35549, Tucson, AZ 85704: Free catalog ❖ Astronomy books.

Paladin Press, P.O. Box 1307, Boulder, CO 80306: Catalog $2 ❖ Books on self defense, how to establish privacy and personal security, history of weapons, locksmithing, military and police science, and martial arts. 303–443–7250.

Penfield Press, 215 Brown St., Iowa City, IA 52245: Free catalog ❖ Books on ethnic interests. 800–728–9998; 319–337–9998 (in IA).

Peri Lithon Books, Box 9996, San Diego, CA 92169: Catalog $2 ❖ Out-of-print, rare, and other books about gemstones, minerals, fossils, jewelry, and geology. 619–488–6904.

Pet Bookshop, P.O. Box 507, Oyster Bay, NY 11771: Free catalog ❖ Books on birds, dogs, cats, fish, reptiles, and other pets. 800–676–0067.

Pieces of History, P.O. Box 4470, Cave Creek, AZ 85331: Catalog $2 ❖ Military history books. 602–488–1377.

Bud Plant Comic Art, P.O. Box 1689, Grass Valley, CA 95945: Free catalog ❖ Graphic novels, comic strip collections, history of comics and comic creators, limited editions, prints, and other comic book-related material. 916–273–2166.

Players Press, P.O. Box 1132, Studio City, CA 91614: Information $1 ❖ Books on the theater, films, television, costumes, and puppets. 818–789–4980.

Portrayal Press, P.O. Box 1190, Andover, NJ 07821: Catalog $3 ❖ Hard-to-find books on 20th-century subjects. 201–579–5781.

The Potters Shop, 31 Thorpe Rd., Needham Heights, MA 02194: Free catalog ❖ Books on pottery and ceramics. 617–449–7687.

Pruett Publishing Company, 2928 Pearl St., Boulder, CO 80301: Free catalog ❖ Books about the history and people of the American West, outdoor adventures, railroads, cooking, and horticulture. 303–449–4919.

Puett Electronics, P.O. Box 28572, Dallas, TX 75228: Catalog $5 (refundable) ❖ Antique radio publications, from 1902 to the 1960s.

Pyramid Collection, P.O. Box 3333, Chelmsford, MA 01824: Free catalog ❖ Jewelry, books, fragrance items, video tapes, recordings, and other gifts. 800–333–4220.

Que Corporation, 201 W. 103rd St., Indianapolis, IN 46290: Free information ❖ Computer books. 317–581–3500.

Quilting Books Unlimited, 1911 W. Wilson, Batavia, IL 60510: Catalog $1 ❖ Quilting books. 708–406–0237.

Random House, 201 E. 50th St., New York, NY 10022: Free catalog ❖ Calendars, puzzles, video cassettes, and fiction, travel guides, hobbies, references, and other books for adults and children. 212–751–2600.

Reader's Digest, P.O. Box 107, Pleasantville, NY 10571: Free catalog ❖ Books on gardening, crafts and hobbies, travel, science and nature, cooking, health, history, geography, religion, and archeology. 914–241–7445.

Rizzoli International Publications, 300 Park Ave. South, New York, NY 10010: Catalog $3 ❖ Books on architecture, interior design, home crafts, decorating, and renovating techniques. 212–387–3534.

Roberts Rinehart Publishers, P.O. Box 666, Niwot, CO 80544: Free information ❖ Books about natural history, Native Americans, the West, and Irish history and culture. 303–652–2921.

Rodale Press Inc., 33 E. Minor St., Emmaus, PA 18098: Free information ❖ Health information books. 610–967–8545.

John M. Santarelli, Civil War Books, 226 Paxson Ave., Glenside, PA 19038: Free information with two 1st class stamps ❖ Civil War books. 215–576–5358.

The Scholar's Bookshelf, 110 Mekrich Rd., Cranbury, NJ 08512: Free catalog ❖ Old and new World War II books.

Schumacher & Company, 1800 Century Park East, Ste. 1250, Los Angeles, CA 90067: Free information ❖ Easy-to-understand books on estate planning and living trusts. 310–284–8866.

Scott Publications, 30595 W. 8 Mile Rd., Livonia, MI 48152: Free catalog ❖ Books for the ceramist, china painter, and doll-maker. 313–477–6650.

The Self Awareness Institute, 219 Broadway, Ste. 417, Laguna Beach, CA 92651: Free catalog ❖ Yoga books and audio tapes on awakening and evolving consciousness. 714–491–3356.

Self-Counsel Press Inc., 1704 N. State St., Bellingham, WA 98225: Free catalog ❖ Self-help books on law, business, psycholgy, and other areas. 800–663–3007.

Jackie Shaw Studio Inc., The Old Stone Mill, 13306 Edgemont Rd., Smithsburg, MD 21783: Catalog $1 ❖ Craft books. 301–824–7592.

Show-Biz Services, 1735 E. 26th St., Brooklyn, NY 11229: Free list ❖ Books for magicians. 718–336–0605.

Sierra Club Books, 100 Bush St., 13th Floor, San Francisco, CA 94104: Free catalog ❖ Books about ecology, natural history, environment, wildlife, outdoor activities, and nature photography. 415–291–1600.

Skipjack Press Inc., 637 Drexel Ave., Drexel Hill, PA 19026: Free information ❖ Books on blacksmithing. 610–284–7693.

Sky Publishing Corporation, P.O. Box 9111, Belmont, MA 02178: Free information ❖ Astronomy books, posters, and videos. 800–253–0245.

Small Press Distribution Inc., 1814 San Pablo Ave., Berkeley, CA 94702: Free catalog ❖ Contemporary literature and books from publishers in the United States, Canada, and Great Britain. 510–549–3336.

Samuel Patrick Smith, P.O. Box 769, Tavares, FL 32778: Free information ❖ How-to books on theatrical marketing, writing letters, entertaining children, performing better on the stage, advertising, and other topics.

Smithsonian Institution Press, 470 L'Enfant Plaza, Ste. 7100, Washington, DC 20560: Free catalog ❖ Books on art, aviation, anthropology, archaeology, and museum studies. 202–287–3738.

Special Needs Project, 3463 State St., Ste. 282, Santa Barbara, CA 93105: Free catalog ❖ Special needs books for persons with physical and mental disabilities. 805–683–9633.

Specialty Books Company, P.O. Box 616, Croton-on-Hudson, New York 10520: Free catalog ❖ Books on wine, wine regions, travel, wine and food, and other topics. 800–274–4816.

Springer-Verlag New York, 175 5th Ave., New York, NY 10010: Free information ❖ Books on medicine and science. 212–460–1500.

Springhouse Publishing Company, 1111 Bethlehem Pike, P.O. Box 908, Springhouse, PA 19044: Free catalog ❖ Books on nursing and consumer health. 215–646–8700.

Squadron/Signal Publications Inc., 1115 Crowley Dr., Carrollton, TX 75011: Free catalog ❖ Books on aviation, armor, ships, and military history. 800–527–7427.

Stampede Investments, P.O. Box 1772E, North Riverside, IL 60546: Free catalog ❖ Fine books and autographs for historical enthusiasts. 708–788–9022.

Sterling Publishing Company Inc., 387 Park Ave. South, New York, NY 10016: Free catalog ❖ Books on body building, hobbies, crafts, occult, herbs and gardening, science, cooking, health, sports, music, theater, self-defense, and books for children. 212–532–7160.

Storey Communications Inc., Schoolhouse Rd., P.O. Box 445, Pownal, VT 05261: Free catalog ❖ How-to books on gardening, woodworking and building, cooking, country skills, animals, crafts, nature, home improvement, animals, and the outdoors. 800–441–5700.

Fred Struthers Books, P.O. Box 2706, Fort Bragg, CA 95437: Catalog $2.50 ❖ Hard-to-find books on costumes, textiles, etiquette, sewing, and needlecrafts. 707–964–8662.

Sun Designs, 173 E. Wisconsin Ave., Oconomowoc, WI 53066: Catalog $9.95 ❖ Idea books and plans for building gazebos, bridges, doghouses, furniture, swings and other outdoor play structures, and birdhouses. 414–567–4255.

Sybex Computer Books, 2021 Challenger Dr., Alameda, CA 94501: Free catalog ❖ Computer books. 800–227–2346; 510–523–8233 (in CA).

Tab Books Inc., Division McGraw Hill, 13311 Montrey Ln., Blue Ridge Summit, PA 17294: Free catalog ❖ How-to books on electronics, computers, aviation, science, hobbies, automobiles, crafts, and other subjects. 800–233–1128.

Tartan Book Sales, 500 Arch St., Williamsport, PA 17705: Free catalog ❖ Nonfiction and fiction books. 800–233–8467.

The Taunton Press, 63 S. Main St., P.O. Box 5506, Newtown, CT 06470: Free information ❖ Books, videos, and magazines on sewing, patterns, fabrics, gardening, woodworking and other crafts. 800–888–8286.

Tennant's Aviation Books, P.O. Box 1695, Auburn, WA 98071: Catalog $3 ❖ New, used, and out-of-print books on aviation. 206–833–7506.

That Patchwork Place, P.O. Box 118, Bothell, WA 98041: Free information ❖ Quilting books. 206–483–3313.

Theatre Communications Group, 355 Lexington Ave., New York, NY 10017: Free catalog ❖ Books about the theater and performing arts. 212–697–5230.

Thomas Brothers Maps, 17731 Cowan St., Irvine, CA 92714: Free catalog ❖ Atlases, street guides, and maps. 714–863–1984.

Time-Life Books, P.O. Box 85563, Richmond, VA 23285: Free catalog ❖ Educational and entertainment videos and books. 800–854–1681.

Timeless Books, P.O. Box 3543, Spokane, WA 99220: Free catalog ❖ Books, audiotapes, and videos on yoga, Buddhism, and Eastern philosophy. 509–838–6652.

The Tool Chest, 45 Emerson Plaza East, Emerson, NJ 07630: Catalog $2 (refundable) ❖ Books for the home craftsman. 201–261–8665.

Tools of the Trade, P.O. Box 23556, Lexington, KY 40523: Free catalog ❖ Books on desktop publishing, writing, editing, and graphic design.

Top of the World Books, 20 Westview Circle, Williston, VT 05495: Free catalog ❖ New and used books on mountaineering. 802–878–8737.

Travel Keys Books, Travel Books Worldwide, P.O. Box 160691, Sacramento, CA 95816: Free information ❖ Travel guides. 916–452–5200.

Travelers Bookstore, 22 W. 52nd St., New York, NY 10019: Catalog $2 ❖ Maps and books on travel, student opportunities, adventure, trekking, hiking, biking, kayaking, and mountaineering. 800–755–8728; 212–664–0995 (in NY).

Unicorn Books & Crafts Inc., 1338 Ross St., Petaluma, CA 94954: Catalog $3 ❖ Books on basketry, color, costumes, dolls, dyeing, embroidery, fabric decoration, historic and ethnic textiles, jewelry, knitting and crochet, lace, machine knitting, paper crafting, rug hooking, sewing, weaving, and spinning. 800–289–9276; 707–762–3362 (in CA).

Uniquity, P.O. Box 10, Galt, CA 95632: Free catalog ❖ Books on mental health, aggression release, child abuse, play therapy, sexuality, and other subjects. 209–745–2111.

The University of Alabama Press, Box 870380, Tuscaloosa, AL 35487: Free information ❖ Books about the Civil War, anthropology, archaeology, contemporary Native Americans, and Judaic studies. 205–348–1568.

University of South Carolina Press, 205 Pickens St., Columbia, SC 29208: Free information ❖ World War II books. 800–768–2500.

University Press of Kansas, 2501 W. 15th St., Lawrence, KS 66049: Free information ❖ Books on American and military history, presidential studies, Western Americana, the Great Plains, and Midwest. 913–864–4154.

Vestal Press Ltd., P.O. Box 97, Vestal, NY 13851: Catalog $2 ❖ Posters, recordings, and books on carousels, music boxes, player pianos and other music machines, antique radios and phonographs, early movie stars, and radio personalities. 607–797–4872.

Vintage '45 Press, P.O. Box 266, Orinda, CA 94563: Free brochure ❖ Books about older women and mid-life problems. 510–254–7266.

War Room, 31 McKinley Ave., Washington, NJ 07882: Catalog $2 ❖ Used, rare, and out-of-print books on World War II. 908–689–8256.

Warbirds & Warriers Military Books, P.O. Box 266, Leicester, NY 14481: Price list $1 (specify subject area) ❖ Out-of-print American military history books, specializing in World War II aviation and armor studies. 716–382–3234.

Barbara Weindling, 69 Ball Pond Rd., Danbury, CT 06811: Catalog $2 ❖ Cookbooks. 203–746–2514.

Western Horseman Books, P.O. Box 7980, Colorado Springs, CO 80933: Free information ❖ Books on horsemanship and training, barrel racing, team and calf roping, reining, cutting, health problems, horse breaking, and horseshoeing. 800–874–6774; 719–633–0700 (in CO).

Western Publishing Company Inc., 1220 Mound Ave., Racine, WI 53404: Free catalog ❖ Golden Field Guides on birds, reptiles, rocks and minerals, seashells, astronomy, trees, insects, fishes, fossils, and weather. 414–631–5158.

Westwater Books, Box 2560, Evergreen, CO 80439: Free catalog ❖ Books for river runners. 800–628–1326.

Willmann-Bell Inc., P.O. Box 35025, Richmond, VA 23235: Catalog $1 ❖ Astronomy books. 804–320–7016.

Wolfe Publishing Company, 6471 Airpark Dr., Prescott, AZ 86301: Free catalog ❖ Sporting books. 800–899–7810.

Wood Violet Books, 3814 Sunhill Dr., Madison, WI 53704: Catalog $2 ❖ Books on gardening and herbs.

Woodbine House, 6510 Bells Mill Rd., Bethesda, MD 20817: Free catalog ❖ Consumer reference books and The Special Needs Collection on disabilities for parents, educators, and medical professionals. 800–843–7323; 301–897–3570 (in MD).

WoodenBoat Books, Naskeag Rd., P.O. Box 78, Brooklin, ME 04616: Free information ❖ Calendars, posters, prints, and books about wood boats. 800–225–5205; 207–359–4647 (in ME).

Workman Publishing Company Inc., 708 Broadway, New York, NY 10003: Free catalog ❖ Cooking, food and wine, travel, homes and gardens, space, humor, exercise and health, pregnancy and babies, sports and television, games, hobbies and handicrafts, computer, and children's books. 212–254–5900.

Writer's Digest Books, 1507 Dana Ave., Cincinnati, OH 45207: Free catalog ❖ Self-help and how-to books for writers, fine and graphic artists, songwriters, musicians, photographers, homemakers, and children. 513–531–2222.

Zenith Books, 1000 Milwaukee Ave., Glenview, IL 60025: Free catalog ❖ Books

about ragwings, supersonic spy planes, and other aircraft; video tapes on military aircraft, plastic and radio control modeling, warplanes, and aviation history; and calendars. 708–391–7000.

Zephyr Press, P.O. Box 66006, Tucson, AZ 85728: Free catalog ❖ Innovative learning materials for teacher-friendly hands-on activities. 602–322–5090.

Zon International Publishing Company, P.O. Box 47, Millwood, NY 10546: Free information ❖ Guides and books about carousels, cowboy antiques, and other collectibles. 800–266–5767; 914–245–2926 (in NY).

Large-Print & Braille Books

American Printing House for the Blind, 1839 Frankfort Ave., P.O. Box 6085, Louisville, KY 40206: Free catalog ❖ Books in braille for the visually impaired. 502–895–2405.

Grey Castle Press, Pocket Knife Square, Lakeville, CT 06039: Free catalog ❖ Large-print books on literary classics, and books about wildlife, the Civil War, world literature, for children, American biographies, sports, citizenship, and foreign countries. 203–496–2565.

G.K. Hall, 70 Lincoln St., Boston, MA 02111: Free catalog ❖ Best sellers in large-print. 617–423–3990.

The William A. Thomas Braille Bookstore, Division Braille International Inc., 3290 SE Slater St., Stuart, FL 34997: Free catalog ❖ Books in braille and large-print. 800–336–3142.

Thorndike Press, P.O. Box 159, Thorndike, ME 04986: Free catalog ❖ Large-print books. 800–223–6121.

Religious Books

Abingdon Press, 201 8th Ave. South, Nashville, TN 37202: Free information ❖ Religious books. 615–749–6451.

Augsburg Fortress Publishers, 426 S. 5th St., Box 1209, Minneapolis, MN 55440: Free catalog ❖ Books, curriculum materials, music, gifts, audiovisuals, ecclesiastical arts items. 800–328–4648; 612–330–3300 (in MN).

Baker Book House, P.O. Box 6287, Grand Rapids, MI 49516: Free catalog ❖ Religious books for the home, church, and school. 616–676–9185.

Behrman House Publishers Inc., 235 Watchung Ave., West Orange, NJ 07052: Free information ❖ Books on Jewish subjects for children and adults. 201–669–0447.

Dharma Publishing, 2910 San Pablo Ave., Berkeley, CA 94702: Free information ❖ Buddhist books and art reproductions. 510–548–5407.

God's World Publications, Box 2330, Asheville, NC 28802: Free catalog ❖ Selected books from Christian and secular publishers. 704–253–8063.

Immaculata Bookstore, P.O. Box 159, St. Mary's, KS 66536: Free catalog ❖ Educational and inspirational books, and music tapes, compact disks, full score music books of great composers, and other Catholic publications. 913–437–2409.

Israel Book Export Institute, 3 Station Plaza, P.O. Box 101, Woodmere, NY 11598: Free information ❖ History, political, and religion books for adults and children, in Hebrew and English. 516–569–0830.

Jewish Publication Society, 1930 Chestnut St., Philadelphia, PA 19103: Free information ❖ Books about Judaica. 800–234–3151.

Lion Publishing Corporation, 20 Lincoln Ave., Elgin, IL 60120: Free information ❖ Christian books for children and adults. 708–741–4256.

The Liturgical Press, St. John's Abbey, Collegeville, MN 56321: Free information ❖ Catholic and general Christian books on scripture, theology, and liturgy. 612–363–2533.

Thomas Nelson Publishers, Nelson Place at Elm Hill Pike, Nashville, TN 37214: Free catalog ❖ Bibles and religious books. 615–889–9000.

1–800–Judaism, America's Jewish Bookstore, 2028 Murray Ave., Pittsburgh, PA 15217: Free catalog ❖ Current and classic Jewish books for adults and children. 1–800–JUDAISM.

Orbis Books, Walsh Building, Box 308, Maryknoll, NY 10545: Free catalog ❖ Religious books. 914–941–7636.

Riverside-World, P.O. Box 370, Iowa Falls, IA 50126: Free catalog ❖ Adult and children's religious books, bibles, and other audio products. 800–247–5111.

The University of Alabama Press, Box 870380, Tuscaloosa, AL 35487: Free information ❖ Books about the Civil War, anthropology, archaeology, contemporary Native Americans, and Judaic studies. 205–348–1568.

Zondervan, 5300 Patterson Ave. SE, Grand Rapids, MI 49530: Free information ❖ Bibles and religious books. 616–698–6900.

Used Books

Benedikt & Salmon Record Rarities, 3020 Meade Ave., San Diego, CA 92116: Free catalogs, indicate choice of (1) rare books and autographs; (2) classical; (3) jazz; big bands and blues and (4) personalities, soundtracks and country music ❖ Autographed memorabilia and rare books on music and the performing arts, antique phonographs and cylinders, and rare recordings from the 1890s to date. 619–281–3345.

Michael Dennis Cohan Bookseller, 502 W. Alder St., Missoula, MT 59802: Free catalog ❖ Out-of-print and rare books on geology, mining, and related subjects. 406–721–7379.

Editions, Boiceville, NY 12412: Catalog $2 ❖ Used, old, and rare books. 914–657–7000.

Historical Technology Inc., 6 E. Mugford St., Marblehead, MA 01945: Annual catalog subscription $12 ❖ Rare books and antique scientific instruments. 617–631–2275.

Imperial Fine Books, 790 Madison Ave., Room 200, New York, NY 10021: Catalog $3 ❖ Antique leatherbound books in full sets or singles. 212–861–6620.

Herbert A. Luft, 46 Woodcrest Dr., Scotia, NY 12302: Free list ❖ Rare and current astronomy books.

McGowan Book Company, P.O. Box 16325, Chapel Hill, NC 27516: Catalog $3 ❖ Rare, out-of-print Civil War books. 919–968–1121.

David Meyer Magic Books, Box 427, Glenwood, IL 60425: Catalog $1 ❖ New and old books on magic.

Old Hickory Bookshop Ltd., 20225 New Hampshire Ave., Brinklow, MD 20862: Free catalog ❖ Used medical books. 301–924–2225.

Bud Plant Illustrated Books, P.O. Box 1689, Grass Valley, CA 95945: Free catalog ❖ Rare and out-of-print children's books, art monographs and history of book illustrating, and books about comics, comic strips, and their creators. 916–273–2166.

Wallace D. Pratt, Bookseller, 1801 Gough St., San Francisco, CA 94109: Free catalog ❖ Out-of-print and rare books about the Civil War, Indian Wars, and naval history. 415–673–0178.

Red Lancer, P.O. Box 8056, Mesa, AZ 85214: Catalog $6 ❖ Rare books, Victorian-era campaign medals and helmets, toy soldiers, and original 19th-century military art. 602–964–9667.

Unicorn Books & Crafts Inc., 1338 Ross St., Petaluma, CA 94954: Catalog $3 ❖ Books on basketry, color, costumes, dolls, dyeing, embroidery, fabric decoration, historic and ethnic textiles, jewelry, knitting and crochet, lace, machine knitting, paper crafting, rug hooking, sewing, weaving, and spinning. 800–289–9276; 707–762–3362 (in CA).

Wooden Porch Books, Box 262, Middlebourne, WV 26149: Catalog $3 ❖ Out-of-print books on fiber arts.

BOOK SEARCH SERVICES

American Indian Books & Relics, P.O. Box 16175, Huntsville, AL 35802: Free catalog with long SASE ❖ Search service for books about Native Americans. 205–881–6727.

Avonlea Books, P.O. Box 74, Main Station, White Plains, NY 10602: Free information ❖ Search service for hard-to-find and out-of-print books. 914–946–5923.

Book Associates, Bob Snell, P.O. Box 687, Orange, CT 06477: Free information ❖ Search service for hard-to-find and out-of-print books. 203–795–3107.

Book Hunters, P.O. Box 7519, North Bergen, NJ 07047: Free information ❖ Search service for hard-to-find and out-of-print books.

Book Trader, P.O. Box 603, Fairmont, NC 28340: Free information with long SASE ❖ Searches for out-of-print books.

Michael Dennis Cohan Bookseller, 502 W. Alder St., Missoula, MT 59802: Free catalog ❖ Search service for books on geology, mining, and related subjects. 406–721–7379.

Goodspeed's, 7 Beacon St., Boston, MA 02108: Catalog $2 ❖ Search service for hard-to-find and out-of-print books. 617–523–5970.

Harvard Cooperative, 1400 Massachusetts Ave., Cambridge, MA 02238: Free information ❖ Search service for hard-to-find and out-of-print books. 617–499–2000.

Richard A. LaPosta, 154 Robindale Dr., Kensington, CT 06037: Information $1 ❖

Searches for out-of-print, first editions, and other Civil War books. 203–828–0921.

Rose Lasley Estate Books, 5827 Burr Oak, Berkeley, IL 60163: Free information ❖ Search service for hard-to-find and out-of print books.

NightinGale Resources, P.O. Box 322, Cold Spring, NY 10516: Catalog $3 ❖ Search service for out-of-print and rare cookbooks.

Out-of-State-Book-Service, Box 3253, San Clemente, CA 92674: Free information ❖ Search service for hard-to-find and out-of-print books. 714–492–1976.

Ellen Roth, 47 Truman Dr., Marlboro, NJ 07746: Free information ❖ Search service for hard-to-find and out of print books. 908–536–0850.

Significant Books, P.O. Box 9248, Cincinnati, OH 45209: Free information ❖ Search service for hard-to-find and out-of print books.

George Tramp Books, 709 2nd St., Jackson, MI 49203: Free list ❖ Search service for hard-to-find and out of print books. 517–784–1057.

BOOKS ON TAPE

Audio Diversions, 306 Commerce St., Occoquan, VA 22125: Catalog $2 ❖ Best selling books on tape. 800–628–6145.

Audio Editions, Books on Cassette, 1133 High St., Auburn, CA 95603: Free catalog ❖ Best sellers and all-time favorites, books for young people, classics, drama and poetry, languages, books on cassettes, and personal growth, business, and management titles. 916–888–7803.

Books on Tape Inc., P.O. Box 7900, Newport Beach, CA 92658: Free catalog ❖ Books recorded on cassettes. 800–626–3333.

Brilliance Corporation, 1810 Industrial, Grand Haven, MI 49417: Free catalog ❖ Cassette recordings of books. 616–846–5256.

Dercum Audio Press Ltd., P.O. Box 1425, West Chester, PA 19355: Free information ❖ Mysteries, science fiction, classics, and other audio books for adults and children. 215–430–8889.

A Gentle Wind, P.O. Box 3103, Albany, NY 12203: Free information ❖ Music and story cassettes for children, age 1 to 12. 518–436–0391.

KEBA International, P.O. Box 15131, Columbus, OH 43215: Free catalog ❖ Books,

books-on-tape, and other tapes on drugs, cooking, diet and nutrition, parenting, and stress. 800–847–847; 614–457–1301 (in OH).

Recorded Books Inc., 270 Skipjack Rd., Prince Frederick, MD 20678: Free catalog ❖ Unabridged books on cassettes. 800–638–1304.

BOOMERANGS

Australian Dreaming Inc., P.O. Box D, Middletown, RI 02842: Free information ❖ Boomerangs. 800–390–BOOM.

Boomerang Man, 1806 N. 3rd St., Monroe, LA 71201: Free catalog ❖ Contest and sport boomerangs. 318–325–8157.

Colonel Gerrish Boomerangs, 4885 SW 78th Ave., Portland, OR 97225: Free information ❖ Boomerangs. 503–292–5697.

Into the Wind/Kites, 1408 Pearl St., Boulder, CO 80302: Free catalog ❖ Boomerangs and kites. 800–541–0314.

What's Up Kites, 4500 Chagrin River Rd., Chagrin Falls, Ohio 44022: Free information ❖ Boomerangs, kites, air toys, and books. 216–247–4222.

BOWLING
Clothing

Collegiate Specialty Company, 444 River St., P.O. Box 1079, Troy, NY 12181: Free catalog ❖ Bowling apparel.

Converse Inc., 1 Fordham Rd., North Reading, MA 01864: Free information ❖ Shoes. 800–428–2667; 508–664–1100 (in MA).

Eastern Bowling/Hy-Line Inc., 4717 Stenton Ave., Philadelphia, PA 19144: Free information ❖ Shoes. 800–523–0140; 215–438–9000 (in PA).

King Louie International, 13500 15th St., Grandview, MO 64030: Free information ❖ Jackets, shirts, and blouses. 800–521–5212; 816–765–5212 (in MO).

National Sporting Goods Corporation, 25 Brighton Ave., Passaic, NJ 07055: Free information ❖ Shoes. 201–779–2323.

Nike Footwear Inc., One Bowerman Dr., Beaverton, OR 97005: Free information ❖ Shoes, shirts, blouses, and bowling ball bags. 800–344–6453.

Saucony/Hyde, 13 Centennial Dr., Peabody, MA 01961: Free information ❖ Shoes. 800–365–7282.

Shaffer Sportswear, 224 N. Washington, Neosho, MO 64850: Free information ❖ Jackets and shirts. 417–451–9444.

Universal Bowling, Golf & Billiard Supplies, 619 S. Wabash Ave., Chicago, IL 60605: Free catalog ❖ Shirts, one-and two-ball bags, and women's shoes. 800–523–3037.

Wa-Mac Inc., Highskore Products, P.O. Box 128, Carlstadt, NJ 07410: Free information ❖ Shoes, gloves, bowling ball and shoe bags, grips, novelties, and towels. 800–447–5673; 201–438–7200 (in NJ).

Windjammer, 525 N. Main St., Banger, PA 18013: Free information ❖ Jackets, shirts, T-shirts, sweat suits, and other sportswear. 800–441–6958.

Wolverine Boots & Shoes, 9341 Courtland Dr., Rockford, MI 49351: Free information ❖ Shoes. 800–543–2668.

Equipment

Ajay Leisure Products Inc., 1501 E. Wisconsin St., Delavan, WI 53115: Free information with list of retailers ❖ Bowling ball bags, grips, novelties, and towels. 800–558–3276; 414–728–5521 (in WI).

The Bag Company, 3508 De La Cruz Blvd., Santa Clara, CA 95050: Free information ❖ Bags. 800–531–0700; 800–556–8008 (CA).

Bowling's Bookstore, Tech-Ed Publishing Company, P.O. Box 4, Deerfield, IL 60015: Free information ❖ Books and videos on bowling. 800–521–BOWL.

Cosom Sporting Goods, Division Mantua Industries, Grandview Ave., Woodbury Heights, NJ 08097: Free information ❖ Bowling balls. 800–328–5635; 609–853–0300 (in NJ).

Ebonite International Inc., 1813 W. 7th St., Box 746, Hopkinsville, KY 42240: Free information ❖ Bags, balls, and wrist supports. 800–626–8350; 502–886–5261 (in KY).

Hilco Inc., Hilsport Division, 2102 Fair Park Blvd., Harlingen, TX 78550: Free information ❖ Bowling ball and shoe bags. 512–423–1885.

J-S Sales Company Inc., 5 S. Fulton Ave., Mt. Vernon, NY 10550: Free information ❖ Bowling ball bags, grips, towels, and novelties. 800–431–2944; 914–668–8051 (in NY).

Kansas Industries for the Blind, State Department of Social & Rehabilitation Services, 2700 W. 6th, 1st Floor, Biddle

Building, Topeka, KS 66606: Free price list ❖ Products made by people with visual impairments. 913–296–3211.

KR Industries Inc., 200 N. Artesian, Chicago, IL 60612: Free information ❖ Bags. 800–621–6097; 312–666–1100 (in IL).

Master Industries Inc., 17222 Von Karman Ave., Irvine, CA 92713: Free information ❖ Bags, balls, grips, novelties, and towels. 800–854–3794; 714–660–0644 (in CA).

Nike Footwear Inc., One Bowerman Dr., Beaverton, OR 97005: Free information ❖ Bowling ball bags, shoes, shirts, and blouses. 800–344–6453.

Pin Breaker Inc., P.O. Box 218, Lockport, IL 60441: Catalog $1 (refundable) ❖ Bowling balls and other equipment. 800–442–2903.

Sports Calc Division, Cygnus of South Florida Inc., 1290 Weston Rd., Ste. 300, Fort Lauderdale, FL 33326: Free information ❖ Easy-to-use pocket-size computer to record bowling scores. 800–624–6022; 305–384–1281 (in FL).

Sports Technologies Inc., 145 Rand St., Box 1574, Sanford, NC 27331: Free information ❖ Bags, balls, and wrist supports. 800–322–3962; 919–776–9544 (in NC).

Universal Bowling, Golf & Billiard Supplies, 619 S. Wabash Ave., Chicago, IL 60605: Free catalog ❖ Bowling equipment. 800–523–3037.

Universal Trav-Ler, 359 Wales Ave., Bronx, NY 10454: Free information ❖ Bowling ball and shoe bags. 800–833–3026; 212–993–7100 (in NY).

Wa-Mac Inc., Highskore Products, P.O. Box 128, Carlstadt, NJ 07410: Free information ❖ Bowling ball and shoe bags, grips, novelties, towels, shoes, and gloves. 800–447–5673; 201–438–7200 (in NJ).

BOXING

Clothing

Adidas USA, 5675 N. Blackstock Rd., Spartanburg, SC 29303: Free information ❖ Shoes. 800–423–4327.

Alpha Sportswear Inc., 20660 Nordoff St., Chatsworth, CA 91311: Free information ❖ Trunks. 818–775–4555.

Butwin Sportswear Company, 3401 Spring St. NE, Minneapolis, MN 55413: Free information ❖ Robes. 800–328–1445.

Converse Inc., 1 Fordham Rd., North Reading, MA 01864: Free information ❖ Shoes. 800–428–2667; 508–664–1100 (in MA).

Eisner Brothers, 75 Essex St., New York, NY 10002: Free information ❖ Trunks. 212–475–6868.

Faber Brothers, 4141 S. Pulaski Rd., Chicago, IL 60632: Free information ❖ Bags, gloves, and head guards. 312–376–9300.

Franklin Sports Industries Inc., 17 Campanelli Parkway, P.O. Box 508, Stoughton, MA 02072: Free information ❖ Bags and gloves. 617–344–1111.

G & S Sporting Goods, 43 Essex St., New York, NY 10002: Free price list ❖ Trunks, robes, gloves, training equipment, and protective gear. 212–777–7590.

Genesport Industries Ltd., Hokkaido Karate Equipment Manufacturing Company, 150 King St., Montreal, Quebec, Canada H3C 2P3: Free information ❖ Robes, shoes, trunks, punching bags, skip ropes, and boxing rings. 514–861–1856.

Markwort Sporting Goods, 4300 Forest Park Ave., St. Louis, MO 63108: Catalog $8 ❖ Bags, gloves, and headguards. 314–652–3757.

Otomix, 431 N. Oak St., Inglewood, CA 90302: Free information ❖ Fitness clothing, shoes, and martial arts equipment. 310–330–0750.

Pony USA Inc., 676 Elm St., Concord, MA 01742: Free information ❖ Shoes. 800–654–7669; 508–287–0052 (in MA).

Tuf-Wear USA, P.O. Box 239, Sidney, NE 69162: Free information ❖ Robes, shoes, and trunks. 800–445–5210; 308–254–4011 (in NE).

Equipment

Betlin Manufacturing, 1445 Marion Rd., Columbus OH 43207: Free information ❖ Robes and trunks. 614–443–0248.

Cannon Sports, P.O. Box 11179, Burbank, CA 91510: Free information with list of retailers ❖ Punching bags and skip ropes. 800–362–3146; 818–753–5940 (in CA).

Everlast Sports Manufacturing Corporation, 750 E. 132nd St., Bronx, NY 10454: Free information ❖ Punching bags, boxing rings, skip ropes, gloves, headguards, helmets, and tooth and mouth protectors. 800–221–8777; 212–993–0100 (in NY).

Faber Brothers, 4141 S. Pulaski Rd., Chicago, IL 60632: Free information ❖ Clothing for boxers. 312–376–9300.

G & S Sporting Goods, 43 Essex St., New York, NY 10002: Free price list ❖ Trunks, robes, gloves, training equipment, and protective gear. 212–777–7590.

Genesport Industries Ltd., Hokkaido Karate Equipment Manufacturing Company, 150 King St., Montreal, Quebec, Canada H3C 2P3: Free information ❖ Punching bags, skip ropes, boxing rings, robes, shoes, trunks, gloves, headguards, helmets, and tooth and mouth protectors. 514–861–1856.

Gladiator Sports, 3499 Cowes Mewes, Woodbridge, VA 22193: Free information ❖ Gloves, protective gear, punching bags, and dummies. 703–878–9434.

Ivanko Barbell Company, P.O. Box 1470, San Pedro, CA 90731: Free information with list of retailers ❖ Punching bags and skip ropes. 800–247–9044; 310–514–1155 (in CA).

Macho Products Inc., 10045 102nd Terr., Sebastian, FL 32958: Free catalog ❖ Equipment and clothing. 800–327–6812; 407–388–9892 (in FL).

NDL Products Inc., 2313 NW 30th Pl., Pompano Beach, FL 33069: Free information ❖ Punching bags and skip ropes. 800–843–3021; 305–942–4560 (in FL).

Tuf-Wear USA, P.O. Box 239, Sidney, NE 69162: Free information ❖ Punching bags, skip ropes, boxing rings, robes, shoes, trunks, gloves, headguards, helmets, and tooth and mouth protectors. 800–445–5210; 308–254–4011 (in NE).

BREAD MAKING

Dough Kneader, AA1 Manufacturing, 1457 Bassett Ave., Bronx, NY 10461: Free information ❖ Easy-to-use kneaders for making bread at home. 212–828–4510.

BRIDGE

Baron/Barclay Bridge Supplies, 3600 Chamberlain Ln., Ste. 230, Louisville, KY 40201: Free catalog ❖ Bridge supplies and books. 800–274–2221; 502–426–0410.

Timeless Expectations, P.O. Box 1180, Fairfield, IA 52556: Free information ❖ Scrabble, chess, bridge, backgammon, gin, cribbage, and other electronic and regular board games, books, and gifts. 800–622–1558.

BRUSHES

Ace Wire Brush Company Inc., 30 Henry St., Brooklyn, NY 11201: Free brochure ❖ Brushes and brooms. 718–624–8032.

Fuller Direct, One Fuller Way, Great Band, KS 67530: Free catalog ❖ Brooms and brushes, space-saving organizers, and other home aids. 800–522–0499.

BUMPER STICKERS

Carswell's Creations, 3476 Alward Rd., Pataskala, OH 43062: Catalog $1 ❖ Automobile-related bumper stickers, buttons, magnets, mirrors, rubber stamps, note cards, and award certificates. 614–927–5224.

Lancer Label, P.O. Box 3637, Omaha, NE 68103: Free catalog ❖ Bumper stickers and labels in rolls, sheets, and pinfeed for computers. 800–228–7074.

Magic Systems Inc., P.O. Box 23888, Tampa, FL 33623: Free information ❖ Easy-to-use portable bumper sticker printing machine and supplies. 813–886–5495.

Royal Graphics Inc., 3117 N. Front St., Philadelphia, PA 19133: Free information ❖ Bumper stickers, posters, and show cards. 215–739–8282.

N.G. Slater Corporation, 220 W. 19th St., New York, NY 10011: Free catalog ❖ Advertising novelties, T-shirts, clips and pins, I.D. cards, bumper stickers, and equipment for making imprinted buttons. 212–924–3133.

BUSINESS CARDS, ID CARDS & CARD CASES

Advanced Products, 11201 Hindry Ave., Los Angeles, CA 90045: Free catalog ❖ Plastic ID cards, calendars, and Rolodex cards. 800–421–2858; 213–410–9965 (in CA).

Artistic Greetings Inc., 409 William St., P.O. Box 1623, Elmira, NY 14902: Free catalog ❖ Business cards, memo and informal note cards, and personalized stationery. 607–733–9076.

Arthur Blank & Company Inc., 225 Rivermoor St., Boston, MA 02132: Free information ❖ Plastic credit, ID, membership, and other cards. 800–776–7333; 617–325–9600 (in MA).

The Business Book, 41 W. 8th Ave., Oshkosh, WI 54906: Free catalog ❖ Pressure sensitive labels, mailing labels, stampers, envelopes, stationery, speed letters, memo pads, business cards and forms, greeting cards, books, and other office supplies. 414–231–4886.

Business Cards Plus, 14560 Manchester, Ballwin, MO 63011: Free information ❖ Color photo business cards. 800–966–2545.

Business Envelope Manufacturers Inc., 900 Grand Blvd., Deer Park, NY 11729: Free catalog ❖ Business cards, imprinted envelopes, forms, stationery, and labels. 516–667–8500.

CFT Business Cards, P.O. Box 3368, Brooksville, FL 34606: Free catalog ❖ Thermographed business cards. 904–683–9808.

Colorfast, 9522 Topanga Canyon Blvd., Chatsworth, CA 91311: Free information ❖ Full-color photo business cards. 818–407–1881.

Comprehensive Identification Products Inc., Middlesex Tpke., Burlington, MA 01803: Free catalog ❖ Instant photo ID system cameras and equipment for making photo ID cards and badges, badge holders, and luggage tags. 617–229–8780.

Cowens, 215 NE 59th St., Miami, FL 33137: Free information ❖ Vinyl card cases. 800–442–0244.

Custom Business Cards, 656 Axminister Dr., St. Louis, MO 63026: Free information ❖ Full-color photo business cards. 800–325–9541; 314–343–0178 (in MO).

Day-Timers, One Willow Ln., East Texas, PA 18046: Free catalog ❖ Business cards, stationery, forms, and office supplies. 215–395–5884.

Enfield Stationers, 215 Moody Rd., Enfield, CT 06082: Free catalog ❖ Business cards, calendars, and gifts. 203–763–3980.

Fantastic Impressions, 20 Lucon Dr., Deer Park, NY 11729: Catalog $15 ❖ Business cards, letterheads, and envelopes. 516–242–9199.

Grayarc, P.O. Box 2944, Hartford, CT 06104: Free catalog ❖ Stationery, business cards, forms, labels, and envelopes. 800–562–5468.

Hodgins Engraving, P.O. Box 597, Batavia, NY 14021: Free catalog ❖ Thermographed business cards. 800–666–8950.

Jackson Marketing Products, Brownsville Rd., Mt. Vernon, IL 62864: Free information ❖ Business cards and supplies for making rubber stamps. 800–STAMP–CALL.

Lee's Company Inc., 1717 N. Bayshore Dr., Unit 4145, Miami, FL 33132: Free information ❖ Photo business cards. 800–LEES–023.

Mid-South Business Cards, P.O. Box 2183, Jackson, TN 38302: Free catalog ❖ Thermographed business cards.

Photo Card Specialists Inc., 1726 Westgate Rd., Eau Claire, WI 54703: Free information ❖ Full-color photo business cards. 800–727–4488; 715–839–9102 (in WI).

Photo Images, 554 Park Dr., Jackson, MS 39208: Free information ❖ Photo business cards. 800–637–1440.

Prolitho Inc., 630 New Ludlow Rd., South Hadley, MA 01075: Free information ❖ Thermographed business cards and stationery and envelopes with flat and raised printing. 413–532–9473.

Pronto Business Cards, Box 548, Safety Harbor, FL 34695: Free catalog ❖ Raised business cards.

Supreme Cards Inc., P.O. Box 5578, Clearwater, FL 34618: Free catalog ❖ Business cards. 800–771–5273.

ZIP Business Cards, P.O. Box 935, Norwalk, OH 44857: Free information ❖ Thermographed business cards. 419–668–0930.

BUTTERFLIES

American Butterfly Company, 3609 Glen Ave., Baltimore, MD 21215: Free information ❖ Imported and domestic butterfly specimens.

Brown's Edgewood Gardens, 2611 Corrine Dr., Orlando, FL 32803: Catalog $2 ❖ Butterfly-attracting plants, herbs, and organic gardening products. 407–896–3203.

The Butterfly Company, 50–01 Rockaway Beach Blvd., Far Rockaway, NY 11691: Catalog $2 ❖ Butterflies, moths, other insects, kits, boards, mounting pins, display cases, books, and chemicals. 718–945–5400.

Scientific, P.O. Box 307, Round Lake, IL 60073: Catalog $1 ❖ Exotic moths, butterflies, and other insects. 708–546–3350.

CABINETS
Bathroom Cabinets

Decora, P.O. Box 420, Jasper, IN 47546: Free information ❖ Bathroom cabinets, knobs, and pulls. 812–634–2288.

NuTone Inc., P.O. Box 1580, Cincinnati, OH 45201: Catalog $3 ❖ Bathroom cabinets, other fixtures, and decor accessories. 800–543–8687.

Sonoma Woodworks Inc., 1285 S. Cloverdale Blvd., Cloverdale, CA 95425: Brochure $1 ❖ Solid oak cabinets, medicine and vanity cabinets, high-tank pull chain toilets, and other bathroom furniture. 800–659–9003.

General Purpose Cabinets

Campbell Cabinets, 39 Wall St., Bethlehem, PA 18018: Brochure $1. 215–835–7775.

Iberia Millwork, P.O. 12139, New Iberia, LA 70562: Free information. 318–365–8129.

La Pointe Cabinetmaker, 41 Gulf Rd., Pelham, MA 01002: Free information. 413–256–1558.

Kitchen Cabinets

American Woodmark Corporation, Box 1980, Winchester, VA 22601: Free information. 800–388–2483.

Aristokraft, P.O. Box 420, Jasper, IN 47547: Free information. 812–482–2527.

Crystal Cabinet Works Inc., 1100 Crystal Dr., Princeton, MN 55371: Free information. 612–389–4187.

Decora, P.O. Box 420, Jasper, IN 47546: Free information. 812–634–2288.

Fieldstone Cabinetry Inc., P.O. Box 109, Northwood, IA 50459: Free information. 515–324–2114.

Haas Cabinet Company Inc., 625 W. Utica St., Sellersburg, IN 47172: Free information. 800–457–6458.

Heritage Custom Kitchens, 215 Diller Ave., New Holland, PA 17557: Free information. 717–354–4011.

Hirsh Company, 8051 Central Ave., Skokie, IL 60076: Free information. 708–673–6610.

HomeCrest Corporation, P.O. Box 595, Goshen, IN 46526: Free information. 219–533–9571.

J & M Custom Cabinets & Millworks, 2750 North Bauer Rd., St. Johns, MI 48879: Catalog $2. 517–593–2244.

Kitchen Kompact Inc., P.O. Box 868, Jeffersonville, IN 47130: Free information. 812–282–6681.

KraftMaid Cabinetry Inc., 16052 Industrial Pkwy., P.O. Box 1055, Middlefield, OH 44062: Catalog $4. 800–654–3008.

Merillat Industries Inc., P.O. Box 1946, Adrian, MI 49221: Free information. 800–624–1250.

Plain 'n Fancy Kitchens, P.O. Box 519, Schaefferstown, PA 17088: Free information. 800–447–9006.

Quaker Maid, Rt. 61, Leesport, PA 19533: Free information. 215–926–3011.

Rutt Custom Cabinetry, P.O. Box 129, Goodville, PA 17528: Catalog $7. 215–445–6751.

Triangle Pacific Corporation, 16803 Dallas Pkwy., Dallas, TX 75266: Free information. 214–931–3000.

WCI Cabinet Group, P.O. Box 1567, Richmond, IN 47374: Free information. 317–935–2211.

Wilsonart, 600 General Bruce Dr., Temple, TX 76504: Free information. 800–322–3222.

Wood-Hu Kitchens Inc., 343 Manly St., West Bridgewater, MA 02379: Free information. 800–343–7919; 800–344–8777 (in MA).

Wood-Mode Cabinets, 1 Second St., Kreamer, PA 17833: Free information. 717–374–2711.

CALENDARS

Cedco Publishing Company, 2955 Kerner Blvd., San Rafael, CA 94901: Free catalog ❖ Calendars, datebooks, and soft-cover books. 415–457–3893.

Down East Books & Gifts, Rt. One Roxmont, Rockport, ME 04856: Free catalog ❖ Calendars, books, and crafts from Maine and New England. 800–766–1670.

Enfield Stationers, 215 Moody Rd., Enfield, CT 06082: Free catalog ❖ Business cards, calendars, and gifts. 203–763–3980.

Georgi Publishers, P.O. Box 6059, Chelsea, MA 02150: Free catalog ❖ Fine art and photo art calendars. 617–387–7300.

Heirloom Editions, Box 520–B, Rt. 4, Carthage, MO 64836: Catalog $4 ❖ Lithographs, greeting cards, stickers, miniatures, stationery, framed prints, and other turn-of-the-century art and paper collectibles. 800–725–0725.

Kar-Ben Copies Inc., 6800 Tildenwood Lane, Rockville, MD 20852: Free catalog ❖ Calendars. 800–452–7236.

Lang Calendars & Cards, P.O. Box 99, Delafield, WI 53018: Catalog $2 ❖ Country-style calendars and greeting cards. 414–646–2211.

Naval Institute Press, Customer Service, 2062 Generals Hwy., Annapolis, MD 21401: Free information ❖ Calendars. 800–233–8764.

Sormani Calendars Inc., P.O. Box 6059, Chelsea, MA 02150: Free catalog ❖ Art-photo illustrated calendars. 800–622–6612.

Starwood Publishing, 5230 MacArthur Blvd. NW, Washington, DC 20016: Free catalog ❖ Calendars with pictures of famous cities, dinosaurs, and garden scenes. 202–362–7404.

Thoroughbred Racing Catalog, Warsaw, VA 22572: Catalog $2 ❖ Calendars with pictures of winning thoroughbred race horses, mailboxes, doormats, sweat shirts and T-shirts, mugs, glasses, jewelry, and wall clocks. 800–777–RACE.

Tide-Mark Press Ltd., P.O. Box 280311, East Hartford, CT 06108: Catalog $2 ❖ Calendars and desk diaries. 203–289–0363.

Zenith Books, 1000 Milwaukee Ave., Glenview, IL 60025: Free catalog ❖ Calendars, books, and video tapes about aviation. 708–391–7000.

CALLIGRAPHY

Ken Brown Studio, P.O. Box 637, Hugo, OK 74743: Free information with long SASE ❖ Birthday card-making kit.

The Calligraphy Shoppe, P.O. Box 715, Safety Harbor, FL 34695: Free information ❖ Pen holders. 813–726–1954.

Coit Pen System, Coit Calligraphics Inc., P.O. Box 239, Georgetown, CT 06829: Free brochure ❖ Single and multiple line pens, instruction books, and pen cleaner. 203–938–9081.

Laurie Cook, 1480 Howell Prairie Rd. SE, Salem, OR 97301: Free brochure ❖ Adjustable ruling pen. 503–588–8547.

Creative Calligraphy, 1701 E. Lincoln Hwy., P.O. Box 943, DeKalb, IL 60115: Catalog $2 ❖ Framed personal remembrances and heirloom and family treasures. 800–545–3928; 815–756–6900 (in IL).

Ebersole Arts & Crafts Supply, 11417 West Hwy. 54, Wichita, KS 67209: Catalog $2 ❖

Calligraphy and other art supplies. 316–722–4771.

Hunt Manufacturing Company, 230 S. Broad St., Philadelphia, PA 19102: Free information ❖ Fountain pens and sets, nibs, inks, and calligraphy papers, markers, and kits. 800–765–5669.

Mernick House, Calligraphy by Kit, P.O. Box 453, Peking, IL 61555: Free information ❖ Framed calligraphy prints. 309–347–4742.

Nasco, 901 Janesville Ave., Fort Atkinson, WI 53538: Free catalog ❖ Calligraphy supplies and greeting cards. 800–558–9595.

John Neal, Bookseller, 1833 Spring Garden St., Greensboro, NC 27403: Free information ❖ Calligraphy and marbling supplies, books, and bookbinding. 800–369–9598.

Pendragon, P.O. Box 1995, Arlington Heights, IL 60006: Catalog $2 ❖ Calligraphy supplies. 800–775–7367.

Pyramid of Urbana, 2107 N. High Cross Rd., Urbana, IL 61801: Catalog $5 ❖ Calligraphy and lettering supplies, office and school equipment, and other art and craft supplies. 217–328–3099.

CAMCORDERS & ACCESSORIES

Retailers

A/V Solutions, Division Sara International Inc., 5890 Point West, Houston, TX 77036: Free information ❖ Camcorders, VCRs, editing equipment, and other electronics. 713–988–1522.

Abe's of Maine Camera & Electronics, 1957 Coney Island Ave., Brooklyn, NY 11223: Free information ❖ Video equipment, camcorders, and photography equipment. 800–992–2379; 718–645–1818 (in NY).

Camera Sound of Pennsylvania, 1104 Chestnut St., Philadelphia, PA 19107: Free information ❖ Camcorders, VCRs, editing equipment, and other electronics. 800–477–0022.

Camera World, 4619 W. Market St., Greensboro, NC 27407: Catalog $1 ❖ Video equipment, camcorders, and photography equipment. 800–634–0556.

Camera World of Oregon, Camera World Building, 500 SW 5th Ave., Portland, OR 97204: Free information ❖ Camcorders and tapes. 503–227–6008.

DataVision, 40 Exchange Pl., New York, NY 10005: Free information ❖ Video cameras

and editing equipment. 800–482–7466; 212–825–1990 (in NY).

Digital Distributors, 1274 49th St., Ste. 129, Brooklyn, NY 11219: Free information ❖ Video cameras, editing equipment, batteries and chargers, and other electronics. 718–768–0609.

The Electronic Mailbox, 10–12 Charles St., Glen Cove, NY 11542: Free information ❖ Video editing and lighting equipment. 800–323–2325.

Electronic Wholesalers, 1160 Hamburg Tnpk., Wayne, NJ 07470: Free information ❖ Camcorders, TVs, cassette players, receivers, CD and laser players, and telephones. 201–696–6531.

Free Trade Video, 1864 48th St., Brooklyn, NY 11204: Free information ❖ Camcorders and editing equipment. 718–435–4151.

Genesis Camera Inc., 814 W. Lancaster Ave., Bryn Mawr, PA 19010: Free information ❖ Camcorders. 800–879–9438; 215–527–5261 (in PA).

Global Video, 1260 W. Swedesford Rd., Berwyn, PA 19312: Free information ❖ Video cameras and editing equipment. 800–420–5050.

Haven Electronics, 46–23 Crane St., Long Island City, NY 11101: Free information ❖ Video equipment and camcorders. 800–231–0031.

Marine Park Camera & Video Inc., 3126 Avenue U, Brooklyn, NY 11229: Free information ❖ Video equipment and VCRs. 800–448–8811; 718–891–1878 (in NY).

Markertek Video Supply, 4 High St., Saugerties, NY 12477: Free catalog ❖ Video equipment. 800–522–2025; 914–246–3036 (in NY).

Mibro Cameras Inc., 64 W. 36th St., New York, NY 10018: Free information ❖ Camcorders, lighting equipment, battery packs, wireless microphones, and photography equipment. 800–223–0322; 212–967–2353 (in NY).

New West Electronics, 4120 Meridian, Bellingham, WA 98226: Free information ❖ VCRs, Camcorders, TVs and monitors, disc players, audio components and speakers, and other electronics. 800–488–8877.

Newtech Video & Computers, 350 7th Ave., New York, NY 10001: Free information ❖ Video equipment, computers and peripherals,

software, cellular phones, fax machines, and office equipment. 800–554–9747.

PowerVideo, 4413 Blue Bonnett, Stafford, TX 77477: Free information ❖ Camcorders, TVs, cassette players, and video equipment. 713–240–3202.

Prime Time Video & Cameras, 100 Main St., P.O. Box 54269, Southeastern, PA 19105: Free information ❖ Video cameras and editing equipment. 800–477–8445.

Profeel Video, 42 Main St., Monsey, NY 10952: Free information ❖ Video cameras and editing equipment. 800–433–5214; 914–425–2070 (in NY).

Professional Video Warehouse, 575 SE Ashley Pl., Grants Pass, OR 97526: Free information ❖ Video equipment. 800–736–6677.

Sixth Avenue Electronics, 331 Rt. 4W, Paramus, NJ 07652: Free information ❖ Video and audio equipment, TVs, monitors, camcorders, laser players, and other electronics. 201–467–0100.

Sunshine Video & Computers, 22191 Powerline Rd., Boca Raton, FL 33433: Free information ❖ Video cameras. 407–394–3742.

Supreme Video, 1562 Coney Island Ave., Brooklyn, NY 11230: Free information ❖ Video editing equipment. 800–332–2661; 718–692–4110 (in NY).

Thrifty Distributors, 641 W. Lancaster Ave., Frazer, PA 19355: Information $1 ❖ Video cameras, editing equipment, batteries, wireless microphones, lights, and other video accessories. 800–342–3600.

Tri-State Camera, 650 6th Ave., New York, NY 10011: Free information ❖ Audio and video equipment, camcorders, video tape cassettes, fax machines, and other equipment. 800–537–4441; 212–633–2290 (in NY).

Universal Video & Camera, P.O. Box 54269, Southeastern, PA 19105: Free information ❖ Video cameras and editing equipment. 800–477–1003.

Video Direct Distributors, 116 Production Dr., Yorktown, VA 23693: Free catalog ❖ Video and audio equipment, TVs, monitors, camcorders, microphones, carrying cases, and other electronics. 800–368–5020.

Video Wholesaler, 726 7th Ave., New York, NY 10019: Free information ❖ Camcorders and video tapes. 800–331–5423; 212–245–3152 (in NY).

Videonics, 1370 Dell Ave., Campbell, CA 95008: Free information ❖ Video editing equipment. 408–866–8300.

Vidicomp Distributors Inc., 232 W. 38th St., Houston, TX 77018: Free information ❖ Video cameras and editing equipment. 800–622–6599; 713–694–6400 (in TX).

Westcoast Discount Video, 5201 Eastern Ave., Baltimore, MD 21224: Catalog $5 ❖ Camcorders. 800–344–7123; 410–633–0508 (in MD).

Manufacturers

Allsop, P.O. Box 23, Bellingham, WA 98227: Free information ❖ Camcorders. 800–426–4303; 206–734–9090 (in WA).

Azden Corporation, 147 New Hyde Park Rd., Franklin Square, NY 11010: Free information ❖ Camcorders, headphones, and other electronics. 516–328–7500.

Bib America, 10497 Centennial Rd., Littleton, CO 80127: Free information ❖ Camcorders. 800–325–0853; 303–972–0410 (in CO).

Canon, One Canon Plaza, Lake Success, NY 11042: Free information ❖ Cassette players, camcorders, and other electronics. 516–488–6700.

Casio, 570 Mount Pleasant Ave., P.O. Box 7000, Dover, NJ 07801: Free information ❖ Camcorders. 201–361–5400.

Chinon America Inc., 1065 Bristol Rd., Mountainside, NJ 07092: Free information ❖ Camcorders. 908–654–0404.

Discwasher, 2950 Lake Emma Rd., Lake Mary, FL 32746: Free information ❖ Camcorders. 800–325–0573; 407–333–0200 (in FL).

Eastman Kodak Company, Kodak Information Center, 343 State St., Rochester, NY 14650: Free information ❖ Camcorders. 800–462–6495.

Emerson Radio Corporation, 1 Emerson Ln., North Bergen, NJ 07047: Free information ❖ Camcorders, monitors, receivers, cassette and CD players, and TVs. 800–922–0738.

Fisher, 21350 Lassen St., Chatsworth, CA 91311: Free information ❖ Speakers, cassette and CD players, camcorders, TVs, and other electronics. 818–998–7322.

Hitachi Sales Corporation, 401 W. Artesia Blvd., Compton, CA 90220: Free information

❖ Cassette and CD players, camcorders, TVs, and other electronics. 310–537–8383.

Instant Replay, 2601 S. Bayshore Dr., Miami, FL 33133: Free information ❖ Camcorders and cassette players. 305–854–6777.

JVC, 41 Slater Dr., Elmwood Park, NJ 07407: Free information ❖ CD and cassette players, camcorders, receivers, amplifiers, TVs, and headphones. 201–794–3900.

Memorex, 1600 II Tandy Center, Fort Worth, TX 76102: Free information ❖ Camcorders. 800–548–8308.

Minolta, 101 Williams Dr., Ramsey, NJ 07446: Free information ❖ Cassette players and camcorders. 201–825–4000.

Mitsubishi Electronics, 5665 Plaza Dr., Cypress, CA 90630: Free information ❖ Audio and video systems, cassette and CD players, camcorders, and TVs. 800–843–2515.

NAP Consumer Electronics, 1 Phillips Dr., Knoxville, TN 37914: Free information ❖ Camcorders, TVs, CD and cassette players, and other electronics. 615–521–4391.

NEC Home Electronics, 1255 Michael Dr., Wood Dale, IL 60191: Free information ❖ Speakers, CD and players, receivers, amplifiers, TVs, camcorders, and other electronics. 708–860–9500.

Olympus Corporation, 145 Crossways Park, Woodbury, NY 11797: Free information ❖ Camcorders. 800–221–3000.

Panasonic, Panasonic Way, Secaucus, NJ 07094: Free information ❖ Audio and video systems, cassette and CD players, TVs, camcorders, headphones, and other electronics. 201–348–7000.

Pentax Corporation, 35 Inverness Dr. East, Englewood, CO 80112: Free information ❖ Cassette players, camcorders, and other electronics. 303–799–8000.

Quasar, 1707 N. Randall Rd., Elgin, IL 60123: Free information ❖ Audio and video systems, CD and cassette players, camcorders, and TVs. 708–468–5600.

Radio Shack, Division Tandy Corporation, One Tandy Center, Fort Worth, TX 76102: Free information ❖ Cassette and CD players, camcorders, universal remotes, computers, and other electronics. 817–390–3011.

RCA Sales Corporation, 600 N. Sherman Dr., Indianapolis, IN 46201: Free information ❖ Audio and video systems, cassette and CD

players, TVs, camcorders, and other electronics. 800–336–1900.

Ricoh Consumer Products Group, 180 Passaic Ave., Fairfield, NJ 07004: Free brochure ❖ Camcorders. 201–882–7762.

Sanyo, 21350 Lassen St., Chatsworth, CA 91311: Free information ❖ Cassette and CD players, camcorders, TVs, and other electronics. 818–998–7322.

Sharp Electronics, Sharp Plaza, Mahwah, NJ 07430: Free information ❖ Cassette and CD players, camcorders, TVs, and other electronics. 800–BE-SHARP.

Sony Consumer Products, 1 Sony Dr., Park Ridge, NJ 07656: Free information ❖ Camcorders, speakers, CD and cassette players, headphones, and other electronics. 201–930–1000.

CAMPING & BACKPACKING
Clothing & Shoes

Academy Broadway Corporation, 5 Plant Ave., Vanderbilt Industrial Park, Smithtown, NY 11787: Free information ❖ Clothing and rainwear. 516–231–7000.

Adidas USA, 5675 N. Blackstock Rd., Spartanburg, SC 29303: Free information ❖ Hiking and climbing shoes. 800–423–4327.

Asolo Boots, 8141 W. I-70 Frontage Rd. North., Arvada, CO 80002: Free information ❖ Outdoor footwear. 303–425–1200.

Eddie Bauer, P.O. Box 3700, Seattle, WA 98124: Free catalog ❖ Men and women's active and casual clothes, footwear, and goose down outerwear. 800–426–8020.

L.L. Bean Inc., Freeport, ME 04033: Free catalog ❖ Clothing for hiking, camping, fishing, sports, outdoor activities. 800–221–4221.

Bowhunter Supply Inc., 1158 46th St., P.O. Box 5010, Vienna, WV 26105: Free information ❖ Rainwear and hiking shoes. 800–289–2211; 304–295–8511 (in WV).

Brenco Enterprise Inc., 1003 6th Ave. South, Seattle, WA 98134: Free information ❖ Climbing and hiking shoes.

Brigade Quartermasters Inc., 1025 Cobb International Blvd., Kenesaw, GA 30144: Free catalog ❖ Clothing and rainwear. 404–428–1234.

Browning Company, Dept. C006, One Browning Pl., Morgan, UT 84050: Catalog $2 ❖ Clothing, rainwear, and hiking shoes. 800–333–3288.

Campmor, P.O. Box 700, Saddle River, NJ 07458: Free catalog ❖ Outdoor clothing and equipment for climbing, camping, hiking, backpacking, and biking. 800–230–2151.

Coleman Outdoor Products Inc., 250 N. Saint Francis, Wichita, KS 67202: Free information ❖ Clothing, hiking and climbing shoes, and equipment. 800–835–3278.

Crescent Down Works, 500 15th Ave. East, Seattle, WA 98112: Catalog $1 ❖ Parkas with goose down and weather-resistant Gore-Tex. 206–328–3696.

Damart, 3 Front St., Rollinsford, NH 03805: Free information ❖ Thermal underwear. 800–258–7300.

Dorfman-Pacific, 2615 Boeing Way, Stockton, CA 95206: Free information ❖ Clothing and rainwear. 800–367–3626; 209–982–1400 (in CA).

Ex Officio Outdoor Sport, 1419–A Elliott Ave. West, Seattle, WA 98119: Free information ❖ Outdoor clothing.

Fabiano Shoe Company, 850 Summer St., South Boston, MA 02127: Free information with long SASE ❖ Insulated hiking and climbing shoes. 617–268–5625.

Hi-Tec Sports USA Inc., 4801 Stoddard Rd., Modesto, CA 95356: Free information ❖ Hiking and climbing boots. 800–521–1698.

Hiker's Hut, 126 Main St., Box 542, Littleton, NH 03561: Free information ❖ Boots and other footwear. 603–444–6532.

Integral Designs, P.O. Box 40023, Highfield Postal Outlet, Calgary, Alberta, Canada T2G 5G5: Free information ❖ Sleeping bags and outerware. 403–640–1445.

Kirkham's Outdoor Sports Products, 3125 S. State St., Salt Lake City, UT 84115: Free catalog ❖ Outdoor clothing. 801–486–4161.

Leisure Outlet, 421 Soquel Ave., Santa Cruz, CA 95062: Free catalog ❖ Camping equipment and clothing. 800–322–1460.

Leisure Unlimited, P.O. Box 308, Cedarburg, WI 53012: Free information ❖ Clothing and rainwear. 800–323–5118; 414–377–7454 (in WI).

Lowe Alpine, P.O. Box 1449, Broomfield, CO 80038: Free information ❖ Outdoor clothing and backpacks. 303–465–0522.

Marathon Rubber Products Company Inc., 510 Sherman St., Wausau, WI 54401: Free information ❖ Rainwear. 715–845–6255.

Martin Archery Inc., Rt. 5, Box 127, Walla Walla, WA 99362: Free information ❖ Hiking shoes. 306–757–1221.

Mekan Boots, 3900 S. 2070 East, Salt Lake City, UT 84124: Free information ❖ Hiking and climbing boots. 800–657–2884; 801–272–4710 (in UT).

Merrell Footwear, P.O. Box 4249, South Burlington, VT 05406: Free information ❖ Outdoor footwear. 800–869–3348.

O.H. Mullen Sales Inc., RR 2, Oakwood, OH 45873: Free information ❖ Clothing and rainwear. 800–258–6625; 800–248–6625 (in OH).

New Balance Athletic Shoe Inc., 38 Everett St., Boston, MA 02134: Free information ❖ Hiking shoes. 800–343–4648; 617–783–4000 (in MA).

Nike Footwear Inc., One Bowerman Dr., Beaverton, OR 97005: Free information ❖ Climbing shoes. 800–344–6453.

North by Northeast, 181 Conant St., Pawtucket, RI 02862: Free information ❖ Clothing and rainwear. 800–556–7262.

North Face, 999 Harrison St., Berkeley, CA 94710: Free information ❖ Clothing and rainwear. 510–527–9700.

One Sport Outdoor Footwear, 1003 6th Ave. South, Seattle WA 98134: Free information ❖ Outdoor footwear. 206–621–9303.

Only the Lightest Camping Equipment, P.O. Box 266, Troutdale, OR 97060: Catalog $1 ❖ Lightweight clothing and camping equipment. 503–666–9365.

Orvis Manchester, Historic Rt. 7A, Manchester, VT 05254: Free catalog ❖ Outdoor clothing and equipment. 800–548–9548.

Pachmayr Ltd., 1875 S. Mountain Ave., Monrovia, CA 91016: Free catalog ❖ Shooting and hunting accessories, clothing, camping equipment, books, and video tapes. 800–423–9704.

Patagonia Mail Order, P.O. Box 8900, Bozeman, MT 59715: Free catalog ❖ Outdoor clothing. 800–336–9090.

Rainshed Outdoor Fabrics, 707 NW 11th, Corvallis, OR 97330: Catalog $1 ❖ Outdoor fabrics, hardware, webbing, patterns, and other supplies. 503–753–8900.

Ramsey Outdoor Store, 226 Rt. 17, P.O Box 1689, Paramus, NJ 07653: Free catalog ❖ Outdoor apparel and equipment. 800–526–7436; 201–261–5000 (in NJ).

REI Recreational Equipment Company, Sumner, WA 98352: Free catalog ❖ Outdoor equipment and clothing, exercise and walking shoes, shoes, rainwear, packs that convert to tents, ski equipment, knives and cooking utensils, sunglasses, and foods. 800–426–4840.

Rettinger Importing Company, 125 Enterprise, Secaucus, NJ 07094: Free information ❖ Clothing, hiking shoes, and rainwear. 800–526–3142; 201–432–7400 (in NJ).

Sierra Trading Post, 5025 Campstool Rd., Cheyenne, WY 82007: Free catalog ❖ Outdoor clothing and equipment. 307–775–8000.

Solstice, 6 NW Davis, Portland, OR 97209: Free information ❖ Outdoor clothing. 503–227–1039.

Sportif US Inc., 445 E. Glendale Ave., Sparks, NV 89431: Free information ❖ Outdoor clothing. 800–776–7843.

Tecnica USA, 19 Technology Dr., West Lebanon, NH 03784: Free information ❖ Outdoor footwear. 800–258–3897.

Vasque Boots, 314 Main St., Red Wing, MN 55066: Free information ❖ Hiking boots. 801–972–5220.

Jack Wolfskin, P.O. Box 2487, Binghamton, NY 13902: Free catalog ❖ Outerwear, packs, sleeping bags, tents, travel luggage, and other outdoor equipment. 607–779–2755.

Wyoming River Raiders, 601 Wyoming Blvd., Casper, WY 82609: Free catalog ❖ Clothing, books, and equipment for camping, river expeditions, fishing, hiking, and other outdoor activities. 800–247–6068; 307–235–8624 (in WY).

Equipment

Adventure Outfitters, Box 2830, Cambridge, MA 02238: Free information ❖ Outdoor equipment. 617–497–7818.

All Outdoors Mountain Equipment Inc., 321 Elm St., Manchester, NH 03101: Free information ❖ Equipment for climbing, hiking, kayaking, canoeing, skiing, and camping. 800–624–1468.

Backpacks Unlimited, 27665 Forbes Rd., Laguna Miguel, CA 92677: Free brochure ❖ Backpacks, mountaineering rucksacks, and travel packs. 714–348–2881.

Bass Pro Shops, 1935 S. Campbell, Springfield, MO 65807: Free information ❖ Camping and backpacking equipment. 800–227–7776.

Bay Archery Sales, 1001 N. Johnson St., Bay City, MI 48708: Free catalog ❖ Camping and backpacking equipment and survival supplies. 517–894–0777.

L.L. Bean Inc., Freeport, ME 04033: Free catalog ❖ Tents, backpacks, bicycles, boats, and other outdoor equipment. 800–221–4221.

Bear Archery Inc., 4600 SW 41st Blvd., Gainesville, FL 32608: Free information ❖ Backpacks, eating utensils, knives, camping tools, lanterns and flashlights, and other equipment. 800–874–4603; 904–376–2327 (in FL).

Bianchi International, 100 Calle Cortez, Temecula, CA 92390: Catalog $3 ❖ Backpacks, knives, camping tools, and sleeping bags. 714–676–5621.

Bibler Tents, 5441 Western, Boulder, CO 80301: Catalog $1 ❖ Easy-to-set-up tents. 303–449–7351.

Bowhunter Supply Inc., 1158 46th St., P.O. Box 5010, Vienna, WV 26105: Free information ❖ Backpacks and equipment. 800–289–2211; 304–295–8511 (in WV).

Brunton U.S.A., 620 E. Monroe, Riverton, WY 82501: Information $1 ❖ Pocket transits, compasses, binoculars, and knives. 307–856–6559.

Buck Knives, P.O. Box 1267, El Cajon, CA 92022: Free information ❖ Knives. 800–326–2825; 619–449–1100 (in CA).

Cabela's, 812 13th Ave., Sidney, ME 69160: Free catalog ❖ Tents, sleeping bags, outdoor clothing, footwear, and hunting equipment. 800–237–4444.

Camel Outdoor Products, 5988 Peachtree Corners East, Norcross, GA 30071: Free information ❖ Camping equipment and easy-to-set-up dome tents. 800–251–9412.

Camp Trails, P.O. Box 966, Binghamton, NY 13902: Free information ❖ Backpacks, eating utensils, sleeping bags, and other equipment. 800–848–3673.

Camping World, Three Springs Rd., Bowling Green, KY 42102: Free information ❖ Camping equipment. 800–626–5944.

Campmor, P.O. Box 700, Saddle River, NJ 07458: Free catalog ❖ Clothing and equipment for climbing, camping, hiking, backpacking, and biking. 800–230–2151.

Caribou Mountaineering Inc., 46 Loren Ave., Chico, CA 95928: Free information ❖ Backpacks, sleeping bags, tents, shoulder bags, travel packs, and soft luggage. 800–824–4153.

Casco Sports Medicine, 80 Common Rd., Dresden, ME 04342: Free catalog ❖ Sleeping bags, clothing, moccasins, and other camping equipment. 800–327–9285; 207–737–8516 (in ME).

Coghlan's, The Outdoor Accessory People, 121 Irene St., Winnipeg, Manitoba, Canada R3T 4C7: Free information ❖ Camping, fishing, hunting, backpacking, trailering, and boating equipment. 204–284–9550.

Coleman Outdoor Products Inc., 250 N. Saint Francis, Wichita, KS 67202: Free information ❖ Backpacks, dining utensils, knives, camping tools, lanterns and flashlights, sleeping bags, and other equipment. 800–835–3278.

Colorado Tent Company, 2228 Blake St., Denver, CO 80205: Free information ❖ Tents and sleeping bags. 800–354–TENT.

Comtrad Industries, 2820 Waterford Lake Dr., Ste. 106, Midlothian, VA 23113: Free information ❖ Portable refrigerator with optional built-in food warmer. 800–992–2966.

Dana Designs, 1950 N. 19th Ave., Bozeman, MT 59715: Free information ❖ Backpacks and external frames for men and women. 406–587–4188.

Diamond Brand Canvas Products, P.O. Box 249, Naples, NC 28760: Free information ❖ Two- and four-person tents and backpacks for men, women, and children. 800–258–9811.

Discount Camping Equipment, 421 Soquel Ave., Santa Cruz, CA 95062: Free catalog ❖ Camping equipment.

Duluth Tent & Awning, 1610 W. Superior St., P.O. Box 16024, Duluth, MN 55816: Free catalog ❖ Backpacks, bags, and luggage. 218–722–3898.

Early Winters, P.O. Box 4333, Portland, OR 97208: Free catalog ❖ Camping and backpacking clothing and equipment. 800–458–4438.

Eastern Mountain Sports Inc., One Vose Farm Rd., Peterborough, NH 03458: Free information ❖ Camping equipment and outdoor clothing. 603–924–6154.

Eastpak, 50 Rogers Rd., P.O. Box 8232, Ward Hill, MA 01835: Free information ❖

Backpacks that convert to a suitcase. 508–373–1581.

Envirogear Ltd., 127 Elm St., Cortland, NY 13045: Free information ❖ All-weather, all-terrain sleeping enclosures. 607–753–8801.

Eureka Tents, P.O. Box 968, Binghamton, NY 13902: Free catalog ❖ Self-supporting tents with shock-corded frames. 800–848–3673.

Feathered Friends Mail Order, 2013 4th Ave., Seattle, WA 98121: Free information ❖ Sleeping bags in short, regular, and long sizes, with Gore-Tex, down collar, overfill, and underfill options. 206–443–9549.

Flaghouse Camping Equipment, 150 Macquesten Pkwy., Mt. Vernon, NY 10550: Free catalog ❖ Outdoor equipment. 800–221–5185.

Four Seasons Tentmasters, 4221 Livesay Rd., Sand Creek, MI 49279: Catalog $2 ❖ Tents, cooking utensils, and other camping equipment. 517–436–6245.

Frank's Center Inc., P.O. Box 530, Nevada, MO 64772: Free information with long SASE ❖ Backpacking, camping, rescue/rappelling equipment, and sportshooting guns. 417–667–9190.

Gander Mountain Inc., P.O. Box 248, Gander Mountain, Wilmot, WI 53192: Free catalog ❖ Outdoor equipment, boats, archery supplies, knives, rifle reloading equipment and scopes, camping equipment, and hunting and fishing videos. 414–862–2331.

Gold-Eck of Austria, 6313 Seaview Ave. NW, Seattle, WA 98107: Free information ❖ Sleeping bags. 206–781–0886.

Gordon's Easy Trails, 1519 Alpha Ln., Anaheim, CA 92805: Catalog $1 (refundable) ❖ Camping equipment. 714–776–5965.

Gregory Mountain Products, 100 Calle Cortez, Temecula, CA 92390: Free information ❖ External-frame backpacks. 800–477–3420.

Henderson Camp Products Inc., Raleigh Rd., Box 867, Henderson, NC 27536: Free information ❖ Tents and sleeping bags. 800–547–4605; 919–492–6061 (in NC).

High Sierra, H. Bernbaum Import Export, 880 Corporate Woods, Vernon Hills, IL 60061: Free information ❖ Backpacks, dining utensils, sleeping bags, and other equipment. 800–323–9590; 708–913–1100 (in IL).

Igloo Products Corporation, P.O. Box 19322, Houston, TX 77024: Free catalog ❖

Outdoor cookers and ice chests. 713–465–2571.

Integral Designs, P.O. Box 40023, Highfield Postal Outlet, Calgary, Alberta, Canada T2G 5G5: Free information ❖ Sleeping bags and outerwear. 403–640–1445.

JanSport Inc., 10411 Airport Rd., Everett, WA 98204: Free information ❖ Backpacks and sleeping bags. 800–552–6776.

Kelly's Camping, P.O. Box 602, Lindsay, CA 93247: Free catalog ❖ Backpacking, camping, and optical equipment. 800–69–KELLY.

Kelty Packs Inc., 1224 Fern Ridge Pkwy., Creve Coeur, MO 63141: Free catalog ❖ Sleeping bags and cordura nylon backpacks that convert to luggage. 800–423–2320.

Koolatron Industries Ltd., 2 Treadeasy Ave., Batavia, NY 14020: Free catalog ❖ Portable refrigerators and coolers.

Lafuma Camping Equipment, P.O. Box 812, Farmington, GA 30638: Free information ❖ Sleeping bags, backpacks, and two-, three-, and four-person tents. 404–769–6627.

Leisure Outlet, 421 Soquel Ave., Santa Cruz, CA 95062: Free catalog ❖ Camping equipment and clothing. 800–322–1460.

Leki Sport USA, 60 Earhart Dr., Williamsville, NY 14221: Free information ❖ Trekking poles. 800–255–9982.

Lowe Alpine, P.O. Box 1449, Broomfield, CO 80038: Free information ❖ Outdoor clothing, mountaineering fleecewear, and backpacks. 303–465–0522.

Madden USA, 2400 Central Ave., Boulder, CO 80301: Free information ❖ Backpacks and other equipment. 303–442–5828.

Mark One Distributors, 515 W. 16th St., Bloomington, IN 47404: Free catalog ❖ Camping equipment, sporting goods, hardware and outdoor maintenance products, and safety aids. 800–869–9058; 812–333–7923 (in IN).

Marmot Mountain Works Ltd., 3049 Adeline Ave., Berkeley, CA 94703: Free information ❖ Sleeping bags. 800–MARMOT-9.

Midwest Company, 9043 S. Western Ave., Chicago, IL 60620: Free information ❖ Leather backpacks with roomy cargo sections and expandable outside pockets. 312–445–6166.

Moonstone Mountaineering, 5350 Ericson Way, Arcata, CA 95521: Free information ❖ Sleeping bags. 707–822–2985.

Moss Tents Inc., P.O. Box 309, Camden, ME 04843: Free information ❖ One-, two-, three-, and four-person tents. 207–236–8368.

Mountain Equipment Inc., 4776 E. Jensen, Fresno, CA 93725: Free information ❖ Adjustable backpacks. 209–486–8211.

Mountainsmith, 18301 W. Colfax Ave., Heritage Square, Bldg. P, Golden, CO 80401: Free information ❖ Backpacks, external frames, and two-, four-, and eight-person tents. 800–426–4075.

O.H. Mullen Sales Inc., RR 2, Oakwood, OH 45873: Free information ❖ Backpacks, dining utensils, knives, camping tools, sleeping bags, and other equipment. 800–258–6625; 800–248–6625 (in OH).

Nalge Company, P.O. Box 20365, Rochester, NY 14624: Free catalog ❖ Outdoor equipment. 716–586–8800.

North Face, 999 Harrison St., Berkeley, CA 94710: Free information ❖ Backpacks, camping equipment, and sleeping bags. 510–527–9700.

Northwest River Supplies Inc., 2009 S. Main, Moscow, ID 83843: Free catalog ❖ Backpacks and equipment. 800–635–5202.

Only the Lightest Camping Equipment, P.O. Box 266, Troutdale, OR 97060: Catalog $1 ❖ Lightweight clothing and camping equipment. 503–666–9365.

Osprey Packs, P.O. Box 539, Dolores, CO 81323: Free information ❖ External-frame backpacks. 303–882–2221.

Outbound, 1580 Zephyr, Haywood, CA 94545: Free information ❖ Backpacks, sleeping bags, and two-, three-, and four-person tents. 800–866–9880.

Pachmayr Ltd., 1875 S. Mountain Ave., Monrovia, CA 91016: Free catalog ❖ Shooting and hunting accessories, clothing, camping equipment, books, and video tapes. 800–423–9704.

Paddle & Pack Outfitters Inc., P.O. Box 50299, Nashville, TN 37205: Free catalog ❖ Canoeing, kayaking, and backpacking equipment. 800–786–5565.

Premier International Inc., 901 N. Stuart St., Ste. 84, Arlington, VA 22203: Free information ❖ Backpacks. 800–354–5420.

Ramsey Outdoor Store, 226 Rt. 17, P.O. Box 1689, Paramus, NJ 07653: Free catalog ❖ Camping and backpacking equipment. 800–526–7436; 201–261–5000 (in NJ).

Ranger Manufacturing Company Inc., P.O. Box 14067, Augusta, GA 30919: Free information ❖ Camouflage clothing. 800–847–3469; 404–738–2023 (in GA).

REI Recreational Equipment Company, Sumner, WA 98352: Free catalog ❖ Exercise and walking shoes, Gore-Tex rain gear, day packs that convert to tents, shoes, ski equipment, gifts, knives and other utensils, sunglasses, and camping foods. 800–426–4840.

Remington Outdoor Products, 14760 Santa Fe Trail Dr., Lenexa, KS 66215: Free information ❖ Backpacks, sleeping bags, and two-, three-, and four-person tents. 913–492–3200.

Rettinger Importing Company, 125 Enterprise, Secaucus, NJ 07096: Free information ❖ Backpacks, sleeping bags, and other equipment. 800–526–3142; 201–432–7400 (in NJ).

A.G. Russell Knife Company, 1705 Hwy. 71 B North, Springdale, AR 72764: Catalog $2 ❖ Knives and cutlery. 800–255–9034.

Siemens, P.O. Box 6032, Camarillo, CA 93010: Free information ❖ Rechargeable solar-operated lantern. 800–ARCO-SOL.

Sierra Trading Post, 5025 Campstool Rd., Cheyenne, WY 82007: Free catalog ❖ Outdoor clothing and equipment. 307–775–8000.

Sims Stoves, P.O. Box 21405, Billings, MT 59104: Free information ❖ Folding camp stoves, tents, packsaddles, books, and other equipment. 800–736–5259.

Slumberjack Inc., P.O. Box 7048, St. Louis, MO 63177: Free information ❖ Insulated sleeping bags. 314–576–8000.

The Sportsman's Kitchen Inc., 3038 John Young Pkwy., Orlando, FL 32804: Free information ❖ Refrigerators, cooking equipment, tables, and knives. 800–435–9787.

The Survival Center, P.O. Box 234, McKenna, WA 98558: Catalog $2 ❖ Survival equipment for outdoor activities. 206–458–6778.

Suunto USA, 2151 Las Palmas Dr., Carlsbad, CA 92009: Free information ❖ Compasses. 619–931–6788.

Swallow's Nest, 2308 6th Ave., Seattle, WA 98121: Free catalog ❖ Backpacking, climbing, and mountaineering equipment. 800–676–4041; 206–441–4100 (in WA).

Taymor/Outbound, Outdoors Division, 1580 Zephyr St., Hayward, CA 94545: Free information ❖ Camping tools, backpacks, dining utensils, knives, sleeping bags, and other equipment. 800–338–8143; 510–783–0412 (in CA).

Tents & Trails, 21 Park Pl., New York, NY 10007: Free information ❖ Camping and mountaineering equipment and clothing. 800–237–1760; 212–227–1760 (in NY).

Tentsmiths, Box 496, North Conway, NH 03860: Catalog $2 (refundable) ❖ Authentic period-style tents. 603–447–2344.

Texsport, P.O. Box 55326, Houston, TX 77255: Free information ❖ Backpacks, dining utensils, knives, camping tools, lanterns and flashlights, sleeping bags, and other equipment. 800–231–1402; 713–464–5551 (in TX).

Timberwolf Outdoors, 4606 E. 11th, Tulsa, OK 74112: Free catalog ❖ Camping and canoeing equipment. 800–444–1177.

U.S. Cavalry, 2855 Centennial Ave., Radcliff, KY 40160: Catalog $3 ❖ Camping equipment. 800–777–7732.

Walrus Inc., 929 Camelia St., Berkeley, CA 94710: Free information ❖ One-, two-, three-, and four-person tents. 510–526–8961.

Wenzek, P.O. Box 7048A, St. Louis, MO 63177: Free information ❖ Padded shoulder strap-adjustable frame back pack. 800–325–4121.

Wiggy's Inc., 2842 Industrial Blvd., Grand Junction, CO 81505: Free information ❖ Sleeping bags and insulated clothing. 303–241–6465.

Wild Country USA, 624 Main St., Center Conway, NH 03818: Free catalog ❖ Tents. 603–447–1961.

Wilderness Experience, 20721 Dearborn St., Chatsworth, CA 91311: Free information ❖ External-frame backpacks. 818–341–5774.

Jack Wolfskin, P.O. Box 2487, Binghamton, NY 13902: Free catalog ❖ Outerwear, backpacks, sleeping bags, tents, travel luggage, and other outdoor equipment. 607–779–2755.

Wyoming River Raiders, 601 Wyoming Blvd., Casper, WY 82609: Free catalog ❖ Clothing, camping, and river expedition equipment. 800–247–6068; 307–235–8624 (in WY).

Food

Adventure Foods, Rt. 2, Whittier, NC 28789: Free brochure ❖ Camping foods and stoves. 704–497–4113.

AlpineAire, P.O. Box 1600, Nevada City, CA 95959: Free information ❖ Freeze-dried and concentrated foods. 800–322–6325.

Backpack Gourmet, P.O. Box 334, Underhill, VT 05489: Free information ❖ Freeze-dried foods. 802–899–5445.

Backpacker's Pantry, 6350 Gunpark Dr., Boulder, CO 80301: Free catalog ❖ Lightweight, quick, and easy-to-prepare freeze-dried foods. 303–581–0518.

Clear Water Trader, 637 Fairview Dr., Woodland, CA 95695: Free information ❖ Freeze-dried foods. 916–661–1507.

Myers Meats, Rt. 1, Box 132, Parshall, ND 58770: Free information ❖ Original or peppered beef jerky and beef stick. 800–635–3759.

Nitro-Pak Preparedness Center, 151 N. Main St., Heber City, UT 84032: Catalog $3 ❖ Survival equipment and other supplies, freeze-dried and dehydrated foods, books, and videos. 800–866–4876.

Outdoor Kitchen, Box 1600, Nevada City, CA 95959: Free catalog ❖ Additive-free freeze-dried foods. 800–322–MEAL.

Piragis Northwoods Company, 105 N. Central Ave., Ely, MN 55731: Catalog $2 ❖ Canoes, boating gear, boats, videos and tapes, and trail foods. 800–223–6565.

REI Recreational Equipment Company, Sumner, WA 98352: Free catalog ❖ Exercise and walking shoes, Gore-Tex rain gear, day packs that convert to tents, shoes, ski equipment, gifts, knives and other utensils, sunglasses, and camping foods. 800–426–4840.

Richmoor Corporation, P.O. Box 8092, Van Nuys, CA 91409: Free information ❖ Freeze-dried and concentrated foods. 800–423–3170; 818–787–2510 (in CA).

Stow-A-Way Industries, P.O. Box 957, East Greenwich, RI 02818: Free catalog ❖ Lightweight foods.

Survival Supply, Box 1745, Shingle Springs, CA 95682: Catalog $1 ❖ Freeze-dried and storage foods. 916–621–3836.

Trail Foods Company, P.O. Box 9309, North Hollywood, CA 91609: Free catalog ❖ Two- and four-person meal pouches. 818–897–4370.

Uncle John's Foods, P.O. Box 489, Fairplay, CO 80440 Free information ❖ Freeze-dried foods. 800–530–8733.

Wee-Pak, P.O. Box 562, Sun Valley, ID 83353: Free information ❖ Freeze-dried foods. 800–722–2710.

CANDLES & CANDLE MAKING

American Candle Classics, 19 E. Martin St., Allentown, PA 18103: Free brochure ❖ Classic-style candles with a choice of scents and colors. 215–791–7768.

B & B Honey Farm, Rt. 2, Box 245, Houston, MN 55943: Free catalog ❖ Beekeeping and candle-making supplies. 507–896–3955.

B & R Candles, P.O. Box 1584, Piscataway, NJ 08855: Free information ❖ Hand-poured candles in different sizes, shapes, and scents. 908–463–0963.

Barker Enterprises Inc., 15106 10th Ave. SW, Seattle, WA 98166: Catalog $2 ❖ Candle-making supplies and molds. 800–543–0601.

The Candle Factory, 4411 South I.H. 35, Georgetown, TX 78626: Free catalog ❖ Hand-dipped tapers, dinner and novelty candles, machine made and molded decorative pillars, and wax potpourri chips. 512–863–6025.

Candlechem Products, P.O. Box 705, Randolph, MA 02368: Catalog $2 ❖ Oils, perfume oils, dyes, and other scents for making candles and perfumery items. 617–986–7541.

Candlewic Company, 35 Beulah Rd., New Britain, PA 18901: Catalog $2 (refundable) ❖ Candle-making supplies. 215–348–9285.

Gardens Past, P.O. Box 1846, Estes Park, CO 80517: Catalog $1 ❖ Soaps and soap making supplies, dried flowers, potpourri, herbs, candles, and aromatherapy items. 303–586–0400.

The Glowing Candle Factory, 672 8th Ave., San Diego, CA 92101: Free information ❖ Handcrafted decorated candles. 800–622–6353; 619–231–0054 (in CA).

Jack-Be-Nimble Candleworks, 561 Church Ln., Reading, PA 19606: Free price list ❖ Hand-dipped candles. 800–462–2031.

K & L Candles, 12 Barden Ln., P.O. Box 322, Warren, RI 02885: Catalog $3 (refundable) ❖ In-stock and custom candles. 401–245–4460.

Mann Lake Supply, County Rd. 40 & 1st St., Hackensack, MN 56452: Free catalog ❖ Beekeeping and honey production equipment, protective clothing, candle molds and kits, and how-to books. 800–233–6663.

Mountain Crafts, 163 E. Main St., Little Falls, NJ 07424: Free catalog ❖ Candle-making supplies, tumbled gemstones, wire tree-making supplies, and woodworking patterns. 201–256–3669.

Nasco, 901 Janesville Ave., Fort Atkinson, WI 53538: Free catalog ❖ Candle-making supplies. 800–558–9595.

Pourette Manufacturing, 6910 Roosevelt Way NE, Seattle, WA 98115: Catalog $2 (refundable) ❖ Candles and candle- and soap-making supplies. 206–525–4488.

Pyramid of Urbana, 2107 N. High Cross Rd., Urbana, IL 61801: Catalog $5 ❖ Candle-making and other craft, office, art, and school supplies. 217–328–3099.

Southern Glo Candle Company, 811 E. Plano Pkwy., Plano, TX 75074: Free information ❖ Decorative fragrant candles. 800–437–3147; 214–423–2736 (in TX).

Traditional Country Crafts, Box 111, Landisville, PA 17538: Brochure $1 ❖ Pennsylvania Amish-dipped candles in old-fashioned colors and sizes. 717–653–5969.

CANDY MAKING & CAKE DECORATING

Assouline & Ting Inc., 314 Brown St., Philadelphia, PA 19123: Free information ❖ Cocoa powder and chocolate couverture. 800–521–4491; 215–627–3000 (in PA).

Cooking Craft Inc., 1415 W. Main, Valley Shopping Center, St. Charles, IL 60174: Free catalog ❖ Chocolate and candy-making supplies. 708–377–1730.

Holcraft Collection, 211 El Cajon Ave., P.O. Box 792, Davis, CA 95616: Catalog $2 ❖ Molds for making chocolate candy. 916–756–3023.

Lorann Oils, P.O. Box 22009, Lansing, MI 48909: Free information ❖ Supplies for making suckers and other hard candies. 800–248–1302.

Maid of Scandinavia, 3244 Raleigh Ave., Minneapolis, MN 55416: Free catalog ❖

Utensils, kitchen tools, cake tins, and candy-making molds and ingredients. 800–851–1121.

Meadow's Chocolate & Cake Supplies, P.O.Box 448, Richmond Hill, NY 11419: Catalog $2 ❖ Candy-making and cake-decorating supplies. 718–835–3600.

Paradigm, 5775 SW Jean Rd., Lake Oswego, OR 97034: Catalog $1 (refundable) ❖ Chocolate for bakers and candy makers. 800–234–0250.

Petit Fleurs, 4696 Creekwood Dr., Fremont, CA 94555: Information 50¢ ❖ Cake decorating supplies. 510–745–9405.

Albert Uster Imports Inc., 9211 Gaither Rd., Gaithersburg, MD 20877: Free catalog ❖ Chocolate couverture, cocoa powder, disposable pastry bags, and candy boxes. 800–231–8154; 301–258–7350 (in MD).

Wilton Enterprise Inc., 2240 W. 75th St., Woodbridge, IL 60517: Catalog $6 (refundable) ❖ Supplies for making candies, cookies, and cakes. 708–963–963–7100.

CANES, WALKERS & HIKING STICKS

Able Walker Ltd., 1122 Fir Ave., Blaine, WA 98230: Free brochure ❖ Folding, adjustable walker with a shopping basket, convertible seat, and locking hand brakes. 800–663–1305.

American Foundation for the Blind Inc., Product Center, 3342 Melrose Ave., Roanoke, VA 24017: Free catalog ❖ Canes, watches and clocks, household and personal care supplies, and other aids for visually impaired persons. 800–829–0500.

American Health Manufacturing, P.O. Box 16287, Baltimore, MD 21210: Free catalog ❖ Walkers. 800–232–3044.

American Walker Inc., 742 Market St., Oregon, WI 53575: Free information ❖ Walkers and walk-a-cycles for rough terrains.

Cascade Designs Inc., 400 1st Ave. South, Seattle, WA 98134: Free information ❖ Adjustable walking staffs. 800–531–9531.

Catalog of Canes & Walking Sticks, 767 Old Onion Mountain Rd., Wilderville, OR 97543: Brochure $1 ❖ Walking sticks and staffs in wrist, elbow, and shoulder lengths. 800–458–5920.

DutchGuard, P.O. Box 411687, Kansas City, MO 64141: Free catalog ❖ Gadget and flask canes and secrecy sticks in lustrous

hardwoods and exotics, and optional silver, brass, gold, and wood heads. 800–821–5157.

ETAC USA, 2325 Parklawn Dr., Ste. J, Waukesha, WI 53186: Free brochure ❖ Walking aids, bath safety equipment, wheelchairs, and other aids to make daily living easier. 800–678–3822.

The Gathering Place, 868 15th St., P.O. Box 163, Otsrego, MI 49078: Free information ❖ Hiking and walking sticks, bamboo and cedar birdhouses, and bird feeders. 616–694–4477.

Guardian Products Inc., 12800 Wentworth St., Arleta, CA 91331: Free catalog ❖ Walkers, crutches, canes, home activity aids, beds, lifters, ramps, and transporting equipment. 800–255–5022; 818–504–2820 (in CA).

Miles Kimball Company, 41 W. 8th Ave., Oshkosh, WI 54906: Free catalog ❖ Canes and other aids for people with physical disabilities. 800–546–2255.

Leki Sport USA, 60 Earhart Dr., Williamsville, NY 14221: Free information ❖ Trekking poles. 800–255–9982.

Poestenkill Hiking Staff, P.O. Box 300, Poestenkill, NY 12140: Catalog $1 ❖ Victorian-style cane replicas. 518–279–3011.

Tracks Walking Staffs, 4000 1st Ave. South, Seattle, WA 98134: Free information ❖ Telescoping walking staffs. 800–527–1527.

The Umbrella Shop, P.O. Box 804, Chicago, IL 60690: Catalog $2 ❖ Umbrellas and walking sticks. 312–861–1806.

Uncle Sam Umbrella Shop, 161 W. 57th St., New York, NY 10019: Free catalog ❖ Umbrellas, canes, and walking sticks. 212–247–7163.

Walk Easy Inc., 2915 S. Congress Ave., Delray Beach, FL 33445: Free brochure ❖ Crutches, walkers, commode chairs, and regular, tripod, and quad canes. 800–441–2904.

Whistle Creek, 5050 Quorum, Dallas, TX 75240: Free information ❖ Handcrafted hardwood hiking and walking sticks. 214–239–0220.

CANNING & PRESERVING

Berry-Hill Limited, 75 Burwell Rd., St. Thomas, Ontario, Canada N5P 3R5: Catalog $2 ❖ Canning supplies, weather vanes, cider press, and garden tools. 519–631–0480.

Canning Supply, P.O. Box 1158, Ramona, CA 92065: Catalog $1 ❖ Canning supplies.

Farmer Seed & Nursery Company, 818 NW 4th St., Faribault, MN 55021: Free catalog ❖ Canning supplies. 507–334–2017.

Gardener's Supply Company, 128 Intervale Rd., Burlington, VT 05401: Free catalog ❖ Garden carts, composters, sprayers, watering systems, weeding and cultivating tools, organic fertilizers and other chemical preparations, leaf mulchers, canning and preserving supplies, and furniture. 800–688–5510.

Gurney Seed & Nursery Company, 110 Capitol St., Yankton, SD 57079: Free catalog ❖ Canning supplies. 605–665–1671.

Earl May Seeds & Nursery Company, N. Elm St., Shenandoah, IA 51603: Free catalog ❖ Canning supplies. 712–246–1020.

Mellinger's Inc., 2328 W. South Range Rd., North Lima, OH 44452: Free catalog ❖ Canning supplies. 216–549–9861.

Modern Homesteader, 1825 Big Horn Ave., Cody, WY 82414: Free catalog ❖ Canning supplies. 800–443–4934; 307–587–5946 (in WY).

CARNIVAL SUPPLIES

Oriental Trading Company Inc., P.O. Box 2308, Omaha, NE 68103: Free catalog ❖ Toys, gifts, novelties, fund raisers, holiday and seasonal items, and other carnival supplies. 800–228–0475.

Sally Distributors Inc., 4100 Quebec Ave. North, Minneapolis, MN 55427: Free catalog ❖ Balloons, toys, greeting cards, gifts, and carnival merchandise. 612–533–7100.

U.S. Toy Company Inc., 1227 E. 119th St., Grandview, MO 64030: Catalog $3 ❖ Carnival supplies, prizes, and games. 800–448–7830; 816–761–5900 (in MO).

CAROUSEL FIGURES & ART

Americana Antiques, Rusty & Emmy Donohue, P.O. Box 650, Oxford, MD 21654: Brochure $4 ❖ Antique wood carousel horses and menagerie figures. 410–226–5677.

Amusement Arts, P.O. Box 1158, Burlington, CT 06013: Free price list with long SASE ❖ Antique carousel figures. 203–675–7653.

Antiques & Collectables, Dave Boyle, 36 Andrews Trace, New Castle, PA 16102: Free information with long SASE ❖ Carousel figure display stands. 412–656–8181.

Brass Ring Graphics, Phil & Molly Rader, 2277 Ogden Rd., Wilmington OH 45177: Free information with long SASE ❖ Carousel T-shirts, sweatshirts, and prints. 513–382–3266.

Carousel Antiques, P.O. Box 47, Millwood, NY 10546: Free information ❖ Antique carousel animals. 914–245–2926.

The Carousel at Casino Pier, Boardwalk & Sherman Ave., Seaside Heights, NJ 08751: Free brochure ❖ Carousel reproductions, music boxes, books, T-shirts, cotton throws, miniatures, and jewelry. 908–830–4183.

Carousel Corner, Jon Abbott, Box 420, Clarkston, MI 48016: Free price list ❖ Carousel animals. 810–625–1233.

Carousel Fantasies, The Village Green at Smithville, 615 E. Moss Mill Rd., Smithville, NJ 08201: Free information with long SASE ❖ Carousel art from brass rings to full-size figures. 609–748–0011.

The Carousel Man, P.O. Box 455, Rexburg, ID 83440: Price list $1 with long SASE ❖ Carousel do-it-yourself horse kits, from one-third scale to full size.

Carousel Shopper, P.O. Box 47, Millwood, NY 10546: Catalog $2.50 ❖ Carousel collectibles. 914–245–2926.

Carousel Magic!, P.O. Box 1466, Mansfield, OH 44901: Catalog $1 ❖ Handcarved carousel figures and carousel carving kits. 419–526–4009.

Dreamtex Collectibles, 8835 Shirley Ave., Northridge, CA 91324: Catalog $2.50 (refundable) ❖ Miniature replicas of carousel horses and menagerie animals. 800–733–8464.

Manny Frank, 6428 Coral Lake Ave., San Diego, CA 92119: Free information ❖ Carousel horses. 619–463–3711.

Guyot Arts, 2945 SE 140th St., Portland, OR 97236: Free brochure with long SASE ❖ Miniature handcarved carousel figures. 503–761–9519.

A Horse of a Different Color Showroom, 22829 NE 54th St., Redmond, WA 98053: Free list with long SASE ❖ American antique carousel figures. 206–868–9344.

Layton's Studio, RD 4, P.O. Box 163, New Castle, PA 16101: Free information ❖ Replica carousel figures, art paintings, and prints. 412–924–2916.

Merry-Go-Round Antiques, Al Rappaport, 29541 Roan Dr., Warren, MI 48093: Free

information with long SASE ❖ Antique carousel figures. 313–751–8078.

Raymarie Carousels, 8485 Sunshine Grove Rd., Brooksville, FL 34613: Catalog $3 with long SASE ❖ Ready-to-paint fiberglass carousel reproductions, wood horses, and decor pieces. 904–596–4137.

Shriver's Carving Kits, 502 Barclay, Dewey, OK 74029: Free catalog with long SASE ❖ Kits for carving carousel miniatures with base and hardware for mounting. 918–534–2730.

The Spirited Steeds, 610 N. Alma School Rd., Ste. 18, Chandler, AZ 85224: Catalog $3 ❖ Carousel art. 602–786–6465.

Total Restorations, Ken Gross, 311–315 E. McGaffey, Roswell, NM 88201: Free information ❖ Handcarved original and reproduction carousel horses, band organ figures, and circus wagons. 505–623–9091.

Vestal Press Ltd., P.O. Box 97, Vestal, NY 13851: Catalog $2 ❖ Posters, recordings, and books about carousels. 607–797–4872.

The Wooden Horse, Marianne Stevens, 920 W. Mescalero Rd., Roswell, NM 88201: Free information ❖ Carousel art. 505–622–7397.

CERAMIC & POTTERY SUPPLIES

A.R.T. Studio Clay Company, 1555 Louis Ave., Elk Grove Village, IL 60007: Catalog $5 ❖ Ceramic supplies. 800–323–0212; 708–593–6060 (in IL).

Aardvark Clay & Supplies, 1400 E. Pomoma St., Santa Ana, CA 92705: Price list $1 ❖ Ceramic supplies. 714–541–4157.

Aegean Sponge Company Inc., 4722 Memphis Ave., Cleveland, OH 44144: Free catalog ❖ Ceramic supplies. 216–749–1927.

Africana Colors, Batavia, OH 45103: Free information ❖ Textured stains. 513–625–9486.

Aim Kiln, 369 Main St., Ramona, CA 92065: Free information ❖ Electric kilns. 800–647–1624; 800–222–KILN (in CA).

Alberta's Molds Inc., P.O. Box 2018, Atascadero, CA 93423: Catalog $6 ❖ Ceramic molds. 805–466–9255.

AMACO, 4717 W. 16th St., Indianapolis, IN 46222: Free catalog ❖ Underglaze colors for brush application on bisque or greenware. 800–374–1600; 317–244–6871 (in IN).

American Art Clay Company Inc., 4717 W. 16th St., Indianapolis, IN 46222: Free catalog ❖ Clays, kilns, pottery-making equipment, glazes, tools, coloring materials, and metal enameling supplies. 800–374–1600; 317–244–6871 (in IN).

Art Decal Company, 1145 Loma Ave., Long Beach, CA 90804: Free information ❖ Ceramic decals. 800–742–0270; 310–494–4744 (in CA).

Astro Artcraft Supply, 1026 W. 44th St., Norfolk, VA 23508: Free information ❖ Ceramic supplies. 800–USA–COST; 804–440–1373 (in VA).

Atlantic Mold Corporation, 55 Main St., Trenton, NJ 08620: Catalog $6.50 ❖ Ceramic molds. 609–581–0880.

Axner Pottery Supply, P.O. Box 1484, Oviedo, FL 32765: Free information ❖ Pottery-making and metal enamelling supplies. 800–843–7057.

Badger Air-Brush Company, 9128 W. Belmont Ave., Franklin Park, IL 60131: Brochure $1 ❖ Air brushes. 708–678–3104.

Bailey Ceramic Supply, Box 1577, Kingston, NY 12401: Free catalog ❖ Ceramic supplies. 800–431–6067.

Bennett's Pottery & Ceramic Supplies, 431 Enterprise St., Ocoee, FL 34761: Free information ❖ Kilns, glazes, potter wheels, clay, slip, tools, and other supplies. 407–877–6311.

Black Magic Cleaners, P.O. Box 404, Burlington, WI 53105: Free information ❖ Greenware cleaner. 414–642–7121.

Blue Diamond Kiln Company, P.O. Box 172, Metarie, LA 70004: Free information ❖ Automatic kilns. 800–USA–KILN; 504–835–2035 (in LA).

Bluebird Manufacturing Inc., P.O. Box 2307, Fort Collins, CO 80522: Free information ❖ Potter wheels. 303–484–3243.

Boothe Mold Company, 767 Mark Sharon Industrial Ct., St. Louis, MO 63125: Catalog $7 ❖ Ceramic molds. 800–782–0512.

Brent Potter's Equipment, 4717 W. 16th St., Indianapolis, IN 46222: Free information ❖ Potter wheels, ware carts, slab rollers, hand extruders, and other equipment. 317–244–6871.

Brickyard House of Ceramics, 4721 W. 16th St., Speedway, IN 46222: Free information ❖ Glazes, stains, underglazes,

brushes, tools, molds, kiln and potter wheel repair parts, and kilns. 317–244–5230.

Brush Country Molds, Catalog Department, 4218 Callicoatte, Corpus Christi, TX 78410: Catalog $5 ❖ Ceramic molds. 512–241–7586.

Byrne Ceramics, 95 Bartley Rd., Flanders, NJ 07836: Free information ❖ Wheels, kilns, tools, brushes, colors, oxides, porcelains, glazes, and other supplies. 201–584–7492.

C & F Wholesale Ceramics, 3241 E. 11th Ave., Hialeah, FL 33013: Catalog $4 ❖ Ceramic supplies, stains and glazes, brushes, tools, music boxes, clock works, and air brushes. 305–835–8200.

Carols Imported Decals, 13008 Eureka, Southgate, MI 48195: Catalog $5 ❖ Ceramic decals. 313–281–1820.

Cedar Heights Clay Company Inc., 50 Portsmouth Rd., Oak Hill, OH 45656: Free information ❖ Foundry and ceramic clay. 614–682–7794.

Central Penn Ceramic Center, 1 Campbell Pl., Camp Hill, PA 17011: Catalog $7 ❖ Ceramic molds.

Cer Cal Decals Inc., 626 N. San Gabriel Ave., Azusa, CA 91702: Free brochure ❖ Ceramic decals. 818–969–1456.

Cerami Corner, P.O. Box 1206, Grants Pass, OR 97526: Catalog $6 ❖ Ceramic molds, decals, china paints, and brushes. 800–423–8543.

Ceramic/Art Distributors, 7576 Clairemont Mesa Blvd., San Diego, CA 92111: Catalog $4.50 ❖ Ceramic projects and supplies. 619–279–4437.

Ceramic Supply of NY/NJ, 7 Rt. 46 West, Lodi, NJ 07644: Catalog $4 ❖ Electric and gas kilns, clays, colors, slip casting and sculpting equipment, potter wheels, and glazes. 800–7–CERAMIC; 201–340–3005 (in NJ).

Ceramichrome, P.O. Box 327, Stanford, KY 40484: Catalog $6.50 ❖ Ceramic molds, colors, and supplies. 800–544–0764.

Chaselle Inc., 9645 Gerwig Ln., Columbia, MD 21046: Catalog $4 ❖ Art software and books, brushes and paints, tempera colors, acrylics, pastels, ceramic molds and kilns, sculpture equipment, silk-screen painting supplies, and other art and craft supplies. 800–242–7355.

Clay Magic Ceramic Products Inc., 21201 Russell Dr., P.O. Box 148, Rockwood, MI

48173: Catalog $3.50 ❖ Ceramic molds. 313–379–4944.

Cohol's Sponges & Decals, 445 Park Ave., Poland, OH 44514: Catalog $3.50 ❖ Decals and sponges. 216–758–1167.

Columbus Clay Company, 1049 W. 5th Ave., Columbus, OH 43212: Free catalog ❖ Clays, glazes, kilns, and other supplies. 614–294–1114.

Continental Clay Company, 1101 Stinson Blvd., Minneapolis, MN 55413: Catalog $4 ❖ Ceramic supplies. 800–432–CLAY.

Creative Hobbies, 900 Creek Rd., Bellmawr, NJ 08031: Free catalog ❖ Ceramic supplies. 800–THE–KILN; 609–933–2540 (in NJ).

Cress Manufacturing Company Inc., 1718 Floradale Ave., South El Monte, CA 91733: Free catalog ❖ Automatic and manual operated kilns for ceramics, porcelain crafts, stoneware, china painting, and lost wax process. 800–423–4585.

Cridge Inc., Box 210, Morrisville, PA 19067: Catalog $2 ❖ Jewelry supplies for decorating ceramics. 215–295–3667.

Crusader Kilns, American Art Clay Company Inc., 4717 W. 16th St., Indianapolis, IN 46222: Free information with long SASE ❖ Energy-saving kilns. 800–374–1600; 317–244–6871 (in IN).

D & R Molds, P.O. Box 5311, Scottsdale, AZ 85271: Catalog $3 ❖ Ceramic molds. 602–968–9234.

Debcor, 513 W. Taft Dr., South Holland, IL 60473: Free information ❖ Drying and damp cabinets, kiln carts and stands, wedging boards, clay carts, and other craft-working furniture.

Doc Holliday Molds Inc., 125 MacArthur Ct., Nicholasville, KY 40356: Catalog $7.50 ❖ Ceramic molds. 606–887–1427.

Dona's Molds Inc., P.O. Box 145, West Milton, OH 45383: Catalog $7.50 ❖ Ceramic molds and coloring materials. 513–947–1333.

Dove Brushes, 280 Terrace Rd., Tarpon Springs, FL 34689: Catalog $2.50 ❖ Brushes. 800–334–3683; 813–934–5283 (in FL).

Evenheat Kiln Inc., 6949 Legion Rd., Caseville, MI 48725: Free catalog ❖ Kilns. 517–856–2281.

Ex-Cel Inc., 1011 N. Hollywood, Memphis, TN 38108: Free information ❖ Slip for ceramic casting. 800–238–7270; 901–324–3851 (in TN).

Fash-en-Hues, 118 Bridge St., Piqua, OH 45356: Free information ❖ Translucent colors for staining ceramic and porcelain crafts. 513–778–8500.

G & J Enterprises, 4199 State Road 144, Mooresville, IN 46158: Catalog $2 (refundable) ❖ Ceramic and electrical supplies.

Gare Incorporated, 165 Rosemont St., P.O. Box 1686, Haverhill, MA 01830: Catalog $9 ❖ Ceramic molds, fired colors, stains, stonewashed glazes, brushes, tools, and kilns. 508–373–9131.

Gator Ceramic Molds, 128 Eisenhower Ct., Nicholasville, KY 40356: Free information ❖ Ceramic molds. 606–885–1994.

Georgie's Ceramic & Clay Company, 756 NE Lombard, Portland, OR 97211: Supplies catalog $5.50; mold catalog $5 ❖ Ceramic supplies and molds. 800–999–2529.

Frank Gleason Ceramic Molds Inc., 1219 N. Jesse James Rd., Excelsior Springs, MO 64024: Free information ❖ Ceramic molds. 800–821–5684; 816–637–3800 (in MO).

Highlands Ceramic Supply, 465 Oak Circle, Sebring, FL 33872: Free information ❖ Ceramic molds, kilns and kiln parts, pouring equipment, slip, clay, and greenware. 813–385–6656.

Hill Decal Company, 5746 Schutz St., Houston, TX 77032: Catalog $2 ❖ Floral decals for ceramics and glass. 713–449–1942.

Holland Mold Inc., 1040 Pennsylvania Ave., P.O. Box 5021, Trenton, NJ 08638: Catalog $7 ❖ Ceramic molds. 609–392–7032.

House of Caron, 10111 Larrylyn Dr., Whittier, CA 90603: Price list $2.50 ❖ Molds and supplies for miniature dolls. 310–947–6753.

House of Ceramics Inc., 1011 N. Hollywood, Memphis, TN 38108: Free catalog ❖ Molds for ceramics and chinaware crafting. 901–324–3851.

Iandola Mold Company, P.O. Box 5507, Trenton, NJ 08638: Catalog $3 ❖ Ceramic molds. 609–396–8832.

Indiana Hobby Molds, P.O. Box 1074, Newburgh, IN 47629: Catalog $4 ❖ Ceramic molds. 812–853–5938.

International Technical Ceramics Inc., P.O. Box 1726, Ponte Vedra, FL 32004: Free information ❖ Kilns and parts for repair. 904–285–0200.

Jay-Kay Molds, P.O. Box 2307, Quinlan, TX 75474: Catalog $5 ❖ Ceramic molds. 903–356–3416.

Jones Mold Company, 416 Harding Industrial Dr., Nashville, TN 37211: Catalog $6.25 ❖ Ceramic molds. 615–333–0683.

K-Ceramic Imports, 732 Ballough Rd., Daytona Beach, FL 32114: Catalog $10 ❖ European decals, sponges, and brushes. 904–252–6530.

Kelly's Ceramics Inc., 3016 Union Ave., Pennsauken, NJ 08109: Free information ❖ Ceramic supplies and molds. 609–665–4181.

Kemper Tools & Doll Supplies Inc., 13595 12th St., Chino, CA 91710: Free catalog ❖ Pottery, sculpting, craft, and art tools. Also doll-making supplies. 800–388–5367.

Kerry Specialties, P.O. Box 5129, Deltona, FL 32728: Free information ❖ Brushes and cleaning tools. 407–574–6209.

Kimple Mold Corporation, 415 Industrial, Goddard, KS 67052: Catalog $7 ❖ Ceramic molds. 316–794–8621.

Laguna Clay Company, 14400 Lomitas Ave., City of Industry, CA 91746: Free information ❖ Clays, glazes, tools, equipment, and other supplies. 800–4–LAGUNA.

Lamp Specialties Inc., Box 240, Westville, NJ 08093: Catalog $3 (refundable) ❖ Electrical supplies for ceramic crafting. 800–225–5526.

Lee's Ceramic Supply, 103 Honeysuckle Dr., West Monroe, LA 71291: Catalog $2 (refundable) ❖ Ceramic supplies, molds, decals, and kits. 800–424–LEES.

Lehman Manufacturing Company Inc., P.O. Box 46, Kentland, IN 47951: Free information ❖ Casting and mixing machines, parts, and slip. 800–348–5196.

Lotties Ceramics & Clay, P.O. Box 189, St. Thomas, PA 17252: Free information ❖ Ceramic molds. 717–369–4941.

Marjon Ceramics Inc., 426 W. Alturas, Tucson, AZ 85706: Free information ❖ Ceramic supplies and tools. 602–624–2872.

Marx Brush Manufacturing Company Inc., 130 Beckwith Ave., Paterson, NJ 07503: Catalog $2 ❖ Ceramic adhesive for mending greenware, bisque, fastening greenware to bisque, adding pieces, mending hairline cracks, and repairing broken stilts and hard spots. 800–654–6279.

Mayco Molds, 4077 Weaver Ct. South, Hilliard, OH 43026: Free information with long SASE ❖ Ceramic molds. 614–876–1171.

Miami Clay Company, 270 NE 183rd St., North Miami, FL 33179: Catalog $2 ❖ Pottery supplies. 305–651–4695.

Mike's Ceramic Molds Inc., 5217 8th Ave. South, St. Petersburg, FL 33707: Catalog $6 ❖ Ceramic molds. 813–321–3725.

Mile Hi Ceramics Inc., 77 Lipan, Denver, CO 80223: Free catalog ❖ Clays and other ceramic supplies. 303–825–4570.

Minnesota Ceramic Supply, 962 Arcade St., St. Paul, MN 55106: Free catalog ❖ Ceramic molds and supplies. 800–652–9724.

Mr. & Mrs. of Dallas, 1301 Ave. K, Plano, TX 75074: Free catalog ❖ Ceramics and china painting supplies. 214–881–1699.

Mug Merchant, 982 N. Batavia St., Ste. B-11, Orange, CA 92667: Free information ❖ Ceramics and glass decals. 800–662–MUGS.

Nasco, 901 Janesville Ave., Fort Atkinson, WI 53538: Free catalog ❖ Ceramic supplies, potter's tools, glazes, and kilns. 800–558–9595.

National Artcraft Company, 23456 Mercantile Rd., Beachwood, OH 44122: Catalog $4 ❖ Ceramic supplies. 800–793–0152.

Nowell's Molds, 1532 Pointer Ridge Rd., Bowie, MD 20716: Catalog $3 ❖ Ceramic molds. 301–249–0846.

Ohio Ceramic Supply Inc., 2881 State Rt. 59, Kent, OH 44240: Free information ❖ Ceramic supplies. 216–296–3815.

Olympic Enterprises, P.O. Box 321, Campbell, OH 44405: Catalog $5 ❖ Ceramic supplies, decals, chinaware, and brushes. 216–755–2726.

Olympic Kilns, Division Haugen Manufacturing Inc., 6301 Button Gwinnett Dr., Atlanta, GA 30340: Free catalog ❖ Kilns. 404–441–5550.

Paragon Industries, 2011 S. Town East Blvd., Mesquite, TX 75149: Free catalog ❖ Kilns. 800–876–4328; 214–288–7557 (in TX).

PCM Molds, P.O. Box 2167, Riverview, MI 48192: Catalog $6.50 ❖ Ceramic molds. 313–283–0722.

Pierce Tools, 1610 Parkdale Dr., Grants Pass, OR 97527: Free catalog ❖ Ceramic, pottery, doll, and sculpting tools. 503–476–1778.

Pine Tree Molds, 14596 S. Main St., Mill Village, PA 16427: Catalog $5 ❖ Ceramic molds. 800–346–4428.

PolyCrafts, 1839 61st St., Sarasota, FL 34243: Free information ❖ Ceramic molds and other supplies. 813–355–9755.

Provincial Ceramic Products, 140 Parker Ct., Chardon, OH 44024: Brochure $6 ❖ Ceramic supplies and molds. 216–286–1277.

Pyramid of Urbana, 2107 N. High Cross Rd., Urbana, IL 61801: Catalog $5 ❖ Ceramic supplies and tools. 217–328–3099.

R-Molds, 18711 St. Clair Ave., Cleveland, OH 44110: Catalog $7.50 ❖ Ceramic molds. 216–531–9185.

Red Barn Ceramics Inc., Rt. 13 South, Cortland, NY 13045: Catalog $3 (refundable) ❖ Ceramic equipment and electrical supplies. 607–756–2039.

Carol Reinert Ceramics, 1100 Grosser Rd., Gilbertsville, PA 19525: Free information ❖ Molds and ceramic supplies. 215–367–4373.

Riverview Molds Inc., 2141 P Ave., Williamsburg, IA 52361: Catalog $7 ❖ Ceramic molds. 319–668–9800.

Schafer's Wholesale, 9401 E. 81st St., Raytown, MO 64138: Free information ❖ Ceramic supplies. 816–353–7239.

Heinz Scharff Brushes, P.O. Box 746, Fayetteville, GA 30214: Free catalog ❖ Brushes for ceramic and tole painting, china and decorative painting, and other crafts. 404–461–2200.

Scioto Ceramic Products Inc., 2455 Harrisburg Pike, Grove City, OH 43123: Catalog $5.95 ❖ Ceramic molds. 614–871–0090.

Scott Publications, 30595 W. 8 Mile Rd., Livonia, MI 48152: Free catalog ❖ Books for the ceramist, china painter, and doll maker. 313–477–6650.

Sheffield Pottery Inc., US Rt. 7, P.O. Box 399, Sheffield, MA 01257: Free catalog ❖ Kilns, stains, other equipment and supplies, and moist, screened fire, and slip clays. 413–229–7700.

Skutt Ceramic Products, 2618 SE Steele St., Portland, OR 97202: Free brochure ❖ Electric kilns. 503–231–7726.

Southern Oregon Pottery & Supply, 111 Talent Ave., Box 158, Talent, OR 97540: Free brochure ❖ Manual, automatic, and electronic 110– and 240–volt kilns. 503–535–6700.

Star Stilts, P.O. Box 367, Feasterville, PA 19053: Free catalog ❖ Stilts and other supports. 215–357–1893.

Stewart's of California Inc., 16055 Heron Ave., La Mirada, CA 90638: Catalog $2 ❖ Ceramic supplies. 714–523–2603.

Sugar Creek Industries Inc., P.O. Box 354, Linden, IN 47955: Free catalog ❖ Ceramic equipment. 317–339–4641.

Tampa Bay Mold Company, 2724 22nd St. North, St. Petersburg, FL 33713: Catalog $2 ❖ Ceramic molds. 800–359–0534.

Tari Tan Ceramic & Craft Supply, 3919 N. Greenbrooke SE, Grand Rapids, MI 49512: Free information ❖ Ceramic molds and supplies. 616–698–2460.

Trenton Mold Boutique, 329 Whitehead Rd., Trenton, NJ 08619: Catalog $5 ❖ Ceramic molds. 609–890–0606.

VIP Molds Inc., 1819 German St., Erie, PA 16503: Catalog $8 ❖ Ceramic molds. 814–455–3396.

Weaver's Ceramic Mold Inc., 684 W. Main St., New Holland, PA 17557: Catalog $2 ❖ Ceramic molds. 717–354–4491.

Weidlich Ceramics Inc., 2230 W. Camplain Rd., Somerville, NJ 08876: Free information ❖ Greenware, kilns, and fired and non-fired colors. 908–725–8554.

Wise Screenprint Inc., 1011 Valley St., Dayton, OH 45404: Free information ❖ Decals for ceramics and glass. 513–223–1573.

The Wishing Well, 221 W. 8th, Box 226, Cozad, NE 69130: Free information ❖ Liquid suede kits and water soluble, non-toxic ceramic paints. 308–784–3100.

Yozie Molds Inc., RD 1, Box 415, Dunbar, PA 15431: Catalog $12 ❖ Ceramic molds. 412–628–3693.

Zembillas Sponge Company Inc., P.O. Box 24, Campbell, OH 44405: Catalog $3.50 ❖ Decals, brushes, and tools. 216–755–1644.

CHAIR CANING

A & H Brass & Supply, 126 W. Main St., Johnson City, TN 37604: Catalog $1 ❖ Chair caning restoration materials. 615–928–8220.

Al Con Enterprises, P.O. Box 1060, Quincy, FL 32351: Free catalog ❖ Macrame, chair weaving, and crochet supplies. 800–523–4371; 904–627–6996 (in FL).

Barap Specialties, 835 Bellows Ave., Frankfort, MI 49635: Catalog $1 ❖ Caning supplies and tools, lamp parts, turned wood items, and other craft supplies. 800–3–BARAP–3.

Cane & Basket Supply Company, 1283 S. Cochran, Los Angeles, CA 90019: Catalog $2 ❖ Reeds, fiber and rush, Danish seat cord, raffia, rattan seagrass, and other caning and basket-making supplies. 213–939–9644.

Caning Shop, 926 Gilman St., Berkeley, CA 94710: Catalog $1 (refundable) ❖ Caning and basket-making supplies and tools. 510–527–5010.

Country Seat, RD 2, Box 24A, Kempton, PA 19529: Price list $1 ❖ Basket-making and chair-caning supplies and books. 215–756–6124.

Frank's Cane & Rush Supply, 7252 Heil Ave., Huntington Beach, CA 92647: Free information ❖ Cane, rush, other basket-making supplies, and wood parts. 714–847–0707.

Furniture Restoration Supply Company, 5498 Rt. 34, Oswego, IL 60543: Catalog $2 (refundable) ❖ Upholstery, chair caning, and wicker repair supplies. 800–432–2745.

Go-Cart Shop, 168 Main St., Fairhaven, MA 02719: Catalog 25¢ ❖ Chair cane, woven cane, flat and oval reeds, basket reeds, imitation rush, caning pegs, and how-to books. 508–992–5811.

Jack's Upholstery & Caning Supplies, 5498 Rt. 34, Oswego, IL 60543: Catalog $2 (refundable) ❖ Upholstery, basket-making, and chair caning supplies. 708–554–1045.

Newell Workshop, 19 Blaine Ave., Hinsdale, IL 60521: Free catalog ❖ Caning kits and restoration materials. 708–323–7367.

Peerless Rattan & Reed, 222 Lake Ave., Yonkers, NY 10701: Catalog 50¢ ❖ Caning supplies. 914–968–4046.

H.H. Perkins Company, 10 S. Bradley Rd., Woodbridge, CT 06525: Free catalog ❖ Seat weaving and basket-making supplies, macrame supplies, and how-to books. 800–462–6660.

Royalwood Ltd., 517 Woodville Rd., Mansfield, OH 44907: Catalog $1 ❖ Caning and basket-making supplies, tools, kits, and dyes. 419–526–1630.

Snapvent Company, 147 W. Baxter Ave., Knoxville, TN 37917: Free price list with long SASE ❖ Basket and chair caning supplies. 615–523–6784.

Veterans Caning Shop, 550 W. 35th St., New York, NY 10001: Free catalog ❖ Caning supplies. 212–868–3244.

CHEERLEADING

Apsco Inc., 1st Ave. & 50th St., Building 57, Brooklyn, NY 11232: Free information ❖ Caps, hats, pennants, banners, and sweaters. 718–965–9500.

Asics Tiger Corporation, 10540 Talbert Ave., West Bldg., Fountain Valley, CA 92708: Free information ❖ Shoes. 800–766–ASICS; 714–962–7654 (in CA).

Betlin Manufacturing, 1445 Marion Rd., Columbus, OH 43207: Free information ❖ Jackets, skirts, and uniforms. 614–443–0248.

Butwin Sportswear Company, 3401 Spring St. NE, Minneapolis, MN 55413: Free information ❖ Jackets. 800–328–1445.

CAMBER Universal Sportswear, 36 N. 3rd St., Philadelphia, PA 19106: Free information ❖ Jackets, skirts, and uniforms. 800–345–7518; 215–922–1488 (in PA).

Cran Barry Inc., 130 Condor St., Box 488, East Boston, MA 02128: Free information ❖ Caps, hats, megaphones, pom poms, and sweaters. 800–992–2021.

Danskin, 111 W. 40th St., 18th Floor, New York, NY 10018: Free information ❖ Uniforms. 800–288–6749; 212–764–4630 (in NY).

Dodger Industries, 1702 21st St., Eldora, IA 50627: Free information ❖ Sweaters. 800–247–7879; 515–858–5464 (in IA).

Fancy Pants, 3360 Sports Arena Blvd., Ste. G, San Diego, CA 92110: Free information ❖ Skirts and uniforms. 800–755–9565; 619–222–1104 (in CA).

Wm. Getz Corporation, 1024 S. Linwood Ave., Santa Ana, CA 92705: Free information ❖ Pom poms and megaphones. 800–854–7447; 714–835–0100 (in CA).

Hatchers Manufacturing Inc., 130 Condor St., Box 424, East Boston, MA 02128: Free information ❖ Megaphones, pom poms, and sweaters. 800–225–6842; 617–568–1262 (in MA).

Johnny Jones Jr. Company, 6633 Hamilton Ave., Pittsburgh, PA 15206: Free information ❖ Pom poms. 800–245–4252; 412–363–4600 (in CA).

Markwort Sporting Goods, 4300 Forest Park Ave., St. Louis, MO 63108: Catalog $8 with list of retailers ❖ Pom poms. 314–652–3757.

Dick Martin Sports Inc., 181 E. Union Ave., P.O. Box 7381, East Rutherford, NJ 07073: Free information ❖ Megaphones. 800–221–1993; 201–438–5255 (in NJ).

Pepco Poms, Hwy. 60, P.O. Box 950, Wharton, TX 77488: Free information ❖ Megaphones and pom poms. 800–527–1150; 800–992–1048 (in TX).

Plastimayd Corporation, 14450 SE 98th Ct., P.O. Box 1550, Clackamas, OR 97015: Free information ❖ Uniforms. 503–654–8502.

Recreonics Corporation, 4200 Schmitt Ave., Louisville KY 40213: Free information ❖ Megaphones. 800–428–3254.

Shaffer Sportswear, 224 N. Washington, Neosho, MO 64850: Free information ❖ Jackets and uniforms. 417–451–9444.

Sportime, 1 Sporting Way, Atlanta, GA 30340: Free information ❖ Megaphones. 800–444–5700; 404–449–5700 (in GA).

Valley Decorating Company, P.O. Box 9470, Fresno, CA 93792: Free catalog ❖ Pom poms. 209–275–2500.

Wear-Ever Lace & Braid, 90 Cherry St., Hudson, MA 01749: Free information ❖ Pom poms. 508–562–4155.

CHEESE MAKING

Cheesemaking Supply Outlet, 9155 Madison Rd., Montville, OH 44064: Free catalog ❖ Cheese-making supplies. 216–968–3770.

New England Cheesemaking Supply Company, 85 Main St., Ashfield, MA 01330: Catalog $1 ❖ Supplies for making cheese, butter, yogurt, and buttermilk. 413–628–3808.

CHESS

Chessmen of Antiquity, P.O. Box 803241, Santa Clarita, CA 91380: Brochure $2 ❖ Olmec style pre-Columbian and other styles of chess sets. 805–270–0008.

U.S. Chess Federation, 186 Rt. 9W, Newburgh, NY 12550: Free catalog ❖ Conventional and computer chess sets, books, and competition supplies. 914–562–8350.

CHINA PAINTING & METAL ENAMELING

Allcraft Tool & Supply Company, 666 Pacific St., Brooklyn, NY 11207: Catalog $5 ❖ Metal enameling tools and supplies. 800–645–7124; 718–789–2800 (in NY).

American Art Clay Company Inc., 4717 W. 16th St., Indianapolis, IN 46222: Free catalog ❖ Clays, kilns, pottery-making equipment, glazes, tools, coloring materials, and metal enameling supplies. 800–374–1600; 317–244–6871 (in IN).

Axner Pottery Supply, P.O. Box 1484, Oviedo, FL 32765: Free information ❖ Pottery-making and metal enameling supplies. 800–843–7057.

Cerami Corner, P.O. Box 1206, Grants Pass, OR 97526: Catalog $6 ❖ Ceramic molds, decals, china paints, and brushes. 800–423–8543.

Charlie's Rock Shop, 620 J St., Penrose, CO 81240: Free catalog ❖ Metal enameling tools and supplies. 800–336–6923.

Chaselle Inc., 9645 Gerwig Ln., Columbia, MD 21046: Catalog $4 ❖ Art software and books, brushes and paints, tempera colors, acrylics and sets, pastels, ceramic molds and kilns, sculpture equipment, and screen painting supplies. 800–242–7355.

The China Warehouse, 4919 E. 38th Ave., Denver, CO 80207: Catalog $1.50 ❖ China for painting. 303–377–0762.

Cridge Inc., Box 210, Morrisville, PA 19067: Catalog $2 ❖ Gold and silver settings, bisque and glazed porcelain insets, and other china painting supplies. 215–295–3667.

Evenheat Kiln Inc., 6949 Legion Rd., Caseville, MI 48725: Free information ❖ Kilns. 517–856–2281.

Firemountain Gems, 28195 Redwood Highway, Cave Junction, OR 97523: Catalog $3 ❖ Metal enameling tools and supplies. 800–423–2319.

Greater New York Trading, 81 Canal St., New York, NY 10002: Free brochure ❖ Silver, china, and glassware. 212–226–2808.

T.B. Hagstoz & Son Inc., 709 Sansom St., Philadelphia, PA 19106: Catalog $5 (refundable with $25 order) ❖ Metal enameling tools and supplies. 800–922–1006; 215–922–1627 (in PA).

House of Clay Inc., 1100 NW 30th, Oklahoma City, OK 73118: Catalog $3 (refundable) ❖ China, kilns, and other supplies. 405–524–5610.

Maryland China Company, 54 Main St., Reisterstown, MD 21136: Free catalog ❖ China painting supplies. 800–638–3880.

Mr. & Mrs. of Dallas, 1301 Ave. K, Plano, TX 75074: Free catalog ❖ Ceramics and china painting supplies. 214–881–1699.

Nasco, 901 Janesville Ave., Fort Atkinson, WI 53538: Free catalog ❖ Metal enameling supplies. 800–558–9595.

National Artcraft Company, 23456 Mercantile Rd., Beachwood, OH 44122: Catalog $4 ❖ Tiles, china, paints and other coloring preparations, and brushes. 800–793–0152.

Paragon Industries, 2011 S. Town East Blvd., Mesquite, TX 75149: Free catalog ❖ Kilns. 800–876–4328; 214–288–7557 (in TX).

Rynne China Company, 222 W. 8 Mile Rd., Hazel Park, MI 48030: Free information ❖ Decals, books, china and glass paints, overglaze, kilns, brushes, and other supplies. 800–468–1987.

Southern Oregon Pottery & Supply, 111 Talent Ave., Box 158, Talent, OR 97540: Free brochure ❖ Manual, automatic, and electronic 110– and 240–volt kilns. 503–535–6700.

CHINA, POTTERY & STONEWARE

William Ashley, 50 Boor St. West, Toronto, Ontario, Canada M4W 3L8: Free information ❖ China, crystal, and silver. 800–268–1122.

Baccarat, 625 Madison Ave., New York, NY 10022: Free information ❖ Crystal and china Baccarat. 212–826–4100.

Barrons, P.O. Box 994, Novi, MI 48376: Free information ❖ China, crystal, and silver. 800–538–6340.

Mildred Brumback, P.O. Box 132, Middletown, VA 22645: Free information ❖ Discontinued china and crystal. 703–869–1261.

Lis Burrows Pots, Pots, Pots, 4836 King Solomon Dr., Annandale, VA 22003: Free information ❖ Lead-free oven-, microwave-, and dishwasher-safe stoneware. 703–323–8675.

China & Crystal Marketing, P.O. Box 33, Cheltenham, PA 19012: Free information ❖ Discontinued and other China, earthenware, and crystal patterns. 215–342–7919.

China & Crystal Matchers Inc., 2379 John Glenn Dr., Chamblee, GA 30341: Free information ❖ Discontinued china and crystal. 404–455–1162.

The China Cabinet, P.O. Box 426, Clearwater, SC 29822: Free information with long SASE ❖ China and crystal. 803–593–9655.

China Cabinet Inc., 24 Washington St., Tenafly, NJ 07670: Free information with long SASE ❖ China, crystal, flatware, and other gifts. 201–567–2711.

The China Connection, Box 972, Pineville, NC 28134: Free information ❖ Inactive fine and everyday china. 800–421–9719; 704–889–8198 (in NC).

The China Hutch, 1333 Ivey Dr., Charlotte, NC 28205: Free information ❖ Discontinued china. 800–524–4397.

China Replacement Service, 1415 Michigan Ave., Saint Cloud, FL 34769: Free information ❖ Replacement and discontinued china. 800–222–7357.

China Replacements, 2263 Williams Creek Rd., High Ridge, MO 63049: Free information with long SASE ❖ Discontinued china and crystal. 800–562–2655; 677–5577 (in St. Louis).

The China Warehouse, Box 21797, Cleveland, OH 44121: Free information ❖ China, crystal, and flatware. 800–321–3212.

Clintsman International, 20855 Watertown Rd., Waukesha, WI 53186: Free information ❖ Discontinued china, crystal, and flatware. 414–798–0440.

Cowboy Exchange, P.O. Box 27, Elfrida, AZ 85610: Free information ❖ Western-style decorated china. 602–824–3540.

Crystal Lalique, 680 Madison Ave., New York, NY 10021: Free information ❖ Crystal and china Lalique. 800–214–2738; 212–355–6550 (in NY).

Dining Elegance Ltd., Box 4203, St. Louis, MO 63163: Free catalog ❖ Fine china and crystal. 314–865–1408.

East Knoll Pottery, 46 Albrecht Rd., Torrington, CT 06790: Brochure $1 ❖ Hand-thrown and decorated reproduction yellowware.

Eastside Gifts & Dinnerware Inc., 351 Grand St., New York, NY 10002: Free information ❖ China, crystal, flatware, and other gifts. 800–443–8711; 212–982–7200 (in NY).

Michael C. Fina, 580 5th Ave., New York, NY 10036: Free catalog ❖ Sterling serving pieces, tea sets, crystal stemware, bone china, and pewter. 800–BUY–FINA; 718–937–8484 (in NY).

The Five Seasons Corporation, 1901 Rt. 332, Canandaigua, NY 14425: Free information ❖ Handpainted personalized stoneware crocks. 800–724–4064; 716–396–2021 (in NY).

Flat Earth Clay Works Inc., 5760 N. Broadway, Wichita, KS 67219: Brochure $2 ❖ Lead-free microwave- and oven-safe earthenware pottery. 800–654–8695.

Fortunoff Fine Jewelry, P.O. Box 1550, Westbury, NY 11590: Free catalog ❖ China, silverplate and stainless steel serving pieces, and sterling flatware. 800–937–4376.

Greater New York Trading, 81 Canal St., New York, NY 10002: Free brochure ❖ Silver, china, and glassware. 212–226–2808.

Groundhog Blues Pottery, Box 183, Reeders, PA 18352: Free information ❖ In-stock and custom hand-thrown pottery. 717–629–0208.

Jacquelyn Hall, 10629 Baxter, Los Altos, CA 94022: Free information ❖ Lenox china and crystal. 408–739–4876.

Kelley Haney Art Gallery, P.O. Box 103, Seminole, OK 74868: Free brochure with long SASE ❖ Original Native American paintings, sculpture, jewelry, baskets, and pottery. 405–382–3915.

Hartstone Inc., P.O. Box 2626, Zanesville, OH 43701: Free information ❖ Hand decorated dinnerware and accessories. 614–452–9992.

House of 1776, 3110 S. Jupiter, Garland, TX 75041: Free information ❖ China place settings and open stock, tableware, and gifts. 800–989–1776; 214–864–1776 (in TX).

Jacquelynn's China Matching Service, 219 N. Milwaukee St., Milwaukee, WI 53202: Free information with long SASE ❖ Discontinued American and English dinnerware. 414–272–8880.

Jepson Studios Inc., P.O. Box 36, Harveyville, KS 66431: Brochure $2 (refundable) ❖ Country ceramics. 913–589–2481.

Karlin Pottery, 662 Minkin Dr., Traverse City, MI 49684: Brochure $1 ❖ Country pottery and stoneware. 616–275–5649.

Kitchen Accessories Etc., P.O. Box 1560, North Hampton, NH 03862: Free catalog ❖ Kitchen aids, serving pieces, china, and silverplate. 603–964–5174.

Lanac Sales, 73 Canal St., New York, NY 10002: Free catalog ❖ China, crystal, sterling, and gifts. 212–925–6422.

Le Fanion, ZED International Ltd., 299 W. 4th St., Greenwich Village, New York, NY 10014: Free catalog ❖ French country antique and contemporary pottery. 212–463–8760.

Lenox Collections, P.O. Box 3020, Langhorne, PA 19047: Free catalog ❖ China, crystal, and porcelain sculptures. 800–225–1779.

Locators Inc., 908 Rock St., Little Rock, AR 72202: Free information ❖ Discontinued china, crystal, and silver. 800–367–9690.

Midas China & Silver, 4315 Walney Rd., Chantilly, VA 22021: Free catalog ❖ Silverware, table settings, gifts, and china. 800–368–3153.

Mole Hill Pottery, 5011 Anderson Pike, Signal Mountain, TN 37377: Catalog $1 ❖ Signed and dated stoneware lamps and pottery. 615–886–4926.

Mountain Meadows Pottery, P.O. Box 163, South Ryegate, VT 05069: Free catalog ❖ Functional stoneware and humorous and sentimental plaques. 800–639–6790.

Teresita Naranjo, Santa Clara Pueblo, Rt. 1, Box 455, Espanola, NM 87532: Free information with long SASE ❖ Ceremonial and melon bowls, wedding vases, and other traditional Santa Clara black and red pottery. 505–753–9655.

Noritake China Replacements, 2635 Clearbrook Dr., Arlington Heights, IL 60005: Free information ❖ Noritake china replacements. 800–562–1991.

Old Patagonia Pottery, Marty Frolick, 36 W. Clark St., Hermitage, PA 16148: Free information ❖ Fine American art pottery. 412–981–9706.

Olympus Cove Antiques, 179 E. 300 South, Salt Lake City, UT 84111: Free information ❖ Discontinued china. 800–284–8046.

Past & Presents, 65–07 Fitchett St., Rego Park, NY 11374: Free information ❖ China, crystal, and flatware. 718–897–5515.

Pfaltzgraff Factory Outlet, 2900 Whiteford Rd., York, PA 17402: Catalog $1 (refundable) ❖ Dinnerware, baking and serving pieces, decor accessories, and other stoneware irregulars. 800–999–2811; 717–757–2200 (in PA).

Replacements Ltd., 1089 Knox Rd., P.O. Box 26029, Greensboro, NC 27420: Free information with long SASE ❖ Discontinued china, earthenware, and crystal. 800–562–4462.

Robin Importers, 510 Madison Ave., New York, NY 10022: Brochure $1 with long SASE ❖ China, crystal, and stainless steel flatware. 800–223–3373; 212–753–6475 (in NY).

Rogers & Rosenthal, 22 W. 48th St., Room 1102, New York, NY 10036: Free information with long SASE ❖ China, crystal, and stainless steel. 212–827–0115.

Ross-Simons Jewelers, 9 Ross Simons Dr., Cranston, RI 02920: Free information ❖ Sterling and china. 800–556–7376.

Rowe Pottery Works, 404 England St., Cambridge, WI 53523: Free catalog ❖ Salt-glazed stoneware in early authentic folk designs. 800–356–5003.

Rudi's Pottery, Silver & China, 176 Rt. 17, Paramus, NJ 07652: Free information with long SASE ❖ Glass stemware, china, and gifts. 201–265–6096.

Nat Schwartz & Company, 549 Broadway, Bayonne, NJ 07002: Free catalog ❖ Crystal, sterling, and china. 800–526–1440.

Shannon, Box 22361, Houston, TX 77227: Free information ❖ China. 800–742–7766.

Silver Lane, P.O. Box 322, San Leandro, CA 94577: Free information ❖ Discontinued crystal and china patterns, and current and obsolete silver. 510–483–0632.

Spode, 1265 Glen Ave., Moorestown, NJ 08057: Free information ❖ China and accessories Spode. 609–866–2900.

Tetbury Castle, 10200 NW 73rd Terr., Weatherby Lake, MO 64152: Catalog $3 ❖ Old English style goblets, mugs, and other gifts. 816–746–7406.

Thurber's, 2256 Dabney Rd., Ste. C, Richmond, VA 23230: Free information ❖ China and sterling. 800–848–7237.

Van Ness China Company, 601 Shenandoah Village Dr., Waynesboro, VA 22980: Free information ❖ Discontinued and current English bone china. 703–942–2827.

Carol Vigil, P.O. Box 443, Jemez Pueblo, NM 87024: Free information with long SASE ❖ Carved and painted Jemez pottery.

Waterford Crystal Inc., 41 Madison Ave., New York, NY 10010: Free brochure ❖ Crystal and china.

Wedgwood, 41 Madison Ave., New York, NY 10010: Brochure $2 ❖ China.

Wesson Trading Company, 1316 Willow Street Dr., Woodstock, GA 30188: Catalog $2 ❖ Handcrafted pottery, textiles, and folk art. 404–928–6145.

White's Collectables & Fine China, 516 E. 1st., P.O. Box 680, Newborg, OR 97132: Free information ❖ Collectible plates and new and discontinued china patterns. 503–538–7421.

Wisconsin Pottery, W3199 Hwy. 16, Columbus, WI 53925: Free catalog ❖ Handcrafted and hand-decorated salt-glazed stoneware and redware pottery. 800–669–5196.

Workshops of David T. Smith, 3600 Shawhan Rd., Morrow, OH 45152: Catalog $5 ❖ Reproduction furniture, pottery, lamps, and chandeliers. 513–932–2472.

CHOIR GOWNS

Lyric Choir Gown Company, P.O. Box 16954, Jacksonville, FL 32245: Free catalog ❖ Professionally tailored choir gowns. 904–725–7977.

CHRISTMAS DECORATIONS & ORNAMENTS

D. Blumchen & Company Inc., P.O. Box 1210, Ridgewood, NJ 07451: Catalog $3 ❖ Reproductions of antique holiday decorations. 201–652–5595.

Christmas Treasures, P.O. Box 53, Dewitt, NY 13214: Catalog $3 ❖ Reproductions of old Christmas decorations.

The Cracker Box, Solebury, PA 18963: Catalog $4.50 ❖ Christmas ornament kits. 215–862–2100.

The Dough-Nut, 8172 Danneffel Rd., Watervliet, MI 49098: Catalog $1 ❖ Personalized ornaments. 616–463–3864.

European Imports & Gifts, 7900 N. Milwaukee Ave., Niles, IL 60648: Free information ❖ Art collectibles, porcelain, Christmas ornaments, pewter, and other gifts. 708–967–5253.

The Faith Mountain Company, P.O. Box 199, Sperryville, VA 22740: Free catalog ❖ Kitchen utensils, folk art reproductions, toys and dolls, handmade Appalachian baskets, and Christmas decorations. 800–822–7238.

Marilou's Children, 717 Lingo, Ste. 209, Richardson, TX 75081: Catalog $1 ❖ Handmade ornaments. 214–699–3845.

Schaefer's Bakery, P.O. Box 264, Evergreen, CO 80439: Brochure $2 ❖ Personalized Christmas ornaments. 303–431–5952.

The Silver Sleigh, 55 Pittsfield Rd., Lenox, MA 01240: Free information ❖ Handcrafted ornaments. 413–637–3522.

Victor Trading & Manufacturing Works, 114 S. 3rd, P.O. Box 53, Victor, CO 80860: Catalog $3 ❖ Hard-to-find Victorian Christmas decorations. 719–689–2346.

Wooden Soldier, P.O. Box 800, North Conway, NH 03860: Free catalog ❖ Christmas decorations and ornaments and designer clothing for children. 603–356–6343.

CLOCKS & CLOCK MAKING

Alpha Supply, P.O. Box 2133, Bremerton, WA 98310: Catalog $3 ❖ Clocks, clock movements and parts, and engraving tools. 206–373–3302.

Armor Products, P.O. Box 445, East Northport, NY 11731: Free catalog ❖ Replacement movements for mantel, banjo, and grandfather clocks. 800–292–8296.

B & J Rock Shop, 14744 Manchester Rd., Ballwin, MO 63011: Catalog $3 ❖ Quartz clock movements and kits. 314–394–4567.

Beemans Clock Manufacturing, 109 W. Van Buren, Centerville, IA 52544: Catalog $2 ❖ Quartz clock movements and other parts.

Cas-Ker Company, Box 2347, Cincinnati, OH 45201: Catalog $1 ❖ Clock movements, parts, and tools. 513–241–7073.

Charlie's Rock Shop, 620 J St., Penrose, CO 81240: Free catalog ❖ Clocks, movements and parts, beads, jewelry-making supplies, display boxes, and faceted gemstones. 800–336–6923.

Chelsea Clock Company, 284 Everett Ave., Chelsea, MA 02150: Brochure $2 ❖ Clocks and parts. 617–884–0250.

Clock Repair Center, 33 Boyd Dr., Westbury, NY 11590: Catalog $6 ❖ Clock movements, parts, and tools. 516–997–4810.

Clocks Etc., 3401 Mt. Diablo Blvd., Lafayette, CA 94549: Brochure $1 ❖ Old and new clocks, antique furniture, and other gifts. 510–284–4720.

Craftsman Wood Service, 1735 W. Cortland Ct., Addison, IL 60101: Catalog $2 ❖

Kiln-dried and imported rare woods, veneers, hand and power tools, hardware, finishing materials, clock movements and kits, and lamp parts. 708–629–3100.

Ebersole Lapidary Supply, 11417 West Hwy. 54, Wichita, KS 67209: Catalog $2 ❖ Clocks, clock-making parts, tools, findings and mountings, cabochons and rocks, and jewelry kits. 316–722–4771.

Ed's House of Gems, 7712 NE Sandy Blvd., Portland, OR 97211: Free information with long SASE ❖ Clocks, clock-making parts, crystals, minerals, gemstones, and lapidary equipment. 503–284–8990.

Eloxite Corporation, 806 10th St., Wheatland, WY 82201: Catalog $1 ❖ Clock-making parts, tools, gemstones, belt buckles, mountings, equipment for rock hounds, and other craft supplies. 307–322–3050.

Emperor Clock Company, Emperor Industrial Park, P.O. Box 1089, Fairhope, AL 36533: Catalog $1 ❖ Grandfather clocks, kits, and parts. 800–542–0011; 205–928–2316 (in AL).

R. Engels & Company, 4031 Chicago Dr., P.O. Box 235, Grandville, MI 49418: Catalog $5 ❖ Wall, mantel, and grandfather clocks. 800–637–1118.

Hare Hollow, 322 Broad St., Milford, PA 18337: Brochure $2 ❖ Handpainted country-style wall clocks. 717–296–5757.

Haskell's Handcraft, 40 College Ave., Waterville, ME 04901: Catalog $6 ❖ Quartz clock movements, parts, kits and assembled clocks, and electrical supplies. 207–873–5070.

Hearth & Home Clocks, RFD 2, Box 118, Meredith, LA 03253: Free information ❖ Battery-operated country-style clocks. 603–366–5126.

It's About Time, 7151 Ortonville Rd., Clarkston, MI 48016: Catalog $5 (refundable) ❖ Grandfather, wall, self-chiming, and other clocks. 800–423–4225.

Heinz Jauch Inc., P.O. Box 405, Fairhope, AL 36532: List $1 ❖ Grandfather clock kits. 205–928–0467.

Klockit, P.O. Box 636, Lake Geneva, WI 53147: Free catalog ❖ Grandfather and other clock kits, quartz and mechanical movements, parts, wood-finishing supplies, and tools. 800–556–2548.

Kraftkit, P.O. Box 636, Lake Geneva, WI 53147: Free catalog ❖ Clocks and

clock-making, other crafts, and needlework supplies. 414–248–1150.

Kuempel Chime, 1195 Minnetonka Blvd., Excelsior, MN 55331: Catalog $3 ❖ Kits and plans for grandfather clocks with bells or chimes, hand-painted moon wheels, and handcrafted pendulums. 800–328–6445.

S. LaRose Inc., 3223 Yanceyville St., P.O. Box 21208, Greensboro, NC 27420: Catalog $2.50 ❖ Clock replacement movements and motors, other parts, and tools. 910–621–1936.

Mason & Sullivan, 586 Higgins Crowell Rd., West Yarmouth, MA 02673: Catalog $1 ❖ Clock kits, parts, hardware, and books. 617–778–1056.

Merritt's Antiques Inc., P.O. Box 277, Douglassville, PA 19518: Catalog $3 ❖ Clock repair supplies and reproduction antique grandfather, wall, and shelf clocks. 215–689–9541.

Howard Miller Clock Company, 860 E. Main St., Zeeland, MI 49464: Catalog $5 ❖ Parts for building and repairing clocks. 616–772–9131.

Modern Technical Tool & Supply Company, 211 Nevada St., Hicksville, NY 11801: Catalog $3.50 ❖ Clock-making parts. 516–931–7875.

Precision Movements, P.O. Box 689, Emmaus, PA 18049: Free catalog ❖ Clock kits, quartz movements, and parts. 800–533–2024; 215–967–3156 (in PA).

Red & Green Minerals Inc., 7595 W. Florida Ave., Lakewood, CO 80226: Free information ❖ Clocks, movements, parts, and rock specimens from worldwide sources. 303–985–5559.

Richardson's Recreational Ranch Ltd., Gateway Route, Box 440, Madras, OR 97741: Free information ❖ Clocks, parts, movements, and rock specimens from worldwide sources. 503–475–2680.

Selva-Borel, 126 2nd St., P.O. Box 796, Oakland, CA 94604: Free information ❖ Clocks, clock kits, and parts. 510–832–0356.

Simply Country Furniture, HC 69, Box 147, Rover, AR 72860: Brochure $2 ❖ Grandfather clocks. 501–272–4794.

Steebar, P.O. Box 463, Andover, NJ 07821: Catalog $3 ❖ Clock kits, quartz clock and music box movements, and parts. 201–383–1026.

Stitches 'N Pine, P.O. Box 710, Eldersburg, MD 21784: Brochure $1 ❖ Country-style quartz movement clocks and accent pieces. 410–795–1801.

Time Gallery, 3121 Battleground Ave., Greensboro, NC 28603: Free information ❖ Grandfather clocks. 800–683–TIME.

Turncraft Clock Imports Company, P.O. Box 100, Mound, MN 55364: Catalog $3.50 ❖ Clock kits and parts.

M.G. Warren Company, 940 Douglas Ave., Altamonte Springs, FL 32714: Free information ❖ Handcarved Black Forest cuckoo clocks from Germany. 407–862–7491.

Yankee Ingenuity, P.O. Box 113, Altus, OK 73522: Brochure $1 ❖ Handcrafted clocks and clock-making parts. 405–477–2191.

CLOSETS & STORAGE SYSTEMS

Clairson International, 720 SW 17th St., Ocala, FL 32674: Free information ❖ Modular shelving for room, closet, and other storage areas. 800–874–0008; 904–351–6100 (in FL).

Closetmaid, 720 SW 17th St., Ocala, FL 32674: Free information ❖ Wire basket caddies. 904–622–6627.

Do+Able Products, 15320 E. Salt Lake Ave., City of Industry, CA 91745: Free information ❖ Closet components. 818–336–4886.

Elfa Closet Storage Accessories, 300–3A Rt. 17 South, Lodi, NJ 07644: Free information ❖ Epoxy-covered steel shelves, bins, and other accessories for storage rooms and closets. 201–777–1554.

Hirsh Company, 8051 Central Ave., Skokie, IL 60076: Free information ❖ Easy-to-install closet organizers and shelf units. 708–673–6610.

Journeyman Products Ltd., 303 Najoles Rd., Millersville, MD 21108: Free information ❖ Stackable tray and box storage system. 800–248–8707.

Kasten Inc., 5080 N. Ocean Dr., Singer Island, FL 33404: Free information ❖ Bedside, footend, and under-the-bed slide-n-hide support for heavy luggage and TVs. 407–845–1087.

Laminations Inc., 3311 Laminations Dr., Holland, MI 49424: Free information ❖ Easy-to-install storage units, shelves, and rods. 800–562–4257.

Lee/Rowan Company, 6333 Etzel Ave., St. Louis, MO 63133: Free information ❖ Wire shelving units for closets. 800–325–6150.

Rubbermaid, 1147 Akron Rd., Wooster, OH 44691: Free information ❖ Closet and storage room accessories. 216–264–6464.

Rutt Custom Cabinetry, P.O. Box 129, Goodville, PA 17528: Catalog $7 ❖ Storage room and closet cabinets. 215–445–6751.

Schulte Corporation, 12115 Ellington Ct., Cincinnati, OH 45249: Free information ❖ Closet and room storage organizers. 800–669–3225.

White Home Products, 2401 Lake Park Dr., Atlanta, GA 30080: Free information ❖ Automatic revolving carousels for closets. 404–431–0900.

CLOTHING
Bridal Fashions

Badhir Trading Inc., 8429 Sisson Hwy., Eden, NY 14057: Catalog $2.50 (refundable) ❖ Beaded, sequined, and jeweled appliques and trims for dresses, costumes, and bridal clothing. 800–654–9418.

Bridesmaids Direct, 142 Woodburn Dr., Dothran, AL 36301: Catalog $3 (refundable) ❖ Bridesmaid gowns. 800–844–7117.

Country Elegance, 7353 Greenbush Ave., North Hollywood, CA 91605: Catalog $3 ❖ Bridal fashions. 818–765–1551.

Peter Fox Bridal Shoes, 105 Thompson St., New York, NY 10012: Catalog $3 ❖ Bridal boots and shoes. 800–338–3430.

Illusions of Grandeur, P.O. Box 735, Colverdale, CA 95425: Free catalog ❖ Make-them-yourself kits for headpieces, veils, and other bridal accessories.

Impression Bridal, 10850 Wilcrest, Houston, TX 77099: Free information ❖ Wedding gowns, headpieces, and veils. 800–274–3251; 713–530–6695 (in TX).

P.C. Mary's Inc., P.O. Box 722902, Houston, TX 77272: Brochure $3 ❖ Bridal headpieces. 713–933–9878.

Jessica McClintock Bridal, Mail Order Department, P.O. Box 44393, San Francisco, CA 94144: Catalog $6 ❖ Bridal fashions.

J.C. Penney Company Inc., Catalog Division, Milwaukee, WI 53263: Free information ❖ Petite and misses clothing for brides and attendants. 800–222–6161.

San Martin Bridal Fashions, 3353 Verdugo Rd., Los Angeles, CA 90065: Free catalog ❖ Bridal fashions.

Children's Clothing

After the Stork, 1501 12th St. NW, Albuquerque, NM 87104: Free catalog ❖ Natural fiber clothing for infants and children up to age 7. 800–333–5437.

The Alice Dress Company, P.O. Box 1664, Orleans, MA 02653: Catalog $2 ❖ Children's clothing. 617–240–0401.

Hanna Anderson, 1010 NW Flanders, Portland, OR 97209: Free catalog ❖ Children's clothing. 800–222–0544.

Baby Clothes Wholesale, 70 Ethel Rd. West, Piscataway, NJ 08854: Catalog $3 ❖ Clothing for babies and children. 800–568–1930.

Bemidji Woolen Mills, P.O. Box 277, Bemidji, MN 56601: Free brochure ❖ Woolen outerwear for men, women, and children. 218–751–5166.

Biobottoms, P.O. Box 6009, Petaluma, CA 04953: Free catalog ❖ Cotton outerwear and dress-up clothing for infants, toddlers, and older children. 800–766–1254; 707–778–7152 (in CA).

Brights Creek, Bay Point Pl., Hampton, VA 23653: Free catalog ❖ Clothing for infants and children up to age 12. 800–622–9202.

The B2 Products, Ingram Dr., P.O. Box 1108, Haymarket, VA 22069: Free brochure with long SASE ❖ Clothing for infants. 800–695–7073.

Cherry Tree Clothing, 166 Valley St., Providence, RI 02909: Free information ❖ Children's outerwear. 800–869–7742.

Childcraft, P.O. Box 29149, Mission, KS 66201: Free catalog ❖ Play clothes for boys, sizes 4 to 16; girls, sizes 4 to 6X and 7 to 14. 800–631–5657.

Children's Wear Digest, 31333 Agoura Rd., Westlake Village, CA 91361: Free catalog ❖ Children's clothing for school, playtime, dressing-up, and keeping warm. 800–433–1895.

Esprit, 499 Illinois St., San Francisco, CA 94107: Free catalog ❖ Fashionable clothing for children and their mothers. 415–648–6900.

Garnet Hill, 262 Main St., Franconia, NH 03580: Free catalog ❖ Adult sleepwear, maternity clothing, natural fiber underwear, and sleepwear and outerwear for children. 800–622–6216.

Gerber Childrenswear Inc., P.O. Box 301, Greenville, SC 29602: Free information ❖

Baby's sleepwear in small, medium, and large. 803–240–2890.

Just for Kids, P.O. Box 29141, Shawnee, KS 66201: Free catalog ❖ Infant and children's clothing, toys, and gifts. 800–443–5827.

Lands' End Inc., 1 Lands' End Ln., Dodgeville, WI 53595: Free catalog ❖ Children's clothing for school and playtime. 800–356–4444.

Maggie Moore Inc., 170 Ludlow St., Yonkers, NY 10705: Catalog $2 ❖ Clothing for infants and other children up to size 14. 914–968–0600.

The Natural Baby Company, 114 W. Franklin, Pennington, NJ 08534: Free information ❖ Children's clothing. 609–388–BABY.

Oshkosh Direct, Division Oshkosh B'Gosh Inc., P.O. Box 2222, Monroe, WI 53566: Free catalog ❖ Oshkosh clothing for babies and older children, from newborn to 6x/7. 800–MY-BGOSH.

Patagonia Mail Order, P.O. Box 8900, Bozeman, MT 59715: Free catalog ❖ Children's clothing. 800–336–9090.

J.C. Penney Company Inc., Catalog Division, Milwaukee, WI 53263: Free information ❖ Children's clothing in large sizes. 800–222–6161.

Pleasant Company, P.O. Box 620190, Middleton, WI 53562: Free catalog ❖ Classic clothing for little girls. 800–845–0005.

Red Flannel Factory, 73 S. Main, P.O. Box 370, Cedar Springs, MI 49319: Free catalog ❖ Clothing for children and adults. 616–696–9240.

Rubens & Marble Inc., P.O. Box 14900, Chicago, IL 60614: Free brochure with long SASE ❖ Clothing and bedding for infants. 312–348–6200.

Spencer's Inc., 238 Willow St., Mt. Airy, NC 27030: Free information ❖ Infant and children's underwear, sleepwear, playwear, fleece-wear, and gift sets. 910–789–9111.

Spiegel, P.O. Box 6340, Chicago, IL 60680: Free information ❖ Children's clothing, shoes, and toys. 800–345–4500.

Storybook Heirlooms, 1215 O'Brien Dr., Menlo Park, CA 94025: Free catalog ❖ Children's clothing and gifts. 800–899–7666.

Strasburg Lace, 12310 S. Memorial Pkwy., Huntsville, AL 35803: Catalog $5 ❖ French

hand-sewn children's clothing. 800–866–4717; 205–880–0400 (in AL).

Talbots for Kids, 175 Beal St., Hingham, MA 02043: Free catalog ❖ Clothing for boys, sizes 4 to 12; sizes 4 to 14 for girls. 800–543–7123.

Tortellini, P.O. Box 2515, Sag Harbor, NY 11963: Free catalog ❖ Children's dressing-up and fun-to-wear clothing. 800–527–8725; 516–725–9285 (in NY).

Wooden Soldier, P.O. Box 800, North Conway, NH 03860: Free catalog ❖ Children's designer clothing. 603–356–6343.

Exercise Clothing

Adidas USA, 5675 N. Blackstock Rd., Spartanburg, SC 29303: Free information ❖ Men and women's shorts and singlets, aerobic and workout shoes, socks, and warm-up suits. 800–423–4327.

Austad's, 4500 E 10th St., P.O. Box 5428, Sioux Falls, SD 57196: Free catalog ❖ Equipment and clothing for most major sports. 800–444–1234.

Body Wrappers, Attitudes in Dressing Inc., 1350 Broadway, Ste. 304, New York, NY 10018: Free information ❖ Exercise suits, leotards, headbands, leg warmers, women's shorts, and warm-up suits. 800–323–0786; 212–279–3492 (in NY).

California Best, 970 Broadway, Ste. 104, Chula Vista, CA 91911: Free catalog ❖ Men and women's exercise and fitness clothing. 800–438–9327.

Champion Products Inc., 475 Corporate Square Dr., Winston Salem, NC 27105: Free information ❖ Exercise clothing, leotards, shorts, and singlets for men and women.

Danmar Products Inc., 221 Jackson Industrial Dr., Ann Arbor, MI 48103: Free catalog ❖ Hydrofitness products and soft swim boots for sensitive feet. 800–783–1998; 313–761–1990 (in MI).

Danskin, 111 W. 40th St., 18th Floor, New York, NY 10018: Free information ❖ Exercise suits, headbands, leg warmers, leotards, singlets for women, warm-up suits, and wrist bands. 800–288–6749; 212–764–4630 (in NY).

Ellesse USA Inc., 1430 Broadway, New York, NY 10018: Free information ❖ Exercise suits, headbands, aerobic and workout shoes, leotards, shorts and singlets for men and women, warm-up suits, and wrist

bands. 800–345–9036; 212–840–6111 (in NY).

Freed of London Inc., 922 S. 7th Ave., New York, NY 10019: Free price list ❖ Exercise clothing, gym shoes, and other footwear for women and men. 212–489–1055.

Gold's Gym, 360 Hampton Dr., Venice, CA 90291: Free information ❖ Gloves, headbands, leotards, aerobic and workout shoes, shorts, singlets, and warm-up suits. 800–457–5375; 213–392–3005 (in CA).

Hind Sportswear, 3765 S. Higuera St., San Luis Obispo, CA 93401: Free information ❖ Exercise suits, gloves, leotards, shorts, socks, and singlets for men and women. 800–235–4150.

Jazzertogs, 1050 Joshua Way, Vista, CA 92083: Free catalog ❖ Exercise clothing. 800–FIT-ISIT.

Jet Trends, P.O. Box 110937, Miami, FL 33011: Free information ❖ Men and women's clothing for jet skiing and other water activities. 800–231–9279; 305–635–2411 (in FL).

Leo's Dancewear Inc., 1900 N. Narragansett Ave., Chicago, IL 60639: Free cataog with request on school stationery ❖ Leg warmers, leotards, workout shoes, and headbands. 312–889–7700.

Gilda Marx Industries, 5340 Allard Rd., Los Angeles, CA 90066: Free information ❖ Exercise suits, leotards, headbands, leg warmers, shorts, and warm-up suits. 800–876–6279; 310–578–6279 (in CA).

New Balance Athletic Shoe Inc., 38 Everett St., Boston, MA 02134: Free information ❖ Exercise suits, leotards, workout shoes, shorts and singlets for men and women, and warm-up suits. 800–343–4648; 617–783–4000 (in MA).

Pony USA Inc., 676 Elm St., Concord, MA 01742: Free information ❖ Exercise suits, headbands, leotards, aerobic and workout shoes, shorts, singlets, and warm-up suits. 800–654–7669; 508–287–0053 (in MA).

Puma USA Inc., 147 Centre St., Brockton, MA 02403: Free information with long SASE ❖ Exercise suits, headbands, leg warmers, leotards, shorts, socks, aerobic and workout shoes, singlets, and warm-up suits. 508–583–9100.

Royal Textile Mills Inc., P.O. Box 250, Yanceyville, NC 27379: Free information ❖ Exercise suits, head and wrist bands, leg warmers, leotards, socks, and warm-up suits. 800–334–9361; 910–694–4121 (in NC).

Softouch Company Inc., 1167 NW 159th Dr., Miami, FL 33169: Free information ❖ Headbands, leg warmers, leotards, women's shorts, and socks. 800–327–1539; 305–624–5581 (in FL).

Spalding Sports Worldwide, 425 Meadow St., P.O. Box 901, Chicopee, MA 01201: Free information with list of retailers ❖ Exercise suits, headbands, leotards, shorts and singlets for men and women, and warm-up suits. 800–225–6601.

Full-Figured Women's Clothing

Brownstone Studio Inc., 685 3rd Ave., New York, NY 10017: Free catalog ❖ Clothing. 800–322–2991.

Lane Bryant, P.O. Box 8301, Indianapolis, IN 46283: Free catalog ❖ Misses clothing in size 14 to 20, half sizes 12½ to 34½, and size 36 to 60; shoes, size 6 to 12, AA to EEE. 800–777–0016.

Dion Jones Ltd., 3226 S. Aberdeen, Chicago, IL 60608: Free catalog ❖ Skirts, dresses, pants, jackets, and coats for full-figured women. 312–927–1113.

Just My Size, P.O. Box 748, Rural Hall, NC 27098: Free catalog ❖ Lingerie for full-figured women. 800–522–0889.

Just Right Clothing, 30 Tozer Rd., Beverly, MA 01915: Free catalog ❖ Clothing, size 14 and up. 800–767–6666.

Lerner New York, Midwest Distribution Center, P.O. Box 8380, Indianapolis, IN 46283: Free catalog ❖ Clothing in half sizes, 12½ to 34½; women's sizes 34 to 54; misses sizes 12 to 24; and shoes, size 6 to 12, AA to EEE. 800–288–4009.

Old Pueblo Traders, Palo Verde at 34th, P.O. Box 27800, Tucson, AZ 85726: Free catalog ❖ Women's clothing in misses, full-figured, and half sizes. 602–748–8600.

J.C. Penney Company Inc., Catalog Division, Milwaukee, WI 53263: Free information ❖ Clothing for full-figured and tall women, in sizes up to 32W. 800–222–6161.

Premiere Editions, Hanover, PA 17333–0012: Free catalog ❖ Sportswear and casual clothing for misses and petites. 717–633–3311.

Regalia, Palo Verde at 34th, P.O. Box 27800, Tucson, AZ 85726: Free catalog ❖ Large and

half-size clothing for full-figured women and shoes in hard-to-fit sizes. 602–747–5000.

Roaman's, P.O. Box 8360, Indianapolis, IN 46283: Free catalog ❖ Clothing for full-figured women: sizes 12 to 26 for misses, 34 to 56 for full-figured women, and half sizes; shoes and boots in hard-to-fit sizes. 800–274–7130.

Jill Saunders, 435 5th Ave., New York, NY 10016: Free catalog ❖ Women's fashions, from size 16 to 26. 212–685–8545.

Showcase of Savings, P.O. Box 748, Rural Hall, NC 27098: Free catalog ❖ Large-size lingerie for full-figured women. 910–744–1790.

Silhouettes, 340 Poplar St., Hanover, PA 17333: Free catalog ❖ Sportswear and casual clothing in large sizes. 717–633–3311.

Spiegel, P.O. Box 6340, Chicago, IL 60680: Free information ❖ Sportswear and casual clothing in large sizes. 800–345–4500.

Nicole Summers, Winterbrook Way, P.O. 3003, Meredith, NH 03253: Free catalog ❖ Clothing for women, sizes 10 to 20. 800–642–6786.

Lingerie & Underwear

Beauty by Spector Inc., McKeesport, PA 15134: Free catalog ❖ Women's wigs and hairpieces, men's toupees, jewelry, and exotic lingerie. 412–673–3259.

Lane Bryant, P.O. Box 8301, Indianapolis, IN 46283: Free catalog ❖ Intimate clothing, outerwear, dresses, blouses, coordinates, sweaters, and footwear. 800–777–0016.

Chock Catalog Corporation, 74 Orchard St., New York, NY 10002: Catalog $2 ❖ Lingerie, hosiery, and underwear for women, men, and children. 212–473–1929.

Damart, 3 Front St., Rollinsford, NH 03805: Free information ❖ Thermal underwear for men and women. 800–258–7300.

Decent Exposures, 2202 NE 115th St., Seattle, WA 98125: Free information ❖ Women's underwear in 100 percent cotton. 800–524–4949; 206–364–4540 (in WA).

Frederick's of Hollywood, P.O. Box 229, Hollywood, CA 90099: Free catalog ❖ Intimate clothing and lingerie, casual clothing, swim wear, jewelry, and shoes. 310–637–7770.

Gohn Brothers, 105 S. Main, P.O. Box 111, Middlebury, IN 46540: Free information with long SASE ❖ Men and women's Amish

clothing, underwear, and hosiery. 219–825–2400.

Goldman & Cohen Inc., 55 Orchard St., New York, NY 10002: Free information with long SASE ❖ Women's lingerie and hosiery. 212–966–0737.

Green Pond Company, 3731 Northcreft Rd., Ste. 12, Atlanta, GA 30340: Free brochure ❖ Men's boxer shorts. 800–827–POND.

Intimate Appeal, Palo Verde at 34th, P.O. Box 27800, Tucson, AZ 85726: Free catalog ❖ Intimate clothing for women who have had mastectomies. 602–748–8600.

Jeffries Socks Sources, P.O. Box 1680, Burlington, NC 27216: Free catalog ❖ Hosiery and socks for men, women, and children. 800–637–SOCK.

Just My Size, P.O. Box 748, Rural Hall, NC 27098: Free catalog ❖ Lingerie for full-figured women. 800–522–0889.

L'eggs Brands Inc., Outlet Catalog, P.O. Box 748, Rural Hall, NC 27098: Free catalog ❖ L'eggs, Hanes, Bali, and Playtex lingerie and hosiery. 910–744–1790.

National Wholesale Company Inc., 400 National Blvd., Lexington, NC 27294: Free catalog ❖ Hosiery and lingerie. 704–249–4202.

Newport News Fashions, Avon Ln., Newport News, VA 23630: Free catalog ❖ Daytime and nighttime intimate clothing. 800–688–2830.

Night 'n Day Intimates, Hanover, PA 17333–0022: Free catalog ❖ Women's intimate clothing and casual fashions. 717–633–3311.

No Nonsense Direct, P.O. Box 26095, Greensboro, NC 27420: Free catalog ❖ Hosiery. 800–677–5995.

Petticoat Express, 318 W. 39th St., New York, NY 10018: Free information ❖ Lingerie. 212–594–1276.

Primary Layer, P.O. Box 6697, Portland, OR 97228: Free catalog ❖ Undergarments for men and women, in sizes to fit almost everyone. 800–282–8206.

Roby's Intimates, 386 Cedar Ln., Teaneck, NJ 07666: Catalog $1 ❖ Bras, lingerie, hosiery, and other intimate clothing. 800–8788–BRA; 201–836–0630 (in NJ).

Sambar Hosiery, 55 Orchard St., New York, NY 10002: Free information ❖ Hosiery. 212–925–9650.

Secret Passions, P.O. Box 8870, Chapel Hill, NC 27515: Free catalog ❖ Intimate clothing, lingerie, and hosiery. 800–334–5474.

Showcase of Savings, P.O. Box 748, Rural Hall, NC 27098: Free catalog ❖ Lingerie for full-figured women. 910–744–1790.

The Smart Saver, P.O. Box 209, Wasco, IL 60183: Free catalog ❖ Women's intimate apparel. 800–554–4453.

Socks Galore, 220 2nd Ave. South, Franklin, TN 37064: Free catalog ❖ Women's hosiery and socks for men, women, and children. 800–626–7625; 615–790–7625 (in TN).

Undergear, 101 Kindig Ln., Hanover, PA 17333: Free catalog ❖ Men's clothing and underwear. 717–633–3300.

Victoria's Secret, North American Office, P.O. Box 16589, Columbus, OH 43216: Free catalog ❖ Women's lingerie, other intimate wear, formal and casual clothing, and outerwear. 800–888–1500.

Mendell Weiss Inc., 91 Orchard St., New York, NY 10002: Free brochure ❖ Women's lingerie and lounging clothing. 212–925–6815.

Maternity Clothing

Bosom Buddies, P.O. Box 6138, Kingston, NY 12401: Free catalog ❖ Maternity clothing for fashion-conscious women. 914–338–2038.

5th Avenue Maternity, 415 Pike, Seattle, WA 98101: Catalog $2 ❖ Stylish clothing for pregnant women. 800–426–3569; 206–343–9470 (in WA).

Garnet Hill, 262 Main St., Franconia, NH 03580: Free catalog ❖ Natural fiber maternity clothing, sleepwear, underwear, and outerwear. 800–622–6216.

Dan Howard's Maternity Factory Outlet, 710 W. Jackson Blvd., Chicago, IL 60661: Free catalog ❖ Sportswear, casual and informal fashions, career wear, coordinates, sweaters, intimate wear, and maternity fashions. 800–468–6700.

Mother's Place, P.O. Box 94512, Cleveland, OH 44101: Free catalog ❖ Casual, active, dress-up, and sleepwear for mothers-to-be. 800–829–0080; 216–826–1712 (in OH).

Mothers Work, 1309 Noble St., 5th Floor, Philadelphia, PA 19123: Catalog $3 ❖ Maternity suits and dresses. 215–625–9259.

Motherwear, P.O. Box 114, Northampton, MA 01061: Free catalog ❖ Easy access clothing for nursing mothers. 800–633–0303.

Holly Nicolas Nursing Collection, P.O. Box 7121, Orange, CA 92613: Free information with long SASE ❖ Clothing for mothers-to-be. 714–639–5933.

J.C. Penney Company Inc., Catalog Division, Milwaukee, WI 53263: Free information ❖ Career and casual maternity clothing in petite, misses, tall, and regular sizes. 800–222–6161.

Reborn Maternity, 1449 3rd Ave., New York, NY 10028: Catalog $2 ❖ Clothing for mothers-to-be. 212–737–7676.

Men's & Women's Clothing

Allen Allen USA, Attn: Catalog Order, 20003 S. Rancho Way, Rancho Dominguz, CA 90220: Free catalog ❖ Women's sportswear, casual clothing, and swimwear. 800–422–0466.

American View, Division Hanover Direct Pennsylvania, Hanover, PA 17333–0001: Free catalog ❖ Casual clothing for men. 717–633–3333.

Andover Shop, 127 Main St., P.O. Box 5127, Andover, MA 01810: Free catalog ❖ Handmade silk ties. 508–475–2252.

Johnny Appleseed, 30 Tozer Rd., P.O. Box 1020, Beverly, MA 01915: Free catalog ❖ Clothing for women, size 4 to 18. 800–767–6666.

Armoire, 408 Pasadena Ave., Ste. 5, Pasadena, CA 91105: Free catalog ❖ Women's casual clothing. 800–528–3131.

Array, 33 Hill St., P.O. Box 1025, Beverly, MA 01915: Free catalog ❖ Women's formal and casual clothing and separates. 800–767–6776.

Laura Ashley Inc., Mail Order, P.O. Box 18413, Memphis, TN 38181: Free information ❖ Women's clothing. 800–367–2000.

Athletic Supply, 10812 Alder Cir., Dallas, TX 75238: Free catalog ❖ Men and women's sportswear, jackets, T-shirts, memorabilia, and figurines. 416–971–5222.

Adrian Avery for Brownstone Studio, 685 3rd Ave., New York, NY 10017: Free information ❖ Women's clothing. 800–221–2468.

Bachrach Clothing Catalog, 1 Bachrach Ct., Decatur, IL 62524: Free catalog ❖ Men's clothing. 800–637–5840.

Eddie Bauer, P.O. Box 3700, Seattle, WA 98124: Free catalog ❖ Active and casual clothing for men and women. 800–426–8020.

L.L. Bean, Freeport, ME 04033: Free catalog ❖ Outdoor clothing, footwear, and sporting accessories for men and women. 800–221–4221.

Beau Ties Ltd. of Vermont, 19 Gorham Ln., Middlebury, VT 05753: Free brochure ❖ Hand-stitched, 100 percent silk free-style bow ties. 800–488–TIES.

Bedford Fair, 421 Landmark Dr., Wilmington, NC 28410: Free catalog ❖ Women's casual and career clothing and swimwear. 800–964–1000.

Bemidji Woolen Mills, P.O. Box 277, Bemidji, MN 56601: Free brochure ❖ Woolen outerwear for men, women, and children. 218–751–5166.

Atelier Biamón, P.O. Box 55–7848, Miami, FL 33255: Catalog $3 ❖ Designer haute couture clothing, sizes 6 to 14. 305–663–1577.

Bila of California, 324 W. Venice Blvd., Los Angeles, CA 90015: Free catalog ❖ Women's casual clothing and jewelry. 800–824–3541; 213–746–4190 (in CA).

The Bow Tie Club, P.O. Box 20420, Baltimore, MD 21284: Free catalog ❖ Handmade bow ties. 800–269–5668.

Brooks Brothers, 350 Campus Plaza, P.O. Box 4016, Edison, NJ 08818: Free catalog ❖ Men and women's sportswear, casual clothing, and shoes. 800–274–1815.

Brownstone Studio Inc., 685 3rd Ave., New York, NY 10017: Free catalog ❖ Women's sportswear, lounging attire, casual and career clothing, and sleepwear. 800–322–2991.

Lane Bryant, P.O. Box 8301, Indianapolis, IN 46283: Free catalog ❖ Women's outerware, dresses and blouses, sweaters, intimate clothing, and footwear. 800–777–0018.

Bullock & Jones, P.O. Box 883124, San Francisco, CA 94188: Free catalog ❖ Men and women's clothing. 800–227–3050.

Cable Car Clothiers, 246 Sutter St., San Francisco, CA 94108: Catalog $3 ❖ Men's clothing. 415–397–4740.

Camp Beverly Hills, 9640 Santa Monica Blvd., Beverly Hills, CA 90210: Catalog 50¢ ❖ Sportswear for men and women. 310–858–3925.

Canari Cycle Wear, 10025 Huennekens St., San Diego, CA 92121: Free information ❖ Winter apparel for bikers. 800–929–2925; 619–455–8245 (in CA).

Carabella Collections, 1852 McGaw Ave., Irvine, CA 92714: Catalog $3 ❖ Women's swimwear, casual clothing, and activewear. 714–263–2300.

Casco Bay Fine Woolens, 192 Stevens Ave., Portland, ME 04102: Free brochure ❖ Handcrafted wool capes. 800–788–9842.

Cashmeres Etc., 854 Madison Ave., New York, NY 10021: Free catalog ❖ Men and women's cashmere, silk, and cotton clothing. 800–441–7743; 212–772–8350 (in NY).

Chadwick's of Boston, One Chadwick Pl., Box 1600, Brockton, MA 02403: Free catalog ❖ Casual and career clothing for women. 508–583–7200.

Clifford & Wills, One Clifford Way, Asheville, NC 28810: Free catalog ❖ Career and casual clothing for women. 800–922–1035.

Joan Cook, 119 Foster St., P.O. Box 6008, Peabody, MA 01961: Free catalog ❖ Women's classic clothing. 800–935–0971.

Creative Designs by Mary Jane, 6022 Monroe Pl., West New York, NJ 07093: Free information ❖ Handmade tie-dye clothing in 100 percent cotton.

J. Crew Outfitters, One Ivy Crescent, Lynchburg, VA 24513: Free catalog ❖ Casual clothing for men and women. 800–932–0043.

Mark Cross, 645 5th Ave., New York, NY 10022: Catalog $2 ❖ Men and women's clothing. 212–421–3000.

Deerskin Place, 283 Akron Rd., Ephrata, PA 17522: Catalog $1 ❖ Cowhide, sheepskin, and deerskin clothing. 717–733–7624.

Deerskin Trading Post, 119 Foster St., Box 6008, Peabody, MA 01961: Free catalog ❖ Leather shoes and slippers, gloves, shoulder bags, and boots. 508–532–4040.

DEVA Lifewear, Box 266, Westhope, ND 58793: Free catalog ❖ * Cotton clothing for men and women. 800–222–8024.

Doneckers at Home, 409 N. State St., Ephrata, PA 17522: Free catalog ❖ Classic fashions for women and men. 800–377–2205.

Early Winters, P.O. Box 4333, Portland, OR 97208: Free catalog ❖ Ski clothing, leisure separates, and other outdoor clothing for men and women. 800–458–4438.

Essence by Mail, P.O. Box 62, Hanover, PA 17333: Free catalog ❖ Women's clothing. 717–633–3333.

Extrasport Inc., 5305 NW 35th Ct., Miami, FL 33142: Free catalog ❖ All-terrain clothing and sportswear. 800–633–0837.

Fashion Galaxy, P.O. Box 26, Hanover, PA 17333: Free catalog ❖ Women's career and casual clothing, lingerie, swimwear, shoes and sandals, and tops. 713–633–3311.

Filson, P.O. Box 34020, Seattle, WA 98124: Free information ❖ Outdoor clothing. 800–624–0201.

The Finals, 21 Minisink Ave., Port Jervis, NY 12771: Free catalog ❖ Bicycling, aerobic, swimming, running, sweats, and exercise clothing. 914–856–5291.

Frederick's of Hollywood, P.O. Box 229, Hollywood, CA 90099: Free catalog ❖ Intimate clothing and lingerie, casual clothing, swim wear, jewelry, and shoes. 310–637–7770.

Garnet Hill, 262 Main St., Franconia, NH 03580: Free catalog ❖ Natural fiber adult sleepwear, maternity clothing, underwear, and sleepwear and outerwear for children. 800–622–6216.

Gerry Sportswear, 1051 1st Ave. South, Seattle, WA 98134: Free information ❖ Men and women's outerwear. 800–934–3779.

Gelber's Menswear, 1001 Washington Ave., St. Louis, MO 63101: Free information with long SASE ❖ Men's designer clothing. 314–421–6698.

Gohn Brothers, 105 S. Main, P.O. Box 111, Middlebury, IN 46540: Free information with long SASE ❖ Men and women's Amish clothing, underwear, and hosiery. 219–825–2400.

Goose & Gander Country Gift Shop, 6483 E, Seneca Tnpk., Jamesville, NY 13078: Free information with long SASE ❖ Sweatshirt and lace-collar cardigans with matching accessories. 315–492–1266.

Gray-Walsh Capes International, P.O. Box 1912, Amarillo, TX 79105: Catalog $4 ❖ Women's outerwear, shawls, hats, capes, and jackets. 800–999–2212.

Haband, 100 Fairview Ave., Prospect Park, NJ 07530 ❖ Free information ❖ Men's shoes and wash-and-wear clothing.

Heritage House, 611 Church St., Georgetown, TX 78626: Catalog $3 ❖ Blouses, vests, broomstick and wrap skirts, and other fashions. 512–869–1051.

Hermes of Paris Inc., 745 5th Ave., Ste. 800, New York, NY 10151: Free catalog ❖ Hermes scarves from France. 800–441–4488.

His Favorite Tie, 33 Hawthorne Pl., Summit, NJ 07901: Free information ❖ Hand-sewn ties. 800–552–TIES.

The Horchow Collection, P.O. Box 620048, Dallas, TX 75262: Free catalog ❖ Women's casual clothing. 800–395–5397.

Huntington Clothiers, 1285 Alum Creek Dr., Columbus, OH 43209: Free catalog ❖ Traditional fashions for men and women. 800–848–6203.

International Male, Hanover, PA 17333–0075: Free catalog ❖ Men's clothing. 717–633–3300.

Intime for Brownstone Studio, 685 3rd Ave., New York, NY 10017: Free catalog ❖ Women's casual fashions and sleepwear. 800–221–2468.

James River Traders, James River Landing, Hampton, VA 23631: Free catalog ❖ Casual clothing for men and women. 804–827–6000.

Charles Keath Ltd., P.O. Box 48800, Atlanta, GA 30362: Free catalog ❖ Women's casual clothing and jewelry. 800–388–6565; 449–3100 (in Atlanta).

Knights Ltd. Catalog, 2025 Concourse Dr., St. Louis, MO 63146: Free catalog ❖ Women's casual and formal fashions and shoes. 800–445–6811; 314–993–1516 (in MO).

La Costa Products International, 2875 Laker Ave. East, Carlsbad, CA 92008: Free catalog ❖ Men and women's clothing and spa essentials. 800–LA-COSTA.

Landau Woolens, 114 Nassau St., Princeton, NJ 08542: Free catalog ❖ Hand-knit sweaters, Icelandic light wool coats and jackets, blanket throws, sportswear, cotton knits, sleepwear, and shirts. 800–257–9445.

Lands' End Inc., 1 Lands' End Ln., Dodgeville, WI 53595: Free catalog ❖ Men and women's clothing, luggage, belts, knits, flannel shirts, and sweaters. 800–356–4444.

Lee-McClain Company Inc., 1857 Midland Trail, Shelbyville, KY 40065: Free brochure ❖ Men's suits, jackets, coats, and blazers. 502–633–3823.

Lerner New York, Midwest Distribution Center, P.O. Box 8380, Indianapolis, IN

46283 Free catalog ❖ Women's sportswear, casual clothing, sweaters, lingerie, jewelry, shoes and boots, and outerwear. 800–288–4009.

Lewis Creek Company, 3 Webster Rd., Shelburne, VT 05482: Free information ❖ Outerwear. 800–336–4884.

Lite Speed, 3918 W. 1st Ave., Eugene, OR 97402: Catalog $2 ❖ Clothing and rainwear for men, women, and children. 503–345–6665.

Carol Little, Liberty Village Factory Outlet, Store 39A, Flemington, NJ 08822: Free information ❖ Women's designer clothing. 201–884–3432.

Lost Worlds, Box 972, Linden Hill, NY 11354: Catalog $2 ❖ Air force, navy flight, and motorcycle jackets. 212–923–3423.

Madeleine Fashions Inc., 1112 7th Ave., Monroe, WI 53566: Catalog $3 ❖ Women's sportswear, sweaters, shoes, and separates. 800–344–1994.

Lew Magram, 414 Alfred Ave., P.O. Box 2300, Teaneck, NJ 07666: Free catalog ❖ Casual, career, coordinates, and formal fashions for women. 212–695–8148.

Mary Orvis Marbury, 1711 Blue Hills Dr., P.O. Box 12000, Roanoke, VA 24022: Free catalog ❖ Women's career, casual, and evening wear. 800–541–3541.

Philippe Marcel, 6800 Engle Rd., P.O. Box 94610, Cleveland, OH 44101: Free catalog ❖ Women's designer fashions. 800–869–9901.

Mark, Fore & Strike, 6500 Park of Commerce Blvd. NW, P.O. Box 5056, Boca Raton, FL 33431: Free catalog ❖ Classic, casual, and sportswear for men and women. 800–327–3627.

Midwest Trade Imports, 1555 Sherman Ave., Ste. 236, Evanston, IL 60201: Information $2 ❖ Personalized, authentic hand-woven Ashanti Kente cloth stoles and fabrics from Ghana. 800–64–KENTE.

Monarch, One Monarch Pl., Lexington, NC 27294: Free catalog ❖ Women's formal and casual clothing, coordinates, and sleepwear. 800–367–6002.

David Morgan, 11812 Northcreek Pkwy., Ste. 103, Bothell, WA 98011: Free catalog ❖ Hand-braided belts, fur hats, and wool and sheepskin clothing. 800–324–4934.

Nancy's Millinery Plus, 746 W. Upjohn Rd., Ridgecrest, CA 93555: Catalog $3.50 ❖ Hats and bonnets, shoes, corsets, purses, parasols, and hosiery. 619–375–8159.

National Wholesale Company Inc., 400 National Blvd., Lexington, NC 27294: Free catalog ❖ Women's hosiery, panty hose, lingerie, sleepwear, and gowns. 704–249–4202.

Newport News Fashions, Avon Ln., Newport News, VA 23630: Free catalog ❖ Women's swimwear, casual coordinates, shoes, lingerie, sweaters, and sportswear. 800–688–2830.

North Beach Leather, 1335 Columbus Ave., San Francisco, CA 94133: Catalog $3 ❖ Leather clothing and jackets for men and women. 415–346–1113.

Thos. Oak & Sons, 901 Main St., Salem, VA 24156: Free catalog ❖ Clothing, shoes, and gifts for older persons. 703–375–3420.

Olsen's Mill Direct, 1641 S. Main St., Oshkosh, WI 54901: Catalog $2 ❖ Clothing for men, women, and children. 800–537–4979.

Oomingmak Musk Ox Producers' Co-operative, 604 H St., Anchorage, AK 99501: Free information with long SASE ❖ Traditional hand-knitted clothing from rare wools of the domestic Arctic Musk Ox. 907–272–9225.

Orvis Manchester, Historic Rt. 7A, Manchester, VT 05254: Free catalog ❖ Outdoor clothing, sportswear, lingerie, sweaters, and shoes. 800–548–9548.

Outtakes, Division Hanover Direct Pennsylvania, Hanover, PA 17333–0001: Free catalog ❖ Clothing and accessories for men. 717–633–3333.

Pastille, P.O. Box 650503, Dallas, TX 75265: Free catalog ❖ Classic women's fashions for relaxed and formal occasions. 800–727–3900.

Pearl Izumi, 2300 Central Ave., Boulder, CO 80301: Free information ❖ Wind-resistant tights and jerseys with zippers for easy removal of the front panel. 303–938–1700.

Pendleton Shop, Jordan Rd., P.O. Box 233, Sedona, AZ 86336: Catalog $1 ❖ Men and women's sweaters and sportswear. 602–282–3671.

J.C. Penney Company Inc., Catalog Division, Milwaukee, WI 53263: Free information ❖ Women's work clothing, full-figured and extra-tall sizes, and career and casual fashions. 800–222–6161.

J. Peterman Company, 2444 Palumbo Dr., Lexington, KY 40509: Free catalog ❖ Men's clothing. 800–231–7341.

Prime Time Fashions, P.O. Box 10510, Rochester, NY 14610: Free catalog ❖ Clothing for older women with arthritis. Some styles feature velcro fasteners.

Red Flannel Factory, 73 S. Main, P.O. Box 370, Cedar Springs, MI 49319: Free catalog ❖ Clothing for men, women, and children. 616–696–9240.

Carroll Reed, 1001 Washington St., Conshohocken, PA 19428: Free catalog ❖ Women's sportswear and casual clothing. 800–343–5770.

Anthony Richards, 6836 Engle Rd., P.O. Box 94503, Cleveland, OH 44101: Free catalog ❖ Women's fashions. 216–826–1712.

Roaman's, P.O. Box 8360, Indianapolis, IN 46283: Free catalog ❖ Women's casual and career clothing, intimate wear, knits, shoes and boots, sleepwear, and coordinates. 800–274–7130.

A. Rubinstein & Son, 24 E. 17th St., New York, NY 10003: Free brochure ❖ Men's shirts, ties, sportswear, rainwear, and outerwear. 212–924–7817.

Saint Laurie Ltd., 897 Broadway, New York, NY 10003: Catalog $2 ❖ Hand-tailored clothing. 800–221–8660; 212–473–0100 (in NY).

Sarah Glove Company Inc., P.O. Box 1940, Waterbury, CT 06722: Catalog $1 ❖ Work clothes and jeans, shoes and boots, shirts, jackets, and gloves. 203–574–4090.

SER Outfitters, P.O. Box 2051, Savannah, GA 31402: Free catalog ❖ T-shirts, sweats, polo shirts, and hats. 912–232–8800.

Serendipity, Palo Verde at 34th, P.O. Box 27800, Tucson, AZ 85726: Free catalog ❖ Women's formal and casual fashions, coordinates, sweaters, and shoes. 602–748–8600.

Serengeti, P.O. Box 3349, Serengeti Park, Chelmsford, MA 01824: Free catalog ❖ Wildlife apparel and gifts. 800–426–2852.

Shopping International, Palo Verde at 34th, P.O. Box 27800, Tucson, AZ 85726: Free catalog ❖ Mix-and-match blouses, skirts, pants, and other coordinates. 602–748–8600.

Showcase of Savings, P.O. Box 748, Rural Hall, NC 27098: Free catalog ❖ Machine-washable cotton-velour warm-up suits, other fashions, jewelry, and gifts. 910–744–1790.

Sickafus Sheepskins, Rt. 78, Exit 7, Strausstown, PA 19559: Free catalog ❖ Sheepskin clothing. 215–488–1782.

Sidney's, 501 S. Jefferson St., Roanoke, VA 24011: Free catalog ❖ Casual and contemporary fashions for women. 703–563–4415.

Ben Silver, 149 King St., Charleston, SC 29401: Free catalog ❖ Blazer buttons with school designs and monograms, cuff links, suspenders, breast patches, blazers, cotton sweats, neckties, shirts, and trousers. 800–221–4671.

Simply Tops, P.O. Box 12, Hanover, PA 17333: Free catalog ❖ Designer tops. 717–633–3311.

Smith & Hawken, P.O. Box 6907, Florence, KY 41022: Free catalog ❖ Casual clothing for men and women. 800–776–5558.

George Stafford & Sons, 808 Smith Ave., P.O. Box 2055, Thomasville, GA 31799: Free catalog ❖ Men and women's sportswear, casual fashions, and shoes. 912–226–4306.

Paul Stuart, Madison Ave. at 45th St., New York, NY 10017: Catalog $3 ❖ Men and women's casual, career, and formal clothing. 800–678–8278.

Sussex Clothes Ltd., 302 5th Ave., New York, NY 10001: Catalog $2 ❖ Men's clothing. 212–279–4610.

Talbots, 175 Beal St., Hingham, MA 02043: Free catalog ❖ Women's clothing and coordinates. 800–992–9010.

Ann Taylor, P.O. Box 805, New Haven, CT 06503: Free catalog ❖ Women's career, casual, and dress-up fashions. 800–825–6250.

The Territory Ahead, 27 E. Mason St., Santa Barbara, CA 93101: Free catalog ❖ Men's clothing. 805–962–5333.

Thai Silks, 252 State St., Los Altos, CA 94022: Free brochure ❖ Silk clothing. 800–722–SILK; 800–221–SILK (in CA).

Norm Thompson, P.O. Box 3999, Portland, OR 97208: Free catalog ❖ Men and women's clothing and gifts. 800–547–1160.

Tilley Endurables, 300 Lagner Rd, West Seneca, NY 14224: Free catalog ❖ Clothing for travelers with security and secret pockets for theft protection. 800–338–2797.

Tog Shop, Lester Square, Americus, GA 31710: Free catalog ❖ Women's jump suits, shirts, outerwear, skirts and blouses, sleepwear, swimwear, and shoes and sandals. 800–367–8647.

Touch of Class, 1905 N. Van Buren St., Huntingburg, IN 47542: Free catalog ❖ Bathroom accessories, comforters, pillows, shams, window treatments, towels, rugs, and sleepwear for men, women, and children. 800–457–7456.

Trifles, P.O. Box 620048, Dallas, TX 75262: Free catalog ❖ Clothing and jewelry for men, women, and children. 214–556–6055.

Tuttle Golf Collection, P.O. Box 888, Walligford, CT 06492: Free catalog ❖ Sportswear for men and women. 800–882–7511.

Tweeds, One Avery Row, Roanoke, VA 24012: Free catalog ❖ Casual fashions for men and women. 800–999–7997.

The Ujena Company, 1400 N. Shoreline Blvd., Mountain View, CA 04039: Catalog $2 ❖ Women's swimwear and sportswear. 800–227–8318.

Ultimate Outlet, P.O. Box 88251, Chicago, IL 60680: Catalog $2 ❖ Men and women's clothing for swimming, work, or relaxation. 800–332–6000.

Undergear, 101 Kindig Pl., Hanover, PA 17333: Free catalog ❖ Men's clothing and underwear. 717–633–3300.

The Very Thing, Winterbrook Way, P.O. Box 3005, Meredith, NH 03253: Free catalog ❖ Women's clothing. 800–448–4988.

Victoria's Secret, North American Office, P.O. Box 16589, Columbus, OH 43216: Free catalog ❖ Women's clothing, lingerie, sleepwear, slippers, and gifts. 800–888–1500.

Walrus Inc., 929 Camelia St., Berkeley, CA 94710: Free information ❖ Outerwear. 510–526–8961.

WearGuard Corporation, Longwater Dr., Norwell, MA 02061: Free catalog ❖ Clothing for the working man and woman. 800–388–3300.

What on Earth, 2451 Enterprise East Pkwy., Twinsburg, OH 44087: Free catalog ❖ Fun wear and gifts for men, women, and children. 216–425–4600.

Whipp Trading Company, RR 1, Arrasmith Trail, Ames, IA 50010: Free catalog ❖ Sheepskin rugs, slippers, mittens, and hats. 800–533–9447.

Willow Ridge, 421 Landmark Dr., Wilmington, NC 28410: Free catalog ❖ Women's career, dress-up, and casual clothing. 910–343–6900.

Windjammer, 525 N. Main St., Banger, PA 18013: Free information ❖ Jackets, shirts, T-shirts, sweat suits, and other sportswear. 800–441–6958.

WinterSilks, 2700 Laura Ln., P.O. Box 620130, Middleton, WI 53562: Free catalog ❖ Silk turtlenecks, socks and glove liners, longjohns, and ski clothing. 800–621–3229.

Wissota Trader, 1313 1st Ave., Chippewa Falls, WI 54729: Free catalog ❖ Women and men's clothing and shoes in hard-to-fit sizes. 800–962–0160.

Woman Outfitter, P.O. Box 2820, Orleans, MA 02653: Free catalog ❖ Women's clothing for hiking, cycling, paddling, mountaineering, and walking. 800–795–7433.

Natural Fiber Clothing

Garnet Hill, 262 Main St., Franconia, NH 03580: Free catalog ❖ Clothing, bed linens, comforters, blankets, pillows, pillow shams, and towels. 800–622–6216.

JANICE Corporation, 198 Rt. 46, Budd Lake, NJ 07828: Free catalog ❖ Allergy-free clothing, exercise wear, sleepwear, robes, towels, bath and personal grooming aids, and mattresses, pads, quilts, and linens. 800–JANICES.

Mother Hart's Natural Products, P.O. Box 4229, Boynton Beach, FL 33424: Free information ❖ Women and men's clothing. 407–738–5866.

Red Rose Collection, P.O. Box 280140, San Francisco, CA 94128: Free catalog ❖ Natural fiber clothing, books and tapes, art works, jewelry, tools, games, decor accessories, and toiletries. 800–374–5505.

Vermont Country Store, Mail Order Office, P.O. Box 3000, Manchester Center, VT 05255: Free catalog ❖ Clothing and household items. 802–362–4647.

Petite Fashions

The Horchow Collection, P.O. Box 620048, Dallas, TX 75262: Free catalog ❖ Petite women's clothing. 800–395–5397.

Old Pueblo Traders, Palo Verde at 34th, P.O. Box 27800, Tucson, AZ 85726: Free catalog ❖ Dresses, casual fashions, coordinates, outerwear, shoes, lingerie, and sweaters, for women 5'4" and under. 602–748–8600.

J.C. Penney Company Inc., Catalog Division, Milwaukee, WI 53263: Free information ❖ Sportswear, casual fashions, and petite and misses clothing for brides and attendants. 800–222–6161.

Petite Ms, 555 Perkins, Memphis, TN 38117: Catalog $2 ❖ Clothing for women 5'4" and under. 901–685–8362.

Premiere Editions, Hanover, PA 17333–0012: Free catalog ❖ Sportswear and casual clothing for petites. 717–633–3311.

Shopping International, Palo Verde at 34th, P.O. Box 27800, Tucson, AZ 85726: Free catalog ❖ Mix-and-match blouses, skirts, pants, and other clothing for petites. 602–748–8600.

Spiegel, P.O. Box 6340, Chicago, IL 60680: Free information ❖ Career and weekend fashions for women under 5'4". 800–345–4500.

Talbots, 175 Beal St., Hingham, MA 02043: Free catalog ❖ Clothing for petites. 800–992–9010.

Unique Petite, Palo Verde at 34th, P.O. Box 27800, Tucson, AZ 85726: Free catalog ❖ Sweaters, jeans, swim wear, and other fashions for women 5'4" and under; shoes in hard-to-fit sizes. 602–748–8600.

Shirts

Burberry's Limited, 9 E. 57th St., New York, NY 10022: Free catalog ❖ Burberry's classic cotton shirts. 212–371–5010.

Paul Frederick Shirt Company, 223 W. Poplar St., Fleetwood, PA 19522: Free catalog ❖ Men's shirts, with French cut, button-down, tab, or straight collars, and French or button cuffs. 800–247–1417.

Huntington Clothiers, 1285 Alum Creek Dr., Columbus, OH 43209: Free catalog ❖ Men's shirts with optional monograms. 800–848–6203.

James River Traders, James River Landing, Hampton, VA 23631: Free catalog ❖ Men and women's casual clothes, beach attire, shirts, shoes, ties, robes, sweaters, and socks. 804–827–6000.

Lands' End Inc., 1 Lands' End Ln., Dodgeville, WI 53595: Free catalog ❖ Men and women's shirts, blouses, outerwear, sleepwear, casual and career fashions, and sweaters. 800–356–4444.

Quinn's Shirt Shop, Rt. 2, Box 131, North Grosvenordale, CT 06255: Brochure $2 with long SASE ❖ Slightly irregular shirts in regular, big, and for tall men. 508–943–7183.

A. Rubinstein & Son, 24 E. 17th St., New York, NY 10003: Free brochure ❖ Men's shirts, ties, and sportswear, rain wear, and outerwear. 212–924–7817.

Treadwell Shirt Company, 231 Hancock St., Madison, GA 30650: Free brochure ❖ Cotton shirts for men. 800–367–7158.

Special-Needs Clothing

Avenues Unlimited, 1199 Avenida Acaso, Ste. K, Camarillo, CA 93012: Free catalog ❖ Exercise equipment, easy-to-wear clothing, and footwear for men and women in wheelchairs. 800–848–2837.

Danmar Products Inc., 221 Jackson Industrial Dr., Ann Arbor, MI 48103: Free catalog ❖ Special-needs clothing. 800–783–1998; 313–761–1990 (in MI).

Everest & Jennings Ltd., 1199–K Avenita Acaso, Camarillo, CA 93012: Free catalog ❖ Clothing and accessories for people with disabilities. 800–848–2837.

Fashion Ease, Division M & M Health Care, 1541 60th St., Brooklyn, NY 11219: Free catalog ❖ Special-needs clothing and accessories. 800–221–8929; 718–871–8188 (in NY).

MTF Geriatrics, P.O. Box 320, Ellis, KS 67637: Free catalog ❖ Easy-on and easy-off clothing and accessories for the elderly and disabled. 913–726–4807.

Special Clothes, P.O. Box 4220, Alexandria, VA 22303: Free catalog (specify adults or children) ❖ Special-needs clothing. 703–683–7343.

Support Plus, Box 500, Medfield, MA 02052: Free catalog ❖ Medically acceptable support hosiery, personal hygiene and home health care aids, bath safety accessories, and walking shoes. 508–359–2910.

Wardrobe Wagon, 555 Valley Rd., West Orange, NJ 07052: Free catalog ❖ Special-needs clothing. 800–992–2737.

Worldwide Home Health Center Inc., 926 E. Tallmadge Ave., Akron, OH 44310: Free catalog ❖ Ostomy appliances, mastectomy breast forms, special-needs clothing, and skin care products. 800–223–5938; 800–621–5938 (in OH).

Suspenders, Belts & Buckles

Eloxite Corporation, 806 10th St., Wheatland, WY 82201: Catalog $1 ❖ Belt buckles, tools, gemstones, jewelry mountings, and clock-making, rockhounding, and jewelry-making supplies. 307–322–3050.

C. Lifton's Buckles & More, 121 S. 6th St., Stillwater, MN 55082: Catalog $5 ❖ Buckles, leather belts, trophy buckles, and reproductions of Old West badges in sterling silver. 612–439–7208.

David Morgan, 11812 Northcreek Pkwy., Ste. 103, Bothell, WA 98011: Free catalog ❖ Hand-braided belts, wool and sheepskin clothing, and fur hats. 800–324–4934.

Sweaters

Henri Bendel, 712 5th Ave., New York, NY 10019: Free information with long SASE ❖ Casual, outdoor, and dress sweaters for women. 212–247–1100.

J. Crew Outfitters, One Ivy Crescent, Lynchburg, VA 24513: Free catalog ❖ Mock turtlenecks, cardigans, button-down, and other sweaters for men and women. 800–932–0043.

Globetrotter Inc., 17 Lovelace Dr., West Hartford, CT 06117: Catalog $3 ❖ Hand knit cotton sweaters and jackets with ethnic, Western, and whimsical patterns and designs. 800–999–0955; 203–236–8711 (in CT).

James River Traders, James River Landing, Hampton, VA 23631: Free catalog ❖ Men and women's sweaters. 804–827–6000.

Landau Woolens, 114 Nassau St., Princeton, NJ 08542: Free catalog ❖ Men and women's hand knit wool sweaters, Icelandic light wool coats and jackets, blanket throws, wool sportswear, shirts, and cotton knits. 800–257–9445.

Lion's Pride Catalog, P.O. Box 342, Little Cute, WI 54140: Free catalog ❖ Recycled cotton knit sweaters and other clothing for big and tall men. 414–731–4242.

Pendleton Shop, Jordan Rd., P.O. Box 233, Sedona, AZ 86336: Catalog $1 ❖ Men and women's sweaters and sportswear. 602–282–3671.

Peruvian Connection, Canaan Farm, Tonganoxie, KS 66086: Free catalog ❖ Handmade Pima cotton and Alpaca wool sweaters. 800–255–6429.

Wanderings Inc., Warren, NJ 07059: Free catalog ❖ Hand-knit wool sweaters. 908–647–5731.

Winona Knitting Mills, 910 E. 2nd St., Winona, MN 55987: Free catalog ❖ Wool sweaters and other knitwear. 507–454–4381.

WinterSilks, 2700 Laura Ln., P.O. Box 620130, Middleton, WI 53562: Free catalog ❖ Turtlenecks, sweaters, silk long johns, and other fashions. 800–621–3229.

Tall & Big Men's Clothing

Harris Casuals, 110 W. 11th St., Los Angeles, CA 90015: Free information ❖ Casual clothing. 800–533–5066; 213–749–5066 (in CA).

Imperial Wear, 48 W. 48th St., New York, NY 10036: Free catalog ❖ Clothing. 212–719–2590.

King Size Company, P.O. Box 9115, Hingham, MA 02043: Free catalog ❖ Dress shirts to 24 neck, casual shirts to 6XL, jackets and outerwear to 6XL, and slacks and jeans to 72 waist, shoes to 16EEE, and other clothing. 800–846–1600.

Lion's Pride Catalog, P.O. Box 342, Little Cute, WI 54140: Free catalog ❖ Recycled cotton knit sweaters and other clothing for big and tall men. 414–731–4242.

J.C. Penney Company Inc., Catalog Division, Milwaukee, WI 53263: Free information ❖ Shirts, pants, and other clothing. 800–222–6161.

Phoenix Big & Tall, 805 Branch Dr., Alpharetta, GA 30201: Free catalog ❖ Casual and informal fashions, sportswear, outerwear, sleepwear, and other large-size clothing. 800–251–8067.

Rochester Big & Tall, 1301 Avenue of Americas, New York, NY 10019: Free catalog ❖ Suits, casual attire, and shoes. 800–282–8200.

Harry Rothman Clothing, 200 Park Ave. South, New York, NY 10003: Free information with long SASE ❖ Men's clothing in sizes 36 to 56, extra-long, and extra-short. 212–777–7400.

I. Spiewak & Sons Inc., 505 8th Ave., New York, NY 10018: Free brochure ❖ Outerwear for men, sizes 6X to XXXXLT. 800–223–6850; 212–695–1620 (in NY).

Tall Women's Clothing

Long Elegant Legs, 2–1 Homestead Rd., Belle Mead, NJ 08502: Free brochure ❖ Fashionable clothing for tall women. 800–344–2235.

Old Pueblo Traders, Palo Verde at 34th, P.O. Box 27800, Tucson, AZ 85726: Free catalog ❖ Fashions for women, 5'7" and taller. 602–748–8600.

J.C. Penney Company Inc., Catalog Division, Milwaukee, WI 53263: Free information ❖ Sportswear and casual fashions. 800–222–6161.

Tallclassics, Box 15024, Shawnee Mission, KS 66285: Free catalog ❖ Clothing for women 5'10" and taller. 800–345–1958.

T-Shirts & Sweatshirts

Aerie Design, 141 Blackberry Inn, Weaverville, NC 28787: Free catalog ❖ T-shirts with wildlife graphics. 800–233–0229.

Beer Gear, P.O. Box 90318, San Diego, CA 92109: Free information ❖ Cotton T-shirts. 800–582–9440.

Brass Ring' Graphics, Phil & Molly Rader, 2277 Ogden Rd., Wilmington OH 45177: Free information with long SASE ❖ Carousel art T-shirts and sweatshirts. 513–382–3266.

California Cheap Skates, 2701 McMillan Ave., San Luis Obispo, CA 93401: Free catalog ❖ T-shirts, shoes, stickers, skateboards and parts, and safety gear. 800–477–9283.

Counter Fit, P.O. Box 7304–295, North Hollywood, CA 91603: Free catalog ❖ Skateboards, decks, trucks, T-shirts, and other clothing. 818–567–2747.

Crazy Shirts, 99–969 Iwaena St., Aiea, HI 96701: Free catalog ❖ T-shirts and jackets in adult and junior sizes and box tops for adults in small, medium, large, and extra-large. 808–367–7044.

Dallas Alice, 8001 Cessna Ave., Ste. 203, Gaithersburg, MD 20879: Free catalog ❖ Silk-screened T-shirts. 301–948–0400.

Dolan's Sports Inc., 26 Hwy. 547, P.O. Box 26, Farmingdale, NJ 07727: Free catalog ❖ T-shirts with martial arts graphics, training and safety equipment, uniforms, shoes, Samurai swords, bags, and books. 908–938–6656.

Eastern Emblem, Box 828, Union City, NJ 07087: Free catalog ❖ T-shirts, jackets, patches, cloisonne pins, decals, and stickers. 800–344–5112.

Frosty Little, 222 E. 8th St., Burley, ID 83318: Free information ❖ Sweatshirts, T-shirts, pins, and patches with clown graphics. 208–678–0005.

FTC Skate Shop, 1586 Bush St., San Francisco, CA 94109: Free catalog ❖ Skateboards and parts, snowboards, and T-shirts. 415–673–8363.

Hagan/Main Treat, Main St., Tiburon, CA 94920: Free catalog ❖ T-shirts with fine art images for men, women, and children. 415–435–6071.

Just for Kids, P.O. Box 29141, Shawnee, KS 66201: Free catalog ❖ T-shirts and tops for children, toys and games, dolls, arts and crafts, musical instruments, school bags, and videos. 800–443–5827.

Main Treat, 21 Main St., Tiburon, CA 94920: Free information ❖ Fine art posters and prints reproduced on T-shirts and sweats. 415–435–6071.

J. Miller & Sons Outdoor Outfitters, P.O. Drawer 50668, Albany, GA 31705: Free catalog ❖ Nature and environmental T-shirts in 100 percent cotton. 800–344–3323.

Jim Morris Environmental T-Shirts, 5660 Valmont, P.O. Box 18270, Boulder, CO 80308: Free catalog ❖ T-shirts and sweatshirts with environmental and nature graphics. 800–788–5411.

The Nature Company, Catalog Division, P.O. Box 188, Florence, KY 41022: Free catalog ❖ T-shirts with pictures of African animals. 800–227–1114.

Pedigrees Pet Catalog, 1989 Transit Way, P.O. Box 905, Brockport, NY 14559: Free catalog ❖ Carriers, books, pet clothing, collars, toys, and T-shirts with pictures of pets. 800–548–4786.

PiDiDDLE's T-Shirt Factory, P.O. Box 656, Gwynedd Valley, PA 19437: Free information ❖ T-shirts with clown graphics. 215–699–6198.

Ridge Runner Naturals, 130 N. Main St., Waynesville, NC 28786: Free information ❖ Wildlife and nature T-shirts and other nature-related gifts. 704–456–3003.

Scene 1 T-Shirts, 6450 Merriman Rd. SW, Roanoke, VA 24018: Brochure $1 ❖ Wildlife T-shirts. 800–690–0238; 703–772–9373 (in VA).

Schnaubelt Shorts Inc., 1128 4th Ave., Coraopolis, PA 15108: Free information ❖ Silk screened T-shirts and clothing for bikers. 800–782–TEAM.

Shoosh Designs, 476 Arbutus Ave., Morro Bay, CA 93442: Free information ❖ Yoga T-shirts and sweatshirts. 805–772–9253.

Sky Etchings, P.O. Box 855, Syosset, NY 11791: Free brochure with long SASE ❖ T-shirts with aviation history graphics. 800–368–9956.

USA SportWear, 4901 W. Van Buren, Ste. 1, Phoenix, AZ 85043: Catalog $2 ❖ Motorcycle art T-shirts. 800–323–7734.

Vantage Communications Inc., Box 546, Nyack, NY 10960: Free information ❖ T-shirts for adults. 800–872–0068; 914–358–0147 (in NY).

Warner Brothers Catalog, 4000 Warner Blvd., Burbank, CA 91522: Catalog $3 ❖ Bugs Bunny, Looney Tunes, and other T-shirts and sweatshirts, for children and adults. 800–223–6524.

Wireless, P.O. Box 64422, St. Paul, MN 55164: Free catalog ❖ T-shirts, sweatshirts, boxer shorts, toy banks, coffee mugs, and other gifts. 800–669–9999.

Wonderwear, 1441 Rincon Villa Dr., Escondido, CA 92027: Catalog $1 (refundable) ❖ Buddhist, Hindu, Zen, and Taoist T-shirts and sweatshirts. 619–738–1243.

Uniforms

Commodore Uniform & Nautical Supplies, 335 Lower County Rd., Harwichport, MA 02646: Free information ❖ Boating uniforms, insignia, and flags. 800–438–8643; 508–430–7877 (in MA).

Dornan Uniforms, 653 11th Ave., New York, NY 10036: Free catalog ❖ Uniforms. 212–247–0937.

Industrial Uniforms, 906 E. Waterman, Wichita, KS 67202: Free information ❖ Uniforms and work clothing. 800–333–3666; 316–264–2871 (in KS).

Joseph Krasow, P.O. Box 784, Waterbury, CT 06720: Catalog $2 ❖ Uniforms and work clothing. 203–574–0667.

J.C. Penney Company Inc., Catalog Division, Milwaukee, WI 53263: Free information ❖ Women's clothing for health care personnel, in petite, misses, tall, and regular sizes. 800–222–6161.

Smallwoods Yachtwear, 1001 SE 17th St., Fort Lauderdale, FL 33316: Free catalog ❖ Uniforms and casual boating attire. 800–771–2283.

Tafford Manufacturing Inc., 104 Park Dr., P.O. Box 1006, Montgomeryville, PA 18936: Free catalog ❖ Nurse uniforms. 800–283–0065.

Todd Work Apparel, 3668 S. Geyer Rd., St. Louis, MO 63127: Free catalog ❖ Work clothing and uniforms. 800–458–3402.

Western Clothing

Amarillo Western Wear, 818 Rt. 25A, Ste. 114, Northport, NY 11768: Free catalog ❖ Men and women's western-style apparel. 800–368–0602.

Back at the Ranch, 235 Don Gaspar, Santa Fe, NM 87501: Free information ❖ Vintage western clothing, boots, and hats. 505–989–8110.

Buckaroo Bobbins, 377 S. 6300 W., Cedar City, VT 84720: Catalog $1 ❖ Authentic vintage western clothing sewing patterns. 801–865–7922.

Cattle Kate, Box 572, Wilson, WY 83014: Catalog $3 ❖ Contemporary clothing of the Old West for men, women, and children. 307–733–7414.

Cheyenne Outfitters, P.O. Box 12013, Cheyenne, WY 82003: Free catalog ❖ Western-style clothing, jewelry, and gifts. 307–775–7550.

Creations in Leather, 1212 Sheridan Ave., Cody, WY 82414: Brochure $5 ❖ Leather coats, shirts, vests, chaps, chinks, and jackets. 307–587–6461.

Gorlic's Trading Inc., P.O. Box 50, Warwick, NY 10990: Free information ❖ Leather outdoor hunting jackets and traditional cowboy vests. 914–986–8484.

Hobby Horse Clothing Company Inc., 213775 Stockton Ave., Chino, CA 91710: Catalog $2 ❖ Clothing.

Jackson Originals, Box 1049, Mission, SD 57555: Free price list with long SASE ❖ Men, women, and children's leather vests and jackets with bead work designs; denim shirts, vests, and jackets with applique or embroidered designs; and western traditional style Sioux ribbon shirts and dresses. 605–856–2541.

Luskey's Western Stores Inc., 101 N. Houston St., Fort Worth, TX 76102: Free catalog ❖ Western fashions, boots, and hats. 817–335–5833.

The Old Frontier Clothing Company, P.O. Box 691836, Los Angeles, CA 90069: Catalog $3 ❖ Men and women's western clothing. 310–246–WEST.

Red River Frontier Outfitters, P.O. Box 241, Tujunga, CA 91043: Catalog $3 ❖ Reproduction western clothing.

Rod's Western Palace, 3099 Silver Dr., Columbus, OH 43224: Free catalog ❖ Western wear and tack. 800–325–8508.

Roemers, 1920 N. Broadway, Santa Maria, CA 93455: Free catalog ❖ Western-style clothing and gifts for men and women. 800–242–1890; 800–232–1890 (in CA).

Ryon's Saddle & Ranch Supplies, 2601 N. Main, Fort Worth, TX 76106: Free catalog ❖ Western-style clothing and boots for men, women, and children. Also saddles and tack. 817–625–2391.

Sheplers, 6501 W. Kellogg, Wichita, KS 67209: Free catalog ❖ Western clothing. 800–242–6540.

Soda Creek Industries, Box 4343, Steamboat Springs, CO 80477: Free catalog ❖ Western clothing, hats, and dusters for men and women. 800–824–8426; 303–879–3146 (in CO).

Vanderbilt's Mail Order Inc., 500 Lincoln Ave., Wamego, KS 66547: Free catalog ❖ Men, women, and children's western-style clothing. 913–456–9199.

Wild Bills Leather, P.O. Box 13037, Burton, WA 98013: Brochure $2 ❖ Original and authentic frontier leather goods and other historical western items. 206–463–5738.

CLOWN SUPPLIES

Abracadabra Magic Shop, 125 Lincoln Blvd., Middlesex, NJ 08846: Catalog $5 ❖ Magic and juggling equipment, balloons, clown props, costumes, and make-up. 908–805–0200.

Apples & Company, 414 Conant Ave., Union, NJ 07083: Free information ❖ Clown-white make-up. 908–353–2193.

Artistic Clowns, Clown Paraphernalia, P.O. Box 811, Mt. Clemens, MI 48046: Catalog $1 (refundable) ❖ Clown stickers.

Axtell Expressions, 230 Glencrest Circle, Ventura, CA 93003: Catalog $2 ❖ Clown supplies. 805–642–7282.

Bigfoot Stilt Company, 7111 Gardner St., Winter Park, FL 32792: Free information ❖ Custom stilts. 407–677–5900.

Books by Mail, P.O. Box 1444, Corona, CA 91718: Free catalog with two 1st class stamps ❖ Books on clowning. 909–273–0900.

Mike Bornstein Clowns, 319 W. 48th St., New York, NY 10036: Free information with long SASE ❖ Clown props.

Burpo Duh Clown, P.O. Box 160190, Cupertino, CA 95016: Free information ❖ Face-painting rubber stamps and supplies. 408–446–9314.

Chazpro Magic Company, 603 E. 13th, Eugene, OR 97401: Catalog $3 ❖ Clown props, books, juggling equipment, jokes, and novelties. 503–345–0032.

Circus Clowns, 3556 Nicollet Ave., Minneapolis, MN 55408: Catalog $3 ❖ Clown costumes and props. 612–822–4243.

Circus Wagon Balloons, 3424 Belle Terrace, Bakersfield, CA 93309: Free information ❖ Balloons, magic, comedy props and gags, and other clown supplies. 805–837–0252.

Clown City, 1 Inchcliffe Dr., Gales Ferry, CT 06335: Free information ❖ Balloons and clown supplies. 203–464–7116.

The Clown Factory, 5724 N. Meridian, Wichita, KS 67204: Catalog $1 (refundable) ❖ Balloons, magic, comedy props and gags, and other clown supplies. 316–838–0818.

Clown Heaven, 4792 Old State Rd. 37 South, Martinsville, IN 46152: Catalog $3 ❖ Balloons, make-up, puppets, wigs, ministry and gospel items, novelties, magic, clown props, and books. 317–342–6888.

Comanche Clown Shoes Mfg., P.O. Box 551, Mountain View, OK 73062: Free information ❖ Clown shoes. 800–832–3424; 405–347–2817 (in OK).

Cosmar Magic, 6765 El Banquero Pl., San Diego, CA 92119: Catalog $15 ❖ Close-up and stage magic and clown supplies. 619–287–3706.

Costumes by Betty, 2181 Edgerton St., St. Paul, MN 55117: Catalog $5 (refundable) ❖ Clown costumes, make-up, wigs, and shoes. 612–771–8734.

Steve Dawson's Magic Touch, 144 N. Milpitas Blvd., Milpitas, CA 95035: Catalog $3 ❖ Magic and props for clowns and magicians. 408–263–9404.

Dewey's Good News Balloons, 1202 Wildwood, Deer Park, TX 77536: Free catalog ❖ Gospel clown supplies and balloons.

The Entertainers Supermarket, 21 Carol Pl., Staten Island, NY 10303: Free brochure ❖ Props for clowns, magicians, balloon sculpturists, jugglers, face painters, stilt walkers, and other entertainers. 718–494–6232.

Freckles Clown Supplies, 5509 Rossevelt Blvd., Jacksonville, FL 32210: Catalog $5 ❖ Costumes, make-up, clown supplies, puppets, how-to books on clowning and ballooning, and other theatrical supplies. 904–778–3977.

Fun Technicians Inc., P.O. Box 160, Syracuse, NY 13215: Free information ❖ Clown props. 315–492–4523.

Bob Gibbon's Fun Technicians Inc., P.O. Box 160, Syracuse, NY 13215: Free information ❖ Clown props. 315–492–4523.

David Ginn Magic, 4387 St. Michaels Dr., Lilburn, GA 30247: Catalog $10 ❖ Books, props, and how-to magic on video tapes for magicians and clowns.

Graftobian Ltd., 510 Tasman St., Madison, WI 53714: Free information ❖ Face-painting supplies. 800–255–0584.

Holly Sales, 9926 Beach Blvd., Ste. 114, Jacksonville, FL 32246: Free information ❖ Clown stickers. 904–223–5828.

Indianapolis Costume Company Inc., 615–619 Virginia Ave., Indianapolis, IN 46203: Free information ❖ Magic, make-up, balloons, books, wigs, and costumes. 317–634–2229.

John the Clown Shoemaker, 1156 Waukegan Rd., Glenview, IL 60025: Catalog $2 with long SASE ❖ Shoes for clowns. 708–486–0715.

Kidshow Creations, 101 Dorchester Dr., Baltimore, OH 43105: Free information ❖ Books, tapes, comedy props, and other clown supplies for children's shows.

La Rock's Fun & Magic Outlet, 3847 Rosehaven Dr., Charlotte, NC 28205: Catalog $3 ❖ Clown and balloon how-to books, balloon sculpture kits, and magic equipment. 704–563–9300.

Laflin's Magic & Silks, P.O. Box 228, Sterling, CO 80751: Free information ❖ Entertaining and educational magic on video tapes for clowns and magicians. 303–522–2589.

Lynch's Clown Supplies, 939 Howard, Dearborn, MI 48124: Catalog $5 ❖ Wigs, shoes, noses, novelty items, make-up, and costume accessories. 313–565–3425.

Mecca Magic Inc., 49 Dodd St., Bloomfield, NJ 07003: Catalog $10 ❖ Clown equipment, make-up, balloons, magic, costumes and wigs, puppets, ventriloquism and clown props, and juggling supplies. 201–429–7597.

Priscilla Mooseburger Originals, P.O. Box 529, Maple Lake, MN 55358: Catalog $1 ❖ Clown hats and clothing. 612–963–6277.

Morris Costumes, 3108 Monroe Rd., Charlotte, NC 28205: Catalog $20 ❖ Costumes, clown props, masks, joke items,

magic and special effects, novelties, balloons, and books. 704–332–3304.

Novelties Unlimited, 410 W. 21st St., Norfolk, VA 23517: Catalog $5 ❖ Clown supplies, props and gags, magic, balloons, make-up, and party decorations. 804–622–0344.

Ben Nye Makeup, 5935 Bowcroft St., Los Angeles, CA 90016: Catalog $2.50 ❖ Clown make-up. 310–839–1984.

M.E. Persson, The Castles, Rt. 101, Ste. C-7, Brentwood, NH 03833: Catalog $1 ❖ Clown supplies. 603–679–3311.

Potsy & Blimpo Clown Supplies, P.O. Box 2075, Huntington Beach, CA 92647: Free catalog ❖ Clown make-up, wigs, and supplies. 800–897–0749.

Spear's Specialty Shoe Company, 12 Orlando St., Springfield, MA 01108: Brochure $2 ❖ Clown shoes.

Stein's Clown Supplies, P.O. Box 2075, Huntington Beach, CA 92647: Free catalog ❖ Clown make-up, props, and wigs. 714–897–0749.

Under the Big Top, P.O. Box 807, Placentia, CA 92670: Catalog $4 ❖ Clown props, costumes, make-up, juggling equipment, balloons, and party supplies. 800–995–7727.

Up, Up & Away, P.O. Box 159, Beallsville, PA 15313: Catalog $2 ❖ Clown make-up and props. 412–769–5447.

Alan Zerobnick, Tenderfoot Trading Company, P.O. Box 1349, Port Townsend, WA 98368: Catalog $3 ❖ Clown shoes in original designs. 206–385–6164.

COFFEE & ESPRESSO MAKERS

Georgetown Coffee, Tea & Spice, 1330 Wisconsin Ave. NW, Washington, DC 20007: Free catalog ❖ Brewing equipment, coffee filters, replacement beakers, gifts, and imported and domestic coffees, specialty blends, unroasted green beans, sampler assortments, and decaffeinated teas. 800–846–1947.

Mazzoli Coffee Inc., 236 Ave. U, Brooklyn, NY 11223: Catalog 50¢ ❖ Coffee brewers and grinders. 718–449–0909.

Zabar's & Company, 2245 Broadway, New York, NY 10024: Free catalog ❖ Coffee makers, cookware, food processors, microwave ovens, kitchen tools, gourmet foods, and gift baskets. 212–787–2000.

COIN-OPERATED MACHINES

Ancient Slots & Antiques, 3127 Industrial Rd., Las Vegas, NV 89109: Free information ❖ Old slot machines. 800–228–SLOT; 702–796–7779 (in NV).

Antique Slot Machine Part Company, 140 N. Western Ave., Carpentersville, IL 60110: Free catalog ❖ Books and manuals, slot stands and pads, and parts for slot machines, jukeboxes, and pinballs. 708–428–8476.

Bernie Berten, 9420 S. Trumbull Ave., Evergreen Park, IL 60642: Free catalog with two 1st class stamps ❖ Slot machines and parts. 708–499–0688.

Classic Coin-Ops, 7038 Hoke Rd., Clayton, OH 45315: Free information with long SASE ❖ Jukeboxes, slot machines, and coke machines. 513–833–5143.

Coin-Op Amusements Company, Steve Gronowski, RR 2, Bateman Cir., Barrington Hills, IL 60010: Free information with long SASE ❖ Antique penny arcade and slot machines. 708–381–1234.

CSSK Amusements, Box 6214, York, PA 17406: Free list with long SASE ❖ Jukeboxes, other coin-operated collectibles, and parts for jukeboxes and pinball machines. 800–PINBALL.

Durham's Antiques, 909 26th St. NW, Washington, DC 20037: Catalog $2 ❖ Antique coin-operated vending and arcade machines, pinballs, counter-top games, and books. 202–338–1342.

EDI, 3595 Canton Rd., Bldg. A9, Ste. 270, Marietta, GA 30066: Free information ❖ Home and commercial music devices, CD jukeboxes, billiard tables, and other games. 404–516–0833.

Howard J. Fink, 174 Main St., Acton, MA 01720: Free information ❖ Vintage pinball and slot machines for the home. 508–263–6480.

The Gambler, 2574 Hwy. 10 NE, Mounds View, MN 55112: Free information ❖ New and used recreation room games, toys, and casino equipment.

Jian Worldwide Group Ltd., 1033 Franklin Rd., Marietta, GA 30067: Free information ❖ Antique and reproduction music and gaming machines, billiard and snooker tables, coke machines, and other nostalgia. 404–578–4482.

Norm & Mary Johnson, County Home Rd., Bowling Green, OH 43402: Free information with long SASE ❖ Slot machines, old arcade games, peanut and gumball machines, and mechanical and still banks. 419–352–3041.

Jukebox Classics & Vintage Slot Machines Inc., 6742 5th Ave., Brooklyn, NY 11220: Free information ❖ Antique coin-operated machines and jukeboxes. 718–833–8455.

Lloyd's Jukeboxes, 22900 Shaw Rd., Sterling, VA 22170: Free information ❖ Jukeboxes, pinball machines, video games, slot machines, tin toys, advertising signs, and other items from the 1950s. 703–834–6699.

National Jukebox Exchange, Box 460, Mayfield, NY 12117: Free catalog ❖ Antique jukeboxes, slot machines, other arcade machines, and parts. 518–661–5639.

Bob Nelson's Gameroom Warehouse, 826 W. Douglas, Wichita, KS 67203: Free information ❖ Antique coin-operated machines and parts. 316–263–1848.

North Penn Amusement & Vending, 105 N. Main, Souderton, PA 18924: Free information ❖ Jukeboxes, pinball machines, shuffle alleys, vending machines, video games, and pool tables. 215–723–7459.

Orange Trading Company, 57 S. Main St., Orange, MA 01364: Free list with long SASE ❖ Antique jukeboxes, pinballs, and other coin-operated machines. 508–544–6683.

Royal Bell Ltd., 5815 W 52nd Ave., Denver, CO 80212: Catalog $5 ❖ Slot machines and other mechanical memorabilia. 303–431–9266.

St. Louis Slot Machine Company, 2111 S. Brentwood Blvd., St. Louis, MO 63144: Catalog $3 ❖ Common to rare Coca Cola and other coin-operated machines. 314–961–4612.

Alan Sax Slot Machines, 3239 RFD, Long Grove, IL 60047: Free information ❖ Slot machines. 708–438–5900.

Slot-Box Collector, Richard Bueschel, 414 N. Prospect Manor Ave., Mt. Prospect, IL 60056: Free list with seven 1st class stamps ❖ Old saloon artifacts, coin-operated machines, advertising collectibles, and paper memorabilia. 708–253–0791.

COMIC BOOKS

Ray Agricola Comics, P.O. Box 51, Garrett Park, MD 20896: Free information with long SASE ❖ Historical comic books. 301–942–1599.

Bags Unlimited Inc., 7 Canal St., Rochester, NY 14608: Free information ❖ Comic book storage and archival supplies. 800–767–BAGS.

Best Comics Distribution Center, 252–01 Northern Blvd., Little Neck, NY 11362: Free information ❖ Comic books, original comic art, action figures, and trading cards. 800–966–2099; 718–279–2099 (in NY).

Best Rockart Gallery, 2801 Leavenworth St., San Francisco, CA 94133: Free information ❖ Comics, original rock art and posters, toys, and handbills. 800–775–1966.

Bill Cole Enterprises Inc., P.O. Box 60, Randolph, MA 02368: Free information ❖ Comic book archival supplies. 617–986–2653.

College of Comic Book Knowledge, 3151 Hennepin Ave. South, Minneapolis, MN 55408: Catalog $2 (refundable) ❖ Collector comic books. 612–822–2309.

Comic Classics, 365 Main St., Laurel, MD 20707: Free information with long SASE ❖ Comic books, sports cards, and archival supplies. 301–490–9811.

Comic Relief, 2138 University Ave., Berkeley, CA 94704: Free information ❖ Golden and Silver Age comic books. 510–843–5002.

Gary Dolgoff Comics, Brooklyn Navy Yard, Bldg. 280, Ste. 608/609, Brooklyn, NY 11205: Catalog $1 ❖ Collector comic books. 718–596–5719.

Scott Eder Comics, 9 Sedgemere Rd., Center Moriches, NY 11934: Free information ❖ Comic books. 516–878–3023.

Fantasy Distribution Company, 2831 Miller St., San Leandro, CA 94577: Free information ❖ Back issue comic books. 510–352–5832.

Geppi's Comic World Inc., 1966 Greenspring Dr., Ste. 300, Timonium, MD 21093: Free information with long SASE ❖ Comic books and science fiction magazines. 800–783–2981.

Will Gorges Civil War Antiques, 2100 Trent Blvd., New Bern, NC 28560: Catalog $10 ❖ Authentic Civil War uniforms, weapons, photographs, and pre-1964 comic books. 919–636–3039.

Jennings Comic Outlet, 2120 Metro Cir., Huntsville, AL 35801: Free information ❖ Comic books. 205–880–6405.

Joseph Koch, 206 41st St., Brooklyn, NY 11232: Free information with long SASE ❖ Old and new comic books. 718–768–8571.

Philip M. Levine & Sons, Rare & Esoteric Books, P.O. Box 246, Three Bridges, NJ 08887: Free information ❖ Comic books, specializing in pre-1975 issues. 908–788–0532.

Bob Levy Comics, 2456 E. 18th St., Brooklyn, NY 11235: Free catalog ❖ Originals, reprints, special issues, and other comic books. 718–646–4941.

Metropolis, 7 W. 18th St., New York, NY 10011: Free information ❖ Vintage comic books and movie posters. 800–229–6387; 212–627–9691 (in NY).

Mint Condition Comic Books & Baseball Cards Inc., 664 Port Washington Blvd., Port Washington, NY 11050: Free information with long SASE ❖ Current and back issue comic books and sports cards. 516–883–0631.

Moondog's Comicland, 1201 Oakton St., Elk Grove Village, IL 60007: Free information ❖ Comic book archival supplies. 800–344–6060.

New England Comics, P.O. Box 310, Quincy, MA 02169: Catalog $1 ❖ Collectible comic books. 716–774–1745.

Northeast Comic Exchange, 1002 Graham Ave., Windber, PA 15963: Free information ❖ Hard-to-find comic books. 814–467–8837.

Bud Plant Comic Art, P.O. Box 1886, Grass Valley, CA 95945: Free catalog ❖ Comic books, comic strip collections, books about the history of comics and their creators, other limited edition books, and prints. 916–273–2166.

T.J.'s Comics & Cards & Supplies, Lloyds Shopping Center, 330 Rt. 211 East, Middletown, NY 10940: Free information ❖ Comic books, sports and non-sports cards, and hobby supplies. 800–848–848–1482.

Lee Tennant Enterprises Inc., 6963 W. 111th St., Worth, IL 60482: Free information ❖ New issues and collector comic books and archival supplies. 800–356–6401; 708–532–1771 (in IL).

Tomorrow Is Yesterday, 5600 N. 2nd St., Rockford, IL 61111: Free information with long SASE ❖ New and back issue comic books, games, and other collectibles. 815–633–0330.

Unique Dist., 110 Denton Ave., New Hyde Park, NY 11040: Free information ❖ Sports and non-sports cards and comics. 800–294–5901; 516–294–5900 (in NY).

COMPUTERS
Manufacturers

Acer American Corporation, 2641 Orchard Pkwy., San Jose, CA 95134: Free information ❖ IBM compatibles and portables. 408–432–6200.

Advanced Logic Research Inc., 9401 Jeronimo, Irvine, CA 92718: Free information ❖ IBM compatibles and portables. 800–444–4ALR; 714–581–6770 (in CA).

Ager Portable Computers, 18005 Cortney Ct., City of Industry, CA 91748: Free information ❖ IBM compatibles. 800–669–1624.

Airis Computer Corporation, 1824 N. Besly Ct., Chicago, IL 60622: Free information ❖ IBM compatible portables. 312–384–5608.

Altima Systems Inc., 1390 Willow Pass Rd., Ste. 1050, Concord, CA 94520: Free information ❖ IBM compatible portables. 800–356–9990.

American Mitac Corporation, 3797 Spinnaker Ct., Fremont, CA 94538: Free information ❖ IBM compatibles and portables. 800–777–1688; 510–623–5300 (in CA).

American Research Corporation, 1101 Monterey Pass Rd., Monterey Park, CA 91754: Free information ❖ IBM compatible portables. 800–346–3272; 213–265–0835 (in CA).

Apple Compatible Laser Computers, Laser Computer Inc., 800 N. Church St., Lake Zurich, IL 60047: Free information ❖ Apple compatibles, monitors, and laser and dot matrix printers. 708–540–8086.

Apple Computer Inc., 20525 Mariani Ave., Cupertino, CA 95014: Free information ❖ Macintosh computers and portables, printers, and other peripherals. 408–996–1010.

Aquiline Computers Inc., 283 Old London Rd., Latham, NY 12110: Free information ❖ IBM compatible portables. 517–785–6517.

Ares Microdevelopment Inc., 23660–A Research Dr., Farmington Hills, MI 48335: Free information ❖ IBM compatibles. 800–322–3200.

Associated Mega Sub System Inc., 4801 Little John St., Unit A, Baldwin Park, CA 91706: Free information ❖ IBM compatible portables. 818–814–8851.

AST Research Inc., 16215 Alton Pkwy., Irvine, CA 92713: Free information ❖ IBM compatibles and portables. 800–876–4AST.

Atari Computer, 1196 Borregas Ave., Sunnyvale, CA 94088: Free catalog ❖ Atari computers and portables. 408–745–2000.

AT&T/NCR Computers, World Headquarters, 1700 S. Patterson Blvd., Dayton, OH 45479: Free information ❖ IBM compatibles and portables. 800–225–5627.

Austin Computer Systems, 10300 Metric Blvd., Austin, TX 78758: Free information ❖ IBM compatibles and portables. 800–338–1571.

Autotech/Viktron Group, 343 St. Paul Blvd., Carol Stream, IL 60188: Free information ❖ IBM compatible portables. 800–527–2841; 708–668–3355 (in IL).

Auva Computer Inc., 16851 Knott Ave., La Mirada, CA 90638: Free information ❖ IBM compatible portables. 714–562–6999.

Bondwell Industrial Company Inc., 47485 Seabridge Dr., Fremont, CA 94538: Free information ❖ Portable computers. 510–490–4300.

Canon Computer Systems, 123 E. Paularino Ave., P.O. Box 5048, Costa Mesa, CA 92628: Free information ❖ IBM compatible portables. 714–438–3000.

Chaplet Systems, 252 N. Wolfe Rd., Sunnyvale, CA 94086: Free information ❖ IBM compatible portables. 408–732–7950.

Commax Technologies, 2031 Concourse Dr., San Jose, CA 95131: Free information ❖ IBM compatible portables. 800–526–6629; 408–435–5000 (in CA).

Commodore Business Machines Inc., 1200 Wilson Dr., Westchester, PA 19380: Free information ❖ Commodore computers and portables. 800–448–9987; 215–431–9100 (in PA).

Compaq Computer Corporation, P.O. Box 692000, Houston, TX 77269: Free information ❖ IBM compatibles and portables. 713–370–0670.

CompuAdd Corporation, 12303 Technology Blvd., Austin, TX 78727: Free information ❖ IBM compatibles, portables, and monitors. 800–999–9901; 512–250–1489 (in TX).

Comtrade Electronics USA Inc., 15314 E. Valley Blvd., City of Industry, CA 91748: Free information ❖ IBM compatible portables. 800–969–2123.

Core Pacific USA Inc., 197 Meister Ave., Branchburg, NJ 08876: Free information ❖ IBM compatible portables. 201–704–8383.

Data General Corporation, 2400 Computer Dr., Westborough, MA 01580: Free information ❖ IBM compatible portables and dot matrix printers. 800–328–2436; 508–366–8911 (in MA).

Dauphin Technology Inc., 1125 East St. Charles Rd., Lombard, IL 60148: Free information ❖ IBM compatible portables. 800–782–7922; 708–627–4004 (in IL).

Dell Computer Corporation, 9505 Arboretum Blvd., Austin, TX 78759: Free catalog ❖ IBM compatibles and portables. 800–677–4168.

Dolch Computer Systems, 372 Turquoise St., Milpitas, CA 95305: Free information ❖ IBM compatible portables. 800–538–7506; 408–957–6575 (in CA).

Epson America Inc., 20770 Madrona Ave., Torrance, CA 90503: Free information ❖ IBM compatibles, portables, and dot matrix and laser printers. 800–289–3776; 310–782–0770 (in CA).

Ergo Computing, One Intercontinental Way, Peabody, MA 01960: Free information ❖ IBM compatible portables. 800–633–1925; 508–535–7510 (in MA).

Everex Systems Inc., 901 Page Ave., Fremont, CA 94538: Free information ❖ IBM compatibles. 800–821–0806; 510–498–1111 (in CA).

Fora Computers Inc., 308 N. 1st St., San Jose, CA 95113: Free information ❖ IBM compatible portables. 408–944–0393.

Gateway-2000 Computers, 610 Gateway, North Sioux City, SD 57049: Free information ❖ IBM compatibles and portables. 800–523–2000; 605–232–2000 (in SD).

Goldstar Technology, 1000 Sylvan Ave., Englewood, NJ 07632: Free information ❖ IBM compatible portables. 201–816–2200.

The Hewlett-Packard Company, 19091 Pruneridge Ave., Cupertino, CA 95014: Free information and list of retailers ❖ IBM compatible portables, laser printers, and other equipment. 800–752–0900.

Hyundai Electronics America, 1955 Lundy Ave., San Jose, CA 95131: Free information ❖ IBM compatibles and portables. 800–933–3445.

The IBM Corporation, Direct Response Marketing, 3039 Cornwallis Rd., Bldg 203/D17, Research Triangle Park, NC 27709: Free information ❖ IBM computers, portables, dot matrix and laser printers, and peripherals. 800–IBM-2YOU.

Kris Technologies Inc., 260 E. Grand Ave., South San Francisco, CA 94080: Free information ❖ IBM compatible portables. 800–282–5747; 415–875–6729 (in CA).

Leading Edge Products Inc., 117 Flanders Rd., Westborough, MA 01581: Free information ❖ IBM compatibles and portables. 508–836–4800.

The Librex Corporation, 1731 Technology Dr., Ste. 700, San Jose, CA 95110: Free information ❖ IBM compatible portables. 408–441–8500.

Mectel International Inc., 3385 Viso Ct., Santa Clara, CA 95054: Free information ❖ IBM compatible portables. 800–248–0255; 408–980–4709 (in CA).

Micro Express, 1801 Carnegie Ave., Santa Ana, CA 92705: Free information ❖ IBM compatibles and portables. 800–642–7621; 714–852–1400 (in CA).

Micro Generation Computers, 300 McGaw Dr., Edison, NJ 08837: Free information ❖ IBM compatibles and portables. 800–872–2841; 201–225–8899 (in NJ).

Micronics Computers Inc., 232 E. Warren Ave., Fremont, CA 94539: Free information ❖ IBM compatible portables. 510–651–2300.

Midern Computer Inc., 18005 Courtney Ct., City of Industry, CA 91748: Free information ❖ IBM compatible portables. 800–669–1624; 818–964–8682 (in CA).

Midwest Micro, 6910 US Rt. 36 East, Fletcher, OH 45326: Free information ❖ Portable computers, power protection equipment, and peripherals. 800–972–8822.

Mitsuba Computers, 1925 Wright Ave., La Verne, CA 91750: Free information ❖ IBM compatible portables. 800–648–7822; 714–392–2000 (in CA).

Modern Computer Corporation, 1 World Trade Center, Ste. 7967, New York, NY 10048: Free information ❖ IBM compatible portables. 212–488–5916.

NCR Corporation, 1700 S. Patterson Blvd., Dayton, OH 45479: Free information ❖ IBM compatible portables. 513–445–1184.

NEC Technologies Inc., 1414 Massachusetts Ave., Boxborough, MA 01719: Free

information ❖ IBM compatibles, portables, and printers. 800–388–8888; 508–264–8000 (in MA).

Northgate Computer Systems Inc., 7075 Flying Cloud Dr., Eden Prairie, MN 55344: Free information ❖ IBM compatibles and portables. 800–5430–0129.

Olivetti North America Inc., 22425 E. Appleway Ave., Liberty Lake, WA 99019: Free information ❖ IBM compatibles and portables. 800–633–9909; 509–927–5600 (in WA).

Panasonic, Panasonic Way, Secaucus, NJ 07094: Free information ❖ IBM compatible portables. 201–348–7000.

PC Brand Inc., 405 Science Dr., Moor Park, CA 93021: Free information ❖ IBM compatibles and portables. 800–PC-BRAND.

Philips Consumer Electronics, One Philips Dr., Knoxville, TN 37914: Free information ❖ IBM compatible portables. 615–521–4316.

Psion Computers, 5 Concord Farms, 555 Virginia Ave., Concord, MA 01742: Free information ❖ IBM compatible portables. 800–628–7949; 508–371–0310 (in MA).

Quill Computers, 100 Schelter Rd., Lincolnshire, IL 60069: Free information ❖ IBM compatibles. 708–634–6650.

Radio Shack, Division Tandy Corporation, One Tandy Center, Fort Worth, TX 76102: Free catalog ❖ IBM compatibles, portables, monitors, dot matrix and laser printers, and supplies. 817–390–3011.

SAI Systems Laboratories Inc., 911 Bridgeport Ave., Shelton, CT 06484: Free information ❖ IBM compatible portables. 800–331–0488; 203–929–0790 (in CT).

The Sampo Corporation of America, Industrial Products Division, 5550 Peachtree Industrial Blvd., Norcross, GA 30342: Free information ❖ IBM compatible portables. 404–449–6220.

Sharp Electronics, Sharp Plaza, Mahwah, NJ 07430: Free information ❖ IBM compatibles and portables. 800–BE-SHARP.

Swan Technologies, 3075 Research Dr., State College, PA 16801: Free information ❖ IBM compatibles and portables. 800–468–9044.

Tangent Computer Inc., 197 Airport Blvd., Burlingame, CA 94010: Free information ❖ IBM compatibles and portables. 800–800–6060.

TC Computers, 5005 Bloomfield, Jefferson, LA 70121: Free information ❖ IBM compatibles and portables.

Texas Instruments Inc., P.O. Box 202230, Austin, TX 78720: Free information ❖ IBM compatible portables. 800–527–3500.

Toshiba America Information Systems, Computer Systems Division, 9740 Irvine Blvd., Irvine, CA 92718: Free information ❖ IBM compatible portables. 800–334–3445; 714–583–3000 (in CA).

Tri-Star Computer Corporation, 120 S. Weber Dr., Chandler, AZ 85226: Free information ❖ IBM compatibles. 800–800–1929.

United Computer Express, 724 7th Ave., New York, NY 10019: Free information ❖ Desktop and portable computers, peripherals, memory upgrades, printers, and software. 800–448–3738.

Zenith Data Systems, 2150 E. Lake Cook Rd., Buffalo Grove, IL 60089: Free information ❖ IBM compatibles, portables, and monitors. 800–553–0331.

Zeos International Ltd., 1301 Industrial Blvd., Minneapolis, MN 55413: Free information ❖ IBM compatibles and portables. 800–272–8993.

Retailers

ABC Drives, 8714 Darby Ave., Northridge, CA 91325: Free information ❖ Hard and floppy drives, tape backups, and controller cards for IBM compatibles. 818–885–7157.

Acecad, P.O. Box 431, Monterey, CA 93942: Free information ❖ Stylus and touch-sensitive input screen. 800–676–4ACE.

Alltech Electronics Company Inc., 602 Garrison St., Oceanside, CA 92054: Free catalog ❖ Apple disk and hard drives, RAM chips, disks, monitors, expansion cards, cables, and peripherals. 619–721–7733.

American Portable Research Inc., 14261 E. Don Julian Rd., City of Industry, CA 91746: Free information ❖ Portable multimedia computer work stations. 818–855–5290.

APLUS Computer Inc., 398 Lemon Creek Dr., Unit H, Walnut, CA 91789: Free information ❖ Disk and hard drives, portables, peripheral boards, and monitors. 800–443–5373.

The Apple Catalog, One Apple Plaza, P.O. Box 9001, Clearwater, FL 34618: Free catalog ❖ Macintosh computers, printers, scanners, and software. 800–795–1000; 800–755–0601 (TDD).

Apple Computer Inc., 2025 Mariani Ave., Cupertino, CA 95014: Free information ❖ Flatbed scanner. 408–996–1010.

APS Technologies, 6131 Deramus, P.O. Box 4887, Kansas City, MO 64120: Free information ❖ Macintosh storage devices, disk drives, scanners, modems, and other peripherals. 800–874–1429.

Arlington Computer Products Inc., 1970 Carboy, Mt. Prospect, IL 60056: Free information ❖ Computer systems, peripherals, and software. 800–548–5105.

Battery Biz, 31352 Via Colinas, Ste. 104, Westlake Village, CA 91362: Free catalog ❖ Batteries. 800–848–6782.

BayTech, Data Communications Products Division, 200 N. 2nd St., P.O. Box 387, Bay St. Louis, MS 38520: Free information ❖ Printer sharing equipment. 800–523–2702; 601–467–8231 (in MS).

Buffalo Products Inc., 2805 19th St. SE, Salem, OR 97302: Free information ❖ Printer-sharing control units. 800–345–2356.

Bulldog Computer Products, P.O. Box 1459, Evans, GA 30809: Free information ❖ IBM compatible cards and peripherals, disk drives, monitors, mouse devices, modems, software, and laptops. 800–438–6039.

Canon Computer Systems, 123 E. Paularino Ave., P.O.Box 5048, Costa Mesa, CA 92628: Free information ❖ Portable printers. 714–438–3000.

CDW Computer Centers Inc., 1020 E. Lake Cook Rd., Buffalo Grove, IL 60089: Free information ❖ Hardware, software, and peripherals. 800–449–4CDW.

Chinon America Inc., 1065 Bristol Rd., Mountainside, NJ 07092: Free information ❖ CD-ROM drives for the Macintosh. 908–654–0404.

Chip Factory Inc., 151 S. Pfingsten Rd., Deerfield, IL 60015: Free information ❖ Laser printer upgrades and memory chips for IBM compatibles and portables.

CMO Superstore, 101 Reighard Ave., Williamsport, PA 17701: Free information ❖ Computer systems, peripherals, and software. 800–233–8950.

CNF Inc., 17705 Halve Ave., Morgan Hill, CA 95037: Free catalog ❖ Laptop peripherals. 408–778–1160.

Roger Coats, 20200 Nine Mile Rd., St. Clair Shores, MI 48080: Free information ❖ Apple accessories, Laser 128 computers and printers, cards, chips, drives, scanners, modems, system savers, other peripherals, and software. 800–438–2883; 313–774–8240 (in MI).

CompUSA Inc., 15160 Marsh Ln., Dallas, TX 75234: Free catalog ❖ Software, desktop and portable IBM compatibles, peripherals, furniture, books, and other equipment. 800–451–7638.

CompuServe, P.O. Box 20212, Columbus, OH 43220: Free information ❖ PC/AT emulator for the Amiga. 800–848–8990; 614–457–8650 (in OH).

ComputAbility Consumer Electronics, P.O. Box 17882, Milwaukee, WI 53217: Free information ❖ Computer systems, peripherals, other electronics, and software. 800–558–0003.

Computer Friends Inc., 14250 NW Science Park Dr., Portland, OR 97229: Free information ❖ Ribbon re-inkers and inks. 800–547–3303.

Computer Printer Solutions Inc., P.O. Box 869, Oriental, NC 28571: Free information ❖ Printers and supplies. 800–598– 0568; 919–249–0568 (in NC).

Computer Works, 2520 Park Central Blvd., Ste. C-2, Decatur, GA 30035: Free information ❖ Laser computers, disk drives, cards, monitors, printers, modems, cables, and other accessories. 800–969–6757.

DataCal Corporation, 531 E. Elliot Rd., Chandler, AZ 85225: Free catalog ❖ Computer productivity enhancements, software, and keyboard overlays and templates. 800–453–7932.

Daystar Digital, 5556 Atlanta Hwy., Flowery Branch, GA 30542: Free brochure ❖ Peripheral performance upgrades for the Macintosh. 800–942–2077.

Digital Vision Inc., 270 Bridge St., Dedham, MA 02026: Free information ❖ Video equipment for IBM compatible and Macintosh computers. 617–329–5400.

Dirt Cheap Drives, 1110 NASA Rd. 1, Ste. 304, Nassau Bay, TX 77058: Free information ❖ Hard disk, tape, CD-ROM, and optical drives. 800–872–6007; 713–333–9602 (in TX).

DKB Software, 50240 W. Pontiac, Wixom, MI 48393: Free information ❖ Amiga add-on cards. 313–960–8751.

Dynamic Engineering, 435 Park, Ben Lomond, CA 95005: Free information ❖ Macintosh and IBM compatible hardware, software, peripherals, power protection accessories, and add-on memory components. 408–336–8891.

Educational Resources, 1550 Executive Dr., Elgin, IL 60123: Free catalog ❖ Software, diskettes, peripherals, and computers. 800–624–2926; 708–888–8300 (in IL).

Envisions Solutions Technology Inc., 822 Mahler Rd., Burlingame, CA 94010: Free information ❖ Hand-held scanners for IBM compatibles. 800–365–7226.

Epson America Inc., 20770 Madrona Ave., Torrance, CA 90503: Free information ❖ High-resolution color scanners for Amiga computers. 800–289–3776; 310–782–0770 (in CA).

Express Direct, 1801 W. Larchmont Ave., Chicago, IL 60613: Free information ❖ Macintosh systems and peripherals. 800–535–3252.

Fas-Track Computer Products, 7030 Huntley Rd., Columbus, OH 43229: Free information ❖ Software, Apple accessories and peripherals, cards, chips, disk drives, modems, scanners, joysticks, and other peripherals. 800–927–3936.

GCC Technologies, 209 Burlington Rd., P.O. Box 9143, Bedford, MA 01730: Free catalog ❖ Computer peripherals. 800–422–7777.

Global Computer Supplies, 1050 Northbrook Pkwy., Suwanee, GA 30174: Free catalog ❖ Furniture and work stations, hardware, software, peripherals, and printing supplies. 800–745–6225; 404–339–9999 (in GA).

The Grapevine Group Inc., 3 Chestnut St., Suffern, NY 10901: Free information ❖ Amiga chips. 800–292–7445.

Great Valley Products, 600 Clark Ave., King of Prussia, PA 19406: Free information ❖ Amiga peripheral cards and hard drives. 215–337–8770.

Harmony Computers, 1801 Flatbush Ave., Brooklyn, NY 11210: Free information ❖ Computer systems and portables, peripherals, and software. 800–441–1144.

ICS-2–GO, 7000 Broadway, Building 2, Denver, CO 80221: Free information ❖ Memory upgrades for Macintosh, IBM compatible, and portable computers. 303–650–0416.

Insight Computers, 1912 W. 4th St., Tempe, AZ 85281: Free information ❖ Computers, hard and disk drives, modems, printers, cards, software, and CD-ROMs. 800–998–8071.

The Iomega Corporation, 1821 W. 4000 South, Roy, UT 84067: Free information ❖ Hard disk drive with removable disk. 800–456–5522; 801–778–3450 (in UT).

Jameco Electronics, 1355 Shoreway Rd., Belmont, CA 94002: Free catalog ❖ Accessories for Apple, IBM compatible, and Macintosh computers. 800–637–8471.

K-12 MicroMedia Publishing, 6 Arrow Rd., Ramsey, NJ 07446: Free catalog ❖ Teaching aids, software, and accessories for Apple, IBM compatible, Macintosh, and Tandy computers. 800–292–1997; 201–825–8888 (in NJ).

Kenosha Computer Center, 2133 91st St., Kenosha, WI 53140: Free information ❖ Computers, cards, peripherals, and software. 800–255–2989.

Kinson Products Corporation, 482–484 Sunrise Hwy., Rockville Centre, NY 11570: Free information ❖ Transporter cards, disk and hard drives, and other accessories for Apple computers. 516–763–0906.

Laptop Superstore, 2117 Hollywood Blvd., Hollywood, FL 33020: Free information ❖ Portable computers, printers, software, and fax machines. 800–437–4164; 305–923–2245 (in FL).

Lyben Computer Systems, 5545 Bridgewood, P.O. Box 130, Sterling Heights, MI 48311: Free catalog ❖ Computer supplies. 313–268–8100.

MacConnection, 14 Mill St., Marlow, NH 03456: Free information ❖ Macintosh accessories and software. 800–800–2222.

MacDirect, 60 E. Chestnut, Chicago, IL 60611: Free information ❖ Macintosh data storage devices, scanners, monitors, and other peripherals. 800–759–2133.

Macronix Inc., 1348 Ridder Park Dr., San Jose, CA 95131: Free information ❖ Voice and fax mail box accessories. 800–858–5311.

Magellan's, Box 5485, Santa Barbara, CA 93150: Free catalog ❖ Voltage converters, electrical adaptor plugs, modular phone jacks, and other accessories for portable computers. 800–962–4943.

Memory Plus Distributors Inc., 7902 E. Pierce St., Scottsdale, AZ 85257: Free catalog

❖ Accessories for Apple computers. 602–820–8819.

Micro Systems, 1524 County Line Rd., York Springs, PA 17372: Free information ❖ Tandy add-ons. 800–548–5182; 717–528–8802 (in PA).

MicroComputer Accessories Inc., 9920 La Cienega Blvd., Inglewood, CA 90308: Free information ❖ Telephone-related accessories for portable computers. 310–645–9400.

Misco Computers, One Misco Plaza, Holmdel, NJ 07733: Free catalog ❖ Computer supplies. 908–264–5955.

Network Express, 1611 Northgate Blvd., Sarasota, FL 34234: Free information ❖ Computer systems, portables, software, peripherals, and CD-ROMs. 800–333–9899.

Newtech Video & Computers, 350 7th Ave., New York, NY 10001: Free information ❖ Video equipment, computers and peripherals, software, cellular phones, fax machines, and office equipment. 800–554–9747.

Nisca Inc., 1919 Old Denton Rd., Ste. 104, Carrollton, TX 75006: Free information ❖ Hand-held scanner for IBM compatibles. 800–245–7226.

Olivetti North America Inc., 22425 E. Appleway Ave., Liberty Lake, WA 99019: Free information ❖ Scanners and dot matrix printers. 800–633–9909; 509–927–5600 (in WA).

Other World Computing, 224 W. Judd St., Woodstock, IL 60098: Free information ❖ Macintosh and Power-Mac computers, expansion and storage accessories, and software. 815–338–8758.

Panasonic, Panasonic Way, Seacaucus, NJ 07094: Free information ❖ Monitors and printers. 201–348–7000.

Para Systems Inc., 1455 LeMay Dr., Carrollton, TX 75007: Free information ❖ Uninterruptible power supplies. 800–238–7272.

Pen Computer Warehouse Inc., 47 Mall Dr., Commack, NY 11725: Free information ❖ Computer hardware and software. 800–451–4736.

Pinnacle Micro, 19 Technology Dr., Irvine, CA 92718: Free information ❖ Recordable CD-ROM drive for Macintosh and IBM compatible computers. 800–553–7070.

Preferred Computing, 3210 Belt Line Rd., Ste. 154, Dallas, TX 75234: Free catalog ❖ Software, disk drives, modems, peripherals, transporter cards, audio animator boards, joy sticks, and mouse devices.

Procom Technology, 2181 Dupont Dr., Irvine, CA 92715: Free information ❖ CD-ROM drives for the Macintosh. 714–852–1000.

Quality Computers, P.O. Box 349, St. Clair Shores, MI 48080: Free information ❖ Software and peripherals for Macintosh, IBM compatible, and Apple computers. 800–777–3642.

River Computer Inc., P.O. Box 600, Marlow, NH 03456: Free information ❖ Macintosh systems, software, and books. 800–998–0093.

Rose Electronics, P.O. Box 742571, Houston, TX 77274: Free information ❖ Printer-sharing control units. 800–333–9343.

Seiko Instruments USA Inc., Graphic Devices and Systems Division, 1130 Ringwood Ct., San Jose, CA 95131: Free information ❖ Thermal-transfer printer. 800–888–0817.

Shreve Systems, 1200 Marshall, Shreveport, LA 71101: Free information ❖ Apple and Macintosh computer systems, add-ons, and peripherals. 800–227–3971.

Smart Modular Technologies, 45531 Northport Loop West, Fremont, CA 94538: Free information ❖ Memory add-on cards and modules for portable computers. 510–623–1231.

Software House Direct, 2 Riverview Dr., Somerset, NJ 08873: Free information ❖ Software and peripherals for IBM compatibles. 800–777–5014.

Street Electronics Corporation, 6460 Via Real, Carpinteria, CA 93013: Free information ❖ Speech processor for Apple computers. 805–684–4593.

Sunnytech, 17 Smith St., Englewood, NJ 07631: Free information ❖ IBM compatibles, hard and floppy disk drives, system boards, cards, power supplies, keyboards, and monitors. 201–569–7773.

Sunshine Computers, 22191 Powerline Rd., Boca Raton, FL 33433: Free information ❖ Portable computers, memory upgrades, fax modems, carrying cases, mouse devices, and batteries. 800–828–2992.

Supra Corporation, 7101 Supra Dr. SW, Albany, OR 97321: Free information ❖ Hayes-compatible modem, disk and hard drives, RAM expansion cards, and other

accessories for Amiga computers. 800–727–8772.

Tatung Company of America Inc., 2850 El Presidio St., Long Beach, CA 90801: Free information ❖ Monitors. 800–829–2850.

Tenex Computer Express, 56800 Magnetic Dr., Mishawaka, IN 46545: Free catalog ❖ Amiga and Commodore computers and software. 219–259–7051.

Thunderware, 21 Orinda Way, Orinda, CA 94563: Free information ❖ Scanner for use with ImageWriter printers. 510–254–6581.

TMS Peripherals, 1120 Holland Dr., Ste. 16, Boca Raton, FL 33487: Free information ❖ Hardware, add-ons, software, and carrying cases for Apple computers. 800–ASK–4TMS.

Tote-A-Lap, 550 Pilgrim Dr., Foster City, CA 04404: Free information ❖ Portable computers. 800–9–LAPTOP.

Tri-State Computer, 650 6th Ave., New York, NY 10011: Free information ❖ Amiga and Commodore computers, monitors, expansion systems, drives, other peripherals, and software. 800–537–4441; 212–633–2290 (in NY).

Tripp-Lite, 500 N. Orleans, Chicago, IL 60610: Free brochure ❖ Power control center. 312–329–1601.

United Computer Express, 724 7th Ave., New York, NY 10019: Free information ❖ Computer systems, portables, peripherals, and software. 800–448–3788.

USA Micro, 2888 Bluff St., Ste. 257, Boulder, CO 80301: Free information ❖ Apple and IBM compatibles. 800–537–8596; 303–938–9089 (in CO).

Vektron International Inc., 2100 Hwy. 360, Grand Prairie, TX 75050: Free information ❖ Computer systems, peripherals, and other electronics. 800–725–0047.

ViewSonic Corporation, 12130 Mora Dr., Santa Fe Springs, CA 90670: Free information ❖ High-resolution monitors. 800–888–8583.

Vitesse Inc., 13909 Amar Rd., La Puente, CA 91746: Free information ❖ Scanners. 818–813–1270.

Wholesalers Inc., P.O. Box 450, Orchard Park, NY 14127: Free information ❖ Peripherals and upgrades for IBM compatibles. 800–752–9512.

Z-RAM, 22 Morgan, Irvine, CA 92718: Free information ❖ Memory chips. 800–368–4RAM; 714–454–1500 (in CA).

ZIMCO International Inc., 85–39 213th St., Queens Village, NY 11427: Free information ❖ Software, disk drives, modems, cards, monitors, and Apple compatibles. 718–479–7888.

Dust Covers & Cases

Co-Du-Co Computer Dust Covers, 4802 W. Wisconsin Ave., Milwaukee, WI 53208: Free catalog ❖ Dust covers for computers. 800–735–1584.

Furniture

Anthro, 3221 NW Yeon St., Portland, OR 97210: Free catalog ❖ Adjustable computer furniture. 800–325–3841.

CompUSA Inc., 15160 Marsh Ln., Dallas, TX 75234: Free catalog ❖ Desktop and portable IBM compatibles, networking and communications accessories, books, chips, furniture, disk drives, scanners, system savers, add-on cards, peripherals, software, and CD-ROMs. 800–451–7638.

Global Computer Supplies, 1050 Northbrook Pkwy., Suwanee, GA 30174: Free catalog ❖ Furniture and work stations, hardware, software, peripherals, and printing supplies. 800–745–6225; 404–339–9999 (in GA).

Inmac, 2300 Valley View Ln., Irving, TX 75062: Free catalog ❖ Computer supplies, furniture, cables, disks and tapes, and networking and data communications equipment. 800–547–5444.

The PC Zone, 17411 NE Union Hill Rd., Bldg. A, Ste. 140, Redmond, WA 98052: Free catalog ❖ Computer systems, furniture, software, disks, and networking and communications equipment. 800–258–2088.

Scandinavian Computer Furniture Inc., P.O. Box 3217, Redmond, WA 98073: Free catalog ❖ Modular computer furniture. 800–722–6263.

Software (Public Domain, Shareware & CD-ROMs)

Accessible Software, 509 Garden Ln., Rt. 8, East Peoria, IL 61611: Free catalog ❖ Public domain and shareware for IBM compatibles. 800–827–8209.

American Databankers Corporation, 5220 E. 69th Pl., Tulsa, OK 74136: Free brochure

❖ Software libraries on CD-ROMs. 800–775–4232.

The Amish Outlaw Shareware Company, 3705 Richmond Ave., Staten Island, NY 10312: Free catalog ❖ Shareware for IBM compatibles. 800–947–4346.

Big Red Computer Club, 423 Norfolk Ave., Norfolk, NE 68701: Free catalog ❖ Software for Apple computers. 402–379–4680.

BizComp Services, P.O. Box 345, Moorpark, CA 93021: Free catalog ❖ Public domain and user-supported software for IBM compatibles.

Caloke Industries, P.O. Box 18477, Raytown, MO 64133: Free catalog ❖ Apple public domain software. 816–478–6185.

Christella Enterprise, P.O. Box 82205, Rochester, MI 48307: Catalog $2 ❖ Public domain software for Apple computers.

CompuServe, P.O. Box 20212, Columbus, OH 43220: Free information ❖ Public domain software and shareware for IBM compatibles. 800–848–8990; 614–457–8650 (in OH).

Computer Budget Shopper, 2203 Park Ave., Cheyenne, WY 82007: Catalog $3 ❖ Apple public domain and shareware software.

Crazy Bob's Software, 50 New Salem St., Wakefield, MA 01880: Free information ❖ Public domain software, shareware, and CD-ROMs for IBM compatibles. 800–776–5865.

Donnux Shareware, P.O. Box 410, Milford, VA 22514: Free catalog ❖ Shareware for the Macintosh and IBM compatibles. 800–352–3878.

Educorp Computer Services, 7434 Trade St., San Diego, CA 92121: Free information ❖ Public domain software for Macintosh and IBM compatible computers. 800–843–9497; 619–536–9999 (in CA).

International Datawares, 2278 Trade Zone Blvd., San Jose, CA 95131: Free information ❖ Computer accessories and public domain and other selected software. 408–262–6660.

Micro Star, 1945 Camino Vida Roble, Carlsbad, CA 92008: Free information ❖ Public domain software for IBM compatibles. 800–444–1343.

PC Shareware, 1763 Garnet Ave., San Diego, CA 92109: Free catalog ❖ Shareware for IBM compatibles. 800–447–2181.

PC-SIG, 1030 E. Duane Ave., Ste. D, Sunnyvale, CA 94086: Free information ❖

Public domain software for IBM compatibles. 800–245–6717.

Pendragon Software Library, 75 Meadowbrook Rd., East Greenwich, RI 02818: Free catalog ❖ Public domain and shareware for IBM compatibles. 800–828–DISK.

Public Brand Software, P.O. Box 51315, Indianapolis, IN 46251: Free catalog ❖ Public domain software for IBM compatibles. 800–426–3475.

R-A Software, 176 Hyde St., Cranston, RI 02920: Free catalog ❖ Public domain software for IBM compatibles. 401–946–9920.

Raymark Enterprises, P.O. Box 70443, Oakland, CA 94612: Free catalog ❖ Public domain software and shareware for Apple computers. 800–2APPLE2.

Reasonable Solutions, 1221 Disk Dr., Medford, OR 97501: Free information ❖ User-supported software for IBM compatibles. 800–876–3475.

ROM-MAN Technologies, 112 Village Post Rd., Danvers, MA 01923: Free information ❖ Public domain software and shareware for IBM compatibles and CD-ROM disks. 800–334–8666.

SofTec Plus, 4021 E. Grant Rd., Tucson, AZ 85712: Free information ❖ CD-ROM disks for IBM compatibles.

Software Excitement, P.O. Box 1949, Muncie, IN 47308: Free catalog ❖ User-supported software for Apple, Macintosh, Commodore, IBM compatible, and Amiga computers. 800–444–5457.

The Software Labs, Mail Order Department, 100 Corporate Pointe, Ste. 195, Culver City, CA 90231: Free catalog ❖ Public domain software and shareware for IBM compatibles. 800–569–7900.

SoftwareLabs, 8700 148th Ave. NE, Redmond, WA 98052: Free catalog ❖ IBM compatible software. 800–569–7900.

Tallon Software, P.O. Box 27823, Seattle, WA 98125: Free catalog ❖ Shareware for IBM compatibles. 800–346–0139.

Walnut Creek CDROM, 1547 Palos Verdes, Ste. 260, Walnut Creek, CA 94596: Free information ❖ Public domain software and shareware for IBM compatibles and CD-ROMs. 800–786–9907.

Software Publishers

Aatrix Software, 523 N. Washington St., Grand Forks, ND 58203: Free information ❖ Business and home management software for the Macintosh. 800–426–0854.

Abacus Software, 5370 52nd St. SE, Grand Rapids, MI 49508: Free information ❖ Word processing software for the Commodore. Home and business applications and utilities for IBM compatibles. 616–698–0330.

Abracadata, P.O. Box 2440, Eugene, OR 97402: Free catalog ❖ Graphics software for Apple, IBM compatible, and Macintosh computers. Education software, home and business applications, and utilities for the Apple. 800–451–4871.

Accolade Inc., 5300 Stevens Creek Blvd., San Jose, CA 95128: Free information ❖ Software for Amiga, Apple, Atari, Commodore, IBM compatible, and Macintosh computers.

Addison-Wesley Publishing Company, One Jacob Way, Reading, MA 01867: Free information ❖ Software for Amiga, Apple, Commodore, IBM compatible, and Macintosh computers. 617–944–3700.

Adobe Systems Inc., 1585 Charleston Rd., Mountain View, CA 94039: Free information ❖ Desktop publishing and graphics software for IBM compatibles. Desktop publishing, graphics, home and business applications, and productivity software for the Macintosh. 800–83–FONTS; 415–961–4400 (in CA).

Advanced Data Systems Inc., P.O. Box 5717, Winter Park, FL 32793: Free information ❖ Education, home and business applications, programming tools, and productivity software for the Macintosh. 407–657–4805.

After Hours Software, Tri Center Plaza, 5990 Sepulveda Blvd., Van Nuys, CA 91411: Free information ❖ Database, programming tools, and business management software for the Macintosh. 818–780–2220.

Aldus Corporation, 411 1st Ave., Seattle, WA 98104: Free information ❖ Desktop publishing software for IBM compatibles. Desktop publishing, education, graphics, home and business applications, and utilities software for the Macintosh. 800–333–2538.

Allmicro Inc., 18820 US Hwy. 19 North, Ste. 215, Clearwater, FL 34624: Free information ❖ Data recovery software. 800–653–4933.

Alsoft Software Inc., P.O. Box 927, Spring, TX 77383: Free information ❖ Macintosh communications, programming tools, utilities, and health management software. 713–353–4090.

Altsys Corporation, 269 W. Renner Pkwy., Richardson, TX 75080: Free information ❖ Fonts and font-management software for IBM compatibles. 800–477–2131.

American Education Publishing, 150 E. Wilson Bridge Rd., Columbus, OH 43085: Free information ❖ Windows mathematics educational software for young children. 800–542–7833; 614–848–8866 (in OH).

Andromeda Software Inc., P.O. Box 605–G, Amherst, NY 14226: Free catalog ❖ Scientific software for IBM compatibles. 716–6691–4510.

Apex Software Corporation, 4516 Henry St., Pittsburgh, PA 15213: Free information ❖ Entertainment and games for IBM compatibles. 800–858–2739.

Apple Computer Inc., 2025 Mariani Ave., Cupertino, CA 95014: Free information ❖ Database, spreadsheet, and word processing software for Apple and Macintosh computers. 408–996–1010.

Artworx Software Company Inc., 1844 Penfield Rd., Penfield, NY 14526: Free information ❖ Education, entertainment, and games for Amiga, Apple, Commodore, IBM compatible, and Macintosh computers. Home and business applications for the Macintosh. 800–828–6573.

Banner Blue Software, 39500 Stevenson Pl., Fremont, CA 94539: Free information ❖ Windows-supported software for making organization charts. 510–794–6850.

Baudville Inc., 5380 52nd St. SE, Grand Rapids, MI 49512: Free information ❖ Software for Amiga, Apple, Commodore, IBM compatible, and Macintosh computers. 616–698–0888.

Beacon Hill Software, Box 8494, Boston, MA 92114: Free information ❖ Windows-supported utilities and productivity tools software for IBM compatibles. 800–926–2956.

Berkeley Systems, 2095 Rose St., Berkeley, CA 94709: Free information ❖ Software for Apple, Commodore, IBM compatible, and Macintosh computers. 510–540–5535.

Best Choice, 129 Wheeler Ave., Los Gatos, GA 95032: Free information ❖ Macintosh graphics. 800–358–2984; 800–553–2188 (in CA).

Bible Research Systems, 2013 Wells Branch Pkwy., Ste. 304, Austin, TX 78728: Free brochure ❖ Bible education software for Apple, IBM compatible, and Macintosh computers. 800–423–1228.

BibleSoft, 22014 7th Ave. South, Seattle, WA 98198: Free information ❖ Bible-study software for Windows and DOS. 206–824–8360.

Big Red Computer Club, 423 Norfolk Ave., Norfolk, NE 68701: Free catalog ❖ Entertainment, games, utilities, education, productivity, graphics, and programming tools software for Apple computers. 402–379–4680.

Bitstream Inc., 215 1st St., Cambridge, MA 02142: Free information ❖ Windows-supported fonts and font management software for IBM compatibles. 800–522–3668.

Blyth Software, 1065 E. Hillsdale Blvd., Ste. 300, Foster City, CA 94404: Free information ❖ Database and productivity software for the Macintosh. 415–571–0222.

Borland International, 1800 Green Hills Rd., Scotts Valley, CA 95066: Free information ❖ Debugger and assembly software for IBM compatibles. Database, desktop publishing, education, programming tools, and utilities software for the Macintosh. 800–331–0877.

William K. Bradford Publishing Company, P.O. Box 1355, Concord, MA 01742: Free information ❖ Educational software for Apple, IBM compatible, and Tandy computers. 800–421–2009.

Broderbund, 500 Redwood Blvd., Novato, CA 94948: Free catalog ❖ Entertainment and games software and CD-ROMs for IBM compatibles and Macintosh computers. 800–521–6263; 415–382–4700 (in CA).

Bureau Development Inc., 141 New Rd., Parsippany, NJ 07054: Free information ❖ Education CD-ROMs for IBM compatibles and Macintosh computers. 800–828–4766; 201–808–2700 (in NJ).

Califonts, P.O. Box 224891, Dallas, TX 75222: Free information ❖ Calligraphy typeface software for Macintosh and IBM compatible computers. 214–504–8808.

CE Software Inc., 1801 Industrial Cir., West Des Moines, IA 50265: Free information ❖ Macintosh communications, graphics, home and business applications, and utilities software. 515–224–1995.

Centaur Software Inc., P.O. Box 3959, Torrance, CA 90510: Free information ❖ Utilities, entertainment, games, and education software for the Amiga.

Central Point Software Inc., 15220 NW Greenbrier Pkwy., Beaverton, OR 97006: Free catalog ❖ Utilities for IBM compatible and Macintosh computers. 800–278–6657.

ChipSoft Inc., 6256 Greenwich Dr., Ste. 100, San Diego, CA 92122: Free information ❖ Home and business applications for IBM compatibles. 619–453–8722.

The Church of Jesus Christ of Latter-day Saints, Salt Lake Distribution Center, 1999 W. 1700 South, Salt Lake City, UT 84104: Free information ❖ DOS and Macintosh genealogy software. 800–537–5950; 801–240–2584 (in UT).

Claris Corporation, 5201 Patrick Henry Dr., P.O. Box 58168, Santa Clara, CA 95052: Free information ❖ Word processing software for Apple, IBM compatible, and Macintosh computers. 408–987–7000.

Classic Concepts Futureware, P.O. Box 786, Bellingham, WA 98227: Free information ❖ Graphics and word processing software for the Amiga. 206–733–8342.

Cliff's Notes Inc., P.O. Box 80728, Lincoln, NE 68501: Free information ❖ DOS and Macintosh SAT study guide software. 800–228–4078; 402–421–8324 (in NE).

Compton's NewMedia, 2320 Camino Vida Roble, Carlsbad, CA 92009: Free information ❖ Windows-supported Compton's Interactive Encyclopedia for IBM compatibles. 619–929–2500.

Computer Associates International Inc., One Computer Associates Plaza, Islandia, NY 11788: Free information ❖ Windows-supported business and financial management and graphics paint software for IBM compatibles. 800–225–5224.

Computerware, 4403 Manchester Ave., Ste. 101, Encinitas, CA 92024: Free information ❖ Home and business applications for the Amiga.

Cougar Mountain Software, 2609 Kootenai, Box 6886, Boise, ID 83707: Free information ❖ Accounting software for IBM compatibles. 800–344–2540; 208–344–2540 (in ID).

DacEasy Inc., 17950 Preston Rd., Ste. 800, Dallas, TX 75252: Free information ❖ Windows-supported business and financial management software for IBM compatibles. 800–DAC-EASY.

Dariana Inc., 5241 Lincoln Ave., Ste. B5, Cypress, CA 90630: Free information ❖ Diagnostic software for hard drives. 800–892–9950.

Data East USA, 1850 Little Orchard St., San Jose, CA 95125: Free information ❖ Entertainment and games for Amiga, Apple, and Commodore computers. 408–286–7080.

Datawatch Corporation, Triangle Software Division, P.O. Box 51489, Durham, NC 27717: Free information ❖ Macintosh security and other utility software. 919–490–1277.

Davidson & Associates, 19840 Pioneer Ave., Torrance, CA 90503: Free catalog ❖ Education software for Amiga, Apple, Commodore, IBM compatible, and Macintosh computers. 800–545–7677; 310–793–0600 (in CA).

Davka Corporation, 7074 N. Western Ave., Chicago, IL 60645: Free information ❖ Hebrew and Judaic software for IBM compatible, Macintosh, and Apple computers. 800–621–8227; 312–465–4070 (in IL).

Decathlon Corporation, 4100 Executive Park Dr., Cincinnati, OH 45241: Free information ❖ Logo design software for Macintosh and IBM compatible computers. 800–648–5646; 513–421–1938 (in OH).

DeLorne Mapping, Lower Main St., Freeport, ME 04032: Free information ❖ Atlas information-related software for IBM compatibles. 800–452–5931; 207–865–1234 (in ME).

Delrina Corporation, 6830 Via Del Oro, Ste. 240, San Jose, CA 95119: Free information ❖ Fax management software for IBM compatibles. 800–268–6082; 408–363–2345 (in CA).

DeltaPoint, 2 Harris Ct., Ste. B-1, Monterey, CA 93940: Free information ❖ Word processing software for IBM compatibles. 800–446–6955.

Deneba Software, 7400 SW 87th Ave., Miami, FL 33173: Free information ❖ Macintosh productivity, utilities, and graphics software. Graphics software for IBM compatibles. 305–596–5644.

Designing Minds Inc., 3006 N. Main St., Logan, UT 84321: Free information ❖ Education, graphics, and entertainment, and games software for the Amiga. 801–752–2501.

Dialog Information Services Inc., 3460 Hillview Ave., Palo Alto, CA 94304: Free information ❖ Business, science, and technology CD-ROMs. 800–3–DIALOG.

Digital Creations, P.O. Box 97, Ste. 103, Rancho Folsom, CA 95763: Free information ❖ Amiga graphics and productivity software. 916–344–4825.

DigiTech Systems, 34684 Ricard O. Dr., Sterling Heights, MI 48310: Free information ❖ Macintosh graphics. 313–264–3039.

Walt Disney Computer Software, 500 S. Buena Vista St., Buena Vista, CA 91521: Free information with long SASE ❖ Entertainment and games for Apple computers. 818–973–4390.

Dream Maker Software, 925 W. Kenyon Ave., Ste. 16, Englewood, CO 80110: Free information ❖ Clip-art for IBM compatible and Macintosh computers. 800–876–5665.

Dubl-Click Software Inc., 22521 Styles St., Woodland Hills, CA 91367: Free information ❖ Macintosh graphics, fonts, and utilities. 800–266–9525.

Dynamix Software, c/o Sierra On-Line Inc., P.O. Box 485, Coarsegold, CA 93614: Free information ❖ Entertainment and games software for IBM compatibles. 800–326–6654.

East Hampton Industries Inc., 81 Newtown Ln., Box 5069, East Hampton, NY 11937: Free brochure ❖ Software for recipe-collecting, cookbook organizing, and meal planning management. 800–645–1188; 516–324–2224 (in NY).

Edmark Software, P.O. Box 3218, Redmond, WA 98073: Free information ❖ DOS and Macintosh mathematics and other educational software for young children. 206–556–8400.

Educational Activities, 1937 Grand Ave., Baldwin, NY 11510: Free information ❖ Education software for Apple computers. 800–645–3739.

Electronic Arts, 1450 Fashion Island Blvd., San Mateo, CA 94404: Free information ❖ Software for Amiga, Apple, Commodore, IBM compatible, and Macintosh computers. 800–245–4525.

Equilibrium Technologies, 475 Gate Five Rd., Ste. 225, Sausalito, CA 94965: Free information ❖ Graphics software for IBM compatibles. 415–332–4343.

Expert Software, 800 Douglas Rd., Coral Cables, FL 33134: Free information ❖ Windows software for preparing resumes. 800–759–2562; 305–567–9990 (in FL).

Fifth Generation Systems, 10049 N. Reiger Rd., Baton Rouge, LA 70809: Free information ❖ Virus-detection software. 800–873–4384; 504–291–5453 (in LA).

First Byte, 19840 Pioneer Ave., Torrance, CA 90503: Free information ❖ Education software for Macintosh, Amiga, and Apple computers. Desktop publishing software for the Apple; entertainment and games for the Macintosh. 310–793–0610.

1st Desk Systems Inc., 7 Industrial Park Rd., Medway, MA 02053: Free information ❖ Database software for the Macintosh. 800–522–2286.

Fractal Design Corporation, 335 Spreckels Dr., Aptos, CA 95003: Free information ❖ Windows and Macintosh painting and drawing program. 800–647–7443; 408–688–5300 (in CA).

Frame Technology Corporation, 1010 Rincon Cir., San Jose, CA 95131: Free information ❖ Desktop publishing software for IBM compatibles. 408–975–6000.

Free Spirit Software, P.O. Box 158, Trafalgar, IN 46181: Free information ❖ Education, games, entertainment, and other software for Amiga computers.

Gamco Industries, Box 1911, Big Spring, TX 79721: Free information ❖ Education, entertainment, and games software for Apple computers. 800–351–1404; 915–267–6327 (in TX).

Gibson Research Corporation, 35 Journey, Aliso Viejo, CA 92656: Free information ❖ Hard disk diagnostic and repair program. 800–736–0637; 714–362–8800 (in CA).

Good Software Corporation, 4125 Keller Springs Rd., Addison, TX 75244: Free information ❖ Windows-supported financial and general business software for IBM compatibles. 214–713–6370.

Graphics Software Labs, 8572 Kelso Dr., Huntington Beach, CA 92646: Free information ❖ Windows-supported entertainment and games software for IBM compatibles. 714–968–7037.

Great Bear Technology/HealthSoft, 1100 Moraga Way, Ste. 200, Moraga, CA 94556: Free information ❖ Guide to prescription and non-prescription drugs for Windows. 800–795–4325; 510–631–1600 (in CA).

Grolier Electronic Publishing Inc., Sherman Tnpk., Danbury, CT 06816: Free information ❖ The New Grolier Multimedia Encyclopedia for IBM compatibles. 800–356–5590.

Gryphon Software Corporation, 3298 Governor Dr., P.O. Box 221075, San Diego, CA 92122: Free information ❖ Graphics software for IBM compatibles. 619–454–6836.

Gold Disk Inc., 5155 Spectrum Way, Unit 5, Mississauga, Ontario, Canada L4W 5A1: Free information ❖ Desktop publishing, entertainment, games, home, business applications, and graphics software for Amiga computers. 416–602–4000.

Ed Harris' MagiArt Images, PC Concepts, 123 Casa Dr., Haughton, LA 71037: Free information ❖ Clip-art for magicians, clowns, balloon sculpting, and Christmas.

Harvard Associates Inc., 10 Holworthy St., Cambridge, MA 02138: Free information ❖ Home and business applications, graphics, and utilities for IBM compatible and Macintosh computers. 617–492–0660.

Hayes Microcomputer Products Inc., P.O. Box 105203, Atlanta, GA 30348: Free information ❖ Communications software for IBM compatible and Macintosh computers. 800–96–HAYES.

Heizer Software, P.O. Box 232019, Pleasant Hill, CA 94523: Free information ❖ Business management, graphics, communications, computer management, programming tools, spreadsheets, utilities, education, word processing, and home management software for the Macintosh. 800–888–7667.

HowardSoft, 1224 Prospect St., Ste. 150, La Jolla, CA 92037: Free information ❖ Home and business applications and productivity software for IBM compatible and Apple computers. 800–822–4TAX.

HyperGlot Software Company, 314 Erin Dr., Knoxville, TN 37919: Free information ❖ Spanish-teaching program for IBM compatibles. 800–760–4568; 6125–558–8270 (in TN).

Image Club Graphics Inc., U.S. Catalog Fulfillment Center, c/o Publisher's Mail Service, 10545 W. Donges Ct., Milwaukee, WI 53224: Free catalog ❖ IBM compatible and Macintosh clip-art, fonts, photographs, on disk and CD-ROM. 800–661–9410.

Impulse Inc., 8416 Xerxes Ave. South, Brooklyn Park, MN 55444: Free information ❖ Graphics for the Amiga.

Inductel Inc., 5339 Prospect Rd., Ste. 321, San Jose, CA 95129: Free information ❖ Windows-supported Funk and Wagnalls dictionary software for IBM compatibles. 800–367–4497.

Infocom Inc., Division Activision, 11440 San Vincente Blvd., Ste. 300, Los Angeles, CA 90049: Free information ❖ Entertainment and games for Amiga, Apple, Commodore, IBM compatible, and Macintosh computers.

Information Marketing Group, P.O. Box 4715, Los Alamos, NM 87544: Free catalog ❖ Clinical software programs on CD-ROMs. 800–571–5444.

Informix Software Inc., 16011 College Blvd., Lenexa, KS 66219: Free information ❖ Spreadsheet software for the Macintosh. 800–438–7627.

Innovation Advertising & Design, 41 Mansfield Ave., Essex Junction, VT 05452: Free information ❖ IBM compatible and Macintosh clip-art. 800–255–0562.

Interstel Corporation, c/o Electronic Arts, 1450 Fashion Island Blvd., San Mateo, CA 94404: Free information ❖ Entertainment and games for IBM compatible and Amiga computers. 800–245–4525.

Intracorp Inc., 7200 NW 19th St., Ste. 500, Miami, FL 33126: Free information ❖ Desktop publishing, education, entertainment, games, home and business applications, and graphics software for IBM compatible and Amiga computers. Entertainment and games for Apple and Commodore computers.

Intuit, 66 Willow Pl., Menlo Park, CA 94025: Free information ❖ Home and business applications for IBM compatible and Macintosh computers. 800–624–8742.

IQ Software, 3295 River Exchange Dr., Ste. 550, Norcross, GA 30092: Free information ❖ Word processing software for IBM compatibles. 800–458–0386; 404–446–8880 (in GA).

IVI Publishing, 7500 Flying Cloud Dr., Minneapolis, MN 55344: Free information ❖ CD-ROM Windows and Macintosh Mayo Clinic Family Health Book reference guide and other health care programs. 612–996–6000.

Kabbalah Software, 8 Price Dr., Edison, NJ 08817: Free price list ❖ Word processing software, clip-art, Hebrew fonts for laser printers, fonts and graphics for the Print Shop, Jewish calendar conversion software, and

other Hebrew and Jewish software for IBM compatibles. 908–572–0891.

KEBA International, P.O. Box 15131, Columbus, OH 43215: Free catalog ❖ Self-help, home, financial, and business management software. 800–847–847; 614–457–1301 (in OH).

Knowledge Adventure Inc., 4502 Dyer St., La Crescenta, CA 81214: Free information ❖ United States geography and other educational programs for IBM compatibles. 800–542–4240; 818–542–4200 (in CA).

Krell Software Corporation, P.O. Box 1252, Lake Grove, NY 11755: Free information ❖ Education software for Apple computers. 800–245–7355; 516–689–3500 (in NY).

Lake Forest Logic Inc., 28101 Ballard Rd., Unit E, Lake Forest, IL 60045: Free information ❖ Programming and utilities software for the Amiga. 708–816–6666.

Lattice Inc., 3010 Woodcreek Dr., Ste. A, Downers Grove, IL 60515: Free information ❖ Productivity software and home and business applications for Amiga computers. 800–444–4309; 708–769–4060 (in IL).

Laureate, 110 E. Spring St., Winooski, VT 05404: Free information ❖ Language intervention, cognitive processing, reading, instructional games, and other talking software programs for children 6 months to 8 years of age. 802–655–4755.

Lawrence Productions, 1800 S. 35th St., Galesburg, MI 49053: Free information ❖ Entertainment and games for Amiga and Apple computers. 800–421–4157; 616–665–7075 (in MI).

The Learning Company, 6493 Kaiser Dr., Fremont, CA 94555: Free information ❖ Education and games for Apple, Commodore, IBM compatible, and Macintosh computers. Word processing software for the Apple. 800–852–2255; 510–792–2101 (in CA).

Lionheart Press Inc., P.O. Box 20756, Mesa, AZ 85277: Free information ❖ Amiga home and business applications and productivity software.

Lotus Development Corporation, 55 Cambridge Pkwy., Cambridge, MA 02142: Free information ❖ Communications, desktop publishing, education, graphics, home and business applications, productivity, utilities, and word processing software for IBM compatibles. 800–828–7086.

Mallard Software Inc., 3207 Justin Rd., Flower Mound, TX 75028: Free information ❖ Entertainment and games for IBM compatibles. 800–WEB-FEET.

Maris Multimedia Software, 3871 Piedmont Ave., Oakland, CA 94611: Free information ❖ Windows and Macintosh astronomy software. 510–652–7430.

Masque Publishing, P.O. Box 5223, Englewood, CO 80155: Free information ❖ Windows-supported entertainment and games software for IBM compatibles. 800–765–4223.

Maxwell Electronic Publishing, 124 Mt. Auburn, Cambridge, MA 02138: Free information ❖ Children's education CD-ROMS for IBM compatibles. 800–342–1338.

MECA Software Inc., 55 Walls Dr., P.O. Box 912, Fairfield, CT 06430: Free information ❖ Financial management, tax planning and management, and investment tracking software for IBM compatibles. 800–288–6322; 203–255–1441 (in CT).

MECC Software, 6160 Summit Dr. North, Minneapolis, MN 55430: Free information ❖ Education software for Apple computers. 800–685–MECC; 612–569–1500 (in MN).

MediClip, 1245 16th St., Ste. 100, Santa Monica, Ca 90404: Free information ❖ Medical anatomy graphics for Macintosh and IBM compatible computers. 800–998–8705.

Metro Imagebase Inc., 18623 Ventura Blvd., Ste. 210, Tarzana, CA 91356: Free information ❖ Disk and CD-ROM clip-art for IBM compatible and Macintosh computers. 800–525–1552.

Micricom Inc., 500 River Ridge Dr., Norwood, MA 02062: Free information ❖ Communications software for Windows and DOS. 800–822–8224.

Micrografx Inc., 1303 E. Arapaho Rd., Richardson, TX 75081: Free information ❖ IBM compatible art/coloring program for children ages 3 to 6. 800–733–3729; 214–234–1769 (in TX).

MicroIllusions, 13464 Washington Blvd., Marina Del Ray, CA 90291: Free information ❖ Entertainment, games, and education software for Amiga, Apple, Commodore, and IBM compatible computers. Home and business applications and graphics for the Amiga.

MicroLogic Software, 1351 Ocean Ave., Emeryville, CA 94608: Free information ❖

Tru-type fonts for DOS and Windows. 800–888–9078.

MicroMaps Software, P.O. Box 757, Lamberville, NJ 08530: Free brochure ❖ Clip-art maps for IBM compatible and Macintosh computers. 800–334–4291.

MicroProse Software Inc., 180 Lakefront Dr., Hunt Valley, MD 21030: Free information ❖ Entertainment and games for IBM compatible, Amiga, Apple, Atari, and Commodore computers. 800–879–7529.

MicroSearch Inc., 9000 US 59 South, Ste. 330, Houston, TX 77074: Free information ❖ Desktop publishing, graphics and word processing software for Amiga computers.

Microsoft Corporation, One Microsoft Way, Redmond, WA 98052: Free information ❖ Productivity software for the Amiga and Macintosh. Education software for the Apple. Database, entertainment, games, graphics, home and business applications, productivity and programming tools, and spreadsheet software for the Macintosh. 800–426–9400.

MicroTac Software, 4375 Jutland Dr., Ste. 110, San Diego, CA 92117: Free information ❖ German, French, Spanish, and Italian translation programs for IBM compatibles. 619–272–5700.

Midisoft, P.O. Box 1000, Bellevue, WA 98052: Free information ❖ Music educations windows software. 800–776–6434; 206–881–7176 (in WA).

Milliken Publishing, 1100 Research Blvd., P.O. Box 21579, St. Louis, MO 63132: Free information ❖ Desktop publishing, entertainment, and games software for the Apple. 800–643–0008; 314–991–4220 (in MO).

Mindplay Software, A Software Toolworks Company, 60 Leveroni Ct., Novato, CA 94949: Free information ❖ Education software for IBM compatibles. 415–883–3000.

New Horizons Software Inc., P.O. Box 164260, Austin, TX 78746: Free information ❖ Graphics and word processing software for the Amiga. 512–328–6650.

New Vision Technologies Inc., Presentation Task Force, 38 Auriga Dr., Nepean, Ontario, Canada K2E 8A5: Free information ❖ Graphics for IBM compatibles. 613–727–8184.

Nolo Press, 950 Parker St., Berkeley, CA 94710: Free catalog ❖ Home, business, and productivity software for Apple, IBM

compatible, and Macintosh computers. 800–992–6656; 510–549–1976 (in CA).

Nova Cube, 1900 Superline Ln., Wilmington, DE 19802: Free brochure ❖ Letters, numbers, and punctuation clip-art graphics. 800–728–5052.

Odyssey Computing, 1515 S. Melrose Dr., Ste. 90, Vista, CA 92083: Free brochure ❖ Windows-supported software for recipe, cookbook, and meal planning management. 619–599–0823.

Odyssey Development, 650 S. Cherry St., Ste. 220, Denver, CO 80222: Free information ❖ Windows- and DOS-supported information retrieval software for WordPerfect and other word processing programs. 800–992–4797.

OnLine Computer Systems Inc., 20251 Century Blvd., Germantown, MD 20874: Free catalog ❖ CD-ROM networking software and single and multi-drive CD-ROM storage units. 800–922–9204.

One Mile Up Inc., 7011 Evergreen Ct., Annandale, VA 22003: Free information ❖ Government-related clip-art. 800–258–5280; 703–642–1177 (in VA).

Orange Cherry, New Media Schoolhouse, 69 Westchester Ave., P.O. Box 390, Pound Ridge, NY 10576: Free catalog ❖ Educational software on disks and CD-ROMs for the Macintosh and IBM compatibles. Software on disks for Apple and Commodore C-64 computers. 800–672–6002.

Orange Micro Inc., 1400 N. Lakeview Ave., Anaheim, CA 92807: Free information ❖ Communications and education software for Apple computers. 714–779–2772.

Origin Systems Inc., P.O. Box 161750, Austin, TX 78716: Free information ❖ Entertainment and games for IBM compatible and Amiga computers.

Oxxi Inc., P.O. Box 90309, Long Beach, CA 90309: Free information ❖ Amiga entertainment, games, home and business applications, and graphics software. 310–427–1227.

Pangaea Scientific, RR 5, Brockville, Ontario, Canada K6V 5T5: Free catalog ❖ Geological software. 613–342–1513.

Parsons Technology, One Parsons Dr., P.O. Box 100, Hiawatha, IA 52233: Free information ❖ Virus-detection, business, financial, entertainment, games, and educational software. 800–223–6925; 319–395–9626 (in IA).

PC-Kwik Corporation, 15100 SW Koll Pkwy., Beaverton, OR 97006: Free information ❖ Diagnostic software for hard drives. 800–759–5945.

Peachtree Software, 1505 Pavilion Pl., Norcross, GA 30093: Free information ❖ Windows-supported business and financial management software for IBM compatibles. 800–247–3224.

Pinnacle Publishing Inc., 1800 72nd Ave. South, Ste. 217, Kent, WA 98032: Free information ❖ Windows-supported graphics, charts, and presentation software for IBM compatibles. 800–788–1900

Power Industries, 37 Walnut St., Wellesley Hills, MA 02181: Free information ❖ Graphics and productivity software for Apple computers. 800–395–5009; 617–235–7733 (in MA).

Power Up Software, P.O. Box 7600, San Mateo, CA 94403: Free catalog ❖ Communications, database, desktop publishing, education, graphics, home and business applications, productivity, programming tools, spreadsheets, word processing, and utilities software for IBM compatibles. 800–851–2917.

Precision Type, 47 Mall Dr., Commack, NY 11725: Free information ❖ Macintosh graphics. 800–248–3668.

Print Shop Users Club, P.O. Box 150, Renton, WA 98057: Free information ❖ Clip-art for Apple computers. 206–251–6570.

Psygnosis, 29 Saint Marys Ct., Brookline, MA 02146: Free information ❖ Entertainment and games for the Amiga computer. 617–731–3553.

Quality Computers, P.O. Box 349, St. Clair Shores, MI 48080: Free information ❖ Education and productivity software for Apple computers. 800–777–3642.

Quanta Press Inc., 1313 5th St. NE, Minneapolis, MN 55414: Free information ❖ Education CD-ROMs for IBM compatibles. 612–379–3956.

Quarterdeck Office Systems, 150 Pico Blvd., Santa Monica, CA 90405: Free information ❖ Memory manager software for IBM compatibles. 800–354–3222.

Que Software, Macmillan Publishing, 201 W. 103rd St., Indianapolis, IN 46290: Free information ❖ Windows-supported education and word processing software for IBM compatibles. 800–992–0244.

Quinsept Inc., P.O. Box 216, Lexington, MA 02173: Free information ❖ Home and business applications for Apple, IBM compatible, and Macintosh computers. 800–637–7668; 617–641–2930 (in MA).

Radio Shack, Division Tandy Corporation, One Tandy Center, Fort Worth, TX 76102: Free information ❖ Software for Tandy and IBM compatible computers. 817–390–3011.

ReadySoft Inc., 30 Wertheim Ct., Unit 2, Richmond Hill, Ontario, Canada L4B 1B9: Free information ❖ Entertainment and games CD-ROMs for IBM compatibles. 416-731-4175.

Rockware Inc., The Rockware Building, 2221 East St., Golden, CO 80401: Free catalog ❖ Software for the earth sciences. 800–775–6745.

RT Computer Graphics Inc., 602 San Jyan de Rio, Rio Rancho, NM 87124: Free information ❖ Native American and southwest clip-art for Macintosh and IBM compatible computers. 505–891–1600.

Safe Harbor Computers, 2120 E. Moreland Blvd., Waukesha, WI 53186: Free information ❖ Amiga software and hardware. 800–544–6599.

SBT Corporation, One Harbor Dr., Sausalito, CA 94965: Free information ❖ Home and business applications for the Macintosh. 415–331–9900.

Scholastic Software, 2931 E. McCarty St., P.O. Box 7502, Jefferson City, MO 65102: Free information ❖ Education, utilities, programming tools, and word processing software for Apple and IBM compatible computers. 800–541–5513.

Sierra On-Line Inc., P.O. Box 485, Coarsegold, CA 93614: Free information ❖ Software for Amiga, Apple, Atari, IBM compatible, and Macintosh computers. 800–757–7707.

Silicon Beach Software, 9770 Carroll Center Rd., Ste. J, San Diego, CA 92126: Free information ❖ Education, entertainment, games, information management, desktop publishing, graphics, and utilities software for the Macintosh. 619–695–6956.

SmartSoft Inc., P.O. Box 50178, Phoenix, AZ 85076: Free information ❖ Word processing, fonts, grammar correction, and other software for Amiga computers. 800–824–6785.

Tom Snyder Productions, 80 Coolidge Rd., Watertown, MA 02172: Free information ❖

Education software for Apple, IBM compatible, and Macintosh computers. 800–342–0236.

SofNet Inc., 1110 Northchase Pkwy., Ste. 150, Marietta, GA 30067: Free information ❖ Fax management software for IBM compatibles. 404–984–8088.

Soft Logik Corporation, 11131 S. Towne Square, Ste. F, St. Louis, MO 63123: Free information ❖ Desktop publishing software for the Amiga. 314–894–8608.

Softdisk Publishing, P.O. Box 30008, Shreveport, LA 71130: Free catalog ❖ Software for Apple, Commodore, IBM compatible, and Macintosh computers. 800–831–2694.

SoftKey International Inc., 201 Broadway, Cambridge, MA 02139: Free information ❖ Windows painting and drawing program for IBM compatibles. 800–323–8088; 617–494–1200 (in MA).

SoftLogic Solutions Inc., One Perimeter Rd., Manchester, NH 03103: Free information ❖ Diagnostic software for hard drives. 800–272–9900.

SoftSpoken, P.O. Box 18343, Raleigh, NC 27619: Free information ❖ Software for exchanging Appleworks data files with most popular MS-DOS software. Converts word processing, database, and spreadsheet files. 919–870–5694.

Software Advantage Consulting Corporation, 388442 Gail St., Clinton Township, MI 48036: Free information ❖ Amiga home and business applications software.

Software Marketing Corporation, 9830 S. 51st St., Phoenix, AZ 85044: Free information ❖ Health management and information software for DOS, Windows, and Macintosh computers. 602–893–3377.

The Software Toolworks, 60 Leveroni Ct., Novato, CA 94949: Free information ❖ Education, entertainment, and games software for Amiga, IBM compatible, and Macintosh computers. 415–883–3000.

Spectrum Holobyte, 2490 Mariner Square Loop, Alameda, CA 94501: Free information ❖ Software for Amiga, Apple, Commodore, IBM compatible, and Macintosh computers. 510–522–3584.

Spinnaker Software Corporation, 201 Broadway, Cambridge, MA 02139: Free catalog ❖ Software for Amiga, Apple,

Commodore, IBM compatible, and Macintosh computers. 617–494–1200.

StatSoft, 2325 E. 13th St., Tulsa, OK 74104: Free information ❖ Statistical data management and graphic illustration program for the Macintosh. 918–583–4149.

Streetwise Software, 2216 Wilshire Blvd., Ste. 230, Santa Monica, CA 90403: Free brochure ❖ WordPerfect and MS-Word add-on desktop publishing programs. 800–743–6765.

SubLOGIC Corporation, 501 Kenyon Rd., Champaign, IL 61820: Free information ❖ Entertainment and games for Amiga, Apple, Commodore, IBM compatible, and Macintosh computers. 800–637–4983.

SuperMac Technology, 215 Moffett Park Dr., Sunnyvale, CA 94089: Free information ❖ Graphics for the Macintosh. 408–541–6100.

SWFTE International Ltd., Stone Mill Office Park, 722 Yorklyn Rd., Hockessin, DE 19707: Free information ❖ Windows-supported fonts and font management software for IBM compatibles. 800–237–9383.

Sylvan Software, 5144 N. Academy Blvd., Ste. 531, Colorado Springs, CO 80918: Free information ❖ Medical, technical, scientific, and legal spelling dictionaries and utilities software for IBM compatibles. 800–235–9455.

Symantec Corporation, 10201 Torre Ave., Cupertino, CA 95014: Free information ❖ Graphics, productivity, communications, and utilities software for the Macintosh. 800–441–7234.

Synergistic Systems, 442 3rd St., Neptune Beach, FL 32266: Free information ❖ Business management software for IBM compatibles. 904–249–0201.

T/Maker Company, 1390 Villa St., Mountain View, CA 94041: Free information ❖ Education, graphics, productivity, and word processing software for Macintosh and IBM compatible computers. 800–395–0195.

TechPool Studios, 1463 Warrensville Rd., Cleveland, OH 44121: Free catalog ❖ Anatomy, dental, and emergency medical clip-art for Macintosh and IBM compatible computers. 800–777–8930.

Teleware, 300 Roundhill Dr., Rockaway, NJ 07866: Free information ❖ Accounting software for the Macintosh. 800–227–5638.

3G Graphics, 114 2nd Ave. South, Ste. 104, Edmonds, WA 98020: Free information ❖ Clip-art for Macintosh and IBM compatible computers. 800–456–0234; 206–774–3518 (in WA).

Timeworks Inc., 625 Academy Dr., Northbrook, IL 60062: Free information ❖ Software for Apple, Atari, Commodore, IBM compatible, and Macintosh computers. 800–535–9497.

Totem Graphics Inc., 6200 Capitol Blvd., Tumwater, WA 98501: Free information ❖ Full-color clip-art in 13 subject areas for Macintosh and IBM compatible computers. 206–352–1851.

True BASIC Inc., 12 Commerce Ave., West Lebanon, NH 03784: Free information ❖ Communications, desktop publishing, education, graphics, programming tools, and productivity software for the Macintosh. Amiga education and programming tools. 800–872–2742.

Unicorn Software Company, 6000 S. Eastern Ave., Bldg. 610, Ste. I, Las Vegas, NV 89119: Free information ❖ Education software for Amiga, Commodore, Apple, IBM compatible, and Macintosh computers. Games and entertainment for the Apple and Macintosh. 702–597–0818.

Viacom New Media, 648 S. Wheeling Rd., Wheeling, IL 60090: Free information ❖ Windows-supported graphics software for IBM compatibles. 800–877–4266.

Villa Crespo Software, 1725 McGovern St., Highland Park, IL 60035: Free information ❖ Entertainment and games software. 708–433–0500.

Virginia Systems Software Services, 5509 W. Bay Ct., Midlothian, VA 23112: Free information ❖ Macintosh word processing software. 804–739–3200.

The Voyager Company, 1351 Pacific Coast Hwy., Santa Monica, CA 90401: Free information ❖ Programming tools, utilities, and education software for the Macintosh. 800–443–2001.

Roger Wagner Publishing Inc., 1050 Pioneer Way, El Cajon, CA 92020: Free information ❖ Software for the Apple. 800–421–6526.

WayForward Technologies Inc., 119 E. Alron Ave., Ste. D, Santa Ana, CA 92707: Free information ❖ Windows-supported entertainment and games software for IBM compatibles. 800–959–GAME.

Wizardware Ltd., 918 Delaware Ave., Bethlehem, PA 18015: Free information ❖ WordPerrfect 6.0 CD-ROM clip art graphics. 800–548–7969; 215–866–9613 (in PA).

WordPerfect Corporation, 1555 N. Technology Way, Orem, UT 84057: Free information ❖ Word processing software for Amiga, Apple, Commodore, IBM compatible, and Macintosh computers. 800–451–5151.

The Writers' Computer Store, 11317 Santa Monica Blvd., Los Angeles, CA 90025: Free catalog ❖ Writer's software. 310–479–7774.

Software & CD-ROM Disk Retailers

CD Source, 13502 Whittier Blvd., Ste. H-133, Whittier, CA 90605: Free information ❖ CD-ROM disks. 800–424–0035; 310–902–8137 (in CA).

Chips & Bits, P.O. Box 234, Rochester, VT 05767: Free information ❖ Software and hardware for IBM compatibles. 800–699–4263.

Roger Coats, 20200 Nine Mile Rd., St. Clair Shores, MI 48080: Free information ❖ Apple accessories, Laser 128 computers and printers, scanners, cards, chips, drives, modems, system savers, software, and other peripherals. 800–438–2883; 313–774–8240 (in MI).

CompUSA Inc., 15160 Marsh Ln., Dallas, TX 75234: Free catalog ❖ Software, desktop and portable IBM compatibles, peripherals, furniture, books, and other equipment. 800–451–7638.

ComputAbility Consumer Electronics, P.O. Box 17882, Milwaukee, WI 53217: Free information ❖ Software and CD-ROM disks. 800–558–0003.

Computer Basics, 1490 N. Hermitage Rd., Hermitage, PA 16148: Free information ❖ Software and peripherals for Amiga computers. 412–962–0533.

Computer Express, 31 Union Ave., Sudbury, MA 01776: Free information ❖ Software and hardware for IBM compatibles. 508–443–6125.

Creative Computers, 4453 Redondo Beach Blvd., Lawndale, CA 90260: Free information ❖ Software and peripherals for Amiga computers. 310–542–2292.

DataCal Corporation, 531 E. Elliot Rd., Chandler, AZ 85225: Free catalog ❖ Computer productivity enhancements, CD-ROM disks, and software. 800–453–7932.

Dell Computer Corporation, 9505 Arboretum Blvd., Austin, TX 78759: Free catalog ❖ Software and peripherals for IBM compatibles. 800–677–4168.

Dr. Mac, 11050 Randall St., Sun Valley, CA 91352: Free information ❖ Macintosh software. 818–504–2159.

Dustin Discount Software, 21010 Superior St., Chatsworth, CA 91311: Free price list ❖ Business and personal software for IBM compatibles. 800–200–0602.

Educational Resources, 1550 Executive Dr., Elgin, IL 60123: Free catalog ❖ Software, diskettes, peripherals, cards, and computers. 800–624–2926; 708–888–8300 (in IL).

Fas-Track Computer Products, 7030 Huntley Rd., Columbus, OH 43229: Free information ❖ Software, Apple accessories and peripherals, cards, chips, disk drives, modems, scanners, joysticks, and other peripherals. 800–927–3936.

Global Computer Supplies, 1050 Northbrook Pkwy., Suwanee, GA 30174: Free catalog ❖ Work stations and furniture, hardware, software, peripherals, and printing supplies. 800–745–6225; 404–339–9999 (in GA).

Mac Warehouse, 1720 Oak St., P.O. Box 3013, Lakewood, NJ 08701: Free catalog ❖ Macintosh software. 800–255–6227.

The Mac Zone, 17411 NE Union Hill Rd., Redmond, WA 98052: Free information ❖ Macintosh software. 800–248–0800.

MacConnection, 14 Mill St., Marlow, NH 03456: Free information ❖ Macintosh accessories and software. 800–800–3333.

Media Magic, P.O. Box 598, Nicasio, CA 94946: Free catalog ❖ Education and entertainment software, computer books, and video tapes. 415–662–2426.

Newtech Video & Computers, 350 7th Ave., New York, NY 10001: Free information ❖ Video equipment, computers and peripherals, software, cellular phones, fax machines, and office equipment. 800–554–9747.

PC Connection, 6 Mill St., Marlow, NH 03456: Free information ❖ Software for IBM compatibles. 800–800–0004.

Peripherals Plus, 5016 Rt. 9 South, Howell, NJ 07731: Free information ❖ Software for IBM compatible and Macintosh computers. 800–444–7369.

Precision Type, 47 Mall Dr., Commack, NY 11725: Free information ❖ Software fonts. 800–248–3668.

The Programmer's Shop, 5 Pond Park Rd., Hingham, MA 02043: Free information ❖ Software for IBM compatibles. 800–421–8006; 617–740–2510 (in MA).

Publisher's Toolbox, 8845 S. Greenview Dr., Ste. 8, Middleton, WI 53562: Free information ❖ Software and hardware for Macintosh and IBM compatible computers. 800–233–3898.

Softshoppe Inc., P.O. Box 247, Artesia, CA 90701: Free catalog ❖ Software for IBM compatible and Macintosh computers. 800–851–8089.

Software House Direct, 2 Riverview Dr., Somerset, NJ 08873: Free information ❖ Software and peripherals for IBM compatibles. 800–777–5014.

Software Hut, Folcroft East Business Park, 313 Henderson Dr., Sharon Hill, PA 19079: Free information ❖ Commodore and Amiga software, and accessories. 800–93–AMIGA.

Spotlight Software Inc., 1042 S. Oliver, Wichita, KS 67218: Free information ❖ CD-ROM software. 316–683–7272.

Tiger Software, 600 Douglas Entrance, Executive Tower, 7th Floor, Coral Gables, FL 33134: Free information ❖ Software and CD-ROM disks for the Macintosh and IBM compatibles. 800–666–2562 (Macintosh information); 800–888–4437 (IBM compatibles and DOS information).

Supplies

Action Computer Supplies, 6100 Stewart Ave., Fremont, CA 94538: Free catalog ❖ Computer supplies, furniture, software, and hardware. 800–822–3132; 510–651–0626 (in CA).

American Ribbon Company, 2895 W. Prospect Rd., Fort Lauderdale, FL 33309: Free information ❖ Printer ribbons, laser toner cartridges, and inkjet refills. 800–327–1013.

Best Computer Supplies, 4980 Longley Ln., Ste. 104, Reno, NV 89502: Free catalog ❖ Computer supplies, furniture, cables, disks, printer ribbons, cleaning and maintenance products, back-up systems, and drives.

Chenesko Products Inc., 2221 5th Ave., Ste. 4, Ronkonkoma, NY 11779: Free catalog ❖ Recharge kits for laser printer and copier toner cartridges. 800–221–3516; 516–467–3205 (in NY).

Dayton Computer Supply, 6501 State Rt. 123 North, Franklin, OH 45005: Free information ❖ Printer ribbons. 800–735–3272.

Global Computer Supplies, 1050 Northbrook Pkwy., Suwanee, GA 30174: Free catalog ❖ Work stations and furniture, hardware, software, peripherals, and printing supplies. 800–745–6225; 404–339–9999 (in GA).

Idea Art, P.O. Box 291505, Nashville, TN 37229: Free catalog ❖ Preprinted laser/copier/offset paper with ready-to-use designs. 800–433–2278.

Inmac, 2300 Valley View Ln., Irving, TX 75062: Free catalog ❖ Computer supplies, furniture, cables, disks and tapes, and networking and data communications equipment. 800–547–5444.

Island Computer Supply, 305 Grand Blvd., Massapequa Park, NY 11762: Catalog $1 (refundable) ❖ Printer ribbons and diskettes. 516–798–6500.

MEI/Micro Center, 1160 Steelwood Rd., Columbus, OH 43212: Free information ❖ Disks, disk cases, ribbons, surge protectors, and accessories. 800–468–0545.

National Computer Ribbons, 9566 Deereco Rd., Timonium, MD 21093: Free information ❖ Printer ribbons. 800–292–6272; 410–561–0200 (in MD).

Paper Access, 23 W. 18th St., New York, NY 10011: Free information ❖ Over 500 choices of paper for laser printers. 800–PAPER-01.

Paper Direct Inc., 100 Plaza Dr., Secaucus, NJ 07094: Free catalog ❖ Laser printer, desktop publishing, and copier paper. 800–A-PAPERS.

Pendle Company Inc., N35 W23770 Capitol Dr., Pewaukee, WI 53072: Free information ❖ Toner cartridges. 800–869–7973; 414–691–5858 (in WI).

RAMCO Computer Supplies, P.O. Box 475, Manteno, IL 60950: Free information ❖ Printer and heat transfer ribbons, printer paper, and other supplies. 800–522–6922.

Ribbon Land, P.O. Box 4894, Philadelphia, PA 19124: Free catalog ❖ Printer ribbons and paper, laser cartridges, auto-inkers, T-shirt iron-ons and software, and disks. 215–744–9761.

COOKIE CUTTERS

D.D. Dillon, 850 Meadow Ln., Camp Hill, PA 17011: Free information ❖ Handcarved cookie and shortbread molds. 717–761–6895.

The Little Fox Factory, 931 Marion Rd., Bucyrus, OH 44820: Catalog $1 ❖ Handcrafted cookie cutters. 419–562–5420.

The Lyphon & Gryphon, 3779 Schindler Rd., Fallon, NV 89406: Catalog $4 (refundable) ❖ Cookie cutters. 702–867–4574.

Maid of Scandinavia, 3244 Raleigh Ave., Minneapolis, MN 55416: Free catalog ❖ Utensils, kitchen tools, and cake, cookie, and candy-making molds and supplies. 800–851–1121.

Sur La Table, Pike Place Farmers Market, Seattle, WA 98101: Free information ❖ Handcarved, thistle-pattern wood shortbread molds. 206–448–2244.

Wilton Enterprise Inc., 2240 W. 75th St., Woodridge, IL 60517: Catalog $6 (refundable) ❖ Supplies for making cookies, candies, and cakes. 708–963–7100.

COPIERS & FAX MACHINES

A V Distributors, 16451 Space Center Blvd., Houston, TX 77058: Free information ❖ Fax machines and audio, video, stereo, and TV equipment. 800–843–3697.

Computability Consumer Electronics, P.O. Box 17882, Milwaukee, WI 53217: Free catalog ❖ Fax machines and copiers. 800–558–0003.

Computerlane, 7500 Topanga Canyon Blvd., Canoga Park, CA 91304: Free information ❖ Fax machines, computers, and software. 800–526–3482; 818–884–8644 (in CA).

Crutchfield, 1 Crutchfield Park, Charlottesville, VA 22906: Free catalog ❖ Fax machines, telephones and answering machines, word processors, personal copiers, computers, and software. 800–955–9009.

Factory Direct, 131 W. 35th St., New York, NY 10001: Free information ❖ Fax machines and audio, video, stereo, and TV equipment. 800–428–4567.

Fax City Inc., P.O. Box 38182, Greensboro, NC 27438: Free catalog ❖ Fax machines and copiers. 800–426–6499.

Newtech Video & Computers, 350 7th Ave., New York, NY 10001: Free information ❖ Video equipment, computers and peripherals, software, cellular phones, fax machines, and office equipment. 800–554–9747.

Olden Video, 1265 Broadway, New York, NY 10001: Free information ❖ Telephones, copiers, and photographic equipment. 212–725–1234.

Reliable Home Office, P.O. Box 1501, Ottawa, IL 61350: Catalog $2 ❖ Computer accessories and furniture, filing and storage systems, and fax machines. 800–869–6000.

Sound City, Meadtown Shopping Center, Rt. 23, Kinnelon, NJ 07405: Free information ❖ Audio and video equipment, cassette and CD players, camcorders, TVs, fax machines, processors, telephones, and other electronics. 800–542–7283.

Staples Inc., Attention: Marketing Services, P.O. Box 9328, Framingham, MA 01701: Free catalog ❖ Fax machines, typewriters, word processors, office supplies and furniture, computer supplies, and drafting equipment. 800–333–3330.

Tri-State Camera, 650 6th Ave., New York, NY 10011: Free information ❖ Fax machines, copiers, audio and video equipment, camcorders, and photography equipment. 800–537–4441; 212–633–2290 (in NY).

COSMETICS & SKIN CARE

B & B Honey Farm, Rt. 2, Box 245, Houston, MN 55943: Free catalog ❖ Natural products for hair, skin, hygiene, and health care. 507–896–3955.

Barth Vitamins, 865 Merrick Ave., Westbury, NY 11590: Free catalog ❖ Natural vitamins, health foods, mineral supplements, cosmetics, and home health aids. 800–645–2328; 800–553–0353 (in NY).

Baudelaire Fine Imported Cosmetics Inc., Forest Rd., Marlow, NH 03456: Free information ❖ Imported European therapeutic bath oils rich in herbal extracts and essential oils. 800–327–2324.

Beautiful Visions, 1233 Montauk Hwy., P.O. Box 9000, Oakdale, NY 11769: Free catalog ❖ Women and men's nationally advertised cosmetics and toiletries. 800–645–1030.

Beauty Boutique, 6836 Engle Rd., P.O. Box 94520, Cleveland, OH 44101: Free catalog ❖ Cosmetics, toiletries, skin care items, costume jewelry, and women's fashions. 216–826–3008.

Bioenergy Nutrients, 6565 Odell Pl., Boulder, CO 80301: Catalog $1 ❖ Nutritional supplements, homeopathic medicines, antioxidants, and all-natural skin care products. 800–627–7775.

The Body Shop Inc., Attention: Catalog Department, 45 Horsehill Rd., Hanover Technical Center, Cedar Knolls, NJ 07927: Catalog $2 ❖ Toiletries and cosmetics. 800–541–2535.

Caswell-Massey Company Ltd., Catalog Division, 100 Enterprise Place, Dover, DE 19901: Catalog $1 ❖ Toiletries, cosmetics, and personal care products. 800–326–0500.

Cats in the Cradle, Rt. 140, Alton, NH 03809: Free brochure with long SASE ❖ Herbal soaps, creams, lotions, and salves.

Cosmetics Plus, 275 W. 27th St., New York, NY 10001: Free information with long SASE ❖ Private brand and other cosmetics and toiletries. 212–924–3493.

Crabtree & Evelyn Limited, P.O. Box 167, Woodstock Hill, CT 06281: Catalog $3.50 ❖ Soaps and shampoos, bath gels and oils, colognes and toilet waters, creams, lotions, talcum powders, sponges, brushes, combs, from England, France, and Switzerland. 203–928–2761.

Esse Salon & Spa, Altid Park, P.O. Box 6529, Chelmsford, MA 01824: Free catalog ❖ Cosmetic and skin care products. 800–879–3773.

Essential Products Company Inc., 90 Water St., New York, NY 10005: Free catalog ❖ Copies of fragrances for men and women. 212–344–4288.

Famous Smoke Shop Inc., 55 W. 39th St., New York, NY 10018: Free catalog ❖ Women and men's cosmetic fragrances. 800–672–5544.

The Florist Shop, 703 Madison Ave., New York, NY 10021: Free catalog ❖ Hand-milled soaps, bath oils, body milk, talc, room fragrances, and potpourris. 800–J-FLORIS.

Fredericksburg Herb Farm, P.O. Drawer 927, Fredericksburg, TX 78624: Catalog $2 ❖ Herb plants, seeds, flowers, toiletries, oils, and seasonings. 512–997–8615.

Gabrieana's Herbal & Organic Products, P.O. Box 215322, Sacramento, CA 95821: Free catalog ❖ Skin care and bath care items, essential oils, dried herbs, and other organic products. 800–684–4372.

General Nutrition Catalog, Puritan's Pride, 105 Orville Dr., Bohemia, NY 11716: Free catalog ❖ Vitamins, health foods, natural cosmetics, books, and gifts. 800–645–1030.

Gold Medal Hair Products Inc., 1 Bennington Ave., Freeport, NY 11520: Free catalog ❖ Wigs for black men and women, hair and beauty preparations, hair styling equipment, and jewelry. 516–378–6900.

Gayle Hayman Beverly Hills, 8306 Wilshire Blvd., Beverly Hills, CA 90211: Free catalog ❖ Cosmetics and jewelry. 800–FOR-GALE.

HealthFest, 74 20th St., Brooklyn, NY 11232: Free catalog ❖ Natural remedies, personal care items, comfort and support aids, cosmetics and toiletries, and handy helpers. 718–768–0010.

Herb & Spice Collection, P.O. Box 118, Norway, IA 52318: Free catalog ❖ Natural herbal body care products, potpourris, culinary herbs and spices, other herbs, and teas. 800–786–1388.

Holzman & Stephanie Perfumes Inc., P.O. Box 921, Lake Forest, IL 60045: Catalog $4.50 (refundable) ❖ Copies of world-famous perfumes. 708–234–7667.

Indiana Botanic Gardens, P.O. Box 5, Hammond, IN 46325: Free catalog ❖ Vitamins, herbs, spices, and personal care products. 219–947–4040.

Island Tan, 360 Hoohana St., Ste. B101, Kahului, HI 96732: Free information ❖ Sunscreens, fragrances, and skin care products with natural ingredients. 800–926–5756; 808–877–0466 (in HI).

Victoria Jackson Cosmetics Inc., National Distribution Center, 16 Paoli Corporate Center, Paoli, PA 19301: Free catalog ❖ Body, bath, hair care, and other cosmetics. 800–392–9250.

Kettle Care Cosmetics, 1535 Eagle Dr., Columbia Falls, MT 59912: Catalog $1 (refundable) ❖ Natural bath and skin care cosmetics and toiletries.

Key West Aloe Inc., P.O. Box 1079, Key West, FL 33041: Free catalog ❖ Men's personal care products and toiletries, and cosmetics and skin care products for women. 800–445–2563.

Kneipp Corporation of America, Valmont Industrial Park, 675 Jaycee Dr., West Hazleton, PA 18201: Free information ❖ Herbal baths and shower gels.

La Costa Products International, 2875 Laker Ave. East, Carlsbad, CA 92009: Free catalog ❖ Hair, skin, and body care products for men and women. 800–LA-COSTA.

Lucky Heart Cosmetics, 138 Huling Ave., Memphis, TN 38103: Free catalog ❖

Cosmetics and skin care products. 800–526–5825.

Katherine March Ltd., P.O. Box 51844, Durham, NC 27717: Free price list ❖ European soaps and luxuries for the bath. 800–87–MARCH.

McKenna's Garden, 2164 Lincoln Ave., San Jose, CA 95125: Free catalog with long SASE ❖ Natural bath and body care products.

Mount Nebo Herbs & Oils, 300 Highland Ave., Athens, OH 45701: Catalog $2 ❖ Essential oils and unscented body and skin care products.

Mountain Rose Herbs, P.O. Box 2000, Redway, CA 95560: Catalog $1 ❖ Natural herbal body care products. 707–923–3941.

Nature Food Centres, One Nature's Way, Wilmington, MA 01887: Free catalog ❖ Vitamins, natural food products, and cosmetics. 800–225–0857.

New York Cosmetics, 318 Brannan St., San Francisco, CA 94107: Catalog $2 ❖ Men and women's fragrances, cosmetics, and skin, nail, hair, and bath care items. 415–543–3880.

Nutrition Headquarters, One Nutrition Plaza, Carbondale, IL 62901: Free catalog ❖ Vitamins and mineral supplements, health and beauty aids, and herbal formulas. 618–457–8100, ext. 229.

Planta Dei Medicinal Herb Farm, Millville, New Brunswick, Canada E0H 1M0: Catalog $2 (refundable) ❖ Biologically grown teas, medicinal herbs, healing tea mixtures, cosmetics, natural ointments, and massage oils. 506–463–8169.

Puritan's Pride, 1233 Montauk Hwy., P.O. Box 9001, Oakdale, NY 11769: Free catalog ❖ Natural vitamins and health and beauty aids. 800–645–1030.

Scente Perfumery, 255 5th Ave., New York, NY 10016: Catalog $2 ❖ Designer fragrances and other cosmetics for men and women. 212–889–8681.

Scents Direct, 24 Turntable Junction, Flemington, NJ 08822: Free catalog ❖ Fragrances, cosmetics, and toiletries from major perfume/cologne manufacturers. 800–772–3687.

A Second Look, 8502 Chapel View Rd., Ellicott City, MD 21043: Free catalog with long SASE ❖ Skin care products. 410–465–6653.

Shield Healthcare Centers, P.O. Box 916, Santa Clarita, CA 91380: Free catalog ❖

Ostomy, urological, skin care, and home diagnostic products

Syd Simons Cosmetics, 2 E. Oak St., Chicago, IL 60611: Free price list ❖ Women's cosmetics and make-up. 312–943–2333.

Soap Opera, 319 State St., Madison, WI 55703: Free price list ❖ Scented glycerin soaps, body lotions and creams, eye care cream, lip balms, suntan lotions, bubble baths and oils, essential oils, designer fragrances, herbs, and perfume bases. 800–251–SOAP.

Star Pharmaceuticals Inc., 1500 New Horizons Blvd., Amityville, NY 11701: Free catalog ❖ Vitamin products, nutritional supplements, toiletries, health care products, and pet supplies. 800–274–6400.

Sunburst Biorganics, 838 Merrick Rd., Baldwin, NY 11510: Free catalog ❖ Nutritional supplements and toiletries. 800–645–8448.

Tropical Botanicals, P.O. Box 1354, Rancho, Santa Fe, CA 92067: Free information ❖ Natural shampoos and skin care products. 800–777–1428; 619–756–1265 (in CA).

The Uncommon Herb Catalog, 731 Main St., Monroe, CT 06468: Catalog $1 ❖ Essential oils, handmade soaps, skin care products, teas, and seasonings. 203–459–0716.

Union Express, 3722 Crater Rd., Honolulu, HI 96816: Free information ❖ Skin care products for men and women. 808–734–0404.

Vineyard Vines, P.O. Box 774, Oak Bluffs, MA 02557: Catalog $1 (refundable) ❖ Dried flowers, herbal skin care products, potpourri and sachets, and other gifts. 508–693–1724.

Wynnewood Pharmacy, Wynnewood Shopping Center, Wynnewood, PA 19096: Free catalog ❖ Perfumes and colognes. 800–966–5999; 215–878–4999 (in PA).

COSTUMES & VINTAGE CLOTHING

Abracadabra Magic Shop, 125 Lincoln Blvd., Middlesex, NJ 08846: Catalog $5 ❖ Close-up and stage magic, juggling equipment, balloons, clown props, costumes, and theatrical supplies. 908–805–0200.

Allstar Costumes, 125 Lincoln Blvd., Middlesex, NJ 08846: Catalog $1 ❖ Costumes for adults and children. 908–805–0200.

Badhir Trading Inc., 8429 Sisson Hwy., Eden, NY 14057: Catalog $2.50 (refundable)

❖ Beaded, sequined, and jeweled appliques, and trims and fringes for dresses, costumes, and bridal fashions. 800–654–9418.

Cattle Kate, Box 572, Wilson, WY 83014: Catalog $3 ❖ Contemporary clothing of the Old West for men, women, and children. 307–733–7414.

Character Costumes, 138 5th Ave., Ste. 143, Pelham, NY 10803: Free brochure ❖ Character costumes.

Circus Clowns, 3556 Nicollet Ave., Minneapolis, MN 55408: Catalog $3 ❖ Clown costumes and props. 612–822–4243.

Clown Heaven, 4792 Old State Rd. 37 South, Martinsville, IN 46152: Catalog $3 ❖ Balloons, make-up, puppets, wigs, ministry and gospel items, novelties, magic, clown props, and books. 317–342–6888.

Confederate Yankee, P.O. Box 192, Guilford, CT 06437: Catalog $2 ❖ Men, women, and children's reproduction Revolutionary and Civil War clothing. 203–453–9900.

The Costume Connection, P.O. Box 4518, Falls Church, VA 22044: Free catalog ❖ Character costumes. 703–237–1373.

Costumes by Betty, 2181 Edgerton St., St. Paul, MN 55117: Catalog $5 (refundable) ❖ Clown costumes, make-up, wigs, and shoes. 612–771–8734.

Dazian's Inc., 2014 Commerce St., Dallas, TX 75201: Free catalog ❖ Costume fabrics and trims, leotards, tights, and other dance wear. 214–748–3450.

Eastern Costume Company, 510 N. Elm St., Greensboro, NC 27401: Free information ❖ Costumes and make-up. 910–379–1026.

Harriet A. Engler, P.O. Box 1363, Winchester, VA 22604: Adult catalog $7; children's catalog $3 ❖ Military and civilian reproduction costumes, uniforms, patterns, and crinolines. 703–667–2541.

Freckles Clown Supplies, 5509 Rosselvelt Blvd., Jacksonville, FL 32210: Catalog $5 ❖ Costumes, make-up, clown supplies, puppets, clowning and ballooning how-to books, and theatrical supplies. 904–778–3977.

Historic Patterns & Slipcovers, P.O. Box 7967, Incline Village, NV 89452: Catalog $5.39 ❖ Victorian gown patterns and wedding accessories. 800–876–2699.

Lacey Costume Wig, 249 W. 34th St., Ste. 707, New York, NY 10001: Free catalog ❖

Wigs, mustaches, beards, and other supplies. 800–562–9911; 212–695–1996 (in NY).

Laidlacker Historical Garments, RD 2, Box 989, Milton, PA 17847: Catalog $3 ❖ Reproduction 18th-, 19th-, and 20th-century clothing for men, women, and children. 717–437–9174.

Lynch's Clown Supplies, 939 Howard, Dearborn, MI 48124: Catalog $5 ❖ Clown wigs, shoes, noses, novelties, make-up, and costumes. 313–565–3425.

Heidi Marsh Patterns, 3494 N. Valley Rd., Greenville, CA 95947: Catalog $3 ❖ Civil War clothing patterns for adults and children.

Mary Ellen & Company, 29400 Rankert Rd., North Liberty, IN 46554: Catalog $3 ❖ Victorian-style clothing, lace-up shoes, hats, fans, parasols, books, and patterns. 219–656–3000.

Maybe It's You Vintage Clothing, 3903 Silsby Rd., Cleveland, OH 44111: Free information ❖ Vintage fashions, from the 1940s to 1960s. 216–252–1537.

Mecca Magic Inc., 49 Dodd St., Bloomfield, NJ 07003: Catalog $10 ❖ Costumes, wigs, and make-up. 201–429–7597.

Morris Costumes, 3108 Monroe Rd., Charlotte, NC 28205: Catalog $20 ❖ Costumes, clown props, masks, joke items, magic tricks and special effects, novelties, and books. 704–332–3304.

National Hair Technologies Ltd., 300 Canal St., Lawrence, MA 01840: Free information ❖ Theatrical character and other wigs. 508–686–2964.

New Columbia, P.O. Box 848, Middleburg, VT 05753: Catalog $4.50 ❖ Reproduction military uniforms, from 1845 to 1945. 217–348–5927.

The 1909 Company, 70 Greenwich Ave., Ste. 309, New York, NY 10011: Catalog $2 ❖ Recreated wearable vintage clothing. 800–331–1909.

Northwest Traders Inc., 5055 W. Jackson Rd., Enon, OH 45323: Catalog $1 ❖ Frontier clothing and related items. 513–767–9244.

Raiments, P.O. Box 93095, Pasadena, CA 91109: Catalog $5 ❖ Books, under pinnings, and patterns for historical costumes, from the middle ages to the 1950s. 818–797–2723.

Reflections of the Past, P.O. Box 40361, Bay Village, OH 44140: Catalog $4 ❖ Men, women, and children's American and

European antique fashions, from the 17th- to 19th-century. 216–835–6924.

Rubie's Costume Company, 120–08 Jamaica Ave., Richmond Hill, Queens, NY 11418: Free information ❖ Costumes, make-up, hair goods, and special effects. 718–846–1008.

Salt Lake Costume Company, 1701 S. 1100 East, Salt Lake City, UT 84105: Free catalog ❖ Historical costumes and make-up. 801–467–7494.

Alan Sloane & Company Inc., 80 Kean St., West Babylon, NY 11704: Free catalog ❖ Clown costumes, props, and other theatrical items. 800–252–6266; 516–643–2262 (in NY).

James Townsend & Son Inc., 133 N. 1st St., P.O. Box 415, Pierceton, IN 46562: Catalog $2 ❖ Historical clothing, hats, lanterns, tomahawks, knives, tents, guns, and blankets. 219–594–5852.

Under the Big Top, P.O. Box 807, Placentia, CA 92670: Catalog $4 ❖ Costumes, clown props, make-up, juggling equipment, and party supplies. 800–995–7727.

COUNTRY CRAFTS

Adirondack Store & Gallery, 109 Saranac Ave., Lake Placid, NY 12946: Free information ❖ Country-style twig furniture, stoneware and pottery, rugs, fireboards, lawn and other wood furniture, baskets, and pillows. 518–523–2646.

Amish Country Collection, Sunset Valley Rd., RD 5, New Castle, PA 16105: Catalog $5 (refundable) ❖ Amish-style pillows, quilts, wall hangings, rugs, cribs and beds, and other household items. 412–458–4811.

Arts-Nic & Old Lace, P.O. Box 587215, Alsip, IL 60658: Free information ❖ Signed and dated Early American-style mantel clocks with folk art designs. 708–424–0937.

Baskets & Things, 136 Miller Ln., London, KY 40741: Brochure $1 (refundable) ❖ Hand-woven baskets. 800–847–5983.

Bayou Country Store, 823 E. Jackson St., Pensacola, FL 32501: Free catalog ❖ Country crafts and decor accessories. 800–262–5403; 904–432–5697 (in FL).

Beki's Garden Gallery, P.O. Box 2566, Boca Raton, FL 33427: Free catalog ❖ Handcrafted garden and home items. 407–482–2024.

Berea College Crafts, CPO 2347, Berea, KY 40404: Catalog $2 ❖ Handmade woodwork, weavings, and iron and pottery crafts. 606–986–9341.

Brown's Country Creations, Rt. 1, Box 1228, Dunnegan, MO 65640: Catalog $2.50 ❖ Handcrafted bathroom ensembles and hanging towel and matching table sets. 800–338–7696; 417–326–4880 (in MO).

Brush Strokes, 19312 Haviland Dr., South Bend, IN 46637: Brochure $3 ❖ Signed and numbered limited edition prints reproduced from original oil paintings, with a choice of mats and frames. 219–277–5414.

Carpenter's General Store, 6347 Fair Ridge Rd., Hillsboro, OH 45133: Brochure $3 ❖ Country-style wood decor accessories. 800–345–5615.

Chriswill Forge, 2255 Manchester Rd., North Lawrence, OH 44666: Catalog $2 ❖ Country-style floor lamps with a heavy-duty steel plate base and a choice of designs for the top. 216–832–9136.

Cinnamon & Spice by the Sea, Broadway at 7th St., Barnegat Light, NJ 08006: Catalog $1 ❖ Handcrafted Victorian country-style gifts. 609–494–5413.

Classics by Simply Country, P.O. Drawer 656, Wytheville, VA 24382: Brochure $2 (refundable) ❖ Wallhangings, throws, pillows, clothing, and afghans. 800–537–8911.

Colonial Casting Company Inc., 68 Liberty St., Haverhill, MA 01832: Catalog $3 ❖ Handcrafted lead-free pewter miniature castings. 508–374–8783.

Colonial Collections of New England Inc., 202 Idlewood Dr., Stamford, CT 06905: Catalog $1 ❖ Weather vanes, cupolas, sundials, mailboxes, door knockers, personalized and date plaques, lanterns, and other home and garden decor items. 203–322–0078.

Conewago Junction, 1255 Oxford Rd., New Oxford, PA 17350: Catalog $2 ❖ Colonial chests, cupboards, wood buckets, tools, afghans, tinware, household items, and other handcrafted reproductions. 717–624–4786.

The Cotton Gin Inc., Deep Creek Farm, P.O. Box 24, Jarvisburg, NC 27947: Free catalog ❖ Country collectibles, southern-style clothing, and fine antiques. 800–637–2446.

Country Accents, P.O. Box 437, Montoursville, PA 17754: Catalog $5 ❖ Museum tin replicas and accent pieces. 717–478–4127.

Country Bouquet, P.O. Box 233, Kellogg, MN 55945: Brochure $2 ❖ Candle holders and sconces, Raggedy Ann and Andy dolls, folk items, stenciled aprons, ornaments, and shelves, pegboards, and wall cupboards. 800–328–5598; 507–767–2230 (in MN).

Country Frames, Box 284, Rochert, MN 56578: Free information ❖ Country-style frames. 800–253–9993.

Country Lane Stenciling, P.O. Box 517, West Chester, OH 45069: Brochure $2 ❖ Hand-stenciled rolling kitchen furniture, cotton valances, tie backs, and table runners. 513–777–7027.

Country Loft, Mail Order Department, 2165 N. Forbes Ave., Tucson, AZ 85745: Free catalog ❖ Lamps and chandeliers, cupboards and cabinets, crocks and carriers, Shaker reproductions, whimsical folk art, whirligigs, baskets, buckets, pillows, and braided rugs. 800–225–5408.

Country Manor, Mail Order Dept., Rt. 211, P.O. Box 520, Sperryville, VA 22740: Catalog $3 ❖ Handwoven cotton rugs, kitchen utensils, other craft items, and decor accessories. 800–344–8354.

Country Punchin', 14757 Glenn Dr., Whittier, CA 90604: Brochure $1 ❖ Hand-punched, tarnish-proof name signs and plaques in solid copper or pewter-like metal. 310–944–1038.

The Country Store, 28 James St., Geneva, IL 60134: Catalog $2 ❖ Punched tin and turned wood chandeliers, ceiling lights, outlet covers, country-style decor accessories, braided rugs, and stoneware. 708–879–0098.

Country Store Crafts, 5925 Country Ln., P.O. Box 990, Greendale, WI 53129: Free catalog ❖ Country gifts for men, women, and children. 800–558–1013.

The Country Touch, 8 Bonnywick Dr., Harrisburg, PA 17111: Brochure $2 ❖ Handcrafted wood country crafts and gifts. 717–566–6711.

Creative Crafts, 308 S. Todd, McComb, OH 45858: Brochure $2 ❖ Handcrafted earthenware pottery. 419–293–3838.

Custom Country Wood Products, Rt. 2, Box 108, Greenville, TX 75402: Free information ❖ Country-style furniture with a whitewash stain or unfinished. 903–455–0542.

Darowood Farms, 4614 School Rd., P.O. Box 470, Egg Harbor, WI 54209: Brochure $2 ❖ Handcrafted country wood items. 800–228–3908.

D.D. Dillon, 850 Meadow Ln., Camp Hill, PA 17011: Free information ❖ Handcarved cookiem and shortbread molds and wall hangings. 717–761–6895.

Dilworthy Country Store, 275 Brinton's Bridge Rd., West Chester, PA 19382: Free information ❖ Country-style gifts, decor accessories, folk art, herbs and dried flowers, colonial furnishings, and 18th-century reproductions. 215–399–0560.

The Faith Mountain Company, P.O. Box 199, Sperryville, VA 22740: Free catalog ❖ Kitchen utensils, country-style gifts, folk art reproductions, toys and dolls, handmade Appalachian baskets, and Christmas decorations. 800–822–7238.

Floating Turtle Creek Woodworks, P.O. Box 156, Steens, MS 39766: Free brochure ❖ Authentic reproduction spice cabinets. 601–328–5075.

Gard Woodworking, 121 N. Walnut, Colfax, IA 50054: Brochure $1 ❖ Wood country crafts and decor accessories. 515–674–3060.

Grunewald Folk Art, P.O. Box 721, Wauconda, IL 60084: Catalog $2 ❖ Signed and numbered limited edition lithographs of pen and ink drawings of animals and people in rural American settings. 708–526–1417.

Heart of the Woods Inc., P.O. Box 185, Ely, MN 55731: Catalog $1 (refundable) ❖ Wood country-style decor accessories. 800–852–2075.

Holst Inc., 1118 W. Lake, Box 370, Tawas City, MI 48764: Free catalog ❖ Country items, decor accessories, sundials and weather vanes, housewares, figurines, and holiday decorations. 517–362–5664.

Home Sweet Home, 218 Hilldrop, Caldwell, ID 83605: Catalog $1.50 with long SASE ❖ Traditional country-style stoneware, dolls, and holiday decorations. 208–459–3813.

Homestead Creations, 4920 Highwood Circle, Middleton, WI 53562: Catalog $2 ❖ Country crafts and decor accessories. 608–836–6035.

Independence Forge, Rt. 1, Box 1, Whitakers, NC 27891: Brochure $1 ❖ Furniture, chandeliers, floor lamps, table and wall lamps, and other country-style handcrafted iron pieces. 919–437–2931.

Jepson Studios Inc., P.O. Box 36, Harveyville, KS 66431: Brochure $2 (refundable) ❖ Country ceramics. 913–589–2481.

Karlin Pottery, 662 Minkin Dr., Traverse City, MI 49684: Brochure $1 ❖ Country pottery and stoneware. 616–275–5649.

Lambs Farm, P.O. Box 520, Libertyville, IL 60048: Free catalog ❖ Country crafts, specialty foods, nuts, candies, and gifts for pets. 800–52-LAMBS.

Mapleleaf Workshop, P.O. Box 0218, Stanford, IL 61774: Free catalog ❖ Country-style wood crafts, tin ware, kitchen accent pieces, placemats, hot pads, decor items, and sweatshirts. 800–354–5501.

McVay's Limited, P.O. Box 553, Leslie, MI 49251: Brochure $2 ❖ Wall accent pieces, gameboards, weather vanes, and other handcrafted household and gift items. 517–589–5312.

Orleans Carpenters, P.O. Box 217, Orleans, MA 02653: Catalog $3 ❖ Shaker-style oval bentwood boxes and other small wood crafts. 508–255–2646.

The Owl's Nest, 112 SCT Dr., White House, TN 37188: Catalog $2 ❖ Traditional country crafts. 615–672–9383.

Pesta's Country Store, 300 Standard Ave., Mingo Junction, OH 43938: Price list $1 ❖ Country crafts for decorating. 614–535–1873.

Raindrops on Roses Rubber Stamp Company, 4808 Winterwood Dr., Raleigh, NC 27613: Catalog $3 ❖ Country-style rubber stamp sets with brush markers. 919–846–8617.

RBL Publications, Beki's Garden Gallery, P.O. Box 2566, Boca Raton, FL 33427: Free catalog ❖ Home and garden accessories, pet items, birdhouses and feeders, wind chimes, and books. 407–482–2024.

Redwood Unlimited, P.O. Box 2344, Valley Center, CA 92082: Brochure $2 ❖ Wall- and post-mounted mailboxes with ornamental scrolls, posts, and weather vanes. 800–283–1717.

Rocking Horse Crafts, 529 Plymouth St., Bridgewater, MA 02324: Free catalog ❖ Shadow boxes, decor pieces, toys, doll clothes, furniture, stuffed animals, and personalized signs. 508–697–7046.

Shaker Shops West, 5 Inverness Way, Inverness, CA 94937: Catalog $3 ❖ Reproductions of traditional music boxes, country-style furniture, candles, accessories for the home, teas and herbs, and books on the lifestyles, traditions, and history of the Shakers. 415–669–7256.

Simply Country Furniture, HC 69, Box 147, Rover, AR 72860: Brochure $2 ❖ Grandfather clocks. 501–272–4794.

Stitches 'N Pine, P.O. Box 710, Eldersburg, MD 21784: Brochure $1 ❖ Country-style quartz movement clocks and accent pieces. 410–795–1801.

Studio Workshop, 2808 Tucker St., Omaha, NE 68112: Catalog $2 ❖ Oak and walnut bathroom and decor accessories and furniture. 800–383–7072.

Sutter Creek Antiques, 28 Main St., Box 699, Sutter Creek, CA 95685: Free brochure with long SASE ❖ Antique country-style lamps, pottery, and carved wood items. 209–267–0230.

Sweet Antiques Galleries, 131 S. Main St., P.O. Box 563, Barre, VT 05641: Free brochure ❖ Reproduction antique-style tin signs, recycled glass bottles, wood items, oven-and dishwasher-safe enamelware, and toys. 802–476–3302.

Eve Tenny, Santons De France, P.O. Box 536, Wiscasset, ME 04578: Catalog $1.50 ❖ Handcrafted, terra cotta, peasants, craftsmen, and creche figures made in Provence from antique molds. 207–882–7010.

Three Rivers Pottery Productions Inc., 125 N. 2nd St., P.O. Box 462, Coshocton, OH 43812: Free information ❖ Oven-, microwave-, and dishwasher-safe pottery. 614–622–4154.

Tin Bin, 20 Valley Rd., Neffsville, PA 17601: Catalog $2.50 ❖ Handcrafted antiqued copper and brass country-style chandeliers. 717–569–6210.

A Touch of Country, P.O. Box 653, Palos Heights, IL 60463: Catalog $2 ❖ Country-style, handpainted wood ceiling fan and light pulls. 708–361–0142.

Vaillancourt Folk Art, 145 Armsby Rd., Sutton, MA 01590: Catalog $3 ❖ Reproduction antique American grandfather clocks. 508–865–9183.

Wesson Trading Company, 1316 Willow Street Dr., Woodstock, GA 30188: Catalog $2 ❖ Pottery, textiles, and folk art. 404–928–6145.

Westwinds, 3540 76th St. SE, Caledonias, MI 49316: Free brochure ❖ Weather vanes, signs, sundials, and birdbaths. 800–635–5262.

Will Woodworking, 23376 Rd. R, Fort Jennings, OH 45844: Catalog $2 ❖

Country-style wood crafts and decor accessories. 419–286–2298.

Wink's Woods, 1225 W. US 2, Crystal Falls, MI 49920: Free information with long SASE ❖ Country-style wood decor accessories. 906–875–3750.

Wood Concepts, 23565 Reedy Dr., Elkhart, IN 46514: Free information with long SASE ❖ Easy-to-assemble solid oak country-style furniture and decor accessories. 219–262–3457.

The Wood Shed, P.O. Box 27383, Knoxville, TN 37927: Free information ❖ Handmade wood items, quilted products, jellies, and cornhusk dolls.

Woodworks Unlimited, 208 Breckenridge Dr., West Monroe, LA 71292: Free information ❖ Pine furniture, accent pieces, and lamps. 318–325–2350.

Worthy Works, 1220 Rock St., Rockford, IL 61101: Brochure $2 ❖ Ceramic knobs for cabinets, kitchens, bathrooms, furniture, and accessories. 815–968–5858.

Zimmerman Handcrafts, 254 E. Main St., Leola, PA 17540: Brochure $1 ❖ Country-style decor items and traditional crafts. 717–656–8290.

CRAFT SUPPLIES

Activa Products, Box 472, Westford, MA 01886: Free information ❖ Art and craft supplies. 508–692–9300.

Arrow Fastener Company Inc., 271 Mayhill St., Saddle Brook, NJ 07662: Free information ❖ Hot melt glue guns.

The Art Store, 935 Erie Blvd. East, Syracuse, NY 13210: Price list $3 ❖ Supplies for fabric dyeing, screen printing, marbling, and other crafts. 800–669–2787.

Artistic Airbrush, P.O. Box 3318, Portland, OR 97208: Free information ❖ Art and craft supplies. 800–547–9750.

Atlas Art & Stained Glass, P.O. Box 76084, Oklahoma City, OK 73147: Catalog $3 ❖ Kaleidoscopes, frames, lamp bases, and art and craft, stained glass, jewelry-making, and foil-crafting supplies. 405–946–1230.

Barap Specialties, 835 Bellows Ave., Frankfort, MI 49635: Catalog $1 ❖ Lamp parts, chair caning supplies, turned wood parts, and other craft supplies. 800–3-BARAP-3.

Baubanbea Enterprises, P.O. Box 1205, Smithtown, NY 11787: Catalog $1 ❖

Rhinestones, sequins, beads, jewels, lace, appliques, fringe, trim, feathers, imported and domestic fabrics, and silk flowers. 516–724–4661.

Bersted's Hobbycraft, 1303 Tuscaloosa Ave. SW, Birmingham, AL 35211: Free catalog ❖ Hobby and craft supplies.

Bolek's Craft Supplies, 330 N. Tuscarawas Ave., P.O. Box 465, Dover, OH 44622: Catalog $1.50 ❖ Craft supplies, tools, and kits. 216–364–8878.

Brian's Crafts Unlimited, 1421 S. Dixie Freeway., New Smyrna, FL 32168: Catalog $1 (refundable) ❖ Craft supplies. 904–672–2726.

Carolan Craft Supplies, P.O. Box 9920, Cleveland, OH 44142: Catalog $3 ❖ Darice beads, plastic canvas, craft books, stencils, basket-making supplies, jewelry, quilts and needle crafts, pom poms, bears, dolls, and wire crafts. 216–362–0340.

Chaselle Inc., 9645 Gerwig Ln., Columbia, MD 21046: Catalog $4 ❖ Ceramic- and pottery-making equipment, and supplies for art, sculpting, stained glass, weaving, leather crafting, etching, and other crafts. 800–242–7355.

Circle Craft Supply, P.O. Box 3000, Dover, FL 33527: Catalog $1 ❖ Art and craft supplies. 813–659–0992.

Craft Catalog, 6095 McNaughten Centre, Columbus, OH 43232: Catalog $2 ❖ Art and craft supplies. 800–777–1442.

Craft King Mail Order Dept., P.O. Box 90637, Lakeland, FL 33804: Catalog $2 ❖ Craft, needlework, and macrame supplies. 813–648–0433.

Craft Resources Inc., Box 828, Fairfield, CT 06430: Catalog $1 ❖ String art, basket-making, metal and wood crafting, stained glass, and other craft supplies; and needlework kits for latch hooking, needlepoint, cross-stitching, and crewel. 203–254–7702.

Craft Time Catalog, 211 S. State College Blvd., Ste. 341, Anaheim, CA 92806: Catalog $2 ❖ Ready-to-paint plastercraft figurines. 714–671–1639.

Crafty's Featherworks, P.O. Box 370, Overton, NV 89040: Free information ❖ Feathers for floral arrangements, Native American and other crafts, millinery, fly-tying, and accent pieces. 702–397–8211.

Lou Davis Wholesale Ceramics & Crafts, N3211 Hwy. H North, Lake Geneva, WI 53147: Free catalog ❖ Craft supplies. 800–748–7991.

Design Originals, 2425 Cullen St., Fort Worth, TX 76107: Free information ❖ Supplies for making rag rugs, baskets, wood crafts, belts, fabric crafts, cross stitching, and other crafts. 800–877–7820.

Discount Bead House, P.O. Box 186, The Plains, OH 45780: Catalog $5 ❖ Leather, seed beads, findings, wood items, tools, and modeling supplies. 800–793–7592.

Earth Guild, 33 Haywood St., Asheville, NC 28801: Free catalog ❖ Basket-making, weaving, spinning, dyeing, pottery, woodcarving, hand and machine knitting, rug-making, netting, and chair-caning supplies. 800–327–8448.

Eastern Art Glass, P.O. Box 341, Wyckoff, NJ 07481: Catalog $2 (refundable) ❖ Stained glass kits, glass-etching equipment, glass coloring materials, fabric dyes, mirror-removing and wood-burning supplies, and how-to videos. 201–847–0001.

Enterprise Art, P.O. Box 2918, Largo, FL 34649: Free catalog ❖ Art and craft supplies. 813–536–1492.

Factory Direct Craft Supplies, 440 Conover Dr., P.O. Box 16, Franklin, OH 45005: Catalog $2 ❖ Art and craft supplies. 513–743–5855.

Fairfield Processing Corporation, P.O. Box 1130, Danbury, CT 06813: Free information ❖ Fiberfill and batting products. 800–442–2271; 203–371–1901 (in CT).

Freudenberg/Pellon, 1040 Avenue of Americas, New York, NY 10018: Free information ❖ Supplies for bonding fabrics to fabric, cardboard, wood, and other porous surfaces. 800–223–5275; 212–391–6308 (in NY).

Grey Owl Indian Craft Company, P.O. Box 468, Jamaica, NY 11434: Catalog $3 ❖ Supplies and kits for making Native American crafts. 718–341–4000.

Guildcraft Company, 100 Firetower Dr., Tonawanda, NY 14150: Free catalog ❖ Supplies for crafting with foil, chair caning, basket-making, plaster crafts, candle and wood crafting, leather and egg crafting, and fabric dyeing. 716–743–8336.

House of Crafts & Stuff, 5157 Gall Blvd., Zephyrhills, FL 33541: Catalog $2 ❖

Needlework, bead-crafting, doll-making, and other craft supplies.

Kathy's Discount Craft Supply, P.O. Box 18025, Fountain Hills, AZ 85269: Free catalog ❖ Craft, floral, wicker, and wedding supplies.

Kirchen Brothers, Box 1016, Skokie, IL 60076: Catalog $2 ❖ Art and craft supplies. 708–647–6747.

Luv 'n Stuff, P.O. Box 85, Poway, CA 92074: Catalog $2 ❖ Sewing supplies, rubber stamps, and patterns for dolls, stuffed animals, holiday decorations, and ornaments. 619–748–8060.

Mountain Crafts, 163 E. Main St., Little Falls, NJ 07424: Free catalog ❖ Craft kits, candle-making supplies, and gemstones. 201–256–3669.

Nasco, 901 Janesville Ave., Fort Atkinson, WI 53538: Free catalog ❖ Supplies for art projects, calligraphy, leather crafting, metal enameling, ceramics, photography, and needle crafts. 800–558–9595.

National Artcraft Company, 23456 Mercantile Rd., Beachwood, OH 44122: Catalog $4 ❖ Tools and supplies for floral crafting and for making clocks, lamps, dolls, candles, and jewelry. 800–793–0152.

Oppenheim's, 120 E. Main St., North Manchester, IN 46962: Free catalog ❖ Sewing notions, fabrics, and craft supplies. 219–982–6848.

Pyramid of Urbana, 2107 N. High Cross Rd., Urbana, IL 61801: Catalog $5 ❖ Art and craft supplies, office and school equipment, and calligraphy and lettering supplies. 217–328–3099.

Red Hill Corporation, P.O. Box 4234, Gettysburg, PA 17325: Free catalog ❖ Hot melt glue sticks, glue guns, and sandpaper belts, sheets, and discs. 800–822–4003.

Ribbons & Lace, Box 30070, Mesa, AZ 85272: Catalog $3 (refundable) ❖ Laces, ribbons, craft supplies, and beads.

Sax Arts & Crafts, P.O. Box 51710, New Berlin, WI 51710: Free catalog ❖ Art and craft supplies. 800–558–6696; 414–784–6880 (in WI).

Schrock's Crafts & Hobby World, 1527 E. Amherst Rd., P.O. Box 1136, Massillon, OH 44648: Catalog $3 ❖ Art and craft and needlework supplies. 216–837–8845.

Suncoast Discount Arts & Crafts Warehouse, 9015 US 19 North, Pinellas Park, FL 34666: Catalog $1 ❖ Art and craft supplies. 813–572–1600.

Sunshine Discount Crafts, 12335 62nd St. North, Largo, FL 34643: Catalog $2 ❖ Art and craft supplies. 813–538–2878.

Supplies 4 Less, 13001 Las Vegas Blvd., Las Vegas, NV 89124: Catalog $3.50 ❖ Laces, appliques, ribbons, other craft supplies, flowers, and how-to books.

United Supply Company Inc., P.O. Box 9219, Fort Wayne, IN 46899: Free catalog ❖ Art and craft supplies, books, and tools. 800–322–3247.

Vanguard Crafts Inc., P.O. Box 340170, Brooklyn, NY 11234: Free catalog ❖ Art and craft supplies. 800–662–7238; 718–377–5188 (in NY).

Warscokins, 17930 Magnolia, Fountain Valley, CA 92708: Catalog $3.50 ❖ Art and craft supplies. 800–225–6356; 714–962–8991 (in CA).

Weaving Works, 4717 Brooklyn Ave. NE, Seattle, WA 98105: Catalog $4.50 ❖ Supplies for making baskets, dyeing, weaving, spinning, and knitting. 206–524–1221.

West Mountain Gourd Farm, Rt. 1, Box 853, Gilmer, TX 75644: Information $2 ❖ Ready-to-paint gourds. 903–734–5204.

Zimmerman's Discount Craft Supplies, 2884 34th St. North, St. Petersburg, FL 33713: Catalog $2 ❖ Art and craft supplies. 813–526–4880.

CRICKET

American Sports Inc., 735 S. Mansfield Ave., Los Angeles, CA 90036: Free information with list of retailers ❖ Bats, balls, and gloves. 800–922–8939.

General Sportcraft Company Ltd., 140 Woodbine Rd., Bergenfield, NJ 07621: Free information ❖ Bats, balls, and gloves. 201–384–4242.

Genesport Industries Ltd., Hokkaido Karate Equipment Manufacturing Company, 150 King St., Montreal, Quebec, Canada H3C 2P3: Free information ❖ Bats, balls, and gloves. 514–861–1856.

Don Jagoda Associates Inc., 1 Underhill Blvd., Syosset, NY 11791: Free information ❖ Bats, balls, and gloves. 516–496–7300.

CROQUET

Cannon Sports, P.O. Box 11179, Burbank, CA 91510: Free information with list of retailers ❖ Croquet sets. 800–362–3146; 818–753–5940 (in CA).

Clarkpoint Croquet Company, P.O. Box 457, Southwest Harbor, ME 04679: Free information with long SASE ❖ Croquet sets. 207–244–9284.

Escalade Sports, P.O. Box 889, Evansville, IN 47706: Free information ❖ Croquet accessories. 800–457–3373; 812–467–1200 (in IN).

Forster Manufacturing Company, P.O. Box 657, Wilton, ME 04294: Free information ❖ Croquet sets. 800–341–7574; 207–645–2574 (in ME).

Indian Industries Inc., P.O. Box 889, Evansville, IN 47706: Free catalog ❖ Sets. 800–457–3373; 812–467–1200 (in IN).

Market Square, P.O. Box 1188, Westbrook, ME 04098: Free information ❖ Croquet sets. 800–675–8203.

Olympia Sports, 745 State Cir., Ann Arbor, MI 48106: Free information ❖ Croquet sets. 800–521–2832; 313–761–5135 (in MI).

Pennsylvania Sporting Goods, 1360 Industrial Hwy., P.O. Box 451, Southhampton, PA 18966: Free information ❖ Croquet accessories. 800–535–1122.

Porter Athletic Equipment Company, 2500 S. 25th Ave., Broadview, IL 60153: Free information ❖ Croquet sets. 708–338–2000.

Regent Sports Corporation, 45 Ranick Rd., Hauppage, NY 11788: Free information ❖ Croquet sets. 516–234–2800.

Russell Corporation, Russell Athletic Division, P.O. Box 272, Alexander City, AL 35010: Free information ❖ Croquet sets. 205–329–4000.

Spalding Sports Worldwide, 425 Meadow St., P.O. Box 901, Chicopee, MA 01201: Free information ❖ Croquet accessories. 800–225–6601

Sportime, 1 Sporting Way, Atlanta, GA 30340: Free information ❖ Croquet accessories. 800–444–5700; 404–449–5700 (in GA).

CRYSTAL & GLASSWARE

Alberene Crystal, 3222 M St. NW, Washington, DC 20007: Free information ❖ Edinburgh and Thomas Webb crystal and Perthshire paperweights. Includes

discontinued items. 800–843–9078.

Baccarat, 625 Madison Ave., New York, NY 10022: Free information ❖ Crystal and china Baccarat. 212–826–4100.

Barrons, P.O. Box 994, Novi, MI 48376: Free information ❖ China, crystal, and silver. 800–538–6340.

Mildred Brumback, P.O. Box 132, Middletown, VA 22645: Free information ❖ Discontinued china and crystal patterns. 703–869–1261.

China & Crystal Marketing, P.O. Box 33, Cheltenham, PA 19012: Free information ❖ Discontinued china and crystal. 215–342–7919.

The China Cabinet, P.O. Box 426, Clearwater, SC 29822: Free information with long SASE ❖ China and crystal. 803–593–9655.

China Replacements, 2263 Williams Creek Rd., High Ridge, MO 63049: Free information with long SASE ❖ Discontinued china and crystal. 800–562–2655; 677–5577 (in St. Louis).

The China Warehouse, Box 21797, Cleveland, OH 44121: Free information ❖ China, crystal, and flatware. 800–321–3212.

Clintsman International, 20855 Watertown Rd., Waukesha, WI 53186: Free information ❖ Discontinued china, crystal, and flatware. 414–798–0440.

Crystal d'Arques, Durand International, P.O. Box 5001, Millville, NJ 08332: Free information ❖ Crystal d'Arques from France. 800–334–5014.

Crystal Lalique, 680 Madison Ave., New York, NY 10021: Free information ❖ Crystal and china Lalique. 800–214–2738; 212–355–6550 (in NY).

Dartington Crystal, 77 Ivy Way, Port Washington, NY 11050: Free information ❖ Crystal Dartington.

Dining Elegance Ltd., Box 4203, St. Louis, MO 63163: Free catalog ❖ China and crystal. 314–865–1408.

Greater New York Trading, 81 Canal St., New York, NY 10002: Free brochure ❖ Silver, china, and glassware. 212–226–2808.

Jacquelyn Hall, 10629 Baxter, Los Altos, CA 94022: Free information ❖ Lenox china and crystal replacements. 408–739–4876.

Heirloom Completions, 1620 Venice, Granite, IL 62040: Free information ❖

Matching china and silverplate replacement pieces. 618–931–4333.

Hoya Crystal Gallery, 450 Park Ave., New York, NY 10022: Catalog $5 ❖ Art sculptures, vases, bowls, glass stemware, ornamental pieces, and crystal clocks. 800–462–HOYA.

Iittala Crystal, Rt. 6, Mahopac, NY 10541: Free information ❖ Iittala glass from Finland. 800–678–2667.

Lanac Sales, 73 Canal St., New York, NY 10002: Free catalog ❖ Crystal, china, and sterling. 212–925–6422.

Lenox Collections, P.O. Box 3020, Langhorne, PA 19047: Free catalog ❖ China, crystal, and porcelain sculptures. 800–225–1779.

Locators Inc., 908 Rock St., Little Rock, AR 72202: Free information ❖ Discontinued china, crystal, and silver. 800–367–9690.

Luigi Crystal, 7332 Frankford Ave., Philadelphia, PA 19136: Catalog $2 ❖ Table lamps, cut crystal chandeliers, hurricane lamps, sconces, other crystal accessories, and decor pieces. 215–338–2978.

Miki's Crystal Registry, Box 22506, Robbinsdale, MN 55422: Free information ❖ Fostoria crystal matching service. 800–628–9394.

Orrefors Kosta Boda USA, 58 E. 57th St., New York, NY 10022: Free information ❖ Orrefors crystal. 800–351–9842; 212–753–3442 (in NY).

Past & Presents, 65–07 Fitchett St., Rego Park, NY 11374: Free information ❖ Replacement crystal, china, and flatware. 718–897–5515.

Replacements Ltd., 1089 Knox Rd., P.O. Box 26029, Greensboro, NC 27029: Free information with long SASE ❖ Discontinued bone china, earthenware, and crystal. 800–562–4462.

Robin Importers, 510 Madison Ave., New York, NY 10022: Brochure $1 with long SASE ❖ China, crystal, and stainless steel flatware. 800–223–3373; 212–753–6475 (in NY).

Rogers & Rosenthal, 22 W. 48th St., Room 1102, New York, NY 10036: Free information with long SASE ❖ Crystal, china, silver, silver plate, and stainless steel. 212–827–0115.

Rudi's Pottery, Silver & China, 176 Rt. 17, Paramus, NJ 07652: Free information with long SASE ❖ Glass stemware, china, and gifts. 201–265–6096.

Scandinavian Specialties Ltd., 12768 Ripple Creek Ct., Woodbridge, VA 22192: Free catalog ❖ Gränna Glas, 100 percent lead crystal from Sweden. 703–497–4317.

Steuben Glass, Customer Relations, Corning Glass Center, Corning, NY 14831: Catalog $8 ❖ Steuben crystal and other gifts. 800–424–4240.

Waterford Crystal Inc., 41 Madison Ave., New York, NY 10010: Free brochure ❖ Crystal and china.

Zucker's Fine Gifts, 151 W. 26th St., New York, NY 10001: Free catalog ❖ Hummel, Swarovski silver and crystal, Waterford crystal, Lladro porcelain, and other gifts. 212–989–1450.

CURTAINS, DRAPES & BLINDS

Blinds & Window Shades

All States Decorating Network, 810 Main St., Toms River, NJ 08753: Free information ❖ Blinds and verticals. 800–334–8590.

American Blind & Wallpaper Factory, 28237 Orchard Lake Rd., Farmington Hills, MI 48018: Free information ❖ Roller and pleated shades and wood, micro and mini, and vertical blinds. 800–735–5300.

Blind Center USA, 7013 3rd Ave., Brooklyn, NY 11209: Free information ❖ Vertical, mini, micro, duettes, and wood blinds. 800–676–5029.

Blinds 'N Things, 516 Jefferson Blvd., Birmingham, AL 35217: Free information ❖ Micro and mini blinds and other window treatments. 205–849–9045.

Colorel Blinds, 8200 E. Park Meadows Dr., Littleton, CO 80124: Free information ❖ Window treatments. 800–877–4800.

Custom Windows & Walls, 32525 Stephenson Hwy., Madison Heights, MI 48071: Free information ❖ Mini blinds. 800–772–1947.

Devenco Products Inc., Box 700, Decatur, GA 30031: Free brochure ❖ Period reproductions of wood blinds and plantation-style, traditional, and movable shutters. Also exterior shutters. 800–888–4597; 404–378–4597 (in GA).

Goodman Fabrications, P.O. Box 8164, Prairie Village, KS 66208: Free brochure ❖ Roller shades, draperies, curtains, and wood venetian blinds. 816–942–0832.

Headquarters Windows & Walls, 8 Clinton Pl., Morristown, NJ 07960: Free information ❖ Wall coverings and micro, mini, verticals, and pleated blinds. 800–338–4882.

Hunter Douglas Window Fashions, 2 Duette Way, Broomfield, CO 80020: Free information ❖ Window coverings. 800–32–STYLE.

Kestrel Manufacturing, P.O. Box 12, Saint Peters, PA 19470: Information $2 ❖ Knock-down and ready-to-hang folding screens and interior and exterior shutters. 610–469–6444.

National Blind & Wallpaper Factory, 400 Galleria, Southfield, MI 48034: Free information ❖ Window blinds. 800–477–8000.

Peerless Wallpaper & Blind Depot, 39500 14 Mile Rd., Walled Lake, MI 48390: Free information ❖ Wallcoverings and blinds. 800–999–0898.

The Shutter Depot, Rt. 2, Box 157, Greenville, GA 30222: Free brochure ❖ Interior and exterior raised panel and fixed louver shutters. 706–672–1214.

Shuttercraft, 282 Stepstone Hill Rd., Guilford, CT 06437: Free brochure ❖ Moveable door fixed louver and raised panel shutters. 203–453–1973.

Silver's Wholesale Club, 3001–15 Kensington Ave., Philadelphia, PA 19134: Free information ❖ Wallcoverings, blinds, and verticals. 800–426–6600.

3 Day Blinds, Attn: Mail Order, 2220 E. Cerrit Ave., Anaheim, CA 92806: Free information ❖ Pleated shades and vertical, mini, and wood blinds. 800–966–3DAY.

USA Blind Factory, 1312 Live Oak, Houston, TX 77003: Free information ❖ Vertical, pleated, mini, micro, and wood blinds. 800–275–3219.

Wallpaperxpress, P.O. Box 4061, Naperville, IL 60567: Free information ❖ Wallcoverings, fabrics, and mini blinds. 800–288–9979.

Wells Interiors, 7171 Amador Valley Plaza Rd., Dublin, CA 95468: Free catalog ❖ Kits for energy-efficient Roman shades or adding fabric to existing decor arrangements and mini, wood, vertical, pleated, and woven wood blinds. 800–547–8982.

Wholesale Verticals, P.O. Box 305, Baldwin, NY 11510: Free information ❖ Minis, verticals, pleated shades, duettes, wood blinds, and drapery hardware. 800–762–2748.

Window Scapes, 11211 Sorrento Valley Rd., San Diego, CA 92121: Free information ❖ Vertical, pleated, mini, micro, and wood blinds. 800–786–3021.

Worldwide Wallcoverings & Blinds Inc., 333 Skokie Blvd., Northbrook, IL 60062: Free information with long SASE ❖ Wallcoverings and blinds. 800–322–5400.

Curtains & Drapes

Martin Albert Interior Inc., 288 Grand St., New York, NY 10002: Free information ❖ Drapery hardware and window treatments. 212–226–4047.

Bucks Trading Post, 930 Old Bethlehem Pike, Sellersville, PA 18960: Catalog $2 ❖ European lace curtains and matching tablecloths and doilies. 800–242–0738; 215–453–0623 (in PA).

Caroline's Country Ruffles, 420 W. Franklin Blvd., Gastona, NC 28052: Catalog $2 ❖ Curtains. 800–426–1039.

Country Curtains, Red Lion Inn, Stockbridge, MA 01262: Free catalog ❖ Cotton muslin or permanent-press country-style curtains. 413–243–1474.

Curtains Up, 2709 S. Park Rd., Louisville, KY 40219: Free information ❖ Drapery accessories. 502–969–1464.

Designer Secrets, P.O. Box 529, Fremont, NE 68025: Catalog $2 (refundable) ❖ Window treatments, wall coverings, fabrics, bedspreads, and furniture. 800–955–2559.

Dianthus Ltd., P.O. Box 870, Plymouth, MA 02362: Catalog $6 ❖ Curtains with a country look. 508–747–4179.

Dimestore Cowboys, 4500 Hawkins NE, Albuquerque, NM 87109: Catalog $7 ❖ Door sets, cabinet pulls, shutters, bathroom accessories, curtain rods and rings, and other handcrafted hardware. 505–345–3933.

Dorothy's Ruffled Originals Inc., 8112 Market St., Wilmington, NC 28405: Catalog $4 ❖ Ruffled curtains and other window treatments. 800–367–6849.

Especially Lace, 202 5th St., West Des Moines, IA 50265: Catalog $4.50 ❖

European lace curtains and ready-to-hang valances. 515–277–8778.

Fabric Shop, 120 N. Seneca St., Shippensburg, PA 17257: Free information with long SASE ❖ Draperies, antique satins, and fabrics for slipcovers and upholstery. 800–233–7012; 717–532–4150 (in PA).

Fabrics by Phone, P.O. Box 309, Walnut Bottom, PA 17266: Brochure and samples $3 ❖ Draperies, antique satins, and slipcover and upholstery fabrics. 800–233–7012; 717–532–4150 (in PA).

Faith's Lacery, 89 W. Main St., Dundee, IL 60118: Catalog $2 ❖ Valances, cafes, swags, door panels, country lace and Victorian curtains, runners, and table overlays.

Virginia Goodwin, Rt. 2, Box 770, Boone, NC 28607: Information $1 ❖ Window valances, hand-tied fishnet bed canopies, dust ruffles, and bed spreads. 800–735–5191.

Harding's Custom Sheers, 807 S. Auburn, Grass Valley, CA 95945: Free brochure ❖ Pleated seamless sheers. 800–228–0825.

Linen & Lace, 4 Lafayette, Washington, MO 63090: Catalog $2 ❖ Linen and imported Bavarian lace curtains, runners, and accent pillows. 800–332–5223.

London Lace, 167 Newbury St., Boston, MA 02116: Catalog $2.50 ❖ Lace window coverings. 800–926–LACE.

Mather's Department Store, 31 E. Main St., Westminster, MD 21157: Free catalog ❖ Country-style curtains and other window treatments. 410–848–6410.

Rue de France, 78 Thames St., Newport, RI 02840: Catalog $3 ❖ Lace curtains, tablecloths, runners, and pillows. 800–777–0998.

Seraph, 5606 State Route 37, Delaware, OH 43015: Catalog $4 ❖ Bed hangings and window treatments with coordinating rugs and accessories. 614–369–1817.

South Bound Millworks, P.O. Box 349, Sandwich, MA 02563: Catalog $1 (refundable) ❖ Wood curtain rods and brackets and wrought-iron accessories. 508–477–9355.

Vintage Valances, P.O. Box 43326, Cincinnati, OH 45243: Catalog $12 ❖ Ready-to-hang period-style drapes, bed hangings, and window shades, from 1800 to 1930. 513–561–8665.

Window Quilt, P.O. Box 975, Brattleboro, VT 05301: Information $1 ❖ Insulating window shades. 800–257–4501.

DANCING
Ballet Barres

Alva Barres, 1417 W. 8th St., San Pedro, CA 90732: Free brochure ❖ Wall-mounted and free-standing ballet barres. 213–519–1314.

Ballet Barres Inc., P.O. Box 261206, Tampa, FL 33685: Free catalog ❖ Dance shoes, bodywear, legwear, and ballet barres. 800–767–1199.

Victoria's Dance-Theatrical Supply, 1331 Lincoln Ave., San Jose, CA 95125: Catalog $2 ❖ Portable wall-mounted ballet barres, dance shoes, dancewear, and make-up. 408–295–9317.

Clothing & Costumes

Apparel Warehouse, 6010 Yolanda St., Tarzana, CA 91356: Free catalog ❖ Briefs, leotards, dance belts, leg warmer socks, and cotton, shiny, and spandex tights. 800–245–8434; 818–344–3224 (in CA).

Ballet Barres Inc., P.O. Box 261206, Tampa, FL 33685: Free catalog ❖ Dance shoes, bodywear, legwear, and ballet barres. 800–767–1199.

Baum's Inc., 106 S. 11th St., Philadelphia, PA 19107: Free catalog with request on school stationery ❖ Costumes, leotards, shoes, fabrics, and majorette items. 215–923–2244.

Carushka Inc., 7716 Kester Ave., Van Nuys, CA 91406: Catalog $2 ❖ Women's bodywear, leotards, tank tops, trunks, and bike tights. 818–904–0574.

Chatila Dance & Gymnastic Fashions, P.O. Box 508, Staten Island, NY 10304: Free catalog with request on school stationery ❖ Bodywear, lyrical dresses, and tap, ballet, and jazz shoes. 718–720–3632.

Cicci Dance Supplies, 3594 Washington Ave., Finleyville, PA 15332: Free catalog with request on school stationery ❖ Dance costumes. 412–348–7359.

Costume Gallery, 1604 South Rt. 130, Burlington, NJ 08016: Free catalog with request on school stationery ❖ Costumes and other dancewear.

The Costume Shop, 253 Broad St., P.O. Box 1497, Manchester, CT 06045: Free catalog with request on school stationery ❖ Dance costumes. 203–646–5758.

Curtain Call Costumes, 333 E. 7th Ave., P.O. Box 709, York, PA 17405: Free catalog ❖ Dancing attire. 717–852–6910.

Dance Shop, 2485 Forest Park Blvd., Fort Worth, TX 76110: Free catalog ❖ Shoes and bodywear.

Dansant Boutique, 6623 Old Dominion Dr., McLean, VA 22101: Free catalog ❖ Dancewear, leotards, tights, and shoes. 703–448–9655.

Danskin, 111 W. 40th St., 18th Floor, New York, NY 10018: Free information ❖ Leotards, tights, costumes, ballet shoes, swimsuits, lingerie, and hosiery. 800–288–6749; 212–764–4630 (in NY).

Dazian's Inc., 2014 Commerce St., Dallas, TX 75201: Free catalog ❖ Leotards, tights, other dancewear, costume fabrics, trimmings, and novelties. 214–748–3450.

Freed of London Inc., 922 S. 7th Ave., New York, NY 10019: Free price list ❖ Soft ballet slippers, leotards and ballroom attire, exercise wear, and pointe, jazz, character, and gym shoes. 212–489–1055.

Hoctor Products, P.O. Box 38, Waldwick, NJ 07463: Free catalog ❖ Costumes, records, dance routines, videos, cassettes, phonographs and cassette players, and video recorders. 201–652–7767.

Illinois Theatrical, P.O. Box 34284, Chicago, IL 60634: Free catalog with request on school stationery ❖ Costumes. 800–745–3777.

Instructor's Choice, Oakbrook Sales Corporation, 1750 Merrick Ave., Merrick, NY 11566: Free information ❖ Tights, leotards, and unitards. 800–622–7667.

Kling's Theatrical Shoe Company, 218 S. Wabash Ave., Chicago, IL 60604: Catalog 50¢ ❖ Shoes and dancewear. 312–427–2028.

Lebo's of Charlotte Inc., 4118 E. Independence Blvd., Charlotte, NC 28205: Free catalog with request on school stationery ❖ Costumes, footwear, leotards, tights, fabrics, record players, tapes, and records. 704–535–5000.

Leo's Dancewear Inc., 1900 N. Narragansett Ave., Chicago, IL 60639: Free catalog with request on school stationery ❖ Dance costumes. 312–889–7700.

Loshin's Dancewear, 260 W. Mitchell Ave., Cincinnati, OH 45232: Free catalog with request on school stationery ❖ Costumes, leotards, tights, sequin trimmings, tiaras, hats, and shoes. 513–541–5400.

Lynch's Clown Supplies, 939 Howard, Dearborn, MI 48124: Catalog $5 ❖ Dancewear, shoes, super tone taps, sequin appliques and trim, sequin fabrics, rhinestones, hats, and make-up. 313–565–3425.

Physical Fashions, 289 Allwood Rd., Clifton, NJ 07012: Free information ❖ Dancewear for children and adults. 800–24–DANCE; 201–773–3887 (in NJ).

Repetto Dance Shoes, 30 Lincoln Plaza, New York, NY 10023: Free information ❖ Classical ballet and contemporary dancewear and shoes. 212–582–3900.

Rising House Boutique, 56 Grand Summit Rd., Cambridge, KS 67023: Catalog $2 ❖ Leotards, tights, and pointe, ballet, and jazz shoes. 316–467–4251.

H.W. Shaw Inc., P.O. Box 4034, Hollywood, FL 33083: Free catalog ❖ Dancewear. 800–327–9548; 305–989–1300 (in FL).

Star Styled Dancewear, P.O. Box 1805, Hialeah, FL 33011: Free information ❖ Bodywear for dancers. 800–634–4628.

Art Stone Dancewear, 1795 Express Dr. North, Smithtown, NY 11787: Free catalog with request on school stationery ❖ Bodywear and footwear for dancers. 516–582–9500.

Taffy's-by-Mail, 701 Beta Dr., Cleveland, OH 44143: Catalog $3 ❖ Dancewear, shoes, videos, and books. 216–461–3360.

Victoria's Dance-Theatrical Supply, 1331 Lincoln Ave., San Jose, CA 95125: Catalog $2 ❖ Portable wall-mounted ballet barres, dance shoes, dancewear, and make-up. 408–295–9317.

Weissman's Designs for Dance, 1600 Macklind Ave., St. Louis, MO 63110: Free catalog with request on school stationery ❖ Costumes. 314–773–9000.

R.B. Williams Company Inc., 157 6th Ave. NE, St. Petersburg, FL 33701: Free information ❖ Dance sweat pants in small, medium, and large. 800–843–7346; 813–822–1602 (in FL).

A Wish Come True, 2500 Pearl Buck Rd., Bristol, PA 19007: Free catalog with request on school stationery ❖ Costumes. 215–781–2022.

Music

Dansounds, P.O. Box 27618, Philadelphia, PA 19118: Free information ❖ Music for ballet dance classes.

Hoctor Products, P.O. Box 38, Waldwick, NJ 07463: Free catalog ❖ Records, cassettes, dance routines, cassette players, video recorders, phonographs, and books. 201–652–7767.

Hot Pink Productions, 304 Trindale Rd., High Point, NC 27263: Free information ❖ All-original dance music. 919–431–2017.

Jay Distributors, Box 191332, Dallas, TX 75219: Free information ❖ Records and tapes. 800–793–6843.

Lebo's of Charlotte Inc., 4118 E. Independence Blvd., Charlotte, NC 28205: Free catalog with request on school stationery ❖ Costumes, dancewear, footwear, leotards and tights, fabrics, record players, tapes, and records. 704–535–5000.

Ray Records, 754 New Ballas Rd., Creve Coeur, MO 63141: Free brochure ❖ Tap dancing music. 314–432–3890.

Roper Records, P.O. Box 4386, Long Island City, NY 11104: Free catalog ❖ Ballet and ballroom dance music.

Shoes

A Pied Manufacturing Company, 2821 N. 4th St., Milwaukee, WI 53212: Free catalog ❖ Ballet shoes. 800–762–3138.

Capezio Factory Store, Southwest Outlet Center, I-35 Northeast, Ste. 107, Hillsboro, TX 76645: Free information with long SASE ❖ Shoes. 817–582–7396.

Chatila Dance & Gymnastic Fashions, P.O. Box 508, Staten Island, NY 10304: Free catalog with request on school stationery ❖ Bodywear, lyrical dresses, and tap, ballet, and jazz shoes. 718–720–3632.

Coast Shoes Inc., 13401 Saticoy, North Hollywood, CA 91605: Free brochure ❖ Tap, jazz, ballet, and character dance shoes. 800–262–7851.

Danskin, 111 W. 40th St., 18th Floor, New York, NY 10018: Free information ❖ Ballet shoes, costumes, leotards, tights, swimsuits, lingerie, and hosiery. 800–288–6749; 212–764–4630 (in NY).

Freed of London Inc., 922 S. 7th Ave., New York, NY 10019: Free price list ❖ Pointe shoes, soft ballet slippers, jazz and character shoes, ballet accessories, and leotards. 212–489–1055.

Grishko, 1320 Huntsman Ln., Glaywyne, PA 19035: Free information ❖ Glove leather and long-wearing canvas dancing shoes. 215–527–9553.

Kling's Theatrical Shoe Company, 218 S. Wabash Ave., Chicago, IL 60604: Catalog 50¢ ❖ Shoes and dancewear. 312–427–2028.

La Mendola, 1795 Express Dr. North, Smithtown, NY 11787: Free information ❖ Lyrical/ballet shoes. 516–582–3230.

La Ray, 633 Alacci Way, River Vale, NJ 07675: Free information ❖ Toe shoes and ballet slippers. 201–664–5882.

Loshin's Dancewear, 260 W. Mitchell Ave., Cincinnati, OH 45232: Free catalog with request on school stationery ❖ Costumes, leotards, tights, sequin trimmings, tiaras, hats, and shoes. 513–541–5400.

Lynch's Clown Supplies Inc., 939 Howard, Dearborn, MI 48124: Catalog $5 ❖ Dancewear, shoes, super tone taps, sequin appliques and trim, sequin fabrics, rhinestones, hats, and make-up. 313–565–3425.

Miguelito's Dancewear, 7315 San Pedro Ave., San Antonio, TX 78216: Free information ❖ Ballet shoes, flamenco boots, and gymnastic wear. 210–349–2573.

Repetto Dance Shoes, 30 Lincoln Plaza, New York, NY 10023: Free information ❖ Classical ballet and contemporary dancewear and shoes. 212–582–3900.

Rising House Boutique, 56 Grand Summit Rd., Cambridge, KS 67023: Catalog $2 ❖ Leotards, tights, and pointe, ballet, and jazz shoes. 316–467–4251.

Sansha, 1733 Broadway, New York, NY 10019: Free information ❖ Soft ballet and pointe shoes and jazz shoes and boots. 212–246–6212.

Soloist & Company USA, 60 Brown Ave., Springfield, NJ 07081: Free information ❖ Pointe shoes. 201–912–8808.

Art Stone Dancewear, 1795 Express Dr. North, Smithtown, NY 11787: Free catalog with request on school stationery ❖ Bodywear and footwear for dancers. 516–582–9500.

Taffy's-by-Mail, 701 Beta Dr., Cleveland, OH 44143: Catalog $3 ❖ Tap, jazz, pointed, and ballet shoes, and jazz boots, and dancewear. 216–461–3360.

Victoria's Dance-Theatrical Supply, 1331 Lincoln Ave., San Jose, CA 95125: Catalog $2 ❖ Portable wall-mounted ballet barres, dance shoes, dancewear, and make-up. 408–295–9317.

DARTS

Accudart, 160 E. Union Ave., East Rutherford, NJ 07073: Free catalog ❖ Darts and dart boards. 800–526–0451; 201–438–9000 (in NJ).

Al's American Dartboards, 18 Weaver Ave., Waterford, NY 12188: Free information ❖ Darts and dartboards. 518–235–4012.

American Dartlines, 2350 S. Meredith Ln., Santa Maria, CA 93455: Free information ❖ Darts. 805–922–5445.

Amerola Sports Inc., 4719 Hatfield St., Pittsburgh, PA 15201: Free information ❖ Dart boards and cabinets, dart-making supplies, and sets. 800–426–3765.

Buck Knives, P.O. Box 1267, El Cajon, CA 92022: Free information ❖ Darts and dartboards. 800–326–2825; 619–449–1100 (in CA).

Dart Mart Inc., 2255 Computer Ave., Willow Grove, PA 19090: Free information ❖ Dart boards, cabinets, dart-making supplies, and sets. 800–423–3220; 215–830–0501 (in PA).

Dart World Inc., P.O. Box 845, Lynn, MA 01904: Free information ❖ Dart boards, cabinets, dart-making supplies, and sets. 800–225–2558; 617–581–6035 (in MA).

Darts Unlimited, 282 N. Henry St., Brooklyn, NY 11222: Free information ❖ Dart boards, cabinets, dart-making supplies, and sets. 718–389–7755.

Dunlop Stazenger Corporation, P.O. Box 3070, Greenville, SC 29602: Free information ❖ Darts and dartboards. 800–845–8794; 803–271–9767 (in SC).

Escalade Sports, P.O. Box 889, Evansville, IN 47706: Free catalog ❖ Dartboards, darts, and cabinets. 800–457–3373; 812–467–1200 (in IN).

Franklin Sports Industries Inc., 17 Campanelli Pkwy., P.O. Box 508, Stoughton, MA 02072: Free information ❖ Dart boards, cabinets, and sets. 617–344–1111.

General Sportcraft Company Ltd., 140 Woodbine Rd., Bergenfield, NJ 07621: Free information ❖ Dart boards, cabinets, dart-making supplies, and sets. 201–384–4242.

Great Lakes Dart Distributors Inc., 3125 S. 108th St., West Allis, WI 53227: Free information ❖ Darts. 800–225–7593.

Horizon Dart Supply, 2415 S. 50th St., Kansas City, MO 66106: Free information ❖ Darts and dartboards. 913–236–9111.

Indian Industries Inc., P.O. Box 889, Evansville, IN 47706: Free catalog ❖ Dart boards, cabinets, dart-making supplies, and sets. 800–457–3373; 812–467–1200 (in IN).

Don Jagoda Associates Inc., 1 Underhill Blvd., Syosset, NY 11791: Free information ❖ Boards, cases, darts, and dart-making supplies. 516–496–7300.

Marksman Products, 5482 Argosy Dr., Huntington Beach, CA 92649: Free information ❖ Dart boards, cabinets, dart-making supplies, and sets. 714–898–7535.

Mueller Sporting Goods Inc., 4825 S. 16th, Lincoln, NE 68512: Free catalog ❖ Billiard and dart supplies. 800–925–7665; 402–423–8888 (in NE).

Pennray Billiard & Recreational Products, 6400 W. Gross Point Rd., Niles, IL 60714: Free catalog ❖ Darts, billiards, and soccer equipment. 800–523–8934.

Pennsylvania Sporting Goods, 1360 Industrial Hwy., P.O. Box 451, Southampton, PA 18966: Free information ❖ Dart boards, cabinets, dart-making supplies, and sets. 800–535–1122.

Regent Sports Corporation, 45 Ranick Rd., Hauppage, NY 11788: Free information ❖ Darts and dartboards. 516–234– 2800.

Spalding Sports Worldwide, 425 Meadow St., P.O. Box 901, Chicopee, MA 01021: Free information with list of retailers ❖ Dart boards, cabinets, dart-making supplies, and sets. 800–225–6601.

Sportime, 1 Sportime Way, Atlanta, GA 30340: Free information ❖ Darts and dartboards. 800–444–5700; 404–449–5700 (in GA).

Tide-Rider Inc., P.O. Box 429, Oakdale, CA 95361: Free information ❖ Dart boards, cabinets, dart-making supplies, and sets. 209–848–4420.

Valley Recreation Products Inc., Box 656, Bay City, MI 48707: Free information ❖ Dart boards. cabinets, dart-making supplies, and sets. 800–248–2837; 517–892–4536 (in MI).

DECALS, EMBLEMS & PATCHES

A.T. Patch Company, Littleton, NH 03561: Free catalog ❖ Embroidered emblems, decals, and enameled pins. 603–444–3423.

Adhatters, Box 667, Effingham, IL 62401: Free information ❖ Patches, pins, and decals. 800–225–7642.

Conrad Industries, P.O. Box 695, Weaverville, NC 28787: Free catalog ❖ Embroidered emblems. 704–064–3015.

Eastern Emblem, Box 828, Union City, NJ 07087: Free catalog ❖ Patches, cloisonne pins, decals, stickers, T-shirts, caps, and jackets. 800–344–5112.

Fagel EMS Specialties, 68 Canterbury, Aurora, IL 60506: Free catalog ❖ Embroidered emblems and reflective/vinyl decals. 708–897–9068.

Hoover's Manufacturing Company, 4015 Progress Blvd., Peru, IL 61354: Free catalog ❖ Dog tag key rings, beer and coffee mugs, Zippo lighters, belt buckles, patches, flags, and Vietnam, Korea, and World War II hat pins. 815–223–1159.

HSU Patches, P.O. Box 700310, San Jose, CA 95170: Free information ❖ Embroidered patches. 408–252–0162.

Frosty Little, 222 E. 8th St., Burley, ID 83318: Free information ❖ Sweatshirts, T-shirts, pins, and patches with clown graphics. 208–678–0005.

Microscale Industries Inc., P.O. Box 11950, Costa Mesa, CA 92627: Catalog $2 ❖ Microscale decals for decorating miniatures.

Mr. Ed The Sign Man, P.O. Box 303, Crystal Beach, FL 34681: Free information ❖ Magnetic signs, name badges, and vinyl lettering.

Musashi International, 1842 S. Grand Ave., Santa Ana, CA 92705: Free information ❖ Patches. 714–557–4274.

Namark Cap & Emblem Company, 6325 Harrison Dr., Las Vegas, NV 89120: Free information ❖ Screen-printed emblems, caps, T-shirts, and jackets. 800–634–6271.

Phoenix Emblems, 71 Tinker St., Woodstock, NY 12498: Free information ❖ Embroidered patches. 908–287–9482.

Recco Maid Embroidery Company, 4626 W. Cornelia Ave., Chicago, IL 60641: Free catalog ❖ Embroidered emblems. 800–345–3458; 312–286–6333 (in IL).

Southern Emblem, P.O. Box 8, Toast, NC 27049: Free catalog ❖ Embroidered emblems, emblematic jewelry, badges, flags, and screen printing supplies. 910–789–3348.

Squadron Flight Shop, 843 Broadway, Revere, MA 02151: Catalog $2 ❖ Flight jackets, helmet bags, art, and air force, navy, and marine patches, emblems, and other insignia. 617–284–9500.

Stadri Emblems, 71 Tinker, Woodstock, NY 12498: Free catalog ❖ Embroidered emblems, pins, and decals. 914–679–6600.

DECORATIVE ITEMS

Amish Country Collection, Sunset Valley Rd., RD 5, New Castle, PA 16105: Catalog $5 (refundable) ❖ Amish-style pillows, quilts, wall hangings, rugs, beds and cribs, and other crafts. 412–458–4811.

Baldwin Hardware Corporation, P.O. Box 15048, Reading, PA 19612: Bathroom accessories brochure 75¢; lighting fixtures brochure $3; door hardware brochure 75¢; decor hardware brochure 75¢ ❖ Brass dead bolts and door hardware, bathroom accessories, and lighting fixtures. 800–346–5128.

Ballard Designs, 1670 DeFoor Ave. NW, Atlanta, GA 30318: Catalog $3 ❖ Furniture, pillows, prints, and decor accessories for indoor room arrangements and outdoor landscaping. 404–351–5099.

Basketville Inc., Main St., P.O. Box 710, Putney, VT 05364: Catalog $2 ❖ Woven baskets for home decor arrangements. 802–387–5509.

Betsy's Place, 323 Arch St., Philadelphia, PA 19106: Brochure $3 ❖ Sundials and stands, trivets, and brass reproduction door knockers. 800–452–3524; 215–922–3536 (in PA).

The Country Mouse, Box 17___ CT 06791: Free catalog ❖ An___ decor accessories. 203–485–1___

Country Manor, Mail Order Dept., Rt. 211, P.O. Box 520, Sperryville, VA 22740: Catalog $3 ❖ Kitchen utensils, decor accessories, rugs, and carpets. 703–987–8372.

Crafts Manufacturing Company, 72 Massachusetts Ave., Lunenburg, MA 01462: Catalog $2.50 ❖ Early American handmade tinware, lamps, candle holders, trays, and sconces. 508–342–1717.

Shepard Eberly Decor, 5056 Forest Dr., Rome, OH 44085: Free information ❖ Wall plaques, mirrors, ceramics, and switch plates. 216–563–9849.

Farmer's Daughter, P.O. Box 1071, Nags Head, NC 27959: Catalog $2 ❖ Country accessories, pottery potpourri burners, potpourri candles, and electric candle lamps. 800–423–2196.

Garbe's, 4137 S. 72nd E. Ave., Tulsa, OK 74145: Free catalog ❖ Decor accessories for home and office. 800–735–2241; 918–627–0284 (in OK).

Glen Arbor City Limits, 6610 Western Ave., Box 444, Glen Arbor, MI 49636: Free information ❖ Decor accessories. 616–334–4424.

Historic Housefitters Company, Farm to Market Rd., Brewster, NY 10509: Catalog $3 ❖ Hand-forged ironwork for 18th-century decor settings. 914–278–2427.

Home Decorators Collection, 2025 Concourse Dr., St. Louis, MO 63146: Free catalog ❖ Decor hardware, switch plates, mail boxes, weather vanes, plant stands, furniture, clocks, light fixtures, chandeliers, bathroom accessories, and wicker items. 800–245–2217; 314–993–6045 (in MO).

Hoya Crystal Gallery, 450 Park Ave., New York, NY 10022: Catalog $5 ❖ Art sculptures, vases, bowls, glasses, ornamental pieces, and crystal clocks. 800–462–HOYA.

Interiors, 320 Washington St., Mt. Vernon, NY 10553: Free catalog ❖ Art and other furnishings for the home. 800–228–5215.

Just Between Us, 41 W. 8th Ave., Oshkosh, WI 54906: Free catalog ❖ Decor items for the home. 800–546–2255.

John R. Keyser, 160 W. Meadowlark Ln., Corrales, NM 87048: Free information ❖ Decor accessories. 505–897–0468.

Marble Arch, Box 833, High Point, NC 27261: Catalog $4 ❖ Brass and crystal finials and other decor accessories. 800–723–1328.

A.J. Munzinger & Company, 1454 S. Devon, Springfield, MO 65809: Brochure $1 ❖ Antique housewares. 417–887–4335.

Museum Collections, 586 Higgins Crowell Rd., West Yarmouth, MA 02673: Free catalog ❖ Decorative glass accent accessories. 800–442–2460.

Museum of Modern Art New York, Mail Order Department, P.O. Box 2534, West Chester, PA 19380: Free catalog ❖ Contemporary items for homes, offices, or gifts. 212–708–9888.

Prairie Town Products Inc., P.O. Box 1426, Sedalia, MO 65301: Brochure $1 ❖ Solid wood switch plates with hand-painted ornaments and walnut finish. 816–826–4208.

The Renovator's Supply, P.O. Box 2660, North Conway, NH 03860: Free catalog ❖ Reproduction antique hardware, lighting and plumbing fixtures, curtains, and decor accessories. 800–659–2211.

Rose & Gerard, 55 Sunnyside, Mill Valley, CA 94941: Free catalog ❖ Dinnerware and glasses, plant stands, pottery, serving pieces, place mats and napkins, lanterns, Dhurrie rugs, baskets, and candles. 415–383–6399.

Touch of Class, 1905 N. Van Buren St., Huntingburg, IN 47542: Free catalog ❖ Bedroom furnishings, decor and bathroom accessories, and draperies. 800–457–7456.

Allan Waller Ltd., 3800 Ivy Rd. NE, Atlanta, GA 30305: Free information ❖ Imported tapestries. 404–233–1926.

Wild Wings, South Hwy. 61, Lake City, MN 55041: Free catalog ❖ Home furnishings and decor accessories with a wildlife theme. 800–445–4833.

Yield House, P.O. Box 2525, Conway, NH 03818: Free catalog ❖ Furniture and decor accessories in a Shaker tradition. 800–258–4720.

Zimmerman Handcrafts, 254 E. Main St., Leola, PA 17540: Brochure $1 ❖ Country-style decor accessories. 717–656–8290.

DECOUPAGE

Adventures in Crafts, P.O. Box 6058, Yorkville Station, New York, NY 10128: Catalog $3.50 ❖ Decoupage supplies and projects. 212–410–9793.

Harrower House, P.O. Box 274, Hope, NJ 07844: Catalog $2 ❖ Decoupage supplies and tools. 908–459–5765.

DECOYS

Beaver Dam Decoys, 3311 State Rt. 305, P.O. Box 40, Cortland, OH 44410: Catalog $2 ❖ Decoys and carving supplies. 216–637–4007.

Birds in Wood, P.O. Box 2649, Meriden, CT 06450: Catalog $2 (refundable) ❖ Decoy carving kits.

The Decoy, P.O. Box 3652, Carmel, CA 93921: Free brochure ❖ Handcarved wood birds, antique decoys, limited edition prints, and original art. 800–332–6988.

Decoy Den Galleries, P.O. Box 412, Columbia, IL 62236: Free brochure ❖ Handcarved wood geese, ducks, swans, shorebirds, and other decoys. 800–255–0551.

Decoys Unlimited, 518 N. 9th St., Clinton, IA 52732: Catalog $1 ❖ Decoy kits. 319–243–3948.

Dux' Dekes, Decoy Company, RD 2, Box 66, Greenwich, NY 12834: Free information ❖ Goose, duck, loon, shorebird, and other carving blanks. 800–553–4725; 518–692–7703 (in NY).

Will Kirkpatrick Shorebird Decoys Inc., 124 Forest Ave., Hudson, MA 01749: Catalog $2 ❖ Hand-carved and hand-painted shorebird decoy reproductions. 508–562–7841.

Penn's Woods Products Inc., 19 W. Pittsburgh St., Delmont, PA 15626: Free information ❖ Decoys. 412–468–8311.

DEPARTMENT STORES

The department stores listed below publish general merchandise/seasonal special edition catalogs. There is often a nominal charge for these catalogs, although the price may be waived or refunded if you satisfy minimum purchase requirements. For information on how to obtain these catalogs, write or call the stores directly.

Bennett Brothers Inc., 30 E. Adams St., Chicago, IL 60603. 312–263–4800.

Bergdorf Goodman, 754 5th Ave., New York, NY 10019. 800–662–5455.

Bloomingdales's by Mail Ltd., Federated Department Stores, 475 Knotter Dr., Cheshire, CT 06410. 800–777–0000.

Burdines Florida, P.O. Box 5060, Miami, FL 33101. 305–835–5151.

Carson Pirie Scott & Company, 1 S. State St., Chicago, IL 60603. 312–372–6800.

Cassidy Cosgrove, 127 E. Saint Paul St., Spring Valley, IL 61362. 815–663–2251.

Filene's, 426 Washington St., Boston, MA 02101. 800–345–3637.

Gucci, CSB 3168, Department 846, Melville, NY 11747. 800–221–2590.

Gump's, 1707 Falcon Dr., Ste. 102, Desoto, TX 75115. 800–284–8677.

Hecht's, 685 N. Glebe Rd., Arlington, VA 22203. 703–524–5100.

I. Magnin, P.O. Box 2096, Oakland, CA 94604. 800–227–1125.

Jordan Marsh, 450 Washington St., Boston, MA 02107. 617–357–3000.

Lord & Taylor, 424 5th Ave., New York, NY 10018. 212–391–3300.

Macy's, Herald Square, New York, NY 10001. 212–971–6000.

Marshall Field, 111 N. State St., Chicago, IL 60601. 800–323–1717.

Neiman-Marcus, 221 E. Walnut Hill Ln., Irving, TX 75039: Catalog $6.50. 800–825–8000.

J.C. Penney Company Inc., Catalog Division, Milwaukee, WI 53263. 800–222–6161.

Rich's, P.O. Box 4236, Atlanta, GA 30302. 404–586–2322.

Saks Fifth Ave., Folio Collections Inc., 557 Tuckahoe Rd., Yonkers, NY 10710. 800–345–3454.

Service Merchandise Catalog, Mail Order, P.O. Box 25130, Nashville, TN 37202. 800–251–1212.

Spiegel, P.O. Box 6340, Chicago, IL 60680. 800–345–4500.

Whole Earth Access, 822 Anthony St., Berkeley, CA 94710. 800–829–6300.

DIABETIC SUPPLIES

AD-RX Pharmacy, 6256 Wilshire Blvd., Los Angeles, CA 90048: Free information ❖ Diabetic supplies. 800–435–1992.

Atwater-Carey Ltd., 5505 Central Ave., Boulder, CO 80301: Free information ❖ Purse-size and belt-pack carry-all cases for diabetic supplies. 800–359–1646.

Boehringer Mannhaim Corporation, Patient Care Systems, 9115 Hague Rd., P.O.

Box 50100, Indianapolis, IN 46250: Free information ❖ Glucose monitoring system. 800–858–8072.

Bruce Medical Supply, 411 Waverly Oaks Rd., P.O. Box 9166, Waltham, MA 02154: Free catalog ❖ Health supplies for diabetics, ostomy patients, sick rooms, and first aid. 800–225–8446.

Cases Plus, 290 Rickenbacker Cir., #300, Livermore, CA 94550: Free information ❖ Compact, watertight travel case for diabetic supplies. 800–982–1880.

DERATA Corporation, 1840 Berkshire Ln., Minneapolis, MN 55441: Free information ❖ Medi-Jector EZ needle-free insulin injection system. 800–328–3074; 612–553–1102 (in MN).

Diabetes Supplies, 8181 N. Stadium Dr., Houston, TX 77054: Free catalog ❖ Insulin, blood glucose monitoring equipment, test strips, and other health care supplies. 800–622–5587.

The Diabetic & Nutrition Health Center, 122 University Ave., San Diego, CA 92103: Free information ❖ Blood glucose monitoring systems. 619–491–0106.

Diabetic Depot of America, 1426 E. Fletcher Ave., Tampa, FL 33612: Free information ❖ Insulin, blood glucose monitoring equipment, test strips, and other heath care supplies. 800–537–0404.

Diabetic Express, 2406 W. Tuscarawas, Canton, OH 44708: Free information ❖ Insulin, blood glucose monitoring equipment, test strips, and other health care supplies. 800–338–4656.

Diabetic Promotions, P.O. Box 5400, Willowick, OH 44095: Free catalog ❖ Insulin, blood glucose monitoring equipment, test strips, and other health care supplies. 800–433–1477.

Diabetic Warehouse, 1334 Brommer St., Ste. B1, Santa Cruz, CA 95062: Free information ❖ Diabetic supplies. 800–995–4308.

Gainor Medical U.S.A. Inc., P.O. Box 353, McDonough, GA 30253: Free information ❖ Easy-to-use lancets that provide protection from accidental puncture and risks associated with cross-infection of blood-borne illnesses. 800–825–8282; 404–474–0474 (in GA).

GEM Edwards Inc., P.O. Box 429, Hudson, OH 44236: Free information ❖ Diabetic supplies. 800–793–1995.

H-S Medical Supplies, P.O. Box 42, Whitehall, PA 18052: Free information ❖ Blood glucose meters, test strips, and other supplies for diabetics. 800–344–7633.

Health-o-meter, Division Continental Scale Corporation, 7400 W. 100th Pl., Bridgeview, IL 60455: Free information ❖ Automated method of converting ounces and grams to diabetic food exchanges. 800–323–8363; 708–598–9100 (in IL).

Healthway Inc., 4830 Old Hickory Blvd., Hermitage, TN 37076: Free information ❖ Nutritional management system for diabetics. 800–438–7481.

Hospital Center Pharmacy, 433 Brookline Ave., Boston, MA 02215: Free information ❖ Insulin, blood glucose monitoring equipment, test strips, and other health care supplies. 800–824–2401.

Liberty Medical Supply, P.O. Box 1966, Palm City, FL 34990: Free information ❖ Blood glucose meters, test strips, lancets, monolets, and other diabetic supplies. 800–762–8026.

Mada Medical, 60 Commerce Rd., Carlstadt, NJ 07072: Free information ❖ Vitajet Needleless Injector for dosage accuracy and ease of insulin administration. 201–460–0454.

Medi-Ject Corporation, 1840 Berkshire Ln., Plymouth, MN 55441: Free information ❖ Needle-free insulin injectors. 800–328–3074.

Medicool Inc., 23761 Madison St., Torrance, CA 90505: Free information ❖ Insulin protector for use while traveling. 800–433–2469; 800–654–1565 (in CA).

MediSense Inc., 266 2nd Ave., Waltham, MA 02154: Free information ❖ Blood glucose monitoring systems. 800–316–7952.

Miles Inc., Diagnostics Division, P.O. Box 2001, Mishawaka, IN 46544: Free information ❖ Glucometer blood glucose monitoring system. 800–445–5901.

MiniMed Technologies, 12744 San Fernando Rd., Sylmar, CA 91342: Free information ❖ MiniMed pumps for insulin therapy control. 800–843–6687; 800–826–2099 (in CA).

Penny Saver Medical Supply, 1851 W. 52nd Ave., Denver, CO 80221: Free catalog ❖ Blood glucose monitors and test strips, syringes, lancets and lancet devices, insulin, and other health care supplies. 800–748–1909.

Source International, 8216 Ridgeview Dr., Ben Lomond, CA 95005: Free information ❖

Diabetic, ostomy, and other medical supplies. 800–237–6696.

Thrif-Tee Home Diabetic Center, 4818 Starkey Rd., Roanoke, VA 24014: Free information ❖ Diabetic supplies. 800–258–9559.

Ulster Scientific Inc., P.O. Box 819, New Paltz, NY 12561: Free information ❖ Autojector which inserts the needle and injects insulin automatically and almost without pain. 800–431–8233.

Vitajet Corporation, 27075 Cabot Rd., #102, Laguna Hills, CA 92653: Free information ❖ Needle-free injector. 800–848–2538.

DISPLAY FIXTURES & PORTABLE EXHIBITS

Aftosa, 1034 Ohio Ave., Richmond, CA 94804: Free catalog ❖ Clear acrylic plate stands and bowl holders. 800–231–0397.

Bluegrass Case Company, 272 Airport Rd., Box 386, Stanton, KY 40380: Free information ❖ Collector and display frames. 606–663–9871.

Classic Displays, P.O. Box 44057, Houston, TX 77244: Free information ❖ Display cases with engraved nameplates, acrylic covers, black acrylic bases with gold risers, and wood bases. 800–275–8574.

Columbus Show Case Company, 850 5th Ave., Columbus, OH 43212: Free information ❖ Display fixtures. 800–848–3573; 614–299–3161 (in OH).

Display Fixtures Company, P.O. Box 7245, Charlotte, NC 28241: Free catalog ❖ Display fixtures. 704–588–0880.

Emerson Wood Works Inc., 2640 E. 43rd Ave., Denver, CO 80216: Free brochure ❖ Drawers and cases for collectors. 303–295–1360.

ESV Lighting Inc., 525 Court St., Pekin, IL 61554: Free information ❖ Lighting systems for displays. 800–225–5378.

The Fixture Factory, 835 N.E. 8th St., Gresham, OR 97030: Free information ❖ Display fixtures. 503–661–6525.

Franklin Fixtures Inc., 59 Commerce Park Rd., Brewster, MA 02631: Free catalog ❖ Display fixtures. 508–896–3713.

Global Fixtures Inc., 4121 Rushton St., Florence, AL 35631: Free catalog ❖ Display fixtures. 205–767–5200.

Graphic Display Systems, 1243 Lafayette St., Lebanon, PA 17042: Free information ❖ Lightweight, easy-to-set-up display system, complete with base, leg adjusters, and clips. 800–848–3020; 717–274–3954 (in PA).

Handy Store Fixtures, 337 Sherman Ave., Newark, NJ 07114: Free catalog ❖ Display fixtures. 800–676–1913.

Model Display & Fixture Company Inc., 1405 E. McDowell Rd., Phoenix, AZ 85006: Free information ❖ Display fixtures. 800–528–5306; 800–876–6335 (in AZ).

Melvin S. Roos & Company Inc., 4465 Commerce Dr. SW, Atlanta, GA 30336: Free information ❖ Display fixtures. 800–241–6897; 800–282–9110 (in GA).

Ruddles Mills Products, 19 S. Main St., Cynthiana, KY 41031: Free information ❖ Handcrafted hardwood display cases in solid oak, walnut, or cherry. 606–234–9224.

Schacht Lighting, 5214 Burleson Rd., Austin, TX 78744: Free brochure ❖ Track lighting supplies, replacement bulbs, and craft-show lights. 800–256–7114.

Showbest Fixture Corporation, 2300 Magnolia Rd., P.O. Box 25336, Richmond, VA 23260: Free catalog ❖ Display fixtures. 804–643–3600.

DOLLHOUSES & MINIATURES

A-C's Emporium of Miniatures, Box 802, McMurray, PA 15317: Catalog $15 ❖ Miniatures. 412–942–4120.

Acquisto Silver Company, 8901 Osuna Rd. NE, Albuquerque, NM 87111: Free brochure with long SASE ❖ Sterling silver miniatures. 505–292–0910.

American Home Stencils Inc., 10007 S. 76th St., Franklin, WI 53132: Catalog $2.75 (refundable) ❖ Miniature stencils.

Angel Children, 4977 Sparr Rd., Gaylord, MI 49735: Catalog $2 ❖ Miniature porcelain dolls. 517–732–1931.

Angela's Miniature World, 2237 Ventura Blvd., Camarillo, CA 93010: Free information with long SASE ❖ Miniatures, dollhouses, building materials, and other collectibles. 805–482–2219.

Architectural Etcetera, 888 Tower Rd., Mundelein, IL 60060: Catalog $3 ❖ Bookshelves, fireplaces, doors, windows, and other architectural details. 708–949–0041.

B.H. Miniatures, 20805 N. 19th Ave., Ste. 5, Phoenix, AZ 85027: Catalog $5 ❖ Prepasted wallpaper, coordinated print and solid color fabrics, velvet carpeting, and furniture in kits or assembled. 602–582–3385.

Barnstable Originals, 50 Harden Ave., Camden, ME 04843: Free information with long SASE ❖ Handcrafted sterling silver miniatures and other miniatures and room settings. 207–236–8162.

Bauder-Pine Ltd., P.O. Box 518, Langhorne, PA 19047: Catalog $4 ❖ Furniture and kits. 215–355–2033.

Beauvais Castle, 141 Union St., P.O. Box 4060, Manchester, NH 03108: Catalog $3 ❖ Miniatures. 800–282–8944.

Betty's Mini Creations, 596 Knollwood Rd., Severna Park, MD 21146: Catalog $6 ❖ Miniatures and other collectibles. 410–544–6388.

Bob's Doll House Shop, 2822 NW 63rd St., French Market Mall, Oklahoma City, OK 73116: Free information with long SASE ❖ Dollhouses and miniatures. 405–843–1094.

Cape May Miniatures, 208 Ocean St., Cape May, NJ 08204: Free information ❖ Dollhouses, furniture and accessories, lighting, and building supplies. 609–884–7999.

Cardinal Incorporated, 400 Markley St., Port Reading, NJ 07064: Catalog $7.50 (refundable) ❖ Miniature dollhouse furniture and porcelain collectible dolls. 800–888–0936.

Carlisle Miniatures, 703 N. Elm, Creston, IA 50801: Free catalog with long SASE ❖ Handcrafted furniture, from the 1930s and 1940s.

Catworkz...and DOGS' too Inc., P.O. Box 1789, New York, NY 10163: Free brochure with long SASE and two 1st class stamps ❖ Miniature cats, dogs, and accessories.

Elizabeth Chambers, P.O. Box 352, Bristol, NH 03222: Free information ❖ Dedham pottery miniatures. 603–744–5135.

Chan's Hobbies, 2450 Van Ness Ave., San Francisco, CA 94109: Free information with long SASE ❖ Miniatures. 415–885–2899.

Chez Riche, 1616 Grinstead Dr., Louisville, KY 40204: Free catalog ❖ Miniatures, dollhouses, lumber, lighting, and other collectibles. 502–587–6338.

Cindy's Workshop, 1609 Stanford Dr., Columbia, MO 65203: Price list $3

(refundable) ❖ Miniature reproductions of European-style furniture. 314–445–2446.

Cir-Kit Concepts Inc., 407 NW 14th St., Rochester, MN 55901: Catalog $4 ❖ Electrical miniatures and wiring kits for dollhouses. 507–288–0860.

CJ Originals, P.O. Box 538, Bridgeville, PA 15017: Catalog $4 ❖ Miniature needlework cross-stitch kits. 412–221–5797.

The Company Mouse, 4932 Elm St., Bethesda, MD 20814: Free information ❖ Dollhouse miniatures. 301–654–1222.

Country Cottage, 5628 W. Broadway, Richmond, IL 60071: Free information with long SASE ❖ Country-style miniatures. 815–678–4428.

Country Miniature Stoneware, Jane Graber, RR 5, Box 111, Nashville, TN 47448: Free price list ❖ Country-style stoneware and redware miniatures. 812–988–8014.

Country Store Miniatures, 813 Main, Vancouver, WA 98660: Free information ❖ Dollhouses, other buildings, and miniatures. 206–695–1425.

Craft Creative Kits, 2200 Dean St., St. Charles, IL 60174: Catalog $1.50 ❖ Dollhouse kits, miniatures, wallpaper patterns, and books. 708–584–9600.

CraftSmyths, 546 Foxwood Ln., Paoli, PA 19301: Price list $1 with long SASE ❖ Miniature handcrafted floral arrangements. 215–647–7289.

Create Your Own, 932 East Blvd., Alpha, NJ 08865: Free brochure ❖ Miniature cross-stitch and needlepoint rug kits. 908–454–3044.

Dawn's Artistic Treasures, 2801 Willow Creek Rd., Prescott, AZ 86301: Price list $3 (refundable) ❖ Miniature musical instruments. 602–778–5707.

DD's Dollhouse, 931 Fennell Ave. East, Hamilton, Ontario, Canada L8V 1W9: Catalog $10 ❖ Dollhouses and accessories. 416–574–2942.

Diminutive Specialties, 10337 Ellsworth Dr., Roscoe, IL 61073: Catalog $5 ❖ Miniature photos. 815–623–2011.

The Dollhouse, 6107 N. Scottsdale Rd., Scottsdale, AZ 85253: Free information with long SASE ❖ Miniatures and dollhouses. 800–398–3981.

Dollhouse Delights, 11 Starboard Dr., Taney Town, MD 21787: Catalog $1 (refundable) ❖

Miniatures for dollhouse gardens. 410–756–2062.

The Dollhouse Factory, 157 Main St., Lebanon, NJ 08833: Catalog $5.50 ❖ Dollhouses, miniatures, tools, books, and plans. 908–236–6404.

Dollhouses & Miniatures of Myrtle Beach, 10127 North Hwy. 17, Myrtle Beach, SC 29572: Free information with long SASE ❖ Dollhouses, furnishings, and other miniatures. 803–272–0478.

Donna's Dollhouses of Frankfort, 51 W. Clinton St., Ste. 102, Frankfort, IN 46041: Information $1 ❖ Everything for dollhouses. 317–654–9075.

Dwyer's Doll House, 1944 Warwick Ave., Warwick, RI 02889: Catalog $10 ❖ Dollhouses, building supplies, and miniatures. 800–248–3655.

Elena's Dollhouses & Miniatures, 5565 Schueller, Burlington, Ontario, Canada L7L 3T1: Free information ❖ Dollhouses and miniatures. 905–333–3402.

Enchanted Doll House, Rt. 7A, Manchester Center, VT 05255: Catalog $2 ❖ Dollhouses and kits, furniture, dolls, stuffed animals, and other toys. 802–362–1327.

Fantasy Fabrications, P.O. Box 164, Turner, OR 97392: Brochure $2.50 ❖ Victorian, Art Deco, and original miniatures.

Favorite Things, York & Monton Rds., Hereford, MD 21111: Free information with long SASE ❖ Dollhouse furnishings, dollhouses, and English, Scottish, and American miniatures. 410–343–0400.

Favorites from the Past, P.O. Box 739, Newan, GA 30264: Catalog $3 ❖ Furniture, lumber, tools, patterns, and electrical wiring. 404–427–3921.

Fred's Dollhouse & Miniature Center, Rt. 7, Pittsford, VT 05763: Catalog $4 ❖ Dollhouses and kits, building supplies, and furniture. 802–483–6362.

Freda's Fancy, 295 Fairview Ave., Bayport, NY 11705: Brochure $3 with long SASE ❖ Dollhouse miniatures. 516–472–0078.

G.E.L. Products Inc., 19 Grove St., Vernon, CT 06066: Free information ❖ Dollhouse kits. 203–872–6539.

Garden Path, 174 Blair Ln., Palatine, IL 60067: Price list $1 with long SASE ❖ Miniature flowers, Christmas ornaments, and original watercolors from England. 708–358–3030.

Greenhouse Miniature Shop, 6616 Monroe St., Sylvania, OH 43560: Catalog $3 ❖ Miniatures. 419–882–8259.

Handcraft Designs Inc., 63 E. Broad St., Hatfield, PA 19440: Free information with long SASE ❖ Miniature upholstered furniture. 215–855–3022.

Happy House Miniatures, 135 N. Main St., Mocksville, NC 27028: Catalog $5 (refundable) ❖ Dollhouses and accessories. 704–634–1424.

Harvey's Miniatures & Dollhouses, P.O. Box 340, Ada, MI 49301: Free information ❖ Dollhouses and kits, building supplies, and furniture. 616–676–3071.

Haslam's Doll Houses, 7208 S. Tamiami Trail, Sarasota, FL 34231: Free information with long SASE ❖ Dollhouses, miniatures, and building supplies. 813–922–8337.

Hearth Song, Mail Processing Center, 6519 N. Galena Rd., P.O. Box 1773, Peoria, IL 61656: Free catalog ❖ Dollhouse miniatures, books for children, toiletries for babies, cuddly dolls, party decorations, art supplies, and games. 800–325–2502.

Heirloom Toys, 8393 Strato Dr., Sandy, UT 84093: Brochure $1 ❖ Barbie-sized doll house kits and furniture.

J. Hermes, P.O. Box 4023, El Monte, CA 91734: Catalog $3 ❖ Dollhouse kits.

His & Her Hobbys, 15 W. Busse Ave., Mt. Prospect, IL 60056: Free information ❖ Dollhouses and kits, furniture kits or assembled, wallpaper and fabrics, building and landscaping supplies, and lighting accessories. 708–392–2668.

Hobby Craft, 6632 Odama Rd., Madison, WI 53719: Free information ❖ Dollhouses, furniture and furniture kits, wallpaper, lighting, and building materials. 608–833–4944.

The Hobby Gallery Miniature Loft, 1810 Meriden Rd., Wolcott, CT 06716: Free information with long SASE ❖ Dollhouses, miniatures, plush animals, and dolls. 203–879–2316.

The Hobby Suite, P.O. Box 613, McComb, MS 39648: Catalog $18.50 ❖ Kits and assembled miniatures, dollhouses, tools, rugs, wallpaper, and electrical supplies.

Hobby World Miniatures, 5450 Sherbrooke St. West, Montreal, Quebec, Canada H4A 1V9: Free catalog ❖ Dollhouses and miniatures. 514–481–5434.

House of Caron, 10111 Larrylyn Dr., Whittier, CA 90603: Price list $2.50 ❖ Molds and supplies for miniature dolls. 310–947–6753.

Houseworks, 2388 Pleasantdale Rd., Atlanta, GA 30340: Free catalog and list of retailers ❖ Dollhouse building components, hardware, lighting, flooring, and furniture. 404–448–6596.

Ideal Gifts, 81 William St., Portsmouth, RI 02871: Catalog $5 ❖ Dollhouse furniture.

In a Nutshell Miniatures, 305 Lakeshore Rd. East, Oakville, Ontario, Canada L6J 1J3: Catalog $6 ❖ Miniatures and other collectibles. 416–338–9631.

Innovative Photography, 1724 NW 36th, Lincoln City, OR 97367: Catalog $2.50 ❖ Miniature photographs and framed Victorian-style prints, from the 1920s to 1930s. 503–994–9421.

It's A Small World, 560 Green Bay Rd., Winnetka, IL 60093: Catalog $7 ❖ Dollhouses and miniatures. 708–446–8399.

Jan's Dollhouse, 6600 Dixie Hwy., Rt. 4, Fairfield, OH 45014: Catalog $18.95 ❖ Miniatures, dolls, bears, and dollhouses. 513–860–0595.

Jeepers Miniatures, Meridian Village Plaza, 1315 S. Rangeline Rd., Carmel, IN 46032: Catalog $20 ❖ Miniatures and finished or ready-to-wire and paint dollhouses. 317–846–6708.

Janna Joseph, P.O. Box 1262, Dunedin, FL 34697: Catalog $4.95 ❖ Miniature doll molds. 813–784–1877.

Karen's Miniatures, 6020 Doniphan, Ste. B1, El Paso, TX 79932: Catalog $6 ❖ Architectural mouldings and cast metal miniature kits. 508–589–2371.

Karin's Mini Garden, 6128 McLeod NE, Apt. 15, Albuquerque, NM 87109: Catalog $1.50 (refundable) ❖ Indoor and outdoor miniature plants, cacti, succulents, and floral arrangements. 505–883–4561.

Keshishian Carpets, Box 3002, San Clemente, CA 92674: Brochure $3 ❖ Carpets for dollhouses.

Kimberly House Miniatures, 3867 S. Valley View, Las Vegas, NV 89103: Free information ❖ Landscaping miniatures. 702–253–9790.

The Lawbre Company, 888 Tower Rd., Mundelein, IL 60060: Catalog $4 ❖

Reproduction period-designed dollhouses and miniatures. 708–949–0031.

Lilliput Land, 89 Lisa Dr., Northport, NY 11768: Brochure $4 ❖ English, French, and American handcrafted miniatures. 516–754–5511.

Little Goodies, P.O. Box 1004, Lewisville, TX 75067: Catalog $2 ❖ Miniature pre-cut paper flowers in kits.

Little House of Miniatures on Chelsea Lane, 621½ Sycamore St., Waterloo, IA 50703: Catalog $15 (refundable) ❖ Dollhouses, furniture, dolls, wallpaper, carpets, electric wiring, and building supplies. 319–233–6585.

Little Lincoln's, County Rd. 550, Box 262, Marquette, MI 49855: Brochure $1 ❖ Log cabin dollhouses in the style of homes, from 1850 to 1880. 527–366–5263.

Littlethings, 129 Main St., Irvington, NY 10533: Free list with long SASE ❖ Miniature paintings, dollhouses, furniture, bears, and other collectibles. 914–591–9150.

Littletown USA, 94th St. Ocean Plaza Mall, Ocean City, MD 21842: Free information ❖ Dollhouse supplies, building materials, and miniatures. 410–524–5450.

Lolly's, 1054 Dundee Ave., Elgin, IL 60120: Catalog $21.50 ❖ Dollhouses and miniatures. 708–697–4040.

Lookingglass Miniatures, P.O. Box 830, Winchester, OR 97495: Catalog $4 ❖ Miniature kits. 503–673–5445.

Lucille's Little House, 1504 Hancock St., Quincy, MA 02169: Free newsletter ❖ Building materials for dollhouses, miniatures, and dolls. 617–479–1141.

MacDoc Designs, 405 Tarrytown Rd., White Plains, NY 10607: Free information and list of retailers ❖ Miniature oriental rugs. 914–376–2156.

Maison des Maisons, 460 S. Marion Pkwy., Denver, CO 30209: Price list $5 with long SASE ❖ Southwest Indian furniture and other miniatures. 303–871–0731.

The Ken Manning Collection, 15486 85th Ave., Surrey, British Columbia, Canada V3S 6W1: Brochure $1 ❖ Miniature musical instruments. 604–597–2991.

Mary Elizabeth Miniatures, 49–04 39th Ave., Woodside, NY 11377: Free brochure with long SASE ❖ Handcrafted miniature ice cream parlor furnishings. 718–429–4114.

Mel's Miniz, 290 Rt. 18, East Brunswick, NJ 08753: Free information ❖ Dollhouses and kits, furniture, other furnishings, building and electrical supplies, and tools. 908–545–0706.

Microscale Industries Inc., P.O. Box 11950, Costa Mesa, CA 92627: Catalog $2 ❖ Microscale decals for decorating miniatures.

Mini Splendid Things, 626 Main St., Covington, KY 41011: Catalog $18.95 ❖ Dollhouses and miniatures. 606–261–5500.

Mini Temptations, 3633 W. 95th, Overland Park, KS 66206: Catalog $7 ❖ Dollhouse accessories, miniatures, and other collectibles. 913–648–2050.

Mini-Facets, 7707 Indian Springs Dr., Nashville, TN 37221: Catalog $3 ❖ Handcrafted miniatures. 615–646–0695.

Mini-tiques, P.O. Box 683, 140 S. Main St., Thiensville, MN 53092: Catalog $3 ❖ Miniatures and accessories. 414–242–8053.

Miniature Estates, 1451 S. Robertson Blvd., Los Angeles, CA 94510: Free information with long SASE ❖ Dollhouses and miniatures. 310–552–2200.

Miniature Grand Pianos, Ralph E. Partelow, P.O. Box 3314, Littleton, CO 80161: Catalog $2 ❖ Miniature keyboard instruments. 303–798–5014.

The Miniature Kingdom of River Row, 182 Front St., P.O. Box 39, Oswego, NY 13827: Catalog $2 ❖ Dollhouses and handcrafted miniatures. 607–687–5601.

Miniature Makers' Workshop, 4515 N. Woodward Ave., Royal Oak, MI 48073: Catalog $10 ❖ Furniture, dolls, and dollhouses. 313–549–0633.

miniature MINIATURES, 7 Madison St., Port Washington, NY 11050: Catalog $3 ❖ Miniature dollhouses for regular-size dollhouses.

The Miniature Shop, 1115 4th Ave., Huntington, WV 25701: Catalog $10 ❖ Dollhouses, furniture kits, and electrical and decorating supplies. 304–523–2418.

Miniature Village, 1725 50th St., Kenosha, WI 53140: Catalog $7.50 ❖ Dollhouses, furniture, and electrical accessories. 800–383–0188.

Miniatures In-Your-Mailbox, P.O. Box 32496, Cleveland, OH 44132: Free price list with long SASE and two 1st class stamps ❖ Dollhouses, furniture, building and electrical supplies, wall and floor coverings, and tools. 800–283–8191.

MiniGraphics, 2975 Exon Ave., Cincinnati, OH 45241: Catalog $6 ❖ Over-stuffed velvet furniture, wallpaper, coordinated fabrics, carpeting, drapes, and other accessories. 513–563–8600.

Miss Elaineous, 2904 Selwyn Ave., Charlotte, NC 28209: Free information with long SASE ❖ Dollhouses, furniture, and draperies. 704–375–8774.

Mosaic Press, 358 Oliver Rd., Cincinnati, OH 45215: Catalog $3 ❖ Hand-bound miniature books made with traditional binding methods. 513–761–5977.

Mother Muck's Minis, 755 Lacey Way, North Salt Lake, UT 84954: Catalog $3 ❖ Miniatures.

Mott Miniatures & Doll House Shop, 7700 Orangethorpe Ave., Ste. 8, Buena Park, CA 90621: Free catalog ❖ Furniture, dolls, dollhouses and kits, and building materials. 800–874–6222.

The Mountain Valley Miniature Shop, 199 Union St., P.O. Box 94, Occoquan, VA 22125: Free information ❖ Dollhouses, finishing supplies, furniture, kits, and books. 703–690–1144.

Muskoka Miniatures, 510 Muskoka Rd. North, Box 218, Gravenhurst, Ontario, Canada P0C 1G0: Free information with long SASE ❖ Miniatures. 705–687–3351.

My Dollhouse, 7 S. Broadway, Nyack, NY 10960: Free information with long SASE ❖ Dolls, dollhouses, and miniatures. 914–358–4185.

My Sister's Shoppe Inc., 1671 Penfield Rd., Rochester, NY 14625: Catalog $3 (refundable) ❖ Victorian furniture miniatures. 800–821–0097.

Nana's Attic, P.O. Box 56, Medicine Park, OK 73557: Catalog $15 (refundable with $100 order) ❖ Dollhouse building supplies, furniture, and miniatures. 405–529–2225.

New Hampshire Woodworkers, 515 Winnacunnet Rd., Hampton, NH 03842: Free information with long SASE ❖ Miniature fences for landscape settings.

Ni-Glo Lamps by Nicole, 5684 Sterling Rd., Hamburg, NY 14075: Information $5 ❖ Miniature hand-painted china lamps with replaceable bulbs. 716–627–4644.

North Country Gardens, P.O. Box 277, Northport, MI 49670: Catalog $7 ❖ Miniatures. 616–386–7003.

Northeastern Scale Models Inc., P.O. Box 727, Methuen, MA 01844: Catalog $1 ❖ Materials for constructing dollhouses. 508–688–6019.

The Oakridge Corporation, P.O. Box 247, Lemont, IL 60439: Catalog $2 (specify dollhouses, furniture, or accessories) ❖ Dollhouse kits, building supplies, and furniture. 800–594–5115.

Old World Craftsmen Dollhouses Inc., 643 Industrial Dr., Hartland, WI 53029: Brochure $2 ❖ Custom-made or in-stock dollhouses. 800–234–4748; 414–367–2753 (in WI).

Once Upon A Time, 120 Church St. NE, Vienna, VA 22180: Free information ❖ Miniature wire wicker furniture. 703–255–3285.

P.J.'s Miniatures, 5818 Hwy. 74 West, Monroe, NC 28110: Catalog $14.95 ❖ Miniatures. 704–821–9144.

Patti's Miniature World, 4114 Hwy. 70 SW, Hickory, NC 28602: Free information with long SASE ❖ Miniatures. 704–328–5088.

Peg's Dollhouse, 4019 Sebastopol Rd., Santa Rosa, CA 95407: Information $1 (refundable) ❖ Miniatures and dollhouses. 707–546–6137.

Petite Innovations, 243 High St., Burlington, NJ 08016: Free information with long SASE ❖ Dollhouses and furnishings, lighting supplies, building materials, and miniatures. 609–386–7476.

Pinocchio's Miniatures, 465 S. Main St., Frankenmuth, MI 48734: Catalog $19.50 ❖ Handmade miniatures. 517–652–2751.

Precious Little Things, The Fieldwood Company, P.O. Box 6, Chester, VT 05143: Catalog $3.50 ❖ Handcrafted miniature furnishings. 802–875–4127.

Puffer Lane Petites, 52 Puffer Ln., Sudbury, MA 01776: Free information ❖ Miniature plants and foods. 617–424–8044.

Enrique Quintanar, 210 Post St., Studio 813, San Francisco, CA 94108: Brochure $1 (refundable) ❖ Sterling silver miniatures. 415–398–5678.

R & N Miniatures, 458 Wythe Creek Rd., Poquoson, VA 23662: Price list $2 ❖ Everything to finish and furnish dollhouses. 804–868–7103.

Rondel Wood Products, 2679 Washington Rd., Waldoboro, ME 04572: Brochure $2 ❖ Wagon and carriage kit miniatures. 207–832–6837.

Rose's Doll House Store, 5826 W. Bluemound, Milwaukee, WI 53213: Free catalog ❖ Dolls and dollhouse miniatures. 414–259–9965.

Saloon Originals, 746 W. Upjohn Rd., Ridgecrest, CA 93555: Catalog $3.50 & Battery-operated, miniature arcade-type amusement, and music machines. 619–375–8159.

Scientific Models Inc., 340 Snyder Ave., Berkeley Heights, NJ 07922: Catalog $1 ❖ Easy-to-assemble, museum-quality dollhouse furniture.

Second Childhood Miniatures, Rt. 1, Box 180, Willis, VA 24380: Catalog $10 ❖ Miniatures. 703–789–4262.

Shaker Workshops, P.O. Box 1028, Concord, MA 01742: Catalog $1 ❖ Furniture and dolls, Shaker furniture in kits or assembled. 617–646–8985.

Shenandoah Designs Inc., P.O. Box 313, Brookfield, CT 06804: Price list $1 ❖ Kits and assembled furniture.

Shoda's Miniature Wonderland, 3504 Wells St., Fort Wayne, IN 46808: Free information with long SASE ❖ Miniatures, music boxes, dolls, and figurines. 219–484–7167.

Sierra Miniatures, 912 Loyola St., Carson City, NV 89705: Catalog $15 plus $1.50 postage ❖ Miniatures and other collectibles. 702–883–6830.

Simms Miniatures Ltd., P.O. Box 291, Williamsburg, VA 23187: Catalog $3 ❖ Tools and furniture, silver and gold miniatures. 804–220–3319.

Sir Thomas Thumb, 1398 Oregon Rd., Leola, PA 17540: Catalog $1 with long SASE ❖ Handcrafted miniatures. 717–656–8838.

Small Houses, 8064 Columbia Rd., Olmsted Falls, OH 44138: Catalog $6 ❖ Dollhouse kits, furniture, wallpaper, and building supplies.

Small Ideas, 35 Koefferam, Old Greenwich, CT 06870: Catalog $5 ❖ Museum-quality, 18th-century miniatures. 203–637–4264.

The Squirrel's Nest Miniatures, 401 Buckingham Rd., Pittsburgh, PA 15125: Free information with long SASE ❖ Sterling silver miniatures, Early American accessories, and dollhouse building supplies. 800–852–3156.

C. Ann Struck, 17080 Seven Springs Way, Mockingbird Canyon, CA 92504: Free information ❖ Petit point rugs. 714–780–5564.

Sundance Potters, 6479 Dodge Rd., White City, OR 97503: Catalog $2 (refundable) ❖ Handcrafted pottery miniatures. 503–826–8641.

T & T Creative Enterprise, 1932 Palisades Dr., Pacific Palisades, CA 90272: Free information with long SASE ❖ Handcrafted English pewter miniatures, jointed dolls, toys, and animals. 213–573–1114.

Tammy's Tiny Treasures, 158 Bloomingdale St., Chelsea, MA 02150: Free brochure ❖ Hard-to-find miniature furnishings. 617–381–7345.

Tanglewald Miniatures, P.O. Box 449, Dallas, OR 97338: Brochure $2 ❖ Dollhouses, furniture, wall racks, and miniature porcelains. 503–623–2649.

Teri's Mini Workshop, P.O. Box 387, Goldenrod, FL 32733: Catalog $1 with long SASE ❖ Miniatures for dollhouses and other settings.

This Old House, 1342 S. 8th St., Fargo, ND 58103: Catalog $2.50 ❖ Miniature willow furniture and country-style accessories.

Thistle Seed Collection, 101 Leland Hill Rd., Sutton, MA 01527: Free brochure ❖ Stained glass miniature windows and assembled post-and-beam dollhouses or kits. 508–865–4387.

Thomaston Miniature Works, Ginger Graham, 111 Main St., P.O. Box 272, Thomaston, ME 04861: Price list $1.50 with long SASE ❖ Food, clothing, tools, and other miniatures. 207–354–0211.

The Thumbeline Touch, 8009 Parks Ln., Baltimore, MD 21207: Catalog $7 ❖ Miniatures for dollhouses and other settings. 410–964–9217.

Tiny Dollhouse, 1146 Lexington Ave., New York, NY 10021: Free information ❖ Miniatures, building supplies, lighting accessories, pewter, brass, silver, furniture and kits, wallpaper, and dollhouses. 212–744–3719.

Marie Toner Lighting Designs Inc., 725 Inverness Dr., Horsham, PA 19044: Catalog $1 with long SASE ❖ Easy-to-install miniature ceiling and wall light fixtures.

The Toy Box, 4657 South US 1, Rockledge, FL 32955: Catalog $4 ❖ Dollhouses and kits, building and electrical supplies, furniture, and books. 407–632–2411.

Val-Le of the Dolls, 840 Hamilton Ave., Waterbury, CT 06706: Catalog $12 ❖ Dollhouses, miniatures, furnishings, and building supplies. 203–754–1622.

Vernon Pottery, 441 Bethune Dr., Virginia Beach, VA 23452: Catalog $2 ❖ Reproduction 19th-century salt-glazed stoneware miniatures. 804–486–5147.

Vicki's Miniatures, P.O. Box 142407, Anchorage, AK 99514: Free brochure ❖ Handcrafted miniature weight training equipment.

Village Emporium, 828 Professional Pl., West Chesapeake, VA 23320: Free quarterly newsletter ❖ Dollhouses and kits, furniture and kits, and building and electrical supplies. 804–547–5814.

Village Miniatures, Box 142, Queenston, Ontario, Canada L0S 1L0: Catalog $5 ❖ Miniatures, dollhouses and dollhouse kits, tools, landscaping materials, wallpaper and floor coverings, and building materials. 416–262–4779.

W & D Mini Homes, P.O. Box 1654, Bloomington, IN 47402: Brochure $1 with long SASE and two 1st class stamps ❖ Native American miniatures. 812–332–2499.

The Ward Warehouse, 1050 Ala Moana Blvd., Honolulu, HI 96814: VHS video catalog $10 ❖ Handcrafted miniatures. 808–521–8803.

Warling Miniatures, 22453 Covello St., West Hills, CA 91307: Brochure $1 with long SASE and two 1st class stamps ❖ Victorian to modern wicker furniture kits. 818–340–9855.

Wharton Wholesalers Ltd., 3256 Chaparral Dr., Idaho Falls, ID 83404: Free information ❖ Gifts, novelties, fine jewelry, and miniatures. 208–529–5260.

Wood Shoppe, 2908 Simmons Rd., Edmond, OK 73034: Free information with long SASE ❖ Country classics in miniature. 405–341–2991.

DOLL MAKING & DOLL CLOTHING

Adopt-A-Doll, 1041 Lincoln Ave., San Jose, CA 95125: Catalog $3 ❖ Old and new dolls, doll-making supplies, clothing, shoes, and hats. 408–298–DOLL.

All About Dolls, 16905 San Fernando Mission Blvd., Granada Hills, CA 91344: Free price list with long SASE ❖ Porcelain for making dolls, kilns, eyes, wigs, and other supplies. 818–368–8422.

Ann's Doll Patterns, P.O. Box 16946, Portland, OR 97216: Catalog $3 ❖ Patterns for doll clothing. 503–829–2603.

Annette's Antique Dolls, P.O. Box 5227, Bellingham, WA 98227: Free information ❖ Antique dolls, teddy bears, and toys. 206–758–2476.

BB Doll Supplies, 4216 Grandview Rd., Kansas City, MO 64137: Catalog $6 (refundable) ❖ Supplies to start, finish, and dress a doll. 800–227–3655.

Bekk Ceramics, P.O. Box 120127, Clermont, FL 34712: Catalog $8 ❖ Antique reproduction and modern doll molds and supplies. 904–394–2175.

Broadview Ceramics, 5247 State Rd., Parma, OH 44134: Catalog $4 ❖ Doll bisque kits and other doll-making supplies. 216–661–4856.

Brown House Dolls, 3200 N. Sand Lake Rd., Allen, MI 49227: Catalog $2 ❖ Easy-to-sew patterns for doll clothing. 517–849–2833.

Carolee Creations, 787 Industrial Dr., Elmhurst, IL 60126: Catalog $2 ❖ Paper patterns for cloth dolls and accessories. Also hair materials, yarns, books, and other supplies. 708–530–7175.

Carver's Eye Company, P.O. Box 16692, Portland, OR 97216: Catalog $1 ❖ Glass and plastic eyes, noses, joints, growlers, and eye glasses for dolls and bears. 503–666–5680.

Collectible Doll Company, 1421 N. 34th, Seattle, WA 98103: Free information ❖ Doll clothes, molds, and supplies for making dolls. 800–468–DOLL; 206–634–3131 (in WA).

CR's Crafts, Box 8, Leland, IA 50453: Catalog $2 ❖ Doll- and bear-making supplies, kits, and patterns for making jointed bears. 515–567–3652.

D & L Dolls & Supplies, 224–228 Admiral St., Providence, RI 02908: Free information ❖ Soft-fired greenware, wigs, eyes, shoes, patterns, and other supplies. 401–421–7558.

Lou Davis Doll Supply, N3211 Hwy. H North, Lake Geneva, WI 53147: Free catalog ❖ Doll-making supplies. 800–748–7991.

Dee's Place of Dolls, 140 E. College St., Covina, CA 91723: Free information ❖ Doll-making supplies and dolls. 818–915–1005.

Deja Vu Originals, P.O. Box 55375, Riverside, CA 92517: Catalog $1 ❖ Costumes for dolls. 714–780–7405.

Doll Crafting Depot, 4224 Louis Ave., Holiday, FL 34691: Free catalog ❖ Wigs, eyes, shoes, socks, clothing, and other supplies. 800–526–3655.

Doll Creations, 1987 Santa Rita Rd., Pleasanton, CA 94566: Free information ❖ Greenware, doll-making supplies and clothes, and paper dolls. 510–846–6120.

Doll Gallery/Hospital, 1137 Susan St., Columbia, SC 29210: Free information with long SASE ❖ Doll-making supplies. 803–798–7044.

Dollspart Supply Company, 8000 Cooper Ave., Bldg. 28, Glendale, NY 11385: Free catalog ❖ Wigs, glass eyes, doll stands, shoes, other doll parts and bodies, ceramic supplies, clothing, patterns, and books. 718–326–4587.

Elaine's Doll House, 537 W. Harding Way, Stockton, CA 95204: Free catalog with long SASE ❖ Doll-making supplies. 209–948–1193.

Elizabeth's Dollware, 1875 Ellard Pl., Concord, CA 94521: Free list with long SASE ❖ Soft-fired greenware. 510–687–1323.

Angela Eoriatti, 8511 N Beaver Dr., Johnston, IA 50131: Catalog $5.50 ❖ Patterns for doll clothing. 515–276–3234.

Fabric Chalet, Windchime Center, Colorado Springs, CO 80919: Information $5 ❖ Clothing patterns, sewing supplies, and fabrics. 719–522–1214.

Fun Stuff, P.O. Box 999, Yuma, AZ 85366: Free list with long SASE ❖ Artist vinyl and porcelain kits. 602–726–1513.

Global Dolls Corporation, 1903 Aviation Blvd., Lincoln, CA 95648: Catalog $2.50 ❖ Doll wigs. 800–GLOBAL-7.

Ali Hansen's Childhood Fantasies, 1914 Walnut Plaza, Carrollton, TX 75006: Catalog $3 (refundable) ❖ Bisque kits, patterns, and supplies. 214–416–4262.

Haskell's Handcraft, 40 College Ave., Waterville, ME 04901: Catalog $6 ❖ Doll-making and clock-building supplies. 205–873–5070.

Heartcraft Gifts, 3855 South Hwy. 79, Ste. 113, Rapid City, SD 57701: Catalog $4 ❖ Porcelain doll kits.

Hello Dolly, 6550 Mobile Hwy., Pensacola, FL 32526: Catalog $5 ❖ Doll-making supplies. 800–438–7227.

Herb's Porcelain Doll Studio, 1208 E. 15th St., Plano, TX 75074: Price list $2 (refundable) ❖ Bisque kits for making dolls. 800–628–4696; 214–578–1128 (in TX).

Hickory Dickory Dolls, 124 E. Aurora Rd., Northfield, OH 44067: Free price list ❖ Dolls, clothing, and shoes. 800–468–2085.

House of Caron, 10111 Larrylyn Dr., Whittier, CA 90603: Price list $2.50 ❖ Miniature doll molds and doll-making supplies. 310–947–6753.

Huston Dolls, 7960 US Rt. 23, Chillicothe, OH 45601: Catalog $2 ❖ Handmade porcelain dolls and make-them-yourself kits. 614–663–2881.

International Manufacturing Company, 1130 Live Oak St., Lillian Springs, FL 32351: Catalog $1 ❖ Doll-making and other craft supplies, pine cones, and potpourri materials. 904–875–2918.

Jennell's Doll House, 7662 Krosp Rd., Millington, TN 38053: Catalog $2 (refundable) ❖ Doll kits, supplies, pre-sewn bodies, and clothes. 901–872–1664.

Jo's Dolls-N-Fine Porcelain, 111 Army Post Rd., Des Moines, IA 50315: Catalog $7.95 ❖ Doll-making supplies. 800–323–4689.

Jomac Dolls & Supplies, 702 Crenshaw, Pasadena, TX 77504: Free information ❖ Doll-making supplies, bisque and wax kits, and greenware. 713–944–8221.

Janna Joseph, P.O. Box 1262, Dunedin, FL 34697: Catalog $4.95 ❖ Miniature doll molds. 813–784–1877.

Joyce's Doll House, 20188 Williamson, Mt. Clemens, MI 48403: Catalog $1 ❖ Doll parts, wigs, natural straw hats, eyes, and sewing supplies.

Judis Dolls, P.O. Box 607, Port Orchard, WA 98366: Catalog $2 ❖ Patterns and supplies for cloth dolls. 206–895–2779.

Kari & Judy's Creations, 5014 Argus Dr., Los Angeles, CA 90041: Free price list with long SASE ❖ Finished and unfinished composition doll bodies. 213–257–8219.

Kay Jay's Doll Emporium & Hospital, 18 E. 9th St., New Jersey Plaza, Ocean City, NJ 08226: Free information ❖ Antique and designer dolls and doll-making supplies. 609–399–5632.

Karen Kay Porcelain Arts, P.O. Box 4028, El Paso, TX 79914: Free information ❖ Doll-making kits. 915–751–0966.

Kemper Tools & Doll Supplies Inc., 13595 12th St., Chino, CA 91710: Free catalog ❖ Pottery, sculpting, craft, and art tools. Also doll-making supplies. 800–388–5367.

Kirchen Brothers, Box 1016, Skokie, IL 60076: Catalog $2 ❖ Doll-making supplies and kits, ready-to-wear and ready-to-sew clothing, shoes and socks, and other craft supplies and kits. 708–647–6747.

Ledgewood Studio, 6000 Ledgewood Dr., Forest Park, GA 30050: Catalog $2 with long SASE and three 1st class stamps ❖ Dress patterns, period clothing, fabrics, supplies for antique dolls, and sewing notions.

Victor H. Levy Inc., 1355 S. Flower St., Los Angeles, CA 90015: Catalog $5 ❖ Doll- and jewelry-making supplies. 800–421–8021; 213–749–8247 (in CA).

Linda's Dreamland, P.O. Box 113, Roseburg, OR 97470: Free information ❖ Doll-making supplies, wigs, stockings, shoes, eyes, and stands. 503–459–5184.

Magic Cabin Dolls, Rt. 2, Box 39, Westby, WI 54667: Free catalog ❖ Natural fiber doll-making supplies, kits and patterns, skin-tone cotton knits, yarns, and handmade dolls. 608–634–2848.

Marl & Barbie, 5707 39th Street Circle East, Bradenton, FL 34203: Catalog $5 ❖ Barbie doll fashions, from 1959 to the present. 813–751–6275.

Maybelle's Doll Works, 140 Space Park Dr., Nashville, TN 37211: Catalog $6 ❖ Doll-making supplies and molds. 615–831–0661.

Mimi's Books & Supplies, P.O. Box 662, Point Pleasant, NJ 08742: Free catalog ❖ Doll-making tools, supplies, and books. 800–521–5512.

Mini World, 9919 E. 63rd St., Raytown, MO 64133: Catalog $3 ❖ Doll-making supplies. 800–762–3318; 816–353–6999 (in MO).

Minnie's Doll House, Knight Rd., Rt. 3, Box 527, Lake Providence, LA 71254: Brochure $1.50 ❖ Original doll clothes. 318–559–2857.

Monique Trading Corporation, 270 Oyster Point Blvd., South San Francisco, CA 94080: Catalog $3 ❖ Doll wigs. 800–621–4338.

Pierce Tools, 1610 Parkdale Dr., Grants Pass, OR 97527: Free catalog ❖ Tools for the

dollmaker, ceramist, potter, and sculptor. 503–476–1778.

Mary Radbill Doll Supplies, 4512 Eden St., Philadelphia, PA 19114: Catalog $3 ❖ Doll-making supplies. 215–632–4606.

Karen Raum's Fantasy Dolls, 202 Ridgeview Ln., Boulder, CO 80302: Catalog $3.75 ❖ Doll-making supplies. 800–879–3655.

Thelma Resch, 89 Purple Martin Dr., Murrells Inlet, SC 29576: Brochure $2 ❖ Original doll molds. 803–651–0596.

Rivendell Inc., 8209 Proctor Rd., Painesville, OH 44077: Catalog $4 ❖ Supplies for porcelain dolls. 216–254–4088.

Sandcastle Creations, P.O. Box 563, Newport, OR 97365: Free information ❖ Wig-making supplies, kits, and clothing. 503–265–2499.

Seeley's, P.O. Box 669, Oneonta, NY 13820: Free catalog ❖ Doll-making supplies.

Shoppe Full of Dolls, 39 N. Main St., New Hope, PA 18938: Catalog $2 ❖ Dolls and clothing. 215–862–5524.

Standard Doll Company, 23–83 31st St., Long Island City, NY 11105: Catalog $3 ❖ Supplies for making and repairing dolls, clothing, doll stands, shoes and socks, buttons, wigs, books, and sewing notions. 800–543–6557.

Diane Stec's All About Dolls, 49 Lakeside Blvd., Hopatcong, NJ 07843: Catalog $2 ❖ Doll kits, blanks, and supplies. 201–770–3228.

Regina A. Steele Antique Dolls, 23 Wheatfield Dr., Wilmington, DE 19810: Free list with long SASE ❖ Antique dolls. 302–475–5374.

Sugar Creek Industries Inc., P.O. Box 354, Linden, IN 47955: Free catalog ❖ Porcelain pouring equipment and supplies. 317–339–4641.

Tallina's Doll Supplies Inc., 15790 Southeast Hwy. 224, Clackamas, OR 97015: Catalog $1 ❖ Doll-making supplies. 503–658–6148.

TM Ceramic Service, Division T.M. Porcelain, 108 N. Henry, Bay City, MI 48706: Catalog $5 ❖ Slip, molds, doll bodies, arms, legs, reproduction and character heads, and other supplies. 517–893–3526.

The Ultimate Collection Inc., 12783 Forest Hill Blvd., Ste. 1208, West Palm Beach, FL

33414: Catalog $6 (refundable) ❖ Doll and accessory molds. 407–790–0137.

Unicorn Studios, Box 370, Seymour, TN 37865: Catalog $1 ❖ Easy-to-install windup and electronic music box movements, winking light units, and voices for dolls and bears. 615–984–0145.

DOLLS

Adopt-A-Doll, 1041 Lincoln Ave., San Jose, CA 95125: Catalog $3 ❖ Old and new dolls, doll-making supplies, clothing, shoes, and hats. 408–298–DOLL.

Alpha's Dolls & Gifts, 161 Ferguson Village Shopping Center, Dallas, TX 75228: Free list with long SASE ❖ Current and retired Barbie dolls, porcelains, Bob Mackies, and other collectible dolls. 214–328–2729.

Angel Children, 4977 Sparr Rd., Gaylord, MI 49735: Catalog $2 ❖ Miniature porcelain dolls. 517–732–1931.

Anything Goes Inc., 9801 Gulf Dr., Anna Maria, FL 34216: Quarterly newsletter $2 ❖ Current Barbie dolls. 813–778–4456.

Aurelia's World of Dolls Inc., 2025 Merrick Rd., Merrick, NY 11566: Free newsletter ❖ Dolls by U.S. and international artists. 516–378–2556.

Baby Me, 730 Boston Rd., Rt. 3A, Billerica, MA 01821: Free information ❖ Dolls. 508–667–1187.

Be'be' House of Dolls, 247 3rd Ave., Chula Vista, CA 91910: Free information with long SASE ❖ Dolls. 619–476–0680.

Best of Everything, 8301 5th Ave., Brooklyn, NY 11209: Free information ❖ Felt dolls and other collectibles. 718–238–9626.

Biggs Limited Editions, 5517 Lakeside Ave., Richmond, VA 23228: Free information with long SASE ❖ Limited edition artist and other dolls. 800–637–0704.

Cabbages & Kings, 6330 Lawrenceville Hwy., Tucker, GA 30084: Free information with long SASE ❖ Dolls. 404–934–0055.

Calico Corner, 3082 Niagara Falls Blvd., North Tonawanda, NY 14120: Free information with long SASE ❖ Dolls. 716–694–7575.

Cardinal Incorporated, 400 Markley St., Port Reading, NJ 07064: Catalog $7.50 (refundable) ❖ Miniature dollhouse furniture and porcelain collectible dolls. 800–888–0936.

Celia's Dolls & Collectibles, 800 E. Halland Beach Blvd., Hallandale, FL 33009: Catalog $5 ❖ Dolls. 305–458–0661.

CJ's Dolls & Dreams, 5 Plaistow Rd., Rt. 125, Plaistow, NH 03865: Free information ❖ Artist dolls. 603–382–3449.

Corbett's Collectable Dolls, 123 Creek Rd., Mount Laurel, NJ 08054: Free information ❖ Artist and manufacturer dolls. 609–866–9787.

Country House, 424 Broad St., Elmer, NJ 08318: Free information with long SASE ❖ Dolls and bears. 609–358–2048.

Marl Davidson Dolls, 5707 39th Street Circle East, Bradenton, FL 34203: Free list with 9x12 envelope and three 1st class stamps ❖ Barbie dolls and clothing, from 1959 to the present. 813–751–6275.

Doll Centre, P.O. Box 2188, Placerville, CA 95667: Free catalog ❖ Limited edition dolls. 800–231–5111.

Doll City USA, 2040 S. Harbor Blvd., Anaheim, CA 92802: Price list $2 ❖ Dolls.

Doll Cottage, 427 Meeting St., West Columbia, SC 29169: Free information ❖ Dolls. 803–794–2119.

Doll Den, 231 W. Douglas, El Cajon, CA 92020: Free information with long SASE ❖ Dolls and stuffed animals. 619–444–2198.

Doll Emporium, P.O. Box 1000, Studio City, CA 91604: Free information ❖ Antique dolls. 818–763–5937.

The Doll Gallery, 81 Glasgow St., Clyde, NY 14433: Free price list with long SASE ❖ Dolls.

The Doll House, 5022 N. May, Oklahoma City, OK 73112: Free information ❖ Collectible dolls. 405–943–1498.

The Doll Palace, 51 George St., Pataskala, OH 43062: Free information ❖ Artist and manufacturer dolls. 800–999–9680.

Doll Parlor, 7 Church Street, Allentown, NJ 08501: Free information with long SASE ❖ Dolls. 609–259–8118.

Doll Showcase, 104 Front St., Marietta, OH 45750: Free price list with long SASE ❖ Artist and manufacturer dolls. 800–93–DOLLS.

Dollmakers Originals International, 1230 Pottsdown Pike, Glenmoore, PA 19343: Free information with long SASE ❖ Handmade porcelain dolls. 215–458–1120.

Dolls - Gone - Bye Company, Jennifer DeHay, 157 Pomfret Rd., Brooklyn, CT 06234: Free information ❖ Antique dolls. 203–779–1866.

Dollsville Dolls & Bearsville Bears, 461 N. Palm Canyon Dr., Palm Springs, CA 92262: Catalog $2 ❖ Dolls. 619–325–2241.

Dwyer's Doll House, 1944 Warwick Ave., Warwick, RI 02889: Catalog $10 ❖ Dolls, dollhouses, miniatures, and dollhouse building supplies. 800–248–3655.

Enchanted Doll House, Rt. 7A, Manchester Center, VT 05255: Catalog $2 ❖ Dolls, miniatures, bears, stuffed animals, and other toys. 802–362–1327.

Enesco Corporation, 1 Enesco Plaza, Elk Grove Village, IL 60007: Free information and list of retailers ❖ Barbie dolls. 708–640–3566.

Ernie's Toyland, 671 Colusa Ave., Yuba City, CA 95991: Free information ❖ Barbies and other dolls. 800–367–1233.

Fabric Creations, Rt. 3, Box 96, Crocker, MO 65452: Free brochure with long SASE ❖ Fabric dolls. 314–736–5733.

GiGi's Dolls & Sherry's Teddy Bears Inc., 6029 N. Northwest Hwy., Chicago, IL 60631: Free catalog ❖ Bears, dolls, plush toys, and miniatures.

Grandma's Attic, Joyce Kekatos, 3132 Ampere Ave., Bronx, NY 10465: Free information with long SASE ❖ Antique French and German bisque dolls. 718–863–0373.

Guys 'N Dolls, 614 S. 2nd St., Wilmington, NC 28401: Free information with long SASE and three 1st class stamps ❖ Barbie dolls. 910–251–9501.

David Hammon Dolls & Toys, 1117 E. 1st St., Long Beach, CA 90802: List $1 ❖ Imported Japanese fashion dolls fom Takara, ma-ba, and Bandai. 310–436–6444.

Heirloom Dolls & Treasures, 226 S. Washington St., Naperville, IL 60540: Free price list with long SASE ❖ Dolls. 708–717–5995.

Hickory Dickory Dolls, 124 E. Aurora Rd., Northfield, OH 44067: Free price list ❖ Dolls, clothing, and shoes. 800–468–2085.

The Hobby Gallery Miniature Loft, 1810 Meriden Rd., Wolcott, CT 06716: Free information with long SASE ❖ Dolls, dollhouses, miniatures, and plush animals. 203–879–2316.

Iron Horse Gifts, Rt. 9, Latham, NY 12110: Free information ❖ Designer dolls. 518–785–3735.

Jan Dolls, 5204 Godfrey Rd., Godfrey, IL 62035: Free newsletter ❖ Artist dolls. 618–466–0080.

Kay Jay's Doll Emporium & Hospital, 18 E. 9th St., New Jersey Plaza, Ocean City, NJ 08226: Free information ❖ Antique and designer dolls and doll-making supplies. 609–399–5632.

Lane's Toyland & Gifts, 1301 Magnolia, Texarkana, TX 75501: Free catalog ❖ Barbies and other dolls. 800–421–8697.

Lee's Collectibles, P.O. Box 19133, Sacramento, CA 95819: Free information with long SASE ❖ Wood, cloth, and other contemporary artist dolls. 916–457–4308.

Seymour Mann, 225 5th Ave., New York, NY 10010: Catalog $7.50 ❖ Dolls.

Marj's Doll Sanctuary, 5238 Plainfield Ave. NE, Grand Rapids, MI 49505: Free catalog with three 1st class stamps ❖ Dolls and bears.

Marl & Barbie, 5707 39th Street Circle East, Bradenton, FL 34203: Catalog $5 ❖ Barbie dolls and clothing, from 1959 to the present. 813–751–6275.

Mary D's Dolls & Bears & Such, 8407 W. Broadway, Brooklyn Park, MN 55445: Catalog $1 ❖ Dolls. 612–424–4375.

Mary Stolz Doll Shop, RD 6, Box 6767, East Stroudsburg, PA 18301: Free catalog ❖ Barbies and other collectible dolls. 717–588–7566.

Melton's Antiques, 4201 Indian River Rd., Chesapeake, VA 23325: Free information with long SASE ❖ Antique dolls. 804–420–9226.

Lee Middleton Original Dolls Inc., 1301 Washington Blvd., Belpre, OH 45714: Catalog $3 ❖ Original dolls and bears. 800–843–9572.

Monarch Collectibles, 2121 NW Military Hwy., San Antonio, TX 78213: Free information ❖ Dolls. 512–341–DOLL.

Not Just Dolls, 2447 Gus Thomasson Rd., Dallas, TX 75228: Price list $2 ❖ Artist and manufacturer dolls. 214–321–0412.

Original Appalachian Artworks Inc., P.O. Box 714, Cleveland, GA 30528: Free information ❖ Cabbage Patch dolls. 706–865–2171.

J. Parker, Box 34, Midland, Ontario, Canada L4R 4K6: Catalog $3 (refundable) ❖ Porcelain doll kits.

Pewter Classics, 3635 28th St. SE, Eastbrook Mall, Grand Rapids, MI 49512: Free information with long SASE ❖ Dolls, bears, and other collectibles. 800–833–3655.

Playhouse, Zane Plaza Mall, 1080 N. Bridge St., Chiliccothe, OH 45601: Free list with long SASE ❖ Artist dolls and bears. 614–774–3655.

Pleasant Company, P.O. Box 620190, Middleton, WI 53562: Free catalog ❖ Dolls. 800–845–0005.

Poppets Inc., Annapolis Harbor Center, Annapolis, MD 21403: Free information with long SASE ❖ New dolls and out-of-production specials. 410–266–7713.

Rainbow Factory, 131 W. Vienna St., Clio, MI 48420: Free information with long SASE ❖ Dolls, miniatures, carrousels, music boxes, and bears. 313–687–1351.

Rose's Doll House Store, 5826 W. Bluemound, Milwaukee, WI 53213: Free catalog ❖ Dolls, bears, and dollhouse furnishings. 414–259–9965.

Samurai Antiques, 229 Santa Ynez Ct., Santa Barbara, CA 93103: Price list $1 with long SASE ❖ Japanese antique dolls by Samurai, Emperor, and Empress. 805–965–9688.

Sandy's Dolls & Collectables Inc., 11224 SW Hwy., Palos Hills, IL 60465: Price list $1 ❖ Artist and limited edition dolls. 708–423–0070.

Second Childhood Inc., Bay Run Farm, RR 2, Box 179, West Branch, IA 52358: Catalog $4 ❖ Traditional Japanese dolls. 319–643–2441.

Shirley's Doll House, 20509 North Hwy. 21, P.O. Box 99A, Wheeling, IL 60090: Free information with long SASE ❖ Dolls, bears, antiques, doll house furniture, wigs, clothing, shoes, and socks. 708–537–1632.

Shoppe Full of Dolls, 39 N. Main St., New Hope, PA 18938: Catalog $2 ❖ Dolls and clothing. 215–862–5524.

Simply Lovely Gift Shoppe, 572 New Brunswick Ave., Fords, NJ 08863: Free price list with long SASE ❖ Dolls. 908–738–4181.

Society's Child, 28686 W. Northwest Hwy., Barrington, IL 60010: Free information with long SASE ❖ Artist and limited edition dolls. 800–232–DOLL.

Sutter Street Emporium, 731 Sutter St., Folsom, CA 95630: Free information ❖ Limited edition, original artist, and other dolls. 800–255–6243; 916–985–4647 (in CA).

Theriault's, P.O. Box 151, Annapolis, MD 21404: Free newsletter ❖ Antique and other collectible dolls. 410–224–3655.

Those Swell Doll Guys, 1421 36th Ave. South, Seattle, WA 98144: Information $1 ❖ Vintage Barbie dolls and clothing.

Thru Children's Eyes, 708 Thousand Oaks Blvd., Thousand Oaks, CA 91360: Free list with long SASE ❖ Vintage Barbies, Ginnys, and other collectible dolls. 805–494–4500.

Tide-Rider Inc., P.O. Box 429, Oakdale, CA 95361: Free information ❖ Handcrafted felt dolls with detailed facial features and costuming. 209–848–4420.

Toy Shoppe, 1003 Sycamore Square, P.O. Box 28, Midlothian, VA 23113: Free information ❖ Collectible portrait dolls by English doll makers, Philip and Christine Heath. 800–447–7995.

Ryan Twist Gallery, 430 Teaneck Rd., Ridgefield Park, NJ 07660: Free information with long SASE ❖ Dolls. 800–421–0171.

Your Old Friends Doll Shop, Carmen & Mike Tickal, 21 5th St. SW, Mason City, IA 50401: Catalog $5 ❖ Barbie dolls, fashions, and accessories. 515–424–0984.

DRAFTING SUPPLIES

Alvin Drafting, Engineering & Graphic Arts Supplies, P.O. Box 188, Windsor, CT 06095: Free catalog ❖ Drafting, engineering, and graphic art supplies. 800–444–ALVIN; 203–243–8991 (in CT).

Co-Op Artists' Materials, P.O. Box 53097, Atlanta, GA 30355: Free catalog ❖ Painting, drafting, drawing, airbrushing, and other graphic art supplies. 800–877–3242.

Fairgate Rule Company Inc., 22 Adams Ave., P.O. Box 278, Cold Spring, NY 10516: Free catalog ❖ Rulers, other measuring devices, stencils, and drawing aids. 800–431–2180; 914–265–3677 (in NY).

Hearlihy & Company, 714 W. Columbia St., Springfield, OH 45504: Free catalog ❖ Drafting and graphics equipment, computer software for computer-aided designing, drawing and drafting instructional aids, videos, plotters, and furniture. 800–622–1000.

Nasco, 901 Janesville Ave., Fort Atkinson, WI 53538: Free catalog ❖ Drawing and drafting supplies. 800–558–9595.

Norton Products, Box 2012, New Rochelle, NY 10802: Free information ❖ Craft projector that projects an image onto most surfaces. 800–453–3326.

Professional Graphics, 23 Omni Cir., P.O. Box 1327, Auburn, ME 04211: Free information ❖ Drafting equipment. 207–783–9132.

Pyramid of Urbana, 2107 N. High Cross Rd., Urbana, IL 61801: Catalog $5 ❖ School equipment and drawing, drafting, crafts, office, and art supplies. 217–328–3099.

DUMBWAITERS

Aid-O-Maid Company, P.O. Box 3, Waco, TX 76703: Free information ❖ Dumbwaiters for houses. 817–752–8702.

Econol Lift Corporation, 2513 Center St., Box 854, Cedar Falls, IA 50613: Free information ❖ Dumbwaiters, residential elevators, and vertical, wheelchair, and stair-riding lifts. 319–277–4777.

Inclinator Company of America, P.O. Box 1557, Harrisburg, PA 17105: Free information ❖ Dumbwaiters. 717–234–8065.

Miller Manufacturing Inc., 165 Cascade Ct., Rohnert Park, CA 94928: Free information ❖ Commercial and residential manual-operated dumbwaiters. 800–232–2177.

Whitco/Vincent Whitney Company, 60 Liberty Ship Way, Sausalito, CA 94966: Free information ❖ Residential and commercial hand-operated dumbwaiters. 800–332–3286.

EGG CRAFTING

Dennis Brand Handcrafted Eggs, 13236 Crenshaw Blvd., Gardena, CA 90249: Free information ❖ Handcrafted eggs made from polished stones. 800–553–6855; 310–327–2323 (in CA).

Olesky Enterprises, W6742 #12 Rd., Wallace, MI 49803: Free information with long SASE ❖ Decorated chicken and goose eggs for decorating. 906–227–3051.

Schiltz Goose Farm, 7 W. Oak St., P.O. Box 267, Sisseton, SD 57262: Free information ❖ Decorating supplies, tools, and blown goose, duck, quail, and turkey eggs in jumbo, X-large, large, and regular sizes. 605–698–7651.

Woods of the World Inc., 897 North Bend Rd., Cincinnati, OH 45224: Brochure $1 ❖ Over 150 egg-shaped different woods from worldwide sources.

ELECTRICAL SUPPLIES

Coghlin Electric & Electronics, 155 Summer St., P.O. Box 150858, Worcester, MA 01615: Free catalog ❖ Electronic and electrical supplies, test equipment, and tools. 508–791–7861.

Marlin P. Jones & Associates, P.O. Box 12685, Lake Park, FL 33403: Free catalog ❖ Electrical and electronic components. 407–848–8236.

Wiremold Company, 60 Woodlawn St., West Hartford, CT 06110: Free information ❖ Fixtures, switches, controls, and grounding outlets for installation without having to break into walls or ceilings. 800–621–0049.

ELECTRIC GENERATORS & ENGINES

China Diesel Imports, 15749 Lyons Valley Rd., Jamul, CA 92035: Free catalog ❖ Diesel generators and parts for an economical power source. 619–699–1995.

Generac Corporation, Box 8, Waukesha, WI 53187: Free information ❖ Emergency electricity-generating source. 414–544–4811.

ELECTRONICS EQUIPMENT
Components & Equipment

Accord Electronic Systems Inc., 1001 W. Cypress Creek Rd., Fort Lauderdale, FL 33309: Free information ❖ Electronic components. 800–998–2242; 305–772–2242 (in FL).

Ace Communications, 6975 Hillsdale Ct., Indianapolis, IN 46250: Free information ❖ Electronic equipment. 800–445–7717.

Active Micro, 1891 Obispo Ave., Signal Hill, CA 90804: Free information ❖ Integrated circuits, memory chips, eproms, circuit boards, diodes, transistors, and LED's. 310–494–4851.

All Electronics Corporation, P.O. Box 567, Van Nuys, CA 91408: Free catalog ❖ New and surplus electronic parts and supplies. 800–826–5432; 818–904–0524 (in CA).

Allied Electronics, 7410 Pebble Dr., Fort Worth, TX 76118: Free catalog ❖ Electronic parts, tools, and books. 800–433–8700.

Alltronics, 2300 Zanker Rd., San Jose, CA 95131: Free catalog ❖ Electronic components and test equipment. 408–943–9773.

American Design Components, 400 County Ave., Secaucus, NJ 07094: Free catalog ❖ New, reconditioned, and used electro-mechanical and electronic equipment. 800–776–3800.

American Electronics Inc., 164 Southpark Blvd., P.O. Box 301, Greenwood, IN 46142: Free information ❖ Electronic components. 800–872–1373.

ARS Electronics, 7110 de Celis Pl., P.O. Box 7323, Van Nuys, CA 91409: Free brochure ❖ Replacement electronic tubes.

Battery-Tech Inc., 28–25 215th Pl., Bayside, NY 11360: Free information ❖ Replacement batteries. 800–442–4275.

Brigar Electronics, 79 Alice St., Binghamton, NY 13904: Free information ❖ Electronic parts. 607–723–3111.

Calcera, P.O. Box 489, Belmont, CA 94002: Free information ❖ Surplus electronic components. 800–257–5549.

Capital Electronics Inc., 5451 N. Broadway Ave., Chicago, IL 60640: Free information ❖ Printed circuit boards. 312–271–9510.

Circuit Specialists Inc., 220 S. Country Club Dr., Mesa, AZ 85210: Free catalog ❖ Electronic equipment. 800–528–1417.

Consolidated Electronics Inc., 705 Watervliet Ave., Dayton, OH 45420: Catalog $5 ❖ Electronic equipment. 800–543–3568.

Contact East, 335 Willow St. South, North Andover, MA 01845: Free catalog ❖ Tools and equipment for testing, repairing,and assembling electronic equipment. 800–225–5370; 508–682–2000 (in MA).

Crump Electronics, 6340 W. Mississippi Ave., Lakewood, CO 80226: Free catalog ❖ New and used electronic parts. 303–936–4407.

Crystek Corporation, 2371 Crystal Dr., Fort Myers, FL 33907: Free information ❖ Crystals for radio operation and experimenters. 813–936–2109.

Dalbani Electronics, 2733 Carrier Ave., Los Angeles, CA 90040: Free catalog ❖ Electronic components. 800–325–2264; 213–727–0054 (in CA).

Daliban, 4225 NW 72nd Ave., Miami, FL 33166: Free catalog ❖ Electronic components. 800–325–2264; 305–716–1016 (in FL).

Debco Electronics, 4025 Edwards Rd., Cincinnati, OH 45209: Free information ❖ Components and tools. 800–423–4499.

Derf Electronics, 1 Biehn St., New Rochelle, NY 10801: Free information ❖ Surplus electronic components. 800–431–2912.

Digi-Key Corporation, Hwy. 32 South, Thief River Falls, MN 56701: Free catalog ❖ Electronic components. 800–346–5144.

The Electronic Goldmine, P.O. Box 5408, Scottsdale, AZ 85261: Free catalog ❖ Electronic components. 602–451–7454.

Fair Radio Sales Company Inc., P.O. Box 1105, Lima, OH 45802: Free information ❖ Surplus electronic parts. 419–227–6573.

H & R Company, 18 Canal St., Bristol, PA 19007: Free catalog ❖ Electronic components, tools, computer equipment, power supplies, test equipment, and meters. 215–788–5583.

Halted Electronic Supply, 3500 Ryder St., Santa Clara, CA 95051: Catalog $1 ❖ Electronic equipment. 800–442–5833.

Haltek Electronics, 1062 Linda Vista Ave., Mountain View, CA 94043: Free information ❖ New, used, and surplus electronic equipment. 408–744–1333.

Hosfelt Electronics Inc., 2700 Sunset Blvd., Steubenville, OH 43952: Free catalog ❖ Electronic components. 800–524–6464.

Jameco Electronics, 1355 Shoreway Rd., Belmont, CA 94002: Free catalog ❖ Electronic components, kits, and testing and computer equipment. 800–637–8471.

Jan Crystals, P.O. Box 06017, Fort Myers, FL 33906: Free catalog ❖ Crystals for radio operation and experimenters. 800–JAN-XTAL; 813–936–2397 (in FL).

JDR Microdevices, 1850 S. 10th St., San Jose, CA 95112: Free information ❖ Electronic components, micro-devices, tools, chips, and computer equipment. 800–538–5000.

Marlin P. Jones & Associates, P.O. Box 12685, Lake Park, FL 33403: Free catalog ❖ Electrical and electronic components. 407–848–8236.

Joseph Electronics, 8830 N. Milwaukee Ave., Niles, IL 60648: Free catalog ❖ Electronic components, test instruments, tools, and soldering equipment. 800–323–5925; 708–297–4200 (in IL).

K & F Electronics Inc., 33041 Groesbeck, Fraser, MI 48026: Free information ❖ Etched and drilled printed circuit boards. 313–294–5999.

K & K Electronics, 170 E. Market St., Alliance, OH 44601: Free information ❖ Printed circuit boards. 216–821–6478.

Kelvin Electronics, 10 Hub Dr., Melville, NY 11747: Free information ❖ Electronic components and test equipment. 800–645–9212; 516–756–1750 (in NY).

McGee's Electronics, 1901 McGee St., Kansas City, MO 64108: Free catalog ❖ Speakers and electronic parts. 800–842–5092.

MCM Electronics, 650 Congress Park Dr., Centerville, OH 45459: Free catalog ❖ Test equipment, computer and telephone accessories, TV and electronic components, and speakers. 800–824–TECH.

Mendelson Electronics Company Inc., 340 E 1st St., Dayton, OH 45402: Free catalog ❖ Electronic components. 800–422–3525; 513–461–3525 (in OH).

MFJ Enterprises Inc., P.O. Box 494, Mississippi State, MS 39762: Free catalog ❖ Equipment for electronic experimenters and amateur radio operators. 800–647–1800.

Mouser Electronics, 2401 Hwy. 287 North, Mansfield, TX 76063: Free catalog ❖ Electronic components. 800–992–9943.

New England Circuit Sales, 292 Cabot St., Beverly, MA 01915: Free information ❖ Surplus electronic components. 800–922–NECS.

Ocean State Electronics, 6 Industrial Dr., Westerly, RI 02891: Catalog $2 ❖ Amateur radio and electronic components and kits, books, and other hard-to-find equipment. 401–596–3080.

Parts Express, 340 E. 1st St., Dayton, OH 45042: Free catalog ❖ Parts for electronic projects, repair, experimentation, and research. 800–338–0531; 513–222–0173 (in OH).

RA Enterprises, 2260 De La Cruz Blvd., Santa Clara, CA 95050: Free information ❖ Surplus and new test equipment, electro-mechanical devices, and other electronics. 408–986–8286.

Radio Shack, Division Tandy Corporation, One Tandy Center, Fort Worth, TX 76102: Free information ❖ Electronic components, science kits, computers, stereo equipment, toys and games, and other equipment. 817–390–3011.

RF Parts, 435 S. Pacific St., San Marcos, CA 92069: Free information ❖ Power transistors and parts for amateur, marine, and commercial radio operation. 619–744–0700.

Scanner World USA, 10 New Scotland Ave., Albany, NY 12208: Free information ❖ Scanners. 518–436–9606.

Sescom Inc., 2100 Ward Dr., Henderson, NV 89015: Free information ❖ Sheet metal boxes for electronics construction. 702–565–3400.

Soft Light Manufacturing, 501 Simpson Chapel Rd., Bloomington, IN 47404: Free information ❖ Solderless breadboards. 800–365–2575.

Southpaw Electronics, P.O. Box 886, New Hyde Park, NY 11040: Free information ❖ Electronic components. 516–775–5045.

Surplus Traders, Winters Ln., P.O. Box 276, Alburg, VT 05440: Free catalog ❖ Surplus electronic parts. 514–739–9328.

2M Electronics Inc., 4503 Walzem, San Antonio, TX 78218: Free information ❖ Electronic components and new and used test equipment. 800–433–0554.

3M Electronic Specialty Products, Attention: Electronics Dept., 6801 River Place Blvd., Austin, TX 78769: Free information ❖ Solderless breadboards. 800–328–0411.

Tucker Surplus Store, 1717 Reserve St., Garland, TX 75042: Free information ❖ Surplus electronic equipment. 800–527–4642.

The Ultimate Saving Source, 2733 Carrier Ave., Los Angeles, CA 90040: Free catalog ❖ Electronic components. 800–325–2264; 213–727–0054 (in CA).

Unicorn Electronics, 10000 Canoga Ave., Chatsworth, CA 91311: Free information ❖ Electronic components, lasers, robotic kits, and other supplies. 818–341–8833.

Visitect Inc., P.O. Box 14156, Fremont, CA 94539: Free information ❖ Miniature transmitters and receivers. 510–651–1425.

W & W Associates, 29–11 Parsons Blvd., Flushing, NY 11354: Free catalog ❖ Batteries. 800–221–0732; 718–961–2103 (in NY).

Kits & Plans

Amazing Concepts, Box 716, Amherst, NH 03031: Catalog $1 ❖ Easy-to-assemble sub-miniature FM transmitters for telephones and voice transmission. 603–673–4730.

Consumertronics, 2011 Crescent Dr., P.O. Drawer 537, Alamogordo, NM 88310:

Catalog $2 ❖ Electronic kits and parts. 505–434–0234.

DC Electronics, P.O. Box 3203, Scottsdale, AZ 85271: Free information ❖ Electronic kits. 800–423–0070.

Edlie Electronics, 2700 Hempstead Tnpk., Levittown, NY 11756: Free catalog ❖ Electronic kits, parts, and test equipment. 516–735–3330.

The Electronic Goldmine, P.O. Box 5408, Scottsdale, AZ 85261: Free catalog ❖ Easy-to-assemble kits. 602–451–7454.

Electronic Rainbow, 6254 LaPas Trail, Indianapolis, IN 46268: Free information ❖ Easy-to-assemble kits. 317–291–7262.

Graymark, P.O. Box 2015, Tustin, CA 92681: Free catalog ❖ Easy-to-build robotic kits. 800–854–7393.

Heath Company, 455 Riverview Dr., Benton Harbor, MI 49022: Free catalog ❖ Electronic kits. 616–925–6000.

Information Unlimited Inc., Box 716, Amherst, NH 03031: Catalog $1 ❖ Electronic projects. 603–673–4730.

Jameco Electronics, 1355 Shoreway Rd., Belmont, CA 94002: Free catalog ❖ Electronic kits, test equipment, and computer equipment. 800–637–8471.

Krystal Kits, P.O. Box 445, Bentonville, AR 72712: Catalog $1 ❖ Electronic kits and plans for amateur science experimenters. 501–273–5340.

LNS Technologies, 20993 Foothill Blvd., Hayward, CA 94541: Catalog $1 ❖ Electronic kits.

Mark V Electronics Inc., 8019 E. Slauson Ave., Montebello, CA 90640: Free catalog ❖ Electronic kits for beginning, intermediate, and advanced experimenters. 213–888–8988.

Meredith Instruments, P.O. Box 1724, Glendale, AZ 85301: Free catalog ❖ Lasers and other optical equipment, parts, and accessories. 602–934–9387.

Midwest Laser Products, P.O. Box 2187, Bridgeview, IL 60455: Free catalog ❖ Laser equipment. 708–460–9595.

MWK Industries, 1269 W. Pomona Rd., #112, Corona, CA 91720: Free catalog ❖ Laser equipment, power supplies, other optics, light shows, and books. 909–278–0563.

Ocean State Electronics, 6 Industrial Dr., Westerly, RI 02891: Catalog $2 ❖

Educational kits and electronic equipment. 401–596–3080.

Quantum Research, 17919 77th Ave., Edmonton, Alberta, Canada T5T 2S1: Catalog $4 (refundable) ❖ Voice disguiser, lie detector, lasers, transmitters, and other electronic devices in kits or assembled.

Radio Shack, Division Tandy Corporation, One Tandy Center, Fort Worth, TX 76102: Free information ❖ Electronic components, science kits, computers, stereo equipment, toys and games, and other equipment. 817–390–3011.

Ramsey Electronics Inc., 793 Canning Pkwy., Victor, NY 14564: Free information ❖ Test equipment and easy-to-assemble electronic kits. 716–924–4560.

Silicon Valley Surplus, 1273 Industrial Pkwy., Ste. 460, Hayward, CA 94544: Free information ❖ Light and motion projects, laser applications, computer interface equipment, and other kits. 510–582–6602.

Townsend Electronics Inc., P.O. Box 415, Pierceton, IN 46562: Catalog $1 ❖ Kits for amateur radio equipment, ham radio books, and other publications. 219–594–3661.

Unicorn Electronics, 10000 Canoga Ave., Chatsworth, CA 91311: Free information ❖ Electronic components, lasers, robotics kits, and other supplies. 818–341–8833.

Xandi Electronics, Box 25647, Tempe, AZ 85285: Free catalog ❖ Satellite TV receiver, voice disguiser, FM bug, telephone transmitter, phone snoop, and other easy-to-build kits. 800–336–7389.

Test Equipment

Alfa Electronics, 741 Alexander Rd., Princeton, NJ 08540: Free catalog ❖ Multipurpose test equipment. 800–526–2532; 609–520–2002 (in NJ).

Wm. B. Allen Supply Company, Allen Square, 300 Block N. Rampart St., New Orleans, LA 70112: Free information ❖ Multipurpose test equipment, replacement probes, and electronic components. 800–535–9593; 800–462–9520 (in LA).

Alltronics, 2300 Zanker Rd., San Jose, CA 95131: Free catalog ❖ Test equipment and electronic components. 408–943–9773.

Amprobe Test Equipment, Box 329, Lynbrook, NY 11563: Free catalog ❖ Multimeters, volt-amp-ohmmeters, and other test equipment. 516–593–5600.

BMC Electronics, 20 Highpoint, Dove Canyon, CA 92630: Free catalog ❖ Test equipment. 800–532–3221.

C & H Sales Company, 2176 E. Colorado Blvd., Pasadena, CA 91107: Free catalog ❖ Test equipment. 800–325–9465.

C & S Sales Inc., 1245 Rosewood, Deerfield, IL 60015: Free catalog ❖ Test equipment. 800–292–7711; 708–541–0710 (in IL).

Contact East, 335 Willow St. South, North Andover, MA 01845: Free catalog ❖ Tools for testing, repairing, and assembling electronic equipment. 800–225–5370; 508–682–2000 (in MA).

Danbar Sales Company, 14455 N. 79th St., Scottsdale, AZ 85260: Free catalog ❖ Test equipment. 602–483–6202.

Davilyn Corporation, 13406 Saticoy St., North Hollywood, CA 91605: Free information ❖ Multipurpose test equipment. 800–235–6222; 818–787–3334 (in CA).

Electro Tool Inc., 9103 Gillman, Livonia, MI 48150: Free information ❖ Tools and electronic test equipment. 800–772–3455.

Global Specialties, 70 Fulton Terrace, New Haven, CT 06512: Free information ❖ Compact multi-meters that measure AC and DC voltage, current, resistance, and check diodes and continuity. 800–572–1028.

JDR Microdevices, 1850 S. 10th St., San Jose, CA 95112: Free information ❖ Multipurpose test equipment. 800–538–5000.

Joseph Electronics Inc., 8830 N. Milwaukee Ave., Niles, IL 60648: Free catalog ❖ Multipurpose test equipment. 800–323–5925; 708–297–4200 (in IL).

Kelvin Electronics, 10 Hub Dr., Melville, NY 11747: Free information ❖ Electronic components and test equipment. 800–645–9212; 516–756–1750 (in NY).

MCM Electronics, 650 E. Congress Park Dr., Centerville, OH 45459: Free catalog ❖ Test equipment, computer and telephone accessories, speakers, and other parts. 800–824–TECH.

R & S Surplus, 1050 E. Cypress St., Covina, CA 91724: Free information ❖ Surplus test equipment. 818–967–0846.

Tech-Systems, 1309 Hwy. 71, Belmar, NJ 07719: Free information ❖ Used electronic test equipment. 800–435–1516.

Toronto Surplus & Scientific, 608 Gordon Baker Rd., Willowdale, Ontario, Canada

M2H 3B4: Free information ❖ Test equipment and other electronics. 416–490–8865.

2M Electronics Inc., 4503 Walzem, San Antonio, TX 78218: Free information ❖ Electronic components and new and used test equipment. 800–433–0554.

Westcon Inc., 5101 N. Interstate Ave., Portland, OR 97217: Free catalog ❖ Test probes. 800–547–4515.

Western Test Systems, 530 Compton St., Unit C, Broomfield, CO 80020: Free information ❖ New and used test equipment. 800–538–1493.

Tools & Accessories

Craig Laboratories Inc., 16744 W. Bernardo Dr., San Diego, CA 92127: Free catalog ❖ Environmentally-safe electronic chemicals and soldering equipment. 619–451–1799.

Electro Tool Inc., 9103 Gillman, Livonia, MI 48150: Free information ❖ Tools and electronic test equipment. 800–772–3455.

W.S. Jenks & Son, 1933 Montana Ave. NE, Washington, DC 20002: Free catalog ❖ Hand and power tools for electronics. 202–529–6020.

Jensen Tools Inc., 7815 S. 46th St., Phoenix, AZ 85044: Free catalog ❖ Precision tools for electronics. 800–426–1194; 602–968–6231 (in AZ).

Joseph Electronics, 8830 N. Milwaukee Ave., Niles, IL 60648: Free catalog ❖ Electronic components, test instruments, tools, and soldering equipment. 800–323–5925; 708–297–4200 (in IL).

ELECTROPLATING

American Bronzing Company, P.O. Box 6504, Bexley, OH 43209: Free information ❖ Bronzing and two-tone antique finish for baby's shoes. 800–345–8112.

Edmund Scientific Company, Edscorp Bldg., Barrington, NJ 08007: Free catalog ❖ Electroplating kits. 609–573–6260.

Hiles Plating Company Inc., 2030 Broadway, Kansas City, MO 64108: Free brochure ❖ Silver and gold plating and refinishing with brass, copper, and pewter. 816–421–6450.

New England International Gems, 188 Pollard St., Billerica, MA 01862: Free catalog ❖ Casting and plating equipment. 508–667–7394.

The Orum Silver Company, 51 S. Vine St., Meriden, CT 06450: Free information ❖ Old silver metal finishing. 203–237–3037.

Plating Service, N3503 Hwy. 55, Chilton, WI 53014: Free information with long SASE ❖ Electroplating services.

River Road Industries, 12806 River, Plano, IL 60545: Free information with long SASE ❖ Electroplating services.

Strassen Plating Company, 3619 Walton Ave., Cleveland, OH 44113: Free information ❖ Metal polishing and brass, nickel, and chrome plating. 216–961–1525.

Texas Platers Supply, 2453 W. Five Mile Pkwy., Dallas, TX 75233: Free information ❖ Electroplating kits.

Tropic House, Box 95, Palm Bay, FL 32906: Free information ❖ How to plate with gold, silver, copper, nickel, chromium, tin, zinc, cadmium, antimony, other metals, and brass, bronze, and black nickel alloys.

ENERGY CONSERVATION

Energy Savers, Solar Components Corporation, 121 Valley St., Manchester, NH 03103: Catalog $2 ❖ Energy-saving products. 603–668–8186.

Real Goods, 966 Mazzoni St., Ukiah, CA 95482: Free catalog ❖ Solar-operated tankless water heater, water-saving appliances, composting toilets, gas appliances, and recycled paper products. 800–762–7325.

Save Energy Company, 2410 Harrison St., San Francisco, CA 94110: Free catalog ❖ Home and garden products that conserve energy, resources, and money. 800–326–2120.

ENGRAVING & ETCHING

Alpha Supply, P.O. Box 2133, Bremerton, WA 98310: Catalog $3 ❖ Engraving and jewelry-making tools and supplies, and casting, faceting, and lapidary equipment. 206–373–3302.

B. Rush Apple Company, 3855 W. Kennedy Blvd., Tampa, FL 33609: Free price list ❖ Engraving tools. 813–870–3180.

Brownells Inc., 200 S. Front St., Montezuma, IA 50171: Free catalog ❖ Engraving tools. 515–623–5401.

James R. DeMunck, 3012 English Rd., Rochester, NY 14616: Free information with long SASE ❖ Engraving tools. 813–385–0647.

Eastern Art Glass, P.O. Box 341, Wyckoff, NJ 07481: Catalog $2 (refundable) ❖ Stained glass kits and glass etching, engraving, and crafting supplies. 201–847–0001.

Hand Engravers Supply Company, 601 Springfield Dr., Albany, GA 31707: Free catalog ❖ Engraving tools. 912–432–9683.

Indian Jewelers Supply Company, P.O. Box 1774, Gallup, NM 87305: Catalog $5 ❖ Precious and base metals, precious and base metal findings, metal-working equipment, lapidary and engraving tools and supplies, semiprecious stones, shells, and coral. 505–722–4451.

Ken Jantz Supply, P.O. Box S84, Davis, OK 73030: Catalog $4 ❖ Engraving tools. 405–369–2316.

J.M. Ney Company, Neycraft Division, 13553 Calimesa Blvd., Yucaipa, CA 92399: Free information ❖ Engraving tools. 714–795–2461.

EXERCISE EQUIPMENT

Ajay Leisure Products Inc., 1501 E. Wisconsin St., Delavan, WI 53115: Free information with list of retailers ❖ Monitoring aids and weight training, body building, and exercise equipment. 800–558–3276; 414–728–5521 (in WI).

All Pro Exercise Products, 135 Hazelwood Dr., Jericho, NY 11753: Free information with list of retailers ❖ Home exercise equipment. 800–735–9287; 516–938–9287 (in NY).

American Athletic Inc., 200 American Ave., Jefferson, IA 50129: Free information ❖ Monitoring aids, home gymnasiums, and weight training, body building, and exercise equipment. 800–247–3978; 515–386–3125 (in IA).

American Sports Inc., 735 S. Mansfield Ave., Los Angeles, CA 90036: Free information with list of retailers ❖ Home exercise equipment. 800–922–8939.

Aspire Fitness Products, 3545 Scarlet Oak Blvd., St. Louis, MO 63122: Free information ❖ Body building and fitness equipment.

Austin Athletic Equipment Corporation, 705 Bedford Ave., Box 423, Bellmore, NY 11710: Free information ❖ Monitoring aids, home gymnasiums, and weight training, body building, and exercise equipment. 516–785–0100.

Badger Fitness Equipment, 1010 Davis Ave., South Milwaukee, WI 53172: Free information ❖ Weight-lifting equipment and home gymnasiums. 414–764–4068.

Better Health Fitness, 5201 New Utrecht Ave., Brooklyn, NY 11219: Free information with long SASE ❖ Home gymnasium and exercise equipment. 718–436–4693.

Bio-Dyne Corporation, 5400 Bucknell Dr. SW, Atlanta, GA 30336: Free information with list of retailers ❖ Home exercise equipment. 800–845–2575; 404–346–3100 (in GA).

Body Masters Sports Industries Inc., Box 259, Rayne, LA 70578: Free information ❖ Home exercise equipment. 800–325–8964; 318–334–9611 (in LA).

Bollinger Fitness Products, 222 W. Airport Freeway, Irving, TX 75062: Free information ❖ Home gymnasiums, trampolines, monitoring aids, and weight training, body building, and exercise equipment. 800–527–1166; 214–445–0386 (in TX).

California Gym Equipment Company, 14829 Salt Lake Ave., City of Industry, CA 91748: Free information with list of retailers ❖ Home gymnasiums, monitoring aids, and weight training, body building, and exercise equipment. 800–824–5210; 818–961–6564 (in CA).

Cannon Sports, P.O. Box 11179, Burbank, CA 91510: Free information with list of retailers ❖ Monitoring aids, home gymnasiums, trampolines, and weight-lifting and exercise equipment. 800–362–3146; 818–753–5940 (in CA).

Chattanooga Group Inc., 4717 Adams Rd., P.O. Box 489, Hixson, TN 37343: Free information with list of retailers ❖ Adjustable, compact exerciser for therapeutic calisthenics while standing, seated, kneeling, or lying down. 800–529–7329.

Concept II Inc., RR 1, Box 1100, Morrisville, VT 05661: Free information with list of retailers ❖ Total body exercise machine. 800–245–5676.

Creative Health Products Inc., 5148 Saddle Ridge Rd., Plymouth, MI 48170: Free catalog ❖ Exercise bicycles, rowing machines, stethoscopes, thermometers, digital blood pressure units, scales, lung capacity testers, and pulse monitors. 800–742–4478.

Dunlop Stazenger Corporation, P.O. Box 3070, Greenville, SC 29602: Free information ❖ Home exercise equipment. 800–845–8794; 803–271–9767 (in SC).

Dynamic Classics Ltd., 230 5th Ave., Ste. 1510, New York, NY 10001: Free information ❖ Gymnastic bars, home gymnasiums, and weight training, body building, and exercise equipment. 212–571–0267.

Enduraciser, 1149 N. Main, Monticello, UT 84535: Free information ❖ Total body workout and aerobic exerciser. 800–424–8137.

Escalade Sports, P.O. Box 889, Evansville, IN 47706: Free catalog ❖ Home fitness equipment. 800–457–3373; 812–467–1200 (in IN).

Everlast Sports Manufacturing Corporation, 750 E. 132nd St., Bronx, NY 10454: Free information ❖ Home exercise equipment. 800–221–8777; 212–993–0100 (in NY).

Fitness Master Inc., 504 Industrial Blvd., Waconia, MN 55387: Free brochure with list of retailers ❖ Cardiovascular fitness and body tone exerciser. 800–328–8995.

Fitness To Go Inc., P.O. Box 266, Independence, MO 64501: Free information ❖ Motorized and mechanical isokinetic treadmills. 800–821–3126.

Flaghouse, 150 N. MacQuesten Pkwy., Mt. Vernon, NY 10550: Free catalog ❖ Physical fitness and gymnastic equipment and equipment for camping, playgrounds, and other outdoor activities. 800–793–7900.

GameTime, P.O. Box 121, Fort Payne, AL 35967: Free information ❖ Playground/backyard play systems and outdoor fitness equipment. 205–845–5610.

Gold's Gym, 360 Hampton Dr., Venice, CA 90291: Free information ❖ Home exercise equipment. 800–457–5375; 213–392–3005 (in CA).

HealthMax, 677 Connecticut Ave., Norwalk, CT 06854: Free information with list of retailers ❖ Total body fitness systems. 203–866–0101.

Heart-Rate Inc., 3188 Airway Ave., Ste. E, Costa Mesa, CA 92626: Free brochure ❖ Total body aerobic exercise machine. 800–237–2271.

Hi Products, Hofmann Industries Inc., P.O. Box 2147, Sinking Spring, PA 19608: Free information ❖ Home gymnasiums and weight training, body building, and exercise equipment. 215–678–2626.

Hoist Fitness Systems, 9990 Empire St., Ste. 130, San Diego, CA 92126: Free information with list of retailers ❖ Home exercise equipment. 800–548–5438; 619–578–7676 (in CA).

Holabird Sports Discounters, 9008 Yellow Brick Rd., Rossville Industrial Park, Baltimore, MD 21237: Free catalog ❖ Exercise equipment and clothing for basketball, tennis, running and jogging, golf, racquetball, and other sports. 410–687–6400.

Ivanko Barbell Company, P.O. Box 1470, San Pedro, CA 90731: Free information with list of retailers ❖ Weight-lifting equipment. 800–247–9044; 310–514–1155 (in CA).

Jayfro Corporation, Unified Sports Inc., 976 Hartford Tnpk., P.O. Box 400, Waterford, CT 06385: Free catalog ❖ Wall-mounted gyms and other physical fitness and exercise equipment. 203–447–3001.

M.W. Kasch Company, 5401 W. Donges Bay Rd., Mequon, WI 53092: Free information ❖ Home gymnasiums and weight training, body building, and exercise equipment. 414–242–5000.

LifeFitness Inc., 10601 W. Belmont Ave., Franklin Park, IL 60131: Free brochure with list of retailers ❖ Home fitness equipment. 708–288–3300.

Lifegear Inc., 300 Round Hill Dr., Rockaway, NJ 07876: Free information ❖ Home exercise equipment. 800–882–1113; 201–627–3065 (in NJ).

Mongoose Bicycles, 3400 Kashiwa St., Torrance, CA 90505: Free information ❖ Lightweight fitness bicycles. 310–539–8860.

New York Barbell, P.O. Box 3473, Elmira, NY 14905: Free information ❖ Home gymnasium and exercise equipment. 800–446–1833; 607–733–8038 (in NY).

NordicTrack, 104 Peavey Rd., Chaska, MN 55318: Free brochure ❖ Total body exercisers and other exercise equipment. 800–328–5888.

Olympia Sports, 745 State Cir., Ann Arbor, MI 48106: Free information ❖ Home exercise equipment. 800–521–2832; 313–761–5135 (in MI).

PCA Industries Inc., 5642 Natural Bridge, St. Louis, MO 63120: Free information ❖ Gymnastic bars and other floor equipment. 800–727–8180.

Precore USA, P.O. Box 3004, Bothell, WA 98041: Free information with list of retailers

❖ Off-snow, cross-country skier exercise machine. 800–786–8404.

Professional Gym Inc., P.O. Box 188, Marshall, MO 65340: Free brochure ❖ Weight training, body building, and exercise equipment. 800–821–7665; 800–892–2616 (in MO).

Quinton Instrument Company, 2121 Terry Ave., Seattle, WA 98121: Free information with list of retailers ❖ Fitness bicycles and an upper and lower body workout exercise machine. 800–426–0337; 206–223–7373 (in WA).

Ross Bicycles USA, 51 Executive Blvd., Farmingdale, NY 11735: Free information ❖ Home exercise equipment. 800–338–7677; 516–249–6000 (in NY).

Sentry Pack, 696 Plank Rd., Waterbury, CT 06705: Free information ❖ Home exercise equipment. 203–753–7170.

Spalding Sports Worldwide, 425 Meadow St., P.O. Box 901, Chicopee, MA 01021: Free information with list of retailers ❖ Home gymnasiums, trampolines, monitoring aids, and weight training, body building, and exercise equipment. 800–225–6601.

Sports America Fitness Equipment, 9100 Bank St., Valley View, OH 44125: Free information ❖ Home gymnasium and exercise equipment. 800–669–1672.

Trampolking Sporting Goods, P.O. Box 3828, Albany, GA 31708: Free brochure ❖ Home gymnasiums, trampolines, weight training, body building, and exercise equipment. 800–841–4351; 912–435–2101 (in GA).

Trimax, 20 S. Main St., Janesville, WI 53545: Free brochure ❖ Fitness and exercise machine. 800–866–5676.

True Fitness Technology Inc., 865 Hoff Rd., O'Fallon, MO 63366: Free information with list of retailers ❖ Home fitness equipment. 314–272–7100.

Universal Gym Equipment, P.O. Box 1270, Cedar Rapids, IA 52406: Free catalog ❖ Weight and exercise equipment, treadmills, computerized aerobic and exercise machines, and gymnastic bars. 800–553–3906; 319–365–7561 (in IA).

Vectra Fitness Inc., 15135 NE 90th St., Remond, WA 98052: Free information with list of retailers ❖ Home gymnasium equipment. 800–2–VECTRA; 206–867–1500 (in WA).

Voit Sports, 1451 Pittstand-Victor Rd., 100 Willowbrook Office Park, Fairport, NY 14450: Free information ❖ Home exercise equipment. 800–444–VOIT.

WaterRower Inc., 255 Armistice Blvd., Pawtucket, RI 02860: Free brochure with list of retailers ❖ Water resistance-operated exercise rowing machine. 401–728–1966.

FABRIC PAINTING, DYEING & OTHER DECORATING

Aljo Dyes, 81 Franklin St., New York, NY 10013: Free catalog ❖ Fabric dyes. 212–226–2878.

The Art Store, 935 Erie Blvd. East, Syracuse, NY 13210: Price list $3 ❖ Fabric dyeing, screen printing, marbling, and other craft supplies. 800–669–2787.

Badger Air-Brush Company, 9128 W. Belmont Ave., Franklin Park, IL 60131: Brochure $1 ❖ Air brushes and fabric paints. 708–678–3104.

Blueprint-Printables, 1504 Industrial Way, Belmont, CA 94002: Catalog $3 ❖ Fabrics, T-shirts, and blueprinting kits. 800–356–0445.

Cerulean Blue Ltd., P.O. Box 21168, Seattle, WA 98111: Free catalog ❖ Dyes for wool and silk, how-to books, natural fiber fabrics, and supplies for blueprinting on silk. 800–676–8602.

Createx Colors, 14 Airport Park Rd., East Granby, CT 06026: Free information ❖ Fabric dyes. 800–243–2712.

Decart Inc., P.O. Box 309, Morrisville, VT 05661: Free information ❖ Permanent, machine washable, dry-cleanable fabric paints, air brushing paints, and water-based enamels. 802–888–4217.

DecoArt, P.O. Box 370, Stanford, KY 40484: Free information ❖ Easy-to-apply acrylics for fabric decorating.

Dharma Trading Company, P.O. Box 150916, San Rafael, CA 94902: Free catalog ❖ Dyes and fabric paints. 800–542–5227.

Duncan, 5673 E. Shields Ave., Fresno, CA 93727: Free information ❖ Easy-to-apply iron-on-patterns, foil transfers, and glitter. 800–438–6226; 209–291–4444 (in CA).

Eastern Art Glass, P.O. Box 341, Wyckoff, NJ 07481: Catalog $2 (refundable) ❖ Fabric painting kits and supplies. 201–847–0001.

Gabrieana's Herbal & Organic Products, P.O. Box 215322, Sacramento, CA 95821: Free catalog ❖ Skin care and bath care items, essential oils, dried herbs, and other organic products. 800–684–4372.

Gramma's Graphics Inc., 20 Birling Gap, Fairport, NY 14450: Free information ❖ Sun-printing kits for fabrics and paper. 716–223–4309.

Ivy Crafts Imports, 12213 Distribution Way, Beltsville, MD 20705: Catalog $3.95 ❖ Fabric paints, resists, and applicators. 301–595–0550.

MS Associates, P.O. Box 868032, Plano, TX 75086: Catalog $2 (refundable) ❖ Silk painting supplies.

Nasco, 901 Janesville Ave., Fort Atkinson, WI 53538: Free catalog ❖ Fabric and silk painting supplies, textile dyes, and other decorating supplies. 800–558–9595.

Photographers Formulary, P.O. Box 950, Condon, MT 59826: Free catalog ❖ Supplies for blueprinting on fabric. 800–922–5255.

PRO Chemical & Dye Inc., P.O. Box 14, Somerset, MA 02726: Free information ❖ Fabric dyes. 508–676–3838.

Qualin International, P.O. Box 31145, San Francisco, CA 94131: Free catalog with long SASE and two 1st class stamps ❖ Silk fabrics, scarf blanks, and silk painting supplies. 415–333–8500.

Rupert, Gibbon & Spider Inc., P.O. Box 425, Healdsburg, CA 95448: Free catalog ❖ Textile dyes and paints, brushes, resists, silk and cotton fabrics for printing and dyeing. 800–442–0455.

Sequin Imports, 3265 E. Tropicana, Las Vegas, NV 89121: Catalog $2 ❖ Sequin appliques.

Silkpaint Corporation, P.O. Box 18, Waldron, MO 64092: Free information ❖ Fabric dyes for silk painting. 816–891–7774.

SLF Trading Corporation, 9850 Sandlefoot Blvd., Ste. 440, Boca Raton, FL 33428: Catalog $1 (refundable) ❖ Iron-on transfers with easy-to-apply sequins.

Soho South, P.O. Box 1324, Cullman, AL 35056: Catalog $2.50 (refundable) ❖ Beads and findings, fabric dyes and paints, silk scarves and fabrics, and marbling supplies. 205–739–6114.

FABRICS & TRIM
Fabrics

ABC Decorative Fabrics, 2410 298th Ave. North, Clearwater, FL 34621: Free information ❖ Decorator fabrics. 800–548–3499.

AK Sew & Serge, 1602 6th St. SE, Winter Haven FL 33880: Catalog $5 ❖ Designer and other fabrics, smocking, Battenberg lace, and sewing notions. 800–299–8096; 813–299–3080 (in FL).

Alexandra's Homespun Textile & Seraph Textile Collection, P.O. Box 500, Sturbridge, MA 01566: Catalog $2 ❖ Hand woven homespuns and reproduction museum fabrics for household furnishings and upholstery. 508–347–2241.

Aurora Silk, 5806 N. Vancouver Ave., Portland, OR 97217: Brochure and color chart $15 ❖ Naturally dyed silk. 503–286–4149.

Baltazor's, 3262 Severen Ave., Metairie, LA 70002: Catalog $2 ❖ Lace and lace-making supplies, fabrics, smocking, and bridal fashion-making supplies. 800–532–LACE.

Barbeau Fine Fabrics, 1308 Birch St., Fort Collins, CO 80521: Information $12 ❖ Silks, wools, cottons, and other fabrics. 800–766–5588; 303–221–9697 (in CO).

Bridals International, 45 Albany St., Cazenovia, NY 13035: Catalog $8.50 (refundable with $50 purchase) ❖ Imported fabrics and lace for bridal fashions. 800–752–1171.

Calico House, Rt. 4, Box 16, Scottsville, VA 24590: Catalog $6 ❖ French and English lace, Swiss eyelets, and embroideries.

California Bridal Fabrics, 729 E. Temple St., Los Angeles, CA 90012: Catalog $10 ❖ Satins, taffeta, French and domestic lace, brocades, sheers, embroideries, trimmings, and crowns. 213–626–5123.

Carolina Mills Factory Outlet, Hwy. 76 West, P.O. Box V, Branson, MO 65616: Free brochure ❖ Designer fabrics. 417–334–2291.

Cerulean Blue Ltd., P.O. Box 21168, Seattle, WA 98111: Free catalog ❖ Dyes for wool and silk, how-to books, natural fiber fabrics, and supplies for blueprinting on silk. 800–676–8602.

Classic Cloth, 34930 US 19 North, Palm Harbor, FL 34684: Swatches $5 ❖ Cotton fabrics. 800–237–7739; 813–785–6593 (in FL).

Classic Whites by Etceteras, 7310 Bucknell Dr., Austin, TX 78723: Catalog $4 (refundable with $20 order) ❖ Fabrics, laces, and trims. 512–928–3217.

Clearbrook Woolen Shop, P.O. Box 8, Clearbrook, VA 22624: Free information with long SASE ❖ Wool fabrics. 703–662–3442.

Cotton Express, 4400 Country Club Dr., Wilson, NC 27893: Information $4 ❖ Jersey, interlock, cotton mesh, and other 100 percent cotton fabrics. 919–399–7639.

D'Anton Leathers, 3079 NE Oasis Rd., West Branch, IA 52358: Catalog $1.50 ❖ Garment leathers and suede. 319–643–2568.

Dazian's Inc., 2014 Commerce St., Dallas, TX 75201: Free catalog ❖ Satin brocade, nylon net, organdy, stretch materials, unbleached muslin, lame, metallic, and other costume fabrics. 214–748–3450.

Denham Fabrics, P.O. Box 241275, Memphis, TN 38124: Fabric portfolio $8 ❖ Polyester and cotton fabrics. 901–683–4574.

Designer Home Fabrics, P.O. Box 2560, Cinnaminson, NJ 08077: Catalog $2 (refundable) ❖ Traditional and contemporary cotton prints, chintzes, damasks, tapestries, solids, and other fabrics. 800–666–4202.

Dharma Trading Company, P.O. Box 150916, San Rafael, CA 94902: Free catalog ❖ Clothing blanks and silk, cotton, and rayon fabrics. 800–542–5227.

DK Sports, Division Daisy Kingdom, 134 NW 8th Ave., Portland, OR 97209: Free information ❖ Rainwear and outerwear fabrics and sewing notions. 503–222–9033.

Exotic Silks, 1959 Leghorn St., Mountain View, CA 94043: Brochure 25¢ ❖ Natural silks and scarves in white, solid colors, and printed patterns. 800–845–SILK; 415–965–7760 (in CA).

Fabric Center, P.O. Box 8212, Fitchburg, MA 01420: Catalog $2 ❖ Decorator fabrics. 508–343–4402.

Fabric Chalet, Windchime Center, Colorado Springs, CO 80936: Information $5 ❖ China silk, cotton velveteen, English cotton, silk taffeta and organza, and Swiss lawn, organdy, and batiste. 719–522–1214.

Fabric Editions Ltd., 25 Kenwood Cir., Ste. 4, Franklin, MA 02038: Catalog $3 (refundable) ❖ Fabric prints and solids. 800–242–5684.

Fabric Gallery, 146 W. Grand River, Williamson, MI 48895: Information $8 ❖ Imported and domestic silks, wools, cottons, blends, and synthetics. 517–655–4573.

The Fabric Outlet, P.O. Box 2417, South Hamilton, MA 01982: Free information ❖ Decorator fabrics. 800–635–9715.

Fabric Shop, 120 N. Seneca St., Shippensburg, PA 17257: Free information with long SASE ❖ Antique satins and decorative drapery, slipcover, and upholstery fabrics. 800–233–7012; 717–532–4150 (in PA).

Fabric Wholesalers Inc., 13400 Riverside Dr., Sherman Oaks, CA 91423: Free price list ❖ Fabrics and sewing notions for clothes, draperies, curtains, and upholstering furniture. 818–995–7000.

Fabrics by Phone, P.O. Box 309, Walnut Bottom, PA 17266: Brochure and samples $3 ❖ Antique satins and decorative drapery, slipcover, and upholstery fabrics. 800–233–7012; 717–532–4150 (in PA).

Fabrics Unlimited, 5015 Columbia Pike, Arlington, VA 22204: Free information ❖ Fabrics from designer cutting rooms, ultrasuede, and imported silks, wools, and cottons. 703–671–0324.

Felt People, Box 135, Bloomingdale, NJ 07403: Information $2 (refundable) ❖ Wool felt. 800–631–8968; 201–838–1100 (in NJ).

Michel Ferree, P.O. Box 958, Niwot, CO 80544: Samples $12 (refundable) ❖ Silk fabrics. 800–488–6170.

Fishman's Fabrics, 1101–43 S. Desplaines St., Chicago, IL 60607: Free information ❖ Designer woolens, cottons, linens, and silks. 800–648–5161.

G Street Fabrics, Mail Order Service, 12240 Wilkins Ave., Rockville, MD 20852: Free catalog ❖ Decorator, clothing, and drapery fabrics. 800–333–9191.

Green Pepper, 3918 W. 1st Ave., Eugene, OR 97402: Catalog $2 ❖ Rainwear and outerwear fabrics, spandex fabrics, sewing notions, and patterns. 503–345–6665.

Gutcheon Patchworks Inc., 917 Pacific Ave., #305, Tacoma, WA 98402: Information and fabric samples $3 ❖ Coordinating plain color fabrics and 100 percent cotton prints. 206–383–3047.

Hancock Fabrics, 3841 Hinkleville Rd., Paducah, KY 42001: Free information ❖ Quilting supplies, fabrics, and sewing notions. 800–626–2723.

Home Fabric Mills Inc., 882 S. Main St., Cheshire, CT 06410: Free brochure ❖ Velvets, upholstery and drapery fabrics, prints, sheers, antique satins, and thermal fabrics. 203–272–6686.

Heirloom Creations, 431 Rena Dr., Lafayette, LA 70503: Free information ❖ Swiss and silk batiste, linen, velveteen, cotton corduroy, and lace. 318–984–8949.

Homespun Fabrics & Draperies, P.O. Box 3223, Ventura, CA 93006: Catalog $2 ❖ 100 percent natural cotton fabrics. 805–642–8111.

Homespun Weavers, 55 S. 7th St., Emmaus, PA 18049: Brochure 50¢ ❖ Cotton fabrics. 215–967–4550.

House of Laird, Box 23778, Lexington, KY 40523: Free information ❖ Silk and blends, wool, and rayon suitings. 800–338–4618.

International Fabric Collection, 3445 W. Lake Rd., Erie, PA 16505: Catalog $3 ❖ Fabrics from Italy, India, Japan, Holland, Africa, and other worldwide sources. Also quilting and embroidery books. 800–462–3891; 814–838–0740 (in PA).

Jehlor Fantasy Fabrics, 730 Andover Park West, Seattle, WA 98188: Catalog $3.60 ❖ Costume fabrics and trims. 206–575–8250.

Judy's Heirloom Sewing, 13650 E. Zayante Rd., Felton, CA 95018: Catalog $5 ❖ Imported fabrics and laces, patterns and trims, and smocking supplies. 408–335–4684.

Labours of Love, 3760 Old Clayburn Rd., Abbotsford, British Columbia, Canada V2S 6B7: Catalog $2 ❖ French val lace, Swiss batiste and embroideries, patterns, books, videos, notions, and silk ribbons. 604–853–9132.

Lace Heaven, P.O. Box 50150, Mobile, AL 36605: Catalog $3 (refundable) ❖ Lingerie fabrics, ribbons and trim, stretch lace, elastic, and notions. 205–478–5644.

Landau Woolen Company Inc., 561 7th Ave., New York, NY 10018: Free information ❖ Worsted wools, merino jerseys, luxury fibers, rayons, and cottons. 800–553–2292; 212–391–8371 (in NY).

Ledgewood Studio, 6000 Ledgewood Dr., Forest Park, GA 30050: Catalog $2 with long SASE and three 1st class stamps ❖ Dress patterns for antique dolls, supplies for recreating period costumes, braids, French lace, silk ribbons and taffeta, China silk, Swiss batiste, trims, and notions.

Donna Lee's Sewing Center, 25234 Pacific Hwy. South, Kent, WA 98032: Catalog $4 ❖ Swiss and imperial batiste, China silk, silk charmeuse, French val lace, English lace,

Swiss embroideries, trims and yardage, silk ribbon, ribbons, smocking, doll patterns, books, and sewing notions. 206–941–9466.

Samuel Lehrer & Company Inc., 7 Depinedo Ave., Stamford, CT 06902: Free information ❖ Wool flannels, gabardines, linen blends, pinstripes, and plaids for men and women's clothing. 800–221–2433.

S. Levine & Sons Inc., P.O. Box 148, Allentown, PA 18105: Free information ❖ Fabrics, pound goods, and remnants. 800–523–9452; 215–398–2204 (in PA).

Linen & Lace, 4 Lafayette, Washington, MO 63090: Catalog $2 ❖ Linen and lace fabrics. 800–332–5223.

The Linen Fabric World, 1246 Bird Rd., Miami, FL 33146: Information $5 ❖ Imported linen fabrics. 305–663–1577.

The Linen Lady, 6011 Folson Blvd., Sacramento, CA 95819: Catalog $3 ❖ Fabrics and trims. 916–457–6718.

Lisa's Heirloom Shop, 14 Melrose Pl., West Caldwell, NJ 07006: Free price list with two 1st class stamps and long SASE ❖ Fabrics, antique laces, smocking pleaters, and books. 201–226–LACE.

Marlene's Decorator Fabrics, 301 Beech St., Hackensack, NJ 07601: Free brochure with long SASE ❖ Decorator and upholstery fabrics. 800–992–7325.

The Material World, 5700 Monroe St., Sylvania, OH 43560: Free information ❖ Fabrics. 419–885–5416.

Midwest Trade Imports, 1555 Sherman Ave., Ste. 236, Evanston, IL 60201: Information $2 ❖ Personalized, authentic hand-woven Ashanti Kente Cloth stoles and assorted fabrics from Ghana, West Africa. 800–64–KENTE.

Monterey Mills Outlet, P.O. Box 271, Janesville, WI 53545: Brochure $4 ❖ Fake furs, deep pile fabrics, and stuffing. 608–754–8309.

Mylace, 3530 Dogwood Valley, Tallahassee, FL 32312: Catalog $5.50 ❖ Fabrics and trims.

Nancy's Notions, P.O. Box 683, Beaver Dam, WI 53916: Free catalog ❖ Sewing notions, threads, books, patterns, how-to videos, and interlock knits, fleece, gabardines, sweater knits, challis, and other fabrics. 800–833–0690.

Oppenheim's, 120 E. Main St., North Manchester, IN 46962: Free catalog ❖

Sewing notions, fabrics, and craft supplies. 219–982–6848.

Outdoor Wilderness Fabrics, 16195 Latah Dr., Nampa, ID 83651: Free price list ❖ Coated and uncoated nylon fabrics, fleece and blends in coat weights, waterproof fabrics, webbing, patterns, and sewing notions. 208–466–1602.

The Patchworks, 126 E. Main, Boseman, MT 59715: Catalog $1 ❖ Reproduction cotton fabrics for quilts and clothing. 406–587–2112.

Martha Pullen Company Inc., 518 Madison St., Huntsville, AL 35801: Catalog $2 ❖ Fabrics and trims. 800–547–4176.

Qualin International, P.O. Box 31145, San Francisco, CA 94131: Free catalog with long SASE and two 1st class stamps ❖ Silk fabrics, scarf blanks, and silk painting supplies. 415–333–8500.

Rainshed Outdoor Fabrics, 707 NW 11th, Corvallis, OR 97330: Catalog $1 ❖ Outdoor fabrics, hardware, webbing, and patterns. 503–753–8900.

Rubin & Green, 290 Grand St., New York, NY 10002: Free information with long SASE ❖ Upholstery and decorator fabrics. 212–226–0313.

Donna Salyers' Fabulous-Furs, 700 Madison Ave., Covington, KY 41011: Catalog $1 ❖ Alternatives to natural furs and leather, kits, and patterns. 800–848–4650.

Sawyer Brook Fabrics, P.O. Box 909, Boylston, MA 01505: Catalog $7.50 ❖ Natural fiber fabrics, polyesters and blends, wools, silks, and cotton prints. 800–290–2739.

Seattle Fabrics, 3876 Bridge Way North, Seattle, WA 98103: Price list $3 (refundable) ❖ Outdoor and recreation fabrics. 206–632–6022.

Shama Imports, Box 2900, Farmington Hills, MI 48018: Free brochure ❖ Hand-embroidered crewel fabric from India. 313–478–7740.

Silk Surplus, 235 E. 58th St., New York, NY 10022: Free information with long SASE ❖ Discontinued and closeout drapery, upholstery, and other fabrics. 212–753–6511.

Slipcovers of America, East Broad & Wood Sts., Dept. 128, Bethlehem, PA 18016: Free catalog ❖ Slipcovers, matching draperies, and fabrics. 215–867–7581.

Smocking Bonnet, P.O. Box 555, Cooksville, MD 21723: Catalog $3 ❖ English smocking,

French handsewing, fabrics, and lace. 800–524–1678.

Soho South, P.O. Box 1324, Cullman, AL 35056: Catalog $2.50 (refundable) ❖ Beads and findings, fabric dyes and paints, silk scarves and fabrics, and marbling supplies. 205–739–6114.

Specialties, 4425 Cotton Hanlon Rd., Montour Falls, NY 14865: Catalog $2 ❖ Lingerie fabrics, notions, and patterns. 607–594–2021.

Stretch & Sew, 8697 La Mesa Blvd., La Mesa, CA 91941: Catalog $3 ❖ Fabrics, patterns, and notions. 619–589–8880.

Taylor's Cutaways & Stuff, 2802 E. Washington St., Urbana, IL 61801: Brochure $1 ❖ Satins, lace, velvet, cottons felt, calico, trims, polyester squares, sewing notions, other craft supplies, books, and patterns.

Testfabrics Inc., P.O. Box 420, Middlesex, NJ 08846: Free catalog ❖ Cotton, linen, silk, wool, blend, synthetics, muslin, satin, twill, and other fabrics. 201–469–6446.

Thai Silks, 252 State St., Los Altos, CA 94022: Free catalog ❖ Silk fabrics and linen/cotton and wool gabardine. 800–722–SILK; 800–221–SILK (in CA).

Threads at Gingerbread Hill, 356 E. Garfield, Aurora, OH 44202: Information and samples $8 ❖ Imported and domestic silks, wools, cottons, synthetics, and other fabrics. 216–562–7100.

L.P. Thur Fabrics, 126 W. 23rd St., New York, NY 10011: Free information ❖ Costume, designer, craft, theatrical, and other fabrics. 212–243–4913.

Tioga Mill Outlet, 200 S. Hartman St., York, PA 17403: Free brochure ❖ Damasks, crewel, tapestry, linen, cotton, and other upholstery and drapery fabrics. 717–843–5139.

Ultramouse Ltd., 3433 Bennington Ct., Bloomfield Hills, MI 48301: Catalog $2 ❖ Sewing notions and ultrasuede and other fabric scraps. 800–225–1887.

The Unique Needle, 539 Blossom Way, Hayward, CA 94541: Brochure $1.50 ❖ Imported Swiss fabrics and embroideries, French lace, other fabrics, trims, patterns, books, and supplies. 415–727–9130.

Utex Trading, 710 9th St., Ste. 5, Niagara Falls, NY 14301: Free brochure with long SASE ❖ Imported silk fabrics and sewing supplies. 716–282–8211.

Victorian Treasures, 12148 Madison St. NE, Blaine, MN 55434: Catalog $3.50 (refundable) ❖ Imported lace, fabrics, Swiss embroideries, and notions. 612–755–6302.

Lace & Ribbon

Baltazor's, 3262 Severen Ave., Metairie, LA 70002: Catalog $2 ❖ Lace and lace-making supplies, fabrics, smocking, and bridal fashion-making supplies. 800–532–LACE.

Beggars' Lace, P.O. Box 481223, Denver, CO 80248: Catalog $2 (refundable) ❖ Lace-making materials and kits. 303–722–5557.

Cindy's Stitches, 588 Roger Williams Ave., Highland Park, IL 60035: Catalog $2 ❖ Lace-making and needlework equipment and books. 708–433–5183.

Classic Whites by Etceteras, 7310 Bucknell Dr., Austin, TX 78723: Catalog $4 (refundable with $20 order) ❖ Fabrics, laces, and trims. 512–928–3217.

Elsie's Exquisiques, 208 State St., St. Joseph, MI 49085: Free information ❖ Silk and novelty ribbons, trims, and ribbon roses. 616–982–0449.

Fabric Barn, 3121 E. Anaheim St., Long Beach, CA 90804: Free catalog ❖ Ribbon and lace. 800–544–9374; 310–498–0285 (in CA).

Famous Trading Company, 237 W. 37th St., New York, NY 10018: Free catalog ❖ Lace and trims, elastic, jacket zippers, ribbons, plastic scarves and doilies, velcro hooks and loop tape, sequins, and other notions. 800–326–6878; 212–768–9647 (in NY).

Ginsco Trims, 242 W. 38th, New York, NY 10018: Catalog $5 (refundable) ❖ Fashion trims and braids.

Glimakra Looms & Yarns Inc., 1338 Ross St., Petaluma, CA 94954: Catalog $2.50 ❖ Weaving equipment, looms, yarns, and lace-making equipment. 800–289–9276; 707–762–3362 (in CA).

Heirloom Creations, 431 Rena Dr., Lafayette, LA 70503: Free information ❖ Laces, Swiss and silk batiste, linen, velveteen, and cotton corduroy. 318–984–8949.

Lace Corner, Box 1224, Weaverville, CA 96093: Catalog $3 (refundable) ❖ Ruffled, flat, ribbon, and other laces.

Lace Heaven, P.O. Box 50150, Mobile, AL 36605: Catalog $3 (refundable) ❖ Lingerie fabrics, ribbons and trim, stretch lace, elastic, and notions. 205–478–5644.

Lacis, 3163 Adeline St., Berkeley, CA 94703: Catalog $4 ❖ Hairpin lace looms. 510–843–7178.

Lisa's Heirloom Shop, 14 Melrose Pl., West Caldwell, NJ 07006: Free price list with two 1st class stamps and long SASE ❖ Fabrics, antique laces, smocking pleaters, and books. 201–226–LACE.

The Ribbon Outlet Inc., 3434 Rt 22 West, Ste 110, Summerville, NJ 08876: Free catalog ❖ Ribbons and trims. 800–766–BOWS.

Ribbons & Lace, Box 30070, Mesa, AZ 85272: Catalog $3 (refundable) ❖ Laces, ribbons, craft supplies, and beads.

Sew Fine, 9659 Reseda Blvd., Northridge, CA 91324: Free information with long SASE ❖ Smocking and sewing supplies, French and English lace, buttons, ribbons, and Swiss embroideries. 818–886–1108.

Viv's Ribbons & Laces, 212 Virginia Hills Dr., Martinez, CA 94553: Catalog $3.50 ❖ Old and new French and English cotton laces.

Warscokins, 17930 Magnolia, Fountain Valley, CA 92708: Catalog $3.50 ❖ Lace, ribbon, and sewing notions. 800–225–6356; 714–962–8991 (in CA).

YLI Corporation, 482 N. Freedom Blvd., Provo, UT 84601: Catalog $2.50 ❖ Silk, spark organdy, synthetic silk, ribbons, silk thread, and other craft supplies. 800–854–1932; 801–377–3900 (in UT).

FANS

AAA-Vacuum Cleaner Center, 1230 N. 3rd, Abilene, TX 79601: Brochure $2 (refundable) ❖ Ceiling fans and vacuum cleaners. 915–677–1311.

Casablanca Fan Company, 450 N. Baldwin Park Blvd., City of Industry, CA 91746: Free information ❖ Ceiling fans. 818–369–6441.

Fan Fair, 2251 Wisconsin Ave. NW, Washington, DC 20007: Free information ❖ Fans. 202–342–6290.

The Fan Man, 1914 Abrams Pkwy., Dallas, TX 75214: Restored fans brochure $2; parts catalog $3 ❖ New and restored antique fans. 214–826–7700.

Hunter Fan Company, 2500 Fisco Ave., Memphis, TN 38114: Catalog $1 ❖ Ceiling fans, remote control units, light fixtures, and electronic thermostats. 901–745–9222.

Lamp Warehouse, 1073 39th St., Brooklyn, NY 11219: Free information with long SASE

❖ Ceiling fans and light fixtures.
800–52–LITES; 718–436–8500 (in NY).

FAUCETS & PLUMBING FIXTURES

American Standard Inc., P.O. Box 6820,
Piscataway, NJ 08854: Free information ❖
Bathroom and kitchen faucets and other
plumbing fixtures. 800–821–7700.

Antique Baths & Kitchens, 2220 Carlton
Way, Santa Barbara, CA 93109: Catalog $2
❖ Reproduction Victorian-style plumbing
fixtures. 805–962–8598.

Chicago Faucet Company, 2100 S.
Clearwater Dr., Des Plaines, IL 60018: Free
information ❖ Bathroom plumbing fixtures.
708–803–5000.

Delta Faucet Company, 55 E. 111th St.,
Indianapolis, IN 46280: Free information ❖
Solid brass plumbing fixtures. 317–848–1812.

Elkay Manufacturing Company, 2222
Camden Ct., Oak Brook, IL 60521: Free
information ❖ Faucets with retractable
nozzles. 708–574–8484.

Kohler Company, 444 Highland Dr., Kohler,
WI 53041: Free information ❖ Solid brass
faucets and other plumbing fixtures.
800–456–4537.

MAC the Antique Plumber, 6325 Elvas
Ave, Sacramento, CA 95819: Catalog $6
(refundable) ❖ Plumbing fixtures in a 1900s
style. 916–454–4507.

Moen Inc., 377 Woodland Ave., Elyria, OH
44036: Free information ❖ Single- and
double-handle faucets for bathrooms and
kitchens. 800–347–6636.

The Renovator's Supply, P.O. Box 2660,
North Conway, NH 03860: Free catalog ❖
Plumbing fixtures, light fixtures, and
hardware. 800–659–2211.

FENCES & GATES

Alcan Pipe/Kroy Industries, Sales Office,
P.O. Box 14166, Albany, NY 12212: Free
information ❖ White vinyl rail fencing.
518–869–6078.

Architectural Iron Company, Schocopee
Rd., P.O. Box 126, Milford, PA 18337:
Catalog $4 ❖ Reproduction cast-iron 18th-
and 19th-century gates, fences, and fountains.
800–442–4766.

Bamboo Fencer, 31 Germania St., Jamaica
Plain, MA 02130: Catalog $3 ❖ Fences,
gates, and other construction materials.
617–524–6137.

Bufftech Inc., 2525 Walden Ave., Buffalo,
NY 14225: Free brochure ❖
Maintenance-free vinyl fence. 800–333–0569.

California Redwood Association, 405
Enfrente Dr., Ste. 200, Novato, CA 94949:
Free information ❖ Redwood fences.
415–382–0662.

Central Tractor Farm & Family Center,
3915 Delaware, Des Moines, IA 50313: Free
catalog ❖ Fencing supplies. 800–247–1760;
515–266–3101 (in IA).

Comtrad Industries, 2820 Waterford Lake
Dr., Ste. 106, Midlothian, VA 23113: Free
information ❖ Electric invisible pet
containment systems. 800–992–2966.

Custom Ironwork Inc., P.O. Box 180,
Union, KY 41091: Catalog $1 ❖
Reproduction cast- and wrought-iron fencing
in Victorian and other styles. 606–384–4122.

Delgard Fence, 8600 River Rd., Delair, NJ
08110: Free information ❖ Weather-resistant
aluminum fences. 800–235–0185.

Elite Aluminum Fence Products, 6675
Burroughs, Sterling Heights, MI 48314: Free
information ❖ Aluminum fencing with a
baked-on enamel finish. 313–731–1331.

Freedom Fence Inc., Box 02061, River Rd.,
North Adams, MA 01247: Free information
❖ Underground invisible pet containment
fence. 800–828–9089.

Furman Lumber Inc., P.O. Box 130,
Nutting Lake, MA 01865: Free information ❖
Factory-assembled picket fences.
800–843–9663.

Heritage Fence Company, P.O. Box 121,
Skippack, PA 19464: Catalog $2 ❖
Reproduction wood colonial and Victorian
fences. 215–584–6710.

Invisible Fencing, 300 Berwyn Park, Ste.
215, Berwyn, PA 19312: Free information ❖
Invisible electronic pet containment fence.
215–651–0999.

Jerith Manufacturing Company Inc., 3939
G. St., Philadelphia, PA 19124: Free brochure
❖ Rust-proof, high-strength aluminum alloy
fences with a baked on enamel finish.
800–344–2242.

LouverRail, Box 507, Concordville, PA
19331: Free information ❖ Adjustable louver
panels for fences. 215–558–3515.

LPD Fantastic Inc., 27565 Fantastic Lane,
Castaic, CA 91310: Free information ❖ Solid
wood fencing with polyethylene covering.
800–521–3633; 805–257–3450 (in CA).

Moultrie Manufacturing, P.O. Drawer 1179,
Moultrie, GA 31776: Catalog $3 ❖
Reproduction "Old South" gates and fences.
800–841–8674.

Pool Fence Company, 1791–907 Blount Rd.,
Pompano Beach, FL 33069: Free brochure ❖
Swimming pool protection-against-entry
fences. 800–992–2206.

Radio Fence, 230 E. Russell St., Fayetteville,
NC 28301: Free information ❖ Easy-to-install
electronic invisible pet containment systems.
800–775–8404.

Southeastern Wood Products Company,
P.O. Box 113, Griffin, GA 30224: Free
brochure ❖ Wire and wood fences, plant
supports, and cold frames. 800–722–7486;
404–227–7486 (in GA).

Stewart Iron Works Company, P.O. Box
2612, Covington, KY 41012: Catalog $3 ❖
Victorian-style fences and gates.
606–431–1985.

Texas Standard Picket Company, 606 W.
17th St., Austin, TX 78701: Information
$4.50 ❖ Reproduction Victorian fence pickets.

West Virginia Fence Corporation, US Rt.
219, Lindside, WV 24951: Free catalog ❖
Permanent and portable electric pet
containment fences. 800–356–5458;
304–753–4387 (in WV).

FENCING

American Fencers Supply Company, 1180
Folsom St., San Francisco, CA 94103: Free
information ❖ Gloves, masks, shoes,
uniforms, blades, epees, foils, rapiers, and
sabers. 415–863–7911.

Blade Fencing Equipment Inc., 212 W. 15th
St., New York, NY 10011: Free information
❖ Gloves, masks, shoes, uniforms, blades,
epees, foils, rapiers, and sabers.
212–620–0114.

Genesport Industries Ltd., Hokkaido Karate
Equipment Manufacturing Company, 150
King St., Montreal, Quebec, Canada H3C
2P3: Free information ❖ Gloves, masks,
uniforms, blades, and sabers. 514–861–1856.

Mid-Lakes Corporation, 3304 Rifle Range
Rd., Knoxville, TN 37918: Free information
❖ Fencing equipment. 615–687–7341.

Renaissance Ltd., 3170 Hwy. 60, P.O. Box
418, Jackson, WI 53037: Free information ❖
Gloves, masks, uniforms and shoes, blades,
epees, foils, rapiers, and sabers.
414–677–4113.

George Santelli, 465 S. Dean St., Englewood, NJ 07631: Free catalog ❖ Fencing equipment. 201–871–3105.

Sportime, 1 Sportime Way, Atlanta, GA 30340: Free information ❖ Fencing equipment. 800–444–5700; 404–449–5700 (in GA).

FIREPLACES
Accessories & Tools

The Adams Company, 100 E. 4th St., Dubuque, IA 52001: Free catalog ❖ Solid brass and black cast-iron fireplace tool sets, baskets, screens, fire backs, lighters, and fenders. 800–553–3012.

Danny Alessandro, Edwin Jackson Inc., 307 E. 60th St., New York, NY 10022: Catalog $5 ❖ Antique and reproduction fireplace accessories and 18th-century limestone, wood, and marble mantels. 212–421–1928.

Art Marble & Stone, 5862 Peachtree Industrial Blvd., Atlanta, GA 30341: Free brochure ❖ Glass doors, tools, mantels, and gas logs with glowing embers for natural or LP gas. 800–476–0298.

Bona Decorative Hardware, 3073 Madison Rd., Cincinnati, OH 45209: Price list $2 ❖ Solid brass hardware for fireplaces, bathrooms, doors, cabinets, furniture, and kitchens. 513–321–7877.

Century Fireplace Furnishings Inc., P.O. Box 248, Wallingford, CT 06492: Free information ❖ Fireplace screens. 800–284–4328.

Coppersmith Sheet Metal, 40136 Enterprises Dr., Bldg. 18–A, Oakhurst, CA 93644: Free brochure ❖ Fireplace hoods, cupolas, mailboxes, and dormers. 209–658–8909.

Country Iron Foundry, P.O. Box 600, Paoli, PA 19301: Catalog $2 ❖ Handcrafted colonial-style and other firebacks. 215–353–5542.

Crowfutt Inc., 94 Bethlehem Pike, Philadelphia, PA 19118: Free brochure ❖ Reproduction fireplace accessories. 215–242–8818.

Fireside Distributors Inc., 4013 Atlantic Ave., Raleigh, NC 27604: Free information ❖ Fireplace accessories. 800–333–3473; 919–872–4434 (in NC).

Grate Fires, P.O. Box 351, Athens, GA 30603: Free brochure ❖ Authentic English gas coal fires. 706–353–8281.

Hallidays America Inc., P.O. Box 731, Sparta, NJ 07871: Free information ❖ Fireplace accessories, handcarved mantels, and wood moldings. 201–729–8876.

Hearth Realities, P.O. Box 38093, Atlanta, GA 30334: Free information with long SASE ❖ Cast-iron fireplace accessories. 404–627–3719.

William H. Jackson Company, 210 E. 58th St., New York, NY 10022: Free brochure ❖ Antique fireplace accessories and mantels. 212–753–9400.

Kayne & Son Custom Hardware, 100 Daniel Ridge Rd., Candler, NC 28715: Catalog $4.50 ❖ Fireplace tools and hand-forged hardware. 704–667–8868.

Lemee's Fireplace Equipment, 815 Bedford St., Bridgewater, MA 02324: Catalog $2 ❖ Fireplace equipment. 508–697–2672.

Jon Leonard, Antique Hardware, 509 Tangle Dr., Jamestown, NC 27282: Catalog $2 ❖ 18th- and 19th-century wrought iron fireplace equipment. 919–454–3583.

Liberty Forge, 40128 Industrial Park North, Georgetown, TX 78626: Free information ❖ Fireplace screens. 512–869–2830.

New England Firebacks, 161 Main St., P.O. Box 268, Woodbury, CT 06798: Catalog $5 ❖ Solid, hand-cast iron fireback reproductions. 203–263–5737.

Robert H. Peterson Company, 530 N. Baldwin Park Blvd., City of Industry, CA 91744: Free catalog ❖ Stone built-in and outdoor barbecues, handcrafted fireplace accessories, and ceramic radiant heat gas logs. 818–369–5085.

Plow & Hearth, 301 Madison Rd., P.O. Box 830, Orange, VA 22960: Free catalog ❖ Fireplace accessories, gardening tools, birdhouses and feeders, and porch and lawn furniture. 800–627–1712.

Portland Willamette, P.O. Box 13097, Portland, OR 97213: Free brochure ❖ Fireplace screens. 503–288–7511.

Seymour Manufacturing Company Inc., 500 N. Broadway, P.O. Box 248, Seymour, IN 47274: Free brochure ❖ Fireplace tools, stove and fireplace repair accessories, brooms, bellows, and fire-starting supplies. 812–522–3320.

Fireplaces & Fireplace Kits

Charmaster Products Inc., 2307 Hwy. 2 West, Grand Rapids, MN 55744: Free brochure ❖ Fireplaces and wood-burning, wood-gas, and wood-oil furnaces and conversion units. 800–542–6360.

Custom Hardwood Productions, 917 York, Quincy, IL 62301: Free catalog ❖ Handcrafted, reproduction 19th-century English-style cast-iron fireplaces. 217–224–7013.

Fourth Bay, 10500 Industrial Dr., Garrettsville, OH 44231: Free brochure ❖ Reproduction cast iron fireplaces. 216–527–4343.

Grate Fires, P.O. Box 351, Athens, GA 30603: Free brochure ❖ Authentic English gas-coal fireplace unit. 706–353–8281.

Heat-N-Glo, 6665 W. Hwy. 13, Savage, MN 55378: Free brochure ❖ Fireplaces and accessories. 800–669–4328.

Heatilator Inc., 1915 W. Saunders St., Mt. Pleasant, IA 52641: Free information ❖ Wood-burning stoves and fireplace inserts. 800–247–6798.

Jotul USA, P.O. Box 1157, Portland, ME 04104: Free brochure ❖ Stoves and fireplaces. 800–535–2995.

Lopi International Ltd., Travis Industries, 10850 117th Pl. NE, Kirkland, WA 98033: Free information ❖ Fireplace inserts. 800–425–3915.

Majestic, 1000 E. Market St., Huntington, IN 46750: Free information ❖ Fireplaces and accessories. 800–525–1898.

Nu-Tec Incorporated, P.O. Box 908, East Greenwich, RI 02818: Free brochure ❖ Wood burning stoves and fireplace inserts. 800–822–0600.

Superior Fireplace, 4325 Artesia Ave., Fullerton, CA 92633: Free information ❖ Fireplaces and accessories. 714–521–7302.

Tulikivi Natural Stone Fireplaces, Tulikivi Group North America, P.O. Box 300, Schulyer, VA 22969: Free information ❖ Baking ovens, cookstoves, and natural stone fireplaces. 800–843–3473; 804–831–2228 (in VA).

Vermont Castings Inc., 7095 Prince St., Randolph, VT 05060: Free information ❖ Energy-efficient, easy-to-install fireplaces. 800–227–8683.

Mantels

A.D.I. Corporation, 5000 Nicholson Ct., North Bethesda, MD 20895: Free information ❖ Wood mantels. 301–564–1550.

Danny Alessandro, Edwin Jackson Inc., 307 E. 60th St., New York, NY 10022: Catalog $5 ❖ Antique and reproduction fireplace accessories and 18th-century limestone, wood, and marble mantels. 212–421–1928.

Architectural Paneling Inc., 979 3rd Ave., New York, NY 10022: Catalog $10 (refundable) ❖ Handcarved wood mantels and moldings. 212–371–9632.

Bradley Custom Mantels & Woodworking, 518 13th Ave., Prospect Park, PA 19076: Free brochure ❖ Mantels and other millwork. 215–586–3528.

Brill & Walker Associates Inc., P.O. Box 731, Sparta, NJ 07871: Catalog $4 ❖ Handcrafted English-style mantels. 201–729–8876.

Bryant Stove Inc., Box 2048, Thorndike, ME 04986: Free brochure ❖ Wood mantels and ornamental trim. 207–568–3665.

By-Gone Days Antiques Inc., 3100 South Blvd., Charlotte, NC 28209: Free information ❖ Mantels, restored door hardware, and other architectural antiques. 704–568–7537.

Decorators Supply Corporation, 3610 S. Morgan St., Chicago, IL 60609: Free information ❖ Wood mantels, capitals, brackets, medallions, plaster cornices, and moldings. 312–847–6300.

Driwood Ornamental Wood Moulding, P.O. Box 1729, Florence, SC 29503: Catalog $6 (refundable) ❖ Mantels, embossed wood moulding, raised paneling, curved stairs, and doors. 803–669–2478.

Hallidays America Inc., P.O. Box 731, Sparta, NJ 07871: Free information ❖ Fireplace accessories, handcarved mantels, and wood moldings. 201–729–8876.

Heritage Mantels Inc., P.O. Box 240, Southport, CT 06490: Catalog $3 ❖ Reproduction antique marble composition mantels. 203–335–0552.

House of Moulding, 15202 Oxnard St., Van Nuys, CA 91411: Catalog $5 ❖ Fireplaces, mantels, wood moldings and trim, and ceiling medallions. 800–327–4186; 800–675–1952 (in CA).

William H. Jackson Company, 210 E. 58th St., New York, NY 10022: Free brochure ❖ Antique fireplace accessories and mantels. 212–753–9400.

Maizefield Mantels, P.O. Box 336, Port Townsend, WA 98368: Free brochure ❖

Mantels with carved ornamentation. 206–385–6789.

Mantels of Yesteryear Inc., W. Tennessee Ave., Box 908, McCaysville, GA 30555: Free information ❖ Restored antique mantels. 706–492–5534.

Mountain Woodcarvers Mantels, P.O. Drawer R, Branson, MO 65616: Free information ❖ Handcarved mantels and fireplace accessories. 417–334–1843.

Nevers Oak Fireplace Mantels, 933 Rancheros Dr., St. B, San Marcos, CA 92069: Catalog $7.50 ❖ Handcarved mantels. 619–745–8841.

Piedmont Mantel & Millwork, 4320 Interstate Dr., Macon, GA 31210: Catalog $3 ❖ Colonial-style mantels and salvaged heart-pine flooring. 912–477–7536.

Plantation Mantels, 220 N. Carrollton, New Orleans, LA 70119: Catalog $2.25 ❖ Handcrafted wood mantels. 504–486–6822.

Readybuilt Products Company, P.O. Box 4425, Baltimore, MD 21223: Catalog $2 ❖ Hand-carved wood mantels in American and English styles, electric/gas fireplace logs, facings, and fireplaces. 800–626–2901; 410–233–5833 (in MD).

Roman Marble Company, 120 W. Kinzie, Chicago, IL 60610: Free brochure ❖ Pedestals, statuary, and Victorian, French, and English-style mantels. 312–337–2217.

Urban Artifacts, 4700 Wissahickon Ave., Philadelphia, PA 19144: Free information ❖ Antique carved wood and marble mantels. 800–621–1962.

The Wood Factory, 901 Harvard, Houston, TX 77008: Catalog $2 ❖ Ornamental trim, mantels, doors, and other reproduction millwork. 713–863–7600.

FIRE SAFETY

Escape Ladders

American LaFrance, Box 7146, Charlottesville, VA 22906: Free information ❖ Escape ladders. 804–973–4361.

Jomy Safety Ladder Company, 1728 16th St., Ste. 201, Boulder, CO 80302: Free information ❖ Collapsible fire escape ladder. 800–255–2591.

Ladder Man Inc., 3005 Silver Dr., Columbus, OH 43224: Free catalog ❖ Safety equipment, attic and fire escape equipment, and specialty, articulating, and stairwell ladders. 800–783–8887.

Fire Extinguishers

American LaFrance, Box 7146, Charlottesville, VA 22906: Free information ❖ Fire extinguishers. 804–973–4361.

Black & Decker, 6 Armstrong Rd., Shelton, CT 06484: Free information ❖ Fire extinguishers. 203–926–3000.

Blair-Jaeger Industrial Group, 32841 8 Mile Rd., Livonia, MI 48152: Free information ❖ Combination fire extinguisher and emergency automobile tire inflator.

Fireboy Halon Systems, P.O. Box 152, Grand Rapids, MI 49502: Free information ❖ Fire extinguishers for boats. 616–454–8337.

First Alert, 780 McClure Rd., Aurora, IL 60404: Free information ❖ Fire extinguishers. 800–323–9005.

Walter Kidde, Division Kidde Inc., 1394 S. 3rd St., Mebane, NC 27302: Free information ❖ Fire extinguishers. 919–563–5911.

Smoke Detectors

Black & Decker, 6 Armstrong Rd., Shelton, CT 06484: Free information ❖ Smoke alarms. 203–926–3000.

First Alert, 780 McClure Rd., Aurora, IL 60404: Free information ❖ Smoke alarms. 800–323–9005.

Jameson Home Products Inc., 2820 Thatcher Rd., Downers Grove, IL 60515: Free information ❖ Smoke alarms. 708–963–2850.

Radio Shack, Division Tandy Corporation, One Tandy Center, Fort Worth, TX 76102: Free information ❖ Smoke alarms. 817–390–3011.

Sanyo Electric, 200 Riser Rd., Little Ferry, NJ 07643: Free information with long SASE ❖ Electrostatic air cleaner/ionizer with a smoke sensor. 201–641–2333.

Sprinkler Systems

ASCOA Fire Systems, Box 418012, Cleveland, OH 44141: Free information ❖ Residential sprinkler systems. 216–526–8980.

Central Fire Sprinkler Corporation, 451 N. Cannon Ave., Lansdale, PA 19446: Free information ❖ Residential sprinkler systems. 215–362–0700.

Grinnel Fire Protection Systems Company, 1341 Elmwood Ave., Cranston, RI 02910: Free information ❖ Residential sprinkler systems. 401–941–8000.

Reliable Sprinkler Company, 525 N. MacQuestern Pkwy., Mount Vernon, NY 10552: Free information ❖ Residential sprinkler systems. 914–668–3470.

FIREWORKS

Because regulations governing the purchase and use of fireworks vary from state to state, consumers should read applicable regulations before ordering them from the companies listed below. Consumers should also make certain that they buy fireworks only from licensed or certified vendors who meet the requirements governing the sale of fireworks. Using fireworks illegally can result in substantial fines and possible jail sentences.

"Backyard" Fireworks

Ace Fireworks, P.O. Box 221, Conneaut, OH 44030: Catalog $1 ❖ Class C "backyard" fireworks. 800–344–4ACE.

Alonzo Fireworks, 12 Country Rd. 75, Mechanicsville, NY 12118: Free information ❖ Class C "backyard" fireworks. 518–664–9994.

Amazing Fireworks, 852 Drift Rd., Westport, MA 02790: Free information ❖ Class C "backyard" fireworks. 508–636–2221.

Bethany Sales Company, P.O. Box 248, Bethany, IL 61914: Free catalog ❖ Class C "backyard" fireworks. 217–665–3396.

Fireworks of America, 8550 Rt. 224, Deerfield, OH 44411: Free catalog ❖ Class C "backyard" fireworks. 800–423–1776.

Fireworks Unlimited, P.O. Box 764, Plainsboro, NJ 08536: Free information ❖ Class C "backyard" fireworks. 609–799–9475.

Neptune Fireworks Company Inc., 768 E. Dania Beach Blvd., P.O. Box 398, Dania, FL 33004: Free catalog ❖ Class C "backyard" fireworks. 800–456–2264; 305–920–6770 (in FL).

New England Fireworks, P.O. Box 3504, Stamford, CT 06905: Free information with long SASE ❖ Class C "backyard" fireworks. 203–324–5159.

Old Southern Trading Post, RD 1, Allendale, SC 29810: Free information ❖ Class C "backyard" fireworks. 803–584–3981.

Olde Glory Fireworks, P.O. Box 2863, Rapid City, SD 57709: Free catalog ❖ Class C "backyard" fireworks. 800–843–8758.

Phantom Fireworks, B.J. Alan Company, 555 Martin Luther King Blvd., Youngstown, OH 44502: Free information ❖ Class C "backyard" fireworks. 800–777–1699; 216–746–1064 (in OH).

Premium Fireworks, 207 Pike St., P.O. Box 703, Covington, KY 41011: Free information with long SASE ❖ Class C "backyard" fireworks. 606–431–0606.

Tall Paul Inc., P.O. Box 248, Eagleville, MO 64442: Catalog $3 ❖ Class C "backyard" fireworks. 800–525–4461; 816–867–3354 (in MO).

Fireworks Display Specialists

Atlas Enterprises Inc., Rt. 25, Box 93, Fort Worth, TX 76135: Free information ❖ Class B display fireworks. 817–237–3372.

Fireworks by Grucci, One Grucci Ln., Brookhaven, NY 11719: Free information ❖ Class B display fireworks. 800–227–0088; 516–286–0088 (in NY).

Pyro Spectaculars, P.O. Box 2329, Rialto, CA 92377: Free information ❖ Class B display fireworks. 714–874–1644.

Zambelli Internationale, P.O. Box 801, New Castle, PA 16103: Free information ❖ Class B display fireworks. 800–245–0397.

Fireworks Memorabilia

American Fireworks News, Star Route Box 30, Dingmans Ferry, PA 18328: Free brochure ❖ Books, manuals, and other information for people who collect and research fireworks and fireworks memorabilia. 717–828–8417.

Collectors Trading Service, 1849 E. Guadalupe, #101–103, Tempe, AZ 85283: Price list $1.50 ❖ Fireworks collectibles, patriotic paper Americana, labels, posters, catalogs, advertising items, empty boxes, and signs. 602–839–7842.

Dennis C. Manochio, Curator, 4th of July Americana & Fireworks Museum, P.O. Box 2010, Saratoga, CA 95070: Free information ❖ Old fireworks catalogs, packages and boxes of fireworks, literature, toys, and other memorabilia. 408–996–1963.

FISHING & FLY-TYING

Equipment

Abel Reels, 165 Avlador St., Camarillo, CA 93010: Free information ❖ Precision-engineered fly reels. 805–484–8789.

Abu-Garcia, 21 Law Dr., Fairfield, NJ 07006: Catalog $1 ❖ Saltwater spinning reels and rods, plug and bait casting and spin casting reels, and fishing lines. 201–227–7666.

Acme Tackle Company, 69 Bucklin St., Providence, RI 02907: Free information ❖ Saltwater lures for casting, jigging, and trolling.

All Star Graphite Rods Inc., 9750 Whithorn, Houston, TX 77095: Free catalog ❖ Plug and bait casting rods. 713–855–9603.

Allied Signal Inc., P.O. Box 31, Petersburg, VA 23804: Free information ❖ Braided fishing line. 804–520–3242.

Ande Inc., 1310 53rd St., West Palm Beach, FL 33407: Free brochure ❖ Fishing lines. 407–842–2474.

George Anderson's Yellowstone Angler, Hwy. 89 South, P.O. Box 660, Livingston, MT 59047: Free catalog ❖ Tackle, fly-fishing supplies, and fishing and hunting videos. 406–222–7130.

Andrus Bait Company, 708 W. Main St., Millville, NJ 08332: Free information ❖ Striped bass lures.

Angler's Workshop, P.O. Box 1044, Woodland, WA 98674: Free information ❖ Fishing and hunting videos and rods, tackle, reels, and other equipment. 206–225–6359.

Fred Arbogast Company, 313 W. North St., Akron, OH 44303: Free information ❖ Multi-purpose lures for pike, muskie, and large- and smallmouth bass. 800–252–5873; 216–253–2177 (in OH).

Area Rule Engineering, 32232 Azores Rd., Laguna Niguel, CA 92677: Free information ❖ Big-game trolling lures.

Atlantis, 30 Barnet Blvd., New Bedford, MA 02745: Free catalog ❖ Foul weather gear and clothing for yachtsmen and fishermen. 508–995–7000.

B'n'M Pole Company, Box 231, West Point, MS 39773: Free information ❖ Graphite and fiberglass poles and rods for crappie fishing. 800–647–6363; 601–494–5092 (in MS).

Bagley Baits, P.O. Box 810, Winter Haven, FL 33880: Free information ❖ Crayfish-simulating lures for panfish and smallmouths. 813–294–4271.

Dan Bailey's Fly Shop, P.O. Box 1019, Livingston, MT 59047: Free catalog ❖ Tackle, fly-tying supplies, and fishing and hunting videos. 800–356–4052.

The Bass Pond, P.O. Box 82, Littleton, CO 80160: Catalog $1 ❖ Flies, fly-tying components, fly rods, reels, lines, leaders, floats, and clothing.

Bass Pro Shops, 1935 S. Campbell, Springfield, MO 65898: Free information ❖ Float fishing equipment and other outdoor equipment. 800–227–7776.

Bead Tackle, 600 Main St., Monroe, CT 06468: Catalog $1 ❖ Spinning rods and saltwater lures. 203–459–1213.

L.L. Bean, Freeport, ME 04033: Free catalog ❖ Fly-tying supplies, fishing and hunting videos, and fly-, bass, and saltwater fishing equipment. 800–221–4221.

Bennett Video Group, 730 Washington St., Marina del Rey, CA 90292: Catalog $2.50 ❖ Boating, sailing, fishing, scuba diving, other watersports, travel, and other videos. 310–821–3329.

Berkeley Inc., One Berkeley Dr., Spirit Lake, IA 51360: Free catalog ❖ Fishing and fly lines, fly leaders, and spinning, plug and bait casting, and saltwater rods. 800–237–5539; 712–336–1520 (in IA).

Best American Duffel, 2601 Elliot Ave., Ste 4317, Seattle, WA 98121: Free information ❖ Tackle bags. 800–424–BAGS.

Bitterroot River Products, 20390 Carlton Creek Rd., Florence, MT 59833: Free information ❖ Tackle bags. 800–523–9834.

Blue Fox Tackle, 645 N. Emerson, Cambridge, MN 55008: Free information ❖ High-speed trolling lures. 612–869–3402.

Blue Ribbon Flies, Box 1037, West Yellowstone, MT 59758: Free catalog ❖ Fly-tying materials.

Bomber Bait, c/o PRADCO, Box 1587, Fort Smith, AR 72901: Free information ❖ High-speed trolling lures. 800–422–FISH.

Braid Products Inc., 616 E. Avenue P, Palmdale, CA 93550: Free information ❖ Trolling lures.

Charlie Brewer's Slider Company, P.O. Box 130, Lawrenceburg, TN 38464: Free information ❖ Soft plastic crawfish lures. 815–762–4700.

Browning Company, Dept. C006, One Browning Pl., Morgan, UT 84050: Catalog $2 ❖ Saltwater spinning reels, spinning rods, and plug and bait casting reels and rods. 800–333–3288.

BSI Sporting Goods, P.O. Box 5010, Vienna, WV 26105: Free catalog ❖ Firearm and muzzleloading supplies, optics, clothing, and archery, fishing, and hunting equipment. 304–295–8511.

C & H Lures Ultimate Tackle, 142 Mill Creek Rd., Jacksonville, FL 32211: Free information ❖ Lures for king mackerel fishing.

Cabela's, 812 13th Ave., Sidney, NE 69160: Free catalog ❖ Float fishing supplies and hunting and outdoor equipment. 800–237–4444.

Capt. Harry's Fishing Supplies, 100 NE 11th St., Miami, FL 33132: Catalog $3 ❖ Fly-fishing, saltwater fishing, bass fishing, and fly-tying supplies. 305–374–4661.

Cold Spring Anglers, P.O. Box 129, Carlisle, PA 17013: Catalog $2 ❖ Flies, tackle, and fly-tying supplies. 717–245–2646.

Cortland Line Company, P.O. Box 5588, Cortland, NY 13045: Free information ❖ Fly reels, lines, and leaders. 607–756–2851.

Creme Lure Company, P.O. Box 6162, Tyler, TX 75711: Free information ❖ Adjustable lures. 903–561–0522.

D.O.A. Lures, 3461–B Palm City School Ave., Palm City, FL 34990: Free information ❖ Soft-plastic lures filled with shrimp and baitfish particles.

Daiwa Corporation, 7421 Chapman Ave., Garden Grove, CA 92641: Catalog $1 ❖ Plug and bait casting reels and rods, saltwater reels and rods, and spin casting reels. 714–895–6662.

Donart Tackle, 302 Guy Lombardo, Freeport, NY 11520: Catalog $3 (refundable with $30 order) ❖ Rods and tackle components. 516–378–89921.

Double D Lures, 2500 Chinook Trail, Maitland, FL 32751: Free information ❖ Multi-purpose bass lures. 407–628–9648.

Eagle Claw Fishing Tackle, P.O. Box 16011, Denver, CO 80216: Catalog 50¢ ❖ Reels, rods, and fishing hooks. 303–321–1481.

EdgeWater Fishing Products, 35 N. 1000 West, Clearfield, UT 84015: Free catalog ❖ Handmade flies and fly-tying supplies. 800–584–7647.

Egger's, P.O. Box 1344, Cumming, GA 30130: Free catalog ❖ Fly-tying supplies, tools, and net kits.

Fenwick Corporation, 5242 Argosy Dr., Huntington Beach, CA 92649: Catalog $1 ❖ Saltwater spinning reels and spinning, plug and bait casting, and fly rods. 714–897–1066.

Fish 'n' Shack, P.O. Box 1080, Camdenton, MO 65020: Free catalog ❖ Freshwater fishing supplies. 314–346–4044.

Flies Only, 78 North Rt. 303, Congers, NY 10920: Free catalog ❖ Flies for cold and warm water fishing.

The Fly Box, 923 SE 3rd St., Bend, OR 97702: Catalog $1 ❖ Fly-fishing supplies and fishing and hunting videos. 503–388–3330.

The Fly Shop, 4140 Churn Creek Rd., Redding, CA 96002: Free information ❖ Fly-fishing supplies, tackle, and fishing and hunting videos. 800–669–3474.

Gander Mountain Inc., P.O. Box 248, Gander Mountain, Wilmot, WI 53192: Free catalog ❖ Outdoor sports equipment and clothing for fishing, hunting, and camping. 414–862–2331.

Gudebrod, P.O. Box 357, Pottsdown, PA 19464: Free information ❖ Braided fishing line. 215–327–4050.

Harrison-Hoge Industries Inc., Panther Martin, 200 Wilson St., Port Jefferson Station, NY 11776: Free catalog ❖ Fishing lures. 800–852–0925.

Hart Tackle Company Inc., P.O. Box 898, Stratford, OK 74872: Free information ❖ Bass lures. 800–543–0774.

Hook & Tackle Company, 7 Kaycee Loop Rd., Plattsburgh, NY 12901: Free catalog ❖ Fly-fishing tackle, fly-tying and fly rod-building supplies, hand-tied flies, clothing, and wading boots. 800–552–8342.

Hopkins Fishing Tackle, 1130 Boissevain Ave., Norfolk, VA 23507: Free information ❖ Saltwater lures. 804–622–0977.

Hunter's Angling Supplies, One Central Square Box 300, New Boston, NH 03070: Catalog $3 ❖ Fly-fishing, bass fishing, saltwater fishing, and fly-tying supplies. 603–487–3388.

Izorline International Inc., 813 Gardena Blvd., Gardena, CA 90247: Free information ❖ Braided fishing line. 310–324–1159.

J & J Tackle, P.O. Box 718, Belmar, NJ 07719: Catalog $1.50 ❖ Lures for fresh and saltwater fishing. 908–280–0200.

Jann's Sportsman's Supplies, P.O. Box 4315, Toledo, OH 43609: Free catalog ❖ Lures, rods, and fly-tying supplies.

Jawtec Worms, P.O. Box 1181, Forney, TX 75126: Free information ❖ Plastic crawfish lures. 800–544–4842.

Jerry's Bait & Tackle, 604 12th St., Highland, IL 62249: Free catalog ❖ Fly-fishing and fly-tying supplies, tackle, and fishing and hunting videos. 618–654–3235.

Johnson Fishing Inc., 1531 E. Madison Ave., Mankato, MN 56002: Free information ❖ Lures for large- and smallmouth bass. 507–345–4623.

Kaufmann's Streamborn, P.O. Box 23032, Portland, OR 97223: Free catalog ❖ Fly-fishing, bass fishing, saltwater fishing, and fly-tying supplies. 800–442–4FLY.

Bill Lewis Lures, P.O. Box 7959, Alexandria, LA 71306: Free information ❖ Fishing tackle and multi-purpose lures for crappie, bass, bluegill, walleye, and white bass. 318–487–0352.

Li'l Mac, P.O. Box 6325, Spokane, WA 99207: Catalog $2 ❖ Fishing sinker molds. 509–466–3545.

G. Loomis Company, P.O. Box 957, Woodland, WA 98674: Catalog $1 ❖ Spinning, fly, and plug and bait casting rods. 206–225–6516.

Lure-Craft Industries Inc., P.O. Box 35, Solsberry, IN 47459: Catalog $2 ❖ Plastic worm- and lure-making supplies. 812–825–9088.

Madison River Fishing Company, Box 627, Ennis, MT 59729: Free catalog ❖ Fresh and saltwater fly tackle, fly-tying materials, rod-building supplies, and books. 800–227–7127.

Magna Strike Inc., P.O. Box 69, Freeport, NY 11520: Catalog $1 ❖ Fresh- and saltwater lures. 516–378–1913.

Main Stream Fly-fishing, 8260 Market St., Boardman, OH 44512: Free catalog ❖ Fresh and saltwater fly-fishing and fly-tying equipment. 216–792–3744.

Mann's Bait Company, 604 State Docks Rd., Eufaula, AL 36027: Free information ❖ High-speed trolling lures. 205–687–5716.

Marble Hall Inc., 1426 N. 27th Ln., Phoenix, AZ 85009: Free information ❖ Natural-looking baitfish-like lures. 602–269–0708.

Marriott's Flyfishing Store, 2700 W. Orangethorpe, Fullerton, CA 92633: Catalog $3 ❖ Fly-, bass, saltwater fishing, and fly-tying supplies. 714–525–1827.

Martin Reel Company, P.O. Box 6554, Yorkville Station, New York, NY 10128: Free information ❖ Fly reels. 315–866–1690.

Mason Tackle Company, 11273 N. State Rd., P.O. Box 56, Otisville, MI 48463: Free information ❖ Braided fishing line. 313–631–4571.

Mikes Fly Desk, 2395 S. 150 East, Bountiful, UT 84010: Free catalog ❖ Fly-tying materials. 801–292–4736.

Mister Twister Inc., P.O. Drawer 996, Minden, LA 71058: Free information ❖ Fresh water lures. 318–377–8818.

Netcraft Company, Box 5151, Toledo, OH 43613: Free catalog ❖ Rods, reels, marine electronics, rod and lure building components, and fly-tying supplies. 419–472–9826.

Normark, 10395 Yellow Circle Dr., Minnetonka, MN 55423: Free information ❖ High-speed trolling lures. 612–833–7060.

On the Fly, 3628 Sage Dr., Rockford, IL 61111: Free catalog ❖ Fly-fishing and fly-tying supplies. 815–877–0090.

Orvis Manchester, Historic Rt. 7A, Manchester, VT 05254: Free catalog ❖ Fly-fishing rods, reels, leaders, neoprene waders, tackle boxes, and lures. 800–548–9548.

Owner American Corporation, 17965 Von Karman, Ste. 111, Irvine, CA 92714: Free information ❖ Hooks.

Pace Industries Inc., P.O. Box 5127, Fort Lauderdale, FL 33310: Free information ❖ Rod handles, floats, bait bodies, and other supplies. 305–975–6333.

Penn Fishing Tackle, 3028 W. Hunting Park Ave., Philadelphia, PA 19132: Catalog $2 ❖ Saltwater spinning reels, spinning rods, plug and bait casting reels, and saltwater reels and rods. 215–229–9415.

Pradco, P.O. Box 1587, Fort Smith, AR 72902: Free information ❖ Fishing line and tackle. 800–422–FISH.

Proven Pattern, 1932 Del Amo Blvd., Torrance, CA 90501: Free information ❖ Casting and offshore trolling lures.

R.J. Tackle Inc., 5719 Corporation Cir., Unit 1, Fort Meyers, FL 33905: Free information ❖ Lures. 813–693–7070.

Ramsey Outdoor Store, 226 Rt. 17, P.O. Box 1689, Paramus, NJ 07653: Free catalog ❖ Fly-tying, other fishing supplies, and fishing and hunting videos. 800–526–7436; 201–261–5000 (in NJ).

Red Eye Tackle, 661 Orchard Rd., Elba, NY 14058: Free information ❖ Lures for bass and walleye.

Rizuto's Fly Shop, P.O. Box 6309, Navajo Dam, NM 87414: Free catalog ❖ Fly-fishing equipment and supplies.

Roaring River Lodge, Hwy. 112 South, Cassville, MO 65625: Free information ❖ Fly-fishing supplies, tackle, and fishing and hunting videos. 417–847–2330.

Ryobi America Corporation, 5201 Pearman Dairy Rd., Anderson, SC 29625: Free information ❖ Plug and bait casting reels and rods, saltwater reels and rods, and spin casting reels. 800–323–4615.

Sadu Blue Water Inc., 4669 122nd Dr. North, Royal Palm Beach, FL 33411: Free information ❖ Offshore trolling lures.

Scientific Anglers, 3M Center, Bldg. 225–3N–04, St. Paul, MN 55144: Free information ❖ Reels and other fishing accessories, and how-to cassettes on bass fishing, fly-fishing, deer hunting, waterfowl hunting, and turkey hunting. 612–733–0973.

Scott Powr-Ply Company, 707 Heinz St., Berkeley, CA 94710: Free information ❖ Graphite fly rods. 510–841–2444.

Senco Inc., Box 306, Marquette, MI 49855: Free information ❖ Recreational shelters, portable hunting blinds and ice fishing houses, and greenhouses. 407–589–6563.

Shakespeare Company, 3801 Westmore Dr., Columbia, SC 29223: Catalog $1 ❖ Plug and bait casting reels and rods, spin casting reels, and fishing lines. 803–754–7000.

Sheldon's Inc., 626 Center St., Antigo, WI 54409: Free information ❖ Freshwater lures. 715–623–2382.

Shimano American Corporation, One Shimano Dr., P.O. Box 19615, Irvine, CA 92713: Catalog $1 ❖ Plug and bait casting reels and rods, saltwater reels and rods, and other accessories. 714–951–5003.

Silstar America Corporation, 1411 Silstar Rd., West Columbia, SC 29179: Catalog $2 ❖ Saltwater spinning reels and rods, plug and bait casting reels and rods, and other accessories.

Smithwick, P.O. Box 1587, Fort Smith, AR 72902: Free information ❖ Minnow lures.

Snag Proof, 11387 Deerfield Rd., Cincinnati, OH 45232: Free information ❖ Bass and northern pike lures. 800–762–4773.

South Bend Sporting Goods, 1950 Stanley St., Northbrook, IL 60065: Catalog $2 ❖ Saltwater spinning reels and rods, plug and bait casting rods, and high-speed trolling lures. 708–564–1900.

South Creek Ltd., P.O. Box 981, Lyons, CO 80540: Catalog $1 ❖ Fishing accessories and 1–, 2–, and 3–piece bamboo rods. 800–354–5050.

Storm Manufacturing Company, Box 720265, Norman, OK 73070: Free information ❖ High-speed trolling lures. 405–329–5894.

Stren Fishing Lines, c/o Dupont, 6207 Brandywine Building, Wilmington, DE 19898: Free information ❖ Braided fishing line. 302–773–0156.

Strike King Lure Company, 174 Hwy. 72 West, Collierville, TN 38017: Free information ❖ Multi-purpose spinnerball lures. 901–853–1455.

Tackle-Craft, 1440 Kennedy Rd., Chippewa Falls, WI 54729: Free catalog ❖ Fly- and jig-tying supplies, spinner-making tools, and other fishing aids. 715–723–3645.

The Tackle Shop, Box 830369, Richardson, TX 75080: Free catalog ❖ Tackle and rod-building supplies, lure components, plastic lures, and fishing and hunting videos. 214–231–5982.

R.D. Taylor Rodmakers, P.O. Box 54, Turners Falls, MA 01376: Free brochure ❖ Handcrafted bamboo fly rods. 413–863–8608.

Thomas & Thomas, P.O. Box 32, Turner Falls, MA 01376: Catalog $3 (refundable) ❖ Fly-tying equipment. 413–863–9727.

Thorn Brothers, 7500 University Ave. NE, Minneapolis, MN 55432: Free information ❖ Graphite ice fishing rods.

Tournament Tackle Inc., P.O. Box 372820, Satellite Beach, FL 32937: Free information ❖ Offshore trolling lures.

Triple Fish Fishing Line, 321 Enterprise Dr., Ocoee, FL 34761: Free information ❖ Braided fishing line. 407–656–7834.

Westbank Anglers, P.O. Box 523, Teton Village, WY 83025: Free catalog ❖ Fly-fishing supplies. 307–733–6483.

R.L. Winston Rod Company, Drawer T, Twin Bridges, MT 59754: Free catalog ❖ Salt water salmon rods and handcrafted bamboo, glass, and graphite fly rods. 406–684–5674.

Wyoming River Raiders, 601 Wyoming Blvd., Casper, WY 82609: Free catalog ❖ Fishing gear, clothing for outdoors, books, and camping, river expedition, and hiking equipment. 800–247–6068; 307–235–8624 (in WY).

Yakima Bait Company, P.O. Box 310, Granger, WA 98932: Free information ❖ High-speed trolling lures. 509–854–1311.

Yeagers Sporting Goods & Marine, 3101 Northwest Ave., Bellingham, WA 98225: Free information ❖ Fishing supplies, tackle, and fishing and hunting videos. 206–733–1080.

Zebco Corporation, P.O. Box 270, Tulsa, OK 74101: Free catalog ❖ Saltwater spinning reels and rods, plug and bait casting reels and rods, and spin casting reels. 918–836–5581.

Fish-Finding Electronics

Computrol Inc., 499 E. Corporate Dr., Meridian, ID 83642: Free information ❖ Depthfinders for locating fish. 208–887–1000.

Eagle Electronics Inc., 12000 E. Skelly Dr., Tulsa, OK 74128: Free information ❖ Depthfinders for locating fish. 918–437–6881.

Fish Hawk Electronic Corporation, P.O. Box 340, Crystal Lake, IL 60039: Free information ❖ Depthfinders for locating fish.

Furuno USA, P.O. Box 2343, South San Francisco, CA 94083: Free information ❖ Depthfinders for locating fish. 415–873–9393.

Interphase Technologies Inc., 1201 Shaffer Rd., Santa Cruz, CA 95060: Free information ❖ Depthfinders for locating fish. 408–426–2007.

Lowrance Electronics, 12000 E. Skelly Dr., Tulsa, OK 74070: Free information ❖ Depthfinders for locating fish. 800–324–4737.

Magellan Systems Corporation, 960 Overland Ct., San Dimas, CA 91773: Free information ❖ Depthfinders for locating fish. 909–394–5000.

Marinetek, 2076 Zanker Rd., San Jose, CA 95141: Free information ❖ Depthfinders for locating fish. 408–441–1661.

Si-Tex Marine Electronics, P.O. Box 6700, Clearwater, FL 34618: Free information ❖ Depthfinders for locating fish. 813–535–4681.

Techsonic Industries Inc., One Humminbird Ln., Eufaula, AL 36027: Free information ❖ Depthfinders for locating fish. 205–687–6613.

Uniden, 4700 Amon Carter Blvd., Fort Worth, TX 76155: Free information ❖ Depthfinders for locating fish. 817–858–3300.

FLAGS & FLAG POLES

American Flag & Gift, 737 Manuela Way, Arroyo Grande, CA 93420: Catalog $2 ❖ Flags, banners, bunting, and flag poles. 805–473–0395.

American Flagpoles & Flags, 109–F Lumber Ln., Goose Creek, SC 29445: Free catalog ❖ Flagpoles and United States, state, international, nautical, and historical flags. 800–777–1706.

Banner Fabric, Kite Studio, 5555 Hamilton Blvd., Wescosville, PA 18106: Free information ❖ Fabrics, notions, and hardware for kites, flags, banners, and windsocks. 610–395–3560.

Banner Ideas, 10625 Trade Rd., Richmond, VA 23236: Catalog $2 (refundable) ❖ Special occasion decorating flags. 804–379–0335.

Broward Flag Company, P.O. Box 8593, Asheville, NC 28814: Catalog $2 (refundable) ❖ Flag poles, pennants, banners, decals, and United States, state and territorial, foreign, historic, display, church, marine, confederate, and other flags. 704–258–9295.

Carija & Plona, 36 Water St., Mystic, CT 06355: Free brochure ❖ Flagpole sets with optional decorative brackets. 800–582–8676.

Carrot-Top Industries Inc., P.O. Box 820, Hillsborough, NC 27278: Free catalog ❖ Ready-made and made-to-order flags, banners, and decorations. 800–628–3524.

Central Mass Discount Flag, 66 West St., Leominster, MA 01453: Free information ❖ Flags and flagpoles. 800–356–4232.

Flag America Company, 2708 Long Beach Blvd., Ship Bottom, NJ 08008: Free information ❖ Flags, banners, windsocks, and flag poles. 609–494–2626.

Flag Fables Inc., P.O. Box 60701, Longmeadow, MA 01116: Free catalog ❖ Flags for every occasion. 800–257–1025; 413–747–0525 (in MA).

Flags & Flagpoles, Division Associated Builders Specialties, 7106 Mapleridge, Houston, TX 77081: Free information ❖ Flags and fiberglass flagpoles. 713–666–2371.

Frontier Flags, 1761 Owl Creek Rt., Thermopolis, WY 82443: Catalog $3 ❖ Hand-sewn historic flag reproductions. 800–921–9218.

Glory Flag & Pole Company, RR 3, Box 67, Fort Dodge, IA 50501: Free catalog ❖ Flag poles and U.S., state, foreign, religious, military, and other flags and banners. 800–841–8206.

Hennessy House, P.O. Box 57, Sierra City, CA 96125: Free brochure ❖ Handmade wood flag poles and flags. 800–285–2122.

House of Flags, P.O. Box 8410, Warwick, RI 02888: Free brochure ❖ Flagpoles, weather vanes, eagles, and United States, historical, state, foreign, holiday, seasonal, nautical, and other flags. 800–45–FLAGS.

International Distribution, 434 DeAnza St., San Carlos, CA 94070: Free catalog ❖ Decorative holiday and garden flags. 800–392–7476.

B.J. Lindsy Flag & Banner Company, 44 Chapman St., Greenfield, MA 01302: Catalog $3 (refundable) ❖ Flags, banners, and accessories. 800–360–6512; 413–774–5807 (in MA).

Martin's Flag Company, P.O. Box 1118, Fort Dodge, IA 50601: Free catalog ❖ Flags and accessories. 800–992–3524; 515–576–0481 (in IA).

Marvin Display, 322 Boston Post Rd., Milford, CT 06460: Free information ❖ Flagpoles, hardware, and United States, historical, state, foreign, nautical, and fun flags. 800–322–8587.

Montgomery Flag Works, P.O. Box 240391, Montgomery, AL 36124: Free catalog ❖ Reproduction Civil War flags.

Old Glories Vintage Design, P.O. Box 33077, Cincinnati, OH 45233: Free brochure ❖ Flag poles and United States, Confederate, and pre-revolutionary flags. 513–941–7425.

Safety Flag Company of America, P.O. Box 1088, Pawtucket, RI 02862: Free catalog ❖ Flags and safety equipment for boats. 401–722–0900.

U.S. Flag Service, 5741 Elmer Derr Rd., Frederick, MD 21701: Free information ❖ Flags and accessories. 800–USA-FLAG.

Vaughn Display, 5050 W. 78th St., Minneapolis, MN 55435: Free catalog ❖ Flagpoles, floor stands, holders, brackets, religious flags, bunting, pennants, and United States, foreign, state, territorial, and other flags. 800–328–6120.

Windborne Kites, 585 Cannery Row, Monterey, CA 93940: Free catalog ❖ Kites and accessories, windsocks, and flags. 408–373–7422.

FLOWERS & PLANTS
Artificial Flowers

Bailey's Wholesale Floral Supply, P.O. Box 591, Arcadia, IN 46030: Catalog $3 (refundable) ❖ Silk flowers. 317–984–3663.

Fine Design, P.O. Box 310704, New Braunfels, TX 78131: Free information ❖ Silk rose arrangements. 800–200–2224.

Gardens Past, P.O. Box 1846, Estes Park, CO 80517: Catalog $1 ❖ Soaps and soap making supplies, potpourri, dried flowers, herbs, candles, and aromatherapy items. 303–586–0400.

International Manufacturing Company, 1130 Live Oak St., Lillian Springs, FL 32351: Catalog $1 ❖ Silk plants, trees, flower arranging supplies, potpourri, and other art and craft supplies. 904–875–2918.

May Silk, 13262 Moore St., Cerritos, CA 90701: Free catalog ❖ Silk plants, trees, and flowers. 800–282–7455; 310–926–7172 (in CA).

Meadows Direct, 13805 Hwy. 136, Onslow, IA 52321: Free list ❖ Dried and preserved leaves and flowers. 800–542–9771.

Petals, 1 Aqueduct Rd., White Plains, NY 10606: Free catalog ❖ Silk floral arrangements, flowers, plants, and trees. 914–637–3825.

Riverside Gardens, 300 E. Riverside, Timberville, VA 22853: Free price list ❖ Dried flowers and plants. 800–847–6449; 703–896–9859 (in VA).

Shady Acres Herb Farm, 7815 Hwy. 212, Chaska, MN 55318: Free list with long SASE ❖ Dried plants and herbal vinegars. 612–466–3391.

Silk-kit, 27 Union Ave., Ronkonkoma, NY 11779: Catalog $2 (refundable) ❖ Silk flower arrangement kits and supplies.

Waters of the South, P.O. Box 726, Minden, LA 71058: Free brochure ❖ Realistic looking garden greenery. 800–782–5480; 318–377–9394 (in LA).

Dried Flowers

Caswell-Massey Company Ltd., Catalog Division, 100 Enterprise Pl., Dover, DE 19901: Catalog $1 ❖ Potpourri and pomander mixes, dried flowers, herb plants, essential oils, and perfumery supplies. 800–326–0500.

Fieldstone Farm, 3500 Elderhill Rd., Driftwood, TX 78619: Catalog $1 (refundable) ❖ Fresh-dried flowers and herbs.

The Gathered Herb & Greenhouse, 12114 N. State Rd., Otisville, MI 48463: Catalog $2 ❖ Dried flowers, herbs, herb tea, perennials, and potpourri supplies. 313–631–6572.

Goodwin Creek Gardens, P.O. Box 83, Williams, OR 97544: Catalog $1 ❖ Dried floral arrangements, seeds and plants, trees, shrubs, and perennial flowers. 503–846–7357.

Hartman's Herb Farm, Old Dana Rd., Barre, MA 01005: Catalog $2 ❖ Herbs and herb products, potpourri, and essential oils. 508–355–2015.

Herbs-Liscious, 1702 S. 6th St., Marshalltown, IA 50158: Catalog $2 (refundable) ❖ Dried flowers, herbs and spices, oils and fragrances, and potpourri.

Hummingbird Hills Herbal Nursery, 17201 S. Hawkinds, Ashland, MO 65010: Catalog $1 ❖ Dried flowers, perennials, everlastings, and organically grown herbs. 314–657–2082.

Meadow Everlastings, 16464 Shabbona Rd., Malta, IL 60150: Catalog $2 (refundable) ❖ Dried flowers, wreath kits, and potpourri.

Mountain Farms Inc., 307 Number 9 Rd., Fletcher, NC 28732: Free catalog ❖ Dried floral products and herbs. 704–628–4709.

J. Page Basketry, 820 Albee Rd. West, Nokomis, FL 34275: Catalog $2 (refundable) ❖ Dried flowers and herbs, books, and pine needle, wheat weaving, and basket-making supplies and tools. 813–485–6730.

Tom Thumb Workshops, Rt. 13, P.O. Box 357, Mappsville, VA 23407: Catalog $1 ❖ Potpourri, herbs, spices, essential oils, dried flowers, and other art and craft supplies. 804–824–3507.

Vineyard Vines, P.O. Box 774, Oak Bluffs, MA 02557: Catalog $1 (refundable) ❖ Dried flowers, herbal skin care products, potpourri and sachets, and other gifts. 508–693–1724.

Warmbier Farms, 7328 Buck Rd., Freeland, MI 48623: Free brochure ❖ Dried flowers. 517–695–5044.

Well-Sweep Herb Farm, 317 Mt. Bethel Rd., Port Murray, NJ 07865: Catalog $2 ❖ Potpourri and pomander mixes, dried flowers, and herb. 908–852–5390.

FOIL CRAFTS

Atlas Art & Stained Glass, P.O. Box 76084, Oklahoma City, OK 73147: Catalog $3 ❖ Kaleidoscopes, frames, lamp bases, and art and craft, stained glass, jewelry-making, and foil crafting supplies. 405–946–1230.

Guildcraft Company, 100 Firetower Dr., Tonawanda, NY 14150: Free catalog ❖ Colored metal foils and supplies. 716–743–8336.

FOOD PROCESSORS

A Cook's Wares, 211 37th St., Beaver's Falls, PA 15010: Catalog $2 ❖ Food processors, cutlery, bakeware, porcelain, French copper pans, and other kitchen aids. 412–846–9490.

Cuisinarts Cookware, 150 Milford Rd., East Windsor, NJ 08520: Free information ❖ Food processors and attachments. 800–726–9499.

European Home Products, 136 Washington St., Norwalk, CT 06854: Free catalog ❖ Replacement parts for food processors and other kitchen appliances. 800–225–0760.

Oreck Corporation, 100 Plantation Rd., New Orleans, LA 70123: Free information ❖ Small kitchen appliances and food processors. 800–989–4200.

Vita-Mix Corporation, 8615 Usher Rd., Cleveland, OH 44138: Free information ❖ Vita-Mix food processor. 800–848–2649.

Zabar's & Company, 2245 Broadway, New York, NY 10024: Free catalog ❖ Cookware, food processors, microwave ovens, kitchen tools, and coffee makers. 212–787–2000.

FOODS

Apple Cider

Berry-Hill Limited, 75 Burwell Rd., St. Thomas, Ontario, Canada N5P 3R5: Catalog $2 ❖ Cider press, canning equipment, weather vanes, and garden equipment. 519–631–0480.

Happy Valley Ranch, 16577 W327, Paola, KS 66071: Catalog $1 ❖ Home cider presses and fruit grinders. 913–849–3103.

Jaffrey Manufacturing Company, Box 23527, Shawnee Mission, KS 66223: Brochure $1 ❖ Apple cider and wine presses, assembled or as a kit. 913–849–3139.

Breads & Rolls

Balducci's, Shop from Home Service, 42–25 12th St., Long Island City, NY 11101: Catalog $3 ❖ Bread and other food specialties. 800–225–3822.

Baldwin Hill Bakery, Baldwin Hill Rd., Phillipston, MA 01331: Free brochure ❖ Bread. 508–249–4691.

Boudin Sourdough Bakery, 132 Hawthorne, San Francisco, CA 94107: Free information ❖ Sourdough bread and other specialties. 415–882–1800.

Bread Alone, Rt. 28, Boiceville, NY 12412: Free information ❖ Hearth-baked bread made with organic flours and whole grains. 914–657–3328.

Burnt Cabins Grist Mill, P.O. Box 65, Burnt Cabins, PA 17215: Free brochure ❖ Old-fashioned buckwheat and wheat flours, roasted and regular cornmeal, and pancake and muffin mixes. 800–BRT-MILL.

C'est Croissant Inc., 22138 S. Vermont Ave., Unit A, Torrance, CA 90502: Free brochure ❖ Plain, fluffy French almond, chocolate, and all-butter croissants. 800–633–2767.

Daily Bread Company Inc., P.O. Box 1901, Portsmouth, NH 03802: Free information ❖ Honey-oatmeal, onion dill, and nine-grain easy-to-make bread mixes. 603–436–2722.

Dean & DeLuca Mail-Order, 560 Broadway, New York, NY 10012: Free information ❖ Bread. 800–221–7714.

Deborah's Country French Bread, 954 W. Washington Blvd., Chicago, IL 60607: Free brochure ❖ Overnight delivery of bread from the Poilane bakery in Paris. 800–952–1400.

DiCamillo Bakery, 811 Linwood Ave., Niagara Falls, NY 14305: Free catalog ❖ Italian bread and other specialties. 800–634–4363; 716–282–2341 (in NY).

Dunham Hill Bakery, P.O. Box 125, Woodstock, VT 05091: Free catalog ❖ European-style bread and pastries. 800–281–3121; 802–457–3121 (in VT).

Genie's Kitchen, 150 Magic Ln., Box 456, Wibaux, MT 59353: Free information (request list of retail sources) ❖ Low-fat, no cholesterol muffin mixes. 406–795–2228.

H & H Bagels, 2239 Broadway, New York, NY 10024: Free catalog ❖ Bagels. 800–NY-BAGEL; 212–595–8000 (in NY).

HeartyMix Company, 1231 Madison Hill Rd., Rahway, NJ 07065: Free catalog ❖ Mixes for bread machines. 908–382–3010.

The J.B. Dough Company, 200 Paw Paw Ave., Benton Harbor, MI 49022: Free price list ❖ Mixes for bread machines or for making by hand. 800–528–6222.

The King Arthur Flour Baker's Catalog, P.O. Box 876, Norwich, VT 05055: Free information ❖ Sourdough starter for bread, pancakes, biscuits, and cakes. 800–827–6836.

Moishe's Homemade Kosher Bakery, 181 E. Houston St., New York, NY 10002: Free information ❖ Corn bread, challah, and bagels. 212–475–9624.

Native Grains Inc., 101 1st St. West, Fosston, MN 56542: Free information ❖ Mixes for easy-to-make natural organic bread. 800–845–2486.

Orwasher's Bakery, 308 E. 78th St., New York, NY 10021: Free information ❖ Bread and other specialties. 212–288–6569.

Plantation Pride Bakeries, 1002 Apperson Dr., Salem, VA 24153: Free information ❖ High-fiber bread. 800–729–2732.

The Pletzel Company, 2660 Walnut St., Denver, CO 80205: Free information ❖ Bagel chips in a variety of flavors. 800–765–4243; 303–296–4132 (in CO).

R.F. Nature Farm Foods Inc., 850 NBC Center, Lincoln, NE 68508: Free information (request list of retail sources) ❖ All-natural bread mixes for bread machines and oven-baking. 800–222–FARM; 402–474–7576 (in NE).

Rubschlager Baking Corporation, 3320 W. Grand Ave., Chicago, IL 60651: Free information ❖ European-style whole rye and stone-ground wheat bread. 312–826–1245.

Sunberry Baking Company, 757 Kohn St., Norristown, PA 19401: Free information ❖ Fresh-baked sourdough bread. 800–833–4090.

Sunrise Gourmet Foods & Gifts, 1813 3rd Ave. East, Hibbing, MN 55746: Free information ❖ Bread and other specialties. 800–782–6736.

Wanda's Nature Farm Foods, 850 NBC Center, Lincoln, NE 68508: Free catalog ❖ All-natural bread, muffin, pancake, waffle, and double-chocolate cake mixes. 800–222–FARM.

Wolferman's, One Muffin Ln., P.O. Box 15913, Lenexa, KS 66215: Free catalog ❖ English muffins, crumpets, scones, and bagels. 800–999–1910.

Ye Olde Sweet Shoppe Bakery, 100 W. German St., P.O. Box 1672, Shepherdstown, WV 25443: Free information ❖ Home-baked bread, strudels, German stollen, and other specialties. 800–922–5379.

Cakes & Cookies

Ariola Foods Inc., 218–38 97th Ave., Queens Village, NY 11429: Free information ❖ Cannoli shells, cheesecakes, and other Italian pastries. 800–443–0777.

Aunt Goldie's Goldies Inc., 305 E. 40th St., New York, NY 10016: Free information ❖ Preservative-free butterscotch and chocolate brownies. 212–599–1791.

Beth's Fine Desserts, 1201 Andersen Dr., San Rafael, CA 94901: Free information ❖ Gourmet cookies. 800–425–BETH.

Bette's Oceanview Diner, 4240 Hollis St., Emeryville, CA 94608: Free information ❖ Scone and pancake mixes. 510–601–6980.

Bittersweet Pastries, 17 S. Greenbush Rd., Orangeburg, NY 10962: Free information (request list of retail sources) ❖ All-natural bittersweet chocolate truffle cakes, tarts, and other pastries. 914–359–5580.

Boston Coffee Cake Company, 16 Henshaw St., Woburn, MA 01801: Free information ❖ Coffee cakes. 800–434–0500.

Brass Ladle Products, 14 Olde Ridge Rd., Chadds Ford, PA 19317: Free information ❖ All-natural gourmet cake mixes. 610–558–4171.

Browniepop Inc., 1405 SW 6th Ct., Ste. F, Pompano Beach, FL 33069: Free information ❖ Gourmet brownies. 800–825–3743.

Buckley's Fancy Foods & Confections Ltd., P.O. Box 14119, Baton Rouge, LA 70898: Free catalog ❖ Cookies, toffee and brittle, pretzels, coffee, tea, and holiday specialties. 800–445–3957.

Byrd Cookie Company, 2233 Norwood Ave., Savannah, GA 31406: Free brochure ❖ Preservative-free, Southern-style cookies and confections by Savannah's cookie maker, Benjamin "Cookie" Byrd. 912–355–1716.

Cafe Beaujolais, Box 730, Mendocino, CA 95460: Free catalog ❖ Pastries and desserts. 707–937–0443.

The Cake Stylist/Granny's Cheesecakes, 5842 Maurice Ave., Maspeth, NY 11378: Free information (request list of retail sources) ❖ Gourmet cheese cakes, layer cakes, petit fours, and other pastries. 718–894–3494.

Carol's Heirloom Cookies, Division Dillon Marketing, 850 Meadow Ln., Camp Hill, PA 17011: Free information ❖ Springerle cookies. 717–761–6895.

Celia's Sweets Inc., P.O. Box 424, Grand Ledge, MI 48837: Free information (request list of retail sources) ❖ Italian wafer cookies. 517–627–1910.

Champlain Chocolate Company, 431 Pine St., Burlington, VT 05401: Free information ❖ Candy. 800–634–8105.

Charleston Cake Lady, 774 Woodward Rd., Charleston, SC 29407: Free catalog ❖ Cakes made with fresh, natural ingredients. 800–488–0830.

Cheesecake Lady, P.O. Box 584, Hopland, CA 95449: Free brochure ❖ Cheesecakes and a low-fat, low-cholesterol lemon cake. 800–225–3523.

Cheesecake Royale, 9016 Garland Rd., Dallas, TX 75218: Free information with long SASE ❖ Cheesecakes. 800–328–9102; 214–328–9102 (in TX).

Choc-O-Lea's Chocolate Creations, 1300 Jez Rd., Ladysmith, WI 54848: Free price list ❖ Brownies, cookies, and fudge. 800–437–0431.

Chocolate Catalogue, 3983 Gratiot, St. Louis, MO 63110: Free catalog ❖ Petit fours double-dipped in chocolate, with a choice of fillings. 800–325–8881; 314–534–2402 (in MO).

Chops of Iowa Inc., 105 SW Locust, P.O. Box 190, Earlham, IA 50072: Free catalog ❖ Corn-fed beef, honey-cured sliced ham, cheesecakes, and cheese. 800–242–4692.

Collin Street Bakery, P.O. Box 79, Corsicana, TX 75151: Free brochure ❖ Fruitcakes, cheesecakes, pecan pies, and other bakery favorites. 903–872–8111.

Crabtree & Evelyn Limited, P.O. Box 167, Woodstock Hill, CT 06281: Catalog $3.50 ❖ English biscuits and cookies, gingerbread, ginger and butter-ginger cookies, Scottish shortbread, Belgian chocolates, cheese wafers and biscuits from Holland, Italian biscuits, preserves, marmalades, jellies, honey, English sauces, spices and condiments, herbs, tea, and candy. 203–928–2761.

Cryer Creek Kitchens, P.O. Box 9003, Corsicana, TX 75151: Free catalog ❖ Cheesecakes, pecan and pecan-fudge pies, fruitcakes, cookies, and pecan, macadamia, and rum cakes. 903–872–8411.

Delancy Dessert Company, P.O. Box 6035, New York, NY 10128: Free information ❖ All-natural, kosher rugelach and other baked goods. 212–996–4194.

DiCamillo Bakery, 811 Linwood Ave., Niagara Falls, NY 14305: Free catalog ❖ Almond macaroons, sesame-coated red wine and finger biscuits, butter cookies, cakes, and bread. 800–634–4363; 716–282–2341 (in NY).

Divine Delights Bakery & Cafe, 1125 Magnolia Ave., Larkspur, CA 94939: Free information ❖ Triple-chocolate petit fours. 800–4–HEAVEN; 415–461–2999 (in CA).

Dunham Hill Bakery, P.O. Box 125, Woodstock, VT 05091: Free catalog ❖ European-style bread and pastries. 800–281–3121; 802–457–3121 (in VT).

Duo Delights, 4400 N. Big Spring, Ste. C-31, Midland, TX 79705: Free information ❖ Lemon crunch cookies and other favorites. 915–684–6166.

Eilenberger's Butter Nut Baking Company, P.O. Box 710, Palestine, TX 75802: Free brochure ❖ Cakes and other pastries. 903–729–2253.

Essentially Chocolate, 1501 14th St. NW, Washington, DC 20005: Free information ❖ Chocolate candy and gourmet food gifts. 800–387–6994; 202–387–6994 (in Washington, DC).

Europa Foods Ltd., 170 Commerce Dr., Hauppage, NY 11788: Free information (request list of retail sources) ❖ All-natural butter shortbreads. 516–273–0456.

The Famous Pacific Dessert Company, 2414 SW Andover St., Seattle, WA 98106: Free information ❖ Tortes, cheesecakes, and other baked goods. 206–935–1999.

Food of our Own Design, 1988 Springfield Ave., Maplewood, NJ 07040: Free information ❖ Brownie pie, rugelach, and apricot, raspberry, toffee, and truffle crunch bars. 800–722–2328.

Gloria's Kitchen, P.O. Box 1415, Guilford, CT 06437: Free price list ❖ Almond marzipan tea cake mixes. 800–680–9944.

Godiva Direct, P.O. Box 945, Clinton, CT 06413: Free catalog ❖ Cakes, other pastries, and chocolate candy. 800–643–7551.

Grandma's Fruit Cake, Division Metz Baking Company, Box 457, Beatrice, NE 68310: Free brochure ❖ Fruitcake. 800–228–4030; 402–223–2358 (in NE).

Grandma's Recipe Rugelach, P.O. Box 303, Gracie Station, New York, NY 10028: Free information ❖ Low-calorie, whole wheat rugelach with natural fruit spreads and other Kosher rugelach. 800–538–5055.

William Greenberg Desserts Inc., 1377 3rd Ave., New York, NY 10021: Free catalog ❖ Brownies, butter cookies, cheese straws, pound cake, schnecken, Danish pastries, kugelhopf, coffee and chocolate yeast loaves, muffins, pecan rings, angel food cake, and carrot cake. 800–255–8278; 212–861–1340 (in NY).

Harry & David, P.O. Box 712, Medford, OR 97501: Free catalog ❖ Cakes, baklava, cinnamon pastries, tortes, candy, preserves, fresh and dried fruits, and other specialties. 800–345–5655.

HeartyMix Company, 1231 Madison Hill Rd., Rahway, NJ 07065: Free catalog ❖ Salt-free bread, wheat-free products, and preservative-, cholesterol-, and saturated fat-free baking mixes for cookies and cakes. 908–382–3010.

Holey Moses Foods, P.O. Box 37, North Kingstown, RI 02852: Free price list ❖ Cheesecakes.

Hunt Country Foods Inc., P.O. Box 876, Middleburg, VA 22117: Free information ❖ Shortbread cookies. 703–364–2622.

Immaculate Heart Hermitage, Big Sur, CA 93920: Free brochure ❖ Date-nut and fruitcakes. 408–667–2456.

Indian Hill Farms, 213 Old Indian Rd., Milton, NY 12547: Free catalog ❖ Smoked whole turkey and turkey breast, Kosher turkey, smoked ham, Norwegian smoked salmon, and brandied fruitcake. 914–795–2700.

La Tempesta Bakery Confections, 439 Littlefield Ave., South San Francisco, CA 94080: Free information ❖ Biscotti favorites. 415–873–8944.

Linn's Fruit Bin, 2485 Village Ln., Cambria, CA 93428: Free catalog ❖ Fresh-fruit pies, fruit-filled muffins, and cookies. 800–676–1670.

Mary of Puddin Hill, P.O. Box 241, Greenville, TX 75403: Free catalog ❖ Fruitcakes, other cakes, pies, and candy. 800–545–8889.

Matthews 1812 House, 250 Kent Rd., P.O. Box 15, Cornwall Bridge, CT 06754: Free brochure ❖ Original fruit, holiday, and other special occasion cakes. 800–662–1812.

Monastery Bakery, Holy Cross Abbey, Rt. 2, Box 3870, Berryville, VA 22611: Free information ❖ Traditional fruitcakes baked by Trappist Monks. 703–955–1425.

Moravian Sugar Crisp Company Inc., 4643 Friedberg Church Rd., Clemmons, NC 27012: Free brochure ❖ Handmade cookies flavored with sugar, ginger, lemon, butterscotch, or chocolate. 910–764–1402.

Mother Myrick's Confectionary, P.O. Box 1142, Manchester Center, VT 05255: Free brochure ❖ Hot fudge sauce, maple cheesecake, linzer torte, stollen, fudge, buttercrunch, truffles, and caramels. 802–362–1560.

My Grandma's of New England Coffee Cake, 231 Bussey St., Dedham, MA 02026: Free brochure ❖ Regular and low-fat coffee cakes. 800–847–2636.

Northwest Specialty Bakers, 15425 SW Koll Pkwy., Beaverton, OR 97006: Free information ❖ Baking mixes. 503–643–2351.

One Cookie Place, P.O. Box 160756, Altamone Springs, FL 32716: Free brochure ❖ Cookies and gift baskets. 407–774–9433.

Paradigm, 5775 SW Jean Rd., Lake Oswego, OR 97034: Catalog $1 (refundable) ❖ Scone and Belgian waffle mixes, fruit spreads, and dessert sauces. 800–234–0250.

Pennysticks, 5200 6th Ave., Altoona, PA 16602: Free information ❖ Lightly salted or unsalted, all-natural, and cholesterol- and sugar-free oat bran pretzel nuggets. 800–344–GIFT.

Pittman & Davis, 843 N. Expressway 77, Harlingen, TX 78552: Catalog $1 ❖ Fruitcakes, cheese, smoked hams, turkeys, ruby-red grapefruit, oranges, citrus fruit packs, and pecans. 210–423–2154.

Arnold Reuben Jr's Cheese Cakes, 158 S. 12th Ave., Mt. Vernon, NY 10550: Free information ❖ Cheesecakes. 800–648–2253.

Rhino Foods Inc., 79 Industrial Pkwy., Burlington, VT 05401: Free information ❖ Creamy cheesecakes and cheesecake cookies. 800–639–3350; 802–862–0252 (in VT).

Rowena's, 758 W. 22nd, Norfolk, VA 23517: Free information ❖ Almond pound cake, preserves and jams, and cooking sauces. 800–296–0022.

Santa Fe Cookie Company, 3905 San Mateo NE, Albuquerque, NM 87110: Free brochure ❖ Gourmet and sugar-free cookies, spicy snacks, pretzels, crackers, and nut mixes. 800–873–5589.

Stringham & Smith, 5699–B SE International Way, Milwauee, OR 97222: Free brochure ❖ Brownies. 800–888–1487.

Stuart's Products Inc., RR. 2, Box 192, Walpole, NH 03608: Free catalog ❖ All-butter shortbread, English dessert bread, Scottish oat cakes, and other baked goods. 603–756–3925.

Sugar Spoon All Natural Cheesecake, 451 N. 66th St., #1, Lincoln, NE 68505: Free catalog ❖ Gourmet cheesecakes. 800–228–0052; 402–464–2829 (in NE).

The Sweetery, P.O. Box 243, Anderson, SC 29622: Free brochure ❖ Cheesecakes, butter pecan chews, chocolate chip cookies, carrot cake, fruitcakes, and brownies. 803–752–1188.

TZ Enterprises Inc., 1345 Dussel Dr., Maumee, OH 43537: Free information ❖ Ginger-spice cookies. 419–893–8777.

Albert Uster Imports Inc., 9211 Gaither Rd., Gaithersburg, MD 20877: Free catalog ❖ Ready-to-serve, petite-size pastries. 800–231–8154; 301–258–7350 (in MD).

Walkers Shortbread Ltd., P.O. Box 1328, New York, NY 10185: Free information ❖ Shortbread cookies.

Ye Olde Sweet Shoppe Bakery, 100 W. German St., P.O. Box 1672, Shepherdstown, WV 25443: Free information ❖ Home-baked bread, strudels, German stollen, and other specialties. 800–922–5379.

Candy & Dessert Sauces

American Maple Products, Newport, VT 05855: Free price list ❖ Fudge and maple syrup, candy, sugar, and butter. 800–343–0837; 800–548–1221 (in VT).

Andre's Boillier Ltd., 5018 Main St., Kansas City, MO 64112: Free brochure ❖ Handmade truffles and chocolate candy. 816–561–3440.

Aplets & Cotlets Factory, P.O. Box C, Cashmere, WA 98815: Catalog $1 (refundable) ❖ Aplets and Cotlets,

Washington's famous fruit and nut confection. 509–782–2191.

Arkansas Blue Heron Farms, Rt. 2, Box 323, Lowell, AR 72745: Free catalog ❖ Blueberry jam and marmalades, Amaretto dessert sauce, and other specialties. 800–225–6849.

Astor Chocolate Corporation, 4825 Metropolitan Ave., Glendale, NY 11385: Free brochure ❖ Chocolate dessert shells, mocha and liqueur cups, dinner mints, truffles, and chocolate greeting cards. 718–386–7400.

Aunt Leah's Fudge, P.O. Box 981, Nantucket, MA 02554: Free brochure ❖ Homemade fudge and other Nantucket favorites. 800–824–6330.

Buckley's Fancy Foods & Confections Ltd., P.O. Box 14119, Baton Rouge, LA 70898: Free catalog ❖ Cookies, toffee and brittle, pretzels, coffee, tea, and holiday specialties. 800–445–3957.

Karl Bissinger's French Confections, 3983 Gratiot, St. Louis, MO 63110: Free catalog ❖ Chocolates, fruit and nut bars, jellies, jams, cheese, meat, and tea. 800–325–8881.

Maude Borup, 20 W. 5th St., St. Paul, MN 55102: Free catalog ❖ Homemade candy. 612–293–0530.

Chocoholics, P.O. Box 890, Trinidad, CA 95570: Free information (request list of retail sources) ❖ Low-calorie chocolate butter sauce. 707–677–3405.

Chocolate Catalogue, 3983 Gratiot, St. Louis, MO 63110: Free catalog ❖ Handmade chocolates and petit fours double dipped in chocolate. 800–325–8881; 314–534–2402 (in MO).

The Chocolate Lady Inc., 2716 Pestalozzi St., St. Louis, MO 63118: Free information ❖ Handmade chocolate specialties. 800–242–5283; 314–773–3834 (in MO).

Chocolate Photos, 637 W. 27th St., New York, NY 10001: Free catalog ❖ Molded chocolate wedding novelties. 212–714–1880.

Clearbrook Farms, 5514 Fair Ln., Fairfax, OH 45227: Free brochure ❖ Semi-sweet chocolate sauces, marmalades, and preserves. 800–222–9966; 513–271–2053 (in OH).

Cocoloco, 1525 15th St., Denver, CO 80202: Free brochure ❖ European-style truffles and gourmet chocolates. 800–305–8768.

Community Products Inc., RD 2, Box 1950, Montpelier, VT 05602: Free information ❖

Butter confection with tropical cashews and Brazil nuts. 802–229–1840.

Da Vinci Fine Chocolates Inc., 623 Yale Ave. North, Seattle, WA 98109: Free information ❖ Syrups for baked goods, beverages, desserts, and pancake toppings. 206–682–4682.

Essentially Chocolate, 1501 14th St. NW, Washington, DC 200054: Free information ❖ Chocolate candy and brownies. 800–387–6994; 202–387–6994 (in Washington, DC).

Estee Candy Company Inc., 169 Lackawanna Ave., Parsippany, NJ 07054: Free catalog ❖ Sugarless candy and cookies. 201–335–1000.

Ethel-M Chocolates Mail-order, P.O. Box 98505, Las Vegas, NV 89195: Free catalog ❖ Milk and dark chocolate truffles, buttercreams, nuts, and other candy. 800–438–4356.

Fannie May Candy Shops Inc., 1137 W. Jackson Blvd., Chicago, IL 60607: Free brochure ❖ Chocolates, nuts and nut candy, hard candy, and other favorites. 800–999–3629.

Figi's, 3200 S. Maple, Marshfield, WI 54404: Free catalog ❖ Candy and other specialties. 715–384–6101.

Fralinger's Inc., 1325 Boardwalk, Atlantic City, NJ 08401: Free brochure ❖ Saltwater taffy, mints, fudge, peanut butter chews, chocolates, chocolate covered marshmallows, and almond macaroons. 609–345–2177.

Fran's Chocolates, 1300 E. Pike St., Seattle, WA 98122: Free information ❖ Dessert sauces and candy. 800–422–FRAN.

Godiva Direct, P.O. Box 945, Clinton, CT 06413: Free catalog ❖ Chocolate candy and pastries. 800–643–7551.

Gourmand Candy, 636 S. Pickett St., Alexandria, VA 22304: Free information ❖ Imported Valrhona chocolates. 703–461–0600.

Green Mountain Chocolate Company, RR 2, Box 1447, Waterbury, VT 05676: Free brochure ❖ Handmade truffles. 800–686–8783.

Hammond Candy Company, 2550 W. 29th Ave., Denver, CO 80211: Free information ❖ Hard candy. 303–455–2320.

Harbor Candy Shop, P.O. Box 498, Ogunquit, ME 03907: Free catalog ❖ Chocolate-covered fruit and dark or

milk-chocolate pecan- or cashew-caramel turtles. 207–646–8078.

Harbor Sweets Inc., Palmer Cove, 85 Leavitt St., Salem, MA 01970: Free catalog ❖ Handmade chocolates. 508–745–7648.

Harry & David, P.O. Box 712, Medford, OR 97501: Free catalog ❖ Candy, cakes, baklava, cinnamon pastries, tortes, preserves, fresh and dried fruits, and other specialties. 800–345–5655.

Hershey's Mailorder, P.O. Box 801, Hershey, PA 17033: Free catalog ❖ Hershey specialties and candy novelties. 800–544–1347.

Indian Wells Date Gardens & Chocolatier, 74–774 Hwy. 111, Indian Wells, CA 92210: Free catalog ❖ Candy, nuts, dates, and date specialties. 619–346–2914.

Jinil Au Chocolat, 414 Central Ave., Cedarhurst, NY 11516: Free information ❖ Kosher chocolate specialties and gift baskets. 516–295–2550.

Kendall Cheese Company, P.O. Box 686, Atascadero, CA 93423: Free information ❖ Creme Fraiche dessert topping. 805–466–7252.

Knudsen's Candy & Nut Company, 25067 Viking St., Hayward, CA 94545: Free catalog ❖ Buttercream caramels, triple-chocolate truffles, and dessert sauces. 800–748–6271; 415–655–8414 (in CA).

Koppers Chocolate Specialty Company Inc., 39 Clarkson St., New York, NY 10014: Free information (request list of retail sources) ❖ Cordials, chocolate-covered fruits and nuts, and other gourmet candies. 800–325–0026; 212–243–0220 (in NY).

Lammes Candy, P.O. Box 1885, Austin, TX 78767: Free catalog ❖ Pecan pralines. 800–252–1885; 512–835–6791 (in TX).

Liberty Orchards Company Inc., P.O. Box 179, Cashmere, WA 98815: Catalog $1 ❖ Aplets and Cotlets and other handmade all-natural candy and fruit specialties. 800–888–5696.

The Licker Company, P.O. Box 21, Winslow, AZ 86047: Free catalog ❖ Handmade lollipops.

Harry London Candies Inc., 1281 S. Main St., North Canton, OH 44720: Free information ❖ Melt-away mint candy. 216–494–0833.

Maggie Lyon Inc., 6000 Peachtree Industrial Blvd., Norcross, GA 30071: Free information (request list of retail sources) ❖ Regular and sugar-free truffles. 800–969–3500; 404–446–2191 (in GA).

Margaret's Superior Desserts, P.O. Box 908, Marquette, MI 49855: Free information ❖ Liqueur-flavored truffles. 906–226–9001.

Marshall's Fudge Shops, 308 E. Central Ave., Mackinaw City, MI 49701: Free catalog ❖ Preservative-free fudge, other homemade candy, and nuts. 800–343–8343; 616–436–5082 (in MI).

Mary of Puddin Hill, P.O. Box 241, Greenville, TX 75403: Free catalog ❖ Candy, fruitcakes, pies, and other baked goods. 800–545–8889.

Matthews 1812 House, 250 Kent Rd., P.O. Box 15, Cornwall Bridge, CT 06754: Free brochure ❖ Candies, dessert sauces, maple syrup, nuts and snacks, and other gourmet specialties. 800–662–1812.

Moonshine Trading Company, P.O. Box 896, Winters, CA 95694: Free catalog ❖ Semisweet, white, and milk chocolate nut spreads. 916–753–0601.

Mother Myrick's Confectionary, P.O. Box 1142, Manchester Center, VT 05255: Free brochure ❖ Hot fudge sauce, maple cheesecake, linzer torte, stollen, fudge, buttercrunch, truffles, and caramels. 802–362–1560.

Mrs. London's Confections, P.O. Box 529, Lexington, MA 02173: Free price list ❖ Preservative-free handmade toffee. 800–452–8162; 508–371–3074 (in MA).

Neubaus Candy, 2 Secatoag Ave., Fort Washington, NY 11050: Free information ❖ Belgian truffles. 516–883–7400.

New Canaan Farms, P.O. Box 386, Dripping Springs, TX 78620: Free brochure ❖ Ice cream toppings, jellies, and mustard. 800–727–5267.

Nunes Farms Almonds, 4012 Pete Miller Rd., P.O. Box 311, Newman, CA 95360: Free information ❖ Almonds, almond candy, and English toffee. 800–255–1641.

Paradigm, 5775 SW Jean Rd., Lake Oswego, OR 97034: Catalog $1 (refundable) ❖ Scone and Belgian waffle mixes, fruit spreads, and dessert sauces. 800–234–0250.

Plimoth Lollipop Company, P.O. Box 6223, North Plymouth, MA 02362: Free information ❖ Old-fashioned, hand-poured lollipops. 800–777–0115.

Plumbridge, P.O. Box 55, Montvale, NJ 07645: Free catalog ❖ Chocolates, mints, spiced nuts, candied fruits, and other favorites. 201–391–3394.

Ann Raskas Candies, P.O. Box 13367, Kansas City, KS 66113: Free information ❖ Candy for dieters, 14 calories each piece. 913–422–7230.

Sarris Candies, 511 Adams Ave., Canonsburg, PA 15317: Free catalog ❖ Candy made with all-natural ingredients. 800–255–7771.

See's Candies, P.O. Box S, Culver City, CA 90231: Free catalog ❖ Chocolate candy, seasonal and holiday specialties, lollipops, and assortments. 800–347–7337.

Select Origins, 11–10 Old Dock Rd., Yaphank, NY 11980: Free catalog ❖ Dessert sauces, oils, vinegars, sauces, marinades, relishes and condiments, herbs and spices, coffee, tea, and preserves. 516–924–5447.

Seroogy's Chocolates, P.O. Box 143, De Pere, WI 54115: Free catalog ❖ Candy and nut assortments. 800–776–0377; 414–336–1383 (in WI).

Standard Candy Company, P.O. Box 101025, Nashville, TN 37210: Free catalog ❖ Tennessee's Goo Goo Cluster, an original combination of chewy caramel, creamy marshmallow, roasted peanuts, and milk chocolate. 615–889–6360.

Teuscher Chocolates of Switzerland, 620 5th Ave., New York, NY 10020: Free catalog ❖ Chocolates flown in weekly from Switzerland. 212–246–4416.

Things of Good Taste, P.O. Box 455, Waynesboro, VA 22980: Free information (request list of retail sources) ❖ Cakes, fruit butters, candies, nuts, and dip and seasoning mixes. 800–248–2591.

Top Hat Company, Box 66, Wilmette, IL 60091: Free brochure ❖ Dessert sauces. 708–256–6565.

Trappistine Creamy Caramels, Abbey of Our Lady of the Mississippi, RR 3, Dubuque, IA 52001: Free brochure ❖ Caramels and creamy mints. 319–556–6330.

Trappistine Quality Candy, Mount Saint Mary's Abbey, 300 Arnold St., Wrentham, MA 02093: Free brochure ❖ Butternut munch, caramels, chocolate fudge, and penuche. 617–528–1282.

West Fork Creations Inc., P.O. Box 27, Red Lodge, MT 59068: Free information ❖

Bittersweet chocolate, espresso, and orange-flavored dessert sauces. 800–962–6555.

World of Chantilly, 4302 Farragut Rd., Brooklyn, NY 11203: Free information (request list of retail sources) ❖ Certified kosher French pastries, chocolate candy, and gift baskets. 718–859–1110.

Young Pecans, c/o Pecan Plantations, P.O. Drawer 6709, Florence, SC 29502: Free catalog ❖ Butter roasted and salted pecans and cashews, double-dipped chocolate pecan halves, butter toffee pecan popcorn, pecan divinity logs, and praline, sugar and orange, sugar and spiced, and Cheddar cheese pecans. 800–729–8004.

Caviar

Assouline & Ting Inc., 314 Brown St., Philadelphia, PA 19123: Free information ❖ Imported and domestic caviar, smoked fish, snails, and other specialties. 800–521–4491; 215–627–3000 (in PA).

Caviar & Caviar, 12307 Washington Ave., Rockville, MD 20852: Free information ❖ American sturgeon and Russian Beluga caviar. 800–472–4456; 301–231–0700 (in MD).

Caviar House Inc., 687 NE 79th St., Miami, FL 33138: Free catalog ❖ Caviar, smoked Sottish salmon, foie gras, and truffles. 800–522–8427.

Caviarteria Inc., 29 E. 60th St., New York, NY 10022: Free catalog ❖ Smoked fish and American whitefish, sturgeon, salmon, Beluga, and Sevruga caviar. 800–4–CAVIAR; 212–759–7410 (in NY).

Hansen Caviar Company, 93D S. Railroad Ave., Bergenfield, NJ 07621: Free information ❖ American sturgeon and Russian Beluga caviar. 800–735–0441; 201–385–6221 (in NJ).

J & K Trading Company, 10808 Garland Dr., Culver City, CA 90230: Free price list ❖ Lump fish caviar, crab meat, escargots, hearts of palm, and button mushrooms. 310–836–3334.

Petrossian Shop, 182 W. 58th St., New York, NY 10019: Free information ❖ Caviar, foie gras, truffles, and smoked salmon. 800–828–9241.

Poriloff Caviar, Purepak Foods Inc., 47–39 49th St., Woodside, NY 11377: Free information ❖ American sturgeon and Russian Beluga caviar. 800–323–4180; 718–784–3344 (in NY).

Cheese

Bandon Cheese Inc., P.O. Box 1668, Bandon, OR 97411: Free brochure ❖ Jalapeno and Monterey Jack, and medium and aged sharp Baja, sharp, garlic, onion Cheddar, and Cajun Cheddar cheese. 800–548–8961.

Cabot Creamery, P.O. Box 128, Cabot, VT 05647: Free information ❖ All-natural cheese with half the fat and cholesterol and 33 percent fewer calories than Cheddar. 800–639–3198; 802–563–2650 (in VT).

Calef's Country Store, P.O. Box 57, Barrington, NH 03825: Free brochure ❖ Homemade cheese, maple syrup, and candy. 800–462–2118.

Dan Carter Inc., Box 106, Mayville, WI 53050: Free information ❖ Black Diamond Canadian Cheddar cheese and other specialties. 414–387–5740.

Chops of Iowa Inc., 105 SW Locust, P.O. Box 190, Earlham, IA 50072: Free catalog ❖ Corn-fed beef, honey sliced hams, homemade cheesecakes, and cheese. 800–242–4692.

Coach Dairy Goat Farm, 105 Mill Hill Rd., Pine Plains, NY 12567: Free information ❖ Goat cheese and yogurt. 518–398–5325.

Crowley Cheese, Healdville, VT 05758: Free brochure ❖ Mild, medium, and sharp Crowley cheese and Spiced Crowley Cheese with garlic, hot pepper, caraway, or dill. 802–259–2340.

Formagg, Galaxy Foods, 2441 Viscount Rd., Orlando, FL 32809: Free information ❖ Low-fat and low-cholesterol cheese. 800–441–9419.

Gerber Cheese Company Inc., 1500 Summer St., Stanford, CT 06905: Free information ❖ Imported Swiss cheese and other cheese products. 203–323–9239.

Gourm-E-Co Imports, 405 Glenn Dr., Sterling, VA 20164: Free information ❖ Imported cheese. 800–899–5616.

Grafton Village Cheese Company, P.O. Box 87, Grafton, VT 05146: Free brochure ❖ Cheddar cheese. 802–843–2221.

The Granville Country Store, P.O. Box 141, Granville, MA 01034: Free information ❖ Aged Cheddar cheese. 800–356–3141.

Heluva Good Cheese Inc., 6152 Barclay Rd., P.O. Box C, Sodus, NY 14551: Free catalog ❖ Gourmet cheese specialties. 800–445–0269.

Hickory Farms, P.O. Box 75, Maumee, OH 43537: Free brochure ❖ Cheese, smoked meat, and other specialties. 800–222–4438.

Ideal Cheese Shop, 1205 2nd Ave., New York, NY 10021: Catalog $2 ❖ Imported and domestic cheese. 212–688–7579.

Imperia Foods, 234 St. Nicholas Ave., South Plainfield, NJ 07080: Free information ❖ Imported regular, reduced fat, and low-cholesterol grated Romano and Parmesan cheese. 908–756–7333.

Kolb-Lena Cheese Company, 301 W. Railroad St., Lena, IL 61048: Free catalog ❖ Imported and domestic cheese. 815–369–4577.

Mackenzie Limited, 2900–D Whittington Ave., Baltimore, MD 21230: Free brochure ❖ Imported seafood specialties and English cheese. 800–858–7100.

Marin French Cheese Company, P.O. Box 99, Petaluma, CA 94953: Free brochure ❖ French Camembert, Schloss, Breakfast, and Fromage De Brie cheese. 707–762–6001.

Maytag Dairy Farms Inc., P.O. Box 806, Newton, IA 50208: Free catalog ❖ Cheddar cheese spreads and blue, natural white Cheddar, brick, baby Swiss, Edam, and other cheeses. 800–247–2458; 800–258–2437 (in IA).

Mozzarella Company, 2944 Elm St., Dallas, TX 75226: Free brochure ❖ Queso fresco, a crumbly cheese that resembles farmer's cheese; and rindless crescenza, semisoft herb-like caciotta, creamy mascarpone, and other cheeses made from cow's, goat's, and sheep's milk. 214–741–4072.

Nauvoo Cheese Company, P.O. Box 188, Nauvoo, IL 62354: Free brochure ❖ Blue cheese specialties. 217–453–2213.

Plymouth Cheese Corporation, P.O. Box 1, Plymouth, VT 05056: Free catalog ❖ Aged and naturally cured Vermont granular curd cheese. 802–672–3650.

Smith's Country Cheese, 20 Otter River Rd., Winchendon, MA 01475: Free information ❖ Gouda and Cheddar cheese. 508–939–5738.

Sonoma Cheese Factory, 2 Spain St., Sonoma, CA 95476: Free brochure ❖ Lite garlic, hot pepper, and Jack cheese with reduced fat, cholesterol, calories, and salt. 800–535–2855.

Soyco Foods, Division Galaxy Cheese Company, 2441 Viscount Row, Orlando, FL 32809: Free information ❖ Casein-free cheese alternative. 800–441–9419.

Swiss Cheese Shop, 1725 Lake Dr., Monroe, WI 53566: Free catalog ❖ Blue cheese, muenster and caraway muenster, smoked Swiss cheese, brick, limburger, port salut, Colby, Monterey Jack, Cheddar, and hot pepper cheese. 608–325–3493.

Swiss Colony, Catalog Request Department, Madison, WI 53793: Free catalog ❖ Cheese, meat, sausages, pastries, nuts, candy, and snacks.

WSU Creamery, Washington State University, Troy Hall 101, Pullman, WA 99164: Free brochure ❖ Cheddar, Cougar Gold, mild flavored Viking, and Hot Pepper cheese. 509–335–4014.

Wisconsin Cheeseman, P.O. Box 1, Madison, WI 53701: Free catalog ❖ Aged Wisconsin natural cheese, sausage, cookies and pastries, fruits, nuts, and other specialties. 608–837–4100.

Creole & Cajun

Comeaux's Grocery & Market, 118 Canaan Dr., Lafayette, LA 70508: Free information ❖ Andouille, boudin (regular, crawfish, and seafood), tasso, and other Cajun specialties. 800–323–2492; 318–989–1528 (in LA).

Community Kitchens, P.O. Box 2311, Baton Rouge, LA 70821: Free catalog ❖ Cajun spices, Creole seasonings, French Quarter binet mix, Louisiana corn bread mix, jambalaya seasoning, tea, and coffee. 800–535–9901.

Creole Delicacies, 533 Saint Ann St., New Orleans, LA 70116: Free brochure ❖ Pecan pralines, remoulade sauce, hot pepper jelly, Creole seasonings, and specialties from Brennan's restaurant. 800–523–6425.

Luzianne Blue Plate Foods, P.O. Box 60296, New Orleans, LA 70160: Free brochure ❖ Luzianne coffee and tea, and New Orleans-style jambalaya, gumbo, Creole, and etouffee dinners. 800–692–7895.

Ethnic

Don Alfonso Foods, P.O. Box 201988, Austin, TX 78720: Catalog $1 ❖ Salsa, sauces, seasonings, and chiles. 800–456–6100.

The Amishman, P.O. Box 128, Mount Holly Springs, PA 17065: Free brochure ❖ Amish food specialties.

Anzen Importers, 736 NE Union Ave., Portland, OR 97232: Free information ❖ Thai specialties. 503–233–5111.

Bangkok Produce, 966 San Julian St., Los Angeles, CA 90015: Free information ❖ Thai food specialties. 213–689–7933.

Basic American Foods, P.O. Box 39, Las Cruces, NM 88004: Free information ❖ Canned and frozen green chiles. 505–523–6959.

Bayou to Go Seafood Inc., P.O. Box 20104, New Orleans, LA 70141: Free catalog ❖ Cajun food, spices, gumbo, sausage, and seafood. 800–541–6610.

Bet-Del Foods Inc., 5619 Brassvalley, Houston, TX 77096: Free information ❖ Sauces for enchiladas, burritos, nachos, and other Mexican dishes. 713–777–0770.

Cavanna Foods Enterprises, 2810 Thousand Oaks, Ste. 275, San Antonio, TX 78232: Free information ❖ Salsa and other condiments. 800–772–3698.

Chattahoochee Foods Inc., P.O. Box 17948, Raleigh, NC 27619: Free information ❖ Pasta and Creole sauces. 919–876–3330.

CMC Company, P.O. Box 322, Avalon, NJ 08202: Free catalog ❖ Mexican, Thai-Indonesian, and Szechuan-Chinese cooking ingredients. 800–CMC-2780.

Coyote Cafe General Store, 132 W. Water St., Santa Fe, NM 87501: Free catalog ❖ Food products and specialty items from the Southwest. 505–982–2454.

De Wildt Imports Inc., 30 Compton Way, Hamilton Square, NJ 08690: Free catalog ❖ Oriental, Dutch, and Indonesian foods. 800–338–3433.

Delancy Dessert Company, P.O. Box 6035, New York, NY 10128: Free information ❖ All-natural kosher rugelach and other baked goods. 212–996–4194.

Duangrat Market, 5888 Leesburg Pike, Falls Church, VA 22041: Free information ❖ Oriental foods. 703–578–0622.

El Paso Chile Company, 909 Texas Ave., El Paso, TX 79901: Free information ❖ Medium-hot cactus salsa made from vine-ripened tomatillos, onions, fresh cilantro, mild chiles, fiery jalapeno, vinegar, spices, and nopalitos. 915–544–3434.

Epicurean International, P.O. Box 13242, Berkeley, CA 94701: Free information ❖ Thai food specialties. 510–268–0209.

Ferrara Foods & Confections Inc., 195 Grand St., New York, NY 10013: Free brochure ❖ Coffee, candy, syrups, sauces, breadsticks, vegetables, pastas, and other Italian specialties. 212–226–6150.

Fortuna's Sausage Company, 975 Greenville Ave., Greenville, RI 02828: Free catalog ❖ Fresh and dry-cured sausages and other Italian specialties. 800–427–6879

Frieda's by Mail, P.O. Box 58488, Los Angeles, CA 90058: Free catalog ❖ Habaneras and other fresh and dried chiles. 800–241–1771; 714–826–6100 (in CA).

Gallina Canyon Ranch, 144 Camino Escondido, Santa Fe, NM 87501: Free information ❖ Smoked pasillas and other chiles. 505–982–4149.

Gaston Dupre Inc., 7904 Hopi Pl., Tampa, FL 33634: Free information ❖ Beet, tomato and basil, lemon and pepper, tarragon and chives, chocolate, wild mushroom, saffron, squid ink, and curry-flavored rolled fettucine and angel hair pasta. 800–937–9445.

Global Village, Box 51115, Seattle, WA 98115: Free information ❖ Thai food specialties. 800–745–5226.

GNS Spices, P.O. Box 90, Walnut, CA 91788: Free information ❖ Dried, flaked, pureed, brined, ground, and fresh Habaneras. 909–594–9505.

Grandma's Recipe Rugelach, P.O. Box 303, Gracie Station, New York, NY 10028: Free information ❖ Low-calorie, whole wheat rugelach with natural fruit spreads and other Kosher rugelach. 800–538–5055.

The Great Valley Mills, 1774 County Line Rd., Bartow, PA 19504: Free brochure ❖ Pennsylvania Dutch country cheese, ham, bacon, sausage, beef, preserves, fruitcakes, stollen, flour, cereals, and meals. 800–688–6455.

Hallbourgh Land & Cattle Company, 8138 E. Gail Rd., Scottsdale, AZ 85260: Free catalog ❖ Chili fixings, barbecue sauces, condiments, salsa and hot sauces, and salad dressings. 800–552–1500.

Hard Times Chili, 310 Commerce St., Alexandria, VA 22314: Free information ❖ Texas Roadhouse and Cincinnati Chile mixes. 703–836–7449.

Jardine's Texas Foods, 1 Chisholm Trail, Buda, TX 78610: Free catalog ❖ Chili fixings, salsas, hand-stuffed olives, and spicy Bloody Mary mix. 800–544–1880.

Katagiri Market, 224 E. 59th St., New York, NY 10022: Free information ❖ Japanese and Oriental and Asian gourmet cooking specialties. 212–755–3566.

Kosher Cornucopia, P.O. Box 326, Jeffersonville, NY 12748: Free catalog ❖ Gourmet foods and gifts. 800–756–7437; 914–482–3118 (in NY).

L.A. Specialty Produce, 2838 S. Alameda, Vernon, CA 90058: Free information ❖ Thai food specialties. 213–235–0955.

La Cour de Ferme Ltd., 1019 Delcambre Rd., Breaux Bridge, LA 70517: Free information ❖ Barbecue sauce, Cajun cayenne juice, chow chow, Cajun powder, and other condiments. 800–467–3613; 318–332–3613 (in LA).

Lioni Bufala Corporation, 78–19 15th Ave., Brooklyn, NY 11228: Free information ❖ Italian specialty products. 800–5–BUFALA.

Louisiana's Cajun Marketplace, 10557 Cherry Hill Ave., Baton Rouge, LA 70816: Free price list ❖ Jambalaya, etouffee, creole gumbo, other Creole specialties, and quick-to-fix Cajun mixes. 800–321–5571.

Malibu Greens, P.O. Box 6286, Malibu, CA 90264: Free information ❖ Thai specialties. 800–383–1414.

Manganaro Foods, 488 9th Ave., New York, NY 10018: Free information ❖ Italian salami, prosciutto ham, cheese, panettone, amaretti, colomba, torrone desserts, and other specialties. 800–472–5264.

Morisi's Pasta, 647 5th Ave., Brooklyn, NY 11215: Catalog $2.50 (refundable) ❖ All-natural pasta. 800–253–6044.

Mrs. Mazzula's Food Products Inc., P.O. Box 4427, Linden, NJ 07036: Free information ❖ All-natural Italian sun-dried tomatoes. 908–862–5400.

Native Sun Southwestern Foods Inc., 235 Davis Ave., Staten Island, NY 10310: Free information ❖ Corn tamales made with beans and cheese, sweet potato and apple, eggplant and hickory smoked garlic, and sun dried tomatoes with cheese. 718–876–8337.

Old Southwest Trading Company, P.O. Box 7545, Albuquerque, NM 87194: Free catalog ❖ Habanero and other exotic and domestic chiles. 505–836–0168.

The Oriental Market, 2002 S. Wentworth Ave., Chicago, IL 60616: Free information ❖ Oriental and other Asian specialties for gourmet cooking. 312–949–1060.

The Oriental Pantry, 423 Great Rd., Acton, MA 01720: Free catalog ❖ Oriental foods, exotic spices, sauces, and other specialties. 800–828–0368.

Pendery's Inc., 1221 Manufacturing St., Dallas, TX 75207: Catalog $2 ❖ Mexican spices, seasonings, flavorings, and other specialties. 800–533–1870; 214–741–1870 (in TX).

Petra Foods International Inc., 1350 Beverly Rd., McLean, VA 22101: Free information ❖ All-natural imported Japanese, Kosher, Middle Eastern, Greek, and other international foods. 800–356–1807.

G.B. Ratto & Company, International Grocers, 821 Washington St., Oakland, CA 94607: Free catalog ❖ Imported ethnic and other foods. 800–228–3515.

Rossi Pasta, P.O. Box 759, Marietta, OH 45750: Free brochure ❖ Handmade black olive, linguine, garlic fettuccini, saffron linguine, and other pastas. 800–227–6774.

Sanctuary Much Inc., 6280 W. Oakton St., Morton Grove, IL 60053: Free information ❖ Jamaican hot sauce, papaya chutney, and all-natural, hot marinade for grilling, roasting, baking, or stir-frying. 708–470–9112.

Schaller & Weber Inc., 22–35 46th St., Long Island City, NY 11105: Free catalog ❖ German-style smoked bacon, ham, salami, and sausage. 718–879–3047.

2nd Avenue Deli, 156 2nd Ave., New York, NY 10003: Free catalog ❖ Delicatessen favorites, baked goods, and other specialties. 800–692–3354.

Sorrenti Family Farms, 1630 Main St., Escalon, CA 95320: Free information ❖ California wild rice and pasta combinations. 209–838–1127.

Start Fresh Weight Control Program, 4813 12th Ave., Brooklyn, NY 11219: Free catalog ❖ Prepared Kosher meals for weight loss. 800–226–5000.

Sultan's Delight Inc., P.O. Box 090302, Brooklyn, NY 11209: Free catalog ❖ Middle East coffee, baked goods, candy, nuts, and grains. 718–745–6844.

Texas Tamale Company, 7070 Allensby, Houston, TX 77022: Free brochure ❖ Tamales, chili, queso, sauces, condiments, and other Mexican specialties. 713–694–0600.

The Thai Chef, 770 Lexington Ave., Ste. 1200, New York, NY 10021: Free information ❖ Thai food specialties. 212–838–5350.

Tipiak Inc., 54 Middlebury St., Stanford, CT 06902: Free information ❖ Boil-in-the-bag couscous. 203–961–9117.

Wolsk's Gourmet Confections, 81 Ludlow St., New York, NY 10002: Free information ❖ Low-calorie, sugar-free, kosher cookies, crackers, biscuits, gourmet confections, dried fruits, nuts, coffee and tea, and international specialties. 800–692–6887.

World of Chantilly, 4302 Farragut Rd., Brooklyn, NY 11203: Free information (request list of retail sources) ❖ Certified kosher French pastries, chocolate candy, and gift baskets. 718–859–1110.

Fruits & Vegetables

Apricot Farm Inc., 2620 Buena Vista Rd., Hollister, CA 95023: Free catalog ❖ Dried fruit. 800–233–4413; 408–637–6388 (in CA).

Atkinson's Vidalia Onions, Box 121, Garfield, GA 30425: Free information ❖ Vidalia onions. 800–241–3408; 912–763–2149 (in GA).

Aux Delices des Bois, 4 Leonard St., New York, NY 10013: Free information ❖ Black truffles. 212–334–1230.

Bess' Beans, P.O. Box 1542, Charleston, SC 29402: Free brochure ❖ Bean soups and other specialties. 800–233–2326.

Bland Farms, P.O. Box 506, Glennville, GA 30427: Free catalog ❖ Vidalia onions, marinated mushrooms, relishes, sauces, pickled items, salad dressings, meat, peanuts, nut candy and fudge, and pecans. 800–843–2542.

Blue Heron Fruit Shippers, 3221 Bay Shore Rd., Sarasota, FL 34234: Free brochure ❖ Tree-ripened citrus fruit, candy, marmalades, pecans, gourmet Southern foods, stone crab claws, and honey. 813–355–6946.

Delegeane Garlic Farms, P.O. Box 2561, Yountville, Napa Valley, CA 94599: Free brochure ❖ Fresh garlic, chili ristras, salt-free herb seasonings, and wildflower honeys. 707–944–8019.

Delftree Farm, 234 Union St., North Adams, MA 01247: Free price list ❖ Fresh shiitake mushrooms. 800–CHEFSHAT.

Desert Glory, P.O. Box 453, Devine, TX 78016: Free information ❖ Cocktail tomatoes. 800–44–SALAD.

Florida's Gift Fruit Shippers, P.O. Box 620000, Orlando, FL 32891: Free information ❖ Navel oranges and red grapefruit. 800–428–4423.

G.I.M.M. Dry Yard, P.O. Box 1016, Winters, CA 95964: Free catalog ❖ Dried fruit. 916–795–2919.

Georgia "Sweets" Brand Inc., 1606 W. North St., Vidalia, GA 30474: Free information ❖ Jumbo and sandwich-size Vidalia onions. 800–552–9902.

Giant Artichoke Company, 11241 Merritt St., Castroville, CA 95012: Free price list ❖ Fresh artichokes and artichoke specialties. 408–633–2778.

Gracewood Fruit Company, 9075 17th Pl., P.O. Box 2590, Vero Beach, FL 32961: Free information ❖ Navel oranges and ruby red grapefruit. 800–678–1154.

Susan Green's California Cuisine, Catalog Order Center, P.O. Box 596, Maumee, OH 43537: Free catalog ❖ Dried and fresh fruit, nuts, delicatessen favorites, baked goods, hams, and candy. 800–753–8558.

Hadley Fruit Orchards, P.O. Box 495, Cabazon, CA 92230: Free catalog ❖ Dried fruit, nuts, candy, honey, and jellies. 800–854–5655.

Hale Indian River Groves, Indian River Plaza, P.O. Box 217, Wabasso, FL 32970: Free catalog ❖ Jumbo navel oranges, sweet ruby red grapefruit, and nova tangelos. 800–289–4253.

Harry & David, P.O. Box 712, Medford, OR 97501: Free catalog ❖ Oregold peaches, Alphonse LaValle grapes, Royal Riviera pears, Crisp Mountain apples, other fruits, and other specialties. 800–345–5655.

Harry's Crestview Farms, 9030 17th Pl., Vero Beach, FL 32966: Free catalog ❖ Tree-ripened ruby red grapefruit, oranges, and other gifts. 800–285–8488.

Hart's Crestview Groves, 9030 17th Pl., Vero Beach, FL 32966: Free information ❖ Oranges and tree-ripened ruby-red grapefruit. 800–285–8488.

Hendrix Farms, P.O. Box 175, Metter, GA 30439: Free information ❖ Vidalia onions. 800–752–1551.

Hyatt Fruit Company, Box 639, Vero Beach, FL 32961: Free catalog ❖ Oranges, grapefruit, candy, and jellies. 800–327–5810; 407–567–3766 (in FL).

Jaffe Brothers Natural Foods, P.O. Box 636, Valley Center, CA 92082: Free catalog ❖ Grains and grain products, nuts, fruit, honey, and other natural foods. 619–749–1133.

Lone Star Farms, P.O. Box 685, Mercedes, TX 78570: Free information ❖ Sweet onions. 800–552–1015.

The Maples Fruit Farm, P.O. Box 167, Chewsville, MD 21721: Catalog $1 (refundable) ❖ Dried fruit, nuts, coffee, other specialties, and gift baskets. 301–733–0777.

Mission Orchards, Catalog Order Center, P.O. Box 546, Maumee, OH 43537: Free catalog ❖ Comice pears, red dessert grapes, navel oranges, red grapefruit, cherries, plums, tangelos, pineapples, and kiwi fruit. Also cheese, candy, dried fruit, nuts, truffles, fruit cakes and pastries, and smoked meat and seafood. 419–893–5149.

Mrs. Mazzula's Food Products Inc., P.O. Box 4427, Linden, NJ 07036: Free information ❖ All-natural Italian sun-dried tomatoes. 908–862–5400.

Neill's Farm, 2709 McNeill Rd., Fort Pierce, FL 34981: Free catalog ❖ Fresh-picked tomatoes. 800–441–6740.

New Penny Farm, P.O. Box 448, Presque Isle, ME 04769: Free catalog ❖ Organic-grown potatoes. 800–827–7551.

Newbern Groves Gift Shop, 15315 N. Nebraska Ave., Tampa, FL 33682: Free information ❖ Navel oranges, tangelos, and sweet red grapefruit. 800–486–0441; 971–0440 (in Tampa).

Oasis Date Gardens, P.O. Box 757, Thermal, CA 92274: Free information ❖ Medjool and Noor dates, dried figs, and candied apricots. 800–827–8017.

Old Southwest Trading Company, P.O. Box 7545, Albuquerque, NM 87194: Free catalog ❖ Habanero and other exotic and domestic chiles. 505–836–0168.

The Onion Country Store Inc., P.O. Box 1043, Vidalia, GA 30474: Free information ❖ Vidalia onions. 912–583–2294.

Pezzini Farms, P.O. Box 1276, Castroville, CA 95012: Free information ❖ Artichokes and artichoke dipping and pasta sauces. 800–347–6118.

Pinnacle Orchards, 444 S. Fir, Medford, OR 97501: Free catalog ❖ Comice pears and other specialties. 800–879–7327.

Pittman & Davis, 843 N. Expressway 77, Harlingen, TX 78552: Catalog $1 ❖ Ruby red grapefruit, oranges, pecans, fruit cakes, cheese, smoked hams, and turkeys. 210–423–2154.

Red Cooper, Rt. 3, Box 10, Alamo, TX 78516: Free catalog ❖ Grapefruit, oranges, pineapples, avocados, apples, persimmons, tangelos, dates, pears, and dried fruit. 800–876–4733.

Sphinx Date Ranch, 3039 N. Scottsdale Rd., Scottsdale, AZ 85251: Free brochure ❖ Date-pecan loaves, trail mixes, fruit cakes, jellies, nuts, and Medjool dates, pitted and hand-dipped in creamy milk chocolate, stuffed with walnuts, rolled in powdered sugar, or for cooking. 800–482–3283; 602–941–2261 (in AZ).

Spyke's Grove, 7250 Griffin Rd., Davie, FL 33314: Free catalog ❖ Oranges, mangos, avocados, and grapefruit. 305–583–0426.

Sullivan Victory Groves, P.O. Box 10, Cocoa, FL 32923: Free brochure ❖ Navel oranges. 800–ORANGE-1.

Sweet Energy, 4 Acorn Ln., Colchester, VT 05446: Free catalog ❖ Apricots and other fruit. 802–655–4440.

Timber Crest Farms, 4791 Dry Creek Rd., Healdsburg, CA 95448: Free catalog ❖ Dried fruit, dried tomato products, fruit butters, nuts, and trail mixes. 707–433–8251.

Urbani Truffle, 29–24 40th Ave., Long Island City, NY 11101: Free information ❖ White truffles. 718–392–5050.

USA Evans Farm, P.O. Box 913, Fort Valley, GA 31030: Free brochure ❖ Tree-ripened peaches. 800–321–0640.

Walla Walla Gardener's Association, 210 N. 11th Ave., Walla Walla, WA 99362: Free information ❖ Sweet Walla Walla onions. 800–553–5014; 509–525–7070 (in WA).

Zarda Bar-B-Q & Catering Company, 214 N. Hwy. 7, Blue Springs, MO 64014: Free information ❖ Barbecue-flavored oven-baked beans with chopped beef. 800–776–6427; 816–229–9999 (in MO).

Gift Assortments & Gourmet Specialties

Ace Specialty Foods, 281 West 83rd St., Burr Ridge, IL 60521: Free catalog ❖ Cakes, fruit gifts, candies, and nuts. 800–323–9754; 708–325–9700 (in IL).

America: State by State, 5699 Kanan, Agoura, CA 91301: Free brochure ❖ Specialty foods from across America. 800–706–4438.

The Antique Mall & Crown Restaurant, P.O. Box 540, Indianola, MS 38751: Free catalog ❖ Smoked catfish specialties and other gourmet favorites. 800–833–7731; 601–887–2522 (in MS).

Ash Enterprises Inc., P.O. Box 40113, Tucson, AZ 85717: Free information ❖ Food gift assortments. 602–795–1644.

Balducci's, Shop From Home Service, 42–25 12th St., Long Island City, NY 11101: Catalog $3 ❖ Breads and food specialties. 800–225–3822.

Bean Bag Mail Order Company, 818 Jefferson St., Oakland, CA 94607: Catalog $1 ❖ Gourmet seasonings and bean specialties. 800–845–2326.

BelCanto Fancy Foods Ltd., 555 2nd Ave., New York, NY 10016: Free information (request list of retail sources) ❖ Imported olive specialties. 212–689–4433.

Belmont General Store, P.O. Box 287, Belmont Rd., Belmont, VT 05730: Free catalog ❖ Vermont food favorites and gifts. 800–262–9430.

Black Shield Inc., 5356 Pan American Freeway NE, Albuquerque, NM 87109: Free information ❖ Popcorn gift packs. 800–6-JEWELS.

Bland Farms, P.O. Box 506, Glennville, GA 30427: Free catalog ❖ Vidalia onions, marinated mushrooms, relishes, sauces, pickled items, salad dressings, meat, peanuts, nut candy, fudge, and Georgia pecans. 800–843–2542.

Blue Heron Fruit Shippers, 3221 Bay Shore Rd., Sarasota, FL 34234: Free brochure ❖ Tree-ripened citrus fruit, candy, marmalades, pecans, gourmet Southern foods, stone crab claws, and honey. 813–355–6946.

Bogland Inc., P.O. Box 565, Gloucester, MA 01930: Free information ❖ Cranberry salsa, grilling sauce, catsup, and other specialties. 508–281–2898.

Brittigan's Specialty Soups, 74 Tracey Rd., Huntington Valley, PA 19006: Free brochure ❖ Gourmet soups. 215–830–0942.

Brumwell Flour Mill, P.O. Box 126, South Amana, IA 52334: Free brochure ❖ Maple syrup, sorghum, apple butter, and pancake, muffin, biscuit, and granola mixes. 319–622–3455.

Burberry's Limited, 9 E. 57th St., New York, NY 10022: Free catalog ❖ International tea, preserves and marmalades, chutney, mustards, horseradish sauces, cakes, and shortbread biscuits. 212–371–5010.

Burnt Cabins Grist Mill, P.O. Box 65, Burnt Cabins, PA 17215: Free brochure ❖ Old-fashioned buckwheat and wheat flours, roasted and regular cornmeal, and pancake and muffin mixes. 800–BRT-MILL.

Callaway Gardens Country Store, Pine Mountain, GA 31822: Free catalog ❖ Southern-style bacon, ham, other meats, and jellies. 800–282–8181.

Cavanaugh Lakeview Farms Ltd., P.O. Box 580, Chelsea, MI 48118: Free information ❖ Honey-cured and smoked poultry, smoked ham and bacon, fresh-frozen poultry, steaks, game, smoked seafood, desserts, and popcorn. 800–243–4438.

Coastal Express Food & Spirits, 1501 14th St. NW, Washington, DC 20005: Free catalog ❖ Fruit, chocolates, cakes, spirits and wines, and other favorites. 800–243–7466; 202–387–6492 (in DC).

Community Kitchens, P.O. Box 2311, Baton Rouge, LA 70821: Free catalog ❖ Imported coffee and tea, Cajun spices, Creole seasonings, French Quarter binet mix, Louisiana corn bread mix, jambalaya seasoning, and candy. 800–535–9901.

Country Maid, 1919 S. Kinnickinnic Ave., Milwaukee, WI 53204: Free information ❖ Potato baskets. 414–383–3970.

Dakin Farm, Rt. 7, Ferrisburg, VT 05456: Free catalog ❖ Vermont smoked ham and bacon, maple syrup, and aged Cheddar cheese. 800–993–2546.

Deli Direct, 9254 Seton Ct., Wheeling, IL 60090: Free brochure ❖ Delicatessen meats, aged Wisconsin cheese spreads, barbecue sauce, and condiments. 800–321–3354; 708–520–1020 (in IL).

Discovery Kitchen, P.O. Box 6325, Woodland Hills, CA 91365: Free brochure ❖ Cheese, apple butter, honeys, smoked fish, jams, mustard, and spices. 818–887–2007.

Dufour Pastry Kitchens Inc., 808 Washington St., New York, NY 10014: Free information ❖ Gourmet hors d'oeuvres. 212–929–2800.

S. Wallace Edwards & Sons Inc., P.O. Box 25, Surry, VA 23883: Free catalog ❖ Virginia meats, seafood selections, candy and nuts, and gourmet baked specialties. 800–222–4267.

Essentially Chocolate, 1501 14th St. NW, Washington, DC 200054: Free information ❖ Chocolate candy and gourmet food gifts. 800–387–6994.

Festive Foods of the Rockies Inc., P.O. Box 49172, Colorado Springs, CO 80949: Free catalog ❖ Belgian Callebaut chocolate specialties, Spanish saffron, herbs and spices, coffees and teas, exotic vanilla beans, and other gourmet products. 719–594–6768.

Figi's, 3200 S. Maple, Marshfield, WI 54404: Free catalog ❖ Baked goods, meat, cheese, candy, jams and jellies, and nuts. 715–384–6101.

Fin 'n Feather, P.O. Box 487, Smithfield, VA 23430: Free catalog ❖ Smoked meats, poultry, pastries, candies, and other regional specialties. 800–628–2242.

Fraser-Morris Fine Foods, 1264 3rd Ave., New York, NY 10021: Free catalog ❖ Meat, cookies and other pastries, candy, fruit, seafood, cheese, nuts, preserves, coffee and tea, caviar, pates, soups, spices and other condiments, mustards, truffles, and mushrooms. 212–288–2727.

Frieda's By Mail, P.O. Box 58488, Los Angeles, CA 90058: Free catalog ❖ Gift baskets of exotic fruits and vegetables. 800–241–1771; 714–826–6100 (in CA).

G & R Farms of Georgia, Rt. 3, Box 35A, Glennville, GA 30427: Free catalog ❖ Fruits and vegetables, baked goods, popcorn specialties, salad dressings, Georgia pecans and peanuts, nut candy, sauces, and condiments. 800–522–0567.

Gazin's Cajun Creole Foods, 2910 Toulouse St., P.O. Box 19221, New Orleans, LA 70179: Catalog 50¢ ❖ Specialties from New Orleans. 800–262–6410; 504–482–0302 (in LA).

Goodies from Goodman, 13390 Grissom Ln., Dallas, TX 75229: Free catalog ❖ Fruit, cheese, nuts, candy, popcorn specialties, and smoked meat and fish. 800–535–3136.

The Great Valley Mills, 1774 County Line Rd., Bartow, PA 19504: Free brochure ❖ Pennsylvania Dutch country cheese, ham, bacon, sausage, beef, preserves, fruitcakes, stollen, flour, cereals, and meals. 800–688–6455.

Susan Green's California Cuisine, Catalog Order Center, P.O. Box 596, Maumee, OH 43537: Free catalog ❖ Candy, dried fruits, sourdough bread, nuts, seasonings and condiments, farm-fresh crops, cheese, meat, seafood, and pastries. 800–753–8558.

Hagensborg Foods U.S.A. Inc., P.O. Box 6058, Kent, WA 98064: Free information ❖ Smoked salmon, shrimp, and regular salmon ready-to-spread pates. 800–851–1771; 206–622–8025 (in WA).

Harman's Cheese & Country Store, Main St., Box H624, Sugar Hill, NH 03585: Free catalog ❖ Cheddar cheese, maple syrup, fruit preserves, salad dressings, plain and smoked salmon, crab meat, honey, smoked herring fillets, pancake mixes, maple butter, and candy. 603–823–8000.

Harrington Ham Company, Main St., Richmond, VT 05477: Free information ❖ Spiral-sliced, cob-smoked, maple-glazed hams and other smoked bacon, turkey breast, and pheasant. Also cheese, maple syrup, pastries, plum pudding, fruitcakes, and dried fruit. 802–434–4444.

Harry & David, P.O. Box 712, Medford, OR 97501: Free catalog ❖ Fruit, cakes, baklava, cinnamon pastries, tortes, candy, preserves, and gift packages. 800–345–5655.

Hasty-Bake, P.O. Box 471285, Tulsa, OK 74147: Free catalog ❖ Gourmet foods, charcoal ovens, and grill accessories. 800–426–6836.

Heartland/Minnesota, 1791 Glen Lake Station, Minnetonka, MN 55345: Free catalog ❖ Swedish baked goods, apple-cider syrup, wild rice sausage, smoked pheasant, apple-smoked hams, preserves, and wild turkey. 800–544–8661.

Hickin's, Black Mountain Rd., RR 1, Box 293, Brattleboro, VT 05301: Free catalog ❖ Jams and jellies, pickles, fruit syrups, maple syrup, fruit cakes, candy, and cheese. 802–254–2146.

Hickory Farms, P.O. Box 75, Maumee, OH 43537: Free brochure ❖ Cheese, meat, candy, pastries, deli specialties, seafood, nuts, truffles, fruit and liqueur cakes, tea and coffee, dried fruit, jellies and preserves, fresh fruit, and popcorn. 800–222–4438.

House of Webster, P.O. Box 488, Rogers, AR 72757: Catalog $1 ❖ Preserves and jellies, cheese, country cured and smoked bacon, biscuit and pancake mixes, candy, syrups, wild honey, and country sorghum. 501–636–4640.

J & K Trading Company, 10808 Garland Dr., Culver City, CA 90230: Free price list ❖ Escargots, crab meat, lump fish caviar, hearts of palms, button mushrooms, and other specialties. 310–836–3334.

Knott's Berry Farm, P.O. Box 1989, Placentia, CA 92670: Free catalog ❖ Jellies and preserves, cheese, sausage, candy, cakes, cookies, and dried fruit. 800–877–6887.

Kozlowski Farms, 5566 Gravenstein Hwy., North Forestville, CA 95436: Free brochure ❖ Marmalades, jams, preserves, honey, mustards, barbecue sauce, fruit butters, sugar-free berry vinegars, conserves, and chutney. 707–887–1587.

Lambs Farm, P.O. Box 520, Libertyville, IL 60048: Free catalog ❖ Country crafts, specialty foods, nuts, candies, and gifts for pets. 800–52–LAMBS.

Stew Leonard's, 100 Westport Ave., Norwalk, CT 06851: Free catalog ❖ Fruit, cakes and cookies, cheese, breads, candies, nuts, and meats. 800–729–7839.

Les Trous Petits Cochons Pate Company, 453 Greenwich St., New York, NY 10013: Free information ❖ Gourmet pates. 212–219–1230.

Maison Glass Delicacies, 111 E. 58th St., New York, NY 10022: Catalog $5 ❖ Smoked meat and fish. 800–822–5564; 212–755–3316 (in NY).

The Maples Fruit Farm Inc., 13144 Pennsylvania Ave., Hagerstown, MD 21742: Free catalog ❖ Dried fruit, nuts, coffee, other specialties, and gift baskets. 301–733–0777.

Market Square Food Company Inc., 1642 Richfield Ave., Highland Park, IL 60035: Free information ❖ Wild rice from Minnesota, smoked sockeye salmon from Alaska, oils, vinegars, sauces, and baked goods. 708–831–2228.

Matthews 1812 House, 250 Kent Rd., P.O. Box 15, Cornwall Bridge, CT 06754: Free brochure ❖ Cakes, nuts, chocolates, jams, tea, condiments, and smoked meat. 800–662–1812.

Mississippi Product Sales Inc., 208 W. Washington St., Greenwood, MS 38930: Free catalog ❖ Gourmet gift baskets and other unique Southern gifts. 800–467–7763.

New England Harvest, 25 Mountain View St., Bristol, VT 05443: Free price list ❖ Dried fruits, fruit and nut snack mix, nut butters, chocolate covered cherries and nuts, and other specialties. 802–453–3098.

Northern Lakes Wild Rice Company, P.O. Box 592, Teton Village, WY 83025: Free information ❖ Wild rice. 307–733–7192.

Oregon Territory Company, 8065 SW Cirrus Dr., Beaverton, OR 97005: Catalog $1 (refundable) ❖ Gourmet foods, gift

assortments and baskets, and other Northwest specialties. 800–247–0727.

Pepperidge Farm, P.O. Box 917, Clinton, CT 06413: Free catalog ❖ Soups, cookies and other pastries, crackers, candy, cheese, sausage, popcorn, and breakfast mixes. 800–243–9314.

Petrossian Shop, 182 W. 58th St., New York, NY 10019: Free information ❖ Caviar, foie gras, truffles, and smoked salmon. 800–828–9241.

Pfaelzer Brothers, 281 W. 83rd St., Burr Ridge, IL 60521: Free catalog ❖ Gourmet food specialties and gift baskets. 800–621–0226.

Pinnacle Orchards, 444 S. Fir, Medford, OR 97501: Free catalog ❖ Comice pears and other specialties. 800–879–7327.

Pueblo to People, P.O. Box 2545, Houston, TX 77252: Information $2 ❖ Nuts, dried fruit, ceramics, jewelry, coffee, and gift baskets. 713–956–1172.

Purely American, 1060 W. 35th St., Norfolk, VA 23508: Free information (request list of retail sources) ❖ Gift-packaged food mixes. 800–359–7873.

Rossi Pasta, P.O. Box 759, Marietta, OH 45750: Free brochure ❖ Handmade black olive, linguine, garlic fettuccini, saffron linguine, and other pastas. 800–227–6774.

S.E. Rykoff & Company, 3501 Taylor Dr., Ukiah, CA 95482: Free catalog ❖ Foods and professional cookware for home chefs. 800–333–1448.

Salsa Express, P.O. Box 3985, Albuquerque, NM 87190: Free catalog ❖ Salsa, dips, condiments, nuts, snack foods, chile peppers, and other spicy food specialties. 800–437–2572.

Sambet's Cajun Store, 8644–E Spicewood Springs Rd., Austin, TX 78759: Catalog $2 ❖ Pepper sauces, marinades, Cajun seasonings and spices, specialty coffees, barbecue sauces, jellies and jams, beignet mixes, and Cajun cookbooks. 800–472–6238.

San Antonio River Mill, 129 E. Gunther, San Antonio, TX 78204: Free catalog ❖ Chili, biscuit and other baking mixes, preserves, jellies, and cooking equipment. 800–235–8186.

Sea Island Mercantile, 928 Bay St., P.O. Box 100, Beaufort, SC 29901: Free information ❖ She-Crab soup and other

Carolina low-country foods and gifts. 800–735–3215.

Seyco Fine Foods, 1645 Donlon St., Ste. 106, Ventura, CA 93003: Catalog $2 ❖ Pates, sauces, preserves, desserts, soups, olives, pickles and relishes, sweet pickled fruit, oils, vinegars, dressings, jellies and marmalades, spirited fruits, candy, and nuts. 805–644–9937.

A Southern Season, Eastgate, Chapel Hill, NC 27514: Free catalog ❖ Irish whiskey cake, shortbread, imported coffee, nuts, candy, fruit cakes and other baked goods, condiments, preserves, and pastas. 800–253–3663; 919–929–7133 (in NC).

Southwest Delectables, 2766 N. Country Club Rd., Tucson, AZ 85716: Free information ❖ Southwest food specialties, chile favorites, other condiments, and seasonings. 602–323–3322.

Splurge Inc., 1223 Wilshire Blvd., Santa Monica, CA 90403: Free information ❖ Low-fat, no-guilt snacks and confections. 310–451–2506.

The Squire's Choice, Mail Order Department, 2250 W. Cabot Blvd., Langhorne, PA 19047: Free catalog ❖ Food gifts. 800–523–6163.

Sutton Place Gourmet, 10323 Old Georgetown Rd., Bethesda, MD 20814: Free catalog ❖ International and domestic seafoods, coffee and tea, fruit, caviar, foie gras, champagnes, nuts, wild rices, condiments, meat, dried fruit, cheese, deli specialties, sauces, candy, and wines. 800–346–8763.

Swiss Colony, Catalog Request Department, Madison, WI 53793: Free catalog ❖ Cheese, meat, sausages, pastries, nuts, candy, and snacks.

Tillamook Cheese, P.O. Box 313, Tillamook, OR 97141: Free catalog ❖ Cheese, exotic delicacies, candy, meat and fowl, smoked fish, jellies, and preserves. 503–842–4481.

Todaro Brothers, 555 2nd Ave., New York, NY 10016: Catalog $1 ❖ Cheese, pastas, breads, meat, confections, spices, coffee, and other specialties. 212–679–7766.

Whet Your Appetite, P.O. Box 2069, Dublin, CA 94568: Free catalog ❖ Gift assortments from around the world. 800–228–9438.

Wolsk's Gourmet Confections, 81 Ludlow St., New York, NY 10002: Free information ❖ Low-calorie, sugar-free, kosher cookies, crackers, biscuits, gourmet confections, dried fruits, nuts, coffee and tea, and international specialties. 800–692–6887.

World of Chantilly, 4302 Farragut Rd., Brooklyn, NY 11203: Free information (request list of retail sources) ❖ Certified kosher French pastries, chocolate candy, and gift baskets. 718–859–1110.

Zabar's & Company, 2245 Broadway, New York, NY 10024: Free catalog ❖ Smoked fish, condiments and spices, candy, crackers, and other specialties. Also cookware, food processors, microwave ovens, kitchen tools, and coffee makers. 212–787–2000.

Zingerman's Delicatessen, 422 Detroit St., Ann Arbor, MI 48104: Free catalog ❖ Domestic and imported cheese, ethnic and low-fat specialties, condiments, baked goods, and pasta. 313–663–3400.

Health & Natural

Allergy Resources Inc., 195 Huntington Beach Dr., Colorado Springs, CO 80921: Free catalog ❖ Wheat- and gluten-free products and other organic foods. 719–488–3630.

American Spoon Foods, 1668 Clarion Ave., P.O. Box 566, Petoskey, MI 49770: Free information ❖ Pancake and waffle mix made with organic-grown Indian blue corn, wild rice, wild berry preserves, and wild pecans. 800–222–5886.

Blue Heron Farm, P.O. Box 68, Rumsey, CA 95679: Free information ❖ Oranges, other citrus fruits, and nuts. 916–796–3799.

Brumwell Flour Mill, P.O. Box 126, South Amana, IA 52334: Free brochure ❖ Maple syrup, sorghum, apple butter, and pancake, muffin, biscuit, and granola mixes. 319–622–3455.

Cabot Creamery, P.O. Box 128, Cabot, VT 05647: Free information ❖ All-natural cheese with half the fat and cholesterol and 33 percent fewer calories than Cheddar. 800–639–3198; 802–563–2650 (in VT).

Cascadian Farm, 719 Metcalf St., Cedro Wooley, WA 98284: Free information ❖ Canned fruit juices, vegetables, and other foods. 206–855–0100.

Dakota Lean Meats Inc., P.O. Box 434, Winner, SD 57580: Free information ❖ Hormone-free meat. 800–727–5326.

Deer Valley Farm, RD 1, Box 173, Guilford, NY 13780: Catalog 50¢ ❖ Natural and organic foods. 607–764–8556.

Diabetic Food Emporium Ltd., 51 Cleveland St., Hackensack, NJ 07601: Free information ❖ Diabetic foods. 800–285–3210.

Diamond Organics, P.O. Box 2159, Freedom, CA 95019: Free information ❖ Lettuce, greens, roots, herbs, and fruits. 800–922–2396.

Eden Foods, 701 Tecumseh, Clinton, MI 49236: Free information ❖ Low-sodium and organic soy sauces. 517–456–7424.

Fatwise, 1130 E. Linden Ave., Colina, NJ 07036: Free catalog ❖ Fat-free foods and snacks. 908–862–3886.

Fiddler's Green Farm, RR 1, Box 656, Belfast, ME 04915: Free information ❖ Pancake, muffin, and spice cake mixes, and a breakfast gift package that includes pancake and muffin mixes, maple syrup, and honey. 207–338–3872.

Gold Mine Natural Food Company, 1947 30th St., San Diego, CA 92110: Free information ❖ Organic brown rice and beans. 800–475–FOOD.

Golden Acres Orchard, Rt. 2, Box 2450, Front Royal, VA 22630: Free information ❖ Apples, apple cider vinegar, and apple juice. 703–636–9611.

Gluten-Free Pantry, P.O. Box 881, Glastonbury, CT 06033: Free information ❖ Gluten-free baking mixes. 203–633–3826.

Hardscrabble Enterprises Inc., Box 42, Cherry Grove, WV 26804: Catalog $3 (refundable) ❖ Shiitake mushrooms. 304–567–2727.

Harvest Direct Inc., P.O. Box 4514, Decatur, IL 62525: Free catalog ❖ All-natural products for vegetarians. 800–835–2867; 217–422–3324 (in IL).

International Yogurt Company, 628 N. Doheny Dr., Los Angeles, CA 90069: Free catalog ❖ Yogurt tablets, acidophilus capsules, yogurt culture, acidophilus milk culture, cheese culture, and Kefir grains and culture. 310–274–9917.

Jaffe Brothers Natural Foods, P.O. Box 636, Valley Center, CA 92082: Free catalog ❖ Preservative- and chemical additive-free dried foods. 619–749–1133.

Living Farms, Box 50, Tracey, MN 56175: Free information ❖ Grains, beans, rice, wheat, sunflowers, and alfalfa, clover, and radish sprouting seeds. 800–533–5320.

Morgan's Mills, RD 2, Box 4602, Union, ME 04862: Free information ❖ Salt-free

mixes for pancakes, waffles, and bran muffins. 800–373–2756.

Mountain Ark Trading Company, P.O. Box 3170, Fayetteville, AR 72702: Free information ❖ Vegetables, miso, seasonings, rice, pasta, fruit, spreads, oils, beans, and soups. 800–643–8909.

Organic Foods Express Inc., 12050 Parklawn Dr., Rockville, MD 20852: Free catalog ❖ Grains, beans, cheese, milk, meat, breads, juices, coffees, snacks, vegetables, and fruits. 301–816–4944.

Southern Brown Rice, P.O. Box 185, Weiner, AR 72479: Free catalog ❖ Rice products fresh from the farm. 800–421–7423.

Soyco Foods, Division Galaxy Cheese Company, 2441 Viscount Row, Orlando, Fl 32809: Free information ❖ Casein-free cheese alternative. 800–441–9419.

Timber Crest Farms, 4791 Dry Creek Rd., Healdsburg, CA 95448: Free catalog ❖ Dried fruit, dried tomato products, fruit butters, nuts, and trail mixes. 707–433–8251.

Walnut Acres Natural Foods, 438 White Oak Rd., Penns Creek, PA 17862: Free catalog ❖ Fresh and canned vegetables, canned and dried fruit, grains, baked goods, natural cheese, fruit and vegetable juices, nuts, jams, preserves, and other specialties. 800–433–3998.

Wanda's Nature Farm Foods, 850 NBC Center, Lincoln, NE 68508: Free catalog ❖ All-natural bread, muffin, pancake, waffle, and double-chocolate cake mixes. 800–222–FARM.

Wax Orchards, 22744 Wax Orchards Rd. SW, Vashon, WA 98070: Free information (request list of retail sources) ❖ Conserves, fruit butters and syrups, dessert toppings, and other food products sweetened with concentrated natural fruit juices. 800–634–6132.

Maple Syrup

Auger's Sugarmill Farm, Rt. 16, Box 26, Barton, VT 05822: Free catalog ❖ Vermont maple syrup. 800–688–7978.

Butternut Mountain Farm, P.O. Box 381, Johnson, VT 05656: Free information ❖ Maple syrup and sugar. 800–828–2376.

Cleary Evergreens, P.O. Box 425, Derby Line, VT 05830: Free information ❖ Maple syrup and maple products. 800–465–5148.

Grafton Village Apple Company, 703 Main St., Weston, VT 05161: Free catalog ❖ Maple syrup and sugar. 800–843–4822.

Green Mountain Sugar House, Box 341, Ludlow, VT 05149: Free catalog ❖ Maple syrup, maple sugar candy, nut brittle, cheese, smoked slab bacon, fudge, pancake mix, mincemeat, Vermont grist mill products, and homemade jams. 802–228–7151.

Maple Grove Farms of Vermont, 167 Portland St., St. Johnsbury, VT 05819: Free information ❖ Maple sugar and syrup. 802–748–3136.

Spring Tree Corporation, P.O. Box 1160, Brattleboro, VT 05302: Free information ❖ Additive- and preservative-free, 100 percent pure maple syrup. 802–254–8784.

Vermont Country Maple Inc., P.O. Box 53, Jericho Center, VT 05465: Free information ❖ Maple sugar and syrup. 802–864–7519.

Wood's Cider Mill, RFD 2, Box 477, Springfield, VT 05156: Free catalog with long SASE ❖ Maple syrup, cider jelly and syrup, and boiled cider. 802–263–5547.

Meats

Aidells Sausage Company, 1575 Minnesota St., San Francisco, CA 94107: Free catalog ❖ Filler- and preservative-free fresh and hickory-smoked sausage. 415–285–6660.

Amana Meat Shop & Smokehouse, P.O. Box 158, Amana, IA 52203: Free brochure ❖ Ham, bacon, sausage, cheese, and other specialties. 800–373–MEAT; 319–622–3111 (in IA).

Basse's Choice Plantation, P.O. Box 1, Smithfield, VA 23430: Free information ❖ Cured, smoked, and aged Smithfield ham, or the less salty Williamsburg ham. 804–292–2773.

Bluescreek Farm, 14141 Hillview Rd., Marysville, OH 43040: Free information ❖ American-grown, lean, low-cholesterol Belgian blue beef. 513–644–2583.

Boyle Meat Packing Company, 500 E. 3rd St., Kansas City, MO 64106: Free brochure ❖ Hand-carved rib eye steaks and other meats. 800–821–3626; 842–5852 (in Kansas City).

Broadbent's B & B Food Products, 6321 Hopkinsville Rd., Cadiz, KY 42211: Free catalog ❖ Jams, jellies, cheese, and smoked, hand-cured country hams, bacon, and sausage. 800–841–2202; 502–235–5294 (in KY).

Broadleaf Venison USA, 11030 Randall St., Sun Valley, CA 91352: Free information ❖ Farm-raised venison, buffalo, lamb, and pheasant. 800–336–3844.

Broken Arrow Ranch, P.O. Box 530, Ingram, TX 78025: Free brochure ❖ Venison, smoked wild boar, antelope, emu, and other exotic meats. 800–962–4263.

B3R Country Meats Inc., 2100 W. Hwy. 287, P.O. Box 374, Childress, TX 79201: Free information ❖ Hormone-, antibiotic-, and growth stimulant-free beef. 817–937–3668.

Burgers' Ozark Country Cured Hams Inc., Rt. 3, Box 3248, California, MO 65018: Free catalog ❖ Barbecued chickens, sausage, cheese, and hickory-smoked-sugar-cured ham and ham steaks, bacon, and turkeys. 800–624–5426; 314–796–4111 (in MO).

Cavanaugh Lakeview Farms Ltd., P.O. Box 580, Chelsea, MI 48118: Free information ❖ Honey-cured and smoked poultry, smoked hams and bacons, fresh-frozen poultry, steaks, game, and smoked seafood. 800–243–4438.

Certified Prime, 9139 Francisco, Aberdeen Park, IL 60642: Free information ❖ Meats. 800–257–2977.

Chops of Iowa Inc., 105 SW Locust, P.O. Box 190, Earlham, IA 50072: Free catalog ❖ Corn-fed beef, honey sliced hams, homemade cheesecakes, and cheese. 800–242–4692.

Classic Country Rabbit Company, P.O. Box 1412, Hillsboro, OR 97123: Free catalog ❖ Rabbit specialties. 800–821–7426.

Classic Steaks, 4430 S. 110th St., Omaha, NE 68137: Free catalog ❖ USDA choice steaks. 800–288–2783.

Critchfield Meat, 2254 Vandale Center, Lexington, KY 40503: Free catalog ❖ Old-fashioned sugar-cured country ham and other meats. 800–86–MEATS; 606–276–4965 (in KY).

D'Artagnan, 399–419 St. Paul Ave., Jersey City, NJ 07306: Free catalog ❖ Fresh American foie gras, Muscovy duck, other game birds, rabbit, and venison. 800–327–8246.

Dakin Farm, Rt. 7, Ferrisburg, VT 05456: Free catalog ❖ Smoked ham and bacon, maple syrup, and Cheddar cheese. 800–993–2546.

Denver Buffalo Company, 1120 Lincoln St., Ste. 905, Denver, CO 80203: Free catalog ❖ All-natural buffalo meat and smoked sausage

products. 800–289–2833; 303–831–1299 (in CO).

Edes Custom Meats Inc., 6700 W. McCormick Rd., Amarillo, TX 79118: Free information with long SASE ❖ Sausage, ham, bacon, beef jerky, grain fed and aged USA choice beef, lamb, and turkey. 800–537–5902; 806–622–0205 (in TX).

S. Wallace Edwards & Sons Inc., P.O. Box 25, Surry, VA 23883: Free catalog ❖ Preserves from the Blue Ridge Mountains, seafood from the Eastern Shore, and hickory-smoked Virginia hams, bacon, and sausage. 800–222–4267.

Faire Game, P.O. Box 7026, Loveland, CO 80537: Free information ❖ Farm-raised exotic game meats. 800–889–6328.

Fiddler's Creek Farm, Hunter Rd., RD 2, Box 188, Titusville, NJ 08560: Free information ❖ Country-cured and hickory-smoked premium meats, turkey, chicken, pork, and bacon. 609–737–0685.

Folk's Folly Prime Cut Shoppe, 551 S. Mendenhall, Memphis, TN 38117: Free catalog ❖ Meats. 800–467–0245.

Fortuna's Sausage Company, 975 Greenville Ave., Greenville, RI 02828: Free catalog ❖ Fresh and dry-cured Italian sausages and other Italian specialties. 800–427–6879

Gaspar's Sausage Company, 384 Faunce Corner Rd., North Dartmouth, MA 02747: Free information ❖ Hot and mild Portuguese-style sausage, sweet breads, and sliced meat. 508–998–2012.

Gerhard's, 901 Enterprise Way, Napa, CA 94558: Free information (request list of retail sources) ❖ Low-fat and low-cholesterol chicken sausage. 707–252–4116.

Golden Trophy, 1101 Perimeter Dr., Ste. 210, Schaumberg, IL 60173: Free catalog ❖ Gourmet meats. 800–835–6607.

The Great Valley Mills, 1774 County Line Rd., Bartow, PA 19504: Free brochure ❖ Pennsylvania Dutch country cheese, ham, bacon, sausage, beef, preserves, fruitcakes, stollen, flour, cereals, and meals. 800–688–6455.

Greenberg Smoked Turkeys Inc., P.O. Box 4818, Tyler, TX 75712: Free information ❖ Smoked turkeys. 903–595–0725.

Harrington Ham Company, Main St., Richmond, VT 05477: Free information ❖ Cheese, maple syrup, pastries and fruitcakes, plum pudding, dried fruit, and cob-smoked maple-glazed hams and smoked bacon, turkey breast, and pheasant. 802–434–4444.

High Valley Farm Inc., 3221 Commerce St., Castle Rock, CO 80104: Free catalog ❖ Hickory-smoked poultry. 719–634–2944.

Hoffman's Quality Meats, 13225 Cearfoss Pike, Hagerstown, MD 21740: Free brochure ❖ Country ham and bacon, Delmonico and boneless New York strip steaks, and country sausage. 800–356–3193.

Honey Baked Ham Company Inc., 4501 Erskin, Ste. 120, Cincinnati, OH 45242: Free brochure ❖ Smoked turkey and turkey breasts, barbecued pork back ribs, Canadian-style bacon, and hickory-smoked hams with a honey-spice glaze. 513–984–9600.

Indian Hill Farms, 213 Old Indian Rd., Milton, NY 12547: Free catalog ❖ Smoked whole turkey and turkey breast, Kosher turkey, smoked ham, Norwegian smoked salmon, and brandied fruitcake. 914–795–2700.

Inman Wild Game, Box 616, Aberdeen, SD 57401: Free brochure ❖ Fresh, frozen, and smoked pheasant, wild turkey, buffalo sausage, quail, and partridge. 800–843–1962.

Jamison Farm, 161 Jamison Ln., Latrobe, PA 15650: Free brochure ❖ Young milk-fed lamb. 800–237–LAMB.

Klement's Sausage Company, 207 E. Lincoln Ave., Milwaukee, WI 53207: Free catalog ❖ Gourmet sausages. 800–KLEMENT; 744–5554 (in Milwaukee area).

R. Lefebvre & Son Smokehouse Meats, P.O. Box 278, South Barre, VT 05670: Free information ❖ Maple-cured smoked ham and smoked bacon. 800–457–6066.

Maurice's Flying Pig, P.O. Box 6847, West Columbia, SC 29171: Free catalog ❖ Hickory pit-cooked all-ham barbecue and barbecue sauce. 800–MAURICE.

Meadow Farms Country Smokehouse, P.O. Box 1387, Bishop, CA 93515: Free brochure ❖ Mahogany-smoked ham and fowl, slab bacon, loin chops, whole Tom turkey breast, sirloin beef tip, sausage, beef jerky, Polish Kolbase, Cheddar cheese, knockwurst, Italian salami, and hot sticks. 619–873–5311.

Myers Meats, Rt. 1, Box 132, Parshall, ND 58770: Free information ❖ Country-style sausage, beef jerky, country-cured dried beef,

beef sticks, and other specialties. 800–635–3759.

New Braunfels Smokehouse, P.O. Box 311159, New Braunfels, TX 78131: Free catalog ❖ Bin-cured and hickory-smoked turkeys, ham, sausage, bacon, chicken, and beef. 800–537–6932.

New Skete Farms, P.O. Box 128, Cambridge, NY 12816: Catalog $1 ❖ Smoked whole ducks and chickens, turkey and chicken breasts, bacon, ham, and sausage, Cheddar cheese, and cheese spreads. 518–677–3928.

Newsom's Old Mill Store, 208 E. Main St., Princeton, KY 42445: Free information ❖ Hickory-smoked ham. 502–365–2482.

Noble Farms Inc., P.O. Box 1612, Sedalia, MO 65301: Free information ❖ Whole-smoked pheasant and smoked pheasant breast. 800–827–5907.

North Country Smokehouse, Airport Rd., P.O. Box 1415, Claremont, NH 03743: Free brochure ❖ All-natural, old-fashioned cob-smoked meat, ham, slab and Canadian bacon, pork chops, sausage, spareribs, boneless lamb, whole turkeys and turkey breasts, duck, pheasant, and smoked sharp Vermont and mozzarella cheese. 800–258–4304.

Nueske's Hillcrest Farm Meats, RR 2, Wittenberg, WI 54499: Free brochure ❖ Smoked hams, sausage, bacon, smoked shanks, pork loins, pork chops, duck, turkeys and turkey breasts, chicken and chicken breasts, and cornish game hens. 800–382–2266.

Oak Grove Smokehouse Inc., 17618 Old Jefferson Hwy., Prairieville, LA 70769: Free catalog ❖ Smoked meat and Cajun and Creole mixes. 504–673–6857.

Oakridge Smokehouse Restaurant, P.O. Box 146, Schulenburg, TX 78956: Free information ❖ Peppered beef tenderloins, smoked pork tenderloins, and baby-back smoked pork spare ribs. 800–548–6325.

Omaha Steaks International, 4400 S. 96th St., Omaha, NE 68127: Free catalog ❖ Aged steaks and beef. 800–228–9055.

Ozark Mountain Smoke House Inc., P.O. Box 37, Farmington, AR 72730: Free catalog ❖ Smoked poultry and meat. 800–643–3437; 800–632–0155 (in AR).

Pfaelzer Brothers, 281 W. 83rd St., Burr Ridge, IL 60521: Free catalog ❖ Gourmet

meats, fruit and gift baskets, desserts, and other specialties. 800–621–0226.

Pittman & Davis, 843 N. Expressway 77, Harlingen, TX 78552: Catalog $1 ❖ Ruby red grapefruit, oranges, pecans, fruit cakes, cheese, smoked hams, and turkeys. 210–423–2154.

The Sausage Maker Inc., 26 Military Rd., Buffalo, NY 14207: Free catalog ❖ Equipment and supplies for making sausage at home. 716–876–5521.

Schaller & Weber Inc., 22–35 46th St., Long Island City, NY 11105: Free catalog ❖ German-style smoked bacon, ham, salami, and sausage. 718–879–3047.

Schiltz Goose Farm, 7 W. Oak St., P.O. Box 267, Sisseton, SD 57262: Free information ❖ Geese, shipped early October through the holidays, packaged for the freezer. 605–698–7651.

Scott Hams, 1301 Scott Rd., Greenville, KY 42345: Free information ❖ Aged country hams. 502–338–3402.

Sinai Kosher Foods Corporation, 1000 W. Pershing Rd., Chicago, IL 60609: Free information ❖ Kosher beef, lamb, veal, roasts, steaks, chops, and ground beef. 800–621–5044; 312–650–6330 (in IL).

Smithfield Ham & Products Company, P.O. Box 487, Smithfield, VA 23430: Free catalog ❖ Country-style Red Eye and Amber Smithfield hams, smoked game birds, hams and other meat, cheese, jellies, jams, and cookies. 800–628–2242; 804–357–2121 (in VA).

Spice 'n Slice, P.O. Box 2605, Phoenix, AZ 85068: Free information ❖ How-to and supplies for making venison sausage. 602–861–4094.

Stock Yards Packing Company, 340 N. Oakley Blvd., Chicago, IL 60612: Free catalog ❖ Foods and meat specialties. 800–621–3687.

Summerfield Farm, HCR 4, Box 195A, Brightwood, VA 22715: Free brochure ❖ Veal. 703–948–3100.

Summers, P.O. Box 34, Lamar, IN 47550: Catalog $2 ❖ Sausage-making supplies and how-to information.

Texas Tamale Company, 7070 Allensby, Houston, TX 77022: Free brochure ❖ Bean- and tomato-free Texas beef chili and chicken, beef, bean, and spinach-cheese tamales. 713–694–0600.

Texas Wild Game Cooperative, P.O. Box 530, Ingram, TX 78025: Free catalog ❖ Venison, antelope, wild boar, and other exotic meats. 800–962–4263.

Thundering Herd Buffalo Products, P.O. Box 1051, Reno, NV 89504: Free catalog ❖ Ranch-raised buffalo meat. 800–525–9730.

Unique Meats, P.O. Box 427, Pittsfield, NH 03263: Free information ❖ Farm-raised venison, buffalo, pheasant, rabbit, and other game. 800–990–7878.

Usinger's Famous Sausage, 1030 N. Old World 3rd St., Milwaukee, WI 53203: Free catalog ❖ Over 75 varieties of sausage. 800–558–9999; 414–276–9105 (in WI).

Virginia Diner, P.O. 310, Wakefield, VA 23888: Free catalog ❖ Virginia bacon and ham, fudge, homemade jellies and jams, peanuts, and peanut specialties. 800–868–NUTS; 804–899–3196 (in VA).

The Daniel Weaver Company, P.O. Box 525, Lebanon, PA 17042: Free catalog ❖ Pennsylvania Dutch smoked meats. 800–932–8377; 717–274–6100 (in PA).

Wild Game Inc., 2315 W. Huron, Chicago, IL 60612: Free information ❖ Organically raised geese. 312–278–1661.

Wimmer's Meat Products, 126 W. Grant, West Point, NE 68788: Free catalog ❖ Hams, sausage, bacon, and other meat cured using old-world spice recipes. 800–358–0761.

Wolfe's Neck Farm, 10 Burnett Rd., Freeport, ME 04032: Free catalog ❖ Natural Angus beef. 207–865–4469.

Wylie Hill Farm, P.O. Box 3, Craftsbury Common, VT 05827: Free brochure ❖ Pheasant, pheasant pate, venison, and other game meat. 800–884–2887.

Nuts

A & B Milling Company Inc., Box 327, Enfield, NC 27823: Free information ❖ Shelled and fried peanuts, chocolate peanut clusters, and other nut favorites. 800–843–0105.

Ace Pecan Company, 485 Crossroads Pkwy., Bolingbrook, IL 60440: Free catalog ❖ Pecans and pecan candy. 800–323–9754.

Almond Plaza, Catalog Order Center, P.O. Box 426, Maumee, OH 43537: Free catalog ❖ Almonds, candy, and herbs. 800–225–6887.

Assouline & Ting Inc., 314 Brown St., Philadelphia, PA 19123: Free information ❖

Nut and gourmet nut specialties. 800–521–4491; 215–627–3000 (in PA).

Azar Nut Company, 1800 Northwestern Dr., El Paso, TX 79912: Free information ❖ Mixed nuts, jumbo and honey-roasted cashews, pistachios, roasted pecans, honey-roasted peanuts, and macadamia nuts. 800–351–8178; 915–877–4079 (in TX).

Bates Nut Farm Inc., 15954 Woods Valley Rd., Valley Center, CA 92082: Free price list ❖ Walnuts, pecans, cashews, macadamias, pistachios, fresh apricots, prunes, dates, candy, granolas, dried fruit, preserves, and honey. 800–642–0348; 619–749–3333 (in CA).

Buchanan Hollow Nut Company, 6510 Minturn, Le Grand, CA 95333: Free information ❖ Fresh-roasted pistachios. 800–532–1500; 209–389–4594 (in CA).

Carolyn's Pecans, P.O. Box 1221, Concord, MA 01742: Free brochure ❖ Sweet, salt-flavored, salt-free, and chocolate covered pecans. 800–656–2940; 508–369–2940 (in MA).

Country Estate Pecans, P.O. Box 7, Sahuarita, AZ 85629: Free information ❖ Pecans. 800–327–3226.

Dasher Pecan Company, P.O. Box 5366, Valdosta, GA 31603: Free information ❖ Pecans, cashews, mixed nuts, and nut specialties. 800–992–2688.

Durey-Libby Nuts Inc., 100 Industrial Rd., Carlstadt, NJ 07072: Free brochure ❖ Walnuts, cashews, pecans, macadamias, almonds, and pistachios. 201–939–2775.

Farmington Filberts, P.O. Box 424, Hillsboro, OR 97123: Free information ❖ Fertilizer- and pesticide-free shelled hazelnuts.

Fran's Pecans, P.O. Box 98, Harlem, GA 30814: Free brochure ❖ Honey-roasted and cinnamon-sugar pecan specialties, and praline, roasted and salted, and pecan halves. 800–476–6887.

From the Rainforest, 1133 Broadway, Ste. 1129, New York, NY 10010: Free information ❖ Preservative-free roasted cashews and a papaya, banana chip, mango, Brazil nut, cashew, pineapple, and coconut snack mix. 800–EAR-TH96.

Golden Kernel Pecan Company Inc., Box 613, Cameron, SC 29030: Free brochure ❖ Pecans and pecan specialties. 800–845–2448; 803–823–2311 (in SC).

Goodbee Pecans, c/o Pecan Plantations, P.O. Box 6709, Florence, SC 29502: Free catalog ❖ Pecans and pecan specialties. 800–729–7004.

House of Almonds, P.O. Box 2930, Bakersfield, CA 93303: Free catalog ❖ Almond and chocolate specialties. 800–225–6663.

Houston's Peanut Outlet, P.O. Box 160, Dublin, NC 28332: Free brochure ❖ Extra-large, raw, blanched, salted-in-the-shell, and oil-roasted peanuts. 800–334–8383.

Lane Pecans, P.O. Box 716, Fort Valley, Georgia 31030: Free brochure ❖ Shelled and unshelled pecans. 800–277–3224.

The Maples Fruit Farm, P.O. Box 167, Chewsville, MD 21721: Catalog $1 (refundable) ❖ Nuts, nut assortments, candy, and fruits. 301–733–0777.

Mariani Nut Company, P.O. Box 664, Winters, CA 95694: Free information ❖ Cholesterol-free almonds.

Mauna Loa Macadamia Nut Corporation, Mainland Expediting Center, 6523 N. Galena Rd., P.O. Box 1772, Peoria, IL 61656: Free catalog ❖ Milk or dark chocolate-coated, honey-roasted, salted and unsalted macadamia nuts, truffles, other candy, and Kona coffee. 800–832–9993.

Missouri Dandy Pantry, P.O. Box A, Stockton, MO 65785: Free brochure ❖ Cashews, pistachios, black walnuts, other nuts, and candy. 800–872–6879.

Nunes Farms Almonds, 4012 Pete Miller Rd., P.O. Box 311, Newman, CA 95360: Free information ❖ Fresh, roasted-salted, honey-glazed, and Cheddar cheese almonds. 800–255–1641.

Nuts D'Vine, P.O. Box 589, Edenton, NC 27932: Free catalog ❖ Peanut brittle, farm-fresh in the shell, and roasted, salted, unsalted, and red skin peanuts. 800–334–0492.

Peanut Patch Inc., 111 N. Main St., P.O. Box 186, Courtland, VA 23837: Free brochure ❖ Peanut and peanut candy assortments, and raw peanuts in bulk. 800–544–0896.

Pecan Plantations, P.O. Box 6709, Florence, SC 29502: Free catalog ❖ Pecans, pecan candies, and other nut specialties. 800–729–8004.

Pecan Producers International, P.O. Box 1301, Corsicana, TX 75110: Free information ❖ Pecans and pistachios. 903–872–1337.

Priester's Pecans, 227 Old Fort Dr., Fort Deposit, AL 36032: Free catalog ❖ Nut brittle, pecan candy, pecan brownies and pie, sugar-free pecan clusters, and roasted, salted, and salt-free pecans. 800–277–3226.

Pueblo to People, P.O. Box 2545, Houston, TX 77252: Information $2 ❖ Nuts, dried fruit, ceramics, jewelry, coffee, and gift baskets. 713–956–1172.

Ross-Smith Pecan Company Inc., 710 Oak St., McRae, GA 31055: Free brochure ❖ Pecans. 800–841–5503; 912–868–5693 (in GA).

Santa Fe Cookie Company, 3905 San Mateo NE, Albuquerque, NM 87110: Free brochure ❖ Gourmet and sugar-free cookies, spicy snacks, pretzels, crackers, and nut mixes. 800–873–5589.

Senor Pistachio, 23320 Ave. 95, Terra Bella, CA 93720: Free information ❖ Salted and unsalted roasted pistachios. 800–468–1319; 800–437–8067 (in CA).

J.H. Sherard, P.O. Box 75, Sherard, MS 38669: Free brochure ❖ Shelled and unshelled pecans, pistachios, and other nuts. 800–647–5518; 205–627–7211 (in MS).

Society Hill Snacks, 2121 Gillingham St., Philadelphia, PA 19124: Free information (request list of retail sources) ❖ Butter-toasted pecans, cashews, almonds, peanuts, pistachios, and mixed nuts. 800–673–7867.

The Squire's Choice, Mail Order Department, 2250 W. Cabot Blvd., Langhorne, PA 19047: Free catalog ❖ Nuts, coffee, and other specialties. 800–523–6163.

Sunburst Farms, P.O. Box 983, Tifton, GA 31793: Free brochure ❖ Pecans and peanuts. 800–358–9412.

Sunnyland Farms Inc., P.O. Box 8200, Albany, GA 31706: Free catalog ❖ Pecans, other nuts, candy, baked specialties, dried fruits, maple syrup, honey, jellies, and gift assortments. 912–883–3085.

Sun River Packing Company, 1329 Hazeldean Rd., Waterford, CA 95386: Free information ❖ Fresh, blanched, and hickory-smoked almonds. 800–334–NUTS.

Tanner Pecan Company, P.O. Box 7188, Mobile, AL 36670: Free catalog ❖ Pecans and pecan confections. 800–635–3651.

H.M. Thames Pecan Company, P.O. Box 2206, Mobile, AL 36652: Free catalog ❖ Nuts and nut specialties, candy, baked goods, pralines, and fruit cake. 800–633–1306.

Things of Good Taste, P.O. Box 455, Waynesboro, VA 22980: Free information (request list of retail sources) ❖ Cakes, fruit butters, candies, nuts, and dip and seasoning mixes. 800–248–2591.

Vetsch Farms, P.O. Box 9126, Bakersfield, CA 93389: Free information ❖ Farm-fresh shelled almonds. 805–831–3094.

Virginia Diner, P.O. 310, Wakefield, VA 23888: Free catalog ❖ Peanuts, peanut specialties and pie, homemade jellies and jams, Virginia bacon and ham, and fudge. 800–642–NUTS; 804–899–3196 (in VA).

Young Pecans, c/o Pecan Plantations, P.O. Box 6709, Florence, SC 29502: Free catalog ❖ Toffee-pecan popcorn, pecan cake, pecan divinity logs, cashews, pecan halves, and butter-roasted, salted, chocolate coated, praline, sugar-orange, sugar-spice, and Cheddar cheese pecans. 800–729–8004.

Whitley Peanut Factory, Hwy. 17, P.O. Box 647, Gloucester County, Hayes, VA 23072: Free information ❖ Virginia peanuts. 804–642–7688.

Popcorn

Black Shield Inc., 5356 Pan American Freeway NE, Albuquerque, NM 87109: Free information ❖ Popcorn gift packs. 800–6–JEWELS.

Fisher's Popcorn, 200 S. Boardwalk, Ocean City, MD 21842: Free brochure ❖ Caramel popcorn. 410–289–5638.

Mallard Pond Farms, 746 Mallard Pond Dr., Boulder, CO 80303: Free catalog ❖ Popping corn, popcorn flour, popcorn bread, and wildflower seed mix. 303–494–3551.

Popcorn Factory, Mail Order Dept., One Harvest Ln., Peoria, IL 61614: Free catalog ❖ Butter-flavored, Cheddar cheese, homemade caramel, and other popcorn favorites. 800–541–2676.

Popcorn World Inc., 2303 Princeton Rd., P.O. Box 507, Trenton, MO 64683: Free brochure ❖ Butter, caramel, cheese, cinnamon, cinnamon with almonds and pecans, vanilla butter with almonds, and popcorn with pecans. 800–443–8226.

Preserves, Jellies & Honey

American Marketing Team, 300 Broadacres Dr., Bloomfield, NJ 07003: Free information ❖ Sugar-free, low-calorie fruit spreads sweetened with NutraSweet. 201–338–0300.

American Spoon Foods, 1668 Clarion Ave., P.O. Box 566, Petoskey, MI 49770: Free information ❖ Fruit preserves and jelly, pumpkin butter, rhubarb marmalade, and fruit conserves. 800–222–5886.

Arkansas Blue Heron Farms, Rt. 2, Box 323, Lowell, AR 72745: Free catalog ❖ Blueberry jam and marmalades, and Amaretto dessert sauce. 800–225–6849.

Bainbridge's Festive Foods, P.O. Box 50805, Nashville, TN 37215: Free information ❖ Fruit preserves. 615–383–5157.

Baranof Berry Patch, P.O. Box 452, Sitka, AK 99835: Free information ❖ Wild berry jellies and jams. 907–747–3031.

Blackberry Patch, Rt. 7, Box 918C, Tallahassee, FL 32308: Free information (request list of retail sources) ❖ Jellies, fresh fruit jams, syrups, honeys, and salad dressings. 800–8–JELLY–8; 904–893–3183 (in FL).

Cascade Conserves Inc., P.O. Box 8306, Portland, OR 97207: Free brochure ❖ All-natural, low-sugar conserves and fruit syrups. 800–846–7396; 503–243–3608 (in OR).

Clearbrook Farms, 5514 Fair Ln., Fairfax, OH 45227: Free brochure ❖ Semi-sweet chocolate sauce, fruit sauces, and marmalades. 800–222–9966; 513–271–2053 (in OH).

Crabtree & Evelyn Limited, P.O. Box 167, Woodstock Hill, CT 06281: Catalog $3.50 ❖ English biscuits and cookies, gingerbread, ginger and butter-ginger cookies, Scottish shortbread, Belgian chocolates, cheese wafers and biscuits from Holland, Italian biscuits, preserves, marmalades, jellies, honey, English sauces, spices and condiments, herbs, tea, and candy. 203–928–2761.

Harold P. Curtis Honey Company, P.O. Box 1012, LaBelle, FL 33935: Free brochure ❖ Honey specialties. 813–675–2187.

Das Peach Haus Inc., Rt. 3, Box 118, Fredericksburg, TX 78624: Free brochure ❖ Jams, jellies, and mustard. 800–369–9257; 210–997–7194 (in TX).

Delight Industries Inc., 7939 State Hwy. 76 East, Kirbyville, MO 65679: Free information ❖ Apple butter, pumpkin butter, and preserves. 417–334–5356.

Glorybee Honey & Supplies, P.O. Box 2744, Eugene, OR 97402: Catalog 50¢ ❖ Beekeeping and honey processing supplies, honey, honey-prepared foods, and gift assortments. 800–456–7923; 503–689–0913 (in OR).

Grandma's Spice Shop, P.O. Box 472, Odenton, MD 21113: Free catalog ❖ Teas, coffees, cocoa, spices, fruit preserves, butters, spreads, essential oils, and herbal potpourris. 410–672–0933.

Hadley Fruit Orchards, P.O. Box 495, Cabazon, CA 92230: Free catalog ❖ Jams and jellies, dried fruits, nuts, candy, and honey. 800–854–5655.

Harry & David, P.O. Box 712, Medford, OR 97501: Free catalog ❖ Fruit preserves, fruits, baked specialties, other desserts, and gift assortments. 800–345–5655.

Honey Acres, Hwy. 67, Ashippun, WI 53003: Free information ❖ Honey, honey-fruit spreads, candy, beeswax candles, mustards, gifts, and cookbooks. 800–558–7745.

Knott's Berry Farm, P.O. Box 1989, Placentia, CA 92670: Free catalog ❖ Jellies and preserves, cheese, sausage, candy, cakes, cookies, and dried fruit. 800–877–6887.

Kozlowski Farms, 5566 Gravenstein Hwy., North Forestville, CA 95436: Free brochure ❖ Marmalades, jams, preserves, honey, mustards, barbecue sauce, fruit butters, sugar-free berry vinegars, conserves, and chutney. 707–887–1587.

Latta's Oregon Delicacies, P.O. Box 1377, Newport, OR 97365: Free catalog ❖ Homemade preserves, seafood, dried fruits, and nuts. 503–265–7675.

Limited Edition Presents, 3106 N. Big Spring, Ste. 100, Midland, TX 79705: Free information (request list of retail sources) ❖ Honey butters. 915–686–2008.

Linn's Fruit Bin, 2485 Village Ln., Cambria, CA 93428: Free catalog ❖ Low-sugar preserves and sugar-free fruit spreads. 800–676–1670.

Lollipop Tree Inc., 319 Vaughan St., Portsmouth, NH 03801: Free information (request list of retail sources) ❖ All-natural preserves, condiments, and baking mixes. 603–436–8196.

Maury Island Farm, P.O. Box L, Vashon, WA 98070: Free brochure ❖ Preserves. 800–356–5880.

The Mayhaw Tree, P.O. Box 3430, Peachtree City, GA 30269: Free information ❖ Sauces, mustard, preserves, and mayhaw berry jelly, sauce, and syrup. 800–262–9429.

Midway Plantation, HC-62, Box 17, Waterproof, LA 71375: Free information ❖ Country-fresh jams and jellies. 800–336–JAMS.

Moon Shine Trading Company, P.O. Box 896, Winters, CA 95694: Free catalog ❖ Almond butter; semisweet chocolate crunch, white chocolate cashew creme, white chocolate almond, and milk chocolate almond crunch nut spreads; and sweet clover, yellow star thistle, sunflower, and eucalyptus honey. 916–753–0601.

New Canaan Farms, P.O. Box 386, Dripping Springs, TX 78620: Free brochure ❖ Ice cream toppings, jellies and jams, mustard, and other specialties. 800–727–5267.

Old Southern Touch Muscadine, 2212 B St., Meridian, MS 39301: Free catalog ❖ Sugar-free muscadine jams, jellies, preserves, toppings, syrups, and sauces. 800–233–1736.

Oregon Apiaries, P.O. Box 1078, Newberg, OR 97132: Free information ❖ Honey specialties. 503–538–8546.

Oregon Hill Farms Inc., 32861 Pittsburgh Rd., St. Helens, OR 97051: Free information ❖ All-natural fruit jams. 800–243–4541; 503–397–2791 (in OR).

Pan Handler Products Inc., RR 4, Box 399, Stowe, VT 05672: Free brochure ❖ Conserves, jams, and jellies. 800–338–5354.

Pine Ridge Country Honey, Box 9A, Crawford, NE 69339: Free brochure ❖ Natural creamed honeys flavored with lemon and spices. 800–658–3285.

Rocky Top Farms, RR 1, Essex Rd., Ellsworth, MI 49729: Free information ❖ All-natural, additive-free preserves and fruit butters. 800–862–9303.

Rowena's, 758 W. 22nd, Norfolk, VA 23517: Free information ❖ Almond pound cake, preserves and jams, and cooking sauces. 800–296–0022.

St. Dalfour Conserves, 2180 Oakdale Dr., Philadelphia, PA 19125: Free information ❖ All-natural, sugar-free, pure fruit conserves imported from France.

Sarabeth's Kitchen, 169 W. 78th St., New York, NY 10024: Free brochure ❖ Marmalades, preserves, additive- and preservative-free fruit butter, chunky apple butter, and cranberry relish. 800–552–JAMS; 212–580–8335 (in NY).

This Blooming Island, P.O. Box 31, Deer Harbor, WA 98243: Free information ❖

Homemade marmalades and jams. 206–376–4972.

Victorian Cupboard, P.O. Box 1852, Chelsea Station, NY 10113: Free catalog ❖ Flower and herb vinegars, preserves and jellies, fruits in liqueur, and scone mixes. 800–653–8033.

Virginia Diner, P.O. 310, Wakefield, VA 23888: Free catalog ❖ Homemade jellies and jams, Virginia bacon and ham, fudge, peanuts, and peanut specialties. 800–642–NUTS; 804–899–3196 (in VA).

Wood's Cider Mill, RFD 2, Box 477, Springfield, VT 05156: Free catalog with long SASE ❖ Maple syrup, cider jelly and syrup, and boiled cider. 802–263–5547.

Salt-free

Avalon Foods Corporation, 2914 Coney Island Ave., Brooklyn, NY 11235: Free brochure ❖ Salt-free cakes and cookies and low-calorie and sugar-free foods. 718–332–6000.

Ener-G Foods, P.O. Box 84487, Seattle, WA 98124: Free information ❖ Low-sodium, gluten-free, low-protein, and non-allergenic foods. 800–331–5222.

HeartyMix Company, 1231 Madison Hill Rd., Rahway, NJ 07065: Free catalog ❖ Preservative-, cholesterol-, and saturated fat-free baking mixes for cookies, cakes and other pastries, salt-free bread, and wheat-free items. 908–382–3010.

Seafood

Assouline & Ting Inc., 314 Brown St., Philadelphia, PA 19123: Free information ❖ Imported and domestic caviar, smoked fish, snails, and other specialties. 800–521–4491; 215–627–3000 (in PA).

Baycliff Company Inc., 242 E. 72nd St., New York, NY 10021: Free information ❖ Sushi-making kits. 212–772–6078.

Blue Heron Fruit Shippers, 3221 Bay Shore Rd., Sarasota, FL 34234: Free brochure ❖ Tree-ripened citrus fruit, candy, marmalades, pecans, gourmet Southern foods, stone crab claws, and honey. 813–355–6946.

Byrd's Famous Seafood, P.O. Box 547, Crisfield, MD 21817: Free brochure ❖ Chesapeake Bay blue crabs, lump crab meat, and backfin, claw, and crab fingers. 410–968–1666.

Captain's Choice, HCR 78, Box 464, Naselle, WA 98638: Free information ❖ Smoked sturgeon. 206–484–3805.

Carolina Mountain, Rt. 1, Box 287, Andrews, NC 28901: Free information ❖ Fresh and smoked salmon and trout. 800–722–9477.

Carolina Smoked Specialties Inc., 118 S. Cypress, Mullins, SC 29574: Free information ❖ Hand-cut oak-apple-smoked trout fillets. 800–800–776–8731.

Caviar House Inc., 687 NE 79th St., Miami, FL 33138: Free catalog ❖ Smoked Scottish salmon, caviar, foie gras, and truffles. 800–522–8427.

Chesapeake Express, Rt. 1, Box 38, Centreville, MD 21617: Free brochure ❖ Maryland's Eastern Shore backfin meat crab cakes, oysters, and soft shell crabs. Delivered ready to heat and serve. 800–282–2722.

Chief Seattle Seafood, 672 S. Orcas, Seattle, WA 98108: Free information ❖ Indian-style smoked Pacific Northwest smoked salmon. 800–426–0001; 206–762–4165 (in WA).

Clambake Celebrations, 9 West Rd., Skaket Corners, Orleans, MA 02653: Free information ❖ Cape Cod seafood dinners with live lobsters, shellfish, and fresh corn. Ready to cook, they are shipped air direct to your door. 800–423–4038.

Cook's Bay Seafoods, P.O. Box 100506, Anchorage, AK 99510: Free information ❖ Alaskan salmon and halibut steaks and fillets. 800–97–FRESH.

Cotuit Oyster Company, P.O. Box 563, Cotuit, MA 02635: Free catalog ❖ New England oysters and cherrystone clams. 508–428–6747.

Crawford Lobster Company, 62 Badgers Island, Kittery, ME 03904: Free catalog ❖ Lobsters, clams, salmon, and oysters. 207–439–0920.

Down East Direct, 77 Atlantic Ave., Boothbay Harbor, ME 04538: Free information ❖ Fresh live lobsters shipped overnight. 800–972–1454.

Downeast Seafood Express, Rt. 176, Box 138, Brooksville, ME 04617: Free brochure ❖ Live Maine lobsters, ocean-fresh lobster meat, fresh Maine crab meat, fresh sea scallops, and Maine steamer clams (when available). 800–556–2326.

Ducktrap River Fish Farm Inc., 57 Little River Dr., Belfast, ME 04915: Free brochure ❖ Preservative- and additive-free smoked salmon, rainbow trout, and a seafood sampler of mussels and scallops. 800–828–3825.

Dutchess Farms, Old Indian Rd., RD 1, Box 95, Milton, NY 12547: Free catalog ❖ Imported Norwegian salmon and other delicacies. 914–795–2175.

S. Wallace Edwards & Sons Inc., P.O. Box 25, Surry, VA 23883: Free catalog ❖ Preserves from the Blue Ridge Mountains, seafood from the Eastern Shore, and hickory-smoked Virginia hams, bacon, and sausage. 800–222–4267.

Fisherman's Finest, 3318 N. 26th St., Tacoma, WA 98407: Free information ❖ Smoked Alaskan sockeye salmon. 206–759–7163.

Graffam Brothers, Box 340, Rockport, ME 04856: Free information ❖ Live Maine lobsters. 207–236–3396.

Great Northern Trading Company, P.O. Box 662, Monroe, WA 98272: Free information (request list of retail sources) ❖ Smoked salmon fillets. 800–707–8606; 206–794–8606 (in WA).

Green Turtle Cannery, P.O. Box 585, Islamorada, Florida Keys 33036: Free information ❖ Turtle soup, and Manhattan clam, New England fish, and New England clam chowders. 305–664–9595.

Grossman's Seafood Inc., P.O. Box 205, West Mystic, CT 06388: Free information ❖ Steamers, mussels, shelled sea scallops, oysters (in the shell), seafood dinners, and clambakes. Features next day shipping. 800–742–5511.

Hagensborg Foods U.S.A. Inc., P.O. Box 6058, Kent, WA 98064: Free information ❖ Smoked and regular salmon and shrimp pates. 800–851–1771; 206–622–8025 (in WA).

Handy Softshell Crawfish, P.O. Box 309, Crisfield, MD 21817: Free brochure ❖ Softshell crabs and crawfish. 800–426–3977.

Hat Creek Fish Company, Division Napa Valley Trading Company, 6540 Washington St., Yountville, CA 94599: Free information ❖ Smoked trout, goat cheese and smoked trout mousse, and other specialties. 800–688–7233; 707–944–9101 (in CA).

Hegg & Hegg, 801 Marine Dr., Port Angeles, WA 98362: Free information ❖ Pacific Northwest smoked salmon, nova-style smoked salmon, Puget Sound red sockeye salmon steaks, sturgeon, shrimp, baby clams, tuna, smoked shad, and dungeness crab meat seafood appetizers and sampler assortments. 800–435–3474; 206–457–3344 (in WA).

Homarus Inc., 76 Kisco Ave., Mount Kisco, NY 10549: Free brochure ❖ Cured salmon smoked in pastrami spices, smoked trout, and Norwegian smoked salmon. 800–23–SALMON.

Horton's Seafood, P.O. Box 430, Waterboro, ME 04087: Free catalog ❖ Naturally smoked Maine salmon, mussels, trout, shrimp, mackerel, and blue fish. 800–346–6066.

Indian Hill Farms, 213 Old Indian Rd., Milton, NY 12547: Free catalog ❖ Smoked whole turkey and turkey breast, Kosher turkey, smoked ham, Norwegian smoked salmon, and brandied fruitcake. 914–795–2700.

J & K Trading Company, 10808 Garland Dr., Culver City, CA 90230: Free price list ❖ Crab meat, lump fish caviar, escargot, hearts of palm, and button mushrooms. 310–836–3334.

Josephson's Smokehouse & Dock, 106 Marine Dr., Astoria, OR 97103: Free catalog ❖ Smoked salmon and oysters, scallops, boneless trout and sturgeon, salmon steaks, and sturgeon caviar. 800–772–3474.

Kirkland Custom Seafoods, P.O. Box 2040, Kirkland, WA 98083: Free brochure ❖ Smoked and canned salmon, oysters, sturgeon, trout, and pates. 800–321–3474.

Latta's Oregon Delicacies, P.O. Box 1377, Newport, OR 97365: Free catalog ❖ Homemade preserves, seafood, dried fruit, and nuts. 503–265–7675.

Legal Sea Foods, 33 Everett St., Allston, MA 02134: Free brochure ❖ Smoked salmon from Ireland and smoked bluefish pate. 800–343–5804.

The Lobster Company, P.O. Box 445, Seabreeze Ave., Stonington, ME 04681: Free brochure ❖ Features overnight shipment of live lobsters and frozen lobster products. 800–442–8262.

Lopez Seafoods, Rt. 2, Box 3305A, Lopez Island, WA 98261: Free information ❖ Smoked seafood specialties. 206–468–3706.

Mackenzie Limited, 2900–D Whittington Ave., Baltimore, MD 21230: Free brochure ❖ Imported seafood specialties and English cheese. 800–858–7100.

Mountain Springs, P.O. Box 861, Prineville, OR 97754: Free brochure ❖ Low-salt and smoke-flavored rainbow trout fillets. 800–542–2303.

Nantucket Specialty Seafood Company, Box 487, Nantucket, MA 02554: Free information ❖ Fresh bay scallops. 508–257–6160 (from November to March).

Nelson Crab Inc., P.O. Box 520, Tokeland, WA 98590: Free brochure ❖ Dungeness crab, smoked sturgeon, albacore tuna, chinook and blueback salmon, minced razor clams, smoked shad, and Pacific shrimp. 800–262–0069; 206–267–2911 (in WA).

New England Smoked Seafood, 46 Hazel St., Rutland, VT 05701: Free brochure ❖ Smoked rainbow trout, Norwegian salmon, and other specialties. 802–773–4628.

Persona Farms Food Specialties, 350 Andover Sparta Rd., Andover, NJ 07821: Free information ❖ Smoked Atlantic salmon. 800–762–8569; 201–729–6161 (in NJ).

Petrossian Shop, 182 W. 58th St., New York, NY 10019: Free information ❖ Smoked salmon, caviar, foie gras, truffles, and other specialties. 800–828–9241.

Pharr Pointe Seafood, Box 509, Wrightsville Beach, NC 28480: Free brochure ❖ Never frozen, fresh jumbo shrimp and lump crab meat shipped overnight. 800–722–0035.

Port Chatham Smoked Seafood, 632 NW 46th St., Seattle, WA 98107: Free brochure ❖ Hand-packed smoked Sockeye and Coho and kipper-smoked salmon, salmon pate, smoked rainbow trout and rainbow trout pate, smoked sturgeon, Pacific Northwest oysters, and Dungeness crab. 800–872–5666; 206–783–8200 (in Seattle area).

Rent Mother Nature, P.O. Box 193, Cambridge, MA 02238: Free catalog ❖ Clam, lobster, mussels, cod, onion, potato, and corn (when in season) seafood dinners for two and four persons, in a reusable enamelled pot. 617–354–5430.

Sea Island Mercantile, 928 Bay St., P.O. Box 100, Beaufort, SC 29901: Free information ❖ She-Crab soup and other Carolina Low-country foods. 800–735–3215.

SeaBear, 605 30th St., P.O. Box 591, Anacortes, WA 98221: Free catalog ❖ Alderwood-smoked Pacific Northwest sockeye salmon and oysters. 800–645–3474.

Seafood Direct, P.O. Box 1836, Woodinville, WA 98072: Free brochure ❖ Canned fresh sockeye salmon, kippered salmon, trout pate, smoked trout, salmon pate, and smoked oysters. 800–732–1836.

The Seasoned Traveler, P.O. Box 111641, Tacoma, WA 98411: Free information ❖ Smoked Alaska sockeye salmon.

Silver Lining Seafood, Division NorQuest Seafood Inc., P.O. Box 6092, Ketchikan, AK 99901: Free catalog ❖ Smoked, fresh, and frozen salmon specialties. 907–225–9865.

Simply Shrimp, 7794 NW 44th St., Fort Lauderdale, FL 33351: Free information ❖ Seafood from the Gulf and around the world and Florida stone-crab claws (when in season). 800–833–0888.

Totem Smokehouse, 1906 Pike Place Market, Seattle, WA 98101: Free brochure ❖ Alderwood-smoked salmon and other seafood. 800–9–SALMON; 206–443–1710 (in WA).

Villa Tatra Colorado, 729 Pinewood Dr., Lyons, CO 80540: Free information ❖ Preservative-free, all-natural smoked salmon, trout, and sausage. 800–430–4003.

Weathervane Seafoods, Public Landing, Belfast, ME 04915: Free information ❖ Live Maine lobsters and mussels. 207–338–1777.

Wisconsin Fishing Company, P.O. Box 965, Green Bay, WI 54305: Free catalog ❖ Shrimp, lobster, crab, and other seafood. 414–437–3582.

Seasonings & Condiments

Almond Plaza, Catalog Order Center, P.O. Box 426, Maumee, OH 43537: Free catalog ❖ Herbs, almonds, and candy. 800–225–6887.

Alyce's Herbs, 4950 Femrite Dr., Madison, WI 53715: Brochure $2 ❖ Herb vinegars and herb-infused oils for cooking and salads. 800–276–4911.

Assouline & Ting Inc., 314 Brown St., Philadelphia, PA 19123: Free information ❖ Fruit and nut extracts, vinegars and olive, nut, and specialty oils. 800–521–4491; 215–627–3000 (in PA).

Charles Baldwin & Sons, 1 Center St., West Stockbridge, MA 01266: Price list $1 ❖ Pure vanilla extract made from the Madagascar Bourbon Vanilla Bean. 413–232–7785.

Bean Bag Mail Order Company, 818 Jefferson St., Oakland, CA 94607: Catalog $1 ❖ Gourmet seasonings and bean specialties. 800–845–2326.

Norman Bishop, P.O. Box 2451, San Jose, CA 95113: Free brochure ❖ Low-sodium, preservative-free mustards and mayonnaise. 408–292–1089.

Blackberry Patch, Rt. 7, Box 918C, Tallahassee, FL 32308: Free information (request list of retail sources) ❖ Jellies, fresh fruit jams, syrups, honeys, and salad dressings. 800–8–JELLY–8; 904–893–3183 (in FL).

Blanchard & Blanchard Ltd., P.O. Box 1080, Norwich, VT 05055: Free information ❖ Preservative-free natural salad dressings, dessert sauces, mustards, glazes, and marinades. 800–334–0268; 802–649–1327 (in VT).

Blue Crab Bay Company, P.O. Box 180, Onancock, VA 23417: Free catalog **F129Mv** All-natural seafood seasonings, seafood marinade, and clam pasta sauces. 800–221–2722; 804–787–3602 (in VA).

Boetje's Foods Inc., 2736 12th St., Rock Island, IL 61201: Free information ❖ Stone-ground mustards. 309–788–4352.

Bootlegger & Buckaroo Foods, 2905 San Gabriel, Ste. 207, Austin, TX 78705: Free information ❖ Peach salsa and other food specialties. 800–972–1119.

Caesar & Me Specialty Foods, 1142 Manhattan Ave., Manhattan Beach, CA 90254: Free information ❖ Salsa for dipping, cooking, marinades, and salad dressing. 310–798–7223.

Calypso Queen Foods Inc., P.O. Box 35347, Charlotte, NC 28235: Free information ❖ Caribbean-style salsa, barbecue and steak sauces, marinades, and salad dressings. 704–527–1464.

Campagna Distinctive Flavors, Box 1607, Eugene, OR 97440: Free information ❖ Herb and pepper jellies and chive, dill, and peppercorn vinegars. 800–959–4372; 503–343–1425 (in OR).

Chef Jeffs Chutney, 215 MacFarlane Dr., Delray Beach, FL 33483: Free information ❖ Chutney specialties. 800–279–9655.

Colorado Spice Company, 5030 Nome St., Unit A, Denver, CO 80239: Free catalog ❖ Culinary spices and herbs, hot sauce, spice blends, chilies, salsa, and other specialty sauces. 303–373–0141.

Commissariat Imports Inc., 2641 Veteran Ave., Los Angeles, CA 90064: Free information ❖ Curry, ginger, chutney, and other condiments for Indian-style cooking. 310–475–5628.

Crabtree & Evelyn Limited, P.O. Box 167, Woodstock Hill, CT 06281: Catalog $3.50 ❖ English mustards and chutney, herbs and spices, French mustard and mustard sauces, oils and vinegars, fruit vinegars and syrups, preserves, biscuits and cookies, and candy. 203–928–2761.

Cuisine Express, 1784 Deer Trail Rd., Boulder, CO 80302: Free catalog ❖ All-natural spices and seasonings. 303–444–4302.

Culinary Arts Ltd., P.O. Box 2157, Lake Oswego, OR 97035: Free catalog ❖ Gourmet vinegars, mustards, and liqueurs.

Das Peach Haus Inc., Rt. 3, Box 118, Fredericksburg, TX 78624: Free brochure ❖ Jams, jellies, and mustard. 800–369–9257; 210–997–7194 (in TX).

De Medici Imports, 221 W. 57th St., New York, NY 10019: Free information ❖ Condiments and other food specialties. 212–974–8101.

Delegeane Garlic Farms, P.O. Box 2561, Yountville, Napa Valley, CA 94599: Free brochure ❖ Fresh garlic, chili ristras, salt-free herb seasonings, and California wildflower honeys. 707–944–8019.

Desert Rose Foods Inc., P.O. Box 5391, Tucson, AZ 85703: Free brochure ❖ Salsa, spicy mesquite honey-based barbecue sauce, spicy Italian peppers, and tortilla chips. 800–937–2572.

Dilly Dames Inc., P.O. Box 141, Howard, OH 43028: Catalog $1 ❖ Herbal wine vinegars and seasonings.

Eden Foods, 701 Tecumseh, Clinton, MI 49236: Free information ❖ Low-sodium and organic soy sauces. 517–456–7424.

El Paso Chile Company, 909 Texas Ave., El Paso, TX 79901: Free information ❖ Chili and spice blends. 915–544–3434.

Essex Street Pickle Corporation, 35 Essex St., New York, NY 10002: Free information ❖ Sauerkraut, horseradish, tomatoes and hot peppers, olives, herring, and sour, half-sour, and hot pickles. 800–252–GUSS.

Fitzgerald Fairfield Inc., P.O. Box 3151, Palm Beach, FL 33480: Free information ❖ Herb blends and seasonings. 407–848–6261.

Fox Hollow Farm, 10 Old Lyme Rd., Hanover, NH 03755: Free information ❖ Gourmet mustard. 603–643–6002.

Fredericksburg Herb Farm, P.O. Drawer 927, Fredericksburg, TX 78624: Catalog $2 (does not include herb plants) ❖ Herb plants, seeds, flowers, toiletries, oils, and seasonings. 512–997–8615.

Helen's Tropical Exotics, 3316B Hamilton Blvd., Atlanta, GA 30354: Free brochure ❖ Dips, marinades, sauces, Jamaican pimentos, tropical spices, and hot peppers. 800–544–JERK.

Herb & Spice Collection, P.O. Box 118, Norway, IA 52318: Free catalog ❖ Culinary herbs and spices, herbs and tea, natural herbal body care products, and potpourris. 800–786–1388.

Judyth's Mountain, 1737 Lorenzen Dr., San Jose, CA 95124: Free information ❖ Sauces and condiments for use with meat, cheese, chicken, lamb, or beef. 408–264–3330.

GNS Spices, P.O. Box 90, Walnut, CA 91788: Free information ❖ Dried, flaked, pureed, brined, ground, and fresh Habaneras. 909–594–9505.

Gorilla Gardens, 10153–1/2 Riverside Dr., Toluca Lake, CA 91602: Free information ❖ Additive- and preservative-free, all-natural herb-infused vinegars and oils. 818–752–3455.

Grandma's Spice Shop, P.O. Box 472, Odenton, MD 21113: Free catalog ❖ Teas, coffees, cocoa, spices, fruit preserves, butters, spreads, essential oils, and herbal potpourri. 410–672–0933.

Hall Mock Productions, 212 S. Main, Colfax, WA 99111: Free information ❖ Gourmet condiments. 509–397–2137.

Hallbourgh Land & Cattle Company, 8138 E. Gail Rd., Scottsdale, AZ 85260: Free catalog ❖ Chili fixings, barbecue sauces, condiments, salsa and hot sauces, and salad dressings. 800–552–1500.

Henkel's Food Corporation, 419 Rose Ln., Rockville Center, NY 11570: Free catalog ❖ Gourmet mustard. 800–222–1899.

Hope Springs Seasonings, P.O. Box 8096, Newport Beach, CA 92658: Free information ❖ Preservative-free natural seasonings. 714–721–1651.

Huy Fong Foods Inc., 5001 Earle Ave., Rosemead, CA 91770: Free information ❖ Hot chili sauces. 818–286–8328.

The Juarez Chile Company, P.O. Box 33695, San Antonio, TX 78265: Free catalog ❖ All-natural salsa, sauces, and condiments. 800–221–3578.

Kelchner's, P.O. Box 245, Dublin, PA 18917: Free information ❖ Horseradish cocktail, horseradish tartar, and hot mustard with horseradish sauces.

Kozlowski Farms, 5566 Gravenstein Hwy., North Forestville, CA 95436: Free brochure ❖ Condiments and mustards, sugar-free berry vinegars, barbecue sauce, conserves, chutney, jams, marmalades, honey, and salad dressings. 707–887–1857.

Lots of Hots & Fiery Foods, 39 Pebble Hill Rd., Fairport, NY 14450: Free catalog ❖ Hot salsa, sauces, condiments, and spices. 800–836–1677; 716–425–7556 (in NY).

Luciano Foods Inc., 150 Whitestone, Cedar Park, TX 78613: Free information ❖ Sauces, salsa, salad dressings, spices, and other Mexican and southwestern favorites. 800–653–6425.

Manusow's, 10 Old Lyme Rd., Hanover, NH 03755: Free information ❖ Gourmet mustard. 800–4–MANUSO; 708–323–0858 (in IL).

Maui Jelly Factory, 1464 Lower Main St., Wailuku, Maui, HI 96793: Free information ❖ Onion jelly, onion mustard, chili pepper water, and other gourmet food products. 800–803–8343.

The Mayhaw Tree, P.O. Box 3430, Peachtree City, GA 30269: Free information ❖ Sauces, mustard, preserves, and mayhaw berry jelly, sauce, and syrup. 800–262–9429.

McIlhenny Company, Avery Island, LA 70513: Free information ❖ Tabasco and barbecue sauces and other Louisiana favorites.

Mendocino Mustard, 1260 N. Main, Fort Bragg, CA 95437: Free brochure ❖ Gourmet mustard. 707–964–2250.

Mo Hotta-Mo Betta, P.O. Box 4136, San Luis Obispo, CA 93403: Free catalog ❖ Chili pepper and other hot pepper sauces, pickled products, spicy condiments, barbecue sauces, seasonings and spices to shake on, curries and chutney, soups, dried chilies, cooking sauces and pastes, and snacks. 800–462–3220.

Morris Farms, Rt. 1, Hwy. 56 East, Uvalda, GA 30473: Free catalog ❖ Vidalia onion relish, relish with mustard, barbecue sauce, onion pickles, and sweet onion vinaigrette. 800–447–9338.

Mount Horeb Mustard Museum, P.O. Box 72, Mount Horeb, WI 53572: Catalog $5 ❖ Gourmet mustard. 603–643–6002.

Nantucket Off-Shore Seasonings Inc., P.O. Box 1437, Nantucket, MA 02554: Free information ❖ Salt-free seasonings for grilled or broiled fish, meat, and poultry. 508–228–9292.

Napa Valley Mustard Company, P.O. Box 125, Oakville, CA 94562: Free information ❖ Cholesterol-free, low-sodium mustard-spiced oil and mustard. 707–944–8330.

New Canaan Farms, P.O. Box 386, Dripping Springs, TX 78620: Free brochure ❖ Ice cream toppings, jellies and jams, mustard, and other specialties. 800–727–5267.

No-Salt-Salt, P.O. Box 3151, Palm Beach, FL 33480: Free information (request list of retail sources) ❖ All-natural sauces and herb dips. 800–955–4372.

Old Southwest Trading Company, P.O. Box 7545, Albuquerque, NM 87194: Free catalog ❖ Habanero and other exotic and domestic chiles. 505–836–0168.

The Olive Company, 11746 Rt. 108, Clarksville, MD 21029: Free information (request list of retail sources) ❖ Olive specialties. 410–531–5332.

The Tony Packo Food Company, 1902 Front St., Toledo, OH 43605: Free catalog ❖ Pickles, relishes, salsa, sauces, and other condiments. 800–366–4218; 419–691–1953.

Panola Pepper Corporation, Rt. 2, Box 148, Lake Province, LA 71254: Free price list ❖ Gourmet sauces. 318–559–1774.

Pendery's Inc., 1221 Manufacturing St., Dallas, TX 75207: Catalog $2 ❖ Spices, seasonings, and flavorings for Mexican cooking. 800–533–1870; 214–741–1870 (in TX).

Penzey's Spice House, P.O. Box 1633, Milwaukee, WI 53201: Free information ❖ Fresh-ground spices. 414–768–8799.

Pezzini Farms, P.O. Box 1276, Castroville, CA 95012: Free information ❖ Artichokes and artichoke dipping and pasta sauces. 800–347–6118.

Phamous Phloyd's Inc., 2998 S. Steele St., Denver, CO 80210: Free information ❖ Barbecue sauce, marinade, and dry rub-on condiments. 303–757–3285.

Pikled Garlic Company, P.O. Box 846, Pacific Grove, CA 93950: Free information ❖ Jalapeno, red chili, lemon dill, smoke-flavored, and mild marinated garlic specialties. 800–775–9788; 408–372–7944 (in CA).

Popie's Brands Inc., 1414 N. Burnside, Gonzales, LA 70737: Free information ❖ Cajun sauces. 800–223–3495.

Rafal Spice Company, 2521 Russell, Detroit, MI 48207: Free catalog ❖ Spices,

decaffeinated coffee beans, tea, and flavoring extracts. 313–259–6373.

Ranch O Casados, P.O. Box 1149, San Juan Pueblo, NM 87566: Free price list ❖ Chile powder and other local chile and corn products. 505–852–4482.

Rapazzini Winery, P.O. Box 247, Gilroy, CA 95021: Free information ❖ Mustard and spices, cooking wines, bordelaise sauce, olives, and other garlic-flavored specialties. 408–842–5649.

Ray's Brand Products Inc., 1920 S. 13th St., P.O. Box 1000, Springfield, IL 62705: Free information ❖ Chile with beans and all-beef hot dog sauce. 217–523–2777.

The Rosemary House, 120 S. Market St., Mechanicsburg, PA 17055: Catalog $2 ❖ Spices. 717–697–5111.

Rowena's, 758 W. 22nd, Norfolk, VA 23517: Free information ❖ Almond pound cake, preserves and jams, and cooking sauces. 800–296–0022.

The Royers' Round Top Cafe, On the Square, Round Top, TX 78954: Free information ❖ Pepper sauce and herbal vinegars. 800–86–ROYERS; 409–249–3611 (in TX).

San Francisco Herb Company, 250 14th St., San Francisco, CA 94103: Free catalog ❖ Cooking herbs and spices. 800–227–4530; 800–622–0768 (in CA).

San Francisco Mustard Company, 4049 Petaluma Blvd. North, Petaluma, CA 94952: Free information ❖ All-natural, salt-free whole seed mustards. 707–769–0866.

Santa Barbara Olive Company, P.O. Box 1570, Santa Ynez, CA 93460: Free information ❖ Handpicked olives, olive oil, salad dressings, garlic nectar, and other condiments. 800–624–4896.

Santa Cruz Chili & Spice Company, Box 177, Tumacacori, AZ 85640: Free information ❖ Chili paste for flavoring meat and chicken. 602–398–2591.

Santa Fe Exotix, DeVargas Center, Ste. G473, Santa Fe, NM 87501: Free catalog ❖ Gourmet condiments.

Scott's Food Products, 122 S. Guadalupe Ave., Ste. 4, Redondo Beach, CA 90277: Free information (request list of retail sources) ❖ Sauces, marinades, and spice blends. 310–374–1900.

Select Origins, 11–10 Old Dock Rd., Yaphank, NY 11980: Free catalog ❖

Kitchen-tested vanilla, cooking sweets, dessert sauces, oils, vinegars, sauces, marinades, relishes and condiments, herbs and spices, coffee and tea, and preserves. 516–924–5447.

Shady Acres Herb Farm, 7815 Hwy. 212, Chaska, MN 55318: Free list with long SASE ❖ Dried plants and herbal vinegars. 612–466–3391.

Spice Merchant, P.O. Box 524, Jackson Hole, WY 83001: Free catalog ❖ Spices, herbs, and flavoring condiments from China, Japan, Indonesia, Thailand, and other countries. 800–551–5999.

Sweet Adelaide Enterprises, 12918 Cerise Ave., Hawthorne, CA 90250: Free information ❖ Low-salt, all-natural herb vinegars and herb seasonings with no sugar, MSG or other additives and preservatives. Also cold-pressed French walnut oil and red-hot pecan oil. 310–970–7840.

Talk O'Texas, 1610 Roosevelt St., San Angelo, TX 76905: Free information ❖ Hot and mild crisp okra pickles. 800–749–6572.

Tommy Tang's Thai Seasonings, P.O. Box 46700, Los Angeles, CA 90046: Free information ❖ MSG- and artificial ingredients-free seasonings. 213–874–3883.

Things of Good Taste, P.O. Box 455, Waynesboro, VA 22980: Free information (request list of retail sources) ❖ Cakes, fruit butters, candies, nuts, and dip and seasoning mixes. 800–248–2591.

The Uncommon Herb Catalog, 731 Main St., Monroe, CT 06468: Catalog $1 ❖ Essential oils, handmade soaps, skin care products, teas, and seasonings. 203–459–0716.

Victorian Cupboard, P.O. Box 1852, Chelsea Station, NY 10113: Free catalog ❖ Flower and herb vinegars, preserves and jellies, fruits in liqueur, and scone mixes. 800–653–8033.

Watkins Manufacturing, 150 Liberty St., P.O. Box 5570, Winona, MN 55987: Free catalog ❖ Seasonings, spices, flavorings, and extracts. 800–553–8018.

Wild Thyme Farm, Medussa, NY 12120: Free information ❖ Gourmet mustard. 518–239–4756.

Sugar-free & Dietetic

Calco Food Company Inc., 3540 W. Jarvis, Skokie, IL 60076: Free catalog ❖ Sugar-free gourmet diet foods. 800–325–5409.

Estee Candy Company Inc., 169 Lackawanna Ave., Parsippany, NJ 07054: Free catalog ❖ Sugarless candy and cookies. 201–335–1000.

Hearty Mix Company, 1231 Madison Hill Rd., Rahway, NJ 07065: Free catalog ❖ Preservative-, cholesterol-, and saturated fat-free baking mixes for cookies, cakes and other pastries, salt-free bread, and wheat-free items. 908–382–3010.

Ann Raskas Candies, P.O. Box 13367, Kansas City, KS 66113: Free information ❖ Candy for dieters, with 14 calories each piece. 913–422–7230.

Tea, Coffee & Cocoa

Alaska Herb Tea Company, P.O. Box 110289, Anchorage, AK 99520: Free information ❖ Dried fruit and wild herb tea. 800–654–2664.

Assouline & Ting Inc., 314 Brown St., Philadelphia, PA 19123: Free information ❖ Whole bean gourmet coffees. 800–521–4491; 215–627–3000 (in PA).

Baronet Gourmet Coffee, P.O. Box 987, Hartford, CT 06143: Free catalog ❖ Coffee and brewing equipment. 800–253–7374.

Bean Bag, 10400 Old Georgetown Rd., Bethesda, MD 20814: Free catalog ❖ Exotic blends of coffee and tea. 301–530–8090.

The Beverly Hills Coffee Company, 369 S. Doheny Dr., Beverly Hills, CA 90211: Free catalog ❖ Imported and domestic coffee. 800–576–1674.

Brothers Gourmet Coffee, P.O. Box 812124, Boca Raton, FL 33481: Free catalog ❖ Flavored and non-flavored, caffeinated and decaffeinated, 100 percent Arabica coffee, and espresso makers, grinders, filters, thermal carafes, and gift baskets. 800–284–5776.

Buckley's Fancy Foods & Confections Ltd., P.O. Box 14119, Baton Rouge, LA 70898: Free catalog ❖ Cookies, toffee and brittle, pretzels, coffee and tea, and holiday treats. 800–445–3957.

Cafe La Semeuse, P.O. Box 429, Brooklyn, NY 11222: Free brochure ❖ Regular or water-processed whole bean decaffeinated coffee. 800–242–6333.

Coffee Caboodle, 525 Maple Ave. West, Vienna, VA 22180: Free price list ❖ Coffee and tea from worldwide sources. 800–541–2469; 703–281–5599 (in VA).

Cordon Brew, 3339 55th St., San Diego, CA 92105: Free price list ❖ Brewing equipment

and regular, blended, and decaffeinated coffee. 800–232–6793.

Dean & DeLuca Mail-Order, 560 Broadway, New York, NY 10012: Free information ❖ Bensdorp and Droste cocoa for chocolate and dessert creations. 800–221–7714.

Desert Mountain Tea Company, Box 328, Whitehorn, CA 95489: Free information ❖ Caffeine- and alkaloid-free wild herb tea. 800–955–4832.

First Colony Coffee & Tea Company, 204–222 W. 22nd St., Norfolk, VA 23517: Free information ❖ Raspberry, peach orchard, apple orchard, orange and cinnamon, black current, tangy apricot, and strawberry patch tea. 800–446–8555; 804–622–2224 (in VA).

Don Francisco Coffee Traders, P.O. Box 58271, Los Angeles, CA 90058: Free catalog ❖ Coffee from worldwide sources. 800–697–5282.

Gevalia Kaffe, P.O. Box 11046, Des Moines, IA 50336: Free catalog ❖ Exotic coffee from around the world. 800–678–2687.

Georgetown Coffee, Tea & Spice, 1330 Wisconsin Ave. NW, Washington, DC 20007: Free catalog ❖ Imported coffee, unroasted green beans, herbal bulk tea, decaffeinated tea, brewing equipment, filters, and replacement beakers. 800–846–1947.

Gillies Coffee Company, 150 19th St., Brooklyn, NY 11232: Free brochure ❖ Imported coffee and tea from around the world. 800–344–5526.

Grace Tea Company, 50 W. 17th St., New York, NY 10011: Free information ❖ Tea. 212–255–2935.

Grandma's Spice Shop, P.O. Box 472, Odenton, MD 21113: Free catalog ❖ Teas, coffees, cocoa, spices, fruit preserves, butters, spreads, essential oils, and herbal potpourris. 410–672–0933.

Green Mountain Coffee Roasters, 33 Coffee Ln., Waterbury, VT 05676: Free catalog ❖ Freshly roasted Colombian coffee. 800–223–6768.

Green Tea Products, Box 332, Piermont, NY 1096: Free information with long SASE ❖ Green tea and green tea blends. 201–894–7746.

Harney & Sons Tea Company, P.O. Box 676, Salisbury, CT 06068: Free price list ❖ Tea that is available loose, in tea bags, gift

canisters, and hotel-style packaging. 800–832–8463.

Kobricks Coffee Company, 693 Henderson St., Jersey City, NJ 07302: Free catalog ❖ Flavored specialty and espresso coffee. 201–656–6313.

Mackinlay Teas, 5025 Venture Dr., Ann Arbor, MI 46108: Free information ❖ Decaffeinated tea in exotic flavors. 800–TEA–FOR–U.

McNultys Tea & Coffee Company, 109 Christopher St., New York, NY 10014: Free brochure ❖ Imported tea and coffee from the around world and brewing equipment. 800–356–5200; 212–242–5351 (in NY).

Northwestern Coffee Mills, 217 N. Broadway, Milwaukee, WI 53202: Catalog 50¢ ❖ Imported and domestic coffee and tea. 414–276–1031.

O'Mona International Tea Company, 9 Pine Ridge Rd., Rye Brook, NY 10573: Catalog $1 ❖ Tea from worldwide sources. 914–937–8858.

Paulig USA, P.O. Box 474, Willernie, MN 55090: Free information ❖ Tea.

Rafal Spice Company, 2521 Russell, Detroit, MI 48207: Free catalog ❖ Coffee, coffee beans, tea, spices, and flavoring extracts. 313–259–6373.

The Republic of Tea, 2165 E. Francisco Blvd., Ste. E, San Rafael, CA 94901: Free information ❖ Tea. 415–721–2170.

Schapira Coffee Company, 117 W. 10th St., New York, NY 10011: Free information ❖ Coffee. 212–675–3733.

Simpson & Vail Inc., 38 Clinton St., P.O. Box 309, Pleasantville, NY 10570: Free catalog ❖ Coffee and flavored tea. 914–747–1336.

Stash Tea, 9040 SW Burnham, Tigard, OR 97223: Free catalog ❖ Traditional, herb, decaffeinated, and spiced tea. Also tea accessories and gifts. 800–826–4218.

Steamer Hot Cocoa Inc., 3 Westchester Plaza, Elmsford, NY 10523: Free information ❖ All-natural hot chocolate and a white hot chocolate mix. 800–444–5860.

Sunberry Farms, 1830 Jefferson St., Napa, CA 94559: Free catalog ❖ Sugar- and artificial sweetener-free low-fat cocoa mix and natural caffeinated or decaffeinated ice tea mixes. 800–622–8800.

Torrefazione Italia Inc., 320 Occidental Ave. South, Seattle, WA 98104: Free information ❖ Coffee. 800–827–2333; 206–624–5773 (in WA).

The Uncommon Herb Catalog, 731 Main St., Monroe, CT 06468: Catalog $1 ❖ Essential oils, handmade soaps, skin care products, teas, and seasonings. 203–459–0716.

Upton Tea Imports, P.O. Box 159, Upton, MA 01568: Free information ❖ Tea. 800–234–TEAS.

Mark T. Wendell, P.O. Box 1312, West Concord, MA 01742: Free information ❖ Tea. 508–369–3709.

Williams-Sonoma, Mail Order Department, P.O. Box 7456, San Francisco, CA 94120: Free information ❖ Pernigotti and Dark Jersey cocoa for chocolate and dessert creations. 415–541–1262.

FOOTBALL
Clothing

AlliedSignal Fibers, 1411 Broadway, New York, NY 10018: Free information ❖ Clothing for players and coaches. 212–391–5000.

Apsco Inc., 1st Ave. & 50th St., Building 57, Brooklyn, NY 11232: Free information ❖ Clothing for players. 718–965–9500.

Betlin Manufacturing, 1445 Marion Rd., Columbus, OH 43207: Free information ❖ Clothing for players and coaches. 614–443–0248.

Bomark Sportswear, P.O. Box 2068, Belair, TX 77402: Free information ❖ Clothing for players and coaches. 800–231–3351.

DeLong, 733 Broad St., P.O. Box 189, Grinnell, IA 50112: Free information ❖ Clothing for players and coaches. 800–733–5664; 515–236–3106 (in IA).

Empire Sporting Goods Manufacturing Company, 443 Broadway, New York, NY 10013: Free information ❖ Clothing for players and coaches. 800–221–3455; 212–966–0880 (in NY).

Fab Knit Manufacturing, Division Anderson Industries, 1415 N. 4th St., Waco, TX 76707: Free information ❖ Clothing for players and coaches. 800–433–3380; 817–752–2511 (in TX).

Shaffer Sportswear, 224 N. Washington, Neosho, MO 64850: Free information ❖ Jackets, pants, and uniforms. 417–451–9444.

Southland Athletic Manufacturing Company, P.O. Box 280, Terrell, TX 75160: Free information ❖ Jackets and uniforms. 214–563–3321.

Speedline Athletic Wear, 1804 N. Habana, Tampa, FL 33607: Free information ❖ Jackets, pants, and uniforms. 813–876–1375.

Venus Knitting Mills Inc., 140 Spring St., Murray Hill, NJ 07974: Free information ❖ Clothing for players and coaches. 800–955–4200; 908–464–2400 (in NJ).

Wilson Sporting Goods, 8700 Bryn Mawr, Chicago, IL 60631: Free information ❖ Clothing for players and coaches. 800–272–6060; 312–714–6400 (in IL).

Equipment

Adams USA, 810 S. Jefferson, P.O. Box 489, Cookeville, TN 38501: Free information ❖ Protective gear. 800–251–6857; 615–526–2109 (in TN).

Alchester Mills Company Inc., 314 S. 11th St., Camden, NJ 08103: Free information ❖ Protective gear. 609–964–9700.

Ampac Enterprises Inc., All Star Division, Box 1356, Shirley, MA 01464: Free information ❖ Field and playing equipment and protective gear. 800–777–3810; 508–425–6266 (in MA).

The Athletic Connection, 1901 Diplomat, Dallas, TX 75234: Free information ❖ Footballs, goal posts, kicking tees, and other equipment. 800–527–0871; 214–243–1446 (in TX).

Austin Athletic Equipment Corporation, 705 Bedford Ave., Box 423, Bellmore, NY 11710: Free information ❖ Goal posts, markers, and marking machines. 516–785–0100.

Baden Sports Inc., 34114 21st Ave. South, Federal Way, WA 98003: Free information ❖ Leather, rubber-covered, synthetic, and juvenile footballs. 800–544–2998; 206–925–0500 (in WA).

Bike Athletic Company, P.O. Box 666, Knoxville, TN 37901: Free information ❖ Protective gear. 615–546–4703.

Body Glove International, 530 6th St., Hermosa Beach, CA 90254: Free information ❖ Protective gear. 800–678–7873; 310–374–4074 (in CA).

H.D. Brown Enterprise Ltd., 23 Beverly St. East, St. George, Ontario, Canada N0E 1N0: Free information ❖ Footballs. 519–448–1381.

Cannon Sports, P.O. Box 11179, Burbank, CA 91510: Free information with list of retailers ❖ Protective gear. 800–362–3146; 818–753–5940 (in CA).

Casco Sports Medicine, 80 Common Rd., Dresden, ME 04342: Free catalog ❖ Protective gear. 800–327–9285; 207–737–8516 (in ME).

Gerry Cosby & Company, 3 Pennsylvania Plaza, Madison Square Garden, New York, NY 10001: Free information ❖ Protective gear. 800–548–4003; 212–563–6464 (in NY).

Cougar Sports, 14827 Martin Dr., Eden Prairie, MN 55344: Free information ❖ Protective gear. 800–445–2664; 612–934–5384 (in MN).

Cramer Products Inc., P.O. Box 1001, Gardner, KS 66030: Free information ❖ Protective gear. 800–345–2231; 913–884–7511 (in KS).

Franklin Sports Industries Inc., 17 Campanelli Pkwy., P.O. Box 508, Stoughton, MA 02072: Free information ❖ Leather, rubber-covered, synthetic, and juvenile footballs. 617–344–1111.

Gared Sports Inc., 1107 Mullanphy St., St. Louis, MO 63106: Free information ❖ Goal posts, markers, and marking machines. 800–325–2682.

GeorGI-Sports, P.O. Box 1107, Lancaster, PA 17603: Free information ❖ Leather, rubber-covered, synthetic, and juvenile footballs, and protective gear. 800–338–2527; 717–291–8924 (in PA).

Marty Gilman Inc., P.O. Box 97, Gilman, CT 06336: Free information ❖ Blockers and chargers, charging and blocking sleds, kicking cages, and tackling dummies. 800–243–0398; 203–889–7334 (in CT).

Grid Inc., NDL Products, 2313 NW 30th Pl., Pompano Beach, FL 33069: Free information ❖ Protective gear. 800–843–3021; 305–942–4560 (in FL).

Hutch Sports USA, 1835 Airport Exchange Blvd., Erlanger, KY 41018: Free information ❖ Footballs, helmets, and shoulder guards. 800–727–4511; 606–282–9000 (in KY).

Jayfro Corporation, Unified Sports Inc., 976 Hartford Tnpk., P.O. Box 400, Waterford, CT 06385: Free catalog ❖ Goals, training equipment, and field markers. 203–447–3001.

Leisure Marketing Inc., 2204 Morris Ave., Ste. 202, Union, NJ 07083: Free information

❖ Leather, rubber-covered, synthetic, and juvenile footballs. 908–851–9494.

Markwort Sporting Goods, 4300 Forest Park Ave., St. Louis, MO 63108: Catalog $8 with list of retailers ❖ Footballs, face masks, gloves, helmets, and shoulder guards. 314–652–3757.

Dick Martin Sports Inc., 181 E. Union Ave., P.O. Box 7381, East Rutherford, NJ 07073: Free information ❖ Footballs. 800–221–1993; 201–438–5255 (in NJ).

McDavid Sports Medical Products, 5420 W. Roosevelt Rd., Chicago, IL 60650: Free information ❖ Protective gear. 800–237–8254; 312–626–7100 (in IL).

Molten USA Inc., 1095 Spice Island Dr., Sparks, NV 89431: Free information ❖ Leather, rubber-covered, synthetic, and juvenile footballs. 800–666–5836; 702–353–4000 (in NV).

Mueller Sports Medicine Inc., One Quench Dr., Prairie du Sac, WI 53578: Free information ❖ Protective gear. 800–356–9522; 608–643–8530 (in WI).

New South Athletic Company Inc., 301 E. Main, P.O. Box 604, Dallas, NC 28034: Free information ❖ Protective gear. 800–438–9934; 704–922–1557 (in NC).

Olympia Sports, 745 State Cir., Ann Arbor, MI 48106: Free information ❖ Blockers and chargers, charging and blocking sleds, kicking cages, and tackling dummies. 800–521–2832; 313–761–5135 (in MI).

Pennsylvania Sporting Goods, 1360 Industrial Hwy., P.O. Box 451, Southampton, PA 18966: Free information ❖ Protective gear. 800–535–1122.

Rawlings Sporting Goods Company, P.O. Box 22000, St. Louis, MO 63126: Free information ❖ Leather, rubber-covered, synthetic, and juvenile footballs, and protective gear. 314–349–3500.

Reda Sports Express, 44 N. 2nd St., P.O. Box 68, Easton, PA 18044: Free information ❖ Footballs and protective equipment. 800–444–REDA; 215–258–5271 (in PA).

Regent Sports Corporation, 45 Ranick Rd., Hauppage, NY 11788: Free information ❖ Leather, rubber-covered, synthetic, and juvenile footballs. 516–234–2800.

Riddell Inc., 3670 N. Milwaukee Ave., Chicago, IL 60641: Free information ❖ Helmets, kicking tees, protective gear,

footballs, and other equipment. 800–445–7344; 312–794–1994 (in IL).

Royal Textile Mills Inc., P.O. Box 250, Yanceyville, NC 27379: Free information ❖ Protective gear. 800–334–9361; 910–694–4121 (in NC).

Spalding Sports Worldwide, 425 Meadow St., P.O. Box 901, Chicopee, MA 01021: Free information with list of retailers ❖ Leather, rubber-covered, synthetic, and juvenile footballs. 800–225–6601.

Star Specialty Knitting Company Inc., 266 Union Ave., 2nd Floor, Laconia, NH 03246: Free information ❖ Protective gear. 603–528–STAR.

Venus Knitting Mills Inc., 140 Spring St., Murray Hill, NJ 07974: Free information ❖ Clothing for players and coaches and protective gear. 800–955–4200; 908–464–2400 (in NJ).

Voit Sports, 1451 Pittstand-Victor Rd., 100 Willowbrook Office Park, Fairport, NY 14450: Free information ❖ Leather, rubber-covered, synthetic, and juvenile footballs. 800–444–VOIT.

Wilson Sporting Goods, 8700 Bryn Mawr, Chicago, IL 60631: Free information ❖ Clothing for players and coaches and leather, rubber-covered, synthetic, and juvenile footballs. 800–272–6060; 312–714–6400 (in IL).

Wolvering Sports, 745 State Circle, Box 1941, Ann Arbor, MI 48106: Catalog $1 ❖ Baseball, basketball, field hockey, soccer, football, and other athletic and recreation equipment. 313–761–5691.

FOUNTAINS

Moultrie Manufacturing, P.O. Drawer 1179, Moultrie, GA 31776: Catalog $3 ❖ Cast-aluminum tables, chairs, settees, planters, urns, fountains, chaises, and light fixtures. 800–841–8674.

FRAMES

American Frame Corporation, 400 Tomahawk Dr., Maumee, OH 43537: Free information ❖ Metal picture frames. 800–537–0944.

Artemis Wood Products Inc., P.O. Box 766, Jefferson City, TN 37760: Free catalog ❖ Handcrafted hardwood frames. 615–475–5669.

Atlas Art & Stained Glass, P.O. Box 76084, Oklahoma City, OK 73147: Catalog $3 ❖ Kaleidoscopes, frames, lamp bases, and art

and craft, stained glass, jewelry-making, and foil crafting supplies. 405–946–1230.

Colorado Frame Manufacturing, 1230 Blue Spruce Dr., Fort Collins, CO 80524: Free information ❖ Wholesale supplier of frames and framing materials. 303–493–5966.

Contemporary Frame Company, 346 Scott Swamp Rd., P.O. Box 514, Farmington, CT 06032: Free information ❖ Aluminum section frames. 203–677–7787.

Country Frames, Box 284, Rochert, MN 56578: Free information ❖ Country-style frames. 800–253–9993.

Creative House Frames, 1200 N. Palafox St., Pensacola, FL 32501: Free information ❖ Ready-to-assemble wood frame kits. 800–521–6023.

Crown Art Products, 90 Dayton Ave., Passaic, NJ 07055: Free catalog ❖ Metal section frames and framing supplies. 201–777–6010.

Cupid's Bow Frames, 1668 Bishop, Saline, MI 48176: Free information ❖ Antique replica picture frames. 313–429–7894.

DAB Studio, 31 N. Terrace, P.O. Box 96, Maplewood, NJ 07040: Free catalog ❖ Stained glass picture frames. 800–682–6151.

Decor Frame Company, 4307 Metzger Rd., Fort Pierce, FL 34947: Free catalog ❖ Aluminum section frames with hardware and optional springs and hangers. 800–826–7969.

Discount Framesource USA Inc., One Frame Plaza, P.O. Box 4592, Archdale, NC 27263: Free information ❖ Frames. 800–493–7263.

Documounts, 3709 W. 1st Ave., Eugene, OR 97402: Free information ❖ Wood picture frames and bevel-edge mats. 800–942–9191.

Dreamtime Carousel, Rt 25, Box 697, Tyler, TX 75707: Free information ❖ Handpainted ceramic frames. 903–566–3302.

Exposures, 1 Memory Ln., P.O. Box 3615, Oshkosh, WI 54903: Free catalog ❖ Albums and frames. 800–572–5750.

Fletcher-Terry Company, 65 Spring Ln., Farmington, CT 06032: Free information ❖ Easy-to-use picture framing tool that won't tear or dent backing materials or cause frames to split. 800–THE-FTCO; 203–677–7331 (in CT).

Florida Frames Inc., 12011 44th St. North, Clearwater, FL 34622: Free catalog ❖ Solid oak and teak frames. 800–878–3946.

Frame Factory, 1909 W. Diversey Pkwy., Chicago, IL 60614: Free catalog ❖ Frames and framing supplies. 800–621–6570.

Frame Fit Company, P.O. Box 8926, Philadelphia, PA 19135: Free information ❖ Aluminum picture frames and hangers. 800–523–3693.

Frames by Mail, 11551 Adie Rd., St. Louis, MO 63043: Free catalog ❖ Wood and metal picture frames.

Franken Frames, 609 W. Walnut, Johnson City, TN 37604: Free catalog ❖ Frames and moldings. 800–322–5899.

Gold Leaf Studios, P.O. Box 50156, Washington, DC 20004: Free brochure with long SASE ❖ Frames. 202–638–4660.

Graphik Dimensions Ltd., 2103 Brentwood St., High Point, NC 27263: Free information ❖ Frames and framing supplies. 800–221–0262.

David Howell & Company, 405 Adams St., Bedford Hills, NY 10507: Free catalog ❖ Frames inspired by museum collections. 914–666–4080.

M.J. Galleries, 1250 E. Wayzata Blvd., Wayzata, MN 55391: Brochure $1 ❖ Handcrafted museum reproduction frames.

The Mettle Company, P.O. Box 525, Fanwood, NJ 07023: Free information ❖ Aluminum frames. 800–621–1329.

Old Tyme Picture Frames, P.O. Box 2308, Temecula, CA 92593: Catalog $1 ❖ Reproduction antique frames. 714–699–9622.

Plaid Enterprises, P.O. Box 7600, Norcross, GA 30091: Free information ❖ Frame-making supplies and accessories. 404–923–8200.

Pootatuck, P.O. Box 24, Windsor, VT 05089: Free information ❖ Framing accessories. 802–674–5984.

Press-On-Products, 1020 S. Westgate, Addison, IL 60101: Free catalog ❖ Framing accessories and mat boards. 800–323–1745.

Putnum Distributors, P.O. Box 477, Westfield, NJ 07091: Free catalog ❖ Frames. 800–631–7330; 908–232–9200 (in NJ).

S & W Framing Supplies Inc., 120 Broadway, P.O. Box 340, Garden City Park, NY 11040: Free catalog ❖ Framing supplies and tools. 800–645–3399; 516–746–1000 (in NY).

Daniel Smith Art Supplies, 4150 1st Ave. South, Seattle, WA 98134: Free catalog ❖ Framing supplies. 800–426–6740.

Stu-Art Supplies, 2045 Grand Ave., Baldwin, NY 11510: Free catalog ❖ Mats, plastic and glass, pre-assembled frames, aluminum and wood frame-making components, shrink wrap, plastic picture saver panels, and other framing supplies. 516–546–5151.

Taylor Frame Company, 677 Anita St., Ste. D-6, Chula Vista, CA 91911: Free catalog ❖ Frames and framing supplies. 800–423–2620.

Tennessee Moulding & Frame Company, 1188 Antioch, Nashville, TN 37211: Catalog $5 ❖ Mats, framing equipment, and tools, and metal, wood, laminates, and formica frames. 800–821–5483.

Wayne Frame Products Inc., 5832 Lakeside Ave., Toledo, OH 43611: Free information ❖ Panorama-style frames. 419–729–4006.

Wholesale Frame Service-USA, P.O. Box 11047, High Point, NC 27265: Free catalog ❖ Wood frames in colorful rustics, traditional wood tones, weathered driftwood, and gold and silver. 800–522–3726.

Wild West Supply, P.O. Box 5678, Borgel, TX 79008: Free price list ❖ Canvasses, art supplies, and picture frames. 806–274–4455.

FUND-RAISING

Ace Pecan Company, 485 Crossroads Pkwy., Bolingbrook, IL 60440: Free catalog ❖ Fund-raising programs selling nuts and nut specialties. 800–323–9754.

Acme Premium Supply Corporation, 4100 Forest Park, St. Louis, MO 63108: Free catalog ❖ Specialty merchandise for fund-raising, carnivals, and premium programs, and bingo. 800–325–7888.

America's Best, P.O. Box 91717, Mobile, AL 36691: Free information ❖ Fund-raising programs. 800–633–6750.

Classic American Fund Raisers, Cookbook Plan, 11184 Antioch, Ste. 415, Overland Park, KS 66210: Free information with long SASE ❖ Fund-raising cookbook plan. 800–821–5745.

Cookbook Publishers Inc., P.O. Box 15920, Lenexa, KS 66285: Free information ❖ Fund-raising programs with personalized cookbooks. 800–227–7282.

Cookbooks by Morris Press, P.O. Box 1681, Kearney, NE 68848: Free information ❖

Fund-raising cookbook plan. 800–445–6621; 308–236–7888 (in NE).

Foreign Candy Company Inc., 451 Black Forest Rd., Hull, IA 51239: Free catalog ❖ Fund-raising programs. 712–439–1496.

Fundcraft, P.O. Box 340, Collierville, TN 38017: Free information ❖ Fund-raising program with personalized cookbooks. 800–351–7822.

Hale Indian River Groves, Indian River Plaza, P.O. Box 217, Wabasso, FL 32970: Free catalog ❖ Fund-raising program with oranges and grapefruit. 800–289–4253.

Krum's Chocolatier, 4 Dexter Plaza, Pearl River, NY 10965: Free catalog ❖ Fund-raising program with kosher chocolates. 800–ME-CANDY.

Mascot Pecan Company, P.O. Box 765, Glennville, GA 30427: Free information ❖ Fund-raising program with pecans and pecan candy. 800–841–3985; 912–654–2195 (in GA).

Nestle-Beich, P.O. Box 2914, Bloomington, IN 61702: Free information ❖ Fund-raising program with boxed chocolates and other candy. 800–431–1248.

Oriental Trading Company Inc., P.O. Box 2308, Omaha, NE 68103: Free catalog ❖ Fund raising merchandise, toys, gifts, novelties, carnival supplies, and holiday and seasonal items. 800–228–0475.

Profit Potentials, 451 Black Forest Rd., Hull, IA 51239: Free catalog ❖ Fund-raising programs. 800–543–5480.

Revere Company, N. South Rd., Scranton, PA 18504: Free catalog ❖ Fund-raising program with household items. 800–876–9967.

Spirit of America Fund Raisers, P.O. Box 621, Montgomery, AL 36101: Sample $2 ❖ Fund-raising program featuring daily planners with memo pads. 800–628–3671.

Treasure Chest Fund Raising, Division Enesco Corporation, P.O. Box 295, Elk Grove Village, IL 60009: Free catalog ❖ Fund-raising programs. 800–438–3203.

U.S. Pen Fund Raising Company, P.O. Box 1027, Montgomery, AL 36101: Free information ❖ Fund-raising program for schools, churches, and other organizations selling home, office, and school products. 800–633–8738.

Walter's Cookbooks, 215 5th Ave. SE, Waseca, MN 56093: Free information ❖

Fund-raising program with cookbooks. 800–447–3274.

FURNACES, HEATING SYSTEMS & CONTROLS

Carrier Corporation, P.O. Box 4808, Syracuse, NY 13221: Free information ❖ Combination gas and electric heating and cooling system, gas and electric furnaces, heat pumps, and air conditioners. 800–CARRIER.

Central Boiler Inc., Greenbrush, MN 56726: Free brochure ❖ Outdoor wood furnaces. 800–210–6207; 218–782–2575 (in MN).

Central Environmental Systems, York International Corporation, P.O. Box 1592, York, PA 17405: Free information ❖ Gas furnaces. 717–771–7890.

Charmaster Products Inc., 2307 Hwy. 2 West, Grand Rapids, MN 55744: Free brochure ❖ Fireplaces and wood-burning, wood-gas, and wood-oil furnaces and conversion units. 800–542–6360.

Friedrich Air Conditioning & Refrigeration Company, P.O. Box 1540, San Antonio, TX 78295: Free brochure ❖ Room air conditioners, air cleaners, heat pumps, and electric heaters. 512–225–2000.

G.E. Appliances, General Electric Company, Appliance Park, Louisville, KY 40225: Free information ❖ Air conditioners and heat pumps. 800–626–2000.

Heatway Radiant Floors & Snowmelting, 3131 W. Chestnut Expwy., Springfield, MO 65802: Free information ❖ Heating systems for installation under frame or slab floors. 800–255–1996.

Hunter Fan Company, 2500 Fisco Ave., Memphis, TN 38114: Catalog $1 ❖ Electronically programmable thermostats, ceiling fans, light fixtures, air conditioners, and dehumidifiers. 901–745–9222.

Intertherm Inc., P.O. Box 46911, St. Louis, MO 63146: Free brochure ❖ Portable heaters. 800–422–4328.

Jameson Home Products, 2820 Thatcher Rd., Downers Grove, IL 60515: Free information ❖ Programmable, electronic thermostats. 708–963–2850.

Light Associates, Ridge Rd. & Park Ave., Perkasie, PA 18944: Free information ❖ Under-the-floor and driveway radiant heating equipment. 215–453–9228.

Northwest Energy, 7500 212th SW, Edmonds, WA 98026: Free information ❖

Under-the-floor and driveway radiant heating equipment. 206–778–7277.

Orbit Manufacturing Company, 1507 Park Ave., Perkasie, PA 18944: Free information ❖ Residential electric heating equipment. 215–257–0727.

Panelectric, 1100 Winchester Rd., Irvine, KY 40336: Free information ❖ In-ceiling radiant heating systems. 800–228–9022.

Radiant Technology Inc., 11 Farber, Dr., Bellport, NY 11713: Free information ❖ Hot water baseboard heating equipment. 516–286–0900.

Radiantec, Box 1111, Lyndonville, VT 05851: Free information ❖ Under-the-floor heating systems. 800–451–7593; 802–626–8045 (in VT).

Tarm USA, One Branch St., Medford, NJ 08055: Free information ❖ Wood-burning furnace with automatic oil or gas back-up. 800–782–9927.

Taylor Manufacturing, P.O. Box 518, Elizabethtown, NC 28337: Free information ❖ Outdoor wood heating systems. 800–545–2293.

York International Corporation, P.O. Box 1592, York, PA 17405: Free information ❖ Gas furnaces. 717–771–7890.

FURNITURE

Beds

American Starbuck, P.O. Box 15376, Lenexa, KS 66215: Free catalog ❖ Pencil post beds. 913–894–1567.

Amish Country Collection, Sunset Valley Rd., RD 5, New Castle, PA 16105: Catalog $5 (refundable) ❖ Early American rustic bedroom furniture. 412–458–4811.

Bartley Collection Ltd., 29060 Airpark Dr., Easton, MD 21601: Free catalog ❖ Kits for reproduction 18th-century beds. 410–820–7722.

The Bed Factory, P.O. Box 791, Westerville, OH 43081: Catalog $5 ❖ Heirloom wood, iron, and brass beds. 419–468–3861.

Bedlam Brass, 530 River Dr., Garfield, NJ 07026: Free catalog ❖ Brass beds and mirrors, tables, coat racks, and quilt and blanket racks. 201–546–0100.

Bedpost Inc., 32 S. High St., East Bangor, PA 18013: Catalog $2 ❖ Brass beds and furnishings. 215–588–3824.

Brass Bed Factory, P.O. Box 335, Galion, OH 44833: Catalog $2 ❖ Brass and white iron beds and daybeds. 419–468–3861.

Brass Bed Shoppe, 12421 Cedar Rd., Cleveland, OH 44106: Catalog $1 ❖ Brass beds. 216–229–4900.

Brass Beds Direct, 4866 W. Jefferson Blvd., Los Angeles, CA 90016: Free catalog ❖ Brass beds. 800–727–6865.

Carpenter's Brothers Furniture, Box 425, Sunderland, MA 01375: Free information ❖ Desks, dressers, bookcases, other furniture, and bunk, twin, full, and queen-size beds. 800–777–BUNK.

Cohasset Colonials, 10 Churchill Rd., Hingham, MA 02043: Catalog $3 ❖ Kits for Early American, Shaker, Queen Anne, Chippendale beds, and other furniture. 800–288–2389.

Country Bed Shop, Richardson Rd., RR 1, Box 65, Ashby, MA 01431: Catalog $4 ❖ Handcrafted reproductions of 17th- and 18th-century American beds, chairs, tables, and other furniture. 508–386–7550.

Hollingsworth Furniture, P.O. Box 2592, Wilmington, NC 28402: Free brochure ❖ Handpainted, stained, or unfinished American, country-style reproduction pencil post and sleigh beds and other furniture. 910–251–0280.

Leonard's Reproductions & Antiques, 600 Taunton Creek, Seekonk, MA 02771: Catalog $4 ❖ Original and reproduction antique beds. 508–336–8585.

Osborne Wood Products, Rt. 3, Box 551, Toccoa, GA 30577: Free information ❖ Easy-to-assemble pencil post beds. 800–849–8876.

Rainbow Woodworks, P.O. Box 308, Henderson, MN 56044: Brochure $3 ❖ Solid oak bedroom and other furniture. 612–248–9670.

Charles P. Rogers Beds, 899 1st Ave., New York, NY 10022: Catalog $1 ❖ Original 19th- and 20th-century solid brass and iron beds. 800–272–7726; 212–935–6900 (in NY).

Room & Board, 4800 Olson Memorial Hwy., Minneapolis, MN 55422: Free information ❖ Handcrafted steel beds and tables. 800–486–6554.

Sico Incorporated, Room Makers Division, 7525 Cahill Rd., P.O. Box 1169, Minneapolis, MN 55440: Free information ❖ Wallbeds with mattresses and box springs. 800–328–6138.

Thomasville Furniture, P.O. Box 339, Thomasville, NC 27360: Catalog $3.50 ❖ Early American-style beds and other furniture. 800–225–0265.

A Touch of Brass, 9339 Baltimore National Pike, Ellicott City, MD 21042: Catalog $3 ❖ Reproduction iron and solid brass beds. 800–BRASS-34.

Lisa Victoria Brass Beds, 17106 S. Crater Rd., Petersburg, VA 23805: Catalog $4 ❖ Brass beds. 804–862–1491.

Beds, Adjustable

American Health Manufacturing, P.O. Box 16287, Baltimore, MD 21210: Free catalog ❖ Adjustable beds with electric hand controls. 800–232–3044.

Craftmatic Beds, 2500 Interplex Dr., Trevose, PA 19047: Free information ❖ Adjustable beds with electric hand controls. 800–677–8200.

Electropedic Products, 907 Hollywood Way, Burbank, CA 91505: Free brochure ❖ Adjustable beds with electric hand controls. 800–662–4548.

Ultimate Home Care Company, 3250 E. 19th St., Long Beach, CA 90804: Free information ❖ Regular and adjustable beds for unassisted transfers from wheel chairs.

Wonderbed Manufacturing Company, P.O. Box 1551, Roswell, GA 30077: Free price list ❖ Adjustable beds with electric hand controls. 800–543–0600.

Children's Furniture

A & B Furniture, 11710 Baltimore Ave., Beltsville, MD 20705: Free information ❖ Cribs, chests, and dressers. 301–210–4994.

A Baby Carriage, 5617 W. Belmont, Chicago, IL 60634: Free catalog ❖ Strollers for twins and triplets, stroller parts, and cribs. 800–228–8946; 312–237–4300 (in IL).

Boston & Winthrop, 2 E. 93rd St., New York, NY 10128: Free catalog ❖ Handpainted furniture. 212–410–6388/617–593–8248.

H.U.D.D.L.E. Furniture for Kids, 11159 Santa Monica Blvd., Los Angeles, CA 90025: Free catalog ❖ Adjustable, convertible, expandable, transformable, and climbable furniture. 213–479–4769.

Little Colorado Inc., 15866 W. 7th Ave., Golden, CO 80401: Catalog $2 ❖ Handmade solid wood furniture. 303–278–2451.

Woodfields, 5800 Merle Hay Rd., P.O. Box 466, Johnston, IA 50131: Brochure $1 ❖ Country-style rocking chairs for children. 515–270–6825.

Furniture Kits

Adams Wood Products Inc., 974 Forest Dr., Morristown, TN 37814: Free catalog ❖ Ready-to-assemble furniture. 615–587–2942.

Andover Wood Products, P.O. Box 38, Andover, ME 04216: Free information ❖ Ready-to-assemble American Heritage Windsor chairs. 207–392–2101.

Bartley Collection Ltd., 29060 Airpark Dr., Easton, MD 21601: Free catalog ❖ Antique reproduction furniture kits. 410–820–7722.

Cohasset Colonials, 10 Churchill Rd., Hingham, MA 02043: Catalog $3 ❖ Kits for Early American, Shaker, Queen Anne, Chippendale beds, and other furniture. 800–288–2389.

Cypress Street Center, 350 Cypress St., Fort Bragg, CA 95437: Free catalog ❖ Easy-to-assemble outdoor chairs with matching love seats, foot rests, side carts, and tables. 800–222–0343.

Emperor Clock Company, Emperor Industrial Park, P.O. Box 1089, Fairhope, AL 36533: Catalog $1 ❖ Build-it-yourself grandfather clocks and furniture kits. 800–542–0011; 205–928–2316 (in AL).

F. Hayden Designs Inc., 394 Moyer Rd., Souderton, PA 18964: Brochure $1 with long SASE ❖ Shaker furniture kits. 215–721–4983.

Pacific Wood Products, 5150 Edison Ave., Chino, CA 91710: Catalog $1 ❖ Macrame furniture kits. 800–421–2781; 800–262–1638 (in CA).

Shaker Workshops, P.O. Box 1028, Concord, MA 01742: Catalog $1 ❖ Shaker furniture in kits or assembled, needlecrafts, dolls, and dollhouse furniture. 617–646–8985.

Wood Classics, Osprey Ln., Gardner, NY 12525: Catalog $2 ❖ Teak and mahogany outdoor furniture in kits or assembled. 914–255–5599.

Yield House, P.O. Box 2525, Conway, NH 03818: Free catalog ❖ Pre-sanded furniture kits. 800–258–4720.

Home Furnishings

Stephen Adams, Furnituremaker, P.O. Box 130, Rt. 160, Denmark, ME 04022: Catalog $5 ❖ Period furniture reproductions. 207–452–2378.

Adriance Furniture Makers, 288 Gulf Rd., South Dartmouth, MA 02748: Catalog $3 ❖ Classic New England designed furniture. 508–993–4800.

American Furniture Galleries, P.O. Box 60, Montgomery, AL 36101: Brochure $1 ❖ Handcrafted reproduction Victorian furniture. 800–547–5240.

American Log Furniture Designs, 2709 N. Woodward Ave., Royal Oak, MI 48073: Free information ❖ Bedroom, family room, and dining room contemporary log furniture. 800–435–LOGS.

Amish Country Collection, RD 5, Sunset Valley Rd., New Castle, PA 16105: Catalog $5 (refundable) ❖ Amish-style oak and hickory twig furniture, rugs, quilts, and wall hangings. 412–458–4811.

Antiquaria, 60 Dartmouth St., Springfield, MA 01109: Catalog $4 ❖ Victorian-style furniture. 413–781–6927.

Antiquarian Traders, 4851 S. Alameda St., Los Angeles, CA 90058: Catalog $15 ❖ American Renaissance, revival Victorian, American oak, country French, English-style, and other furniture. 213–687–4000.

Antiquity, W329 S6975 Oak Knoll, Mukwonago, WI 53149: Catalog $5 ❖ Handcrafted reproduction 18th-century furniture. 414–392–9566.

Atlanta Furniture Craftsmen, 1780 Hembree Rd., Alpharetta, GA 30201: Free brochure ❖ Handcrafted bedroom sets, dining room tables, and other furniture. 404–475–8300.

Backwoods Furnishings, Box 161, Indian Lake, NY 12842: Free brochure ❖ Rustic-style tables and chairs, rocking chairs, four-poster beds, and desks. 518–251–3327.

Bargain John's Antiques, 700 S. Washington, Lexington, NE 68850: Free information ❖ Antique Victorian furniture, from 1840 to 1900. 303–324–4576.

Barnes & Barnes Fine Furniture, 190 Commerce Ave., Southern Pines, NC 28387: Free brochure ❖ Home furnishings. 800–334–8174.

C.H. Becksvoort, Box 12, New Gloucester, ME 04260: Catalog $5 ❖ Handmade furniture in classic, contemporary, and Shaker designs. 207–926–4608.

Bentwood Building, 21 Addison Square, Kalispell, MT 59901: Catalog $4 ❖ Log spiral stairways and furniture.

Best Furniture Distributors Inc., 16 W. Main, P.O. Box 489, Thomasville, NC 27360: Free information ❖ Home furnishings. 800–334–8000.

Blackwelder's, RR 18–8, Statesville, NC 28677: Free information with long SASE ❖ Home furnishings. 800–438–0201.

Blake Industries, P.O. Box 155, Abington, MA 02351: Free information ❖ Outdoor and indoor teak furniture, ornamental cast-iron pole lights, and fixtures. 617–337–8772.

Bombay Company, P.O. Box 161009, Fort Worth, TX 76161: Free catalog ❖ Antique furniture reproductions. 800–829–7789.

Bonita Furniture Galleries, P.O. Box 9143, Hickory, NC 28603: Free information with long SASE ❖ Home furnishings. 704–324–1992.

Brentwood Manor Furnishings, 316 Virginia Ave., Clarksville, VA 23927: Free brochure ❖ Home furnishings, clocks, draperies, and mirrors. 800–225–6105.

Teri M. Browning, The Wentworth Collection, P.O. Box 131, Wentworth, NH 03282: Catalog $6 ❖ Furniture reproductions. 603–764–9395.

Curtis Buchanan, Windsor Chairmaker, 208 E. Main St., Jonesborough, TN 37659: Brochure $2 with long SASE ❖ Windsor chairs. 615–753–5160.

Michael Camp, Cabinetmaker, 495 Amelia, Plymouth, MI 48170: Catalog $3 ❖ Reproduction 18th- and 19th-century furniture. 313–459–1190.

Candlertown Chairworks, P.O. Box 1630, Candler, NC 28715: Catalog $2 ❖ Handbuilt country-style adult and children's chairs, benches, bar stools, and other furniture. 704–667–4844.

Carpenter's Brothers Furniture, Box 425, Sunderland, MA 01375: Free information ❖ Desks, dressers, bookcases, other furniture, and bunk, twin, full, and queen-size beds. 800–777–BUNK.

CCSI Furniture, 13509 Method St., Dallas, TX 75243: Free information with long SASE ❖ Deacon's benches and other rustic country-style furniture. 214–231–7178.

Cherry Hill Furniture, Box 7405, Furnitureland Station, High Point, NC 27264: Information $5 ❖ Home furnishings. 800–888–0933.

Cherry Pond Designs, P.O. Box 6, Jefferson, NH 03583: Catalog $10 ❖ Shaker furniture. 800–643–7384; 603–586–7795 (in NH).

Classic Wicker, 8532 Melrose Ave., Los Angeles, CA 90069: Catalog $6 ❖ Vintage wicker and reproduction Victorian- style furniture. 213–659–1121.

Clear Lake Furniture, 250 Whipple Rd., Tewksbury, MA 01876: Catalog $5 ❖ Handcrafted furniture.

Coffey Furniture Galleries, Box 141, Granite Falls, NC 28630: Free information ❖ Home furnishings. 704–396–2900.

Cohasset Colonials, 10 Churchill Rd., Hingham, MA 02043: Catalog $3 ❖ Reproduction furniture in kits or assembled, fabrics, paints and stains, brass and pewter items, and light fixtures. 800–288–2389.

Cole's Appliance & Furniture Company, 4026 Lincoln Ave., Chicago, IL 60618: Free information with long SASE ❖ Home furnishings, audio and video equipment, TVs, and kitchen appliances. 312–525–1797.

Colonial Williamsburg, 201 5th Ave., Williamsburg, VA 23187: Catalog $14.65 ❖ Williamsburg-style furniture reproductions. 800–446–9240.

Cornucopia, P.O. Box 44, Harvard, MA 01451: Catalog $2 ❖ Early American and primitive style rocking and Windsor chairs, settees, tables, and hutches. 508–772–0023.

Countree Living, 18002 County Line Rd., Elkhart Lake, IN 53020: Catalog $9.95 ❖ Handcrafted log furniture. 414–894–7985.

Country Bed Shop, Richardson Rd., RR 1, Box 65, Ashby, MA 01431: Catalog $4 ❖ Handcrafted reproductions of 17th- and 18th-century American beds, chairs, and tables. 508–386–7550.

Country Store Furniture, P.O. Box 17696, Whitefish Bay, WI 53217: Catalog $2 ❖ Willow furniture. 414–263–1919.

Country Workshop, 95 Rome St., Newark, NJ 07105: Catalog $1 ❖ Finished and ready-to-finish furniture. 800–526–8001; 201–589–3407 (in NJ).

Gerald Curry, Cabinetmaker, Pound Hill Rd., Union, ME 04862: Free brochure ❖ Reproduction 18th-century furniture. 207–785–4633.

Custom Country Wood Products, Rt. 2, Box 108, Greenville, TX 75402: Free information ❖ Country-style furniture with a whitewash stain or unfinished. 903–455–0542.

D.H.M. Cabinetmakers Inc., Rt. 4, Box 173, Floyd, VA 24091: Catalog $4 ❖ Handmade furniture in the style of 1750 to 1825. 703–745–3825.

Frederick Dackloe & Bros. Inc., P.O. Box 427, Portland, PA 18351: Catalog $6 ❖ Handcrafted Windsor chairs, rockers, benches, and bar stools. 717–897–6172.

Davis Cabinet Company, P.O. Box 60444, Nashville, TN 37206: Free information with long SASE ❖ Bedroom and other custom built furniture. 800–578–5426.

Decorum, 235 Commercial St., Portland, ME 04101: Free information ❖ Antique lighting and period lamps, roll-top and other desks, file cabinets, recycled cabinet and door hardware, and plumbing and bathroom fixtures. 207–775–3346.

The Deep River Trading Company, 2436 Willard Rd., High Point, NC 27265: Free information ❖ 18th-century reproductions. 910–885–2436.

Designer Secrets, P.O. Box 529, Fremont, NE 68025: Catalog $2 (refundable) ❖ Home furnishings, wall coverings, fabrics, bedspreads, and window treatments. 800–955–2559.

Dubrow Antiques, P.O. Box 128, Bayside, NY 11361: Free information ❖ American-style 19th-century furniture. 718–767–9758.

Charles Durfee Cabinetmaker, RD 1, Box 1132, Woolwich, ME 04579: Brochure $1 ❖ Shaker- and Early American-style solid wood furniture. 207–442–7049.

E.P. Woodworks, Lance & Vicki Munn, P.O. Box 271, Bloomfield, IN 47424: Free information with long SASE ❖ Handcrafted hardwood furniture in red oak, black walnut, and wild cherry. 812–384–4806.

Edgar B Furniture, Box 849, Clemmons, NC 27012: Catalog $15 (refundable) ❖ Home furnishings. 800–255–6589; 910–766–7321 (in NC).

Flynt & Son Hardwoods, 11335 W. Reed Valley Rd., Fayetteville, AR 72703: Free catalog ❖ Butcher block tables. 501–361–2983.

Frontier Furniture, 815 Montana Hwy. 82, Somers, MT 59932: Catalog $4 ❖ Handcrafted log furniture. 406–857–3525.

Functional Art, P.O. Box 80744, Billings, MT 59108: Brochure $2 ❖ Western-style lamps and tables. 406–656–6901.

The Furniture Barn, 1190 Hwy. 74 Bypass, Spindale, NC 28160: Free brochure ❖ Home furnishings. 704–287–7106.

Furniture Connection of Carolina, P.O. Box 21497, Hilton Head, SC 29925: Free information ❖ Home furnishings. 800–869–5664.

The Furniture Patch of Calabash Inc., P.O. Box 4970, Calabash, NC 28467: Free brochure ❖ Home furnishings. 910–579–2001.

The Furniture Showcase, 1190 Hwy. 74 Bypass, Spindale, NC 28160: Free brochure with long SASE ❖ Home furnishings. 919–638–2121.

Furnitureland South Inc., P.O. Box 790, High Point, NC 27261: Free brochure ❖ Home furnishings. 919–841–4328.

Gardner's Farm & Wood Products, Box 1193, Eagle Rock, MO 65641: Free information ❖ Country-style rockers, tables, swings, and other furniture. 417–271–3999.

Genada Imports, P.O. Box 204, Teaneck, NJ 07666: Catalog $1 ❖ Modern Danish furniture. 201–790–7522.

Great American Log Furniture, Box 3360, Ketchum, ID 83340: Catalog $4 ❖ Handcrafted log furniture. 800–624–5779.

Great Meadows Joinery, P.O. Box 392, Wayland, MA 01778: Catalog $4 ❖ Handmade reproduction Shaker-style furniture. 508–358–4370.

Habersham Plantation, P.O. Box 1209, Toccoa, GA 30577: Catalog $12 ❖ Reproduction 17th- and 18th-century country and contemporary furniture. 800–241–0716.

Harden Furniture, McConnellsville, NY 13401: Catalog $2 ❖ Handcrafted chairs.

Harvest House Furniture, P.O. Box 1440, Denton, NC 27239: Free information: Free information with long SASE ❖ Home furnishings. 704–869–5181.

Heirloom Reproductions, 1834 W. 5th St., Montgomery, AL 36106: Free catalog ❖ Victorian and French period furniture reproductions. 800–288–1513.

Hickory Furniture Mart, 2220 Highway 70E, Hickory, NC 28602: Free information ❖ Traditional and contemporary furniture. 704–324–1776.

Hollingsworth Furniture, P.O. Box 2592, Wilmington, NC 28402: Free brochure ❖ American country furniture reproductions. 910–251–0280.

Holton Furniture Company, P.O. Box 280, Thomasville, NC 27360: Free information ❖ Home furnishings. 800–334–3183; 919–472–0400 (in NC).

Homeway Furniture Company, P.O. Box 1548, Mt. Airy, NC 27030: Free information ❖ Home furnishings. 800–334–9094; 910–786–6151 (in NC).

Martha M. House, 1022 S. Decatur St., Montgomery, AL 36104: Catalog $3 ❖ Victorian sofas, chairs, tables, dining room, and bedroom furniture. 205–264–3558.

House Dressing Furniture, 2212 Battleground, Greensboro, NC 27408: Free information ❖ Home furnishings. 800–322–5850.

Hudson's Discount Furniture, P.O. Box 2547, Hickory, NC 28603: Free information ❖ Home furnishings. 704–322–5717.

Hunt Galleries Inc., P.O. Box 2324, Hickory, NC 28603: Catalog $5 ❖ Sofas, upholstered chairs, ottomans, benches, lounges, headboards, and other furniture. 800–248–3876.

IKEA Inc., Plymouth Commons, Plymouth Meeting, PA 19462: Catalog $3 ❖ Swedish designed furniture, flooring, wallpaper, bed linens, and tablewares. 215–834–0150.

Ian Ingersoll, Cabinetmakers, Main St., West Cornwall, CT 06796: Brochure $3 ❖ Reproduction Shaker furniture and chairs. 800–237–4926.

Interior Furnishings Ltd., Box 1644, Hickory, NC 28603: Free brochure ❖ Home furnishings. 704–328–5683.

Irion Company Furniture Makers, 1 S. Bridge St., Christiana, PA 17509: Free brochure ❖ Handmade 18th-century furniture reproductions. 215–593–2153.

Jennifer's Trunk Antiques & General Store, 201 N. Riverside, Dr., St. Clair, MI 48079: Free brochure ❖ Victorian-style antique furniture, books, jewelry, lamps and shades, and other gifts. 810–329–2032.

John-Michael Furniture, 2113 Hickory Blvd., Hudson, NC 28638: Free information ❖ Home furnishings. 800–669–3801; 704–728–2944 (in NC).

Jones' Oak Furniture, P.O. Box 400, Talbott, TN 37877: Catalog $3 ❖ Solid oak and cherry, country-style coffee and end tables. 800–752–5543; 615–581–6031 (in TN).

Kestrel Manufacturing, P.O. Box 12, Saint Peters, PA 19470: Information $2 ❖ Knock-down and ready-to-hang folding screens and interior and exterior shutters. 610–469–6444.

Klein Design Inc., 99 Sadler St., Gloucester, MA 01930: Free brochure ❖ Rockers, chairs, love-seats, sofas, and side tables. 800–451–7247.

Knight Galleries, P.O. Box 1254, Lenoir, NC 28645: Free information ❖ Home furnishings. 800–334–4721.

Lanier Furniture Company, P.O. Box 3576, Wilmington, NC 28406: Free information ❖ Handcrafted reproduction Shaker furniture. 800–453–1362.

Leather Interiors, Box 9305, Hickory, NC 28603: Free information ❖ Traditional and contemporary leather furniture. 800–627–4526.

Lenoir Furniture Market Inc., 2034 Hickory Blvd., Lenoir, NC 28645: Free information with long SASE ❖ Indoor and outdoor furniture, beds, and bedding. 704–728–2946.

Levenger, P.O. Box 1256, Delray Beach, FL 33447: Free catalog ❖ Books, furniture, pens, briefcases, and other gifts for serious readers. 800–545–0242.

Liberty Hall, P.O. Box 236, 104 Fremont St., Burgaw, NC 28425: Catalog $3 (refundable) ❖ Armoires and entertainment centers. 800–255–9704.

Loftin-Black Furniture Company, 111 Sedgehill Dr., Thomasville, NC 27360: Free catalog ❖ Home furnishings. 800–334–7398; 910–472–6117 (in NC).

Mack & Rodel Cabinet Makers, Leighton Rd., RR 1, Box 88, Pownal, ME 04069: Catalog $4 ❖ Home furnishings. 207–688–4483.

Daniel Mack Rustic Furnishings, 14 Welling Ave., Warwick, NY 10990: Free information ❖ Furniture from branches, saplings, and logs.

Magnolia Hall, 725 Andover, Atlanta, GA 30327: Catalog $3 ❖ Carved furniture. 404–237–9725.

Mallory's Furniture, P.O. Box 1150, Jacksonville, NC 28546: Free brochure ❖ Home furnishings. 919–353–1828.

Mark Sales Company, 609 E. 81st St., Brooklyn, NY 11236: Catalog $2 ❖ Ready-to-paint or stain hand-carved country French, Italian, and French Provincial chairs. 718–763–2591.

Emphraim Marsh Furniture Catalog, P.O. Box 266, Concord, NH 28026: Catalog $5 ❖ Reproduction 18th-century cherry and mahogany furniture. 800–992–8322.

Maynard House Antiques, 11 Maynard St., Westborough, MA 01581: Brochure $2 ❖ Handcrafted American country sofas and wing chairs, from the 1780s to 1820s. 508–366–2073.

MidAmerica Furniture, P.O. Box 112, Hamburg, AR 71646: Free brochure ❖ Home furnishings. 800–259–7897.

Miya Shoji & Interiors Inc., 109 W. 17th St., New York, NY 10011: Free brochure ❖ Japanese Shoji screens. 212–243–6774.

Thos. Moser Cabinetmakers, 72 Wright's Landing, Auburn, ME 04211: Catalog $10 ❖ Handcrafted furniture for homes and offices. 800–862–1973.

Moultrie Manufacturing, P.O. Drawer 1179, Moultrie, GA 31776: Catalog $3 ❖ Southern-style furniture reproductions for homes and gardens. 800–841–8674.

Murrow Furniture Galleries, P.O. Box 4337, Wilmington, NC 28406: Free brochure ❖ Home furnishings. 910–799–4010.

Nite Furniture Company, 611 S. Green St., P.O. Box 249, Morgantown, NC 28655: Free brochure ❖ Home furnishings. 704–437–1491.

North Carolina Discount Furniture, 3302 Clarendon Blvd., Hwy. 17 South, New Bern, NC 28652: Catalog $7.50 ❖ Home furnishings. 919–638–2121.

North Carolina Furniture Sales, P.O. Box 2802, Hickory, NC 28603: Free brochure ❖ Home furnishings. 800–248–6237.

North Woods Chair Shop, 237 Old Tilton Rd., Canterbury, NH 03224: Catalog $3 ❖ Handcrafted Shaker furniture. 603–783–4595.

Northwestern Exposure Furniture, 39027 Shelburn Dr., Scio, OR 97374: Catalog $3 ❖

Stick furniture. 800–448–3434; 503–394–2463 (in OR).

Old Wagon Factory, P.O. Box 1427, Clarksville, VA 23927: Catalog $2 ❖ Chippendale furniture, Victorian railings and brackets, and Victorian and Chippendale storm screen doors. 804–374–5787.

Robert A. Oluzen, 35 S. Platt Rd., Milan, MI 48160: Catalog $2 ❖ Windsor chairs.

Orleans Carpenters, P.O. Box 217, Orleans, MA 02653: Catalog $3 ❖ Shaker and colonial furniture reproductions. 508–255–2646.

Out-Of-The-West Furniture, 1000 W. Armitage, Chicago, IL 60614: Brochure $3 ❖ Western-style furniture. 312–404–9378.

Parkway Furniture Galleries, Hwy. 105 South, Box 2450, Boone, NC 28607: Free information ❖ Home furnishings. 704–264–3993.

Plexi-Craft Quality Products, 514 W. 24th St., New York, NY 10011: Catalog $2 ❖ Lucite and Plexiglas furniture. 212–924–3244.

Priba Furniture Sales & Interiors, 210 Stage Coach Trail, Greensboro, NC 27409: Free information ❖ Home furnishings. 910–855–9034.

Rhoney Furniture, 2401 Hwy. 70 SW, Hickory, NC 28602: Free information ❖ Traditional and contemporary furniture. 704–328–2034.

Dana Robes Wood Craftsmen, Lower Shaker Village, P.O. Box 707, Enfield, NH 03748: Catalog $5 ❖ Shaker reproduction furniture. 800–722–5036.

The Rocker Shop of Marietta, 1421 White Circle NW, P.O. Box 12, Marietta, GA 30061: Free information ❖ Handmade cane rocking chairs. 800–531–3635; 404–427–2618 (in GA).

Mario Rodriguez Cabinetmaker, 1 E. Ridge Rd., Warwick, NY 10990: Catalog $3.50 ❖ Handcrafted reproduction 18th-century furniture. 914–986–6636.

William James Roth, P.O. Box 355, Yarmouthport, MA 02675: Catalog $4 ❖ Handcrafted period furniture reproductions. 508–362–9235.

St. Charles Furniture, 5828 High Point Rd., Greensboro, NC 27407: Free information ❖ Home furnishings. 800–545–3287.

Shaker Workshops, P.O. Box 1028, Concord, MA 01742: Catalog $1 ❖ Shaker

furniture in kits or assembled, needlecrafts, dolls, and dollhouse furniture. 617–646–8985.

Shaw Furniture Galleries, P.O. Box 576, Randleman, NC 27317: Free brochure ❖ Home furnishings. 910–498–2628.

The Shop Woodcrafters Inc., P.O. Box 1450, Quitman, TX 75783: Catalog $4 ❖ Stained white pine furniture. 903–763–5491.

Simply Country Furniture, HC 69, Box 147, Rover, AR 72860: Brochure $2 ❖ Country-style furniture. 501–272–4794.

John C. Snedeker, 711 Meeting St., Charleston, SC 29403: Free information ❖ Handmade Charleston furniture reproductions. 803–722–6411.

Sobol House of Furnishings, Richardson Blvd., Black Mountain, NC 28711: Free brochure ❖ Home and office furnishings. 704–669–8031.

Southampton Antiques, 172 College Way, Rt. 10, Southampton, MA 01073: Video catalog $25 ❖ Antique American oak and Victorian furniture. 413–527–1022.

Southern Country Furniture, 40 Lewis Ln., Pearl River, LA 70452: Free information ❖ Country-style furniture. 504–863–7232.

M. Star Antler Designs, P.O. Box 3093, Lake Isabella, CA 93240: Catalog $5 ❖ Antler-designed chandeliers, lamps, furniture, mirrors, and other deco accessories. 619–379–5777.

Stevens Furniture, 1258 Hickory Blvd. SW, Lenoir, NC 28645: Free information ❖ Home furnishings. 704–728–5511.

Stuckey Brothers Furniture, Rt. 1, Box 527, Stuckey, SC 29554: Free information with long SASE ❖ Indoor and outdoor furniture. 803–558–2591.

Sutton-Council Furniture, P.O. Box 3288, Wilmington, NC 28406: Catalog $5 ❖ Home furnishings. 910–799–1990.

Sweet Water Ranch, P.O. Drawer 398, Cody, WY 82414: Free information ❖ Western style home furnishings and accessories. 800–357–CODY.

T-M Cowboy Classics, 364 Main St., Longmont, CO 80501: Brochure $3 ❖ Western style furniture. 303–776–3394.

Taos Furniture, 232 Galisteo St., Taos, NM 87501: Free brochure ❖ Handmade drum tables, pedestals, and Indian chairs.

Timberline Log Furniture, 6868 Thorpe Rd., Belgrade, MT 83113: Brochure $3 ❖ Rustic-looking log furniture. 406–388–2035.

R. Trammell & Son Cabinetmakers, 8519–1/2 Chestnut Ave., Historic Old Bowie, MD 20715: Catalog $3 ❖ American Shaker furniture in cherry or aged milk-painted finishes. 301–745–9347.

Marion Travis, P.O. Box 1041, Statesville, NC 28677: Catalog $1 ❖ Handwoven fiber rush seats on native hardwood. 704–528–4424.

Trott Furniture Company, P.O. Box 7, Richlands, NC 28574: Catalog $5 ❖ Oriental rugs and 18th-century style furniture. 800–682–0095; 910–324–3660 (in NC).

Turner-Tolson Inc., P.O. Drawer 1507, New Bern, NC 28560: Free brochure ❖ Home furnishings. 800–334–6616; 919–638–2121 (in NC).

Valley Furniture Shop, 20 Stirling Rd., Watchung, NJ 07060: Catalog $5 ❖ Reproduction 18th-century furniture. 908–756–7623.

Village Furniture House, 146 West Ave., Kannapolis, NC 28081: Free brochure ❖ Home furnishings. 704–938–9171.

Walpole Woodworkers, 767 East St., Walpole, MA 02081: Catalog $6 ❖ Handcrafted natural cedar New England-style furniture. 800–343–6948.

Charles Webb, Six Story St., Harvard Square, Cambridge, MA 02138: Catalog $4 ❖ Designer furniture. 617–547–2100.

Wellington's Furniture, P.O. Box 2178, Boone, NC 28607: Free catalog ❖ Leather furniture. 800–262–1049; 704–264–1049 (in NC).

Eldred Wheeler, 60 Sharp St., Hingham, MA 02043: Catalog $5 ❖ Reproduction 18th-century furniture. 617–337–5311.

Willsboro Wood Products, South Ausable St., Keeseville, NY 12944: Free brochure ❖ Fold-away Adirondack chairs, rocking chairs, and other country-style furniture. 800–342–3373.

Windrift Furniture Gallery, P.O. Box 1507, New Bern, NC 28563: Free catalog ❖ Home furnishings. 910–273–1886.

Wood Concepts, 23565 Reedy Dr., Elkhart, IN 46514: Free information with long SASE ❖ Easy-to-assemble solid oak country-style furniture. 219–262–3457.

Workshops of David T. Smith, 3600 Shawhan Rd., Morrow, OH 45152: Catalog $5 ❖ Reproduction furniture, pottery, lamps, and chandeliers. 513–932–2472.

Lift Chairs

American Health Manufacturing, P.O. Box 16287, Baltimore, MD 21210: Free catalog ❖ Lift chairs. 800–232–3044.

American Stair-Glide Corporation, 4001 E. 138th St., Grandview, MO 64030: Free brochure ❖ Cushioned chairs that rise to a standing position. 800–383–3100.

Ortho-Kinetics, The Independence Company, 1 Mobility Centre, P.O. Box 1647, Waukesha, WI 53187: Free information ❖ Combination power recliner/lounger/lift chair. 800–446–4522.

Whitakers, 1 Odell Plaza, Yonkers, NY 10703: Free catalog ❖ Lifts for transporting people with physical disabilities up and down and into the bathtub. 800–44–LIFTS; 800–924–LIFT (in NY).

Office Furniture

Alfax Wholesale Furniture, 370 7th Ave., Ste. 1101, New York, NY 10001: Free catalog ❖ Office furniture. 800–221–5710; 212–947–9560 (in NY).

American Security Products Company, 11925 Pacific Ave., Fontana, CA 92337: Free information ❖ Gun and other safes for homes and offices. 800–421–6142.

Basil & Jones Cabinetmakers, 2712 36th St. NW, Washington, DC 20007: Free brochure ❖ Wood or leather-finished stand-up desks in period and contemporary styles. 202–337–4369.

Business & Institutional Furniture Company, 611 N. Broadway, Milwaukee, WI 53202: Free catalog ❖ Office furniture. 800–558–8662; 414–272–0248 (in WI).

Frank Eastern Company, 599 Broadway, New York, NY 10012: Catalog $1 ❖ Office furniture. 212–219–0007.

National Business Furniture Inc., 222 E. Michigan St., Milwaukee, WI 53202: Free catalog ❖ Office furniture. 800–558–1010.

Office Furniture Center, 322 Moody St., Waltham, MA 02154: Free catalog ❖ Office furniture. 617–893–7300.

PAR Seating Specialists, 310 Main St., New Rochelle, NY 10802: Free catalog ❖ Office chairs and automotive seats. 800–367–7270.

Pyramid of Urbana, 2107 N. High Cross Rd., Urbana, IL 61801: Catalog $5 ❖ Office furniture, art and craft supplies, and school equipment. 217–328–3099.

Reliable Home Office, P.O. Box 1501, Ottawa, IL 61350: Catalog $2 ❖ Office furniture. 800–869–6000.

Safe Specialties Inc., 10932 Murdock & Lovell Rd., Knoxville, TN 37932: Catalog $2 ❖ Office and home safes. 800–695–2815.

The Stand-Up Desk Company, 5207 Baltimore Ave., Bethesda, MD 20816: Free brochure ❖ Handcrafted stand-up desks and stools. 301–657–3630.

Staples Inc., Attention: Marketing Services, P.O. Box 9328, Framingham, MA 01701: Free catalog ❖ Office furniture, drafting equipment, fax machines, typewriters, and supplies. 800–333–3330.

Stuart-Townsend-Carr Furniture, P.O. Box 373, Limington, ME 04049: Free information ❖ Classic furniture for offices and dens. 800–637–2344.

Outdoor Furniture

Adirondack Designs, 350 Cypress St., Fort Bragg, CA 95437: Free catalog ❖ Redwood chairs, love seats, swings, and tables. 800–222–0343.

Adirondack Store & Gallery, 109 Saranac Ave., Lake Placid, NY 12946: Free information ❖ Oak and maple outdoor furniture. 518–523–2646.

AK Exteriors, 298 Leisure Ln., Clint, TX 79836: Catalog $4 ❖ Cast-aluminum Victorian-style outdoor furniture and light fixtures. 915–851–2594.

Alfresco Porch Swing Company, P.O. Box 1336, Durango, CO 81302: Free brochure ❖ Redwood porch swings, Adirondack chairs, and garden benches. 303–247–9739.

Amish Country Collection, RD 5, Sunset Valley Rd., New Castle, PA 16105: Catalog $5 (refundable) ❖ Amish-style twig furniture, rugs, quilts, and wall hangings. 412–458–4811.

Barlow Tyrie, 1263 Glen Ave., Ste. 230, Moirestown, NJ 08057: Free brochure ❖ English-style teak outdoor furniture. 609–273–7878.

Blake Industries, P.O. Box 155, Abington, MA 02351: Free information ❖ Outdoor and indoor teak furniture, ornamental cast-iron pole lights, and fixtures. 617–337–8772.

Brown-Jordan, P.O. Box 5688, El Monte, CA 91734: Free information ❖ Aluminum furniture. 818–443–8971.

Charleston Battery Bench, 191 King St., Charleston, SC 29401: Catalog $1 ❖ Reproduction cast-iron and cypress benches from the 1880s. 803–722–3842.

Clapper's, P.O. Box 2278, West Newton, MA 02165: Free catalog ❖ Teak furniture for gardens, patios, and breezeways. 617–244–7900.

Coppa Woodworking Inc., 1231 Paraiso Ave., San Pedro, CA 90731: Free catalog ❖ Adirondack chairs and screen doors. 310–548–4142.

Country Casual, 17317 Germantown Rd., Germantown, MD 20874: Catalog $3 ❖ Teak benches, swings, chairs, tables, and planters. 301–540–0040.

Country Wood, P.O. Box 314, Sugar Loaf, NY 10981: Free information ❖ Adirondack rockers and chairs.

Cypress Street Center, 350 Cypress St., Fort Bragg, CA 95437: Free catalog ❖ Easy-to-assemble outdoor chairs with matching love seats, foot rests, side carts, and tables. 800–222–0343.

Diversified Overseas Marketing, 200 Main St., Coraopolis, PA 15108: Free information ❖ Cast aluminum furniture with all-weather cushions. 412–269–2690.

DuMor Inc., P.O. Box 142, Mifflintown, PA 17059: Free catalog ❖ Outdoor furniture. 717–436–2106.

Fib-Con Corporation, Box 3387, Silver Spring, MD 20918: Free catalog ❖ Reinforced fiberglass planters, benches, waste receptacles, and patio furniture. 301–572–5333.

Flanders Industries Inc., P.O. Box 1788, Fort Smith, AR 72902: Free brochure ❖ Casual and outdoor pool furniture. 800–843–7532.

Gardenside Ltd., 999 Andersen Dr., Ste. 140, San Rafael, CA 94901: Free catalog ❖ Teak garden furniture. 415–455–4500.

Green Enterprises, 43 S. Rogers St., Hamilton, VA 22068: Brochure $1 ❖ Swings, gliders, tables, and benches. 703–338–3606.

Holiday Pool & Patio, P.O. Box 727, Hudson, NC 28638: Free information ❖ Patio furniture. 704–728–2637.

Kelly-Grayson Woodcarving & Design, 5111 Todd Rd., Sebastopol, CA 95472: Brochure $1 ❖ Handcarved furniture and accessories. 707–829–7764.

Kingsley-Bate Ltd., 5587 Guinea Rd., Fairfax, VA 22032: Catalog $2 ❖ Teak planters, window boxes, and garden furniture. 703–978–7200.

Kramer Brothers, P.O. Box 255, Dayton, OH 45404: Free catalog ❖ Garden furniture and ornaments. 513–228–4194.

Landscape Forms Inc., 431 Lawndale Ave., Kalamazoo, MI 49001: Free information ❖ Outdoor furniture and garden planters. 800–521–2546; 616–381–0396 (in MI).

Lenoir Furniture Market Inc., 2034 Hickory Blvd., Lenoir, NC 28645: Free information with long SASE ❖ Indoor and outdoor furniture, beds, and bedding. 704–728–2946.

Kenneth Lynch & Sons, 84 Danbury Rd., Wilton, CT 06897: Catalog $4 ❖ Outdoor benches, gates, fountains, and pools. 203–762–8363.

MacMillan-Bloedel, 5895 Windward Pkwy., Ste. 200, Alpharetta, GA 30201: Free information ❖ Unfinished, Western red cedar outdoor furniture. 800–432–6226.

McKinnon & Harris Inc., P.O. Box 4885, Richmond, VA 23220: Catalog $4 ❖ Garden furniture. 804–358–2385.

Mel-Nor Industries, 303 Gulf Bank, Houston, TX 77037: Information $1 ❖ Hanging lawn and porch swings, park benches, and old-time lamp posts. 713–445–3485.

Moultrie Manufacturing, P.O. Drawer 1179, Moultrie, GA 31776: Catalog $3 ❖ Indoor and outdoor aluminum furniture. 800–841–8674.

Nebraska Plastics Inc., P.O. Box 45, Cozad, NE 69130: Free information ❖ Rose trellises, garden arbors, picnic tables, and other outdoor furniture and accessories. 800–445–2887.

Old Hickory Furniture Company, 403 S. Noble St., Shelbyville, IN 46176: Free catalog ❖ Casual and outdoor furniture. 317–398–3151.

The Patio, P.O. Box 925, San Juan, Capistrano, CA 92693: Catalog $2 ❖ Outdoor patio furniture. 800–81–PATIO.

Pittman & Davis, 843 N. Expressway 77, Harlingen, TX 78552: Catalog $1 ❖ Folding tables and outdoor furniture. 210–423–2154.

Plow & Hearth, 301 Madison Rd., P.O. Box 830, Orange, VA 22960: Free catalog ❖ Porch and lawn furniture, birdhouses and feeders, and fireplace accessories. 800–627–1712.

Pompeian Studios, 90 Rockledge Rd., Bronxville, NY 10708: Catalog $10 ❖ Original sculptures, ornaments, and forged furniture for patio or garden. 800–457–5595.

Roberts Furniture, 115 E. Putnam Ave., P.O. Box 433, Greenwich, CT 06836: Catalog $6 ❖ Brown Jordan furniture. 800–899–4610.

Robinson Iron Corporation, P.O. Box 1119, Alexander City, AL 35010: Catalog $5 ❖ Cast-iron benches. 205–329–8486.

Smith & Hawken, P.O. Box 6907, Florence, KY 41022: Free catalog ❖ Garden furniture. 800–776–5558.

Southerlands for Leisure Living, 10 Biltmore Ave., Asheville, NC 28801: Free catalog ❖ Outdoor furniture and garden accessories. 704–252–0478.

Victor Stanley Inc., P.O. Box 144, Dunkirk, MD 20754: Free information ❖ Indoor and outdoor furniture. 800–368–2573; 301–855–8300 (in MD).

Stuckey Brothers Furniture, Rt. 1, Box 527, Stuckey, SC 29554: Free information with long SASE ❖ Indoor and outdoor furniture. 803–558–2591.

Sun Designs, 173 E. Wisconsin Ave., Oconomowoc, WI 53066: Catalog $9.95 ❖ Plans for gazebos, bridges, doghouses, arbors, lawn furniture, swings and other outdoor play structures, and birdhouses. 414–567–4255.

Telescope Casual Furniture, P.O. Box 299, Granville, NY 12832: Free information ❖ Outdoor furniture. 518–642–1100.

Tidewater Workshop, Rt. 9, Oceanville, NJ 08231: Free information ❖ Outdoor furniture. 800–666–TIDE.

Tropitone Furniture Company, P.O. Box 3197, Sarasota, FL 33578: Catalog $3 ❖ Patio and casual furniture. 813–355–2715.

Walpole Woodworkers, 767 East St., Walpole, MA 02081: Catalog $6 ❖ Porch and children's swings and other handcrafted lawn and garden cedar furniture. 800–343–6948.

Wicker Works Furniture, 267 8th St., San Francisco, CA 94103: Free information ❖ Outdoor furniture. 415–626–6730.

Windsor Designs, 37 Great Valley Pkwy., Malvern, PA 19355: Free information ❖ Traditional furniture in teak, hardwood, and cast aluminum. 800–783–5434; 215–640–1212 (in PA).

Wood Classics, Osprey Ln., Gardner, NY 12525: Catalog $2 ❖ Teak and mahogany outdoor furniture in kits or assembled. 914–255–5599.

Wicker & Rattan

Classic Wicker, 8532 Melrose Ave., Los Angeles, CA 90069: Catalog $6 ❖ Vintage wicker and reproduction Victorian-style furniture. 213–659–1121.

Deutsch Inc., 31 E. 32nd St., New York, NY 10016: Catalog $3 ❖ Rattan furniture. 800–223–4550; 212–683–8746 (in NY).

Dovetail Antiques, 474 White Pine Rd., Columbus, NJ 08022: Catalog $5 ❖ Antique wicker furniture. 609–298–5245.

Ellenburg's Furniture, P.O. Box 5638, Statesville, NC 28687: Catalog $6 ❖ Wicker and rattan furniture with optional upholstered cushions, padding, and covers. 800–841–1420.

Fran's Basket House, 295 Rt. 10, Succasunna, NJ 07876: Catalog 50¢ ❖ Wicker and rattan furniture. 201–584–2230.

Lloyd/Flanders Industries, 3010 10th St., Menominee, MI 49858: Free information ❖ All-weather wicker furniture. 906–863–4491.

Masterworks, P.O. Box M, Marietta, GA 30061: Catalog $2.50 ❖ Indoor, outdoor, children's, and bent-willow furniture. 404–426–6538.

Rattan Factory Outlet, 13396 Preston Rd., Dallas, TX 75240: Free information with long SASE ❖ Rattan tables, chairs, and other furniture. 214–386–6484.

Wicker Gallery, 8009 Glenwood Ave., Raleigh, NC 27612: Free brochure ❖ Wicker and rattan furniture. 919–781–2215.

Wicker Warehouse Inc., 195 S. River St., Hackensack, NJ 07601: Catalog $5 (refundable) ❖ Wicker and rattan furniture. 800–274–8602.

Wicker Works of High Point, 213 E. Fairfield Rd., High Point, NC 27263: Catalog $3 ❖ Country, contemporary, Victorian, and traditional wicker furniture. 910–431–7455.

GARAGE DOORS & OPENERS

Atlas Roll-Lite, P.O. Box 593949, Orlando, FL 32859: Free information ❖ Insulated raised-panel garage doors. 407–857–0680.

Clopay Corporation, Consumer Affairs Department, 101 E. 4th St., Cincinnati, OH 45202: Free information ❖ Garage doors with raised panels. 800–225–6729.

Overhead Door, P.O. Box 809046, Dallas, TX 75380: Free information ❖ Insulated steel overhead garage doors and opener with a microprocessor controller program to detect obstructions. 800–543–2269.

Philips Home Products, 22790 Lake Park Blvd., Alliance, OH 44601: Free information ❖ Garage door openers with an option for controlling house lights. 800–654–3643.

Raynor Garage Doors, P.O. Box 448, Dixon, IL 61021: Free information ❖ Wood-grained steel garage doors with raised panels. 800–545–0455.

Ridge Doors, New Rd., Monmouth, NJ 08852: Free information ❖ Solid wood garage doors with carved or plain panels and optional trims and glass. 800–631–5656; 800–872–4980 (in NJ).

Wayne-Dalton Corporation, P.O. Box 67, Mount Hope, OH 44660: Free information ❖ Insulated steel garage doors. 216–674–7015.

GARDENING EQUIPMENT & SUPPLIES

Beneficial Insects & Organisms

Applied Bionomics, 11074 W. Saanich Rd., Sidney, British Columbia, Canada V8L 3X0: Free brochure ❖ Beneficial insects. 604–656–2123.

Arbico Inc., P.O. Box 4247, Tucson, AZ 85738: Free catalog ❖ Beneficial insects. 800–767–2847.

Arrigo, P.O. Box 4247, Tucson, AZ 85738: Free catalog ❖ Beneficial insects. 602–825–9785.

Beatrice Farms, Dawson, GA 31742: Free information ❖ Redworms for soil improvement and composting.

Bozeman Bio-Tech, P.O. Box 3146, Bozeman, MT 59772: Free catalog ❖ Beneficial insects and other pest control products. 406–587–5891.

W. Atlee Burpee & Company, 300 Park Ave., Warminster, PA 18974: Free catalog ❖ Beneficial insects. 215–674–1793.

Cape Cod Worm Farm, 30 Center Ave., Buzzards Bay, MA 02532: Free information ❖ Redworms for soil improvement and composting. 508–759–5664.

D & R Rabbits, 2111 N. Century Blvd., McDavid, FL 32568: Free information ❖ Redworms for soil improvement and composting. 904–256–2845.

Farmer Seed & Nursery Company, 818 NW 4th St., Faribault, MN 55021: Free catalog ❖ Beneficial organisms. 507–334–2017.

Henry Field's Seed & Nursery, 415 N. Burnett, Shenandoah, IA 51602: Free catalog ❖ Beneficial organisms. 605–665–4491.

Gardener's Supply Company, 128 Intervale Rd., Burlington, VT 05401: Free catalog ❖ Beneficial insects. 800–688–5510.

Garden-Ville, 8648 Old Bee Caves Rd., Austin, TX 78735: Free catalog ❖ Organic gardening supplies, beneficial insects, other pest controls, and tools. 512–288–6115.

Gardens Alive, 5100 Schenley Pl., Lawrenceburg, IN 47025: Free catalog ❖ Beneficial insects and organisms. 812–537–8650.

Harmony Farm Supply, P.O. Box 460, Graton, CA 95444: Catalog $2 (refundable) ❖ Beneficial insects. 707–823–9125.

M & R Durango Inc., P.O. Box 886, Bayfield, CO 81122: Free catalog ❖ Beneficial insects. 800–526–4075; 303–259–3521 (in CO).

Mellinger's, 2328 W. South Range Rd., North Lima, OH 44452: Free catalog ❖ Beneficial organisms. 216–549–9861.

Natural Gardening Company, 217 San Anselmo Ave., San Anselmo, CA 94960: Free catalog ❖ Beneficial insects, organic gardening supplies, pest controls, drip irrigation equipment, and wildflower seeds. 707–766–9303.

Natural Gardening Research Center, Hwy. 48, P.O. Box 149, Sunman, IN 47041: Free catalog ❖ Beneficial organisms. 800–755–4769.

Nature's Control, P.O. Box 35, Medford, OR 97501: Free catalog ❖ Beneficial insects and organisms. 503–899–8318.

Necessary Trading Company, One Natures Way, New Castle, VA 24127: Free catalog ❖ Beneficial insects. 800–447–5354.

Orcon, 5132 Venice Blvd., Los Angeles, CA 90019: Free brochure ❖ Beneficial insects. 213–937–7444.

Peaceful Valley Farm Supply, P.O. Box 2209, Grass Valley, CA 95945: Catalog $2 (refundable) ❖ Beneficial organisms. 916–272–4769.

Rincon-Vitova Insectaries Inc., P.O. Box 95, Oak View, CA 93022: Free brochure ❖ Beneficial insects. 800–248–2847; 805–643–5407 (in CA).

Territorial Seed Company, P.O. Box 157, Cottage Grove, OR 97424: Free catalog ❖ Organic fertilizers, natural insecticides, biological pest controls, and vegetable, herb, and flower seeds. 503–942–9547.

Unique Insect Control, 5504 Sperry Dr., Citrus Heights, CA 95621: Free brochure ❖ Beneficial insects. 916–961–7945.

Carts

Ames Lawn & Garden Tools, P.O. Box 1774, Parkersburg, WV 26102: Free information ❖ Easy-to-roll lawn cart. 800–624–2654.

BCS America, 13601 Providence Rd., Matthews, NC 28105: Free catalog ❖ Garden carts, chippers and shredders, tillers, sprayers, mowers, and tractors. 704–846–1040.

Classic Design Carts, 22 Robertsville Rd., Marlboro, NJ 07746: Free brochure ❖ Garden carts, assembled or kits. 800–743–2278; 816–753–2278 (in NJ).

Country Manufacturing, P.O. Box 104, Fredericktown, OH 43019: Free catalog ❖ Quick-dump carts, lawn brooms, pressure sprayers, turf spreaders, wagons, and trailers. 614–694–9926.

Garden Way, 9th Ave. & 102nd St., Troy, NY 12180: Free information ❖ Carts, tillers, clippers, sickle bar mowers, garden composters, and other equipment. 800–345–4454.

Gardener's Supply Company, 128 Intervale Rd., Burlington, VT 05401: Free catalog ❖ Garden carts, composters, sprayers, watering systems, weeding and cultivating tools, organic fertilizers and other chemical preparations, leaf mulchers, and canning and preserving supplies. 800–688–5510.

Homestead Carts, 2396 Perkins St. NE, Salem, OR 97303: Free brochure ❖ Garden carts and composters. 800–825–1925; 503–393–3973 (in OR).

Norway Industries, 143 W. Main St., Stoughton, WI 53589: Free brochure ❖ Garden carts. 608–873–8664.

Chippers & Shredders

Amerind MacKissic Inc., P.O. Box 111, Parker Ford, PA 19457: Free information ❖ Gasoline-operated chipper/shredder. 215–495–7181.

Crary Bear Cat, P.O. Box 849, West Fargo, ND 58078: Free information ❖ Chippers and chipper-shredders with optional blower and vacuum attachments, hydraulic feeds, tow hitches, and other optional accessories.

Flowtron Outdoor Products, 2 Main St., Melrose, MA 02176: Free information ❖ Electric chipper/shredder. 617–321–2300.

Garden Way, 9th Ave. & 102nd St., Troy, NY 12180: Free information ❖ Compact chipper/shredder. 800–345–4454.

Gardener's Supply Company, 128 Intervale Rd., Burlington, VT 05401: Free catalog ❖ Gasoline-powered chipper/shredder. 800–688–5510.

Kemp Company, 160 Koser Rd., Lititz, PA 17543: Free information ❖ Chipper/shredder. 717–627–7979.

The Kinsman Company, River Rd., Point Pleasant, PA 18950: Free catalog ❖ Electric chipper/shredder. 800–733–4146.

Mantis Manufacturing Company, 1028 Street Rd., Southampton, PA 18966: Free information ❖ Gasoline and electric-powered chipper/ shredders. 800–366–6268.

Mighty Mac, Mackissic Inc., P.O. Box 111, Parker Ford, PA 19457: Free information ❖ Chippers, tillers, blowers, and sprayers.

Snapper Power Equipment, P.O. Box 777, McDonough, GA 30253: Free information ❖ Shredder. 404–954–2706.

White Outdoor Products Company, P.O. Box 361131, Cleveland, OH 44136: Free information ❖ Gasoline-powered chipper/shredder.

Farm Equipment & Supplies

Erth-Rite, RD 1, Box 243, Gap, PA 17527: Free information ❖ Natural organic fertilizers for farmers, homeowners, and commercial growers. 800–332–4171; 717–442–4171 (in PA).

Naturally Scientific, 5925 Imperial Pkwy., Ste. 130, Mulberry, FL 33860: Free catalog ❖ Environmentally responsible pesticides and fertilizers for home garden and farm use. 800–248–9970.

Sutton Agricultural Enterprises Inc., 746 Vertin Ave., Salinas, CA 93901: Free brochure ❖ Seed planters, measuring devices, field supplies, and bird control products. 408–422–9693.

Fertilizers & Plant Food

Erth-Rite, RD 1, Box 243, Gap, PA 17527: Free information ❖ Natural organic fertilizers for farmers, homeowners, and commercial growers. 800–332–4171; 717–442–4171 (in PA).

Garden-Ville, 8648 Old Bee Caves Rd., Austin, TX 78735: Free catalog ❖ Organic gardening supplies, beneficial insects, other pest controls, and tools. 512–288–6115.

Garden City Seeds, 1324 Red Crow Rd., Victor, MT 59875: Information $1 ❖ Fertilizers. 406–961–4837.

Gardener's Supply Company, 128 Intervale Rd., Burlington, VT 05401: Free catalog ❖ Garden carts, composters, sprayers, watering systems, weeding and cultivating tools, organic fertilizers and other chemical preparations, leaf mulchers, canning and preserving supplies, and furniture. 800–688–5510.

Greenleaves, 24045 Frampton Ave., Harbor City, CA 90710: Free information ❖ Plant foods. 800–678–8844.

Natural Gardening Research Center, Hwy. 48, P.O. Box 149, Sunman, IN 47041: Free catalog ❖ Organic fertilizers, plant foods, application equipment, propagation aids, foods for attracting insect-eating birds, and pest barriers. 800–755–4769.

Naturally Scientific, 5925 Imperial Pkwy., Ste. 130, Mulberry, FL 33860: Free catalog ❖ Environmentally responsible pesticides and fertilizers for home garden and farm use. 800–248–9970.

Necessary Trading Company, One Natures Way, New Castle, VA 24127: Free catalog ❖ Soil testing supplies, plant nutrients, fertilizers, and pest control preparations. 800–447–5354.

Ohio Earth Food, 5488 Swamp St. SE, Hartville, OH 44362: Free information ❖ Organic fertilizers. 216–877–9356.

Ringer, 9959 Valley View Rd., Eden Prairie, MN 55344: Free catalog ❖ Chemical treatments and fertilizers, tools, growing aids, propagation aids, and pest control preparations. 800–654–1047.

Schultz Company, 14090 Riverport Dr., Maryland Heights, MO 63043: Free information ❖ Plant and flower food, insect sprays, and other nutrient preparations.

Shore Fertilizer Company, 307 S. Evers St., Plant City, FL 33566: Free information with long SASE ❖ Lawn and garden fertilizers. 813–754–3577.

Stern's Miracle-Gro, P.O. Box 888, Port Washington, NY 11050: Free information ❖ Sprayers, chemical treatments, and fertilizers. 516–883–6550.

Territorial Seed Company, P.O. Box 157, Cottage Grove, OR 97424: Free catalog ❖ Organic fertilizers, natural insecticides, biological pest controls, and vegetable, herb, and flower seeds. 503–942–9547.

Greenhouses

Creative Structures, 1765 Walnut Ln., Quakerstown, PA 18951: Catalog $1 ❖ Sun room and greenhouse kits. 215–538–2426.

Cropking Inc., P.O. Box 310, Medina, OH 44258: Catalog $3 ❖ Greenhouses. 216–725–5656.

Dixie Greenhouse Manufacturing Company, Rt. 1, Box 339, Alapaha, GA 31622: Free information ❖ Build-it-yourself greenhouse kits. 800–346–9902; 912–532–4600 (in GA).

Elite Greenhouses Ltd., P.O. Box 22960, Rochester, NY 14962: Free information ❖ Aluminum frame greenhouses. 800–544–7938.

Farm Wholesale Inc., 2396 Perkins St. NE, Salem, OR 97303: Free catalog ❖ Easy-to-assemble greenhouses. 800–825–1925.

Four Seasons Solar Products, 5005 Veterans Memorial Hwy., Holbrook, NY 11741: Free information ❖ Greenhouses. 800–368–7732.

Fox Hill Farm/Hoop House, 20 Lawrence St., Vernon, CT 06066: Free catalog ❖ Greenhouse kits. 203–875–6676.

Gardener's Supply Company, 128 Intervale Rd., Burlington, VT 05401: Free catalog ❖ Greenhouses. 800–688–5510.

Geneva Greenhouse Systems, 64 Airport Rd., West Milford, NJ 07480: Information $3 ❖ Greenhouses. 800–FLORIAN.

Gothic Arch Greenhouses, P.O. Box 1564, Mobile, AL 36633: Free brochure ❖ Redwood/ fiberglass greenhouse kits. 800–628–4974.

Greenhouse Designs, Division San Antonio Tent & Awning Company, P.O. Box 200426, San Antonio, TX 78220: Free information ❖ Build-it-yourself greenhouse kits. 800–531–7230.

GreenTech, 1201 Minters Chapel Rd., Building A-1, Grapevine, TX 76051: Free information ❖ Indoor greenhouses. 800–844–3665.

Jacobs Greenhouse Manufacturing, 371 Talbot Rd., Delhi, Ontario, Canada N4B 2A1: Catalog $2 ❖ Greenhouses with tempered glass and automatic roof vents. 519–582–2880.

Janco Greenhouses, 9390 Davis Ave., Laurel, MD 20707: Brochure $5 ❖ Greenhouses. 800–323–6933.

Lindal Cedar Homes, P.O. Box 24426, Seattle, WA 98124: Catalog $15 ❖ Greenhouses and sunrooms. 800–426–0536.

National Greenhouse Company, P.O. Box 100, Pana, IL 62557: Free catalog ❖ Greenhouses. 800–826–9314; 217–562–9333 (in IL).

Northwest Eden Greenhouses, 14219 NE 167th St., Woodenville, WA 98072: Free information ❖ Greenhouses. 800–545–3336.

Progressive Building Products, P.O. Box 866, East Longmeadow, MA 01028: Catalog $5.95 ❖ Greenhouse and solarium components. 800–776–2534.

Santa Barbara Greenhouses, 721 Richmond Ave., Oxnard, CA 93030: Free catalog ❖ Redwood greenhouses. 800–544–5276.

Senco Inc., Box 306, Marquette, MI 49855: Free information ❖ Recreational shelters, portable hunting blinds and ice fishing houses, and greenhouses. 407–589–6563.

Skytech Systems, P.O. Box 763, Bloomsburg, PA 17815: Catalog $3 ❖ Free-standing and window greenhouses, solariums, and sunrooms. 717–752–1111.

Solar Components Corporation, 121 Valley St., Manchester, NH 03103: Brochure $1 ❖ Lean-to and free-standing build-it-yourself greenhouse kits. 603–668–8186.

Southeastern Insulated Glass, 6477–B Peachtree Industrial Blvd., Atlanta, GA 30360: Free information ❖ Greenhouse and sun room kits, sliding glass doors, and skylights. 800–841–9842; 404–455–8838 (in GA).

Sturdi-Built Manufacturing Company, 11304 SW Boones Ferry Rd., Portland, OR 97219: Free catalog ❖ Greenhouses, cold frames, and sunrooms. 503–244–4100.

Sun Room Company, P.O. Box 301, Leola, PA 17540: Free information ❖ Window and free-standing greenhouses and solariums. 800–426–2737.

Sun System Greenhouses, 75 Austin Blvd., Commack, NY 11725: Free catalog ❖ Aluminum, double pane-covered greenhouses. 516–543–7600.

Sun-Porch Structures, P.O. Box 1353, Stamford, Ct. 06904: Catalog $2 ❖ Solar greenhouses. 203–324–0010.

Sundome Greenhouses, 42125 Blackhawk Plaza Circle, Danville, CA 94506: Free brochure ❖ Portable greenhouses. 800–252–5346.

Sunglo Solar Greenhouses, 4441 26th Ave. West, Seattle, WA 98199: Free brochure ❖ Solar greenhouses and solariums. 800–647–0606; 206–284–8900 (in WA).

Texas Greenhouse Company, 2524 White Settlement Rd., Fort Worth, TX 76107: Free catalog ❖ Greenhouses. 800–227–5447.

Troy-Bilt Manufacturing Company, 9th Ave & 102nd St., Troy, NY 12179: Free information ❖ Greenhouses. 800–438–6969.

Turner Greenhouses, Hwy. 117 South, P.O. Box 1260, Goldsboro, NC 27530: Free catalog ❖ Greenhouses. 800–672–4770.

Under Glass Manufacturing Corporation, P.O. Box 323, Wappingers Falls, NY 12590: Catalog $3 ❖ Indoor window greenhouses, other greenhouses, and solariums. 914–298–0645.

Victory Garden Supply, 1428 E. High St., Charlottsville, VA 22901: Free brochure ❖ Aluminum-frame greenhouses with double strength glass and space-saving sliding doors. 804–293–2298.

View-Light Window Shelves, 9144 Emperor Ave., San Gabriel, CA 91775: Free catalog ❖ Easy-to-install indoor window shelf for plants. 818–287–7633.

Hydroponic Gardening Supplies

Alternative Garden Supply Inc., 297 N. Barrington Rd., Streamwood, IL 60107: Free catalog ❖ Hydroponic supplies. 800–444–2837.

American Hydroponics, 824 L St., Arcata, CA 95521: Free brochure ❖ Hydroponic supplies and kits for beginners. 800–458–6543; 707–822–5777 (in CA).

Applied Hydroponics, 3135 Kerner Blvd., San Rafael, CA 94901: Free catalog ❖ Hydroponic equipment. 800–634–9999; 415–459–7898 (in CA).

Aqua Culture Inc., 700 1st St., Tempe, AZ 85281: Free catalog ❖ Hydroponic systems, lights, and plant food. 800–633–2137.

Aqua-Ponics International, P.O. Box 411736, Los Angeles, CA 90041: Free information ❖ Hydroponic supplies.

Brew & Grow, 8179 University Ave. NE, Fridley, MN 55432: Free information ❖ Hydroponic equipment and home brewing supplies for making beer. 612–780–8191.

Cropking Inc., P.O. Box 310, Medina, OH 44258: Catalog $3 ❖ Hydroponic supplies. 216–725–5656.

Diamond Lights, 628 Lindaro St., San Rafael, CA 94901: Free catalog ❖ Hydroponic nutrients and other supplies. 800–331–3994.

Discount Garden Supply Inc., 14109 E. Sprague, Spokane, WA 99216: Free catalog ❖ Hydroponic systems, lights, nutrients and fertilizers, and propagation aids. 800–444–4378.

East Coast Hydroponics, 432 Castleton Ave., Staten Island, NY 10301: Free catalog ❖ Hydroponic and outdoor gardening supplies. 800–255–0121; 718–727–9300 (in NY).

Eco Enterprises, 1240 NE 175th St., Seattle, WA 98155: Free catalog ❖ Hydroponic equipment. 800–426–6937.

Foothill Hydroponics, 10705 Burbank Blvd., North Hollywood, CA 91601: Free catalog ❖ Nutrients, growlights, climate control and test equipment, rock wool, and irrigation equipment. 818–760–0688.

Frank's Magic Crops, 2402 Edith Ave., Burlington, Ontario, Canada L7R 1N8: Free information ❖ Hydroponic systems. 416–333–3282.

General Hydroponics, 15 Koch Service Rd., Corte Madera, CA 94925: Free information ❖ Hydroponic systems. 800–37–HYDRO; 415–924–3390 (in CA).

Gold Coast Greenhouse, 7390 Bird Rd., Miami, FL 33155: Free information ❖ Hydroponic supplies and lighting equipment. 800–780–6805.

Green Fire, 347 Nord Ave., Chico, CA 95926: Free brochure ❖ Natural liquid fertilizers and hydroponic equipment. 916–895–8301.

Green Gardens, 12748 Bel-Red Rd., Bellevue, WA 98005: Free catalog ❖ Hydroponic and indoor garden supplies. 206–454–5731.

Green Thumb Hydro-Gardens, 3312 Lakeshore Dr., Sheboygan, WI 53081: Free catalog ❖ Automatic, programmable closed-loop hydroponic gardens. 414–459–8405.

Halide of Oregon, 9220 SE Stark, Portland, OR 97216: Free information ❖ Hydroponic systems. 800–433–6805; 503–256–2400 (in OR).

Hamilton Technology Corporation, 14902 S. Figueroa St., Gardena, CA 90248: Free catalog ❖ Lights, hydroponic systems, and gardening supplies. 800–447–9797.

Harvest Moon Hydroponics Inc., Airport Plaza, 4214 Union Rd., Cheektowaga, NY 14225: Free catalog ❖ Hydroponic supplies. 800–635–1383.

Heartland Hydroponics, Vernon Plaza, 115 Townline Rd., Vernon Hills, IL 60061: Free catalog ❖ Hydroponic supplies. 800–354–GROW.

Home Harvest Garden Supply Inc., 13426 Occoquan Rd., Woodbridge, VA 22191: Free information ❖ Indoor horticultural light systems and hydroponic equipment. 800–348–4796.

Hydrofarm, 3135 Kerner Blvd., San Rafael, CA 94901: Free catalog ❖ Lights and other hydroponic supplies. 800–634–9999.

Light Manufacturing Company, 1634 SE Brooklyn, Portland, OR 97202: Free catalog ❖ Hydroponic systems, lights, and nutrient controls. 800–NOW-LITE.

MAH Nursery, 115 Commerce Dr., Hauppage, NY 11788: Free information ❖ Hydroponic equipment.

New Earth Inc., 3623 East Hwy. 44, Sheperdsville, KY 40165: Free catalog ❖

Hydroponic and outdoor gardening supplies. 800–462–5953; 502–543–5933 (in KY).

Superior Growers Supply, 4870 Dawn Ave., East Lansing, MI 48823: Free catalog ❖ Hydroponic supplies. 800–227–0027.

Virginia Hydroponics, 114 W. Mercury Blvd., Hampton, VA 23669: Free information ❖ Hydroponic supplies. 804–766–1324.

Wilder Agriculture Products Company Inc., P.O. Box 406, Pulaski, PA 16143: Free catalog ❖ Hydroponic nutrients for cloning, seed modification, and tissue culture preparation. 800–462–8102.

Worm's Way, 3151 South Hwy. 446, Bloomington, IN 47401: Free catalog ❖ Hydroponic and organic gardening supplies. 800–274–9676.

Indoor Gardening Supplies

Alternative Garden Supply Inc., 297 N. Barrington Rd., Streamwood, IL 60107: Free catalog ❖ Indoor lighting systems, growing kits, and biological pest controls. 800–444–2837.

Floralight, 6–620 Supertest Rd., North York, Ontario, Canada M3J 2M5: Free information ❖ Indoor light gardens, lamps, and supplies. 416–665–4000.

Florist Products Inc., 2242 N. Palmer Dr., Schaumburg, IL 60173: Catalog $10 (refundable) ❖ Horticultural supplies and tools. 800–828–2242.

Indoor Gardening Supplies, P.O. Box 40567, Detroit, MI 48240: Free catalog ❖ Indoor gardening supplies, stands, lights, and books. 313–426–9080.

Plant Collectibles, 103 Kenview Ave., Buffalo, NY 14217: Free catalog with two 1st class stamps ❖ Garden and greenhouse supplies and light stands. 716–875–1221.

Urban-Tek Growers Supply Inc., 2911 W. Wilshire, Oklahoma City, OK 73116: Free catalog ❖ Organic gardening supplies and lighting equipment for greenhouses and indoor gardens. 405–843–1888.

Landscaping Stone

Allan Block, 7400 Metro Blvd., Ste. 125, Edina, MN 55435: Free brochure ❖ Mortar-less concrete blocks for retaining walls, curves, corners, stairways, and terraces. 612–835–5309.

Conn Stone Supplies, 311 Post Rd., Orange, CT 06477: Free information ❖ New cobblestone for edging, paving, and other landscaping projects. 203–795–9767.

Di Giacomo Inc., 612 S. Duggan Ave., Azusa, CA 91702: Free information ❖ Custom-made artistic rock formations. 818–334–8211.

Eurocobble, 4265 Lemp Ave., Studio City, CA 91604: Free information ❖ Cobblestone in modules and single sets. 213–877–5012.

Fabra-Tech Manufacturing Inc., 35 E. Pierson St., Greenfield, IN 46140: Free information ❖ Waterfall kits and landscaping and light rocks. 317–462–6686.

Stone Company Inc., Rt. 1, Eden, WI 53019: Free information ❖ Natural building and landscaping cobblers, granite boulders, wall stone, steppers, and flagstone. 414–477–2521.

Urdl's Waterfall Creations Inc., 1010 NW 1st St., Delray Beach, FL 33444: Free information ❖ Manufactured hollow concrete rocks for landscaping and waterfall settings. 305–278–3320.

Lawn Ornaments & Statues

Armchair Shopper, P.O. Box 130, Indianapolis, IN 46206: Free catalog ❖ Classic old-world style sundials, wind chimes, and lawn ornaments. 800–558–2376.

Ballard Designs, 1670 DeFoor Ave. NW, Atlanta, GA 30318: Catalog $3 ❖ Castings for indoor and outdoor settings, furniture, lamps, fireplace accessories, pillows, and art prints. 404–351–5099.

The BB Brass, 10151 Pacific Mesa Blvd., San Diego, CA 92121: Free catalog ❖ Brass fountains and sculptures. 800–536–0987.

BowBends, P.O. Box 900, Bolton, MA 01740: Catalog $3 ❖ Arbors, bridges, gazebos, and other garden structures. 508–779–6464.

Robert Compton Ltd., RD 3, Box 3600, Bristol, VT 05443: Brochure $2 ❖ Original stone fountains. 802–453–3778.

Continental Bridge, 8301 State Hwy. 29 North, Alexandria, MN 56308: Free information ❖ Prefab bridges for garden settings. 800–328–2047; 612–852–7500 (in MN).

Cross Vinyl Lattice, 3174 Marjan Dr., Atlanta, GA 30341: Free information ❖ Trellises, arbors, and fencing. 404–457–5125.

Excel Bridge Manufacturer, 12001 Shoemaker Ave., Santa Fe Springs, CA 90670: Free information ❖ Easy-to-install,

pre-fabricated bridges. 800–548–0054; 310–944–0701 (in CA).

Flora Fauna, P.O. Box 578, Gualala, CA 95445: Free information ❖ Lattice panels, columns, arches, and sundials. 800–358–9120.

Florentine Craftsmen, 46–24 28th St., Long Island City, NY 11101: Catalog $5 ❖ Ornamental sculpture, fountains, birdbaths, and furniture. 718–937–7632.

FrenchWyres, P.O. Box 131655, Tyler, TX 75713: Catalog $3 ❖ Trellises, topiary frames, urns, plant stands, cachepots, window boxes, and arches. 903–597–8322.

Garden Accents, 4 Union Hill Rd., West Conshohocken, PA 19428: Free information ❖ Antique and contemporary garden ornaments. 800–296–5525; 610–825–5525 (in PA).

The Garden Architecture Group, 631 N. 3rd St., Philadelphia, PA 19123: Catalog $3 ❖ Easy-to-assemble garden decor settings. 215–627–5552.

Garden Concepts Collection, P.O. Box 241233, Memphis, TN 38124: Catalog $5 ❖ Handcrafted furniture and trellises. 901–756–1649.

The Garden Gate, 5122 Morningside Dr., Houston, TX 77005: Catalog $10 ❖ Imported classical English cast stone statuary. 800–861–8141; 713–528–2654 (in TX).

Garden Ornaments Stone, P.O. Box 1451, Roswell, GA 30077: Catalog $10 ❖ Statues, mantlepieces, fountains, benches, tables, and other decor ornamentals.

Gingerbread Man Woodworks, Factory Outlet Store, P.O. Box 59, Noel, MO 64854: Catalog $5 ❖ Gazebos, garden structures, and ornamental trim. 417–775–2553.

Haddonstone (USA) Ltd., 201 Heller Pl., Bellmawr, NJ 08031: Catalog $10 ❖ English garden ornaments and architectural stonework. 609–931–7011.

Hardwicke Gardens, 254 Boston Turnpike Rd., Westboro, MA 01581: Catalog $2 (refundable) ❖ Garden pool supplies and statuary.

Hen-Feathers & Company Inc., 250 King Manor Dr., King of Prussia, PA 19406: Free catalog ❖ Hand-cast architectural and decor garden accents. 800–282–1910.

Hermitage Gardens, P.O. Box 361, Canastota, NY 13032: Catalog $1 ❖ Fiberglass rocks and waterfalls, redwood

water wheels, wood bridges, garden pools, and bubbling fantasias. 315–697–9093.

Kestrel Manufacturing, P.O. Box 12, Saint Peters, PA 19470: Information $2 ❖ American and English garden accessories. 215–469–6370.

Kramer Brothers, P.O. Box 255, Dayton, OH 45404: Free catalog ❖ Garden furniture and ornaments. 513–228–4194.

Lazy Hill Farm Designs, Rt. 1, Box 235, Colerain, NC 27924: Free information ❖ Handcrafted garden accessories. 919–356–2828.

Legendary Lighting by Copper Sculptures, 1016 N. Flowood Dr., Jackson, MS 39208: Free brochure ❖ Handcrafted gas lanterns and architectural accent pieces. 601–936–4200.

Machin Designs by Amdega, P.O. Box 7, Glenview, IL 60025: Catalog $10 ❖ English-style conservatories constructed in either western red cedar or aluminum and garden ornaments. 800–922–0110.

Mister Boardwalk, P.O. Box 789, Pt. Pleasant, NJ 08742: Free catalog ❖ Do-it-yourself, easy-to-assemble carpentry- and permit-free walkways. 800–999–7136.

Mt. Fuji Stone Lanterns, 12500 132nd Ave. NE, Kirkland, WA 98034: Free catalog ❖ Pagodas, lanterns, stone basins and bridges, and other stone formations for Japanese garden settings.

Nebraska Plastics Inc., P.O. Box 45, Cozad, NE 69130: Free information ❖ Rose trellises, garden arbors, picnic tables, and other outdoor furniture and accessories. 800–445–2887.

New England Garden Ornaments, 38 E. Brookfield Rd., North Brookfield, MA 01535: Catalog $8 ❖ Garden ornaments and furniture. 508–867–4474.

Park Place, 2251 Wisconsin Ave. NW, Washington, DC 20007: Catalog $2 ❖ Classic outdoor furnishings and architectural products. 202–342–6294.

Pompeian Studios, 90 Rockledge Rd., Bronxville, NY 10708: Catalog $10 ❖ Original sculptures, ornaments, and forged furniture for patio or garden. 800–457–5595.

Rivertown Products, 3812 River Rd., P.O. Box 5174, St. Joseph, MO 64505: Brochure $1 ❖ Handcrafted arbors and other outdoor products. 816–232–8822.

Sculpture Placement Ltd., P.O. Box 9709, Washington, DC 20016: Free catalog ❖ Bronze life-size sculptures. 202–362–9310.

Southerlands for Leisure Living, 10 Biltmore Ave., Asheville, NC 28801: Free catalog ❖ Outdoor furniture and garden accessories. 704–252–0478.

Southern Statuary & Stone, 901 33rd St. North, Birmingham, AL 35222: Catalog $5 ❖ Stone castings for garden landscaping. 205–322–0379.

Stickney's Garden Houses, One Thompson Square, P.O. Box 34, Boston, MA 02129: Catalog $3 ❖ Handcrafted garden houses with optional seats. 617–242–1711.

Stone Forest, P.O. Box 2840, Santa Fe, NM 87504: Catalog $3 ❖ Fountains, lanterns, water basins, birdbaths, pedestals, and other handcarved granite statuary. 505–986–8883.

Strassacker Bronze America Inc., P.O. Box 931, Spartanburg, SC 29304: Catalog $15 ❖ Contemporary and abstract bronze sculptures, fountains, and lighting equipment. 803–573–7438.

Sun Garden Specialties, P.O. Box 52382, Tulsa, OK 74152: Free information ❖ Wood decor items for gardens.

Sun Source Inc., P.O. Box 4191A, Metuchen, NJ 08840: Catalog $2 (refundable) ❖ Modular trellis, fan trellis, and arbor systems.

Toscano Design, 15 E. Campbell St., Arlington Heights, IL 60005: Catalog $5 ❖ Hand-cast replica artifacts and sculpture. 800–525–0733.

Unit Structures, 5724 Koppers Rd., Morrisville, NC 27560: Free information ❖ Easy-to-assemble prefabricated pedestrian and vehicular shelters and bridges. 800–777–UNIT.

Victorian Replicas, P.O. Box 866, Menlo Park, CA 94026: Free catalog ❖ Cast-iron urns, benches, tables, and other replicas. 415–365–8637.

Samuel Welch Sculpture Inc., P.O. Box 55, Cincinnati, OH 45201: Catalog $10 ❖ Large-scale sculpture in bronze, aluminum, steel, concrete, marble, and granite. 513–321–8882.

Western Wood Structures Inc., P.O. Box 130, Tualatin, OR 97062: Free information ❖ Pedestrian, equestrian, and golf course bridges, from 20– to 100–foot spans. 503–692–6900.

Zachariasen Studio, N659 Drumm Rd., Denmark, WI 54208: Free brochure ❖ Handmade ceramic birdbaths, fountains, and other garden ornaments. 414–776–1778.

Mowers, Trimmers & Blowers

Agri-Fab Inc., 303 W. Raymond St., Sullivan, IL 61951: Free information ❖ Walk-behind mowers.

American Lawn Mower Company, P.O. Box 369, Shelbyville, IN 46176: Free information ❖ Push-type lawn mowers. 800–633–1501.

Ariens Company, 655 W. Ryan St., Brillion, WI 54110: Free information ❖ Self-propelled and riding mowers with electric start engines. 414–756–2141.

BCS America, 13601 Providence Rd., Matthews, NC 28105: Free catalog ❖ Garden carts, chippers and shredders, tillers, sprayers, lawn and garden tractors, and mowers. 704–846–1040.

Black & Decker, P.O. Box 798, Hunt Valley, MD 21030: Free information ❖ Portable vacuums and blowers in gasoline-powered and cordless electric models, electric hedge trimmers, and electric lawn mowers. 800–762–6672; 410–683–7000 (in MD).

Country Home Products, Ferry Rd., Box 89, Charlotte, VT 05445: Free information ❖ Power trimmer on wheels. 802–446–8746.

Dixon Industries Inc., P.O. Box 1569, Coffeyville, KS 67337: Free information ❖ Riding mowers. 316–251–2000.

Echo Inc., 400 Oakwood Rd., Lake Zurich, IL 60047: Free catalog ❖ Trimmers, blowers, hedge clippers, sprayers, chain saws, and shredders. 708–540–8400.

Excel Industries Inc., P.O. Box 7000, Hesston, KS 67062: Free information ❖ Riding mowers that mow, shred, edge, or vacuum. 316–327–4911.

Garden Way, 9th Ave. & 102nd St., Troy, NY 12180: Free information ❖ Carts, tillers, clippers, sickle bar mowers, garden composter, and other equipment. 800–345–4454.

The Grasshopper Company, One Grasshopper Trail, P.O. Box 637, Moundridge, KS 67107: Free information ❖ Riding mowers. 316–345–8621.

Homelite Sales, Box 7047, Charlotte, NC 28273: Free information with long SASE ❖ Push and riding mowers, lawn tractors, electric and gasoline-operated trimmers,

hedge trimmers, gasoline-powered blowers, vacuums, sprayers, cutoff saws, and snow removal equipment. 800–242–4672.

Husqvarna Power Products, Perimeter Woods Dr., Charlotte, NC 28216: Free information ❖ Walk-behind and riding mowers. 800–438–7297.

Kubota Tractor Corporation, P.O. Box 2992–C, Torrance, CA 90509: Free information ❖ Walk-behind mowers.

Lawn-Boy, Lyndale Ave. South, Bloomington, MN 55420: Free information ❖ Walk-behind and riding mowers, lawn and garden tractors, and power-operated tillers. 800–526–6937.

Mainline of North America, P.O. Box 526, London, OH 43140: Free information ❖ All-gear driven tiller with no belts or chains and optional sickle bar, hydraulic log splitter, cart, and snow thrower. 614–852–9733.

MTD Products Inc., P.O. Box 368022, Cleveland, OH 44136: Free information ❖ Walk-behind mowers with optional mulching and bagging attachments. 216–225–2600.

Poulan, 5020 Flournoy-Lucas Rd., Shreveport, LA 71129: Free information ❖ Gasoline-powered, hand-held blowers and lawn trimmer. 318–683–3546.

Simplicity Manufacturing Inc., P.O. Box 997, Port Washington, WI 53074: Free information ❖ Walk-behind and riding mowers. 414–284–8669.

Snapper Power Equipment, P.O. Box 777, McDonough, GA 30253: Free information ❖ Walk-behind and riding mowers. 404–954–2706.

Toro Company, 8111 Lyndale Ave., Bloomington, MN 55420: Free information ❖ Riding trimmers. 800–321–8676.

White Outdoor Products Company, P.O. Box 361131, Cleveland, OH 44136: Free information ❖ Walk-behind and riding mowers.

Organic Gardening Supplies

Bountiful Gardens, 18001 Shafer Ranch Rd., Willits, CA 95490: Free catalog ❖ Seeds for vegetables, compost crops, herbs, and flowers. Also books and organic gardening supplies. 707–459–6410.

Bricker's Organic Farm Inc., Sandbar Ferry Rd., Augusta, GA 30901: Catalog $1 ❖ Organic fertilizer and other gardening supplies. 800–200–5110.

Brown's Edgewood Gardens, 2611 Corrine Dr., Orlando, FL 32803: Catalog $2 ❖ Butterfly-attracting plants, herbs, and organic gardening products. 407–896–3203.

Gabrieana's Herbal & Organic Products, P.O. Box 215322, Sacramento, CA 95821: Free catalog ❖ Skin care and bath care items, essential oils, dried herbs, and other organic products. 800–684–4372.

Garden-Ville, 8648 Old Bee Caves Rd., Austin, TX 78735: Free catalog ❖ Organic gardening supplies, beneficial insects, other pest controls, and tools. 512–288–6115.

Gardens Alive, 5100 Schenley Pl., Lawrenceburg, IN 47025: Free catalog ❖ Organic gardening supplies. 812–537–8650.

Green Earth Organics, c/o Soil Conditioning, P.O. Box 206, Zillah, WA 98953: Free information ❖ Environmentally-safe fertilizers and nutrients for grasses, shrubs, flowers, and vegetables.

A High Country Garden, 2902 Rufina St., Santa Fe, NM 87501: Free catalog ❖ Organic gardening products and flowering plants. 800–925–9387.

Koos Inc., 4500 13th Ct., Kenosha, WI 53141: Free information ❖ Fertilizers, herbicides, insecticides, and organic plant foods. 414–654–5301.

Natural Gardening Company, 217 San Anselmo Ave., San Anselmo, CA 94960: Free catalog ❖ Beneficial insects, organic gardening supplies, pest controls, drip irrigation equipment, and wildflower seeds. 707–766–9303.

Nitron Industries Inc., P.O. Box 1447, Fayetteville, AR 72702: Free catalog ❖ Organic fertilizers, enzyme soil conditioners, natural pest controls, and pet care products. 800–835–0123.

Urban-Tek Growers Supply Inc., 2911 W. Wilshire, Oklahoma City, OK 73116: Free catalog ❖ Organic gardening supplies and lighting equipment for greenhouses and indoor gardens. 405–843–1888.

Pots & Planters

Cambridge Designs, P.O. Box 765, Hillsdale, MI 49242: Free catalog ❖ Landscaping benches, planters, receptacles, fountains, and pedestrian control screens. 517–439–4348.

Kingsley-Bate Ltd., 5587 Guinea Rd., Fairfax, VA 22032: Catalog $2 ❖ Hand-carved and traditional teak planters,

window boxes, and garden furniture. 703–978–7200.

Landscape Forms Inc., 431 Lawndale Ave., Kalamazoo, MI 49001: Free information ❖ Outdoor furniture and garden planters. 800–521–2546; 616–381–0396 (in MI).

Plant Collectibles, 103 Kenview Ave., Buffalo, NY 14217: Free catalog with two 1st class stamps ❖ Plastic pots, hanging baskets, starter trays, watering equipment, plant foods, insecticide sprays, and lighting units. 716–875–1221.

Planters International, 2635 Noble Rd., Cleveland, OH 44121: Free information ❖ Easy-to-use, no assembly self-watering planters. 800–341–2673; 216–382–3539 (in OH).

Products Plus Inc., 9655 SW Sunshine Ct., #100, Beaverton. OR 97005: Free information ❖ Park bench planter. 800–999–7136.

Pull 'N Feed, P.O. Box 8392, Madison, WI 53708: Free information ❖ Adjustable hanger for indoors and outdoors. 608–222–3699.

Syracuse Pottery, 6551 Pottery Rd., Warners, NY 13164: Free catalog ❖ Stoneware, ceramic, brass, and terra cotta indoor and outdoor planters. 315–487–6066.

TerraCast, 4700 Mitchell St. North, Las Vegas, NV 89030: Free information ❖ Unbreakable, lightweight planters for indoor and outdoor gardens. 800–423–8539; 702–643–2644 (in NV).

Violet House of Pots, Box 1274, Gainesville, FL 32601: Free catalog ❖ Indoor and outdoor plastic pots, hanging baskets, seeds for growing African violets, insecticides, potting soils, fertilizers, perlite, vermiculite, books, and trays. 904–377–8465.

Soil Testing

Cook's Consulting, RD 2, Box 13, Lowville, NY 13367: Free information ❖ Low-cost tests.

Freedom Soil Lab, P.O. Box 1144, Freedom, CA 95019: Free information ❖ Soil and garden testing services. 408–724–4427.

Necessary Trading Company, One Natures Way, New Castle, VA 24127: Free catalog ❖ Soil and garden testing services, testing supplies and equipment, plant nutrients, fertilizers, and pest control preparations. 800–447–5354.

Soil & Plant Laboratory, 4173–18 Joe Miller Rd., Malaga, WA 98828: Free information ❖ Soil and garden testing services.

Tillers

Ariens Company, 655 W. Ryan St., Brillon, WI 54110: Free information ❖ Power-operated tillers. 414–756–2141.

BCS America, 13601 Providence Rd., Matthews, NC 28105: Free catalog ❖ Garden carts, chippers and shredders, tillers, sprayers, lawn and garden tractors, and mowers. 704–846–1040.

Black & Decker, P.O. Box 798, Hunt Valley, MD 21030: Free information ❖ Power-operated tillers. 800–762–6672; 410–683–7000 (in MD).

Ford New Holland Inc., 500 Diller Ave., Holland, PA 17557: Free information ❖ Power-operated tillers. 717–355–1371.

Garden Way, 9th Ave. & 102nd St., Troy, NY 12180: Free information ❖ Power-operated tiller and composter for small gardens. 800–345–4454.

Husqvarna Power Products, Perimeter Woods Dr., Charlotte, NC 28216: Free information ❖ Power-operated tillers. 800–438–7297.

Kubota Tractor Corporation, P.O. Box 2992–C, Torrance, CA 90509: Free information ❖ Power-operated tillers.

Lawn-Boy, Lyndale Ave. South, Bloomington, MN 55420: Free information ❖ Walk-behind and riding mowers, lawn and garden tractors, and power-operated tillers. 800–526–6937.

Mainline of North America, P.O. Box 526, London, OH 43140: Free information ❖ Hydraulic log splitter, carts, snow throwers, and an all-gear driven tiller with optional sickle bar and no belts or chains. 614–852–9733.

Mantis Manufacturing Company, 1028 Street Rd., Southampton, PA 18966: Free information ❖ Electric-powered tiller with optional border edger, planter furrower, lawn aerator, and thatch remover. 800–366–6268.

Mighty Mac, Mackissic Inc., P.O. Box 111, Parker Ford, PA 19457: Free information ❖ Chippers, tillers, blowers, and sprayers.

Poulan, 5020 Flournoy-Lucas Rd., Shreveport, LA 71129: Free information ❖ Gasoline-powered hand-held blowers and lawn trimmer. 318–683–3546.

Roto-Hoe, P.O. Box 792, 345 15th St. NW, Barberton, OH 44203: Free information ❖ Easy-handling tillers. 216–753–2288.

White Outdoor Products Company, P.O. Box 361131, Cleveland, OH 44136: Free information ❖ Power-operated tillers.

Tools & Sprayers

Alsto Company, P.O. Box 1267, Galesburg, IL 61401: Catalog $1 ❖ Tools, pet products, kitchen aids, and other convenience items. 800–447–0048.

American Arborist Supplies Inc., 882 S. Matlack St., Unit A, West Chester, PA 19382: Catalog $4 (refundable) ❖ Tools for "backyard" gardeners.

Amerind MacKissic Inc., P.O. Box 111, Parker Ford, PA 19457: Free information ❖ Sprayers for fruit trees, shrubs, gardens, and lawns. 215–495–7181.

Ames Lawn & Garden Tools, P.O. Box 1774, Parkersburg, WV 26102: Free information ❖ Hand garden tools. 800–624–2654.

Arborist Supply House Inc., P.O. Box 23607, Fort Lauderdale, FL 33307: Free catalog ❖ Equipment, tools, and books.

Brookstone Company, Order Processing Center, 1655 Bassford Dr., Mexico, MO 65265: Free catalog ❖ House and garden tools. 800–926–7000.

W. Atlee Burpee & Company, 300 Park Ave., Warminster, PA 18974: Free catalog ❖ Tools, other equipment, and growing aids. 215–674–1793.

Carter Heirlooms, 15383 Nixon Rd., Mt. Vernon, OH 43050: Free information ❖ Red cedar potting bench. 614–892–3883.

Charley's Greenhouse Supply, 1569 Memorial Hwy., Mt. Vernon, WA 98273: Catalog $2 ❖ Shading materials, fans, watering and misting equipment, and propagating aids. 206–428–2626.

Clapper's, P.O. Box 2278, West Newton, MA 02165: Free catalog ❖ Spreaders, sprayers, sprinkling and full-flow watering systems, outdoor furniture, landscaping ornaments, and outdoor lighting. 617–244–7900.

Creative Enterprises Inc., P.O. Box 3452, Idaho Falls, ID 83403: Free information ❖ Hand garden tools. 208–523–0526.

Duraco Products, 109 E. Lake St., Streamwood, IL 60103: Free information ❖ Garden accessories. 800–888–POTS.

Environmental Concepts, 710 NW 57th St., Fort Lauderdale, FL 33309: Free brochure ❖

Meters that measure soil temperature, pH, light intensity, and the need for fertilizer. 305–491–4490.

Garden Tools of Maine, RR 2, Box 2208, East Holden, ME 04429: Free information ❖ Hand garden tools. 207–843–6271.

Gardener's Eden, Circulation Department, 100 N. Point St., n Francisco, CA 94133: Catalog $2 ❖ Tools, landscaping accessories, growing and transplanting aids, and furniture. 800–822–9600.

Gardener's Supply Company, 128 Intervale Rd., Burlington, VT 05401: Free catalog ❖ Composters, pest control sprayers, watering systems and controls, weeding and cultivating tools, organic fertilizers, garden carts, leaf mulchers, canning and preserving supplies, and furniture. 800–688–5510.

E.C. Geiger, Rt. 63, Box 285, Harleysville, PA 19438: Free catalog ❖ Greenhouse and other gardening supplies and tools.

Gro-Tek, 518 Rt. 81, Killingworth, CT 06417: Catalog 50¢ ❖ Seedling starter kits, tools, and supplies for greenhouses, solariums, and home gardening.

Harris Seeds, P.O. Box 22960, Rochester, NY 14692: Free catalog ❖ Gardening equipment, seeds, and plants. 716–594–9411.

Home Gardener Manufacturing Company, 30 Wright Ave., Littiz, PA 17543: Free information ❖ Easy-to-use compost-makers. 800–880–2345.

House of Wesley, 1704 Morrisey Dr., Bloomington, IL 61704: Free catalog ❖ Tools, plants, and seeds. 309–663–8551.

Indoor Gardening Supplies, P.O. Box 40567, Detroit, MI 48240: Free catalog ❖ Supplies, lights, and books. 313–426–9080.

Johnny's Selected Seeds, 310 Foss Hill Rd., Albion, ME 04910: Free catalog ❖ Tools, growing aids, and other gardening supplies. 207–437–9294.

Kemp Company, 160 Koser Rd., Lititz, PA 17543: Free information ❖ Composters. 717–627–7979.

The Kinsman Company, River Rd., Point Pleasant, PA 18950: Free catalog ❖ Composters, compost bins, chipper-shredders, rose arbors, garden arches, plant supports, and tools. 800–733–4146.

Langenbach Fine Tool Company, P.O. Box 453, Blairstown, NJ 07825: Free catalog ❖ Tools. 800–362–1991.

A.M. Leonard Inc., P.O. Box 816, Piqua, OH 45356: Free catalog ❖ Tools, sprayers, and gardening supplies. 800–543–8955; 513–773–2694 (in OH).

MacKenzie Nursery Supply Inc., P.O. Box 322, Perry, OH 44081: Free brochure ❖ Tools and supplies. 800–777–5030.

Mainline of North America, P.O. Box 526, London, OH 43140: Free information ❖ All-gear driven tiller with no belts or chains and optional sickle bar, hydraulic log splitter, cart, and snow thrower. 614–852–9733.

Mantis Manufacturing Company, 1028 Street Rd., Southampton, PA 18966: Free information ❖ Portable sprayer for gardens, washing windows and outside walls, and other uses. 800–366–6268.

Mellinger's, 2328 W. South Range Rd., North Lima, OH 44452: Free catalog ❖ Tools, plants and seeds, and growing aids. 216–549–9861.

Mighty Mac, Mackissic Inc., P.O. Box 111, Parker Ford, PA 19457: Free information ❖ Chippers, tillers, blowers, and sprayers.

Modern Homesteader, 1825 Big Horn Ave., Cody, WY 82414: Free catalog ❖ Gardening equipment, clothing and hats, tools, truck and automotive accessories, and canning equipment. 800–443–4934; 307–587–5946 (in WY).

Natural Gardening Company, 217 San Anselmo Ave., San Anselmo, CA 94960: Free catalog ❖ Tools, seeds, fertilizers, pest controls, birdhouses, and books. 707–766–9303.

Niwa Tool, 1333 San Pablo Ave., Berkeley, CA 94702: Catalog $2 ❖ Handcrafted Japanese garden and bonsai tools. 800–443–5512.

L.L. Olds Seed Company, P.O. Box 7790, Madison, WI 53707: Catalog $2.50 ❖ Tools, growing aids, seeds, and plants. 608–249–9291.

Park Seed Company, Cokesbury Rd., P.O. Box 46, Greenwood, SC 29648: Free catalog ❖ Tools, plants and seeds, and growing aids. 803–223–7333.

PeCo Inc., P.O. Box 1197, Arden, NC 28704: Free information ❖ Battery-powered sprayer with charger and wand. 800–438–5823; 704–684–1234 (in NC).

Pinetree Garden Seed, Box 300, New Gloucester, ME 04260: Free catalog ❖ Sprayers. 207–926–3400.

Plow & Hearth, 301 Madison Rd., P.O. Box 830, Orange, VA 22960: Free catalog ❖ Tools, outdoor furniture, bird houses and feeders, and birdbaths. 800–627–1712.

Poulan, 5020 Flournoy-Lucas Rd., Shreveport, LA 71129: Free information ❖ Gasoline-powered, hand-held blowers and lawn trimmer. 318–683–3546.

Ringer, 9959 Valley View Rd., Eden Prairie, MN 55344: Free catalog ❖ Tools, chemical treatments and fertilizers, growing aids, propagation aids, compost-making equipment, lawn care supplies, and planters. 800–654–1047.

Smith & Hawken, P.O. Box 6907, Florenced, KY 41022: Free information ❖ Tools, sprayers, and greenhouse supplies. 800–776–5558.

Stern's Miracle-Gro, P.O. Box 888, Port Washington, NY 11050: Free information ❖ Sprayers, chemical treatments, and fertilizers. 516–883–6550.

Stokes Seeds Inc., Box 548, Buffalo, NY 14240: Free catalog ❖ Greenhouse tools and supplies. 416–688–4300.

V & B Manufacturing, P.O. Box 268, Walnut Ridge, AR 72476: Free information ❖ Landscaping tools. 800–443–1987.

Topiary Frames & Supplies

Fox Hill Farm, 444 W. Michigan Ave., Box 9, Parma, MI 49269: Catalog $1 ❖ Herbal topiary standards and supplies. 517–531–3179.

FrenchWyres, P.O. Box 131655, Tyler, TX 75713: Catalog $3 ❖ Trellises, topiary frames, urns, plant stands, cachepots, window boxes, and arches. 903–597–8322.

The Kinsman Company, River Rd., Point Pleasant, PA 18950: Free catalog ❖ Topiary forms. 800–733–4146.

Rabbit Shadow Farm, 2880 E. Hwy. 402, Loveland, CO 80537: Free information ❖ Herbs, roses, topiary supplies, and scented geraniums. 303–667–5531.

Topiary Inc., 41 Bering, Tampa, FL 33606: Free brochure ❖ Geometric and animal topiary shapes. 813–837–2841.

Tractors

Ariens Company, 655 W. Ryan St., Brillon, WI 54110: Free information ❖ Lawn and garden tractors. 414–756–2141.

BCS America, 13601 Providence Rd., Matthews, NC 28105: Free catalog ❖ Lawn and garden tractors, garden carts, chippers and shredders, tillers, sprayers, and mowers. 704–846–1040.

Club Cadet Corporation, Box 368023, Cleveland, OH 44136: Free information ❖ Easy-to-operate tractor with optional snow thrower and bagging attachment. 216–273–4550.

Ford New Holland Inc. 500 Diller Ave., Holland, PA 17557: Free information ❖ Lawn and garden tractors. 717–355–1371.

Garden Way, 9th Ave. & 102nd St., Troy, NY 12180: Free information ❖ Lawn and garden tractors. 800–345–4454.

Husqvarna Power Products, Perimeter Woods Dr., Charlotte, NC 28216: Free information ❖ Lawn and garden tractors. 800–438–7297.

Kubota Tractor Corporation, P.O. Box 2992–C, Torrance, CA 90509: Free information ❖ Lawn and garden tractors.

Lawn-Boy, Lyndale Ave. South, Bloomington, MN 55420: Free information ❖ Walk-behind and riding mowers, lawn and garden tractors, and power-operated tillers. 800–526–6937.

Poulan, 5020 Flournoy-Lucas Rd., Shreveport, LA 71129: Free information ❖ Lawn and garden tractors. 318–683–3546.

Simplicity Manufacturing Inc., P.O. Box 997, Port Washington, WI 53074: Free information ❖ Lawn and garden tractors. 414–284–8669.

Snapper Power Equipment, P.O. Box 777, McDonough, GA 30253: Free information ❖ Lawn and garden tractors. 404–954–2706.

White Outdoor Products Company, P.O. Box 361131, Cleveland, OH 44136: Free information ❖ Lawn and garden tractors.

Yamaha Outdoor Power Equipment Division, 6555 Katella Ave., Cypress, CA 90630: Free information ❖ Lawn and garden tractors.

Water Gardening Supplies

Bareebo Inc., 3840 Main Rd. East, Emmaus, PA 18049: Free information ❖ Aerating fountain equipment. 800–AERSTER; 215–965–6018 (in PA).

Cambridge Designs, P.O. Box 765, Hillsdale, MI 49242: Free catalog ❖ Landscaping benches, planters, receptacles, fountains, and pedestrian control screens. 517–439–4348.

Dolphin Outdoors, Dolphin Pet Village, 1808 W. Campbell Ave., Campbell, CA 95008: Free brochure with long SASE ❖ Fiberglass ponds for water gardens, filters, plants, and fish. 408–379–7600.

Fabra-Tech Manufacturing Inc., 35 E. Pierson St., Greenfield, IN 46140: Free information ❖ Waterfall kits and landscape and light rocks. 317–462–6686.

Grovac Inc., 4310 N. 126th St., Brookfield, WI 53005: Free information ❖ Power-operated aerating equipment for water gardens. 414–781–5020.

Hardwicke Gardens, 254 Boston Turnpike Rd., Westboro, MA 01581: Catalog $2 (refundable) ❖ Garden pool supplies and statuary.

Hermitage Gardens, P.O. Box 361, Canastota, NY 13032: Catalog $1 ❖ Fiberglass rocks and waterfalls, redwood water wheels, wood bridges, garden pools, and bubbling fantasias. 315–697–9093.

Laboratories Corporation, Box 630, Cibolo, TX 78108: Free information ❖ Garden pool products. 512–658–3503.

Lilypons Water Gardens, P.O. Box 10, Buckeystown, MD 21717: Catalog $5 ❖ Supplies for aquatic gardens. 800–723–7667.

Maryland Aquatic Nurseries, 3427 N. Furnace Rd., Jarrettsville, MD 21084: Catalog $5 (refundable) ❖ Plants for water garden settings, ornamental grasses, and Japanese irises. 410–557–7615.

Paradise Water Gardens, 32 May St., Whitman, MA 02382: Free catalog ❖ Fountains, pools, pumps, goldfish, aquatic plants, and books. 617–447–4711.

Patio Garden Ponds, 7919 S. Shields, Oklahoma City, OK 73149: Catalog $3 ❖ Patio garden pond liners, pumps, filters and filter media, water lilies, nitrifying aids, and bacteria. 405–634–7663.

Pets Unlimited, 1888 Drew, Clearwater, FL 34625: Information $2 ❖ Water pond supplies. 813–442–2197.

Rock & Waterscape Systems Inc., 11 Whatney, Irvine, CA 92718: Free information ❖ Custom rock and water arrangements. 714–770–1936.

S. Scherer & Sons, 104 Waterside Rd., Northport, NY 11768: Free price list ❖ Water lilies, aquatic plants, pools, pumps, waterfalls, and fish. 516–261–7432.

Slocum Water Gardens, 1101 Cypress Gardens Rd., Winter Haven, FL 33884: Catalog $3 ❖ Water garden supplies. 813–293–7151.

Somethin' Fishy, 5103 Kingston Pike, Knoxville, TN 37919: Catalog $2 ❖ Water garden supplies. 615–584–1925.

Tetra Pond, 201 Tabor Rd., Morris Plains, NJ 07950: Free brochure ❖ Pool liners, plants, fish and food, and water treatments.

Urdl's Waterfall Creations Inc., 1010 NW 1st St., Delray Beach, FL 33444: Free information ❖ Manufactured hollow concrete rocks for landscaping and waterfall settings. 305–278–3320.

Van Ness Water Gardens, 2460 N. Euclid, Upland, CA 91786: Catalog $2 ❖ Water lilies, other aquatic plants, waterfalls, and garden supplies. 714–982–2425.

Waterford Gardens, 74 E. Allendale Rd., Saddle River, NJ 07458: Catalog $5 ❖ Water lilies, lotus and bog plants, pools, and fish. 201–327–0721.

Windy Oaks, W377 S10677 Betts Rd., Eagle, WI 53119: Free catalog ❖ Water garden supplies. 414–594–2803.

Watering & Irrigation Equipment

Acu-Drip Water System, Wade Manufacturing Company, P.O. Box 8769, Portland, OR 97208: Free brochure ❖ Easy-to-install drip watering systems. 800–222–7246.

Full Circle, P.O. Box 6, Redway, CA 95560: Catalog $2 ❖ Watering system kits, outdoor irrigation supplies, and soaker hoses. 800–426–5511.

Harmony Farm Supply, P.O. Box 460, Graton, CA 95444: Catalog $2 (refundable) ❖ Watering system kits, outdoor irrigation supplies, and soaker hoses. 707–823–9125.

Hunter Sprinklers, 1940 Diamond St., San Marcos, CA 92069: Free information ❖ Water-efficient sprinkler systems. 619–744–5240.

International Aeration Systems (Irrigo), 1555 3rd Ave., P.O. Box 360, Niagara Falls, NY 14304: Free information ❖ Micro-porous irrigation systems for home gardeners and commercial growers. 905–688–4093.

International Aeration Systems (Oxyflo), 1555 3rd Ave., P.O. Box 360, Niagara Falls, NY 14304: Free information ❖ Micro-porous aeration systems for fish farming and general aeration applications. 905–688–4093.

Irrigro, 1555 3rd Ave., P.O. Box 360, Niagara Falls, NY 14304: Free information ❖ Drip irrigation systems. 416–688–4090.

Mel-Nor Industries, 303 Gulf Bank, Houston, TX 77037: Information $1 ❖ Time-controlled sprinklers, hose reel carts, hanging lawn and porch swings, park benches, and old-time lamp posts. 713–445–3485.

Moss Products Inc., P.O. Box 72, Palmetto, FL 33561: Free catalog ❖ Watering systems for gardens. 813–729–5433.

Natural Gardening Company, 217 San Anselmo Ave., San Anselmo, CA 94960: Free catalog ❖ Beneficial insects, organic gardening supplies, pest controls, drip irrigation equipment, and wildflower seeds. 707–766–9303.

Plastic Plumbing Products, 17005 Manchester Rd., P.O. Box 186, Grover, MO 63040: Catalog $1 (refundable) ❖ Drip irrigation systems, outdoor irrigation supplies, and soaker hoses. 314–458–2226.

Raindrip Inc., 21305 Itasca St., Chatsworth, CA 91313: Free catalog ❖ Watering system kits, outdoor irrigation supplies, and soaker hoses. 800–225–3747.

Ramsey Irrigation Systems, 7711 Knoxville Dr., Lubbock, TX 79423: Free information ❖ Drip irrigation equipment. 800–477–2347.

Skagit Gardens, 1695 Johnson Rd., Mt. Vernon, WA 98273: Catalog $2 ❖ Watering system kits, outdoor irrigation supplies, and soaker hoses. 206–424–6760.

Submatic Irrigation Systems, P.O. Box 246, Lubbock, TX 79048: Free information ❖ Irrigation systems. 800–692–4100.

Urban Farmer Store, 2833 Vicente St., San Francisco, CA 94116: Catalog $1 ❖ Watering system kits, outdoor irrigation supplies, and soaker hoses. 800–753–3747; 415–661–2204 (in CA).

VC & C Products, Rt. 3, Box 438, Hereford, TX 79045: Free catalog ❖ Adjustable lawn and garden sprinkler. 806–276–5338.

Weiss Brothers Nurseries, 11690 Colfax Hwy., Grass Valley, CA 95945: Free catalog ❖ Drip irrigation supplies. 916–272–7657.

GARDENING—PLANTS & SEEDS
African Violets & Gesneriads

Alice's Violets, Rt. 6, Box 233, Waynesville, MO 65583: Free catalog with long SASE ❖ Single, double, semi-double, miniature, and semi-miniature African violets. 314–336–4763.

Cape Cod Violetry, 28 Minot St., Falmouth, MA 02540: Catalog $2 (refundable) ❖ African violet plants and leaves. 508–548–2798.

Davidson-Wilson Greenhouses, Rt. 2, Box 168, Crawfordsville, IN 47933: Catalog $3 ❖ African violets, houseplants, and geraniums. 317–364–0556.

DoDe's Gardens Inc., 1490 Saturn St., Merritt Island, FL 32953: Free catalog with two 1st class stamps ❖ African violets and growing supplies. 407–452–5670.

Florals of Fredericks, 155 Spartan Dr., Maitland, FL 32751: Catalog $2 ❖ African violets and growing supplies. 800–771–0899.

JoS Violets, 2205 College Dr., Victoria, TX 77901: Free list with long SASE ❖ Standard, semi-miniature, miniature, and trailing African violets and growing supplies. 512–575–1344.

Judy's Violets, 9 Graeler Dr., Creve Coeur, MO 63146: Catalog $1 ❖ African violets. 314–997–2859.

Kartuz Greenhouses, 1408 Sunset Dr., Vista, CA 92083: Catalog $2 ❖ Gesneriads, begonias, miniature terrarium, and unusual tropical plants. 619–941–3613.

Lauray of Salisbury, 432 Undermountain Rd., Salisbury, CT 06068: Catalog $2 ❖ Gesneriads, begonias, orchids, cacti and succulents, and other plants. 203–435–2263.

Les Violettes Natalia, P.O. Box 206, Beecher Falls, VT 05902: Catalog $2 ❖ African violet cuttings.

Lyndon Lyon Greenhouses Inc., 14 Mutchler St., Dolgeville, NY 13329: Catalog $2 ❖ African violets and exotic houseplants. 315–429–8291.

D. Mendoza African Violets, 160 N. Montgomery St., San Jose, CA 95110: Free catalog ❖ African violets. 408–279–8411.

Midland Violets, Don & Jean Ness, 3667 Midland Ave., White Bear Lake, MN 55110: Free catalog with long SASE ❖ Standard, miniature, and semi-miniature African violets. 612–429–4109.

Mighty Minis, 7318 Sahara Ct., Sacramento, CA 95828: Catalog $1 (refundable) ❖ Miniature African violet plants and leaves. 916–421–7284.

Pleasant Hill African Violets, Rt. 1, Box 73, Brenham, TX 77833: Price list $1.50 ❖ Standard and miniature African violets. 409–836–9736.

Rob's Mimi-o-lets, P.O. Box 9, Naples, NY 14152: Catalog $1 (refundable) ❖ Miniature African violets and gesneriads.

Spirit North, 3690 Townline Rd., Eagle River, WI 54521: Free list with 1st class stamp ❖ Hybridized African violets. 715–479–2927.

Tinari Greenhouses, P.O. Box 190, Huntingdon Valley, PA 19006: Catalog 50c ❖ Standard, miniature, trailer, and variegated African violets. 215–947–0144.

Travis Violets, P.O. Box 42, Ochlochnee, GA 31773: Catalog $1 (refundable) ❖ Hybrid African violets, growing supplies, and pots. 912–574–5167.

Violet Creations, 5520 Wilkins Rd., Tampa, FL 33619: Free catalog ❖ African violets, gesneriads, and growing supplies. 813–626–6817.

Violet Express, Everett Rd., Eagle River, WI 54521: Catalog $2 ❖ African violet leaf cuttings.

Violet Showcase, 3147 S. Broadway, Englewood, CO 80110: Catalog $1 ❖ Standards, trailers, pinwheels, miniatures, and other African violet plants. 303–761–1770.

Violets by Appointment, Bill & Kathryn Paauwe, 45 3rd St., West Sayville, NY 11796: List $1.50 (refundable) ❖ African violets. 516–589–2724.

Volkmann Bros. Greenhouses, 2714 Minert St., Dallas, TX 75219: Free catalog ❖ African violets and growing supplies. 214–526–3484.

Aquatic Plants

Eco-Gardens, P.O. Box 1227, Decatur, GA 30031: Price list $1 ❖ Water garden plants, perennials, wildflowers, ferns, daylilies, trees, shrubs, and ferns. 404–294–6468.

Kester's Birdseed Inc., P.O. Box 516, Omro, WI 54963: Catalog $2 ❖ Aquatic plants. 800–558–8815; 414–685–2929 (in WI).

Maryland Aquatic Nurseries, 3427 N. Furnace Rd., Jarrettsville, MD 21084: Catalog

$5 (refundable) ❖ Marginal and bog plants for aquatic gardens. 410–557–7615.

S. Scherer & Sons, 104 Waterside Rd., Northport, NY 11768: Free price list ❖ Water lilies, other aquatic plants, pools, pumps, waterfalls, fish, liners, and other supplies. 516–261–7432.

William Tricker Inc., 7125 Tanglewood Dr., Independence, OH 44131: Catalog $2 ❖ Water lilies, aquatic plants, exotic fish for indoor and outdoor water gardens, and pumps, liners, and other supplies. 800–524–3492.

Waterford Gardens, 74 E. Allendale Rd., Saddle River, NJ 07458: Catalog $5 ❖ Water lilies, lotus and bog plants, and pools. 201–327–0721.

Wicklein's Aquatic Farm & Nursery Inc., 1820 Cromwell Bridge Rd., Baltimore, MD 21234: Catalog $1 ❖ Water lilies, other aquatic plants, and perennials. 410–823–1335.

Azaleas & Rhododendrons

Carlson's Gardens, Box 305, South Salem, NY 10590: Catalog $3 ❖ Dwarf rhododendrons and landscape-size azaleas. 914–763–5958.

Crownsville Nursery, P.O. Box 797, Crownsville, MD 21032: Catalog $10 ❖ Ferns, wildflowers, azaleas, ornamental grasses, and perennials. 410–923–2212.

Cummins Garden, 22 Robertsville Rd., Marlboro, NJ 07746: Catalog $2 (refundable) ❖ Dwarf rhododendrons, evergreens and deciduous azaleas, dwarf conifers, and companion plants. 908–536–2591.

Daystar, Rt. 2, Box 250, Litchfield, ME 04350: Catalog $1 ❖ Perennials, rhododendrons, trees, shrubs, and other plants. 207–724–3369.

Eco-Gardens, P.O. Box 1227, Decatur, GA 30031: Price list $1 ❖ Azaleas, perennials, wildflowers, ferns, daylilies, water garden plants, trees, and shrubs. 404–294–6468.

Flora Lan Nursery, Rt. 1, Box 357, Forest Grove, OR 97116: Free catalog ❖ Azaleas and rhododendron hybrids. 503–357–3500.

Girard Nurseries, P.O. Box 428, Geneva, OH 44041: Free catalog ❖ Azaleas and rhododendrons. 216–466–2881.

The Greenery, 14450 NE 16th Pl., Bellevue, WA 98007: Catalog $1 (refundable) ❖ Azaleas and rhododendrons. 206–641–1458.

Greer Gardens, 1280 Goodpasture Island Rd., Eugene, OR 97401: Catalog $3 ❖ Azaleas and rhododendrons, trees, shrubs, Japanese maples, and bonsai. 503–686–8266.

Roslyn Nursery, 211 Burrs Ln., Dix Hills, NY 11746: Catalog $3 ❖ Rhododendrons. 516–643–9347.

Bamboo

David C. Andrews, P.O. Box 358, Oxon Hill, MD 20750: Free price list ❖ Bamboo plants.

Bamboo Sourcery, 666 Wagnon Rd., Sebastopol, CA 95472: Catalog $2 ❖ Bamboo plants. 707–823–5866.

Kurt Bluemel Inc., 2740 Greene Ln., Baldwin, MD 21013: Catalog $2 ❖ Bamboo plants, perennials, ferns, and ornamental grasses. 410–557–7229.

Burt Associates, P.O. Box 719, Westford, MA 01886: Catalog $2 ❖ Bamboo plants. 508–692–3240.

Endangered Species, P.O. Box 1830, Tustin, CA 92681: Catalog $6 ❖ Giant, medium-sized, dwarf-green, and variegated bamboo plants and other rare plants. 714–544–9505.

Garden World's Exotic Plants, 2503 Garfield St., Laredo, TX 78043: Catalog $1 ❖ Bamboo, bananas, citrus trees, cacti, and other tropical growing stock. 512–724–3951.

Gardens of the Blue Ridge, P.O. Box 10, Pineola, NC 28662: Catalog $3 (refundable) ❖ Bamboo plants. 704–733–2417.

Louisiana Nursery, Rt. 7, Box 43, Opelousas, LA 70570: Catalog $6 ❖ Bamboo plants, and other rare, unusual, and hard-to-find plants and books. 318–948–3696.

New England Bamboo Company, P.O. Box 358, Rockport, MA 01966: Catalog $5 (refundable) ❖ Bamboo plants. 508–546–3581.

Orion Trading Company, 820 Coventry Rd., Kensington, CA 94707: Catalog $1 ❖ Bamboo poles. 510–540–7136.

Steve Ray's Bamboo Gardens, 909 79th Pl. South, Birmingham, AL 35206: Catalog $2 ❖ Bamboo plants. 205–833–3052.

Tradewinds Bamboo Nursery, 28446 Hunter Creek Loop, Gold Beach, OR 97444: Catalog $2 ❖ Bamboo plants and books.

Tripple Brook Farm, 37 Middle Rd., Southampton, MA 01073: Free catalog ❖

Bamboo plants, exotic fruits, trees, perennials, and shrubs. 413–527–4626.

Banana Plants

The Banana Tree, 715 Northampton St., Easton, PA 18042: Catalog $3 ❖ Banana and other tropical plants and seeds.

Garden World's Exotic Plants, 2503 Garfield St., Laredo, TX 78043: Catalog $1 ❖ Bamboo, bananas, citrus trees, cacti, and other tropical growing stock. 512–724–3951.

Begonias

Antonelli Brothers, 2545 Capitola Rd., Santa Cruz, CA 95062: Catalog $1 ❖ Tuberous and miniature begonias. 408–475–5222.

Fairyland Begonia Garden, 1100 Griffith Rd., McKinleyville, CA 95521: Price list 50¢ ❖ Hybrid begonias.

Glasshouse Works Greenhouses, P.O. Box 97, Stewart, OH 45778: Catalog $3 ❖ Begonias and rare tropical plants. 614–662–2142.

Kartuz Greenhouses, 1408 Sunset Dr., Vista, CA 92083: Catalog $2 ❖ Begonias, miniature terrarium plants, and tropical plants. 619–941–3613.

Kay's Greenhouses, 207 W. Southcross, San Antonio, TX 78221: Price list $2 ❖ Cane and rhizomatous begonias.

Lauray of Salisbury, 432 Undermountain Rd., Salisbury, CT 06068: Catalog $2 ❖ Begonias, gesneriads, orchids, cacti and succulents, and other plants. 203–435–2263.

Berry Plants

Ahrens Strawberry Nursery, P.O. Box 145, Huntingburg, IN 47542: Free catalog ❖ Fruit trees, grapevines, rhubarb, currants, and strawberry, gooseberry, raspberry, blueberry, and blackberry plants. 612–683–3055.

Allen Plant Company, P.O. Box 310, Fruitland, MD 21826: Free catalog ❖ Registered virus-free strawberry plants and blueberries, raspberries, thornless blackberries, and asparagus. 410–742–7122.

Vernon Barnes & Son Nursery, P.O. Box 250, McMinnville, TN 37110: Free catalog ❖ Berry plants, shrubs, hedges, vines, wildflowers, and flowering, shade, fruit, and nut trees. 615–668–8576.

Bear Creek Nursery, P.O. Box 41175, Northport, WA 99157: Catalog $1 ❖ Blueberry plants. 509–732–6219.

Blueberry Hill, RR 1, Maynooth, Ontario, Canada K0L 2S0: Free catalog ❖ Hardy, native lowbush blueberry plants for cold climates.

Boston Mountain Nurseries, Rt. 2, Box 405–A, Mountainburg, AR 71946: Free catalog with 1st class stamp ❖ Plants for strawberries, blueberries, cane berries, and table grapes. 501–369–2007.

Brittingham Plant Farms, P.O. Box 2538, Salisbury, MD 21801: Free catalog ❖ Strawberry, blueberry, raspberry, thornless blackberry, grape, and asparagus plants. 410–749–5148.

W. Atlee Burpee & Company, 300 Park Ave., Warminster, PA 18974: Free catalog ❖ Berry plants, seeds, bulbs, and gardening supplies. 215–674–1793.

Champlain Isle Farm, Isle La Motte, VT 05463: Free information ❖ Vermont-certified virus-free, greenhouse-grown raspberries. 802–928–3425.

The Conner Company, P.O. Box 534, Augusta, AR 72006: Free catalog ❖ Strawberry plants. 501–347–2561.

Country Carriage Nurseries & Seed Inc., P.O. Box 548, Hartford, MI 49057: Free catalog ❖ Vegetable and herb seeds, fruit trees, and berry plants. 616–621–2491.

DeGrandchamp's Blueberry Farm, 15575 77th St., South Haven, MI 49060: Free catalog ❖ Blueberry plants. 616–637–3915.

Dutch Mountain Nursery, 7984 N. 48th St., Augusta, MI 49012: Free catalog with long SASE ❖ Berry plants. 616–731–5232.

Dyke Blueberry Farm & Nursery Inc., Rt. 1, Box 251, Vincent, OH 45758: Free catalog with long SASE ❖ Blueberry growing stock. 800–732–7869; 614–678–2192 (in OH).

Emlong Nurseries, 2671 Marquette Woods Rd., Stevensville, MI 49127: Free catalog ❖ Thornless blackberries, other berry plants, shrubs, flowers, landscaping plants, roses, and dwarf and standard fruit, nut, and ornamental trees. 616–429–3431.

Enoch's Berry Farm, Rt. 2, Box 227, Fouke, AR 71837: Free price list ❖ Blackberry plants and root cuttings. 501–653–2806.

Farmer Seed & Nursery Company, 818 NW 4th St., Faribault, MN 55021: Free catalog ❖ Berry plants, vegetable seeds, flowering bulbs, fruit and shade trees, ornamental shrubs and hedges, and roses. 507–334–2017.

Henry Field's Seed & Nursery, 415 N. Burnett, Shenandoah, IA 51602: Free catalog ❖ Strawberry and other berry plants, vegetable and flower seeds, hedges, ornamental shrubs, roses, and fruit, nut, and shade trees. 605–665–4491.

Fig Tree Nursery, P.O. Box 124, Gulf Hammock, FL 32639: Catalog $1 ❖ Berry plants, ornamentals, and grapes for southern climates. 904–486–2930.

Fruit Testing Association Nursery, P.O. Box 462, Geneva, NY 14456: Catalog $10 ❖ Berry plants. 315–787–2205.

Harris Seeds Inc., P.O. Box 22960, Rochester, NY 14692: Free catalog ❖ Berry plants and seeds. 716–594–9411.

Hartmann's Plantation, P.O. Box E, Grand Junction, MI 49056: Catalog $2.25 (refundable) ❖ Blueberry plants. 616–253–4281.

Highlander Nursery, P.O. Box 177, Pettigrew, AR 72752: Free catalog ❖ Hardy, low-chill blueberry plants. 501–677–2300.

Ison's Nursery, Rt. 1, Brooks, GA 30205: Free catalog ❖ Fruit and nut trees, muscadine grapevines, and blackberry, blueberry, raspberry, and strawberry plants. 800–733–0324.

Johnny's Selected Seeds, 310 Foss Hill Rd., Albion, ME 04910: Free catalog ❖ Strawberry plants, flower and vegetable seeds for northern climates, gardening tools, and growing supplies. 207–437–9294.

Johnson Nursery, Rt. 5, Box 296, Ellijay, GA 30540: Free catalog ❖ Strawberry plants, grapevines, and apple, plum, pear, cherry, apricot, and walnut and almond nut trees. 404–276–3187.

Kelly Nurseries, 1708 Morrissey Dr., Bloomington, IL 61704: Free catalog ❖ Berry plants, grapevines, heavily rooted fruit and nut trees, landscaping trees, shrubs, ornamentals, and flowers. 309–663–9551.

Krohne Plant Farms, Rt. 6, Box 586, Dowagiac, MI 48197: Free information ❖ Strawberry plants. 616–424–3450.

Lewis Strawberry Nursery Inc., P.O. Box 24, Rocky Point, NC 28457: Free catalog ❖ Strawberry plants. 800–453–5346.

Makielski Berry Nursery, 7130 Platt Rd., Ypsilanti, MI 48197: Free catalog ❖ Plants for raspberries, thornless blackberries, strawberries, rhubarb, currants, gooseberries, and blueberries. 313–434–3673.

Earl May Seeds & Nursery Company, N. Elm St., Shenandoah, IA 51603: Free catalog ❖ Vegetable and flower seeds, bulbs, fruit and nut trees, roses, berry plants, grapevines, shade and ornamental trees, flowering shrubs, other plants, and gardening supplies. 712–246–1020.

Mellinger's, 2310 W. South Range Rd., North Lima, OH 44452: Free catalog ❖ Fruit and nut trees, ornamental and shade trees, flowering shrubs and hedges, perennials, wildflowers, berry plants, and gardening supplies. 216–549–9861.

J.E. Miller Nurseries, 5060 West Lake Rd., Canandaigua, NY 14424: Free catalog ❖ Berry plants, fruit trees, and grapevines. 800–836–9630.

Nichols Garden Nursery, 1190 Pacific West, Albany, OR 97321: Free catalog ❖ Vegetable and herb seeds, strawberry plants, and saffron crocus, garlic, and shallot growing stock. 503–928–9280.

North Star Gardens, 19060 Manning Trail North, Marine, MN 55047: Free catalog ❖ Currants, gooseberries, raspberries, and blackberries. 612–227–9842.

Nourse Farms, 41 River Rd., South Deerfield, MA 01373: Free information ❖ Raspberry, strawberry, asparagus, and rhubarb plants. 413–665–2568.

Pacific Berry Works, 963 Thomas Rd., Bow, WA 98232: Free list ❖ Raspberries, strawberries, and blackberries for northern climates. 206–757–4385.

Park Seed Company Inc., Cokesbury Rd., P.O. Box 46, Greenwood, SC 29648: Free catalog ❖ Strawberry plants, seeds and bulbs, tools, and gardening supplies. 803–223–7333.

Patrick's Nursery, P.O. Box 130, Ty Ty, GA 31795: Free catalog ❖ Vegetable seeds for southern climates, fruit and nut trees, berry plants, and grapevines. 912–386–1122.

Peaceful Valley Farm Supply, P.O. Box 2209, Grass Valley, CA 95945: Catalog $2 (refundable) ❖ Berry plants. 916–272–4769.

Rayner Brothers Inc., P.O. Box 1617, Salisbury, MD 21801: Free catalog ❖ Dwarf fruit trees, evergreen seedlings, and strawberry, raspberry, blueberry, and asparagus plants. 410–742–1594.

Savage Farms Nursery, P.O. Box 125, McMinnville, TN 37110: Free catalog ❖ Berry plants, evergreens, gardening supplies, and shrubs, fruit, shade, and flowering trees. 615–668–8902.

R.H. Shumway Seedsman, P.O. Box 1, Graniteville, SC 29829: Free catalog ❖ Berry plants, fruit trees, roses, seeds and bulbs, ornamental shrubs and plants, and gardening supplies.

Stark Bro's. Nurseries & Orchards Company, P.O. Box 10, Louisiana, MO 63353: Free catalog ❖ Berry plants, gardening supplies, and fruit, nut and shade trees. 800–325–4180.

Thompson & Morgan Inc., P.O. Box 1308, Jackson, NJ 08527: Free catalog ❖ Strawberry plants and vegetable and flower seeds. 800–274–7333.

White Flower Farm, Rt. 63, Litchfield, CT 06759: Free catalog ❖ Bulbs, perennials, shrubs, strawberry plants, other seeds and plants, books, tools, and gardening supplies. 800–888–7756.

Bonsai

Artistic Plants, P.O. Box 1165, Burleson, TX 76028: Catalog $1 ❖ Bonsai, bonsai pots and tools, succulents, terrarium mixtures, and gardening supplies. 817–295–0802.

Avid Gardener, Box 200, Hamburg, IL 62045: Catalog $2 ❖ Dwarf conifers, companion shrubs, ground covers, and potential bonsai.

Bonsai Associates Inc., 3000 Chestnut Ave., Baltimore, MD 21211: Catalog $2 ❖ Books, plants, tools, soil components, and wire. 301–235–5336.

Bonsai Farm, P.O. Box 130, Lavernia, TX 78121: Catalog $1 ❖ Bonsai trees, indoor and outdoor bonsai plants, books, tools, and pots. 512–649–2109.

Bonsai of Brooklyn, 2443 McDonald Ave., Brooklyn, NY 11223: Free price list ❖ Potted and established bonsai, trained and semi-trained pre-bonsai stock, tools, books, pottery, and other supplies. 800–8–BONSAI; 718–339–8252 (in NY).

Bonsai of Florida, 6812 Coralberry Ln. North, Jacksonville, FL 32244: Catalog $1 ❖ Bonsai tools, wire, containers, and other supplies. 904–779–7698.

Bonsai Northwest, 5021 S. 144th St., Seattle, WA 98168: Catalog $2 ❖ Bonsai pots and tools. 206–242–8244.

Bonsai Products, Jim Barrett, 480 Oxford Dr., Arcadia, CA 91006: Free information with long SASE ❖ Bonsai supplies. 818–445–4529.

The Bonsai Shop, 43 William St., Smithtown, NY 11787: Catalog $2 ❖ Bonsai, growing supplies, tools, and books. 516–724–3055.

Bonsai West, 100 Great Rd., P.O. Box 1291, Littleton, MA 01460: Free information with long SASE ❖ Bonsai growing supplies, pots, tools, and books. 508–486–3556.

Brussel's Bonsai Nursery, 8365 Center Hill Rd., Olive Branch, MS 38654: Catalog $1 (refundable) ❖ Bonsai, pots, growing supplies. 601–895–7457.

Dallas Bonsai Garden, P.O. Box 801565, Dallas, TX 75380: Free catalog ❖ Bonsai and supplies. 800–982–1223.

Electra Tech International Inc., 2302 Parkside, Irving, TX 75061: Free catalog ❖ Bonsai containers and other pottery from China. 214–986–0706.

Flowertown Bonsai, 207 E. Luke St., Summerville, SC 29483: Free price list ❖ Bonsai and pottery. 803–821–8347.

Forestfarm, 990 Tetherow Rd., Williams, OR 97544: Catalog $3 ❖ Plants, ornamental trees, shrubs, and perennials for bonsai. 503–846–6963.

Girard Nurseries, P.O. Box 428, Geneva, OH 44041: Free catalog ❖ Bonsai and ornamental trees, shrubs, and evergreen seeds and trees. 216–466–2881.

Greer Gardens, 1280 Goodpasture Island Rd., Eugene, OR 97401: Catalog $3 ❖ Bonsai, azaleas and rhododendrons, trees, shrubs, Japanese maples, and succulents. 503–686–8266.

Jiu San Bonsai Company, P.O. Box 151, Old Bethpage, NY 11804: Free information ❖ Bonsai and supplies. 516–293–9246.

Jope's Bonsai, P.O. Box 594, Wenham, MA 01984: Catalog $2 ❖ Unusual dwarf plants, tools, pots, growing supplies, and books. 508–468–2249.

Keystone Arts, 131 Morewood Ave., Pittsburgh, PA 15213: Free catalog ❖ Bonsai stands, pots, and tools. 412–682–8066.

Lone Pine Connection, P.O. Box 1338, Forestville, CA 95436: Catalog $3 ❖ Bonsai starters.

Marrs Tree Farm, P.O. Box 375, Payallup, WA 98373: Catalog $1 (refundable) ❖ Bonsai plants.

Matsu-Momiji Nursery, P.O. Box 11414, Philadelphia, PA 19111: Catalog $2 ❖

Japanese maple, black pine, and spruce trees for bonsai training. 215–722–6286.

Miami Tropical Bonsai, 14775 SW 232nd St., Homestead, FL 33170: Free price/availability list ❖ Imported tropical and indoor bonsai. 305–258–0865.

Miniature Plant Kingdom, 4125 Harrison Grade Rd., Sebastopol, CA 95472: Catalog $2.50 ❖ Miniature roses and Japanese maples, conifers, and other plants for bonsai. 707–874–2233.

Monastery Greenhouse, 2625 Hwy. 212 SW, Conyers, GA 30208: Catalog $3 (refundable) ❖ Bonsai tools and pots. 404–918–9661.

Mt. Si Bonsai, 43321 SE Mt. Si Rd. North, Bend, WA 98045: Catalog $1 ❖ Indoor and outdoor bonsai, pots, tools, and bonsai starters. 206–888–0350.

Mountain Maples, 5901 Spyrock Rd., Laytonville, CA 95454: Catalog $1 ❖ Japanese maples for bonsai. 707–984–6522.

New England Bonsai Gardens, 914 S. Main St., Bellingham, MA 02019: Free information with long SASE ❖ Tropical, sub-tropical, and juniper bonsai in ceramic bonsai pots, and pots, tools, and other supplies. 508–883–2666.

Niwa Garden Tool Catalog, 2661 Bloomfield Ct., Fairfield, CA 94533: Catalog $2 ❖ Handcrafted Japanese gardening and bonsai tools. 800–443–5512.

Northland Gardens, West Mountain Rd., Box 315, Queensbury, NY 12804: Information $2 ❖ Bonsai, starter stock, books, pottery, tools, and growing aids. 800–4–BONSAI.

Northridge Gardens Nursery, 9821 White Oak Ave., Northridge, CA 91325: Catalog $1 (refundable) ❖ Cacti, bonsai-usable, and other rare and unusual plants. 818–349–9798.

Pen Y Bryn, RR 1, Box 1313, Forksville, PA 18616: Free catalog ❖ Pre-bonsai trees and growing supplies.

Petals & Buds, 10798 County Rd. 3101, Winona, TX 75792: Catalog $2 ❖ Blossoming apple trees, a replica of Japanese bonsai. 903–877–3724.

Pine Garden Pottery, 20331 SR 530 NE, Arlington, WA 98223: Catalog $2 ❖ Stoneware bonsai containers. 206–435–5995.

Prime Material & Supply Corporation, P.O. Box 681685, Houston, TX 77268: Free information ❖ Haydite aggregate selected and graded for bonsai. 713–353–1230.

Rakestraw's Gardens, 3094 S. Term St., Burton, MI 48529: Catalog $1 ❖ Bonsai and perennials. 313–742–2685.

Riverside Bonsai, P.O. Box 633, Columbus, NC 28722: Catalog $1.50 ❖ Bonsai supplies. 704–894–3735.

Secret Garden Bonsai, 1230 North B St., Lake Worth, FL 33460: Free price list ❖ Tropical and indoor bonsai and pre-bonsai. 407–586–2541.

Shanti Bithi Nursery, 3047 High Ridge Rd., Stamford, CT 06903: Free catalog ❖ Bonsai plants, growing supplies, tools, and pots. 203–329–0768.

Spring Hill Nurseries, 6523 N. Galena Rd., P.O. Box 1758, Peoria, IL 61656: Free catalog ❖ Bonsai, perennials, roses, annuals, ground covers, small fruits, houseplants, other seeds and plants, and gardening supplies. 800–582–8527.

Waterstone, P.O. Box 671143, Houston, TX 77267: Free information ❖ Bonsai wire. 617–444–5911.

Wee World of Bonsai, P.O. Box 375, Newberg, OR 97132: Free catalog ❖ Bonsai pottery, tools, books, and supplies. 503–538–6071.

Wildwood Gardens, 14488 Rock Creek Rd., Chardon, OH 44024: Catalog $1 ❖ Imported and domestic bonsai and pre-bonsai plants. 216–286–3714.

Woodview Gardens, HC 68, Box 405H, St. Francisville, LA 70775: Catalog $1 ❖ Bonsai, pre-bonsai plants, pots, tools, and supplies. 504–635–4220.

Cacti & Succulents

Abbey Garden, 4620 Carpinteria Ave., Carpinteria, CA 93013: Catalog $2 (refundable) ❖ Cacti and succulents. 805–684–5112.

Brudy's Exotics, Box 820874, Houston, TX 77282: Free catalog ❖ Exotic seeds, plumerias, gingers, ornamental bananas, bougainvillea, hibiscus, and dwarf cannas. 800–926–7333.

Cactus by Mueller, 10411 Rosedale Hwy., Bakersfield, CA 93312: Catalog $2 ❖ Cacti and succulents. 805–589–2674.

Desert Nursery, 1301 S. Copper, Deming, NM 88030: Free list with 1st class stamp ❖ Cacti and succulents. 505–546–6264.

Epi World, 10607 Glenview Ave., Cupertino, CA 95014: Catalog $2 ❖ Orchid cacti. 408–865–0566.

Flechsig Cacti & Succulents, 619 Opheus Ave., Encinitas, CA 92024: Catalog $1 (refundable) ❖ Nursery-grown cacti, aloes, cerepegias, and other succulents. 619–753–5942.

Garden World's Exotic Plants, 2503 Garfield St., Laredo, TX 78043: Catalog $1 ❖ Bamboo, bananas, citrus trees, cacti, and other tropical growing stock. 512–724–3951.

Greenlife Mailorder Nursery, 101 County Line Rd., Griffin, GA 30223: Catalog $2 ❖ Succulents and cacti plants.

Grigsby Cactus Gardens, 2354 Bella Vista, Vista, CA 92084: Catalog $2 ❖ Rare cacti and succulents. 619–727–1323.

Henrietta's Nursery, 1345 N. Brawley, Fresno, CA 93722: Catalog 50¢ ❖ Cacti and succulents. 209–275–2166.

Highland Succulents, 1446 Bear Run Rd., Galipolis, OH 45631: Catalog $2 ❖ Succulents. 614–256–1428.

Intermountain Cactus, 1478 N. 750 East, Kaysville, UT 84037: Price list $1 ❖ Winter-hardy cacti. 801–546–2006.

Lauray of Salisbury, 432 Undermountain Rd., Salisbury, CT 06068: Catalog $2 ❖ Cacti and succulents, begonias, gesneriads, and orchids. 203–435–2263.

Mesa Garden, Box 72, Belen, NM 87002: Catalog $1 ❖ Cacti and succulent seeds and plants. 505–864–3131.

Northridge Gardens Nursery, 9821 White Oak Ave., Northridge, CA 91325: Catalog $1 (refundable) ❖ Cacti, bonsai-usable, and other rare and unusual plants. 818–349–9798.

Rainbow Gardens, 1444 E. Taylor St., Vista, CA 92084: Catalog $2 ❖ Cacti, hoyas, and books on cacti. 619–758–4290.

Rocky Waters Farm, 4383 Pool Rd., Winston, GA 30187: Catalog $1 (refundable) ❖ Cacti and succulent seedlings, root cuttings, and mature plants. 404–942–3114.

The Seed Shop, Tongue River Stage, Miles City, MT 59301: Price list $2 ❖ Seed for cacti and succulents.

Succulenta, P.O. Box 480325, Los Angeles, CA 90048: Catalog $1 ❖ Rare and unusual cacti and succulents. 213–933–8676.

Tropiflora, 3530 Tallevast Rd., Sarasota, FL 34243: Free information ❖ Tillandsias, bromeliads, caudiciform, and other rare plants. 813–351–2267.

Carnivorous Plants

Carolina Exotic Gardens, Rt. 5, Box 283–A, Greenville, NC 27834: Catalog $1 ❖ Carnivorous plants and seeds and terrarium plant groupings. 919–758–2600.

Peter Pauls Nurseries, 4665 Chapin Rd., Canandaigua, NY 14424: Free catalog ❖ Carnivorous and woodland terrarium plants. 716–394–7397.

Chrysanthemums

Dooley Gardens, 210 N. High St., Hutchinson, MN 55350: Free list ❖ New and old chrysanthemums. 612–587–3050.

Huff's Garden Mums, 710 Juniatta, Burlington, KS 66839: Catalog $1 (refundable) ❖ Chrysanthemums. 800–279–4675.

King's Chrysanthemums, P.O. Box 368, Clements, CA 94227: Catalog $2 (refundable) ❖ Rooted cuttings. 209–759–3571.

Lamb Nurseries, 101 E. Sharp Ave., Spokane, WA 99202: Catalog $1 ❖ Chrysanthemums, perennials, and rock garden plants. 509–328–7956.

Thon's Garden Chrysanthemums, Oak St., Crystal Lake, IL 60014: Free catalog ❖ Exhibition, football, and spider chrysanthemums. 815–923–4644.

Citrus & Exotic Fruits

Alberts & Merkel Brothers Inc., 2210 S. Federal Hwy., Boynton Beach, FL 33435: Catalog $1 ❖ Citrus and exotic fruits. 305–732–2071.

The Banana Tree, 715 Northampton St., Easton, PA 18042: Catalog $3 ❖ Citrus and exotic fruits. 215–253–9589.

W. Atlee Burpee & Company, 300 Park Ave., Warminster, PA 18974: Free catalog ❖ Exotic fruits. 215–674–1793.

Crockett's Tropical Plants, P.O. Box 1150, Harlingen, TX 78551: Catalog $3 ❖ Container-grown ornamentals, citrus, and palms.

Edible Landscaping, P.O. Box 77, Afton, VA 22920: Free catalog ❖ Exotic fruits. 800–524–4156.

Exotica Rare Fruit Nursery, P.O. Box 160, Vista, CA 92083: Free mail order price list ❖ Tropical fruit, nut, palm, and other trees and plants. 619–724–9093.

Henry Field's Seed & Nursery, 415 N. Burnett, Shenandoah, IA 51602: Free catalog ❖ Exotic fruits. 605–665–4491.

Fig Tree Nursery, P.O. Box 124, Gulf Hammock, FL 32639: Catalog $1 ❖ Exotic fruits. 904–486–2930.

Garden of Delights, 14560 SW 14th St., Davie, FL 33325: Catalog $2 (refundable) ❖ Tropical fruits and nuts. 305–370–9004.

Garden World's Exotic Plants, 2503 Garfield St., Laredo, TX 78043: Catalog $1 ❖ Exotic fruits. 512–724–3951.

Glasshouse Works Greenhouses, P.O. Box 97, Stewart, OH 45778: Catalog $3 ❖ Citrus and exotic fruits. 614–662–2142.

Gurney Seed & Nursery Company, 110 Capitol St., Yankton, SD 57079: Free catalog ❖ Citrus and exotic fruits. 605–665–1671.

House of Wesley, 1704 Morrisey Dr., Bloomington, IL 61704: Free catalog ❖ Citrus and exotic fruits. 309–663–8551.

Kartuz Greenhouses, 1408 Sunset Dr., Vista, CA 92083: Catalog $2 ❖ Citrus and exotic fruits. 619–941–3613.

Logee's Greenhouses, 141 North St., Danielson, CT 06239: Catalog $3 (refundable) ❖ Citrus and exotic fruits. 203–774–8038.

Mellinger's, 2310 W. South Range Rd., North Lima, OH 44452: Free catalog ❖ Citrus and exotic fruits. 216–549–9861.

Northwoods Retail Nursery, 27635 S. Oglesvy Rd., Canby, OR 97013: Free catalog ❖ Citrus and exotic fruits. 503–266–5432.

Pacific Tree Farms, 4301 Lynnwood Dr., Chula Vista, CA 92010: Catalog $1.50 ❖ Citrus and exotic fruits. 619–422–2400.

Peaceful Valley Farm Supply, P.O. Box 2209, Grass Valley, CA 95945: Catalog $2 (refundable) ❖ Citrus fruits. 916–272–4769.

Raintree Nursery, 391 Butts Rd., Morton, WA 98356: Free information ❖ Citrus and exotic fruits. 206–496–6400.

South Seas Nursery, P.O. Box 4974, Ventura, CA 93007: Free catalog with long SASE ❖ Tropical and subtropical fruit trees. 805–647–6990.

Tripple Brook Farm, 37 Middle Rd., Southampton, MA 01073: Free catalog ❖ Bamboo plants, exotic fruits, trees, perennials, and shrubs. 413–527–4626.

Daffodils

Cascade Daffodils, P.O. Box 10626, White Bear Lake, MN 55110: Catalog $2 ❖ Standard, miniature, and show daffodils. 612–426–9616.

The Daffodil Mart, Rt. 3, Box 794, Gloucester, VA 23061: Free catalog ❖ Novelty, miniature, hybridized, and species daffodils. 804–693–3966.

Grant Mitsch Novelty Daffodils, P.O. Box 218, Hubbard, OR 97032: Catalog $3 (refundable) ❖ Exhibition and garden varieties of pink and hybrid daffodils. 503–651–2742.

Oregon Trail Daffodils, 41905 SE Louden Rd., Corbett, OR 97019: Free catalog ❖ New and novelty daffodils. 503–695–5513.

Quality Dutch Bulbs, 50 Lake Dr., P.O. Box 225, Hillsdale, NJ 07642: Free catalog ❖ Daffodils, irises, tulips, and other bulbs. 201–391–6586.

Dahlias

B.J. Dahlias, 130 Taylor Loop Rd., Selah, WA 98942: Free catalog with two 1st class stamps ❖ Dahlias. 509–697–6089.

Connell's, 10616 Waller Rd. East, Tacoma, WA 98446: Catalog $2 ❖ Exhibition and garden varieties of dahlias from worldwide sources. 206–531–0292.

Cornellis, 10216 40th Ave. East, Tacoma, WA 98446: Catalog $2 (refundable) ❖ Dahlias from worldwide sources.

Evergreen Acres Dahlia Gardens, 682 Pulaski Rd., Greenlawn, NY 11740: Catalog 50¢ ❖ Established dahlia cultivars and new introductions from the United States, England, Canada, Japan, and New Zealand. 516–261–1024.

Garden Valley Dahlias, 406 Lower Garden Valley, Roseburg, OR 97470: Free catalog ❖ Dahlias. 503–673–8521.

Kordonowy's Dahlias, 401 Quick Rd., Castle Rock, WA 98611: Free catalog ❖ Dahlias.

Swan Island Dahlias, P.O. Box 700, Canby, OR 97013: Catalog $3 (refundable) ❖ Dahlias. 503–266–7711.

Ferns

Kurt Bluemel Inc., 2740 Greene Ln., Baldwin, MD 21013: Catalog $2 ❖ Ferns, perennials, bamboo plants, and ornamental grasses. 410–557–7229.

Busse Gardens, 13579 10th St. NW, Cokato, MN 55321: Catalog $2 (refundable with $25 order) ❖ Ferns, other seeds and plants, and Siberian irises. 612–286–2654.

Conley's Garden Center, 145 Townsend Ave., Boothbay Harbor, ME 04538: Catalog $1.50 (refundable) ❖ Hardy wildflowers and seeds, ferns, native perennials, bulbs, orchids, and ground covers. 207–633–5020.

Crownsville Nursery, P.O. Box 797, Crownsville, MD 21032: Catalog $10 ❖ Ferns, wildflowers, azaleas, ornamental grasses, and perennials. 410–923–2212.

Foliage Gardens, 2003 128th Ave. SE, Bellevue, WA 98005: Catalog $2 ❖ Indoor and outdoor ferns.

Gardens of the Blue Ridge, P.O. Box 10, Pineola, NC 28662: Catalog $3 (refundable) ❖ Wildflower seeds, ferns, trees, plants, shrubs, and bulbs. 704–733–2417.

Gilson Gardens Inc., 3059 US Rt. 20, P.O. Box 277, Perry, OH 44081: Free catalog ❖ Ground covers, perennials, and ferns.

Russell Graham Plants, 4030 Eagle Crest Rd. NW, Salem, OR 97304: Catalog $2 ❖ Ferns, ornamental grasses, lily bulbs, irises, daffodils, and other plants. 503–362–1135.

Griffey's Nursery, 16870 Hwy. 25–70, Marshall, NC 28753: Free catalog ❖ Appalachian wildflowers, ferns and vines, rock and bog plants, and orchids. 704–656–2334.

Jerry Horne, 10195 SW 70th St., Miami, FL 33173: Free list with long SASE ❖ Aroids, bromeliads, cycads, ferns, and palms. 305–270–1235.

Lamb Nurseries, 101 E. Sharp Ave., Spokane, WA 99202: Catalog $1 ❖ Perennials, ferns, other plants, and shrubs. 509–328–7956.

Limerock Ornamental Grasses Inc., RD 1, Box 111, Port Matilda, PA 16870: Catalog $3 ❖ Ornamental and native grasses, companion perennials, and nursery-grown hardy ferns. 814–692–2272.

Orchid Gardens, 2232 139th Ave. NW, Andover, MN 55304: Catalog 75¢ ❖ Ferns and wildflowers. 612–755–0205.

Rice Creek Gardens, 11506 Hwy. 65, Minneapolis, MN 55434: Catalog $2 ❖ Ferns, vines, ornamental shrubs, rock garden plants, and gardening supplies.

Varga's Nursery, 2631 Pickertown Rd., Warrington, PA 18976: Price list $1 ❖ Ferns.

Wildflower Nursery, 1680 Hwy. 25–70, Marshall, NC 28753: Free catalog ❖ Ferns.

Geraniums

Clark's Greenhouse & Herbal Country, RR 1, Box 15B, San Jose, IL 62682: Catalog $2 ❖ Herbs, everlasting plants, and scented geraniums. 309–247–3679.

Cook's Geranium Nursery, 712 N. Grand, Box 523, Lyons, KS 67554: Catalog $1 (refundable) ❖ New, old, and unusual geraniums. 316–257–2836.

Dabney Herbs, P.O. Box 22061, Louisville, KY 40222: Catalog $2 ❖ Ginseng, herbs, scented geraniums, perennials, and wildflowers. 502–893–5198.

Davidson-Wilson Greenhouses, Rt. 2, Box 168, Crawfordsville, IN 47933: Catalog $3 ❖ African violets, geraniums, and houseplants. 317–364–0556.

Fox Hill Farm, 444 W. Michigan Ave., Box 9, Parma, MI 49269: Catalog $1 ❖ Easy-to-grow geraniums. 517–531–3179.

Good Hollow Greenhouse & Herbarium, Rt. 1, Box 116, Taft, TN 38488: Catalog $1 ❖ Herbs, perennials, wildflowers, scented geraniums, essential oils and potpourris, teas, dried herbs, and spices. 615–433–7640.

Happy Hollow Nursery, 221 Happy Hollow Rd., Villa Rica, GA 30180: Catalog $1 (refundable) ❖ Scented geraniums and herb plants. 404–459–4144.

Holbrook Farm & Nursery, P.O. Box 368, Fletcher, NC 28732: Free catalog ❖ Geraniums, native wildflowers, trees, shrubs, garden perennials, and hostas. 704–891–7790.

Lily of the Valley Herb Farm, 3969 Fox Ave., Minerva, OH 44657: Price list $1 (refundable) ❖ Herbs and herbal products, everlasting, perennials, and scented geranium plants. 216–862–3920.

Sandy Mush Herb Nursery, Surret Cove, Rt. 2, Leicester, NC 28748: Catalog $4 ❖ Geraniums. 704–683–2014.

Rabbit Shadow Farm, 2880 E. Hwy. 402, Loveland, CO 80537: Free information ❖ Herbs, roses, topiary supplies, and scented geraniums. 303–667–5531.

Rasland Farm, N.C. 82 at US 13, Godwin, NC 28344: Catalog $2.50 ❖ Herb plants, scented geraniums, and dried flowers. 910–567–2705.

Shady Hill Gardens, 821 Walnut St., Batavia, IL 60510: Catalog $2 (refundable) ❖ Geraniums. 708–879–5665.

Sunnybrook Farms Nursery, P.O. Box 6, Chesterland, OH 44026: Catalog $1 (refundable) ❖ Geraniums, herb plants, ivies, and houseplants. 216–729–7232.

Well-Sweep Herb Farm, 317 Mt. Bethel Rd., Port Murray, NJ 07865: Catalog $2 ❖ Geraniums. 908–852–5390.

Wheeler Farm Gardens, 171 Bartlett St., Portland, CT 06480: Free brochure ❖ Flowering balcony geraniums. 203–342–2374.

Wilson Plant Sales, 202 S. Indiana St., Roachdale, IN 46172: Free catalog ❖ Geraniums, African violets, and exotic houseplants. 317–522–1320.

Young's Mesa Nursery, 2755 Fowler Ln., Arroyo Grande, CA 93420: Catalog $2 (refundable) ❖ Miniature and regular-size geraniums. 805–489–0548.

Ginseng

American Ginseng Gardens, 404 Mountain Meadow Ln., Flag Pond, TN 37657: Information $1 ❖ Ginseng and goldenseal roots and seeds.

William H. Collins Gardens, Box 48, Viola, IA 52350: Free information ❖ Ginseng seed roots.

Dabney Herbs, P.O. Box 22061, Louisville, KY 40222: Catalog $2 ❖ Ginseng, herbs, scented geraniums, perennials, and wildflowers. 502–893–5198.

The Homestead, Kimbolton, OH 43749: Free information ❖ Ginseng planting stock.

HSU's Ginseng Enterprises Inc., P.O. Box 509, Wausau, WI 54402: Free information ❖ American and Canadian stratified ginseng seed, rootlets, and ginseng health products and extracts. 800–826–1577; 715–675–2325 (in WI).

Gladioli

Connell's, 10616 Waller Rd. East, Tacoma, WA 98446: Catalog $2 ❖ Gladioli bulbs. 206–531–0292.

Kingfisher Glads, 11734 Road 33–1/2, Madera, CA 93638: Free catalog ❖ New gladioli and older cultivars. 209–645–5329.

Mellinger's, 2310 W. South Range Rd., North Lima, OH 44452: Free catalog ❖ Gladioli, fruit and nut trees, shade and ornamental trees, flowering shrubs, hedges, irises, wildflowers, and gardening equipment. 216–549–9861.

Skolaski's Glads & Flowers, 4821 County Trunk Hwy. Q, Waunakee, WI 53597: Catalog $1 ❖ Gladioli bulbs, lilies, and perennials. 608–836–4822.

Waushara Gardens, Rt. 2, Box 570, Plainfield, WI 54966: Free catalog ❖ Gladioli. 715–335–4462.

Gourds

H. Bankhead Gourds, Rt. 2, Box 60, Roscoe, TX 79545: Free information with long SASE ❖ Seeds for large luffa gourds.

Lena Braswell Gourds, Rt. 1, Box 73, Wrens, GA 30833: Free information with long SASE ❖ Gourds. 404–547–6784.

J.L. Hudson, Seedsman, Box 1058, Redwood City, CA 94064: Catalog $1 ❖ Gourd seeds.

Nichols Garden Nursery, 1190 N. Pacific Hwy., Albany, OR 97321: Free catalog ❖ Gourd seeds. 503–928–9280.

West Mountain Gourd Farm, Rt. 1, Box 853, Gilmer, TX 75644: Information $2 ❖ Ready-to-paint gourds in all shapes and sizes. 903–734–5204.

Frank Wheeler Gourds, 8285 Johnstown-Utica Rd., Johnstown, OH 43031: Free information with long SASE ❖ Basketball, cannon ball, and martin house gourd seeds.

Grapes

Ahrens Strawberry Nursery, P.O. Box 145, Huntingburg, IN 47542: Free catalog ❖ Strawberry, gooseberry, raspberry, blueberry, and blackberry plants; and fruit trees, grapevines, rhubarb, and currants. 612–683–3055.

Boordy Nursery, P.O. Box 38, Riderwood, MD 21139: Free catalog with 1st class stamp ❖ Wine grapes.

California Nursery Company, P.O. Box 2278, Fremont, CA 94536: Free catalog ❖ Table and wine grapevines, fruit and nut trees, and gardening supplies. 510–797–3311.

Fig Tree Nursery, P.O. Box 124, Gulf Hammock, FL 32639: Catalog $1 ❖ Berry plants, ornamentals, and grapes for southern climates. 904–486–2930.

Ison's Nursery, Rt. 1, Brooks, GA 30205: Free catalog ❖ Muscadine grapevines, berries, and fruit and nut trees. 800–733–0324.

Earl May Seeds & Nursery Company, N. Elm St., Shenandoah, IA 51603: Free catalog ❖ Grapevines, berry plants, fruit and nut trees, roses, shade and ornamental trees, flowering shrubs, and gardening supplies. 712–246–1020.

J.E. Miller Nurseries, 5060 West Lake Rd., Canandaigua, NY 14424: Free catalog ❖ Grapevines, berry plants, and fruit trees. 800–836–9630.

W.K. Morse & Son, Rt. 2, Boxford, MA 01921: Free brochure ❖ Grapevines and strawberry and raspberry plants. 617–352–2633.

Patrick's Nursery, P.O. Box 130, Ty Ty, GA 31795: Free catalog ❖ Grapevines, vegetable seeds, berry plants, and fruit and nut trees. 912–386–1122.

Lon J. Rombough, 13113 Ehlen Rd., Aurora, OR 97002: Free catalog with long SASE ❖ Grapevine cuttings. 503–678–1410.

Grasses & Ground Covers

Avid Gardener, Box 200, Hamburg, IL 62045: Catalog $2 ❖ Dwarf conifers, companion shrubs, ground covers, and potential bonsai.

Barbour Bros. Inc., RD 2, Stoneboro, PA 16153: Free catalog ❖ Ground covers.

Kurt Bluemel Inc., 2740 Greene Ln., Baldwin, MD 21013: Catalog $2 ❖ Ornamental grasses, water garden plants, and perennials. 410–557–7229.

Bluestone Perennials, 7211 Middle Ridge Rd., Madison, OH 44057: Free catalog ❖ Ground covers. 800–852–5243.

W. Atlee Burpee & Company, 300 Park Ave., Warminster, PA 18974: Free catalog ❖ Ornamental grasses. 215–674–1793.

Classic Groundcovers Inc., 405 Belmont Rd., Athens, GA 30605: Free catalog ❖ Ground covers. 800–248–8424; 404–543–0145 (in GA).

Conley's Garden Center, Boothbay Harbor, ME 04538: Catalog $1.50 (refundable) ❖ Ground covers, wildflowers, ferns, and vines. 207–633–5020.

Crownsville Nursery, P.O. Box 797, Crownsville, MD 21032: Catalog $10 ❖ Ferns, wildflowers, azaleas, ornamental grasses, and perennials. 410–923–2212.

Double D Nursery, Arnoldsville, GA 30619: Free catalog ❖ Ground covers. 800–438–7685.

Evergreen Nursery, 1220 Dowdy Rd., Athens, GA 30606: Free catalog ❖ Bare root and potted ground covers. 800–521–7267; 404–548–7781 (in GA).

Gilson Gardens Inc., 3059 US Rt. 20, P.O. Box 277, Perry, OH 44081: Free catalog ❖ Ground covers, perennials, and ferns.

Russell Graham Plants, 4030 Eagle Crest Rd. NW, Salem, OR 97304: Catalog $2 ❖ Ferns, ornamental grasses, lily bulbs, irises, daffodils, and other plants. 503–362–1135.

Greenlee Nursery, 301 E. Franklin Ave., Pomona, CA 91766: Free catalog ❖ Ornamental grasses. 714–629–9045.

Heritage Gardens, 1 Meadow Ridge Rd., Shenandoah, IA 51601: Free catalog ❖ Ornamental grasses, perennials, foliage plants, hostas, shade and rock garden plants, ferns, lilies, shrubs, azaleas and rhododendrons, roses, and flowering trees. 605–665–5188.

Limerock Ornamental Grasses Inc., RD 1, Box 111, Port Matilda, PA 16870: Catalog $3 ❖ Ornamental and native grasses, companion perennials, and nursery-grown hardy ferns. 814–692–2272.

Maryland Aquatic Nurseries, 3427 N. Furnace Rd., Jarrettsville, MD 21084: Catalog $5 (refundable) ❖ Water garden plants, ornamental grasses, and Louisiana and Japanese irises. 410–557–7615.

J.E. Miller Nurseries, 5060 W. Lake Rd., Canandaigua, NY 14424: Free catalog ❖ Fruit and nut trees, vines, ornamentals, and ground covers. 800–836–9630.

Park Seed Company Inc., Cokesbury Rd., P.O. Box 46, Greenwood, SC 29648: Free catalog ❖ Ornamental grasses. 803–223–7333.

Plants of the Southwest, Rt. 6, Box 11A, Santa Fe, NM 87501: Catalog $3.50 ❖ Native trees, grasses, wildflowers, shrubs, and other plants. 505–471–2212.

Prairie State Commodities, P.O. Box 6, Trilla, IL 62469: Catalog $1 ❖ Seeds for annuals, perennial rye grass and Park Kentucky bluegrass, corn, clover, and alfalfa. 217–235–4322.

Prentiss Court Ground Covers, P.O. Box 8662, Greenville, SC 29604: Catalog $1 ❖ Ground covers. 803–277–4037.

Rocknoll Nursery, 7812 Mad River Rd., Hillsboro, OH 45133: Catalog $1 ❖ Ground covers, rock garden plants, wildflowers, perennials, dwarf evergreens, flowering shrubs, and ivies. 513–393–5545.

Thompson & Morgan Inc., P.O. Box 1308, Jackson, NJ 08527: Free catalog ❖ Ornamental grasses. 800–274–7333.

Van Hise Nursery, 30688 SE Waybill Rd., Boring, OR 97009: Free information ❖ Ground covers, perennials, and shrubs. 503–663–6123.

Zoysia Farm Nurseries, General Offices & Store, 3617 Old Taneytown Rd., Taneytown, MD 21787: Free information ❖ Zoysia plugs.

Herbs

ABC Herb Nursery, 121 Anna St., St. James, MO 65559: Free price list with 1st class stamp ❖ Herb plants.

Aphrodesia Products, 264 Bleeker St., New York, NY 10014: Catalog $3 ❖ Dried herbs, herb products, and books. 800–221–6898; 212–989–6440 (in NY).

Bo's Nursery, 12743 Gillard Rd., Winter Garden, FL 34787: Information $2 (refundable) ❖ Herb and native plants, perennials, and old roses. 407–656–1959.

Bountiful Gardens, 18001 Shafer Ranch Rd., Willits, CA 95490: Free catalog ❖ Seeds for vegetables, compost crops, herbs, and flowers. Also books and organic gardening supplies. 707–459–6410.

Brown's Edgewood Gardens, 2611 Corrine Dr., Orlando, FL 32803: Catalog $2 ❖ Butterfly-attracting plants, herbs, and organic gardening products. 407–896–3203.

Capriland's Herb Farm, 534 Silver St., Coventry, CT 06238: Free catalog with long SASE ❖ Plants, seeds, books, and potpourri. 203–742–7244.

Catnip Acres Herb Nursery, 67 Christian St., Oxford, CT 06483: Free information ❖ Herb plants and scented geraniums. 203–888–5649.

Clark's Greenhouse & Herbal Country, RR 1, Box 15B, San Jose, IL 62682: Catalog $2 ❖ Herbs, everlasting plants, and scented geraniums. 309–247–3679.

Companion Plants, 7247 N. Coolville Ridge, Athens, OH 45701: Catalog $2 ❖ Seeds for exotic, herb, and native plants. 614–592–4643.

Comstock, Ferre & Company, 263 Main St., Wethersfield, CT 06109: Catalog $2 ❖ Vegetable, flower, and herb seeds. 203–571–6590.

Country Carriage Nurseries & Seed Inc., P.O. Box 548, Hartford, MI 49057: Free catalog ❖ Vegetable and herb seeds, fruit trees, and berry plants. 616–621–2491.

Dabney Herbs, P.O. Box 22061, Louisville, KY 40222: Catalog $2 ❖ Ginseng, herbs, scented geraniums, perennials, and wildflowers. 502–893–5198.

T. DeBaggio Herbs, 923 N. Ivy St., Arlington, VA 22201: Catalog $1 ❖ Herbs. 703–243–2498.

Dutch Mill Herb Farm, Rt. 2, Box 190, Forest Grove, OR 97116: Free catalog with long SASE ❖ Herbs. 503–357–0924.

Flowery Branch, P.O. Box 1330, Flowery Branch, GA 30542: Catalog $2 ❖ Rare and exotic herb seeds. 404–536–8380.

Fox Hill Farm, 444 W. Michigan Ave., Box 9, Parma, MI 49269: Catalog $1 ❖ Culinary, medicinals, fragrants, everlastings, and other container-grown herb plants. 517–531–3179.

The Gathered Herb & Greenhouse, 12114 N. State Rd., Otisville, MI 48463: Catalog $2 ❖ Herbs, herb teas, perennials, dried flowers, and potpourri supplies. 313–631–6572.

Good Hollow Greenhouse & Herbarium, Rt. 1, Box 116, Taft, TN 38488: Catalog $1 ❖ Herbs, perennials, wildflowers, scented geraniums, essential oils, potpourris, teas, and dried herbs and spices. 615–433–7640.

Goodwin Creek Gardens, P.O. Box 83, Williams, OR 97544: Catalog $1 ❖ Dried floral arrangements, herb plants, container-grown native American trees, shrubs, and perennial flowers. 503–846–7357.

The Gourmet Gardener, 8650 College Blvd., Overland Park, KS 66210: Catalog $2 ❖ Herb, vegetable, and edible flower seeds from around the world. 913–345–0490.

Greenfield Herb Garden, Depot & Harrison, P.O. Box 437, Shipshewana, IN 46565: Catalog $1.50 ❖ Herb books and plants. 219–768–7110.

Happy Hollow Nursery, 221 Happy Hollow Rd., Villa Rica, GA 30180: Catalog $1 (refundable) ❖ Scented geraniums and herb plants. 404–459–4144.

Hartman's Herb Farm, Old Dana Rd., Barre, MA 01005: Catalog $2 ❖ Herbs and herb products, potpourri, essential oils, and wreaths. 508–355–2015.

The Herbfarm, 32804 Issaquah-Fall City Rd., Fall City, WA 98024: Information $1 ❖

Herb plants, seed, and herbal items. 800–866–4372.

Hummingbird Hills Herbal Nursery, 17201 S. Hawkinds, Ashland, MO 65010: Catalog $1 ❖ Organically grown herbs, perennials, everlastings, and dried flowers. 314–657–2082.

Indiana Botanic Gardens, P.O. Box 5, Hammond, IN 46325: Free catalog ❖ Herbs, essential oils, and herb seeds. 219–947–4040.

Le Jardin du Gourmet, P.O. Box 75, St. Johnsbury Center, VT 05863: Catalog $1 ❖ Herb plants and seeds and vegetable seeds. 802–748–1446.

Lily of the Valley Herb Farm, 3969 Fox Ave., Minerva, OH 44657: Price list $1 (refundable) ❖ Herb plants, everlastings, perennials, scented geraniums, and herbal products. 216–862–3920.

Lost Prairie Herb Farm, 46655 Terrace Dr., Neskowin, OR 97149: Catalog $2 (refundable) ❖ Herb plants.

Meadowbrook Herb Gardens, 93 Kingstown Rd., Wyoming, RI 02898: Catalog $1 ❖ Herb seeds. 401–539–7603.

Meadowsweet Herb Farm, 729 Mount Holly Rd., Shrewsbury, VT 05738: Catalog $1 ❖ Potpourris, ornamental herbs, seeds for windowsill herbs, dried flowers, and scented basils. 802–492–3565.

Sandy Mush Herb Nursery, Surret Cove, Rt. 2, Leicester, NC 28748: Catalog $4 ❖ Culinary and tea herbs, other herbs, scented geraniums, and flowering perennials. 704–683–2014.

Nichols Garden Nursery, 1190 Pacific West, Albany, OR 97321: Free catalog ❖ Seeds, plants, and herbal products. 503–928–9280.

Perennial Pleasures Nursery, 2 Brickhouse Rd., East Hardwock, VT 05836: Catalog $2 (refundable) ❖ Heirloom herbs and flowers. 802–472–5104.

Planta Dei Medicinal Herb Farm, Millville, New Brunswick, Canada E0H 1M0: Catalog $2 (refundable) ❖ Biologically grown teas, medicinal herbs, healing tea mixtures, cosmetics, natural ointments, and massage oils. 506–463–8169.

Rabbit Shadow Farm, 2880 E. Hwy. 402, Loveland, CO 80537: Free information ❖ Herbs, roses, topiary supplies, and scented geraniums. 303–667–5531.

Rasland Farm, N.C. 82 at U.S. 13, Godwin, NC 28344: Catalog $2.50 ❖ Herb plants, scented geraniums, dried flowers, and herbal products. 910–567–2705.

Redwood City Seed Company, P.O. Box 361, Redwood City, CA 94064: Catalog $1 ❖ Herb and vegetable seeds from worldwide sources. 415–325–7333.

The Rosemary House, 120 S. Market St., Mechanicsburg, PA 17055: Catalog $2 ❖ Plants, seeds, herb products, and books. 717–697–5111.

Seeds of Change, P.O. Box 15700, Sante Fe, NM 87506: Free information ❖ Open-pollinated, organically grown herb seeds. 505–438–8080.

Story House Herb Farm, Rt. 7, Box 246, Murray, KY 42071: Catalog $2 (refundable) ❖ Organically-grown herb plants. 502–753–4158.

Sunnybrook Farms Nursery, P.O. Box 6, Chesterland, OH 44026: Catalog $1 (refundable) ❖ Herb plants, ivies, scented geraniums, other seeds, and herbal products. 216–729–7232.

Taylor's Herb Garden, 1535 Lone Oak Rd., Vista, CA 92084: Catalog $1 ❖ Ornamental and cooking herb plants and seeds. 619–727–3485.

Tinmouth Channel Farm, Box 428B, Tinmouth, VT 05773: Catalog $2 ❖ Vermont-certified organic plants and seeds. 802–446–2812.

Well-Sweep Herb Farm, 317 Mt. Bethel Rd., Port Murray, NJ 07865: Catalog $2 ❖ Seeds for herbs, plants, and perennials. 908–852–5390.

Wrenwood of Berkeley Springs, Rt. 4., Box 361, Berkeley Springs, WV 25411: Catalog $2 ❖ Herbs and perennials. 304–258–3071.

Hostas

American Daylily & Perennials, P.O. Box 210, Grain Valley, MO 64029: Catalog $3 (refundable) ❖ Hostas, dwarf cannas, and daylilies. 800–770–2777.

Caprice Farm Nursery, 15425 SW Pleasant Hill Rd., Sherwood, OR 97140: Free catalog ❖ Peonies, irises, daylilies, and hostas. 503–625–7241.

Carroll Gardens, 444 E. Main St., P.O. Box 310, Westminster, MD 21157: Catalog $3 (refundable) ❖ Hostas plants and cultivars. 800–638–6334.

Crownsville Nursery, P.O. Box 797, Crownsville, MD 21032: Catalog $10 ❖ Hosta plants and cultivars. 410–849–2212.

Holbrook Farm & Nursery, P.O. Box 368, Fletcher, NC 28732: Free catalog ❖ Geraniums, native wildflowers, trees, shrubs, perennials, and hostas. 704–891–7790.

Klehm Nursery, 4210 N. Duncan Rd., Champaign, IL, 61821: Catalog $2 ❖ Peonies, irises, daylilies, hostas, and perennials. 800–553–3715.

Rocknoll Nursery, 7812 Mad River Rd., Hillsboro, OH 45133: Catalog $1 ❖ Hosta plants and cultivars, perennials, ivies, dwarf plants, and ground covers. 513–393–5545.

Savory's Gardens Inc., 5300 Whiting Ave., Edina, MN 55439: Catalog $2 ❖ Hostas. 612–941–8755.

Andre Viette Nurseries, Rt. 1, Box 16, Fisherville, VA 22929: Catalog $2 ❖ Hosta plants and cultivars. 703–943–2315.

Walnut Hill Gardens, 999 310th St., Atalissa, IA 52720: Price list $2 ❖ Daylilies, hostas, and Siberian irises. 319–946–3471.

Wayside Gardens, 1 Garden Ln., Hodges, SC 29695: Free catalog ❖ Hosta plants and cultivars. 800–845–1124.

Houseplants & Indoor Gardens

Avid Gardener, Box 200, Hamburg, IL 62045: Catalog $2 ❖ Dwarf conifers, companion shrubs, ground covers, and potential bonsai.

Belisle's Violet House, P.O. Box 111, Radisson, WI 54867: Catalog $2 ❖ Miniature sinninglas tubers and plants. 715–945–2687.

Brudy's Exotics, Box 820874, Houston, TX 77282: Free catalog ❖ Exotic seeds, plumerias, gingers, ornamental bananas, bougainvillea, hibiscus, and dwarf cannas. 800–926–7333.

Coda Gardens, P.O. Box 8417, Fredericksburg, VA 22404: Catalog $2 ❖ Miniature sinninglas plants.

Crockett's Tropical Plants, P.O. Box 1150, Harlingen, TX 78551: Catalog $3 ❖ Container-grown ornamentals, citrus, and palms.

Davidson-Wilson Greenhouses, Rt. 2, Box 168, Crawfordsville, IN 47933: Catalog $3 ❖ Exotic houseplants. 317–364–0556.

Gardener's Choice, Country Rd. 687, P.O. Box 8000, Hartford, MI 49057: Free catalog ❖ Houseplants, vegetables, flowers, and trees. 800–274–4096.

Glasshouse Works Greenhouses, Church St., Box 97, Stewart, OH 45778: Catalog $3 ❖ Windowsill jasmine plants. 614–662–2142.

Golden Lake Greenhouses, 10782 Citrus Dr., Moorpark, CA 93021: Price list $1 ❖ Bromeliads, tillandsias, ephylliums, hoyas, and other plants.

Lauray of Salisbury, 432 Undermountain Rd., Rt. 41, Salisbury, CT 06068: Catalog $2 ❖ Begonias, orchids, cacti, and succulents. 203–435–2263.

Logee's Greenhouses, 141 North St., Danielson, CT 06239: Catalog $3 (refundable) ❖ Begonias, geraniums, exotics, herbs, and other houseplants. 203–774–8038.

Lyndon Lyon Greenhouses Inc., 14 Mutchler St., Dolgeville, NY 13329: Catalog $2 ❖ African violets and exotic houseplants. 315–429–8291.

Merry Gardens, P.O. Box 595, Camden, ME 04843: Catalog $2 ❖ Houseplants. Flowering plants, herbs, ivies, gesneriads, ferns and mosses, impatiens, jasmines, and geraniums. 207–236–9064.

Michael's Bromeliads, 1365 Canterbury Rd. North, St. Petersburg, FL 33710: Free catalog ❖ Species and hybrid bromeliads. 813–347–0349.

Pacific Southwest Nursery, P.O. Box 985, National City, CA 91951: Catalog $3 ❖ Miniature sinninglas plants.

The Plumeria People, P.O. Box 820014, Houston, TX 77282: Catalog $2 ❖ Jasmine and other tropical houseplants.

Rhapis Palm Growers, 31350 Alta Vista, Redlands, CA 92373: Catalog $2 with long SASE ❖ Rhapis palms. 714–794–3823.

Spring Hill Nurseries, 6523 N. Galena Rd., P.O. Box 1758, Peoria, IL 61656: Free catalog ❖ Houseplants, perennials, roses, annuals, ground covers, and bonsai. 800–582–8527.

Stallings Nursery, 910 Encinatas Blvd., Encinatas, CA 92024: Catalog $3 ❖ Windowsill jasmine plants.

Sunnybrook Farms Nursery, P.O. Box 6, Chesterland, OH 44026: Catalog $1 (refundable) ❖ House and herb plants, ivies, scented geraniums, seeds, and herbal products. 216–729–7232.

Well-Sweep Herb Farm, 317 Mt. Bethel Rd., Port Murray, NJ 07865: Catalog $2 ❖ Windowsill jasmine plants. 908–852–5390.

Wilson Plant Sales, 202 S. Indiana St., Roachdale, IN 46172: Free catalog ❖ Exotic houseplants, geraniums, and African violets. 317–522–1320.

Hoyas

Golden Lake Greenhouses, 10782 Citrus Dr., Moorpark, CA 93021: Price list $1 ❖ Bromeliads, tillandsias, ephylliums, and hoyas.

Rainbow Gardens, 1444 E. Taylor St., Vista, CA 92084: Catalog $2 ❖ Cacti, hoyas, and books on cacti. 619–758–4290.

Ivies & Vines

Bluestone Perennials, 7211 Middle Ridge Rd., Madison, OH 44057: Free catalog ❖ Ivies and vines, perennial flowers, and ground covers. 800–852–5243.

Conley's Garden Center, Boothbay Harbor, ME 04538: Catalog $1.50 (refundable) ❖ Vines and ivies, wildflowers, ferns, and gardening supplies. 207–633–5020.

Park Seed Company Inc., Cokesbury Rd., P.O. Box 46, Greenwood, SC 29648: Free catalog ❖ Vines, strawberry plants, seeds, bulbs, and gardening tools. 803–223–7333.

Rice Creek Gardens, 11506 Hwy. 65, Minneapolis, MN 55434: Catalog $2 ❖ Rock garden plants, vines, ferns, and ornamental shrubs.

Rocknoll Nursery, 7812 Mad River Rd., Hillsboro, OH 45133: Catalog $1 ❖ Rock garden plants, ivies, perennials, dwarf plants, and ground covers. 513–393–5545.

Sunnybrook Farms Nursery, P.O. Box 6, Chesterland, OH 44026: Catalog $1 (refundable) ❖ Ivies, scented geraniums, herb plants, seeds, herbal products, and gardening supplies. 216–729–7232.

Lilacs

Hastings, P.O. Box 115535, Atlanta, GA 30310: Free catalog ❖ Lilacs. 404–755–6580.

Marigolds

W. Atlee Burpee & Company, 300 Park Ave., Warminster, PA 18974: Free catalog ❖ Marigolds. 215–674–1793.

Hastings, P.O. Box 115535, Atlanta, GA 30310: Free catalog ❖ Marigolds. 404–755–6580.

Park Seed Company, Cokesbury Rd., P.O. Box 46, Greenwood, SC 29648: Free catalog ❖ Marigolds. 803–223–7333.

Stokes Seeds Inc., Box 548, Buffalo, NY 14240: Free catalog ❖ Marigolds. 416–688–4300.

Thompson & Morgan Inc., P.O. Box 1308, Jackson, NJ 08527: Free catalog ❖ Marigolds. 800–274–7333.

Mushrooms

Far West Fungi, P.O. Box 428, South San Francisco, CA 94083: Free catalog with long SASE ❖ Mushroom-growing supplies, kits, and spawn for shiitake, button, tree-oyster, almond, and other mushrooms. 415–871–5424.

Field & Forest Products Inc., N3296 Kuzuzek Rd., Peshtigo, WI 54157: Catalog $2 (refundable) ❖ Mushroom-growing supplies. 715–582–4997.

Fungi Perfecti, P.O. Box 7634, Olympia, WA 98507: Catalog $3 ❖ Mushroom-growing supplies and spawn. 206–426–9292.

Gourmet Mushrooms, P.O. Box 515, Graton, CA 95444: Free information ❖ Morel mushroom spawn for backyard gardens. 707–829–7301.

Hardscrabble Enterprises Inc., Box 42, Cherry Grove, WV 26804: Catalog $3 (refundable) ❖ Shiitake mushroom-growing supplies. 304–567–2727.

Mushroom-people, P.O. Box 220, Summertown TN 38483: Catalog $3 ❖ Mushroom-growing kits and how-to books. 615–964–2200.

Western Biologicals, Box 283, Aldergrove, British Columbia, Canada V0X 1A0: Catalog $3 ❖ Spawn, cultures, kits, books, and cultivation supplies.

Nurseries

The companies in this section offer a wide variety of seeds and plants, gardening supplies, tools, and equipment.

W. Atlee Burpee & Company, 300 Park Ave., Warminster, PA 18974: Free catalog ❖ 215–674–1793.

Henry Field's Seed & Nursery, 415 N. Burnett, Shenandoah, IA 51602: Free catalog ❖ 605–665–4491.

Harris Seeds Inc., P.O. Box 22960, Rochester, NY 14692: Free catalog ❖ 716–594–9411.

J.W. Jung Seed Company, 335 High St., Randolph, WI 53957: Free catalog ❖ 414–326–4100.

Orol Ledden & Sons, P.O. Box 7, Sewell, NJ 08080: Free catalog ❖ 609–468–1000.

Letherman's Seeds, 1221 Tuscarawas St. East, Canton, OH 44702: Free catalog ❖ 216–452–5704.

Earl May Seeds & Nursery Company, N. Elm St., Shenandoah, IA 51603: Free catalog ❖ 712–246–1020.

Mellinger's, 2310 W. South Range Rd., North Lima, OH 44452: Free catalog ❖ 216–549–9861.

Nichols Garden Nursery, 1190 Pacific West, Albany, OR 97321: Free catalog ❖ 503–928–9280.

L.L. Olds Seed Company, P.O. Box 7790, Madison, WI 53707: Catalog $2.50 ❖ 608–249–9291.

Park Seed Company Inc., Cokesbury Rd., P.O. Box 46, Greenwood, SC 29648: Free catalog. 803–223–7333.

Shady Oaks Nursery, 112 10th Ave. SE, Waseca, MN 56093: Information $1 ❖ 507–835–5033.

R.H. Shumway Seedsman, P.O. Box 1, Graniteville, SC 29829: Free catalog.

Stark Bro's. Nurseries & Orchards Company, P.O. Box 10, Louisiana, MO 63353: Free catalog ❖ 800–325–4180.

Otis Twilley Seed Company, P.O. Box 65, Trevose, PA 19047: Catalog $1 ❖ 800–622–7333.

Orchids

Adagent Acres, 2245 Floral Way, Santa Rosa, CA 95403: Free catalog with 1st class stamp ❖ Hybrid orchids. 707–575–4459.

Alberts & Merkel Brothers Inc., 2210 S. Federal Hwy., Boynton Beach, FL 33435: Catalog $1 ❖ Orchid plants and growing supplies. 407–732–2071.

Carter & Holmes Inc., P.O. Box 668, Newberry, SC 29108: Catalog $1.50 (refundable) ❖ Unusual hybrids and orchid growing supplies. 803–276–0579.

Epi World, 10607 Glenview Ave., Cupertino, CA 95014: Catalog $2 ❖ Orchid cactus starter collections and other hybrids.

Fennell's Orchid Company, 2650 SW 27th Ave., Miami, FL 33133: Free catalog ❖

Easy-to-grow orchids for indoors or outside. 800–344–2457.

Fox Orchids, 6615 W. Markham, Little Rock, AR 72205: Free price list ❖ Orchids, staghorn ferns, bromeliads, fertilizers, potting mixes, and books. 501–663–4246.

G & B Orchid Laboratory & Nursery, 2426 Cherimoya Dr., Vista, CA 92084: Free catalog ❖ Growing supplies, flasking media, chemical supplies, laboratory glassware, fertilizers, seedlings, and orchid species. 619–727–2611.

Golden Orchid, 9100 Fruitville Rd., Sarasota, FL 34240: Free brochure ❖ Cattleyas, cattleya-like mericlones, and a few vandas, phalaenopsis, epidendrums, dendrobiums, and other orchid hybrids. 813–377–1058.

Greenleaf Orchids, 158 S. Winterset Ave., Crystal River, FL 32629: Catalog $2 ❖ Cattleya, angraecum, vandas, phalaenopsis, miniatures, and dwarf orchids. 904–795–3785.

Huronview Nurseries, RR 1, Bright's Grove, Ontario, Canada N0N 1C0: Free catalog ❖ Easy-to-grow orchids.

J & L Orchids, 20 Sherwood Rd., Easton, CT 06612: Catalog $1 ❖ Hybrid orchids, rare and unusual species, and easy-to-grow miniatures. 203–261–3772.

J.E.M. Orchids, 6595 Morikami Park Rd., Delray Beach, FL 33446: Catalog $2 (refundable) ❖ Mini-cats, oncidium intergenerics, catasetum, and species-breeding orchids.

Kensington Orchids, 3301 Plyers Mill Rd., Kensington, MD 20895: Price list $1 (refundable) ❖ Orchid plants. 301–933–0036.

Krull-Smith Orchids, 2815 Ponkan Rd., Apopka, FL 32712: Free catalog ❖ Easy-to-grow orchids.

Lauray of Salisbury, 432 Undermountain Rd., Salisbury, CT 06068: Catalog $2 ❖ Orchids, begonias, gesneriads, cacti, and succulents. 203–435–2263.

Rod McLellan Company, 1450 El Camino Real, South San Francisco, CA 94080: Catalog $2 ❖ Orchid plants and growing supplies. 415–871–5655.

Mellinger's, 2310 W. South Range Rd., North Lima, OH 44452: Free catalog ❖ Orchids, daylilies, gladioli, irises, trees, shrubs, and gardening equipment. 216–549–9861.

The Orchid Club, Box 463, Baldwinsville, NY 13027: Free brochure ❖ Club members receive a different plant each month with instructions for care. 800–822–9411.

Orchid Thoroughbreds, 731 W. Siddondsburg Rd., Dillsburg, PA 17019: Free catalog ❖ Easy-to-grow orchids.

Orchids by Hauserman Inc., 2N134 Addison Rd., Villa Park, IL 60181: Catalog $1.25 ❖ Orchid plants and growing supplies. 708–543–6855.

Palestine Orchids Inc., Rt. 1, Box 312, Palestine, WV 26160: Free information ❖ Easy-to-grow orchids. 304–275–4781.

Sunswept Laboratories, P.O. Box 1913, Studio City, CA 91614: Catalog $2 ❖ Artificially propagated rare and endangered orchid species. 818–506–7271.

Teas Nursery Company, 4400 Bellaire Blvd., Bellaire, TX 77401: Catalog $1 (refundable) ❖ Orchid starter collections, growing supplies, and books. 713–664–4400.

Wildflower Nursery, 1680 Hwy. 25–70, Marshall, NC 28753: Free catalog ❖ Native orchids.

Palms

Crockett's Tropical Plants, P.O. Box 1150, Harlingen, TX 78551: Catalog $3 ❖ Container-grown ornamentals, citrus, and palms.

Floribunda Palms, Box 635, Mt. View, HI 96771: Free information with long SASE ❖ Palms from worldwide sources.

The Green Escape, P.O. Box 1417, Palm Harbor, FL 34682: Catalog $6 (refundable) ❖ Indoor, cold-hardy, and tropical palm species.

Green World Enterprises Inc., 1723 Avenida Del Sol, Boca Raton, FL 33432: Free brochure ❖ Exotic table top coconut palms. 407–362–8343.

Rhapis Gardens, P.O. Box 287, Gregory, TX 78359: Catalog $2 ❖ Green, variegated, and other dwarf indoor rhapis excella plants. 512–643–2061.

Rhapis Palm Growers, 31350 Alta Vista, Redlands, CA 92373: Catalog $2 with long SASE ❖ Rhapis palms. 714–794–3823.

Peonies, Irises & Daylilies

Aitken's Salmon Creek Garden, 608 NW 119th St., Vancouver, WA 98685: Catalog $2 ❖ Tall bearded, medians, Japanese, Siberian, and other irises.

American Daylily & Perennials, P.O. Box 210, Grain Valley, MO 64029: Catalog $3 (refundable) ❖ Daylilies, hostas, and dwarf cannas. 800–770–2777.

B & D Lilies, 330 P St., Port Townsend, WA 98368: Catalog $3 ❖ Species and hybrid lilies and special heirloom collections. 206–385–1738.

Big Tree Daylily Garden, 777 General Hutchinson Pkwy., Longwood, FL 32750: Catalog $1 (refundable) ❖ Daylilies. 407–831–5430.

Bloomingfields Farm, Box 565, Gaylordsville, CT 06755: Catalog $1 (refundable) ❖ Daylilies. 203–354–6951.

Borbeleta Gardens, 15980 Canby Ave., Faribault, MN 55021: Catalog $3 ❖ Daylilies, bearded and Siberian irises, and lilies. 507–334–2807.

Lee Bristol Nursery, Bloomingfields Farm, Rt. 55, Gaylordsville, CT 06755: Free catalog ❖ Daylilies. 203–354–6951.

Busse Gardens, 13579 10th St. NW, Cokato, MN 55321: Catalog $2 (refundable with $25 order) ❖ Siberian irises and ferns. 612–286–2654.

Caprice Farm Nursery, 15425 SW Pleasant Hill Rd., Sherwood, OR 97140: Free catalog ❖ Peonies, irises, daylilies, and hostas. 503–625–7241.

Comanche Acres Iris Gardens, Rt. 1, Box 258, Gower, MO 64454: Catalog $3 ❖ Tall-bearded and intermediate irises. 816–424–6436.

Cooley's Gardens, 11553 Silverton Rd. NE, P.O. Box 126, Silverton, OR 97381: Catalog $2 (refundable) ❖ Irises. 800–225–5391.

Cordon Bleu Farms, P.O. Box 2017, San Marcos, CA 92079: Catalog $1 ❖ Daylilies and irises.

Cottage Gardens, 266 17th Ave., San Francisco, CA 94121: Free catalog ❖ New tall-bearded irises.

Daylily Discounters, One Daylily Plaza, Alachua, FL 32615: Free catalog ❖ Award-winning daylilies. 904–462–1539.

Daylily World, P.O. Box 1612, Sanford, FL 32772: Catalog $5 (refundable) ❖ Daylilies. 407–322–4034.

Eco-Gardens, P.O. Box 1227, Decatur, GA 30031: Price list $1 ❖ Perennials, wildflowers, ferns, daylilies, water garden plants, trees, shrubs, and ferns. 404–294–6468.

Greenwood Daylily Gardens Inc., 5595 E. 7th St., Long Beach, CA 90804: Catalog $5 ❖ Daylilies. 310–494–8944.

The Iris Pond, 7311 Churchill Rd., McLean, VA 22101: Price list $1 ❖ Tall bearded, Japanese, Siberians, table irises, and other species.

Jernigan Gardens, Rt. 6, P.O. Box 593, Dunn, NC 28334: Free price list with long SASE ❖ Lilies, hostas, and irises. 910–567–2135.

Johnson Daylily Garden, 70 Lark Ave., Brooksville, FL 34601: Free price list with 1st class stamp ❖ Daylilies. 904–544–1319.

Klehm Nursery, 4210 N. Duncan Rd., Champaign, IL, 61821: Catalog $2 ❖ Peonies, irises, hostas, daylilies, and perennials. 800–553–3715.

Long's Garden, P.O. Box 19, Boulder, CO 80306: Free catalog ❖ Tall, intermediate, and dwarf irises. 303–442–2353.

Louisiana Nursery, Rt. 7, Box 43, Opelousas, LA 70570: Catalog $3 ❖ Daylily and iris cultivars. 318–948–3696.

Marietta Gardens, P.O. Box 70, Marietta, NC 28362: Free catalog ❖ Daylilies. 910–628–9466.

Maryland Aquatic Nurseries, 3427 N. Furnace Rd., Jarrettsville, MD 21084: Catalog $5 (refundable) ❖ Water garden plants, ornamental grasses, and Louisiana and Japanese irises. 410–557–7615.

Maryott's Gardens, 1073 Bird Ave., San Jose, CA 95125: Catalog $1 (refundable) ❖ Bearded, ruffled, and laced irises. 408–971–0444.

Mellinger's, 2310 W. South Range Rd., North Lima, OH 44452: Free catalog ❖ Daylilies, gladioli, irises, other plants, and gardening equipment. 216–549–9861.

The New Peony Farm, P.O. Box 18235, St. Paul, MN 55118: Free brochure ❖ Peony cultivars in singles, doubles, semi-doubles, and Japanese varieties. 612–457–8994.

Oakes Daylilies, 8204 Monday Rd., Corryton, TN 37721: Free catalog ❖ Daylily cultivars. 615–687–3770.

Quality Dutch Bulbs, 50 Lake Dr., P.O. Box 225, Hillsdale, NJ 07642: Free catalog ❖ Irises, daffodils, tulips, and other ornamental bulbs. 201–391–6586.

Roris Gardens, 8195 Bradshaw Rd., Sacramento, CA 95829: Catalog $2 (refundable) ❖ Irises. 916–689–7460.

Schreiner's Gardens, 3625 Quinaby Rd. NE, Salem, OR 97303: Catalog $4 ❖ Dwarf and tall-bearded irises. 800–525–2367.

Serendipity Gardens, 3210 Upper Bellbrook Rd., Bellbrook, OH 45305: Free catalog ❖ Daylilies. 513–426–6596.

Skolaski's Glads & Flowers, 4821 County Trunk Hwy. Q, Waunakee, WI 53597: Catalog $1 ❖ Gladiolius bulbs, lilies, and perennials. 608–836–4822.

Smirnow's Son, 11 Oakwood Dr. West, Rt. 1, Huntington, NY 11743: Catalog $2 ❖ Tree peonies. 516–421–0836.

Tischler Peony Gardens, 1021 E. Division St., Faribault, MN 55021: Free catalog ❖ Herbaceous peonies. 507–334–7242.

Tranquil Lake Nursery, 45 River St., Rehoboth, MA 02769: Catalog $1 ❖ Daylilies and irises. 508–252–4002.

Walnut Hill Gardens, 999 310th St., Atalissa, IA 52720: Price list $2 ❖ Daylilies, hostas, and Siberian irises. 319–946–3471.

Wayside Gardens, 1 Garden Ln., Hodges, SC 29695: Free catalog ❖ Siberian irises. 800–845–1124.

White Flower Farm, Rt. 63, Litchfield, CT 06759: Free catalog ❖ Herbaceous peonies. 800–888–7756.

Gilbert H. Wild & Son Inc., P.O. Box 338, Sarcoxie, MO 64862: Catalog $3 (refundable) ❖ Peonies, irises, and daylilies. 417–548–3514.

Windmill Gardens, P.O. Box 351, Luverne, AL 36049: Catalog $2 ❖ Daylilies. 205–335–5568.

Perennials & Ornamentals

Agua Fria Nursery, 1409 Agua Fria St., Santa Fe, NM 87501: Free catalog ❖ Containerized western wildflowers, perennials, and shrubs.

Kurt Bluemel Inc., 2740 Greene Ln., Baldwin, MD 21013: Catalog $2 ❖ Perennials, ferns, bamboo plants, and ornamental grasses. 410–557–7229.

Bluestone Perennials, 7211 Middle Ridge Rd., Madison, OH 44057: Free catalog ❖ Perennial flowers, ground covers, ivies, and vines. 800–852–5243.

Bo's Nursery, 12743 Gillard Rd., Winter Garden, FL 34787: Information $2 (refundable) ❖ Herb and native plants, perennials, and old roses. 407–656–1959.

Canyon Creek Nursery, 3527 Dry Creek Rd., Oroville, CA 95965: Catalog $1 ❖ Perennials. 916–533–2166.

Country Heritage Nurseries Inc., P.O. Box 536, Hartford, MI 49057: Free catalog ❖ Strawberries, raspberries, fruit trees, and ornamentals. 616–621–2491.

Crownsville Nursery, P.O. Box 797, Crownsville, MD 21032: Catalog $10 ❖ Ferns, wildflowers, azaleas, ornamental grasses, and perennials. 410–923–2212.

Daystar, Rt. 2, Box 250, Litchfield, ME 04350: Catalog $1 ❖ Perennials, trees, shrubs, and rhododendrons. 207–724–3369.

Eco-Gardens, P.O. Box 1227, Decatur, GA 30031: Price list $1 ❖ Perennials, wildflowers, ferns, daylilies, water garden plants, trees, and shrubs. 404–294–6468.

Fieldstone Gardens Inc., 620 Quaker Ln., Vassalboro, ME 04989: Catalog $1.50 ❖ Nursery-propagated perennials. 207–923–3836.

Garden Place, 6780 Heisley Rd., P.O. Box 388, Mentor, OH 44061: Catalog $1 ❖ Perennials. 216–255–3705.

Gilson Gardens Inc., 3059 US Rt. 20, P.O. Box 277, Perry, OH 44081: Free catalog ❖ Ground covers, perennials, and ferns.

Good Hollow Greenhouse & Herbarium, Rt. 1, Box 116, Taft, TN 38488: Catalog $1 ❖ Herbs, perennials, wildflowers, scented geraniums, essential oils and potpourris, teas, and dried herbs and spices. 615–433–7640.

The Gourmet Gardener, 8650 College Blvd., Overland Park, KS 66210: Catalog $2 ❖ Herb, vegetable, and edible flower seeds from around the world. 913–345–0490.

Heaths & Heathers, P.O. Box 850, Elma, WA 98541: Free information with long SASE ❖ Easy-to-grow heathers. 206–482–3258.

Heritage Gardens, 1 Meadow Ridge Rd., Shenandoah, IA 51601: Free catalog ❖ Perennial plants for all climates, ornamental grasses, foliage plants, hostas, shade garden plants, ferns, lilies, rock garden plants, shrubs, azaleas and rhododendrons, roses, and flowering trees. 605–665–5188.

Hummingbird Hills Herbal Nursery, 17201 S. Hawkinds, Ashland, MO 65010: Catalog $1 ❖ Organically grown herbs, perennials, everlastings, and dried flowers. 314–657–2082.

Klehm Nursery, 4210 N. Duncan Rd., Champaign, IL, 61821: Catalog $2 ❖ Peonies, irises, daylilies, hostas, and perennials. 800–553–3715.

Lamb Nurseries, 101 E. Sharp Ave., Spokane, WA 99202: Catalog $1 ❖ Perennials, ferns, shrubs, and other plants. 509–328–7956.

Lily of the Valley Herb Farm, 3969 Fox Ave., Minerva, OH 44657: Price list $1 (refundable) ❖ Herb, everlasting, perennial, and scented geranium plants. 216–862–3920.

Limerock Ornamental Grasses Inc., RD 1, Box 111, Port Matilda, PA 16870: Catalog $3 ❖ Ornamental and native grasses, companion perennials, and nursery-grown hardy ferns. 814–692–2272.

Mellinger's, 2310 W. South Range Rd., North Lima, OH 44452: Free catalog ❖ Perennials, wildflowers, berry plants, orchids, trees, shrubs, and gardening equipment. 216–549–9861.

Milaeger's Gardens, 4838 Douglas Ave., Racine, WI 53402: Catalog $1 ❖ Perennials. 800–669–9956.

J.E. Miller Nurseries, 5060 W. Lake Rd., Canandaigua, NY 14424: Free catalog ❖ Fruit and nut trees, vines, ornamentals, and ground covers. 800–836–9630.

Mohns Inc., P.O. Box 2301, Atascadero, CA 93423: Free catalog with two 1st class stamps ❖ Perennial poppies for western gardens. 805–466–4362.

Niche Gardens, 1111 Dawson Rd., Chapel Hill, NC 27516: Catalog $3 ❖ Nursery-propagated wildflowers, perennials, trees, and shrubs. 919–967–0078.

Patrick's Nursery, P.O. Box 130, Ty Ty, GA 31795: Free catalog ❖ Perennials, vegetables, fruit and nut trees, berry plants, and grapevines for southern climates. 912–386–1122.

Perennial Pleasures Nursery, 2 Brickhouse Rd., East Hardwock, VT 05836: Catalog $2 (refundable) ❖ Heirloom herbs and flowers. 802–472–5104.

Rakestraw's Gardens, 3094 S. Term St., Burton, MI 48529: Catalog $1 ❖ Bonsai supplies and perennials for rock gardens. 313–742–2685.

Riverhead Perennials, 5 Riverhead Ln., East Lyme, CT 06333: Catalog $2 (refundable) ❖ Perennials. 203–437–7828.

Rocknoll Nursery, 7812 Mad River Rd., Hillsboro, OH 45133: Catalog $1 ❖ Perennials, ivies, dwarf plants, ground covers, and plants for rock gardens. 513–393–5545.

Skolaski's Glads & Flowers, 4821 County Trunk Hwy. Q, Waunakee, WI 53597: Catalog $1 ❖ Gladiolius bulbs, lilies, and perennials. 608–836–4822.

Spring Hill Nurseries, 6523 N. Galena Rd., P.O. Box 1758, Peoria, IL 61656: Free catalog ❖ Perennials, roses, annuals, ground covers, bonsai, and houseplants. 800–582–8527.

Surry Gardens, P.O. Box 145, Surry, ME 04684: Free information ❖ Herbaceous borders and rock garden supplies. 207–667–4493.

Twombly Inc., 163 Barn Hill Rd., Monroe, CT 06468: Catalog $4 ❖ Dwarf conifer miniatures and other rare and unusual plants and trees. 203–261–2133.

Van Bourgondien Bros., 245 Farmingdale Rd., P.O. 1000, Babylon, NY 11702: Free catalog ❖ Perennials. 800–622–9997.

Van Hise Nursery, 30688 SE Waybill Rd., Boring, OR 97009: Free information ❖ Perennials, ground covers, and shrubs. 503–663–6123.

Vandenberg, Black Meadow Rd., Chester, NY 10918: Free catalog ❖ Perennials, hybrid lilies, seeds, and bulbs. 914–469–2633.

Andre Viette Nurseries, Rt. 1, Box 16, Fisherville, VA 22939: Catalog $2 ❖ Flowering and rock garden perennials, woodland plants, and daylilies. 703–943–2315.

Wayside Gardens, 1 Garden Ln., Hodges, SC 29695: Free catalog ❖ Perennials, trees, shrubs, ground covers, and gardening supplies. 800–845–1124.

Weiss Brothers Nursery, 11690 Colfax Hwy., Grass Valley, CA 95945: Free catalog ❖ Perennials and drip irrigation supplies. 916–272–7657.

Wildflower Nursery, 1680 Hwy. 25–70, Marshall, NC 28753: Free catalog ❖ Perennials.

Wrenwood of Berkeley Springs, Rt. 4., Box 361, Berkeley Springs, WV 25411: Catalog $2 ❖ Perennials and herbs. 304–258–3071.

Rock Gardens

Carroll Gardens, 444 E. Main St., P.O. Box 310, Westminster, MD 21157: Catalog $3 (refundable) ❖ Rock garden and alpine plants. 800–638–6334.

Daystar, Rt. 2, Box 250, Litchfield, ME 04350: Catalog $1 ❖ Rock garden plants and growing supplies. 207–724–3369.

Endangered Species, P.O. Box 1830, Tustin, CA 92681: Catalog $6 ❖ Rare and unusual rock garden plants. 714–544–9505.

Rice Creek Gardens, 11506 Hwy. 65, Minneapolis, MN 55434: Catalog $2 ❖ Rock garden plants, gardening supplies, vines, ferns, and ornamental shrubs.

Rocknoll Nursery, 7812 Mad River Rd., Hillsboro, OH 45133: Catalog $1 ❖ Rock garden plants, ivies, perennials, dwarf plants, ground covers, and gardening supplies. 513–393–5545.

Siskiyou Rare Plant Nursery, 2825 Cummings Rd., Medford, OR 97501: Catalog $2 ❖ Dwarf and other plants for rock gardens and woodland and alpine settings. 503–772–6846.

Twombly Inc., 163 Barn Hill Rd., Monroe, CT 06468: Catalog $4 ❖ Dwarf conifer miniatures and other rare and unusual plants and trees for water gardens. 203–261–2133.

We-Du Nursery, Rt. 5, Box 724, Marion, NC 28752: Catalog $2 ❖ Plants and rock garden supplies. 704–738–8300.

Roses

Antique Rose Emporium, Rt. 5, Box 143, Brenham, TX 77833: Catalog $5 ❖ Antique roses for southern climates. 800–441–0002.

Blossoms & Bloomers, E. 11415 Krueger Rd., Spokane, WA 99207: Catalog $1 ❖ Old-fashioned roses. 509–922–1344.

Bo's Nursery, 12743 Gillard Rd., Winter Garden, FL 34787: Information $2 (refundable) ❖ Herb and native plants, perennials, and old roses. 407–656–1959.

Edmunds Roses, 6235 SW Kahle Rd., Wilsonville, OR 97070: Free catalog ❖ Exhibition and European roses. 503–682–1476.

Gloria Del, 36 East Rd., High Falls Park, High Falls, NY 12440: Free catalog ❖ New miniature roses. 914–687–9981.

Heirloom Old Garden Roses, 24062 NE Riverside Dr., St. Paul, OR 97137: Catalog $5

❖ Old garden, English, and winter-hardy roses. 503–538–1576.

Jackson & Perkins, P.O. Box 1028, Medford, OR 97501: Free catalog ❖ Roses. 800–292–4769.

Lowe's Own Root Roses, 6 Sheffield Rd., Nashua, NH 03062: Catalog $2 ❖ Custom-grown 17th-, 18th-, and 19th-century roses. 603–888–2214.

Earl May Seeds & Nursery Company, N. Elm St., Shenandoah, IA 51603: Free catalog ❖ Roses, shade and ornamental trees, flowering shrubs, vegetable and flower seeds, bulbs, and gardening supplies. 712–246–1020.

The Mini-Rose Garden, Mini-Rose Bldg., Cross Hill, SC 29332: Free catalog ❖ Miniature roses for indoor and outdoor growing. 800–996–4647.

Miniature Plant Kingdom, 4125 Harrison Grade Rd., Sebastopol, CA 95472: Catalog $2.50 ❖ Miniature roses and Japanese maples, conifers, and other plants for bonsai. 707–874–2233.

Nor'East Miniature Roses Inc., 58 Hammond St., Rowley, MA 01969: Free catalog ❖ Miniature roses. 508–948–7964.

Oregon Miniature Roses, 8285 SW 185th Ave., Beaverton, OR 97007: Catalog $1 ❖ Micro-mini, climbing miniature, and miniature tree roses. 503–649–4482.

Rabbit Shadow Farm, 2880 E. Hwy. 402, Loveland, CO 80537: Free information ❖ Herbs, roses, topiary supplies, and scented geraniums. 303–667–5531.

Rosehill Farm, Gregg Neck Rd., Galena, MD 21635: Free catalog ❖ Roses. 410–648–5538.

Roses by Fred Edmunds, 6235 SW Kahle Rd., Wilsonville, OR 97070: Free catalog ❖ Roses. 503–682–1476.

Roses of Yesterday & Today, 803 Brown's Valley Rd., Watsonville, CA 95076: Catalog $4 ❖ Old, rare, and unusual roses. 408–724–3537.

Savage Farms Nursery, P.O. Box 125, McMinnville, TN 37110: Free catalog ❖ Roses. 615–668–8902.

Sequoia Nursery/Moore Miniature Roses, 2519 E. Noble Ave., Visalia, CA 93277: Catalog $1 ❖ Miniatures, tree roses, climbing miniatures, and roses for hanging baskets. 209–732–0190.

R.H. Shumway Seedsman, P.O. Box 1, Graniteville, SC 29829: Free catalog ❖

Roses, berry plants, fruit trees, seeds and bulbs, ornamental shrubs and plants, and gardening supplies.

Spring Hill Nurseries, 6523 N. Galena Rd., P.O. Box 1758, Peoria, IL 61632: Free catalog ❖ Perennials and annuals, trees and shrubs, ground covers, bonsai, houseplants, and old roses, miniatures, and other roses. 800–582–8527.

Texas Mini Roses, P.O. Box 267, Denton, TX 75202: Free catalog ❖ Miniature rose plants. 817–566–3034.

Vintage Gardens, 3003 Pleasant Hill Rd., Sebastopol, CA 95472: Catalog $4 ❖ Antique roses. 707–829–5342.

Sassafras

Vernon Barnes & Son Nursery, P.O. Box 250, McMinnville, TN 37110: Free catalog ❖ Vines, wildflowers, hedges and shrubs, berry plants, and shade, sassafras, flowering, fruit, and nut trees. 615–668–8576.

Dutch Mountain Nursery, 7984 N. 48th St., Augusta, MI 49012: Free catalog with long SASE ❖ Sassafras trees. 616–731–5232.

Forestfarm, 990 Tetherow Rd., Williams, OR 97544: Catalog $3 ❖ Sassafras trees. 503–846–6963.

Louisiana Nursery, Rt. 7, Box 43, Opelousas, LA 70570: Catalog $6 ❖ Sassafras trees and other rare, unusual, and hard-to-find plants. 318–948–3696.

Seeds & Bulbs

Abundant Life Seed Foundation, P.O. Box 772, Port Townsend, WA 98368: Catalog $2 ❖ Organic and untreated vegetable, grain, herb, wildflower, and other seeds. 206–385–5660.

Jacques Amand, P.O. Box 59001, Potomac, MD 20859: Free catalog ❖ Imported rare and unsual bulbs from England. 800–452–5414.

Amaryllis Inc., P.O. Box 318, Baton Rouge, LA 70821: Catalog $1 ❖ Amaryllis bulbs. 504–924–5560.

American Horticultural Society, 7931 East Blvd. Dr., Alexandria, VA 22308: Free list for members ❖ Heirloom and other hard-to-find seeds. 703–768–5700.

Archia's Seed Store, 106 E. Main St., Sedalia, MO 65301: Free catalog ❖ Vegetable and flower seeds, gardening supplies, nursery stock, and beekeeping equipment. 816–826–1330.

The Banana Tree, 715 Northampton St., Easton, PA 18042: Catalog $3 ❖ Seeds from temperate and tropical climates.

Bountiful Gardens, 18001 Shafer Ranch Rd., Willits, CA 95490: Free catalog ❖ Seeds for vegetables, compost crops, herbs, and flowers. Also books and organic gardening supplies. 707–459–6410.

Breck's Dutch Bulbs, Mail Order Reservation Center, 6523 N. Galena Rd., P.O. Box 1757, Peoria, IL 61656: Free catalog ❖ Holland spring-flowering bulbs. 309–691–4616.

John Brudy Exotics, Box 820874, Houston, TX 77280: Catalog $2 (refundable) ❖ Seeds for the rare Adenium plant, trees, and shrubs. 800–926–7333.

Bundles of Bulbs, 112 Greenspring Valley Rd., Owings Mills, MD 21117: Catalog $2 ❖ Spring-flowering bulbs. 410–363–1371.

W. Atlee Burpee & Company, 300 Park Ave., Warminster, PA 18974: Free catalog ❖ Seeds and bulbs. 215–674–1793.

D.V. Burrell Seed Company, P.O. Box 150, Rocky Ford, CO 81067: Free catalog ❖ Seeds, gardening supplies, and tools. 719–254–3318.

Butterbrooke Farm, 78 Barry Rd., Oxford, CT 06483: Free catalog ❖ Chemically untreated, open-pollinated, short-maturity seeds. 203–888–2000.

Caladium World, P.O. Drawer 629, Sebring, FL 33871: Free catalog ❖ Caladium bulbs. 813–385–7661.

Comstock, Ferre & Company, 263 Main St., Wethersfield, CT 06109: Catalog $2 ❖ Vegetable, flower, and herb seeds. 203–571–6590.

The Cook's Garden, P.O. Box 535, Londonberry, VT 05148: Catalog $1 ❖ Seeds for baby and Italian-style vegetables. 802–824–3400.

The Daffodil Mart, Rt. 3, Box 794, Gloucester, VA 23061: Free catalog ❖ Daffodils, tulips, autumn flowering and forcing bulbs, other bulbs, and growing supplies. 804–693–3966.

Dan's Garden Shop, 5821 Woodwinds Cir., Frederick, MD 21701: Free catalog ❖ Seeds for annuals, perennials, and vegetables. 301–695–5966.

DeGiorgi Seed Company Inc., 6011 N St., Omaha, NE 68117: Catalog $2 ❖ Seeds. 402–731–3901.

deJager Bulb Company, Box 2010, South Hamilton, MA 01982: Free catalog ❖ Dutch bulbs. 508–468–4707.

Dutch Gardens Inc., P.O. Box 200, Adelphia, NJ 07710: Free information ❖ Tulip, hyacinth, crocus, iris, amaryllis, and other bulbs. 800–818–3861.

Evergreen Y.H. Enterprises, P.O. Box 17538, Anaheim, CA 92817: Catalog $2 (refundable) ❖ Gardening tools, cookbooks, and vegetable seeds from China, Japan, and other countries.

Fancy Plants Farms, P.O. Box 989, Lake Placid, FL 33852: Free information ❖ Caladium bulbs. 800–869–0953.

Far North Gardens, 16785 Harrison, Livonia, MI 48154: Catalog $2 (refundable) ❖ Rare flower seeds from worldwide sources. 313–422–0747.

Farmer Seed & Nursery Company, 818 NW 4th St., Faribault, MN 55021: Free catalog ❖ Vegetable seeds, flowering bulbs, fruit and shade trees, ornamental shrubs and hedges, berry plants, and roses. 507–334–2017.

Henry Field's Seed & Nursery, 415 N. Burnett, Shenandoah, IA 51602: Free catalog ❖ Vegetable and flower seeds, berry plants, hedges, ornamental shrubs, roses, and fruit and nut and shade trees. 605–665–4491.

Fisher's Garden Store, P.O. Box 236, Belgrade, MT 59714: Free catalog ❖ Vegetable and flower seeds for high altitude gardening and short growing seasons. 406–388–6052.

The Fragrant Path, P.O. Box 328, Fort Calhoun, NE 68023: Catalog $2 ❖ Seeds for prairie wildflowers, grasses, ferns, trees and shrubs, and climbing plants.

Garden City Seeds, 1324 Red Crow Rd., Victor, MT 59875: Information $1 ❖ Untreated seeds, many organically grown, for gardens in northern climates. 406–961–4837.

Garden Solutions, 617 Garden Terrace, Holland, MI 49422: Free catalog ❖ Bulbs, flowering perennials, trees, vines, shrubs, hedges, and other plants.

Gardener's Choice, Country Rd. 687, P.O. Box 8000, Hartford, MI 49057: Free catalog ❖ Seeds for vegetables, flowers, house plants, and trees. 800–274–4096.

Gleckler Seedmen, Metamora, OH 43540: Free catalog ❖ Unusual seed varieties.

Russell Graham Plants, 4030 Eagle Crest Rd. NW, Salem, OR 97304: Catalog $2 ❖ Ferns, ornamental grasses, lily bulbs, irises, daffodils, and other plants. 503–362–1135.

Greenleaf Seeds, P.O. Box 98, Conway, MA 01341: Catalog 50¢ ❖ Seeds for root and green leafy vegetables.

Gurney Seed & Nursery Company, 110 Capitol St., Yankton, SD 57079: Free catalog ❖ Seeds, bulbs, and semi-dwarf and standard varieties of apple trees. 605–665–1671.

Happiness Farms, 704 CR 621 East, Lake Placid, FL 33852: Free catalog ❖ Caladium bulbs. 813–465–0044.

Harris Seeds, P.O. Box 22960, Rochester, NY 14692: Free catalog ❖ Seeds and gardening supplies. 716–594–9411.

Hastings, P.O. Box 115535, Atlanta, GA 30310: Free catalog ❖ Seeds for vegetables and plants for southern climates. 404–755–6580.

Heirloom Garden Seeds, P.O. Box 138, Guerneville, CA 95446: Price list $2.50 ❖ Rare, culinary, and ornamental seeds.

Holland Bulb Farms, 423 Broad St., P.O. Box 220, Tatamy, PA 18085: Free catalog ❖ Imported bulbs from Holland. 800–283–5082.

J.L. Hudson, Seedsman, Box 1058, Redwood City, CA 94064: Catalog $1 ❖ Seeds from around the world.

Imported Dutch Bulbs, P.O. Box 32, Cavendish, VT 05142: Free catalog ❖ Daffodils, tulips, and other bulbs. 802–226–7653.

Jackson & Perkins, P.O. Box 1028, Medford, OR 97501: Free catalog ❖ Seeds, plants, and roses. 800–292–4769.

Johnny's Selected Seeds, 310 Foss Hill Rd., Albion, ME 04910: Free catalog ❖ Strawberry plants and flower and vegetable seeds for cool northern climates. 207–437–9294.

J.W. Jung Seed Company, 335 High St., Randolph, WI 53957: Free catalog ❖ Seeds and gardening supplies. 414–326–4100.

Kitazawa Seed Company, 1111 Chapman St., San Jose, CA 95126: Free price list ❖ Chinese and Japanese vegetable seeds.

D. Landreth Seed Company, P.O. Box 6426, Baltimore, MD 21230: Catalog $2 ❖ Vegetable and flower seeds. 410–727–3922.

Le Jardin du Gourmet, P.O. Box 75, St. Johnsbury Center, VT 05863: Catalog $1 ❖

Seeds for vegetables and herb plants. 802–748–1446.

Orol Ledden & Sons, P.O. Box 7, Sewell, NJ 08080: Free catalog ❖ Seeds for cantaloupes, corn, and tomatoes. 609–468–1000.

Letherman's Seeds, 1221 Tuscarawas St. East, Canton, OH 44707: Free catalog ❖ Landscaping tools, gardening supplies, and vegetable, flower, and grass seeds. 216–452–5704.

Liberty Seed Company, P.O. Box 806, New Philadelphia, OH 44663: Free catalog ❖ Flower and vegetable seeds. 216–364–1611.

Lindenberg Seeds Ltd., 803 Princess Ave., Brandon, Manitoba, Canada R7A 0P5: Catalog $1 ❖ Vegetable and flower seeds and gardening supplies.

Marlborough Greenhouses Inc., P.O. Box 32, Marlborough, NH 03455: Catalog $1 ❖ Preplanted flowering dutch bulbs. 603–876–4397.

Earl May Seeds & Nursery Company, N. Elm St., Shenandoah, IA 51603: Free catalog ❖ Vegetable and flower seeds, bulbs, fruit and nut trees, roses, grapes, and flowering shrubs. 712–246–1020.

Mellinger's, 2310 W. South Range Rd., North Lima, OH 44452: Free catalog ❖ Vegetable and flower seeds, flowering shrubs and hedges, perennials, wildflowers, berry plants, and fruit, nut, ornamental, and shade trees. 216–549–9861.

Michigan Bulb Company, 1950 Waldorf NW, Grand Rapids, MI 49550: Free catalog ❖ Bulbs, perennials, foliage plants, trees and shrubs, exotic house plants, hedges and climbers, and roses. 616–771–9500.

Netherland Bulb Company, 13 McFadden Rd., Easton, PA 18042: Free catalog ❖ Imported Dutch bulbs. 215–253–8879.

Nichols Garden Nursery, 1190 N. Pacific West, Albany, OR 97321: Free catalog ❖ Vegetable seeds, herb seeds and plants, saffron crocus, garlic and shallots, and strawberry plants. 503–928–9280.

L.L. Olds Seed Company, P.O. Box 7790, Madison, WI 53707: Catalog $2.50 ❖ Vegetable, herb, and flower seeds. 608–249–9291.

Oregon Bulb Farms, 2300 SW 1st Ave., #104, Portland, OR 97201: Catalog $2 (refundable) ❖ Lily bulbs.

Park Seed Company, Cokesbury Rd., P.O. Box 46, Greenwood, SC 29648: Free catalog

❖ Bulbs, vegetable and flower seeds, and gardening tools and supplies. 803–223–7333.

Patrick's Nursery, P.O. Box 130, Ty Ty, GA 31795: Free catalog ❖ Vegetable and flower seeds, fruit and nut trees, berry plants, and grapevines for southern climates. 912–386–1122.

Pepper Gal, P.O. Box 23006, Fort Lauderdale, FL 33307: Price list $1 ❖ Seeds for peppers. 305–537–5540.

Pinetree Garden Seed, Box 300, New Gloucester, ME 04260: Free catalog ❖ Seeds for vegetables, herbs, flowers, house plants, and perennials. 207–926–3400.

Pleasant Valley Glads, P.O. Box 494, Agawam, MA 01001: Free catalog ❖ Gladioli bulbs. 413–789–0307.

Pony Creek Nursery, P.O. Box 16, Tilleda, WI 54978: Catalog $1 (refundable) ❖ Seeds for vegetables and flowers, trees and shrubs, and gardening supplies. 715–787–3889.

Porter & Son Seedsmen, P.O. Box 104, Stephenville, TX 76401: Free catalog ❖ Seeds for vegetables, fruits, and flowers. 817–965–5600.

Quality Dutch Bulbs, 50 Lake Dr., P.O. Box 225, Hillsdale, NJ 07642: Free catalog ❖ Iris, daffodil, tulip, and other bulbs. 201–391–6586.

Rex Bulb Farms, P.O. Box 774, Port Townshend, WA 98368: Catalog $1 (refundable) ❖ Lily bulbs for garden and greenhouse-growing. 206–385–4280.

John Scheepers Inc., P.O. Box 700, Bantam, CT 06750: Free catalog ❖ Flowering bulbs. 203–567–0838.

Seeds Blum, Idaho City Stage, Boise, ID 83706: Catalog $3 ❖ Hybrid and heirloom vegetable seeds. 208–343–2202.

Seeds of Change, P.O. Box 15700, Santa Fe, NM 87506: Free information ❖ Open-pollinated seeds. 505–438–8080.

Seedway Inc., Box 250, Hall, NY 14463: Free catalog ❖ Hybrid vegetable and flower seeds. 716–526–6391.

Select Seeds, 180 Stickney Hill Rd., Union, CT 06076: Catalog $3 ❖ Seeds for foxgloves, mignonetta, balloon flowers, hollyhocks, sweet peas, nicotiana, and other "old-fashioned" flowers. 203–689–9310.

Shepherd's Garden Seeds, 30 Irene St., Torrington, CT 06790: Catalog $1 ❖ Seeds

for baby, Mexican, Italian, Oriental, and French vegetables. 203–482–3638.

Seymour's Selected Seeds, P.O. Box 1346, Sussex, VA 23884: Free catalog ❖ Rare and familiar flower seed varieties. Includes many imported from England.

R.H. Shumway Seedsman, P.O. Box 1, Graniteville, SC 29829: Free catalog ❖ Seeds and bulbs, berry plants, fruit trees, roses, ornamental shrubs and plants, and gardening supplies.

Southern Exposure Seed Exchange, P.O. Box 170, Earlysville, VA 22936: Catalog $2 (refundable) ❖ Seeds for vegetables, flowers, herbs, and other plants. 804–973–4703.

Southern Oregon Organics, 1130 Tetherow Rd., Williams, OR 97544: Free catalog ❖ Open-pollinated vegetable seeds. 503–846–7173.

Southern Seeds, P.O. Box 2091, Melbourne, FL 32902: Catalog $1 ❖ Seeds for bananas, passion fruit, papaya, and other edible exotics. 407–727–3662.

Stark Bros. Nurseries & Orchards Company, P.O. Box 10, Louisiana, MO 63353: Free catalog: Grapevines and berry plants, ornamentals, roses, and fruit, nut, and shade trees. 800–325–4180.

Stokes Seeds, Box 548, Buffalo, NY 14240: Free catalog ❖ Vegetable and flower seeds. 416–688–4300.

Sunrise Enterprises, P.O. Box 330058, West Hartford, CT 06110: Catalog $2 (refundable) ❖ Seeds for Oriental vegetables and other plants. 203–666–8071.

Territorial Seed Company, P.O. Box 157, Cottage Grove, OR 97424: Free catalog ❖ Organic fertilizers, natural insecticides, biological pest controls, and vegetable, herb, and flower seeds. 503–942–9547.

Thompson & Morgan Inc., P.O. Box 1308, Jackson, NJ 08527: Free catalog ❖ Vegetable and flower seeds. 800–274–7333.

Otis Twilley Seed Company, P.O. Box 65, Trevose, PA 19047: Catalog $1 ❖ Seeds for fruits, vegetables, and flowers. 800–622–7333.

U.S. Bulb Reservation Center, Louisiana, MO 63353: Free catalog ❖ Dutch bulbs. 314–754–4525.

Van Bourgondien Bros., 245 Farmingdale Rd., P.O. 1000, Babylon, NY 11702: Free catalog ❖ Holland flower bulbs. 800–622–9959.

Van Engelen Inc., Stillbrook Farm, 313 Maple St., Litchfield, CT 06759: Free catalog ❖ Tulips, daffodils, narcissi, crocuses, hyacinths, irises, muscari, and other imported Dutch bulbs. 203–567–8734.

Mary Mattison Van Schaik, P.O. Box 32, Cavendish, VT 05142: Catalog $1 ❖ Novelty and miniature tulip, daffodil, and hyacinth bulbs. 802–226–7653.

Vandenberg, Black Meadow Rd., Chester, NY 10918: Free catalog ❖ Perennials, hybrid lilies, seeds, and imported bulbs. 914–469–2633.

Vermont Bean Seed Company, Garden Ln., Fair Haven, VT 05743: Free catalog ❖ Untreated bean seeds.

Vesey Seeds Ltd., P.O. Box 9000, Charlottetown, Prince Edward Island, Canada C1A 8K6: Free catalog ❖ Early maturing vegetable and flower seeds.

Wayside Gardens, 1 Garden Ln., Hodges, SC 29695: Free catalog ❖ Bulbs. 800–845–1124.

White Flower Farm, Rt. 63, Litchfield, CT 06759: Free catalog ❖ Bulbs, shrubs, strawberry plants, books, tools, and gardening supplies. 800–888–7756.

Willhite Seed Company, P.O. Box 23, Poolville, TX 76076: Free catalog ❖ Seeds. 817–599–8656.

Wyatt-Quarles Seed Company, P.O. Box 739, Garner, NC 27529: Free catalog ❖ Seeds. 919–832–0551.

Shrubs

Agua Fria Nursery, 1409 Agua Fria St., Santa Fe, NM 87501: Free catalog ❖ Containerized western wildflowers, perennials, and shrubs.

Farmer Seed & Nursery Company, 818 NW 4th St., Faribault, MN 55021: Free catalog ❖ Ornamental shrubs and hedges, vegetable seeds, flowering bulbs, fruit and shade trees, berry plants, and roses. 507–334–2017.

Holbrook Farm & Nursery, P.O. Box 368, Fletcher, NC 28732: Free catalog ❖ Herbaceous perennials, trees and shrubs, and native wildflowers. 704–891–7790.

Inter-State Nurseries, Catalog Division, P.O. Box 10, Louisiana, MO 63353: Free catalog ❖ Plants, shrubs, trees, and flowering bulbs. 314–754–4525.

Lamb Nurseries, 101 E. Sharp Ave., Spokane, WA 99202: Catalog $1 ❖ Plants, shrubs, perennials, ferns, and gardening supplies. 509–328–7956.

Rice Creek Gardens, 11506 Hwy. 65, Minneapolis, MN 55432: Catalog $2 ❖ Ornamental shrubs, vines, ferns, rock garden plants, and gardening supplies.

R.H. Shumway Seedsman, P.O. Box 1, Graniteville, SC 29829: Free catalog ❖ Ornamental shrubs and plants, berry plants, fruit trees, roses, seeds and bulbs, and gardening supplies.

Stark Bros. Nurseries & Orchards Company, P.O. Box 10, Louisiana, MO 63353: Free catalog ❖ Plants and shrubs. 800–325–4180.

Van Hise Nursery, 30688 SE Waybill Rd., Boring, OR 97009: Free information ❖ Shrubs, perennials, and ground covers. 503–663–6123.

Terrariums

Carolina Exotic Gardens, Rt. 5, Box 283–A, Greenville, NC 27834: Catalog $1 ❖ Carnivorous plants, seeds, terrarium plants, and soil. 919–758–2600.

Kartuz Greenhouses, 1408 Sunset Dr., Vista, CA 92083: Catalog $2 ❖ Begonia plants and rare and tropical miniature terrarium flowering and foliage plants. 619–941–3613.

Peter Pauls Nurseries, 4665 Chapin Rd., Canandaigua, NY 14424: Free catalog ❖ Woodland terrarium and carnivorous plants. 716–394–7397.

Trees

Adams County Nursery Inc., P.O. Box 108, Aspers, PA 17304: Free catalog ❖ Dwarf and standard size plum and antique apples trees. 717–677–8105.

Ames' Orchard & Nursery, 18292 Wildlife Rd., Rt. 5, Box 194, Fayettville, AR 72701: Free information ❖ Apple, pear, and peach trees. 501–443–0282.

Vernon Barnes & Son Nursery, P.O. Box 250, McMinnville, TN 37110: Free catalog ❖ Wildflowers, hedges and shrubs, vines, berry plants, and sassafras, flowering, shade, fruit, and nut trees. 615–668–8576.

Bear Creek Nursery, P.O. Box 41175, Northport, WA 99157: Catalog $1 ❖ Fruits, nuts, and old apples. 509–732–6219.

Burford Brothers, Rt. 1, Monroe, VA 24574: Catalog $2 ❖ Modern and antique apples. 804–929–4950.

California Nursery Company, P.O. Box 2278, Fremont, CA 94536: Free catalog ❖ Fruit and nut trees, table and wine grapevines, and other growing stock. 510–797–3311.

Carino Nurseries, P.O. Box 538, Indiana, PA 15701: Free catalog ❖ Christmas trees, seedlings, and transplants. 800–223–7075.

Chestnut Hill Nursery Inc., Rt. 1, Box 341, Alachua, FL 32615: Free information ❖ Oriental persimmons and hybrid American-Chinese chestnuts. 904–462–2820.

Colvos Creek Nursery, P.O. Box 1512, Vashon Island, WA 98070: Catalog $2 (refundable) ❖ Trees, shrubs, bamboo, and other rare and unusual plants. 206–441–1509.

Country Carriage Nurseries & Seed Inc., P.O. Box 548, Hartford, MI 49057: Free catalog ❖ Vegetable and herb seeds, fruit trees, and berry plants. 616–621–2491.

Cumberland Valley Nurseries Inc., P.O. Box 471, McMinnville, TN 37110: Free catalog ❖ Fruit trees. 800–492–0022; 615–668–4153 (in TN).

Daystar, Rt. 2, Box 250, Litchfield, ME 04350: Catalog $1 ❖ Perennials, trees and shrubs, and rhododendrons. 207–724–3369.

Eco-Gardens, P.O. Box 1227, Decatur, GA 30031: Price list $1 ❖ Perennials, wildflowers, ferns, daylilies, water garden plants, trees, and shrubs. 404–294–6468.

Edible Landscaping, P.O. Box 77, Afton, VA 22920: Free catalog ❖ Dwarf citrus trees. (Does not ship to California.) 800–524–4156.

Farmer Seed & Nursery Company, 818 NW 4th St., Faribault, MN 55021: Free catalog ❖ Fruit and shade trees, vegetable seeds, flowering bulbs, ornamental shrubs and hedges, berry plants, and roses. 507–334–2017.

Henry Field's Seed & Nursery, 415 N. Burnett, Shenandoah, IA 51602: Free catalog ❖ Berry plants, hedges and ornamental shrubs, roses; dwarf, standard, and seedling apple trees; and fruit, nut, and shade trees. 605–665–4491.

Four Wind Growers, P.O. Box 3538, Fremont, CA 94539: Free brochure ❖ Dwarf citrus trees. (Does not ship to Arizona, Florida, or Texas.) 510–656–2591.

Fowler Nurseries Inc., 525 Fowler Rd., Newcastle, CA 95658: Catalog $3 ❖ Asian

pear trees, berry plants, and vines. 916–645–8191; 800–675–6075 (in CA).

Fruit Testing Association Nursery, P.O. Box 462, Geneva, NY 14456: Catalog $10 ❖ Apple and other fruit trees. 315–787–2205.

Frysville Farms, 300 Frysville Rd., Ephrata, PA 17522: Free catalog ❖ Trees. 800–422–FRYS.

Garden World's Exotic Plants, 2503 Garfield St., Laredo, TX 78043: Catalog $1 ❖ Citrus trees, bamboo, bananas, cacti, and pineapples. 512–724–3951.

Gardener's Choice, Country Rd. 687, P.O. Box 8000, Hartford, MI 49057: Free catalog ❖ Vegetables, flowers, house plants, and trees. 800–274–4096.

Girard Nurseries, P.O. Box 428, Geneva, OH 44041: Free catalog ❖ Baby evergreen seeds and seedlings, shade trees, and flowering shrubs. 216–466–2881.

Goodwin Creek Gardens, P.O. Box 83, Williams, OR 97544: Catalog $1 ❖ Container-grown native American trees, shrubs, and perennial flowers. 503–846–7357.

Gossler Farms Nursery, 1200 Weaver Rd., Springfield, OR 97478: Catalog $2 ❖ Magnolias and new, rare, and unusual trees and shrubs that include maples, stewartias, and styrax. 503–746–3922.

Greer Gardens, 1280 Goodpasture Island Rd., Eugene, OR 97401: Catalog $3 ❖ Asian pear trees. 503–686–8266.

Grimo Nut Nursery, RR 3, Niagara-on-the-Lake, Ontario, Canada L0S 1J0: Catalog $2 (refundable) ❖ Grafted and seed varieties of nut trees.

Gurney Seed & Nursery Company, 110 Capitol St., Yankton, SD 57079: Free catalog ❖ Semi-dwarf and standard varieties of apple trees. 605–665–1671.

Harmony Farm Supply, P.O. Box 460, Graton, CA 95444: Catalog $2 (refundable) ❖ Miniature and standard size fruit and nut trees. 707–823–9125.

Hollydale Nursery, P.O. Box 68, Pelham, TN 37366: Free list ❖ Peach trees.

Inter-State Nurseries, Catalog Division, P.O. Box 10, Louisiana, MO 63353: Free catalog ❖ Shrubs, berry plants, roses, perennials, and flowering, shade, and fruit trees. 314–754–4525.

Ison's Nursery, Rt. 1, Brooks, GA 30205: Free catalog ❖ Muscadine grapevines, berry plants, and apple, pear, fig, peach, walnut and pecan trees. 800–733–0324.

Johnson Nursery, Rt. 5, Box 296, Ellijay, GA 30540: Free catalog ❖ Strawberry plants, grapevines, and apple, plum, pear, cherry, apricot, walnut, almond, and other fruit and nut trees. 404–273–3187.

Kelly Nurseries, 1708 Morrissey Dr., Bloomington, IL 61704: Free catalog ❖ Heavily rooted fruit and nut trees, landscaping trees and shrubs, ornamentals, berry plants, grapevines, and flowers. 309–663–9551.

Lawson's Nursery, Rt. 1, Box 294, Ball Ground, GA 30107: Free list ❖ Antique apple trees. 404–893–2141.

Henry Leuthardt Nurseries, Box 666, East Moriches, NY 11940: Free catalog ❖ Dwarf fruit trees that grow full-size fruit. 516–878–1387.

Living Tree Center, P.O. Box 10082, Berkeley, CA 94709: Catalog $4 ❖ Trees and other growing stock for pomegranates, figs, almonds, grapes, and apples.

Earl May Seeds & Nursery Company, N. Elm St., Shenandoah, IA 51603: Free catalog ❖ Flowering shrubs, berry plants, roses, seeds for vegetables and fruit, and fruit, nut, shade, and ornamental trees. 712–246–1020.

Mellinger's, 2310 W. South Range Rd., North Lima, OH 44452: Free catalog ❖ Flowering shrubs and hedges, perennials, wildflowers, berry plants, gardening supplies, and fruit, nut, ornamental, and shade trees. 216–549–9861.

J.E. Miller Nurseries, 5060 W. Lake Rd., Canandaigua, NY 14424: Free catalog ❖ Berry plants, grapevines, spring and fall varieties of semi-dwarf hybrid antique apples, and other fruit and nut trees. 800–836–9630.

Musser Forests, P.O. 340, Indiana, PA 15701: Free catalog ❖ Evergreen hardwood seedlings and transplants, other trees and shrubs, and ground covers. 412–465–5685.

National Arbor Day Foundation, 100 Arbor Ave., Nebraska City, NE 68410: Free catalog ❖ Berry plants, flowering shrubs and trees, evergreens, flowering bulbs, nut trees, and standard and dwarf fruit trees and nut trees. 402–474–5655.

Niche Gardens, 1111 Dawson Rd., Chapel Hill, NC 27516: Catalog $3 ❖ Nursery-propagated wildflowers, trees and shrubs, and perennials. 919–967–0078.

Nolin River Nut Tree Nursery, 797 Port Wooden Rd., Upton, KY 42784: Free price list ❖ Grafted or budded Black and Persian walnut, pecan, chestnut, heartnut, and butternut trees. 502–369–8551.

Northwoods Retail Nursery, 27635 S. Oglesvy Rd., Canby, OR 97013: Free catalog ❖ Growing stock for figs, persimmons, kiwis, Asian pears, passion fruit, and pomegranates. 503–651–5432.

Oikos Tree Crops, P.O. Box 19425, Kalamazoo, MI 49019: Free information ❖ Trees and other growing stock for nuts and native fruits.

Pacific Tree Farms, 4301 Lynnwood Dr., Chula Vista, CA 92010: Catalog $1.50 ❖ Miniature trees, genetic dwarf avocados, and exotic ornamentals. 619–402–2400.

Patrick's Nursery, P.O. Box 130, Ty Ty, GA 31795: Free catalog ❖ Vegetable seeds for southern climates, fruit and nut trees, berry plants, and grapevines. 912–386–1122.

Peaceful Valley Farm Supply, P.O. Box 2209, Grass Valley, CA 95945: Catalog $2 (refundable) ❖ Miniature fruit and nut trees, tools, propagation supplies, seeds, and farming equipment. 916–272–4769.

Raintree Nursery, 391 Butts Rd., Morton, WA 98356: Free information ❖ Asian pear trees. 206–496–6400.

Savage Farms Nursery, P.O. Box 125, McMinnville, TN 37110: Free catalog ❖ Flowering trees and shrubs, evergreens, berry plants, gardening supplies, and fruit and shade trees. 615–668–8902.

F.W. Schumacher Company, 36 Spring Hill Rd., Sandwich, MA 02563: Free catalog ❖ Fir and other evergreen trees. 508–888–0659.

Sonoma Antique Apple Nursery, 4395 Westside Rd., Healdsburg, CA 95448: Catalog $2 ❖ Old-time apple and pear trees on semi-dwarf root stocks. 707–433–6420.

Southmeadow Fruit Gardens, Lakeside, MI 49116: Catalog $9 ❖ Apples, rare grapes and gooseberries, mediars, nectarines, pears, peaches, cherries, plums, apricots, currants, quince, and other trees and shrubs. 616–469–2865.

Stark Bros. Nurseries & Orchards Company, P.O. Box 10, Louisiana, MO 63353: Free catalog ❖ Berry plants, gardening supplies, and fruit, nut, and shade trees. 800–325–4180.

TEC Trees, P.O. Box 539, Osseo, MN 55369: Free catalog ❖ Seedlings and transplants.

Tripple Brook Farm, 37 Middle Rd., Southampton, MA 01073: Free catalog ❖ Bamboo plants, exotic fruits, trees, perennials, and shrubs. 413–527–4626.

Twombly Inc., 163 Barn Hill Rd., Monroe, CT 06468: Catalog $4 ❖ Dwarf conifer miniatures and other rare and unusual plants and trees. 203–261–2133.

Vans Pines Inc., 7550 144th Ave., West Olive, MI 49460: Free catalog ❖ Evergreen and deciduous trees. 616–399–1620.

Waynesboro Nurseries, P.O. Box 987, Waynesboro, VA 22980: Free information ❖ Ornamentals and dwarf and standard antique apple, fruit and nut, flowering, and shade trees. 703–942–4141.

Wayside Gardens, 1 Garden Ln., Hodges, SC 29695: Free catalog ❖ Container-grown trees ready for transplanting. 800–845–1124.

Western Maine Nurseries, One Evergreen Dr., Fryeburg, ME 04037: Free catalog ❖ Evergreen trees. 800–447–4745; 207–935–2161 (in ME).

Wildflower Nursery, 1680 Hwy. 25–70, Marshall, NC 28753: Free catalog ❖ Trees and shrubs.

Womack's Nursery Company, Rt. 1, Box 80, De Leon, TX 76444: Free catalog ❖ Peach, pear, apricot, fig, plum, and persimmon trees. 817–893–6497.

Vegetable Plants

Brown's Omaha Plant Farms Inc., P.O. Box 787, Omaha, TX 75571: Catalog 25¢ ❖ Onion, cauliflower, cabbage, broccoli, and brussel sprouts plants. 903–884–2421.

Country Carriage Nurseries & Seed Inc., P.O. Box 548, Hartford, MI 49057: Free catalog ❖ Vegetable and herb seeds, fruit trees, and berry plants. 616–621–2491.

Delegeane Garlic Farms, P.O. Box 2561, Yountville, Napa Valley, CA 94599: Free brochure ❖ Garlic cloves for planting. 707–944–8019.

Dixondale Farms, P.O. Box 127, Carrizo Springs, TX 78834: Free information ❖ Onion plants. 210–876–2430.

Enchanted Seeds, P.O. Box 6087, Las Cruces, NM 88006: Free information ❖ Seeds for rare and exotic chilies. 505–523–6058.

Evergreen Y.H. Enterprises, P.O. Box 17538, Anaheim, CA 92817: Catalog $2 (refundable) ❖ Oriental vegetable seeds.

Fedco Seeds, 52 Mayflower Hill Dr., Waterville, ME 04901: Free information ❖ Heirloom hybrid vegetable and herb seeds.

Filaree Productions, Rt. 2, Box 162, Okanogan, WA 98840: Catalog $2 ❖ Garlic varieties. 509–422–6940.

Fred's Plant Farm, P.O. Box 707, Dresden, TN 38225: Free information ❖ Sweet potato seeds and plants. 901–364–3754.

Golden River Farm, P.O. Box 73568, Fairbanks, AK 99707: Free information ❖ Organic certified seed potatoes. 907–456–5876.

The Gourmet Gardener, 8650 College Blvd., Overland Park. KS 66210: Catalog $2 ❖ Herb, vegetable, and edible flower seeds from around the world. 913–345–0490.

Horticultural Enterprises, P.O. Box 810082, Dallas, TX 75381: Free catalog ❖ Hot and sweet peppers, jicama, and herbs for Mexican cooking.

Hurov's Tropical Seeds, P.O. Box 1596, Chula Vista, CA 92012: Price list $1 ❖ Seeds for exotic plants from worldwide locations.

Illinois Foundation Seeds, Box 722, Champaign, IL 61824: Free price list ❖ Seeds for sweet corn. 217–485–6260.

Jersey Asparagus Farms Inc., RD 5, Box 572, Newfield, NJ 08344: Free brochure ❖ Seeds and crowns for all-male asparagus. 609–358–2548.

Kalmia Farm, P.O. Box 3881, Charlottsville, VA 22903: Free catalog ❖ Shallots, multiplier onions, and garlic varieties.

Lockhart Seeds Inc., P.O. Box 1361, Stockton, CA 92505: Free catalog ❖ Asparagus cultivars and hybrids.

Long Island Seed Company, 1368 Flanders Rd., Flanders, NY 11901: Free catalog ❖ Lettuce, heirloom tomatoes, hot peppers, pole beans, and other seeds. 516–369–0257.

Moose Tubers, 52 Mayflower Hill Dr., Waterville, ME 04901: Free information ❖ Maine-certified seed potatoes.

Piedmont Plant Company, P.O. Box 424, Albany, GA 31703: Free catalog ❖ Field-grown pepper, onion, tomato, cabbage, cauliflower, and broccoli plants. 912–883–7029.

Redwood City Seed Company, P.O. Box 361, Redwood City, CA 94064: Catalog $1 ❖ Herb and vegetable seeds from worldwide sources. 415–325–7333.

Ronniger's Seed Potatoes, Star Rt. 54, Moyie Springs, ID 83845: Catalog $2 ❖ Heirloom and European varieties of seed potatoes.

Roswell Seed Company Inc., P.O. Box 725, Roswell, NM 88202: Free price list with long SASE ❖ Chile pepper seed.

Seeds Blum, Idaho City Stage, Boise, ID 83706: Catalog $3 ❖ Seed potatoes. 208–343–2202.

Southern Oregon Organics, 1130 Tetherow Rd., Williams, OR 97544: Free catalog ❖ Open-pollinated vegetable seeds. 503–846–7173.

Steele Plant Company, 212 Collins St., P.O. Box 191, Gleason, TN 38229: Free catalog with two 1st class stamps ❖ Sweet potato plants for northern and southern climates and brussel sprouts, onion, cabbage, cauliflower, and broccoli plants. 901–648–5476.

Tomato Growers Supply Company, P.O. Box 2237, Fort Myers, FL 33902: Free catalog ❖ Tomatoes, peppers, books, and gardening supplies.

The Tomato Seed Company Inc., P.O. Box 1400, Tryon, NC 28782: Free catalog ❖ Tomato seeds and heirloom vegetables.

Totally Tomatoes, P.O. Box 1626, Augusta, GA 30903: Free catalog ❖ Tomato seeds.

Wildflowers & Native Plants

Allgrove, P.O. Box 459, East Wakefield, NH 03830: Catalog 50¢ ❖ Wildflower plants.

Applewood Seed Company, P.O. Box 10761, Edgemont Station, Golden, CO 80401: Free catalog ❖ Wildflower seeds and mixture packets. 303–431–6283.

Agua Fria Nursery, 1409 Agua Fria St., Santa Fe, NM 87501: Free catalog ❖ Containerized western wildlowers, perennials, and shrubs.

Vernon Barnes & Son Nursery, P.O. Box 250, McMinnville, TN 37110: Free catalog ❖ Wildflowers, nut and sassafras trees, hedges, vines, and berry plants. 615–668–8576.

Conley's Garden Center, 145 Townsend Ave., Boothbay Harbor, ME 04538: Catalog $1.50 (refundable) ❖ Wildflowers and seeds, ferns, native perennials, bulbs, orchids, ground covers, and vines. 207–633–5020.

Crownsville Nursery, P.O. Box 797, Crownsville, MD 21032: Catalog $10 ❖ Ferns, wildflowers, azaleas, ornamental grasses, and perennials. 410–923–2212.

Dabney Herbs, P.O. Box 22061, Louisville, KY 40222: Catalog $2 ❖ Ginseng, herbs, scented geraniums, perennials, and wildflowers. 502–893–5198.

E & H Products, 78260 Darby Rd., Bermuda Dunes, CA 92201: Free information ❖ Individual species and mixes of wildflower seeds. 619–345–0147.

Far North Gardens, 16785 Harrison, Livonia, MI 48154: Catalog $2 (refundable) ❖ Rare plants, herbs, ornamentals, and plants for woodland settings, prairies, and rock gardens. 313–422–0747.

Forestfarm, 990 Tetherow Rd., Williams, OR 97544: Catalog $3 ❖ Native and unusual ornamental American plants, shrubs, and trees. 503–846–6963.

The Fragrant Path, P.O. Box 328, Fort Calhoun, NE 68023: Catalog $2 ❖ Seeds for prairie wildflowers and grasses, ferns, trees and shrubs, and climbing plants.

Gardens of the Blue Ridge, P.O. Box 10, Pineola, NC 28662: Catalog $3 (refundable) ❖ Wildflower seeds, ferns, trees, plants, shrubs, and bulbs. 704–733–2417.

Good Hollow Greenhouse & Herbarium, Rt. 1, Box 116, Taft, TN 38488: Catalog $1 ❖ Herbs, perennials, wildflowers, scented geraniums, essential oils and potpourris, teas, dried herbs, and spices. 615–433–7640.

Green Horizons, 218 Quinlan, Ste. 571, Kerrville, TX 78028: Free brochure ❖ Texas wildflower seeds and books. 210–257–5141.

Griffey's Nursery, 16870 Hwy. 25–70, Marshall, NC 28753: Free catalog ❖ Appalachian wildflowers, rock and bog plants, and ferns and vines. 704–656–2334.

Holbrook Farm & Nursery, P.O. Box 368, Fletcher, NC 28732: Free catalog ❖ Geraniums, native wildflowers, trees, shrubs, perennials, and hostas. 704–891–7790.

Lafayette Home Nursery, LaFayette, IL 61449: Catalog 25¢ ❖ Seeds for prairie plants, grasses, and flowers. 309–995–3311.

Las Pilitas Nursery, Star Rt., Box 23, Santa Margarita, CA 93453: Catalog $4 ❖ Native plants and seeds from California.

Mellinger's, 2310 W. South Range Rd., North Lima, OH 44452: Free catalog ❖ Wildflowers, trees, flowering shrubs and hedges, perennials, berry plants, vegetable seeds, and gardening supplies. 216–549–9861.

Midwest Wildflowers, P.O. Box 64, Rockton, IL 61072: Catalog 50¢ ❖ Woodland wildflowers.

Native Gardens, 5737 Fisher Ln., Greenback, TN 37742: Catalog $2 ❖ Nursery-propagated wildflowers. 615–856–0220.

Natural Gardening Company, 217 San Anselmo Ave., San Anselmo, CA 94960: Free catalog ❖ Beneficial insects, organic gardening supplies, pest controls, drip irrigation equipment, and wildflower seeds. 707–766–9303.

New England Wildflower Society, Garden in the Woods, 180 Hemenway Rd., Framingham, MA 01701: Free catalog with long SASE and two 1st class stamps ❖ Wildflower seeds native to New England. 508–877–7630.

Niche Gardens, 1111 Dawson Rd., Chapel Hill, NC 27516: Catalog $3 ❖ Nursery-propagated wildflowers, perennials, trees, and shrubs. 919–967–0078.

Orchid Gardens, 2232 139th Ave. NW, Andover, MN 55304: Catalog 75¢ ❖ Wildflower and fern plants. 612–755–0205.

Plants of the Southwest, Rt. 6, Box 11A, Santa Fe, NM 87501: Catalog $3.50 ❖ Wildflowers and native plants from the southwest. 505–471–2212.

Prairie Moon Nursery, Rt. 3, Box 163, Winona, MN 55987: Catalog $2 ❖ Plants and seeds for prairie wildflowers and grasses. 507–452–1362.

Prairie Nursery, P.O. Box 306, Westfield, WI 53964: Catalog $3 ❖ Plants and seeds for prairie wildflowers and grasses. 608–296–3679.

Prairie Ridge Nursery, 9738 Overland Rd., Mount Horeb, WI 53572: Catalog $3 (refundable) ❖ Wildflowers. 608–437–5245.

The Primrose Path, RD 2, Box 110, Scottsdale, PA 15683: Catalog $2 ❖ Alpine and woodland plants. 412–887–6756.

Putney Nursery Inc., Rt. 5, Putney, VT 05346: Catalog $1 (refundable) ❖ Wildflowers, ferns, herbs, perennials, orchids, and gardening supplies. 802–387–5577.

Rice Creek Gardens, 11506 Hwy. 65, Minneapolis, MN 55432: Catalog $2 ❖ Wildflower seeds and mixtures for meadow growing, dwarf conifers, ground covers,

colorful rock garden plants, and rhododendrons.

Clyde Robin Seed Catalog, P.O. Box 2366, Castro Valley, CA 94546: Catalog $2 ❖ Wildflower seeds, trees, and shrubs. 510–785–0425.

Sunlight Gardens, Rt. 1, Box 600, Andersonville, TN 37705: Catalog $3 ❖ Nursery-grown wildflowers for the north and south, planting in the sun or shade, or for wet and dry locations. 615–494–8237.

Vermont Wildflower Farm, Rt. 7, P.O. Box 5, Charlotte, VT 05455: Free catalog ❖ Seeds for wildflowers, annuals, and perennial flowers. 802–425–3500.

We-Du Nursery, Rt. 5, Box 724, Marion, NC 28752: Catalog $2 ❖ Japanese and American wildflowers, woodland and rock garden plants, unusual perennials, and irises. 704–738–8300.

Wildflower Nursery, 1680 Hwy. 25–70, Marshall, NC 28753: Free catalog ❖ Wild native flowering plants.

Wildseed Inc., P.O. Box 308, Eagle Lake, TX 77434: Free catalog ❖ Wildflower seeds. 409–234–7353.

GAZEBOS & OTHER GARDEN STRUCTURES

Amish Country Gazebos, 2900 E. Miraloma, Unit B, Anaheim, CA 92806: Free information ❖ Easy-to-assemble gazebo kits. 714–630–3944.

Walter J. Bass Company, 1432 W. Grand River, P.O. Box 397, Williamston, MI 48895: Free information ❖ Easy-to-assemble gazebo kits. 800–345–5735.

BowBends, P.O. Box 900, Bolton, MA 01740: Brochure $3 ❖ Easy-to-assemble gazebos, bridges, and arbors. 508–779–6464.

Caldera Spas, 1080 W. Bradley Ave., El Cajon, CA 92020: Free information ❖ Build-it-yourself gazebo kits. 619–562–5120.

California Redwood Association, 405 Enfrente Dr., Ste. 200, Novato, CA 94949: Free information ❖ Easy-to-build redwood gazebos. 415–382–0662.

Cedar Gazebo Inc., 10432 Lyndale, Melrose Park, IL 60164: Brochure $2 ❖ Handcrafted western red cedar gazebos with optional screens. 708–455–0928.

Cumberland Woodcraft Company Inc., P.O. Drawer 609, Carlisle, PA 17013: Catalog $4.50 ❖ Gazebo kits, in 10–, 12–, and

16–foot diameters. 800–446–8560; 717–243–0063 (in PA).

Dalton Pavilions Inc., 20 Commerce Dr., Telford, PA 18969: Catalog $5 ❖ Western red cedar gazebos. 800–532–5866; 215–721–1492 (in PA).

Gazebos by Leisure Designs, 1991 Friendship Dr., El Cajon, CA 92020: Free information ❖ Gazebos and spa enclosures. 619–562–8988.

Gazebos Ltd., 1844 Stonecrest Dr., Milford, MI 48381: Free information ❖ Build-it-yourself gazebo kits. 810–624–8990.

Gingerbread Man Woodworks, Factory Outlet Store, P.O. Box 59, Noel, MO 64854: Catalog $5 ❖ Gazebos, garden structures, and ornamental trim. 417–775–2553.

Handy Home Products, 6400 E. 11 Mile Rd., Warren, MI 48091: Free information ❖ Build-it-yourself gazebo kits. 800–221–1849.

Heritage Garden Houses, City Visions Inc., 311 Seymour, Lansing, MI 48933: Catalog $3 ❖ Pool houses, potting sheds, tool storage, hot tub enclosures, colonnades, seats, cabinets, gazebos, and classical, Victorian, Japanese, and other garden retreats. 517–372–3385.

Kloter Farms Inc., 216 West Rd., Ellington, CT 06029: Brochure $3 ❖ Handcrafted gazebos. 203–871–1048.

Leisure Woods Inc., P.O. Box 177, Genoa, IL 60135: Free information ❖ Colonial and Victorian-style gazebos. 815–784–2497.

Litchfield Industries Inc., 4 Industrial Dr., P.O. Box 317, Litchfield, MI 49252: Free catalog ❖ Garden shelters. 800–542–5282.

Sun Designs, 173 E. Wisconsin Ave., Oconomowoc, WI 53066: Catalog $9.95 ❖ Plans for gazebos, bridges, doghouses, arbors, lawn furniture, swings and other outdoor play structures, and birdhouses. 414–567–4255.

Thaxted Cottage, Gardener, 121 Driscoll Way, Gaithersburg, MD 20878: Free information ❖ Redwood cottage with trellis sides and built-in seat. 301–330–6211.

Vintage Wood Works, Hwy. 34 South, Box R, Quinlan, TX 75474: Catalog $2 ❖ Pre-assembled gazebos with bolt-together solid wood panels. 903–356–2158.

Vixen Hill Gazebos, Main St., Elverson, PA 19520: Catalog $4 ❖ Pre-engineered gazebos for easy assembly by non-carpenters. 800–423–2766.

GENEALOGY
State Offices & Genealogical Associations

Alabama

State of Alabama Archives & History, 624 Washington Ave., Montgomery, AL 36130. 205–261–4361.

State of Alabama Historical Association, P.O. Box 870380, Tuscaloosa, AL 35487.

State of Alabama Genealogical Society Inc., Samford University Library, American Genealogical Society Depository & Headquarters, 800 Lakeshore Dr., Birmingham, AL 35229. 205–870–2749.

Alaska

State of Alaska Archives & Records Management, Division of Libraries & Archives, Department of Education, 141 Willoughby, Juneau, AK 99801. 907–465–2275.

State of Alaska Historical Library & Museum, P.O. Box G, State Office Building, 8th Floor, Juneau, AK 99811. 907–465–2925.

State of Alaska Genealogical Society, 7030 Dickerson Dr., Anchorage, AK 99504.

Arizona

Arizona Archives & Public Records, Arizona Library Department, Research Division, State Capitol, 1700 W. Washington, Phoenix, AZ 85007. 602–542–3942.

State of Arizona Historical Society, 949 E. 2nd St., Tucson, AZ 85719. 602–628–5774.

State of Arizona Genealogical Society, P.O. Box 42075, Tucson, AZ 85733.

Arkansas

History Commission of Arkansas, 1 Capitol Mall, Little Rock, AR 72201. 501–682–6900.

State of Arkansas Historical Society, University of Arkansas, Department of History, Old Main 416, Fayetteville, AR 72701. 501–575–5884.

State of Arkansas Genealogical Society, P.O. Box 908, Hot Springs, AR 71902.

California

State of California Archives, Office of the Secretary of State, 1020 O St., Room. 130, Sacramento, CA 95814. 916–653–0066.

State Library of California, California Section, P.O. Box 942837, Sacramento, CA 94237. 916–654–0176.

State of California Historical Society, 2099 Pacific Ave., San Francisco, CA 94109.

State of California Genealogical Society, P.O. Box 77105, San Francisco, CA 94107. 415–777–9936.

Colorado

Colorado Division of Archives & Public Records, Colorado Department of Administration, 1313 Sherman St., Denver, CO 80203. 303–866–2358.

State Library of Colorado, 201 E. Colfax Ave., Denver, CO 80203. 303–866–6728.

State of Colorado Historical Society, Stephen H. Hart Library, 1300 Broadway, Denver, CO 80203. 303–866–2305.

State of Colorado Genealogical Society, P.O. Box 9218, Denver, CO 80209.

Connecticut

State Library of Connecticut, History & Genealogy Unit, 231 Capitol Ave., Hartford, CT 06106. 302–566–3690.

State of Connecticut Historical Society, 1 Elizabeth St., Hartford, CT 06105. 203–236–5621.

State of Connecticut Society of Genealogists, P.O. Box 435, Glastonbury, CT 06433. 203–569–0002.

District of Columbia

Office of Public Records of the District of Columbia, 1300 Naylor Ct. NW, Washington, DC 20001. 202–727–2054.

Historical Society of the District of Columbia, 1307 New Hampshire Ave. NW, Washington, DC 20036. 202–785–2068.

Florida

State Archives of Florida, Bureau of Archives & Records Management, Division of Library & Information Services, Public Services Section, R.A. Gray Building, 500 S. Bronough St., Tallahassee, FL 32399. 904–487–2073.

State of Florida Historical Society, University of South Florida Library, P.O. Box 3645, University Station, Gainesville, FL 32601. 813–974–3815.

Florida Genealogical Society, P.O. Box 18624, Tampa, FL 33679.

State of Florida Genealogical Society, P.O. Box 10249, Tallahassee, FL 32302.

Georgia

Georgia Department of Archives & History, Secretary of State, Search Room, 330 Capitol Ave. SE, Atlanta, GA 30334. 404–656–2350.

State of Georgia Historical Society, 501 Whittaker St., Savannah, GA 31499. 912–651–2128.

State of Georgia Genealogical Society, P.O. Box 38066, Atlanta, GA 30334. 404–475–4404.

Hawaii

Hawaii Division of Archives, Dept. of Accounting & General Services, Iolani Palace Grounds, 478 S. King St., Honolulu, HI 96813. 808–586–0329.

State of Hawaii Historical Society, 560 Kawaiahao St., Honolulu, HI 96813. 808–537–6271.

State of Hawaii Genealogy Society, Genealogical Resource Center, Native Hawaiian Libraries Project, 1024 Mapunapuna St., Honolulu, HI 96819. 808–836–8940.

Idaho

State of Idaho Historical Society, Library of Genealogy, 450 N. 4th St., Boise, ID 83702. 208–334–2305.

State of Idaho Genealogical Society, 4620 Overland Rd., Boise, ID 83705. 208–384–0542.

Illinois

State of Illinois Archives Division, Secretary of State, Archives Building, Capitol Complex, Springfield, IL 62756. 217–782–4682.

State of Illinois Historical Society, Old State Capitol, Springfield, IL 62701. 217–782–4836.

State of Illinois Genealogical Society, P.O. Box 2225, Springfield, IL 62791.

Indiana

State of Indiana Library, William Henry Smith Memorial Library, 140 N. Senate Ave., Indianapolis, IN 46204. 317–232–3686.

State of Indiana Historical Society, Indiana State Library & Historical Building, P.O. Box 88255, Indianapolis, IN 46202. 317–232–1884.

State of Indiana Genealogical Society, P.O. Box 10507, Fort Wayne, IN 46852.

Iowa

State of Iowa Archives, Capitol Complex, E. 12th St. & Grand Ave., Des Moines, IA 50319.

Historical Iowa State Society, Library-Archives Bureau, Iowa State Historical Building, 600 E. Locust, Des Moines, IA 50319. 515–281–6200.

State of Iowa Genealogical Society, P.O. Box 7735, Des Moines, IA 50322.

Kansas

State Library of Kansas, Statehouse, 3rd Floor, Topeka, KS 66612. 913–296–3296.

State of Kansas Historical Society, Division of Archives, Reference Services, Memorial Building, 120 W. 10th St., Topeka, KS 66612. 913–296–4776.

Kansas State Genealogical Society, P.O. Box 103, Dodge City, KS 67801.

Kentucky

State Archives of Kentucky, Kentucky Department of Archives & Library, Division of Public Records, 300 Coffee Tree Rd., 1st Floor, Frankfort, KY 40602. 502–875–7000.

Kentucky State Historical Society, Old Capitol Annex, 300 Broadway, P.O. Box H, Frankfort, KY 40602. 502–564–3016.

State of Kentucky Genealogical Society, P.O. Box 153, Frankfort, KY 40602. 502–223–0492.

Louisiana

Le Comité des Archives de la Louisiane, P.O. Box 44370, Capitol Station, Baton Rouge, LA 70804. 504–355–9906.

State of Louisiana Archives & Records, Office of the Secretary of State, P.O. Box 94125, Baton Rouge, LA 70804. 504–922–1206.

Genealogical & Historical Society of Louisiana, P.O. Box 3454, Baton Rouge, LA 70821. 504–766–3018.

Maine

Maine State Archives, State House Station, Augusta, ME 04333. 207–289–5795.

Historical Society of Maine, 485 Congress St., Portland, ME 04111. 207–774–1822.

State of Maine Genealogical Society, P.O. Box 221, Farmington, ME 04938.

Maryland

State Archives of Maryland, Hall of Records Building, 350 Rowe Blvd., Annapolis, MD 21401. 410–974–3914.

Maryland Historical Society, 201 W. Monument St., Baltimore, MD 21201. 410–685–3750.

Maryland State Genealogy Society, 201 W. Monument St., Baltimore, MD 21201.

Massachusetts

Commonwealth of Massachusetts Archives, Reference Desk, 220 Morrissey Blvd., Boston, MA 02125. 617–727–2816.

State of Massachusetts Historical Society, 1154 Boylston St., Boston, MA 02215. 617–536–1608.

New England Historic Genealogical Society, 101 Newbury St., Boston, MA 02116.

Michigan

Michigan State Archives, Bureau of History, State Department, 717 W. Allegan, Lansing, MI 48918. 517–373–1408.

Michigan Historical Society, 2117 Washtenaw Ave., Ann Arbor, MI 48104. 313–769–1828.

Michigan Genealogical Council, P.O. Box 80953, Lansing, MI 48908.

Minnesota

Minnesota Historical Society, Library & Archives Division, 160 John Ireland Blvd., St. Paul, MN 55102. 612–296–6980.

State of Minnesota Historical Society, 690 Cedar St., St. Paul, MN 55101. 612–296–2143.

State of Minnesota Genealogical Society, P.O. Box 16069, St. Paul, MN 55116. 612–222–6929.

Mississippi

Mississippi Archives & History Department, Archives & Library Division, P.O. Box 571, Jackson, MS 39205. 601–359–6876.

Mississippi History and Genealogy Association, 618 Avalon Rd., Jackson, MS 39206.

Genealogical Society of Mississippi, P.O. Box 5301, Jackson, MS 39296.

Missouri

Missouri State Archives, P.O. Box 778, Jefferson City, MO 65102. 314–751–3280.

Historical Society of Missouri, 1020 Lowry St., Columbia, MO 65201. 314–882–7083.

Missouri State Genealogical Association, P.O. Box 833, Columbia, MO 65205. 816–747–9330.

Montana

State Library of Montana, 1515 E. 6th Ave., Helena, MT 59620. 406–444–3004.

Montana Historical Society, Memorial Building, 225 N. Roberts St., Helena, MT 59620.

Genealogical Society of Montana, P.O. Box 555, Chester, MT 59522.

Nebraska

State Historical Society of Nebraska, Archives Division, Reference Services, P.O. Box 82554, Lincoln, NE 68501. 402–471–4771.

Nebraska State Genealogical Society, P.O. Box 5608, Lincoln, NE 68505. 402–266–8881.

Nevada

State of Nevada Library & Archives, Archives & Records Division, 100 Stewart St., Carson City, NV 89710. 702–687–5210.

State of Nevada Historical Society, 1650 N. Virginia St., Reno, NV 89503. 702–688–1190.

Nevada Genealogical State Society, P.O. Box 20666, Reno, NV 89515.

New Hampshire

New Hampshire Division of Records Management & Archives, New Hampshire Department of State, 71 S. Fruit St., Concord, NH 03301. 603–271–2236.

New Hampshire State Historical Society, 30 Park St., Concord, NH 03301. 603–225–3381.

New Hampshire Society of Genealogists, P.O. Box 633, Exeter, NH 03833. 603–432–8137.

New Jersey

New Jersey State Department of Archives, CN 307, Trenton, NJ 08625. 609–292–6260.

New Jersey State Library, Genealogy Section, CN 520, Trenton, NJ 08625. 609–292–6274.

State of New Jersey Historical Society, 230 Broadway, Newark, NJ 07104. 201–483–3939.

New Mexico

New Mexico Archives & Records Center, 404 Montezuma St., Santa Fe, NM 87501.

New Mexico Historical Society, P.O. Box 4638, Santa Fe, NM 87501.

New Mexico State Genealogical Society, P.O. Box 8283, Albuquerque, NM 87198. 505–281–3133.

New York

New York State Archives, Department of Education, Cultural Education Center, Albany, NY 12230. 518–474–1195.

State Historical Association of New York, P.O. Box 800, Cooperstown, NY 13326. 607–547–2533.

State of New York Genealogical & Biographical Society, 122–126 E. 58th St., New York, NY 10022. 212–755–8532.

North Carolina

North Carolina State Archives, Department of Cultural Resources, Archives & History Division, State Library Building, 109 E. Jones St., Raleigh, NC 27601. 919–733–3952.

North Carolina Society of Historians, P.O. Box 848, Rockingham, NC 28379.

State of North Carolina Genealogical Society, P.O. Box 1492, Raleigh, NC 27602.

Ohio

Ohio State Library, Genealogy Section, 65 S. Front St., Columbus, OH 43266. 614–644–6966.

State of Ohio Historical Society, Library Division of Archives, 1982 Velma Ave., Columbus, OH 43211. 614–297–2510.

State Genealogical Society of Ohio, Library Section, P.O. Box 2625, Mansfield, OH 44906.

Oklahoma

Oklahoma Department of Libraries, Office of Archives & Records, 200 NE 18th St., Oklahoma City, OK 73105. 405–521–2502.

Oklahoma Historical Society, Division of Library Resources, Wiley Post Historical Building, 2100 N. Lincoln Blvd., Oklahoma City, OK 73105. 405–521–2491.

Genealogy Society of Oklahoma, P.O. Box 12986, Oklahoma City, OK 73157.

Oregon

Archives Division of Oregon, Secretary of State, 800 Summer St. NE, Salem, OR 97310. 503–373–0701.

Oregon Historical Society, 1230 SW Park Ave., Portland, OR 97205. 503–222–1741.

Genealogy Society of Oregon, Library, 1410 SW Morrison St., Room 812, Portland, OR 97205. 503–227–2398.

Pennsylvania

Pennsylvania State Archives, Reference Division, P.O. Box 1206, Harrisburg, PA 17108.

Pennsylvania Historical & Genealogy Society, 1300 Locust St., Philadelphia, PA 19107. 215–545–0391.

Rhode Island

Rhode Island State Archives, State House, Room 43, 82 Smith, Providence, RI 02903.

State of Rhode Island Historical Society, 121 Hope St., Providence, RI 02906. 401–331–8575.

Rhode Island State Genealogical Society, 13 Countryside Dr., Cumberland, RI 02864.

South Carolina

South Carolina Department of Archives & History, P.O. Box 11669, Columbia, SC 29211. 803–734–8577.

South Carolina Historical Society, 100 Meeting St., Charleston, SC 29401. 803–723–3225.

State of South Carolina Genealogy Society, P.O. Box 16355, Greenville, SC 29606.

South Dakota

South Dakota Archives, Cultural Heritage Center, 900 Governors Dr., Pierre, SD 57501. 605–773–3804.

State of South Dakota Historical Society, Cultural Heritage Center, 900 Governors Dr., Pierre, SD 57501. 605–773–3804.

South Dakota Genealogical Society, P.O. Box 490, Winner, SD 57580.

Tennessee

Tennessee State Archives & Library, 403 7th Ave. North, Nashville, TN 37243. 615–741–2764.

Historical Society of Tennessee, War Memorial Building, Ground Floor, 300 Capital Blvd., Nashville, TN 37234. 615–741–8934.

Tennessee Genealogical Society, 3340 Poplar Ave., Ste. 327, Memphis, TN 38111. 901–327–3273.

Texas

Texas State Library, P.O. Box 12927, Capital Station, Austin, TX 78711. 512–463–5463.

Historical Association of Texas, 2.306 SRH, University Station, Austin, TX 78712.

State of Texas Genealogy Society, 2507 Tannehill, Houston, TX 77008. 713–864–6862.

Utah

Utah Archives & Record Services, Archives Building, State Capitol, Salt Lake City, UT 84114. 801–538–3013.

Utah State Historical Society, 300 Rio Grande, Salt Lake City, UT 84101. 801–533–5808.

Family History Library of The Church of Jesus Christ of Latter-day Saints, 35 N. West Temple, Salt Lake City, UT 84150. 801–240–2331.

Utah Genealogical Association, P.O. Box 1144, Salt Lake City, UT 84110. 801–262–7263.

Vermont

State of Vermont Archives, Office of the Secretary of State, 26 Terrace St., Redstone Building, Montpelier, VT 05609. 802–828–2308.

Historical Society of Vermont, Pavilion Office Building, 109 State St., Montpelier, VT 05609. 802–828–2291.

Genealogy Society of Vermont, P.O. Box 422, Pittsford, VT 05763. 802–483–2957.

Virginia

Virginia State Library & Archives, Genealogy & Archives Section, 11th Street at Capitol Square, Richmond, VA 23219. 804–786–2306.

Historical Society of Virginia, P.O. Box 7311, Richmond, VA 23211. 804–342–9677.

Virginia Genealogical Society, P.O. Box 7469, Richmond, VA 23221. 804–770–2306.

Washington

Archives & Records Management of Washington, Office of the Secretary of State, State Archives & Records Center Building, 1120 Washington St SE, EA-11, Olympia, WA 98504. 206–586–1492.

State of Washington Historical Society, Hewitt Library, State Historical Building, 315 N. Stadium Way, Tacoma, WA 98403. 206–593–2830.

Washington State Genealogical Society, P.O. Box 1422, Olympia, WA 98507. 206–352–0595.

West Virginia

Archives & History Division of West Virginia, West Virginia Library Commission, Department of Culture & History, Science & Cultural Center, Capitol Complex, Charleston, WV 25305. 304–348–2277.

State of West Virginia Genealogy Society, P.O. Box 249, Elkview, WV 25071.

Wisconsin

Wisconsin Department of Public Instruction, Library Sciences Division, Interlibrary Loan & Resource Sharing Bureau, 21209 S. Stoughton Rd., Madison, WI 53716. 608–221–6160.

Wisconsin State Historical Society, 816 State St., Madison, WI 53706. 608–264–6535.

Genealogy Society of Wisconsin, 21209 20th Ave., Monroe, WI 53566. 608–325–2609.

Wyoming

State Archives of Wyoming, Research Division, Barrett Building, 2301 Capitol Ave., Cheyenne, WY 82002. 307–777–7281.

State Library of Wyoming, Supreme Court Building, 2301 Capitol Ave., Cheyenne, WY 82002. 307–777–7281.

Retail Sources & Publishers

Civil War Genealogy, T.L. Murphy, P.O. Box 3542, Gettysburg, PA 17325: Free brochure with long SASE ❖ Confederate and Union Pension, prisoner of war and service records, and capsule unit histories.

Consumer Information Center, Pueblo, CO 81009: Free catalog ❖ Offers publications that contain genealogical information: Military Service Records in the National Archives (50¢); Using Records in the National Archives for Genealogical Research (50¢); Where to Write for Vital Records ($2.25); and Your Right to Federal Records (50¢). 719–948–4000.

Genealogical Publishing Company Inc., 1001 N. Calvert St., Baltimore, MD 21202: Free catalog ❖ General reference and how-to books, manuals, directories and finding aids, and state guides. 800–296–6687.

Genealogy Unlimited Inc., P.O. Box 537, Orem, UT 84059: Free catalog ❖ Genealogical books, forms, archival supplies, and historical, topographic, and modern European maps. 800–666–4363.

Goodspeed's, 7 Beacon St., Boston, MA 02108: Catalog $2 ❖ Genealogy books and other publications. 617–523–5970.

Heritage Books Inc., 1540 E. Pointer Ridge Place, Ste. 180, Bowie, MD 20716: Free catalog ❖ Books and periodicals arranged by state and subject. 301–390–7709.

David Morgan, 11812 Northcreek Pkwy., Ste. 103, Bothell, WA 98011: Free catalog ❖ Maps of Great Britain for travel or genealogy research. 800–324–4934.

National Archives & Records Administration, National Archives Books, Washington, DC 20408: Paperbound book $19 ❖ Guide to Genealogical Research in the National Archives that describes census records, military service information, passenger ship arrival lists, and other information for genealogical research. 202–523–3164.

The Ships Chandler, Wilmington, VT 05363: Free catalog ❖ Thousands of names from 32 countries in report form, genealogical paintings, plaques, and needlepoints. 813–355–3000.

GIFTS

Children's Gifts

Daisy Kingdom Inc., 134 NW 8th Ave., Portland, OR 97209: Catalog $2 ❖ Apparel, bedding, and other sew-it-yourself kits or ready-mades. 503–222–9033.

Hand in Hand, Rt. 26, RR 1, Box 1425, Oxford, ME 04270: Free catalog ❖ Teaching toys, travel items, videos, and nursery room furniture that helps nurture, teach, and protect children. 800–872–9745.

Hearth Song, Mail Processing Center, 6519 N. Galena Rd., P.O. Box 1773, Peoria, IL 61656: Free catalog ❖ Books for children, doll house miniatures, toiletries for babies, dolls, party decorations, back yard play structures, art supplies, kites, games, and musical instruments. 800–325–2502.

Just for Kids, P.O. Box 29141, Shawnee, KS 66201: Free catalog ❖ Toys and games, dolls and doll houses, things for babies, science gadgets, arts and crafts, musical instruments, T-shirts, bathing aids, sports and learning toys, school bags, and videos. 800–443–5827.

Lilly's Kids, Lillian Vernon Corporation, Virginia Beach, VA 23479: Free catalog ❖ Games, science sets, art, backyard and other outdoor toys, dolls, animal toys, and rainy day and traveling fun things. 800–285–5555.

McGill's, 9007 F St., Omaha, NE 68127: Free brochure ❖ Gifts and novelties for twins. 402–592–0000.

Metropolitan Museum of Art, 255 Gracie Station, New York, NY 10028: Catalog $1 ❖ Books, cassettes, records, cards, games, and toys. 800–468–7386.

Out of the Woodwork, 2120 Timber Pointe Rd., Charlottsville, VA 22901: Free brochure ❖ Handcrafted solid hardwood, personalized educational gifts for children of all ages. 804–973–3376.

Right Start Catalog, Right Start Plaza, 5334 Sterling Center Dr., Westlake Village, CA 91361: Catalog $2 ❖ Music and videos, strollers and car seats, swings, crib sets, personal care aids, clothing, bathtime aids, highchairs, and infant, toddler, and preschool toys and games. 800–548–8531.

Storybook Heirlooms, 1215 O'Brien Dr., Menlo Park, CA 94025: Free catalog ❖ Clothing and gifts. 800–899–7666.

Troll Learn & Play, 100 Corporate Dr., Mahwah, NJ 07430: Free catalog ❖ Toys and games, arts and crafts, and books with an educational slant. 800–247–6106.

Twincerely Yours, 748 Lake Ave., Clermont, FL 34711: Free catalog with long SASE ❖ Gifts, novelties, and T-shirts for twins and their families. 904–394–5493.

Miscellaneous Gifts

Alex & Ivy Country, 550 Bailey Ave., Ste. 660, Fort Worth, TX 76107: Free catalog ❖ Country-style gifts for the home. 800–359–2539.

Amazon Drygoods, 2218 E. 11th St., Davenport, IA 52803: Catalog $7 ❖ Victorian style clothing, toiletries, books, toys, hats, fans, and garden and home accessories. 800–798–7979.

Ambassador, Palo Verde at 34th St., P.O. Box 28807, Tucson, AZ 85726: Free catalog ❖ Women's clothing and jewelry. 602–748–8600.

American National Parks, 1100 Hector St., Ste. 105, Conshohocken, PA 19428: Free catalog ❖ Gifts that commemorate American history. 800–821–2903.

Anticipations by Ross Simons, 9 Ross Simons Dr., Cranston, RI 02920: Free catalog ❖ Decor accessories, jewelry, rugs, sterling silver flatware, crystal, furniture, artwork, china, gifts for babies, quilts, and porcelain dinnerware. 800–556–7376; 401–463–3100 (in RI).

Anyone Can Whistle, P.O. Box 4407, Kingston, NY 12401: Free catalog ❖ Bird feeders, wind chimes, and other musical gifts. 800–435–8863.

Armchair Shopper, P.O. Box 130, Indianapolis, IN 46206: Free catalog ❖ Classic, old-world style sundials, windchimes, and lawn ornaments. 800–558–2376.

Art from the Heartland, 9 W. Stimson Ave., Athens, OH 45701: Free catalog ❖ Handcrafted art, crafts, and gourmet foods. 800–536–8116.

Art Institute of Chicago, The Museum Shop, 111 S. Michigan Ave., Chicago, IL 60603: Catalog $1 ❖ Museum reproductions and publications that relate to the Institute's collections. 800–621–9337.

Artistic Greetings Inc., 409 William St., P.O. Box 1623, Elmira, NY 14902: Free catalog ❖ Personalized stationery, memo and informal note cards, toys and puzzles, kitchen accessories, and gifts for pets. 607–733–9076.

Laura Ashley Inc., Mail Order, P.O. Box 18413, Memphis, TN 38181: Free information ❖ Clothing for mothers and children, calendars, note cards, tapestry kits, decor accessories, perfumes and sachets, and fine soaps. 800–367–2000.

Attitudes, Subsidiary of IDEC Corporation, P.O. Box 61148, Sunnyvale, CA 94088: Free catalog ❖ Decor accessories, high-tech electronics, sporting equipment, bicycle gadgets, barbecue accessories, telescopes, toys, computer games, and personal care, travel, bathroom, and kitchen aids. 800–241–1107.

Auto Motif Inc., 2968 Atlanta Rd., Smyrna, GA 30080: Catalog $3 ❖ Car models, gifts and collectibles with an automotive theme, books, prints, puzzles, office accessories, lamps, original art, and posters. 800–367–1161.

William Barthman Jewelers, 174 Broadway, New York, NY 10038: Free information ❖ Jewelry, watches, porcelain, crystal, and sterling. 800–727–9782; 212–227–3524 (in NY).

Beki's Garden Gallery, P.O. Box 2566, Boca Raton, FL 33427: Free catalog ❖ Wind chimes, birdhouses, feeders, kitchenwares, soaps, ironwork, plaques, and handcrafted garden and home items. 407–482–2024.

Bennett Brothers Inc., 30 E. Adams St., Chicago, IL 60603: Free catalog ❖ Rings, pins and bracelets, pearls, semiprecious and precious stones, lockets, charms, electronic gifts, toys, cameras, and leather goods. 312–263–4800.

Bergsma Gift Gallery, Bellis Fair Mall, Bellingham, WA 98226: Free information ❖ Statuary and figurines, plates, dolls, and other porcelain collectibles. 206–733–2073.

Biggs Limited Editions, 5517 Lakeside Ave., Richmond, VA 23228: Free information ❖ Statuary and figurines, plates, dolls, and other porcelain collectibles. 800–637–0704.

Bits & Pieces, Stevens Point, WI 54481–7199: Free catalog ❖ Jigsaw puzzles, books, games, and other gifts for adults and children. 800–884–2637.

The Blarney Gift Catalogue, Blarney Woollen Mills Inc., 373D Rt. 46 West, Fairfield, NJ 07004: Free catalog ❖ Waterford crystal, Belleek china, jewelry, and other Irish gifts. 800–451–8720.

Joan Bogart, 1392 Old Northern Blvd., Rosilyn, NY 11576: Free information ❖ Victorian style antiques, gifts, and gas chandeliers and other lighting devices, from 1840 to 1900. 516–621–2454.

Bruce Bolind, P.O. Box 9751, Boulder, CO 80301: Free catalog ❖ Novelty and gift merchandise for adults, children, and pets. 303–443–9688.

Brainstorms, Division Anatomical Chart Company, 8221 Kimball, Skokie, IL 60076: Catalog $3 ❖ Mind-boggling and creative gift ideas and fun items. 800–621–7500; 708–679–4700 (in IL).

Brielle Galleries, P.O. Box 475, Brielle, NJ 08730: Free catalog ❖ Watches, jewelry, paperweights, and crystal, silver, bronze, pewter, and porcelain items. 800–542–7435.

Brookstone Company, Order Processing Center, 1655 Bassford Dr., Mexico, MO 65265: Free catalog ❖ Homewares, tools, travel aids, and other gifts. 800–926–7000.

Buffalo Bill Historical Center, Museum Selections Gift Shop, P.O. Box 2630, Cody, WY 82414: Free catalog ❖ Untamed western frontier-style decor accessories. 800–533–3838.

Burberry's Limited, 9 E. 57th St., New York, NY 10022: Free catalog ❖ Clothing, handbags, luggage, silk scarves and shawls, belts, hats, shoes, and toiletries. 212–371–5010.

Camalier & Buckley, P.O. Box 303, Wye Mills, MD 21679: Free catalog ❖ Desk accessories, luggage, jewelry, and travel items. 800–233–5000.

Camellia & Main, 102 W. Main St., P.O. Box 1709, Fort Valley, GA 31030: Free catalog ❖ All-occasion gifts for everyone. 800–993–4438.

Harriet Carter, North Wales, PA 19455: Free catalog ❖ Unusual gifts for everyone. 215–361–5122.

Cash's of Ireland, Mail Order Courier Center, P.O. Box 158, Plainview, NY 11803: Catalog $3 ❖ China, crystal, walking sticks, wool stoles and cardigans, pottery, frames, serving pieces, lamps and chandeliers, and other gifts from Ireland. 800–223–8100.

Casual Living, 5401 Hangar Ct., P.O. Box 32173, Tampa, FL 33631: Free catalog ❖ Toys, books, furniture, watches and clocks, puzzles, kitchen accessories, hand-painted portraits made from photographs, lamps, mailboxes, music boxes, model construction kits, and computer games. 800–843–1881.

The Celebration Fantastic, 1620 Montgomery St., Ste. 250, San Francisco, CA 94111: Free catalog ❖ Romantic, whimsical, and imaginative gifts for special occasions. 800–527–6566.

Chiasso, P.O. Box 10399, Chicago, IL 60610: Free catalog ❖ Housewares, jewelry, toys, telephones, clocks, and home office items. 312–245–0120.

CitiShopper, P.O. Box 1016, Trumbull, CT 06611: Free catalog ❖ High-tech and electronic devices, toys, playroom furniture, optics and cameras, luggage, furniture, clothing, comforters and bed furnishings, decor accessories, household aids, bicycles, telephones, watches, and computers. 800–TEL-SHOP.

Clocks, Etc., 3401 Mt. Diablo Blvd., Lafayette, CA 94549: Brochure $1 ❖ Old and new clocks, antique furniture, and other gifts. 510–284–4720.

Coach Leatherware Company, 410 Commerce Blvd., Carlstadt, NJ 07072: Free catalog ❖ Leather bags, belts, wallets, briefcases, and other accessories. 201–460–4716.

The Coca-Cola Catalog, 2515 E. 43rd St., P.O. Box 182264, Chattanooga, TN 37422: Free catalog ❖ Coca-Cola theme gifts for men, women, and children. 800–872–6531.

Coldwater Creek, 1123 Lake St., Sandpoint, ID 83864: Free catalog ❖ Nature-related and Native American jewelry, clothing, decor accessories, art, pottery, wind chimes, and other gifts. 800–262–0040.

Collector's Armoury, 800 Slaters Ln., P.O. Box 59, Alexandria, VA 22313: Free catalog ❖ Western and Civil War collectibles and gifts. 800–544–3456.

Colonial Casting Company Inc., 68 Liberty St., Haverhill, MA 01832: Catalog $3 ❖ Handcrafted lead-free pewter miniature castings. 508–374–8783.

Colonial Williamsburg, 201 5th Ave., Williamsburg, VA 23187: Catalog $14.65 ❖ Reproduction colonial furnishings and decor accessories. 800–446–9240.

Colorful Images, 1401 S. Sunset St., Longmont, CO 80501: Free catalog ❖ Decor accessories, watches and jewelry, pens, note cards, cookie jars, wind chimes, desk accessories, novelty telephones, fancy kitchen mugs, calculators, and paperweights. 303–651–6111.

The Company of Women Inc., 102 Main St., P.O. Box 742, Nyack, NY 10960: Free catalog ❖ Gifts for women. 800–937–1193.

Country Loft, Mail Order Department, 2165 N. Forbes Blvd., Tucson, AZ 85745: Free catalog ❖ Lamps and chandeliers, cupboards, cabinets, crocks and carriers, Shaker reproductions, whimsical folk art, whirligigs, baskets, buckets, pillows, braided rugs, and other gifts. 800–225–5408.

Country Store Gifts, 5925 Country Ln., P.O. Box 990, Greendale, WI 53129: Free catalog ❖ Country-style gifts and crafts. 800–558–1013.

Crate & Barrel, P.O. Box 9059, Wheeling, IL 60090: Free catalog ❖ Personalized stationery, kitchen aids, storage systems, sound equipment, and decor accessories. 800–323–5461.

The Crow's Nest Birding Shop, 159 Sapsucker Woods Rd., Ithaca, NY 14850: Free catalog ❖ Books and gifts for bird enthusiasts. 607–254–2400.

Cumberland General Store, Rt. 3, Box 81, Crossville, TN 38555: Catalog $3 ❖ Cooking ranges, gardening tools, cast-iron ware, farm bells, buggies, blacksmithing equipment, harnesses, and other old-fashioned gifts. 800–334–4640.

The Daily Planet, P.O. Box 1313, New York, NY 10013: Free catalog ❖ Novelties, gifts, stationery, musical instruments, T-shirts, jewelry, reproduction memorabilia from the past, toys, and other items from worldwide locations. 212–334–0006.

Dilworthy Country Store, 275 Brinton's Bridge Rd., West Chester, PA 19382: Free information ❖ Country-style gifts, folk art, herbs and dried flowers, colonial furnishings, and 18th-century reproductions. 215–399–0560.

The Walt Disney Catalog, One Disney Dr., P.O. Box 29144, Shawnee Mission, KS 66201: Free catalog ❖ Disney-theme gifts and clothing for men, women, and children. 800–237–5751.

Down East Books & Gifts, Rt. One Roxmont, Rockport, ME 04856: Free catalog ❖ Calendars, books, and crafts from Maine and New England. 800–766–1670.

Down's Collectors Showcase, 1617 S. 101st St., Milwaukee, WI 53214: Free catalog ❖ Collectible figurines, miniatures, thimbles, music boxes, mugs and steins, country crafts, plates, art, and porcelain. 800–558–4200.

DR Marketing, P.O. Box 251, Stratford, CT 06497: Free catalog ❖ Unusual, practical, and handy gift items.

Walter Drake & Sons, Drake Building, Colorado Springs, CO 80940: Free catalog ❖ Personalized stationery, toys, household items, clothing, decor and office accessories, and hundreds of other items. 800–525–9291.

The Early West, Box 9292, College Station, TX 77842: Free catalog ❖ Western-style gifts, books, and videos. 409–775–6047.

Early Winters Inc., P.O. Box 4333, Portland, OR 97208: Free catalog ❖ Men and women's outdoor gifts and equipment, ski wear and accessories, and other clothing. 800–458–4438.

Eastside Gifts & Dinnerware Inc., 351 Grand St., New York, NY 10002: Free information ❖ China, crystal, flatware, and other gifts. 800–443–8711; 212–982–7200 (in NY).

El Paso Saddleblanket Company Inc., 601 N. Oregon, El Paso, TX 79901: Free information ❖ Pottery, folk art, jewelry, antiques, Native American arts and crafts, kachina dolls, baskets, Zapotec rugs, beaded items, leather goods, clothing, weavings, and other hand-loomed items.

European Imports & Gifts, 7900 N. Milwaukee Ave., Niles, IL 60714: Free catalog ❖ Imported and other gifts and collectibles. 708–967–5253.

Eximious, 1000 Greenbay Rd., Winnetka, IL 60093: Free catalog ❖ Travel aids, desk and office accessories, garden aids, and American crafts. 800–221–9464.

Expressions from Potpourri, 120 N. Meadows Rd., Medfield, MA 02052: Free catalog ❖ Toys and puzzles for children and adults, jewelry and watches, note cards and stationery, and decor accessories. 800–688–8051.

The Faith Mountain Company, P.O. Box 199, Sperryville, VA 22740: Free catalog ❖ Herbs and flowers, clothing, home furnishings, garden accessories, and American crafts. 800–822–7238.

Falcon Press, P.O. Box 1718, Helena, MT 59624: Free catalog ❖ Outdoor gifts. 800–582–2665.

Fingerhut, Box 2500, St. Cloud, MN 56395: Free catalog ❖ Kitchen aids, china and flatware, cookware, furniture, curtains and draperies, pillows and bedroom coordinates, bathroom furnishings, jewelry and watches, clothing, decor accessories, tools, high-tech electronics, and toys. 612–259–2500.

Finishing Touches, 586 Higgins Crowell Rd., West Yarmouth, MA 02673: Free catalog ❖ Kitchen and bathroom accessories, handmade finials and brass ornaments, oil paintings, music boxes, lamps and other light fixtures, telephones, architectural accouterments, country crafts, and decor accessories. 508–775–4643.

For Convenience Sake, 4092B Howard Ave., Kensington, MD 20895: Free catalog ❖ Leisure and recreation, household helpers, dressing and grooming, kitchen, and other comfort items. 800–242–9763.

Fox Ridge Outfitters Inc., 400 N. Main St., P.O. Box 1700, Rochester, NH 03867: Free catalog ❖ Clothing, guns, solid pine carvings, cookware, knives and cutlery, and other items for outdoor sportsmen. 800–243–4570.

Frontgate, 396 Wards Corner Rd., Ste. 200, Loveland, OH 45140: Free catalog ❖ Housewares, mailboxes, kitchen accessories, outdoor furniture, gardening tools, barbecue and charcoal ovens, gifts for pets, intercoms, scales, dart boards, automobile gadgets, sports equipment, heaters, and floor registers. 800–626–6488.

Geary's, 351 N. Beverly Dr., Beverly Hills, CA 90210: Free catalog ❖ Silver sculptures,

Lladro porcelain, Christofle French silverplate, Halcyon enamels, tapestries, dinnerware, desk accessories, and Waterford, Baccarat and Lalique crystal. 800–243–2797; 310–273–3344 (in CA).

Good Catalog Company, 5456 SE International Way, Portland, OR 97222: Free catalog ❖ All-occasion gifts for everyone. 800–225–3870.

Good Idea!, P.O. Box 955, Vail, CO 81658: Free catalog ❖ All-occasion gifts for everyone. 800–538–6690.

W.M. Green & Company, Hwy. 64 East, P.O. Box 278, Robersonville, NC 27871: Free catalog ❖ Gifts for adults and children. 800–482–5050.

Haitian Art Company, 600 Frances St., Key West, FL 33040: Free information with long SASE ❖ Paintings, wood sculptures, steel cut-outs, papier-mache crafts, spirit flags, and other gifts. 305–296–8932.

Hammacher Schlemmer, 9180 LeSaint Dr., Fairfield, OH 45014: Free catalog ❖ Gifts for the entire family. 800–233–4800.

Hanover House, P.O. Box 2, Hanover, PA 17333: Free catalog ❖ Clothing, gardening supplies, household aids, jewelry, and novelties. 717–633–3366.

Heartland America, 6978 Shady Oak Rd., Eden Prairie, MN 55344: Free catalog ❖ High-tech electronics, household accessories, telephones, computers, tools, leather goods and luggage, games, office and home furniture, and audio and stereo, optics and astronomy, and exercise equipment. 800–229–2901.

Herrington, 3 Symmes Dr., Londonderry, NH 03053: Free catalog ❖ Automotive gadgets and tools, photographic and video equipment, compact disks, disk and cassette storage cabinets, gifts for music lovers, and astronomy equipment. 603–437–4638.

Hitching Post Supply, 10312 210th St. SE, Snohomish, WA 98290: Free catalog ❖ Gifts for horse owners. 206–668–2349.

Hoffritz, 515 W. 24th St., New York, NY 10011: Catalog $1 ❖ Optics, knives and scissors, kitchen aids, clocks, travel aids, luggage, flashlights, calculators, games, yogurt makers, and other gifts from worldwide sources. 212–924–7300.

Holst Inc., 1118 W. Lake, Box 370, Tawas City, MI 48764: Free catalog ❖ Country items, sundials and weather vanes,

housewares, figurines, and holiday decorations. 517–362–5664.

The Horchow Collection, P.O. Box 620048, Dallas, TX 72262: Free catalog ❖ Home furnishings and accessories, dishes and serving pieces, rugs, bedroom linens, and lamps. 800–395–5397.

House of Tyrol, P.O. Box 909, Alpenland Center, Helen Highway/75 North, Cleveland, GA 30528: Free catalog ❖ Musical cuckoo clocks, crystal, porcelain, lamps, music boxes, pillows, knitted items, decor accessories, bar accessories, collector plates, pewter, tapestries, cards, Alpine hat pins, Christmas decorations, and folk music videos. 800–241–5404.

Jennifer's Trunk Antiques & General Store, 201 N. Riverside, Dr., St. Clair, MI 48079: Free brochure ❖ Victorian-style antique furniture, books, jewelry, lamps and shades, and other gifts. 810–329–2032.

The Jompole Company Inc., 330 7th Ave., New York, NY 10001: Free information with long SASE ❖ Balloons and lollipops to diamonds and furs, fine china, writing instruments, table settings, and other giftwares. 212–594–0440.

David Kay Inc., One Jenni Ln., Peoria, IL 61614: Free catalog ❖ Planters, bird houses, furniture, pool and backyard toys, fireplace accessories, games, sculptures, and wind chimes. 800–535–9917.

Charles Keath Ltd., P.O. Box 48800, Atlanta, GA 30362: Free catalog ❖ Women's clothing, jewelry, watches, decor and fireplace accessories, and luggage and purses. 800–388–6565; 449–3100 (in Atlanta).

Kemp & George, 301 Madison Rd., P.O. Box 511, Orange, VA 22960: Free catalog ❖ Gifts for the home. 800–967–3310.

Miles Kimball Company, 41 W. 8th Ave., Oshkosh, WI 54906: Free catalog ❖ Hundreds of gifts and gadgets from around the world. 800–546–2255.

Lane Luggage, 1146 Connecticut Ave. NW, Washington, DC 20036: Free catalog ❖ Luggage, electronic gadgets, toys and games, and desk and decor accessories. 202–452–1146.

Lefthanders International, P.O. Box 8249, Topeka, KS 66608: Catalog $2 ❖ Items for lefties. 913–234–2177.

Lembick, 2559 Scott Blvd., Santa Clara, CA 95050: Free catalog ❖ Collectible miniatures, kitchen and table accessories, serving pieces,

pottery, music box cake tops, jewelry, children's gifts, and decor accents. 800–825–1237.

Levenger, P.O. Box 1256, Delray Beach, FL 33447: Free catalog ❖ Books, furniture, pens, briefcases, and other gifts for serious readers. 800–545–0242.

Lifestyle Fascination Gifts, 55 Progress Pl., Jackson, NJ 08527: Free catalog ❖ High-tech and other innovative and unusual gifts. 800–669–8875.

C. Lifton's Buckles & More, 121 S. 6th St., Stillwater, MN 55082: Catalog $5 ❖ Harley Davidson-theme money clips, belt buckles, badges, desk accessories, and other gifts. 612–439–7208.

The Limited of Michigan Ltd., 10861 Paw Paw Dr., Holland, MI 49424: Free catalog ❖ Old and new Hummel figurines, back-issue plates, bells, and other gifts. 800–355–6363.

Lynchburg Hardware & General Store, 39 Main St., Lynchburg, TN 37352: Catalog $1 ❖ Gifts, novelty items, housewares, tools, and gardening supplies. 615–759–7184.

Mature Wisdom, P.O. Box 28, Hanover, PA 17333: Free catalog ❖ Kitchen and bathroom aids, baby gifts, desk accessories, shoes, lingerie and clothing, and travel aids. 717–633–3323.

May Silk, 13262 Moore St., Cerritos, CA 90701: Free catalog ❖ Silk plants, gifts, housewares, and jewelry. 800–282–7455; 310–926–7172 (in CA).

Metropolitan Museum of Art, 255 Gracie Station, New York, NY 10028: Catalog $1 ❖ Greeting and note cards, ornaments, books, jewelry, ties, frames, calendars, and other reproductions from museum collections. 800–468–7386.

Minneapolis Institute of Art, 2400 3rd Ave. South, Minneapolis, MN 55404: Catalog $1 ❖ Art reproductions and other gifts. 612–870–3029.

Moby Dick Marine Specialties, 27 William St., New Bedford, MA 02740: Catalog $5 ❖ Nautical gifts, decor accessories, and scrimshaw. 800–343–8044.

Claire Murray Inc., P.O. Box 390, Ascutney, VT 05030: Catalog $5 (refundable) ❖ Handpainted ceramics, quilts, and hand-hooked rugs. 800–252–4733.

Museum Collections, 586 Higgins Crowell Rd., West Yarmouth, MA 02673: Free catalog ❖ Museum replicas. 800–442–2460.

Museum of Fine Arts Boston, Catalog Sales Dept., P.O. Box 244, Avon, MA 02322: Free catalog ❖ Museum replicas. 800–225–5592.

Museum of Modern Art New York, Mail Order Department, P.O. Box 2534, West Chester, PA 19380: Free catalog ❖ Museum replicas. 212–708–9888.

Museum Replicas Limited, P.O. Box 840, Conyers, GA 30207: Catalog $1 (refundable) ❖ Reproductions of historic weapons and period battle wear.

Music Stand, 1 Rockdale Plaza, Lebanon, OH 03766: Free catalog ❖ Gifts with a music theme, candies, gift baskets, trophies, plaques, and certificates. 800–515–5010.

Mystic Seaport Museum Stores, Greemanville Ave., Mystic, CT 06355: Free catalog ❖ Gifts with a seafaring theme. 800–248–1066.

National Geographic Society, 1145 17th St. NW, Washington, DC 20036: Free catalog ❖ Books, games, videos, maps and globes, travel aids, and magazine subscriptions. 800–447–0647.

The Nature Company, Catalog Division, P.O. Box 188 Florence, KY 41022: Free catalog ❖ Jewelry made from natural materials, high-tech devices, science gadgets, T-shirts, books, sculptures, optics, clocks, garden accessories, puzzles and toys, and archaeological reproductions. 800–227–1114.

New Mexico Catalog, 1700 Shalem Colony Trail, P.O. Box 261, Fairacres, NM 88033: Free catalog ❖ Native American, Hispanic, and Anglo-American arts and crafts, gifts, and foods. 800–678–0585; 1–525–0585 (in NM).

Northstyle Gifts, P.O. Box 1360, Minocqua, WI 54548: Free catalog ❖ Nature-influenced gifts. 800–336–5666.

O'Grady Presents, 150 E. Huron St., Ste. 1200, Chicago, IL 60611: Free catalog ❖ Gifts for the holidays, young at heart, and adults. 800–548–5759; 312–642–2000 (in IL).

Oriental Trading Company Inc., P.O. Box 2308, Omaha, NE 68103: Free catalog ❖ Toys, giftwares, novelties, carnival supplies, and holiday and seasonal items. 800–228–0475.

Orvis Manchester, Historic Rt. 7A, Manchester, VT 05254: Free catalog ❖ Men and women's clothing, country gifts, rugs, fireplace accessories, gifts for the family pet, kitchen accessories, luggage, lamps, and fishing equipment. 800–548–9548.

Out of the Woodwork, 2120 Timber Pointe Rd., Charlottsville, VA 22901: Free brochure ❖ Personalized educational gifts for children of all ages. 804–973–3376.

Pandora's Box Mail Order, 1820 S. West Ave., Ste. 150A, Freeport, IL 61032: Catalog $5 (refundable) ❖ Radar and laser detectors and other items for the home office and car. 815–369–4047.

The Paragon Gifts, 89 Tom Harvey Rd., Westerly, RI 02891: Free catalog ❖ Casual clothing, housewares, decor accessories, games and toys, and bathroom items. 800–343–3095.

Personal Creations, 530 Executive Dr., Burr Ridge, IL 60521: Free catalog ❖ Frames, office and desk accessories, leather goods, and gifts. 800–326–6626.

The Personal Touch, One Artistic Plaza, P.O. Box 1999, Elmira, NY 14902: Catalog $2 ❖ Personalized stationery and gifts. 800–227–0946; 607–733–5541 (in NY).

Pigxies Enterprises Inc., 1030 Calle Sombra, Ste C, San Clemente, CA 92673: Free catalog ❖ Everything for pig lovers and collectors. 800–752–6901.

Pitt Petri, 378 Delaware Ave., Buffalo, NY 14202: Free catalog ❖ Crystal, silverware and silver serving pieces, Lladro porcelain, porcelain and china, ceramics, children's clothing, dolls, and home and bar, decor, and personal care aids. 800–345–0053.

Plow & Hearth, 301 Madison Rd., P.O. Box 830, Orange, VA 22960: Free catalog ❖ Gardening tools, birdhouses and feeders, porch and lawn furniture, fireplace accessories, and gifts for pets. 800–627–1712.

Plummer-McCutcheon, A Hammacher Schlemmer Company, 9180 LeSaint Dr., Fairfield, OH 45014: Free catalog ❖ Distinctive and unusual gifts for everyone. 800–233–4800.

Post Scripts from Joan Cook, 119 Foster St., P.O. Box 6008, Peabody, MA 01961: Free catalog ❖ Women and children's clothing, toys, home accessories, luggage, personal care items, and electronic gadgets. 508–532–4040.

Potpourri, 120 N. Meadows Rd., Medfield, MA 02052: Free catalog ❖ Jewelry, clothing, party items, games, and decor accessories. 800–688–8051.

Pottery Barn, Mail Order Dept., P.O. Box 7044, San Francisco, CA 94120: Free catalog ❖ Gifts for the home. 800–922–5507.

Pueblo to People, P.O. Box 2545, Houston, TX 77252: Information $2 ❖ Nuts, dried fruit, ceramics, jewelry, coffee, and gift baskets. 713–956–1172.

Pyramid Collection, P.O. Box 3333, Chelmsford, MA 01824: Free catalog ❖ Unforgettable gifts with an accent on personal growth and exploration. 800–333–4220.

Rand McNally & Company, Catalog Operations Center, 2515 E. 43rd St., P.O. Box 182257, Chattanooga, TN 37422: Free catalog ❖ Gifts for sports enthusiasts, health and exercise equipment, maps, world globes, books, videos, clocks, prints, travel aids, and watches. 800–234–0679.

Recap Universal, 283 Rhode Island, Buffalo, NY 14213: Free catalog ❖ Gifts, jewelry, leather goods, luggage, kitchen tools, toys, handmade originals. miniatures, musicals and collectibles in porcelain, and wood, brass, and stone items. 800–292–6338.

Red Cross Gifts, 122 Walnut St., Spooner, WI 54801: Free information ❖ Collectible plates, Ashton-Drake dolls, and other gifts and collectibles. 800–344–9958.

Red Rose Collection, P.O. Box 280140, San Francisco, CA 94128: Free catalog ❖ Books and tapes, art works, jewelry, tools, games, natural fiber clothing, decor accessories, and toiletries. 800–374–5505.

Ridge Runner Naturals, 130 N. Main St., Waynesville, NC 28786: Free information ❖ Wildlife and nature T-shirts and other nature-related gifts. 704–456–3003.

Rodco Products, 2565 16th Ave., Columbus, NE 68601: Catalog 50¢ ❖ High-tech equipment for the home and office. 800–323–2799.

Leonard Rue Enterprises, 138 Millbrook Rd., Blairstown, NJ 07825: Free catalog ❖ Books, video tapes, equipment, and other gifts for photographers and outdoor enthusiasts. 908–362–6616.

Sally Distributors Inc., 4100 Quebec Ave. North, Minneapolis, MN 55427: Free catalog ❖ Balloons, toys, greeting cards, gifts, novelties, and carnival supplies. 612–533–7100.

Schrader Enterprises Inc., 230 S. Abbe Rd., Fairview, MI 48621: Catalog $1 ❖ Gifts for the railroad enthusiast. 517–848–2225.

The Scope Catalog, 50 Oser Ave., Hauppauge, NY 11788: Free catalog ❖ Serving pieces, kitchen gadgets, personal care items, toys, tools, travel aids, and high-tech, sporting, pool and beach, outdoor, and video and audio equipment. 800–695–4848.

Scotty's Gifts & Accessories, 1500 Dixie Hwy., Park Hills, KY 41011: Free catalog ❖ Jewelry and art, collectibles, clothing, stationery, and other gifts. 606–431–1262.

Scully & Scully Inc., 504 Park Ave., New York, NY 10126: Free catalog ❖ Handcrafted reproductions of 18th-century enamels by English artisans, figurines, furniture, books and games, men's clothing, crystal, and home office aids. 800–223–3717; 212–755–2590 (in NY).

Seacraft Classics, 7850 E. Evans Rd., Ste. 109, Scottsdale, AZ 85260: Free information ❖ Handmade detailed models of 19th-century ships and boats, with hardwood display stands and brass name plates. 800–356–1987; 602–998–4988 (in AZ).

Seasons, P.O. Box 64545, St. Paul, MN 55164: Free catalog ❖ All-occasion gifts for everyone. 800–776–9677.

Serengeti, P.O. Box 3349, Serengeti Park, Chelmsford, MA 01824: Free catalog ❖ Wildlife apparel and gifts. 800–426–2852.

Service Merchandise Catalog, Mail Order, P.O. Box 25130, Nashville, TN 37202: Free catalog ❖ Homewares, toys and games, hobby supplies, and jewelry. 800–251–1212.

SGF Gifts & Furnishings Catalog, P.O. Box 620047, Dallas, TX 75262: Catalog $3 ❖ Serving pieces, linens, furniture, luggage and attache cases, children's gifts, and jewelry. 214–484–1517.

Sharper Image, 650 Davis St., San Francisco, CA 94111: Free catalog ❖ Health and exercise equipment, toys, watches and clocks, pet products, calculators, telephones, and sunglasses. 800–344–4444.

Ship's Hatch, 10376 Main St., Fairfax, VA 22030: Brochure $1 ❖ Military patches, pins and insignia, official USN ship ball caps, ship's clocks, hatchcover tables, nautical and military gifts, jewelry, lamps and lanterns, ship's wheels, and other gifts. 703–691–1670.

Showcase of Savings, P.O. Box 748, Rural Hall, NC 27098: Free catalog ❖ Machine-washable cotton-velour warm-up suits, other fashions, jewelry, and gifts. 910–744–1790.

Signals Catalog, P.O. Box 64428, St. Paul, MN 55114: Free catalog ❖ Books, T-shirts, sweat shirts, video and cassette tapes, and other gifts. 800–669–5225.

Signatures, 19465 Brennan Ave., Perris, CA 92599: Free catalog ❖ All-occasion gifts for everyone. 909–943–2021.

Smithsonian Catalogue, 7955 Angus Ct., Springfield, VA 22153: Free catalog ❖ Gifts, toys, games, books, puzzles, and replicas from the Smithsonian Institution's collections. 800–322–0344.

Soccer International Inc., P.O. Box 7222, Arlington, VA 22207: Catalog $2 ❖ Gifts and novelties with a soccer motif. 703–524–4333.

Solutions, P.O. Box 6878, Portland, OR 97228: Free catalog ❖ Home accessories, tableware, jewelry, exercise equipment, and travel aids. 800–342–9988.

Sophisticats Catalog, P.O. Box 4564, North Hollywood, CA 91607: Free catalog ❖ Gift items decorated with cat artwork. 818–879–0339.

Sound Exchange, 45 N. Industry Ct., Deer Park, NY 11729: Free catalog ❖ Music, gifts, and collectibles. 800–521–0042.

Sporty's Preferred Living Catalog, Clermont Airport, Batavia, OH 45103: Free catalog ❖ Garden aids, outdoor furniture, sundials, mailboxes, gourmet meat smokers, portable refrigerators, kitchen aids and cutlery, embroidered shirts, automotive aids, sports equipment, games and toys, optics, gifts for pets, and weather forecasting equipment. 800–543–8633.

George Stafford & Sons, 808 Smith Ave., P.O. Box 2055, Thomasville, GA 31799: Free catalog ❖ Jewelry, luggage, books on the outdoors, mugs and dishes, and men and women's clothing and shoes. 912–226–4306.

Starcrest of California, 19465 Brennan Ave., Perris, CA 92599: Free catalog: Gifts and novelties. 909–657–2793.

STIK-EES, 1165 Joshua Way, P.O. Box 9630, Vista, CA 92085: Free catalog ❖ Reusable static cling, pre-cut vinyl stickers for decorating gifts, windows, and other surfaces. 619–727–7011.

Sturbridge Yankee Workshop, P.O. Box 9797, Portland, ME 04104: Free catalog ❖ Home furnishings, Victorian- and Shaker-style items, kitchen and bathroom accessories, and country crafts. 800–343–1144.

Sugar Hill, 1037 Front Ave., Columbus, GA 31902: Free catalog ❖ Bedroom linens, furniture, mirrors, lamps, and other gifts. 800–344–6125.

Sundance Catalog, Customer Service Center, 1909 S. 4250 West, Salt Lake City, UT 84106: Free catalog ❖ Sculptures, lamps, stoneware, jewelry, decor accessories, and Western and Native American gifts. 800–422–2770.

Super Locomotion Inc., 1213 Elko Dr., Sunnyvale, CA 94708: Free catalog ❖ High-tech and children's gifts, automotive accessories, travel aids, and games. 800–525–2468.

Tapestry, P.O. Box 46, Hanover, PA 17333: Free catalog ❖ Decor accessories, Americana, imported gifts, fun and fantasy items, and holiday specials. 717–633–3319.

Taylor Gifts, 355 E. Conestoga Rd., Wayne, PA 19093: Free catalog ❖ Gifts and novelties. 215–293–3613.

Tender Heart Treasures Ltd., 10525 J St., Omaha, NE 68127: Free catalog ❖ Gifts for homes, offices, friends, and family. 800–443–1367; 402–593–1313 (in NE).

Tetbury Castle, 10200 NW 73rd Terr., Weatherby Lake, MO 64152: Catalog $3 ❖ Old English-style goblets, mugs, and other gifts. 816–746–7406.

Think Big, 390 W. Broadway, New York, NY 10012: Free catalog ❖ Unusual and oversized gags and gifts. 800–487–4244.

Norm Thompson, P.O. Box 3999, Portland, OR 97208: Free catalog ❖ Kitchen and bathroom aids, automotive accessories, storage and closet organizers, clothing, shoes and boots, and high-tech gadgets. 800–547–1160.

Thoroughbred Racing Catalog, Warsaw, VA 22572: Catalog $2 ❖ Calendars and limited edition prints with pictures of famous racing horses and horse-decorated mailboxes, doormats, sweat shirts and T-shirts, mugs and glasses, jewelry, and wall clocks. 800–777–RACE.

Tiffany & Company, Customer Service, 801 Jefferson Rd., Parsippany, NJ 07054: Catalog $1 ❖ Jewelry, crystal, watches, cultured pearls and settings, other jewelry, serving pieces, pens and pencils, and desk accessories. 201–428–0570.

Touchstone, Order Processing Center, 3589 Broad St., Atlanta, GA 30341: Free catalog ❖ Decor and desk accessories, furniture and lamps, and other traditional American-style gifts. 800–962–6890.

Trifles, P.O. Box 620048, Dallas, TX 75262: Free catalog ❖ Jewelry, coffee and tea service sets, stationery, porcelain and bone china, linens, toys, fireplace accessories, crystal, luggage, furniture, and clothing for men, women, and children. 214–556–6055.

Troll Family Gift Catalog, 100 Corporate Dr., Mahwah, NJ 07430: Free catalog ❖ Clocks, electronic baby sitters, photo albums, stationery, kitchen gadgets, toys, books, cassettes, and other gifts. 800–247–6106.

Unicef, P.O. Box 182233, Chattanooga, TN 37422: Free catalog ❖ Greeting and note cards, toys, limited edition plates, postcards, and other gifts. 800–553–1200.

United States Purchasing Exchange, United States Purchasing Exchange Bldg., North Hollywood, CA 91611: Free catalog ❖ Household aids, novelties and toys, personal care items, clothing and lingerie, telephones, clocks, kitchen accessories, jewelry, automotive aids, tools, and bathroom furnishings.

Vermont Country Store, Mail Order Office, P.O. Box 3000, Manchester Center, VT 05255: Free catalog ❖ Clothing, shoes, purses, watches, pillows and linens, bed coverings, travel aids, throw rugs, stove top potpourris, cleaning aids, kitchen accessories, and other gifts from New England. 802–362–4647.

Lillian Vernon, Virginia Beach, VA 23479: Free catalog ❖ Holiday specialties, clothing, electronic gadgets, jewelry, closet organizers, toys, baby care items, kitchen and cooking aids, and luggage and leather accessories. 800–285–5555.

Weekender, P.O. Box 1499, Burnsville, MN 55337: Free catalog ❖ Garden and landscaping supplies, outdoor cooking aids, clothing and gloves, security devices and alarms, and high-tech electronics. 800–438–5480.

Weston Bowl Mill, P.O. Box 218, Weston, VT 05161: Catalog $1 ❖ Wood bowls, crafts, and kitchen and dining room accessories. 800–824–6219.

Wharton Wholesalers Ltd., 3256 Chaparral Dr., Idaho Falls, ID 83404: Free information ❖ Gifts, novelties, fine jewelry, and miniatures. 208–529–5260.

What on Earth, 2451 Enterprise East Pkwy., Twinsburg, OH 44087: Free catalog ❖ Gifts for men, women, and children. 216–425–4600.

Wild Wings, South Hwy. 61, Lake City, MN 55041: Free catalog ❖ Art prints, gun

cabinets, solid oak wall clocks, gifts for fishermen and animal lovers, and note cards. 800–445–4833.

Williams-Sonoma, Mail Order Dept., P.O. Box 7456, San Francisco, CA 94120: Free catalog ❖ Kitchenware, gourmet foods, and other gifts. 800–541–1262.

Williamsburg Pottery Factory Catalog, P.O. Box 8733, Williamsburg, VA 23187: Free catalog ❖ Country crafts, pottery and stoneware, bone china, gourmet foods and Smithfield hams, toys, holiday decorations, quilts, miniatures, Civil War memorabilia, novelties and other collectibles, rugs, prints and frames, and lamps. 800–768–8379.

Winterthur Museum & Gardens, Catalog Division, 100 Enterprise Pl., Dover, DE 19901: Free catalog ❖ American art, jewelry, playing cards, lamps, dinnerware, clocks, planters, wind chimes, garden sculptures, and reproductions from the Henry Francis du Pont Winterthur Museum. 800–767–0500.

Wireless, P.O. Box 64422, St. Paul, MN 55164: Free catalog ❖ T-shirts and sweat shirts, old time radio broadcasts, toy banks, coffee mugs, Disney cartoons on video, books, wind chimes, and electronics. 800–669–9999.

World Wildlife Fund Catalog, P.O. Box 224, Peru, IN 46970: Free catalog ❖ Wildlife theme clothing, books, games, coasters, coffee mugs, puzzles, note pads, kitchen accents, carryall bags, candlesticks, sculptures, wind chimes, braided door rugs, bird feeders, place mats, and umbrellas. 800–833–1600.

Carol Wright Gifts, 340 Applecreek Rd., P.O. Box 8503, Lincoln, NE 68544: Free catalog ❖ Gifts for homes, offices, friends, and family. 402–474–5174.

The Write Touch, The Rytex Company, 5850 W. 80th St., P.O. Box 68188, Indianapolis, IN 46268: Free catalog ❖ Stationery, writing aids, and other gifts. 800–288–6824.

Writewell Company, P.O. Box 68186, Indianapolis, IN 46268: Free catalog ❖ Decor accessories, household items, stationery, books, home office supplies, games, rubber stamps, videos, business cards, and other gifts. 800–968–5850.

Your Exceptional Home, W.M. Green & Company, Hwy. 64 East, P.O. Box 278, Robersonville, NC 27871: Free catalog ❖ Home accessories and gifts. 800–482–5050.

Zucker's Fine Gifts, 151 W. 26th St., New York, NY 10001: Free catalog ❖ Hummel, Swarovski silver and crystal, Waterford crystal, Lladro porcelain, and other gifts. 212–989–1450.

Religious Gifts

A & L Designs, 201 E. Tabor Rd., Philadelphia, PA 19120: Price list $3 ❖ Needlepoint and cross-stitch religious designs. 215–329–7321.

Abbey Press, 371 Hill Dr., St. Meinrad, IN 47577: Free catalog ❖ Religious gifts and other items for people of Christian faith. 812–357–8251.

Augsburg Fortress Publishers, 426 S. 5th St., Box 1209, Minneapolis, MN 55440: Free catalog ❖ Books, curriculum materials, music, gifts, audiovisuals, and ecclesiastical arts items. 800–328–4648; 612–330–3300 (in MN).

Biblical Archaeology Society, 3000 Connecticut Ave. NW, Ste. 300, Washington, DC 20008: Free catalog ❖ Biblical-theme gifts. 202–387–8888.

California Stitchery, 6015 Sunnyslope Ave., Van Nuys, CA 91401: Free catalog ❖ Judaic-design needlepoint, embroidery, and latch hook kits. 800–345–3332.

Ergo Media, 668 Front St., P.O. Box 2037, Teaneck, NJ 07666: Free catalog ❖ Award-winning videos on all aspects of Jewish life. 800–695–3746.

Gallerie Robin, 345 Harpeth Ridge Rd., Nashville, TN 37221: Free information ❖ Judaic art, graphics, and handcrafted gifts. 800–635–8279.

A Glimpse of Judaica, 9219 W. Pico Blvd., Los Angeles, CA 90035: Free catalog ❖ Original handcrafted Judaica. 800–546–1776; 310–275–1355 (in CA).

Hamakor Judaica Inc., Mail Order Department, P.O. Box 48836, Niles, IL 60714: Free catalog ❖ Kosher foods, kitchen accessories, Jewish art, watches and pendants, seder dishes, mezuzahs, candelabras, and other items. 800–426–2567.

Judaic Folk Art, Lois Kramer, 8101 Timber Valley Ct., Dunn Loring, VA 22027: Free brochure ❖ Judaic folk art. 703–560–2914.

Old Village Shop, Hanover, PA 17333–0008: Free catalog ❖ Toys, religious gifts, kitchen aids, clothing and intimate apparel, novelties, and other unusual and classic gifts. 717–633–3311.

Shasta Abbey Buddhist Supplies, P.O. Box 199, Mt. Shasta, CA 96067: Catalog $2 ❖ Buddhist meditation supplies and gifts. 916–926–6682.

The Source for Everything Jewish, P.O. Box 48836, Niles, IL 60714: Free catalog ❖ Ritual and ceremonial objects, books, fine art, Kosher gourmet food, and audio and video cassettes. 800–426–2567.

GLASS COLLECTIBLES

Ruth S. Jordan, Meridale, NY 13806: Free list with long SASE ❖ American brilliant period cut glass. 607–746–2082.

GLOBES

George F. Cram Company Inc., 301 S. LaSalle St., Indianapolis, IN 46201: Free catalog ❖ Maps, atlases, globes, and charts. 800–227–4199; 317–635–5564 (in IN).

Creative Imaginations, 10879 Portal Dr., Los Alamitos, CA 90720: Free information ❖ Inflatable globes. 800–942–6487.

National Geographic Society, 1145 17th St. NW, Washington, DC 20036: Free catalog ❖ Books, games, videos, maps and globes, travel aids, and magazine subscriptions. 800–447–0647.

Omni Resources, 1004 S. Mebane St., P.O. Box 2096, Burlington, NC 27216: Free catalog ❖ Fossils, rocks, hiking and topography maps, and globes. 800–742–2677.

Rand McNally & Company, Catalog Operations Center, 2515 E. 43rd St., P.O. Box 182257, Chattanooga, TN 37422: Free catalog ❖ Gifts for sports enthusiasts, health and exercise equipment, maps, world globes, books, videos, clocks, prints, travel aids, and watches. 800–234–0679.

Replogle Globes Inc., 2801 S. 25th Ave., Broadview, IL 60153: Free catalog ❖ Earth and space globes in desk and floor models. 708–343–0900.

Trippensee Transparent Globes, 301 Cass St., Saginaw, MI 48602: Free catalog ❖ World globes in desk and floor models. 517–799–8102.

GO KARTS & MINICARS

Kart World, 1488 Mentor Ave., Painsville, OH 44077: Catalog $3 ❖ Go karts and minicars, engines, kits, and parts. 216–357–5569.

Performance Speedway, 2810–C Algonquin Ave., Jacksonville, FL 32210: Catalog $5 ❖ Electric cars, golf cars, mopeds, and parts, how-to manuals, and other books.

GOLF
Clothing

A.B. Emblem Corporation, P.O. Box 695, Weaverville, NC 28787: Free information ❖ Caps, hats, shirts, and sweaters. 800–438–4285; 704–645–3015 (in NC).

All Star Pro Golf Company Inc., 120 9th St. SW, Clarion, IA 50525: Free information ❖ Caps, hats, gloves, jackets, visors, sweaters, and shirts. 800–247–4830; 515–532–2864 (in IA).

Tommy Armour Golf Company, 8350 N. Lehigh Ave., Morton Grove, IL 60053: Free information ❖ Gloves, shirts, skirts, slacks, sweaters, and visors. 800–723–4653.

Bogner of America, Bogner Dr., Newport, VT 05855: Free information ❖ Caps, hats, gloves, jackets, shirts, skirts, slacks, sweaters, and visors. 800–451–4417; 802–334–6507 (in VT).

Broder Brothers, 45555 Port St., Plymouth, MI 48170: Free information ❖ Jackets, shirts, sweaters, and visors. 800–543–4482; 313–589–1919 (in MI).

Ellesse USA Inc., 1430 Broadway, New York, NY 10018: Free information ❖ Jackets, shirts, skirts, slacks, sweaters, and visors. 800–345–9036; 212–840–6111 (in NY).

M. Handelsman Company, 1323 S. Michigan Ave., Chicago, IL 60605: Free information ❖ Caps, hats, shirts, socks, sweaters, and visors. 800–621–4454; 312–427–0784 (in IL).

King Louie International, 13500 15th St., Grandview, MO 64030: Free information ❖ Caps, hats, jackets, shirts, sweaters, and visors. 800–521–5212; 816–765–5212 (in MO).

Le Coq Sportif, 28 Engelhard Dr., Cranbury, NJ 08512: Free information ❖ Caps, hats, shoes, shirts, skirts, slacks, socks, and sweaters. 800–524–2377; 609–655–1515 (in NJ).

Lily's, 4910–B W. Rosecrans Ave., Hawthorne, CA 90250: Free information ❖ Caps, hats, shoes, shirts, skirts, slacks, socks, sweaters, and visors. 800–421–4474.

MacGregor Golf Clubs, 1601 S. Slappey Blvd., Albany, GA 31708: Free information ❖ Caps, hats, shoes, gloves, shirts, skirts, slacks, socks, sweaters, and visors. 800–841–4358; 912–888–0001 (in GA).

Marcia Originals, 18324–3 Oxnard St., Tarzana, CA 91356: Free information ❖ Jackets, shirts, skirts, slacks, and sweaters. 800–423–5208; 818–881–3588 (in CA).

Ortho-Vent Inc., 11851 30th Ct. North, St. Petersburg, FL 33716: Free catalog ❖ Shoes. 800–678–4601.

Spalding Sports Worldwide, 425 Meadow St., P.O. Box 901, Chicopee, MA 01021: Free information with list of retailers ❖ Caps, hats, gloves, jackets, shirts, skirts, slacks, socks, sweaters, and vests. 800–225–6601.

T-Shirt City, 4501 W. Mitchell Ave., Cincinnati, OH 45232: Free information ❖ Caps, hats, jackets, shirts, sweaters, socks, and visors. 800–543–7230.

Tuttle Golf Collection, P.O. Box 888, Wallingford, CT 06492: Free catalog ❖ Sportswear for men and women. 800–882–7511.

Equipment Manufacturers

Accuform Golf Clubs, 6380 Viscount Rd., Mississaugua, Toronto, Ontario, Canada L4B 1H3: Free information. 800–668–7873.

Tommy Armour Golf Company, 8350 N. Lehigh Ave., Morton Grove, IL 60053: Free information. 800–723–4653.

Bridgestone Golf Clubs, 15320 Industrial Park Blvd. NE, Covington, GA 30209: Free information. 800–358–6310; 404–787–7400 (in GA).

Browning Golf Clubs, 2346 W. 1000 South, Salt Lake City, UT 84104: Free information. 800–666–6033.

Callaway Golf Clubs, 2285 Rutherford Rd., Carlsbad, CA 92008: Free information. 800–228–2767; 619–931–1771 (in CA).

Carbite Golf Company, 3675 Ruffin Rd., Ste. 315, San Diego, CA 92123: Free information. 800–272–4325.

Cobra Golf Clubs, 1812 Ashton Ave., Carlsbad, CA 92008: Free information. 800–223–3537.

Ray Cook Golf Company, 2233 Faraday Ave., Carlsbad, CA 92008: Free information. 800–531–7252.

Cubic Balance Golf Technology, 30231 Tomas Rd., Santa Margarita, CA 92668: Free information. 800–727–7775.

Daiwa Corporation, 7421 Chapman Ave., Garden Grove, CA 92641: Catalog $1. 503–222–9033.

Dunlop Stazenger Corporation, Box 3070, Greenville, SC 29602: Free information. 800–845–8794; 803–271–9767 (in SC).

Dynacraft Gold Products Inc., 71 Maholm St., Newark, OH 43055: Free information. 800–425–2968.

Founders Club, 1780 La Costa Meadows Dr., San Marcos, CA 92069: Free information. 800–654–9295.

Goldentouch Golf Inc., 1116 E. Valencia Dr., Fullerton, CA 92631: Free information. 800–423–2220.

GolfGear International, 16782 Burke Ln., Huntington Beach, CA 92647: Free information. 800–955–6440; 714–375–0545 (in CA).

Head Golf, 1200 W. Berry Rd., Fort Worth, TX 76110: Free information. 800–432–3430; 817–924–6161 (in TX).

Hillerich & Bradsby Company Inc., P.O. Box 35700, Louisville, KY 40232. Free information. 502–585–5226.

Hurricane Sports Inc., 1130 Commerce Blvd. North, Sarasota, FL 34243: Free information. 800–749–8848.

Lynx Golf Clubs, 16017 E. Valley Blvd., City of Industry, CA 91749: Free information. 800–233–5969; 818–961–0222 (in CA).

MacGregor Golf Clubs, 1601 S. Slappey Blvd., Albany, GA 31708: Free information. 800–841–4358; 912–888–0001 (in GA).

Maxfli Golf Division, 728 N. Pleasantburg Dr., Greenville, SC 29602: Free information. 803–241–2200.

Mitsushiba Golf Clubs, 210 W. Baywood Ave., Orange, CA 92665: Free information. 800–722–4061.

Mizuno Corporation, 5125 Peachtree Industrial Blvd., Norcross, GA 30092: Free information. 800–333–7888.

Northwestern Golf Clubs, 4701 N. Ravenswood, Chicago, IL 60640: Free catalog. 312–275–0500.

Pal Joey Golf Inc., 99 S. Pine St., Newark, OH 43055: Free information. 614–344–6985.

Palm Springs Golf, 74824 Lennon Pl., Palm Desert, CA 92255: Free information. 619–341–3220.

Pinseeker Golf Clubs, 3502 S. Susan St., Santa Ana, CA 92704: Free information. 714–979–4500.

Joe Powell Golf Inc., 1781 Barber Rd., Sarasota, FL 34240: Free information. 800–237–4660.

Ram Golf Clubs, 2020 Indian Boundary Dr., Melrose Park, IL 60160: Free information. 800–833–4653.

Riley Golf, 875 W. Market St., Salinas, CA 93901: Free information. 408–373–8855.

Ryobi-Toski Golf Clubs, 160 Essex St., Box 576, Newark, OH 43055: Free information. 800–848–2075.

Sasse Golf Inc., 2101 Sandhills Blvd., Southern Pines, NC 28387: Free information. 800–334–3451; 910–692–2205 (in NC).

Spalding Sports Worldwide, 425 Meadow St., Chicopee, MA 01021: Free information with list of retailers. 800–225–6601.

Taylor Made Golf Clubs, 2271 Cosmos Ct., Carlsbad, CA 92009: Free information. 619–931–1991.

Titleist Golf Clubs, 333 Bridge St., Fairhaven, MA 02719: Free information. 800–225–8500.

Wood Wand Putters, 2101 Sandhills Blvd., Southern Pines, NC 28387: Free information. 800–334–3451; 910–692–2205 (in NC).

Yamaha Sporting Goods Division, 6600 Orangethorpe Ave., Buena Park, CA 90620: Free information. 800–541–6514; 714–522–9011 (in CA).

Yonex Corporation, 350 Challenger St., Torrance, CA 90503: Free information. 800–449–6639.

Zett Sports Marketing International, P.O. Box 25847, Greenville, SC 29616: Free information. 803–233–7933.

Equipment Retailers

All Star Pro Golf Company Inc., 120 9th St. SW, Clarion, IA 50525: Free information ❖ Grips, head covers, clubs, bags, and bag covers. 800–247–4830; 515–532–2864 (in IA).

Austad's, 4500 E. 10th St., P.O. Box 5428, Sioux Falls, SD 57196: Free catalog ❖ Golfing, other sports equipment, and clothing. 800–444–1234.

Custom Golf Clubs Inc., 11000 N. Interstate Hwy. 35, Austin, TX 78753: Free catalog ❖ Repair supplies, clothing, gloves, bags, and other equipment. 800–456–3344; 512–837–4810 (in TX).

Dorson Sports Inc., 1 Roebling Ct., Ronkonkona, NY 51779: Free information ❖ Bags and bag covers, grips, head covers, tubes, and other equipment. 800–645–7215; 516–585–5440 (in NY).

Duffer's Golf Depot, 1415 N. Federal Hwy., Fort Lauderdale, FL 33304: Free information ❖ Golf clubs and other equipment. 305–568–2489.

Essex Manufacturing, 330 5th Ave., New York, NY 10001: Free information ❖ Golf umbrellas. 800–648–6010; 212–239–0080 (in NY).

Foxbat Golf Equipment Outlet, 15105 Surveyor, Addison, TX 75244: Free information with long SASE ❖ Discontinued and closeout golf equipment. 800–933–2775; 214–239–5200 (in TX).

Golf Day, 135 American Legion Hwy., Revere, MA 02151: Free catalog ❖ Bags and bag covers, clubs, shoes, gloves, clothing, grips, head covers, tubes, and other equipment. 800–669–8600.

Golf Haus, 700 N. Pennsylvania, Lansing, MI 48906: Free catalog ❖ Clubs, bags, clothing, umbrellas, and scorekeepers. 517–482–8842.

Golfsmith, 11000 N. Interstate Hwy. 35, Austin, TX 78753: Free catalog ❖ Golf club-making supplies. 800–925–7709.

The Golfworks, P.O. Box 3008, Newark, OH 43055: Free catalog ❖ Supplies for customizing and assembling golf clubs, how-to books, and video and audio tapes. 800–848–8358.

Harris International Inc., 9999 NE Glisan St., Portland, OR 97220: Free information ❖ Head covers, other equipment, and clubs, bags, and bag covers. 800–547–2880; 503–256–2302 (in OR).

Holabird Sports Discounters, 9008 Yellow Brick Rd., Rossville Industrial Park, Baltimore, MD 21237: Free catalog ❖ Equipment and clothing for golf, basketball, tennis, running and jogging, racquetball, and other sports. 410–687–6400.

Jayfro Corporation, Unified Sports Inc., 976 Hartford Tnpk., P.O. Box 400, Waterford, CT 06385: Free catalog ❖ Outdoor practice cages, chipping and driving mats, and target baffles. 203–447–3001.

Kangaroo Motorcaddies, 108 Mill Spring Rd., Columbus, NC 28722: Free information ❖ Motorized caddies for golf bags. 800–882–9492 (Mountain/ Pacific);

800–438–3011 (Eastern/Central); 704–894–8241 (in NC).

Larry's Golf Discount Center, 21 W. 35th St., New York, NY 10001: Free information ❖ Golf equipment. 212–563–6895.

Las Vegas Discount Golf & Tennis, 5325 S. Valley View Blvd., Ste. 10, Las Vegas, NV 89118: Free catalog ❖ Equipment, clothing, and shoes for golf, tennis, racquetball, walking and jogging, and other sports. 702–798–7777.

Al Liebers World of Golf, 146 E. 47th St., New York, NY 10017: Free catalog ❖ Golf equipment. 212–242–2895.

Ralph Maltby Enterprises Inc., P.O. Box 3008, Newark, OH 43055: Free catalog ❖ Golf supplies for repair shops, club makers, manufacturers, and do-it-yourselfers. 800–848–8358; 800–762–1831 (in OH).

Masters Golf, 12 Main St., East Islip, NY 11730: Free catalog ❖ Golf clubs, other equipment, and shoes. 800–825–9025.

Richard Metz Golf Studio Inc., 425 Madison Ave., 3rd Floor, New York, NY 10017: Free information ❖ Golf equipment, antique and collectible clubs, video tapes, and books. 212–759–6940.

Mizuno Corporation, 5125 Peachtree Industrial Blvd., Norcross, GA 30092: Free information ❖ Clubs and lightweight, waterproof full-grain leather golf shoes. 800–333–7888.

New York Golf Center, 131 W. 35th St., New York, NY 10001: Free information ❖ Golf equipment. 212–564–2255.

Pennsylvania Sporting Goods, 1360 Industrial Hwy., P.O. Box 451, Southampton, PA 18966: Free information ❖ Golf balls, ball retrievers, ball washers, bags, bag covers, grips, head covers, tubes, and other equipment. 800–535–1122.

Performance Golf Company, 10571 NW 53rd St., Sunrise, FL 33351: Free catalog ❖ Golf equipment. 305–742–8528.

Prima, 5380 S. Valley View Blvd., Las Vegas, NV 89118: Free information ❖ Women's golf clubs. 800–932–1622; 702–736–8801 (in NV).

Pro Shop World of Golf, 8130 N. Lincoln Ave., Skokie, IL 60077: Free catalog ❖ Golf equipment and shoes. 800–323–4047; 708–675–5286 (in IL).

Professional Golf & Tennis Suppliers, 7825 Hollywood Blvd., Pembroke Pines, FL

33024: Free catalog with long SASE ❖ Golf, tennis, and racquetball equipment. 305–981–7283.

Sam's World of Golf, 7547 Mentor Ave., Mentor, OH 44060: Catalog $2 ❖ Golf equipment. 216–946–3392.

SGD Company Inc., P.O. Box 8410, Akron, OH 44320: Free information ❖ Golf balls, ball retrievers, ball washers, and golf course equipment. 216–239–2828.

Taylor Made Golf Clubs, 2271 Cosmos Ct., Carlsbad, CA 92009: Free information ❖ Leather and all-weather gloves, ultra-lightweight bags, and golf clubs. 619–931–1991.

Telepro Golf Shops, 17642 Armstrong Ave., Irvine, CA 92714: Free information ❖ Golf clubs, shoes, carts, and other equipment. 800–333–9903.

UT Golf, 2346 W. 1500 South, Salt Lake City, UT 84104: Free information ❖ Golf club components. 800–666–6033.

Voit Sports, 1451 Pittstand-Victor Rd., 100 Willowbrook Office Park, Fairport, NY 14450: Free information ❖ Bags, bag covers, grips, shafts, head covers, tubes, and golf course equipment. 800–444–VOIT.

Wa-Mac Inc., Highskore Products Inc., P.O. Box 128, Carlstadt, NJ 07410: Free information ❖ Golf balls and ball washers, and golf course equipment. 800–447–5673; 201–438–7200 (in NJ).

Edwin Watts Golf Shops, P.O. Drawer 1806, Fort Walton Beach, FL 32549: Free catalog ❖ Golf clubs, carts, bags, and other equipment. 800–874–0146.

Wittek Golf Supply Company Inc., 3650 N. Avondale, Chicago, IL 60618: Free information ❖ Golf course equipment, grips, head covers, tubes, and clubs, bags, and bag covers. 312–463–2636.

World of Golf, 147 E. 47th St., New York, NY 10017: Free catalog ❖ Equipment for men and women. 212–755–9398.

World of Golf Equipment, 8130 N. Lincoln Ave., Skokie, IL 60077: Free information ❖ Equipment for men, women, and juniors. 800–323–4047.

Left-handed Equipment

Bob Charles, 1972 Williston Rd., South Burlington, VT 05403: Free price list ❖ Golf equipment for lefties. 800–533–8437.

Lefties Only, 1972 Williston Rd., South Burlington, VT 05403: Free price list ❖ Equipment for left-handed persons. 800–533–8437.

Somerton Springs Golf, 53 Bustleton Pike, Feasterville, PA 19047: Free brochure ❖ Left-handed golf clubs, personalized balls, umbrellas, tees, travel covers, putters, jackets, golf bags, and head covers. 800–220–GOLF; 215–355–7276 (in PA).

GREETING CARDS

Associated Photo Company, Box 817, Florence, KY 41022: Free information ❖ Imprinted photo Christmas cards. 606–282–0011.

Anita Beck Collection, 555 W. 78th St., Ste. P, Edina, MN 55439: Free catalog ❖ Seasonal and special occasion greeting cards. 800–328–3894.

Car Collectables, 32 White Birch Rd., Madison, CT 06443: Free brochure ❖ Christmas cards, note cards, and gifts with an automotive theme. 203–245–2242.

Carpenter & Company, 1203 Columbus Cir., Janesville, WI 53545: Catalog $1 ❖ Victorian-style greeting cards. 608–754–2635.

Chesapeake Press Inc., P.O. Box 215, Locust Hill, VA 23092: Free catalog ❖ Automotive Christmas cards. 804–758–4663.

Current Inc., Express Processing Center, Colorado Springs, CO 80941: Free catalog ❖ Greeting cards, stationery, gift wrapping, decorations, toys, calendars, and other gifts. 800–848–2848.

Dalton Advertising, 1014 Main St., P.O. Box 699, Fort Benton, MT 59442: Free catalog ❖ Hand-lettered personalized cartoon greeting cards and notepads. 406–622–3316.

Designs by Denise, P.O. Box 1060, Drexel Hill, PA 19026: Brochure $1 ❖ Birth announcements, thank you notes, invitations, and other greeting cards for twins and multiples. 610–259–1347.

The Drawing Board, P.O. Box 660429, Dallas, TX 75266: Free catalog ❖ Personalized greeting and calendar cards. 800–443–8847.

Kristin Elliott Inc., 6 Opportunity Way, Newburyport, MA 01950: Free catalog ❖ Boxed notes, gift enclosures, Christmas and other greeting cards, desk memos, memo pads, postcards, correspondence cards, and gift wrap. 800–922–1899; 508–465–1899 (in MA).

Enfield Stationers, 215 Moody Rd., Enfield, CT 06082: Free catalog ❖ Greeting cards, calendars, and gifts. 203–763–3980.

Faded Rose, P.O. Box 19575, Portland, OR 97219: Brochure $1 ❖ Recycled paper greeting cards. 503–245–2694.

Handshake Greeting Cards, P.O. Box 9027, Columbus, GA 31908: Free catalog ❖ Personalized greeting cards. 800–634–2134.

Heirloom Editions, Box 520-B, Rt. 4, Carthage, MO 64836: Catalog $4 ❖ Lithographs, greeting cards, stickers, miniatures, stationery, framed prints, and other turn-of-the-century art and paper collectibles. 800–725–0725.

House-Mouse Designs, P.O. Box 48, Williston, VT 05495: Free catalog ❖ Christmas cards, note and recipe cards, magnets, and stickers. 800–242–6423.

Miles Kimball Company, Christmas Cards, 41 W. 8th Ave., Oshkosh, WI 54906: Free catalog ❖ Christmas cards with optional personalization. 800–546–2255.

Nasco, 901 Janesville Ave., Fort Atkinson, WI 53538: Free catalog ❖ Calligraphy supplies and greeting cards. 800–558–9595.

National Wildlife Federation,$INational Wildlife Federation 1400 16th St. NW, Washington, DC 20036: Free catalog ❖ Holiday cards and gifts. 800–432–6564.

New England Card Company, Rt. 41, Box 228, West Ossipee, NH 03890: Free brochure ❖ Greeting cards with scenes of New England. 800–762–5562; 603–539–5200 (in NH).

Reindeer House, 3409 W. 44th St., Minneapolis, MN 55410: Free catalog ❖ Greeting cards and stationery. 800–328–3894.

Renaissance Greeting Cards, P.O. Box 845, Springvale, ME 04038: Catalog $1 ❖ Greeting cards. 800–688–9998; 207–324–4153 (in ME).

Sally Distributors Inc., 4100 Quebec Ave. North, Minneapolis, MN 55427: Free catalog ❖ Balloons, toys, greeting cards, gifts, novelties, and carnival supplies. 612–533–7100.

Trumble Greetings, 6055 Longbow Dr., Boulder, CO 80301: Catalog $1 ❖ Greeting cards that depict America's heritage with country and wildlife scenes. 800–525–0656; 303–530–7768 (in CO).

Unicef, P.O. Box 182233, Chattanooga, TN 37422: Free catalog ❖ Greeting and note

cards, toys, limited edition plates, gifts, and postcards. 800–553–1200.

Victorian Papers, P.O. Box 411332, Kansas City, MO 61141: Catalog $2 ❖ Greeting and note cards for birthdays, holidays, graduation, and other occasions. 816–471–7808.

GUM BALL MACHINES

Norm & Mary Johnson, County Home Rd., Bowling Green, OH 43402: Free information with long SASE ❖ Slot machines, old arcade games, peanut and gumball machines, mechanical and still banks, and other coin-operated machines. 419–352–3041.

KAPS Vending, 593 Lavina Ct., Helmet, CA 92544: Free price list with long SASE ❖ Antique gumball machines, globes, parts, decals, gumballs, candy, and toys. 909–658–4620.

GUNS & AMMUNITION
Air Guns & Supplies

Action Arms Ltd., P.O. Box 9573, Philadelphia, PA 19124: Free brochure ❖ Air guns.

Air Gun Express, RR 2, Box 290, Montezuma, IA 50171: Free information ❖ Airguns. 515–623–3098.

Armsport Inc., 3950 NW 49th St., Miami, FL 33142: Free information ❖ Air rifles and pistols, scopes, pellets and bb ammunition, and targets. 305–635–7850.

Beeman Precision Arms Inc., 3440 Airway Dr., Santa Rosa, CA 95403: Catalog $2 ❖ Air rifles and pistols, scopes, pellets and bb ammunition, and targets. 707–578–7900.

Benjamin Air Rifle Company, 2600 Chicory Rd., Racine, WI 53403: Free catalog ❖ Single shot and repeater air rifles, pistols, scopes, pellets and bb ammunition, and targets. 414–554–7900.

Century International Arms, 48 Lower Newton St., St. Albans, VT 05478: Free information ❖ Air rifles and pistols. 802–527–1252.

Compasseco Inc., 151 Atkinson Hill, Bardstown, KY 40004: Free information ❖ Air rifles and ammunition. 502–349–0181.

Crosman Air Guns, Rt. 5, East Bloomfield, NY 14443: Free information ❖ Air rifles and pistols, scopes, pellets and bb ammunition, and targets. 716–657–6161.

Daisy Manufacturing Company Inc., P.O. Box 220, Rogers, AR 72757: Free information ❖ Air rifles and pistols, pellets

and bb ammunition, scopes, and targets. 501–636–1200.

Dixie Gun Works Inc., P.O. Box 130, Union City, TN 38261: Catalog $4 ❖ Air rifles and pistols. 800–238–6785.

Eastern Sports Supply Ltd., P.O. Box 67, Tremont, PA 17981: Free information ❖ Air rifles and pistols, scopes, pellets and bb ammunition, and targets. 717–695–3113.

Mandall Shooting Supplies, 3616 N. Scottsdale Rd., Scottsdale, AZ 85251: Free information ❖ Air guns, scopes, other equipment, and ammunition. 602–945–2553.

Ammunition & Ammunition-Loading Equipment

ACTIV Industries Inc., 1000 Zigor Rd., P.O. Box 339, Kearneysville, WV 25430: Free brochure ❖ Shotgun shells in a reloadable, all-plastic hull. 304–725–0451.

Alpine Range Supply, 5482 Shelby, Fort Worth, TX 76140: Free information ❖ Reloading equipment. 817–572–1242.

Badger Shooter's Supply Inc., P.O. Box 397, Owen, WI 54460: Free catalog ❖ Sporting firearms and ammunition. 800–424–9069.

Ballistic Products Inc., 20015 75th Ave. North, Corcoran, MN 55340: Catalog $1 ❖ Ammunition supplies. 612–494–9237.

Blount Inc., Sporting Equipment Division, P.O. Box 856, Lewiston, ID 83501: Free information ❖ Big game hunting bullets and ammunition for rifles and handguns. 800–627–3640.

Blue Point Manufacturing, 210 N. Main St., Massena, NY 13662: Free information ❖ Hunting bullets. 613–674–2550.

Broward Shooter's Exchange, 250 S. 60th Ave., Hollywood, FL 33023: Catalog $8 ❖ Shooting, reloading, and muzzleloading supplies. 800–554–9002.

Buffalo Bullet Company, 12637 Los Nietos Rd., Unit A, Santa Fe Springs, CA 90670: Free brochure ❖ Bullets for muzzleloaders and other ammunition. 310–944–0322.

Century International Arms, 48 Lower Newton St., St. Albans, VT 05478: Free information ❖ Ammunition supplies. 802–527–1252.

Colorado Shooter's Supply, P.O. Box 132, Fruita, CO 81521: Free information ❖ Bullet molds. 303–858–9191.

Colorado Sutlers Arsenal, P.O. Box 991, Granby, CO 80446: Free information ❖ Ammunition supplies. 303–887–2813.

Cook Bullets, 1846 Rosemeade Pkwy., Carrollton, TX 75007: Free information ❖ Ammunition supplies. 214–394–8725.

Corbin Manufacturing & Supply Inc., P.O. Box 2659, White City, OR 97503: Information $1 ❖ Ammunition supplies. 503–826–5211.

Dillon Precision Products Inc., 7442 E. Butherus Dr., Scottsdale, AZ 85260: Free catalog ❖ Reloading equipment. 800–223–4570; 602–948–8009 (in AZ).

Eastern Sports Supply Ltd., P.O. Box 67, Tremont, PA 17981: Free information ❖ Ammunition supplies. 717–695–3113.

Federal Cartridge Company, 900 Ehlen Dr., Anoka, MN 55303: Free information ❖ Ammunition supplies. 612–422–2840.

Gander Mountain Inc., P.O. Box 248, Gander Mountain, Wilmot, WI 53192: Free catalog ❖ Reloading supplies. 414–862–2331.

Robert W. Hart & Son Inc., 401 Montgomery St., Nescopeck, PA 18635: Free information ❖ Ammunition supplies. 717–752–3655.

Hogdon Powder Company Inc., P.O. Box 2932, Shawnee Mission, KS 66201: Free information ❖ Powder for muzzleloaders and propellants for rifles, pistols, and shotgun ammunition. 913–362–9455.

Hornady Manufacturing Company, P.O. Box 1848, Grand Island, NE 68802: Catalog $2 ❖ Ammunition supplies. 308–382–1390.

K & T Company, 1027 Skyview Dr., West Carrollton, OH 45449: Free information ❖ Shell reloading equipment and supplies. 513–859–8414.

Lawrence Leather Company, P.O. Box 1479, Lillington, NC 27546: Free information ❖ Ammunition supplies. 910–893–2071.

Lee Precision Inc., 4275 Hwy. U, Hartford, CT 53027: Catalog $1 ❖ Reloading equipment and supplies.

Mayville Engineering Company Inc., 715 South St., Mayville, WI 53050: Free brochure ❖ Shotgun shell reloading equipment. 414–387–4500.

Michaels of Oregon Company, P.O. Box 13010, Portland, OR 97213: Free information ❖ Ammunition supplies. 503–255–6890.

Muzzleload Magnum Products, RR 6, Box 384, Harrison, AR 72601: Free list ❖ Bullets for blackpowder rifles. 501–741–5019.

Nosler Bullets Inc., P.O. Box 671, Bend, OR 97709: Free catalog ❖ Hunting bullets. 503–382–3921.

Pennsylvania Sporting Goods, 1360 Industrial Hwy., P.O. Box 451, Southampton, PA 18966: Free information ❖ Ammunition supplies. 800–523–1122.

Ponsness/Warren, P.O. Box 8, S. 763 Hwy. 41, Rathdrum, ID 83858: Free catalog ❖ Reloading equipment and supplies. 208–687–2231.

Remington Arms Company Inc., 1007 Market St., Wilmington, DE 19898: Free information ❖ Ammunition supplies. 302–773–5292.

Widener's Reloading & Shooting Supply Inc., P.O. Box 3009, Johnson City, TN 37602: Free catalog ❖ Reloading supplies. 615–282–6786.

Antique, Muzzleloading & Replica Guns

Antique Arms Company, 1110 Cleveland, Monett, MO 65708: Free information ❖ Antique muzzleloading guns. 417–235–6501.

Antique Gun Parts Inc., 1118 S. Braddock Ave., Pittsburgh, PA 15218: Free information ❖ Antique muzzleloading guns. 412–241–1811.

Armoury Inc., Rt. 202, New Preston, CT 06777: Free information ❖ Blackpowder handguns and rifles, blackpowder, kits, and replica guns. 203–868–0001.

Armsport Inc., 3950 NW 49th St., Miami, FL 33142: Free information ❖ Antique handguns, rifles, and kits. 305–635–7850.

BSI Sporting Goods, P.O. Box 5010, Vienna, WV 26105: Free catalog ❖ Firearm and muzzleloading supplies, optics, clothing, and archery, fishing, and hunting equipment. 304–295–8511.

Buffalo Arms Company, 123 S. 3rd Ave., Sandpoint, ID 83864: Catalog $1 ❖ Black powder cartridge rifles, target barrels and sights, lead and tin, and other supplies.

Douglas R. Carlson, Antique American Firearms, P.O. Box 71035, Des Moines, IA 50325: Catalog (annual subscription) $20 ❖ Antique firearms.

Cash Manufacturing Company Inc., P.O. Box 130, Waunakee, WI 53507: Free catalog ❖ Muzzleloading equipment. 608–849–5664.

Collector's Armoury, 800 Slaters Ln., P.O. Box 59, Alexandria, VA 22313: Free catalog ❖ Replica and antique guns. 800–544–3456.

Connecticut Valley Arms Inc., 5988 Peachtree Corners East, Norcross, GA 30071: Free catalog ❖ Reproductions of Sam Colt's mid-1880 handguns, other blackpowder handguns, rifles, and kits. 800–251–9412.

Daisy Manufacturing Company Inc., P.O. Box 220, Rogers, AR 72757: Free information ❖ Replica guns. 501–636–1200.

Dixie Gun Works Inc., P.O. Box 130, Union City, TN 38261: Catalog $4 ❖ Antique and replica blackpowder handguns and rifles and blackpowder. 800–238–6785.

Eastern Sports Supply Ltd., P.O. Box 67, Tremont, PA 17981: Free information ❖ Blackpowder rifles and handguns and kits. 717–695–3113.

EMF Company, 1900 E. Warner Ave., Santa Ana, CA 92705: Catalog $1 ❖ Replica U.S. Cavalry and U.S. artillery revolvers. 714–261–6611.

Euroarms of America Inc., P.O. Box 3277, Winchester, VA 22601: Catalog $3 ❖ Blackpowder rifles and handguns, replica guns, and kits. 703–662–1863.

N. Flayderman & Company Inc., P.O. Box 2446, Fort Lauderdale, FL 33303: Catalog $10 ❖ Antique guns, swords, knives, and western, nautical, and other military collectibles. 305–761–8855.

The Frontloader, 16325 Merrill, Fontana, CA 92335: Free information with long SASE ❖ Muzzleloading supplies. 714–829–9077.

Golden Age Arms Company, 115 E. High St., Ashley, OH 43003: Catalog $4 ❖ Muzzleloading guns, parts, and books. 614–747–2488.

J.P. Gubstock Inc., 4508 San Miguel Ave., North Las Vegas, NV 89030: Catalog $2 ❖ Muzzleloading rifles. 702–645–0718.

Kahnke Gunworks, 206 W. 11th St., Redwood Falls, MN 56283: Free information ❖ Muzzleloading handguns. 507–637–2901.

Hansen Cartridge Company, 244 Old Post Rd., Southport, CT 06490: Free information ❖ Replica and antique guns. 203–259–6222.

House of Muskets Inc., P.O. Box 4640, Pagosa Springs, CO 81157: Free information ❖ Replica and antique guns. 303–731–2295.

Log Cabin Shop, Box 275, Lodi, OH 44254: Catalog $4 ❖ Antique and replica guns. 216–948–1082.

Lyman Products Corporation, Rt. 147, P.O. Box 453, Middlefield, CT 06455: Catalog $2 ❖ Blackpowder rifles and handguns and kits. 800–22–LYMAN.

Miltech, P.O. Box 322, Los Altos, CA 94022: Free brochure ❖ Restored vintage military firearms. 415–948–3500.

Mountain State Muzzleloading Supplies Inc., Rt. 2, Box 154–1, Williamstown, WV 26187: Catalog $4 ❖ Blackpowder rifles, handguns, and kits. 304–375–7842.

Mowrey Gun Works, P.O. Box 246, Waldron, IN 46182: Catalog $2 ❖ Handmade rifles, shotguns, and muzzleloaders. 317–525–6181.

Muzzle Loaders Etc. Inc., 9901 Lyndale Ave. South, Bloomington, MN 55420: Free information ❖ Blackpowder and muzzleloading guns. 612–884–1161.

Navy Arms Company, 689 Bergen Blvd., Ridgefield, NJ 07657: Catalog $2 ❖ Blackpowder rifles and handguns, replica guns, kits, and blackpowder. 201–945–2500.

New Orleans Arms Company, 5001 Treasure St., New Orleans, LA 70186: Free information ❖ Antique guns. 504–944–3371.

October Country, P.O. Box 969, Hayden Lake, ID 83835: Catalog $3 (refundable) ❖ Muzzleloading equipment. 208–772–2068.

S & S Firearms, 74–11 Myrtle Ave., Glendale, NY 11385: Free information ❖ Antique guns. 212–497–1100.

Shiloh Rifle Manufacturing Company Inc., 201 Centennial Dr., Big Timber, MT 59011: Free information ❖ Blackpowder and muzzleloading guns. 406–932–4454.

Simmons Gun Specialties Inc., 20241 W. 207th, Spring Hill, KS 66083: Free information ❖ Blackpowder rifles and handguns, kits, and blackpowder. 800–444–0220.

South Bend Replicas Inc., 61650 Oak Rd., South Bend, IN 46614: Catalog $7 ❖ Replica and antique guns. 219–289–4500.

Springfield Sporter Inc., RD 1, Penn Ruth, PA 15765: Catalog $2 ❖ Replica and antique guns. 412–254–9173.

Taylor's & Company Inc., 299 Broad Ave., Winchester, VA 22602: Catalog $1 ❖ Guns from the Revolutionary War through the Civil War. 703–722–2017.

Tennessee Valley Manufacturing, P.O. Box 1175, Corinth, MS 38834: Catalog $3 ❖ Custom rifles. 601–286–5014.

Thompson/Center Arms Company, P.O. Box 5002, Rochester, NH 03867: Free catalog ❖ Muzzleloading rifles, handguns, kits, and blackpowder. 603–332–2394.

Traditions Inc., 500 Main St., P.O. Box 235, Deep River, CT 06417: Free information ❖ Blackpowder rifles and handguns, kits, and replica guns. 203–526–9555.

Warren Muzzleloading Company Inc., Hwy. 21, P.O. Box 100, Ozone, AR 72854: Catalog $2 ❖ Pistol and rifle bullets and muzzleloading supplies. 800–874–3810.

The Winchester Sutler Inc., 270 Shadow Brook Ln., Winchester, VA 22603: Catalog $4 ❖ Reproduction Civil War muskets, carbines, and other reproductions. 703–888–3595.

Racks, Cases & Holsters

Bob Allen Sportswear, 214 SW Jackson, Des Moines, IA 50315: Free information ❖ Carrying cases, holsters, and racks. 515–283–2191.

American Import Company, 1453 Mission St., San Francisco, CA 94103: Free information ❖ Gun racks, soft cases, and slings. 415–863–1506.

American Sales & Manufacturing, Box 677, Laredo, TX 78042: Catalog $3 ❖ Handcrafted gunbelts and holsters. 512–723–6893.

American Security Products Company, 11925 Pacific Ave., Fontana, CA 92337: Free information ❖ Gun and other safes for homes and offices. 800–421–6142.

Americase, Box 271, Waxahachie, TX 75165: Free information ❖ Carrying cases. 800–880–3629.

API Outdoors Inc., P.O. Box 1432, Tallulah, LA 71282: Free information ❖ Gun racks. 800–228–4846

Beeman Precision Arms Inc., 3440 Airway Dr., Santa Rosa, CA 95403: Catalog $2 ❖ Holsters, slings, and soft cases. 707–578–7900.

Bowhunter Supply Inc., 1158 46th St., P.O. Box 5010, Vienna, WV 26105: Free

information ❖ Hard and soft cases and stands for gun storage. 800–289–2211; 304–295–8511 (in WV).

Brauer Brothers Manufacturing Company, 2020 Delmar Blvd., St. Louis, MO 63112: Free information ❖ Soft cases, cabinets, slings, and holsters. 314–231–2864.

Browning Company, Dept. C006, One Browning Pl., Morgan, UT 84050: Catalog $2 ❖ Hard and soft cases, holsters, and slings. 800–333–3288.

Chipmunk Manufacturing Company, Oregon Arms Inc., 164 Schulz Rd., P.O. Box 1104, Central Point, OR 97502: Free information ❖ Gun cases. 503–664–5588.

DeSantis Holster & Leather Company, P.O. Box 2039, New Hyde Park, NY 11040: Free information ❖ Gun holsters. 516–354–8000.

Eastern Sports Supply Ltd., P.O. Box 67, Tremont, PA 17981: Free information ❖ Hard and soft cases, holsters, racks, slings, and stands. 717–695–3113.

A.G. English Inc., 708 S. 12th St., Broken Arrow, OK 74012: Free information ❖ Gun safes. 800–222–7233.

Feline Archery Inc., 229 Rt. 30 West, Ligonier, PA 15658: Free information ❖ Hard and soft cases, holsters, racks, slings, and stands. 412–238–3673.

Fort Knox Security Products, 1051 N. Industrial Park Rd., Orem, UT 84057: Free information ❖ Burglar-proof gun safes. 800–821–5216.

Frontier Safe Company, 1317 Chute St., Fort Wayne, IN 46803: Free information ❖ Gun safes. 219–422–4801.

G-S Sales Company, P.O. Box 514, Kent, OH 44240: Free information ❖ Gun safes. 800–544–1102; 216–678–3023 (in OH).

Don Hume Leathergoods, Box 351, Miami, OK 74354: Catalog $1 ❖ Holsters. 800–331–2686; 918–542–6604 (in OK).

Liberty Safe, 316 W. 700 South, Provo, UT 84601: Free brochure ❖ Gun safes. 800–247–5625.

National Security Safe Company, P.O. Box 39, American Fork, UT 84003: Free brochure ❖ Gun safes with double steel walls. 800–544–3829.

Penguin Industries Inc., Airport Industrial Mall, Coatesville, PA 19320: Free information ❖ Gun cases and cabinets. 215–384–6000.

Rhino Gun Cases Inc., 4960 SW 52nd St., Ste. 408, Davie, FL 33314: Free information ❖ Aluminum gun cases and ported chokes.

Safariland Leather Products, 3120 E. Mission Blvd., P.O. Box 51478, Ontario, CA 91761: Free information ❖ Gun holsters. 800–347–1200.

Shooting Systems, 1075 Headquarters Park, Fenton, MO 63026: Free information ❖ Canvas carrying and gun storage cases, holsters, and slings. 800–325–3049; 314–343–3575 (in MO).

Southern Security Safes, 1700 Oak Hills Dr., Kingston, TN 37763: Free information ❖ Gun safes with protective bolt-locking systems. 800–251–9992.

Sun Welding Safe Company, 290 Easy St., Ste. 3, Simi Valley, CA 93065: Free brochure ❖ Gun safes. 800–776–1908.

Tread Corporation, 1764 Granby St., Roanoke, VA 24032: Free information ❖ Security gun chests. 703–982–6881.

Whiteside Safe Sales Company, P.O. Box 11283, Prescott, AZ 86304: Free information ❖ Gun safes. 800–433–7024.

Wild Bills Leather, P.O. Box 13037, Burton, WA 98013: Brochure $2 ❖ Authentic reproduction holsters, gunbelts, and accessories. 206–463–5738.

Wilson Case Company, P.O. Box 1106, Hastings, NE 68902: Free information ❖ Gun cases. 800–322–5493.

Scopes, Mounts & Sights

Aimpoint, 580 Herndon Pkwy., Herndon, VA 22070: Free brochure ❖ Electronic red-dot sight with an optional 3x scope attachment. 703–471–6828.

American Import Company, 1453 Mission St., San Francisco, CA 94103: Free information ❖ Scopes, mounts, and storage racks. 415–863–1506.

B-Square Company, P.O. Box 11281, Fort Worth, TX 76110: Free catalog ❖ Scope mounts for handguns, rifles, and shotguns. 800–433–2909.

Bausch & Lomb, 9200 Cody, Overland Park, KS 66214: Free information ❖ Spotting scopes and mounts. 800–423–3537.

Maynard P. Buehler, 17 Orinda Way, Orinda, CA 94563: Free catalog ❖ Mounting

bases and rings for rifle and handgun scopes. 510–254–3201.

Burris Company Inc., P.O. Box 1747, Greeley, CO 80632: Free catalog ❖ Mounts and spotting scopes. 303–356–1670.

Conetrol Scope Mounts, Hwy. 123 South, Sequin, TX 78155: Free information ❖ Scope mounting systems. 800–CONETROL.

Europtik Ltd., P.O. Box 319, Dunmore, PA 18509: Free information ❖ Binoculars and riflescopes. 717–347–6049.

Inventive Technology, 554 S. 100 West, American Fork, UT 84003: Free information ❖ Sighting systems. 801–756–6017.

Keng's Firearms Specialty Inc., 875 Wharton Dr., Atlanta, GA 30336: Free information ❖ Scope mounts. 800–848–4671.

Kowa Optimed Inc., 20001 S. Vermont Ave., Torrance, CA 90502: Free information ❖ Spotting scopes. 213–327–1913.

Leupold & Stevens Inc., P.O. Box 688, Beaverton, OR 97075: Free catalog ❖ Low-light rifle scope with variable power settings. 503–526–5196.

Millett Industries, 16131 Gothard St., Huntington Beach, CA 92647: Catalog $1 ❖ Gun sights. 714–842–5575.

Redfield Company, 5800 E. Jewell Ave., Denver, CO 80224: Catalog $2 ❖ Rifle scopes. 303–757–6411.

Simmons Outdoor Company, 201 Plantation Oak Dr., Thomasville, GA 31792: Catalog $2 ❖ Rifle scopes. 904–878–5100.

Tasco Sales Inc., P.O. Box 520080, Miami, FL 33152: Free information ❖ Gun scopes. 305–591–3670.

Warne Manufacturing Company, 9039 SE Jannsen Rd., Clackamas, OR 97015: Free information ❖ Easy-to-install, detachable rifle scope mounts. 503–657–5590.

Williams Gun Sight Company, 7389 Lapeer Rd., P.O. Box 329, Davison, MI 48423: Free information ❖ Scope mounts for rifles, shotguns, and black powder guns. 313–653–2131.

Sportshooting Rifles & Handguns

American Derringer Corporation, 127 N. Lacy Dr., Waco, TX 76705: Free information ❖ Sport shooting automatic pistols, derringers, and revolvers.

Armoury Inc., Rt. 202, New Preston, CT 06777: Free information ❖ Guns for sport shooting. 203–868–0001.

Badger Shooter's Supply Inc., P.O. Box 397, Owen, WI 54460: Free catalog ❖ Sporting firearms and ammunition. 800–424–9069.

Billingsley & Brownell Rifle Metalsmith, Box 25, Dayton, WY 82836: Brochure $2 ❖ Rifle accessories. 307–655–9344.

Brownells Inc., 200 S. Front St., Montezuma, IA 50171: Free catalog ❖ Gunsmithing supplies and tools. 515–623–5401.

Browning Company, Dept. C006, One Browning Pl., Morgan, UT 84050: Catalog $2 ❖ Bolt and lever action guns, semiautomatics and single shot rifles, and over/under, side-by-side, and single barrel shotguns. 800–333–3288.

Century International Arms, 48 Lower Newton St., St. Albans, VT 05478: Free information ❖ Bolt and lever action guns, semiautomatic rifles, and single shot rifles. 802–5277–1252.

Clark Custom Guns Inc., 11462 Keatchie Rd., P.O. Box 530, Keithville, LA 71047: Catalog $1 ❖ Handguns. 318–925–0836.

Claro Walnut Gunstock Company, 1235 Stanley Ave., Chico, CA 95928: Free price list ❖ Blanks for rifles, shotguns, and black powder guns. 916–342–5188.

Davis Industries, 11186 Venturte Dr., Mira Loma, CA 91752: Catalog $2 ❖ Double-barreled derringers.

Douglas Barrels Inc., 5504 Big Tyler Rd., Charleston, WV 25313: Free information ❖ Rifle barrels. 304–776–1341.

Eagle Arms Inc., 131 E. 22nd Ave., P.O. Box 457, Coal Valley, IL 61240: Free information ❖ Parts and complete rifles. 800–336–0184.

Eastern Sports Supply Ltd., P.O. Box 67, Tremont, PA 17981: Free information ❖ Automatic pistols, blank pistols, derringers, shotguns, revolvers, and bolt and lever action, target, semiautomatic, and single shot rifles. 717–695–3113.

EMF Company, 1900 E. Warner Ave., Santa Ana, CA 92705: Catalog $1 ❖ United States and foreign revolvers, rifles, pistols, and shotguns. 714–261–6611.

Feline Archery Inc., 229 Rt. 30 West, Ligonier, PA 15658: Free information ❖

Lever and bolt action, semiautomatic, single shot, and target rifles. 412–238–3673.

Frank's Center Inc., P.O. Box 530, Nevada, MO 64772: Free information with long SASE ❖ Sportshooting guns and backpacking, camping, and rescue/rappelling equipment. 417–667–9190.

Gun Parts Corporation, Williams Ln., West Hurley, NY 12491: Catalog $5.95 ❖ Commercial, military, antique, and foreign gun parts. 914–679–2417.

Half Moon Rifle Shop, 490 Halfmoon Rd., Columbia Falls, MT 59912: Catalog $1 (refundable) ❖ Gunsmithing supplies. 406–892–4409.

Gil Hebard Guns, 125 Public Square, Knoxville, IL 61448: Free catalog ❖ Pistols. 309–289–2700.

Interarms, 10 Prince St., Alexandria, VA 22314: Free information ❖ Bolt and lever action, target, semiautomatic, and single shot rifles. 703–548–1400.

Harry Lawson Company, 3328 N. Richey Blvd., Tucson, AZ 85716: Catalog $1 ❖ Rifles. 602–326–1117.

Liberty Mountain Sports, 9325 SW Barber St., Wilsonville, OR 97070: Free information ❖ Automatic and blank pistols, derringers, revolvers and autoloading, automatic, over/under, semiautomatic, side-by-side, and single barrel shotguns. 503–685–9600.

Marlin Firearms Company, P.O. Box 248, North Haven CT 06473: Catalog $1 ❖ Semi-automatic, single shot, and bolt and lever action rifles. 203–239–5621.

Midway Arms Inc., 5875 W. Van Horn Tavern Rd., Columbia, MO 65203: Free catalog ❖ Handguns, rifles, and ammunition. 800–243–2506.

O.F. Mossberg & Sons Inc., 7 Grasso Ave., P.O. Box 497, North Haven, CT 06473: Free information ❖ Shotguns.

Mowrey Gun Works, P.O. Box 246, Waldron, IN 46182: Catalog $2 ❖ Handmade rifles, shotguns, and muzzleloaders. 317–525–6181.

Navy Arms Company, 689 Bergen Blvd., Ridgefield, NJ 07657: Catalog $2 ❖ Automatic pistols, blank guns, revolvers, and target, bolt and lever action, semiautomatic, and single shot rifles. 201–945–2500.

Precision Sales International, Box 1776, Westfield, MA 01086: Free information ❖ Firearms.

Remington Arms Company Inc., 1007 Market St., Wilmington, DE 19898: Free information ❖ Autoloading, automatic, over/under, and semi-automatic shotguns. 302–773–5292.

Savage, 100 Springdale Rd., Westfield, MA 01085: Free information ❖ Sporting firearms for deer hunting. 413–568–7001.

Sherwood, 14830 Alondra Blvd., La Mirada, CA 90638: Free information ❖ Parts for guns. 800–962–3203.

Simmons Gun Specialties Inc., 20241 W. 207th, Spring Hill, KS 66083: Free information ❖ Automatic pistols, revolvers, derringers, and target, bolt and lever action, semiautomatic, and single shot rifles. 800–444–0220.

Smith & Wesson, Box 2208, Springfield, MA 01102: Free information ❖ Firearms.

Springfield Armory, 420 W. Main St., Geneseo, IL 61254: Catalog $3 ❖ Pistols, handguns, and rifles. 309–944–5631.

Sturm, Ruger & Company Inc., 11 Lacey Pl., Southport, CT 06490: Free catalog ❖ Semiautomatic and single shot, bolt and lever action, and target rifles. 203–259–7843.

Tar-Hunt Rifles Inc., RR 3, Box 572, Bloomsburg, PA 17815: Free information ❖ Left- and right-handed sport shooting slug guns. 717–784–6368.

Ultra Light Arms Inc., P.O. Box 1270, Granville, WV 26534: Free information ❖ Sporting firearms for deer hunting. 304–599–5687.

U.S. Repeating Arms Company, 275 Winchester Ave., New Haven, CT 06511: Free information ❖ Firearms.

Weatherby Inc., 2781 Firestone Blvd., South Gate, CA 90280: Free information ❖ Sporting firearms for deer hunting. 213–569–7186.

Targets & Range Supplies

Beeman Precision Arms Inc., 3440 Airway Dr., Santa Rosa, CA 95403: Catalog $2 ❖ Targets and range equipment. 707–578–7900.

Caswell International Corporation, 1221 Marshall St. NE, Minneapolis, MN 55413: Free information ❖ Range supplies and target carriers. 612–379–2000.

Crosman Air Guns, Rt. 5, East Bloomfield, NY 14443: Free information ❖ Targets and range equipment. 716–657–6161.

Daisy Manufacturing Company Inc., P.O. Box 220, Rogers, AR 72757: Free information ❖ Targets and range equipment. 501–636–1200.

Marksman Products, 5482 Argosy Dr., Huntington Beach, CA 92649: Free information ❖ Targets and range equipment. 714–898–7535.

National Target Company, 47690 Wyaconda Rd., Rockville, MD 20852: Free information ❖ Targets and range equipment. 301–770–7060.

NRA Sales Department, P.O. Box 5000, Kearneysville, WV 25430: Free information ❖ Life-size game targets.

Outers Laboratories Inc., Division Blount Inc., Rt. 2, Onalaska, WI 54650: Free information ❖ Targets and range equipment. 608–781–5800.

Peterson Instant Targets Inc., 147 West St., Middlefield, CT 06801: Free information ❖ Targets. 203–349–3421.

Trap & Clay Target Shooting

Ballistic Products Inc., 20015 75th Ave. North, Corcoran, MN 55340: Catalog $1 ❖ Targets and traps. 612–494–9237.

Beeman Precision Arms Inc., 3440 Airway Dr., Santa Rosa, CA 95403: Catalog $2 ❖ Targets and traps. 707–578–7900.

Briley, 1230 Lumpkin, Houston, TX 77043: Free information ❖ Replacement chokes. 800–331–5718; 713–932–6995 (in TX).

Claymate Inc., 257 Chestnut St., Wrentham, MA 02093: Free information ❖ Voice activated trap release. 508–758–2747.

Eastern Sports Supply Ltd., P.O. Box 67, Tremont, PA 17981: Free information ❖ Launchers, targets, and traps. 717–695–3113.

The Hunters Pointe, Rt. 1, Box 166, Augusta, KS 67010: Free information ❖ Manual and automatic traps for clay targets. 316–778–1122.

Midwest Sports, 9350 East O Ave., Kalamazoo, MI 49001: Free information ❖ Automatic trap machines. 616–665–4736.

Omark Industries, Blount Sporting Equipment Division, 2299 Snake River Ave., Lewiston, ID 83501: Free information ❖ Launchers, traps, and targets. 208–746–2351.

Rhino Gun Cases Inc., 4960 SW 52nd St., Ste. 408, Davie, FL 33314: Free information ❖ Aluminum gun cases and ported chokes.

Simmons Gun Specialties Inc., 20241 W. 207th, Spring Hill, KS 66083: Free information ❖ Traps, launchers, and targets. 800–444–0220.

Trius Inc., P.O. Box 25, Cleves, OH 45002: Free catalog ❖ Portable traps and other range equipment. 513–941–5682.

HAMMOCKS & SWINGS

Adirondack Store & Gallery, 109 Saranac Ave., Lake Placid, NY 12946: Free information ❖ Oak and maple porch swings, lawn furniture, and picnic table sets. 518–523–2646.

Alfresco Porch Swing Company, P.O. Box 1336, Durango, CO 81301: Free brochure ❖ Porch swings, Adirondack chairs, and garden benches. 303–247–9739.

Brushy Mountain Bee Farm, Rt. 1, P.O. Box 135, Moravian Falls, NC 28654: Free catalog ❖ Porch swings, birdhouses and feeders, and beekeeping supplies. 800–BEESWAX.

Country Casual, 17317 Germantown Rd., Germantown, MD 20874: Catalog $3 ❖ Porch swings and classic British-style solid teak garden seats. 301–540–0040.

Gardner's Farm & Wood Products, Box 1193, Eagle Rock, MO 65641: Free information ❖ Country-style rockers, tables, swings, and other furniture. 417–271–3999.

Gazebo & Porchworks, 728 9th Ave. SW, Puyallup, WA 98371: Catalog $2 ❖ Outdoor swings and backyard play structures. 206–848–0502.

Grand ERA Reproductions, P.O. Box 1026, Lapeer, MI 48446: Catalog $2 ❖ Porch swings. 810–664–1756.

Green Enterprises, 43 S. Rogers St., Hamilton, VA 22068: Brochure $1 ❖ Swings, gliders, tables, and benches. 703–338–3606.

Hangouts Handwoven Hammocks, 1328 Pearl St., Boulder, CO 80302: Free brochure ❖ Handwoven hammocks. 800–426–4688.

King Wood Products, P.O. Box 398, Newport, RI 02840: Free brochure ❖ Classic glider and porch swings. 800–848–0793.

Lazy Day Hammocks, 8225 Hwy. 64 East, Knightdale, NC 27545: Free brochure ❖ Hand-woven cotton rope hammocks, hammock chairs, and swings. 919–266–2819.

Mel-Nor Industries, 303 Gulf Bank, Houston, TX 77037: Information $1 ❖ Hanging lawn and porch swings, park benches, and old-time lamp posts. 713–445–3485.

O'Connor's Woodworks, P.O. Box 712, Washington, LA 70589: Brochure $2 ❖ Solid cypress porch swings. 800–786–1051.

Sun Designs, 173 E. Wisconsin Ave., Oconomowoc, WI 53066: Catalog $9.95 ❖ Plans for gazebos, bridges, doghouses, arbors, lawn furniture, swings and other outdoor play structures, and birdhouses. 414–567–4255.

Marion Travis, P.O. Box 1041, Statesville, NC 28677: Catalog $1 ❖ Wood porch swings. 704–528–4424.

Twin Oaks Hammocks, Rt. 4, P.O. Box 169, Louisa, VA 23093: Free brochure ❖ Woven rope hammocks and other furniture. 800–688–8946.

Unique Simplicities, 93 Anderson Rd., Gardiner, NY 12525: Free catalog ❖ Easy-to-install hammocks. 800–845–1119.

Walpole Woodworkers, 767 East St., Walpole, MA 02081: Catalog $6 ❖ Porch and covered swings, swing sets for children, chairs, tables, and picnic table sets. 800–343–6948.

HANDBALL

Adidas USA Inc., 5675 N. Blackstock Rd., Spartanburg, SC 29303: Free information ❖ Balls. 800–423–4327.

Baden Sports Inc., 34114 21st Ave. South, Federal Way, WA 98003: Free information ❖ Balls. 800–544–2998; 206–925–0500 (in WA).

Cannon Sports, P.O. Box 11179, Burbank, CA 91510: Free information ❖ Balls and eyeguards. 800–362–3146; 818–753–5940 (in CA).

Ektelon, 8929 Serio Dr., San Diego, CA 92123: Free information ❖ Eyeguards and gloves. 800–854–2958.

Professional Gym Inc., P.O. Box 188, Marshall, MO 65340: Free brochure ❖ Eyeguards. 800–821–821–7665; 800–892–2616 (in MO).

Spalding Sports Worldwide, 425 Meadow St., P.O. Box 901, Chicopee, MA 01021: Free information with list of retailers ❖ Balls. 800–225–6601.

Unique Sports Products Inc., 840 McFarland Rd., Alpharetta, GA 30201: Free information ❖ Eyeguards and gloves. 800–554–3707; 404–442–1977 (in GA).

Wa-Mac Inc., Highskore Products Inc., P.O. Box 128, Carlstadt, NJ 07410: Free

information ❖ Balls and gloves. 800–447–5673; 201–438–7200 (in NJ).

HARDWARE

A & B Industries Inc., 1160 Industrial Ave., Petaluma, CA 94952: Free catalog ❖ Brass and bronze hardware.

A & H Brass & Supply, 126 W. Main St., Johnson City, TN 37604: Catalog $1 ❖ Restoration furniture hardware. 615–928–8220.

Acorn Manufacturing Company Inc., 457 School St., P.O. Box 31, Mansfield, MA 02048: Catalog $6 ❖ Reproduction colonial hardware, sconces, hurricane lamps, fireplace tools, and bathroom accessories. 800–835–0121; 508–339–4500 (in MA).

American Home Supply, P.O. Box 697, Campbell, CA 95009: Catalog $2 ❖ Victorian and contemporary style knobs, cabinet hardware and locks, roll top and other desk hardware, door handles and dead bolts, faucets and bathroom hardware, grills and registers, and restoration items. 408–246–1962.

Anglo-American Brass Company, P.O. Box Drawer 9487, San Jose, CA 95157: Catalog $2 ❖ Solid brass reproduction hardware. 408–246–0203.

Antique Brass Works, 290 Port Richmond Ave., Staten Island, NY 10302: Free brochure ❖ Restored brass and other metal light fixtures and hardware. 718–273–6030.

Antique Hardware Store, Easton Rd., Kintnersville, PA 18930: Catalog $3 ❖ Antique hardware, pedestal sinks, faucets, high tank toilets, cabinet hardware, weather vanes, brass bar rails, and tin and wood chandeliers. 800–422–9982.

Antique Trunk Supply Company, 3706 W. 169th St., Cleveland, OH 44111: Catalog $1 ❖ Trunk repair parts. 216–941–8618.

Armor Products, P.O. Box 445, East Northport, NY 11731: Free catalog ❖ Hardware, lamp parts, wood turnings and parts for toys and other crafts, and replacement clock movements for mantel, banjo, and grandfather clocks. 800–292–8296.

Baldwin Hardware Corporation, P.O. Box 15048, Reading, PA 19612: Bathroom accessories brochure 75¢; lighting fixtures brochure $3; door hardware brochure 75¢; decor hardware brochure 75¢ ❖ Brass dead bolts and door hardware, bathroom accessories, and lighting fixtures. 800–346–5128.

Ball & Ball, 463 W. Lincoln Hwy., Exton, PA 19341: Catalog $7 (refundable) ❖ Brass and wrought-iron reproductions of 1680s to 1900s American hardware. 610–363–7330.

Bathroom Machineries, 495 Main St., P.O. Box 1020, Murphys, CA 95247: Catalog $3 ❖ Solid brass reproduction Victorian door and cabinet hardware. 209–728–2031.

Blaine Hardware International, 17319 Blaine Dr., Hagerstown, MD 21740: Free catalog ❖ Grab bars, other aids for people with disabilities, and replacement hardware for doors, screens, and windows. 800–678–1919.

Bona Decorative Hardware, 3073 Madison Rd., Cincinnati, OH 45209: Price list $2 ❖ Solid brass hardware for bathrooms, doors, cabinets, furniture, kitchens, and fireplaces. 513–321–7877.

Brass Menagerie, 524 St. Louis St., New Orleans, LA 70130: Free information ❖ Hardware, light fixtures, and plumbing. 504–524–0921.

The Broadway Collection, 1010 W. Santa Fe, Olathe, KS 66061: Free catalog ❖ Plumbing fittings, brass bowls and bar sinks, grab bars, switch plates, railing systems, and cabinet hardware. 800–766–1966.

By-Gone Days Antiques Inc., 3100 South Blvd., Charlotte, NC 28209: Free information ❖ Mantels, restored door hardware, and other architectural antiques. 704–568–7537.

Camelot Enterprises, Box 65, Bristol, WI 53104: Catalog $2 (refundable) ❖ Bolts, screws, and tools. 414–857–2695.

A Carolina Craftsman, 975 S. Avacado St., Anaheim, CA 92805: Catalog $5 (refundable) ❖ Antique solid brass replacement hardware for houses and furniture. 714–776–7877.

Cirecast Inc., 380 7th St., San Francisco, CA 94103: Brochure $2.50 ❖ Reproduction and custom solid bronze hardware. 415–863–8319.

The Coldren Company, 100 Race St., P.O. Box 668, North East, MD 21901: Catalog $3 ❖ Reproduction 18th- and 19th-century hardware. 410–287–2082.

Constantine, 2050 Eastchester Rd., Bronx, NY 10461: Catalog $1 ❖ Cabinet and furniture wood, hardware, veneers, plans and how-to books, carving tools and chisels, and inlay designs. 800–223–8087; 718–792–1600 (in NY).

Crown City Hardware Company, 1047 N. Allen Ave., Pasadena, CA 91104: Catalog $6.50 ❖ Restoration and decorative hardware.

Dimestore Cowboys, 4500 Hawkins NE, Albuquerque, NM 87109: Catalog $7 ❖ Door sets, cabinet pulls, shutters, bathroom accessories, curtain rods and rings, and other handcrafted hardware. 505–345–3933.

18th Century Hardware Company, 131 E. 3rd St., Derry, PA 15627: Catalog $3 ❖ Early American and Victorian-style hardware in black iron, porcelain, and brass. 412–694–2708.

Elephant Hill Ironworks, RR 1, Box 168, Turnbrige, VT 05077: Catalog $3 ❖ Reproduction 17th-, 18th-, and early 19th-century hardware and ironwork. 802–889–9444.

Elwick Supply Company, 230 Woods Ln., Somerdale, NJ 08083: Free catalog ❖ Stainless steel and brass screws and bolts, high speed drill bits, router accessories, metal tubing, and modeling tools.

Equiparts, 817 Main St., Pittsburgh, PA 15215: Free information ❖ Vintage plumbing, heating, and electrical parts. 800–442–6622.

Faneuil Furniture Hardware Company Inc., 163 Main St., Salem, NH 03079: Catalog $3 ❖ Reproduction brass hardware for cabinets and furniture. 603–898–7733.

Charolette Ford Trunks, P.O. Box 536, Spearman, TX 79081: Catalog $3.50 ❖ Supplies and tools for restoring trunks. 806–659–3027.

Gaston's Wood Finishes & Antiques, 2626 N. Walnut St., Bloomington, IN 47408: Catalog $2.50 ❖ Paint, stains, cabinet hardware, and antique furniture. 800–783–2845.

Hardware Plus, 701 E. Kingsley Rd., Garland, TX 75041: Catalog $5 ❖ Period and restoration colonial, Victorian, nouveau, and deco hardware. 800–522–7336.

Horton Brasses, P.O. Box 120, Cromwell, CT 06416: Catalog $4 ❖ Reproduction Chippendale, Queen Anne, Hepplewhite, Sheraton, Victorian, and early 1900s knobs, drawer pulls, and hardware. 203–635–4400.

Iron Intentions Forge, Box 2399, Spring Grove, PA 17362: Free information ❖ Reproduction 18th-century hardware. 717–229–2665.

Kayne & Son Custom Hardware, 100 Daniel Ridge Rd., Candler, NC 28715:

Catalog $4.50 ❖ Fireplace tools and hand-forged hardware. 704–667–8868.

Phyllis Kennedy Restoration Hardware, 9256 Holyoke Ct., Indianapolis, IN 46268: Catalog $3 ❖ Antique trunk hardware and other supplies. 317–872–6366.

Klockit, P.O. Box 636, Lake Geneva, WI 53147: Free catalog ❖ Hardware, Swiss music box movements and kits and clock-building equipment. 800–556–2548.

Meisel Hardware Specialties, P.O. Box 70, Mound, MN 55364: Catalog $2 ❖ Hardware, wood parts, and plans for musical door harps. 800–441–9870.

Merit Metal Products Corporation, 240 Valley Rd., Warrington, PA 18976: Catalog $10 ❖ Brass locks and hinges, and hardware for doors, furniture, and cabinets. 215–343–2500.

Nexton Industries Inc., 51 S. 1st St., Brooklyn, NY 11211: Free information ❖ Brass decorative hardware and bath accessories. 718–599–3837.

Old Smithy Shop, Box 336, Milford, NH 03055: Catalog $3 ❖ Hand-forged Colonial reproduction hardware and fireplace accessories. 603–673–0132.

Old World Hardware Company, 103 N. Texas, DeLeon, TX 76444: Catalog $4 ❖ Original and antique reproduction hardware. 817–893–3862.

Paxton Hardware Ltd., P.O. Box 256, Upper Falls, MD 21156: Catalog $4 ❖ Cabinet hardware and hinges. 410–592–8505.

Remodelers & Renovators Supplies, P.O. Box 45478, Boise, ID 83711: Catalog $3 ❖ Vintage hardware and plumbing fixtures. 800–456–2135.

The Renovator's Supply, P.O. Box 2660, North Conway, NH 03860: Free catalog ❖ Old-style hardware, plumbing, light fixtures, and decor accessories. 800–659–2211.

The Restoration Place, 305 20th St., Rock Island, IL 61201: Free brochure ❖ Plumbing, hardware, architectural and decor accessories, and light fixtures. 309–786–0004.

Restoration Works Inc., 810 Main St., Buffalo, NY 14205: Catalog $3 ❖ Hardware, ceiling medallions and trims, plumbing fixtures, and bathroom accessories. 800–735–3535.

Rufkahr Hardware, 4207 Eagle Rock Ct., St. Charles, MO 63304: Catalog $2 ❖ Antique reproduction hardware.

Stanley Hardware, 600 Myrtle St., New Britain, CT 06050: Free information ❖ Brass hardware. 800–835–2453.

Stock Drive Products, 2101 Jeritho Tnpk., New Hyde Park, NY 11042: Catalog $5.95 ❖ Hardware and parts in inches and metric sizes. 516–328–0200.

E.P. Titcomb, 17 Jan Sebastian Way, Sandwich, MA 02563: Catalog $3 ❖ Reproduction hardware. 508–833–1168.

Garrett Wade Company, 161 6th Ave., New York, NY 10013: Catalog $4 ❖ English-made, solid brass hardware, with many patterns similar to those of 100 years ago. 800–221–2942.

Watla Brass Company, 3630 Brownsboro Rd., Louisville, KY 40207: Free information ❖ Brass door knockers and cabinet hardware. 502–894–9285.

Wayne's Woods Inc., 39 N. Plains Industrial Rd., Wallingford, CT 06492: Catalog $2 (refundable) ❖ Refinishing supplies and glass, brass, and wood reproduction hardware. 800–793–6208.

Williamsburg Blacksmiths Inc., P.O. Box 1776, Williamsburg, MA 01096: Catalog $5 ❖ Reproduction Early American hardware and wrought-iron furniture. 800–248–1776.

Windy Hill Forge, 3824 Schroeder Ave., Perry Hall, MD 21128: Catalog $3 (refundable) ❖ Custom and restored hardware. 410–256–5890.

Wise Company, 6503 St. Claude Ave., P.O. Box 118, Arabi, LA 70032: Catalog $4 ❖ Antique restoration materials, hardware, and furniture refinishing supplies. 504–277–7551.

Woodworker's Emporium, 4320 W. Bell Dr., Las Vegas, NV 89118: Catalog $3 ❖ Polished iron and brass pull knobs and keyholes. 702–871–0722.

The Woodworkers' Store, 21801 Industrial Blvd., Rogers, MN 55374: Free catalog ❖ Hardware and woodworking supplies. 800–403–9736.

HARMONICAS

Harmonica Music Publishing, P.O. Box 671, Hermosa Beach, CA 90254: Free information ❖ Books, videos, audio cassettes, and instructional tapes on the harmonica. 310–320–0599.

Lee Oskar Harmonicas, P.O. Box 93155, Pasadena, CA 91109: Free information ❖ Harmonicas. 818–441–8874.

HATS

Az-Tex Hat Company, 15044 N. Cave Creek Rd., Phoenix, AZ 85032: Free brochure ❖ Traditionally styled hats from the American Southwest. 800–972–2095.

Back at the Ranch, 235 Don Gaspar, Santa Fe, NM 87501: Free information ❖ Vintage western clothing, boots, and hats. 505–989–8110.

BC Leather Hats, P.O. Box 602, St. Augustine, FL 32085: Free information ❖ Western-style leather hats from Australia. 800–922–4288; 904–794–2008 (in FL).

Caledonia Hats, 300 Chestnut Hill Rd., Stevens, PA 17578: Free information ❖ Western-style hats. 800–338–2410.

Custom Cowboy Shop, 321 N. Main, Sheridan, WY 82801: Free information ❖ Cowboy hats. 800–487–2692.

D. Bar J Hat Company, 3873 Spring Mt. Rd., Las Vegas, NV 89102: Free information ❖ Handmade hats. 800–654–1137; 702–362–4287 (in NV).

D.L. Designs, P.O. Box 27034, Los Angeles, CA 90027: Free catalog ❖ Men and women's hat patterns for costume pieces from the past, bridal headpieces, or contemporary fashions.

Luskey's Western Stores Inc., 101 N. Houston St., Fort Worth, TX 76102: Free catalog ❖ Hats and boots in a western tradition for the entire family. 817–335–5833.

David Morgan, 11812 Northcreek Pkwy., Ste. 103, Bothell, WA 98011: Free catalog ❖ Hand-braided belts, fur hats, and wool and sheepskin clothing. 800–324–4934.

Tonto Rim Trading Company, P.O. Box 463, Salem, IN 47167: Catalog $1 ❖ Western-style boots and hats. 800–253–4287.

Weather Hat Company of Wyoming, 1384 Coffeen Ave., Sheridan, WY 82801: Brochure $1 ❖ Cowboy-style hats. 307–674–6675.

Whipp Trading Company, RR 1, Arrasmith Trail, Ames, IA 50010: Free catalog ❖ Sheepskin rugs, slippers, mittens, and hats. 800–533–9447.

HEALTH CARE SUPPLIES & AIDS

AARP Pharmacy Service Center Catalog, 7609 Energy Pkwy., Baltimore, MD 21226: Free catalog for American Association Retired Persons members ❖ Over-the-counter medications, cosmetics, vitamins, dental needs, sick room and other health care supplies, and personal care items. 800–456–2226.

Allergy Control Products, 96 Danbury Rd., Ridgefield, CT 06877: Free catalog ❖ Air filters, mattress and pillow covers, face masks, dehumidifiers, and books. 800–422–3878; 203–438–9580 (in CT).

Atwater-Carey Ltd., 5505 Central Ave., Boulder, CO 80301: Free information ❖ First aid kits. 800–359–1646.

B & B Company Inc., 2417 Bank Dr., P.O. Box 5731, Boise, ID 83705: Free information ❖ Mastectomy breast forms. 800–262–2789.

BackSaver, 53 Jeffrey Ave., Holliston, MA 01746: Free catalog ❖ Aids for prevention and relief of pain to the back, neck, shoulders, wrists, and arms. 800–251–2225.

BCB Survival Equipment Inc., 7907 NW 53rd, Ste. 310, Miami, FL 33166: Free information ❖ Emergency medical and first aid equipment and survival kits. 305–264–1133.

Bioenergy Nutrients, 6565 Odell Pl., Boulder, CO 80301: Catalog $1 ❖ Nutritional supplements, homeopathic medicines, antioxidants, and all-natural skin care products. 800–627–7775.

Bruce Medical Supply, 411 Waverly Oaks Rd., P.O. Box 649166, Waltham, MA 02154: Free catalog ❖ Health care supplies for ostomy patients, diabetics, sick rooms, post hospital care, and first aid. 800–225–8446.

Chinook Medical Gear Inc., 2805 Wilderness Pl., Ste. 700, Boulder, CO 80301: Catalog $1 (refundable) ❖ Emergency medical and first aid equipment and survival kits. 800–766–1365.

Dr. Clayton's Herbs, Division American Herbal Science Inc., 2717 7th Ave. South, Birmingham, AL 35233: Free catalog ❖ All-natural health care products. 800–633–6286.

Comfortably Yours, 2515 E. 43rd St., P.O. Box 182216, Chattanooga, TN 37422: Free catalog ❖ Mastectomy bras, back support pillows, posture braces, and items for people with physical disabilities. 800–521–0097.

Emergency Medical Products, 9434 Chesapeake Dr., Ste. 1208, San Diego, CA 92123: Free information ❖ First-aid kits. 800–228–1538.

Enrichments, P.O. Box 386, Western Springs, IL 60558: Free information ❖ Health care products, personal care needs, and dressing and comfort aids. 800–323–5547.

ETAC USA, 2325 Parklawn Dr., Ste. J, Waukesha, WI 53186: Free brochure ❖ Walking aids, bath safety equipment, and wheelchairs. 800–678–3822.

Fashion Ease, Division M & M Health Care, 1541 60th St., Brooklyn, NY 11219: Free catalog ❖ Clothing with velcro closures, wheelchair accessories, and incontinence supplies. 800–221–8929; 718–871–8188 (in NY).

Frohock-Stewart Inc., P.O. Box 330, Northborough, MA 01532: Free information ❖ Clamp-on bathtub bench and grip for bathing comfort and safety. 800–343–6059.

Guardian Products Inc., 12800 Wentworth St., Arleta, CA 91331: Free catalog ❖ One-piece, assembly-not-required, height-adjustable shower and commode chair. 800–255–5022; 818–504–2820 (in CA).

Health Center for Better Living, 6189 Taylor Rd., Naples, FL 33942: Free catalog ❖ Herbal health care products. 813–566–2611.

HealthFest, 74 20th St., Brooklyn, NY 11232: Free catalog ❖ Natural remedies, personal care items, comfort and support aids, and cosmetics and toiletries. 718–768–0010.

Healthhouse USA, Box 9034, Jericho, NY 11753: Free catalog ❖ Emergency medical and first aid equipment. 516–334–9754.

Home Diagnostics Inc., 230 Park Ave., New York, NY 10169: Free catalog ❖ Home products for radon testing, water analysis, carbon monoxide and formaldehyde testing, blood pressure monitoring, and diabetes screening. 212–490–7977.

Home Health Products, 949 Seahawk Circle, Virginia Beach, VA 23452: Free catalog ❖ Natural health care products, health care supplies, skin care products, herbal medications, and other preparations. 800–284–9123.

Hyland's Standard Homeopathic Company, 154 W. 131st St., Los Angeles, CA 90061: Free information ❖ Homeopathic medicines. 800–624–9659; 213–321–4284 (in CA).

Independent Living Aids/Can-Do Products, 27 East Mall, Plainview, NY 11803: Free catalog ❖ Health care supplies. 800–537–2118; 516–752–8080 (in NY).

Intimate Appeal, Palo Verde at 34th, P.O. Box 27800, Tucson, AZ 85726: Free catalog

❖ Intimate clothing for women who have had mastectomies. 602–748–8600.

Miles Kimball Company, 41 W. 8th Ave., Oshkosh, WI 54906: Free catalog ❖ Bathroom and kitchen accessories, arthritis aids, clothing, canes, and personal care items for people with disabilities. 800–546–2255.

Dr. Leonard's Health Care Catalog, 74 20th St., Brooklyn, NY 11232: Free catalog ❖ Health care supplies. 718–768–0010.

Maddak Inc., Pequannock, NJ 07440: Free catalog ❖ Aids for daily living, home health care, rehabilitation, personal hygiene and grooming, transportation, recreation, and household activities. 201–628–7600.

Masuen First Aid & Safety, P.O. Box 901, Tonawanda, NY 14151: Free catalog ❖ First aid remedies and kits, and other health care and medical supplies. 800–831–0894.

Nitro-Pak Preparedness Center, 151 N. Main St., Heber City, UT 84032: Catalog $3 ❖ Survival equipment and other supplies, freeze-dried and dehydrated foods, books, and videos. 800–866–4876.

Out N Back, 1797 S. State St., Orem, UT 84058: Free catalog ❖ Survival equipment for outdoor and other recreational activities. 800–533–7415.

Outdoor Research, 1000 1st Ave. South, Seattle, WA 98134: Free information ❖ Outdoor first aid kits. 800–421–2421.

Pillows for Ease, P.O. Box 402113, Miami, FL 33140: Free brochure ❖ Special support pillows, body wedges, back rests, cradles, and other pillow-type supports for chiropractic, orthopedic, and massage therapy-related conditions. 800–347–1486.

J.A. Preston Corporation, P.O. Box 89, Jackson, MI 49204: Free catalog ❖ Exercise equipment, walkers, crutches, mats, positioning aids, perceptual motor accessories, self-help aids, and professional equipment for the doctor's office. 800–631–7277.

Radio Shack, Division Tandy Corporation, One Tandy Center, Fort Worth, TX 76102: Free information ❖ Health care supplies. 817–390–3011.

St. Louis Medical Supply, 10821 Manchester Rd., Kirkwood, MO 63122: Free catalog ❖ Health care and medical supplies. 800–950–6020.

SelfCare Catalog, 5850 Shellmound Ave., Emeryville, CA 94662: Free catalog ❖ Health care supplies. 800–345–3371.

Shield Healthcare Centers, P.O. Box 916, Santa Clarita, CA 91380: Free catalog ❖ Ostomy, urological, skin care, and home diagnostic products.

Source International, 8216 Ridgeview Dr., Ben Lomond, CA 95005: Free information ❖ Diabetic, ostomy, and other medical supplies. 800–237–6696.

Support Plus, Box 500, Medfield, MA 02052: Free catalog ❖ Support hosiery, personal hygiene and home health care aids, bath safety products, and walking shoes. 508–359–2910.

The Survival Center, P.O. Box 234, McKenna, WA 98558: Catalog $2 ❖ Survival equipment for outdoor activities. 206–458–6778.

Walton Way Medical, 948 Walton Way, Augusta, GA 30901: Free catalog ❖ Health care supplies and rehabilitation equipment. 800–241–4636.

Worldwide Home Health Center Inc., 926 E. Tallmadge Ave., Akron, OH 44310: Free catalog ❖ Ostomy appliances, incontinence supplies, mastectomy breast forms, skin care products, and other health care aids. 800–223–5938; 800–621–5938 (in OH).

HEALTH CARE SUPPLIES & AIDS FOR THE DISABLED

Access with Ease Inc., P.O. Box 1150, Chino Valley, AZ 86323: Catalog $1 (refundable) ❖ Self-help products for persons with physical challenges. 602–636–9469.

AccessAble, 111 Cedar St., 3rd Floor, New Rochelle, NY 10801: Free information ❖ Bathroom access products. 800–285–2525.

adaptAbility, P.O. Box 517, Colchester, CT 06415: Free catalog ❖ Mobility, grooming, dressing, bathing, eating and cooking aids, exercise and therapy games, and other adaptive home products for independent living. 800–288–9941.

The Adaptive Design Shop, 12847 Pt. Pleasant Dr., Fairfax, VA 22033: Free brochure ❖ Toilet supports and bath/shower chairs for children and adults. 703–631–1585.

American Foundation for the Blind Inc., Product Center, 3342 Melrose Ave., Roanoke, VA 24017: Free catalog ❖ Describes products available from the American Foundation for the Blind. 800–829–0500.

American Health Manufacturing, P.O. Box 16287, Baltimore, MD 21210: Free catalog ❖ Hospital and adjustable beds, ramps, walkers, electric scooters, wheelchairs, lift chairs, and other aids for the disabled. 800–232–3044.

American Printing House for the Blind, 1839 Frankfort Ave., P.O. Box 6085, Louisville, KY 40206: Free catalog ❖ Braille writing and embossing equipment, electronic devices, reading readiness products, educational aids, and other aids for people with visual handicaps. 502–895–2405.

AMI A]ltimate Medical Inc., 913 S. Washington, Redwood Falls, MN 56283: Free brochure ❖ Standing support and mobility stands. 800–342–8968.

Aqua-Tec Health Care Products, 1003 International Dr., Oakdale, PA 15071: Free catalog ❖ Water pressure-operated, portable bathtub lift for the home. 412–695–2122.

Attainment Company Inc., P.O. Box 930160, Verona, WI 53593: Free catalog ❖ Special needs equipment for children and adults. 800–327–4269.

Barrier Free Lifts Inc., P.O. Box 4163, Manassas, VA 22110: Free information ❖ Battery-operated, multi-directional barrier-free ceiling lift. 800–582–8732; 703–361–6531 (in VA).

Bath-Mate, P.O. Box 80095, Ontario, CA 91758: Free information ❖ Water-powered bathtub lift that pivots outward for safe patient transfer. 800–282–4928.

The Braun Corporation, 1014 S. Monticello, P.O. Box 310, Winamac, IN 46996: Free information ❖ Van conversion and driving accessories, wheelchair lifts, and other equipment. 800–THE-LIFT; 219–946–6153 (in IN).

Bruno Independent Living Aids, 1780 Executive Dr., P.O. Box 84, Oconomowoc, WI 53066: Free information ❖ Wheelchair and scooter lifts. 800–882–8183.

Cleo Inc., 3957 Mayfield Rd., Cleveland, OH 44121: Free catalog ❖ Exercise equipment, blood pressure pillows, walkers and canes, wheelchair accessories, cushions, recreation and rehabilitation aids, heat therapy appliances, bathroom aids, grooming and dressing aids, homemaking and eating aids, and other self-help products for the physically challenged. 800–321–0595; 216–382–9700 (in OH).

Columbia Medical Manufacturing Corporation, P.O. Box 633, Pacific Palisades, CA 90272: Free catalog ❖ Car seats, bath and toilet supports, commodes, exercise equipment, and other rehabilitation products for handicapped children and adults. 800–454–6612.

Columbus McKinnon Corporation, Marketing Communications, 140 John James Audubon Pkwy., Amherst, NY 14228: Free information ❖ Easy-to-operate mobility and lift system.

Comfortably Yours, 2515 E. 43rd St., P.O. Box 182216, Chattanooga, TN 37422: Free catalog ❖ Mastectomy bras, back support pillows, posture braces, and items for people with physical disabilities. 800–521–0097.

Consumer Care Products Inc., P.O. Box 684, Sheboygan, WI 53082: Free catalog ❖ Wheelchair trays, positioning aids, communication and mobility aids, and other supplies for exceptional persons. 414–459–8353.

Crestwood Company, 6625 N. Sidney Pl., Milwaukee, WI 53209: Free catalog ❖ Communication aids for children and adults. 414–352–5678.

Danmar Products Inc., 221 Jackson Industrial Dr., Ann Arbor, MI 48103: Free catalog ❖ Easy-to-hold utensil handles and other arthritis aids. 800–783–1998; 313–761–1990 (in MI).

The Doorman, Parisi Enterprises Inc., 23 Southward Ave., Congers, NY 10920: Free information ❖ No-tools-required, easy-to-install sliding door opener. 914–268–5983.

Eagle Home Medical, 5 W. Main St., Westerville, OH 43081: Free information ❖ Mobility equipment and home health care aids. 800–899–0172.

Equipment Shop, P.O. Box 33, Bedford, MA 01730: Free catalog ❖ Adaptive equipment. 617–275–7681.

ETAC USA, 2325 Parklawn Dr., Ste. J, Waukesha, WI 53186: Free brochure ❖ Walking aids, bath safety equipment, and wheelchairs. 800–678–3822.

Flaghouse, 150 N. MacQuesten Pkwy., Mt. Vernon, NY 10550: Free catalog ❖ Physical education and recreation, sports and play, and other rehabilitation equipment. 800–793–7900.

Grant Waterx Corporation, 986 Bedford St., Stamford, CT 06905: Free information ❖

Pivoting bathtub lift that operates with household water pressure. 800–243–5237.

Guardian Products Inc., 12800 Wentworth St., Arieta, CA 91331: Free catalog ❖ Walkers, crutches, canes, home activity aids, beds, lifts, ramps, and transport assistive equipment. 800–255–5022; 818–504–2820 (in CA).

Handi-Move, 982 Rt. 1, Pine Island, NY 10969: Free information ❖ Remote overhead track or free-standing movable lift. 800–724–5305.

Handi-Ramp Inc., P.O. Box 745, 1414 Armour Blvd., Mundelein, IL 60060: Free catalog ❖ Fixed-in-place and portable ramps for vans and homes. 800–876–RAMP.

T.F. Herceg Inc., 982 Rt. 1, Pine Island, NY 10969: Free information ❖ Remote hand-controlled, overhead track, and free-standing lifts. 800–724–5305.

Homecare Products Inc., 15824 SE 296th St., Kent, WA 98042: Free information ❖ Portable wheelchair ramps. 800–451–1903; 206–631–4633 (in WA).

I-Tec, 5482 Business Dr., Unit C, Huntington Beach, CA 92649: Free information ❖ Ceiling mounted or free-standing electro-mechanical system for in-the-home mobility. 800–622–ITEC; 714–898–9005 (in CA).

Imaginart Communication Products, 307 Arizona St., Bisbee, AZ 85603: Free catalog ❖ Speech, language, and learning materials for special education, speech and language pathology, occupational therapy, geriatric rehabilitation, and early childhood education. 800–828–1376; 602–432–5741 (in AZ).

Independent Living Aids/Can-Do Products, 27 East Mall, Plainview, NY 11803: Free catalog ❖ Self-help products for individuals with vision impairment and physical disabilities/ challenges. 800–537–2118; 516–752–8080 (in NY).

Independent Mobility Systems, 4100 W. Piedras, Farmington, NM 87401: Free information ❖ Automatic door ramp for automotive vehicles.

Miles Kimball Company, 41 W. 8th Ave., Oshkosh, WI 54906: Free catalog ❖ Bathroom and kitchen accessories, arthritis aids, clothing, canes, and personal care items for people with disabilities. 800–546–2255.

Kohler Company, 444 Highland Dr., Kohler, WI 53044: Free information ❖ Low threshold shower stalls for wheelchair accessibility. 800–456–4537.

Laureate, 110 E. Spring St., Winooski, VT 05404: Free information ❖ Talking software programs for children 6 months to 8 years of age. Includes language intervention, cognitive processing, reading, and instructional games. 802–655–4755.

Leckey Support Furniture, 1250 Main St., Waltham, MA 02154: Free information ❖ Adjustable bath chair. 800–LECKEY-O.

Lifestand, P.O. Box 153, Folcroft, PA 19032: Free information ❖ Combination power-assisted standing aid and wheelchair. 800–782–6324.

Lindustries, P.O. Box 295, Auburndale, MA 02166: Free information ❖ Lever convertible adapters for making doors easy to open. 617–237–8177.

Maddak Inc., Pequannock, NJ 07440: Free catalog ❖ Assistive aids for daily living, home health care, rehabilitation, personal hygiene and grooming, transportation, recreation, and household activities. 201–628–7600.

Maxi Aids, P.O. Box 3209, Farmingdale, NY 11735: Free catalog ❖ Aids and appliances for people with visual, hearing, and physical impairments. 800–522–6294.

MTF Geriatrics, P.O. Box 320, Ellis, KS 67637: Free catalog ❖ Easy-on and easy-off clothing and accessories for the elderly and disabled. 913–726–4807.

Open Sesame, 1933 Davis St., #279, San Leandro, CA 94577: Free information ❖ Remote-controlled door systems that open and close automatically from wheelchairs. 800–673–6911.

Power Access Corporation, Bridge St., P.O. Box 235, Collinsville, CT 06022: Free brochure ❖ Easily attached remote or manually operated door opener. 800–344–0088; 693–0751 (in CT).

Relaxo-Back Inc., 319 E. California, P.O. Box 812, Gainesville, TX 76240: Free information ❖ Form-fitting auxiliary seat that can be used to relieve lower back pain. 800–527–5496.

Rock N' Roll Marketing Inc., P.O. Box 1558, Levelland, TX 79336: Free information ❖ Single riders, tandems, and hand and foot-powered cycles with optional seat configurations and custom fitting for individual needs. 800–654–9664.

Sinties Scientific Inc., 5616A S. 122nd East Ave., Tulsa, OK 74146: Free information ❖ Folds-for-storage, adjustable power trainer for arms or legs. 800–852–6869; 918–254–7395 (in OK).

Space Tables Inc., P.O. Box 32082, Minneapolis, MN 55432: Free catalog ❖ Adjustable tables for wheelchairs. 800–328–2580.

Special Designs Inc., P.O. Box 130, Gillette, NJ 07933: Free information ❖ Custom equipment and furniture for "special kids." 908–464–8825.

Stand-Aid of Iowa Inc., Box 386, Sheldon, IA 51201: Free information ❖ Standing aid for disabled persons. 800–831–8580.

Thoele Manufacturing, Rt. 1, Box 116, Montrose, IL 62445: Free information ❖ Pedal-in-place exerciser. 217–924–4553.

Toys for Special Children, 385 Warburton Ave., Hastings-on-Hudson, NY 10706: Free catalog ❖ Enabling and other special devices for the handicapped. 914–478–0960.

Ultimate Home Care Company, 3250 E. 19th St., Long Beach, CA 90804: Free information ❖ Portable, lightweight threshold ramp. Also other folding ramps.

Vantage Mini Vans, 2441 E. Chambers Rd., Phoenix, AZ 85040: Free catalog ❖ Mini-van conversions for the physically challenged. 800–348–VANS.

Walk Easy Inc., 2915 S. Congress Ave., Delray Beach, FL 33445: Free brochure ❖ Crutches, walkers, commode chairs, and canes, tripod canes, and quad canes. 800–441–2904.

Walton Way Medical, 948 Walton Way, Augusta, GA 30901: Free catalog ❖ Medical supplies and rehabilitation equipment. 800–241–4636.

HEARING & COMMUNICATION AIDS

Audio Enhancement, 8 Winfield Point Ln., St. Louis, MO 63141: Free information ❖ Wireless, auditory assistance device for hearing-impaired persons. 314-567-6141.

Audiological Engineering Corporation, 35 Medford St., Somerville, MA 02143: Free information ❖ Infrared and loop hearing systems and other assistive aids for the hearing impaired. 800–283–4601.

General Technologies, 7415 Winding Way, Fair Oaks, CA 95628: Free catalog ❖

Assistive listening devices. 916–962–9225 (voice/TTY).

Harris Communications, 6541 City West Pkwy., Eden Prairie, MN 55344: Free catalog ❖ Closed caption and cable-ready decoder, TDDs, signalers, clocks, and other devices for hearing-impaired persons. 800–825–6758 (voice); 800–825–9187 (TDD).

Hear You Are Inc., 4 Musconetcong Ave., Stanhope, NJ 07874: Free catalog ❖ Doorbell signal, telephone aids, visual and smoke alarms, and other assistive listening devices for hearing-impaired persons. 201–347–7662 (voice/TTY).

Independent Living Aids Inc./Can-Do Products, 27 East Mall, Plainview, NY 11803: Free catalog ❖ Writing aids, low-vision aids and braille items, household items, health care supplies, mobility equipment, and communication aids. 800–537–2118; 516–752–8080 (in NY).

National Captioning Institute Inc., 5203 Leesburg Pike, Falls Church, VA 22041: Free brochure ❖ Closed captioned equipment for people with hearing impairments. 703–845–1992; 703–998–2400 (TTY).

Nationwide Flashing Signal Systems Inc., 8120 Fenton St., Silver Spring, MD 20910: Free catalog ❖ Visual alerting devices and TDDs for hearing-impaired persons. 301–589–6671.

One Video Place, 405 Lowell St., Wakefield, MA 01880: Catalog $3.95 ❖ Closed-captioned movies on video cassettes.

Phone-TTY Inc., 202 Lexington Ave., Hackensack, NJ 07601: Free information ❖ Modems and software for using computers to talk with TDDs. 201–489–7889; 201–489–7890 (TDD).

Phonic Ear Inc., 3880 Cypress Dr., Petaluma, CA 94954: Free catalog ❖ Sound enhancers for group functions and phonic ear personal FM systems for hearing impaired individuals. 800–227–0735; 800–772–3374 (in CA).

Potomac Technology, 1 Church St., Ste. 402, Rockville, MD 20850: Free information ❖ Special needs devices for hearing-impaired persons. 301–762–4005; 301–762–0851 (TDD).

Radio Shack, Division Tandy Corporation, One Tandy Center, Fort Worth, TX 76102: Free catalog ❖ Special needs devices for hearing-impaired persons. 817–390–3011.

Science Products, Box 888, Southeastern, PA 19399: Free catalog ❖ Voice sensory aids and electronics for people with hearing or visual impairments. 800–888–7400; 215–296–2111 (in PA).

Sennheiser, 6 Vista Dr., P.O. Box 987, Old Lyme, CT 06371: Free information ❖ Easy-to-use transmitters and receivers with 16 selectable frequencies for hard-of-hearing persons. 203–434–9190 (voice/TDD).

Siemans Hearing Instruments Inc., 10 Corporate Pl. South, Corporate Park 287, Piscataway, NJ 08854: Free information ❖ Easy-to-install infrared in-home TV listening system. 908–562–6600.

Silent Call, P.O. Box 16348, Clarkston, MI 48016: Free information ❖ Electronically activated wireless personal alert system.

Temasek Telephone Inc., 21 Airport Rd., South San Francisco, CA 94080: Free information ❖ Voice-activated telephones. 800–647–8887.

Ultratec, 450 Science Dr., Madison, WI 53711: Free catalog ❖ All-in-one phone for people with different hearing abilities. 608–238–5400 (voice/TTY).

Weitbrecht Communications Inc., 2656 29th St., Ste. 205, Santa Monica, CA 90405: Free catalog ❖ Assistive listening devices and portable TDDs. 800–233–9130 (voice/TTY).

HEAT EXCHANGERS

Gaylord Industries Inc., P.O. Box 1149, Tualatin, OR 97062: Free information ❖ Air-to-air heat exchangers. 800–547–9696.

HOCKEY, FIELD

Action Sport Systems Inc., P.O. Box 1442, Morgantown, NC 28680: Free information ❖ Uniforms, balls, nets, cages, and leg guards. 800–631–1091; 704–584–8000 (in NC).

American Sports Inc., 735 S. Mansfield Ave., Los Angeles, CA 90036: Free information with list of retailers ❖ Uniforms, balls, nets, cages, leg guards, shoes, and sticks. 800–922–8939.

Austin Athletic Equipment Corporation, 705 Bedford Ave., Box 423, Bellmore, NY 11710: Free information ❖ Nets and cages. 516–785–0100.

Champion Sports Products Company, P.O. Box 138, Sayreville, NJ 08872: Free information ❖ Uniforms, balls, nets, cages, and leg guards. 908–238–0330.

Cran Barry Inc., 130 Condor St., Box 488, East Boston, MA 02128: Free information ❖ Uniforms, balls, nets, cages, leg guards, shoes, and sticks. 800–992–2021.

Doss Shoes, Soccer Sport Supply Company, 1745 1st Ave., New York, NY 10128: Free information ❖ Uniforms, balls, nets, cages, leg guards, shoes, and sticks. 800–223–1010; 212–427–6050 (in NY).

Olympia Sports, 745 State Cir., Ann Arbor, MI 48106: Free information ❖ Balls, goal nets, cages, leg guards, and sticks. 800–521–2832; 313–761–5173 (in MI).

Pennsylvania Sporting Goods, 1360 Industrial Hwy., P.O. Box 451, Southampton, PA 18966: Free information ❖ Balls, nets, cages, leg guards, and sticks. 800–523–1122.

Sportime, 1 Sportime Way, Atlanta, GA 30340: Free information ❖ Balls, goal nets, cages, leg guards, and sticks. 800–444–5700; 404–449–5700 (in GA).

TC Sports, 7251 Ford Hwy., Tecumseh, MI 49286: Free information ❖ Balls, goal nets, and cages. 800–523–1498; 517–451–5221 (in MI).

Wolvering Sports, 745 State Circle, Box 1941, Ann Arbor, MI 48106: Catalog $1 ❖ Baseball, basketball, field hockey, soccer, football, and other athletic and recreation equipment. 313–761–5691.

HOCKEY, ICE

Clothing

Athletic Apparel by Matchfit, Box 13100, Charlotte, NC 28270: Free information ❖ Protective gear and uniforms. 704–847–0896.

Austin Sportsgear, 621 Liberty St., Jackson, MI 49203: Free information ❖ Uniforms. 800–999–7543; 517–784–1120 (in MI).

Betlin Manufacturing, 1445 Marion Rd., Columbus, OH 43207: Free information ❖ Uniforms. 614–443–0248.

Cliff Keen Athletic, 1235 Rosewood, Ann Arbor, MI 48106: Free information ❖ Uniforms. 800–992–0799; 313–769–9555 (in MI).

Majestic Athletic Wear Ltd., 636 Pen Argyl St., Pen Argyl, PA 18072: Free information ❖ Uniforms and other sportswear. 800–955–8555; 215–863–6161 (in PA).

Venus Knitting Mills Inc., 140 Spring St., Murray Hill, NJ 07974: Free information ❖ Uniforms, clothing for ice skaters, and other

sportswear. 800–955–4200; 908–464–2400 (in NJ).

Equipment

Athletic Apparel by Matchfit, Box 13100, Charlotte, NC 28270: Free information ❖ Protective gear and uniforms. 704–847–0896.

Bauer Precision In-Line Skates, Box 716, Swanton, VT 05478: Free information ❖ Gloves, goal nets, cages, protective gear, helmets, pucks, sticks, and skates. 800–622–2189; 802–868–2711 (in VT).

Canstar Sports USA Inc., 50 Jonergin Dr., Swanton, VT 05448: Free information ❖ Figure and hockey ice skates and blade sharpeners. 800–362–3146; 802–868–2711 (in VT).

Cooper International Inc., 501 Alliance Ave., Toronto, Ontario, Canada M6N 2J3: Free information ❖ Guards and pads, helmets, masks, mouth guards, pucks, nets, cages, sticks, figure and hockey ice skates, and blade protectors. 416–763–3801.

Easton Sports, 577 Airport Blvd., Burlingame, CA 94010: Free information ❖ Gloves, goal nets, cages, protective gear, sticks, and skates. 800–347–3901; 415–347–4727 (in CA).

Irwin Sports, 43 Hanna Ave., Toronto, Ontario, Canada M6K 1X6: Free information ❖ Gloves, goal nets, cages, protective gear, pucks, and skates. 800–268–1732.

Lowry's Manufacturing Ltd., 19 Keith Rd., Winnipeg, Manitoba, Canada R3H 0H7: Free information ❖ Figure and hockey ice skates, replacement blades, and blade protectors. 204–633–6359.

Maska USA Inc., 529 Main St., Ste. 205, Boston, MA 02129: Free information ❖ Guards and pads, helmets, masks, pucks, and figure and hockey ice skates. 800–451–4600; 617–242–8600 (in MA).

National Sporting Goods Corporation, 25 Brighton Ave., Passaic, NJ 07055: Free information ❖ Figure and hockey ice skates, blade protectors, and sharpeners. 201–779–2323.

Riedell Shoes Inc., P.O. Box 21, Red Wing, MN 55066: Free information ❖ Blade sharpeners, protectors, and figure, racing, and hockey skates. 612–388–8251.

USA Skate Company, 157 Grant Ave., Islip, NY 11751: Free information ❖ Guards and pads, nets, cages, sticks, and skates. 800–426–3334; 516–277–1000 (in NY).

HOME BUILDING & IMPROVEMENT

Ceilings

AA Abbingdon Affiliates, 2149 Utica Ave., Brooklyn, NY 11234: Brochure $1 ❖ Tin ceiling cornice moldings. 718–258–8333.

Chelsea Decorative Metal Company, 9603 Moonlight Dr., Houston, TX 77096: Catalog $2 ❖ Embossed art deco tin for ceilings and walls. 713–721–9200.

Midwestern Wood Products, 1500 W. Jefferson St., P.O. Box 434, Morton, IL 61550: Free information ❖ Easy-to-install suspended hardwood ceiling panels. 800–441–7493.

W.F. Norman Corporation, P.O. Box 323, Nevada, MO 64772: Catalog $3 ❖ Cornices and sheet metal ornaments for ceilings, wallcoverings, and corner, border, and filler plates. 800–641–4038.

Timberfab Inc., P.O. Box 399, Tarboro, NC 27886: Free information ❖ Exposed beam trusses, timber framing, milled logs, and flooring. 919–641–4141.

Cupolas

Colonial Cupolas, 5902 Buttonwood Dr., P.O. Box 38, Haslett, MI 48840: Brochure $3 ❖ Authentic reproductions of historic cupolas and weather vanes. 517–339–4320.

Coppersmith Sheet Metal, 40136 Enterprise Dr., Bldg. 18–A, Oakhurst, CA 93644: Free brochure ❖ Fireplace hoods, cupolas, mailboxes, and dormers. 209–658–8909.

Crosswinds Gallery, 980 E. Main Rd., Portsmouth, RI 02871: Free catalog ❖ Cupolas with copper roofs and weather vanes. 401–683–7974.

Denninger Cupolas & Weathervanes, RD 1, Box 447, Middletown, NY 10940: Catalog $4 ❖ Redwood cupolas with copper roofs and weathervanes. 914–343–2229.

Outward Signs, 39B Mill Plain Rd., Danbury, CT 06811: Free catalog ❖ Cupolas and copper, iron, and aluminum weather vanes. 800–346–7678.

Sun Designs, 173 E. Wisconsin Ave., Oconomowoc, WI 53066: Catalog $9.95 ❖ Plans for gazebos, bridges, cupolas, and other structures. 414–567–4255.

Town & Country Cupolas, P.O. Box 236, East Conway, NH 03818: Free information ❖ Country-style cupolas, assembled or as a kit. 603–939–2698.

Doors

Accurate Metal Weatherstrip Company, 725 S. Fulton Ave., Mount Vernon, NY 10550: Catalog $3 (refundable) ❖ Weatherstripping for windows and doors. 914–668–6042.

Andersen Windows, P.O. Box 3900, Peoria, IL 61614: Free information ❖ Energy-efficient windows and patio doors. 800–426–4261.

Architectural Components, 26 N. Leverett Rd., Montague, MA 01351: Brochure $5 ❖ Reproduction doors from the 18th and 19th centuries, windows and window frames, and moldings. 413–367–9441.

Arctic Glass & Window Outlet, Rt. 1, Hammond, WI 54015: Catalog $4 ❖ Windows, entryway and patio doors, skylights, and sunrooms. 800–428–9276.

Benchmark Doors, 12842 Pennridge Dr., Bridgeton, MO 63044: Free information ❖ Steel doors with a wood-grain finish. 800–467–2329.

Beveled Glass Works, 23715 W. Malibu Rd., Ste. 351, Malibu, CA 90265: Free information ❖ Wood doors with sidelights and beveled glass. 800–421–0518.

The Bilco Company, P.O. Box 1203, New Haven, CT 06505: Free information ❖ All-steel outside basement doors. 203–934–6363.

Caradco Corporation, 820 Lakeside St., Gurnee, IL 60031: Free information ❖ Hinged, sliding wood, and insulated aluminum doors for entryways and patios. 800–238–1866.

Cascade Woodwork, P.O. Box 316, Ouray, CO 81427: Brochure $1 ❖ Handcrafted storm and screen doors with removable panels, optional hardware, and prefinishing. 303–325–4780.

Ciro Coppa Doors, 1231 Paraiso Ave., San Pedro, CA 90731: Free catalog ❖ Wood screen doors and Adirondack chairs. 310–548–4142.

Colonial Craft, 2772 Fairview Ave., St. Paul, MN 55113: Free catalog ❖ Hardwood windows and doors with removable grilles. 800–727–5187; 612–631–2110 (in MN).

Combination Door Company, P.O. Box 1076, Fond du Lac, WI 54936: Free information ❖ Wood combination storm and screen doors and windows. 414–922–2050.

Creative Openings, 929 N. State St., P.O. Box 4204, Bellingham, WA 98227: Catalog $4 ❖ Historical and traditional style screen and other doors. 206–671–6420.

Crestline, 1725 Indian Wood Cir., Maumee, OH 43537: Free information ❖ French doors with optional glass panels and transoms. 800–552–4111.

Driwood Ornamental Wood Moulding, P.O. Box 1729, Florence, SC 29503: Catalog $6 (refundable) ❖ Doors, embossed wood moulding, raised paneling, mantels, and curved stairs. 803–669–2478.

Elegant Entries, 240 Washington St., Auburn, MA 01501: Free catalog ❖ Mahogany and rosewood exterior and interior doors. 800–343–3432.

Entrances Inc., RFD 1, Box 246A, Poocham Rd., Westmoreland, NH 03467: Catalog $2 ❖ Interior and exterior insulated wood doors, with optional beveled and stained glass. 603–399–7723.

Entry Systems, 911 E. Jefferson, Pittsburgh, KS 66762: Free information ❖ Steel doors with a choice of light and transom designs. 800–835–0364.

Fancy Front Brassiere Company, P.O. Box 2847, Roseville, CA 95746: Catalog $2 ❖ Screen doors, interior and exterior millwork, and other restoration supplies. 916–791–7733.

Fineman Doors Inc., 16020 Valley Wood Rd., Sherman Oaks, CA 91403: Information $2 ❖ Handcrafted solid hardwood entry and interior doors. 818–990–3667.

General Products Company Inc., P.O. Box 7387, Fredericksburg, VA 22404: Free brochure ❖ Steel entry doors. 703–898–5700.

Georgia-Pacific, P.O. Box 2808, Norcross, GA 30091: Free information ❖ Doors and windows. 800–447–2882.

Grand ERA Reproductions, P.O. Box 1026, Lapeer, MI 48446: Catalog $2 ❖ Easy-to-assemble screen and storm door kits. 810–664–1756.

Hess Manufacturing Company, Box 127, Quincy, PA 17247: Free information ❖ Insulated aluminum doors and windows. 800–541–6666; 717–749–3141 (in PA).

Howell's House of Doors, 1103 F St., Salida, CO 81201: Catalog $1 ❖ Victorian-style screen, storm, and other vintage reproduction doors. 719–539–4568.

Hurd Millwork Company, 575 S. Whelen Ave., Medford, WI 54451: Free information

❖ Windows and hinged, sliding wood, and insulated aluminum patio doors. 800–223–4873.

Iberia Millwork, P.O. 12139, New Iberia, LA 70562: Free information ❖ French doors, interior and exterior shutters, and cabinets. 318–365–8129.

International Wood Products, 10883 Thornmint Rd., San Diego, CA 92127: Free information ❖ Single or double wood doors with a choice of transom designs and sidelights. 800–468–3667.

Jeld-Wen, P.O. Box 10266, Portland, OR 97210: Free information ❖ Pre-finished or ready for finishing provincial and colonial-style bi-fold interior doors. 800–877–9482.

Jessup Door Company, 300 E. Railroad St., Dowagiac, MI 49047: Free information ❖ French doors for patios. 616–782–2183.

Joinery Company, P.O. Box 518, Tarboro, NC 27886: Catalog $5 ❖ Reproduction antique entryways and doors. 919–823–3306.

Kenmore Industries, On Thompson Square, Boston, MA 02129: Catalog $3 ❖ Federal and Georgian style doorways. 617–242–1711.

Kirby Millworks, 3269 CR 514, Ignacio, CO 81137: Free brochure ❖ Interior and exterior solid oak doors and moldings. 800–245–3667.

Lamson-Taylor Custom Doors, Tucker Rd., South Acworth, NH 03607: Catalog $2 ❖ Energy-efficient doors. 603–835–2992.

Leslie-Locke Inc., 4501 Circle 75 Pkwy., Ste. D-4300, Atlanta, GA 30339: Free information ❖ Traditional style security storm doors with all-welded steel frames, brass locks, and dead bolts. 404–953–6366.

Mad River Woodworks, P.O. Box 1067, Blue Lake, CA 95525: Catalog $3 ❖ Ready-to-paint or stain reproduction doors from the mid-1800s. 800–446–8560; 707–668–5671 (in CA).

Marvin Windows, P.O. Box 100, Warroad, MN 56763: Free information ❖ Windows and doors with divided light and insulated storm windows and transoms. 800–346–5128.

Morgan Manufacturing, P.O. Box 2446, Oshkosh, WI 54903: Free information ❖ Paneled and carved wood, sliding glass, and hinged patio doors. 800–435–7464.

Old Wagon Factory, P.O. Box 1427, Clarksville, VA 23927: Catalog $2 ❖

Victorian and Chippendale storm screen doors and furniture. 804–374–5787.

Oregon Wooden Screen Door Company, 330 High St., Eugene, OR 97401: Catalog $3 (refundable) ❖ Screen and energy-efficient storm doors.

Peachtree Windows & Doors, P.O. Box 5700, Norcross, GA 30091: Free information ❖ Steel, wood, glass, and aluminum doors and windows. 800–477–6544.

Pease Industries Inc., P.O. Box 14–8001, Fairfield, OH 45014: Information $1 ❖ Steel entryways and hinged patio doors. 800–543–1180.

Remodelers & Renovators Supplies, P.O. Box 45478, Boise, ID 83711: Catalog $3 ❖ Ready-to-stain screen doors. 800–456–2135.

Scherr's Cabinet & Doors, 5315 Burdick Expwy. East, RR 5, Box 12, Minot, ND 58701: Brochure $2 ❖ Raised panel doors for cabinets, drawer fronts, and dovetail drawers. 701–839–3384.

Season-all Industries Inc., 1480 Wayne Ave., Indiana, PA 15701: Free information ❖ Vinyl patio doors. 800–999–1847.

Cole Sewell Corporation, 2288 University Ave., St. Paul, MN 55114: Free information ❖ Reinforced wood storm doors with optional security protection. 612–646–7873.

Sheppard Millwork Inc., 21020 70th Ave. West, Edmonds, WA 98020: Free catalog ❖ Sanded and unfinished doors with optional hardware. 206–771–4645.

Silverton Victorian Millworks, P.O. Box 2987, Durango, CO 81302: Catalog $4 ❖ Doors with stained glass or etched glass inserts. 303–259–5915.

Simpson Door Company, P.O. Box 210, McCleary, WA 98557: Free brochure ❖ Paneled, carved, and standard wood doors. 800–952–4057; 206–495–3291 (in WA).

Southeastern Insulated Glass, 6477–B Peachtree Industrial Blvd., Atlanta, GA 30360: Free information ❖ Greenhouse and sunroom kits, sliding glass doors, and skylights with optional tempered insulated glass. 800–841–9842; 404–455–8838 (in GA).

Stanley Hardware, 600 Myrtle St., New Britain, CT 06050: Free information ❖ Make-your-own sliding closet door kits. 800–835–2453.

Taylor Brothers, P.O. Box 11198, Lynchburg, VA 24506: Catalog $2 ❖

Handcrafted storm screen doors. 800–288–6767.

Temple Products Inc., P.O. Box 1008, Temple, TX 76503: Free information ❖ Paneled and carved entryway and patio doors. 800–634–3667; 800–792–3357 (in TX).

Touchstone Woodworks, P.O. Box 112, Ravenna, OH 44266: Catalog $2 ❖ Authentic Victorian-style screen doors, moldings, porch parts, and ornamental trim. 713–863–7600.

Jack Wallis Door Emporium, Rt. 1, Box 22A, Murray, KY 42071: Catalog $4 ❖ Handcrafted doors with optional stained glass. 502–489–2613.

Weather Shield Mfg. Inc., One Weather Shield Plaza, Medford, WI 54451: Free information ❖ Wood windows, patio doors, and steel entryways. 800–477–6808.

Wing Industries, P.O. Box 38347, Dallas, TX 75238: Free information ❖ Bi-fold French doors for interiors. 800–341–8464.

The Wood Factory, 901 Harvard, Houston, TX 77008: Catalog $2 ❖ Ornamental trim, mantels, screen doors, and other millwork. 713–863–7600.

Woodstone Company, Patch Rd., P.O. Box 223, Westminster, VT 05158: Information $3 ❖ Insulated solid wood doors and single-, double-, or triple-glazed windows, with palladians and straight and fanned transoms. 802–722–9217.

Flooring

Albany Woodworks, P.O. Box 729, Albany, LA 70711: Free information ❖ Antique heart pine and American hardwood flooring. 504–567–1155.

Aspen Specialties, Rt. 2, Box 256A, Longview, TX 75605: Free information ❖ Paneling and decking for interiors. 800–723–4399; 903–663–4399 (in TX).

Authentic Pine Floors Inc., 4042 Hwy. 42, P.O. Box 206, Locust Grove, GA 30248: Free information ❖ Wide plank and heart-pine flooring. 800–283–6038.

Boen Hardwood Flooring Inc., Rt. 5, Box 640, Bassett, VA 24055: Free information ❖ Tongue-and-groove flooring. 703–629–3381.

Bre Lumber/Rare Earth Hardwoods, 6778 E. Traverse Hwy., Traverse City, MI 49684: Free information ❖ Hardwood, other lumber, flooring, and decking. 800–968–0074.

Carlisle Restoration Lumber, 306 W. Johnson, HCR 32, Box 679, Stoddard, NH

03464: Free information ❖ Wide pine flooring and paneling. 603–446–3937.

Castle Burlingame, 10 Stone St., North Plainfield, NJ 07060: Catalog $6.50 ❖ Soft Eastern white pine and re-milled yellow pine antique wide flooring. 908–757–3160.

Centre Mills Antique Wood, P.O. Box 16, Aspers, PA 17304: Free information ❖ Antique flooring, hewn beams, new hardwoods, and some softwoods. 717–334–0249.

Goodwin Lumber, Rt. 2, Box 119, Micanopy, FL 32667: Free information ❖ Heart pine and red cypress flooring, paneling, and beams. 800–336–3116.

Granville Manufacturing Company Inc., Granville, VT 05747: Free brochure ❖ Quartersawn clapboard siding, wide pine and hardwood flooring, and other building materials. 802–767–4747.

Hartco, 900 S. Gay St., Knoxville, TN 37902: Catalog $1 ❖ Oak flooring in parquet, combination, parallel, herringbone, and basket-weave patterns. 615–544–0767.

Joinery Company, P.O. Box 518, Tarboro, NC 27886: Catalog $5 ❖ Antique heart pine tongue-and-groove flooring, paneling, and trim from authentic colonial buildings. 919–823–3306.

Kentucky Wood Floors, P.O. Box 33276, Louisville, KY 40232: Catalog $2 ❖ Walnut, oak, cherry, and ash borders ready for glue-down installation. 502–451–6024.

Launstein Hardwoods, 384 S. Every Rd., Mason, MI 48854: Free information ❖ Easy-to-install and finish pre-sanded hardwood flooring. 517–676–1133.

Livermore Wood Floors, P.O. Box 146, East Livermore, ME 04228: Free information ❖ Cherry, oak, maple, ash, wide pine, walnut, and birch flooring. 207–897–5211.

Memphis Hardwood Flooring Company, 1551 N. Thomas St., P.O. Box 38217, Memphis, TN 38107: Free information ❖ Unfinished and finished oak flooring. 800–346–3010.

Piedmont Mantel & Millwork, 4320 Interstate Dr., Macon, GA 31210: Catalog $3 ❖ Salvaged heart-pine flooring and colonial-style mantels in a choice of woods. 912–477–7536.

J.L. Powell & Company Inc., 600 S. Madison St., Whiteville, NC 28472: Free

information ❖ Antique heart pine flooring. 800–227–2007; 910–642–8989 (in NC).

Quality Woods Ltd., 63 Flanders Bartley Rd., Flanders, NJ 07836: Free brochure ❖ Teak, plywood, teak and Asian rosewood parquet, tongue-and-groove planks, and strip flooring. 201–584–7554.

Timberfab Inc., P.O. Box 399, Tarboro, NC 27886: Free information ❖ Exposed beam trusses, timber framing, milled logs, and flooring. 919–641–4141.

Vintage Lumber Company, 1 Council Dr., Woodsburrow Industrial Park, Woodsburrow, MD 21798: Free information ❖ Remilled antique heart pine, oak, chestnut, oak, cherry, walnut, and poplar flooring. 301–845–2500.

Frames & Beams

Bear Creek Lumber, P.O. Box 669, Winthrop, WA 98862: Brochure $4 ❖ Western red cedar building supplies. 800–597–7191.

Blue Ridge Timber Frame, 2030 Redwood Dr., Christianburg, VA 24073: Brochure $8 ❖ Timber frames for home construction. 800–788–8391; 703–382–1102 (in VA).

E.F. Bufton & Son, Builders Inc., P.O. Box 164, Princeton, MA 01541: Brochure $5 ❖ Oak post and beam frames. 508–464–5418.

Goodwin Lumber, Rt. 2, Box 119, Micanopy, FL 32667: Free information ❖ Heart pine lumber and red cypress flooring, paneling, and beams. 800–336–3118.

Pacific Post & Beam, P.O. Box 13708, San Luis Obispo, CA 93406: Brochure $5 ❖ Handcrafted timber frames. 805–543–7565.

Timberfab Inc., P.O. Box 399, Tarboro, NC 27886: Free information ❖ Exposed beam trusses, timber framing, milled logs, and flooring. 919–641–4141.

Vermont Frames, P.O. Box 100, Hinesburg, VT 05461: Free brochure ❖ Post and beam frames. 802–453–3727.

Paint

Finishing Products, 8165 Big Bend, St. Louis, MO 63119: Catalog $2 ❖ Furniture lacquers, aniline dyes, bronzing powders, and other wood finishing materials. 314–962–7575.

Gaston's Wood Finishes & Antiques, 2626 N. Walnut St., Bloomington, IN 47408: Catalog $2.50 ❖ Paint, stains, cabinet hardware, and antique furniture. 800–783–2845.

Johnson Paint Company Inc., 355 Newbury St., Boston, MA 02115: Catalog $1 ❖ Painting supplies, brushes, and tools. 617–536–4838.

Pintchik Homeworks, 2106 Bath Ave., Brooklyn, NY 11214: Free information ❖ Paints, hardware, and wallpaper, window treatment and flooring supplies. 800–847–4199; 718–996–5580 (in NY).

Paneling

AFCO Industries Inc., 615 E. 40th St., Holland, MI 49423: Free information ❖ Scratch-resistant, waterproof hardwood panels for kitchens and bathrooms. 800–253–4644.

Aspen Specialties, Rt. 2, Box 256A, Longview, TX 75605: Free information ❖ Paneling and decking for interiors. 800–723–4399; 903–663–4399 (in TX).

California Redwood Association, 405 Enfrente Dr., Ste. 200, Novato, CA 94949: Free information with long SASE ❖ Redwood paneling. 415–382–0662.

Driwood Ornamental Wood Moulding, P.O. Box 1729, Florence, SC 29503: Catalog $6 ❖ Embossed wood moulding and raised paneling, mantels, curved stairs, and doors. 803–669–2478.

Georgia-Pacific, P.O. Box 2808, Norcross, GA 30091: Free information ❖ Wall paneling and pre-hung wallpaper on plywood panels. 800–447–2882.

Goodwin Lumber, Rt. 2, Box 119, Micanopy, FL 32667: Free information ❖ Heart pine and red cypress flooring, paneling, and beams. 800–336–3118.

Masonite Corporation, 1 S. Wacker Dr., Chicago, IL 60606: Free information ❖ Hardboard paneling. 800–446–1649.

Simpson Timber, Box 1169, Arcata, CA 95521: Free information ❖ Redwood paneling. 800–637–7077; 707–822–0371 (in CA).

States Industries Inc., P.O. Box 7037, Eugene, OR 97401: Free information ❖ Wood paneling. 800–537–0419.

Restoration Materials

A & H Brass & Supply, 126 W. Main St., Johnson City, TN 37604: Catalog $1 ❖ Wood ornaments, moldings, and veneers. 615–928–8220.

Abatron, 33 Center Dr., Gilberts, IL 60136: Free information ❖ Epoxy restoration supplies and paste fillers. 800–445–1754; 708–426–2200 (in IL).

Accurate Metal Weatherstrip Company, 725 S. Fulton Ave., Mount Vernon, NY 10550: Catalog $3 (refundable) ❖ Weatherstripping and other supplies. 914–668–6042.

Adkins Architectural Antiques, 3515 Fannin, Houston, TX 77004: Free brochure ❖ Salvaged architectural antiques. 713–522–6547.

Architectural Antiquities, Harborside, ME 04642: Free brochure ❖ 18th- and 19th-century Victorian supplies for home building and restoration. 207–326–4938.

Architectural Iron Company, Schocopee Rd., P.O. Box 126, Milford, PA 18337: Catalog $4 ❖ Reproduction 18th- and 19th-century castings and wrought iron accessories. 800–442–4766.

Aristocraft Originals Inc., 6200 Highlands Pkwy. SE, Smyrna, GA 30082: Catalog $5 ❖ Reproduction niches, crown molding, trim, fireplaces, ceiling medallions, corbels, archways, columns, porches, and oak beams. 404–333–9934.

The Bank Architectural Antiques, 1824 Felicity St., New Orleans, LA 70113: Free brochure ❖ Reproduction and repaired New Orleans-style shutters, doors, hardware, and other architectural supplies. 800–274–8883.

Bendix Moldings Inc., 37 Ramland Rd. South, Orangeburg, NY 10962: Free catalog ❖ Decorative wood moldings and ornaments. 800–526–0240; 914–365–1111 (in NY).

Campbellsville Industries Inc., P.O. Box 278, Campbellsville, KY 42718: Free catalog ❖ Aluminum cornices, louvers, cupolas, columns, balustrades, and shutters with an optional baked-on finish. 502–465–8135.

A Carolina Craftsman, 975 S. Avocado St., Anaheim, CA 92805: Catalog $5 (refundable) ❖ Hard-to-find antique replacement parts for houses and furniture. 714–776–7877.

Cathedral Stone Products Inc., 8332 Bristol Ct., Ste. 107, Jessup, MD 20749: Free information ❖ Acrylic- and latex-free bonding agents and restoration mortars. 301–317–4658.

Chadsworth Incorporated, P.O. Box 53268, Atlanta, GA 30355: Catalog $3 ❖ Columns and replacement components in wood, fiberglass, and other materials. 800–394–5177.

Conservation Services, 8 Lakeside Trail, Kinneton, NJ 07405: Free information ❖ Epoxy restoration supplies and paste fillers. 201–836–6412.

Epoxy Technology Inc., 14 Fortune Dr., Billerica, MA 01821: Free information ❖ Epoxy adhesives for artifact restoration. 800–227–2201; 508–667–3805 (in MA).

Fancy Front Brassiere Company, P.O. Box 2847, Roseville, CA 95746: Catalog $2 ❖ Restoration supplies, screen doors, and interior and exterior millwork. 916–791–7733.

Hardware Plus, 701 E. Kingsley Rd., Garland, TX 75041: Catalog $5 ❖ Supplies for restoring old houses and furniture. 800–522–7336.

Kentucky Millwork, 4200 Reservoir Ave., Louisville, KY 40213: Catalog $2 ❖ Architectural supplies for restoring houses. 502–451–3456.

Park Place, 2251 Wisconsin Ave. NW, Washington, DC 20007: Catalog $2 ❖ Classic outdoor furnishings and architectural products. 202–342–6294.

A.F. Schwerd Manufacturing Company, 3215 McClure Ave., Pittsburgh, PA 15212: Free brochure ❖ Wood columns in seasoned northern white pine with matching pilasters and aluminum bases. 412–766–6322.

Tremont Nail Company, P.O. Box 111, Wareham, MA 02571: Free catalog ❖ Old-fashioned cut nails. 800–842–0560.

The Wood Factory, 901 Harvard, Houston, TX 77008: Catalog $2 ❖ Victorian-style moldings, screen doors, porch parts, ornamental trim, and other woodwork. 713–863–7600.

Roofing Materials

C & H Roofing, P.O. Box 2105, Lake City, FL 32056: Free information ❖ Red cedar shingles with a thatched look. 800–327–8115.

Cedar Valley Shingle Systems, 943 San Felipe Rd., Hollister, CA 95023: Free brochure ❖ Cedar shingle panels in regular or rough-sawn textures. 800–521–9523.

CertainTeed, P.O. Box 860, Valley Forge, PA 19482: Free information ❖ Asphalt-based roof shingles that resemble wood shakes. 800–782–8777.

Classic Products, 299 Staunton St., P.O. Box 701, Piqua, OH 45356: Free brochure ❖ Aluminum roofing designed to look like wood. 800–543–8938.

Conklin Metal Industries, P.O. Box 1858, Atlanta, GA 30301: Brochure $3 ❖ Roofing supplies and metal roofing shingles in galvanized steel, copper, and other materials. 404–688–4510.

FibreCem Corporation, P.O. Box 411368, Charlotte, NC 28246: Free brochure ❖ Reinforced cement-base shingles with a slate appearance. 800–346–6147.

Georgia-Pacific, P.O. Box 2808, Norcross, GA 30091: Free information ❖ Easy-to-install shingles with a textured look of cedar. 800–447–2882.

Masonite Corporation, 1 S. Wacker Dr., Chicago, IL 60606: Free information ❖ Wood-fiber shingles with an authentic shake look. 800–446–1649.

Metal Building Components Inc., P.O. Box 38217, Houston, TX 77238: Free catalog ❖ Preformed metal roofs. 713–445–8555.

The New England Slate Company, Burr Pond Rd., RD 1, Sudbury, VT 05733: Free brochure ❖ Recycled roofing slate. 802–247–8809.

Owens-Corning Fiberglas, Fiberglas Tower, Toledo, OH 43659: Free information ❖ Fire-protected fiberglass shingles that resemble wood. 800–ROOF-OCF.

ShakerTown Corporation, 1200 Kerron St., Winlock, WA 98596: Free catalog ❖ Cedar shingles. 800–426–8970.

Supradur Manufacturing Corporation, P.O. Box 908, Rye, NY 10580: Free information ❖ Fireproof roofing shingles with a natural stone look. 800–223–1948.

Tile Roofs Inc., P.O. Box 177, Mokena, IL 60448: Free brochure ❖ New and used slate and tile roofing materials. 708–479–4366.

Westile, 8311 W. Carder Ct., Littleton, CO 80125: Free information ❖ Concrete roofing tiles. 800–433–8450.

Salvaged Building Materials

Aged Woods, 2331 E. Market St., York, PA 17402: Free brochure ❖ Fieldstone, slate, and other antique building materials. 800–233–9307; 717–840–0330 (in PA).

Albany Woodworks, P.O. Box 729, Albany, LA 70711: Free information ❖ Reclaimed antique building materials. 504–567–1155.

Architectural Antique Warehouse, P.O. Box 3065, Station D, Ottawa, Ontario, Canada K1P 6H6: Free information ❖ Reproduction old house parts. 613–526–1818.

Architectural Antiques Exchange, 715 N. 2nd St., Philadelphia, PA 19123: Free brochure ❖ Salvaged building components and trim. 215–922–3669.

Architectural Antiquities, Harborside, ME 04642: Free brochure ❖ Brass lighting fixtures and hardware, Victorian plumbing fixtures, fireplace mantels, doors, windows, stained glass, and other architectural antiquities. 207–326–4938.

Architectural Salvage Company, 726 Anacapa St., Santa Barbara, CA 93101: Free information ❖ Hardware, doors, stained glass, woodwork, mantels, light fixtures, columns, and other architectural antiques. 805–965–2446.

Art Directions, 6120 Delmar Blvd., St. Louis, MO 63112: Catalog $2 ❖ Salvaged building components. 314–863–1895.

The Bank Architectural Antiques, 1824 Felicity St., New Orleans, LA 70113: Free brochure ❖ Salvaged building components. 800–274–8883.

The Brass Knob, 2311 18th St. NW, Washington, DC 20009: Free information ❖ Hardware, garden ornaments, bathroom accessories, fireplace equipment, and antique lighting, from 1870 to 1930. 202–332–3370.

By-Gone Days Antiques Inc., 3100 South Blvd., Charlotte, NC 28209: Free information ❖ Mantels, restored door hardware, and other architectural antiques. 704–568–7537.

Conner's Architectural Antiques, 701 P St., Lincoln, NE 68508: Free information ❖ Interior and exterior architectural antiques. 402–435–3338.

Governor's Antiques and Architectural Materials, 6240 Meadowridge Rd., Mechanicsville, VA 23111: Free brochure ❖ Architectural materials and antiques. 804–746–1030.

Great Gatsby's, 5070 Peachtree Industrial Blvd., Atlanta, GA 30341: Free brochure ❖ Architectural antiquities and ornamental trim. 404–457–1905.

Irreplaceable Artifacts, 14 2nd Ave., New York, NY 10003: Free information ❖ Salvaged building components. 212–777–2900.

Olde Theatre Architectural Salvage, 2045 Broadway, Kansas City, MO 64108: Free brochure ❖ Salvaged building components and decor accessories. 816–283–3740.

Salvage One, 1524 S. Sangamon St., Chicago, IL 60608: Free brochure ❖ Salvaged building components. 312–733–0098.

United House Wrecking Inc., 535 Hope St., Stamford, CT 06906: Free brochure ❖ Doors, mantels, beveled glass, Victorian gingerbread, paneling, light fixtures, dividers, screens, and other salvaged architectural building components and trim. 203–348–8515.

Urban Archaeology, 285 Lafayette St., New York, NY 10012: Free information ❖ Staircases, balconies, plaster moldings, windows and skylights, doors, entryways, and other Victorian and architectural antiques and decor accessories. 212–431–6969.

Wooden Nickel Architectural Antiques, 1410 Central Pkwy., Cincinnati, OH 45210: Free information ❖ Salvaged building components and trims. 513–241–2985.

Shutters

Alside Corporation, P.O. Box 2010, Akron, OH 44309: Free information ❖ Shutter sets. 216–929–1811.

American Heritage Shutters, 2345 Dunn Ave., Memphis, TN 38114: Free brochure ❖ Indoor and exterior panel-style shutters. Also exterior vinyl shutters. 800–541–1186.

Beech River Mill Company, Old Rt. 16, Centre Ossipee, NH 03814: Brochure $5 ❖ Exterior and interior panelled and louvered shutters. 603–539–2636.

Historic Shutter & Restoration Inc., 5700 4th Ave., Key West, FL 33040: Free information ❖ Handcrafted interior and exterior shutters. 305–296–6332.

Historic Windows, P.O. Box 1172, Harrisonburg, VA 22801: Catalog $3 ❖ Handcrafted Victorian-style hardwood shutters. 703–434–5855.

Iberia Millwork, P.O. 12139, New Iberia, LA 70562: Free information ❖ Interior and exterior shutters, cabinets, and French doors. 318–365–8129.

Inter Trade Inc., 3175 Fujita St., Torrance, CA 90505: Free information ❖ Roll shutters that provide security and protection from heat, sun, cold, rain, and noise. 213–515–7177.

Kestrel Manufacturing, P.O. Box 12, Saint Peters, PA 19470: Information $2 ❖ Knock-down and ready-to-hang folding screens and interior and exterior shutters. 610–469–6444.

Perkowitz Window Fashions Inc., 135 Green Bay Rd., Wilmette, IL 60091: Catalog $1 ❖ Moveable louvered shutters. 708–251–7700.

REM Industries, P.O. Box 504, Northborough, MA 01532: Catalog $2 ❖ Interior and exterior shutters. 508–393–8424.

The Shutter Depot, [Shutter] Rt. 2, Box 157, Greenville, GA 30222: Free brochure ❖ Shutter kits and pre-finished and unfinished interior and exterior shutters. 706–672–1214.

Shutter Shop, P.O. Box 11882, Charlotte, NC 28220: Catalog $3 ❖ Interior and exterior shutters. 704–334–8031.

Shuttercraft, 282 Stepstone Hill Rd., Guilford, CT 06437: Free brochure ❖ Unfinished or primed and painted western white pine shutters with movable or fixed louvers. 203–453–1973.

Siding

California Redwood Association, 405 Enfrente Dr., Ste. 200, Novato, CA 94949: Free information with long SASE ❖ Redwood siding. 415–382–0662.

Cedar Valley Shingle Systems, 943 San Felipe Rd., Hollister, CA 95023: Free brochure ❖ Red cedar shingle panels and decorator shingles. 800–521–9523.

Dryvit Systems Inc., P.O. Box 1014, West Warwick, RI 02893: Free information ❖ Siding that looks like stucco. 800–556–7752.

Georgia-Pacific, P.O. Box 2808, Norcross, GA 30091: Free information ❖ Hardboard siding with a colonial wood-grain texture. 800–447–2882.

Granville Manufacturing Company Inc., Granville, VT 05747: Free brochure ❖ Quartersawn clapboard siding, wide pine and hardwood flooring, and other building materials. 802–767–4747.

Louisiana-Pacific Corporation, 111 SW 5th Ave., Portland, OR 97204: Free information ❖ Treated and weatherized wood siding. 503–221–0800.

Stucco Stone Products Inc., P.O. Box 270, Napa, CA 94559: Free information ❖ Manufactured interlocking, lightweight stone components for use as siding. 800–255–7462.

VIPCO, 1441 Universal Rd., P.O. Box 498, Columbus, OH 43216: Free information ❖ Solid-vinyl exterior siding with a look of carved wood clapboard. 800–366–8472.

Ward Clapboard Mill Inc., P.O. Box 1030, Waitsfield, VT 05673: Free information ❖ Spruce quartersawn clapboard siding. 802–496–3581.

Stairways

A.J. Stairs Inc., 1095 Towbin Ave., Lakewood, NJ 08701: Brochure $1 ❖ Easy-to-assemble spiral and curved stairways. 800–425–7824.

American General Products, P.O. Box 395, Ypsilanti, MI 48197: Free catalog ❖ Oak stair parts. 800–STAIRS-1; 313–483–1833 (in MI).

American Ornamental Metal, 5013 Kelley St., P.O. Box 21548, Houston, TX 77026: Free catalog ❖ Iron and wood spiral staircases. 800–231–3693.

Atlantic Stairworks, P.O. Box 244, Newburyport, MA 01950: Catalog $2 ❖ Traditional and contemporary solid wood stairways and handrails. 508–462–7502.

Bentwood Building, 21 Addison Square, Kalispell, MT 59901: Catalog $4 ❖ Log spiral stairways and furniture.

Curvoflite, 205 Spencer Ave., Chelsea, MA 02150: Free information ❖ Spiral and circular oak staircases, paneling, moldings, cabinets, and other millwork. 617–889–0007.

Driwood Ornamental Wood Moulding, P.O. Box 1729, Florence, SC 29503: Catalog $6 ❖ Curved stairs, embossed wood moulding, raised paneling, mantels, and doors. 803–669–2478.

Duvinage Corporation, P.O. Box 828, Hagerstown, MD 21741: Free catalog ❖ Spiral and circular stairways. 800–541–2645.

Goddard Manufacturing, Box 502, Logan, KS 67646: Free information ❖ Spiral staircases with optional wood railings. 913–689–4341.

The Iron Shop, 400 Reed Rd., P.O. Box 547, Broomall, PA 19008: Free brochure ❖ Iron circular stairway kits. 215–544–7100.

David G. Mulder, P.O. Box 1614, Battle Creek, MI 49016: Free information ❖ Circular stairs. 616–965–2676.

Mylen Industries, 650 Washington St., Peekskill, NY 10566: Free brochure ❖ Easy-to-install, space-saving indoor and outdoor spiral stairs. 800–431–2155; 914–739–8486 (IN NY).

Piedmont Home Products Inc., P.O. Box 269, Ruckersville, VA 22968: Free brochure ❖ Handcrafted spiral stairs, rails, balusters,

starting steps, and newel posts. 800–622–3399.

Salter Industries, P.O. Box 183, Eagleville, PA 19408: Free brochure ❖ Easy-to-install spiral stairs. 800–368–8280.

Spiral Manufacturing Inc., 17251 Jefferson Hwy., Baton Rouge, LA 70817: Free brochure ❖ Wood spiral and curved stairway kits. 800–535–9956.

Spiral Stairs of America, 1718 Franklin Ave., Erie, PA 16510: Free brochure ❖ Stairways. 800–422–3700.

Stair-Pak Products, 2575 Rt. 22 West, P.O. Box 3428, Union, NJ 07083: Free information ❖ Wood circular, spiral, and straight stairs. 908–688–1200.

Stair Systems Inc., 1480 E. 6th St., Sandwich, IL 60548: Free information ❖ Easy-to-assemble staircases with factory pre-assembled sections. 800–547–7837.

Stairways Inc., 4166 Pinemont, Houston, TX 77018: Free brochure ❖ Wood and metal stairways. 800–231–0793.

Steptoe & Wife Antiques Ltd., 322 Geary Ave., Toronto, Ontario, Canada M6H 2C7: Catalog $3 ❖ Easy-to-assemble, interior and exterior cast-iron spiral and straight staircases in Victorian design. 416–530–4200.

Visador Company, 7800 Belfort Pkwy., Ste. 170, Jacksonville, FL 32256: Brochure $2 ❖ Red oak curved stairs for homes. 800–847–2367.

York Spiral Stairs, RR 1, Box 945, North Vassalboro, ME 04962: Free brochure ❖ Spiral stairs in red oak, Honduran mahogany, and other hardwoods. 207–872–5558.

Stucco

Stucco Stone Products Inc., P.O. Box 270, Napa, CA 94559: Free information ❖ Building supplies. 800–225–7462.

Tile & Linoleum

Abitibi-Price Corporation, Building Products Division, 3250 Big Beaver Rd., Ste. 200, Troy, MI 48084: Free information ❖ Water-resistant tile board panels for bathrooms and other rooms. 313–649–3300.

American Olean Tile Company, 1000 Cannon Ave., Lansdale, PA 19446: Free information ❖ Easy-to-install ceramic mosaic tiles. 215–855–1111.

Amsterdam Corporation, 150 E. 58th St., 9th Floor, New York, NY 10155: Catalog

$2.50 ❖ Authentic Dutch hand-painted tiles. 212–644–1350.

Armstrong World Industries, P.O. Box 3001, Lancaster, PA 17604: Free information ❖ Tile, linoleum, and other floor coverings with an optional no-wax surface. 717–397–0611.

Laura Ashley, Mail Order, P.O. Box 18413, Memphis, TN 38181: Free information ❖ Floor tiles. 800–367–2000.

Azrock Industries Inc., P.O. Box 696060, San Antonio, TX 78269: Free information ❖ Easy-to-install vinyl tiles.

Color Tile, P.O. Box 749, Fort Worth, TX 76101: Free information ❖ Ceramic tile for bathroom counter tops and walls. 817–870–9409.

Country Floors Inc., 15 E. 16th St., New York, NY 10003: Catalog $6 ❖ Hand-moulded and painted ceramic tiles. 212–627–8300.

Designs in Tile, P.O. Box 358, Mt. Shasta, CA 96067: Brochure $3 ❖ Historic reproductions and contemporary and traditional patterns, and other ceramic tiles, murals, corner blocks, and coordinated borders. 916–926–2629.

Epro Tiles Inc., 156 E. Broadway, Westerville, OH 43081: Free information ❖ Sandstone collection of handmade tiles. 614–882–6990.

Italian Tile Center, 499 Park Ave., New York, NY 10022: Free information ❖ Italian tiles with flowers, fruit, and other patterns. 212–980–1500.

Terra Designs, 241 E. Blackwell St., Dover, NJ 07801: Catalog $1 ❖ Decorator bathroom tiles. 201–539–2999.

Victorian Collectibles, 845 E. Glenbrook Rd., Milwaukee, WI 53217: Catalog $5 ❖ Tiles and matching wallpaper duplicated from 19th-century patterns. 414–352–6971.

Trim & Ornamental Woodwork

Alpine Moulding, 155 Industrial Dr., Burlington, WI 53105: Free information with long SASE ❖ Reproduction and custom mouldings. 414–767–0336.

American Custom Millwork Inc., 3904 Newton Rd., P.O. Box 3608, Albany, GA 31706: Catalog $5 ❖ Embossed and plain architectural moldings and millwork. 912–888–3303.

Anderson-McQuaid Company Inc., 170 Fawcett St., Cambridge, MA 02138: Free price list ❖ Custom and restored moldings, flooring, panelling, and hardwood lumber. 617–876–3250.

Anthony Wood Products Inc., P.O. Box 1081, Hillsboro, TX 76645: Catalog $3 ❖ Handcrafted Victorian gingerbread. 817–582–7225.

Architectural Components, 26 N. Leverett Rd., Montague, MA 01351: Brochure $5 ❖ Custom and reproduction 18th- and 19th-century doors, windows, window frames, moldings, and French doors. 413–367–9441.

Architectural Sculpture Ltd., 242 Lafayette St., New York, NY 10012: Free information ❖ Turn-of-the-century plaster ornaments, plaques, sculptures, and other building and remodeling accoutrements. 212–431–5873.

Aristocraft Originals Inc., 6200 Highlands Pkwy. SE, Smyrna, GA 30082: Catalog $5 ❖ Reproduction niches, crown molding, trim, fireplaces, ceiling medallions, corbels, archways, columns, porches, and oak beams. 404–333–9934.

Arvid's Historic Woods, 2820 Rucker Ave., Everett, WA 98201: Catalog $6 ❖ Interior and exterior historic molding. 800–627–8437.

The Balmer Studios Inc., 9 Codeco Ct., Don Mills. Ontario, Canada M3A 1B6: Catalog $25 ❖ Interior plaster molding patterns. 416–449–2155.

Bendix Moldings Inc., 37 Ramland Rd. South, Orangeburg, NY 10962: Free catalog ❖ Decorative wood moldings and ornaments. 800–526–0240; 914–365–1111 (in NY).

Bryant Stove Inc., Box 2048, Thorndike, ME 04986: Free brochure ❖ Wood mantels and ornamental trim. 207–568–3665.

Campbellsville Industries Inc., P.O. Box 278, Campbellsville, KY 42718: Free catalog ❖ Aluminum cornices, louvers, cupolas, columns, balustrades, and shutters. 502–465–8135.

Chadsworth Incorporated, P.O. Box 53268, Atlanta, GA 30355: Catalog $3 ❖ Columns and replacement components in wood, fiberglass, and other materials. 800–394–5177.

Classic Architectural Specialties, 3223 Canton St., Dallas, TX 75226: Catalog $6 ❖ Colonial, Federal, Greek Revival, and Victorian molding and trim. 214–748–1668.

Cross Vinyl Lattice, 3174 Marjan Dr., Atlanta, GA 30341: Free information ❖ Vinyl decorative lattice panels with diagonal or rectangular patterns. 404–457–5125.

Cumberland Woodcraft Company Inc., P.O. Drawer 609, Carlisle, PA 17013: Catalog $4.50 ❖ Ceiling treatments, corbles, brackets, molding, grilles, and Victorian architectural millwork, carvings, and trims. 800–446–8560; 717–243–0063 (in PA).

Custom Woodturnings, 4000 Telephone Rd., Houston, TX 77087: Catalog $2 ❖ Reproduction Victorian millwork. 713–641–6254.

Decorators Supply Corporation, 3610 S. Morgan St., Chicago, IL 60609: Free information ❖ Wood mantels, capitals, brackets, medallions, plaster cornices, wood moldings, and composition and wood fiber ornaments. 312–847–6300.

Design Toscano, 15 E. Campbell St., Arlington Heights, IL 60005: Catalog $5 ❖ Replica gargoyles and goddesses, classical columns, capitals, table bases, brackets, urns, wall friezes, and other deco objects. 800–525–0733.

Driwood Ornamental Wood Moulding, P.O. Box 1729, Florence, SC 29503: Catalog $6 ❖ Embossed wood molding, raised paneling, mantels, curved stairs, and doors. 803–669–2478.

Empire Woodworks, P.O. Box 717, Blanco, TX 78606: Catalog $3 ❖ Country-style and Victorian trim. 512–833–2119.

Raymond E. Enkeboll Designs, 16506 Avalon Blvd., Carson, CA 90746: Free brochure ❖ Carved and sculptured solid wood architectural accoutrements. 310–532–1400.

Federal Cabinet Company Inc., 409 Highland Ave., Box 190, Middletown, NY 10940: Free brochure ❖ Architectural wood turnings. 914–342–1511.

Felber Ornamental Plastering Corporation, 1000 W. Washington St., Norristown, PA 19404: Catalog $3 ❖ Period-style and other plaster cornices, medallions, sculptures, niches, capitals, brackets, and domes. 610–275–4713.

Fischer & Jirouch Company, 4821 Superior Ave., Cleveland, OH 44103: Catalog $10 ❖ Handcrafted plaster ornaments. 216–361–3840.

Focal Point Inc., P.O. Box 93327, Atlanta, GA 30377: Free information ❖ Ceiling

medallions, cornice moldings, niche caps, and doorway treatments. 800–662–5550.

Gazebo & Porchworks, 728 9th Ave. SW, Puyallup, WA 98371: Catalog $2 ❖ Wood trims, ornamental items, outdoor swings, and backyard play structures. 206–848–0502.

The Gingerbread Man, 327 Industrial Rd., #3, Placerville, CA 95667: Catalog $2 ❖ Victorian-style trim and ornamental woodwork. 916–644–0440.

Gingerbread Man Woodworks, Factory Outlet Store, P.O. Box 59, Noel, MO 64854: Catalog $5 ❖ Gazebos, garden structures, and ornamental trim. 417–775–2553.

Hallidays America Inc., P.O. Box 731, Sparta, NJ 07871: Free information ❖ Fireplace accessories, handcarved mantels, and wood moldings. 201–729–8876.

Heritage Woodcraft, 1230 Oakland St., Hendersonville, NC 28739: Catalog $2 ❖ Corbels, brackets, finials, scrolls, headers, trim, sawn balusters, and turned balusters. 704–692–8542.

House of Moulding, 15202 Oxnard St., Van Nuys, CA 91411: Catalog $5 ❖ Wood mouldings and trim, ceiling medallions, fireplaces, and mantels. 800–327–4186; 800–675–1952 (in CA).

Dimitrios Klitsas, Wood Sculptor, 705 Union St., West Springfield, MA 01089: Free information ❖ Wood sculptures for decorating. 413–732–2661.

Chip La Pointe Cabinetmaker, 41 Gulf Rd., Pelhamn, MA 01002: Catalog $4.50 ❖ Reproduction Victorian trim. 413–256–1558.

Mad River Woodworks, P.O. Box 1067, Blue Lake, CA 95525: Catalog $3 ❖ Corbels, balusters, trims, brackets, spandrels, wood gutters, and railings. 800–446–8560; 707–668–5671 (in CA).

Old World Moulding & Finishing Inc., 115 Allen Blvd., Farmingdale, NY 11735: Catalog $3 ❖ Hard wood mouldings. 516–293–1789.

Pagliacco Turning & Milling, P.O. Box 225, Woodacre, CA 94973: Catalog $6 ❖ Wood balusters, newel and porch posts, railings, and columns. 415–488–4333.

The Porch Factory, P.O. Box 231, White House, TN 37188: Catalog $2 ❖ Victorian, country trim, and ornamental woodwork. 615–672–0998.

The Restoration Place, 305 20th St., Rock Island, IL 61201: Free brochure ❖ Light fixtures and plumbing, hardware, architectural, and decor accessories. 309–786–0004.

River Bend Turnings, RD 1, River Rd., Box 364, Wellsville, NY 14895: Free brochure ❖ Porch turnings, table and chair legs, newel posts, balusters, and finials. 716–593–3495.

A.F. Schwerd Manufacturing Company, 3215 McClure Ave., Pittsburgh, PA 15212: Free brochure ❖ Standard and detailed wood columns in seasoned northern white pine with matching pilasters and aluminum bases. 412–766–6322.

Sepp Leaf Products Inc., 381 Park Ave. South, New York, NY 10016: Free information ❖ Gold and palladium metal leaf, tools, and kits. 212–683–2840.

Silverton Victorian Millworks, P.O. Box 2987, Durango, CO 81302: Catalog $4 ❖ Castings, crowns, corner blocks, doors, bases, wainscot, other architectural accouterments, and Victorian moldings and millwork. 303–259–5915.

Style-Mark, 960 W. Barre Rd., Archbold, OH 43502: Free catalog ❖ Arches, brackets, trim, louvers, window heads, moldings, entryways, other millwork, and architectural accents. 800–446–3040.

M. Swift & Sons Inc., 10 Love Ln., Hartford, CT 06141: Free information ❖ Gold, silver, palladium, aluminum, and composite leaf for decorating and restoring interiors and exteriors of buildings, domes, walls, ceilings, furniture, and works of art. 800–628–0380.

Victorian Interiors, 575 Hayes St., San Francisco, CA 94102: Catalog $2 ❖ Victorian trim and ornamental woodwork. 415–431–7191.

Vintage Wood Works, Hwy. 34 South, Box R, Quinlan, TX 75474: Catalog $2 ❖ Spandrels and shelves, fans, porch posts, balusters, brackets, signs, corbels, headers, gazebos, and other handcrafted Victorian gingerbread. 903–356–2158.

The Woodworkers' Store, 21801 Industrial Blvd., Rogers, MN 55374: Free catalog ❖ Hardware, ornamentals, woodworking supplies, and tools. 800–403–9736.

Wallcoverings

American Blind & Wallpaper Factory, 28237 Orchard Lake Rd., Farmington Hills, MI 48018: Free information ❖ Wallpaper, and roller and pleated shades, and wood, micro, mini, and vertical blinds. 800–735–5300.

American Discount Wallcoverings, 1411 5th Ave., Pittsburgh, PA 15219: Free information ❖ Decorator wallpapers, window treatments, and upholstery fabrics. 800–77–PAPER.

American Wallcovering Distributors, 22600 Rt. 22, Union, NJ 07083: Free information ❖ Wallpaper and fabrics. 800–843–6567.

Laura Ashley, Mail Order, P.O. Box 18413, Memphis, TN 38181 ❖ Wallpaper reproductions of period patterns with complementing borders and coordinating fabrics. 800–367–2000.

Benington's, 1271 Manheim Pike, Lancaster, PA 17601: Catalog $5 ❖ Wallpaper and rugs. 800–252–5060.

Bentley Brothers, 2709 Southpark Rd., Louisville, KY 40219: Free information ❖ Embossed wallcoverings with an ornate look of detailed plasterwork. 800–824–4777.

Best Discount Wallcoverings, P.O. Box 1286, St. Charles, MO 63302: Free information ❖ Wallcoverings. 800–328–5550.

BMI Home Decorating, 33580 Royal Oak Ln., Wildwood, IL 60030: Free information ❖ Decorator fabrics and wallcoverings. 800–999–2091.

Bradbury & Bradbury Wallpapers, P.O. Box 155, Benicia, CA 94510: Catalog $10 ❖ Victorian-style wallpapers, hand-printed borders, friezes, ceiling papers, and coordinated wall frills. 707–746–1900.

J.R. Burrows & Company, P.O. Box 522, Rockland, MA 02370: Catalog $5 ❖ Artistic wallpaper and fabric and period carpet reproductions by special order. 617–982–1812.

Colonial Wallcovering, 707 E. Passyunk Ave., Philadelphia, PA 19147: Free information ❖ Hard-to-get wallpapers and other wallcoverings from worldwide sources. 215–331–9300.

Crown Corporation, 1801 Wynkoop St., Ste. 235, Denver, CO 80202: Catalog $2 ❖ Victorian-style wallcoverings and borders. 800–422–2099.

Designer Secrets, P.O. Box 529, Fremont, NE 68025: Catalog $2 (refundable) ❖ Wallcoverings, fabrics, bedspreads, furniture, and window treatments. 800–955–2559.

Direct Wallpaper Express, 374 Hall St., Phoenixville, PA 19460: Free information ❖ Wallpaper. 800–548–1558.

East Carolina Wallpaper Market, 1106 Pink Hill Rd., Kinston, NC 28501: Free information ❖ Wallpaper, fabrics, and borders. 800–848–7283.

Eisenhart Wallcoverings Company, 1649 Broadway, Hanover, PA 17331: Free information ❖ Wallcoverings and coordinated fabrics. 800–726–3267.

Georgia-Pacific, P.O. Box 2808, Norcross, GA 30091: Free information ❖ Wall paneling and pre-hung wallpaper on plywood panels. 800–447–2882.

Hang-It-Now Wallpaper Stores, 10517–F N. Main St., Archdale, NC 27263: Free information with long SASE ❖ Wallcoverings and decorator fabrics. 800–325–9494; 919–431–6341 (in NC).

Harmony Supply Company Inc., P.O. Box 313, Medford, MA 02155: Free information with long SASE ❖ Wallpaper and fabrics for coordinating wall and window treatments. 617–395–2600.

Headquarters Windows & Walls, 8 Clinton Pl., Morristown, NJ 07960: Free information ❖ Wallcoverings and window blinds. 800–338–4882.

Marlene's Decorator Fabrics, 301 Beech St., Hackensack, NJ 07601: Free brochure with long SASE ❖ Decorator fabrics. 800–992–7325.

Mary's Discount Wallpaper, 111 N. Lansdowne Ave., Lansdowne, PA 19050: Free information ❖ Wallpaper. 800–521–3393.

Carol Mead Wallpapers, RR 3, Box 3396, West Addison, VT 05491: Catalog $5 ❖ Turn-of-the-century historical wallpapers. 802–759–2692.

Nationwide Wallcovering, P.O. Box 40, Hackensack, NJ 07602: Free information ❖ Wallcoverings. 800–488–WALL.

Number One Wallpaper, 2914 Long Beach Rd., Oceanside, NY 11572: Free information ❖ Wallpaper. 800–423–0084; 516–678–4445 (in NY).

Peerless Wallpaper & Blind Depot, 39500 14 Mile Rd., Walled Lake, MI 48390: Free information ❖ Wallcoverings and blinds. 800–999–0898.

Pintchik Homeworks, 2106 Bath Ave., Brooklyn, NY 11214: Free information ❖ Wallpaper, window treatment supplies, paints, floor coverings, and hardware. 800–847–4199; 718–996–5580 (in NY).

Robinson's Wallcoverings, 225 W. Spring St., Titusville, PA 16354: Catalog $2 (refundable) ❖ Wallcoverings and decorator fabrics. 800–458–2426.

Charles Rupert, The Shop, 2004 Oak Bay Ave., Victoria, British Columbia, Canada V8R 1E4: Information $5 ❖ Wallpapers, from the 1770s to 1920s. 604–592–4916.

Sanz International Inc., P.O. Box 1794, High Point, NC 27261: Free information with long SASE ❖ Wallcoverings, decorator fabrics, furniture, lamps, and carpeting. 910–886–7630.

Shibui Wall Coverings, P.O. Box 1268, Santa Rosa, CA 95402: Catalog $4 ❖ Wallcoverings in grasses, jute, cork, and leaf patterns and paper hanging tools and supplies. 800–824–3030; 707–526–6170 (in CA).

Silver's Wholesale Club, 3001–15 Kensington Ave., Philadelphia, PA 19134: Free information ❖ Wallcoverings, blinds, and verticals. 800–426–6600.

Singer Wallcoverings, Box 300, Kings Island, OH 45034: Free information ❖ Vinyl wallcoverings. 800–543–0412; 800–582–1760 (in OH).

Smart Wallcoverings, P.O. Box 2206, Southfield, MI 48037: Free information ❖ Wallcoverings. 800–677–0200.

Southern Discount Wall Covering, 1583 N. Military Trail, West Palm Beach, FL 33409: Free information ❖ Wallcoverings. 800–699–WALL.

Style Wallcovering, P.O. Box 865, Southfield, MI 48037: Free information ❖ Wallcoverings. 800–627–0400.

Victorian Collectibles, 845 E. Glenbrook Rd., Milwaukee, WI 53217: Catalog $5 ❖ Wallpaper in 19th-century patterns with matching tiles. 414–352–6971.

Wallpaper Outlet, 337 Rt. 46, Rockaway, NJ 07866: Free information with long SASE ❖ Wallpaper. 800–291–WALL.

Wallpaper Warehouse Inc., 1434 Ellis Ave., Jackson, MS 39204: Free information ❖ Wallcoverings. 800–523–3503; 800–826–7310 (in MS).

Wallpaperxpress, P.O. Box 4061, Naperville, IL 60567: Free information ❖ Decorator fabrics, mini blinds, and wallcoverings. 800–288–9979.

Worldwide Wallcoverings & Blinds Inc., 333 Skokie Blvd., Northbrook, IL 60062:

Free information with long SASE ❖ Wallcoverings and blinds. 800–322–5400.

Yankee Wallcoverings Inc., 109 Accord Park Dr., Norwell, MA 02061: Free information ❖ Wallcoverings and coordinating fabrics. 800–624–7711.

Yield House, P.O. Box 2525, Conway, NH 03818: Free catalog ❖ Wallcoverings. 800–258–4720.

Yorktowne Wallpaper Outlet, 2445 S. Queen St., York, PA 17402: Free information ❖ Wallcoverings. 800–847–6142.

Windows

Accurate Metal Weatherstrip Company, 725 S. Fulton Ave., Mount Vernon, NY 10550: Catalog $3 (refundable) ❖ Weatherstripping for windows and doors. 914–668–6042.

Allied Window Inc., 2724 W. McMicken Ave., Cincinnati, OH 45214: Free information ❖ Windows. 800–445–5411.

Alside Corporation, P.O. Box 2010, Akron, OH 44309: Free information ❖ Outdoor windows with vinyl trim and insulating glass. 216–929–1811.

Andersen Windows, P.O. Box 3900, Peoria, IL 61614: Free information ❖ Energy-efficient windows, roof windows, and patio doors. 800–426–4261.

Arctic Glass & Window Outlet, Rt. 1, Hammond, WI 54015: Catalog $4 ❖ Windows, entryway and patio doors, skylights, and sunrooms. 800–428–9276.

Art Glass Unlimited Inc., 412 N. Euclid, St. Louis, MO 63108: Free information ❖ Stained and leaded glass windows. 314–361–0474.

Bristolite Skylights, 401 E. Goetz Ave., P.O. Box 2515, Santa Ana, CA 92707: Free catalog ❖ Residential skylights, fixed or with electric and manual openers. 800–854–8618; 800–422–2131 (in CA).

Cherry Creek Enterprises Inc., 3500 Blake St., Denver, CO 80205: Catalog $2 ❖ Beveled glass designs. 303–892–1819.

Colonial Craft, 2772 Fairview Ave., St. Paul, MN 55113: Free catalog ❖ Solid hardwood windows and doors and grilles for regular and sliding patio doors. 800–727–5187; 612–631–2110 (in MN).

Combination Door Company, P.O. Box 1076, Fond du Lac, WI 54936: Free brochure ❖ Wood storm and screen doors, screen

doors, and basement and garage windows. 414–922–2050.

DAB Studio, 31 N. Terrace, P.O. Box 96, Maplewood, NJ 07040: Free catalog ❖ Stained glass windows and decor accessories. 800–682–6151.

Fox Light, 8300 Dayton Rd., Fairborn, OH 45324: Free information ❖ Skylights that can be converted from closed to opening units. 800–233–FOXX.

Georgia-Pacific, P.O. Box 2808, Norcross, GA 30091: Free information ❖ Doors and windows. 800–447–2882.

Great Lakes Windows, P.O. Box 1896, Toledo, OH 43603: Free information ❖ Windows. 419–666–5555.

Louisiana-Pacific Corporation, 111 SW 5th Ave., Portland, OR 97204: Free information ❖ Windows. 503–221–0800.

Marvin Windows, P.O. Box 100, Warroad, MN 56763: Free information ❖ Divided light and insulated storm windows and transoms. 800–346–5128.

Midwest Wood Products, 1051 S. Rolff St., Davenport, IA 52802: Catalog $2 ❖ Divided light insulated storm windows. 319–323–4757.

Perkasie Industries Corporation, 50 E. Spruce St., Perkasie, PA 18944: Free information ❖ Storm window kits for the do-it-yourselfer. 800–523–6747.

Pozzi Wood Windows, P.O. Box 5249, Bend, OR 97708: Free information ❖ Divided-light windows. 800–323–6474.

Rollamatic Roofs Incorporated, 1441 Yosemite Ave., San Francisco, CA 94124: Free brochure ❖ Electrically controlled retractable skylights. 800–345–7392; 415–822–5655 (in CA).

Southeastern Insulated Glass, 6477–B Peachtree Industrial Blvd., Atlanta, GA 30360: Free information ❖ Greenhouse and sunroom kits and sliding glass doors and skylights with optional tempered insulated glass. 800–841–9842; 404–455–8838 (in GA).

Thermo-Press Corporation, 5406 Distributor Dr., Richmond, VA 23225: Information $1 ❖ Storm windows. 804–231–2964.

Velux-America Inc., P.O. Box 5001, Greenwood, SC 29648: Free brochure ❖ Weather-tight roof windows and skylights. 800–283–2831.

Ventarama Skylight Corporation, 303 Sunnyside Blvd., Plainview, NY 11803: Free information ❖ Ventilating, fixed, and motorized skylights. 516–349–8855.

Walsh Screen & Window Inc., 554 E. 3rd St., Mount Vernon, NY 10553: Free information ❖ Screens, windows, storm windows, and doors. 914–668–7811.

Weather Shield Mfg. Inc., One Weather Shield Plaza,, Medford, WI 54451: Free information ❖ Wood windows, patio doors, and steel entryways. 800–477–6808.

Wenco Windows, P.O. Box 1248, Mount Vernon, OH 43050: Free information ❖ Exterior windows with operable sides. 614–397–3403.

Woodstone Company, Patch Rd., P.O. Box 223, Westminster, VT 05158: Information $3 ❖ Insulated solid wood doors and single-, double-, or triple-glazed windows, with palladians and straight and fanned transoms. 802–722–9217.

HOMES & PREFABS
Conventional & Solar Energy Homes

Acorn Structures Inc., Box 1445, Concord, MA 01742: Catalog $15 ❖ Solar energy and other homes. 508–369–4111.

The Beamery, Heiskell, TN 37754: Information $8 ❖ Timber frame homes. 800–BEAMERY.

Classic Post & Beam, P.O. Box 546, York, ME 03909: Catalog $6 ❖ Post and beam homes. 800–872–BEAM.

Davis Frame Company, P.O. Box 361, Brownsville, VT 05037: Brochure $12 ❖ Handcrafted timber frame homes. 802–484–9771.

Deck House, 930 Main St., Acton, MA 01720: Information $20 ❖ Post and beam homes. 800–727–3325.

Deltec Homes, 604 College St., Asheville, NC 28801: Catalog $10 ❖ Pre-engineered panel kits for circular homes. 800–642–2508.

Lindal Cedar Homes, P.O. Box 24426, Seattle, WA 98178: Catalog $15 ❖ Plans for customizing homes or building a new one. 800–426–0536.

Linwood Homes, P.O. Box 20090, Barrie, Ontario, Canada L4M 6E9: Catalog $10 ❖ Post and beam and truss kits. 800–668–6896.

Lumber Enterprises Inc., 75777 Gallatin Rd., Gallatin Gateway, MT 59730: Catalog $5 ❖ Custom homes. 800–235–4321.

Miles Homes, P.O. Box 9495, Minneapolis, MN 55440: Catalog $3 ❖ Homes with pre-cut materials and step-by-step building instructions. 800–343–2884.

Pan Abode Inc., 4350 Lake Washington Blvd. North, Renton, WA 98056: Catalog $15 ❖ Cedar homes. 800–782–2633; 206–255–8260 (in WA).

Powers Steel & Wire, 4118 E. Elwood, Phoenix, AZ 86040: Free brochure ❖ Easy-to-assemble prefabricated utility buildings. 602–437–1160.

Rapid River Rustic Inc., P.O. Box 8, Rapid River, MI 49878: Catalog $10 ❖ Solid cedar homes. 800–422–3327.

Riverbend Timber Framing Inc., P.O. Box 26, Blissfield, MI 49228: Catalog $20 ❖ Timber frame home plans. 517–486–4355.

Timberpeg, Box 1500, Claremont, NH 03743: Information $15 ❖ Post and beam single and multi-level homes. 603–542–7762.

Woodhouse Post & Beam Inc., P.O. Box 219, Mansfield, PA 16933: Catalog $10 ❖ Post and beam homes. 800–227–4311; 717–549–6232 (in PA).

Domes

Daystar Shelter Corporation, 22675 Cedar Dr., Bethel, MN 55005: Free information ❖ Light-weight, easy-to-assemble domes. 612–753–4914.

Oregon Dome Living Inc., 3215 Meadow Ln., Eugene, OR 97402: Catalog $8 ❖ Energy-efficient domes. 800–572–8943.

Timberline Geodesics, 2015 Blake St., Berkeley, CA 94704: Catalog $12 ❖ Easy-to-assemble dome homes. 800–366–3466.

Log Homes

Alpine Log Homes, Box 85, Victor, MT 59875: Free information ❖ Log homes. 406–642–3451.

Alta Industries Ltd., P.O. Box 88, Halcottsville, NY 12438: Catalog $8 ❖ Log homes. 800–926–2582; 914–586–3336 (in NY).

L.C. Andrew Maine Cedar Log Homes, 35 Main St., Windham, ME 04062: Catalog $5 ❖ Log homes. 800–427–5647; 207–892–8561 (in ME).

Appalachian Log Homes, 11312 Station West, Knoxville, TN 37922: Catalog $8 ❖ Log homes in chinked and log-on-log styles. 615–966–6440.

Appalachian Log Structures Inc., P.O. Box 614, Riley, WV 25271: Catalog $7 ❖ Log homes, garages, and other structures. 800–458–9990; 304–372–6410 (in VA).

Asperline Log Homes, Rt. 150, RD 1, Box 240, Lock Haven, PA 17745: Free information ❖ Easy-to-construct log homes. 800–428–4663.

Jim Barna Log Systems, P.O. Box 4529, Oneida, TN 37841: Catalog $7 ❖ Log homes. 800–962–4734.

Beaver Log Homes, P.O. Box 236, Beloit, WI 53512: Catalog $6 ❖ Pre-cut log home kits. 608–365–6833.

Confederation Log Homes, 14200 El Camino Ln., Lenoir City, TN 37771: Catalog $10 ❖ Log homes. 615–986–0021.

Fireside Log Homes, 200 River St., Ellijay, GA 30540: Catalog $8 ❖ Log homes. 800–521–LOGS; 404–635–7373 (in GA).

Garland Homes, P.O. Box 12, Victor, MT 59875: Catalog $10 ❖ Log homes. 800–642–3837.

Gastineau Log Homes Inc., Box 248, New Bloomfield, MO 65063: Catalog $8 ❖ Log homes. 800–654–9253; 314–896–5122 (in MO).

Greatwood Log Homes, P.O. Box 707, Elkhart, WI 53020: Catalog $7.50 ❖ Log homes. 800–558–5812.

Green Mountain Log Homes, Box 428, Chester, VT 05143: Catalog $9 ❖ Log homes. 802–875–2163.

Heartbilt Homes, 1615 Summit Dr., Stockton, IL 61085: Free information ❖ Log homes. 815–947–3244.

Hearthstone Log Homes, 1630 East Hwy., Dandrige, TN 37725: Catalog $12 ❖ Log homes. 800–247–4442.

Heritage Log Homes, P.O. Box 610, Gatlinburg, TN 37738: Catalog $12 ❖ Log homes. 800–456–4663.

Hiawatha Log Homes, P.O. Box 8, Munising, MI 49862: Catalog $6 ❖ Log homes. 800–876–8100.

Highland Log Builders Ltd., P.O. Box 730, Lumby, British Columbia, Canada V0E 2G0: Free information ❖ Cottages, resort lodges, and commercial structures. 604–547–2266.

Holland Log Homes, 13352 Van Buren, Holland, MI 49424: Catalog $7 ❖ Pre-cut log homes. 616–399–9627.

Homestead Log Homes, 6301 Crater Lake Hwy., Medford, OR 97502: Catalog $10 ❖ Pre-cut kits or on-site factory built log homes. 503–826–6888.

Honest Abe Log Homes Inc., Rt. 1, Box 84, Moss, TN 38575: Catalog $8 ❖ Log homes. 800–231–3695.

Katahdin Forest Products, P.O. Box 145, Oakfield, ME 04763: Video catalog $15 ❖ Log homes. 207–757–8278.

Kuhns Brothers Log Homes, RD 2, Box 406A, Lewisburg, PA 17837: Catalog $8 ❖ Log homes. 800–346–7903.

Log Cabin Homes Ltd., P.O. Drawer 1457, Rocky Mount, NC 27802: Catalog $8.95 ❖ Log homes. 919–977–7785.

Lok-N-Logs, P.O. Box 677, Sherburne, NY 13460: Catalog $7.50 ❖ Log homes. 800–343–8928; 607–674–4447 (in NY).

Majestic Log Homes, P.O. Box 772, Fort Collins, CO 80522: Free brochure ❖ Log homes. 303–224–4857.

Montana Log Homes, 3212 Hwy. 93 South, Kalispell, MT 59901: Catalog $7 ❖ Log homes. 406–752–2992.

Mountaineer Log Homes Inc., P.O. Box 248, Morgantown, PA 19543: Catalog $8 ❖ Log homes. 215–286–2005.

New England Log Homes, 2301 State St., P.O. Box 5427, Hamden, CT 06518: Catalog $15 ❖ Log homes. 800–243–3551; 203–562–9981 (in CT).

Northeastern Log Homes, P.O. Box 126, Groton, VT 05046: Information $8 ❖ Log homes. 800–992–6526.

Otsego Cedar Log Homes, P.O. Box 127, Waters, MI 49797: Catalog $6 ❖ Post-and-beam log homes. 517–732–6268.

Pioneer Log Systems Inc., P.O. Box 226, Kingston Springs, TN 37082: Catalog $7 ❖ Log and post-and-beam homes. 615–952–4912.

Ponderosa Log Homes, P.O. Box 1360, Pagosa Springs, CO 81147: Catalog $7.50 ❖ Log houses. 800–999–0832.

Real Log Homes, P.O. Box 202, Hartland, VT 05048: Catalog $9 ❖ Log homes with optional full basements, garages, slabs, crawl spaces, and piers. 800–732–5564.

Rocky Mountain Log Homes, 1883 Hwy. 93 South, Hamilton, MT 59840: Catalog $10 ❖ Log homes. 604–270–2710.

Rustics of Lindbergh Lake Inc., P.O. Box 3240, Silverdale, WA 98383: Catalog $8 ❖ Log homes.

Satterwhite Log Homes, Rt. 2, Box 256, Longview, TX 75605: Free brochure ❖ Log homes. 800–777–7288.

Southern Cypress Log Homes Inc., U.S. Hwy. 19 South, P.O. Box 209, Crystal River, FL 32629: Catalog $4.95 ❖ Log homes. 904–795–0777.

Southland Log Homes, 7521 Broad River Rd., P.O. Box 1668, Irmo, SC 29063: Catalog $7.50 ❖ Log homes. 800–845–3555.

Stonemill Log Homes, 7015 Stonemill Rd., Knoxville, TN 37919: Catalog $6 ❖ Log homes. 615–693–4833.

Timber Log Homes Inc., 639 Old Hartford Rd., Colchester, CT 06415: Brochure $10 ❖ Log homes. 800–533–5906; 203–537–2393 (in CT).

Town & Country Cedar Homes, 4772 US 131 South, Petoskey, MI 49770: Catalog $18.50 ❖ Hand-hewn log homes. 800–968–3178.

Vermont Log Buildings, P.O. Box 202, Hartland, VT 05048: Catalog $8 ❖ Log homes. 802–436–2121.

Ward Log Homes, P.O. Box 72, Houlton, ME 04730: Catalog $8 ❖ Log homes. 800–341–1566; 207–532–6531 (in ME).

Wilderness Log Homes, P.O. Box 902, Plymouth, WI 53073: Catalog $10 ❖ Pre-cut log homes in passive solar and other models. 800–237–8564.

Wisconsin Log Homes Inc., P.O. Box 11005, Green Bay, WI 54307: Catalog $14.95 ❖ Passive solar and other log homes. 800–678–9107.

HORSE & STABLE EQUIPMENT

Health Care & Stable Supplies

Rohn Agri Products, P.O. Box 2000, Peoria, IL 61656: Free information ❖ Heavy-duty horse stalls. 800–447–2264; 309–697–4400 (in IL).

Bargain Corral, P.O. Box 856, Allan, TX 75002: Free information with long SASE ❖ Saddles, stirrups and straps, blankets, spurs, halters, pads, bits, bridles and breast collars,

boots, dusters, and rain slickers. 800–955–5616.

Chick's Saddle, U.S. Rt. 113, Harrington, DE 19952: Free catalog ❖ Horse equipment. 800–444–2441.

Econo-Vet Groom & Health, 8687 Blumenstein Rd., P.O. Box 1191, Minocqua, WI 54548: Free catalog ❖ Health care, grooming, and kennel products for horses. 800–451–4162; 715–369–5591 (in WI).

Farnam Companies Inc., Horse Products Division, P.O. Box 12068, Omaha, NE 68112: Free information ❖ Insect and parasite treatment and repellent products. 800–234–2269.

Drs. Foster & Smith Inc., 2253 Air Park Rd., P.O. Box 100, Rhinelander, WI 54501: Free catalog ❖ Pet and equine products and health care supplies. 800–826–7206.

Happy Jack Inc., Box 475, Snow Hill, NC 28580: Free catalog ❖ Animal health care products. 800–326–5225.

Horsemen's General Store, 345 W. Leffel Ln., Springfield, OH 45506: Catalog $3 ❖ Everything for horse owners, trainers, breeders, riders, and horses. 800–343–0167.

Red River Portable Arenas, P.O. Box 549, Carbon, TX 76435: Free brochure ❖ Portable enclosures for roping, riding and training, and team penning. 800–343–1026.

Joe Roberts Welding, P.O. Box 777, Ringling, OK 73456: Free information ❖ Portable roping arenas. 800–654–4584; 405–662–2071 (in OK).

Texas Outfitters Supply Inc., Rt. 6, Box 25, Sulphur Springs, TX 75482: Catalog $2 (refundable) ❖ Wall tents, folding stoves, panning equipment, saddles, team and driving harnesses, and pack equipment for horses and mules. 903–885–6935.

Valley Vet Supply, P.O. Box 504, Marysville, KS 66508: Free catalog ❖ Equine health products, roping gear, pack equipment, horse blankets, and English, Western, and Arabian tack. 800–468–0059.

Wholesale Vet Supply, 4801 Shepherd Trl., Rockford, IL 61103: Free catalog ❖ Supplies for dogs, cats, rabbits, other household pets, horses, and cattle.

Horse Trailers

Charmac Trailers, Box 205, Twin Falls, ID 83301: Free information ❖ Horse trailers. 208–733–5241.

Featherlite Manufacturing Inc., P.O. Box 387, Grand Meadow, MN 55936: Free information ❖ Horse trailers. 507–754–5171.

4–Star Trailers Inc., Box 75395, Oklahoma City, OK 73147: Free information ❖ Horse trailers. 405–787–9880.

Hillsboro Industries Inc., 220 Industrial Rd., Hillsboro, KS 67063: Free information ❖ Horse trailers. 800–835–0209.

Kiefer Built, Box 88, Kanawha, IA 50447: Free information ❖ Horse trailers. 515–762–3201.

Pierce Sales, Expressway 287, Henrietta, TX 76365: Catalog $1 ❖ Cargo carriers, runabouts, horse trailers, and truck beds. 817–538–5646.

S & H Trailer Manufacturing Company, 800 Industrial Dr., Madill, OK 73446: Free information ❖ Horse, cargo, equipment, stock, RV, utility, and carryall trailers. 405–795–5577.

Sooner Trailers, P.O. Box 1323, Duncan, OK 73534: Free brochure ❖ Horse trailers. 405–255–6979.

Sundowner Trailer Inc., HC61, Box 27, Coleman, OK 73432: Free information ❖ Horse trailers. 800–654–3879; 405–937–4256 (in OK).

W-W Trailer, Box 807, Madill, OK 73446: Free information ❖ Horse trailers. 405–795–5571.

Saddles & Tack

The Australian Stock Saddle Company, P.O. Box 987, Malibu, CA 90265: Catalog $6 ❖ Leather saddles. 818–889–6988.

Bargain Corral, P.O. Box 856, Allan, TX 75002: Free information with long SASE ❖ Saddles, stirrups and straps, blankets, spurs, halters, pads, bits, bridles and breast collars, boots, dusters, and rain slickers. 800–955–5616.

Barstow Pro Rodeo Equipment, P.O. Box 1516, Corsicana, TX 75151: Catalog $2 ❖ Rodeo riding equipment. 903–874–3995.

Bona Allen Saddle Company, 6 Union Dr., Olney, IL 62450: Free catalog ❖ Saddles. 618–392–3858.

Mark Carlton Saddles, P.O. Box J, Harrisonville, MI 64701: Free information ❖ Western saddles. 800–437–9143.

Down Under Saddle Supply, 2306 S. Colorado Blvd., Denver, CO 80222: Free

information ❖ Australian saddles and tack. 303–753–6737.

John M. Fallis Custom Saddles, 29301 County Rd. 3, Elizabeth, CO 80107: Catalog $3 ❖ Saddles. 303–646–4125.

Hitching Post Supply, 10312 210th St. SE, Snohomish, WA 98290: Free catalog ❖ Handmade saddles and horseback riding accessories. 206–668–2349.

Horsemen's General Store, 345 W. Leffel Ln., Springfield, OH 45506: Catalog $3 ❖ Everything for horse owners, trainers, breeders, riders, and horses. 800–343–0167.

K & B Saddle, Rt. 1, Box 21, Council Bluffs, IA 51501: Catalog $1 ❖ Western saddles. 712–366–1026.

Kates Saddle Supply, 3551 S. Monaco Pkwy., Denver, CO 80237: Free information ❖ General purpose and Australian-style saddles. 800–395–8225.

H. Kauffman, 419 Park Ave. South, New York, NY 10016: Catalog $5 ❖ Horseback riding equipment and clothing. 800–872–6687.

Libertyville Saddle Shop Inc., P.O. Box M, Libertyville, IL 60048: Catalog $3 ❖ Saddles and clothing. 800–872–3353.

Mary's Tack & Feed, 3675 Via De La Valle, Del Mar, CA 92014: Catalog $5.95 (refundable) ❖ Saddles and pads, bridles, books, and tack. 800–551–MARY.

Rod's Western Palace, 3099 Silver Dr., Columbus, OH 43224: Free catalog ❖ Western wear and tack. 800–325–8508.

Ryon's Saddle & Ranch Supplies, 2601 N. Main, Fort Worth, TX 76106: Free catalog ❖ Saddles, tack, and Western-style clothing and boots for men, women, and children. 817–625–2391.

Saddle Slicker, P.O. Box 58714, Houston, TX 77258: Free information ❖ Saddle covers. 800–332–1101.

S.S. Schneiders, 8255 E. Washington St., Chagrin Falls, OH 44023: Free information ❖ Saddle, grooming, and tack storage systems. 800–365–1311.

State Line Tack Inc., P.O. Box 1217, Plaistow, NH 03865: Free catalog ❖ English and western riding tack and clothing. 800–228–9208.

Thornhill Enterprises, P.O. Box 3643, Wilmington, DE 19807: Free information ❖ Saddles and tack. 215–444–3998.

C.E. Treon Custom Saddles, P.O. Box 0073, Miami, FL 33256: Catalog $2 ❖ Custom saddles. 305–233–9973.

Valley Vet Supply, P.O. Box 504, Marysville, KS 66508: Free catalog ❖ Equine health products, roping gear, pack equipment, horse blankets, and English, Western, and Arabian tack. 800–468–0059.

Jim White Saddlery & Rodeo Equipment, HC 69, Box 55, Belle Fourche, SD 57717: Free brochure ❖ Saddles and other equipment. 605–692–4482.

HORSESHOES

Cannon Sports, P.O. Box 11179, Burbank, CA 91510: Free information with list of retailers ❖ Horseshoes. 800–362–3146; 818–753–5940 (in CA).

Franklin Sports Industries Inc., 17 Campanelli Pkwy., P.O. Box 508, Stoughton, MA 02072: Free information ❖ Horseshoes. 617–344–1111.

General Sportcraft Company Ltd., 140 Woodbine Rd., Bergenfield, NJ 07621: Free information ❖ Horseshoes. 201–384–4242.

NC Tool Company, 6568 Hunt Rd., Pleasant Garden, NC 27313: Free information ❖ Horseshoeing supplies. 800–446–6498.

Regent Sports Corporation, 45 Ranick Rd., Hauppage, NY 11788: Free information ❖ Horseshoes. 516–234–2800.

Spalding Sports Worldwide, 425 Meadow St., P.O. Box 901, Chicopee, MA 01021: Free information with list of retailers ❖ Horseshoes. 800–225–6601.

Sport Fun Inc., 4621 Sperry St., Los Angeles, CA 90039: Free information ❖ Horseshoes. 800–423–2597; 818–240–6700 (in CA).

Wagon Mound Ranch Supply, Box 218, Wagon Mound, NM 87752: Free catalog ❖ Horseshoeing supplies. 505–666–2489.

HOT TUBS & SAUNAS

Amerec Sauna & Steam, P.O. Box 40569, Bellevue, WA 98004: Free information ❖ Pre-assembled, easy-to-install free-standing modular sauna. 800–331–0349; 206–643–7500 (in WA).

AquaGlass Corporation, P.O. Box 412, Industrial Park, Adamsville, TN 38310: Free information ❖ Whirlpool baths, combination steam showers, lavatories, wall surrounds, and shower floors. 800–238–3940; 901–632–0911 (in TN).

Automatic Steam Products, 43–20 34th St., Long Island City, NY 11101: Free information ❖ Equipment to convert shower stalls into steam rooms. 800–238–3535.

Coleman Spas Inc., P.O. Box 2920, Chandler, AZ 85244: Free information ❖ Spas and hot tubs. 602–895–0598.

Fiat Tubs, Showers & Steam Baths, 1235 Hartrey Ave., Evanston, IL 60202: Free information ❖ Multi-jet tubs, showers, whirlpools, and steam baths. 708–864–7600.

Gazebos by Leisure Designs, 1991 Friendship Dr., El Cajon, CA 92020: Free information ❖ Gazebos and spa enclosures. 619–562–8988.

Helo Saunas from Finland, Box 1339, Minnetonka, MN 55345: Free catalog ❖ Saunas, steambath generators, and accessories. 612–955–2574.

Jacuzzi Whirlpool Bath, P.O. Drawer J, Walnut Creek, CA 94596: Free information ❖ Whirlpool spas and whirlpool baths with hydro massage control. 510–938–7070.

Lyons Industries, P.O. Box 88, Dowagiac, MI 49047: Free information ❖ Whirlpools for space-saving corner installation with optional walls and shatter-proof folding shower stall doors. 800–458–9036.

NEMCO, P.O. Box 17486, Clearwater, FL 34622: Free information ❖ Portable spas with multi-level bench seating.

Nordic Sauna, 937 E. San Carlos Ave., San Carlos, CA 94070: Free information ❖ Build-them-yourself whirlpool, hot tub, and sauna kits. 415–592–1818.

NoviAmerican, P.O. Box 44649, Atlanta, GA 30336: Free information ❖ Extra-deep whirlpool tub with step-by-step, do-it-yourself instructions for installation. 800–521–6080.

Snorkel Stove Company, 4216 6th Ave. South, Seattle, WA 98108: Free information ❖ Power- and plumbing-free, wood-fired hot tubs. 800–962–6208.

Sundance Spas, 13951 Monte Vista Ave., Chino, CA 91710: Free information ❖ Spas. 714–590–1791.

Thermasol, 15148 Bledsoe St., Sylmar, CA 91342: Free information ❖ Self-cleaning whirlpool baths. 800–423–2477.

Universal Rundle, 303 North St., P.O. Box 29, New Castle, PA 16103: Free information ❖ Portable spa that operates by plugging into a standard grounded outlet. 412–658–6631.

Watkins Manufacturing Spas, 1280 Park Center Dr., Vista, CA 92083: Free information ❖ Spas. 800–999–4688.

HOT WATER HEATERS

Controlled Energy Corporation, Fiddler's Green, Waitsfield, VT 05673: Free information ❖ Direct vent room heaters and tankless and mini storage tank instantaneous electric water heaters. 802–496–4436.

HOUSEWARES

Brookstone Company, Order Processing Center, 1655 Bassford Dr., Mexico, MO 65265: Free catalog ❖ Housewares and tools. 800–926–7000.

Chef's Catalog, 3215 Commercial Ave., Northbrook, IL 60062: Free catalog ❖ Professional restaurant equipment for the home chef. 800–338–3232.

Colonial Garden Kitchens, P.O. Box 66, Hanover, PA 17333: Free catalog ❖ Housewares, storage and bathroom accessories, cleaning and cooking aids, furniture, and laundry room aids. 717–633–3330.

Joan Cook, 119 Foster St., P.O. Box 6008, Peabody, MA 01961: Free catalog ❖ Housewares for cooking and home care. 800–935–0971.

Hold Everything, Mail Order Dept., P.O. Box 7807, San Francisco, CA 94120: Free catalog ❖ Clothing and closet organizers, garment protectors, kitchen and laundry aids, bathroom space makers, and bedroom furnishings. 800–421–2285.

HUMIDIFIERS & DEHUMIDIFIERS

Hunter Fan Company, 2500 Fisco Ave., Memphis, TN 38114: Catalog $1 ❖ Electronically programmable thermostats. 901–745–9222.

PetroKem Corporation, 101 Oliver St., P.O. Box 1888, Paterson, NJ 07509: Free information ❖ Non-electric humidifiers for rooms, closets, and other areas. 201–742–6468.

HUNTING
Clothing & Equipment

Amacker Tree Stands, Box 548, Delhi, LA 71232: Free information ❖ Portable and semi-permanent climbing ladders. 800–262–2537.

Ambusher, 2007 W. 7th St., Texarkana, TX 75501: Free information ❖ Portable climbing ladders. 903–793–2609.

API Outdoors Inc., P.O. Box 1432, Tallulah, LA 71282: Free information ❖ Self-climbing tree stands. 800–228–4846.

Archery Corporation, P.O. Box 537, Saddle Brook, NJ 07662: Free information ❖ Portable tree stand safety harnesses and other equipment. 201–843–0159.

L.L. Bean Inc., Freeport, ME 04033: Free catalog ❖ Outdoor clothing. 800–221–4221.

Bear River Industries Inc., 3110 Ranchview Ln., Minneapolis, MN 55447: Free information ❖ Portable tree stands and hunting supplies. 800–536–3337; 612–559–1092 (in MN).

Bowhunter's Discount Warehouse Inc., 1045 Ziegler Rd., Wellsville, PA 17365: Free catalog ❖ Hunting, bow-hunting, camping, and archery equipment. 717–432–8611.

Broward Shooter's Exchange, 250 S. 60th Ave., Hollywood, FL 33023: Catalog $8 ❖ Shooting, reloading, muzzleloading, hunting, and archery equipment. 800–554–9002.

Browning Company, Dept. C006, One Browning Pl., Morgan, UT 84050: Catalog $2 ❖ Camouflage clothing. 800–333–3288.

BSI Sporting Goods, P.O. Box 5010, Vienna, WV 26105: Free catalog ❖ Firearm accessories, muzzleloading supplies, optics, clothing, and archery, fishing, and hunting equipment. 304–295–8511.

Buckshot, P.O. Box 7127, Wilmington, NC 28406: Free information ❖ Lightweight adjustable tree stand. 910–341–7900.

Cabela's, 812 13th Ave., Sidney, NE 69160: Free catalog ❖ Hunting, fishing, and other outdoor equipment. 800–237–4444.

Delta Decoys, 117 E. Kenwood St., Reinbeck, IA 50669: Free information ❖ Life-size ultra-light and collapsible deer decoys. 319–345–6476.

Fieldline, 1919 Vineburn Ave., Los Angeles, CA 90032: Catalog $2 and list of retailers ❖ Fleece packs, pouches, and gaiters for hunters.

Flambeau Products Corporation, 15981 Valplast Rd., Middlefield, OH 44062: Free information ❖ Realistic deer decoys. 800–232–3474.

Gander Mountain Inc., P.O. Box 248, Gander Mountain, Wilmot, WI 53192: Free catalog ❖ Camping equipment, boats, archery supplies, knives, rifle scopes, and hunting videos. 414–862–2331.

Holden Treestands Inc., P.O. Box 563, Marble Falls, TX 78654: Free information ❖ Tree stands with locking device. 210–693–6560.

Loc-On Company, 6903 International Dr., Greensboro, NC 27409: Free information ❖ Portable and semi-permanent climbing ladders. 910–668–3113.

Loggy Bayou Tree Stands, 10397 Rt. 1, Shreveport, LA 71115: Free information ❖ Climbing and hang-on tree stands. 800–544–8733.

Lone Wolf Tree Stands, 5615 S. Pennsylvania Ave., Cudahy, WI 53110: Free information ❖ Self-climbing tree stands. 414–744–4984.

Modern Camouflage, P.O. Box 224785, Dallas, TX 75222: Free catalog ❖ Bow-hunting clothing, winterwear, and rainwear. 800–929–0987.

Natgear, 1200 John Barron Rd., Ste. 303, Little Rock, AR 72205: Free information and list of retailers ❖ Camouflage accessories. 800–590–5590.

Nelson Weather-Rite Clothing, 14760 Santa Fe Trail Dr., Lenexa, KS 66215: Free information ❖ Camouflage clothing.

Nite Lite Company, P.O. Box 777, Clarksville, AR 72830: Free catalog ❖ Clothing for hunters and kennel, training, and hunting supplies for dogs. 501–754–2146.

RealBark Hunting Systems, P.O. Box 2078, Henderson, TX 75653: Free brochure ❖ Blinds, seat tripods, platforms, and game feeders. 800–256–4465.

Rivers Edge, P.O. Box 903, Monticello, MN 55362: Free brochure and list of retailers ❖ Tree stands. 800–450–EDGE.

Senco Inc., Box 306, Marquette, MI 49855: Free information ❖ Recreational shelters, portable hunting blinds and ice fishing houses, and greenhouses. 407–589–6563.

Screaming Eagle, Box 4507, Missoula, MT 59806: Free catalog ❖ Self-climbing tree stands. 800–458–2017.

Skyline, 184 Ellicott Rd., West Falls, NY 14170: Free brochure ❖ Camouflage supplies. 716–655–0230.

Sport Climbers, 2926 75th St., Kenosha, WI 53143: Free catalog ❖ Tree-climbing spikes. 800–877–7025.

Staghorn Treestands, 410 W. Lincoln Ave., Goshen, IN 46526: Free information ❖ Tree stands. 219–534–2234.

Summit Specialties Inc., P.O. Box 786, Decatur, AL 35602: Brochure $1 ❖ Climbing tree stands. 205–353–0634.

Timber Ghost Camouflage, 10022 CR 3070, Rolla, MO 65401: Free information ❖ Camouflage clothing. 314–341–2946.

Timberline Targets, P.O. Box 667, Williston, ND 58802: Free information ❖ 3–D targets. 701–774–0966.

Trailhawk Treestands, 2605 Coulce Ave., La Crosse, WI 54601: Free information ❖ Self-climbing tree stands. 608–787–0500.

Trax America, Box 898, Forrest City, AR 72335: Free information ❖ Self-climbing tree stands. 800–232–2327.

Trebark Camouflage, 3434 Buck Mountain Rd., Roanoke, VA 24014: Free catalog ❖ Camouflage gear for hunters. 800–843–2266; 703–774–9248 (in VA).

Warren & Sweat Manufacturing Company, Box 350440, Grand Island, FL 32735: Free information ❖ Portable and semi-permanent climbing ladders. 904–669–3166.

Whitetail Treestands, 855 Chicago Rd., Quincy, MI 49082: Free information ❖ Self-climbing tree stands. 517–639–3815.

Whitewater Outdoors Inc., W4118 Church St., Highdam, WI 53031: Free information ❖ Camouflage clothing.

Wiley Outdoor Sports, 1808 Sportsman Ln., Huntsville, AL 35816: Catalog $3 (refundable) ❖ Hunting equipment. 205–837–3982.

Woodstream Corporation, P.O. Box 327, Lititz, PA 17543: Free catalog ❖ Hunting and shooting equipment. 800–800–1819; 717–626–2125 (in PA).

Woolrich Clothing, Woolrich, PA 17779: Free information ❖ Camouflage clothing.

Game Calls, Lures & Scents

Abe & Son, 145 S. Broadway, Coos Bay, OR 97420: Free information ❖ Game calls. 800–426–2417.

Rod Benson's Game Calls,
 Benson's Game Calls [Benson's] 1050 Mart St., Muskegon, MI 49440: Free information and list of retailers ❖ Adjustable deer calls. 616–726–3661.

Bowhunter Supply Inc., 1158 46th St., P.O. Box 5010, Vienna, WV 26105: Free information ❖ Game calls, decoys, lures, and scents. 800–289–2211; 304–295–8511 (in WV).

Buck Stop Lure Company Inc., P.O. Box 636, Stanton, MI 48888: Free information ❖ Scents and lures. 800–477–2368; 517–762–5091 (in MI).

Cedar Hill Game Call Company, Rt. 2, Box 236, Downsville, LA 71234: Free information ❖ Game calls. 800–348–3358; 318–982–5632 (in LA).

Deer Run Products Inc., 261 Ridgeview Terrace, Goshen, NY 10924: Free information ❖ Scents and lures. 914–294–9646.

Eastern Sports Supply Ltd., P.O. Box 67, Tremont, PA 17981: Free information ❖ Game calls, decoys, lures, and scents. 717–695–3113.

Golden Eagle Archery, 1111 Corporate Dr., Farmington, NY 14425: Free information ❖ Game calls, lures, and scents. 716–924–1880.

Haydel's Game Calls Inc., 5018 Hazel Jones Rd., Bossier City, LA 71111: Free information ❖ Game calls. 318–746–3586.

Hunter's Specialties Inc., 6000 Huntington Ct. NE, Cedar Rapids, IA 52402: Free information ❖ Game calls, decoys, lures, and scents. 319–395–0321.

James Valley Scents, HCR 1, Box 47, Mellette, SD 57461: Free catalog ❖ Gel and liquid animal scents. 605–887–3125.

Knight & Hale Game Calls, Box 468, Cadiz, KY 42211: Free information ❖ Turkey calls. 502–924–1755.

Lohman Manufacturing Company, Box 220, Neosho, MO 64850: Free information ❖ Game calls. 417–451–4438.

Primos Inc., Box 12785, Jackson, MS 39236: Information $2 ❖ Turkey, deer, elk, waterfowl, and other calls. 800–523–2395.

Quaker Boy Inc., 5455 Webster Rd., Orchard Park, NY 14127: Free information ❖ Turkey calls. 800–544–1600; 716–662–3979 (in NY).

Pete Rickard Inc., RD 1, Box 292, Cobleskill, NY 12043: Free information ❖ Animal scents for deer. 800–282–5663.

Robinson Laboratories, 293 Commercial St., St. Paul, MN 55106: Free information ❖ Deer lure gel. 800–397–1927; 512–224–1927 (in MN).

Scotch Hunting Products Company Inc., 6619 Oak Orchard Rd., Elba, NY 14058: Free information ❖ Game calls. 716–757–9958.

Simmons Gun Specialties Inc., 20241 W. 207th, Spring Hill, KS 66083: Free information ❖ Game calls, decoys, lures, and scents. 800–444–0220.

Johnny Stewart Wild Life Calls Inc., 5100 Fort Ave., Box 7954, Waco, TX 76714: Free information ❖ Game calls. 800–537–0652; 817–772–3261 (in TX).

Sure-Shot Game Calls Inc., Box 816, Groves, TX 77619: Free information ❖ Game calls. 409–962–1636.

Tink's Safariland Hunting Corporation, P.O. Box 244, Madison, GA 30650: Free information ❖ Game calls, decoys, lures, and scents. 800–221–5054; 404–342–1916 (in GA).

Wilderness Sound Productions Ltd., 4015 Main St., Springfield, OR 97478: Free brochure ❖ Game calls. 800–437–0006.

Wildlife Research Center, 4345 157th Ave. NW, Anoka, MN 55304: Free catalog ❖ Scent elimination spray. 800–655–7898; 612–427–3350 (in MN).

Woods Wise Callmasters, P.O. Box 681552, Franklin, TN 37068: Free catalog ❖ Deer, elk, squirrel, and waterfowl game calls. 800–735–8182.

ICE-CREAM MACHINES

Chef's Catalog, 3215 Commercial Ave., Northbrook, IL 60062: Free catalog ❖ Manual, electric-operated, and self-chilling ice-cream makers. 800–338–3232.

Lello Appliances Corporation, 355 Murray Hill Pkwy., East Rutherford, NJ 07073: Free information ❖ Electric-powered ice-cream maker. 800–527–4336.

Sun Appliances, 4554 E. Princess Anne Rd., Norfolk, VA 23502: Free information ❖ Salt and ice, electric-operated ice-cream maker. 800–347–4197.

White Mountain Freezer Inc., P.O. Box 459, Winchendon, MA 01475: Free information ❖ Old-fashioned, rock salt and ice, electric-operated ice-cream maker. 800–343–0065.

Williams-Sonoma, Mail Order Department, P.O. Box 7456, San Francisco, CA 94120: Free catalog ❖ Hand-cranked ice-cream machine. 800–541–1262.

Zabar's & Company, 2245 Broadway, New York, NY 10024: Free catalog ❖ Hand-cranked ice-cream maker. 212–787–2000.

ICE SKATING

Cal Pac Corporation, Triad Bicycles, 5250 Claremont Ave., Stockton, CA 95207: Free information ❖ Skates. 800–477–4734; 209–472–3451 (in CA).

Canstar Sports USA Inc., 50 Jonergin Dr., Swanton, VT 05448: Free information ❖ Figure and hockey skates and blade sharpeners. 800–362–3146; 802–868–2711 (in VT).

Chisco Sports Accessories, 2550 S. 2300 West, Salt Lake City, UT 84119: Free information ❖ Skates. 800–825–4555; 801–972–5656 (in UT).

Cooper International Inc., 501 Alliance Ave., Toronto, Ontario, Canada M6N 2J3: Free information ❖ Figure and hockey skates and blade protectors. 416–763–3801.

First Team Sports/Ultra-Wheels, 2274 Woodale Dr., Mounds View, MN 55112: Free information ❖ Skates. 800–458–2250; 612–780–4454 (in MN).

Lowry's Manufacturing Ltd., 19 Keith Rd., Winnipeg, Manitoba, Canada R3H 0H7: Free information ❖ Figure and hockey skates, replacement blades, and blade protectors. 204–633–6359.

Maska USA Inc., 529 Main St., Ste. 205, Boston, MA 02129: Free information ❖ Figure and hockey skates. 800–451–4600; 617–242–8600 (in MA).

National Sporting Goods Corporation, 25 Brighton Ave., Passaic, NJ 07055: Free information ❖ Figure and hockey skates, blade protectors, and sharpeners. 201–779–2323.

Oberhamer USA, 11975 Portland Ave. South, Ste. 122, Burnsville, MN 55337: Free catalog ❖ Skating attire and skates for men and women. 800–207–OBER; 612–890–1657 (in MN).

Riedell Shoes Inc., P.O. Box 21, Red Wing, MN 55066: Free information ❖ Blade protectors, sharpeners, and figure, racing, and hockey skates. 612–388–8251.

Roller Derby Skate Corporation, Box 930, Litchfield, IL 62056: Free information ❖ Skates. 217–324–3961.

Seneca Sports Inc., 75 Fortune Blvd., Box 719, Milford, MA 01757: Free information ❖ Skates and blade protectors. 508–634–3616.

INCONTINENCE SUPPLIES

Active Living Continence Care Products, Laborie Medical Technologies Corporation, 7 Green Tree Dr., South Burlington, VT 05403: Free catalog ❖ Physician- and nurse-tested incontinent products. 800–522–3393; 802–860–7230 (in VT).

Bruce Medical Supply, 411 Waverly Oaks Rd., P.O. Box 9166, Waltham, MA 02254: Free catalog ❖ Health equipment for disabled and incontinent persons. 800–225–8446.

CarePak, P.O. Box 303, Trabuco Canyon, CA 92679: Free brochure ❖ Underpads, liners, stretch briefs, tissues, and other absorbent aids. 800–697–9737.

Duraline Medical Products, 324 Werner St., P.O. Box 67, Leipsic, OH 45856: Free catalog ❖ Reusable and disposable health care items for children and adults. 800–654–3376.

Fashion Ease, Division M and M Health Care, 1541 60th St., Brooklyn, NY 11219: Free catalog ❖ Incontinence supplies, wheelchair accessories, other health care aids, and clothing with velcro closures for arthritic, elderly, and handicapped persons. 800–221–8929.

Home Delivery Incontinent Supplies Company, 1215 Dielman Industrial Ct., Olivette, MO 63132: Free catalog ❖ Briefs, undergarments, shields, underpads, catheters, and skin care products. 800–538–1036.

Ladies First, P.O. Box 26, Lake Bluff, IL 60044: Free information ❖ Disposable and reusable bladder control protection products for women. 800–215–5151.

Medical Supply Company Inc., P.O. Box 250, Hamburg, NJ 07419: Free price list with long SASE ❖ Underpads, diapers, and disposable briefs. 800–323–9664; 201–209–8448 (in NJ).

Shield Healthcare Centers, P.O. Box 916, Santa Clarita, CA 91380: Free catalog ❖

Ostomy, urological, skin care, and home diagnostic products.

Woodbury Products Inc., 4410 Austin Blvd., Island Park, NY 11558: Free information ❖ Disposable diapers. 800–777–1111.

INDIAN (NATIVE AMERICAN) ARTS & CRAFTS
Alaska

Alaska Legacy Art Gallery, 311 Mill St., Ste. 202, Ketchikan, AK 99901: Free information with long SASE ❖ Northwest Coast masks, paintings, silver and ivory jewelry, baskets, dolls, ivory sculpture, scrimshaw, and other crafts. 907–225–1234.

Chilkat Valley Arts, Box 145, Haines, AK 99827: Free price list with long SASE ❖ Northwest Coast Tlingit Native American silver jewelry. 907–766–2990.

Mardina Dolls, P.O. Box 611, Wrangell, AK 99929: Free information with long SASE ❖ Eskimo dolls in ceremonial robes. 907–874–3854.

Musk Ox Producers Cooperative, 604 H St., Anchorage, AK 99501: Free information with long SASE ❖ Hand-knitted Qiviut scarves, caps, tunics, and other clothing. 907–272–9225.

Nana Museum of the Arctic Craft Shop, P.O. Box 49, Kotzebue, AK 99752: Free information with long SASE ❖ Eskimo dolls, masks, birch bark baskets, ivory and whalebone carvings, and jewelry. 907–442–3304.

St. Lawrence Island Original Ivory Cooperative, P.O. Box 189, Gambell, AK 99742: Free price list with long SASE ❖ Bracelets, cribbage boards, baleen boats, etchings, and ivory carvings of Arctic animals. 907–985–5112.

Savoonga Native Store, P.O. Box 100, Savoonga, AK 99769: Free price list with long SASE ❖ Figurines, scrimshaw, ivory carvings, jewelry, and other crafts.

Taheta Arts & Cultural Group, 605 A St., Anchorage, AK 99501: Catalog $1 ❖ Ivory, stone, wood, and bone carvings; grass, birch bark, and baleen baskets; bead, porcupine, quill, silver, ivory, and baleen jewelry; and Eskimo dance fans, parkas, masks, etchings, and prints. 907–272–5829.

Amos Wallace, P.O. Box 478, Juneau, AK 99802: Free information with long SASE ❖

Carved silver and gold bracelets and earrings. 907–586–9000.

Arizona

Dawa's Hopi Arts & Crafts, P.O. Box 127, Second Mesa, AZ 86043: Free information with long SASE ❖ Hopi overlay silver jewelry. 602–734–2430.

Hatathli Gallery, Navajo Community College Development Foundation, Tsaile, AZ 86556: Free information with long SASE ❖ Jewelry, rugs, sand paintings, and beadwork. 602–724–3311.

Honani Crafts, Hopi Cultural Center, Shop #4, P.O. Box 317, Second Mesa, AZ 86043: Free information with long SASE ❖ Honani silver jewelry, pottery, paintings, and baskets; Navajo rugs; and Zuni, Navajo, and Santa Domingo jewelry. 602–734–2238.

Hopi Arts & Crafts, Silvercraft Cooperative Guild, P.O. Box 37, Second Mesa, AZ 86043: Catalog $2.50 ❖ Hopi overlay jewelry, coiled and wicker baskets, pottery, and paintings. 602–734–2463.

Hopi Kiva, P.O. Box 96, Oraibi, AZ 86039: Free information with long SASE ❖ Hopi silver and gold overlay jewelry. 602–734–2423.

Hopicrafts, P.O. Box 37, Kykotsmovi, AZ 86039: Free information with long SASE ❖ Hopi sterling silver overlay jewelry, kachinas, pottery, baskets, weavings, and Navajo, Zuni, and Santa Domino turquoise jewelry. 602–734–2484.

Kalley Musial, P.O. Box 1335, Flagstaff, AZ 86002: Free information with long SASE ❖ Navajo rugs and beadwork. 602–774–2098; 213–839–4465 (in CA).

Albert Long, P.O. Box 40, Lake Havasu City, AZ 86403: Free information with long SASE ❖ Gold and other jewelry, sand paintings, rugs, baskets, kachina dolls, and pottery. 602–453–5925.

Native Arts, P.O. Box 40342, Mesa, AZ 85274: Free information with long SASE ❖ Apache burden baskets and pottery earrings.

Navajo Arts & Crafts Enterprise, P.O. Drawer A, Window Rock, AZ 86515: Free information with long SASE ❖ Navajo Native American crafts, turquoise and silver jewelry, sand paintings, and pottery. 602–871–4090.

Percharo Jewelry, 313 Pima Ln., Laveen, AZ 85339: Free information with long SASE ❖ Silver and gold jewelry. 602–237–4249.

San Juan Southern Paiute Yingup Weavers Association, P.O. Box 1336, Tuba City, AZ 86045: Free information with long SASE ❖ Paiute baskets. 602–526–7143.

Urshel Taylor's Indian Studio, 2254 W. Calle Comodo, Tucson, AZ 87505: Free information with long SASE ❖ Wood sculptures and oil paintings. 602–887–4021.

Phillip Titla Studio, P.O. Box 497, San Carlos, AZ 85550: Free brochure with long SASE ❖ Woodcarvings, oil and watercolor paintings, etchings, serigraphs, and sculptures in bronze and other metals. 602–475–2361.

Arkansas

Bill & Mary Horn, Rt. 9, Box 227, Pine Bluff, AR 71603: Free information with long SASE ❖ Pottery, baskets, cornhusk dolls, beadwork, wood necklaces, and silver, turquoise, and mother-of-pearl jewelry. 501–879–1066.

California

American Indian Store, 6449 El Cajon Blvd., San Diego, CA 92115: Free catalog ❖ Silver and gold jewelry, Sioux star quilts, ribbon shirts, beadwork, quillwork, dance bustles, war bonnets, Southern Plains metalwork, Pueblo pottery, Navajo rugs, and Hopi kachina dolls. 619–583–5389.

De Luna Jewelers, 521 2nd St., Davis, CA 95616: Free information with long SASE ❖ Pottery, Navajo rugs, jewelry, baskets, paintings, carvings, and beadwork. 916–753–3351.

Going-to-the-Sun Studio, 1063 Hillendale Ct., Walnut Creek, CA 94596: Free information with long SASE ❖ Paintings, bas relief sculptures, tapestries, block-printed fabrics, drums, parfleche containers, dolls, beadwork, ribbon shirts, and shawls. 510–939–8803.

Indian Arts Gift Shop, NCIDC Inc., 241 F St., Eureka, CA 95501: Free information with long SASE ❖ Baskets, silver and shell jewelry, beadwork, paintings, and carvings. 707–445–8451.

Ophelia Johnson's Indian Variety Shop, 10256 Central Ave., Montclair, CA 91763: Free information with long SASE ❖ Silver jewelry, baskets, beadwork, pottery, and dolls. 714–625–2611.

Karok Originals by Vit, P.O. Box 3317, Eureka, CA 95502: Free information with long SASE ❖ Jewelry and wall hangings. 707–442–8800.

Chief George Pierre Trading Post, P.O. Box 3202, Torrance, CA 90510: Free information with long SASE ❖ Rugs, silver and turquoise jewelry, kachina dolls, and beadwork. 213–372–1048.

Tatewin-Petaki American Indian Arts & Crafts, P.O. Box 549, Big Bear City, CA 92314: Free information with long SASE ❖ Beadwork, stitchery items, beaded tapestries, decorated pipes, dolls, and leatherwork. 714–585–1435.

Colorado

Navajo Manufacturing Company, 5801 Logan St., Denver, CO 80216: Catalog $2 ❖ Handmade Navajo and Zuni jewelry. 303–292–8090.

Ben Nighthorse, P.O. Box 639, Ignacio, CO 81137: Free information with long SASE ❖ Contemporary silver, gold, and silver jewelry inlaid with copper, brass, and German silver. 303–563–4623.

Path-Of-The-Sun Images, Gallery & Design Services, 3020 Lowell Blvd., Denver, CO 80211: Free price list with long SASE ❖ Paintings, sculptures, traditional and contemporary crafts, and graphic art. 303–477–8442.

District of Columbia

Naica Collectibles, 5223 Wisconsin Ave. NW, Ste. 138, Washington, DC 20015: Free information with long SASE ❖ Carvings, pottery, beadwork, and sterling silver, turquoise, and gold jewelry. 202–561–1354.

Florida

Me'shiwi, 433 Harrell Dr., Orlando, FL 32828: Free brochure with long SASE ❖ Men and women's gold and sterling silver jewelry inlaid with natural stones and shell, Zuni pottery, kachina dolls, and paintings. 407–568–5162.

This N' That, 204 Brevard Ave., Cocoa Village, FL 32922: Free information with long SASE ❖ Beadwork, jewelry, pottery, carvings, fetishes, baskets, moccasins, dolls, and Navajo rugs.

Idaho

Kamiakin Krafts, P.O. Box 358, Fort Hall, ID 83203: Free price list with long SASE ❖ Beadwork belts, buckles, watch bands, earrings, coin purses, medallion necklaces, moccasins and slippers, men and women's clothing, cedar and raffia baskets, native tanned hides, and other crafts. 208–785–2546.

Trading Post Clothes Horse, P.O. Box 368, Fort Hall, ID 83203: Free brochure with long SASE ❖ Belt buckles, coin purses, earrings, barrettes, bolo ties, gloves, moccasins, dresses, vests, drums, and beaded and tanned buckskin items. 208–237–8433.

Indiana

Tisitsistas Free Traders, RR 1, Box 113, Bunker Hill, IN 46914: Catalog $2 (refundable) ❖ Reproduction Cheyenne household items, leather and beadwork crafts, jewelry, and other crafts. 317–689–5031.

Kansas

Laurie Houseman-Whitehawk, RR 3, Box 155–B, Lawrence, KS 66044: Free information with long SASE ❖ Original paintings in gouache. 913–842–1948.

Louisiana

Native American Arts of the South, P.O. Box 217, Elton, LA 70532: Free price list with long SASE ❖ Pottery and swamp cane, white oak, and long-leaf pine needle baskets. 318–584–5130.

Maine

Basket Bank, Aroostook Micmac Council Inc., 8 Church St., Presque Isle, ME 04769: Free brochure with long SASE ❖ Potato, pack, clothes, fishing, decorative, shopping, cradle, and sewing baskets. 207–764–1972.

Longacre Enterprises Inc., Old Eastport Rd., P.O. Box 196, Perry, ME 04667: Free price list with long SASE ❖ Bow and arrow racks, incense burners, drift wood lamps, other crafts, and Passamaquoddy birch bark, ash, and sweet grass baskets. 207–853–2762.

Nowetah's Indian Store & Museum, Rt. 27, Box 40, New Portland, ME 04954: Free brochure with long SASE ❖ Rugs and wall hangings, beadwork, leatherwork, moccasins, porcupine quill boxes, birch bark baskets, pottery, leatherwork, drums, dolls, masks, Navajo sand paintings, headdresses, peace pipes, and silver and turquoise jewelry. 207–628–4981.

Chief Poolaw Tepee Trading Post, 88 Main St., Old Town, ME 04468: Free information with long SASE ❖ Penobscot sweet grass baskets, Passamaquoddy baskets, baskets by other tribes, pottery, moccasins, beadwork, wood carvings, dolls, war clubs, rugs, and jewelry. 207–827–8674.

Wabanaki Arts, P.O. Box 453, Old Town, ME 04468: Free price list with long SASE ❖ Penobscot carved canes, war clubs, totem poles, stone tomahawks, baskets, beadwork, and quillwork. 207–827–3447.

Maryland

Jewelry by Avery, 5134 Chalk Point Rd., West River, MD 20778: Free information with long SASE ❖ Kachinas, Native American art, precious and semi-precious gemstones, mineral specimens, and handcrafted Zuni, Navajo, and Hopi turquoise jewelry. 410–867–4752.

Massachusetts

Bluebird Indian Crafts, 130 Glenview St., Upton, MA 01568: Free information with long SASE ❖ Porcupine quillwork, beadwork, clothing, and other Native American crafts. 508–473–3708.

Silver Star, Wampanoag Crafts, c/o Anita G. Nielsen, 190 Wood St., P.O. Box 402, Middleboro, MA 02346: Free information with long SASE ❖ Moccasins, beadwork, leather crafts, baskets, quillwork, wall plaques, and other crafts. 617–947–4159.

Three Feathers, c/o Anita G. Nielsen, 190 Wood St., Middleboro, MA 02346: Free information with long SASE ❖ Fingerwoven bags, moccasins, leather pouches, beadwork, baskets, quillwork, and wall plaques. 617–947–6453.

Three Feathers Gifts, c/o Mary Ann Barros, P.O. Box 3354, Plymouth, MA 02361: Free information with long SASE ❖ Fingerwoven bags, moccasins, leather pouches, clothing, beadwork, baskets, and quillwork.

Michigan

Faboriginals by Candi Wesaw Wilcox, 557 Carrier NE, Grand Rapids, MI 49505: Free information with long SASE ❖ Native American portraits and limited edition lithographs. 616–459–8136.

Indian Earth Arts & Crafts Store, 124 W. 1st St., Flint, MI 48502: Free information with long SASE ❖ Paintings, pottery, quillwork, black ash baskets, quilts, beadwork, and moccasins. 313–239–6621.

Indian Hills Trading Company & Indian Art Gallery, 1681 Harbor Rd., Petoskey, MI 49770: Free information with long SASE ❖ Porcupine quill boxes and pendants, traditional drums, beadwork, buckskin baby moccasins, Navajo rugs, Southwestern silver and turquoise jewelry, Pueblo pottery, Eskimo art, and original Native American paintings. 616–347–3789.

Moon Bear Pottery, c/o Shirley M. Brauker, 6135 E. Broadway, #7, Mt. Pleasant, MI 48858: Free brochure with long SASE ❖ Pottery, wall hangings, sculptures, oil paintings and drawings, and dolls. 517–773–2510.

Native American Arts & Crafts Council, Indian Arts & Crafts Store, Goose Creek Rd., P.O. Box 1049, Grayling, MI 49738: Free information with long SASE ❖ Porcupine quill boxes, black ash splint and sweet grass baskets, beadwork, birch bark crafts, paintings and drawings, and leatherwork. 517–348–3190.

Passages Express, 141 W. Tamarack St., Ironwood, MI 49938: Free information with long SASE ❖ Dolls, porcupine quillwork, and leather crafts. 906–932–4108.

Minnesota

Amber Woods Studio, 26570 140th St., Zimmerman, MN 55398: Free information with long SASE ❖ Sculptures, wood relief wall hangings, pipestone and marble carvings, graphics, walking sticks, and paintings. 612–856–2328.

Elk's Camp Society, 214 S. Hiawatha Ave., Pipestone, MN 56164: Free brochure with long SASE ❖ Traditional and contemporary quillwork. 507–825–2052.

Ikwe Marketing, White Earth Indian Reservation, Rt. 1, Osage, MN 56570: Free brochure with long SASE ❖ Birch bark baskets, Ojibway beadwork, star quilts, braided rugs, and quillwork. 218–573–3411.

Lady Slipper Designs, RR 3, Box 556, Bemidji, MN 56601: Free information with long SASE ❖ Beaded charms, moccasins, birch bark birdhouses, other crafts, and birch bark, willow, and black ash baskets. 800–950–5903.

Pipestone Indian Shrine Association, c/o Pipestone National Monument, Box 727, Pipestone, MN 56164: Free brochure with long SASE ❖ Pipes, jewelry, war clubs, arrowheads, buffalo and turtle effigies, and other carvings. 507–825–5463.

Mississippi

Choctaw Museum of the Southern Indian Gift Shop, Rt. 7, Box 21, Philadelphia, MS 39350: Free price list with long SASE ❖ Baskets, beadwork jewelry, moccasins and traditional Choctaw dresses and shirts by special order, dolls, quilts, pottery, stickball rackets and balls, blowguns, and rabbit sticks. 601–656–5251.

Missouri

Turner Art Works, Rt. 3, Box 460, De Soto, MO 63020: Free information with long SASE ❖ Acrylic paintings and handmade traditional and contemporary necklaces, earrings, amulets, and chokers in shell, bone, and crayfish pinchers. 314–586–4105.

Montana

Blackfeet Trading Post, P.O. Box 626, Browning, MT 59417: Free information with long SASE ❖ Moccasins, beadwork, baskets, pottery, shawls, and paintings. 406–338–2050.

Coup Marks, Box 532, Ronan, MT 59864: Free information with long SASE ❖ Paintings, sculptures, ribbon shirts, moccasins, beadwork, dolls, shawls, drums, stick games, wing dresses, and cradleboards. 406–246–3216.

Flathead Indian Museum Trading Post & Art Gallery, P.O. Box 464, St. Ignatius, MT 59865: Free information with long SASE ❖ Moccasins, beaded buckles, medallions, hair ties, silver and turquoise jewelry, earrings, dance costumes, and Native American paintings. 406–745–2951.

Neeney, Box 84, Joplin, MT 59531: Free information with long SASE ❖ Contemporary and traditional beadwork, gemstone necklaces and rings, sacred red rock pipes and fetishes, and native-tanned hides. 406–292–3890.

Northern Plains Indian Crafts Association, P.O. Box E, Browning, MT 59417: Free price list with long SASE ❖ Buckskin vests, gloves, handbags, moccasins, beadwork jewelry and belts, dolls, decorated rawhide items, porcupine hair roaches, and native-tanned hides. 406–338–5661.

The Tipi Gift Shop, Rt. 62, Box 3110E, Livingston, MT 59047: Free information with long SASE ❖ Original paintings, pen and ink sketches, knives, shields, star quilts, and other crafts. 406–222–8575.

Wolf Chief Graphics, 907 C Ave. NW, Great Falls, MT 59404: Free price list with long SASE ❖ Watercolor paintings, alabaster and bronze sculptures, and bone chokers. 406–452–4449.

Nebraska

Pilcher's Indian Store, Rt. 2, Box 348A, Fort Calhoun, NE 68023: Free information with long SASE ❖ Beadwork, peace pipes, dance roaches, bustles, pottery, kachina dolls, and Navajo silver jewelry. 402–468–5131.

Nevada

Arnold Aragon Sculpture & Illustration, Box 64, Schurz, NV 89427: Free information with long SASE ❖ Stone sculptures, drawings, and paintings. 702–773–2542.

Maggi Houten, P.O. Box 265, Nixon, NV 89424: Free information with long SASE ❖ Beadwork hair ties, necklaces, bolo ties, watch bands, belt buckles, belts, moccasins, baby baskets, and coin purses. 702–476–0205.

Malotte Studio, South Fork Reservation, Star Rt., Lee, NV 89829: Free information with long SASE ❖ Original drawings. 702–744–4305.

Winter Moon Trading Company, P.O. Box 189, Schurz, NV 89427: Free information with long SASE ❖ Beaded and silver jewelry, horsehair baskets, pottery, original artwork, and other Native American crafts. 702–773–2510.

New Jersey

Lone Bear Indian Craft Company, 300 Main St., Orange, NJ 07050: Free price list with long SASE ❖ Woodland Native American beadwork, costumes, war bonnets, headdresses, and other Native American collectibles.

New Mexico

Carolyn Bobelu, P.O. Box 443, Zuni, NM 87327: Free information with long SASE ❖ Jewelry with faceted and multi-levels of silver, turquoise, coral, and shell. 505–782–2773.

Chi Nah Bah, P.O. Box 122, Brimhall, NM 87310: Information $1 ❖ Jewelry, Navajo rugs, sand paintings, kachina dolls, leather belts, pottery, baskets, paintings, and other crafts.

Indian Pueblo Cultural Center Inc., 2401 12th St. NW, Albuquerque, NM 87102: Free information with long SASE ❖ Pueblo pottery, baskets, wood carvings, fabrics, stone sculptures, silver and turquoise jewelry, drums, and other crafts. 505–843–7270.

Jicarilla Arts & Crafts Shop/Museum, P.O. Box 507, Dulce, NM 87528: Free brochure ❖ Beadwork, baskets, leather work, and paintings. 505–759–3515.

Lilly's Gallery, P.O. Box 342, Acoma Pueblo, NM 87034: Free information with long SASE ❖ Handcrafted Acoma pottery and figurines. 505–552–9501.

Carol G. Lucero, P.O. Box 319, Jemez Pueblo, NM 87024: Free information with long SASE ❖ Pueblo pottery, baskets, cedar flutes, kachinas, drums, sculptures, Navajo dolls, sand paintings, and other crafts. 505–843–9337.

Mary Laura's, P.O. Box 12615, Albuquerque, NM 87195: Catalog $2 ❖ Native American jewelry from the Zuni Pueblo. 800–662–4848.

Ted Miller Custom Knives, P.O. Box 6328, Santa Fe, NM 87502: Free price list with long SASE ❖ Wood and horn carvings, deer horn pipes, elk horn belt buckles, bolos, and knives with hand-tooled steel blades in elk, stag horn, or bone handles. 505–984–0338.

Teresita Naranjo, Rt. 1, Box 455, Santa Clara Pueblo, Espanola, NM 87532: Free information with long SASE ❖ Santa Clara black and red pottery. 505–753–9655.

Navajo Gallery, P.O. Box 1756, Taos, NM 87571: Free information with long SASE ❖ Paintings, sculptures, lithographs, and drawings. 505–758–3250.

Oke Oweenge Arts & Crafts, P.O. Box 1095, San Juan Pueblo, NM 87566: Free price list with long SASE ❖ Wall hangings, pillows, pottery, dolls, beadwork, silver jewelry, baskets, paintings, and ceremonial mantas, shirts, sashes, vests, and blouses. 505–852–2372.

Oklahoma Indian Crafts Company, 4321 Ellison NE, Albuquerque, NM 87109: Free information with long SASE ❖ War bonnets, headdresses, beadwork, traditional and contemporary buckskin and cloth garments, moccasins and boots, paintings and limited edition prints, and other Native American crafts. 505–345–0796.

Pueblo of Zuni Arts & Crafts, P.O. Box 425, Zuni, NM 87327: Free information with long SASE ❖ Pottery, fetishes, contemporary art, and Zuni turquoise, shell, coral, jet, and silver jewelry. 505–782–4481.

Ramona Sakiestewa Ltd., P.O. Box 2472, Santa Fe, NM 87504: Free brochure with long SASE ❖ Handwoven limited edition fabrics, rugs, blankets, and tapestries. 505–982–8282.

Scripsit, c/o Billy, 3089 Plaza Blanca, Santa Fe, NM 87505: Free information with long SASE ❖ Paper and leather calligraphy crafts. 505–471–1516.

Silver Nugget, 416 Juan Tabu NE, Albuquerque, NM 87123: Catalog $2 ❖ American Native jewelry. 505–293–6861.

Carol Vigil, P.O. Box 443, Jemez Pueblo, NM 87024: Free information with long SASE ❖ Carved and painted Jemez pottery.

Zuni Craftsmen Cooperative Association, P.O. Box 426, Zuni, NM 87327: Information $2 with long SASE ❖ Zuni silver and turquoise jewelry, beadwork, fetishes, pottery, and paintings. 505–782–4425.

New York

Black Bear Trading Post, Rt 9W, P.O. Box 47, Esopus, NY 12429: Free information with long SASE ❖ Baskets, pottery, beadwork, kachina dolls, peace pipes, war clubs, soapstone and woodcarvings, moccasins, cradleboards, paintings, and sterling silver and turquoise jewelry. 914–384–6786.

Chrisjohn Family Arts & Crafts, RD 2, Box 315, Red Hook, NY 12571: Free information with long SASE ❖ Masks and other wood carvings, bone jewelry, silver items, cornhusk dolls, and pipes. 914–758–8238.

Peter B. Jones, Box 174, Versailles, NY 14168: Free information with long SASE ❖ Original works in clay, one-of-a-kind ceramic sculptures, and wall hangings. 716–532–5993.

Little Feather Trading Post, P.O. Box 3165, Jamaica, NY 11431: Free information with long SASE ❖ Beadwork and silver jewelry and leatherwork. 212–658–0576.

Mohawk Impressions, Box 20, Mohawk Station, Hogansburg, NY 13655: Free information with long SASE ❖ Dolls, beadwork, baskets, Mohawk paintings, and other crafts. 518–358–2467.

Seneca-Iroquois National Museum Gift Shop, Broad St. Extension, P.O. Box 442, Salamanca, NY 14779: Free price list with long SASE ❖ Iroquois beadwork, baskets, false face masks, cornhusk masks and dolls, rattles, wampum and scrimshaw jewelry, leather crafts, ribbon shirts, and pottery. 716–945–1738.

Sweetgrass Gift Shop, Akwesasne Museum, Rt. 37, Hogansburg, NY 13655: Free brochure with long SASE ❖ Beadwork, quillwork, cradleboards, and black ash splint and sweet grass baskets. 518–358–2240.

Tuskewe Krafts, 2089 Upper Mountain Rd., Sanborn, NY 14132: Free brochure with long SASE ❖ Women and men's field and box lacrosse sticks. 716–297–1821.

North Carolina

Haliwa-Saponi Tribal Pottery & Arts, P.O. Box 99, Hollister, NC 27844: Free price list with long SASE ❖ Pottery, quilts, beadwork, woodwork, and stonework. 919–586–4017.

Lumbee Indian Arts & Crafts, Rt. 1, Box 310 AA, Rowland, NC 28383: Free information with long SASE ❖ Baskets, beadwork, and leatherwork. 910–521–9494.

Qualla Arts & Crafts Mutual Inc., P.O. Box 277, Cherokee, NC 28719: Free brochure with long SASE ❖ Animal figurines, wood carvings, masks, beadwork, pottery, dolls, metalwork, and river cane, oak splint, and honeysuckle baskets. 704–497–3103.

Sacred Hoop Trading Post, 2701 Homestead Rd., #508, Chapel Hill, NC 27516: Free information with long SASE ❖ Eastern Cherokee baskets, pottery, wood and stone carvings, Lumbee paintings, and other Native American crafts. 919–933–7595.

Tuscarora Indian Handcraft Shop, Rt. 4, Box 172, Maxton, NC 28364: Free price list with long SASE ❖ Leather boots, moccasins, shirts, hats, vests, handbags, pouches, headbands, belts, necklaces, costumes, sterling silver and brass jewelry, and copper bracelets. 910–844–3352.

Wayah'sti Indian Traditions, P.O. Box 130, Hollister, NC 27844: Free price list with long SASE ❖ Beadwork, leather crafts, stone pipes, sculptures, pottery, and other crafts. 919–586–4519.

Robert D. Waynee, P.O. Box 5232, New Bern, NC 28560: Free information with long SASE ❖ Native American wood sculptures. 919–637–2546.

Ohio

American Silver from the Southwest, 5700 Frederick Rd., Dayton, OH 45414: Free information ❖ Native American and contemporary jewelry, pottery, and kachinas. 513–890–0138.

Oklahoma

Adams Studios, Rt. 3, Box 615A, Ponca City, OK 74601: Free price list with long SASE ❖ Watercolors, lithographs, serigraphy, etchings, beadwork key chains, barrettes, and silver and brass buckles, bracelets, and rings decorated with turquoise and other semi-precious stones. 405–765–5086.

American Indian Handicrafts, P.O. Box 533, Meeker, OK 74855: Free brochure with long SASE ❖ Ribbon work blankets, shirts, shawls, beadwork, and feather crafts. 405–279–3343.

Buffalo Sun, 605 E. Central, Box 1556, Miami, OK 74355: Free information with long SASE ❖ Traditional and contemporary Native American blouses, skirts, ribbon shirts, dresses, jackets, vests, coats, moccasins, belts, shawls, and jewelry. 918–542–8870.

Cherokee National Museum Gift Shop, P.O. Box 515, TSA-LA-GI, Tahlequah, OK 74464: Free price list with long SASE ❖ Baskets, weapons, paintings, prints, and sculptures. 918–456–6007.

Crying Wind Gallery & Framing Company, 400 N. Indiana, Oklahoma City, OK 73106: Free information with long SASE ❖ Seminole patchwork, dolls, and watercolor portraits, landscapes, still lifes, and other subjects. 405–235–9991.

The Dancing Rabbit, Designs by Patta LT, 814 N. Jones, Norman, OK 73069: Free information with long SASE ❖ Contemporary jewelry and beadweaving. 405–360–0512.

Five Civilized Tribes Museum Trading Post, Agency Hill, Honor Heights Dr., Muskogee, OK 74401: Free brochure with long SASE ❖ Beaded medallion necklaces, key rings, combs, hair ties, rings, baskets, sculptures, and paintings. 918–683–1701.

The Galleria, 1630 W. Lindsey, Norman, OK 73069: Free information with long SASE ❖ Carvings, paintings, bronzes, baskets, jewelry, beadwork, pottery, drawings, and original prints by Native American artists. 405–329–1225.

Bill Glass Studio, Star Route South, Box 39B, Locust Grove, OK 74352: Free information with long SASE ❖ Original stoneware sculptures and carvings, pottery, and bronzes. 918–479–8884.

Jack Gregory, Rt. 1, Box 79, Watts, OK 74964: Free information with long SASE ❖ Contemporary handmade wood candle holders, bowls, lamps, jewelry, bowls, plates, and other crafts. 918–723–5408.

Kelley Haney Art Gallery, P.O. Box 103, Seminole, OK 74868: Free brochure with long SASE ❖ Original paintings, sculpture, jewelry, baskets, and pottery. 405–382–3915.

Mister Indian's Cowboy Store, 1000 S. Main, Sapulpa, OK 74066: Free information with long SASE ❖ Moccasins, fans, shawls, beadwork, ribbon shirts, rugs, pottery, purses, cradleboards, drums, dolls, silver and

turquoise jewelry, and paintings. 918–224–6511.

Monkapeme, P.O. Box 457, Perkins, OK 74059: Free information with long SASE ❖ Native American contemporary fashions, traditional costumes, moccasins, shawls, headbands, medallions, belts, hair ties, buckskin dresses, leggings, and shirts. 405–547–2948.

Oklahoma Indian Arts & Crafts Cooperative, P.O. Box 966, Anadarko, OK 73005: Free price list with long SASE ❖ Beaded moccasins, belts, ties, pins, dance costume accessories, suede handbags, war dance bustle ensembles, nickel-silver jewelry, hand-sewn and decorated shirts, dolls, and paintings by Southern Plains Native Americans. 405–247–3486.

Connie Seabourn Studio, P.O. Box 23795, Oklahoma City, OK 73132: Free information with long SASE ❖ Original paintings, drawings, and hand-pulled prints. 405–728–3903.

Seabourn Studio, 6105 Covington Ln., Oklahoma City, OK 73132: Free information with long SASE ❖ Lithographs, serigraphs, and etchings. 405–722–1631.

Janet L. Smith, 1929 W. Nashville, Broken Arrow, OK 74012: Free information with long SASE ❖ Traditional and contemporary Cherokee watercolors, original oils, and acrylic paintings. 918–251–8952.

Snake Creek Workshop, P.O. Box 147, Rose, OK 74364: Free brochure with long SASE ❖ Mussel shell gorget necklaces. 918–479–8867.

Supernaw's Oklahoma Indian Supply, P.O. Box 216, Skiatook, OK 74070: Catalog $1 ❖ Feather work, nickel-silver jewelry, beadwork, roaches, women's accessories, and other crafts. 918–396–1713.

Tah-Mels, P.O. Box 1123, Tahlequah, OK 74465: Free information with long SASE ❖ Dolls, beadwork, baskets, quilts, Oochelata pink mussel shell and silver and gold jewelry, oil and watercolor paintings, and woodcarvings. 918–456–5461.

Tiger Art Gallery, 2110 E. Shawnee St., Muskogee, OK 74403: Free information with long SASE ❖ Traditional and contemporary paintings and sculptures. 918–687–7006.

Touching Leaves Indian Crafts, 927 Portland Ave., Dewey, OK 74029: Catalog $1 ❖ Beadwork, German silver jewelry, and leather crafts. 918–534–2859.

Two Feathers Indian Shop & Trading Shop, 1304–A N. Elm Pl., Broken Arrow, OK 74012: Free information with long SASE ❖ Clothing, pottery, baskets, original paintings, moccasins, dance accessories, and other crafts. 918–258–1228.

Zadoka Pottery, 12515 E. 37th St., Tulsa, OK 74146: Free information with long SASE ❖ Earthenware storage vessels, vases, and bowls. 918–663–9455.

Oregon

Ed's House of Gems, 7712 NE Sandy Blvd., Portland, OR 97211: Free information with long SASE ❖ Clocks, clock-making parts, minerals, gemstones, lapidary equipment, mountings, shells, jewelry, and Native American relics. 503–284-8990.

Klahowya! American Indian Gift Shop, 947 S. 1st St., Coos Bay, OR 97420: Free information with long SASE ❖ Beadwork, dolls, earrings, drums, and feather hair ties from various tribes. 503–269–7349.

Quintana's Gallery of Indian & Western Art, 139 NW 2nd Ave., Portland, OR 97209: Free information with long SASE ❖ Northwest Coast art, contemporary western paintings, bronze sculptures, and antique and contemporary Native American art from over 300 tribes. 503–223–1729.

Red Bear Creations, 358 N. Lexington Ave., Brandon, OR 97411: Free information with long SASE ❖ Star quilts, star drum covers, and padded jackets. 503–347–9772.

Spotted Horse Tribal Gifts, P.O. Box 414, Coos Bay, OR 97420: Catalog $2 ❖ Native American craft-making kits, tools, patterns, cassette tapes, books, and other crafts.

Nadine Van Mechelen, Rt. 1, Box 270, Pendleton, OR 97801: Free information with long SASE ❖ Handmade dolls in authentic Native American costumes. 503–276–2566.

Rhode Island

The Turquoise, Rockland Rd., North Scituate, RI 02857: Free information with long SASE ❖ Southwest Native American jewelry, pottery, baskets, rugs, paintings, moccasins, and clothing. 401–647–2579.

South Carolina

Sara Ayers, 1182 Brookwood Cir., West Columbia, SC 29169: Free price list with long SASE ❖ Pottery pipes, vases, pitchers, canoes, candlesticks, bowls, jardinieres, cups, bookends, and other crafts. 803–794–5436.

South Dakota

Contemporary Lakota Fashions by Geraldine Sherman, 235 Curtis, Rapid City, SD 57701: Free information with long SASE ❖ Ribbon shirts, skirts, dresses, shawls, vests, king- and queen-size star quilts, and other crafts. 605–341–7560.

Featherstone Productions, P.O. Box 487, Brookings, SD 57006: Free information with long SASE ❖ Sculptures and original paintings. 605–693–3183.

Jackson Originals, Box 1049, Mission, SD 57555: Free price list with long SASE ❖ Denim shirts, vests and jackets with applique or embroidered designs, Sioux ribbon shirts and dresses, and men, women, and children's leather vests and jackets with beadwork. 605–856–2541.

Lakota Jewelry Visions, 909 E. St. Patrick, Ste. 16, Rapid City, SD 57701: Free information with long SASE ❖ Traditional and contemporary jewelry and dance accessories. 605–343–0603.

Makoce Wanbli, Box 184, Lower Brule, SD 57548: Free information with long SASE ❖ Traditional Plains Native American art, clothing, dolls, weapons, dance accessories, moccasins, drums, and other crafts. 605–473–5622.

Oyate Kin Cultural Cooperative, c/o Wesley Hare, Marty, SD 57361: Free information with long SASE ❖ Beadwork, feather and leather accessories for dance outfits, Native American star quilts, ribbon shirts, and leather crafts.

Rings 'N' Things, P.O. Box 360, Mission, SD 57555: Free information with long SASE ❖ Silver gifts, quillwork, and beadwork. 605–856–4548.

St. Joseph's Lakota Development Council, St. Joseph's Indian School, Chamberlain, SD 57326: Free brochure with long SASE ❖ Dot drawings, jewelry, kachina dolls, leatherwork, beadwork, patchwork quilts, and tote bags. 605–734–6021.

Starboy Enterprises, P.O. Box 33, Rosebud Sioux Reservation, Okreek, SD 57563: Free brochure with long SASE ❖ Star quilts. 605–856–4517.

The Tipi Shop Inc., Box 1542, Rapid City, SD 57709: Catalog $2 ❖ Beaded buckskin moccasins, dance costume accessories, pottery, billfolds, coin purses, beadwork jewelry, quillwork, dolls, parfleche boxes,

willow baskets, and paintings by Sioux artists. 605–343–7851.

Tennessee

Crumbo Indian Arts, 24 Music Square West, Nashville, TN 37203: Free information with long SASE ❖ Original paintings, lithographs, silkscreens, and etchings. 615–244–7900.

Texas

Annesley Studio, P.O. Box 3, Missouri City, TX 77459: Free information ❖ Limited edition bronze sculptures, original 24K gold and silver point drawings, paintings, and pastels. 713–729–8960.

Crazy Crow Trading Post, 107 N. Fannin, P.O. Box 314, Denison, TX 75020: Catalog $2 ❖ Silver items, moccasins, beadwork, and imitation eagle feather war bonnets. 903–463–1366.

Eagle Dancer, 159 Gulf Freeway South, League City, TX 77573: Free information with long SASE ❖ Leatherwork, paintings, wood carvings, sculptures, jewelry, pottery, rugs, dolls, and other crafts. 713–332–6028.

L. David Eveningthunder, Contemporary Native American Art, P.O. Box 1197, Coldspring, TX 77331: Free information with long SASE ❖ Oil paintings, pen and ink drawings, pastels, air-brush items, and portraits. 409–653–2565.

Naranjo's World of American Indian Art, P.O. Box 7973, Houston, TX 77270: Free price list with long SASE ❖ Jewelry, beadwork, leatherwork, pottery, baskets, rugs, dolls, and kachinas. 713–660–9690.

Tribal Enterprise, Alabama-Coushatta Indian Reservation, Rt. 3, Box 640, Livingston, TX 77351: Free information with long SASE ❖ Large and small coiled pine needle and grass baskets, animal effigies, beadwork, pottery, vests, and ribbon shirts. 713–563–4391.

Whitewolf Photography, P.O. Box 297, Redwater, TX 75573: Free information with long SASE ❖ Original photographs with Native American and western themes.

Virginia

The Silver Phoenix Inc., 2946–D Chain Bridge Rd., Oakton, VA 22124: Free information with long SASE ❖ Jewelry, sand paintings, pottery, kachinas, rugs, moccasins, and beadwork. 703–255–3393.

Washington

Bead Lady/Cherokee Rainbows, 315–B Roosevelt, Wenatchee, WA 98801: Free information with long SASE ❖ Beadwork, women and children's moccasins, dance costumes, and other clothing and crafts.

Fran & Bill James, Lummi Indian Craftsmen, 4339 Lummi Rd., Ferndale, WA 98248: Free information with long SASE ❖ Northwest Coast Salish wool blankets and cedar bark baskets. 206–384–5292.

Makah Cultural Research Center, P.O. Box 95, Neah Bay, WA 98357: Free price list with long SASE ❖ Woven baskets, replicas of archaeological artifacts, carved wood masks, totem poles, rattles and bowls, shell jewelry, engraved silver bracelets, miniature basket earrings, painted drums, beadwork, and original serigraphs. 206–645–2711.

Potlatch Gifts, Northwind Trading Company, 708 Commercial Ave., Anacortes, WA 98221: Free brochure with long SASE ❖ Salish-style wood carvings, pottery, jewelry, baskets, wool sweaters, hats, mittens, and socks. 206–293–6404.

Suquamish Museum, P.O. Box 498, Suquamish, WA 98392: Free information with long SASE ❖ Suquamish/Puget Sound Salish clam baskets, dolls, whistles, museum replicas, wood bowls, spoons, canoe bailers, and wood carvings. 206–598–3311.

Templeton Tribal Art, P.O. Box 17941, Seattle, WA 98107: Catalog $3 ❖ Navajo rugs.

Tin-Na-Tit Kin-Ne-Ki Indian Arts & Gifts, P.O. Box 1057, Republic, WA 99166: Free information with long SASE ❖ Jewelry, masks, stone carvings, kachina dolls, baskets, pottery, quillwork, beaded items, sand paintings, and other crafts. 509–775–3077.

Wisconsin

Wa-Swa-Gon Arts & Crafts, P.O. Box 477, Lac du Flambeau, WI 54538: Free information with long SASE ❖ Beadwork, birch bark items, moccasins, finger weavings, traditional and ceremonial clothes, and carvings. 715–588–7636.

Winnebago Public Indian Museum, P.O. Box 441, Wisconsin Dells, WI 53965: Price list $1 ❖ Winnebago baskets, beadwork, deerskin products, pottery, Navajo rugs, and silver items. 608–254–2268.

Wyoming

Fort Washakie Trading Company, 53 N. Fork Rd., P.O. Box 428, Fort Washakie, WY 82514: Free brochure with long SASE ❖ Beaded and quill jewelry, rawhide and smoked skin accessories, dolls, cradleboards, Navajo rugs, southwestern silver and turquoise jewelry, Papago baskets, and Pueblo pottery. 307–332–3557.

La Ray Turquoise Company, P.O. Box 83, Cody, WY 82414: Free information with long SASE ❖ Navajo rugs, Ojibwa beadwork, and Navajo, Zuni, Chippewa, and Hopi silver items. 307–587–9564.

INTERCOMS

Aiphone Communications, 1700 13th Ave. NE, Bellevue, WA 98004: Free information ❖ Voice transmission, entry security control, video, and door answering intercoms. 206–445–0510.

Doorking, 120 Glasgow Ave., Inglewood, CA 90301: Free information ❖ Telephone entry and other access control systems. 800–826–7493.

M & S Systems Inc., 2861 Congressman Ln., Dallas, TX 75220: Free information ❖ Intercom with door chimes and release. 800–877–6631.

Siedle Communication System of America, 780 Parkway, Broomall, PA 19008: Free information ❖ Video intercoms. 215–353–9595.

Talk-A-Phone Company, 5013 N. Kedzie Ave., Chicago, IL 60625: Free information ❖ Intercoms for two-way conversation with optional integration with master system. 312–539–1100.

JET SKIS (PERSONAL WATERCRAFT)

Arizona Jet Ski Center, 2720 E. Bell Rd., Phoenix, AZ 85032: Free information ❖ Jet skis. 800–245–3875; 602–482–9322 (in AZ).

Butch's Jet Ski, 3614 S. Division, Grand Rapids, MI 49508: Free information ❖ Jet skis. 800–54–BUTCH.

Castaic Ski and Sport, 31438 Castaic Rd., P.O. Box 85, Castaic, CA 91310: Free catalog ❖ Personal watercraft. 805–257–3033.

Competition Accessories Inc., Rt. 68 North at Rt. 235, Xenia, OH 45385: Catalog $5 ❖ Personal watercraft accessories. 800–543–3535.

DCT Sports, 4060 Palm, Ste. 602, Fullerton, CA 92635: Free information with long SASE ❖ Personal watercraft. 800–576–9163; 714–526–8415 (in CA).

Decker, P.O. Box 495, Marshfield, WI 54449: Free catalog ❖ Personal watercraft accessories. 715–387–1208.

DG Performance Specialties Inc., 1230 La Loma Cir., Anaheim, CA 92806: Free catalog ❖ Personal watercraft accessories. 714–630–3517.

Dunnavant Performance, 1656 Centerpoint Pkwy., Birmingham, AL 35215: Free information ❖ Jet ski accessories. 800–886–SKIS.

Follansbee Dock Systems, State St., P.O. Box 610, Follansbee, WV 26037: Free information ❖ Personal watercraft lifts in easy-to-assemble kits. 800–223–3444.

Jet Trends, P.O. Box 110937, Miami, FL 33011: Free information ❖ Men and women's clothing for personal watercraft activities. 800–231–9279; 305–635–2411 (in FL).

Jetinetics Racing Products USA, 357 S. Acacia Ave., Fullerton, CA 92631: Free catalog ❖ Personal watercraft. 714–525–9930.

Kawasaki Motor Corporation USA, P.O. Box 25252, Santa Ana, CA 92799: Free information ❖ One- and two-person jet skis. 714–770–0400.

KG Industries, 140 Pacific Dr., Quakertown, PA 18951: Free information ❖ Personal watercraft equipment. 800–531–4252.

Dennis Kirk, 955 Southfield Ave., Rush City, MN 55069: Free catalog ❖ Personal watercraft. 800–328–9280.

L & S Engineering, 9856 Everest, Downey, CA 90242: Free catalog ❖ Jet ski accessories. 310–803–5591.

Laser Jet Performance Inc., 15591 Computer Ln., Huntington Beach, CA 92649: Free information ❖ Personal watercraft.

Lee's Kawasaki, 1538 National Hwy., Thomasville, NC 27360: Free information ❖ Jet ski accessories. 910–889–4667.

Parks Cortland Jet Toys, 3449 State Rt. 5, Cortland, OH 44410: Free information ❖ Personal watercraft. 216–638–8161.

Performance Jet Ski Inc., 4925 E. Hunter, Anaheim, CA 92807: Free information ❖ Personal watercraft. 714–779–8787.

Polaris Industries, 1225 Hwy. 169 North, Minneapolis, MN 55441: Free information ❖ Personal watercraft. 800–POLARIS.

Porta Dock Inc., 100 4th St., P.O. Box 409, Dassel, MN 55325: Information $1 ❖ Single and double, easy-to-assemble personal watercraft lift and canopy. 612–275–3312.

Sano Sports International, P.O. Box 141758, Austin, TX 78714: Free brochure ❖ Traction pads. 512–836–7266.

ShoreLand'r, Midwest Industries Inc., Ida Grove, IA 51445: Free information ❖ Personal watercraft trailers. 712–364–3365.

Tigershark Watercraft, Thief River Falls, MN 56701: Free information ❖ Personal watercraft. 218–681–4999.

Top Gun Kawasaki, Rt. 122 South, P.O. Box 429, Wirtz, VA 24184: Free information ❖ Jet ski parts. 703–721–4900.

Vacation Watercraft, 16277 S. US 41, Fort Myers, FL 33908: Free information ❖ Personal watercraft. 813–489–0053.

VM Boat Trailers, 5200 S. Peach, Fresno, CA 93725: Free information ❖ Jet ski trailers. 209–486–0410.

WetJet International Ltd., 23 Washburne Ave., Paynesville, MN 56362: Free information ❖ Personal watercraft and clothing. 612–243–3311.

White Brothers, 24845 Corbit Pl., Yorba Linda, CA 92687: Catalog $4 ❖ Personal watercraft. 714–692–3404.

Yamaha Motor Corporation, P.O. Box 6555, Cypress, CA 90630: Free information ❖ One- and two-person jet skis. 800–526–6650.

JEWELRY

A.R.C. Traders Inc., Box 3429, Scottsdale, AZ 85257: Free information ❖ Findings, chains, earrings, and sterling silver, gold-filled, and 14k gold beads. 800–528–2374; 602–945–0769 (in AZ).

All Ears, 114 5th Ave., New York, NY 10011: Free catalog ❖ Earrings and other jewelry. 212–675–1273.

The Amber Company, 5643 Cahuenga Blvd., North Hollywood, CA 91601: Free price list ❖ Amber specimens, beads, fossils, jewelry, books, faceting and cabbing rough, and lapidary supplies. 818–509–5730.

American Silver from the Southwest, 5700 Frederick Rd., Dayton, OH 45414: Free information ❖ Native American and contemporary jewelry, pottery, and kachinas. 513–890–0138.

Archive Collection, P.O. Box 1795, Lee's Summit, MO 64063: Catalog $3 ❖ Victorian-style jewelry. 816–525–5183.

Arizona Traders, P.O. Box 2000, El Paso, TX 79950: Free price list ❖ Native American mandellas and handmade turquoise and silver jewelry. 800–351–1674; 915–544–7204 (in AZ).

Arrow Gems & Minerals Inc., P.O. Box 9068, Phoenix, AZ 85068: Free catalog ❖ Pewter figurines, pendants, buckles, beads and findings, mineral specimens, and faceted gemstones. 602–997–6373.

James Avery Craftsman, P.O. Box 1367, Kerrville, TX 78029: Free catalog ❖ Men and women's jewelry. 800–283–1770.

Maurice Badler Jewelry, 578 5th Ave., New York, NY 10036: Catalog $3 ❖ Men and women's jewelry. 800–M-BADLER; 212–575–9632 (in NY).

Beauty by Spector Inc., McKeesport, PA 15134: Free catalog ❖ Women's wigs and hairpieces, men's toupees, jewelry, and exotic lingerie. 412–673–3259.

J.H. Breakell & Company, 69 Mill St., Newport, RI 02840: Catalog $2 ❖ Handcrafted sterling silver and 14k gold jewelry. 800–767–6411.

Circle D Jewelry, 9440 McCombs St., El Paso, TX 79924: Catalog $2 ❖ Sterling silver and 14k gold jewelry. 915–755–4479.

Des Handmade Crafts, 112 Randy Rd., Madison, TN 37115: Free brochure ❖ Handcrafted clay jewelry. 615–868–5279.

Designs by Romeo, 1550 E. Oakland Park Blvd., Fort Lauderdale, FL 33334: Free information ❖ 14k gold rings with semi-precious gemstones. 800–223–7999.

Diamond Essence Company, 6 Saddle Rd., Cedar Knolls, NJ 07927: Free catalog ❖ Men and women's jewelry with simulated diamonds. 201–267–7370.

Diamonds by Rennie Ellen, 15 W. 47th St., Room 401, New York, NY 10036: Catalog $2 ❖ Diamonds, rubies, sapphires, amethysts, emeralds, pearls, opals, tourmaline, and other gemstones, with optional gold or platinum settings. 212–869–5525.

Discoveries, 207 Ramsay Alley, Alexandria, VA 22314: Free information ❖ Handmade pendants, rings, bracelets, earrings, and other

personalized cartouche jewelry. 800–237–3358.

DoPaso Jewelry, P.O. Box 35430, Albuquerque, NM 87176: Free information ❖ Southwestern-style turquoise and sterling silver pins. 800–992–5234.

Eagle Mountain Turquoise Company, 9430 E. Golf Links, Tucson, AZ 85730: Free information ❖ Sterling silver and turquoise jewelry. 800–972–1140; 602–296–1090 (in AZ).

Ed's House of Gems, 7712 NE Sandy Blvd., Portland, OR 97211: Free information with long SASE ❖ Clocks, clock-making parts, minerals, gemstones, lapidary equipment, mountings, shells, jewelry, and Native American relics. 503–284–8990.

Guyot Arts, 2945 SE 140th St., Portland, OR 97236: Free brochure with long SASE ❖ Original sterling silver naturalistic- and abstract-theme jewelry. 503–761–9519.

Harmon's Agate & Silver Shop, Box 94, Crane, MT 59217: Catalog $3 ❖ Montana moss agate, sapphires, and handmade silver and gold jewelry. 406–482–2534.

Gayle Hayman Beverly Hills, 8306 Wilshire Blvd., Beverly Hills, CA 90211: Free catalog ❖ Jewelry and cosmetics. 800–FOR-GALE.

Gray & Sons, 2998 McFarlane Rd., Coconut Grove, FL 33133: Catalog $10 ❖ Pre-owned and restored fine watches. 800–654–0756.

Jaeger-LeCoultre, P.O. Box 1608, Winchester, VA 22604: Free catalog ❖ Jaeger-LeCoultre watches. 800–JLC-TIME.

Jewelry by Avery, 5134 Chalk Point Rd., West River, MD 20778: Free information with long SASE ❖ Kachinas, Native American art, precious and semi-precious gemstones, mineral specimens, and handcrafted Zuni, Navajo, and Hopi turquoise jewelry. 410–867–4752.

K-J-L by Kenneth Jay Lane, 40 W. 37th St., New York, NY 10018: Free information ❖ Copies of famous jewelry made with faux pearls, diamonds, and other gemstones. 800–233–3489.

The Kenya Gem Company, 801 N. Harvard Ave., Ventnor, NJ 08406: Free catalog ❖ Men and women's rings, bracelets, pendants, and other jewelry with simulated diamonds. 800–523–0158.

Lenox Jewelers, 2379 Black Rock Tnpk., Fairfield, CT 06430: Free catalog ❖ Watches, figurines, jewelry, and porcelain, china, and

crystal. 800–243–4473; 203–374–6157 (in CT).

Lewis & Roberts, Scientia Park, P.O. Box 6527, Chelmsford, MA 01824: Free catalog ❖ Men and women's watches and jewelry. 800–933–5335.

Carl Marcus & Company, 815 Connecticut Ave. NW, Washington, DC 20006: Free catalog ❖ Jewelry and Rolex, Patek, Phillippe, Audemars Piguet, Baume Mercier, and Cartier watches. 800–654–7184; 202–331–0671 (in DC).

Mary Laura's, P.O. Box 12615, Albuquerque, NM 87195: Catalog $2 ❖ Native American jewelry from the Zuni Pueblo. 800–662–4848.

J. Mavec & Company, 625 Madison Ave., 2nd Floor, New York, NY 10022: Catalog $3 ❖ Antique jewelry and silver. 212–888–8100.

Merlite Industries Inc., 114 5th Ave., New York, NY 10011: Free catalog ❖ Contemporary and classic jewelry for men and women. 212–924–6440.

Museum of Jewelry, 3000 Larkin St., San Francisco, CA 94109: Free catalog ❖ Handcrafted reproductions of historic jewelry originals. 800–258–0888.

National Watch Exchange, 107 S. 8th St., Philadelphia, PA 19106: Free information ❖ Pre-owned vintage watches. 800–8-WATCHES.

Nature's Jewelry, 222 Mill Rd., Chelmsford, MA 01824: Free catalog ❖ Leaves, shells, and other natural objects transformed into jewelry by preservation in precious metals. 800–333–3235.

Natureworks Bead Company, Four Jonquill Ln., Kings Park, NY 11754: Catalog $2.50 ❖ Exotic beads from worldwide sources and sterling, 14k gold, gold-filled, and natural stone jewelry.

Navajo Manufacturing Company, 5801 Logan St., Denver, CO 80216: Catalog $2 ❖ Turquoise jewelry, novelties, and sunglasses. 303–292–8090.

Niger Bend, 5261 Irish Ridge Rd., Chittenago, NY 13037: Catalog $5 ❖ African beads and jewelry. 315–655–8989.

Olympia Gold, 11540 Wiles Rd., Coral Springs, FL 33076: Free catalog ❖ Necklaces, bracelets, diamond cut charms, filigree rings, and Austrian crystal chain. 800–395–7774.

Oriental Crest Inc., 6161 Savoy Dr., Houston, TX 77036: Free information ❖

Semi-precious gemstone jewelry, other jewelry, bead-stringing supplies, pendant carvings, and earring jackets. 800–367–3954; 713–780–2425 (in TX).

Palancar Jewelers, 1156 E. Alosta Ave., Glendora, CA 91741: Free catalog ❖ Diver's jewelry in 14k gold and sterling. 800–467–9067.

Palm Beach International, 6400 E. Rogers Cir., Boca Raton, FL 33499: Free catalog ❖ Earrings and other jewelry. 800–633–9803.

Pizazz Inc., 770 N. Halstead St., Ste. 107, Chicago, IL 60622: Catalog $3 ❖ Earrings, necklaces, pins, beads, and other jewelry. 312–670–2627.

Q-C Turquoise, 3340 E. Washington, Phoenix, AZ 85034: Free information ❖ Turquoise nugget jewelry, nuggets by the strand or pound, and cutting material and blocks. 602–267–1164.

Joan Rivers Style, P.O. Box 2666, West Chester, PA 19380: Free catalog ❖ Classic designer jewelry. 800–848–1055.

Martin Rochelle Jewelry, 10 Summer St., Pawtucket, RI 02860: Catalog $2 ❖ Designer jewelry from around the world. 800–552–0699.

Ross-Simons Jewelers, 9 Ross Simons Dr., Cranston, RI 02920: Free catalog ❖ China, crystal, flatware, silver, watches, figurines, and diamond, gold, pearl, and gemstone jewelry. 800–556–7376.

Roussels, P.O. Box 476, Arlington, MA 02174: Catalog $1 ❖ Jewelry-making supplies and ready-to-wear jewelry. 508–443–8888.

Script Craft Jewelry, 115 San Jose Ave., Ste. E, Capitola, CA 95010: Free brochure ❖ Personalized gold wire jewelry. 800–777–1169.

Second Look, c/o Silver Works Inc., 3234–B Kirkwood Hwy., Wilmington, DE 19808: Free catalog ❖ Silver and turquoise earrings, bracelets, necklaces, watch bands, and jewelry by Southwest artisans. 800–544–8200.

Cole Sheckler Jewelry, P.O. Box 278, Cato, NY 13033: Free information ❖ Handcrafted gold jewelry with rare gemstones. 315–626–6823.

Silver Nugget, 416 Juan Tabu NE, Albuquerque, NM 87123: Catalog $2 ❖ Native American jewelry. 505–293–6861.

Simply Diamonds, P.O. Box 682, Ardsley, NY 10502: Free catalog ❖ Diamond jewelry

in 14k solid gold mountings. 800–55–CARAT.

Simply Whispers, 33 Riverside Dr., Pembroke, MA 02359: Free catalog ❖ Hypo-allergenic earrings.

Vicky Thaler Designs, Bishops Corner, 8 Crossroads Plaza, West Hartford, CT 06117: Free catalog ❖ Visionary jewelry in 18K and 14k gold and sterling silver. 203–231–7727.

Tiffany & Company, Customer Service, 801 Jefferson Rd., Parsippany, NJ 07054: Catalog $1 ❖ Jewelry, silver, china, crystal, watches and clocks, and other gifts. 201–428–0570.

Tourneau, 488 Madison Ave., New York, NY 10022: Free information ❖ Reconditioned pre-owned Rolex, Patek, Piaget, and other watches. 800–542–2389; 212–758–3671 (in NY).

Vanity Fair, S.A. Peck & Company, 55 E. Washington St., Chicago, IL 60602: Free catalog ❖ Diamond jewelry. 312–977–0300.

Wayfarer Trading Company, 2094 343rd St., Vail, IA 51465: Free brochure ❖ Sterling silver and 18k gold Egyptian cartouche pendants. 712–677–2761.

Wellington Jewels, 4850 Connecticut Ave. NW, Ste. 103, Washington, DC 20008: Free brochure ❖ Fashion jewelry with synthetic diamonds. 800–424–0100.

Wharton Wholesalers Ltd., 3256 Chaparral Dr., Idaho Falls, ID 83404: Free information ❖ Gifts, novelties, fine jewelry, and miniatures. 208–529–5260.

Windsor Collection, 6836 Engle Rd., P.O. Box 94549, Cleveland, OH 44101: Free catalog ❖ Men and women's fashion watches and jewelry. 800–800–0500.

JEWELRY MAKING

A & K Gems & Minerals, 2442 Folsom St., San Francisco, CA 94110: Free information ❖ Rocks, minerals, shells, fossils, tumbled gemstones, geodes, and crystal specimens. 415–282–0196.

A.R.C. Traders Inc., Box 3429, Scottsdale, AZ 85257: Free information ❖ Findings, chains, earrings, other jewelry, and sterling silver, gold-filled, and 14k gold beads. 800–528–2374; 602–945–0769 (in AZ).

Abeada Corporation, 1205 N. Main St., Royal Oak, MI 48067: Free information ❖ Semi-precious gemstone and glass beads, freshwater and cultured pearls, and gold and silver findings. 800–521–6326; 313–399–6642 (in MI).

Ackley's Rocks & Stamps, 3230 N. Stone Ave., Colorado Springs, CO 80907: Catalog $1 (refundable) ❖ Lapidary and silversmithing supplies, mountings, and findings. 719–633–1153.

Aleta's Rock Shop, 1515 Plainfield NE, Grand Rapids, MI 49505: Catalog $1.50 ❖ Jewelry-making supplies, tumblers, lapidary equipment, findings, silicon carbide grits, diamond material, and rocks for cutting, tumbling, and polishing. 616–363–5394.

Allcraft Tool & Supply Company, 666 Pacific St., Brooklyn, NY 11207: Catalog $5 ❖ Lapidary tools and supplies. 800–645–7124; 718–789–2800 (in NY).

Alpha Supply Inc., P.O. Box 2133, Bremerton, WA 98310: Catalog $3 ❖ Casting and faceting equipment, jewelry-making tools, silver rings, wax models, lapidary tools, and clock movements and parts. 206–373–3302.

Amazon Imports, P.O. Box 58, Williston Park, NY 11596: Free price list ❖ Amethyst, aquamarine, emerald, garnet, kunzite, blue topaz, imperial topaz, and tourmaline from Brazil. 516–621–7481.

Ambassador, Palo Verde at 34th St., P.O. Box 28807, Tucson, AZ 85076: Free catalog ❖ Cloisonne, turquoise, sterling silver, 14k gold, and onyx, ruby, emerald, pearl, jade, opal, zirconia, and other semi-precious gemstone settings. 602–748–8600.

The Amber Company, 5643 Cahuenga Blvd., North Hollywood, CA 91601: Free price list ❖ Amber, beads, fossils, jewelry, faceting and cabbing rough, colored stones, and lapidary supplies. 818–509–5730.

Amber Treasure, P.O. Box 20875, Oakland, CA 94620: Catalog $4 ❖ Calibrated and free-form cabochons, amber spheres and beads, polished amber stones, Baltic amber rough, and finished jewelry. 510–547–8660.

Anchor Tool & Supply Company Inc., P.O. Box 265, Chatham, NJ 07928: Catalog $3 (refundable with $10 order) ❖ Tools and supplies for gold- and silversmithing, casting, and blacksmithing. 201–587–8888.

APL Trader, P.O. Box 1900, New York, NY 10185: Catalog $1 ❖ Precious and semi-precious gemstones, cabochons, carvings, and beads. 718–454–2954.

B. Rush Apple Company, 3855 W. Kennedy Blvd., Tampa, FL 33609: Free price list ❖ Jeweler's tools and supplies, casting equipment, and findings. 813–870–3180.

Arizona Gems & Minerals Inc., 6370 East Hwy. 69, Prescott Valley, AZ 86314: Catalog $2 ❖ Chip beads, other beads and findings, silversmithing and lapidary tools, jewelry-making supplies, and mineral specimens. 602–772–6443.

Arrow Gems & Minerals Inc., P.O. Box 9068, Phoenix, AZ 85068: Free catalog ❖ Unusual beads, findings, arrowheads, embedded scorpions, minerals, and faceted gemstones. 602–997–6373.

Art to Wear, 5 Crescent Pl., St. Petersburg, FL 33711: Catalog $1 ❖ Bead-stringing supplies, tools, and jewelry-making kits.

B & J Rock Shop, 14744 Manchester Rd., Ballwin, MO 63011: Catalog $3 ❖ Jewelry-making supplies, beads and bead-stringing supplies, quartz clock movements, clock-building kits, and quartz crystals, amethyst crystal clusters, Brazilian agate nodules, geodes, and other imported and domestic gemstones. 314–394–4567.

Baubanbea Enterprises, P.O. Box 1205, Smithtown, NY 11787: Catalog $1 ❖ Rhinestones, sequins, beads, and gemstones. 516–724–4661.

Bead Depot, Box 673, Novato, CA 94947: Catalog $3 ❖ Findings, earring kits, and beads from worldwide locations. 415–892–6965.

Bead It, P.O. Box 3505, Prescott, AZ 86302: Catalog $4 ❖ Czechoslovakian beads, gemstones, charms, bone, findings, and books. 602–445–9234.

Beada Beada, 4262 N. Woodward Ave., Royal Oak, MI 48073: Free catalog ❖ Semi-precious beads, cabochons, cultured and freshwater pearls, and 14k gold, gold-filled, and sterling findings. 313–549–1005.

Beadbox Inc., 10135 E. Via Linda, Scottsdale, AZ 85258: Catalog $5 ❖ Ready-to-assemble jewelry kits and beads from worldwide sources. 800–232–3269.

Beadworks, 139 Washington St., South Norwalk, CT 06854: Catalog $10 ❖ Glass, wood, metal, porcelain, ceramic, bone, plastic, mother-of-pearl, Swarovski crystal, and other beads. 203–852–9194.

Bejeweled Wholesalers, Box 8096, Pembroke Pines, FL 33084: Catalog $1 (refundable) ❖ Rhinestones, studs, rhinestone and stud setter, and rims. 305–433–5700.

Boone Trading Company, 562 Coyote Rd., Brinnon, WA 98320: Catalog $3 ❖ Ivory, scrimshaw tusks, netsuke, Oriental and Eskimo carvings, and fossilized walrus and mammoth ivory tusks and pieces. 206–796–4330.

Boston Findings & Jewelers Supply, 387 Washington St., 8th Floor, Boston, MA 02108: Catalog $2 ❖ Jewelry findings and supplies. 800–225–2436; 617–357–9599 (in MA).

Bourget Bros., 1636 11th St., Santa Monica, CA 90404: Catalog $5 ❖ Jewelry-making and lapidary tools, gemstones, cabochons, wax patterns, beads, bead-stringing supplies, and sterling silver and gold-filled chains. 310–450–6556.

Brahm Limited, P.O. Box 1, Lake Charles, LA 70602: Catalog $2 ❖ Precious and semi-precious costume and designer beads, rhinestones, and findings.

Brazil Imports, 861 6th Ave., Ste. 700, San Diego, CA 92101: Free price list ❖ Rubies, sapphires, amethysts, emerald cabochons, calibrated emeralds, tanzite, tourmaline, topaz, quartz, and other gemstones from Brazil. 619–234–3675.

Brown Brothers Lapidary, 2248 S. 1st Ave., Safford, AZ 85546: Catalog $1 (refundable) ❖ Gemstones. 602–428–6433.

Bucks County Classic, 73 Coventry Lane, Langhorne, PA 19047: Catalog $2 ❖ Fresh water pearls, Chinese cloisonne, cabachons, findings, and gemstone, handmade, metal, Austrian crystal, and stone accent beads. 800–942–GEMS.

C & R Enterprises Inc., 4833 East Park, Springfield, MO 65809: Free catalog ❖ Sterling silver and 14k gold mountings, lapidary supplies, mineral specimens, belt buckles, beads and beading supplies, and cut stones. 417–866–4843.

Cargo Hold Inc., P.O. Box 239, Charleston, SC 29402: Catalog $3 ❖ Bead-stringing thread. 803–723–3341.

CGM Inc., 19562 Ventura Blvd., Tarzana, CA 91356: Free catalog ❖ Precious and semi-precious gemstones and 14k gold, gold-filled, and sterling silver findings. 818–609–7088.

Charlie's Rock Shop, 620 J St., Penrose, CO 81240: Free catalog ❖ Clocks, clock movements and parts, beads, jewelry-making supplies, and faceted gemstones. 800–336–6923.

Comstock Creations, P.O. Box 2715, Durango, CO 81302: Free information ❖ Cut and polished Brazilian agate and geodes. 800–844–9000; 303–247–3836 (in CO).

Contempo Lapidary, 12257 Foothill Blvd., Sylmar, CA 91342: Free brochure ❖ Lapidary equipment. 800–356–2441; 818–899–1973 (in CA).

The Cotton Ball, 475 Morro Bay Blvd., Morro Bay, CA 93442: Catalog $3 ❖ Charms, ornaments, kits, findings, books, and other jewelry-making supplies.

Covington Engineering Corporation, P.O. Box 35, Redlands, CA 92373: Free catalog ❖ Lapidary equipment. 714–793–6636.

Creative Castle, 2373 Michael Dr., Newbury Park, CA 91320: Free catalog ❖ Bead-making jewelry kits. 805–499–1377.

Crystalite Corporation, 18400 Green Meadows Dr. North, Westerville, OH 43081: Free information ❖ Cabochon machines and other lapidary equipment.

Cupboard Distributing, P.O. Box 148, Urbana, OH 43078: Catalog $2 ❖ Unfinished wood parts for jewelry-making, and projects with crafts, miniatures, toys, tole and decorative painting, and woodworking. 513–390–6388.

Diamond Pacific Tool Corporation, 2620 W. Main St., Barstow, CA 92311: Free catalog ❖ Lapidary, rockhounding, and jewelry-making supplies. 800–253–2954.

Dikra Gem Inc., 56 W. 45th St., Ste. 1005, New York, NY 10036: Free information ❖ Semi-precious gemstones. 800–873–4572.

Discount Agate House, 3401 N. Dodge Blvd., Tucson, AZ 85716: Free information ❖ Rocks and minerals from around the world, lapidary equipment, sterling silver and metalsmithing supplies, and findings. 602–323–0781.

Discount Bead House, P.O. Box 186, The Plains, OH 45780: Catalog $5 ❖ Seed beads, findings, and tools. 800–793–7592.

Dremel Manufacturing, 4915 21st St., Racine, WI 53406: Free information ❖ Tools for grinding, sawing, drilling, carving, shaping, and polishing gemstones. 414–554–1390.

Dyer's Jewelers' Tools & Supplies, 4525 Guadalupe St., Austin, TX 78751: Tool catalog $4; findings catalog $3; wax pattern catalog $4 ❖ Tools, findings, wax and wax patterns, gemstones and rocks, rubber molds, and other supplies. 800–683–1631.

E & W Imports Inc., P.O. Box 157032, Tampa, FL 33684: Price list $1 ❖ Gemstone, cloisonne, and Austrian crystal beads and 14k findings. 813–885–1138.

Eastern Findings Corporation, 19 W. 34th St., New York, NY 10001: Free information ❖ Findings. 800–EFC-6640; 212–695–6640 (in NY).

Ebersole Lapidary Supply Inc., 11417 West Hwy. 54, Wichita, KS 67209: Catalog $2 ❖ Tools, findings, mountings, cabochons and rocks, jewelry-making kits, petrified wood, clocks and clock-making parts, beads, and bead-stringing supplies. 316–722–4771.

Ed's House of Gems, 7712 NE Sandy Blvd., Portland, OR 97213: Free information with long SASE ❖ Clocks, clock-making parts, minerals, gemstones, lapidary equipment, mountings, shells, jewelry, and Native American relics. 503–284–8990.

Eloxite Corporation, 806 10th St., Wheatland, WY 82201: Catalog $1 ❖ Clock-making supplies, tools, gemstones, belt buckles, jewelry mountings, and rockhounding and jewelry do-it-yourself equipment. 307–322–3050.

Embellishments for Designing People, 4793 Telegraph Ave., Oakland, CA 94609: Catalog $2 ❖ Charms, stampings, books, tools, and findings. 510–436–6415.

Firemountain Gems, 28195 Redwood Hwy., Cave Junction, OR 97523: Catalog $3 ❖ Beads, gems, and jewelry-making supplies and tools. 800–423–2319.

Florida Jewelry Crafts Inc., P.O. Box 2620, Sarasota, FL 34230: Catalog $2 (refundable) ❖ Jewelry findings, supplies, and tools. 813–351–9404.

Foredom Electric Company, 16 Stony Hill Rd., Bethel, CT 06801: Free information ❖ Tools for grinding, sawing, drilling, carving, shaping, and polishing gemstones. 203–792–8622.

G & G's Miracle House, 5621 W. Hemlock St., P.O. Box 23234, Milwaukee, WI 53223: Free catalog ❖ Brushes, buffers, rouges, findings, waxes, frames, and burs. 800–558–5513; 800–242–3403 (in WI).

Gem Center U.S.A. Inc., 4100 Alameda Ave., El Paso, TX 79905: Free price list ❖ Geodes and nodules. 915–533–7153.

Gem-Fare, P.O. Box 213, Pittstown, NJ 08867: Price list 50¢ ❖ Rare and unusual gemstones and crystals. 908–806–3339.

Gem-O-Rama Inc., 150 Recreation Park Dr., Hingham, MA 02043: Free catalog ❖ Gemstones, beading supplies, and 14k gold, gold-filled, and sterling silver beads. 617–749–8250.

Gems of Cowee Valley Company, P.O. Box 858, Franklin, NC 28734: Free price list ❖ Emeralds, lapis, beryl, tanzanite, and other gems. 800–2GEMS-99; 704–369–8311 (in NC).

Gemstone Equipment Manufacturing Company, 750 Easy St., Simi Valley, CA 93065: Free information ❖ Vibratory tumblers and other lapidary equipment. 800–235–3375; 805–527–6990 In CA).

Gilman's Lapidary Supply, Durham St., P.O. Box M, Hellertown, PA 18055: Free information ❖ Lapidary equipment, findings and mountings, silver and gold metal crafting supplies, and genuine and synthetic gemstones. 215–838–8767.

Kenneth Glasser, P.O. Box 441, Monsey, NY 10952: Catalog $10 ❖ All types, sizes, and qualities of diamonds. 914–426–1241.

Goodnow's, 3415 S. Hayden St., Amarillo, TX 79109: Free list with long SASE ❖ Gem roughs for faceting, cabbing, and tumbling. 806–352–0725.

Graves Company, 1800 Andrews Ave., Pompano Beach, FL 33069: Free catalog ❖ Lapidary equipment. 800–327–9103.

Grieger's, P.O. Box 93070, Pasadena, CA 91109: Free catalog ❖ Gemstones, lapidary equipment, jewelry-making supplies, mountings, and findings. 800–423–4181.

Griffith Distributors, Box 662, Louisville, CO 80027: Free information ❖ Jewelry-making chemicals. 303–442–8284.

Gryphon Corporation, 101 E. Santa Anita Ave., Burbank, CA 91502: Free information ❖ 10–in-1 multipurpose lapidary workshop tool and other equipment. 818–845–7807.

T.B. Hagstoz & Son Inc., 709 Sansom St., Philadelphia, PA 19106: Catalog $5 (refundable with $25 order) ❖ Metal findings, jeweler's tools, casting equipment, gold and silver solders, and gold, silver, gold-filled, copper, bronze, brass-nickel, silver, and pewter metals. 800–922–1006; 215–922–1627 (in PA).

Hanneman Gemological Instruments, P.O. Box 2453, Castro Valley, CA 94546: Catalog $2 (refundable) ❖ Gemological instruments and tools.

Hardies, P.O. Box 1920, Quartzsite, AZ 85346: Catalog $3 (refundable) ❖ Beads, findings, buckles, bolas, Native American jewelry, gems, rocks, and books. 602–927–6381.

Harmon's Agate & Silver Shop, Box 94, Crane, MT 59217: Catalog $3 ❖ Montana moss agate, sapphires, and handmade silver and gold jewelry. 406–482–2534.

HDM Manufacturing, P.O. Box 691, East Helena, MT 59635: Free brochure ❖ Faceting machines and other equipment. 406–933–5737.

Hong Kong Lapidary Supplies, 2801 University Dr., Coral Springs, FL 33065: Catalog $3 ❖ Semi-precious gemstones and beads. 305–755–8777.

House of Onyx, The Aaron Bldg., Greenville, KY 42345: Free catalog ❖ Jewelry, gemstones, and jewelry-making supplies. 800–844–3100.

Indian Jewelers Supply Company, P.O. Box 1774, Gallup, NM 87305: Catalog $5 ❖ Precious and base metals, findings, metalsmithing and lapidary equipment, semi-precious gemstones, shells, and coral. 505–722–4451.

International Beads, 6200 Savoy, Ste. 308, Houston, TX 77036: Free information ❖ Cabochons and findings. 800–733–1313; 713–783–1855 (in TX).

International Gem Merchants Inc., 4168 Oxford Ave., Jacksonville, FL 32210: Free information ❖ Gemstones, pearls, and synthetic gemstones. 800–633–3653; 904–388–5130 (in FL).

Jarvi Tool Company, 1200 E. Debra Ln., Anaheim, CA 92805: Free information ❖ Lapidary equipment, faceting machines, and other tools. 714–774–9104.

Jewelry Kits by E, P.O. Box 32626, Baltimore, MD 21208: Catalog $2.50 ❖ Jewelry kits. 410–655–3213.

Jewelry Supplies 4 Less, 13001 Las Vegas Blvd. South, Las Vegas, NV 89124: Catalog $4 ❖ Jewelry-making supplies.

Kerr Division of Sybron Corporation, 28200 Wick Rd., P.O. Box 455, Romulus, MI 48174: Catalog $2 ❖ Lapidary equipment, tools, injection wax and molding rubber for making wax patterns, and other supplies. 313–946–7800.

Kikico Beads, P.O. Box 8353, Scottsdale, AZ 85252: Catalog $2 ❖ Beads for jewelry designing. 602–953–2728.

Kingsley North Inc., P.O. Box 216, Norway, MI 49870: Free catalog ❖ Jewelry-making tools and supplies, metal casting and lapidary equipment, and rough, cut, and calibrated opals. 800–338–9280.

Krona Gem Merchants, Box 9968, Colorado Springs, CO 80932: Free price list ❖ Faceted and rare gemstones. 719–597–8779.

Lapcraft Company Inc., 195 W. Olentangy St., Powell, OH 43065: Free information ❖ Lapidary equipment. 614–764–8993.

Lentz Lapidary Inc., 11760 S. Oliver, Rt. 2, Box 134, Mulvane, KS 67110: Catalog $2 ❖ Jewelry, mountings, clocks and parts, rough rock specimens and cabochons, and rockhounding and lapidary equipment. 316–777–1372.

Victor H. Levy Inc., 1355 S. Flower St., Los Angeles, CA 90015: Catalog $5 ❖ Findings, rhinestones, gemstones, braids, and jewelry-making supplies. 800–421–8021; 213–749–8247 (in CA).

Lochs, 312 Main St., Emmaus, PA 18049: Catalog $3 ❖ Faceted and polished gemstones, 14k gold findings, and biron-created emeralds. 215–967–3479.

Lonnie's Inc., 7155 E. Main St., Mesa, AZ 85207: Free findings catalog; tool catalog $5 ❖ Supplies for jewelers, casters, silversmiths, and lapidarists. 602–832–2641.

Lortone Inc., 2856 NW Market St., Seattle, WA 98107: Free catalog ❖ Lapidary equipment. 206–789–3100.

Maxant Industries Inc., P.O. Box 454, Ayer, MA 01432: Catalog $1 ❖ Lapidary equipment. 508–772–0576.

Midwest Fossil Exchange, P.O. Box 681351, Schaumberg, IL 60168: Free price list ❖ Faceted gemstones.

Minnesota Lapidary Supply Corporation, 2825 Dupont Ave. South, Minneapolis, MN 55408: Free catalog ❖ Lapidary equipment. 612–872–7211.

Mohave Industries Inc., 2365 Northern Ave., Kingman, AZ 86401: Brochure $1 ❖ Lapidary equipment. 602–757–2480.

Mountain Crafts, 163 E. Main St., Unit 257, Little Falls, NJ 07424: Free catalog ❖ Candle and wire tree-making supplies, tumbled gemstones, and wood patterns. 201–256–3669.

Nasco, 901 Janesville Ave., Fort Atkinson, WI 53538: Free catalog ❖ Jewelry-making supplies and tools. 800–558–9595.

New England International Gems Inc., 188 Pollard St., Billerica, MA 01862: Free catalog ❖ Brazilian quartz, rocks from India, beads, jewelry-making supplies, tools, and findings. 508–667–7394.

Neycraft, Division of Ney, Ney Industrial Park, Bloomfield, CT 06002: Free information ❖ Tools and other equipment for making jewelry. 800–538–4593.

The NgraveR Company, 67 Wawecus Hill Rd., Bozrah, CT 06334: Catalog $1 (refundable) ❖ Easy-to-use engraving tools and other jewelry-making equipment. 203–823–1533.

Nonferrous Metals, P.O. Box 2595, Waterbury, CT 06723: Catalog $3 (refundable) ❖ Plain and ornamental brass, copper, bronze, and nickel-silver wire. 203–274–7255.

M. Nowotny & Company, 8823 Callaghan Rd., San Antonio, TX 78230: Free information ❖ Gemstones and fossils from worldwide sources, jewelry, pewter figurines, key chains, scarabs, obsidian eggs, and peacock feathers. 800–950– 8276; 512–342–2512 (in TX).

H. Obodda Mineral Specimens, P.O. Box 51, Short Hills, NJ 07078: Free list ❖ Rare and semi-precious gemstones. 201–467–0212.

Optional Extras, 55 San Remo Dr., Burlington, VT 05403: Catalog $2 ❖ Jewelry findings and beads from worldwide sources. 802–608–0013.

Oriental Crest Inc., 6161 Savoy Dr., Houston, TX 77036: Free information ❖ Semi-precious gemstone jewelry, gemstones and findings, bead-stringing supplies, pendant carvings, and earring jackets. 800–367–3954; 713–780–2425 (in TX).

Ornamental Resources Inc., P.O. Box 3010, Idaho Springs, CO 80452: Catalog $25 ❖ Beads, pendants, charms, brass stampings, feathers, chains, rhinestones, antique tassels and trims, and findings. 303–279–2102.

Paradise Diamond Tools, 6267 Becker Way, Paradise, CA 95969: Free information ❖ Diamond carving points and drills. 916–877–2597.

Pearl International, 24 Case Ave., Patchogue, NY 11772: Catalog $5 ❖ Beadworking, jewelry, and lapidary tools. 516–277–6788.

Pikes Peak Rock Shop, 1316 Pecan St., Colorado Springs, CO 80904: Free catalog ❖ Fossils, crystals, tumbled stones, agate products, amethyst, chips, beads, and stands. 800–347–6257.

Pioneer Gem Corporation, P.O. Box 1513, Auburn, WA 98071: Catalog $5 ❖ Cut and polished gemstones. 206–833–2760.

Poly-Metric, Spokane St., Box 400, Clayton, WA 99110: Free information ❖ Faceting instruments. 509–276–5565.

Prospectors Pouch Inc., P.O. Box 112, Kennesaw, GA 30144: Free information ❖ Rocks, gemstones, and jewelry-making supplies. 404–427–6481.

Q-C Turquoise, 3340 E. Washington, Phoenix, AZ 85034: Free information ❖ Turquoise nugget jewelry and nuggets by the strand, pound, cuttings, and blocks. 602–267–1164.

Raytech Industries, 147 West St., P.O. Box 449, Rt. 147, Middlefield, CT 06455: Free information ❖ Lapidary and ultraviolet light equipment. 203–349–3421.

Richardson's Recreational Ranch Ltd., Gateway Route Box 440, Madras, OR 97741: Free information ❖ Rocks and gemstones from worldwide locations, lapidary equipment, and clocks, clock movements, and parts. 503–475–2680.

Rio Grande, 6901 Washington NE, Albuquerque, NM 87109: Free information ❖ Jewelry findings. 800–545–6566.

The Rock Peddler, 58 Wedgewood Rd., Franklin, NC 28734: Catalog $2 (refundable) ❖ Lapidary equipment. 704–524–6042.

Ross Metals, 54 W. 47th St., New York, NY 10036: Free information ❖ Findings, gold and silver wire and spooled chains. 800–654–ROSS; 212–869–1407 (in NY).

Roussels, P.O. Box 476, Arlington, MA 02174: Catalog $1 ❖ Jewelry-making supplies and ready-to-wear jewelry. 508–443–8888.

Running T Trading Company, Hope-Franklin Inc., 1201 Iron Springs Rd., Ste. 11, Prescott, AZ 86301: Free catalog ❖ Prenotched mounts, beads, diamonds, gemstones, chains, safety clasps, and other jewelry-making supplies. 602–778–2739.

Marvin Schwab, 2313 Distribution Cir., Silver Spring, MD 20910: Catalog $3 ❖ Beads and gems, jewelry. findings, and other supplies. 301–652–2588.

SESCO, P.O. Box 21406, Reno, NV 89515: Free catalog ❖ Findings, gemstones, fossils, and novelties. 800–637–3726.

South Pacific Wholesale Company, Rt. 2, P.O. Box 249, East Montpelier, VT 05651: Free price list ❖ Beads, findings, semi-precious gemstone settings, gold and silver bracelets, necklaces, and earrings. 802–223–1354.

Southwest Rock & Gem Company, Rt. 3, Box 10, Hico, TX 76457: Free price list with long SASE ❖ Lapidary supplies. 817–796–4907.

Stardust Gallery, 2501 Jericho Tnpk., Centereach, NY 11720: Catalog $1 ❖ Pearls, Austrian crystals, sequins, findings, appliques, buttons, rhinestones, studs, and other supplies. 516–981–4302.

Stone Age Industries Inc., P.O. Box 383, Powell, WY 82435: Catalog $1.50 ❖ Rough gemstones, slabs, cutting and polishing equipment, and lapidary supplies. 307–754–4681.

Swest Inc., 11090 N. Stemmons Freeway, Dallas, TX 75229: Free information ❖ Jeweler's tools, wax patterns, findings, and gemstones. 214–247–7744.

Tagit, P.O. Box 1534, San Juan Capistrano, CA 92675: Free information ❖ Lapidary equipment. 310–949–8380.

Terrific Little Crafts, 4140 Oceanside Blvd., Oceanside, CA 92056: Catalog $1 ❖ Jewelry findings, quilling and other craft supplies, and paper clay.

Tierracast, 3177 Guerneville Rd., Santa Rosa, CA 95401: Free catalog ❖ Jewelry-making findings. 800–222–9939; 707–545–5787 (in CA).

Tripp's Manufacturing, P.O. Box 1369, Socorro, NM 87801: Free catalog ❖ Pre-notched mounts. 800–545–7962; 505–835–2461 (in NM).

Tru-Square Metal Products, P.O. Box 585, Auburn, VA 98071: Free brochure ❖ Tumblers and other rock polishing equipment. 800–225–1017.

TSI Inc., P.O. Box 9266, Seattle, WA 98109: Free catalog ❖ Jewelry-making tools and supplies. 800–426–9984.

Ultra Tec, 1025 E. Chestnut, Santa Ana, CA 92701: Free brochure ❖ Lapidary equipment. 714–542–0608.

Vibra-Tek Company, 1844 Arroya Rd., Colorado Springs, CO 80906: Free information ❖ Rock polishers. 719–634–8611.

Watch Us Inc., 500 Monroe Tnpk., Ste. 351, Monroe, CT 06468: Free catalog ❖ Contemporary and southwestern watch heads and watch findings. 203–736–0127.

Westbrook Bead Company, 16641 Spring Gulch Dr., Anderson, CA 96007: Catalog $2 ❖ Bead-stringing supplies and gemstone, faceted glass, cobalt blue, old trade, other beads, and other jewelry components for designers and crafts-people. 916–357–3143.

JOKES & NOVELTIES

Chazpro Magic Company, 603 E. 13th, Eugene, OR 97401: Catalog $3 ❖ Clown props, books, juggling equipment, jokes, and novelties. 503–345–0032.

The Fun House, P.O. Box 12250, Newark, NJ 07101: Free catalog with long SASE ❖ Novelties, tricks, jokes, and other fun products.

Global Shakeup Snowdomes, 2265 Westwood Blvd., Ste. 618, Los Angeles, CA 90064: Catalog $2 (refundable) ❖ Snow-filled, hard-to-find imported comical, photo, and other "snow" domes. 213–259–8988.

Klutz Press, 2121 Staunton Ct., Palo Alto, CA 94306: Free information ❖ Novelty and fun merchandise, juggling equipment, and books. 415–857–0888.

Lighter Side Company, 4514 19th St. Court East, P.O. Box 25600, Bradenton, FL 34203: Free catalog ❖ Jokes and novelties, tricks, science equipment, sports equipment, and other hobby supplies. 813–747–2356.

Things You Never Knew Existed, c/o Johnson Smith Company, 4514 19th St. Court East, Bradenton, FL 34203: Free catalog ❖ Novelties, tricks, hobby supplies, and other unusual things. 813–747–2356.

Think Big, 390 W. Broadway, New York, NY 10012: Free catalog ❖ Unusual and oversized gags, gifts, and home furnishings. 800–487–4244.

JUGGLING

Abracadabra Magic Shop, 125 Lincoln Blvd., Middlesex, NJ 08846: Catalog $5 ❖ Close-up and stage magic, clown props,

juggling equipment, balloons, costumes, and theatrical make-up. 908–805–0200.

Books by Mail, P.O. Box 1444, Corona, CA 91718: Free catalog ❖ Books on juggling and clowning. 909–273–0900.

Chazpro Magic Company, 603 E. 13th, Eugene, OR 97401: Catalog $3 ❖ Juggling and clown supplies, books, jokes, and novelties. 503–345–0032.

Brian Dube Inc., 520 Broadway, New York, NY 10012: Free catalog ❖ Juggling equipment and books. 212–941–0060.

The Entertainers Supermarket, 21 Carol Pl., Staten Island, NY 10303: Free brochure ❖ Supplies and props for jugglers, clowns, magicians, balloon sculpturists, face painters, stilt walkers, and other entertainers. 718–494–6232.

Flosso-Hornmann Magic Company, 45 W. 34th St., Room 607, New York, NY 10001: Free information ❖ Magic equipment, juggling supplies, tarot cards, and crystal balls. 212–279–6079.

The Great American Juggling & Fun Company, P.O. Box 227, Pine Forge, PA 19548: Free catalog ❖ Juggling props. 800–3–JUGGLE; 215–367–7926 (in PA).

Juggling Arts, 5535 N. 11th St., Phoenix, AZ 85014: Catalog $1 ❖ Juggling props. 602–266–4391.

Klutz Press, 2121 Staunton Ct., Palo Alto, CA 94306: Free information ❖ Novelty and fun merchandise, juggling equipment, and books. 415–857–0888.

Mecca Magic Inc., 49 Dodd St., Bloomfield, NJ 07003: Catalog $10 ❖ Juggling equipment, theatrical make-up, clown props, balloons, magic, costumes and wigs, puppets, and ventriloquism equipment. 201–429–7597.

Under the Big Top, P.O. Box 807, Placentia, CA 92670: Catalog $4 ❖ Juggling equipment, clown props, costumes, make-up, balloons, and party supplies. 800–995–7727.

JUKEBOXES

Always Jukin', 221 Yesler Way, Seattle, WA 98104: Catalog $2 ❖ Jukebox service manuals, and books about jukeboxes, old phonographs, and radios. 206–233–9460.

Antique Slot Machine Part Company, 140 N. Western Ave., Carpentersville, IL 60110: Free catalog ❖ Books and manuals, slot stands and slot pads, and parts for slot machines, jukeboxes, and pinballs. 708–428–8476.

Classic Coin-Ops, 7038 Hoke Rd., Clayton, OH 45315: Free information with long SASE ❖ Jukeboxes and other slot and coke machines. 513–833–5143.

Coin Machine Trader, P.O. Box 602, Huron, SD 57350: Information $4 ❖ Manuals for most jukeboxes and slot machines. 605–352–7590.

CSSK Amusements, Box 6214, York, PA 17406: Free list with long SASE ❖ Jukeboxes, other coin-operated collectibles, and parts for jukeboxes and pinball machines. 800–PINBALL.

Illinois Antique Slot Machine Company, P.O. Box 542, Westmont, IL 60559: Free information ❖ Antique Wurlitzer jukeboxes, nickelodeons, music boxes, slot machines, and other coin-operated machines. 708–985–2742.

Jukebox Classics & Vintage Slot Machines Inc., 6742 5th Ave., Brooklyn, NY 11220: Free information ❖ Antique jukeboxes and coin-operated machines. 718–833–8455.

Jukebox Junction, P.O. Box 1081, Des Moines, IA 50311: Catalog $2.50 ❖ Antique jukeboxes. 515–981–4019.

Jukebox Memories, 2518 E. Huntington Dr., Duarte, CA 91010: Free information ❖ Jukebox restoration parts. 818–359–8700.

Lloyd's Jukeboxes, 22900 Shaw Rd., Sterling, VA 22170: Free information ❖ Jukeboxes, pinball machines, video games, slot machines, tin toys, advertising signs, and other collectibles from the 1950s. 703–834–6699.

National Jukebox Exchange, 121 Lakeside Dr., Mayfield, NY 12117: Free catalog ❖ Antique jukeboxes, slot machines, arcade machines, and parts. 518–661–5639.

North Penn Amusement & Vending, 105 N. Main, Souderton, PA 18924: Free information ❖ Jukeboxes, pinball machines, shuffle alleys, vending machines, video games, and pool tables. 215–723–7459.

Nostalgic Music Company, 58 Union Ave., New Providence, NJ 07974: Free information ❖ Restored jukeboxes, from the 1940s and 1950s. 908–464–5538.

Orange Trading Company, 57 S. Main St., Orange, MA 01364: Free list with long SASE ❖ Antique coin-operated jukeboxes, pinball and coke machines, and other coin-operated machines. 508–544–6683.

KALEIDOSCOPES

Atlas Art & Stained Glass, P.O. Box 76084, Oklahoma City, OK 73147: Catalog $3 ❖ Kaleidoscopes, frames, lamp bases, and art and craft, stained glass, jewelry-making, and foil crafting supplies. 405–946–1230.

Gemini Kaleidoscopes, 203 Lindsay Rd., Zelienople, PA 16063: Free information ❖ Handcrafted kaleidoscopes. 412–452–8700.

Kaleidoscopes by Laughing Coyote, Claudia & Ron Lee, 25 Upper Butcher Rd., Rockville, CT 06066: Free brochure ❖ Kaleidoscopes for one and two persons. 203–875–5098.

Van Cort Instruments Inc., 29 Industrial Dr., Northampton, MA 01060: Free information ❖ Kaleidoscopes and other optical equipment. 413–586–9800.

KITCHEN UTENSILS & COOKWARE

Alsto Company, P.O. Box 1267, Galesburg, IL 61401: Catalog $1 ❖ Tools, pet products, kitchen aids, and other convenience items. 800–447–0048.

Brookstone Company, Order Processing Center, 1655 Bassford Dr., Mexico, MO 65265: Free catalog ❖ Professional restaurant equipment for home chefs. 800–926–7000.

Chef's Catalog, 3215 Commercial Ave., Northbrook, IL 60062: Free catalog ❖ Calphalon cookware, Cuisinarts electrics, Henckels cutlery, and other professional restaurant equipment for the home chef. 800–338–3232.

Colonial Garden Kitchens, P.O. Box 66, Hanover, PA 17333: Free catalog ❖ Cookware. 717–633–3330.

Commercial Aluminum Cookware Company, P.O. Box 583, Toledo, OH 43697: Free information ❖ Calphalon cookware.

A Cook's Wares, 211 37th St., Beaver's Falls, PA 15010: Catalog $2 ❖ Cookware, cutlery, bakeware, French copper pans, and food processors. 412–846–9490.

Country Manor, Mail Order Department, Rt. 211, P.O. Box 520, Sperryville, VA 22740: Catalog $3 ❖ Kitchen utensils, rugs, carpets, and decor accessories. 800–344–8354.

Crate & Barrel, P.O. Box 9059, Wheeling, IL 60090: Free catalog ❖ Gourmet cooking equipment and appliances. 800–323–5461.

Cuisinarts Cookware, 150 Milford Rd., East Windsor, NJ 08520: Free information ❖ Cookware. 800–726–9499.

Cutco Cutlery, 1116 E. State St., P.O. Box 810, Olean, NY 14760: Catalog $1 ❖ Replacement cutlery. 800–828–0448.

DuFlo Woodcrafts, Mike & Roz DuFlo, Rt. 1, Box 277, St. Joe, AR 72675: Free information ❖ Hardwood kitchen tools. 501–449–6412.

The Faith Mountain Company, P.O. Box 199, Sperryville, VA 22740: Free catalog ❖ Kitchen utensils, country-style gifts, folk art reproductions, toys and dolls, handmade Appalachian baskets, and Christmas decorations. 800–822–7238.

Hoffritz, 515 W. 24th St., New York, NY 10011: Catalog $1 ❖ Optics, knives and scissors, kitchen aids, clocks, yogurt makers, and other gifts. 212–924–7300.

Iron Craft, Old Rt. 28, P.O. Box 369, Ossipee, NH 03864: Catalog $2 ❖ Cast-iron cookware, cookstoves, and coal and wood-heating stoves. 603–539–2807.

Kitchen Accessories Etc., P.O. Box 1560, North Hampton, NH 03862: Free catalog ❖ Kitchen aids, serving pieces, china, and silverplate. 603–964–5174.

Kitchen Bazaar, 4455 Connecticut Ave. NW, Washington, DC 20008: Catalog $1 ❖ Cookware. 202–363–4600.

Lehman Hardware & Appliances Inc., P.O. Box 41, Kidron, OH 44636: Catalog $2 ❖ Kitchen accessories, housewares, stoves for heating and cooking, farming and homesteading items, non-electric appliances, and woodworking and logsmithing tools. 216–857–5757.

Maid of Scandinavia, 3244 Raleigh Ave., Minneapolis, MN 55416: Free catalog ❖ Utensils and kitchen tools, cake molds and cookie cutters, candy-making molds, and ingredients. 800–851–1121.

Microwave Times, P.O. Box 1271, Burnsville, MN 55337: Free catalog ❖ Microwave cookware and cookbooks. 800–328–2846; 612–890–6655 (in MN).

Open House, 200 Bala Ave., Bala-Cynwyd, PA 19004: Free information with long SASE ❖ Flatware, cookware, and other kitchen accessories. 215–664–1488.

Pepperidge Farm, P.O. Box 917, Clinton, CT 06413: Free catalog ❖ Specialty and microwave cookware, tools, kitchen gadgets, glassware, silverware, cookbooks, and gourmet foods. 800–243–9314.

S.E. Rykoff & Company, 3501 Taylor Dr., Ukiah, CA 95482: Free catalog ❖ Professional gourmet cookware and foods for home chefs. 800–333–1448.

Vermont Country Store, Mail Order Office, P.O. Box 3000, Manchester Center, VT 05255: Free catalog ❖ Cookware and other home accessories. 802–362–4647.

Lillian Vernon, Virginia Beach, VA 23479: Free catalog ❖ Kitchen equipment. 800–285–5555.

Williams-Sonoma, Mail Order Department, P.O. Box 7456, San Francisco, CA 94120: Free catalog ❖ Specialty cookware for home gourmet chefs, serving pieces, household accessories, books, and gourmet foods. 800–541–1262.

Wilton Enterprise Inc., 2240 W. 75th St., Woodridge, IL 60517: Catalog $6 (refundable) ❖ Supplies for making cookies, cakes, and candy. 708–963–7100.

Winterthur Museum & Gardens, Catalog Division, 100 Enterprise Pl., Dover, DE 19901: Free catalog ❖ Cookware. 800–767–0500.

Wooden Spoon, P.O. Box 931, Clinton, CT 06413: Free catalog ❖ Cooking utensils, kitchen tools, and gifts. 800–431–2207.

Zabar's & Company, 2245 Broadway, New York, NY 10024: Free catalog ❖ Cookware, food processors, microwave ovens, kitchen tools, coffee makers, and gourmet foods. 212–787–2000.

KITES

Action Kites, 4202 Sorrento Valley Blvd., San Diego, CA 92121: Free information ❖ Kites. 619–452–6151.

Adventures Kites, 29 Hemlock Trail, Sandy Hook, CT 06482: Free catalog ❖ Kites. 203–426–9786.

The Air Circus Corporation, W. Shore Rd., Box 334, Mill Neck, NY 11765: Free information ❖ High-flying kites. 516–922–2053.

Banner Fabric, Kite Studio, 5555 Hamilton Blvd., Wescosville, PA 18106: Free information ❖ Fabrics, notions, and hardware for kites, flags, banners, and windsocks. 610–395–3560.

Big City Kite Company, 1201 Lexington Ave., New York, NY 10028: Catalog $2 ❖ Kites. 212–472–2623.

Catch the Wind, 266 SE Hwy. 101, Lincoln City, OR 97367: Free information ❖ Kites. 800–227–7878.

Chicago Fire Kite Company, 3530 N. Fremont Ave., Chicago, IL 60657: Free information ❖ Easy-to-maneuver high-flying kites. 312–327–6814.

Chinook Winds, P.O. Box 8011, Fort Collins, CO 80526: Free information ❖ Windsocks and wind novelties. 303–223–3584.

Coast Kites Inc., 15953 Minnesota Ave., Paramount, CA 90723: Free information ❖ Kites. 310–634–3630.

The Crystal Kite Company, 1320 Lakeview Dr., La Habra, CA 90631: Free information ❖ Competition stunt kites. 714–870–4546.

Desert Sky Kites, 6850 N. Camino Fray Marcos, Tucson, AZ 85718: Free information ❖ Ultra-performance kites. 602–575–1960.

Dyna-Kite Corporation, P.O. Box 24, Three Rivers, MA 01080: Free information ❖ Kites. 413–283–2555.

Fly-Away Kites, 1108 Main St., Bel Mar, NJ 07719: Free information ❖ Kites, accessories, and windsocks. 800–848–9089.

Gasworks Park Kite Shop, 333 Wallingford, Seattle, WA 98103: Free catalog ❖ Kites and kite-making supplies. 206–633–4780.

Goodwinds Kites, 3333 Wallingford North, Seattle, WA 98103: Free information ❖ Standard and fancy kites. 206–632–6151.

Great Winds Kites, 402 Occidental Ave. South, Seattle, WA 98104: Free catalog ❖ Kites. 206–624–6886.

Hang-Em High Fabrics, 1420 Yale Ave., Richmond, VA 23224: Free information ❖ Kite-making supplies. 804–233–6155.

Hearth Song, Mail Processing Center, 6519 N. Galena Rd., P.O. Box 1773, Peoria, IL 61656: Free catalog ❖ Kites, books, dollhouse miniatures, dolls, and art supplies. 800–325–2502.

Hi Fli Kites Ltd., 12101 E. Iliff, Aurora, CO 80014: Catalog $5 ❖ Kites. 303–755–6105.

Hyperkites, 720 Gateway Center Dr., San Diego, CA 92102: Free catalog ❖ High-performance kites. 619–262–4712.

Bob Ingraham Kites, 315 N. Bayard St., Silver City, NM 88061: Free information ❖ Easy-to-assemble and easy-to-fly delta kites. 505–538–9083.

International Connections, 835 Weldon Rd., Santa Barbara, CA 93109: Free information ❖ Kites, banners, windsocks. 805–963–2964.

Into the Wind/Kites, 1408 Pearl St., Boulder, CO 80302: Free catalog ❖ Kites. 800–541–0314.

Keely's Kites, 240 Commercial St., Provincetown, MA 02657: Free catalog ❖ Kites and wind chimes. 508–746–0555.

Kite Innovations, 1850 Holzwarth, Spring, TX 77388: Free information ❖ Quadrifoil kites. 713–288–5451.

The Kite Loft, P.O. Box 551, Ocean City, MD 21842: Free catalog ❖ Kites. 800–345–KITE.

Kite Sails, 3555 Jubilant Pl., Colorado Springs, CO 80917: Free information ❖ Stunt and miniature kites. 719–596–2332.

The Kite Store, 1201 16th St., Space 338, The Tabor Center, Denver, CO 80202: Free catalog ❖ Kites. 303–595–8800.

Kitty Hawk Kites, Milepost 13, 158 Bypass, Nags Head, NC 27959: Free information ❖ Conventional and stunt kites. 919–441–4124.

Klig's Kites, 811 Seaboard St., Myrtle Beach, SC 29577: Free catalog ❖ Stunt kites, single-line kites, windsocks, banners, and flags. 800–333–5944.

Krazy Kites, 8445 International Dr., Orlando, FL 32819: Free catalog ❖ Stunt kites, single line kites, windsocks, and banners. 800–982–2635.

MacKinaw Kite Company, 116 Washington St., Grand Haven, MI 49417: Free catalog ❖ Stunt kites. 616–846–7501.

Nemesis Kites, 2620 Alveston, Bloomfield Hills, MI 48304: Free information ❖ Easy-to-maneuver high-flying kites. 313–338–8257.

Nevada Kite Company, 947 N. Pecos Rd., Las Vegas, NV 89101: Free information ❖ Kites, windsocks, wind chimes, and other wind toys. 702–642–0254.

NewTech Sports, 7208 McNeil Dr., Ste. 207, Austin, TX 78729: Free information ❖ Stunt and high-flying kites. 800–325–4768.

Peter Powell Kites Inc., 1040 NE 43rd Ct., Fort Lauderdale, FL 33334: Free information

❖ Stunt kites, kite line, and handles. 305–565–5588.

Premier Kites Inc., 8673 Cherry Ln., Laurel, MD 20707: Free catalog ❖ Kites, windsocks, and air toys. 301–604–1881.

Renegade Kites, 3769 Peralta Blvd., Fremont, CA 94536: Free information ❖ High-performance stunt kites. 510–791–5666.

Revolution Enterprises, 6335 Nancy Ridge Dr., San Diego, CA 92121: Free information ❖ Easy-to-maneuver precision team-flying kites. 619–554–1106.

Sky Delight Kites, 1015 Avondale Rd., Austin, TX 78704: Free information ❖ Single line stunt kites that collapse for portability. 512–476–1758.

Sky's the Limit, P.O. Box 3934, Pasco, WA 99301: Free catalog ❖ Kites and windsocks. 509–783–5769.

Top of the Line Sportkites, 3015 St. Charles Pl., San Diego, CA 92110: Free catalog ❖ Kites. 800–637–6371.

Tori Industries, P.O. Box 18183, Salt Lake City, UT 84118: Free catalog ❖ Kites and kite-building supplies. 801–964–8929.

Trlby Kites, 65 New Litchfield St., Torrington, CT 06790: Free information ❖ Stunt kites. 800–328–7529.

What's Up Kites, 4500 Chagrin River Rd., Chagrin Falls, OH 44022: Free information ❖ Ultra-light, stunt, and airfoil kites. 216–247–4222.

Wind Related Inc., 1595 N. 1st, Hamilton, MT 59840: Free information ❖ Handcrafted windsocks. 800–735–1885.

Wind Walker Kites, P.O. Box 225, East Bernard, TX 77435: Free information ❖ High-performance, dual line stunt kites. 409–335–7503.

Windborne Kites, 585 Cannery Row, Monterey, CA 93940: Free catalog ❖ Kites and accessories, windsocks, and flags. 408–373–7422.

KNITTING

Knitting Machines

Brother International Corporation, 200 Cottontail Ln., Somerset, NJ 08875: Free information ❖ Knitting machines.

Fiber Studio, 9 Foster Hill Rd., Box 637, Heniker, NH 03242: Spinning fibers catalog $1; yarn samples $4; equipment catalog $1 ❖ Spinning, weaving, and knitting equipment;

cotton, mohair, wool, alpaca, silk, linen yarns; and spinning fibers. 603–428–7830.

Knitpicky Knitting Machines, 1505 Mayfair, Champaign, IL 61821: Free information ❖ New and used knitting machines and knitter computer interface programs. 217–355–5400.

Krh Knits, P.O. Box 1587, Avon, CT 06001: Catalog $5 ❖ Knitting machines, accessories, how-to information, yarn winders, yarns, fabric paints, finishing tools, crochet accessories, elastic thread, patterns, and notions. 800–248–KNIT.

Mary Lue's Knitting World, 101 W. Broadway, St. Peter, MN 56082: Free information ❖ Refurbished and used Brother knitting machines. 507–931–3702.

Passap, 271 W. 2950 South, Salt Lake City, UT 84115: Free information ❖ Easy-to-use computerized knitting machines. 800–PAS-KNIT.

Sew-Knit Distributors, 9789 Florida Blvd., Baton Rouge, LA 70815: Free information ❖ Sewing and knitting machines. 800–289–5648.

Shannock Tapestry Looms, 10402 NW 11th Ave., Vancouver, WA 98685: Free information ❖ Heavy-duty, professional tapestry looms with roller beams and weaving accessories. 206–573–7264.

Studio Knitting Machines, 11760 Berea Rd., Cleveland, OH 44111: Free information ❖ Easy-to-operate knitting machines. 800–367–0518.

Threads Etc., 61568 Eastlake Dr., Bend, OR 97702: Catalog $2 (refundable) ❖ Knitting machines and accessories, yarns, books, patterns, and kits. 800–208–2046; 503–388–2046 (in OR).

The Weaver's Loft, 308 S. Pennsylvania Ave., Centre Hall, PA 16828: Free information ❖ Knitting, weaving, and spinning yarns. 814–364–1433.

Weaving Works, 4717 Brooklyn Ave. NE, Seattle, WA 98105: Catalog $4.50 ❖ Looms, spinning wheels, hand and machine knitting supplies, traditional and fashion yarns, and books. 206–524–1221.

Yarn-It-All, 2223 Rebecca Dr., Hatfield, PA 19440: Free information ❖ Knitting machines and yarn. 215–822–2989.

Patterns & Accessories

Aura Yarns, Box 602, Derby Line, VT 05830: Free information ❖ Icelandic wool

sweater kits and alpaca, cashmere, mohair, merino, shetland, silk, and cotton yarns.

Cotton Clouds, 5176 S. 14th Ave., Safford, AZ 85546: Catalog $5 (refundable) ❖ Cotton yarns, spinning fibers, tools, books, looms, kits, and patterns. 800–322–7888; 602–428–7000 (in AZ).

Martha Hall, 46 Main St., Yarmouth, ME 04096: Catalog $2 ❖ Easy-to-knit Maine wool sweater kits and hand-dyed silk, mohair, linen, cotton, cashmere, and alpaca yarn. 207–846–9746.

Herrschners Inc., Hoover Rd., Stevens Point, WI 54492: Free catalog ❖ Yarns, knitting accessories, and needle craft, crochet, and hooking kits. 800–441–0838.

Carolin Lowy Needlecraft, 630 Sun Meadows Dr., Kernersville, NC 27284: Free information with long SASE ❖ Needlepoint, knitting, embroidery, and counted cross-stitching patterns. 910–784–7576.

Mary Maxim Inc., 2001 Holland Ave., P.O. Box 5019, Port Huron, MI 48061: Free catalog ❖ Needlecraft kits, yarn, and other supplies. 800–962–9504.

Stitches East, 55 E. 52nd St., New York, NY 10022: Free information ❖ Knitting and needlepoint supplies, yarns, patterns, needles, and canvases. 212–421–0112.

Thumbelina Needlework Shop, P.O. Box 1065, Solvang, CA 93463: Information $1.75 ❖ Books, fabrics, threads, yarns, kits, and other supplies. 805–688–4136.

Wendy's Woolies, P.O. Box 7474, North Port, FL 34287: Brochure $2 ❖ Knitting kits.

Yarns, P.O. Box 434, Uxbridge, MA 01569: Free information ❖ European and American knitting kits. 508–278–7733.

KNIVES & KNIFE MAKING

Arizona Custom Knives, 15442 E. Palomino Blvd., Fountain Hills, AZ 85268: Price list $3 ❖ Handmade knives. 602–837–8157.

Atlanta Cutlery, Box 839, Conyers, GA 30207: Catalog $1 ❖ Knife-making supplies. 800–241–3595.

Hugh E. Bartrug, 505 Rhodes St., Elizabeth, PA 15037: Free information ❖ Knives and folders. 412–384–3476.

L.L. Bean, Freeport, ME 04033: Free catalog ❖ Knives for hunters, fishermen, and campers. 800–221–4221.

Benchmade Knife Company Inc., 15875–G SE 114th St., Clackamas, OR 97015:

Brochure $2 ❖ Folding knives. 503–655–6004.

Beretta U.S.A., 17601 Beretta Dr., Accokeek, MD 20607: Free information ❖ Lightweight, standard, serrated, and other knives. 301–283–2191.

Berkshire Mountain Trading, 92 Bridges Rd., Williamstown, MA 01267: Catalog $2 (refundable) ❖ Knives and cutlery. 413–458–8669.

Blackjack Knives Ltd., 1307 W. Wabash, Effingham, IL 62401: Free information ❖ Knives. 217–347–7700.

Blades 'N' Stuff, 1019 E. Palmer Ave., Glendale, CA 91205: Catalog $5 ❖ Knife-making supplies. 818–956–5110.

Bulldog Brand Knives, P.O. Box 23852, Chattanooga, TN 37422: Free catalog ❖ Knives. 615–894–5102.

Chef's Catalog, 3215 Commercial Ave., Northbrook, IL 60062: Free catalog ❖ Professional kitchen knives by Henckels and Sabatier. 800–338–3232.

Cold Steel, 2128–D Knoll Dr., Ventura, CA 93003: Free catalog ❖ Limited edition, specialty, and closeout knives. 800–255–4716.

Colonial Knife Company, P.O. Box 3327, Providence, RI 02909: Free catalog ❖ Pocket knives.

Custom Knifemaker's Supply, P.O. Box 308, Emory, TX 75440: Catalog $2 ❖ Knives. 903–473–3330.

George Cousino, 7818 Norfolk Dr., Onsted, MI 49265: Brochure $2 ❖ Knives. 517–467–4911.

Cutlery Shoppe, 5461 Kendall St., Boise, ID 83706: Free catalog ❖ Knives and sheaths. 208–376–0430.

Damascus-U.S.A., RR 1, Box 206A, Tyner, NC 27980: Brochure $5 ❖ Forged-to-shape Damascus steel knives. 919–221–2010.

Harvey J. Dean Knives, Rt. 2, Box 137, Rockdale, TX 76567: Brochure $2 ❖ Knives. 512–446–3111.

Dixie Gun Works Inc., P.O. Box 130, Union City, TN 38261: Catalog $4 ❖ Knife-making supplies. 800–238–6785.

Doc Hagen, P.O. Box 58, Pelican Rapids, MN 56572: Catalog $2 ❖ Handmade forged knives with exotic handles. 218–863–1343.

The Edge Company, P.O. Box 826, Brattleboro, VT 05302: Free catalog ❖ Knives and tools. 800–732–9976.

Equip USA Inc., P.O. Box 750, Mancos, CO 81328: Free information ❖ Handmade knives. 303–533–7785.

Foxwood Forge, Keith Kilby, 402 Jackson Trail Rd., Jefferson, GA 30549: Brochure $3 ❖ Damascus, cable, and carbon steel hand-forged knives. 706–367–9997.

Frost Cutlery, P.O. Box 22636, Chattanooga, TN 37422: Free information ❖ Knives. 800–251–7768; 615–894–6079 (in TN).

Gaston Knives, 330 Gaston Dr., Woodruff, SC 29388: Catalog $2 ❖ Knives. 803–439–4766.

Griffin Knives, 9706 Cedardale, Houston, TX 77055: Brochure $2 ❖ Knives. 713–468–0436.

Terry L. Hearn, Rt. 14, Box 7676, Lufkin, TX 75904: Brochure $1 ❖ Knives. 409–632–5045.

Joe Hilliard, P.O. Box 1629, Marysville, CA 95901: Free list with long SASE and three 1st class stamps ❖ Knives. 916–743–6404.

Rick Hinderer Knives, 5423 Kister Rd., Wooster, OH 44691: Brochure $3 ❖ Damascus, stainless, and carbon steel folders and straight knives. 216–263–0962.

Hollett Custom Knives, P.O. Box 255, Fate, TX 75132: Brochure $3 ❖ Knives and edged tools. 214–771–2014.

Ken Jantz Supply, P.O. Box 584, Davis, OK 73030: Catalog $4 ❖ Knife-making supplies. 405–369–2316.

Kauffman Custom Knives, P.O. Box 9041, Helena, MT 59604: Brochure $2 ❖ Knives. 406–442–9328.

Knife & Cutlery Products Inc., P.O. Box 12480, Kansas City, MO 64116: Catalog $2 ❖ Knife-making supplies. 816–454–9879.

Knife & Gun Finishing Supplies, P.O. Box 458, Lakeside, AZ 85929: Catalog $3 ❖ Metal finishing supplies for making knives. 602–537–8877.

R.C. Knipstein, 731 N. Fielder Rd., Arlington, TX 76012: Brochure $2 ❖ Knives. 817–265–2021.

Koval Knives, P.O. Box 26155, Columbus, OH 43226: Catalog $4 ❖ Knife-making supplies. 614–888–6486.

Lile Handmade Knives, 2721 S. Arkansas Ave., Russellville, AR 72801: Free information ❖ Handmade knives. 501–968–2011.

Masecraft Supply Company, 170 Research Pkwy., P.O. Box 423, Meriden, CT 06450: Free information ❖ Stag, pearl, horn, bone, mammoth ivory, and other knife handle materials. 800–682–5489.

Hanford J. Miller Knives, Box 97, Cowdrey, CO 80434: Catalog $3 ❖ Knives.

Northwest Knife Supply, 621 Fawn Ridge Dr., Oakland, OR 97462: Catalog $2 ❖ Knife-making supplies. 503–459–2216.

Lowell R. Oyster Knives, Rt. 1, Box 432, Kenduskeag, ME 04450: Brochure $1 ❖ Handcrafted knives.

Parkers' Knife Collector Service, 6715 Heritage Business Ct., P.O. Box 23522, Chattanooga, TN 37422: Free catalog ❖ Knives. 800–247–0599; 615–892–0448 (in TN).

R & C Knives, P.O. Box 1047, Manteca, CA 95336: Catalog $3 ❖ Knives. 209–239–3722.

Randall-Made Knives, P.O. Box 1988, Orlando, FL 32802: Catalog $2 ❖ Knives. 407–855–8075.

Chris Reeve Knives, 6147 Corporal Ln., Boise, ID 83704: Brochure $2 ❖ Hand-ground knives in 16 blade styles. 208–375–0367.

Dave Ricke Knifemaker, 1209 Adams St., West Bend, WI 53095: Brochure $1 ❖ Knives. 414–334–5739.

Rio Cutlery & Luggage Inc., 10 W. 46th St., New York, NY 10036: Catalog $5 ❖ Custom and antique pocket knives. 212–819–0304.

Robert Schrap, 7024 W. Wells St., Wauwatosa, WI 53213: Free information ❖ Leather knife sheaths. 414–771–6472.

Sheffield Knifemakers Supply, P.O. Box 141, Deland, FL 32721: Catalog $5 ❖ Knife-making supplies. 904–775–6453.

Silver Dollar City Gun & Knife Shop, Branson, MO 65616: Free brochure ❖ Hand-forged knives. 800–282–2489.

Cleston R. Sinyard, Nimo Forge, 27522 Burkhardt Dr., Elberta, AL 36530: Free information ❖ Damascus bladesmith knives. 205–986–7984.

Jim Siska Knives, 6 Highland Ave., Westfield, MA 01085: Free brochure ❖ Knives. 413–568–9787.

Smoky Mountain Knife Works, P.O. Box 4430, Sevierville, TN 37864: Free catalog ❖ Hunting, work, and survival knives. 800–251–9306.

Linder Solingen Knives, 4401 Sentry Dr., Tucker, GA 30084: Information $1 ❖ Knives and knife-making supplies.

Southeast Knife Brokers, Rt. 1, Box 1070, Sautee-Nacoochee, GA 30571: Price list $2 ❖ Old, new, factory-made, and other knives. 706–878–3325.

Special Projects, Customer Service, 2128 Knoll Dr., Unit D, Ventura, CA 93003: Free catalog ❖ Limited edition, cold steel closeout, and new knives. 800–258–1655.

Sportsman's Accessory Manufacturing, 615 Reed St., P.O. Box 18091, Philadelphia, PA 19147: Free information ❖ Knife cases. 215–336–6464.

ST Handmade Knives, Steve Rucker, 3048 Willow Oak, Edgewater, FL 32141: Price information $2 ❖ Handmade knives. 904–427–1659.

Star Sales Company Inc., 1803 N. Central St., P.O. Box 1503, Knoxville, TN 37901: Catalog $2 ❖ Knives. 615–524–0771.

Swiss Armory, 2838 Juniper St., San Diego, CA 92104: Free catalog ❖ Swiss army knives. 800–437–5423.

Texas Knifemakers Supply, P.O. Box 79402, Houston, TX 77279: Catalog $2 ❖ Knife-making supplies. 713–461–8632.

U.S. Cavalry, 2855 Centennial Ave., Radcliff, KY 40160: Catalog $3 ❖ Survival, military, and other pocket-size knives. 800–777–7732

UltraBlade Knives, P.O. Box 710130, Santee, CA 92072: Free information ❖ Pocket knives, folding lock-blades, folding fish fillet knives, non-locking knives for hunters, and fixed-blade sheath knives. 800–735–2825.

Wayne Valachovic Bladesmith, P.O. Box 4219, Kailua-Kona, HI 96745: Brochure $2 ❖ Forged pocket folding, Damascus steel, and high-carbon tool steel knives. 808–325–0203.

Robert J. White Knifemaker, Rt. 1, Gilson, IL 61436: Brochure $1 ❖ Knives. 309–289–4487.

Daniel Winkler Knifemaker, P.O. Box 2166, Blowing Rock, NC 28605: Catalog $2 ❖ Hand-forged knives. 704–295–9156.

LABORATORY & SCIENCE EQUIPMENT

Advance Scientific, 1318 N. Dixie Hwy., Hollywood, FL 33020: Catalog $3 ❖ Laboratory chemicals, glassware, instrumentation, and other supplies. 305–927–2700.

American Science & Surplus, 3605 Howard St., Skokie, IL 60076: Catalog $1 ❖ Surplus science and electro-mechanical supplies, equipment, and kits. 708–982–0870.

Analytical Scientific, 11049 Bandera, San Antonio, TX 78250: Catalog $3 (refundable) ❖ Laboratory glassware, chemicals, equipment, books, and charts. 512–684–7373.

Anatomical Chart Company, 8221 N. Kimball, Skokie, IL 60076: Catalog $2 ❖ Educational anatomical products on health, human anatomy, and other sciences. 800–621–7500; 708–679–4700 (in IL).

ASC Scientific, 2075 Corte del Nogal, Carlsbad, CA 92009: Free catalog ❖ Pocket transit for geologists, hand-held satellite navigator, and other earth science equipment. 800–272–4327.

Bunting Magnetics Company, P.O. Box 468, Newton, KS 67144: Free catalog ❖ Magnets. 800–835–2526; 316–284–2020 (in KS).

Chem-Lab, 1060 Ortega Way, Placentia, CA 92670: Catalog $5 ❖ Chemicals, glassware, scales, microscopes, and other equipment.

Dino Productions, P.O. Box 3004, Englewood, CO 80155: Catalog $2 (refundable) ❖ Fossils, rocks and minerals, ecology and oceanography equipment, and chemistry, general science, astronomy, and biology supplies. 303–741–1587.

Edlie Electronics, 2700 Hempstead Tnpk., Levittown, NY 11756: Free catalog ❖ Electronics kits. 516–735–3330.

Edmund Scientific Company, Edscorp Bldg., Barrington, NJ 08007: Free catalog ❖ Microscopes, magnifiers, weather forecasting instruments, magnets, telescopes, binoculars and other optics, lasers, and other science equipment. 609–573–6260.

The Electronic Goldmine, P.O. Box 5408, Scottsdale, AZ 85261: Free catalog ❖ Science kits. 602–451–7454.

Hagenow Laboratories, 1302 Washington, Manitowoc, WI 54220: Catalog $2 ❖ Chemicals, glassware, and other laboratory accessories. 414–683–3339.

J.L. Hammett Company, Hammett Pl., P.O. Box 9057, Braintree, MA 02184: Free catalog ❖ Science kits, microscopes, laboratory apparatus, rock collections, magnets, astronomy charts, and anatomical models. 800–225–5467; 617–848–1000 (in MA).

Hubbard Scientific Company, 3101 Iris Ave., Boulder, CO 80301: Free catalog ❖ Science equipment for life, earth, and physical science, energy experiments, health and physiology, and topography projects. 800–323–8368.

Magnet Sales & Manufacturing Company, 11248 Playa Ct., Culver City, CA 90230: Free brochure ❖ Flexible strip, flex-dot, button, and bar magnets. 800–421–6692; 310–391–7213 (in CA).

Merrell Scientific/World of Science, 1665 Buffalo Rd., Rochester, NY 14624: Catalog $2 ❖ Chemicals, glassware, and equipment for biology, nature, physical and earth science, rocket, and astronomy experiments. 716–426–1540.

Nasco, 901 Janesville Ave., Fort Atkinson, WI 53538: Free catalog ❖ Science equipment, kits, microscopes and dissection kits, rock collections, magnets, electric motors, ultraviolet light equipment, astronomy charts and star maps, anatomical models, and other equipment. 800–558–9595.

The Nature Company, Catalog Division, P.O. Box 188, Florence, KY 41022: Free catalog ❖ Science supplies, kits, books, toys, novelties, and gifts. 800–227–1114.

Omni Resources, 1004 S. Mebane St., P.O. Box 2096, Burlington, NC 27216: Free catalog ❖ Earth science and other laboratory equipment. 800–742–2677.

LACROSSE

Brine Inc., 47 Sumner St., Milford, MA 01757: Free information ❖ Balls, gloves, goals, protective equipment, sticks, and uniforms. 800–227–2722; 508–478–3250 (in MA).

Wm. T. Burnett & Company Inc., 1500 Bush St., Baltimore, MD 21230: Free information ❖ Balls and gloves, goals, protective gear, and sticks. 800–368–2250.

Cran Barry Inc., 130 Condor St., Box 488, East Boston, MA 02128: Free information ❖ Balls and gloves, goals, protective gear, and sticks. 800–992–2021.

Jayfro Corporation, Unified Sports Inc., 976 Hartford Tnpk., P.O. Box 400, Waterford, CT 06385: Free catalog ❖ Lacrosse and field hockey goals, nets, and other equipment. 203–447–3001.

Olympia Sports, 745 State Cir., Ann Arbor, MI 48106: Free information ❖ Goal nets, balls, and sticks. 800–521–2832; 313–761–5173 (in MI).

Reda Sports Express, 44 N. 2nd St., P.O. Box 68, Easton, PA 18044: Free information ❖ Balls, protective gear, helmets, and sticks. 800–444–REDA; 215–258–5271 (in PA).

Riddell Inc., 3670 N. Milwaukee Ave., Chicago, IL 60641: Free information ❖ Helmets. 800–445–7344; 312–794–1994 (in IL).

Sauk Valley Sports Resort, 10750 Prospect Hill, Brooklyn, MI 49230: Free information ❖ Balls, gloves, goals, helmets, protective equipment, and sticks. 800–USA-SAUK; 517–467–2061 (in MI).

Seneca Sports Inc., 75 Fortune Blvd., Box 719, Milford, MA 01757: Free information ❖ Sticks and balls. 508–634–3616.

STX Inc., 1500 Bush St., Baltimore, MD 21230: Free information ❖ Goal nets, protective gear, gloves, balls, and sticks. 800–368–2250; 410–837–2022 (in MD).

Tuskewe Krafts, 2089 Upper Mountain Rd., Sanborn, NY 14132: Free brochure with long SASE ❖ Women and men's field and box lacrosse sticks. 717–297–1821.

LADDERS

American LaFrance, Box 7146, Charlottesville, VA 22906: Free information ❖ Escape ladders. 804–973–4361.

Jomy Safety Ladder Company, 1728 16th St., Ste. 201, Boulder, CO 80302: Free information ❖ Collapsible fire escape ladder. 800–255–2591.

Ladder Man Inc., 3005 Silver Dr., Columbus, OH 43224: Free catalog ❖ Safety equipment, attic and fire escape equipment, and specialty, articulating, stairway, and stairwell ladders. 800–783–8887.

Putnam Rolling Ladder Company Inc., 32 Howard St., New York, NY 10013: Catalog $1 ❖ Ladders, library carts, and other furniture. 212–226–5147.

LAMPS & LIGHTING

Chandeliers

A.J.P. Coppersmith & Company, 20 Industrial Pkwy., Woburn, MA 01801: Catalog $3 ❖ Chandeliers, sconces, cupolas, weather vanes, and handcrafted copper, tin,

or brass reproduction colonial lanterns. 617–932–3700.

Ala Lite, 380 E. 1700 South, Salt Lake City, UT 84115: Free information ❖ Restored and reproduction antique lamps, shades, chandeliers, and parts. 800–388–5456.

American Lighting, 5211D W. Market St., Ste. 803, Greensboro, NC 27265: Free catalog ❖ Chandeliers. 800–741–0571.

Antique Hardware Store, Easton Rd., Kintnersville, PA 18930: Catalog $3 ❖ Antique chandeliers, indoor and outdoor light fixtures, pedestal sinks, faucets, high tank toilets, cabinet hardware, and weather vanes. 800–422–9982.

Art Directions, 6120 Delmar Blvd., St. Louis, MO 63112: Catalog $2 ❖ Light fixtures and reproduction and restored chandeliers. 314–863–1895.

Authentic Designs, The Mill Rd., West Rupert, VT 05776: Catalog $3 ❖ Handcrafted reproduction 18th-century early American light fixtures and chandeliers in brass, copper, and tin. 802–394–7713.

Ball & Ball, 463 W. Lincoln Hwy., Exton, PA 19341: Catalog $7 (refundable) ❖ Reproduction antique light fixtures and chandeliers. 610–363–7330.

Lester H. Berry & Company, P.O. Box 53377, Philadelphia, PA 19105: Free information ❖ Reproduction 18th-century chandeliers, wall sconces, and coach light accessories. 215–923–2603.

Joan Bogart, 1392 Old Northern Blvd., Rosilyn, NY 11576: Free information ❖ Victorian style antiques, gifts, and gas chandeliers and other lighting accessories, from 1840 to 1900. 516–621–2454.

Brass Light Gallery, 131 S. 1st St., Milwaukee, WI 53204: Free product guide ❖ Interior and exterior lighting. Prairie, Mission, Arts & Crafts, European Country, Original Prismatics. 800–243–9595.

Brass Reproductions, 9711 Canoga Ave., Chatsworth, CA 91311: Catalog $8 (refundable) ❖ Solid brass Victorian and traditional chandeliers, floor and table lamps, and sconces. 818–709–7844.

Brasslight Inc., P.O. Box 695, Nyack, NY 10960: Catalog $4 ❖ Solid brass wall sconces, desk and table lamps, and period chandeliers. 914–353–0567.

Chandelier Warehouse, 40 Withers St., Brooklyn, NY 11211: Catalog $5 ❖ Period style chandeliers. 718–388–6800.

The Coppersmith, Rt. 20, P.O. Box 755, Sturbridge, MA 01566: Catalog $3 ❖ Handcrafted reproduction chandeliers, lanterns, and sconces. 508–347–7038.

Roc Corbett Custom Lighting, P.O. Box 339, Bigfork, MT 59911: Catalog $10 (refundable) ❖ Elk, deer, moose, or caribou antler wagon wheel chandeliers. 406–837–5823.

The Country Store, 28 James St., Geneva, IL 60134: Catalog $2 ❖ Punched tin and turned wood chandeliers, ceiling lights, outlet covers, country-style decor accessories, and braided rugs. 708–879–0098.

Greg Davidson Antique Lighting, 12005 Wilshire Blvd., Los Angeles, CA 90025: Free information ❖ American-style lamps, fixtures, and wall lights, from 1850 to 1930. 310–478–5475.

Gas Light Time, 823 President St., Brooklyn, NY 11215: Catalog $4 ❖ Restored antique gas, combination, and early electric chandeliers and wall sconces, from 1850 to 1925. 718–789–7185.

Golden Valley Lighting, 274 Eastchester Dr., High Point, NC 27260: Catalog $5 ❖ Light fixtures and lamps. 800–735–3377.

Hammerworks, 6 Fremont St., Worcester, MA 01603: Catalog $3 ❖ Handmade reproductions of copper, brass, iron, and tin colonial post lanterns, wall lanterns, chandeliers, and sconces. 508–755–3434.

Howard's Antique Lighting, Rt. 23 West, P.O. Box 472, South Edgemont, MA 01258: Free information ❖ Floor lamps, sconces, and electric, gas, and kerosene chandeliers. 413–528–1232.

Hubbardton Forge & Wood Corporation, P.O. Box 827, Castleton Corners, Castleton, VT 05735: Catalog $3 ❖ Wrought-iron and brass chandeliers, hanging pan racks, bathroom accessories, plant hangers, and table, wall, and candlestick lamps. 802–468–3090.

Iron Apple Forge, P.O. Box 724, Buckingham, PA 18912: Catalog $4 ❖ Traditional wrought iron chandeliers. 215–794–7351.

Jonesborough Power & Light, 144 E. Main St., Old Town Hall, Jonesborough, TN 37659: Free information ❖ Conversion kits, and hard-to-find parts for restoring light fixtures and oil lamps. 615–753–5222.

King's Chandelier Company, P.O. Box 667, Eden, NC 27288: Catalog $3.50 ❖ Chandeliers, candelabras, and crystal sconces. 910–623–6188.

Krusesel's General Merchandise & Auction Company, 22 SW 3rd St., Rochester, MN 55902: Free information ❖ Antique Victorian, art nouveau, and early 20th-century gas, gas-and-electric, and electric ceiling and wall light fixtures. 507–289–8049.

Lamp Warehouse, 1073 39th St., Brooklyn, NY 11219: Free information with long SASE ❖ Ceiling fans and light fixtures. 800–52–LITES; 718–436–8500 (in NY).

Luigi Crystal, 7332 Frankford Ave., Philadelphia, PA 19136: Catalog $2 ❖ Cut crystal accessories, decor table lamps, crystal chandeliers, hurricane lamps, and sconces. 215–338–2978.

Nowell's Inc., 490 Gate 5 Rd., P.O. Box 295, Sausalito, CA 94966: Catalog $5 ❖ Reproduction and restored antique chandeliers and other light fixtures. 415–332–4933.

Olde Village Smithery, P.O. Box 1815, Orleans, MA 02653: Catalog $2.50 ❖ Solid brass chandeliers. 508–255–4466.

Period Lighting Fixtures, 167 River Rd., Clarksburg, MA 01247: Catalog $6.50 ❖ Early American light fixtures, chandeliers, lanterns, and sconces. 800–828–6990.

Ragged Mountain Antler Chandeliers, 897 Bourne Ln., Victor, MT 59875: Free brochure ❖ Chandeliers made from deer antlers.

The Renovator's Supply, P.O. Box 2660, North Conway, NH 03860: Free catalog ❖ Solid brass chandeliers. 800–659–2211.

Roy Electric Company, 1054 Coney Island Ave., Brooklyn, NY 11230: Catalog $6 ❖ Victorian-style and turn-of-the-century chandeliers, sconces, and other light fixtures. 800–366–3347; 718–434–7002 (in NY).

Saltbox Inc., 3004 Columbia Ave., Lancaster, PA 17603: Brochure $2.50 ❖ Handcrafted brass, copper, and tin colonial-style chandeliers, post lights, lanterns, and foyer lights. 717–392–5649.

M. Star Antler Designs, P.O. Box 3093, Lake Isabella, CA 93240: Catalog $5 ❖ Deer antler chandeliers, lamps, furniture, mirrors, and other decor accessories. 619–379–5777.

Studio Steel, 159 New Milford Tnpk., New Preston, CT 06777: Catalog $2 ❖ Lamps, chandeliers, sconces, mirrors, and other handwrought metalwork. 800–800–5217; 203–868–7305 (in CT).

Tin Bin, 20 Valley Rd., Neffsville, PA 17601: Catalog $2.50 ❖ Handcrafted antiqued copper and brass country-style chandeliers. 717–569–6210.

The Tinhorn, 1852 Forest Ln., Crown Point, IN 46307: Catalog $3 ❖ Pewter-like, copper or antiqued copper, punched-heart scalloped chandeliers. 219–988–3332.

Victorian Lighting Works, 251 S. Pennsylvania Ave., P.O. Box 469, Centre Hall, PA 16328: Catalog $5 (refundable) ❖ Victorian-style wall sconces and chandeliers. 814–364–9577.

Village Antique Lighting Company, 847 Ionia NW, Grand Rapids, MI 49503: Free information ❖ Chandeliers and wall lights. 616–451–9945.

Village Lantern, Box 8, North Marshfield, MA 02059: Catalog 50¢ ❖ Handcrafted colonial-style chandeliers. 617–834–8121.

Lt. Moses Willard Inc., 1156 US 50, Milford, OH 45150: Catalog $8.50 ❖ Reproduction chandeliers, wall sconces, exterior lighting units, candle holders, lanterns, and wall and table lamps, from the 1700s. 513–248–5500.

Workshops of David T. Smith, 3600 Shawhan Rd., Morrow, OH 45152: Catalog $5 ❖ Reproduction furniture, pottery, lamps, and chandeliers. 513–932–2472.

Lamps & Fixtures

A.J.P. Coppersmith & Company, 20 Industrial Pkwy., Woburn, MA 01801: Catalog $3 ❖ Handcrafted copper, tin, and brass reproduction colonial lanterns, chandeliers, sconces, cupolas, and weather vanes. 617–932–3700.

Ala Lite, 380 E. 1700 South, Salt Lake City, UT 84115: Free information ❖ Restored and reproduction antique lamps, shades, chandeliers, and parts. 800–388–5456.

Alkco Lighting, 11500 W. Melrose Ave., P.O. Box 1389, Franklin Park, IL 60131: Free information ❖ Indoor light fixtures. 708–451–0700.

Allied Lighting, Drawer E, Trextertown, PA 18087: Free brochure ❖ Light fixtures. 800–241–6111.

American Period Showcase, 3004 Columbia Ave., Lancaster, PA 17603: Brochure $2.50 ❖ Handcrafted, American period lanterns, table lamps, chandeliers, and post lamps. 717–392–5649.

Antique Hardware Store, Easton Rd., Kintnersville, PA 18930: Catalog $3 ❖ Antique-style indoor and outdoor lamps and light fixtures, pedestal sinks, faucets, high tank toilets, cabinet hardware, weather vanes, and tin and wood chandeliers. 800–422–9982.

Antique Lamp Parts & Service, 218 N. Foley Ave., Freeport, IL 61032: Free information with long SASE ❖ Parts for old and new kerosene, electric, and gas lamps. 815–232–8968.

Arroyo Craftsman, 4509 Little John St., Baldwin Park, CA 91706: Catalog $3.50 ❖ Original indoor and outdoor brass light fixtures. 818–960–9411.

Art Directions, 6120 Delmar Blvd., St. Louis, MO 63112: Catalog $2 ❖ Reproduction, restored, and other chandeliers and light fixtures. 314–863–1895.

Aunt Sylvia's Victorian Collections, P.O. Box 67364, Chestnut Hill, MA 02157: Catalog $3 ❖ Traditional and reproduction Victorian-style lamps. 800–231–6644.

Authentic Designs, The Mill Rd., West Rupert, VT 05776: Catalog $3 ❖ Handcrafted reproduction brass, copper, and tin 18th-century early American light fixtures and chandeliers. 802–394–7713.

Baldwin Hardware Corporation, P.O. Box 15048, Reading, PA 19612: Bathroom accessories brochure 75¢; lighting fixtures brochure $3; door hardware brochure 75¢; decor hardware brochure 75¢ ❖ Brass dead bolts and door hardware, bathroom accessories, and light fixtures. 800–346–5128.

Ball & Ball, 463 W. Lincoln Hwy., Exton, PA 19341: Catalog $7 (refundable) ❖ Reproduction light fixtures and chandeliers. 610–363–7330.

Barap Specialties, 835 Bellows Ave., Frankfort, MI 49635: Catalog $1 ❖ Lamp parts, chair caning and other craft supplies, tools, and turned wood parts. 800–3–BARAP–3.

Lester H. Berry & Company, P.O. Box 53377, Philadelphia, PA 19105: Free information ❖ Reproduction 18th-century chandeliers, wall sconces, and coach lighting. 215–923–2603.

Brandon Industries Inc., 4419 Westgrove Dr., Dallas, TX 75248: Free catalog ❖ Wall sconces, aluminum lamp posts, planters, and mailboxes. 214–250–0456.

The Brass Knob, 2311 18th St. NW, Washington, DC 20009: Free information ❖ Antique light fixtures, from 1870 to 1930. 202–332–3370.

The Brass Lion, 5935 S. Broadway, Tyler, TX 75703: Catalog $5 ❖ Reproduction 17th- and 18th-century light fixtures and wall sconces. 903–561–1111.

Brass Menagerie, 524 St. Louis St., New Orleans, LA 70130: Free information ❖ Light fixtures, plumbing, and hardware. 504–524–0921.

Brass Reproductions, 9711 Canoga Ave., Chatsworth, CA 91311: Catalog $8 (refundable) ❖ Solid brass Victorian and traditional chandeliers, floor and table lamps, and sconces. 818–709–7844.

Brasslight Inc., P.O. Box 695, Nyack, NY 10960: Catalog $4 ❖ Wall sconces, desk and table lamps, and solid brass period chandeliers. 914–353–0567.

Brass'n Bounty, 68 Front St., Marblehead, MA 01945: Free information ❖ Antique chandeliers, floor lamps, and sconces, in gas, electric, and combined gas-electric models. 627–631–3864.

Brubaker Metalcrafts, 209 N. Franklin St., Eaton, OH 45320: Catalog $2 ❖ Reproduction 18th-century tin and brass chandeliers, wall sconces, Paul Revere lanterns, and other fixtures. 513–456–5834.

Century Studio, 200 3rd Ave. North, Minneapolis, MN 55401: Brochure $10 (refundable) ❖ Stained glass reproduction Tiffany lamps. 612–339–0239.

City Lights, 2226 Massachusetts Ave., Cambridge, MA 02140: Catalog $5 ❖ Restored antique light fixtures. 617–547–1490.

David L. Claggett, Artistry in Tin, P.O. Box 41, Weston, VT 05161: Catalog $3 ❖ Reproduction light fixtures. 802–824–3194.

The Coppersmith, Rt. 20, P.O. Box 755, Sturbridge, MA 01566: Catalog $3 ❖ Handcrafted reproduction colonial lanterns, sconces, and chandeliers. 508–347–7038.

Elcanco Ltd., P.O. Box 682, Westford, MA 01886: Brochure $1 ❖ Handcrafted electric wax candles with flame-like bulbs. 508–392–0830.

Essex Forge, P.O. Box 423, Essex, CT 06426: Catalog $2 ❖ Reproduction 18th-century indoor and outdoor light fixtures. 203–767–1808.

Fabby, 450 S. La Brea Ave., Los Angeles, CA 90036: Catalog $3 ❖ Ceramic wall sconces and handmade indoor and outdoor light fixtures. 213–839–1388.

Faire Harbour Ltd., 44 Captain Pierce Rd., Scituate, MA 02066: Catalog $2 ❖ One-of-a-kind antique lamps, parts, and oil, early gas, electric, and kerosene lamps. 617–545–2465.

David & Martha Fletcher, Blue Mist Morgan Farm, 68 Liberty St., Haverhill, MA 01830: Catalog $3 ❖ Handcrafted copper lanterns and weather vanes. 508–374–8783.

Functional Art, P.O. Box 80744, Billings, MT 59108: Brochure $2 ❖ Western-style lamps and tables. 406–656–6901.

Gas Light Time, 823 President St., Brooklyn, NY 11215: Catalog $4 ❖ Restored antique gas, combination, and early electric chandeliers and wall sconces, from 1850 to 1925. 718–789–7185.

Genie House, Red Lion Rd., P.O. Box 2478, Vincentown, NJ 08088: Catalog $5 ❖ Handcrafted copper, tin, and brass 17th- and 18th-century reproduction light fixtures. 800–634–3643.

Georgia Lighting Supply Company Inc., 530 14th St. NW, Atlanta, GA 30318: Catalog $12 ❖ Light fixtures in Early American, French, English, and Victorian styles. 404–875–4754.

Dana Gilpin, 2953 S. Detroit, Tulsa, OK 74114: Free information ❖ Lamps and other light fixtures. 918–747–4514.

Brooke Grove Antique & Custom Lighting, 21412 Laytonsville Rd., Laytonsville, MD 20882: Free information ❖ Restored antique light fixtures. 301–948–0392.

Hammerworks, 6 Fremont St., Worcester, MA 01603: Catalog $3 ❖ Handmade reproductions of copper, brass, iron, and tin colonial post lanterns, wall lanterns, chandeliers, and sconces. 508–755–3434.

Hearth Glo, 6 Fremont St., Worcester, MA 01603: Catalog $3 ❖ Handmade Colonial-style light fixtures. 508–755–3434.

Heirloom Reproductions, 1834 W. 5th St., Montgomery, AL 36106: Free catalog ❖ Reproduction French and Victorian lamps and furniture. 800–288–1513.

Home Decorators Collection, 2025 Concourse Dr., St. Louis, MO 63146: Free catalog ❖ Lamp shades and contemporary, traditional, floor, table, halogen lamps, and light fixtures for the bathroom, ceiling, wall, and outdoors. 800–245–2217; 314–993–6045 (in MO).

Howard's Antique Lighting, Rt. 23 West, P.O. Box 472, South Edgemont, MA 01258: Free information ❖ Floor lamps, sconces, and electric, gas, and kerosene chandeliers. 413–528–1232.

Hurley Patentee Lighting, 464 Old Rt. 209, Hurley, NY 12443: Catalog $3 ❖ Handcrafted replica Early American chandeliers, sconces, lanterns, and other lamps. 914–331–5414.

Independence Forge, Rt. 1, Box 1, Whitakers, NC 27891: Brochure $1 ❖ Handcrafted country-style iron furniture, chandeliers, and floor, table, and wall lamps. 919–437–2931.

Jonesborough Power & Light, 144 E. Main St., Old Town Hall, Jonesborough, TN 37659: Free information ❖ Conversion kits, and hard-to-find parts for restoring light fixtures and oil lamps. 615–753–5222.

Juno Lighting Inc., P.O. Box 5065, Des Plaines, IL 60017: Free information ❖ Indoor and outdoor light fixtures. 708–827–9880.

Lamps by Lynne, Durham Rd., Box 190, Pipersville, PA 18947: Free information ❖ Lamps and lampshades. 215–766–7615.

Leviton Manufacturing Company, 59–25 Little Neck Pkwy., Little Neck, NY 11362: Free information ❖ Indoor and outdoor light fixtures. 800–323–8920.

Lighthouse Stained Glass, 1132 W. Cox Ln., Santa Maria, CA 93454: Catalog $3 (refundable) ❖ Stained glass lamps. 805–349–0949.

Lighting Elegance, 147 W. Badillo St., Covina, CA 91723: Catalog $5 ❖ Reproduction 19th-century gas light fixtures. 818–339–7278.

Lightolier, 100 Lighting Way, Secaucus, NJ 07096: Free information ❖ Indoor and outdoor light fixtures. 201–864–3000.

Luigi Crystal, 7332 Frankford Ave., Philadelphia, PA 19136: Catalog $2 ❖ Table lamps, cut crystal chandeliers, hurricane lamps, and sconces. 215–338–2978.

Mole Hill Pottery, 5011 Anderson Pike, Signal Mountain, TN 37377: Catalog $1 ❖

Signed and dated stoneware lamps and pottery. 615–886–4926.

Gates Moore Lighting, 2 River Rd., Silvermine, Norwalk, CT 06850: Catalog $2 ❖ Early American chandeliers, copper lanterns, and wall sconces. 203–847–3231.

Moultrie Manufacturing, P.O. Box 1179, Moultrie, GA 31776: Catalog $3 ❖ Colonial lanterns and other "Old South" reproductions for the home. 800–841–8674.

C. Neri Antiques, 313 South St., Philadelphia, PA 19147: Catalog $5 ❖ Antique light fixtures. 215–923–6669.

Newstamp Lighting Company, 227 Bay Rd., P.O. Box 189, North Easton, MA 02356: Catalog $2 ❖ Handmade replica Early American lamps for indoors and outdoors, sconces, chandeliers, and other light fixtures. 508–238–7071.

Old Lamplighter Shop, At the Musical Museum, Deansboro, NY 13328: Free brochure ❖ Old lamps and parts. 315–841–8774.

Period Lighting Fixtures, 167 River Rd., Clarksburg, MA 01247: Catalog $6.50 ❖ Early American light fixtures, chandeliers, lanterns, and sconces. 800–828–6990.

Progress Lighting, P.O. Box 12701, Philadelphia, PA 19134: Free information ❖ Indoor and outdoor light fixtures.

Rejuvenation Lamp & Fixture Company, 1100 SE Grand Ave., Portland, OR 97217: Free catalog ❖ Reproduction solid brass early 20th-century chandeliers, sconces, and lamps. 503–231–1900.

The Renovator's Supply, P.O. Box 2660, North Conway, NH 03860: Free catalog ❖ Ceiling light fixtures, hanging lamps, table and floor lamps, wall lamps, and replacement glass shades. 800–659–2211.

The Restoration Place, 305 20th St., Rock Island, IL 61201: Free brochure ❖ Plumbing, hardware, architectural and decor accessories, and light fixtures. 309–786–0004.

Roy Electric Company, 1054 Coney Island Ave., Brooklyn, NY 11230: Catalog $6 ❖ Art deco light fixtures. 800–366–3347; 718–434–7002 (in NY).

St. Louis Antique Lighting Company Inc., 801 N. Skinker, St. Louis, MO 63130: Catalog $3 ❖ Handcrafted antique brass reproduction ceiling fixtures, lamps, and sconces. 314–863–1414.

Saltbox Inc., 3004 Columbia Ave., Lancaster, PA 17603: Brochure $2.50 ❖ Handcrafted brass, copper, and tin colonial-style post lights, chandeliers, lanterns, and foyer lights. 717–392–5649.

M. Star Antler Designs, P.O. Box 3093, Lake Isabella, CA 93240: Catalog $5 ❖ Deer antler chandeliers, lamps, furniture, mirrors, and other decor accessories. 619–379–5777.

Studio Steel, 159 New Milford Tnpk., New Preston, CT 06777: Catalog $2 ❖ Lamps, chandeliers, sconces, mirrors, and other handwrought metalwork. 800–800–5217; 203–868–7305 (in CT).

Task Lighting Corporation, P.O. Box 1090, Kearney, NE 68848: Free information ❖ Indoor light fixtures. 800–445–6404.

TSAO + CLS, 31 Grove St., New Canaan, CT 06840: Brochure $1 ❖ Etched glass light fixtures for historic, period, and modern interiors.

Victorian Lightcrafters Ltd., P.O. Box 350, Slate Hill, NY 10973: Catalog $3 (refundable) ❖ Handcrafted Victorian-style light fixtures. 914–355–1300.

Victorian Lighting Works, 251 S. Pennsylvania Ave., P.O. Box 469, Centre Hall, PA 16828: Catalog $5 (refundable) ❖ Victorian-style light fixtures. 814–364–9577.

Washington Copper Works, 49 South St., Washington, CT 06793: Catalog $3 (refundable) ❖ Handcrafted copper lanterns and wall fixtures. 203–868–7527.

Lt. Moses Willard Inc., 1156 US 50, Milford, OH 45150: Catalog $8.50 ❖ Chandeliers, wall sconces, exterior light units, candle holders and lanterns, wall lamps, table lamps, and other reproduction light fixtures from styles of the 1700s. 513–248–5500.

Workshops of David T. Smith, 3600 Shawhan Rd., Morrow, OH 45152: Catalog $5 ❖ Reproduction lamps and chandeliers, furniture, and pottery. 513–932–2472.

Lamp Shades

Ala Lite, 380 E. 1700 South, Salt Lake City, UT 84115: Free information ❖ Restored and reproduction antique lamps, shades, chandeliers, and parts. 800–388–5456.

Brass Light Gallery, 131 S. 1st St., Milwaukee, WI 53204: Catalog $5 ❖ Replacement glass shades and lamps. 800–243–9595.

Burdoch Victorian Lamp Company, 757 N. Twin Oaks Valley Rd., San Marcos, CA

92069: Catalog $5 ❖ Lamp bases and long-fringed lamp shades in satinized-polyester. 800–783–8738.

Campbell Lamp Supply, 1108 Pottsdown Pike, West Chester, PA 19380: Free information ❖ Victorian brocade shades with fringe.

CDR Shade Company, P.O. Box 1030, Great Barrington, MA 01230: Information $2 ❖ Shades for use over lighted candles. 413–528–5050.

Diversified Sales & Marketing, 120 Old Mill Run, Ormond Beach, FL 32174: Free information ❖ Lamp shades. 800–526–7586.

Fantasy Lighting, 7126 Melrose Ave., Los Angeles, CA 90046: Brochure $4 ❖ Victorian shades and lamp bases. 213–933–7244.

Heart Enterprise, 149 Duranta St., Roseville, CA 95678: Catalog $3 ❖ Victorian-style lamp shade kits and supplies. 916–783–4802.

Lamp Glass, P.O. Box 791, Cambridge, MA 02140: Catalog $1 ❖ Replacement glass lamp shades and parts. 617–497–0770.

Lamp Shop, P.O. Box 36, Concord, NH 03302: Catalog $2 ❖ Supplies for making lamp shades. 603–224–1603.

Lamps by Lynne, Durham Rd., Box 190, Pipersville, PA 18947: Free information ❖ Lamps and lamp shades. 215–766–7615.

Lampshades of Antique, P.O. Box 2, Medford, OR 97501: Catalog $4 ❖ Antique-style lamp shades. 503–826–9737.

The Perfect Solution, P.O. Box 964, Easley, SC 29641: Catalog $4 (refundable) ❖ Hand-sewn Victorian-style lamp shades. 803–855–7005.

The Renovator's Supply, P.O. Box 2660, North Conway, NH 03860: Free catalog ❖ Replacement glass shades, ceiling fixtures, and hanging, table, floor, and wall lamps. 800–659–2211

Shades of Olde, 6040 Sherry Lane, Dallas, TX 75225: Catalog $2 ❖ Handmade lamp shades. 214–363–7510.

Shades of Romance, 610 Davis St., Fenton, MI 48430: Information $4 (refundable) ❖ Heirloom fringed lamp shades. 313–750–8103.

Shades of the Past, P.O. Box 206, Fairfax, CA 94930: Catalog $4 ❖ Fringed and beaded lamp shades. 415–459–6999.

Shady Lady, 5020 W. Eisenhower, Loveland, CO 80537: Catalog $3.50 ❖ Lamp shades. 303–669–1080.

Unique Creations, 28 Cherokee Dr., Newark, DE 19713: Catalog 50¢ ❖ Sculptured lamp shades. 302–737–8744.

Yestershades, 4327 SE Hawthorne, Portland, OR 97214: Catalog $3.50 ❖ Victorian-style lamp shades. 503–235–5645.

Outdoor Lighting

AK Exteriors, 298 Leisure Ln., Clint, TX 79836: Catalog $4 ❖ Cast aluminum furniture, light fixtures, and mail boxes. 915–851–2594.

Ameron Pole Products Division, 1020 B St., Fillmore, CA 93015: Free information ❖ Traditional light poles that complement period and modern architectural styles. 800–552–6376.

Authentic Designs, The Mill Rd., West Rupert, VT 05776: Catalog $3 ❖ Outdoor post light units and handcrafted reproduction 18th-century Early American light fixtures, in brass, copper, or tin. 802–394–7713.

Brandon Industries, 4419 Westgrove Dr., Dallas, TX 75248: Free catalog ❖ Cast aluminum street lamps and old-fashioned pedestal mail boxes with solid brass letter slot and cylinder key lock. 214–250–0456.

BRK Electronics, 780 McClure Rd., Aurora, IL 60504: Free information ❖ Controls for converting outdoor lights to an automatic system. 800–323–9005.

Cast Aluminum Reproductions, P.O. Box 1060, St. Elizario, TX 79849: Catalog $2 ❖ Cast aluminum reproduction lamp posts, mail boxes, and benches. 915–764–3793.

Classic & Country Crafts, 5100–1B Clayton Rd., Ste. 291, Concord, CA 94521: Free information ❖ Handmade copper landscape lights. 510–672–4337.

Classic Lamp Posts, 3645 NW 67th St., Miami, FL 33147: Free catalog ❖ Colonial and Victorian-style lamp posts with single or multiple plastic globes. 800–654–5852.

Copper House, RFD 1, Box 4, Epsom, NH 03234: Catalog $3 ❖ Indoor and outdoor light fixtures and handmade copper weather vanes. 603–736–9798.

Josiah R. Coppersmythe, 80 Stiles Rd., Boylston, MA 01505: Catalog $3 ❖ Handcrafted brass or copper Early American indoor and outdoor light fixtures. 508–869–2769.

Doner Design Inc., 2175 Beaver Valley Pike, New Providence, PA 17560: Free brochure ❖ Copper landscape lights. 717–786–8891.

Genie House, P.O. Box 2478, Red Lion Rd., Vincentown, NJ 08088: Catalog $5 ❖ Indoor and outdoor reproduction light fixtures. 800–634–3643.

Great Plains Polymers, 3385 N. 88th Plaza, Omaha, NE 68134: Free brochure ❖ Steel light poles for residential and courtyard lighting. 800–677–1131.

Hanover Lantern, 470 High St., Hanover, PA 17331: Free information ❖ Heavy duty, cast aluminum landscape light fixtures. 717–632–6464.

Heath Company, 455 Riverview Dr., Benton Harbor, MI 49022: Free catalog ❖ Automatic turn-on and turn-off light controls. 616–925–6000.

Heritage Lanterns, 70A Main St., Yarmouth, ME 04096: Catalog $3 ❖ Colonial-style outdoor light fixtures. 800–544–6070.

Herwig Lighting, P.O. Box 768, Russellville, AR 72801: Free brochure ❖ Light fixtures, bollards, street furniture, antique fence posts, street clocks, and post lanterns. 800–643–9523.

Honeywell Inc., Residential Division, 1985 Douglas Dr. North, Golden Valley, MN 55422: Free information ❖ Motion activated light controls. 800–328–5111.

Hubbell Lighting, 2000 Electric Way, Christiansburg, VA 24073: Catalog $5 ❖ Low voltage outdoor lighting systems. 703–382–6111.

Intermatic Lighting Inc., Intermatic Plaza, Spring Grove, IL 60081: Free information ❖ Low voltage outdoor lighting systems. 815–675–2321.

Juno Lighting Inc., P.O. Box 5065, Des Plaines, IL 60017: Free information ❖ Indoor and outdoor light fixtures. 708–827–9880.

KIM Lighting, 16555 E. Gale Ave., P.O. Box 1275, City of Industry, CA 91749: Free information ❖ Landscape lighting equipment. 818–968–5666.

Lamplighter Corner Inc., P.O. Box 235, Edgartown, MA 02539: Free brochure ❖ Handmade solid brass and copper lanterns. 508–627–4656.

Legendary Lighting by Copper Sculptures, 1016 N. Flowood Dr., Jackson, MS 39208: Free brochure ❖ Handcrafted gas lanterns and architectural accent pieces. 601–936–4200.

Leviton Manufacturing Company, 59–25 Little Neck Pkwy., Little Neck, NY 11362: Free information ❖ Indoor and outdoor light fixtures. 800–323–8920.

Lightolier, 100 Lighting Way, Secaucus, NJ 07096: Free information ❖ Indoor and outdoor light fixtures. 201–864–3000.

Liteform Designs, P.O. Box 3316, Portland, OR 97208: Free information ❖ Low voltage, incandescent, and fluorescent garden, driveway, post, and wall mounted light units. 800–458–2505.

Mel-Nor Industries, 303 Gulf Bank, Houston, TX 77037: Information $1 ❖ Park benches, old time lamp posts, and lawn and hanging porch swings. 713–445–3485.

Moultrie Manufacturing, P.O. Box 1179, Moultrie, GA 31776: Catalog $3 ❖ Cast-aluminum indoor and outdoor light fixtures, tables, chairs, settees, planters, urns, fountains, and chaises. 800–841–8674.

Pinckneyville Lighting Standards, 4658 S. Old Peachtree Rd., Pinckneyville, GA 30071: Free information ❖ Light standards. 800–241–4317.

Progress Lighting, P.O. Box 12701, Philadelphia, PA 19134: Free information ❖ Indoor and outdoor light fixtures.

Sentry Electric Corporation, 185 Buffalo Ave., Freeport, NY 11520: Free information ❖ Colonial and early 1900s style cast-aluminum lamp posts and light fixtures. 516–379–4660.

Spring City Electrical Manufacturing Company, P.O. Box 19, Spring City, PA 19475: Free catalog ❖ Heavy-duty cast-iron ornamental lamp posts. 215–948–4000.

Sternberg, 5801 N. Tripp Ave., Chicago, IL 60646: Free catalog ❖ Vintage light fixtures and ornamental poles. 312–478–4777.

Task Lighting Corporation, P.O. Box 1090, Kearney, NE 68848: Free information ❖ Indoor light fixtures. 800–445–6404.

Toro Company, 8111 Lyndale Ave., Bloomington, MN 55420: Free information ❖ Outdoor light units for landscape and security settings, with optional power packs and photo sensors. 800–321–8676.

Tower Lighting Center, P.O. Box 1043, North Adams, MA 01247: Catalog $3 ❖ Hand-wrought copper lanterns. 413–663–7681.

Urban Farmer Store, 2833 Vicente St., San Francisco, CA 94116: Catalog $1 ❖ Low-voltage outdoor lighting. 800–753–3747; 415–661–2204 (in CA).

Valley Iron & Steel Company, 29579 Awbrey Ln., Eugene, OR 97402: Free information ❖ Outdoor light and "streetscaping" fixtures in traditional and futuristic styles. 503–688–7741.

Ultraviolet Light

Alpha Supply Inc., P.O. Box 2133, Bremerton, WA 98310: Catalog $3 ❖ Ultraviolet light, jewelry-making, prospecting, and rockhounding equipment. 206–373–3302.

Bourget Bros., 1636 11th St., Santa Monica, CA 90404: Catalog $3 ❖ Ultraviolet light and rock-polishing equipment, jewelry-making tools, and supplies. 310–450–6556.

Cal-Gold, 2569 E. Colorado Blvd., Pasadena, CA 91107: Free catalog ❖ Ultraviolet light equipment, metal detectors, supplies for miners and geologists, maps, and books. 818–792–6161.

Diamond Pacific Tool Corporation, 2620 W. Main St., Barstow, CA 92311: Free catalog ❖ Ultraviolet light equipment. 800–253–2954.

Ebersole Lapidary Supply Inc., 11417 West Hwy. 54, Wichita, KS 67209: Catalog $2 ❖ Ultraviolet light equipment and jewelry-making, rockhounding, and bead-stringing supplies. 316–722–4771.

Fluorescent Minerals Company, 5106 Walnut Grove Ave., San Gabriel, CA 91776: Free information ❖ Ultraviolet light lamps. 800–833–6757.

Gemstone Equipment Manufacturing Company, 750 Easy St., Simi Valley, CA 93065: Free information ❖ Ultraviolet light and lapidary equipment. 800–235–3375; 805–527–6990 (in CA).

Graves Company, 1800 Andrews Ave., Pompano Beach, FL 33069: Free catalog ❖ Ultraviolet light, rockhounding, and lapidary equipment. 800–327–9103.

Jeanne's Rock & Jewelry, 5420 Bissonet, Bellaire, TX 77401: Price list $1 ❖ Ultraviolet light equipment. 713–664–2988.

Raytech Industries, P.O. Box 449, Rt. 147, Middlefield, CT 06455: Free information ❖ Cabochon machines, trim and slab saws, faceting machines, and ultraviolet light and other equipment. 203–349–3421.

Riviera Lapidary Supply, 30393 Mesquite, Riviera, TX 78379: Catalog $3 ❖ Ultraviolet light equipment. 512–296–3958.

Taiclet Enterprises, 440 Los Encinos Ave., San Jose, CA 95134: Free information ❖ Portable longwave ultraviolet light equipment.

UVP Inc., 5100 Walnut Grove Ave., P.O. Box 1501, San Gabriel, CA 91778: Free information ❖ Short-wave, long-wave, and short/long-wave ultraviolet light equipment. 800–452–6788; 818–285–3123 (in CA).

Wright's Rock Shop, 3612 Albert Pike, Hot Springs, AR 71913: Catalog $2 ❖ Ultraviolet light equipment.

LEATHER CRAFTS

Berman Leathercraft, 25 Melcher St., Boston, MA 02101: Catalog $3 (refundable) ❖ Chamois, suede, and leather for leather crafting. 617–426–0870.

Leather Unlimited, Deershack, 7155 Hwy. B, Belgium, WI 53004: Catalog $2 (refundable) ❖ Leather-crafting supplies and kits. 414–999–9464.

Nasco, 901 Janesville Ave., Fort Atkinson, WI 53538: Free catalog ❖ Leather crafting supplies, tools, and kits. 800–558–9595.

Pyramid of Urbana, 2107 N. High Cross Rd., Urbana, IL 61801: Catalog $5 ❖ Leather-crafting kits, tools, how-to books, other arts and crafts supplies, and office and school equipment. 217–328–3099.

Tandy Leather Company, P.O. Box 2934, Fort Worth, TX 76113: Free catalog ❖ Leather-crafting kits, tools, books, and patterns, and how-to videos.

Veteran Leather Company Inc., 204 25th St., Brooklyn, NY 11232: Free information ❖ Leather-crafting supplies, tools, and kits. 800–221–7565; 718–768–0300 (in NY).

LEFT-HANDED MERCHANDISE

Bob Charles, 1972 Williston Rd., South Burlington, VT 05403: Free price list ❖ Golf equipment for lefties. 800–533–8437.

Left Hand Center, 210 W. Grant, Unit 215, Minneapolis, MN 55403: Catalog $2 ❖ Gifts for left-handers. 612–375–0319.

Left-Handed Solutions, P.O. Box 617, Port Jefferson Station, NY 11776: Catalog $2 ❖ Items for the left-handed person. 516–474–0091.

Lefthanders International, P.O. Box 8249, Topeka, KS 66608: Catalog $2 ❖ Items for lefties. 913–234–2177.

Lefties Only, 1972 Williston Rd., South Burlington, VT 05403: Free price list ❖ Equipment for left-handers. 800–533–8437.

Somerton Springs Golf, 53 Bustleton Pike, Feasterville, PA 19047: Free brochure ❖ Left-handed golf clubs, personalized golf balls, umbrellas, jackets, golf bags, and head covers. 800–220–GOLF; 215–355–7276 (in PA).

LOG SPLITTERS

Bailey's Mail Order Woodsman Supplies, P.O. Box 550, Laytonville, CA 95454: Free catalog ❖ Chain saws, bars, files, protective gear, forestry supplies, log splitters, books, and gifts. 707–984–6133.

Mobile Manufacturing Company, P.O. Box 250, Troutdale, OR 97060: Free brochure ❖ Portable electric- or gasoline-powered saw for cutting logs. 503–666–5593.

Northern Hydraulics, P.O. Box 1219, Burnsville, MN 55337: Free catalog ❖ Log splitters, gas engines, trailer parts, and other tools. 800–533–5545.

Power Equipment Distributors Inc., 3400 Hubbard, Mt. Clemens, MI 48043: Free brochure ❖ Manual hydraulic log splitter. 800–624–2923.

Timberking Inc., 1431 N. Topping, Kansas City, MO 64120: Free information ❖ Portable one-man saw mill. 800–942–4406.

Wood-Mizer, 8180 W. 10th St., Indianapolis, IN 46214: Catalog $2 ❖ Portable sawmills and other tools. 800–553–0219.

LUGGAGE & BRIEFCASES

A to Z Luggage, 4627 New Utrecht Ave., Brooklyn, NY 11219: Free catalog ❖ Luggage and small   leather goods. 800–342–5011; 718–435–2880 (in NY).

Ace Luggage & Gifts, 2211 Ave. U, Brooklyn, NY 11229: Catalog $2 (refundable) ❖ Leather luggage and small leather goods. 718–891–9713.

Al's Luggage, 2134 Larimer St., Denver, CO 80205: Catalog $2 (refundable) ❖ Luggage carts and luggage. 303–295–9009.

Altman Luggage, 135 Orchard St., New York, NY 10001: Free information ❖ Luggage, other leather goods, and pens and pencils. 800–372–3377.

T. Anthony Ltd., 1201 Connecticut Ave. NW, Washington, DC 20036: Free catalog ❖ Leather accessories and luggage. 202–LUGGAGE.

Asics Tiger Corporation, 10540 Talbert Ave., West Bldg., Fountain Valley, CA 92708: Free information ❖ Carry-alls, tote bags, duffles, and shoulder bags. 800–766–ASICS; 714–962–7654 (in CA).

Bally of Switzerland for Ladies, 689 Madison Ave., New York, NY 10021: Free information ❖ Women's shoes, clothing, luggage, and small leather goods. 212–751–2163.

Bally of Switzerland for Men, 711 5th Ave., New York, NY 10022: Free information ❖ Men's shoes, clothing, luggage, and small leather goods. 212–751–9082.

Bettingers Luggage Shop, 80 Rivington St., New York, NY 10002: Free information with long SASE ❖ Luggage, attache and briefcases, and small leather goods. 212–475–1690.

Bondy Export Corporation, 40 Canal St., New York, NY 10002: Free information with long SASE ❖ Luggage and accessories, appliances, typewriters, cameras, TVs, and video equipment. 212–925–7785.

Border Leather, 3800 Main St., Chula Vista, CA 91911: Free catalog ❖ Leather and textile goods. 800–732–6936.

Bottega Veneta, 635 Madison Ave., New York, NY 10022: Free catalog ❖ Wallets, purses and handbags, luggage, and other small leather goods. 212–371–5511.

Classic Designs, P.O. Box 994, Marion, MA 02738: Catalog $1 ❖ Leather accessories. 508–748–2425.

Coach Leatherware Company, 410 Commerce Blvd., Carlstadt, NJ 07072: Free catalog ❖ Leather handbags, gloves, belts, wallets, and briefcases. 201–460–4716.

Creative House, 100 Business Pkwy., Richardson, TX 75081: Free catalog ❖ Luggage, briefcases, attache cases, handbags, and wallets. 800–527–5940; 214–231–3463 (in TX).

Crouch & Fitzgerald, 400 Madison Ave., New York, NY 10017: Free information ❖ Leather goods with optional monogramming. 800–6–CROUCH; 212–755–5888 (in NY).

Dooney & Bourke Inc., 1 Regent St., P.O. Box 841, South Norwalk, CT 06856: Free

catalog ❖ Leather goods and accessories. 800–243–5598.

Eagle International Institute Inc., 1057 E. Henrietta Rd., Rochester, NY 14623: Free catalog ❖ Day planner systems and reminders, open-style and zippered leather binders, office accessories, forms and calendars, and audio and video training programs. 800–273–6111; 716–283–8000 (in NY).

Charolette Ford Trunks, P.O. Box 536, Spearman, TX 79081: Catalog $3.50 ❖ Supplies and tools for restoring trunks. 806–659–3027.

Innovation Luggage, 487 Hackensack Ave., River Edge, NJ 07661: Free information with long SASE ❖ Luggage, briefcases, portfolios, attaché cases, and handbags. 800–722–1800.

Kelty Packs Inc., 1224 Fern Ridge Pkwy., Creve Coeur, MO 63141: Free catalog ❖ Cordura nylon backpacks that convert to luggage. 800–423–2320.

Lodis Corporation, 2261 S. Carme Lina Ave., Los Angeles, CA 90064: Free catalog ❖ Leather luggage, shaving and toilet kits, briefcases, note pads, wallets, and management systems. 800–421–8674; 310–207–6841 (in CA).

The Luggage Center, 960 Remillard St., San Jose, CA 95122: Free information with long SASE ❖ Luggage and accessories. 800–626–6789.

Madden USA, 2400 Central Ave., Boulder, CO 80301: Free information ❖ Carry-alls, tote bags, duffles, and shoulder bags. 303–442–5828.

New England Leather Accessories, 11 Portland St., Rochester, NH 03867: Catalog $5 (refundable) ❖ Leather card cases, diary covers, briefcases and portfolios, small accessories, and handbags and purses. 603–332–0707.

North Beach Leather, 1335 Columbus Ave., San Francisco, CA 94133: Catalog $3 ❖ Men and women's leather clothing. 415–346–1113.

North Face, 999 Harrison St., Berkeley, CA 94710: Free information ❖ Carry-alls, tote bags, duffles, and shoulder bags. 510–527–9700.

Pantos, P.O. Box 585, 74 Rumford Ave., Waltham, MA 02154: Free catalog ❖ Soft-side luggage and travel bags. 617–891–4930.

Rettinger Importing Company, 125 Enterprise, Secaucus, NJ 07096: Free information ❖ Carry-alls, tote bags, duffles, and shoulder bags. 800–526–3142; 201–432–7400 (in NJ).

LUMBER

A & M Wood Specialty Inc., 358 Eagle St. North, Box 3204, Cambridge, Ontario, Canada N3H 5M2: Free catalog ❖ Hardwoods and veneers. 519–653–9322.

Adams Wood Products Inc., 974 Forest Dr., Morristown, TN 37814: Free catalog ❖ Kiln-dried oak, Honduras mahogany, walnut, cherry, maple, pine turning squares, and carving blanks. 615–587–2942.

Albany Woodworks, P.O. Box 729, Albany, LA 70711: Free information ❖ Antique lumber. 504–567–1155.

Allen & Allen Company, P.O. Box 5140, San Antonio, TX 78284: Free information ❖ Hardware, lumber, and mouldings. 512–733–9191.

Anderson-McQuaid Company Inc., 170 Fawcett St., Cambridge, MA 02138: Free price list ❖ Custom and restoration mouldings, flooring, and panelling. 617–876–3250.

Architectural Timber & Millwork, 35 Mount Warner Rd., Hadley, MA 01035: Free information ❖ Kiln-dried antique and new lumber. 413–586–3045.

Barber Lumber Sales Inc., P.O. Box 263, Alachua, FL 32615: Free information ❖ Heart cypress, pine lumber, and other softwood. 904–462–3772.

The Berea Hardwoods Company, 125 Jacqueline Dr., Berea, OH 44017: Free information ❖ Exotic woods for turning and cabinet making. 216–243–4452.

Boulter Plywood Corporation, 24 Broadway, Somerville, MA 02145: Free catalog ❖ Domestic and exotic hardwood, other lumber, and marine plywood. 617–666–1340.

Bre Lumber/Rare Earth Hardwoods, 6778 E. Traverse Hwy., Traverse City, MI 49684: Free information ❖ Hardwood, other lumber, flooring, and decking. 800–968–0074.

Broad-Axe Beam Company, RD 2, Box 417, West Brattleboro, VT 05301: Price list $2 ❖ Wide pine flooring and beaded edge panelling. 802–257–0064.

Catskill Mountain Lumber Company, P.O. Box 450, Swan Lake, NY 12783: Free catalog ❖ Hardwoods. 800–828–9663.

Centre Mills Antique Wood, P.O. Box 16, Aspers, PA 17304: Free information ❖ Antique flooring, hewn beams, new hardwood, and some softwood. 717–334–0249.

Certainly Wood, 11753 Big Tree Rd., East Aurora, NY 14052: Free catalog ❖ Veneers and plywood. 716–655–0206.

Colonial Hardwoods Inc., 7953 Cameron Brown Ct., Springfield, VA 22158: Free information ❖ Hardwood and mouldings. 800–466–5451; 703–451–9217 (in VA).

Maurice L. Condon Company, 248 Ferris Ave., White Plains, NY 10603: Catalog $2 ❖ Exotic woods and plywood. 914–946–4111.

Constantine, 2050 Eastchester Rd., Bronx, NY 10461: Catalog $1 ❖ Cabinet and furniture wood, veneers, plans, hardware, how-to books, carving tools and chisels, inlay designs, and other supplies. 800–223–8087; 718–792–1600 (in NY).

Craftsman Lumber Company, 436 Main St., Groton, MA 01450: Free information ❖ Oak and pine flooring and paneling, in widths up to 30 inches. 508–448–6336.

Craftsman Wood Service, 1735 W. Cortland Ct., Addison, IL 60101: Catalog $2 ❖ Kiln-dried and imported rare woods, veneers, hand and power tools, hardware, finishing materials, and clock movements and kits. 708–629–3100.

CraftWoods, 2101 Greenspring Dr., Timonium, MD 21093: Free catalog ❖ Kiln-dried domestic and exotic woods, and woodworking, wood carving, and power tools. 800–468–7070.

Duluth Timber Company, P.O. Box 16717, Duluth, MN 55816: Free information ❖ Beams, millwork, panelling, and flooring from recycled old-growth timbers from bridges and buildings.

Gilmer Wood Company, 2211 NW St. Helens Rd., Portland, OR 97210: Free information ❖ Exotic wood logs, planks, and squares. 503–274–1271.

Granville Manufacturing Company Inc., Granville, VT 05747: Free brochure ❖ Quartersawn clapboard siding. 802–767–4747.

Groff & Hearne Lumber, 858 Scotland Rd., Quarryville, PA 17566: Free information ❖

Walnut, cherry, and other woods. 717–284–0001.

Handloggers Woods, 135 E. Sir Francis Drake Blvd., Larkspur, CA 94939: Free catalog ❖ Exotic hardwoods. 800–461–1969.

The Harbor Sales Company Inc., 1401 Russell St., Baltimore, MD 21230: Information $1 ❖ Exotic woods. 800–345–1712.

Homecraft Veneer, 901 West Way, Latrobe, PA 15650: Information $1 ❖ Domestic and imported veneers. 412–537–8435.

Joinery Company, P.O. Box 518, Tarboro, NC 27886: Catalog $5 ❖ Reproduction flooring, millwork, cabinets, furniture, and timber frames in antique heart pine. 919–823–3306.

Lane Import Company, 444 Drayton St., Savannah, GA 31401: Free information ❖ Ceylon satinwood turning squares.

Locust Grove Wood Shop, 375 W. Corrine Rd., West Chester, PA 19382: Free information ❖ Walnut, oak, poplar, white ash, maple, mahogany, and other lumber and turning squares. 215–793–1380.

Mountain Lumber, P.O. Box 289, Ruckersville, VA 22968: Free information ❖ Recycled antique heart pine from pre-1900 buildings. 804–985–3646.

Pure Heart Redwood, P.O. Box 830, North Fork, CA 93643: Free information ❖ Old-growth, clear all-heart redwood decking, paneling, beams, windows, doors, and garden furniture. 209–877–4730.

Rand Lumber Company, 511 Wallis Rd., Rye, NH 03870: Free information ❖ Domestic hardwoods and softwoods. 800–436–4494.

Sandy Pond Hardwoods, 921–A Lancaster Pike, Quarryville, PA 17566: Free information ❖ Domestic hardwoods. 800–9–FIGURE; 209–532–1260 (in PA).

Talarico Hardwoods, RD 3, Box 3268, Mohnton, PA 19540: Free catalog ❖ Quartersawn white oak, red oak, and figured lumber. 610–775–0400.

Steve Wall Lumber Company, Box 287, Mayodan, NC 27027: Catalog $1 ❖ Hardwood and woodworking machinery. 800–633–40962; 910–427–0637 (in NC).

Wood-Ply Lumber Corporation, 100 Bennington Ave., Freeport, NY 11520: Free price list ❖ Domestic and exotic hardwoods. 800–354–9002.

Woodcrafters Supply Company, 7703 Perry Hwy., Rt. 19, Pittsburgh, PA 15237: Free information ❖ Domestic and imported woods, veneers, finishes, mouldings, carving stock, hardware, inlays and bandings, plans, books, and tools. 412–367–4330.

Woodhouse Antique Flooring, P.O. Box 7336, Rocky Mount, NC 27804: Brochure $5 ❖ Wide country or quartersawn antique hardwood planks. 919–977–7336.

Woodworker's Dream, Division Martin Guitar Company, 510 Sycamore St., Nazareth, PA 18064: Free information ❖ Exotic and domestic hardwoods and musical instrument woods. 800–345–3103; 215–759–2064 (in PA).

Woodworkers Source, 5402 S. 40th St., Phoenix, AZ 85040: Free information ❖ Exotic and domestic lumber, plywood, veneers, turning squares, and blanks. 800–423–2450; 602–437–4415 (in AZ).

MACRAME

Al Con Enterprises, P.O. Box 1060, Quincy, FL 32351: Free catalog ❖ Macrame, chair weaving, and crochet supplies. 800–523–4371; 904–627–6996 (in FL).

Craft King Mail Order Dept., P.O. Box 90637, Lakeland, FL 33804: Catalog $2 ❖ Craft, needlework, and macrame supplies. 813–648–0433.

Frederick J. Fawcett Inc., 1338 Ross St., Petaluma, CA 94954: Free information ❖ Looms, linen embroidery fabrics, macrame supplies, and linen/cotton and wool yarns and fibers. 800–289–9276.

International Manufacturing Company, 1130 Live Oak St., Lillian Springs, FL 32351: Catalog $1 ❖ Silk plants, trees, flowers, flower-arranging supplies, macrame cord and supplies, beads, and other craft supplies. 904–875–2918.

Pacific Wood Products, 5150 Edison Ave., Chino, CA 91710: Catalog $1 ❖ Macrame-style furniture kits. 800–421–2781; 800–262–1638 (in CA).

H.H. Perkins Company, 10 S. Bradley Rd., Woodbridge, CT 06525: Free catalog ❖ Seat weaving and basket-making supplies, macrame supplies, and how-to books. 800–462–6660.

Wood-Knot Crafts, 36 Chateau Dr., Monorville, NY 11949: Catalog $2 (refundable) ❖ Macrame patterns, supplies, and how-to books.

MAGIC TRICKS & VENTRILOQUISM

Abbott's Magic Company, 124 St. Joseph, Colon, MI 49040: Catalog $12.50 ❖ Magician's props, close-up and stage magic for amateur and professional magicians. 616–432–3235.

Abracadabra Magic Shop, 125 Lincoln Blvd., Middlesex, NJ 08846: Catalog $5 ❖ Magician's props, close-up and stage magic, juggling equipment, balloons, clown accessories, costumes, and make-up. 908–805–0200.

An Amazing Shaners Castle & Magic Museum, 29 Brown & 6th St., Dayton, OH 45402: Free catalog ❖ Books, equipment, props, and accessories for magicians. 513–222–7853.

Axtell Expressions, 230 Glencrest Cir., Ventura, CA 93003: Catalog $2 ❖ Magic for amateur and professional magicians. 805–642–7282.

Books by Mail, P.O. Box 1444, Corona, CA 91718: Free catalog with two 1st class stamps ❖ Books and novelties for clowns, magicians, puppeteers, face painters, and balloon artists. 909–273–0900.

Mike Bornstein Magic, 319 W. 48th St., New York, NY 10036: Free information with long SASE ❖ Magic for amateur and professional magicians.

Captain Dick's Dummy Depot, 2631 NW 95th St., Seattle, WA 98117: Information $3 with long SASE ❖ New and used ventriloquist figures and books. 206–784–0883.

Chazpro Magic Company, 603 E. 13th, Eugene, OR 97401: Catalog $3 ❖ Magic for amateur and professional magicians. 503–345–0032.

Cosmar Magic, 6765 El Banquero Pl., San Diego, CA 92119: Catalog $15 ❖ Close-up and stage magic and clown supplies. 619–287–3706.

Daytona Magic, Harry Allen & Irv Cook, 136 S. Beach St., Daytona, FL 32114: Catalog $10 ❖ Magician's props and close-up and stage magic for amateur and professional magicians. 904–252–6767.

Flosso-Hornmann Magic Company, 45 W. 34th St., Room 607, New York, NY 10001: Free information ❖ Magic tricks, juggling supplies, tarot cards, crystal balls, books, and props. 212–279–6079.

David Ginn Magic, 4387 St. Michaels Dr., Lilburn, GA 30247: Catalog $10 ❖ Books, props, and how-to magic on video tape for magicians and clowns.

Hades' Seattle Magic Sentre, Box 2242, Seattle, WA 98111: Free information ❖ Magic equipment for amateur and professional magicians. 206–624–4287.

Haines House of Cards Inc., 2514 Leslie Ave., Norwood, OH 45212: Free price list ❖ Card magic illusions, trick cards, and books. 513–531–6548.

Klamm Magic, 1412 Appleton, Independence, MO 64052: Small props catalog $2; illusions catalog $3 ❖ Magic equipment for amateur and professional magicians. 816–461–4595.

Jim Kleefeld, 33510 Jennie Rd., Avon, OH 44011: Brochure $2 ❖ Contemporary magic and books for children and adults.

Laflin's Magic & Silks, P.O. Box 228, Sterling, CO 80751: Free information ❖ Entertaining and educational magic on video tape for clowns and magicians. 303–522–2589.

Hank Lee's Magic Factory, Mail Order Division, P.O. Box 789, Medford, MA 02155: Catalog $4.50 ❖ Magic tricks and illusions, books, props, jokes, and novelties. 617–482–8749.

Magic by Bruce Chadwick, P.O. Box 6106, Fort Worth, TX 76115: Catalog $5 ❖ Illusions and transporting cases. 817–927–0581.

Maher Studios, P.O. Box 420, Littleton, CO 80160: Catalog $1 ❖ Ventriloquist dummies, scripts and dialogues, puppets, and how-to books. 303–798–6830.

Mecca Magic Inc., 49 Dodd St., Bloomfield, NJ 07003: Catalog $10 ❖ Magic and ventriloquism accessories, juggling supplies, make-up, clown equipment, balloons, costumes and wigs, puppets, and other props. 201–429–7597.

Steven Meltzer, 670 San Juan, Venice, CA 90291: Free list with long SASE ❖ Marionettes, puppets, and ventriloquist dummies. 310–396–6007.

Meyerbooks Publisher, P.O. Box 427, Glenwood, IL 60425: Free catalog ❖ Books on stage magic history, herbs, health, cooking, and Americana. 708–757–4950.

More than Balloons Inc., 2409 Ravendale Ct., Kissimmee, FL 34758: Free information

❖ Regular balloons, balloons for making sculptures, how-to books, balloon accessories, and magic. 800–BALUNES.

Morris Costumes, 3108 Monroe Rd., Charlotte, NC 28205: Catalog $20 ❖ Magic tricks and special effects, costumes, clown props, masks, jokes, novelties, balloons, and books. 704–332–3304.

Morrissey Magic Ltd., 2882 Dufferin St., Toronto, Ontario, Canada M6B 3S6: Catalog $5 ❖ Magic equipment and entertainment supplies. 416–782–1393.

Quality Used & Rare Magic, Ron Allesi, 364 W. Main St., Fredonia, NY 14063: Catalog $3 ❖ Used, rare, and antique magic apparatus, early magic sets, books, posters, and other magic memorabilia. 716–679–4073.

Sasco Magic Inc., 11609 Proctor Rd., Philadelphia, PA 19116: Free catalog ❖ Coin and other magic tricks. 215–698–2404.

Show-Biz Services, 1735 E. 26th St., Brooklyn, NY 11229: Free list ❖ Books for magicians. 718–336–0605.

Stevens Magic Emporium, 3238 E. Douglas, Wichita, KS 67208: Catalog $7.50 ❖ Professional magic and books. 316–683–9582.

Sun Magic, 1609 E. Bell Rd., #B1, Phoenix, AZ 85022: Catalog $2 ❖ Books and used and collectible close-up, stage, parlor magic, and illusions.

Tannen's Magic, 24 W. 25th St., 2nd Floor, New York, NY 10010: Catalog $15 ❖ Close-up and parlor magic, illusions, books, and props for amateurs and professionals. 212–929–4500.

U.S. Toy Company Inc., 1227 E. 119th St., Grandview, MO 64030: Catalog $3 ❖ Parlor magic, professional illusions, and props for magicians. 800–448–7830; 816–761–5900 (in MO).

Venture Magic, 106 Main St., Milford, OH 45150: Catalog $5 ❖ Antique magic, new magic equipment, and mental illusions for amateur and professional magicians. 513–248–1666.

Wheeler-Tanner Escapes, 3024 E. 35th Ave., Spokane, WA 99223: Catalog $3 ❖ Straitjackets, lock and pick sets, handcuffs, leg irons, trick and specialty items, other accessories for escape artists, and books. 509–448–8457.

Meir Yedid Magic, P.O. Box 55, Rego Park, NY 11374: Catalog $2 ❖ Magic equipment for amateur and professional magicians.

MAILBOXES

Acorn Manufacturing Company Inc., 457 School St., P.O. Box 31, Mansfield, MA 02048: Catalog $6 ❖ Locking, forged iron mailboxes in vertical and horizontal styles. 800–835–0121; 508–339–4500 (in MA).

AK Exteriors, 298 Leisure Ln., Clint, TX 79836: Catalog $4 ❖ Cast aluminum furniture, light fixtures, and mail boxes. 915–851–2594.

Brandon Industries, 4419 Westgrove Dr., Dallas, TX 75248: Free catalog ❖ Old-fashioned cast-aluminum pedestal mailboxes, with solid brass letter slots and cylinder key locks. 214–250–0456.

Cast Aluminum Reproductions, P.O. Box 1060, San Elizario, TX 79849: Catalog $2 ❖ Cast aluminum reproduction lamp posts, mail boxes, and benches. 915–764–3793.

Coppersmith Sheet Metal, 40136 Enterprises Dr., Bldg. 18–A, Oakhurst, CA 93644: Free brochure ❖ Fireplace hoods, cupolas, mailboxes, and dormers. 209–658–8909.

Edisonville Wood Shop, 1916 Edisonville Rd., Strasburg, PA 17579: Brochure $1 ❖ Handcrafted all-wood mailboxes. 717–687–0116.

Frank's Country Store, 162 Washington Ave., North Haven, CT 96473: Free brochure ❖ Handcrafted mailboxes with cedar shingle roofs. 800–875–1960.

Home Decorators Collection, 2025 Concourse Dr., St. Louis, MO 63146: Free catalog ❖ Mailboxes in contemporary and other styles. 800–245–2217; 314–993–6045 (in MO).

Mel-Nor Industries, 303 Gulf Bank, Houston, TX 77037: Information $1 ❖ Mailboxes, park benches, swings, lights, and other landscaping items. 713–445–3485.

Postal Pals, 11242 Playa Ct., Culver City, CA 90230: Free brochure ❖ Redwood address plaques and mail boxes with an animal theme. 800–438–7768; 310–398–7768 (in CA).

Redwood Unlimited, P.O. Box 2344, Valley Center, CA 92082: Brochure $2 ❖ Wall-mounted and post-mounted mail boxes and weather vanes. 800–283–1717.

The Renovator's Supply, P.O. Box 2660, North Conway, NH 03860: Free catalog ❖ Victorian-style solid brass mailboxes, decor accessories, and gifts. 800–659–2211.

Roswell & Company, 9808 Barrows Rd., Huron, OH 44839: Free information with long SASE ❖ Handcrafted personalized antique car mailboxes. 419–433–4709.

MAILING LISTS

Advon, Drawer B, Shelley, ID 83274: Free information ❖ Mixed states mailing lists with adhesive labels. 800–992–3866.

American Business Lists, P.O. Box 27347, Omaha, NE 68127: Catalog $2 ❖ Mailing lists compiled from the Yellow Pages for businesses, consumers, and other groups. 402–331–7169.

American List Counsel Inc., 88 Orchard Rd., CN 5219, Princeton, NJ 08543: Free catalog ❖ Mailing lists, special high interest databases, and telemarketing lists. 800–ALC-LIST.

Cahners Direct Mail Services, 249 W. 17th St., New York, NY 10011: Free information ❖ Mailing lists. 800–537–7930; 212–337–7167 (in NY).

Norman Hill, P.O. Box 1560, Jensen Beach, FL 34958: Free information ❖ Computerized mailing lists. 800–554–LIST; 407–334–5205 (in FL).

List Associates, 116 Kellogg Ave., Ames, IA 50010: Free information ❖ Zip-code sorted mailing lists on pressure-sensitive labels. 515–232–6789.

List-Masters, Box 750, Wantagh, NY 11793: Free information ❖ Mailing lists on adhesive labels. 800–356–8664.

McAfee & Company, 1815 Carpenter St., Bridgeport, TX 76026: Free information ❖ Zip-code sorted mailing lists on pressure-sensitive labels. 800–654–5541; 817–683–2462 (in TX).

Quality Lists, P.O. Box 6060, Seaford, NY 11783: Free information ❖ Computer-generated mailing lists on peel-and-stick labels in zip-code order. 800–356–6392.

MAPS

American Map Corporation, 46–35 54th Rd., Maspeth, NY 11378: Free information ❖ Maps, travel guides, and atlases. 718–784–0055.

Appalachian Mountain Club Books, 5 Joy Street, Boston, MA 02108: Free catalog ❖ Hiking, river, and recreation guides and maps. 617–523–0636.

W. Graham Arader Maps & Prints, 1000 Boxwood Ct., King of Prussia, PA 19406: Free catalog ❖ Rare maps and prints. 215–825–6570.

Bikecentennial, P.O. Box 8308, Missoula, MT 59807: Free catalog ❖ Bike touring maps and books. 800–933–1116.

Carta Nova Publishing, P.O. Box 15, New York, NY 10156: Free information ❖ United States, European, and other maps. 212–730–0518.

Complete Traveler Bookstore, 199 Madison Ave., New York, NY 10016: Catalog $1 ❖ Travel guides, books, and maps. 212–685–9007.

George F. Cram Company Inc., 301 S. LaSalle St., Indianapolis, IN 46201: Free catalog ❖ Maps, atlases, globes, and charts. 800–227–4199; 317–635–5564 (in IN).

Richard Fitch Maps, 2324 Calle Halcon, Santa Fe, NM 87505: Catalog $4 ❖ Antiquarian maps and prints from North America, 16th to 19th-centuries. 505–982–2939.

Forsythe Travel Library Inc., P.O. Box 2975, Shawnee Mission, KS 66201: Free brochure ❖ Travel books, maps, and other publications. 800–367–7984; 913–384–3440 (in KS).

Gabelli U.S. Inc., 605 Lincoln Rd., Ste. 418, Miami Beach, FL 33139: Free information ❖ Colorful and detailed world maps with a simulated three-dimensional image. 800–542–8771.

Genealogy Unlimited Inc., P.O. Box 537, Orem, UT 84059: Free catalog ❖ Genealogical books, supplies, and historical, topographic, and modern European maps. 800–666–4363.

Gold Bug, P.O. Box 588, Alamo, CA 94507: Free brochure ❖ Maps published in the 17th and 18th centuries and reproductions of old maps for prospectors and genealogical research buffs. 510–838–MAPS.

Hammond Incorporated, 515 Valley St., Maplewood, NJ 07040: Free information ❖ Maps and prints, travel guides, road atlases, adult and juvenile references, and books on business. 201–763–6000.

High-Grade Publications, Box 995, Aptos, CA 95001: Catalog $1 ❖ Books and maps on treasure hunting, gold locations, lost mines, ghost towns, gems and minerals, and geology.

Hippocrene Books Inc., 171 Madison Ave., New York, NY 10016: Free catalog ❖ Books on travel and history, dictionaries, maps, and Polish-interest subjects. 212–685–4371.

Hubbard Maps, P.O. Box 760, Chippewa Falls, WI 54729: Free catalog ❖ Framed or unframed United States, world, and national park maps. 800–323–8368.

Interarts Ltd., 15 Mount Auburn St., Cambridge, MA 02138: Free information ❖ Map books and wall maps. 617–354–4655.

LDT Inc., 9375 Dielman Industrial Dr., St. Louis, MO 63132: Free brochure ❖ Hand-held navigator and electronic interstate service directory and interstate travel guide. 800–274–0971.

Map Express, P.O. Box 280445, Lakewood, CO 80228: Free catalog ❖ Maps and photographs from the United States Geological Service. 800–MAP-0039; 303–989–0003 (in CO).

The Map Shack, 968 Main St., Winchester, MA 01890: Free catalog ❖ Topographic, fishing, road, hiking, and other maps. 617–721–4943.

MapLink, 25 E. Mason St., Santa Barbara, CA 93101: Free catalog ❖ Topographic, regional, county, state, city, country, world, and trail maps. 805–965–4402.

David Morgan, 11812 Northcreek Pkwy., Ste. 103, Bothell, WA 98011: Free catalog ❖ Maps of Great Britain for travel or genealogy research. 800–324–4934.

National Geographic Society, 1145 17th St. NW, Washington, DC 20036: Free catalog ❖ Books, games, videos, maps and globes, travel aids, and magazine subscriptions. 800–447–0647.

Kenneth Nebenzahl Inc., Glencove, IL 60022: Catalog $3 ❖ Rare old maps from around the world.

Northern Map Company, 103 Cherokee Cir., Dunnellon, FL 32630: Catalog $1 ❖ Maps from the Civil War, Canadian maps, map kits, and old state, city, railroad, and county maps, from 70 to 120 years old. 904–489–3967.

The Old Print Gallery, 1220 31st St. NW, Washington, DC 20007: Catalog $3 ❖ Prints and maps from the 18th- and 19th-century. 202–965–1818.

Omni Resources, 1004 S. Mebane St., P.O. Box 2096, Burlington, NC 27216: Free

catalog ❖ Fossils, rocks, hiking and topography maps, and globes. 800–742–2677.

Philadelphia Print Shop Ltd., 8441 Germantown Ave., Philadelphia, PA 19118: Catalog $4 ❖ Antique maps, prints, and books. 215–242–4750.

Rand McNally & Company, Catalog Operations Center, 2515 E. 43rd St., P.O. Box 182257, Chattanooga, TN 37422: Free catalog ❖ Gifts for sports enthusiasts, health and exercise equipment, maps, world globes, books, videos, clocks, prints, travel aids, and watches. 800–234–0679.

Raven Maps & Images, 34 N. Central Ave., Medford, OR 97501: Free catalog ❖ Mounted and framed maps. 800–237–0798.

Thomas Brothers Maps, 17731 Cowan St., Irvine, CA 92714: Free catalog ❖ Atlases, street guides, and maps. 714–863–1984.

Travelers Bookstore, 22 W. 52nd St., New York, NY 10019: Catalog $2 ❖ Maps and books on travel. 800–755–8728; 212–664–0995 (in NY).

United Nations Publications, Room DC2–853, New York, NY 10017: Free information ❖ Maps and United Nations publications. 212–963–8323.

MARBLES

Essol's, P.O. Box 176, Sisterville, WV 26175: Free information with long SASE ❖ Toy, Chinese checker, and decorative marbles.

Spice Island Traders, 21546 Golden Triangle Rd., Saugus, CA 91350: Free list with long SASE ❖ Marbles and related items.

MARTIAL ARTS

Academy of Martial Arts Supplies, 405 Black Horse Pike, Haddon Heights, NJ 08035: Free catalog ❖ Uniforms, training equipment, shoes, books, videos, and swords. 609–547–5445.

Artistic Video, 87 Tyler Ave., Sound Beach, NY 11789: Free brochure ❖ Martial arts training videos. 516–744–5999.

Asian World of Martial Arts Inc., 917 Arch St., Philadelphia, PA 19107: Free catalog ❖ Training and protective equipment, weapons, uniforms, and belts. 800–345–2962; 215–925–1161 (in PA).

The Brute Group, 2126 Spring St., P.O. Box 2788, Reading, PA 19609: Free information ❖ Training equipment. 800–397–2788; 215–678–4050 (in PA).

Century Martial Art Supply Inc., 1705 National Blvd., Midwest City, OK 73110: Free information ❖ Sparring gear, belts, and clothing. 800–626–2787.

Co-Mart International, P.O. Box 16194, San Francisco, CA 94116: Catalog $1 ❖ Training equipment, weapons, uniforms, and shoes. 415–759–8640.

Dolan's Sports Inc., 26 Hwy. 547, P.O. Box 26, Farmingdale, NJ 07727: Free catalog ❖ Training and safety equipment, uniforms, shoes, Samurai swords, and books. 201–938–6656.

Dragon International Inc., 12310 Hwy. 99 South, Unit 106, Everett, WA 98204: Catalog $2 ❖ Martial arts equipment. 206–745–5176.

Eagles Proud Products Inc., 614 Bergen Blvd., Fairfield, NJ 07657: Catalog $2 ❖ Martial arts equipment and weaponry. 800–643–5060; 201–943–2121 (in NJ).

ESPYY-TV, 611 Broadway, New York, NY 10012: Free information ❖ Martial art training videos. 800–735–6521.

Genesport Industries Ltd., Hokkaido Karate Equipment Manufacturing Company, 150 King St., Montreal, Quebec, Canada H3C 2P3: Free information ❖ Belts, clothing, and equipment. 514–861–1856.

Honda Martial Arts Supply, 61 W. 23rd St., New York, NY 10010: Free information ❖ Clothing, protective and safety equipment, shoes, books, and training gear. 212–620–4050.

Carson Hurley Enterprises Inc., 2945 Orange Ave. NE, P.O. Box 12783, Roanoke, VA 24028: Free information ❖ Stretching racks. 703–342–7550.

Impact Martial Arts, 336 W. Lacey Rd., Ste. 123, Forked River, NJ 08731: Free information ❖ Competition head gear, shoes, and gloves. 800–851–0045.

Joy Enterprises, Joy Optical Company, 801 Broad Ave., Ridgefield, NJ 07657: Free information ❖ Belts, clothing, and equipment. 800–526–0486; 201–943–5920 (in NJ).

K.P. Sporting Goods, 4141 Business Center Dr., Fremont, CA 94538: Free information ❖ Chop gloves, protective equipment, and kicking targets. 800–227–227–0500.

Karate Mart Supply Center, 1411 W. Indian School Rd., Phoenix, AZ 85013: Catalog $2 ❖ Karate equipment, uniforms, and shoes. 602–265–6858.

Kim Pacific Trading Corporation Inc., 4141 Business Center Dr., Fremont, CA 94538: Free information ❖ Uniforms, shoes, and protective gear. 510–490–0300.

Kiyota Company Inc., 2326 N. Charles St., Baltimore, MD 21218: Free information ❖ Clothing, protective gear, and shoes. 410–366–8275.

Kwon Martial Arts, P.O. Box 888313, Grand Rapids, MI 49588: Free catalog ❖ Martial arts equipment. 800–968–5944.

Macho Products Inc., 10045 102nd Terr., Sebastian, FL 32958: Free catalog ❖ Training equipment, belts, and clothing. 800–327–6812; 407–388–9892 (in FL).

Martial Arts Supplies Company Inc., 10711 Venice Blvd., Los Angeles, CA 90034: Free catalog ❖ Multiple attack stands with lock-in-place hangers, striking bags, belts, and clothing. 213–870–9866.

Ohara Publications Inc., P.O. Box 918, Santa Clarita, CA 91380: Free information ❖ Books on martial arts. 805–257–4066.

Otomix, 431 N. Oak St., Inglewood, CA 90302: Free information ❖ Fitness shoes and martial arts equipment. 310–330–0750.

Panther Productions, 1010 Calle Negocio, San Clemente, CA 92672: Free catalog ❖ Training videos for beginners and advanced students. 800–332–4442.

Pro-Tect Manufacturing Inc., 1251 Ferguson Ave., St. Louis, MO 63133: Free information ❖ Protection and safety gear, uniforms, belts, and kicking shields. 800–325–1652.

RheeMax, 9000 Mendenhall Ct., Columbia, MD 21045: Free catalog ❖ Uniforms, competition equipment, protective gear, and exercisers. 410–381–2900.

Royal Martial Art Supplies, 2605 Peach St., Erie, PA 16508: Catalog $1 ❖ Martial arts supplies. 814–454–2774.

Tiger Mountain, P.O. Box 1712, Wheat Ridge, CO 80033: Catalog $1 ❖ Martial arts, protective, self-defense, and security equipment. 303–431–0573.

MATCHBOOK COVERS

Remember These, P.O. Box 7956, Roanoke, VA 24019: Free information with long SASE ❖ Postcards and matchbook covers. 703–362–3964.

Writewell Company, P.O. Box 68186, Indianapolis, IN 46268: Free information ❖

Loose-leaf matchbook cover albums with padded covers of leather-grained vinyl. 800–968–5850.

MEMORABILIA & COLLECTIBLES (MISCELLANEOUS)

The Az-Tex Cowboy Trading Company & Museum, 220 E. Fremont, P.O. Box 460, Tombstone, AZ 85638: Catalog $5 ❖ Cowboy collectibles. 602–457–3359.

4x1 Imports Inc., 5873 Day Rd., Cincinnati, OH 45251: Free catalog ❖ Nostalgic tin advertising signs and other memorabilia. 513–385–8185.

The Limited of Michigan Ltd., 10861 Paw Paw Dr., Holland, MI 49424: Free catalog ❖ Hard-to-find Disney wood carvings and other collectibles. 800–355–6363.

Russian Gift Shop-Maison Russe, 1720 Ogden Ave., Lisle, ILL 60532: Free information ❖ Russian Matreshka nesting dolls, collectible plates, pre-revolutionary memorabilia, and other collectibles. 708–963–5160.

Philip Sears Disney Collectibles, 1457 Avon Terr., Los Angeles, CA 90026: Free catalog ❖ Walt Disney autographs, animation art, and other memorabilia. 213–666–3740.

SharpeCo Distributors, P.O. Box 522, Kodak, TN 37764: Free catalog ❖ Videos, films, photographs, autographs, toys, books, knives, and other collectibles. 615–933–9387.

Slot-Box Collector, Richard Bueschel, 414 N. Prospect Manor Ave., Mt. Prospect, IL 60056: Free list with seven 1st class stamps ❖ Old saloon artifacts, coin-operated machines, advertising collectibles, and paper memorabilia. 708–253–0791.

Sports Heroes, 550 Kinderkamack Rd., Oradell, NJ 07649: Free information with long SASE ❖ Vintage and unique sports memorabilia. 800–233–4000; 201–262–8020 (in NJ).

METAL CRAFTING & SILVERSMITHING

Ackley's Rock & Stamps, 3230 N. Stone Ave., Colorado Springs, CO 80907: Catalog $1 (refundable) ❖ Silversmithing supplies. 719–633–1153.

Allcraft Tool & Supply Company, 666 Pacific St., Brooklyn, NY 11207: Catalog $5 ❖ Tools and supplies for jewelry-making,

metal crafting and casting, and silversmithing. 800–645–7124; 718–789–2800 (in NY).

Alpha Supply Inc., Box 2133, Bremerton, WA 98310: Catalog $1 (refundable with $15 order) ❖ Copper and silver wire and sheet and other silversmithing supplies. 206–377–5629.

The Amber Company, 5643 Cahuenga Blvd., North Hollywood, CA 91601: Free price list ❖ Silver and silversmithing supplies. 818–509–5730.

American Art Clay Company Inc., 4717 W. 16th St., Indianapolis, IN 46222: Free catalog ❖ Ceramic and metal-enameling supplies, pottery-making equipment, tools, kilns, and coloring materials. 800–374–1600; 317–244–6871 (in IN).

Anchor Tool & Supply Company Inc., P.O. Box 265, Chatham, NJ 07928: Catalog $3 (refundable with $10 order) ❖ Tools and supplies for gold and silversmithing, casting, and blacksmithing. 201–887–8888.

ARE Inc., Rt. 16, Box 8, Greensboro Bend, VT 05842: Catalog $3 ❖ Silver, gold, pewter, base metals, tools, findings, chains, and semiprecious stones. 800–736–4273.

Bourget Bros., 1636 11th St., Santa Monica, CA 90404: Catalog $3 ❖ Silversmithing supplies and copper, gold, and silver wire and sheet. 310–450–6556.

Craig Laboratories Inc., 16744 W. Bernardo Dr., San Diego, CA 92127: Free catalog ❖ Environmentally-safe electronic chemicals and soldering equipment. 619–451–1799.

Campbell Tools Company, 2100 Selma Rd., Springfield, OH 45505: Catalog $2 ❖ Tools, supplies, and brass, aluminum, steel, and other metals. 513–322–8562.

Cannon Foundry & Machine, 309 Hollow Rd., Staatsburg, NY 12580: Free information ❖ Foundry pattern- and mold-making services. 914–889–8390.

Country Accents, P.O. Box 437, Montoursville, PA 17754: Catalog $5 ❖ Handcrafted metal panels, pierced metal kits and patterns, and tools. 717–478–4127.

East West DyeCom, P.O. Box 12294, Roanoke, VA 24024: Catalog $5 (refundable) ❖ Pre-anodized aluminum sheets and colored tubing, dyes, kits, books, and other supplies. 703–345–1489.

Ebersole Lapidary Supply Inc., 11417 West Hwy. 54, Wichita, KS 67209: Catalog $2 ❖ Gold and silver sheet and wire, and silversmithing supplies. 316–722–4771.

Enco Manufacturing Company, 5000 W. Bloomingdale Ave., Chicago, IL 60639: Free catalog ❖ Metal-working tools, machinery, and accessories. 800–USE-ENCO; 312–745–1520 (in IL).

David H. Fell & Company Inc., 6009 Bandini Blvd., City of Commerce, CA 90040: Free information ❖ Precious metals for crafting. 800–822–1996; 213–722–9992 (in CA).

G & G's Miracle House, 5621 W. Hemlock St., P.O. Box 23234, Milwaukee, WI 53223: Free catalog ❖ Metal findings and tools. 800–558–5513; 800–242–3403 (in WI).

T.B. Hagstoz & Son Inc., 709 Sansom St., Philadelphia, PA 19106: Catalog $5 (refundable with $25 order) ❖ Metal findings, jeweler's tools, casting equipment, gold and silver solders, and gold, silver, gold-filled metals, copper, bronze, brass nickel, silver, and pewter. 800–922–1006; 215–922–1627 (in PA).

Indian Jewelers Supply Company, P.O. Box 1774, Gallup, NM 87305: Catalogs $5 ❖ Copper and silver wire and sheet, silversmithing supplies, precious and base metal findings, tools and other supplies, and semiprecious stones, shells, and coral. 505–722–4451.

K & S Engineering, 6917 W. 59th St., Chicago, IL 60638: Catalog $1 ❖ Aluminum and other metal tubing, rods, and sheets. 312–586–8503.

Kingsley North Inc., P.O. Box 216, Norway, MI 49870: Free catalog ❖ Silversmithing supplies, tools, and casting, lapidary, and glass polishing equipment. 800–338–9280.

Lonnie's Inc., 7155 E. Apache Trail, Mesa, AZ 85207: Free findings catalog; tool catalog $5 ❖ Tools, equipment, and supplies for jewelers, casters, silversmiths, and lapidarists. 602–832–2641.

MBM Sales Ltd., 18170 W. Davidson Rd., Brookfield, WI 53045: Catalog $2 ❖ Hard-to-find metals and fasteners in small quantities. 800–657–0721; 414–786–4276 (in WI).

The NgraveR Company, 67 Wawecus Hill Rd., Bozrah, CT 06334: Catalog $1 (refundable) ❖ Easy-to-use engraving tools and other jewelry-making equipment. 203–823–1533.

Nonferrous Metals, P.O. Box 2595, Waterbury, CT 06723: Catalog $3 (refundable) ❖ Plain and ornamental brass, copper, bronze, and nickel-silver wire. 203–274–7255.

Pyramid of Urbana, 2107 N. High Cross Rd., Urbana, IL 61801: Catalog $5 ❖ Kilns, tools, metal enamels, copper shapes and findings, foils and other craft supplies, office accessories, art supplies, and school equipment. 217–328–3099.

Red & Green Minerals Inc., 7595 W. Florida Ave., Lakewood, CO 80226: Free information ❖ Silversmithing supplies. 303–985–5559.

Sculpt-Nouveau, 625 W. 10th Ave., Escondido, CA 92025: Free information ❖ Dyes for coloring metals. 619–432–8242.

Three Feathers Pewter, Box 232, Shreve, OH 44676: Catalog $3 ❖ Original and reproduction pewter items and ornaments. 216–567–2047.

Myronn Toback Inc., 25 W. 47th St., New York, NY 10036: Free information ❖ Tools for metal crafting and silversmithing. 800–223–7550; 800–442–8444 (in NY).

Unique Tool, P.O. Box 34, Miami, NM 87729: Catalog $3 ❖ Silversmithing stamps and tools. 505–483–2940.

M.P. White Hardware, 27 Stuart St., Boston, MA 02116: Free catalog ❖ Hardware, tools, and other supplies for wood and metal working and other shop activities. 800–249–TOOL.

METAL DETECTORS

Alpha Supply Inc., Box 2133, Bremerton, WA 98310: Catalog $1 (refundable with $15 order) ❖ Metal detectors, prospecting equipment, jewelry-making tools, and gem-finishing equipment. 206–377–5629.

Brook's Detectors, P.O. Box 25038, Montgomery, AL 36125: Free catalog ❖ Metal detectors and accessories. 205–281–1806.

C & C Detectors, 2524 E. US Hwy. 14, Janesville, WI 53545: Free catalog ❖ Metal detectors. 800–356–6636; 608–754–0742 (in WI).

Cal-Gold, 2569 E. Colorado Blvd., Pasadena, CA 91107: Free catalog ❖ Metal detectors, supplies for miners and geologists, maps, and books. 818–792–6161.

Clevenger Detector Sales, 8206 N. Oak, Kansas City, MO 64118: Free information ❖ New and used detectors. 800–999–9147.

Cochran & Associates Inc., P.O. Box 20148, Bowling Green, KY 42102: Catalog $5 ❖ Metal detectors for locating ferrous and non-ferrous metals in mineralized soil areas, beaches, and salt water. 502–843–0706.

Compass International Ltd., P.O. Box 488, Forest Grove, OR 97116: Free brochure ❖ Metal detectors and scanners. 800–823–0326; 503–357–2111 (in OR).

D & K Prospecting Headquarters, 13809 Southeast Division, Portland, OR 97236: Free information ❖ Metal detectors and prospecting equipment. 800–542–4653; 503–761–1521 (in OR).

Detector Electronics Corporation, 419 Worcester Rd., P.O. Box 2132, Framingham, MA 01701: Free brochure ❖ Metal detectors. 800–446–0244.

The Detector Warehouse, P.O. Box 6055, Buffalo Grove, IL 60089: Free catalog ❖ Metal detectors, books, tapes, audio tapes, headphones, dredges, and digging tools. 800–828–1455.

Discovery Electronics Inc., 1115 Long St., Sweet Home, OR 97386: Free information ❖ Metal detectors. 503–367–2585.

Dotson Enterprises, 4651 S. Edgerware Ln., Taylorsville, UT 84119: Free information ❖ Automatic gold panner, metal detectors, and other equipment. 801–963–8242.

Fisher Research Laboratory, 200 W. Wilmott Rd., Los Banos, CA 93635: Free information ❖ Metal detectors. 209–826–3292.

JW Fishers Manufacturing Inc., 65 Anthony St., Berkeley, MA 02779: Free information ❖ Underwater metal detectors. 800–822–4644; 508–822–7330 (in MA).

49'er Metal Detectors, 14093 Irishtown Rd., Pine Grove, CA 95665: Free information ❖ Metal detectors. 800–538–7501; 209–296–3544 (in CA).

Garrett Metal Detectors, 1881 W. State St., Garland, TX 75042: Free buyer's guide ❖ Metal detectors. 214–278–6151.

Gettysburg Electronics, 24 Chambersburg St., Gettysburg, PA 17325: Free information ❖ Metal detectors. 717–334–8634.

The Golddigger, 253 N. Main, Moab, UT 84532: Catalog $3 ❖ Metal detectors. 801–259–5150.

House of Treasure Hunters, 5714 El Cajon Blvd., San Diego, CA 92115: Free information ❖ Metal detectors and gold prospecting equipment. 619–286–2600.

K/T Detector Sales, P.O. Box 17015, Fort Worth, TX 76102: Free information ❖ Metal detectors and prospecting equipment. 800–876–3463; 817–498–2228 (in TX).

Kellyco Detector Distributors, 1085 Belle Ave., Winter Springs, FL 32708: Catalog $5 ❖ Metal detectors. 407–699–8700.

Metal Detectors of Minneapolis, 3746 Cedar Ave. South, Minneapolis, MN 55407: Free information ❖ Metal detectors, books and maps, accessories, recovery tools, and audio-video tapes. 612–721–1901.

Mid-America Sales, 5550 Stage Rd., Bartlett, TN 38134: Free information ❖ Metal detectors, books, and accessories. 800–345–6515.

Mid-West Metal Detectors, 8338 Pillsbury Ave. South, Bloomington, MN 55420: Free information ❖ Metal detectors and books. 612–881–5254.

Mississippi River Trading Company Inc., 2980 Austin Peay, Memphis, TN 38128: Free information ❖ Metal detectors and books. 800–535–6868.

Northwoods General Store, 163 Nob Hill East, Colgate, WI 53711: Free price list ❖ Metal detectors. 414–628–0400.

Pacific Detectors, P.O. Box 51158, Pacific Grove, CA 93950: Free information ❖ Metal detectors and books. 800–637–6601.

Pot of Gold, 2616 Griffin Rd., Fort Lauderdale, FL 33312: Free catalog ❖ Metal detector, books, and prospecting equipment. 305–987–2888.

Tesoro Electronics, 715 White Spar Rd., Prescott, AZ 86303: Free information ❖ Easy-to-use, light-weight metal detectors with high gain sensitivity. 800–528–3352.

Thomas Electroscopes, P.O. Box 5058, South Williamsport, PA 17701: Free catalog ❖ Long-range induction metal detectors for treasure hunting and prospecting. 800–323–9275.

White's Electronics, 1011 Pleasant Valley Rd., Sweet Home, OR 97386: Free information ❖ Metal detectors. 800–547–6911.

MICROSCOPES

Chem-Lab, 1060 Ortega Way, Placentia, CA 92670: Catalog $5 ❖ Chemicals, glassware, scales, microscopes, and other equipment.

Edmund Scientific Company, Edscorp Bldg., Barrington, NJ 08007: Free catalog ❖ Microscopes, magnifiers, weather forecasting instruments, magnets, telescopes, binoculars, lasers, and other science equipment. 609–573–6260.

J.L. Hammett Company, Hammett Pl., P.O. Box 9057, Braintree, MA 02184: Free catalog ❖ Science kits, microscopes, laboratory apparatus, rock collections, magnets, astronomy charts, and anatomical models. 800–225–5467; 617–848–1000 (in MA).

Lire La Nature Inc., 1699 Chemin Chandly, Longueuil, Quebec, Canada J4J 3X7: Free price list ❖ Telescopes and accessories, microscopes, and other equipment. 514–463–5072.

Mineralogical Research Company, 15840 E. Alta Vista Way, San Jose, CA 95127: Free list with long SASE and two 1st class stamps ❖ Microscopes, rare mineral specimens, meteorites, micromounts, specimen boxes, and other science equipment. 408–923–6800.

MILITARY MEMORABILIA
General

Dale C. Anderson Company, 4 W. Confederate Ave., Gettysburg, PA 17325: Catalog (6 issues) $12 ❖ Civil War, Indian War, and other militaria.

Aviation Artifacts Inc., 1213 Sandstone Dr., St. Charles, MO 63304: Catalog $2 ❖ Authentic military collectibles.

British Collectibles Ltd., 1727 Wilshire Blvd., Santa Monica, CA 90403: Catalog $10 ❖ Uniforms, wings, flying gear, badges, insignia, and other aviation collectibles. 310–453–3322.

C & D Jarnagin Company, Historical Supply, P.O. Box 1860, Corinth, MS 38834: Catalog $3 ❖ Military memorabilia, from 1750 to 1815. 601–287–4977.

Collector's Armoury, 800 Slaters Ln., P.O. Box 59, Alexandria, VA 22313: Free catalog ❖ Replica model guns, medals, armor, swords, helmets, and other military collectibles. 800–544–3456.

Dixie Leather Works, P.O. Box 8221, Paducah, KY 42002: Catalog $4 ❖ Museum-quality military and civilian reproductions, from 1833 to 1872.

N. Flayderman & Company Inc., P.O. Box 2446, Fort Lauderdale, FL 33303: Catalog $10 ❖ Antique guns, swords, knives, and nautical, western, and other military

collectibles from the Civil War through World War II. 305–761–8855.

Cyrus Galletta, 321 Willow Grove Rd., Stony Point, NY 10980: Catalog $5 ❖ Post Civil War to Vietnam military collectibles. 914–429–1130.

James E. Garcia, 1404 Luthy NE, Albuquerque, NM 87112: Catalog $3 ❖ Vintage aviation collectibles. 505–296–8765.

Hutchinson House, Box 41021, Chicago, IL 60641: Catalog $1 ❖ Full-size, made from the originals, World War I and II and Civil War reproduction war mementos and medals.

Jacques Noel Jacobsen, 60 Manor Rd., Ste. 300, Staten Island, NY 10310: Catalog $10 ❖ Antiques and military collectibles, insignia, weapons, photos and paintings, band instruments, and Native American and Western items. 718–981–0973.

Legendary Arms Inc., P.O. Box 20198, Greeley Square Station, New York, NY 10001: Free information ❖ Reproduction military period knives and swords. 212–532–9055.

Medals, 1929 Fairview Rd., Fountain Inn, SC 29644: Catalog $2 ❖ World War II, Korea, Vietnam military medals, ribbons, badges, and patches.

Military Art China Company Inc., 8 Park Dr., P.O. Box 406, Westford, MA 01886: Catalog $3 ❖ Handcrafted coffee mugs and steins with military crests. 508–392–0751.

The Military Collection, P.O. Box 830970, Miami, FL 33283: Catalog $8 ❖ Aviation and war relics. 305–271–5690.

Museum Replicas Limited, P.O. Box 840, Conyers, GA 30207: Catalog $1 (refundable) ❖ Authentic museum-quality, historical replicas of weapons and period battle wear.

The Noble Collection, P.O. Box 831, Merrifield, VA 22116: Free catalog ❖ Swords, armor, shields, helmets, sidearms, miniatures, and other military collectibles. 703–641–1519.

OWMC Military Memorabilia, 136 E. 7th Dr., Mesa, AZ 85210: Catalog $2 ❖ Pilot jackets, patches, shirts, wings, and other collectibles. 602–964–0794.

Pieces of History, P.O. Box 4470, Cave Creek, AZ 85331: Catalog $2 ❖ Medals from around the world. 602–488–1377.

Red Lancer, P.O. Box 8056, Mesa, AZ 85214: Catalog $6 ❖ Original 19th-century military art, rare books, campaign medals and helmets, and toy soldiers. 602–964–9667.

Regatta Insignia, 1902 Rosecrans, San Diego, CA 92106: Catalog $2 ❖ Medals, ribbons, badges, insignia, and patches.

Sky Etchings, P.O. Box 855, Syosset, NY 11791: Free brochure with long SASE ❖ Replica pins, wings, badges, patches, and aviation collectibles. 800–368–9956.

Civil War

Dale C. Anderson Company, 4 W. Confederate Ave., Gettysburg, PA 17325: Catalog (6 issues) $12 ❖ Civil War, Indian War, and other militaria.

Armchair General's Merchantile, 1008 Adams, Bay City, MI 48708: Catalog $2 (refundable) ❖ Games, miniatures, and books for Civil War enthusiasts. 517–892–6177.

Bohemian Brigade Book Shop, 7347 Middlebrook Pike, Knoxville, TN 37909: Catalog $1 ❖ Civil War books and militaria. 615–694–8227.

Broadfoot Publishing Company, 1907 Buena Vista Cir., Wilmington, NC 28405: Free catalog ❖ Old and new books about the Civil War. 910–686–4816.

C & D Jarnagin Company, Historical Supply, P.O. Box 1860, Corinth, MS 38834: Catalog $3 ❖ Civil War memorabilia, from 1833 to 1865. 601–287–4977.

Cedar Creek Relic Shop, P.O. Box 232, Middletown, VA 22645: Catalog $6 ❖ Civil War relics. 703–869–5207.

Civil War Antiques, P.O. Box 87, Sylvania, OH 43560: Catalog subscription $8 ❖ Civil War antiques. 419–882–5547.

Collector's Armoury, 800 Slaters Ln., P.O. Box 59, Alexandria, VA 22313: Free catalog ❖ Civil War memorabilia, World War II medals, Samurai swords, flags, and replica model guns. 800–544–3456.

Der Dienst, P.O. Box 221, Lowell, MI 49331: Catalog $2 ❖ Replica Civil War medals.

Farnsworth Military Gallery, 401 Baltimore St., Gettysburg, PA 17325: Free information ❖ Art prints and new, used, and rare books on the Civil War. 717–334–8838.

Will Gorges Civil War Antiques, 2100 Trent Blvd., New Bern, NC 28560: Catalog $10 ❖ Authentic Civil War uniforms, weapons, and photographs. Also comic books, pre-1964. 919–636–3039.

Indian Hollow Antiques, 298 W. Old Cross Rd., New Market, VA 22844: Free information with long SASE ❖ Weapons, uniforms, documents, money, buttons, and other Civil War militaria. 703–740–3959.

Bill Mason Books, 104 N. 7th St., Morehead City, NC 28557: Free catalog ❖ Rare, new, and used books, prints, and Civil War, Western Americana, militaria, and nautical collectibles. 919–247–6161.

Northern Map Company, 103 Cherokee Cir., Dunnellon, FL 32630: Catalog $1 ❖ Maps from the Civil War, Canadian maps, map kits, and old state, city, railroad, and county maps, from 70 to 120 years old. 904–489–3967.

Old Sutler John, P.O. Box 174, Westview Station, Binghamton, NY 13905: Catalog $2 ❖ Reproduction Civil War guns, bayonets, swords, uniforms, leather items, and other collectibles. 607–775–4434.

Olde Soldier Books Inc., 18779 N. Frederick Ave., Gaithersburg, MD 20879: Free information ❖ Civil War books, documents, autographs, prints, and Americana. 301–963–2929.

Rapine Bullet Manufacturing Company, P.O. Box 1119, East Greenville, PA 18041: Catalog $2 ❖ Civil War bullet molds. 215–679–5413.

The Regimental Quartermaster, P.O. Box 553, Hatboro, PA 19040: Catalog $2 ❖ Civil War reproductions. 215–672–6891.

Len Rosa Military Collectibles, P.O. Box 3965, Gettysburg, PA 17325: Catalog subscription $6 ❖ Union and Confederate Civil War memorabilia and other artifacts. 717–337–2853.

James Townsend & Son Inc., 133 N. 1st St., P.O. Box 415, Perceton, IN 46562: Catalog $2 ❖ Historical clothing, hats, lanterns, tomahawks, knives, tents, guns, and blankets. 219–594–5852.

The Winchester Sutler Inc., 270 Shadow Brook Ln., Winchester, VA 22603: Catalog $3 ❖ Civil War reproductions. 703–888–3595.

War Medals & Souvenirs

Collector's Armoury, 800 Slaters Ln., P.O. Box 59, Alexandria, VA 22313: Free catalog ❖ Collectible World War II medals, Samurai swords, flags, Civil War memorabilia, and replica model guns. 800–544–3456.

Der Dienst, P.O. Box 221, Lowell, MI 49331: Catalog $2 ❖ Replica Civil War medals.

R. Andrew Fuller Company, Box 2071, Pawtucket, RI 02861: Free catalog ❖ Medals, ribbons, and display cases.

Historical Americana, P.O. Box 310, New York, NY 10028: Free catalog with first class stamp ❖ Military and civilian decorations and medals from the United States and foreign countries, military award certificates, insignias, books, and other collectibles. 718–409–6407.

Hoover's Manufacturing Company, 4015 Progress Blvd., Peru, IL 61354: Free catalog ❖ Dog tag key rings, beer and coffee mugs, belt buckles, patches, flags, pins, patches, and Vietnam, Korea, and World War II hat pins. 815–223–1159.

Martin Lederman, 21 Naples, Brookline, MA 02146: Free list ❖ United States military medals. 617–731–0000.

Sydney B. Vernon, Box 890280, Temecula, CA 92589: Catalog $1 ❖ Military medals and related collectibles.

MIRRORS

Atlantic Glass & Mirror Works, 437 N. 63rd St., Philadelphia, PA 19151: Free information ❖ Antique mirrors and restoration of antique frames. 215–747–6866.

Custom Mirror Gallery, P.O. Box 508–702, Somersville, CT 06072: Catalog $1 ❖ Mirrors and wood moldings. 203–749–2281.

Shepard Eberly Decor, 5056 Forest Dr., Rome, OH 44085: Free information ❖ Wall plaques, mirrors, original ceramics, switch plates, and other decor accessories. 216–563–9849.

La Barge Mirrors, P.O. Box 1769, Holland, MI 49422: Catalog $6 ❖ Handcrafted mirrors with optional decorative complements.

Studio Steel, 159 New Milford Tnpk., New Preston, CT 06777: Catalog $2 ❖ Lamps, chandeliers, sconces, mirrors, and other handwrought metalwork. 800–800–5217; 203–868–7305 (in CT).

MODELS & MODEL BUILDING

Aircraft Models

Ace R/C, 116 W. 19th St., P.O. Box 472, Higginsville, MO 64037: Catalog $2 ❖ Radio controlled gliders. 816–584–7121.

Aerocraft, P.O. Box 553, East Northport, NY 11731: Free information ❖ Easy-to-assemble radio controlled and electric-powered. 516–754–6628.

Aeroloft Designs, 2940 W. Gregg Dr., Chandler, AZ 85224: Free information ❖ Ducted fan-jet airplane models and accessories. 602–838–0447.

Aerotech Inc., 1955 S. Palm St., Ste. 15, Las Vegas, NV 89104: Free information ❖ Rocket launched, radio controlled acrobatic glider. 702–641–2301.

The Airplane Factory Inc., 1880 Pineview, Mandeville, LA 70448: Free information ❖ Quick-building, radio controlled sport-flying airplanes. 800–264–7840.

Airtronics Inc., 11 Autry, Irvine, CA 92718: Free information ❖ Electric sailplane with folding propeller and removable plug-in wing tips. 714–830–8769.

Altech Marketing, P.O. Box 391, Edison, NJ 08818: Free information ❖ Ready-to-fly models. 908–248–8738.

American R/C, 16691 Gothard St., Unit V, Huntington Beach, CA 92647: Free information ❖ Radio controlled gliders. 714–841–4282.

America's Hobby Center Inc., 146 W. 22nd St., New York, NY 10011: Catalog $3 ❖ Model airplanes, radio control equipment, and tools. 212–675–8922.

Anderson Enterprises, 1625 S. Rock Rd., Ste. 129, Wichita, KS 67207: Free information ❖ Handcarved, solid mahogany aircraft models. 800–732–6875.

Aristo-Craft, Polk's Model Craft Hobbies, Inc., 346 Bergen Ave., Jersey City, NJ 07304: Catalog $2 ❖ Radio controlled models. 201–332–8100.

Astro Flight Inc., 13311 Beach Ave., Marina Del Ray, CA 90292: Free information ❖ Electric powered airplanes and engines. 310–821–6242.

Bolar Heli Research, 322 N. 7th St., Leighton, PA 18235: Free information ❖ Helicopter kits. 215–377–4941.

Bridi Aircraft, 23625 Pineforest Ln., Harbor City, CA 90710: Free information ❖ Radio controlled model airplane kits and gliders. 213–549–8264.

Bruckner Hobbies Inc., 2920 Bruckner Blvd., Bronx, NY 10465: Free information ❖ Airplane and automobile kits, radio control equipment, and building supplies.

Byron Originals Inc., P.O. Box 279, Ida Grove, IA 51445: Catalog $4 ❖ Easy-to-assemble model airplanes and jet engines. 712–364–3165.

Century Helicopter Products, 521 Sinclair Frontage Rd., Milpitas, CA 95035: Free information ❖ Radio controlled helicopters. 408–942–9525.

Century Import & Export Inc., 521 Sinclair Frontage Rd., Milpitas, CA 95053: Free information ❖ Helicopter kits. 408–942–9525.

Century Jet Models Inc., 8305 Regency Woods Way, Louisville, KY 40220: Free information ❖ Radio controlled model jet airplane kits. 502–491–4114.

Cermark Electronic & Model Supply, 107 Edward Ave., Fullerton, CA 92633: Free information ❖ Ready-to-fly radio controlled airplanes. 714–680–5888.

Chicago Model International, P.O. Box 170, Deerfield, IL 60015: Free information ❖ Ready-to-fly radio controlled model airplanes. 708–480–5700.

Cleveland Model & Supply Company, 9800 Detroit Ave., Cleveland, OH 44102: Catalog $2 ❖ Airplane models. 216–961–3600.

Combat Models Inc., 8535 Arjons Dr., Ste. R, San Diego, CA 92126: Free information ❖ Radio controlled gliders and almost ready-to-fly radio controlled model airplanes. 619–536–9922.

Coverite, 420 Babylon Rd., Horsham, PA 19044: Free information ❖ Radio controlled model airplane kits, building materials, and tools. 215–672–6720.

Cox Hobbies Inc., 350 W. Rincon St., Corona, CA 91720: Free information ❖ Radio controlled model airplanes and cars. 714–278–2551.

Daron Worldwide Trading Inc., 844 Willis Ave., Albertson, NY 11507: Free catalog ❖ Desktop military and civilian models. 800–776–2324.

Davey Systems Corporation, 675 Tower Ln., West Chester, PA 19380: Free information ❖ Airplane models with electric engines. 215–430–8645.

Discount Radio Control, 5643 W. Charleston, Las Vegas, NV 89102: Free information ❖ Model helicopter kits, radio control equipment, and engines. 702–870–9070.

Dynaflite, P.O. Box 1011, San Marcos, CA 92079: Free information ❖ Radio controlled

airplane models and sailplanes. 619–744–9605.

Easy Built Models, Box 425, Lockport, NY 14095: Free catalog with long SASE ❖ Easy-to-build airplane kits. 716–438–0545.

Evers Toy Store, 204 1st Ave. East, Dyersville, IA 52040: Free information with long SASE ❖ Airplane models and miniature die-cast automobiles. 800–962–9481.

Florio Flyer Corporation, P.O. Box 88, Dagus Mines, PA 15831: Free information ❖ Radio controlled airplane models. 814–885–8360.

G & P Sales, 410 College Ave., Angwin, CA 94508: Information $3 ❖ Radio controlled model airplane kits. 707–965–3866.

Global Hobby Distributors, 10725 Ellis Ave., Fountain Valley, CA 92728: Free information ❖ Radio controlled model airplane kits and gliders. 714–963–0133.

Hobby Barn, P.O. Box 17856, Tucson, AZ 85731: Free catalog ❖ Airplane and boat models. 602–747–3633.

Hobby Dynamics, 4105 Fieldstone Rd., Champaign, IL 61821: Free information ❖ Radio controlled model airplane kits, helicopters, electric powered gliders, and sailplanes. 217–355–0022.

Hobby Horn, 15173 Moran St., P.O. Box 2212, Westminster, CA 92684: Catalog $2 ❖ Electric and fuel-operated airplanes, sailplanes, and radio controlled models. 714–893–8311.

Hobby Lobby International Inc., 5614 Franklin Pike Cir., Brentwood, TN 37027: Catalog $2 ❖ Airplane models. 615–373–1444.

Hobby Shack, 18480 Bandilier Cir., Fountain Valley, CA 92728: Free catalog ❖ Radio control systems and ready-to assemble airplanes and automobiles. 800–854–8471.

Hobby Surplus Sales, P.O. Box 2170, New Britain, CT 06050: Catalog $3 ❖ Airplanes, cars, ships, model trains, radio control equipment, and other craft supplies. Discounts on new and close-out products. 203–223–0600.

Hobby World Ltd. of Montreal, 5450 Sherbrooke St. West, Montreal, Quebec, Canada H4A 1V9: Catalog $5 ❖ Airplanes, helicopters, cars and trucks, ships, military vehicles, and science models. 514–481–5434.

Bob Holman Plans, P.O. Box 741, San Bernardino, CA 92402: Catalog $5 ❖ Radio controlled model airplane kits. 714–885–3959.

Ikon N'wst, P.O. Box 306, Post Falls, ID 83854: Catalog $4 ❖ Giant scale and radio controlled model airplane kits. 208–773–9001.

Indoor Model Supply, Box 5311, Salem, OR 97304: Catalog $2 ❖ Endurance rubber-powered models for indoors and building supplies.

Indy R/C Sales Inc., 10620 N. College Ave., Indianapolis, IN 46280: Free information ❖ Pre-assembled airplane kits. 800–338–4639.

Innovative Model Products Inc., P.O. Box 4365, Margate, FL 33063: Free information ❖ Scale radio controlled airplane model kits. 305–971–8330.

International Hobby Corporation, 413 E. Allegheny Ave., Philadelphia, PA 19134: Catalog $4.98 ❖ Battery powered tools, model airplanes, railroading accessories, and military miniatures. 800–875–1600.

J & K Products, 306 Golden Ave., Long Beach, CA 90806: Free price list ❖ Large-scale models in kits or pre-built. 310–426–8085.

J'Tec, 164 School St., Daly City, CA 94014: Free catalog with long SASE ❖ Model engine mounts, mufflers, engine test stands, and power sticks. 415–756–3400.

K & B Manufacturing Inc., 2100 College Dr., Lake Havasu City, AZ 86403: Free information ❖ Airplane and marine engines.

Kress Jets Inc., 500 Ulster Landing Rd., Saugerties, NY 12477: Free information ❖ Jet engine airplane models. 914–336–8149.

L & R Aircraft Ltd., 13645 Fisher Rd., Burton, OH 44021: Free information ❖ High-performance sport and acrobatic airplanes. 216–834–1578.

Lanier RC, P.O. Box 458, Oakwood, GA 30566: Free catalog with long SASE ❖ Radio controlled model airplane kits, almost ready-to-fly models, and gliders. 404–532–6401.

Leading Edge Models, 170 Oval Dr., Central Islip, NY 11722: Free information ❖ Airplane model kits. 516–234–7264.

Bob Martin R/C Models, 1520–C Acoma Ln., Lake Havasu City, AZ 86403: Free information ❖ Radio controlled gliders. 602–855–6900.

Matney's Models, 11325 Harold Dr., Luna Pier, MI 48157: Free information ❖ Kits for building gliders and radio controlled and other aircraft models. 313–848–8195.

Jim Messer's Model Products, Valley View Dr., Box 43, Allegheny, NY 14706: Free information ❖ Scale radio controlled airplane model kits. 716–372–8408.

Micro Models, Box 1063, Lorain, OH 44055: Catalog $2 ❖ Big flying scale, semi-scale, contest-sport, and outdoor peanut scale kits. 216–282–8354.

Midwest Products Company Inc., 400 S. Indiana St., P.O. Box 564, Hobart, IN 46342: Free information ❖ Giant scale model airplanes. 219–942–1134.

Minimax Enterprise, P.O. Box 2374, Chelan Falls, WA 98816: Free information ❖ Radio controlled gliders. 509–683–1288.

Model Expo Inc., P.O. Box 1000, Industrial Park Dr., Mt. Pocono, PA 18344: Free catalog ❖ Airplane models, tools, automobile and boat kits, and trains. 800–222–3876.

Walt Moucha Models, P.O. Box 112, Menominee, MI 49858: Free information ❖ Radio controlled model airplane kits. 906–863–1225.

MRC Models, 200 Carter Dr., Edison, NJ 08817: Free information ❖ Ready-to-fly airplanes. 908–248–0400.

Pacific Aircraft, 14255 N. 79th St., Scottsdale Airpark, AZ 85260: Free catalog ❖ Handcarved and painted solid mahogany model airplanes. 800–950–9944.

Paul's Flying Stuff, P.O. Box 121, Escondido, CA 92025: Free information ❖ Radio controlled model jet airplanes. 619–743–5458.

Peck-Polymers, Box 710399, Santee, CA 92072: Catalog $4 ❖ Rubber-powered flying model kits and plans. 619–448–1818.

Pica Enterprises, 2657 NE 188th St., Miami, FL 33180: Free information ❖ Radio controlled model airplane kits. 305–935–1436.

Pierce Aero Company, 9626 Jellico Ave., Northridge, CA 91325: Free information ❖ Radio controlled sailplanes. 818–349–4758.

Pirate Models, 13915 Hirschfield, Unit B, Tomball, TX 77375: Free information ❖ Giant scale, jig-built, ready-to-assemble kits. 713–255–8827.

Polk's Model-Craft Hobbies, 346 Bergen Ave., Jersey City, NJ 07304: Catalog $2 ❖ Tools, radio control equipment, building supplies, and airplane, car, and boat models. 201–332–8100.

Proctor Enterprises, 25450 NE Eilers Rd., Aurora, OR 97002: Catalog $4 ❖ Radio controlled model airplane kits and hardware. 503–678–1300.

R.C. Buyers Warehouse, 99 Pines St., Box 646, Nashua, NH 03060: Free information ❖ Helicopter models, parts and supplies, engines, radio control systems, and tools. 603–595–2494.

Robbe Model Sport, 170 Township Line Rd., Belle Mead, NJ 08052: Catalog $5 ❖ Radio controlled model airplane kits, almost ready-to-fly models, gliders, helicopters, and electrical supplies. 908–359–2115.

Royal Products Corporation, 790 W. Tennessee Ave., Denver, CO 80223: Free information ❖ Radio controlled model airplane kits, jet airplane kits, gliders, and electric-powered sailplanes.

Showcase Model Company, P.O. Box 470, State College, PA 16804: Free catalog ❖ Handcrafted aviation display models. 814–238–8571.

SIG Manufacturing Company Inc., 401 S. Front St., Montezuma, IA 50171: Catalog $3 ❖ Radio controlled, control line, and rubber-powered model planes. 515–623–5154.

Square Roundhouse, 1468 Lander, Turlock, CA 95381: Free information with long SASE ❖ Model planes, radio controlled cars, and Lionel trains. 209–668–4454.

Standard Hobby Supply, P.O. Box 801, Mahwah, NJ 07430: Catalog $2 ❖ Ready-to-fly airplanes, off-road buggies and cars, racing cars, and parts. 201–825–2211.

C.B. Tatone Inc., 21658 Cloud Way, Hayward, CA 94545: Free information ❖ Aluminum motor mounts for two- and four-cycle engines and engine mounts. 510–783–4868.

Technopower II Inc., 610 North St., Chagrin Falls, OH 44022: Catalog $3 ❖ Radial-style gas engines. 216–564–9787.

Tower Hobbies, P.O. Box 9078, Champaign, IL 61826: Catalog $3 ❖ Model airplanes, cars, boats, radio control equipment, engines, and building supplies. 800–637–6050.

Vailly Aviation, 18 Oakdale Ave., Farmingville, NY 11738: Catalog $1 ❖ Radio controlled model airplane kits. 516–732–4715.

Vortex R/C Helicopter, 1374 Logan Ave., Costa Mesa, CA 92626: Free information ❖ Radio controlled helicopters. 714–751–6212.

Wing Manufacturing, 306 E. Simmons, Galesburg, IL 61401: Free information ❖ Radio controlled model airplane kits, and building materials. 309–342–3009.

World Hobby Warehouse, 513 Tamarack, Broken Arrow, OK 74012: Catalog $1 ❖ Out-of-production aircraft plastic model kits.

Automobile Models

Accent Models Inc., 26 Diamond Spring Rd., Denville, NJ 07834: Catalog $2 ❖ Collectible car models. 201–625–0997.

Alexandre's Autos, 13020 SW 80th Ave., Miami, FL 33156: Free information ❖ Die cast model cars. 800–779–0576.

America's Hobby Center Inc., 146 W. 22nd St., New York, NY 10011: Catalog $3 ❖ Car model kits. 212–675–8922.

Asheville Diecast, 1446 Patton Ave., Asheville, NC 28806: Free information ❖ Diecast model cars and trucks. 800–343–4685.

Auto Motif Inc., 2968 Atlanta Rd., Smyrna, GA 30080: Catalog $3 ❖ Car models, gifts and collectibles with an automotive theme, books, prints, puzzles, office accessories, lamps, original art, and posters. 800–367–1161.

Auto Toys, P.O. Box 81385, Bakersfield, CA 93380: Free price list with long SASE ❖ Diecast and other scale car models. 805–588–CARS.

Auto World Model Shoppe, 10 Green Ridge St., Scranton, PA 18509: Catalog $5 ❖ Model cars, trucks, slot racing models, radio controlled cars, scratch building supplies, and decals. 717–344–7258.

Autofanatics Ltd., P.O. Box 55158, Sherman Oaks, CA 91413: List $2 ❖ Scale model automobiles in kits or assembled. 818–788–5440.

Automobiles in Scale, 6822 Foxborough Ct., Yorba Linda, CA 92686: Catalog $5 (refundable with $25 order) ❖ Domestic and imported automobile kits, books, super detail products, and wheel and tire kits. 714–970–8328.

Automobilia, 44 Glendale Rd., Park Ridge, NJ 07656: Catalog $3 ❖ Working steam-powered models and cars, trucks, fire engines, and military vehicles. 201–573–0173.

Bruckner Hobbies Inc., 2920 Bruckner Blvd., Bronx, NY 10465: Free information ❖ Automobile and airplane kits, radio control equipment, and building supplies.

Cars & Parts Collectibles, 911 Vandemark Rd., P.O. Box 482, Sidney, OH 45365: Free information ❖ Precision scale car models. 800–448–3611; 800–327–1259 (in OH).

Cox Hobbies Inc., 350 W. Rincon St., Corona, CA 91720: Free information ❖ Radio controlled model airplanes and cars. 714–278–2551.

Crawley Distributing, 4012 Benchmark Trail, Springhill, FL 34609: Free information ❖ Slot cars and accessories. 904–799–4139.

D & R Enterprises, 2013 71st St., Wauwatrosa, WI 53213: Free information with long SASE ❖ Metal and resin kits of British cars.

Dahm's Automobiles, P.O. Box 360, Cotati, CA 94931: Catalog $2 ❖ Racing bodies for radio controlled cars and trucks. 707–792–1316.

DieCast Connection, 411 N. Wahsatch Ave., Ste. 1193D, Colorado Springs, CO 80903: Catalog $5 ❖ Classic and current car models.

Eastwood Automobilia, 580 Lancaster Ave., P.O. Box 3014, Malvern, PA 19355: Free catalog ❖ Transportation collectibles. 800–345–1178.

Edgewood Engineering, 24313 Ox Bow Lane North, Sonora, CA 95370: Catalog $2 ❖ Die cast, resin, plastic kits, and built-up scale race car models. 209–586–2819.

Evers Toy Store, 204 1st Ave. East, Dyersville, IA 52040: Free information with long SASE ❖ Model cars and airplanes. 800–962–9481.

EWA & Miniature Cars USA, 39 Springfield Ave., Berkeley Heights, NJ 07922: Free catalog ❖ Die-cast models, metal and plastic kits, and other model cars. 908–665–7811.

Exoticar Model Company, 2A New York Ave., Framingham, MA 01701: Free catalog ❖ Diecast model cars. 800–348–9159.

High Speed Miniatures, P.O. Box 1011, Taylor, MI 48180: Free list with long SASE ❖ American racing car kits.

Hobby Heaven, P.O. Box 3229, Grand Rapids, MI 49501: Free catalog with long SASE and two 1st class stamps ❖ Ready-to-build model automobiles, from the 1950s, 1960s, and 1970s. 616–453–1094.

Hobby House Inc., 8208 Merriman Rd., Westland, MI 48185: Free information ❖ Model cars and supplies. 313–425–9720.

Hobby Shack, 18480 Bandilier Cir., Fountain Valley, CA 92728: Free catalog ❖ Radio control equipment and ready-to assemble airplanes and automobiles. 800–854–8471.

Hobby Surplus Sales, P.O. Box 2170, New Britain, CT 06050: Catalog $2 ❖ Planes, cars, ships, model trains, radio controlled models, and other craft supplies. 203–223–0600.

Hobby Warehouse of Sacramento, 8950 Osage Ave., Sacramento, CA 95828: Free information ❖ Radio control automobiles and kits. 800–333–3640.

Long Island Train & Hobby Center, 192 Jericho Tnpk., Mineola, NY 11501: Price list $3 ❖ Car models. 516–742–5621.

Merkel Model Car Company, P.O. Box 689, Franklin Park, IL 60131: Catalog $2.95 each (specify type of car model) ❖ Collectible and current car model kits, promotional and pre-assembled cars, die-cast and other models, and building supplies. 708–455–1495.

Mile High Mini Autos, 2002 Spring Dr., Rio Rancho, NM 87124: List $1 ❖ Metal scale models of modern and classic automobiles. 505–892–2124.

Miniatures of the World Inc., 104 May Dr., Harrison, OH 45030: Catalog $3 ❖ Trucks, motorcycles, fire trucks, farm and construction equipment, other collectibles, and race, performance, exotic, and sports cars. 513–367–1746.

MK Model Products, 7209 Balboa Blvd., Van Nuys, CA 91406: Free information ❖ Off-road and on-road car models, chargers, speed controls, and batteries. 800–446–6335; 818–787–5851 (in CA).

Model Car Collectables, 5743 S. Willowbrook Dr., Morrison, CO 80465: Free list with long SASE ❖ Die-cast model cars.

Model Empire, 7116 W. Greenfield Ave., West Allis, WI 53214: Catalog $3 (refundable with $20 order) ❖ Cars, trucks, figures, racers, space and military models, boats, airplanes, and diecast models. 414–453–4610.

Model Expo Inc., Industrial Park Dr., P.O. Box 1000, Mt. Pocono, PA 18344: Free catalog ❖ Detailed scaled models of legendary automobiles, in kits or assembled. 800–222–3876.

The Model Shop, W7982 County Z, Onalaska, WI 54650: Catalog $3 ❖ Model

cars, trucks, and hobby supplies.
608–781–1864.

Motorhead, 1300 SW Campus Dr., Federal Way, WA 98023: Catalog $4 ❖ Scale model cars and kits, art prints, and other collectibles. 800–859–0164.

Munchkin Motors, P.O. Box 266, Eastford, CT 06242: Catalog $3 ❖ Collectible miniature cars. 203–974–2545.

Oakridge Trains, 15800 New Ave., Lemont, IL 60439: Catalog $2 ❖ O-gauge train accessories and die-cast automotive vehicles. 708–257–0909.

Polk's Model-Craft Hobbies, 346 Bergen Ave., Jersey City, NJ 07304: Catalog $2 ❖ Tools, radio control equipment, and airplane, car, and boat models. 201–332–8100.

Sinclair's Auto Miniatures, P.O. Box 8403, Erie, PA 16505: Catalog $1 ❖ Die-cast and handcrafted miniature cars. 814–838–2274.

Merrill Smith Company, Miniature Motors Division, 12634 Angling Rd., Edinboro, PA 16412: Free brochure ❖ Die-cast scale automobiles. 814–734–5631.

Specialty Diecast Company, 370 Miller Rd., Medford, NJ 08055: Free information ❖ Die cast model cars. 800–432–1933.

Square Roundhouse, 1468 Lander, Turlock, CA 95381: Free information with long SASE ❖ Radio controlled cars, Lionel equipment and service, model planes, and rocket equipment. 209–668–4454.

Standard Hobby Supply, P.O. Box 801, Mahwah, NJ 07430: Catalog $2 ❖ Ready-to-fly airplanes, off-road buggies and cars, racing cars, and parts. 201–825–2211.

Stormer Racing, 23 High Speed Rd., P.O. Box 126, Glasgow, MT 59230: Free information ❖ Kits and parts for radio controlled automobiles. 800–255–7223.

Tower Hobbies, P.O. Box 9078, Champaign, IL 61826: Catalog $3 ❖ Model airplanes, cars, boats, radio control equipment, engines, and building supplies. 800–637–6050.

Valley Plaza Hobbies, 2211 Mouton Dr., Carson City, NV 89706: Catalog $6.50 ❖ Miniature car models. 702–887–1131.

Walt's Hobby, 2 Dwight Park Dr., Syracuse, NY 13209: Free information ❖ Radio control equipment and kits. 315–453–2291.

Paper Airplanes

International Paper Airplane Company, P.O. Box 061179, Palm Bay, FL 32906: Free information ❖ Paper airplanes.

Radio Control Equipment

Ace R/C, 116 W. 19th St., Box 472, Higginsville, MO 64037: Catalog $2 ❖ Radio controlled model airplane equipment. 816–584–7121.

Aerocell, 407 Commerce Way, Jupiter, FL 33458: Free information ❖ Flight pack batteries and charger. 407–575–0422.

America's Hobby Center Inc., 146 W. 22nd St., New York, NY 10011: Catalog $3 ❖ Model airplanes, radio control equipment, and tools. 212–675–8922.

B & P Associates, P.O. Box 22054, Waco, TX 76702: Free information ❖ Starter batteries. 817–662–5587.

Bruckner Hobbies Inc., 2920 Bruckner Blvd., Bronx, NY 10465: Free information ❖ Airplane and automobile kits, radio control equipment, and building supplies.

Cannon Electronics, 2828 Cochran St., Ste. 281, Simi Valley, CA 93065: Free information ❖ Radio control systems. 805–581–5061.

Condor R/C Specialties, 1733–G Monrovia Ave., Costa Mesa, CA 92627: Free information ❖ Radio control systems. 714–642–8020.

Custom Electronics, P.O. Box 1332, Alta Loma, CA 91701: Free information ❖ Radio control systems. 714–980–4244.

Discount Radio Control, 5643 W. Charleston, Las Vegas, NV 89102: Free information ❖ Model helicopter kits, radio control equipment, and engines. 702–870–9070.

Futaba Corporation of America, P.O. Box 19767, Irvine, CA 92713: Free information ❖ Radio control systems for cars, trucks, and buggies. 714–455–9888.

Hitec, 10729 Wheatlands Ave., Santee, CA 92071: Free information ❖ Radio control systems. 619–258–4940.

Hobby Shack, 18480 Bandilier Cir., Fountain Valley, CA 92708: Free catalog ❖ Radio control equipment. 800–854–8471.

Horizon Hobby Distributors, 3102 Clark Rd., Champaign, IL 61821: Free information ❖ Radio control systems.

McDaniel R.C. Inc., 1654 Crofton Blvd., Crofton, MD 2114: Free information ❖ Radio control systems. 301–721–6303.

SR Batteries Inc., Box 287, Bellport, NY 11713: Information $3 ❖ Batteries. 516–286–0079.

Walt's Hobby, 2 Dwight Park Dr., Syracuse, NY 13209: Free information ❖ Radio control kits and parts for cars. 315–453–2291.

Rocket Models

Aerotech Inc., 1955 S. Palm St., Ste. 15, Las Vegas, NV 89104: Free information ❖ Rocket launched, radio controlled acrobatic glider. 702–641–2301.

Belleville Wholesale Hobby, 1827 N. Charles St., Bellville, IL 62221: Free information with long SASE ❖ Rocket kits and parts. 618–234–5989.

California Consumer Aeronautics, 7420 Clairemont Mesa Blvd., San Diego, CA 92111: Catalog $2 ❖ Rocket components. 619–581–1546.

Cortriss Technology, 3653 Slopeview Dr., San Jose, CA 95148: Catalog $2 ❖ Kits, parts, and custom accessories.

Countdown Hobbies, 3 P.T. Barnum Square, Bethel, CT 06801: Catalog $2.50 ❖ Rocket and spaceflight equipment. 203–790–9010.

Custom Model Rockets, P.O. Box 2086, Augusta, ME 04338: Free catalog ❖ Model rocket kits. 800–394–4114; 207–623–4114 (in ME).

Dynamic Composites Inc., P.O. Box 85, Boston, PA 15135: Catalog $1 ❖ Rocket kits and components. 412–751–9515.

Estes Industries, 1295 H St., Penrose, CO 81240: Free catalog ❖ Model rocket kits, engines, supplies, and radio control equipment. 719–372–6565.

High Sierra Rocketry, P.O. Box 343, Orem, UT 84059: Catalog $2 ❖ Rocket kits, hardware, and accessories. 801–224–2276.

Hobby Hangar, 153 Lloyd Ave., Florence, KY 41042: Catalog $2 ❖ Parts, plans, radio control equipment, engines, and airplane and helicopter kits. 606–283–5746.

Impulse Aerospace, 22833 Bothell Way SE, Ste. 1148, Bothell, WA 98021: Catalog $2 ❖ Ignition systems. 800–568–2785.

Loc/Precision Inc., P.O. Box 221, Macedonia, OH 44056: Catalog $3 ❖ Rocket kits and components. 216–467–4514.

Magnum Industries, P.O. Box 124, Mechanicsburg, OH 43044: Catalog $2 ❖ Rocket kits and accessories. 513–834–3306.

Merrell Scientific/World of Science, 1665 Buffalo Rd., Rochester, NY 14624: Catalog $2 ❖ Rockets, engines, and igniters. Other items include chemicals, laboratory glassware, and equipment for biology, chemistry, physical and earth science, and astronomy experiments. 716–426–1540.

MRED Industries Inc., P.O. Box 126, Petersburg, NY 12138: Catalog $2 ❖ Rocket systems.

Orion Rocket Works, P.O. Box 232504, Leucadia, CA 92024: Catalog $2 ❖ Rockets and accessories.

Prodyne Inc., P.O. Box 12806, Ogden, UT 84412: Catalog $1 ❖ Rocket equipment and supplies.

Public Missiles Ltd., 38300 Long, Mt. Clemens, MI 48045: Catalog $3 ❖ Rocket kits and accessories. 313–468–3521.

Robby's Rockets, P.O. Box 171, Elkhart, IN 46515: Catalog $3 ❖ Flashbulb igniters, thermalite and supplies, and ejection charges. 219–679–4143.

Rocket R & D, 308 E. Elm St., Urbana, IL 61801: Catalog $1 ❖ Rocket equipment and supplies. 217–344–2449.

Square Roundhouse, 1468 Lander, Turlock, CA 95381: Free information with long SASE ❖ Rocket equipment, radio controlled cars, Lionel train equipment, and model planes. 209–668–4454.

Teleflite Corporation, 11620 Kitching St., Moreno Valley, CA 92387: Catalog $2 ❖ Rocket engine equipment and how-to information.

Tiffany Hobbies of Ypsilanti, P.O. Box 467, Ypsilanti, MI 48197: Free information ❖ Rocket model kits. 800–232–3626.

TNK Aerospace, 2734 Crooks Rd., Royal Oak, MI 48073: Catalog $1 ❖ Rocket equipment and supplies.

Thrust Aerospace, 405 Tarrytown Rd., Unit 203, White Plains, NY 10607: Catalog $1.50 ❖ Model rocket components.

Vaughn Brothers Rocketry, 4575 Ross Dr., Paso Robles, CA 93446: Catalog $1 ❖ Rocket kits and accessories. 805–239–3818.

Ship Models

Alpha USA Inc., 55 Leveroni Ct., Novato, CA 94949: Catalog $3 ❖ Model hover-craft

kits, sailboats, and other models. 800–685–8290.

America's Hobby Center Inc., 146 W. 22nd St., New York, NY 10011: Catalog $3 ❖ Ship building kits. 212–675–8922.

Bluejacket Ship Crafters, P.O. Box 425, Stockton Springs, ME 04981: Catalog $2 (refundable) ❖ Kits, fittings, supplies, and tools. 800–448–5567; 800–834–7608 (in ME).

DPI Leisure Sports, 15500 Wood-Red Rd. NE, Woodinville, WA 98072: Free information and list of retailers ❖ Easy-to-assemble high-performance boats. 206–481–2456.

The Dromedary, Ship Modeler's Center, 6324 Belton Dr., El Paso, TX 79912: Catalog $6 ❖ Books, tools, rigging and fittings, kits, wood, and other boat-building supplies. 915–584–2445.

Dumas Boats, 909 E. 17th St., Tucson, AZ 85719: Free catalog ❖ Radio controlled boat models. 602–623–3742.

A.J. Fisher Inc., 1002 Etowah Ave., Royal Oak, MI 48067: Catalog $3 ❖ Scale brass ship and yacht model fittings. 313–541–0352.

The Floating Drydock, c/o General Delivery, Kresgeville, PA 1833: Catalog $4 ❖ Plans, books, fittings, and other boat-building supplies.

Hobby Barn, P.O. Box 17856, Tucson, AZ 85731: Free catalog ❖ Boat and airplane models. 602–747–3633.

Hobby House Inc., 8208 Merriman Rd., Westland, MI 48185: Free information ❖ Model boats, fittings and supplies, and tools. 313–425–9720.

Hobby Surplus Sales, P.O. Box 2170, New Britain, CT 06050: Catalog $2 ❖ Planes, cars, ships, model trains, and radio controlled models. 203–223–0600.

Hobby World Ltd. of Montreal, 5450 Sherbrooke St. West, Montreal, Quebec, Canada H4A 1V9: Catalog $5 ❖ Airplanes, helicopters, cars and trucks, ships, military vehicles, and science models. 514–481–5434.

International Marine Exchange, 37 Addington Dr., Feasterville, PA 19053: Catalog $4 ❖ Model ships, fittings, and other equipment. 215–322–4773.

K & B Manufacturing Inc., 2100 College Dr., Lake Havasu City, AZ 86403: Free information ❖ Airplane and marine engines.

Laughing Whale, 174 Front St., Bath, ME 04530: Catalog $2 ❖ Kits for classic wood ships. 800–722–0945; 207–443–5732 (in ME).

Model Boats Unlimited, P.O. Box 1135, Haddonfield, NJ 08033: Catalog $11 ❖ Radio control and other boats, electric and sail accessories, fittings, and other supplies. 609–783–9163.

Model Expo Inc., Industrial Park Dr., P.O. Box 1000, Mt. Pocono, PA 18344: Free catalog ❖ Boat kits, airplane models, automobile kits, trains, and tools. 800–222–3876.

Octura Models Inc., 7351 N. Hamlin Ave., Skokie, IL 60076: Free information with long SASE ❖ Radio controlled boats. 708–674–7351.

Polk's Model-Craft Hobbies, 346 Bergen Ave., Jersey City, NJ 07304: Catalog $2 ❖ Tools, radio control equipment, building supplies, and airplane, car, and boat models. 201–332–8100.

Prather Products Inc., 1660 Ravenna Ave., Wilmington, CA 90744: Catalog $2 ❖ High performance epoxy glass boats. 310–835–4764.

Preston's, Main Street Wharf, Greenport, NY 11944: Free catalog ❖ Ship models. 800–836–1165.

Robbe Model Sport Inc., 170 Township Line Rd., Belle Mead, NJ 08502: Catalog $5 ❖ Boats, airplanes, and cars. 908–359–2115.

Rocky Mountain Mini Sports, 6401 N. Broadway, Unit G, Denver, CO 80221: Catalog $3 ❖ Boat-building supplies. 303–426–0110.

The Scale Shipyard, 5866 Orange Ave., #3, Long Beach, CA 90805: Catalog $6 ❖ Fittings and fiberglass model ship hulls, including warships.

Seacraft Classics, 7850 E. Evans Rd., Ste. 109, Scottsdale, AZ 85260: Free information ❖ Handcarved, ready-to-display, detailed classic 19th-century model sailing ships and boats with hardwood display stands and brass name plates. 800–356–1987; 602–998–4988 (in AZ).

Ships N' Things, P.O. Box 605, Somerville, NJ 08876: Catalog $5 (refundable with $25 order) ❖ Competition boats and hardware. 908–722–0075.

Skunkworks Inc., Rt. 2, Box 81–A, Springfield, MO 65802: Video catalog $6 ❖ Radio control model warships. 417–831–2309.

Superboat Marine Products, 320 Convery Blvd., Perth Amboy, NJ 08861: Free information ❖ Powerboat parts. 908–826–6625.

Tower Hobbies, P.O. Box 9078, Champaign, IL 61826: Catalog $3 ❖ Model airplanes, cars, boats, radio control equipment, engines, and building supplies. 800–637–6050.

Trinity Products Inc., 1901 E. Linden Ave., Linden, NJ 07036: Free catalog with long SASE ❖ Electric motors and cooling units for model boats. 908–862–1705.

Victor Model Products, 12260 Woodruff Ave., Downey, CA 90241: Free brochure with long SASE ❖ Radio controlled sailing yachts. 310–803–1897.

Steam-Operated Models

Automobilia, 44 Glendale Rd., Park Ridge, NJ 07656: Catalog $3 ❖ Working steam-powered models and cars, trucks, fire engines, and military vehicles. 201–573–0173.

Diamond Enterprises, Box 537, Alexandria Bay, NY 13607: Catalog $6.95 (refundable) ❖ Kits or assembled live steam models. 613–475–1771.

Graham Industries, P.O. Box 15230, Rio Rancho, NM 87174: Free brochure ❖ Twin cylinder vertical reversing steam engine assembly kit.

Little Engines, 13486 Carapace Ct., Manassas, VA 22111: Catalog $7.50 ❖ Old-time and modern steam engines, accessories, and rolling stock. 703–791–5322.

M.T.H. Electric Trains, 9693 Gerwig Ln., Columbia, MD 21046: Free information ❖ Live steam ready-to-run trains and kits. 410–381–2580.

Tiny Power, Steam Engines & Supplies, P.O. Box 1605, Branson, MO 65615: Catalog $5 ❖ Steam engines and pumps. 417–334–2655.

Supplies, Hardware & Plans

Aerospace Composite Products, P.O. Box 16621, Irvine, CA 92714: Free information ❖ Carbon fiber strips. 714–250–1107.

Aerotrend Products, 31 Nichols St., Ansonia, CT 06401: Free information ❖ Radio controlled model airplane accessories and hardware. 203–734–0600.

Airdrome, P.O. Box 1425, FDR Station, New York, NY 10150: Rolled plans $4;

folded plans $2 ❖ Scale plans for radio controlled historic airplane models.

Balsa USA, P.O. Box 164, Marinette, WI 54143: Free information ❖ Balsa wood and tools. 800–BALSA-US.

Dave Brown Products, 4560 Layhigh Rd., Hamilton, OH 45013: Free information ❖ Radio controlled airplane equipment and building materials. 513–738–1576.

Bruckner Hobbies Inc., 2920 Bruckner Blvd., Bronx, NY 10465: Free information ❖ Airplane and automobile kits, radio control equipment, and building supplies.

Carstens Publications Inc., Fredon-Springdale Rd., Newton, NJ 07860: Free information ❖ Scale model aircraft plans. 201–383–3355.

Chrome-Tech U.S.A., 2914 Ravenswood Rd., Madison, WI 53711: Free brochure with long SASE ❖ Chrome plating for model cars. 608–274–9811.

Coverite, 420 Babylon Rd., Horsham, PA 19044: Free information ❖ Radio controlled model airplane kits, building materials, and tools. 215–672–6720.

Du-Bro Products, 480 Bonner Rd., Wauconda, IL 60084: Free information ❖ Hardware, tools, and building supplies. 312–526–2136.

Gallant Models Inc., 34249 Camino Capistrano, Capistrano Beach, CA 92624: Catalog $2 (refundable) ❖ Full-size model building plans.

Hobby Shack, 18480 Bandilier Cir., Fountain Valley, CA 92728: Free catalog ❖ Model-making supplies and tools. 800–854–8471.

K & S Engineering, 6917 W. 59th St., Chicago, IL 60638: Catalog $1 ❖ Aluminum and other metal tubes, rods, and sheets for model building. 312–586–8503.

Kress Jets Inc., 500 Ulster Landing Rd., Saugerties, NY 12477: Free information ❖ Scale model aircraft plans. 914–336–8149.

Eldon J. Lind Company, 3151 Caravelle Dr., Lake Havasu City, AZ 86403: Free catalog with long SASE ❖ Building jigs, sanders, and accessories. 602–453–7970.

Lone Star Models, 1623 57th St., Lubbock, TX 79412: Free information ❖ Balsa for model building. 806–745–6394.

Northeastern Scale Models Inc., P.O. Box 727, Methuen, MA 01844: Catalog $1 ❖

Basswood and supplies for model and doll house building. 508–688–6019.

Proctor Enterprises, 25450 NE Eilers Rd., Aurora, OR 97002: Catalog $4 ❖ Radio controlled model airplane kits and hardware. 503–678–1300.

Robart Manufacturing, P.O. Box 1247, St. Charles, IL 60174: Free catalog with long SASE ❖ Model airplane accessories and tools. 708–584–7616.

Robbe Model Sport, 170 Township Line Rd., Belle Mead, NJ 08052: Catalog $5 ❖ Radio controlled model airplane kits, almost ready-to-fly models, gliders, helicopters, and electrical supplies. 908–359–2115.

SIG Manufacturing Company Inc., 401 S. Front St., Montezuma, IA 50171: Catalog $3 ❖ Balsa for model building. 515–623–5154.

Sullivan Products, P.O. Box 5166, Baltimore, MD 21224: Free information ❖ Model airplane hardware.

Superior Aircraft Materials, 12020 Centralia, Hawaiian Gardens, CA 90716: Free catalog with long SASE ❖ Balsa, birch, plywood, and other building materials. 310–865–3220.

Tools

Badger Air-Brush Company, 9128 W. Belmont, Franklin Park, IL 60131: Brochure $1 ❖ Tools and supplies for building model airplanes. 312–678–3104.

Campbell Tools Company, 2100 Selma Rd., Springfield, OH 45505: Catalog $2 ❖ Lathes, mills, taps, dies, micrometers, cutting tools, miniature screws, and brass, aluminum, steel, and other supplies. 513–322–8562.

Coverite, 420 Babylon Rd., Horsham, PA 19044: Free information ❖ Radio controlled model airplane kits, building materials, and tools. 215–672–6720.

Dremel Manufacturing, 4915 21st St., Racine, WI 53406: Free information ❖ Power tools for modelers. 414–554–1390.

Du-Bro Products, 480 Bonner Rd., Wauconda, IL 60084: Free information ❖ Hardware, tools, and supplies for building model airplanes. 312–526–2136.

International Hobby Corporation, 413 E. Allegheny Ave., Philadelphia, PA 19134: Catalog $4.98 ❖ Battery powered tools, model airplanes, railroading accessories, and military miniatures. 800–875–1600.

K & S Engineering, 6917 W. 59th St., Chicago, IL 60638: Catalog $1 ❖ Precision tools. 312–586–8503.

Marc's Modelers Tools, 809 Sansom St., Philadelphia, PA 19107: Free catalog ❖ Precision tools. 215–925–4566.

Micro-Mark, 340 Snyder Ave., Berkeley Heights, NJ 07922: Catalog $1 ❖ Miniature and standard size tools. 908–464–6764.

Model Expo Inc., Industrial Park Dr., P.O. Box 1000, Mt. Pocono, PA 18: Free catalog ❖ Modeling tools, train sets, airplane and automobile kits, and wood and plastic ship models. 800–222–3876.

Polk's Model-Craft Hobbies, 346 Bergen Ave., Jersey City, NJ 07304: Catalog $2 ❖ Modeling tools and supplies, radio control equipment, and airplanes, cars, boats, and other craft models. 201–332–8100.

Robart Manufacturing, P.O. Box 1247, St. Charles, IL 60174: Free catalog with long SASE ❖ Model airplane accessories and tools. 708–584–7616.

Sherline Products Inc., 170 Navajo St., San Marcos, CA 92069: Free catalog ❖ Precision-made miniature power-operated tools. 800–541–0735; 619–744–3674 (in CA).

Train Models

All Aboard Train Shoppe, P.O. Box 451, Lincroft, NJ 07738: Free price list ❖ Original post-war Lionel trains. 800–54–TRAIN; 908–842–4744 (in NJ).

Allied Model Trains, 4411 S. Sepulveda Blvd., Culver City, CA 90230: Free catalog ❖ Lionel, American Flyer, LGB, Marklin, and brass rolling stock. 310–313–9353.

American Models, 10088 Colonial Industrial Dr., South Lyon, MI 48178: Free catalog with long SASE ❖ S-gauge trains.

America's Hobby Center Inc., 146 W. 22nd St., New York, NY 10011: Catalog $3 ❖ Kits and equipment for building train layouts. 212–675–8922.

Amro Ltd., 121 Lincolnway West, New Oxford, PA 17350: Free information ❖ Foreign railway models. 717–624–8920.

Aristo-Craft, Polk's Model Craft Hobbies Inc., 346 Bergen Ave., Jersey City, NJ 07304: Catalog $2 ❖ True-to-scale and true-to-life buildings, trestle sets, water towers, and bridges. 201–332–8100.

Arttista Accessories, 1616 S. Franklin St., Philadelphia, PA 19148: Free information

with long SASE ❖ O- and O27–gauge metal figures and accessories. 215–467–2493.

Bookbinder's Trains Unlimited, 84–20 Midland Pkwy., Jamaica, NY 11432: Catalog $5 ❖ Lionel standard and O-gauge trains. 718–657–2224.

Bragdon Enterprises, 2960 Garden Tower Ln., Georgetown, CA 95634: Free information with long SASE ❖ Trees and foliage materials for model train layouts.

Caboose Hobbies, 500 S. Broadway, Denver, CO 80209: Free information ❖ Z and G scale model trains and books. 303–777–6766.

Champion Decal Company, P.O. Box 1178, Minot, ND 58702: Catalog $5 ❖ HO and O scale decals. 701–852–4938.

Christmas Village Company, 4411 Sepulveda Blvd., Culver City, CA 90230: Free catalog ❖ Current and retired Department 56 Snow Village and Heritage buildings, accessories, and model trains. 800–433–7856.

Classic Model Trains, P.O. Box 179, Hartford, OH 44424: Price list $2 ❖ Paints for American Flyer, Ives, and Lionel trains. 216–772–5177.

Classic Models, P.O. Box 1032, Mountainside, NJ 07092: Free catalog with long SASE ❖ O scale building kits and parts for scenery layouts. 908–232–4246.

Collector's Corner Trains, 33 Palace Pl., Port Chester, NY 10573: Free information ❖ Pre- and postwar Lionel trains. 914–939–5511.

Curtis Hi-Rail Products Inc., P.O. Box 385, North Stonington, CT 06359: Free catalog ❖ Handcrafted 3–rail O-gauge switches, track, and other accessories. 800–277–RAIL.

Dallee Electronics, 10 Witmer Rd., Lancaster, PA 17602: Catalog $6.50 ❖ Electronic control equipment for model railroads. 717–392–1705.

Doug's Train World, c/o Valley Junction Train Station, 401 Railroad Pl., West Des Moines, IA 50265: Free price list ❖ Lionel and LGB trains, O-gauge straight and curved track, remote switches, and other accessories. 800–247–5096; 515–274–4424 (in IA).

Anthony F. Dudynski Supply Company, 2036 Story Ave., Bronx, NY 10473: Free information with long SASE ❖ Trains and scenic accessories. 718–863–9422.

Ellie's Lokie Shop, 135 W. Mahanoy Ave., Mahanoy City, PA 17948: Price list $3 ❖

Engines, other rolling stock, and accessories. 800–833–5611; 717–773–2174 (in PA).

Express Station Hobbies Inc., 640 Strander Blvd., Tukwila, WA 98188: Free information ❖ Rolling stock, books, and scenery for train layouts. 206–228–7750.

The Freight Yard, 945 N. Euclid St., Anaheim, CA 92801: Newsletter $1 (specify N or HO scale) ❖ N and HO scale trains. 714–956–1355.

GarGraves Trackage Corporation, RD 1, Box 255, North Rose, NY 14516: Free information ❖ Track for model railroad layouts. 315–483–6577.

Gene's Trains, 159 Primrose Ln., Brick, NJ 08724: Free list with long SASE ❖ Engines and sets. 908–840–9728.

Golden Spike International, 1700 Grand Concourse, Bronx, NY 10457: Catalog $2 ❖ Vintage train models. 212–294–1614.

Grand Central Ltd., 6929 Seward Ave., P.O. Box 29109, Lincoln, NE 68507: Free information with long SASE ❖ Lionel classics and new equipment, operating and layout accessories, and other large gauge items and rolling stock. 402–467–3668.

Hobby Surplus Sales, P.O. Box 2170, New Britain, CT 06050: Catalog $2 ❖ Tools, scenery, other hobby and craft supplies, and Lionel, American Flyer, and HO- and N-gauge accessories. 203–223–0600.

Hobbyland, 343 Lincolnway West, South Bend, IN 46601: Catalog $2 ❖ Trains and scenic accessories. 800–225–6509.

International Hobby Corporation, 413 E. Allegheny Ave., Philadelphia, PA 19134: Catalog $4.98 ❖ Trains and scenic accessories. 800–875–1600.

Island Trains, 4041 Hylan Blvd., Staten Island, NY 10306: Free information with long SASE ❖ Lionel trains. 718–317–0762.

K-Line Electric Trains Inc., P.O. Box 2831, Chapel Hill, NC 27515: Catalog $5 ❖ K-Line electric trains. 800–866–9986.

Leventon's Hobby Supply, P.O. Box 1525, Chehalis, WA 98532: Free train list with long SASE; parts catalog $2 ❖ HO-, S-, O-gauge, and standard gauge parts and rolling stock. 206–748–3643.

Longs Model Railroad Supply, 25070 Alessandro Blvd., Moreno Valley, CA 92553: Free information ❖ Trains and scenic accessories. 714–242–5060.

Donald B. Manlick, 2127 S. 11th St., Manitowoc, WI 54220: Free information with long SASE ❖ Decals for HO, N, O, and S scales.

Miami Valley Products Company, P.O. Box 144, Morrow, OH 45152: Free information with long SASE ❖ HO-, O-, and G-gauge bridge and trestle kits. 513–899–9904.

Mike's Train House, 9693 Gerwig Ln., Columbia, MD 21046: Catalog $2 ❖ Locomotives, cars, and Lionel, Williams rolling stock and accessories. 410–381–2580.

Mike's Trainland Inc., 5661 Shoulder's Hill Rd., Suffolk, VA 23435: Free price list ❖ Model trains and operating equipment. 800–955–4224.

Model Engineering Works, 12600 Frost Rd., Kansas City, MO 64138: Catalog $3.50 ❖ Standard gauge parts and decals.

Model Expo Inc., Industrial Park Dr., P.O. Box 1000, Mt. Pocono, PA 18344: Free catalog ❖ Tools, train sets, and ship, automobile, and airplane kits. 800–222–3876.

Model Railway Post Office, Box 426, Hewitt, NJ 07421: Free information with long SASE ❖ Trains and scenic accessories. 201–728–7595.

Model Rectifier Corporation, 200 Carter Dr., Edison, NJ 08817: Free information ❖ Power control units. 908–248–0400.

North Coast Miniature Motors, 3724 W. 32nd St., Erie, PA 16506: Free information ❖ Antique, classic, racing, promotional models, and other diecast and handbuilt miniature cars. 814–838–1921.

Oakridge Trains, 15800 New Ave., Lemont, IL 60439: Catalog $2 ❖ O-gauge accessories and die-cast automotive vehicles. 708–257–0909.

Owen Upp Railroader's Supply Company, 11300 W. Greenfield Ave., West Allis, WI 53214: Free list with 1st class stamp ❖ Lionel, K-Line and Williams equipment, Gargraves track, books, and videos. 414–771–2353.

P & P Lines, P.O. Box 102, Easton, CT 06612: Catalog $2 ❖ Scenic making supplies. 203–268–3243.

Red Caboose, 16 W. 45th St., 4th Floor, New York, NY 10036: Free information ❖ European scale, American Flyer, and Lionel trains, and other HO-, N-, and O-gauge equipment. 212–354–7349.

Charles Ro Supply Company, 662 Cross St., P.O. Box 100, Malden, MA 02148: Catalog 50¢ ❖ Lionel and LGB trains, HO rolling stock, and other equipment. 617–321–0090.

Roundhouse South, 146 E. International Speedway Blvd., Daytona Beach, FL 32118: Free information with long SASE ❖ Lionel, L.G.B., and Weaver trains. 904–238–7391.

Roundhouse Trains, 12804 Victory Blvd., North Hollywood, CA 91606: Free information with long SASE ❖ LGB, Lionel, American Flyer, Marklin, and HO- and N-gauge equipment. 818–769–0403.

Pat Russo Trains, 51 Vanderbilt Ave., Floral Park, NY 11001: Free information ❖ Trains and engines, other rolling stock and supplies, and track. 516–358–5548.

San Antonio Hobby Shop, 2550 W. El Camino, Mountain View, CA 94040: Free information ❖ Scratch building and brass supplies, books, and HO, N, O, Lionel, LGB, Z and other narrow gauge equipment. 415–941–1278.

Scenery Unlimited, 7236 W. Madison, Forest Park, IL 60130: Catalog $6.95 ❖ Locomotives and rolling stock, tools, and scenery supplies. 708–366–7763.

Charles Siegel's Train City, 3133 Zuck Rd., Erie, PA 16506: Price list $3 ❖ American Flyer, Lionel, MPC, Marx, and other trains. 814–833–8313.

Nicholas Smith Trains, 2343 W. Chester Pike, Broomall, PA 19008: Free information with long SASE ❖ Pola, LGB, and other equipment. 215–353–8585.

Square Roundhouse, 1468 Lander, Turlock, CA 95381: Free information with long SASE ❖ Lionel equipment and other equipment, model planes, rocket equipment, and radio controlled cars. 209–668–4454.

Standard Hobby Supply, P.O. Box 801, Mahwah, NJ 07430: Catalog $2 ❖ Model railroad equipment. 201–825–2211.

T-Reproductions, 227 W. Main St., Johnson City, TN 37603: Catalog $3 (refundable) ❖ Buddy "L" railroad reproductions. 615–926–4287.

Town & Country Hobbies & Crafts, 28 Dewey Ave., Totowa Boro, NJ 07512: Free list with long SASE ❖ Lionel accessories. 201–942–5176.

Toy Trains of Yesteryear, 775 Ravenhill Pl., Ridgefield, NJ 07657: Free information with long SASE ❖ Post- and prewar trains and accessories. 201–945–0223.

Train Express, 4365 W. 96th St., Indianapolis, IN 46268: Free information with long SASE ❖ Lionel train sets, American Flyer equipment, other rolling stock, operating cars and accessories, kits, and track. 800–428–6177.

Train 99, 333 Wilmington Westchester Pike, Glen Mills, PA 19342: Free information with long SASE ❖ Cars and engines, sets, and accessories by Lionel, American Flyer, Williams, and others. 215–TRAIN-99.

The Train Station, 12 Romaine Rd., P.O. Box 381, Mountain Lakes, NJ 07046: Free information ❖ Classic trains and accessories. 201–263–1979.

The Train Works, 251 Hurricane Shoals Rd., Lawrenceville, GA 30245: Free information with long SASE ❖ N- and HO-gauge, American Flyer, Lionel, and other trains. 800–964–8724; 404–339–7780 (in GA).

Train World, 751 McDonald Ave., Brooklyn, NY 11218: Free information ❖ Model railroad equipment. 718–436–7072.

Warren's Model Trains, 20520 Lorain Rd., Fairview Park, OH 44126: Price list $2 ❖ Lionel parts. 216–331–2900.

Watts' Train Shop, 9180 Hunt Club Rd., Zionsville, IN 46077: Free information ❖ Trains and scenic accessories. 800–542–7652.

Whistle Stop, 24900 E. Colorado Blvd., Pasadena, CA 91107: Free information with long SASE ❖ Rolling stock, kits, parts, detailing supplies, tools, building supplies, and brass imports. 818–796–7791.

Williams Electric Trains, 8835–F Columbia 100 Pkwy., Columbia, MD 21045: Free information ❖ Railroad classics, track, and other accessories. 410–997–7766.

Woodland Scenics, P.O. Box 98, Linn Creek, MO 65052: Catalog $1.25 ❖ Trees, turf, foliage, ballast, and scenery supplies. 314–346–5555.

World of Trains, 105–18 Metropolitan Ave., Forest Hills, NY 11375: Free information ❖ Trains and scenic accessories. 718–520–9700.

MOTORCYCLES & MOTOR BIKES

Clothing & Helmets

AGV-MDS, 5711 Industry Ln., Unit 38, Frederick, MD 21701: Catalog $3 ❖ Leather clothing. 800–950–9006.

Arai Helmets Ltd., P.O. Box 9485, Daytona, FL 32120: Brochure $3 ❖ Helmets. 800–766–ARAI.

Bates Leather Shop, P.O. Box 2668, Long Beach, CA 90801: Free catalog ❖ Leather clothing and accessories. 310–435–6551.

Bieffe USA Inc., 1746 Junction Ave., San Jose, CA 95112: Free information ❖ Helmets. 408–436–8098.

Chaparral, 544 S. Crescent Ave., San Bernardino, CA 92410: Free catalog ❖ Clothing, boots, goggles, and soft luggage. 800–841–2960.

Fieldsheer Clothing, 485 E. 17th St., Costa Mesa, CA 92627: Catalog $5 ❖ Leather clothing. 800–347–1010.

FirstGear Clothing, Intersport Fashions West, 333 S. Anita, Ste. 1025, Orange, CA 92668: Free information ❖ Hein Gericke clothing. 714–978–7718.

Langlitz Leathers, 2446 Southeast Division, Portland, OR 97202: Catalog $1 ❖ Leather clothing. 503–235–0959.

Lockhart-Phillips, 991 Calle Negocio St., San Clemente, CA 92672: Catalog $5 ❖ Leather jackets in small to extra-large. 800–821–7291.

Lost Worlds, Box 972, Linden Hill, NY 11354: Catalog $2 ❖ Air Force and Navy flight and motorcycle jackets. 212–923–3423.

Moto Race, P.O. Box 861, Wilbraham, MA 01095: Free information ❖ Boots, vests, gloves, other sportswear, motorcycle accessories, and tires. 800–628–4040.

Motoport USA, 7720 El Camino Real, Ste. 504, Rancho LaCosta, CA 92009: Free information ❖ Touring and biker clothing and accessories for men and women. 800–777–6499; 619–591–0568 (in CA).

Rider Wearhouse, 8 S. 18th Ave., Duluth, MN 55805: Free catalog ❖ Weatherproof motorcycle clothing. 800–222–1994.

Malcom Smith Products, 252 Granite St., Corona, CA 91719: Free information ❖ Motorcycle helmets. 800–854–4742; 909–340–3301 (in CA).

Specialty Sports Limited, 5905 Belding Rd. NE, Rockford, MI 49341: Free brochure ❖ Leather clothing, boots, and gloves. 616–874–5867.

StarCycle Motorcycle Accessories Inc., 7437 Van Nuys Blvd., Van Nuys, CA 91405: Catalog $2 ❖ Clothing, helmets, and parts. 818–782–7223.

Tour Master Riding Gear, 2360 Townsgate Rd., Westlake Village, CA 91361: Free catalog ❖ Sport gloves, Spandex fingerless gloves, knit and leather fingerless gloves, summer gloves, gauntlet gloves, tail and tank bags, clothing, rain suits, rain boots, and dry-knit socks. 800–421–7247; 805–373–6868 (in CA).

Vanson Leathers Inc., 213 Turnpike St., Stoughton, MA 02072: Catalog $8 ❖ Leather clothing. 617–344–5444.

Z Custom Leathers, 15902 Manufacture Ln., Huntington Beach, CA 92649: Free information ❖ Leather clothing. 714–890–5721.

Parts & Accessories

A-1 Used Cycle Parts Inc., 106 E. Arlington, St. Paul, MN 55117: Free information ❖ Honda, Suzuki, Yamaha, and Kawasaki used parts. 800–522–7891.

American Jawa Ltd., 185 Express St., Plainview, Long Island, NY 11803: Free brochure ❖ Motor-cycle side cars. 516–938–3210.

Antique Cycle Supply, Rt. 1, Cedar Springs, MI 49319: Catalog $5 ❖ Harley Davidson obsolete parts, tools, and literature for Flathead, Knucklehead, Panhead, and Shovelhead models. 616–636–8200.

Aritronix Ltd., 5653 Creek Rd., Cincinnati, OH 45242: Free information ❖ Easy-to-install bike alarms. 800–428–0440.

Axxel, 175 N. Branford Rd., Branford, CT 06405: Catalog $2 ❖ Motorcycle performance accessories. 203–481–5771.

Bartels' Performance Products, 3237 Carter Ave., Marina del Ray, CA 90292: Catalog $3 ❖ Harley-Davidson accessories. 310–578–9888.

Blue Moon Cycle, 20 Skin Alley, Norcross, GA 30071: Free catalog ❖ Sidecars and BMW parts. 404–447–6945.

Brickhouse Cycles, 7819 N. Military Hwy., Norfolk, VA 23518: Free information ❖ Used parts for late model Japanese bikes. 800–877–4804; 804–480–4800 (in VA).

California Side Car, 5641 Computer Ln., Huntington Beach, CA 92649: Free information ❖ Motorcycle side cars. 800–824–1523; 714–891–1033 (in CA).

Capital Cycle Corporation, P.O. Box 528, Sterling, VA 22170: Free catalog ❖ BMW parts. 703–444–2500.

Carl's Honda, 9920 Farragut Rd., Brooklyn, NY 11236: Free information ❖ Honda parts. 800–221–7508; 718–257–0602 (in NY).

Chaparral, 544 S. Crescent Ave., San Bernardino, CA 92410: Free catalog ❖ Clothing, boots, goggles, soft luggage, and Dunlop, Metzeler, Michelin, Continental, Bridgestone, Cheng Shin, and other tires. 800–841–2960.

Charleston Custom Cycle, 211 Washington, Charleston, IL 61920: Free information ❖ N.O.S. parts for Harley Davidson Lightweights, American, and other motorcycles, from 1948 to 1978. 217–345–2577.

Clinton Cycle & Used Cars Inc., 6709 Old Branch Ave., Camp Springs, MD 20748: Free price list ❖ Used parts for Honda, Kaw, Yam, and Suz 250 to 1300cc street bikes. 800–332–8264; 301–449–3550 (in MD).

Competition Accessories Inc., Rt. 68 North at Rt. 235, Xenia, OH 45385: Catalog $5 ❖ BMW, Moto Guzzi, Triumph, Yamaha, and Ducati accessories. 800–543–3535.

Competition Werkes, P.O. Box 5233, Rosebud, OR 97470: Free brochure ❖ Motorcycle parts. 800–736–2114.

Covr-Larm, 2554 Lincoln Blvd., Ste. 218, Marina Del Rey, CA 90291: Free information ❖ Security sensor system for vehicle protection. 310–821–7800.

Cycle Outlet, Rt. 3, Box 79, Cumberland, MD 21502: Free information ❖ Used parts and motorcycles. 301–724–6923.

Cycle Re-Cycle, 2117 E. 10th St., Indianapolis, IN 46201: Free information ❖ Used motorcycle parts. 317–634–6645.

Cycle Recyclers, 1538 Park Ave., Chico, CA 95928: Free information ❖ Used motorcycle parts. 800–356–4735.

D & M Sportbike, 2520 Cass St., Fort Wayne, IN 46808: Free information ❖ Used Honda, Yamaha, Kawasaki, and Suzuki parts. 219–483–6833.

Donelson Cycles Inc., 9851 St. Charles Rock Rd., St. Ann, MO 63074: Free information ❖ Clothing, helmets, boots, rain suits, saddlebags, and BMW, Triumph, Norton, and Yamaha parts. 800–325–4144.

East Coast Honda Warehouse, 687 Rt. 1, Edison, NJ 08817: Free information ❖ Honda motorcycles and parts. 800–544–4814.

East Coast Suzuki Warehouse, 687 Rt. 1, Edison, NJ 08817: Free information ❖ Suzuki and Honda motorcycles and parts. 800–544–4814.

Eastern Cycle Salvage Inc., 87 Park St., Beverly, MA 01915: Free information ❖ Used parts for most motorcycles. 617–922–3707.

Golden Triangle Cycle Salvage, 1625 College St., Beaumont, TX 77701: Free information ❖ Motorcycle parts. 409–838–4746.

Gustafson Plastics, P.O. Box 3567, St. Augustine, FL 32085: Free information ❖ Replacement and custom windscreens for cafe, racing, and touring fairings. 904–824–2119.

Honda Parts Warehouse, P.O. Box 1120, Freehold, NJ 07728: Free information ❖ Honda parts. 800–848–2609.

Honda-Suzuki of Greenville, 1918 N. Memorial Dr., Greenville, NC 27834: Free information ❖ Motorcycle parts. 800–888–3084.

Indian Joe Martin's Antique Motorcycle Parts, P.O. Box 3156, Chattanooga, TN 37404: Catalog $5 ❖ Indian and Harley parts. 615–698–1787.

Indian Motorcycle Supply Inc., 264 S. Main St., Sugar Grove, IL 60554: Free information ❖ New parts for Indian Chief, Four Sport Scout, Arrow, VT Scout, and Warrior motorcycles. 708–466–4601.

Kart World, 1488 Mentor Ave., Painesville, OH 44077: Catalog $3 ❖ Parts, engines, and accessories for mini-cars and bikes. 216–357–5569.

Kawasaki of Pittsburgh, 611 Butler St., Pittsburgh, PA 15223: Free information ❖ Kawasaki parts. 800–448–8611; 412–781–8611 (in PA).

Dennis Kirk, 955 Southfield Ave., Rush City, MN 55069: Free information ❖ Motorcycle tires and tubes, accessories, gloves, helmets, luggage racks, carryall bags, and boots. 800–328–9280.

Klempf's British Parts Warehouse, RR 1, Box 85, Dodge Center, MN 55927: Free

catalog ❖ Triumph, BSA, and Norton parts, from the 1960s to the present. 507–374–2222.

Laurel Highlands Accessories Plus, 84 University Dr., Lemont Furnace, PA 15456: Free information ❖ Motorcycle accessories and clothing. 800–332–0670; 412–437–0670 (in PA).

Lockhart-Phillips, 991 Calle Negocio St., San Clemente, CA 92672: Catalog $5 ❖ Motorcycle accessories and windscreens. 800–822–6005; 714–498–9090 (in CA).

M.A.P. Cycle Enterprises, 7165 30th Ave. North, St. Petersburg, FL 33710: Catalog $3 ❖ New, used, stock, and N.O.S. parts for BSA motorcycles. 813–381–1151.

Midwest Action Cycle, 1401 Elkhorn Rd., Lake Geneva, WI 53147: Free information ❖ Suzuki parts. 800–343–9065.

Mike's Cycle Parts, 3511 Boone Rd. SE, Salem, OR 97301: Free information ❖ Used Japanese motorcycle parts. 800–327–7304.

Moores Cycle Supply, 49 Custer St., West Hartford, CT 06110: Catalog $4 ❖ Triumph and BSA parts. 203–953–1689.

Moto Race, P.O. Box 861, Wilbraham, MA 01095: Free information ❖ Tires, brakes, accessories, and clothing. 800–628–4040.

Motorcycle Accessory Warehouse, 925 E. Fillmore St., Colorado Springs, CO 80907: Free information ❖ Tires, helmets, batteries, seats, saddlebags, and sportswear. 800–241–2222.

Motorcycle Salvage Company Inc., 3008 W. Mercury Blvd., Hampton, VA 23666: Free information ❖ Parts for Japanese motorcycles. 804–826–9010.

MR Motorcycle, 996 Patton Ave., Asheville, NC 28806: Free information ❖ Honda, Kawasaki, and Yamaha parts. 800–359–0567.

Performance Motorcycle Center, 8268 Miramar Rd., San Diego, CA 92126: Free information ❖ Motorcycle parts. 619–271–8364.

Rifle Fairings, 3140 El Camino Real, Atascadero, CA 93422: Free information ❖ Rifle windshields for all popular sport bikes. 800–262–1237.

RKA Accessories, Box 1006, Windsor, CA 95492: Free information ❖ Soft luggage for motorcycles. 707–579–5045.

Sam's Motorcycles, 605 Silver, Houston, TX 77007: Free information ❖ Used parts for most motorcycles. 713–862–4026.

David Sarafan Inc., P.O. Box 293, Spring Valley, NY 10977: Free information ❖ Reproduction and N.O.S. parts for Harley-Davidson motorcycles. 914–356–1080.

Satellite Parts Locating System, 3511 Boone Rd. SE, Salem, OR 97301: Free information ❖ New and used Japanese motorcycle parts. 800–327–7304.

Scooterworks USA, 7117 N. Clark St., Chicago, IL 60626: Free information ❖ Scooters and original parts. 312–338–4242.

L. Scot Enterprises, Box 1798, Sulsun City, CA 94585: Free brochure with long SASE ❖ Motorized scooters. 707–422–6755.

Sky Cycle Inc., Rt. 13, Lunenburg, MA 01462: Free information ❖ Used Honda, KAW, Suzuki, and Yamaha parts. 800–345–6115.

Spec II, 9812 Glen Oaks, Sun Valley, CA 91352: Catalog $3 ❖ High performance parts and fairings. 800–235–1236; 818–504–6364 (in CA).

StarCycle Motorcycle Accessories Inc., 7437 Van Nuys Blvd., Van Nuys, CA 91405: Catalog $2 ❖ Clothing, helmets, and parts. 818–782–7223.

Steve's Cycle, Rt. 5, Box 109, Tifton, GA 31794: Free information ❖ Used parts. 912–386–8666.

Storz Performance, 239 S. Olive St., Ventura, CA 93001: Catalog $4 ❖ Performance motorcycle accessories. 805–641–9540.

Superbike, 4140 Oceanside Blvd., Oceanside, CA 92056: Free information ❖ Motorcycle parts and tires. 800–536–8473.

Rich Suski, 7061 County Road 108, Town Creek, AL 35672: Free catalog ❖ Cushman parts for vintage motorbikes and scooters. 205–685–2510.

Suzuki Motorcycle Parts & Accessories, 687 Rt. 1, Edison, NJ 08817: Free information ❖ Suzuki parts. 800–544–4814.

Targa Accessories Inc., 21 Journey, Aliso Viejo, CA 92656: Catalog $5 ❖ Motorcycles and parts. 800–521–7845.

Techne Electronics Limited, 916 Commercial St., Palo Alto, CA 94303: Free brochure ❖ Ready-to-install remote controlled alarms. 800–227–8875.

Tracey's World of Cycles, Ohio River Blvd., Pittsburgh, PA 15202: Free information ❖ Yamaha parts. 800–860–0686.

Tri-City Kawasaki, 1410 Tilghman St., Allentown, PA 18102: Free information ❖ Kawasaki parts. 215–434–7111.

Vance & Hines Motorcycle Center, 14010 Marquardt Ave., Santa Fe Springs, CA 90670: Catalog $3 ❖ Performance accessories. 310–921–7461.

White Brothers, 24845 Corbit Pl., Yorba Linda, CA 92687: Catalog $4 ❖ Performance accessories for all makes of motorcycles. 714–692–3404.

Wolf Cycles, 5413 East Dr., Baltimore, MD 21227: Free information ❖ New and used Amal and Lucas parts. 410–247–7420.

MOUNTAIN & ICE CLIMBING

Adventure 16 Inc., 4620 Alvarado Canyon Rd., San Diego, CA 92120: Free information ❖ Clothing, packs, ropes, and other equipment. 800–854–2672; 800–854–0222 (in CA).

Climb High Inc., 1861 Shelburne Rd., Shelburne, VT 05482: Free information ❖ Boots and clothing, carabiners, packs, ropes, packs, and other equipment. 802–985–5056.

Lowe Alpine, P.O. Box 1449, Broomfield, CO 80038: Free information ❖ Mountain climbing boots and clothing, packs, ropes, and other equipment. 303–465–0522.

Misty Mountain Threadworks, Rt. 4, Box 73, Banner Elk, NC 28604: Free information ❖ Harnesses. 704–963–6688.

Mountain Gear, 2002 N. Division, Spokane, WA 99207: Free information ❖ Mountaineering equipment, clothing, and shoes and boots. 800–829–2009.

Mountain Safety Research, P.O. Box 24547, Seattle, WA 98124: Free information ❖ Mountaineering equipment. 800–877–9MSR.

Mountain Tools, 140 Calle Del Oaks, Monterey, CA 93940: Free information ❖ Equipment and soft goods for mountain and ice climbing. 408–393–1000.

Outdoor Sports Headquarters Inc., 967 Watertower Ln., Dayton, OH 45449: Free information ❖ Mountain climbing boots and clothing, ropes, and other equipment. 515–865–5855.

PMI, P.O. Box 803, LaFayette, GA 30728: Free catalog ❖ Belay devices, harnesses, and other equipment. 800–282–7673.

Ragged Mountain Equipment, Box 130,, Rt. 16–302, Intervale, NH 03845: Free price list ❖ Mountaineering equipment, clothing, and shoes and boots. 603–356–3042.

Ramer Products Ltd., 1803 S. Foothills Hwy., Boulder, CO 80303: Free catalog ❖ Back country ski equipment and clothing, tents, sleeping bags, frame packs, videos, rock and ice climbing gear, caving and winter survival equipment, and books. 303–499–4466.

Swallow's Nest, 2308 6th Ave., Seattle, WA 98121: Free catalog ❖ Backpacking, climbing, and mountaineering equipment. 800–676–4041; 206–441–4100 (in WA).

Tents & Trails, 21 Park Pl., New York, NY 10007: Free information ❖ Camping and mountaineering equipment and clothing. 800–237–1760; 212–227–1760 (in NY).

MOVIE & THEATRICAL MEMORABILIA

American Arts & Graphics Inc., P.O. Box 888, Mukilteo, WA 98275: Catalog $1 ❖ Fun posters for kids; all-star pinup, sports, art, and photo posters; and humorous, animal, art, photo, and scenic calendars. 800–524–3900.

Archival Photography, 14845 Anne St., Allen Park, MI 48101: Free catalog ❖ Classic movie poster and lobby card reproductions. 313–388–5452.

Artrock Posters, 1153 Mission St., San Francisco, CA 94103: Catalog $3 ❖ Original concert posters, T-shirts, books, and other memorabilia.

Authentic Cinema Collectibles, 7726 Girard St., LaJolla, CA 92037: Free information ❖ Autographs, posters, lobby cards, and other collectibles. 619–551–9886.

Barbara's Stars, P.O. Box 723, Smethport, PA 16749: Free catalog with two 1st class stamps ❖ Movie photos. 814–887–5110.

Best Rockart Gallery, 2801 Leavenworth St., San Francisco, CA 94133: Free information ❖ Collectible comics, original rock art and posters, toys, and handbills. 800–775–1966.

Big Screen Collectibles, 753 Woodside Rd., Maitland, FL 32751: Catalog $2 (refundable) ❖ Posters, lobby cards, stills, and photos.

Book City Collectibles, 6631 Hollywood Blvd., Hollywood, CA 90028: Free information ❖ Movie press kits, scripts, photographs, magazines and programs, cinema bios, and books on films. 800–4–Cinema; 213–466–0120 (in CA).

Captain Bijou, P.O. Box 87, Toney, AL 35773: Catalog $4 ❖ Original movie posters, from 1930 to the present. 205–852–0198.

Cinema City, Box 1012, Muskegon, MI 49443: Catalog $3 ❖ Movie posters, photos, autographs, and scripts. 616–722–7760.

Cinema Graphics, P.O. Box 16177, Denver, CO 80216: Catalog $3 ❖ Original movie posters and lobby cards, from 1918 to the 1980s. 303–292–6691.

Cinema Memories, P.O. Box 4517, Key West, FL 33041: Free information with long SASE ❖ Stills, movie posters, and lobby cards. 305–292–0038.

Cinemonde, 1932 Polk St., San Francisco, CA 94109: Free information ❖ Rare movie posters, lobby cards, and books. 415–776–9988.

Dwight Cleveland, P.O. Box 10922, Chicago, IL 60614: Free information ❖ Lobby cards, one-sheets, window cards, glass slides, motion picture heralds, exhibitor's books, and studio annuals. 312–266–9152.

The Collector's Marketplace, 18627 Brookhurst St., Ste. 315, Fountain Valley, CA 92708: Catalog $5 ❖ Posters, promotionals, Disneyana, and other collectibles.

Collectors Warehouse Inc., 5437 Pearl Rd., Cleveland, OH 44129: Catalog $2 ❖ Rare movie posters. 216–842–2896.

Deja Vu Enterprises Inc., 1110 Westwood Blvd., Los Angeles, CA 90024: Free information with long SASE ❖ Original posters from silent movies to the present, lobby cards, and autographed photos. 800–666–9886.

Empire Publishing, Box 717, Madison, NC 27025: Catalog $3 ❖ Movie and TV portraits. 919–427–5850.

Entertainment Heroes, 550 Kinderkamack Rd., Oradell, NJ 07649: Free information ❖ Movie lobby cards. 201–262–8020.

Film Favorites, P.O. Box 133, Canton, OH 73724: Free information with long SASE ❖ Movie stills of hard-to-find scenes from the silents through the classics of the 1980s. 405–886–3358.

Filmart Galleries, P.O. Box 128, Old Bethpage, NY 11804: Free catalog ❖ Contemporary and vintage animation art. 516–935–8493.

Frankly Scarlet, 307 10th St., Augusta, GA 30901: Free catalog with four 1st class stamps

❖ Movie posters and other theatrical memorabilia.

Front Row Photos, Box 29218, Richmond, VA 23242: Catalog $2 ❖ Exclusive concert photos.

Gifted Images Gallery, P.O. Box 34, Baldwin, NY 11510: Free catalog ❖ Cels, drawings, backgrounds, and other animation art. 800–726–6708; 516–536–6886 (in NY).

Gone Hollywood, 172 Bella Vista Ave., Belvedere, CA 94920: Free information ❖ Vintage movie posters. 415–435–1929.

Granada Posters, P.O. Box 64980, Dallas, TX 75206: Free information ❖ Movie posters, lobby cards, black and white stills, and press books. 214–373–9468.

Jim's TV Collectibles, P.O. Box 4767, San Diego, CA 92164: Catalog $2 ❖ Television and theatrical collectibles, from the 1950s through 1990s.

John's Collectible Toys & Gifts, 57 Bay View Dr., Shrewsbury, MA 01545: Catalog $2 ❖ Character toys and other movie and TV collectibles. 508–797–0023.

Richard Kohl, 1848 N. Federal Hwy., Boynton Beach, FL 33435: Free information ❖ Vintage movie posters. 800–344–9103.

La Belle Epoque, 11661 San Vincente Blvd., Ste. 211, Los Angeles, CA 90024: List $4 ❖ Rare posters. 310–442–0054.

Larry's Book Store, 1219 W. Devon Ave., Chicago, IL 60660: Catalog $1 ❖ Movie books and magazines. 312–274–1832.

Last Moving Picture Company, 2044 Euclid Ave., Cleveland, OH 44115: Free information with long SASE ❖ Window cards, lobby cards, inserts, one-sheets, stills, and posters. 216–781–1821.

Werner H. Lehmann, Euro Posters, 531 Clayton St., Denver, CO 80206: Catalog $1 ❖ European movie posters.

The LeMay Company, P.O. Box 480879, Los Angeles, CA 90048: Catalog $1 ❖ Movie posters. 213–933–4465.

Alan Levine Movie & Book Collectibles, P.O. Box 1577, Bloomfield, NJ 07003: Catalog $5 ❖ Movie magazines from 1915 to 1970, movie posters, lobby cards, and celebrity autographs. 201–743–5288.

Rick Lipp, 427 Broadway, Jackson, CA 95642: Free information with long SASE ❖ Stills, lobby sets, inserts, and press kits. 209–296–4754.

Metropolis, 7 W. 18th St., New York, NY 10011: Free information ❖ Vintage comic books and movie posters. 800–229–6387; 212–627–9691 (in NY).

Moe's Movie Madness, 3526 N. Main, P.O. Box 246, Tomsbrook, VA 22660: Free information ❖ Movie posters and memorabilia. 800–382–2501; 703–436–9181 (in VA).

Movie Poster Place Inc., P.O. Box 128, Lansdowne, PA 19050: Catalog $1 (refundable) ❖ Movie posters, stills, press books, and trailers. 610–622–6062.

Movie Star News, 134 W. 18th St., New York, NY 10011: Brochure $5 ❖ Movie photos and posters.

Odyssey Auctions Inc., 510–A S. Corona Mall, Corona, CA 91719: Catalog $20 ❖ Autographed letters, manuscripts, photographs, and documents, from the arts and sciences to politics and entertainment, and other movie memorabilia. 800–395–1359.

Jerry Ohlinger's Movie Material Store Inc., 242 W. 14th St., New York, NY 10011: Free catalog ❖ Stills, movie posters, star photos, magazines, and books. 212–989–0869.

Old Weird Herald's Nostalgia, 2016 NE 65th, Portland, OR 97213: Free information ❖ Movie posters, lobby cards, and other movie, TV, and cartoon memorabilia. 503–287–6779.

One Shubert Alley, 346 W. 44th St., New York, NY 10036: Free information ❖ T-shirts, posters, mugs, jewelry from old and new Broadway shows, and other theatrical memorabilia. 800–223–1320; 212–586–7610 (in NY).

Paper Chase, 2056 Weems Rd., Tucker, GA 30084: Free information ❖ Movie posters, used videos, baseball cards, and comics. 800–433–0025; 404–270–1239 (in GA).

Paper Collectors' Mart, 134 Main St., Suncook, NH 03275: Free information with long SASE ❖ Lobby cards, posters, movie magazines, books, paperbacks, and other memorabilia. 603–485–5856.

Tom Peper, 32 Shelter Cove Lane, #109, Hilton Head Island, SC 29928: Price list $1 ❖ Autographs, lobby cards and posters, animation art and cels, and original comic art. 800–628–7497.

Poster Emporium, P.O. Box 1503, Lee's Summit, MO 64063: Free information ❖ Original movie posters. 816–525–9888.

Posteritati, Sam Sarowitz, 23 E. 10th St., New York, NY 10003: Free information ❖ Vintage movie posters and lobby cards. 212–477–2499.

Reel Memories, 3236 N. Rock Rd., Ste. 150, Wichita, KS 67226: Free information with long SASE ❖ Posters. 316–636–5340.

Rick's Movie Posters, P.O. Box 23709, Gainesville, FL 32602: Catalog $3 ❖ Foreign scripts and original movie posters, from the 1950s through the 1980s. 904–373–7202.

Rogofsky Movie Collectibles, Box 107, Glen Oaks, NY 11004: Catalog $3 ❖ TV and movie magazines, photos, and other collectibles. 718–723–0954 (after 6 pm).

S & P Parker's Movie Market, P.O. Box 1868, Laguna Beach, CA 92652: Free information ❖ Color and black/white movie and TV star photos. 714–376–0326.

Salzer's, 5801 Valentine Rd., Ventura, CA 93003: Free information ❖ Vintage concert posters.

Noel Dean Schiff, 6975 N. Sheridan, Chicago, IL 60626: Free information ❖ Vintage movie posters and lobby cards. 312–262–6011.

Philip Sears Disney Collectibles, 1457 Avon Terr., Los Angeles, CA 90026: Free catalog ❖ Walt Disney autographs, animation art, and other memorabilia. 213–666–3740.

Sport Collectibles, P.O. Box 11171, Chattanooga, TN 37401: Information $1.50 ❖ Posters, lobby cards, and photographs, from the 1970s and 1980s.

Starland Collector's Gallery, P.O. Box 622, Los Olivos, CA 93441: Catalog $2.50 ❖ Sports cards, movie posters, comic art, and hard-to-find movies. 805–686–5122.

Murray A. Summers, 10670 Cliff Mills Dr., Marshall, VA 22115: Catalog $3 (refundable) ❖ Movie posters, and other memorabilia, and scarce movie magazines, from the 1920s to the 1970s.

Jim Szakacs, 55 Maitland St., Apt. 610, Toronto, Ontario, Canada M4Y 1C8: Catalog $3 ❖ Movie memorabilia and miscellaneous paper collectibles.

Theater Poster Exchange, P.O. Box 752302, Memphis, TN 38175: Catalog $3 ❖ Movie posters. 901–795–6383.

Toy Scouts Inc., 137 Casterton Ave., Akron, OH 44303: Catalog $3 ❖ Movie posters, Disney collectibles, and other movie memorabilia. 216–836–0668.

Triton Theatre Posters, 323 W. 45th St., New York, NY 10036: Catalog 50¢ ❖ Current and rare theatrical posters. 800–626–6674; 212–765–2472 (in NY).

Vintage Film Posters, 15925 Van Aken Blvd., Shaker Heights, OH 44120: Free information with long SASE ❖ Vintage posters and other theatrical memorabilia. 216–751–4500.

S. Wallach, 335 Lesmill Rd., Don Mills, Ontario, Canada M3B 2V1: Catalog $2 ❖ Movie posters, lobbies, stills, and trailers. 416–391–0438.

Wex Rex Records & Collectibles, P.O. Box 702, Hudson, MA 01749: Catalog $3 ❖ Movie and theatrical memorabilia, movie and TV show character toys, and other collectibles. 508–229–2662.

Yesterday, 1143 W. Addison St., Chicago, IL 60613: Free information with long SASE ❖ Original stills, lobbies, posters, pressbooks, magazines, and newspapers. 312–248–8087.

MOVIE & TV SCRIPTS

Book City of Burbank, 308 N. San Fernando, Burbank, CA 91502: Catalog $2.50 ❖ Movie and TV scripts. 818–848–4417.

Cinema City, Box 1012, Muskegon, MI 49443: Catalog $3 ❖ Movie scripts, posters, photos, and autographs. 616–722–7760.

Rick's Movie Posters, P.O. Box 23709, Gainesville, FL 32601: Catalog $3 ❖ Foreign scripts and movie posters from the 1950s through the 1980s. 904–373–7202.

Script City, 8033 Sunset Blvd., Hollywood, CA 90046: Free catalog ❖ Movie scripts, TV scripts, film and media books, photos, and posters. 213–871–0707.

MOVIE PROJECTION EQUIPMENT

James M. Hensley, 956 S. Jeff Davis Dr., Fayetteville, GA 30214: Free information ❖ Reconditioned movie projectors and used audio visual equipment. 404–461–0386.

International Cinema Equipment Company, 100 NE 39th St., Miami, FL 33137: Free information ❖ Audiovisual and cinema sound equipment, cameras, sound projectors, and film editing equipment. 305–573–7339.

MOVIES (FILMS)

Alternative Filmworks Inc., 259 Oakwood Ave., State College, PA 16803: Free catalog ❖ Independent and experimental films on video. 800–797–FILM.

Canyon Cinema, 2325 3rd St., Ste. 338, San Francisco, CA 94107: Catalog $15 ❖ Slides and documentary movies. 415–626–2255.

Classic Cinema, P.O. Box 18932, Encino, CA 91416: Catalog $5 ❖ Westerns, mysteries, comedies, and drama on video cassettes. 800–94–MOVIE.

Walt Disney Home Movies, 500 S. Buena Vista, Burbank, CA 91521: Free catalog ❖ Super 8mm movie films. 818–560–5151.

Excalibur Films, 3621 W. Commonwealth, Fullerton, CA 92633: Free catalog ❖ Movie reels and video cassettes. 800–BUY-MOVIES.

Festival Films, 6115 Chestnut Terrace, Shorewood, MN 55331: Free information ❖ 16mm films. 612–470–2172.

Foothill Video, P.O. Box 547C, Tujunga, CA 91043: Free information ❖ Westerns, feature films, serials, and foreign classics on video cassettes. 818–353–8591.

Home Film Festival, P.O. Box 2032, Scranton, PA 18501: Catalog $5 ❖ Hard-to-find films on video cassettes. 800–258–3456.

Laughing House, P.O. Box 8572, Anaheim, CA 92812: Catalog $9 (refundable) ❖ British TV and movie films.

MLR Films International Inc., 301 E. 62nd St., New York, NY 10021: Catalog $5 ❖ Public domain feature films, TV shows, and cartoons. 212–759–1729.

Movies Unlimited, 6736 Castor Ave., Philadelphia, PA 19149: Catalog $7.95 ❖ Silent classics up to the newest releases. 800–523–0823; 215–722–8298 (in PA).

National Cinema Service, P.O. Box 43, Ho-Ho-Kus, NJ 07423: Free list ❖ New and used 16mm full-length features, shorts, and cartoons. 201–445–0776.

National Gallery of Art, Extension Program, Washington, DC 20565: Free catalog ❖ Lends art appreciation films to individuals, schools, and community groups. 202–646–6466.

Pyramid Film & Video, P.O. Box 1048, Santa Monica, CA 90406: Free information ❖ Educational and entertainment films and videos. 800–421–2304.

Richard Semowich, 56 John Smith Rd., Binghamton, NY 13901: Free information ❖ 16mm films. 607–648–4025.

SharpeCo Distributors, P.O. Box 522, Kodak, TN 37764: Free catalog ❖ Westerns, comedies, mysteries, adventure, and other TV shows. 615–933–9387.

Sinister Cinema, P.O. Box 4369, Medford, OR 97501: Free information ❖ Science fiction, horror, mystery, suspense, fantasy, and other films on VHS and beta video cassettes. 503–773–6860.

Starland Collector's Gallery, P.O. Box 622, Los Olivos, CA 93441: Catalog $2.50 ❖ Sports cards, movie posters, comic art, and hard-to-find movies. 805–686–5122.

Hal Stayman, 1000 Savage Ct., Ste. 201, Longwood, FL 32750: List $1 ❖ Hard-to-find VHS movies from the 1940s. 407–331–3004.

Thornhill Entertainment, 2143 Statesville Blvd., Ste. 168, Salisbury, NC 28144: Free information ❖ 16mm films. 704–636–1116.

Video Specialists International, 182 Jackson St., Dallas, PA 18612: Catalog $3 ❖ Lost, rare, and hard-to-find movies, from 1903 to the 1970s. 717–675–0227.

Vintage Video, P.O. Box 53, Leeds Point, NJ 08220: Free information ❖ Saturday matinee and Golden Age of Hollywood movies. 609–748–0368.

MUSIC BOOKS & SHEET MUSIC

Augsburg Fortress Publishers, 426 S. 5th St., Box 1209, Minneapolis, MN 55440: Free catalog ❖ Books, curriculum materials, music, gifts, audiovisuals, and ecclesiastical arts items. 800–328–4648; 612–330–3300 (in MN).

Boston Music Company, 172 Tremont St., Boston, MA 02116: Free catalog ❖ Sheet music. 617–426–5100.

Chinaberry Book Service, 2830 Via Orange Way, Ste. B, Spring Valley, CA 92078: Free catalog ❖ Books and music for children and adults. 800–776–2242.

Empire Publishing Service, P.O. Box 1344, Studio City, CA 91614: Catalog $1 ❖ Entertainment industry and performing art books, other books, plays and musicals, and musical scores. 818–784–8918.

Fun Publishing Company, 2121 Alpine Pl., Cincinnati, OH 45206: Free information ❖ Teach-yourself books for the portable keyboard, piano, and xylophone. 513–533–3636.

Hollywood Sheet Music, Beverly A. Hamer, Box 75, East Derry, NH 03041: Free information with long SASE ❖ Collectible movie sheet music. 603–432–3528.

Patti Music Company, 414 State St., Madison, WI 53703: Free catalog ❖ Music books, sheet music, metronomes, and other teaching aids. 608–257–8829.

Player Piano Company, 704 E. Douglas, Wichita, KS 67202: Free catalog ❖ Player piano music rolls and restoration supplies. 316–263–3241.

Shar Products Company, P.O. Box 1411, Ann Arbor, MI 48106: Free catalog ❖ Music for violins, violas, and cellos. 800–248–7427; 313–665–7711 (in MI).

Willis Music Company, 7380 Industrial Rd., Florence, KY 41042: Free catalog ❖ Sheet music. 606–283–2250.

World Around Songs Inc., 20 Colberts Creek Rd., Burnsville, NC 28714: Free catalog ❖ American and international folk, country, party, and religious music song books. 704–675–5343.

MUSIC BOXES

Klockit, P.O. Box 636, Lake Geneva, WI 53147: Free catalog ❖ Clock-building parts, music box kits, and Swiss music box movements in 144–, 72–, 50–, 36–, and 18–notes. 800–556–2548.

Music Box World, P.O. Box 7577, Rego Park, NY 11374: Catalog $2 ❖ Music boxes and movements. 718–626–8153.

Richter's Music Boxes, 900 N. Point, San Francisco, CA 94109: Free catalog ❖ Music boxes from around the world. 415–441–2663.

San Francisco Music Box Company, Mail Order Dept., P.O. Box 7817, San Francisco, CA 94120: Free catalog ❖ Reproduction antique and other music boxes. 800–227–2190.

Shaker Shops West, 5 Inverness Way, Inverness, CA 94937: Catalog $3 ❖ Reproduction Shaker music boxes and other country crafts. 415–669–7256.

Smocking Bonnet, P.O. Box 555, Cooksville, MD 21723: Catalog $3 ❖ Music box movements. 800–524–1678.

Unicorn Studios, Box 370, Seymour, TN 37865: Catalog $1 ❖ Windup and electronic music box movements, winking light units,

and voice boxes for talking dolls and bears. 615–984–0145.

West Coast Music Box Company, 3924 Camphor Ave., Newbury Park, CA 91320: Free information ❖ Electronic and other music boxes. 805–499–9336.

MUSICAL INSTRUMENTS

Accordion-O-Rama, 307 7th Ave., Ste. 2001, New York, NY 10007: Catalog $1 ❖ New and rebuilt accordions and concertinas. 212–675–9089.

Altenburg Piano House Inc., 1150 E. Jersey St., Elizabeth, NJ 07201: Free information with long SASE ❖ Organs and pianos. 800–526–6979; 908–351–2000 (in NJ).

American Guitar Center, 2446 Reedie Dr., Wheaton, MD 20902: Free catalog ❖ Used and new guitars, amplifiers, and other equipment. 301–946–3043.

American Musical Supply, 235 Franklin Ave., Ridgewood, NJ 07450: Free catalog ❖ Musical instruments. 800–458–4076.

Anyone Can Whistle, P.O. Box 4407, Kingston, NY 12401: Free catalog ❖ Musical instruments, music boxes, windchimes, whistles, and musical-sounding toys. 800–435–8863.

Aquarian Accessories, 1140 N. Tustin Ave., Anaheim, CA 92807: Free information ❖ Drumheads and accessories. 800–473–0231.

Sam Ash Music Corporation, 401 Old Country Rd., Carle Place, NY 11514: Free information with long SASE ❖ Musical instruments. 800–4–SAMASH; 516–333–8700 (in NY).

Atlanta Pro Percussion Inc., 2526 Spring Rd., Smyrna, GA 30080: Free information ❖ Drums, hardware, and accessories. 404–436–3786.

Bell Brass Guitars, 2901 N. Monroe, Spokane, WA 99205: Free information ❖ Resonator guitars. 509–448–7777.

Bill's Music House Inc., 733 Frederick Rd., Baltimore, MD 21228: Free catalog ❖ Used instruments. 410–788–8900.

R.E. Bruné, Luthier, 800 Greenwood St., Evanston, IL 60201: Free catalog ❖ Handmade harpsichords, lutes, and classical and baroque guitars. 708–864–7730.

Callaham Guitars, 114 Tudor Dr., Winchester, VA 22603: Free information ❖ Handmade reproduction guitars. 703–665–8045.

Capri Taurus Folk Music, P.O. Box 153, Felton, CA 95018: Catalog $3 ❖ Ethnic and folk musical instruments. 408–335–4478.

Carvin, 1155 Industrial Ave., Escondido, CA 92025: Free catalog ❖ Guitars, amplifiers, recording mixers, equalizers, crossovers, speakers, microphones, and other equipment. 800–854–2235.

Castiglione Accordion, 13300 E. 11 Mile, Ste. A, Warren, MI 48089: Catalog $5 ❖ New and used accordions and concertinas. 810–755–6050.

CMC Music Inc., 1385 Deerfield Rd., Highland Park, IL 60035: Free information with long SASE ❖ Pianos, synthesizers, and other instruments. 708–831–3252.

Cole Music Company, 70 W. Stockton, Sonora, CA 95370: Free list with long SASE ❖ Vintage guitars. 800–455–COLE.

Cowtown Guitars, 919 E. Dublin Granville Rd., Columbus, OH 43229: Free information ❖ Used and vintage guitars. 614–436–4442.

Discount Music Supply, 41 Vreeland Ave., Totowa, NJ 07512: Free catalog ❖ Guitars and electronic equipment. 201–942–9411.

Discount Reed Company, 24307 Magic Mountain Pkwy., Ste. 181, Valencia, CA 91355: Free catalog ❖ Reeds for clarinets, saxophones, bassoons, oboes, and other instruments. 800–428–5993.

Seymour W. Duncan Antiquity Pickups, 5427 Hollister Ave., Santa Barbara, CA 93111: Free information ❖ Handmade, vintage pickups for electric guitars and basses. 805–964–9610.

Elderly Instruments, P.O. Box 14210, Lansing, MI 48901: Free catalog ❖ Musical instruments, strings, straps, pickups, records, and books. 517–372–7890.

Fitch Brothers Guitars, P.O. Box 469, Fresh Meadows, NY 11365: Free list with long SASE ❖ Vintage and rare guitars. 718–297–5123.

Folkcraft Instruments, Box 807, Winstead, CT 06098: Catalog $1 ❖ Mountain and hammered dulcimers, folk harps, psalteries, books, and recordings. 203–379–9857.

Fork's Drum Closet, 2707 12th Ave. South, Nashville, TN 37204: Free information ❖ New and used drums. 615–383–8343.

Freeport Music, 41 Shore Dr., Huntington Bay, NY 11743: Free catalog ❖ Musical instruments and electronics. 516–549–4108.

Fretted Instrument Workshop, 49 S. Pleasant St., Amherst, MA 01002: Free information ❖ Used musical instruments. 413–256–6217.

Fretware Guitars, 4523 N. Main, Dayton, OH 45405: Free information ❖ Used American-made fretted instruments. 513–275–7771.

Giardinelli Band Instrument Company Inc., 7845 Maltlage Dr., Liverpool, NY 13090: Free catalog ❖ Brass and woodwind instruments. 800–288–2334.

Gruhn Guitars Inc., 410 Broadway, Nashville, TN 37203: Free list ❖ Vintage, used, and new electric and acoustic guitars, banjos, mandolins, and violins. 615–256–2033.

Guitar Guitar, 14270 Ventura Blvd., Sherman Oaks, CA 91423: Free information ❖ Vintage guitars and keyboards. 818–789–1706.

Guitar Villa, John J. Slog, Customer Service, 5440 Monocacy Dr., Bethlehem, PA 18017: Free information ❖ Rare vintage instruments. 215–261–2919.

Guitarmaker's Connection, Martin Guitar Company, Box 329, Nazareth, PA 18064: Catalog $2 ❖ Guitar kits, parts, and exotic and domestic hardwoods. 800–247–6931.

Gulfcoast Guitars, 1820 Gulf Blvd., Englewood, FL 34223: Free list ❖ Vintage and rare guitars. 813–474–6179.

HQ Percussion Products, P.O. Box 430065, St. Louis, MO 63143: Free information ❖ Cymbals, hi-hats, drum set silencers, and other percussion accessories. 314–647–9009.

International Luthiers Supply, Box 580397, Tulsa, OK 74158: Catalog $1 ❖ Violin, banjo, and mandolin-making supplies and books.

International Musical Suppliers, P.O. Box 357, Mount Prospect, IL 60056: Free information ❖ Clarinets and saxophones. 800–762–1116.

International Violin Company, 4026 W. Belvedere Ave., Baltimore, MD 21215: Free catalog ❖ European violins and bows, strings, imported tone wood, tools, varnishes, and parts. 410–542–3535.

Interstate Music Supply, P.O. Box 315, New Berlin, WI 53151: Free catalog ❖ Musical instruments. 800–982–BAND.

Johnson Music Company, P.O. Box 615, Mt. Airy, NC 27030: Brochure $2 ❖ Antique pump organ parts. 919–320–2212.

Kennelly Keys Music Inc., 20505 Hwy. 99, Lynnwood, WA 98036: Free catalog ❖ Musical instruments.

Keyboard Outlet, 14235 Inwood, Dallas, TX 75244: Free information with long SASE ❖ New and used keyboards. 214–490–5397.

Claude Lakey Mouthpieces Inc., P.O. Box 2023, Redmond, WA 98073: Free information ❖ Handcrafted mouthpieces for woodwind players. 206–861–5920.

Latch Lake Music Products, 3115 Mike Collins Dr., St. Paul, MN 55121: Free information ❖ Guitar slides. 800–528–2437; 612–688–7502 (in MN).

Bernard E. Lehmann Stringed Instruments, 34 Elton St., Rochester, NY 14607: Free information ❖ Handmade and vintage guitars, basses, banjos, mandolins, and violins. 716–461–2117.

Victor Litz Music Center, 305 N. Frederick Ave., Gaithersburg, MD 20877: Free catalog ❖ Musical instruments. 301–948–7478.

Lone Star Percussion, 10611 Control Pl., Dallas, TX 75238: Free catalog ❖ Percussion instruments. 214–340–0835.

J.K. Lutherie Guitars, 11115 Sand Run, Harrison. OH 45030: Free catalog ❖ Vintage guitar parts, new and vintage accessories, catalogs and literature, guitar magazines, and out-of-print guitar books. 800–344–8880; 513–353–3320 (in OH).

Luthiers Mercantile, 412 Moore Ln., P.O. Box 774, Healdsburg, CA 95448: Catalog $10 ❖ Banjo and guitar kits. 707–433–1823.

Mandolin Brothers, 629 Forest Ave., Staten Island, NY 10310: Free catalog ❖ Electronic and acoustic mandolins, guitars, autoharps, and banjos. 718–981–3226.

Manny's Musical Instruments & Accessories Inc., 156 W. 48th St., New York, NY 10036: Catalog $2 ❖ Musical instruments.

Metropolitan Music Store, P.O. Box 1415, Stowe, VT 05672: Catalog $1.25 ❖ Violins, violas, cellos, luthier supplies, tools, and wood. 802–253–4814.

Michael's Music, 29 W. Sunrise Hwy., Freeport, NY 11520: Free information ❖ Used guitars. 516–379–4111.

Midwest Percussion, 5402 W. 95th St., Oak Lawn, IL 60453: Free catalog ❖ Drums and hardware. 708–499–0005.

Montans & Lace Vintage Musical Instruments, 15182 Bolsa Chica Rd., Huntington Beach, CA 92649: Free catalog ❖ Vintage guitars, mandolins, and ukuleles. 714–898–2453.

Music Maker Kits, P.O. Box 2117, Stillwater, MN 55082: Catalog $1 ❖ Build-them-yourself musical instrument kits.

Nadine's Music, 18136 Sherman Way, Reseda, CA 91335: Free information ❖ New and used keyboards, guitars, amplifiers, and recording equipment. 800–525–5149.

National Educational Music Company Ltd., P.O. Box 1130, Mountainside, NJ 07092: Free catalog ❖ Imported violins and violas, stands, cases, strings, bows, and brass, woodwind, and percussion instruments. 908–232–6700.

Player Piano Company, 704 E. Douglas, Wichita, KS 67202: Free catalog ❖ Player piano restoration supplies and music rolls. 316–263–3241.

Pro-Mark Corporation, 10707 Craighead Dr., Houston, TX 77025: Free information ❖ Drumsticks and other percussion accessories. 800–233–5250.

Ragtime, 4218 Jessup Rd., Ceres, CA 95307: Catalog $10 ❖ Calliopes, band organs, nickelodeons, player pianos, other Victorian musical instruments, and piano to player conversion kits. 209–668–9704.

Rayburn Musical Instrument Company, 283 Huntington Ave., Boston, MA 02115: Free information ❖ Mouthpieces, reeds, and used woodwind and brass instruments. 617–266–4727.

RIA Mouthpieces, P.O. Box 010359, Staten Island, NY 10301: Free information ❖ Saxophone and clarinet mouthpieces. 800–252–4RIA.

Robinson's Harp Shop, P.O. Box 161, Mt. Laguna, CA 92048: Free catalog ❖ Harp-making parts, plans, strings, hardware, and books. 619–473–8556.

Runyon Products Inc., P.O. Box 590, Lewisburg Rd., Opelousas, LA 70570: Free information ❖ Mouthpieces for soft playing and big band sounds. 800–843–4078.

St. Croix Kits, P.O. Box 2117, Stillwater, MN 55082: Catalog $1 ❖ Kits for harps, guitars, dulcimers, banjos, harpsichords, and bagpipes.

Joe Sax, 55 Roxbury Rd., Dumont, NJ 07628: Free information ❖ Saxophones, clarinets, and flutes. 800–876–8771; 201–384–0833 (in NJ and New York City).

The Saxophone Shop Ltd., 2834 Central St., Evanston, IL 60201: Free information ❖ New and used saxophones, reeds, and mouthpieces. 708–328–5711.

Shar Products Company, P.O. Box 1411, Ann Arbor, MI 48106: Free catalog ❖ Violins, violas, cellos, and music for string instruments. 800–248–7427; 313–665–7711 (in MI).

Stewart-MacDonalds Guitar Shop Supply, 21 N. Shafer St., P.O. Box 900, Athens, OH 45701: Free catalog ❖ Parts, tools, and supplies for building and repairing guitars, violins, banjos, dulcimers, and mandolins. 800–848–2273; 614–592–3021 (in OH).

Stringed Instrument Division, 123 W. Alder, Missoula, MT 59802: Free list with two 1st class stamps ❖ New and vintage banjos, mandolins, acoustic guitars, and electric instruments. 406–549–1502.

Gary Sugal Mouthpieces Inc., 99 South St., Providence, RI 02903: Free information ❖ Saxophone mouthpieces. 800–334–7299; 401–751–2501 (in RI).

Suncoast Music Distributors, P.O. Box 16965, St. Petersburg, FL 33733: Free catalog ❖ Musical instruments. 813–822–4949.

Synthony Music, 3939 E. Campbell, Phoenix, AZ 85018: Free information ❖ Electronic music instruments, midi peripherals, and other equipment. 800–221–KEYS; 602–955–3590 (in AZ).

Tama, P.O. Box 886, Bensalem, PA 19020: Catalog $3 ❖ Drums and accessories.

Thoroughbred Music, 2204 E. Hillsborough Ave., Tampa, FL 33610: Free information ❖ Keyboards, electronics, and drum machines. 800–800–4654.

Used Gear by Mail, Division Daddy's Junky Music Stores Inc., P.O. Box 1018, Salem, NH 03079: Free catalog ❖ Vintage, rare, and collectible used musical equipment. 603–894–6492.

Vintage Drum Center, Rt. 1, Box 129, Libertyville, IA 52567: Free catalog ❖ Vintage drum sets and singles. 800–729–3111; 515–693–3611 (in IA).

Waddell's Drum Center, 1104 S. Leechburg Hill, Leechburg, PA 15656: Free catalog ❖ Drums. 412–845–DRUM.

Weinkrantz Musical Supply Company, 870 Market St., Ste. 1265, San Francisco, CA 94102: Free catalog ❖ Violins, violas, and cellos. 415–399–1201.

West Manor Music, 831 E. Gun Hill Rd., Bronx, NY 10467: Free price list ❖ Brass, woodwind, string, and percussion instruments. 212–655–5400.

Wichita Band Instruments Company, 2525 E. Douglas, Wichita, KS 67211: Free information with long SASE ❖ Musical instruments. 800–835–3006.

Yamaha Music Corporation, Band & Orchestral Division, P.O. Box 899, Grand Rapids, MI 49512: Free information ❖ Electronic key boards.

Zeta Music, 2230 Livingston Ave., Oakland, CA 94606: Free information ❖ Electronic guitars, violins, and controllers. 800–622–6434.

NAMEPLATES

Country Punchin', 14757 Glenn Dr., Whittier, CA 90604: Brochure $1 ❖ Hand-punched tarnish-proof name signs and plaques in solid copper or pewter-like metal. 310–944–1038.

John Hinds & Company, 81 Greenridge Dr. West, Elmira, NY 14905: Free catalog ❖ Aluminum and bronze plaques and signs. 607–733–6712.

Landmark Brass, P.O. Box 150507, Van Brunt Station, Brooklyn, NY 11215: Brochure $1 ❖ Engraved brass architectural plaques. 718–499–0984.

Mr. Ed The Sign Man, P.O. Box 303, Crystal Beach, FL 34681: Free information ❖ Magnetic signs, name badges, and vinyl lettering.

Newman Brothers Inc., 5609 Center Hill Ave., Cincinnati, OH 45216: Free catalog ❖ Handcrafted cast bronze and aluminum plaques. 513–242–0011.

Smith-Cornell Inc., 1545 Holland Rd., Maumee, OH 43537: Free brochure ❖ Brass and aluminum historic markers. 800–325–0248; 419–891–4335 (in OH).

Taylor Graphics, P.O. Box 492, Greencastle, IN 46135: Free catalog ❖ Nameplates, award and recognition plaques, deskplates and doorplates, photo charm products, card cases, and luggage tags. 317–653–8481.

NEEDLE CRAFTS

A & L Designs, 201 E. Tabor Rd., Philadelphia, PA 19120: Price list $3 ❖ Religious designs for needlepoint and cross stitch. 215–329–7321.

Al Con Enterprises, P.O. Box 1060, Quincy, FL 32351: Free catalog ❖ Macrame, chair weaving, and crochet supplies. 800–523–4371; 904–627–6996 (in FL).

American Needlewomen, 2946 SE Loop 820, Fort Worth, TX 76140: Catalog $1 ❖ Needle crafts and supplies from Europe and the United States. 800–433–2231.

Annie's Attic, 106 W. Groves, Big Sandy, TX 75755: Catalog $2 ❖ Sewing and needle craft patterns. 903–636–4303.

Braid-Aid, 466 Washington St., Pembroke, MA 02359: Catalog $4 ❖ Braided rug kits and braiding accessories, wool by the pound or yard, and hooking, basket-making, shirret, spinning, and weaving supplies. 617–826–2560.

Cal Feather Pillow Products, P.O. Box 1117, Armona, CA 93202: Free price list ❖ Polyester pillow filler forms.

California Stitchery, 6015 Sunnyslope Ave., Van Nuys, CA 91401: Free catalog ❖ Judaic-design needlepoint, embroidery, and latch hook kits. 800–345–3332.

The Cotton Patch, 1025 Brown Ave., Lafayette, CA 94549: Catalog $5 ❖ Quilting books, fabric swatches, silk wire ribbon, hand-dyed fabrics, milliners needles, and other supplies. 800–835–4418.

Craft Gallery Ltd., P.O. Box 145, Swampscott, MA 01907: Catalog $2 ❖ Threads, fibers, books, fabrics, and accessories for stitchery, crochet, and other needle crafts. 508–744–2334.

Craft King Mail Order Dept., P.O. Box 90637, Lakeland, FL 33804: Catalog $2 ❖ Needle craft, art and craft, and macrame supplies. 813–648–0433.

Craft Resources Inc., P.O. Box 828, Fairfield, CT 06430: Catalog $1 ❖ Latch-hooking, needlepoint, crewel, cross-stitching kits, and supplies for string art, basket-making, metal and wood crafts, stained glass, and other crafts. 203–254–7702.

Crafts by Donna, P.O. Box 1456, Costa Mesa, CA 92626: Catalog $2 ❖ Threads, other craft supplies, and how-to books for Brazilian embroidery. 714–545–8567.

Creative Yarns, 9 Swan St., Asheville, NC 28803: Catalog $3.50 ❖ Knitting yarns, handpainted canvases, silks, metallics, ribbons, and other supplies. 704–274–7769.

The Cross Eyed Owl, 1552 Rhode Island Ave. North, Golden Valley, MN 55427: Catalog $2.50 ❖ Counted cross-stitch kits. 800–955–1843.

Curriculum Resources Inc., P.O. Box 828, Fairfield, CT 06430: Catalog $1 ❖ Needlepoint, crewel, latch hook, and other stitchery kits. 800–243–2874; 203–254–7702 (in CT).

Custom Needlework Designs Inc., P.O. Box 9, Oreland, PA 19075: Information $2 ❖ Needlecraft patterns and kits. 800–767–6313.

Enchanted Cottage, Brazilian Embroidery Studio, 112 E. Cheyenne Rd., Colorado Springs, CO 80906: Catalog $2 (refundable) ❖ Brazilian rayon threads, books, kits, and designs. 719–475–9244.

Garden Fairies Trading Company, 309 S. Main St., Sebastopol, CA 95472: Catalog $4 ❖ Handmade collar patterns, French and Battenberg lace, Swiss embroideries, smocking and soft toy patterns, books, and designer fabrics. 800–925–9919.

The Greene Needle, 21 Wyndham Rd., Scarsdale, NY 10583: Catalog $3 ❖ Needlepoint kits. 914–723–2920.

Martha Hall, 46 Main St., Yarmouth, ME 04096: Catalog $2 ❖ Easy-to-knit wool sweater kits and hand-dyed silk, mohair, linen, cotton, cashmere, and alpaca yarn. 207–846–9746.

Hedgehog Handworks, P.O. Box 45384, Westchester, CA 90045: Catalog $1 ❖ Semi-precious beads and attachments, sewing notions, gold and silver threads, needlecraft and embroidery supplies, and other accessories. 310–670–6040.

Herr's & Bernat, 70 Eastgate Dr., P.O. Box 630, Danville, IL 61834: Free information ❖ Latch hook kits.

Herrschners Inc., Hoover Rd., Stevens Point, WI 54492: Free catalog ❖ Needlecraft supplies, kits, and yarns. 800–441–0838.

Sue Hillis Designs, P.O. Box 2263, Petersburg, VA 23804: Free information ❖ Counted cross-stitch kits. 800–622–5353.

Homestead Needle Arts, 8036 Holly Rd., Grand Blanc, MI 48439: Catalog $3 (refundable) ❖ Threads, charts, handpainted canvases, books, and accessories. 800–365–1462.

Keepsake Quilting, P.O. Box 1459, Meredith, NH 03253: Free catalog ❖ Quilting books, patterns, notions, fabrics, and batting.

Carolin Lowy Needlecraft, 630 Sun Meadows Dr., Kernersville, NC 27284: Free information with long SASE ❖ Needlepoint, knitting, embroidery, and counted cross-stitch patterns. 910–784–7576.

Maggie's Inc., 1053 Carlisle St., Hanover, PA 17331: Catalog $3 ❖ Art and tole decorating, craft, and needlework supplies and books.

Marnie's Crewel Studio Inc., 6442 E. Otero Pl., Englewood, CO 80112: Free price list with long SASE ❖ Needlepoint kits and supplies.

Mary Maxim Inc., 2001 Holland Ave., P.O. Box 5019, Port Huron, MI 48061: Free catalog ❖ Needlecraft kits, yarn, and accessories. 800–962–9504.

Claire Murray Inc., P.O. Box 390, Ascutney, VT 05030: Catalog $5 (refundable) ❖ Hand-hooked rugs and kits. 800–252–4733.

My Friend & Eye Needlepoint, 6901 Warner Ave., Huntington Beach, CA 92647: Catalog $3 ❖ Needlepoint kits. 714–846–8182.

Nasco, 901 Janesville Ave., Fort Atkinson, WI 53538: Free catalog ❖ Weaving supplies, looms, tools, yarn, and other needlecraft accessories. 800–558–9595.

Needle Arts, 8036 Holly Rd., Grand Blanc, MI 48439: Catalog $3 (refundable) ❖ Threads, charts, handpainted canvases, books, and accessories. 800–365–1462.

The Needle Case, 833 21st St. SE, Cedar Rapids, IA 52403: Free catalog ❖ Fibers, canvases, and other supplies. 319–363–7851.

Needles to Say, 952 Jefferson St., Napa, CA 94559: Catalog $5 ❖ Needlepoint kits and supplies. 707–252–3009.

The Needlecraft Shop, 103 N. Pearl St., Big Sandy, TX 75755: Free catalog ❖ Plastic canvas supplies and patterns. 903–636–4000.

Needlework by Mail, P.O. Box 3766, Springfield, IL 62708: Manufacturer's catalog $3 (specify area of needlework interest) ❖ Needlecraft kits. 217–523–0400.

Pattern Warehouse, P.O. Box 3135, Chicago, IL 60654: Catalog $3 ❖ Cross-stitch and soft craft patterns. 312–828–9634.

Patterncrafts, Box 25639, Colorado Springs, CO 80936: Catalog $2 ❖ Quilt patterns and hoops, counted stitch and sewing projects, stencils, country crafts, wall hangings, needlecrafts, dolls, and stuffed animals. 719–574–2007.

Peacock Alley Needlepoint Crafts, 650 Croswell SE, Grand Rapids, MI 49506: Catalog $2 ❖ Needlecraft kits, supplies, and canvasses. 616–454–9898.

Shay Pendray's Needle Arts Inc., 2211 Monroe, Dearborn, MI 48124: Catalog $2 ❖ Japanese embroidery supplies. 313–278–6266.

Eva Rosenstand, P.O. Box 185, Clovis, CA 93613: Catalog $4.50 ❖ Embroidery supplies.

The Scarlet Letter, P.O. Box 397, Sullivan, WI 53178: Catalog $3 ❖ Museum reproduction counted thread sampler kits, handwoven linens and silks, sewing notions, books, and frames. 414–593–8470.

Shillcraft, 8899 Kelso Dr., Baltimore, MD 21221: Catalog $2 ❖ Needlecraft supplies and latch hook kits for rugs, wall hangings, and other crafts. 410–682–3060.

Sophisticated Stitchery, P.O. Box 263, Carteret, NJ 07008: Catalog $3 ❖ Fibers, designer charts, fabrics, handpainted canvases, and framing supplies. 908–969–0408.

Spinning Wheel, 217 Main St., Fordyce, AR 71742: Catalog $3 (refundable) ❖ Needlepoint, cross stitch, crewel, candle-wicking, and other needle crafts and supplies.

Stitches East, 55 E. 52nd St., New York, NY 10022: Free information ❖ Knitting and other needle craft supplies. 212–421–0112.

Things Japanese, 9805 NE 116th St., Ste. 7160, Kirkland, WA 98034: Free information ❖ Brocade threads and yarns, silk-blend and metallic threads, needlework kits, silk ribbons, embroidery supplies, and other supplies. 206–821–2287.

Thumbelina Needlework Shop, P.O. Box 1065, Solvang, CA 93463: Information $1.75 ❖ Books, fabrics, threads, yarns, and kits. 805–688–4136.

The Weaver's Loft, 308 S. Pennsylvania Ave., Centre Hall, PA 16828: Free information ❖ Knitting, weaving, and spinning supplies and yarn. 814–364–1433.

Web of Thread, 3240 Lone Oak Rd., Ste. 124, Paducah, KY 42003: Catalog $2 ❖ Supplies for serging and embroidery crafts and metallic, rayon, and silk threads for hand and machine embroidery.

Yarn Country, P.O. Box 6500, Concord, CA 94524: Catalog and yarn samples $10.99 ❖ Yarns, other supplies, and books for crochet, cross-stitch, and canvas crafts. 800–441–YARN.

Yarn Shop, 360 N. Westfield St., Feeding Hills, MA 01030: Free brochure ❖ Fashion kits for children and adults and other supplies. 800–525–2685.

NEWSPAPERS & MAGAZINES

American Family Publishers, P.O. Box 62000, Tampa, FL 33662: Free information ❖ Magazine subscriptions. 800–237–2400.

Below Wholesale Magazines, 1909 Prosperity St., Reno, NV 89502: Free brochure ❖ Magazine subscriptions. 800–800–0062.

Box Seat Collectibles, P.O. Box 2013, Halesite, NY 11743: Catalog $5 ❖ Sports and historical newspapers and other memorabilia. 516–423–1025.

Harrowsmith, Camden House Books, Ferry Rd., P.O. Box 1004, Charlotte, VT 05445: Free catalog ❖ Books and magazines on country living, gardening, food, health, crafts, building, and the environment. 800–827–3333.

Claude Held, P.O. Box 515, Buffalo, NY 14225: Price list $1 (specify interest) ❖ Newspaper movie advertisements from the 1940s, pulp magazines, and fantasy and mystery books.

Historic Newspaper Archives, 1582 Hart St., Rahway, NJ 07065: Free catalog ❖ Newspapers for the day on which you were born. 800–221–3221; 908–381–2332 (in NJ).

Larry's Book Store, 1219 W. Devon Ave., Chicago, IL 60660: Catalog $1 ❖ Movie books and magazines. 312–274–1832.

Alan Levine Movie & Book Collectibles, P.O. Box 1577, Bloomfield, NJ 07003: Catalog $5 ❖ Books on collecting, old-time movie posters and lobby cards, and radio, television, and movie magazines. 201–743–5288.

J.K. Lutherie Guitars, 11115 Sand Run, Harrison, OH 45030: Free catalog ❖ Vintage and new guitar parts, catalogs and other literature, guitar magazines, and out-of-print guitar books. 800–344–8880; 513–353–3320 (in OH).

MultiNewspapers, Box 866, Dana Point, CA 92629: Free brochure ❖ English language magazines and newspapers from over 60 countries.

The Overlook Connection, P.O. Box 526, Woodstock, GA 30188: Catalog $1 ❖ Books, audio cassettes, and magazines on horror, science fiction, fantasy, and mystery. 404–926–1762.

Paper Collectors' Mart, 134 Main St., Suncook, NH 03275: Free information with long SASE ❖ Lobby cards, posters, movie magazines, books, paperbacks, and other memorabilia. 603–485–5856.

Steven S. Raab, 2033 Walnut St., Philadelphia, PA 19103: Free catalog ❖ Autographs, signed books and photos, historic newspapers, World War I posters, and other historic memorabilia. 215–446–6193.

Rogofsky Movie Collectibles, Box 107, Glen Oaks, NY 11004: Catalog $3 ❖ TV and movie magazines, photos, and other collectibles. 718–723–0954 (after 6 pm).

Murray A. Summers, 10670 Cliff Mills Dr., Marshall, VA 22115: Catalog $3 (refundable) ❖ Movie magazines from the 1920s to the 1970s, movie posters, and other memorabilia.

Vintage Newspapers, P.O. Box 48621, Los Angeles, CA 90048: Free catalog ❖ Authentic newspapers and magazines, from 1880 to the present. 800–235–1919.

Yesterday, 1143 W. Addison St., Chicago, IL 60613: Free information with long SASE ❖ Original stills, lobbies, posters, pressbooks, magazines, and newspapers. 312–248–8087.

OFFICE & BUSINESS SUPPLIES

Business Forms & Booklets

Adams Business Forms, P.O. Box 91, Topeka, KS 66601: Free information ❖ Manifold books, guest checks, and other forms. 800–444–3508.

Business Forms by Carlson Craft, 1625 Roe Crest Dr., North Mankato, MN 56003: Free information ❖ Business forms. 800–292–9207.

Business Forms of America, 9321 Kirby, Houston, TX 77054: Free catalog ❖ Business forms, stationery, and signs. 800–231–0329; 713–790–1926 (in TX).

Caprock Business Forms Inc., 1211 Ave. F, Lubbock, TX 79401: Free information ❖ Continuous computer forms, letterheads and

envelopes, snap-apart sets, manifold books and pads, and scratch pads. 800–666–3322.

CFO Forms, 2205 Forsyth Rd., Unit L, Orlando, FL 32807: Free price list ❖ Carbonless business forms. 800–451–3676.

Champion Industries Inc., 2450 1st Ave., P.O. Box 2968, Huntington, WV 25728: Free information ❖ Continuous and snap-out forms. 800–624–3431; 304–528–2791 (in WV).

Champion Printing Company, 3250 Spring Grove Ave., Cincinnati, OH 45225: Free information ❖ Self-mailers and bind-ins. 800–543–1957.

Economy Printing Company, 5067 W. 12th St., Jacksonville, FL 32205: Free information ❖ Business forms and booklets. 800–423–1475; 904–786–4070 (in FL).

Grand Forms & Systems Inc., 211 S. Arlington Heights, Arlington Heights, IL 60005: Free information ❖ Business forms. 800–682–1924; 708–259–4600 (in IL).

HG Professional Forms Company, 2020 California St., Omaha, NE 68102: Free catalog ❖ Pre-printed forms, accounting supplies, computer paper, record-keeping systems, binders, report covers, and envelopes. 800–228–1493.

Mattick Business Forms Inc., 333 W. Hintz Rd., Wheeling, IL 60090: Free catalog ❖ Stationery, office and business forms, and labels. 708–541–7345.

Moore Business Products, Catalog Division, P.O. Box 5000, Vernon Hills, IL 60061: Free catalog ❖ Business forms, typewriter and printer ribbons, print wheels, copier supplies, laser printer paper and toner cartridges, fax paper, computer accessories, and other supplies. 800–323–6230.

Morgan Printing Company, 2365 Wyandotte Rd., Willow Grove, PA 19090: Free information ❖ Continuous letterheads, labels, and business forms. 800–435–3892.

Paulton Corporation, 130 Waukegan Rd., Deerfield, IL 60015: Free catalog ❖ Business forms, sales books, and office supplies. 708–948–7270.

Professional Press, P.O. Box 4371, Chapel Hill, NC 27515: Free information ❖ Booklets. 800–277–8960.

Rapidforms Inc., 301 Grove Rd., Thorofare, NJ 08086: Free catalog ❖ Business forms and labels. 800–257–8354.

Shipman Printing Industries, P.O. Box 157, Niagara Falls, NY 14302: Free information ❖ Business forms, letterheads, padded forms, and window-style and other envelopes. 800–462–2114.

Stationery House, 1000 Florida Ave., Hagerstown, MD 21740: Free catalog ❖ Business stationery, business forms, supplies, and gifts. 301–739–4487.

Trade Carbonless, P.O. Box 989, Elfers, FL 34680: Free price list ❖ Edge-glued, carbonless forms. 813–843–0222.

Triangle Printing Company, 325 Hill Ave., Nashville, TN 37210: Free information ❖ Booklets. 800–843–9529.

General Office Supplies

Accountants Supply House, 965 Walt Whitman Rd., Melville, NY 11747: Free catalog ❖ Stationery and envelopes, forms and labels, and adding machines, shipping materials, disk storage cabinets, typewriter and data processing ribbons, furniture, and other supplies. 800–342–5274; 516–561–7700 (in NY).

Ad Lib Advertising, P.O. Box 531, North Bellmore, NY 11710: Free information ❖ Custom Post-It Notes. 800–622–3542.

Alfax Wholesale Furniture, 370 7th Ave., Ste. 1101, New York, NY 10001: Free catalog ❖ General office equipment, furniture, and supplies. 800–221–5710; 212–947–9560 (in NY).

American Loose Leaf Business Products, 4015 Papin, St. Louis, MO 63110: Free catalog ❖ Binders, folders, and indexes. 800–467–7000.

American Thermoplastic Company, 622 2nd Ave., Pittsburgh, PA 15219: Free catalog ❖ Binders, index sets, sheet protectors, clipboards, report and presentation folders, data processing and catalog binders, and cassette albums. 800–456–6602.

Artistic Greetings Inc., 409 Williams St., P.O. Box 1623, Elmira, NY 14902: Free catalog ❖ Stationery and office accessories. 607–733–9076.

Bangor Cork Company Inc., William & D Streets, Pen Argyl, PA 18072: Free catalog ❖ Cork bulletin, marker, and chalkboards. 215–863–9041.

Browncor International, 400 S. 5th St., Milwaukee, WI 53204: Free catalog ❖ Mailing and shipping supplies. 800–327–2278.

The Business Book, 41 W. 8th Ave., Oshkosh, WI 54906: Free catalog ❖ Pressure sensitive labels, stampers, envelopes and stationery, speed letters, memo pads, business cards and forms, greeting cards, books, and other office supplies. 414–231–4886.

Chenesko Products Inc., 2221 5th Ave., Ste. 4, Ronkonkoma, NY 11779: Free catalog ❖ Recharge kits for laser printer and copier toner cartridges. 800–221–3516; 516–467–3205 (in NY).

Copen Press Inc., 303 E. 60th St., New York, NY 10022: Free catalog ❖ Envelopes, order forms, reply cards, and printing, binding, and mailing services. 718–235–4270.

Day-Timers, One Willow Ln., East Texas, PA 18046: Free catalog ❖ Stationery and business cards. 215–395–5884.

Eagle International Institute Inc., 1057 E. Henrietta Rd., Rochester, NY 14623: Free catalog ❖ Day planner systems, open-style and zippered leather binders, office supplies, forms and calendars, and audio and video training programs. 800–273–6111; 716–283–8000 (in NY).

Frank Eastern Company, 599 Broadway, New York, NY 10012: Catalog $1 ❖ Office equipment, furniture, and supplies. 212–219–0007.

Fidelity Products Company, P.O. Box 155, Minneapolis, MN 55440: Free catalog ❖ Office equipment and supplies. 800–328–3034; 612–526–6500 (in MN).

Grayarc, P.O. Box 2944, Hartford, CT 06104: Free catalog ❖ Office equipment and supplies. 800–562–5468.

HG Professional Forms Company, 2020 California St., Omaha, NE 68102: Free catalog ❖ Pre-printed forms, computer paper, record-keeping systems, binders, report covers, and envelopes. 800–228–1493.

Robert James Company Inc., P.O. Box 530, Moody, AL 35004: Free information with long SASE ❖ Office supplies. 800–633–8296; 205–640–7081 (in AL).

Moore Business Products, Catalog Division, P.O. Box 5000, Vernon Hills, IL 60061: Free catalog ❖ Business forms, typewriter and printer ribbons, print wheels, copier supplies, laser printer paper and toner cartridges, fax and computer paper, and binders. 800–323–6230.

Office Depot Inc., 2200 Old Germantown Rd., Delray Beach, FL 33445: Free catalog ❖ Office supplies and equipment. 800–685–8800.

Paper Direct Inc., 100 Plaza Dr., Secaucus, NJ 07094: Free catalog ❖ Laser printer, desktop publishing, and copier paper. 800–A-PAPERS.

Pyramid of Urbana, 2107 N. High Cross Rd., Urbana, IL 61801: Catalog $5 ❖ Office and school equipment, furniture, and art and craft supplies. 800–637–0955; 800–252–1363 (in IL).

Quill Office Supplies, 100 Schelter Rd., Lincolnshire, IL 60197: Free catalog ❖ Office supplies. 708–634–4800.

Science of Business Inc., 8245 Nieman, Ste. 108, Lenexa, KS 66214: Free information ❖ Custom Post-It Notes. 800–POST-ITS.

Staples Inc., Attention: Marketing Services, P.O. Box 9328, Framingham, MA 01701: Free catalog ❖ Office supplies, furniture, computer supplies and paper, drafting equipment, fax machines, and typewriters. 800–333–3330.

The Staplex Company, 777 5th Ave., Brooklyn, NY 11232: Free catalog ❖ Electric staplers. 800–221–0822.

SYNC, Building 42, Hanover, PA 17333: Free catalog ❖ Electronic products and supplies for the office and home. 717–633–3311.

Viking Office Products, 13809 S. Figueroa St., P.O. Box 61144, Los Angeles, CA 90061: Free catalog ❖ Office supplies. 800–421–1222.

Vulcan Binder & Cover, P.O. Box 29, Vincent, AL 35178: Free catalog ❖ Ring binders. 205–672–2241.

J. Williams Company, P.O. Box 72, Covington, GA 30209: Catalog $1 ❖ Office supplies, calculators, and stationery. 800–241–0854.

Labels & Tags

Apple Label, 1120 Old Country Rd., Plainview, NY 11803: Free catalog ❖ Labels, business forms, and other office supplies. 212–786–0100.

Continental Data Forms, 69 Veronica Ave., Somerset, NJ 08873: Free information ❖ Pinfeed pressure-sensitive labels. 800–947–8020.

Data Label Inc., 1000 Spruce St., Terre Haute, IN 47807: Free information ❖ Labels. 800–457–0676.

Ennis Express Label Service, Tag & Label Division, P.O. Box E, Wolfe City, TX 75496: Free information ❖ Labels. 800–527–1008; 903–496–2244 (in TX).

Flamingo Label Company Inc., 18110 14 Mile Rd., Fraser, MI 48026: Free information ❖ Labels in rolls, sheets, and pinfeed for computers. 800–535–6399.

C.J. Fox Company, P.O. Box 6186, Providence, RI 02940: Free information ❖ Labels. 800–556–6868.

GraphComm Services, P.O. Box 220, Freeland, WA 98249: Free catalog ❖ Labels. 800–488–7436.

Graphic Impressions, 8538 W. Grand Ave., River Grove, IL 60171: Free information ❖ Pressure-sensitive labels. 800–451–6658.

Grayarc, P.O. Box 2944, Hartford, CT 06104: Free catalog ❖ Stationery, business cards, forms, labels, envelopes, and other supplies. 800–562–5468.

Hawks Tag Service, P.O. Box 44187, Cincinnati, OH 45244: Free price list ❖ Tags in short run orders. 800–752–5765.

Kay Toledo Tag, 6050 Benore Rd., Toledo, OH 43612: Free brochure ❖ Tags in fluorescent, cloth, vinyl, and other materials. 800–822–8247.

Label Works, 100 Garfield Ave., P.O. Box 8100, North Mankato, MN 56002: Free catalog ❖ Labels. 800–522–3558.

Lancer Label, P.O. Box 3637, Omaha, NE 68103: Free catalog ❖ Bumper stickers and labels in rolls, sheets, and pinfeed. 800–228–7074.

Lixx Labelsz, 2619 14th St. S.W., P.O. Box 32055CC4, Calgary, Alberta, Canada T2T 5X0: Catalog $4 ❖ Labels and bookmarks that combine wildlife designs, calligraphy, eco-action, and recycling. 403–245–2331.

Morgan Printing Company, 2365 Wyandotte Rd., Willow Grove, PA 19090: Free information ❖ Continuous letterheads, labels, and business forms. 800–435–3892.

New York Label, 56 Pentaquit Ave., Bay Shore, NY 11706: Free catalog ❖ Self-adhesive labels in singles, rolls, or sheets. 800–257–2300.

PrintProd Inc., 419 Bainbridge St., Dayton, OH 45410: Free information ❖ Multi-color tags. 800–322–TAGS; 513–228–2181 (in OH).

Short Run Labels, 1681 Industrial Rd., San Carlos, CA 94070: Free catalog ❖ Self-adhesive labels in small orders. 800–522–3583; 415–592–7683 (in CA).

Superfast Label Service, 300 E. 4th St., Safford, AZ 85546: Free information ❖ Labels. 800–767–8566.

U.S. Tag & Label Corporation, 2217 Robb St., Baltimore, MD 21218: Free catalog ❖ Tags and labels. 800–638–1018; 410–467–2633 (in MD).

Writewell Company Inc., P.O. Box 68186, Indianapolis, IN: 46268: Free catalog ❖ Stationery and envelopes, note cards, memo pads, and labels. 800–968–5850.

Receipt Books

Cook Receipt Book Manufacturing Company, Box 2005, Dothan, AL 36302: Free catalog ❖ Receipt books. 800–842–0444.

Herald Multiforms Inc., P.O. Box 1288, Dillon, SC 29536: Free information ❖ Continuous form, check, and snap-out receipt books. 800–845–5050; 803–774–9051 (in SC).

Rapidforms Inc., 301 Grove Rd., Thorofare, NJ 08086: Free catalog ❖ Labels and business forms. 800–257–8354.

Rush Receipt Book Company, 457 Houston South, Mobile, AL 36606: Free price list ❖ Receipt books. 800–654–4237.

Superior Receipt Book Company, 215 S. Clark St., P.O. Box 326, Centreville, MI 49032: Free information ❖ Receipt books. 800–624–2887; 616–467–8265 (in MI).

Shipping Supplies

Automation Fastening Company Inc., 1138 W. 9th St., Cleveland, OH 44113: Free catalog ❖ Shipping and packaging supplies. 216–241–4487.

Chiswick Trading Inc., 33 Union Ave., Sudbury, MA 01776: Free catalog ❖ Shipping and packaging supplies. 800–225–8708; 508–443–9592 (in MA).

Cornell Paper & Box Company Inc., 162 Van Dyke St., Brooklyn, NY 11231: Free catalog ❖ Packaging supplies. 718–875–3202.

U.S. Box Corporation, 1296 McCarter Hwy., Newark, NJ 07104: Catalog $3 ❖ Boxes and other containers. 201–481–2000.

Volk Corporation, 23936 Industrial Park Dr., Farmington Hills, MI 48024: Free information ❖ Marking devices, packaging

supplies, and shipping room equipment. 800–521–6799; 810–477–6700 (in MI).

YAZOO Mills Inc., P.O. Box 369, New Oxford, PA 17350: Free information ❖ Mailing tubes. 800–242–5216.

ORIGAMI (PAPER FOLDING)

The Friends of the Origami Center of America, Room ST-1, 15 W. 77th St., New York, NY 10024: Free list with long SASE and two 1st class stamps ❖ Books, supplies, and origami paper.

OSTOMY SUPPLIES

A-Z Ostomy Supply, 321 W. Main, Marshall, MN 56258: Free catalog ❖ Ostomy supplies. 800–237–4555; 507–532–5754 (in MN).

AARP Ostomy Care Center, 5050 E. Belknap, P.O. Box 14899, Fort Worth, TX 76117: Free catalog ❖ Ostomy supplies. 800–284–4788.

American Ostomy Supplies, W. 223 North 777 Saratoga Dr., Waukesha, WI 53186: Free catalog ❖ Colostomy supplies. 800–858–5858.

Blanchard Ostomy Products, 1510 Raymond Ave., Glendale, CA 91201: Free information ❖ Products for ileostomies, urostomies, and wet colostomies. 818–242–6789.

Bruce Medical Supply, 411 Waverly Oaks Rd., P.O. Box 9166, Waltham, MA 02154: Free catalog ❖ Ostomy supplies. 800–225–8446.

Coloplast Inc., 5610 W. Sligh Ave., Ste, 100, Tampa, FL 33634: Free information ❖ Conseal Colostomy System. 800–237–4555.

Convatec, Bristol-Myers Squibb Company, P.O. Box 5254, Princeton, NJ 08543: Free information ❖ Convatec appliance for ostomates. 800–422–8811.

Edgepark Surgical Inc., 2300 Edison Blvd., Twinsburg, OH 44087: Free catalog ❖ Ostomy supplies. 800–321–0591.

Express Medical Supply Inc., P.O. Box 1164, Fenton, MO 63026: Free catalog ❖ Urostomy and ostomy supplies. 800–633–2139.

Fairs' OPS Inc., Ostomy Prosthesis Support, P.O. Box 5760, Greenway Station, Glendale, AZ 85306: Free information ❖ Undergarments designed by ostomates for ostomates. 602–978–4435.

Family Medical Pharmacy, 851 S. Harbor Blvd., Anaheim, CA 92085: Free information ❖ Ostomy supplies. 714–772–4840; 800–292–3300 (in CA).

Healthcare Prescription Services, 3830 E. Southport Rd., Indianapolis, IN 46237: Free catalog ❖ Ostomy supplies. 800–382–9799; 317–782–3478 (in IN).

Healthfirst Pharmacy, 1000 S. Beckham St., Tyler, TX 75701: Free catalog ❖ Ostomy supplies. 903–531–8830.

Home Health Express, Prinos Ave., Bay 20, Folcroft, PA 19032: Free information ❖ Ostomy supplies. 800–828–7123.

Home Medical Center Hospital Supplies, 7173 W. Cermack, Irwin, IL 60402: Free information ❖ Ostomy supplies. 800–323–2828.

Hospital Drug Store, 200 Loyola, New Orleans, LA 70112: Free information ❖ Ostomy supplies. 800–256–2007; 504–524–2254 (in LA).

King Ostomy Products, 431 W. 13th Ave., Ste. 4, Eugene, OR 97401: Free information ❖ Ostomy health care products. 503–345–0391.

Malloy's Prescription Pharmacy, 901 S. La Brea Blvd., Inglewood, CA 90301: Free information ❖ Ostomy and convalescent supplies. 213–671–6144.

Marc Medical Pharmacy, 6200 Wilshire Blvd., Los Angeles, CA 90048: Free information ❖ Ostomy supplies. 213–938–7131.

Marlen Manufacturing & Development Company, 150 Richmond Rd., Bedford, OH 44146: Free information ❖ Protective adhesive skin barriers for ileostomies, colostomies, and urostomies. 216–292–7060.

Mason Laboratories Inc., P.O. Box 334, Horsham, PA 19044: Free information ❖ Ostomy pouches, pouch odor deodorant, and other supplies. 215–675–6044.

Medic Pharmacy & Surgical, 5100 W. Commercial Blvd., Fort Lauderdale, FL 33319: Free information ❖ Ostomy and medical supplies. 800–888–9417.

Nihan & Martin Pharmacy, 1417 Myott Ave., Rockford, IL 60619: Free catalog ❖ Ostomy appliances. 815–963–8594.

Nu-Hope Laboratories Inc., P.O. Box 3638, Pacoima, CA 91333: Free information ❖ Urostomy pouches. 818–899–7711.

Ostomed Healthcare, 3116 S. Oak Park Ave., Berwyn, IL 60402: Free information ❖ Ostomy supplies. 800–323–1353; 708–795–7701 (in IL).

Ostomy Discount of America, 3600 Laketon Rd., Pittsburgh, PA 15235: Free catalog ❖ Ostomy supplies. 800–443–7828.

Ostomy Supply & Care Center Inc., 502 6th Ave. North, Fargo, ND 58102: Free information ❖ Ostomy supplies. 701–293–0277.

Palisades Pharmaceuticals Inc., 219 County Rd., Tenafly, NJ 07670: Free information ❖ Internal deodorant for patients with colostomies, ileostomies, and incontinence. 800–237–9083.

Parthenon Company Inc., 3311 W. 2400 South, Salt Lake City, UT 84119: Free information ❖ Ostomy supplies. 801–972–5184.

Penny Saver Medical Supply, 1851 W. 52nd Ave., Denver, CO 80221: Free catalog ❖ Ostomy supplies. 800–748–1909.

The Perma-Type Company Inc., 83 Northwest Dr., Plainville, CT 06062: Free catalog ❖ Ileostomy, colostomy, wet colostomy, ileal bladder, and ureterostomy appliances. 203–677–7388.

Salk Company Inc., 119 Braintree St., P.O. Box 452, Boston, MA 02134: Free information ❖ Natural-looking undergarments for active ostomates. 800–343–4497; 617–782–4030 (in MA).

Shield Healthcare Centers, P.O. Box 916, Santa Clarita, CA 91380: Free catalog ❖ Ostomy, urological, skin care, and home diagnostic products.

Source International, 8216 Ridgeview Dr., Ben Lomond, CA 95005: Free information ❖ Diabetic, ostomy, and other medical supplies. 800–237–6696.

Tennessee Home Medical, 117 7th Ave. West, Springfield, TN 37172: Free information ❖ Ostomy supplies. 800–542–2005; 615–384–6093 (in TN).

Torbot Ostomy Center, 1185 Jefferson Blvd., Warwick, RI 02886: Free brochure ❖ Ostomy appliances. 800–545–4254.

Undercover Cover Company, HC 79, 104 BB, Melba, ID 83641: Free information ❖ Appliance undercovers. 208–896–4716.

United Division of Pfizer, 11775 Starkey Rd., Largo, FL 33540: Free catalog ❖ Ostomy supplies. 813–392–1261.

VPI, A Cook Group Company, 127 S. Main St., P.O. Box 266, Spencer, IN 47460: Free information ❖ Non-adhesive systems for colostomy, urostomy, and ileostomy patients. 800–843–4851; 812–829–4891 (in IN).

Worldwide Home Health Center Inc., 926 E. Tallmadge Ave., Akron, OH 44310: Free catalog ❖ Ostomy and incontinence supplies, mastectomy breast forms, and clothing. 800–223–5938; 800–621–5938 (in OH).

Yentl's Secrets, 4415 Mockingbird Ln., Toledo, OH 43623: Free brochure ❖ Pouch covers. 419–841–1752.

PADDLEBALL

Adventure 16 Inc., 4620 Alvarado Canyon Rd., San Diego, CA 92120: Free information ❖ Paddles and balls. 800–854–2672; 800–854–0222 (in CA).

Cannon Sports, P.O. Box 11179, Burbank, CA 91510: Free information with list of retailers ❖ Paddles and balls. 800–362–3146; 818–753–5940 (in CA).

Century Sports Inc., Lakewood Industrial Park, 1995 Rutgers University Blvd., Box 2035, Lakewood, NJ 08701: Free information ❖ Balls and paddles. 800–526–7548; 908–905–4422 (in NJ).

Spalding Sports Worldwide, 425 Meadow St., P.O. Box 901, Chicopee, MA 01021: Free information with list of retailers ❖ Paddles and balls. 800–225–6601.

Sportime, 1 Sportime Way, Atlanta, GA 30340: Free information ❖ Balls and paddles. 800–444–5700; 404–449–5700 (in GA).

Wa-Mac Inc., Highskore Products Inc., P.O. Box 128, Carlstadt, NJ 07410: Free information ❖ Paddles and balls. 800–447–5673; 201–438–7200 (in NJ).

PAPER COLLECTIBLES

Arlington Card, 140 Gansett Ave., Cranston, RI 02910: Free information with long SASE ❖ Non sports cards collectibles and paper wrappers. 401–942–3188.

Box Seat Collectibles, P.O. Box 2013, Halesite, NY 11743: Catalog $3 ❖ Sports and historical newspapers and memorabilia. 516–423–1025.

Buck Hill Associates, Box 501, North Creek, NY 12857: Free catalog ❖ Posters, handbills, historical documents and Americana from America's past, and other paper collectibles. 518–251–2349.

The Cartophilians, 430 Highland Ave., Cheshire, CT 06410: Free information with long SASE ❖ Collectible postcards, trading cards, and other paper ephemera. 203–272–1143.

The Evergreen Press, Box 306, Avalon, CA 90704: Free information with long SASE ❖ Adult and children's books, greeting cards, book marks and bookplates, wedding certificates, calendars, ornaments, paper dolls, postcards, and other 19th- and early 20th-century paper memorabilia. 213–510–1700.

Claude Held, P.O. Box 515, Buffalo, NY 14225: Price list $1 (specify interest) ❖ Newspaper movie advertisements from the 1940s, pulp magazines, and fantasy and mystery books.

Hi-De-Ho Collectibles, P.O. Box 2841, Gaithersburg, MD 20886: Free information ❖ Antique movie posters and lobby cards, cartoon memorabilia, television toys, games, puzzles, and dolls, advertising signs, 3–D figures, and stand-ups. 301–926–4438.

Lynn Galleries, P.O. Box 2907, Tuscaloosa, AL 35403: Free information ❖ Paper collectibles. 205–752–5225.

The Old Print Gallery, 1220 31st St. NW, Washington, DC 20007: Catalog $3 ❖ Paper collectibles. 202–965–1818.

Old Print Shop, 150 Lexington Ave., New York, NY 10016: Free information ❖ Paper collectibles. 212–683–3950.

Original Paper Collectibles, 700 Clipper Gap Rd., Auburn, CA 95603: Free brochure with long SASE ❖ Paper labels and used stock certificates. 916–878–0296.

Tom Peper, 32 Shelter Cove Lane, #109, Hilton Head Island, SC 29928: Price list $1 ❖ Autographs, lobby cards and posters, original comic art, animation art and cels, and other collectibles. 800–628–7497.

Steven S. Raab, 2033 Walnut St., Philadelphia, PA 19103: Free catalog ❖ Autographs, signed books and photos, historic newspapers, World War I posters, and other historic paper memorabilia. 215–446–6193.

Bernard W. Rosen, Fine Paper Collectibles, P.O. Box 286, Amherst, OH 44001: Free catalog ❖ Paper collectibles. 216–282–6790.

Slot-Box Collector, Richard Bueschel, 414 N. Prospect Manor Ave., Mt. Prospect, IL 60056: Free list with seven 1st class stamps ❖ Old saloon artifacts, coin-operated machines,

advertising collectibles, and paper memorabilia. 708–253–0791.

R.M. Smythe, 26 Broadway, New York, NY 10004: Price list $2 ❖ Obsolete stocks and bonds, bank notes, and autographs. 800–622–1880; 212–943–1880 (in NY).

The Sports Alley, 15545 E. Whittier Blvd., Whittier, CA 90603: Free information with long SASE ❖ Hard-to-find sports cards, cancelled checks by sports greats, autographed pictures, world series programs, photographs, and other memorabilia. 310–947–7383.

Jim Szakacs, 55 Maitland St., Apt. 610, Toronto, Ontario, Canada M4Y 1C8: Catalog $3 ❖ Movie memorabilia and miscellaneous paper collectibles.

Mark Vardakis Autographs, Box 1430, Coventry, RI 02816: Catalog $2 ❖ Autographs, paper Americana, pre-1900 stocks, bonds and checks, and other collectibles. 401–823–8440.

Yesterday's Paper, P.O. Box 819, Concrete, WA 98237: Price list 75¢ (specify subject area) ❖ Financial, territorial, and western paper collectibles, documents, and other memorabilia, from 1700 and later. 206–853–8228.

PAPER MAKING & SCULPTING

Aiko's Art Materials Import, 3347 N. Clark St., Chicago, IL 60657: Catalog $1.50 ❖ Japanese handmade paper, Oriental art supplies, fabric dyes, and other art supplies. 312–404–5600.

American Art Clay Company Inc., 4717 W. 16th St., Indianapolis, IN 46222: Free catalog ❖ Modeling clay, self-hardening clay, paper mache, casting compounds, mold-making materials, acrylics, fabric dyes, fillers and patching compounds, wood stains, and metallic finishes. 800–374–1600; 317–244–6871 (in IN).

Gerlachs of Lecha, P.O. Box 213, Emmaus, PA 18049: Catalog $2.25 ❖ Paper sculpting kits. 215–965–9181.

Gold's Artworks Inc., 2100 N. Pine St., Lumberton, NC 28358: Free catalog with long SASE ❖ Paper-making pigments and chemicals, pulp materials, kits, and other supplies. 800–356–2306; 910–739–9605 (in NC).

Holcraft Collection, 211 El Cajon Ave., P.O. Box 792, Davis, CA 95616: Catalog $2 ❖

Molds for papier mache and chalkware crafts and other craft supplies. 916–756–3023.

Lake City Crafts, Rt. 2, Box 637, Highlandville, MO 65669: Catalog $2 ❖ Supplies for paper quilling, crafting, and filigree projects.

Little Goodies, P.O. Box 1004, Lewisville, TX 75067: Catalog $2 ❖ Pre-cut paper flower kits.

Nasco, 901 Janesville Ave., Fort Atkinson, WI 53538: Free catalog ❖ Paper making and sculpting supplies. 800–558–9595.

Ocotillo Arts, 1891 E. Auburn, Tempe, AZ 85283: Sample pack $2 ❖ Rag and non-cotton handmade papers. 602–897–1968.

Papercuttings by Alison, 404 Partridge, Sarasota, FL 34236: Catalog $2.25 ❖ Paper-cutting patterns and supplies. 813–957–0328.

The Pulpers, 1101 N. Highcross Rd., Urbana, IL 61801: Free information ❖ Prepared pulps for making paper and casting. 217–328–0118.

Pyramid of Urbana, 2107 N. High Cross Rd., Urbana, IL 61801: Catalog $5 ❖ Paper-sculpting and paper-making materials, other craft supplies, office and art supplies, and school equipment. 800–637–0955; 800–252–1363 (in IL).

Quill-It, P.O. Box 1304, Elmhurst, IL 60126: Catalog $1 (refundable) ❖ Quilling papers, paper-snipping supplies, kits, books, tools, plaques, frames, fringes, and other supplies.

Terrific Little Crafts, 4140 Oceanside Blvd., Oceanside, CA 92056: Catalog $1 ❖ Quilling supplies, jewelry findings, paper clay, and other craft items.

Tree Toys, Box 492, Hinsdale, IL 60521: Catalog $1 ❖ Silhouette paper-snipping designs on antique parchment or black paper. 708–323–6505.

Twinrocker Papermaking Supplies, P.O. Box 413, Brookston, IN 47923: Free catalog ❖ Paper-making supplies and ready-to-use handmade paper. 800–757–TWIN.

PAPERWEIGHTS

Alberene Crystal, 3222 M St. NW, Washington, DC 20007: Free information ❖ Perthshire paperweights and Thomas Webb and Edinburgh crystal. Includes discontinued items. 800–843–9078.

Brielle Galleries, P.O. Box 475, Brielle, NJ 08730: Free catalog ❖ Watches, jewelry, paperweights, and crystal, silver, bronze, pewter, and porcelain items. 800–542–7435.

L.H. Selman Ltd., 761 Chestnut St., Santa Cruz, CA 95060: Free catalog ❖ Antique, modern, and contemporary paperweights. 800–538–0766.

PARTY DECORATIONS

Anderson's, 4875 White Bear Pkwy., White Bear Lake, MN 55110: Free catalog ❖ Party and prom decorations and supplies. 800–328–9640; 612–426–1667 (in MN).

Birthday Express, 13620 NE 20th, Bellevue, WA 98005: Free catalog ❖ Party decorations, filled favor bags, and gifts. 206–641–0251.

The Cracker Box, Solebury, PA 18963: Catalog $4.50 ❖ Ornament kits. 215–862–2100.

Essentials Unlimited Inc., 909 Burr Oak Ct., Oak Brook, IL 60521: Free catalog ❖ Coordinated paper plates and other party supplies.

Hearth Song, Mail Processing Center, 6519 N. Galena Rd., P.O. Box 1773, Peoria, IL 61656: Free catalog ❖ Party decorations, children's books, doll house miniatures, art supplies, kites, and games. 800–325–2502.

Novelties Unlimited, 410 W. 21st St., Norfolk, VA 23517: Catalog $5 ❖ Magic, balloons, make-up, party decorations, and clown supplies, props, and gags. 804–622–0344.

Paper Wholesaler, 17800 N. State Rd., 9 Drive, North Miami, FL 33162: Catalog $3 ❖ Paper and plastic table wear, party supplies, and gift wrappings. 305–651–4004.

Paradise Products, P.O. Box 568, El Cerrito, CA 94530: Catalog $2 ❖ Party decorations and favors. 510–524–8300.

U.S. Toy Company Inc., 1227 E. 119th St., Grandview, MO 64030: Catalog $3 ❖ Magic equipment and novelties, carnival supplies, and decorations and supplies for holidays, parties, and other celebrations. 800–448–7830; 816–761–5900 (in MO).

Under the Big Top, P.O. Box 807, Placentia, CA 92670: Catalog $4 ❖ Party supplies, costumes, clown props, and balloons. 800–995–7727.

PATIOS & WALKWAYS

Stone Company Inc., Rt. 1, Eden, WI 53019: Free information ❖ Natural building and landscape cobblers, granite boulders, wall stone, steppers, and flagstone. 414–477–2521.

PENS & PENCILS

Altman Luggage, 135 Orchard St., New York, NY 10001: Free information ❖ Writing instruments, luggage, and other leather goods. 800–372–3377.

Arthur Brown & Bros. Inc., P.O. Box 7820, Maspeth, NY 11378: Free catalog ❖ New and contemporary-style fine writing instruments. 800–772–7367; 718–628–0600 (in NY).

Bertram's Inkwell, 11301 Rockville Pike, Kensington, MD 20895: Free catalog ❖ Pens and pencils, desk sets, and other gifts. 800–782–7680; 301–468–6939 (in MD).

H.G. Daniels Company, 1844 India St., San Diego, CA 92101: Free information ❖ Fountain pens and other writing accessories.

Fahrney Pens Inc., 8329 Old Marlboro Pike, Upper Marlboro, MD 20772: Catalog $2 ❖ Writing instruments. 800–336–4775.

Fountain Pen Hospital, 10 Warren St., New York, NY 10007: Free information ❖ Fountain pens, pencils, and other writing accessories. 800–253–PENS; 212–964–0580 (in NY).

The Fountain Pen Shop, 315 W. 5th St., Los Angeles, CA 90013: Catalog $3 ❖ Pens, pencils, and desk sets. 213–626–9387.

Hunt Manufacturing Company, 230 S. Broad St., Philadelphia, PA 19102: Free information ❖ Calligraphy papers, markers, kits and supplies, fountain pens, pen sets, nibs, inks, acrylics, oil paints, and water colors. 800–765–5669.

Menash, 462 7th Ave., New York, NY 10018: Free catalog ❖ Writing instruments and refills. 800–344–PENS.

PERFUMERY SUPPLIES

Angel's Earth, 1633 Scheffer Ave., St. Paul, MN 55116: Catalog $2 ❖ Essential and fragrance oils, potpourri supplies, and perfume-making kits. 612–698–3601.

Aphrodesia Products, 264 Bleeker St., New York, NY 10014: Catalog $3 ❖ Herbs, essential oils, and perfumery supplies. 800–221–6898; 212–989–6440 (in NY).

Candlechem Products, P.O. Box 705, Randolph, MA 02368: Catalog $2 ❖ Essential oils, dyes, and other scenting materials for use in making candles and perfumes. 617–986–7541.

Caswell-Massey Company Ltd., Catalog Division, 100 Enterprise Pl., Dover, DE

19901: Catalog $1 ❖ Herbs, essential oils, and perfumery supplies. 800–326–0500.

East End Import Company, Box 107, Essex St., Montauk, NY 11954: Free information ❖ Essential oils, floral water, lavender products, absolutes, and other perfumery supplies. 516–668–9389.

The Essential Oil Company, P.O. Box 206, Lake Oswego, OR 97034: Free catalog ❖ Essential oils, soap-making molds and supplies, incense materials, potpourri, and aromatherapy items. 800–729–5912.

The Faith Mountain Company, P.O. Box 199, Sperryville, VA 22740: Free catalog ❖ Herbs, essential oils, and perfumery supplies. 800–822–7238.

Gabrieana's Herbal & Organic Products, P.O. Box 215322, Sacramento, CA 95821: Free catalog ❖ Skin care and bath care items, essential oils, dried herbs, and other organic products. 800–684–4372.

The Ginger Tree, 245 Lee Rd., Opelika, AL 36801: Catalog $1 (refundable) ❖ Potpourri, aromatherapy supplies, and essential and fragrance oils. 205–745–4864.

Good Hollow Greenhouse & Herbarium, Rt. 1, Box 116, Taft, TN 38488: Catalog $1 ❖ Herbs, perennials, wildflowers, scented geraniums, essential oils, potpourris, teas, and dried herbs and spices. 615–433–7640.

Grandma's Spice Shop, P.O. Box 472, Odenton, MD 21113: Free catalog ❖ Essential oils and herbal potpourris. 410–672–0933.

Hartman's Herb Farm, Old Dana Rd., Barre, MA 01005: Catalog $2 ❖ Herbs and herb products, potpourri, and essential oils. 508–355–2015.

The Herb Lady, P.O. Box 20, Harpers Ferry, WV 25425: Free catalog ❖ Essential oils, potpourris, sachets, and aromatic blends to simmer on the stovetop. 800–537–1846.

Indiana Botanic Gardens, P.O. Box 5, Hammond, IN 46325: Free catalog ❖ Herbs, fragrances, and essential oils. 219–947–4040.

Lavender Lane, 6715 Donerail, Sacramento, CA 95842: Catalog $2 ❖ Essential and alcohol-free perfume oils and other perfumery supplies and equipment. 916–334–4400.

Meadowbrook Herb Gardens, 93 Kingstown Rd., Wyoming, RI 02898: Catalog $1 ❖ Herbs, essential oils, fragrances, and perfumery supplies. 401–539–7603.

Meg's Garden, P.O. Box 161, Buffalo, NY 14205: Brochure $1 ❖ Potpourris and perfume oils. 716–883–7564.

Mount Nebo Herbs & Oils, 300 Highland Ave., Athens, OH 45701: Catalog $2 ❖ Essential oils and unscented body and skin care products.

Nature's Finest, P.O. Box 10311, Burke, VA 22009: Catalog $2.50 (refundable) ❖ Dried flowers, herbs, spices, oils, fixatives, bottles, books, and other potpourri supplies. 703–978–3925.

Nature's Herb Company, 1010 46th St., Emeryville, CA 94608: Catalog $1 ❖ Herbs, spices, essential oils, perfumery supplies, and supplies for potpourris and sachets. 510–601–0700.

OlFactorium, 401 Euclid Ave., Ste. 155, Cleveland, OH 44114: Free information ❖ Botanical essential and carrier oils. 216–566–8234.

Penn Herb Company, 603 N. 2nd St., Philadelphia, PA 19123: Catalog $1 ❖ Herbs, essential oils, and perfumery supplies. 800–523–9971; 215–925–3336 (in PA).

Soap Opera, 319 State St., Madison, WI 55703: Free price list ❖ Essential oils, rare oils, designer fragrances, herbs, perfume base, and cosmetics and toiletries. 800–251–SOAP.

Tom Thumb Workshops, Rt. 13, P.O. Box 357, Mappsville, VA 23407: Catalog $1 ❖ Potpourri, herbs and spices, essential oils, and dried flowers. 804–824–3507.

The Uncommon Herb Catalog, 731 Main St., Monroe, CT 06468: Catalog $1 ❖ Essential oils, handmade soaps, skin care products, teas, and seasonings. 203–459–0716.

PERSONALIZED & PROMOTIONAL PRODUCTS

AD-CAP Line, 1400 Goldmine Rd., Monroe, NC 28110: Free catalog ❖ T-shirts, banners, bandannas, head bands, tote bags, aprons, and other promotional items. 800–868–7111.

Advertising Ideas Company, 3281 Barber Rd., Barberton, OH 44203: Free catalog ❖ Luggage, desk accessories, caps and T-shirts, badges and holders, toys, and other advertising and promotional novelties. 800–323–6359.

Amsterdam Printing & Litho Corporation, 55 Wallins Corners Rd., Amsterdam, NY 12010: Free catalog ❖ Advertising novelties. 800–543–6882.

Balloon Printing Company, P.O. Box 150, Rankin, PA 15104: Free information ❖ Imprinted balloons. 800–533–5221.

Best Impressions Company, P.O. Box 802, LaSalle, IL 61301: Free catalog ❖ Advertising specialties for promotions, incentives, and gift giving programs. 815–883–3532.

BNN Publications, P.O. Box 126, Nolensville, TN 37135: Free information ❖ Advertising newsletters. 800–673–0799.

Crestline Company Inc., 22 W. 21st St., New York, NY 10010: Free catalog ❖ Badges and ribbons, stickers, buttons, portfolios and presentation folders, pens and pencils, gifts and novelties, and mugs and steins. 212–741–3300.

Hudson Incentives & Imprints Inc., P.O. Box 396, Hudson, OH 44236: Free catalog ❖ Advertising novelties. 800–942–5372; 216–656–1746 (in OH).

The Jompole Company Inc., 330 7th Ave., New York, NY 10001: Free information with long SASE ❖ Balloons and lollipops to diamonds and furs, and other incentive merchandise. 212–594–0440.

Namark Cap & Emblem Company, 6325 Harrison Dr., Las Vegas, NV 89120: Free information ❖ Specialty caps, T-shirts, jackets, and screen-printed emblems. 800–634–6271.

Novelties Unlimited Advertising Specialties, P.O. Drawer 15159, Hattiesburg, MS 39404: Free catalog ❖ Advertising novelties with logos. 800–647–1652; 800–536–7709 (in MS).

Prestige Promotions, 4875 White Bear Pkwy., White Bear Lake, MN 55110: Free information ❖ Pens, coffee mugs, calendars, and bumper stickers. 800–328–9351.

Royal Graphics Inc., 3117 N. Front St., Philadelphia, PA 19133: Free information ❖ Posters, show-cards, and bumper stickers. 215–739–8282.

Sac's & Boxes, 258 Cross Keys Mall, St. Louis, MO 63033: Free information ❖ Printed paper and plastic bags. 800–677–8214.

Sales Guides Inc., 10510 N. Port Washington Rd., Mequon, WI 53092: Free catalog ❖ Pens and pencils, key fobs, memo cubes, desk items, food and candy, games, and gifts. 800–654–6666.

Scratch-It Promotions Inc., 1763 Barnum Ave., Bridgeport, CT 06610: Free information

❖ Scratch-off, pull tabs, and fragrance promotional products. 800–966–9467; 203–367–5377 (in CT).

Shazzam Advertising Specialties, 6325 DeSoto Ave., Woodland Hills, CA 91367: Free information ❖ Promotional advertising specialties. 800–999–8907.

N.G. Slater Corporation, 220 W. 19th St., New York, NY 10011: Free catalog ❖ T-shirts, tote bags, pins, bumper stickers, jewelry, button-making supplies, and other advertising novelties. 212–924–3133.

J.T. Townes Inc., P.O. Box 760, Danville, VA 24543: Free information ❖ Scratch pads. 800–437–PADS; 804–792–3711 (in VA).

PEST CONTROL

Nixalite of America, 1025 16th Ave., P.O. Box 727, East Moline, IL 61244: Free information ❖ Humane bird control products. 800–624–1189.

Sutton Agricultural Enterprises Inc., 746 Vertin Ave., Salinas, CA 93901: Free brochure ❖ Bird control products, seed planters, measuring devices, and field supplies. 408–422–9693.

PETS

Bird Supplies

Apex Feed & Supply, 600 Greene St., Marietta, OH 45750: Free information ❖ Bird food. 800–234–4401.

Audubon Workshop, 1501 Paddock Dr., Northbrook, IL 60062: Free catalog ❖ Bird supplies. 800–325–9464.

AVP/Animal Veterinary Products, Division of U.S. Pet Inc., P.O. Box 1326, Galesburg, IL 61401: Free catalog ❖ Bird supplies. 800–962–1211.

Bird 'N Hand, 40 Pearl St., Framingham, MA 01701: Free information ❖ Birdseed and feeders. 508–879–1552.

C & S Products Company Inc., Box 848, Fort Dodge, IA 50501: Free catalog ❖ Wild bird suet products and suet-related feeders. 515–955–5605.

Bill Chandler Farms, RR 2, Noble, IL 62868: Free price list ❖ Wild bird food. 800–752–BIRD.

Dakota Quality Bird Food, Box 3084, Fargo, ND 58108: Free catalog ❖ Niger thistle, small black sunflower seeds, royal finch mix, safflower seed, and wild birdseed mixes. 800–356–9220.

Duncraft, Penacook, NH 03303: Free catalog ❖ Wild bird supplies, squirrel-proof feeders, birdhouses, bird baths, and books. 603–224–0200.

Hyde Bird Feeder Company, 56 Felton St., P.O. Box 168, Waltham, MA 02254: Free catalog ❖ Bird feeders and wild bird food. 617–893–6780.

Kester's Birdseed Inc., P.O. Box 516, Omro, WI 54963: Catalog $2 ❖ Seed mixes for cockatiels, lovebirds, parakeets, parrots, canaries, and finches. 800–558–8815; 414–685–2929 (in WI).

Lake's Minnesota Macaws Inc., 639 Stryker Ave., St. Paul, MN 55107: Free information ❖ Hand-rearing formulas, feeding syringes, and nutritionally balanced bird food for adult macaws, cockatoos, parakeets, conures, lories, cockatiels, and lovebirds. 800–634–2473; 612–290–0606 (in MN).

Master Animal Care, Division Humboldt Industries Inc., Lake Rd., P.O. Box 3333, Mountaintop, PA 18707: Free catalog ❖ Dog and cat grooming and health care supplies, bird supplies, professional care pet products, toys, books, and gifts. 800–346–0749.

Mellinger's Inc., 2310 W. South Range Rd., North Lima, OH 44452: Free catalog ❖ Thistle, safflower, finch mix, and sunflower birdseed. 216–549–9861.

Pet Warehouse, P.O. Box 310, Xenia, OH 45385: Free catalog ❖ Bird, tropical fish, dog, and cat supplies. 800–443–1160.

Star Pet Supply, 1500 New Horizons Blvd., Amityville, NY 11701: Free catalog ❖ Supplies and grooming aids for dogs, cats, birds, and other pets. 800–274–6400.

UPCO, P.O. Box 969, St. Joseph, MO 64502: Free catalog ❖ Cages, birdseed, supplies, books, toys, and remedies for birds. 816–233–8800.

Volkman Bird Seed, 1040 22nd Ave., Oakland, CA 94606: Free information ❖ Premium birdseed and cuttlebone. 510–261–7780.

Wild Attractions, 2900 Cabin Creek Dr., Burtonsville, MD 20866: Free catalog ❖ Wild bird supplies. 301–384–4308.

Wild Bird Supplies, 4815 Oak St., Crystal Lake IL 60012: Free catalog ❖ Feeders, bird houses, bird baths, birdseed mixes, and books on bird care. 815–455–4020.

Wildlife Nurseries, P.O. Box 2724, Oshkosh, WI 54903: Catalog $3 ❖ Upland game birdseed combinations and gardening supplies. 414–231–3780.

Dog & Cat Supplies

Abeta Products, 5021 Tara Tea Dr., Tega Cay, SC 29715: Catalog $1 ❖ Solid wood furniture for cats. 803–548–1019.

Alsto Company, P.O. Box 1267, Galesburg, IL 61401: Catalog $1 ❖ Tools, pet products, kitchen aids, and other convenience items. 800–447–0048.

AVP/Animal Veterinary Products, Division of U.S. Pet Inc., P.O. Box 1326, Galesburg, IL 61402: Free catalog ❖ Health care supplies for dog and cat breeders, groomers, and kennels. 800–962–1211.

Care-A-Lot, 1617 Diamond Springs Rd., Virginia Beach, VA 23455: Free catalog ❖ Dog and cat supplies. 804–460–9771.

Cedar-al Products Inc., 8353 Hoko-Ozette Rd., Clallam Bay, WA 98326: Free brochure ❖ Pet pillows, cage floor coverings, carpet deodorizer and freshener, pet beds, around the home items, and bathing aids. 800–431–3444; 206–963–2601 (in WA).

Dog-Master Systems, Division Environmental Research Labs, P.O. Box 1250, Agoura Hills, CA 91301: Free catalog ❖ Supplies for raising and training puppies and dogs.

Drs. Foster & Smith Inc., 2253 Air Park Rd., P.O. Box 100, Rhinelander, WI 54501: Free catalog ❖ Pet and equine products and health care supplies. 800–826–7206.

Econo-Vet Groom & Health, 8687 Blumenstein Rd., P.O. Box 1191, Minocqua, WI 54548: Free catalog ❖ Health care, grooming, and kennel products for dogs and cats. 800–451–4162; 715–369–5591 (in WI).

Flexi-Mat Corporation, 2244 South Western Ave., Chicago, IL 60608: Free information ❖ Combination window perch cat bed.

G & G Pet Supplies, 1907 Windish Dr., Galesberg, IL 61401: Catalog $1 ❖ Equipment and supplies for dog grooming and care. 805–489–1111.

J-B Wholesale Pet Supplies, 5 Raritan Rd., Oakland, NJ 07435: Free catalog ❖ Supplies for cats and dogs. 800–526–0388.

Jeffers Vet Supply, P.O. Box 100, Dothan, AL 36302: Free catalog ❖ Books, medications, and other pet supplies. 800–533–3377.

Kennel Vet Corporation, P.O. Box 835, Bellmore, NY 11710: Catalog $1 (refundable) ❖ Vaccines and biologicals, vitamins and nutritional supplements, remedies for common medical conditions, cages, kennels, pet doors, deodorizers and repellents, flea and tick control aids, leashes and leads, toys and rawhide bones, and books about dogs, cats, birds, and horses. 516–783–5400.

Leather Brothers Inc., P.O. Box 700, Conway, AR 72033: Free catalog ❖ Leather and nylon collars and leads, other collars, wire muzzles, dog harnesses, name tags, and training leads. 800–442–5522.

Leatherrite Manufacturing Inc., 261 2nd St. SW, Carmel, IN 46032: Free catalog ❖ Leather, nylon, and vinyl leads, collars, and harnesses. 800–722–5222; 317–844–7241 (in IN).

Leonine Products, Box 657, Springfield, MA 05156: Free catalog ❖ Handcrafted furniture for cats. 802–885–3888.

Master Animal Care, Division Humboldt Industries Inc., Lake Rd., P.O. Box 3333, Mountaintop, PA 18707: Free catalog ❖ Dog and cat grooming and health care supplies, bird supplies, professional care products, toys, books, and gifts. 800–346–0749.

The Natural Pet Care Company, 2713 E. Madison, Seattle, WA 98112: Free catalog ❖ Natural pet care products. 800–962–8266; 206–329–1417 (in WA).

Nite Lite Company, P.O. Box 777, Clarksville, AR 72830: Free catalog ❖ Kennel, training, and hunting supplies for dogs; clothing and accessories for the hunter. 501–754–2146.

Nitron Industries Inc., P.O. Box 1447, Fayetteville, AR 72702: Free catalog ❖ Organic fertilizers, enzyme soil conditioners, natural pest controls, and pet care products. 800–835–0123.

Omaha Vaccine Company Inc., 3030 L St., Omaha, NE 68107: Free catalog ❖ Health, grooming, and training supplies for dogs, cats, other house pets, and horses. 800–367–4444; 402–731–9600 (in NE).

Our Best Friends Pet Catalog, 79 Albertson Ave., Albertson, NY 11507: Free catalog ❖ Pet foods, health and grooming supplies, and pet clothing. 800–852–PETS; 516–742–7400 (in NY).

Pedigrees Pet Catalog, 1989 Transit Way, P.O. Box 905, Brockport, NY 14559: Free catalog ❖ Pet clothing, name tags, collars, leads, feeders, carriers, toys, books, and T-shirts for owners. 800–548–4786.

Pet Warehouse, P.O. Box 310, Xenia, OH 45385: Free catalog ❖ Dog, cat, bird, and tropical fish supplies. 800–443–1160.

Pro Kennel Supply, P.O. Box 25226, Little Rock, AR 72221: Free catalog ❖ Dog and kennel supplies. 800–762–7049.

Star Pet Supply, 1500 New Horizons Blvd., Amityville, NY 11701: Free catalog ❖ Supplies and grooming aids for dogs, cats, birds, and other pets. 800–274–6400.

R.C. Steele Dog Equipment, 1989 Transit Way, Brockport, NY 14420: Free catalog ❖ Dog and kennel supplies. 800–872–4506.

United Pharmacal Company Inc., P.O. Box 969, St. Joseph, MO 64502: Free catalog ❖ Health and medical supplies for dogs, cats, and horses. 816–233–8800.

Vet Express, P.O. Box 155, Hazelhurst, WI 54531: Free catalog ❖ Kennel and other pet supplies. 800–458–7656; 715–356–7221 (in WI).

Wholesale Vet Supply, 4801 Shepherd Trl., Rockford, IL 61103: Free catalog ❖ Supplies for dogs, cats, rabbits, other household pets, horses, and cattle.

Tropical Fish Supplies

Acrylic Creations, 5517 Roan Rd., Sylvania, OH 43560: Free information ❖ Acrylic tanks, reef filters, skimmers, lighting, and other aquarium supplies. 419–882–1287.

American Acrylic Manufacturing, 3330 Market St., San Diego, CA 92102: Free information ❖ Protein skimmers and other aquarium accessories. 619–685–5313.

Anchor Bay Aquarium Inc., 36457 Alfred St., New Baltimore, MI 48047: Catalog $2 ❖ Rare cichlids, catfish, and other exotic tropical fish, books, supplies, and live plants. 313–725–1383.

Anthony Enterprises, P.O. Box 7007, Federal Way, WA 98003: Price list $1 ❖ Mated dwarf seahorses.

Aquarium Design & Engineering Inc., 18159 49th Terrace North, Jupiter, FL 33458: Free information ❖ Water pumps and filtration systems. 407–743–0707.

Aquarium Instruments Inc., 18 Huntington Circle, Shelton, CT 06484: Catalog $2 ❖ Aquarium monitoring products. 203–925–9139.

Aquarium Lights Inc., 1317 Colony Way Ct., Chesterfield, MO 63017: Free price list ❖ Liquid and freeze-dried nutritional products and aquarium light equipment. 800–745–0848.

The Aquarium Mail Order, 4300 Clarcona-Ocose Rd., Ste. 211, Orlando, FL 32810: Free information ❖ Tropical fish supplies. 407–298–1129.

Aquarium Products, 180 Penrod Ct., Glen Burnie, MD 21061: Free information ❖ Medications and water conditioners for tropical fish. 410–761–2100.

Aquarium Systems, 8141 Tyler Blvd., Mentor, OH 44060: Free information ❖ Saltwater aquarium test kits. 800–822–1100; 216–255–1997 (in OH).

Aquatic Life, 7319 Rokeby Dr., Manassas, VA 22110: Free information ❖ Softeners, pH neutralizers, water purifiers, and water testing and treatment systems. 703–369–7124.

Aquatic Specialists, 5201 Kingston Pike, Knoxville, TN 37919: Catalog $5 (refundable) ❖ Net-caught marine fish, marine invertebrates, macro algae, and cured live rock. 615–584–1084.

Aquatic Supply House, 42 Hayes St., Elmsford, NY 10523: Free catalog ❖ Tropical fish supplies, foods and automatic feeding devices, medications, heaters, air pumps, filters, sterilizers, water changers, and books. 800–777–PETS.

Atlantis Aquarium & Pets Inc., 116–06 Queens Blvd., Forest Hills, NY 11375: Free information ❖ Marine and freshwater fish supplies. 718–544–9696.

Buckaroo Marine, 1319 N. Main, Tucson, AZ 85705: Free brochure ❖ Saltwater fish and invertebrates. 800–927–1050.

J.P. Burleson Inc., P.O. Box 32, Frederick, MD 21701: Catalog $3 ❖ Aquarium testing kits, cleansing solutions, water stabilization products, filter media, water conditioners, and conductivity meters. 301–846–4800.

By-Rite Pet Supplies, 23450 Kidder St., Hayward, CA 94545: Catalog $2 ❖ Aquarium supplies. 800–321–3448.

C & B Distributors, P.O. Box 913, Islamorada, FL 33036: Free information ❖ Atlantic and Caribbean tropical fish and live rock. 305–664–4588.

California Reef Specialists, 740 Tioga Ave., Sand City, CA 93955: Catalog $5 (refundable) ❖ Cold water reef fish and invertebrates, aquarium chiller units, wet/dry

filters, acrylic aquariums, protein skimmers, and pumps. 408–394–7271.

Caribbean Creatures, 112 Place Ave., Tavernier, FL 33070: Free information ❖ Hand-caught Caribbean tropical fish, shrimp, snails, crabs, scallops, and plants. 305–852–3991.

Champion Supply Company, 1407 Bethlehem Pike, Flourtown, PA 19031: Free information ❖ Automatic water changing and evaporation control pumps. 800–673–7822; 215–233–1630 (in PA).

Coral Fish Hawaii, 98–810 Moanalua Rd., Aiea, HI 96701: Free price list ❖ Marine fish from worldwide locations. 808–488–8801.

Daleco Master Breeder Products, 3340 Land Dr., Fort Wayne, IN 46809: Catalog $6 ❖ Tropical fish supplies, live food cultures, power filters, purification equipment, medications, lighting and temperature controls, fresh and salt water support systems, and aquariums. 219–747–7376.

Debron Aquatics, 1800 W. Oxford Ave., Ste. 4, Englewood, CO 80110: Free catalog ❖ Tropical fish equipment and supplies. 303–783–9593.

Delaware Aquatic Imports, 18 Anderson Rd., Newark, DE 19713: Free price list ❖ Water-grown aquatic plants. 302–738–4042.

Desert Aquatics, 3355 E. Tropicana Ave., Las Vegas, NV 89121: Free information ❖ Filtration systems for fresh and salt water tropical fish aquariums. 702–459–6000.

Exotic Aquaria Inc., 1672 NE 205th Terrace, North Miami Beach, FL 33179: Free information ❖ Tropical fish, algae, and corals. 800–622–5877.

Exotic Fish, 406 Northside Dr., Valdosta, GA 31602: Catalog $3 ❖ Tropical fish supplies and aquarium accessories. 800–736–0473.

Filtronics, P.O. Box 2457, Oxnard, CA 93033: Free information ❖ Semi-submersible aquarium testers. 805–486–5319.

Hamilton Technology Corporation, 14902 S. Figueroa St., Gardena, CA 90248: Free catalog ❖ Reef tank lights, digital electronic pH meter, and other aquarium equipment. 800–447–9797.

Hawaiian Marine Imports Inc., 10801 Kempwood, Ste. 2, Houston, TX 77043: Free information ❖ Filters and hoses. 713–460–0236.

Hikari Sales USA Inc., 2804 McCone Ave., Hayward, CA 94545: Free information ❖

Algae wafers, micro pellets, sinking wafers, food sticks, and other tropical fish food.

Imperial Discus, P.O. Box 770106, Lakewood, OH 44107: Free information ❖ Tropical fish. 216–234–2320.

Island Eco-Systems, P.O. Box 1102, Tavernier, FL 33070: Free information ❖ Net collected Atlantic Caribbean fish. 305–852–4385.

Dale Jordan, 71 Melon Lea Cove, Winnipeg, Manitoba, Canada R2G 2L4: Free information ❖ Tropical fish. 204–668–9780.

Kent Marine, 915 Raleigh Ct., Marietta, GA 30064: Free information ❖ Saltwater aquarium supplies. 404–427–8870.

Kordon, Division of Novalek Inc., 2242 Davis Ct., Hayward, CA 94545: Free information ❖ Live and frozen brine shrimp, brine shrimp eggs and food, and a salt water mix for brine shrimp.

Lifereef Filter Systems, 4628 S. Ward Way, Morrison, CO 80465: Free catalog ❖ Aquarium filter systems, skimmers, controllers, air dryers, light fixtures, chillers, and water pumps. 303–978–0940.

Living Reef, 9309 Narnia Dr., Riverside, CA 92503: Catalog $2.50 ❖ Tropical fish supplies. 800–788–REEF.

Mail Order Pet Shop, 1338 N. Market Blvd., Sacramento, CA 95834: Free catalog ❖ Filters, heaters, medications, marine supplies, plastic plants, air pumps, water conditioners for tropical fish, and supplies for dogs, cats, birds, and hamsters. 800–326–6677.

Majestic Pet Supply, P.O. Box 88484, Carol Stream, IL 60188: Catalog $2.50 ❖ Tropical fish supplies. 708–682–8867.

Marine Invertebrates, 784 Boston Post Rd., Milford, CT 06460: Catalog $2.50 ❖ Ozone generators, protein skimmers, controllers, water and air pumps, and other equipment. 203–878–2497.

Marine Products, 678 E. Broadway, Milford, CT 06460: Free catalog ❖ Aquarium supplies. 203–877–5002.

Mark's Aquarium & Pet World, 7019 3rd Ave., Brooklyn, NY 11209: Catalog $2 ❖ Tanks, filtration systems, splash guards, stands, and other supplies. 718–833–0755.

Mid-State Pet, Rt. 218, East Brunswick, NJ 08816: Free information ❖ Acrylic aquariums, wet-dry filters, ozonizers, redox controllers, protein skimmers, lighting systems, and UV sterilizers. 908–390–8007.

Mini's Mail Order, 7451 Warner Ave., Huntington Beach, CA 92647: Free information ❖ Tropical fish supplies. 800–382–0077.

Nature's Way, 4411 Bee Ridge Rd., Ste. 195, Sarasota, FL 34233: Free information ❖ Aquarium filters, pumps, and water purification equipment. 800–780–2320.

Nippon Pet Food, 1327 Post Ave., Torrance, CA 90501: Free information ❖ Tropical fish food for cichlids, goldfish, and koi. 310–787–8708.

Now Playing with Fish, 2007 Independence, Cape Girardeau, MO 63701: Free information ❖ Live corals, invertebrates, saltwater fish, and acrylic aquarium accessories. 314–335–1955.

O.S.I. Marine Lab Inc., 3550 Arden Rd., Hayward, CA 94545: Free information ❖ Tropical fish food.

Ocean Warehouse, 12721 Cedar Dr., Leawood, KS 66209: Free information ❖ Ready-to-use and custom acrylic tanks and integrated systems.

Oregon Desert Brine Shrimp, 1335 SE Marion St., Portland, OR 97202: Free information ❖ Brine shrimp and Daphnia. 503–232–4489.

Pet Warehouse, P.O. Box 310, Xenia, OH 45385: Free catalog ❖ Tropical fish, bird, dog, and cat supplies. 800–443–1160.

Pisces Coral & Fish, P.O. Box 772205, Houston, TX 77215: Free information ❖ Multi-colored corallines and macro-algaes for living reef aquariums. 713–272–9938.

Reef Aquarium Designs Inc., 509 Herbert St., Port Orange, FL 32119: Free brochure ❖ Marine, reef, and fresh water aquarium systems. 904–760–0738.

Reef Concepts, 1965 Lake Dr., Winston-Salem, NC 27127: Free information ❖ Ozone generators, pH controllers, trace elements, and other tropical fish aids. 910–788–3017.

Reef Displays, 10925 Overseas Hwy., Marathon, FL 33050: Free catalog ❖ Net-caught Atlantic fish and invertebrates, macro algae, algae snails, Caribbean live rock, and fresh and cured reef rock. 305–743–0070.

Reef Encounter, 1040 River Rd., Edgewater, NJ 07020: Free information ❖ Aquarium accessories. 201–947–7333.

Reef Tech, 6908 Cole St., Arvada, CO 80004: Free information ❖ Aquariums, filters, canopies, and stands. 303–422–3882.

Regal Discus, 2321 N. 9th St., Phoenix, AZ 85006: Free brochure ❖ Aquarium reverse osmosis filter system. 602–531–7532.

San Francisco Bay Brand Inc., 8239 Enterprise Dr., Newark, CA 94560: Free brochure ❖ Frozen and packaged tropical fish foods. 510–792–7200.

Sanders Brine Shrimp Company, 1180 W. 4600 South, Ogden, UT 84405: Free price list ❖ Brine shrimp eggs. 801–393–5027.

Sea-Aquatic International, 1631 S. Dixie Hwy., Pompano Beach, FL 33060: Free price list ❖ Tropical fish and inverts, live rock, and other supplies. 305–784–9278.

Sea-Thru Aquarium Products, 790 Court St., Franklin Lakes, NJ 07417: Free information ❖ Marine filtration equipment. 201–652–5282.

Sea Secrets, 1325 Guilford Dr., Venice, FL 34292: Free price list ❖ Invertebrates, plants, and fish from the Gulf and Florida. 813–488–9474.

Spectacular Sea Systems, 600 NE 42nd St., Pompano Beach, FL 33064: Free information ❖ Aquarium systems. 305–941–3792.

SpectraPure, 738 S. Perry Ln., Tempe, AZ 85281: Free information ❖ Aquarium water purification systems. 800–685–2783.

That Fish Place, 237 Centerville Rd., Lancaster, PA 17603: Free catalog ❖ Aquarium supplies. 800–733–3829.

Tropical Pumps Company, P.O. Box 11342, Spring, TX 77391: Free information ❖ Saltwater-safe pumps, pH testers and controllers, and chemical test kits. 713–251–5273.

Village Wholesale, 704 New Loudon Rd., Latham, NY 12110: Free catalog ❖ Tropical fish and supplies. 518–783–6878.

Willinger Brothers Inc., Wright Way, Oakland, NJ 07436: Free information ❖ Aquarium air pumps.

World Class Aquarium, 2015 Flatbush Ave., Brooklyn, NY 11234: Free information ❖ Aquarium systems, marine and fresh water fish, lights, and other equipment. 718–258–0653.

Carriers

DAFCO, 2411 Grear St., Salem, OR 97301: Free brochure ❖ Lightweight collapsible dog carrier. 800–458–1562.

Kennels & Enclosures

Cal-Formed Plastics Company, 2050 E. 48th St., Los Angeles, CA 90058: Free information ❖ Easy-to-clean, interlocking two-piece dog house with 5–way flow-through ventilation. 800–772–7723.

Central Metal Products Inc., State Rd. 213, North Edge, Windfall, IN 46076: Free catalog ❖ Wire cages for dogs. 317–945–7677.

Horst Company, 101 E. 18th St., Greely, CO 80631: Free catalog ❖ Kennels and runs. 303–353–7724.

Keipper Cooping Company, P.O. Box 249, W224 S8475 Industrial Dr., Big Bend, WI 53103: Free information ❖ All-wire collapsible coops. 414–662–2290.

Kennel-Aire Manufacturing Company, 6651 Hwy. 7, St. Louis Park, MN 55426: Free catalog ❖ Wire animal enclosures. 800–346–0134.

Mason Company, 260 Depot St., Box 365, Leesburg, OH 45135: Free catalog ❖ Kennels and cages for dogs. 800–543–5567.

Pet Castle, P.O. Box 1059, Brownwood, TX 76801: Free information ❖ One-piece molded dog house for indoors and outside. 800–351–1363; 915–643–2517 (in TX).

Pet Logs, 6514 Chapel Hill Rd., Raleigh, NC 27607: Free information ❖ Easy-to-clean cedar log dog houses. 800–334–5530.

Pet Doors

Borwick Innovations Inc., P.O. Box 30345, Santa Barbara, CA 93130: Free information ❖ Easy-to-install screen door that snaps into any screen without screws or bolts. 800–365–5657.

Clearthru Catdoor, P.O. Box 820424, Dallas, TX 75382: Free information ❖ Adjustable catdoor for raised or sliding windows. 214–363–0968.

Hale Security Pet Door, 5622 N. 52nd Ave., Glendale, AZ 85301: Free information ❖ Pet doors for walls and wood doors. 800–888–8914.

Patio Pacific Inc., 1931 N. Gaffey St., San Pedro, CA 90731: Free catalog ❖ Pet door panels for sliding glass doors. 800–826–2871.

Pet-Eze, 862 Southhampton Rd., Benicia, CA 94510: Free brochure ❖ Doors with energy-conserving glass and aluminum insert panel with flexible flap for any size sliding door. 800–331–6702; 707–745–5026 (in CA).

Petdoors U.S.A., 4523 30th St. West, Bradenton, FL 34207: Free brochure ❖ Easy-to-install, self-closing, energy-efficient doors with a security locked see-through panel. 800–749–9609.

Reptiles

American Reptile Inc., 118 S. Main, Dry Ridge, KY 41035: Free information ❖ Iguanas and food. 606–824–0050.

Armstrong's Cricket Farm, P.O. Box 125, West Monroe, LA 71294: Free information ❖ Reptile food. 800–345–8778.

AVTech Systems, 7955 Silverton Ave., Ste. 1217, San Diego, CA 92126: Free information ❖ Incubator-brooder system and other support therapy and critical care equipment. 800–662–6607; 619–695–9640 (in CA).

Birds & Reptiles of Scottsdale, 7904 E. Chaparral, Scottsdale, AZ 85253: Free information ❖ Captive-bred reptiles, snakes, amphibians, and turtles. 602–941–2014.

Carolina Mouse Farm, P.O. Box 382, Salem, SC 29676: Free information ❖ Frozen food for snakes. 803–654–0116.

Custom Cages, i4 Dry Run Rd., River Falls, WI 54022: Free information ❖ Custom and standard-size cages. 715–425–8888.

Glades Herp Inc., P.O. Box 3207, North Fort Myers, FL 33918: Free information ❖ Obscure species, sub-species, and color variations of reptile rarities. 813–543–6100.

Dick Goergen Reptiles, P.O. Box 225, Alden, NY 14004: Free price list ❖ Pythons, boas, tortoises, and other reptiles. 716–681–4518.

Hiss & Hers Reptiles, Jim & Debbie Rouse, 358 Spanish Oak Dr., Canyon Lake, TX 78133: Free price list ❖ Specializes in captive propagation of pythons.

Peter Kahl Reptiles, P.O. Box 6, Long Green, MD 21092: Free price list ❖ Specializes in captive-bred boas and pythons. 410–592–9675.

Lam Distributing Company, P.O. Box 407, Rusk, TX 75785: Free information ❖ Frozen natural food for snakes. 903–683–5212.

Mail Order Pet Shop, 1338 N. Market Blvd., Sacramento, CA 95834: Free catalog ❖ Supplies for herpetoculturists. 800–326–6677.

Neodesha Plastics Inc., Twin Rivers Industrial Park, P.O. Box 371, Neodesha, KS 66757: Free information ❖ Reptile cages. 316–325–3096.

Prehistoric Pets, 5536 E. Philadelphia, Chino, CA 97710: Free price list ❖ Rare and exotic reptiles. 714–465–6085.

Rainbow Mealworms, 126 E. Spruce St., Compton, CA 90220: Free information ❖ Mealworms and crickets for reptiles and amphibians. 800–777–WORM.

Reptile Haven, 2205 E. Valley Pkwy., Escondido, CA 92027: Free information ❖ Captive-produced and imported boas, pythons, tortoises, lizards, and frogs. 619–741–0127.

Reptile Specialties, 10051 Commerce Ave., Tujunga, CA 91042: Free information ❖ Farm-raised imports and captive-bred chameleons and custom cages and terrariums. 818–352–1796.

San Diego Reptile Breeders, P.O. Box 556, Campo, CA 91906: Information $3 with long SASE ❖ Captive-bred boas, pythons, and other snakes. 619–478–5794.

Vince Scheidt Snakes, P.O. Box 22885, San Diego, CA 92192: Free price list with long SASE ❖ Captive-bred snakes. 619–457–3873.

Snake Connection, P.O. Box 173, Largo, FL 34649: Free list ❖ Captive-born boas, pythons, kingsnakes, lizards, and turtles.

Top Hat Cricket Farm Inc., 1919 Forest Dr., Kalamazoo, MI 49002: Free information ❖ Live crickets. 800–638–2555.

Valentine Inc., 4259 S. Western Blvd., Chicago, IL 60609: Free catalog ❖ Supplies for the care and breeding of reptiles and amphibians. 800–GET-STUF.

VJ'S Exotic Reptiles Inc., 10 Avenue O, Brooklyn, NY 11204: Free price list with long SASE ❖ Lizards, snakes, turtles and amphibians, and other exotic reptiles. 718–837–7231.

Zeigler Brothers Inc., P.O. Box 95, Gardners, PA 17324: Free information ❖ Reptile food. 800–841–6800.

PHONOGRAPHS

Kenny Bunny, 480 S. Fair Oaks, Pasadena, CA 91105: Free information ❖ Antique phonographs and parts. 213–733–7733.

Kurluff Enterprises, 4331 Maxson Rd., El Monte, CA 91732: Free information ❖ Antique phonographs and parts. 818–444–7079.

Victorian Talking Machine Company, 261 Robinson Ave., Newburgh, NY 12550: Free information ❖ Antique phonographs and parts. 914–561–0132.

PHOTOGRAPHY
Albums & Photo Mounts

Albums Inc., P.O. Box 81757, Cleveland, OH 44181: Free catalog ❖ Wedding albums, photo mounts, plaques, and frames. 800–662–1000.

Camille Company Inc., 828 Bergen St., Brooklyn, NY 11238: Free catalog ❖ Photo albums. 718–789–0100.

Crown Products, 2178 Superior Ave., Cleveland, OH 44114: Free information ❖ Albums, folios and photo mounts for presentation of wedding, portrait, and other photos. 800–827–0363.

Exposures, 1 Memory Ln., P.O. Box 3615, Oshkosh, WI 54903: Free catalog ❖ Photo mounting supplies, albums, and frames. 800–572–5750.

Memories Inc., P.O. Box 17526, Raleigh, NC 27619: Free information ❖ Handmade wedding books and albums. 800–462–5069; 919–571–1648 (in NC).

Michel Company, 4672 N. Pulaski, Chicago, IL 60630: Free catalog ❖ Albums, photo mounts, and frames. 800–621–6649.

Penn Photomounts, Concord & Tryens Rd., Ashton, PA 19014: Free catalog ❖ Photo mounts, albums, and folios. 800–228–7366; 800–227–7366 (in PA).

Pierce Company, 9801 Nicollet, Minneapolis, MN 55420: Catalog $1 (refundable) ❖ Hand-painted backgrounds for portrait photography, mounts, albums, drapes, and printed forms. 612–884–1991.

Dave Sirken Distributors Inc., 1550 Wentzel St., Rochester, NY 46975: Free information ❖ Frames, folders, and albums. 800–348–2510; 800–223–7263 (in IN).

Backgrounds

Backdrop Outlet, 1524 S. Peoria, Chicago, IL 60608: Free catalog ❖ Handpainted backgrounds. 312–733–7703.

James Bright Backgrounds, 3535 Crenshaw Blvd., Hawthorne, CA 90250: Free information ❖ Handpainted backgrounds. 310–973–8488.

Denny Manufacturing Company Inc., P.O. Box 7200, Mobile, AL 36670: Free catalog ❖ Background scenes and professional backdrops. 800–844–5616.

Photek Backgrounds, 909 Bridgeport Ave., Shelton, CT 06484: Free information ❖ Featherlite, reversible, and washable backgrounds. 800–648–8868; 203–926–1811 (in CT).

Photo-Tech Inc., P.O. Box 9326, North St. Paul, MN 55109: Free information ❖ Easy-to-use background system. 612–771–4438.

Photographers Specialized Services, 650 Amour Rd., P.O. Box 46, Oconomowoc, WI 53066: Catalog $8 ❖ Free-standing, folding background screens and other professional and amateur products. 800–558–0114.

Photographic Products, 13535 Crenshaw Blvd., Hawthorne, CA 90250: Free brochure ❖ Hand-painted backgrounds, motorized roller systems, stools and tables, umbrellas, background cases and stands, strobe lights, and Victorian-style chairs. 800–821–5796; 310–973–8488 (in CA).

Pierce Company, 9801 Nicollet, Minneapolis, MN 55420: Catalog $1 (refundable) ❖ Hand-painted backgrounds for portrait photography, photo supplies, mounts, albums, drapes, and printed forms. 612–884–1991.

Studio Dynamics, 1667 E. 28th St., Long Beach, CA 90806: Free information ❖ Adaptable backgrounds for a wide variety of effects. 310–595–4273.

Bags & Camera Cases

Charles Beseler Company, 1600 Lower Rd., Linden, NJ 07036: Free brochure ❖ Bags for cameras, video equipment, and camcorders. 908–862–7999.

The Camjacket Company, 2610 Adams Ave., San Diego, CA 92116: Free catalog ❖ All-weather cases for cameras and lenses. 800–338–8759.

Coast Manufacturing Company, 200 Corporate Blvd. South, Yonkers, NY 10701: Free information ❖ Camera bags. 800–333–6282; 914–376–1500 (in NY).

Domke, Division Saunders Group, 21 Jet View Dr., Rochester, NY 14624: Free information ❖ Camera bags and other photo equipment. 716–328–7800.

GMI Photographic Inc., 125 Schmitt Blvd., Farmingdale, NY 11735: Free information ❖ Camera bags and equipment cases. 516–752–0066.

Leica USA Inc., 156 Ludlow Ave., Northvale, NJ 07647: Free information ❖ Handcrafted bags for cameras, lenses, binoculars, and other accessories. 201–767–7500.

Lightware, 1541 Platte St., Denver, CO 80202: Free catalog ❖ Camera cases. 303–455–4556.

LowePro, 2194 Northpoint Pkwy., Santa Rosa, CA 95407: Free information ❖ Camera bags. 707–575–4363.

Pelican Products Inc., 2255 Jefferson St., Torrance, CA 90501: Free information ❖ Watertight, unbreakable, corrosion-proof cases. 310–328–9910.

Photoflex, 541 Capitola Rd., Ste. G, Santa Cruz, CA 95062: Free information ❖ Camera bags. 800–486–2674.

Tamrac, 9240 Jordan Ave., Chatsworth, CA 91311: Free catalog ❖ Camera and video bags. 800–662–0717.

TENBA Quality Cases Ltd., 503 Broadway, New York, NY 10012: Free information ❖ Camera equipment bags. 212–966–1013.

Tundra Camjacket, Satter Distributing, P.O. Box 7234, Denver, CO 80207: Free information ❖ Camera bags. 800–525–0196.

Books

Harry N. Abrams Inc., 100 5th Ave., New York, NY 10011: Free information ❖ Books on photography. 212–206–7715.

Aperture, 20 E. 23rd St., New York, NY 10010: Free information ❖ Fine art photography books. 800–929–2323.

John S. Craig, 111 Edward Ave., P.O. Box 1637, Torrington, CT 06790: Free information ❖ Hard-to-find instruction manuals for photography equipment. 203–496–9791.

Eastman Kodak Company, Information Center, 343 State St., Rochester, NY 14650: Free information ❖ Books and other publications on photography. 800–462–6495.

Focal Press, 313 Washington St., Newton, MA 02158: Free catalog ❖ Books on photography. 617–928–2500.

Hudson Hills Press, 230 5th Ave., Ste. 1308, New York, NY 10001: Free information ❖

Books on photography and art.
212–889–3090.

Light Impressions, 439 Monroe Ave.,
Rochester, NY 14607: Free catalog ❖ Books
on photography and supplies for archival
storage of negatives and prints.
800–828–6216.

Camera Manufacturers

Ansco Photo Optical Products, 1801 Touhy
Ave., Elk Grove, IL 60007: Free information.
800–323–6697.

Bronica, GMI Photographic Inc., 125 Schmitt
Blvd., Farmingdale, NY 11735: Free
information. 516–752–0066.

Calumet Photographic, 890 Supreme Dr.,
Bensenville, IL 60106: Free information.
800–225–8638.

Canon, One Canon Plaza, Lake Success, NY
11042: Free information. 516–488–6700.

Chinon America Inc., 1065 Bristol Rd.,
Mountainside, NJ 07092: Free information.
908–654–0404.

Contax, 100 Randolph Rd., CN 6700,
Somerset, NJ 08875: Free information.
201–560–0600.

Eastman Kodak Company, Information
Center, 343 State St., Rochester, NY 14650:
Free information. 800–462–6495.

Fuji Photo Film USA Inc., 555 Taxter Rd.,
Elmsford, NY 10523: Free information.
914–789–8100.

Peter Gowland Cameras, 609 Hightree Rd.,
Santa Monica, CA 90402: Free information.
310–454–7867.

Victor Hasselblad Inc., 10 Madison Rd.,
Fairfield, NJ 07004: Free brochure.
800–338–6477.

Kalimar, 622 Goddard Ave., Chesterfield,
MO 63017: Free information. 314–532–4511.

Konica USA Inc., 440 Sylvan Ave.,
Englewood Cliffs, NJ 07632: Free
information. 201–568–3100.

Leica USA Inc., 156 Ludlow Ave.,
Northvale, NJ 07647: Free information.
201–767–7500.

Mamiya America Corporation, 8
Westchester Plaza, Elmsford, NY 10523: Free
information. 914–347–3300.

Minolta, 101 Williams Dr., Ramsey, NJ
07446: Free information. 201–825–4000.

Nikon, Customer Relations, 19601 Hamilton
Ave., Torrance, CA 90502: Free brochure.
800–645–6687.

Nikonos Cameras, Customer Relations,
19601 Hamilton Ave., Torrance, CA 90502:
Free brochure. 800–645–6687.

Olympus Corporation, 145 Crossways Park,
Woodbury, NY 11797: Free information.
800–221–3000.

Pentax Corporation, 35 Inverness Dr. East,
Englewood, CO 80112: Free brochure.
303–799–8000.

Polaroid Corporation, 549 Technology
Square, Cambridge, MA 02139: Free
information. 617–577–2000.

Ricoh Consumer Products Group, 180
Passaic Ave., Fairfield, NJ 07004: Free
brochure. 201–882–7762.

Ritz Cameras, 6711 Ritzway, Beltsville, MD
20705: Free catalog. 301–784–1441.

Rollei Cameras, HP Marketing, 16 Chapin
Rd., Pine Brook, NJ 07470: Free brochure.
201–808–9010.

Samsung Optical America Inc., 40 Seaview
Dr., Secaucus, NJ 07094: Free information.
201–902–0347.

Sigma Corporation of America, 15
Fleetwood Ct., Ronkonkoma, NY 11779:
Brochure $1. 516–585–1144.

Tamron Industries Inc., P.O. Box 388, Port
Washington, NY 11050: Free brochure.
800–827–8880.

Tokina Optical Corporation, 1512 Kona
Dr., Compton, CA 90220: Free information.
310–537–9380.

Vivitar Corporation, 1280 Rancho Conejo
Blvd., P.O. Box 2559, Newbury Park, CA
91319: Free brochure. 805–498–7008.

Wisner Large Format Cameras, Wisner
Classic Manufacturing Company Inc., P.O.
Box 21, Marion, MA 02738: Free
information. 800–848–0448.

WISTA Large Format Cameras, Foto-Care
Ltd., 132 W. 21st St., New York, NY 10011:
Free information.

Yashica Inc., 100 Randolph Rd., P.O. Box
6802, Somerset, NJ 08875: Free information.
908–560–0060.

Darkroom Equipment & Supplies

Alta Photographic Inc., 1421 International
Dr., Bartlesville, OK 74006: Free information
❖ Darkroom chemicals. 800–688–8688.

Bencher Inc., 831 N. Central Ave., Wood
Dale, IL 60191: Free information ❖
Enlargers, copystands and other darkroom
equipment. 708–238–1183.

Bogen Photo Corporation, 565 E. Crescent
Ave., P.O. Box 506, Ramsey, NJ 07446: Free
information ❖ Dry-mount presses.
201–818–9500.

Century Photo Sales & Service, P.O. Box
1071, Paramus, NJ 07653: Free catalog ❖
Used photo processing and darkroom
equipment. 201–546–2121.

Darkroom Aids Company, 3449 N. Lincoln
Ave., Chicago, IL 60657: Free information ❖
Used darkroom equipment. 312–249–4301.

Darkroom Products Ltd., 2949 11th St.,
Rockford, IL 61109: Free brochure ❖
Photographic developing and enlarging kits
and darkroom supplies. 815–399–0301.

Daylab, 400 E. Main, Ontario, CA 94545:
Free catalog ❖ All-in-one, self-contained
color enlarger, exposure meter, timer, and
developing system. 800–678–3669.

Delta-1, 10830 Sanden Dr., Dallas, TX
75238: Free catalog ❖ Temperature-regulated
sinks and other darkroom supplies.
800–627–0252.

Dimco-Gray, 8200 S. Suburban Rd.,
Centerville, OH 45459: Free brochure ❖
Darkroom timers. 800–333–7608.

Freestyle, 5120 Sunset Blvd., Los Angeles,
CA 90027: Free information ❖ Darkroom
supplies and equipment. 800–292–6137.

GMI Photographic Inc., 125 Schmitt Blvd.,
Farmingdale, NY 11735: Free information ❖
Darkroom chemicals and enlarging papers.
516–752–0066.

Helix, 310 S. Racine Ave., Chicago, IL
60607: Free catalog ❖ Cameras and
accessories, darkroom equipment and
supplies, video equipment, and underwater
photo equipment. 800–33–HELIX;
312–CAMERAS (in IL).

Jobo Fototechnic Inc., P.O. Box 3721, Ann
Arbor, MI 48106: Free information ❖ Photo
processing chemicals and color retouching
dyes for color and black-and-white
photography. 800–664–0344.

KingConcept, Division Amega/Arkay, 191 Shaeffer Ave., Westminster, MD 21157: Free information ❖ Automatic rotary tube film and print processor. 800–777–6634.

Leedal Inc., 1918 S. Prairie Ave., Chicago, IL 60616: Free brochure ❖ Stainless steel darkroom sinks with plumbing and back splash, stands, and shelves. 800–441–6663.

The Maine Photographic Resource, 2 Central St., Rockport, ME 04856: Free catalog ❖ Photography and darkroom equipment. 800–227–1541; 1–236–4788 (in ME).

Omega/Arkay, P.O. Box 2078, 197 Schaeffer Ave., Westminster, MD 21157: Free information ❖ Darkroom equipment and enlargers. 410–857–6353.

The Palladio Company, P.O. Box 28, Cambridge, MA 02140: Free information ❖ Platinum/palladium printing papers. 617–393–0814.

Photo-Therm, 110 Sewell Ave., Trenton, NJ 08610: Free catalog ❖ Temperature controls and temperature baths, modular controls, and film processors. 609–396–1456.

Photographers Formulary, P.O. Box 950, Condon, MT 59826: Free catalog ❖ Photographic chemicals. 800–922–5255.

Porter's Camera Store Inc., Box 628, Cedar Falls, Iowa 50613: Free catalog ❖ Picture-taking equipment, darkroom supplies, and photography novelties and accessories. 800–553–2001.

Seal Products, 550 Spring St., Naugatuck, CT 06770: Free information ❖ Dry-mounting presses. 203–729–5201.

Solar Cine Products Inc., 4247 S. Kedzie Ave., Chicago, IL 60632: Free catalog ❖ Darkroom and other photographic equipment and supplies. 312–254–8310.

TheNewLab, 651 Bryant St., San Francisco, CA 94107: Free brochure ❖ Photo processing equipment.

Yankee Photo Products Inc., 4024 E. Broadway Rd., Phoenix, AZ 85040: Free information ❖ Darkroom equipment and slide trays for most 35mm slide projectors. 602–275–7696.

Zone VI Studios Inc., 698 Elm St., Newfane, VT 05345: Free catalog ❖ Picture-taking equipment and darkroom equipment. 800–457–1114.

Enlargers

Bencher Inc., 831 N. Central Ave., Wood Dale, IL 60191: Free information ❖ Enlargers and darkroom equipment. 708–238–1183.

Charles Beseler Company, 1600 Lower Rd., Linden, NJ 07036: Free brochure ❖ Enlargers, color heads and electronic controls, modular units for color or black-and-white enlarging, and other equipment. 908–862–7999.

Omega/Arkay, P.O. Box 2078, 197 Schaeffer Ave., Westminster, MD 21157: Free information ❖ Darkroom accessories and enlargers. 410–857–6353.

Paterson, Division Saunders Group, 21 Jet View Dr., Rochester, NY 14624: Free catalog ❖ Darkroom equipment and enlargers. 716–328–7800.

The Saunders Group, 21 Jet View Dr., Rochester, NY 14624: Free catalog ❖ Exposure and flash meters, medium format dichroic enlargers and equipment, strobe brackets, tripods, and other equipment. 716–328–7800.

Testrite Instrument Company Inc., 133 Monroe St., Newark, NJ 07105: Free catalog ❖ Enlargers and other equipment. 201–589–6767.

Exposure Meters & Guides

Bogen Photo Corporation, 565 E. Crescent Ave., P.O. Box 506, Ramsey, NJ 07446: Free information ❖ Multi-purpose exposure meters, tripods, enlargers, and other equipment. 201–818–9500.

Harris Photoguides, 83 Rock Beach Rd., Rochester, NY 14617: Free information ❖ Easy-to-use, hand-held dial exposure calculators.

Minolta, 101 Williams Dr., Ramsey, NJ 07446: Free brochure ❖ Exposure meters. 201–825–4000.

Pentax Corporation, 35 Inverness Dr. East, Englewood, CO 80112: Free brochure ❖ Exposure meters. 303–799–8000.

R.T.S. Inc., 40–11 Burt Dr., Deer Park, NY 11729: Free information ❖ Pocket-size exposure meters for incident and reflected light. 516–242–6801.

The Saunders Group, 21 Jet View Dr., Rochester, NY 14624: Free catalog ❖ Exposure and flash meters, medium format dichroic enlargers, strobe brackets, tripods, and other equipment. 716–328–7800.

Sekonic, 40–11 Burt Dr., Deer Park, NY 11729: Free brochure ❖ Standard and full-function digital readout exposure meters. 516–242–6801.

Shepherd Meters, Division Saunders Group, 21 Jet View Dr., Rochester, NY 14624: Free catalog ❖ Exposure meters. 716–328–7800.

Sinar Bron, 17 Progress St., Edison, NJ 08820: Free information ❖ A three-in-one meter that measures color temperature for flash, continuous light sources, flash-duration meter, and lux. 908–754–5800.

Smith-Victor, 301 N. Colfax St., Griffith, IN 46319: Free information ❖ Light meters. 219–924–6136.

Film

Eastman Kodak Company, Information Center, 343 State St., Rochester, NY 14650: Free information ❖ Color slide, color print, black-and-white, infrared, and special process films. 800–462–6495.

Forte Film, GMI Photographic Inc., 125 Schmitt Blvd., Farmingdale, NY 11735: Free information ❖ Black-and-white film. 516–752–0066.

Fuji Photo Film USA Inc., 555 Taxter Rd., Elmsford, NY 10523: Free information ❖ Color slide, color print, and black-and-white film. 914–789–8100.

Ilford Photo Corporation, W. 70 Century Blvd., Paramus, NJ 07652: Free information ❖ Chromogenic black-and-white film. 201–265–6000.

Konica USA Inc., 440 Sylvan Ave., Englewood Cliffs, NJ 07632: Free information ❖ Color print film. 201–568–3100.

MicroTec, P.O. Box 9424, San Diego, CA 92109: Free information ❖ Film for the Minox camera and photo processing. 619–272–8820.

Polaroid Corporation, 549 Technology Square, Cambridge, MA 02139: Free information ❖ Color slide, black-and-white slide, color print pack, and black-and-white pack film. 617–577–2000.

3M Photo Color Systems Division, 3M Center, Bldg. 223–2S-05, St. Paul, MN 55144: Free information ❖ Color slide and print film. 800–695–FILM.

Filters

Aetna Optix, 44 Alabama Ave., Island Park, NY 11558: Free information ❖ Rokunar filters. 516–889–8570.

Cambridge Camera Exchange, 7th Ave. & 13th St., New York, NY 10011: Free information ❖ Cambron filters. 212–675–8600.

Eastman Kodak Company, Information Center, 343 State St., Rochester, NY 14650: Free information ❖ Wratten filters. 800–462–6495.

Schneider Corporation, 400 Crossways Park Dr., Woodbury, NY 11797: Free information ❖ Filters for black-and-white photography, neutral density filters, star and diffraction filters, lens shades, masks for matte boxes, lens reversal rings, tele-converters, and auto-extension tubes. 516–496–8500.

Tiffen Manufacturing, 90 Oser Ave., Hauppage, NY 11788: Free information ❖ Filters. 516–272–2500.

Flash Units & Lighting

Aetna Optix, 44 Alabama Ave., Island Park, NY 11558: Free information ❖ Home portrait equipment. 516–889–8570.

Bogen Photo Corporation, 565 E. Crescent Ave., P.O. Box 506, Ramsey, NJ 07446: Free information ❖ Compact studio electronic flash systems and Metz Mecablitz flash units with a choice of power sources and system accessories. 201–818–9500.

Britek Inc., 12704 Marquardt Ave., Santa Fe Springs, CA 90670: Free information ❖ Professional studio flash and lighting equipment. 800–925–6258.

Paul C. Buff Inc., 2725 Bransford Ave., Nashville, TN 37204: Free information ❖ Compact, lightweight studio flash equipment. 800–443–5542; 615–383–3982 (in TN).

Canon, One Canon Plaza, Lake Success, NY 11042: Free information ❖ Flash units for the Canon cameras. 516–488–6700.

Chimera, 1812 Valtec Ln., Boulder, CO 80301: Free catalog ❖ Portable lighting units and accessories. 800–424–4075.

Courtenay Solaflash, Division Saunders Group, 21 Jet View Dr., Rochester, NY 14624: Free catalog ❖ Professional studio lighting equipment. 716–328–7800.

Creative Light Works, 4633 Mill Rd., Red Wing, MN 55066: Free information ❖ Adjustable light booms. 612–388–5444.

Delta-1, 10830 Sanden Dr., Dallas, TX 75238: Free catalog ❖ Studio lighting and special effects equipment. 800–627–0252.

Dyna-Lite, 311–319 Long Ave., Hillside, NJ 07205: Free information ❖ Professional studio flash and lighting equipment. 908–687–8800.

Foto Tools, 1635 Algonquin, Box 292, Huntington Harbor, CA 92649: Free information ❖ Light reflectors. 714–846–0882.

Konica USA Inc., 440 Sylvan Ave., Englewood Cliffs, NJ 07632: Free brochure ❖ Konica flash equipment and accessories. 201–568–3100.

Larson Enterprises Inc., 365 S. Mountainway Dr., P.O. Box 2150, Orem, UT 84058: Free information ❖ Compact lighting equipment. 801–225–8088.

Lighthouse Photo Products, 1135 Hawthorne Ln., P.O. Box 9426, Charlotte, NC 28299: Free information ❖ Lighting control accessories. 704–334–2682.

Lumiquest, 140 Heimer, Ste. 775, San Antonio, TX 78232: Free information ❖ Tabletop lighting accessories and reflectors. 210–490–1400.

Minolta, 101 Williams Dr., Ramsey, NJ 07446: Free information ❖ Flash units for Minolta cameras. 201–825–4000.

The Morris Company, 1205 W. Jackson Blvd., Chicago, IL 60607: Free information ❖ Lightweight, portable DC flash slave units. 312–421–5739.

Multiblitz Lighting Company, HP Marketing Corporation, 16 Chapin Rd., Pine Brook, NJ 07058: Free information ❖ Studio electronic flash equipment for amateurs and professionals. 201–808–9010.

Nikon, Customer Relations, 19601 Hamilton Ave., Torrance, CA 90502: Free brochure ❖ Flash units and accessories. 800–645–6687.

Nikonos Cameras, Customer Relations, 19601 Hamilton Ave., Torrance, CA 90502: Free brochure ❖ Electronic flash systems for general use and underwater. 800–645–6687.

Novatron of Dallas Inc., 8230 Moberly Ln., Dallas, TX 75227: Free catalog ❖ Studio flash equipment. 214–381–2153.

Olympus Corporation, 145 Crossways Park, Woodbury, NY 11797: Free information ❖ Flash systems for use with Olympus cameras. 800–221–3000.

Pentax Corporation, 35 Inverness Dr. East, Englewood, CO 80112: Free brochure ❖ Electronic flash units for Pentax cameras. 303–799–8000.

Photogenic Machine Company, P.O. Box 3365, Youngstown, OH 44513: Free brochure ❖ Soft lighting equipment for use with studio or small battery-operated strobes. 800–682–7668.

Photographer's Warehouse, P.O. Box 3365, Boardman, OH 44513: Free information ❖ Electronic flash systems. 800–521–4311.

Quantum Instruments Inc., 2075 Stewart Ave., Garden City, NY 11530: Free information ❖ Portable studio-style flash units. 516–222–0611.

Ricoh Consumer Products Group, 180 Passaic Ave., Fairfield, NJ 07004: Free brochure ❖ Flash equipment for Ricoh cameras. 201–882–7762.

Satter Distributing, P.O. Box 7234, Denver, CO 80207: Free information ❖ Electronic flash systems. 800–525–0196.

Sinar Bron, 17 Progress St., Edison, NJ 08820: Free information ❖ A three-in-one FCC meter that measures color temperatures, meter for flash and continuous light sources, a flash-duration meter, and a lux meter. 908–754–5800.

Sonic Research, P.O. Box 850, Bonsall, CA 92003: Free information ❖ Underwater strobe lights. 619–724–4540.

Speedotron Corporation, 310 S. Racine Ave., Chicago, IL 60607: Free information ❖ Lighting equipment for portrait photography. 312–421–4050.

Stage Lighting Distributors, Holt Dr., Stony Point, NY 10980: Free catalog ❖ Lighting equipment. 800–228–0222; 914–947–3034 (in NY).

Studiomate, P.O. Box 626, Gardena, CA 90248: Free information ❖ Studio lighting equipment. 800–283–8346.

Sunpak Division of ToCAD America, 300 Webrow Rd., Parsippany, NJ 07054: Free information ❖ Electronic flash equipment. 201–428–9800.

Testrite Instrument Company Inc., 133 Monroe St., Newark, NJ 07105: Free catalog ❖ Portable light box systems, lightweight aluminum and chrome easels, opaque projectors, and darkroom equipment. 201–589–6767.

Tristar Photo Industrial Inc., 9960 Indiana Ave., Riverside, CA 92503: Free information ❖ Studio lighting equipment, backgrounds, lightstands, brackets and holders, soft boxes, umbrellas, video camera supports, and other equipment. 714–351–8833.

Vivitar Corporation, 1280 Rancho Conejo Blvd., P.O. Box 2559, Newbury Park, CA 91319: Free brochure ❖ Electronic flash equipment, cameras, and lenses. 805–498–7009.

Wein Products Inc., 115 W. 25th St., Los Angeles, CA 90007: Free information ❖ Sound and light-operated wireless meter and switches. 213–749–6049.

F.J. Westcott Company, 1447 Summit St., P.O. Box 1596, Toledo, OH 43603: Free information ❖ Umbrella reflectors and light tents. 419–243–7311.

Woods Electronics Inc., 14781 Pomerado Rd., Poway, CA 92064: Free information ❖ Sound- and infrared-operated remote flash triggering devices. 619–486–0806.

Zone VI Studios Inc., 698 Elm St., Newfane, VT 05345: Free catalog ❖ Lighting and darkroom equipment. 800–457–1114.

Photo Processing

ABC Photo Service, 9016 Prince William St., Manassas, VA 22110: Free information ❖ Black-and-white and color processing. 703–369–1906.

Associated Photo Company, Box 817, Florence, KY 41022: Free information ❖ Photo Christmas cards with name imprint. 606–282–0011.

Brockman Labs Inc., P.O. Box 31, Fayette, MO 65248: Free information ❖ Color and black and white photographic processing. 816–248–3288.

C & C Photo Lab, 125 Walt Whitman Rd., Huntington Station, NY 11746: Free information ❖ Enlargements. 516–421–0492.

Clark Color Labs, P.O. Box 96300, Washington, DC 20090: Free information ❖ Film processing and enlargements.

Color Mate Photo Inc., 2179 W. 6th St., Fayetteville, AR 72701: Free information ❖ Film processing, color enlargements, video transfers, black and white enlargements, and copy negatives. 501–521–7272.

Color Prints by Nordstrom, 576 Powers Dr., El Dorado Hills, CA 95762: Free information ❖ Museum-quality, permanent carbon-pigment color prints. 916–933–3403.

Color Specialist, P.O. Box 112, Ramsey, NJ 07446: Free information ❖ Processing and other services.

Custom Panoramic Lab, 2101 NW 33rd St., Ste. 2700A, Pompano Beach, FL 33069: Free price list ❖ Enlargements, black and white processing, and other services. 305–970–4450.

Custom Quality Studio, P.O. Box 4838, Chicago, IL 60680: Free information ❖ Color film developing and processing, enlargements, slide duplication, black and white processing, duplication and copy services, and hand-coloring of prints.

Dale Laboratories, 2960 Simms St., Hollywood, FL 33020: Free information ❖ Processes slides, prints, and negatives from Kodacolor film. 800–327–1776.

Direct Photo Service, P.O. Box 6789, Hollywood, FL 33081: Free information ❖ Enlargements from color negatives. 305–985–9787.

EMCAX Photo-finishing, P.O. Box 7383, Madison, WI 53707: Free information ❖ Hand-printed Ilfochrome enlargements. 800–497–6544; 608–244–4176 (in WI).

The Enlargement Works Inc., 316 N. Milwaukee St., Ste. 406, Milwaukee, WI 53202: Free information ❖ Handmade color enlargements from slides or negatives. 414–278–1210.

Fuji Anaheim Color Labs, 2665 Woodland Dr., Anaheim, CA 92802: Free information ❖ Fuji color slide and print processing. 800–634–2960.

G-B Color Lab, P.O. Box 562, Hawthorne, NJ 07507: Free brochure ❖ Ilfochrome color prints from slides. 201–427–0460.

General Color Corporation, 604 Brevard Ave., P.O. Box 70, Cocoa, FL 32923: Free brochure ❖ Photo and print processing with enlargements up to 24 x 30 inches. 800–321–1602.

Holland Photo, 1221 S. Lamar, Austin, TX 78704: Free information ❖ Ilfochrome prints from slides or transparencies. 800–477–4024.

Holleman Photo Labs Inc., 3018 N. Lamar, Austin, TX 78705: Free information ❖ Black and white, and color film processing, prints and enlargements, slide duplication, and other services. 412–441–4444.

Imagination Station, 730 NW 2nd St., Grants Pass, OR 97526: Free information ❖ Full color, black and white and sepia antique photo reproductions on paper and fabric. 800–338–3857.

Kelly Color, Box 576, Morgantown, NC 28680: Free information ❖ Proofing, candid and portrait photos, package assortments, copy and restoration services, montages and composites, and display transparencies for light boxes. 704–433–0934.

Lakeside Photography, P.O. Box 370027, Bears Station, Tampa, FL 33697: Free information ❖ Ilfochrome color enlargements. 813–968–9307.

LaserColor Laboratories, P.O. Box 24614, West Palm Beach, FL 33416: Free information ❖ Laser and computer-made color prints. 800–848–2018; 407–848–2000 (in FL).

MicroTec, P.O. Box 9424, San Diego, CA 92109: Free information ❖ Minox format film processing and film for the Minox camera. 619–272–8820.

Minox Processing Laboratories, P.O. Box 1041, New Hyde Park, NY 11040: Free information ❖ Sub-miniature film processing. 800–645–8172; 516–437–5750 (in NY).

Mystic Color Lab, P.O. Box 144, Mystic, CT 06355: Free information ❖ Processes black-and-white and color print film, Kodachrome and Ektachrome slide and movie film, and Kodacolor 35mm, 110, 126, and disc film. 800–367–6061.

Owl Photo Corporation, 701 E. Main St., Weatherford, OK 73096: Free information ❖ Film processing and print-making services. 405–772–3353.

PML Film Processing, P.O. Box 75981, St. Paul, MN 55175: Free price list ❖ Professional black and white film processing. 612–225–9431.

Pro Photo Labs, 213–219 S. Tyler Ave., P.O. Drawer 777, Lakeland, FL 33802: Free information ❖ Film developing, enlarging, and other services. 800–237–6429.

Professional Color Labs, 306 W. 1st Ave., Roselle, NJ 07203: Free information ❖ Photo processing. 908–241–3030.

Shooters of U.S.A. Lab, P.O. Box 8640, Rolling Meadows, IL 60008: Free information ❖ Color enlargements. 708–956–1010.

Silver Image, 4248 Forest Park Blvd., St. Louis, MO 63108: Free information ❖ Black and white negative and print processing. 800–289–9906.

Skrudland Photo, 5311 Fleming Ct., Austin, TX 78744: Free information ❖ Film processing and print-making. 512–444–0958.

The Slideprinter, P.O. Box 9506, Denver, CO 80209: Free information ❖ Color prints and enlargements from slides.

Westside Processing Inc., 1523 26th St., Santa Monica, CA 90404: Free information ❖ Film processing. 310–450–3300.

Photo Restoration

Artex Studio, 6 Forest Ave., Glen Cove, NY 11542: Free information ❖ Black/white and color photo restoration and conversion of black/white photographs to color. 516–676–0376.

Deveraux Photo Restoration, 119 W. 57th St., Ste. 200, New York, NY 10019: Free information ❖ Restoration services for photos, daguerreotypes, tin photographs, and glass negatives. 212–245–1720.

Duplitech, P.O. Box 4154, Salem, OR 97302: Free information ❖ Photo copy services from small or large prints, polaroid prints, tin plates, and others. 503–378–0751.

Elbinger Laboratories Inc., 220 Albert St., East Lansing, MI 48823: Free information ❖ Archival reproduction of photographs in sepia, oil coloring, and black-and-white. 800–332–0302.

Kelly Color, Box 576, Morgantown, NC 28655: Free information ❖ Restoration and copy services, proofing, portraits and machine-processed candid photos, package assortments, montages and composites, and display transparencies for light boxes. 704–433–0934.

Lexington Lensmasters, 1702 Main St., Lexington, MO 64067: Free information with long SASE ❖ Photo restoration services. 816–259–2171.

Modernage Photographic Services, 1150 Avenue of Americas, New York, NY 10036: Free information with long SASE ❖ Photo restoration services. 212–227–4767.

Retail Stores

AAA Camera Exchange Inc., 43 7th Ave., New York, NY 10011: Free information ❖ Cameras and darkroom equipment. 800–221–9521; 212–242–5800 (in NY).

Abbey Camera Inc., 1417 Melon St., Philadelphia, PA 19130: Free information ❖ Photographic equipment, darkroom supplies, and studio equipment. 800–25–ABBEY.

Abe's of Maine Camera & Electronics, 1957 Coney Island Ave., Brooklyn, NY 11223: Free information ❖ Photography equipment. 800–992–2379; 718–645–1878 (in NY).

Abner's by Mail, 5363 Central Ave., St. Petersburg, FL 33710: Free information ❖ Camera equipment. 800–446–4148.

Adorama, 42 W. 18th St., New York, NY 10011: Catalog $3 ❖ Photography, darkroom, and underwater photo equipment. 212–741–0052.

Alfred O's Cameras, 916 Gravier St., New Orleans, LA 70112: Free information ❖ Cameras, movie and studio equipment, binoculars, and projectors. 504–523–2421.

Alkit Pro Camera Inc., 222 Park Ave. South, New York, NY 10003: Free information ❖ Camera equipment. 212–674–1515.

B & H Photo, 119 W. 17th St., New York, NY 10011: Free information ❖ Photo equipment. 212–807–7474.

Beach Camera of Maine, 203 Rt. 22 East, Greenbrook, NJ 08812: Free information ❖ Photography equipment, binoculars, radar detectors, and video equipment. 908–424–1103.

Beach Photo & Video Inc., 604 Main St., Daytona Beach, FL 32118: Free information ❖ Photography equipment and supplies. 800–876–2115; 800–874–2115 (in FL).

Bergen County Camera, 270 Westwood Ave., Westwood, NJ 07675: Free information ❖ Photography equipment. 201–664–4113.

Berger Brothers Camera Exchange, 209 Broadway, Amityville, NY 11701: Free information ❖ Photography equipment. 800–262–4160.

Bi-Rite Photo & Electronics, 15 E. 30th St., New York, NY 10016: Free information ❖ Cameras, darkroom equipment, binoculars, telescopes, and underwater photography equipment. 800–223–1970; 212–685–2130 (in NY).

Bromwell Marketing, 3 Alleghany Center, Pittsburgh, PA 15212: Free catalog ❖ Large-format view cameras, lenses, and tripods. 412–321–4118.

Brooklyn Camera Exchange, 549 E. 26th St., Brooklyn, NY 11210: Free information ❖ New and used cameras and other supplies. 718–462–2892.

Cambridge Camera Exchange, 7th Ave. & 13th St., New York, NY 10011: Free information ❖ Photography equipment. 212–675–8600.

Camera Care, 906 Arch St., Philadelphia, PA 19107: Free information ❖ Photographic equipment. 215–925–7805.

Camera One of Sarasota Inc., 1918 Robinhood St., Sarasota, FL 34231: Free information ❖ Cameras, lenses, filters, enlargers and projectors, binoculars, tripods, cases, and books. 800–759–1302.

Camera Sound of Pennsylvania, 1104 Chestnut St., Philadelphia, PA 19107: Free information ❖ Cameras and accessories, camcorders, laser disk players, and portable audio and high-fidelity equipment. 800–477–0022.

Camera Traders Ltd., 1873 Ocean Pkwy., Brooklyn, NY 11223: Free information ❖ Cameras, lenses, filters, enlargers and projectors, slide duplicators, tripods, copy equipment, flash and lighting equipment, cases, and books. 718–336–6667.

Camera World, 4619 W. Market St., Greensboro, NC 27407: Catalog $1 ❖ Darkroom and other equipment for still, movie, video, and underwater photography. 800–634–0556.

Cameras & Electronics of New Jersey & Maine, 982 River Rd., Edgewater, NJ 07020: Free information ❖ Photography equipment. 201–886–7400.

Canoga Cameras, 22065 Sherman Way, Canoga Park, CA 91303: Free information ❖ Photographic and video equipment for amateurs, professionals, and industrial use. 818–346–5506.

Central Camera Company, 230 S. Wabash Ave., Chicago, IL 60604: Free information ❖ Photography equipment. 800–421–1899; 312–427–5580 (in IL).

Century Photo Sales & Service, P.O. Box 1071, Paramus, NJ 07653: Free catalog ❖ Used photo processing and darkroom equipment. 201–546–2121.

Charlotte Camera Brokers Inc., 2400 Park Rd., Charlotte, NC 28203: Free information ❖ Photography equipment. 704–339–0084.

Don Chatterton of Seattle, P.O. Box 15150, Seattle, WA 98115: Free information ❖ Photographic equipment. 206–525–1100.

Collector Cameras Inc., 3119 E. 25th, Tulsa, OK 74114: Free information ❖ Collectible cameras. 918–749–4021.

Columbus Camera Group Inc., 55 E. Blake, Columbus, OH 43202: Free information ❖ Photography equipment. 614–267–0686.

Custom Photo Manufacturing, 10830 Sanden Dr., Dallas, TX 75238: Free catalog ❖ Darkroom and studio equipment for amateurs, professionals, and industrial use. 800–627–0252.

Del's Camera, 330 E. Canon Perdido, Santa Barbara, CA 93101: Free information ❖ Photographic equipment. 805–962–7557.

Executive Photo & Electronics, 120 W. 31st St., New York, NY 10001: Free information ❖ Photography and video equipment and other electronics. 212–947–5290.

Fields & Views Inc., P.O. Box 132, Old Catham, NY 12136: Free catalog ❖ Wista cameras and accessories. 212–779–1471.

Focus Camera, 4419 13th Ave., Brooklyn, NY 11219: Free information ❖ Cameras and darkroom equipment. 718–436–6262.

47th Street Photo, Mail Order Department, 455 Smith St., Brooklyn, NY 11231: Catalog $2 ❖ Photography and video equipment. 800–221–7774.

Foto Electric Supply Company, 31 Essex St., New York, NY 10002: Free information ❖ Cameras, lenses, and darkroom equipment. 212–673–5222.

Frank's Highland Park Camera, 5715 N. Figueroa St., Los Angeles, CA 90042: Catalog $3 ❖ Cameras, darkroom equipment, underwater photography and video equipment, and books. 800–421–8230; 213–255–0123 (in CA).

Free Trade Photo, 1864 48th St., Brooklyn, NY 11204: Free information ❖ Photographic equipment, camcorders, editing and industrial equipment, and video and audio accessories. 718–435–4151.

Freestyle, 5120 Sunset Blvd., Los Angeles, CA 90027: Free information ❖ Photography and darkroom equipment. 800–292–6137.

G & S Photo & Electronics, 2119 Utica Ave., Brooklyn, NY 11234: Free information ❖ Photographic equipment, camcorders, video and audio accessories, binoculars, and other optical equipment. 800–879–9438; 215–527–5261 (in PA).

Garden State Camera, 101 Kuller Rd., Clifton, NJ 07015: Free information ❖

Photographic equipment, camcorders, video and audio accessories, binoculars, and other optical equipment. 201–742–5777.

Genesis Camera Inc., 814 W. Lancaster Ave., Bryn Mawr, PA 19010: Free information ❖ Photographic equipment, camcorders, editing and industrial equipment, and video and audio accessories. 800–879–9438; 215–527–5261 (in PA).

Gould Trading, 7 E. 17th St., New York, NY 10003: Free catalog ❖ Photography equipment, books, and videos. 212–243–2306.

Helix, 310 S. Racine Ave., Chicago, IL 60607: Free catalog ❖ Cameras, darkroom supplies, and video and underwater equipment. 800–33–HELIX; 312–CAMERAS (in IL).

Hirsch Photo, P.O. Box 684, Hartsdale, NY 10530: Free information ❖ New and used cameras, other optical equipment, and darkroom supplies.

W.B. Hunt Company Inc., 100 Main St., Melrose, MA 02176: Free catalog ❖ Cameras, other optical accessories, and darkroom and studio equipment. 617–662–6685.

Jack's Camera Shop, 300 E. Main, Muncie, IN 47305: Free information ❖ New and used photography equipment. 317–284–6405.

KEH Camera Brokers, P.O. Box 94065, Atlanta, GA 30377: Free catalog ❖ Cameras and accessories. 404–897–2677.

Ken-Mar Camera & Video, 27 Great Neck Rd., Great Neck, NY 11021: Free information ❖ Camera equipment, binoculars, and video equipment. 800–864–0513; 516–482–1025 (in NY).

KOH'S Camera Sales & Service Inc., 2 Heitz Pl., Hicksville, NY 11801: Free information ❖ Cameras, studio accessories, and other optical equipment. 516–933–9790.

Jim Kuehl & Company, 8527 University Blvd., Des Moines, IA 50325: Free information ❖ Leica cameras and other photographic and optical equipment. 515–225–0110.

Le Camera, 4040 Quaker Bridge Rd., Mercerville, NJ 08619: Free information ❖ Camera equipment. 609–588–9090.

Lindahl Specialties Inc., P.O. Box 1365, Elkhart, IN 46515: Free information ❖ Photographic equipment for special effects. 219–264–3560.

Mibro Cameras, 64 W. 36th St., New York, NY 10018: Free information ❖ Camera equipment. 800–223–0322; 212–967–2353 (in NY).

Midwest Photo Exchange, 3313 N. High St., Columbus, OH 43202: Free information ❖ Camera equipment, darkroom supplies, and lighting accessories. 614–261–1264.

New York Camera & Video, 78 S. West End Blvd., Quakertown, PA 18951: Free information ❖ Used cameras and video equipment. 800–448–1613.

Olden Camera & Lens Company Inc., 1265 Broadway, New York, NY 10001: Free information ❖ Photography equipment, supplies, video equipment, computers, and other electronics. 212–725–1234.

Omni Photo, Brooklyn Navy Yard, Bldg. 27, Brooklyn, NY 11205: Free information ❖ Photographic equipment, camcorders, and binoculars. 800–572–5723; 718–875–0779 (in NY).

Peach State Photo, 1706 Chantilly Dr., Atlanta, GA 30324: Free information ❖ Camera and video equipment. 404–633–2699.

Photo Warehouse, 120 Bernoulu, Oxnard, CA 94030: Free catalog with long SASE and two 1st class stamps ❖ Black/white enlarging and color paper, black/white and color film, and other supplies. 805–485–9654.

Photographic Systems, 412 Central SE, Albuquerque, NM 87102: Free catalog ❖ Used equipment. 505–247–9780.

Porter's Camera Store Inc., Box 628, Cedar Falls, Iowa 50613: Free catalog ❖ Photography equipment and darkroom supplies. 800–553–2001.

Reimers Photo Materials Company, 300 E. Bay St., Milwaukee, WI 53207: Free information ❖ Used and new cameras. 800–236–5435; 414–744–4471 (in WI).

Leonard Rue Enterprises, 138 Millbrook Rd., Blairstown, NJ 07825: Free catalog ❖ Books, video tapes, equipment, and other gifts for photographers and outdoor enthusiasts. 908–362–6616.

Samy's Camera, 263 S. La Brea, Los Angeles, CA 90036: Free information ❖ Photographic equipment, flash accessories, and new and used cameras. 800–321–4SAM.

Smile Photo, 29 W. 35th St., New York, NY 10001: Free information ❖ Photography and video equipment and supplies. 212–967–5900.

Solar Cine Products Inc., 4247 S. Kedzie Ave., Chicago, IL 60632: Free catalog ❖ Darkroom and other photographic equipment and supplies. 312–254–8310.

Supreme Camera & Video, 2123 Utica Ave., Brooklyn, NY 11234: Free information ❖ Cameras and accessories. 800–332–2661; 718–692–4110 (in NY).

Tamarkin & Company, 198 Amity Rd., Woodbridge, CT 06525: Free price list ❖ Photographic equipment, flash accessories, and new and used cameras. 800–289–5342; 203–397–7766 (in CT).

Testrite Instrument Company Inc., 133 Monroe St., Newark, NJ 07105: Free catalog ❖ Photography equipment for the darkroom and studio. 201–589–6767.

Tri-State Camera, 650 6th Ave., New York, NY 10011: Free information ❖ Photography equipment. 800–537–4441; 212–633–2290 (in NY).

University Camera Inc., 2030 I-85 Service Rd., Durham, NC 27705: Free information ❖ Photography equipment. 919–477–7225.

The Wall Street Camera, 82 Wall St., New York, NY 10005: Catalog $2.95 (refundable with $50 purchase) ❖ Photography equipment. 212–425–5999.

Woodmere Camera Inc., 337 Merrick Rd., Lynbrook, NY 11563: Free information with long SASE ❖ Photography equipment. 516–599–6013.

Zone VI Studios Inc., 698 Elm St., Newfane, VT 05345: Free catalog ❖ Photography and lighting equipment and darkroom supplies. 800–457–1114.

Slides

Cornell Laboratory of Ornithology, 159 Sapsucker Woods Rd., Ithaca, NY 14850: Free brochure ❖ Slides of North American birds. 607–254–2450.

MMI Corporation, P.O. Box 19907, Baltimore, MD 21211: Catalog $2 ❖ Astronomy 35mm slides. 410–366–1222.

Reel 3-D Enterprises Inc., P.O. Box 2368, Culver City, CA 90231: Free information ❖ Stereo and cardboard slip-in slide mounts. 310–837–2368.

Visuals, P.O. Box 381848, Miami, FL 33238: Free list ❖ Worldwide travel slides from almost 200 countries. 305–681–5379.

Worldwide, 7427 Washburn, Minneapolis, MN 55423: Catalog $1 ❖ Travel slides about

the United States, foreign countries, historic and scenic sites, and nature settings. 612–869–6482.

Storage & Filing Systems

Light Impressions, 439 Monroe Ave., Rochester, NY 14607: Free catalog ❖ Books on photography and supplies for archival storage of negatives and prints. 800–828–6216.

RNI Marketing, P.O. Drawer 638, Ocala, FL 32678: Free information ❖ Light- and heavyweight polyethylene pages for storing, organizing, and displaying slides, prints, and negatives. 800–451–6789; 800–622–0303 (in FL).

20th Century Plastics Inc., 3628 Crenshaw Blvd., Los Angeles, CA 90051: Free catalog ❖ Plastic pages to protect, organize, and display slides, prints, and negatives. 800–767–0777; 213–731–0900 (in CA).

Tripods

Benbo Tripods, Division Saunders Group, 21 Jet View Dr., Rochester, NY 14624: Free catalog ❖ Adjustable tripods. 716–328–7800.

Bogen Photo Corporation, 565 E. Crescent Ave., P.O. Box 506, Ramsey, NJ 07446: Free information ❖ Tripods. 201–818–9500.

Cascade Designs Inc., 4000 1st Ave. South, Seattle, WA 98134: Free information ❖ Walking stick equipped with a universal camera mount that converts to a monopod. 800–531–9531.

Coast Manufacturing Company, 200 Corporate Blvd. South, Yonkers, NY 10701: Free information ❖ Photo and video luggage and tripods. 800–333–6282; 914–376–1500 (in NY).

GMI Photographic Inc., 125 Schmitt Blvd., Farmingdale, NY 11735: Free brochure ❖ Cullman tripods. 516–752–0066.

Karl Heitz Inc., P.O. Box 427, Woodside, NY 11377: Free information ❖ Gitzo monopods. 718–565–0004.

KB Systems, 10407 62nd Pl. West., Mukilteo, WA 98275: Free information ❖ Wood tripods. 206–355–8740.

The Saunders Group, 21 Jet View Dr., Rochester, NY 14624: Free catalog ❖ Tripods, exposure and flash meters, enlargers, strobe brackets, and other equipment. 716–328–7800.

Slik America, 300 Webrow Rd., Parsippany, NJ 07054: Free catalog ❖ Adjustable tripods. 201–428–9800.

Tracks Walking Staffs, 4000 1st Ave. South, Seattle, WA 98134: Free information ❖ Telescoping sectioned walking staffs that convert to a camera monopod. 800–527–1527.

Velbon, 2433 Moreton St., Torrance, CA 90505: Free information ❖ Tripods. 213–530–5446.

Underwater Photography Equipment

AccuGear, 27 William St., New York, NY 10005: Free information ❖ Underwater camera housings. 800–445–4327; 212–825–1856 (in NY).

Adorama, 42 W. 18th St., New York, NY 10011: Catalog $3 ❖ Underwater and other photography equipment. 212–741–0052.

Amphibico Inc., 9563 Cote de Liesse, Dorval, Quebec, Canada H9P 1A3: Free information ❖ Underwater housings and lights for Sony cameras. 514–636–9910.

B & H Photo, 119 W. 17th St., New York, NY 10011: Free information ❖ Underwater photography equipment. 212–807–7474.

Berry Scuba Company, 6674 Northwest Hwy., Chicago, IL 60631: Free catalog ❖ Skin diving and scuba equipment, diving lights, and underwater camera equipment. 800–621–6019; 312–763–1626 (in IL).

Bi-Rite Photo & Electronics, 15 E. 30th St., New York, NY 10016: Free information ❖ Equipment for underwater and other types of photography. 800–223–1970; 212–685–2130 (in NY).

Camera World, 4619 W. Market St., Greensboro, NC 27407: Catalog $1 ❖ Equipment and supplies for still, movie, video, and underwater photography. 800–634–0556.

Divemart, 40 Exchange Pl., Ste. 1515, New York, NY 10005: Free information ❖ Underwater video and other cameras. 800–777–1137.

Frank's Highland Park Camera, 5715 N. Figueroa St., Los Angeles, CA 90042: Catalog $3 ❖ Cameras, darkroom accessories, and underwater photography equipment. 800–421–8230; 213–255–0123 (in CA).

Fuji Photo Film USA Inc., 555 Taxter Rd., Elmsford, NY 10523: Free information ❖ Underwater camera equipment. 914–789–8100.

GMI Photographic Inc., 125 Schmitt Blvd., Farmingdale, NY 11735: Free information ❖ Underwater cameras with electronic flash, close-up lenses, automatic wind and rewind, and built in film coding. 516–752–0066.

Helix, 310 S. Racine Ave., Chicago, IL 60607: Free catalog ❖ Cameras, underwater photography equipment, darkroom supplies, and video equipment. 800–33–HELIX; 312–CAMERAS (in IL).

Ikelite Underwater Systems, 50 33rd St., Indianapolis, IN 46208: Catalog $1 ❖ Underwater housings for most cameras. 317–923–4523.

Merald Vision & Sound, 151 W. 26th., Ste. 11–1, New York, NY 10001: Free information ❖ Underwater video and SLR housings, video and other cameras, and accessories. 800–980–2929.

Minolta, 101 Williams Dr., Ramsey, NJ 07446: Free information ❖ Underwater camera equipment. 201–825–4000.

Nikon, Customer Relations, 19601 Hamilton Ave., Torrance, CA 90502: Free brochure ❖ Underwater camera equipment and lenses. 800–645–6687.

Nikonos Cameras, Customer Relations, 19601 Hamilton Ave., Torrance, CA 90502: Free brochure ❖ Underwater camera equipment and lenses. 800–645–6687.

Pioneer Research Inc., 216 Haddon Ave., Westmont, NJ 08108: Free information ❖ Underwater housings for cameras and video equipment. 800–257–7742; 609–854–2424 (in NJ).

Quest Marine Video, 3176 Pullman St., Ste. 104, Costa Mesa, CA 92625: Free information ❖ Underwater video systems. 714–966–2396.

Sonic Research, P.O. Box 850, Bonsall, CA 92003: Free information ❖ Underwater strobe lights. 619–724–4540.

Vivitar Corporation, 1280 Rancho Conejo Blvd., P.O. Box 2559, Newbury Park, CA 91319: Free brochure ❖ Underwater camera equipment. 805–498–7008.

PINATAS

La Piñata, Number 2 Patio Market, Old Town, Albuquerque, NM 87104: Brochure $1 (refundable) ❖ Pinatas. 800–657–6208; 505–242–2400 (in NM).

PINE CONES

Herbst Mountain Farms, 307 Number 9 Rd., Fletcher, NC 28732: Catalog $1 ❖ Pine cones, pods, and potpourri.

International Manufacturing Company, 1130 Live Oak St., Lillian Springs, FL 32351: Catalog $1 ❖ Pine cones, silk plants, trees and flower arrangements, and flower arranging and other craft supplies. 904–875–2918.

Mountain Farms Inc., 307 Number 9 Rd., Fletcher, NC 28732: Free catalog ❖ Pods, small and large cones, and other foliage supplies. 704–628–4709.

Nature Crafts, 164 Hillside Ave., Livingston, NJ 07039: Catalog $2 (refundable) ❖ Pine cone crafting supplies.

J. Page Basketry, 820 Albee Rd. West, Nokomis, FL 34275: Catalog $2 (refundable) ❖ Pine needle crafting and wheat weaving supplies, dried and preserved flowers and herbs, basket-making supplies, and other craft materials, tools, and books. 813–485–6730.

PLASTICS

Castcraft, Box 16586, Memphis, TN 38186: Free information ❖ How-to information, rubber and plastic materials, and other supplies.

Castolite, 4915 Dean, Woodstock, IL 60098: Catalog $2 ❖ Liquid plastic, mold-making supplies, and how-to books. 815–338–4670.

Magic Systems Inc., P.O. Box 23888, Tampa, FL 33623: Free information ❖ Easy-to-use mold-making kits, coloring materials, and plastic embedding supplies. 813–886–5495.

Synair Corporation, P.O. Box 5269, Chattanooga, TN 37406: Free information ❖ Urethane casting resin and molding systems. 800–251–7642; 615–698–8801 (in TN).

PLATES, COLLECTIBLE

Aftosa, 1034 Ohio Ave., Richmond, CA 94804: Free catalog ❖ Clear acrylic plate stands and bowl holders. 800–231–0397.

Bergsma Gift Gallery, Bellis Fair Mall, Bellingham, WA 98226: Free information ❖ Statuary and figurines, plates, dolls, other porcelain collectibles, and gifts. 206–733–2073.

Biggs Limited Editions, 5517 Lakeside Ave., Richmond, VA 23228: Free information ❖ Statuary and figurines, plates, dolls, other porcelain collectibles, and gifts. 800–637–0704.

Churchills, Twelve Oaks Mall, Novi, MI 48377: Free information ❖ Collectible plates. 800–388–1141.

Dexter & Company, 53 W. 49th St., New York, NY 10020: Free information ❖ Collectible plates. 800–BUY–DEXT; 212–245–7460 (in NY).

Gallery 247, 814 Merrick Rd., Baldwin, NY 11510: Free brochure ❖ Collectible plates and prints. 516–868–4800.

The Plate Hutch, P.O. Box 3364, Midway, WA 98032: Free information ❖ Hard-to-find plates, figurines, dolls, and other collectibles. 206–833–4922.

Red Cross Gifts, 122 Walnut St., Spooner, WI 54801: Free information ❖ Collectible plates, Ashton-Drake dolls, and other gifts and collectibles. 800–344–9958.

Russian Gift Shop-Maison Russe, 1720 Ogden Ave., Lisle, IL 60532: Free information ❖ Russian Matreshka nesting dolls, collectible plates, pre-revolutionary memorabilia, and other gifts. 708–963–5160.

Unicef, P.O. Box 182233, Chattanooga, TN 37422: Free catalog ❖ Stationery, postcards, gifts, and limited edition plates. 800–553–1200.

The Village Plate Collector, 217 King St., Box 1118, Cocoa, FL 32923: Free information ❖ Limited edition plates. 800–752–8371; 407–636–6914 (in FL).

White's Collectables & Fine China, 516 E. 1st., P.O. Box 680, Newborg, OR 97132: Free information ❖ Collectible plates and new and discontinued china patterns. 503–538–7421.

Zaslow's Fine Collectibles, Strathmore Shopping Center, Rt. 34, Matawan, NJ 07747: Free information ❖ Plates, figurines, and other collectibles. 800–526–2355; 908–583–1499 (in NJ).

PLATFORM TENNIS

Century Sports Inc., Lakewood Industrial Park, 1995 Rutgers University Blvd., Box 2035, Lakewood, NJ 08701: Free information ❖ Balls and paddles. 800–526–7548; 908–905–4422 (in NJ).

Cosom Sporting Goods, Division Mantua Industries Inc., Grandview Ave., Woodbury Heights, NJ 08097: Free information ❖ Balls, nets, and paddles. 800–328–5635; 609–853–0300 (in NJ).

Sportime, 1 Sportime Way, Atlanta, GA 30340: Free information ❖ Balls and paddles. 800–444–5700; 404–449–5700 (in GA).

PLAYGROUND EQUIPMENT

BigToys, 7717 New Market, Olympia, WA 98501: Free information ❖ Playground equipment. 800–426–9788.

Cedar Works, P.O. Box 990, Rockport, ME 04856: Free catalog ❖ Wood playsets for backyards and playgrounds. 800–461–3327.

ChildLife Inc., 55 Whitney St., Holliston, MA 01746: Free catalog ❖ Swings and other wood playsets. 800–462–4445.

Florida Playground & Steel Company, 4701 S. 50th St., Tampa, FL 33619: Free brochure ❖ Swings and other equipment for backyards and playgrounds. 800–444–2655; 813–247–2812 (in FL).

GameTime, P.O. Box 121, Fort Payne, AL 35967: Free information ❖ Playground/backyard play systems and outdoor fitness equipment. 205–845–5610.

Gazebo & Porchworks, 728 9th Ave. SW, Puyallup, WA 98371: Catalog $2 ❖ Swings and backyard play structures. 206–848–0502.

GYM-N-I Playgrounds Inc., P.O. Box 310096, Laurel Bend, TX 78131: Free information ❖ Modular playground structures, swing sets, and other equipment. 800–232–3398; 512–629–6000 (in TX).

PCA Industries Inc., 5642 Natural Bridge, St. Louis, MO 63120: Free information ❖ Aluminum playground equipment. 800–727–8180.

Playworld Systems, P.O. Box 505, New Berlin, PA 17855: Free information ❖ Wood and metal play equipment. 800–233–8404; 717–966–1015 (in PA).

Victor Stanley Inc., P.O. Box 144, Dunkirk, MD 20754: Free information ❖ Playground equipment and outdoor furniture. 800–368–2573; 301–855–8300 (in MD).

Sun Designs, 173 E. Wisconsin Ave., Oconomowoc, WI 53066: Catalog $9.95 ❖ Idea books and plans for gazebos, bridges, doghouses, furniture, swings and other outdoor play structures, and birdhouses. 414–567–4255.

Ultra Play Systems Inc., 425 Sycamore St., Anderson, IN 46016: Free information ❖ Outdoor gym equipment. 800–458–5872.

Woodplay, P.O. Box 27904, Raleigh, NC 27611: Free catalog ❖ Redwood backyard play sets. 800–966–3752; 919–231–6080 (in NC).

Woodset Inc., P.O. Box 2127, Waldorf, MD 20601: Free information ❖ Backyard and playground structures. 800–638–9663.

POLITICAL MEMORABILIA

Americana Resources, 18222 Flower Hill Way, Ste. 299A, Gaithersburg, MD 20879: Price list $2 ❖ Political and presidential memorabilia, postcards, advertising memorabilia, photos, books, calendars and almanacs, newspapers, posters and prints, World War I and II items, Nixon and Watergate collectibles, and other Americana. 301–926–8663.

The Campaign Headquarters, P.O. Box 6661, West Palm Beach, FL 33405: Free list with two 1st class stamps ❖ Political memorabilia. 407–582–4705.

Presidential Coin & Antique Company, 6550 Little River Tnpk., Alexandria, VA 22312: Free catalog ❖ Political memorabilia, medals, and tokens; and antiques, coins, and other Americana. 703–354–5454.

Rex Stark-Americana, 49 Wethersfield Rd., Bellingham, MA 02019: Catalog subscription $5 ❖ Political memorabilia, posters, flags, needlework, textiles, china, needlework, folk art, toys, and paintings. 508–966–0994.

PORCELAIN COLLECTIBLES

All God's Children Collectors Club, P.O. Box 8367, Gadsden, AL 35902: Free information ❖ Miss Martha original porcelain dolls. 205–549–0340.

Bergsma Gift Gallery, Bellis Fair Mall, Bellingham, WA 98226: Free information ❖ Statuary and figurines, plates, dolls, other porcelain collectibles, and gifts. 206–733–2073.

Biggs Limited Editions, 5517 Lakeside Ave., Richmond, VA 23228: Free information ❖ Statuary and figurines, plates, dolls, other porcelain collectibles, and gifts. 800–266–7744.

Callahan's Calabash Nautical City, Hwy 179, 9937 Beach Rd., Calabash, NC 28467: Free information ❖ Statuary and figurines, dolls, other porcelain collectibles, and gifts. 800–344–3816.

Down's Collectors Showcase, 1617 S. 101st St., Milwaukee, WI 53214: Free catalog ❖ Figurines, miniatures, thimbles, music boxes, mugs and steins, country items, plates, art, and porcelain. 800–558–4200.

European Imports & Gifts, 7900 N. Milwaukee Ave., Niles, IL 60648: Free information ❖ Art collectibles, porcelains, Christmas ornaments, and pewter. 708–967–5253.

Jan Hagara Collectors Club, 40114 Industrial Park Cir., Georgetown, TX 78626: Free information ❖ Jan Hagara porcelain dolls. 512–863–9499.

Intrigue Gift Shop, 112 E. Elkhorn Ave., P.O. Box 2147, Estes Park, CO 80517: Free information ❖ Statuary and figurines, plates, dolls, other porcelain collectibles, and gifts. 800–735–GIFT.

Lenox Collections, P.O. Box 3020, Langhome, PA 19047: Free catalog ❖ Porcelain sculptures, china, and crystal. 800–225–1779.

The Limited Edition, 2170 Sunrise Hwy., Merrick, NY 11566: Free information ❖ Precious Moments porcelain dolls and statuary. 800–645–2864; 516–623–4400 (in NY).

The Plate Hutch, P.O. Box 3364, Midway, WA 98032: Free information ❖ Hard-to-find plates, figurines, dolls, and other collectibles. 206–833–4922.

The Red Cardinal, 1121 Horsham Rd., Ambler, PA 19002: Free information ❖ Statuary and figurines, plates, dolls, porcelain collectibles, and other gifts. 800–568–2524; 215–628–2524 (in PA).

Red Cross Gifts, 122 Walnut St., Spooner, WI 54801: Free information ❖ Collectible plates, Ashton-Drake dolls, and other gifts and collectibles. 800–344–9958.

Royal Copenhagen Porcelain, 683 Madison Ave., New York, NY 10021: Free brochure ❖ Danish porcelain statuary by the suppliers to the Royal Danish Court since 1775. 800–431–1992.

Zaslow's Fine Collectibles, Strathmore Shopping Center, Rt. 34, Matawan, NJ 07747: Free information ❖ Plates, figurines, and other gifts. 800–526–2355; 908–583–1499 (in NJ).

Zucker's Fine Gifts, 151 W. 26th St., New York, NY 10001: Free catalog ❖ Hummel, Swarovski silver and crystal, Waterford crystal, Lladro porcelain, and other gifts. 212–989–1450.

POSTCARDS

Bernard Aclin Postcards, P.O. Box 330, Bronx, NY 10475: Free information with long SASE ❖ Postcards. 718–549–3305.

Aladin Stamps/Postcards, 2801 Kessler Blvd. East, Indianapolis, IN 46220: Free information with long SASE ❖ Postcards. 317–255–8379.

Alpenglow Collectibles, P.O. Box 211, Brookeville, MD 20833: Free information with long SASE ❖ Postcards. 301–774–7637.

Joan C. Angier, 6365 W. Lost Canyon, Tucson, AZ 85745: Free information with long SASE ❖ Postcards. 602–743–7652.

Atlantis Rising Antique, 545 Warren St., Hudson, NY 12534: Free information with long SASE ❖ Postcards. 518–822–0438.

J.C. Ballentine Postcards, Hatcher Point Mall, P.O. Box 761, Waycross, GA 31501: Free information with long SASE ❖ Postcards. 912–285–3250.

Barry's Postcards, 517 Welcome Way, Anderson, IN 46013: Free information with long SASE ❖ Postcards. 317–643–8455.

George & Ellen Budd Postcards, 6910 Tenderfoot Ln., Cincinnati, OH 45249: Free information with long SASE ❖ Postcards. 513–489–0518.

Edward M. Carter Postcards, P.O. Box 158, Boca Raton, FL 33429: Free information with long SASE ❖ Postcards.

The Cartophilians, 430 Highland Ave., Cheshire, CT 06410: Free information with long SASE ❖ Collectible postcards, trading cards, and other paper ephemera. 203–272–1143.

Agnes Cavalari, 89 Bethlehem Rd., New Windsor, NY 12553: Free information with long SASE ❖ State views, glamour, topicals, foreign, greetings, and other postcards. 914–564–6775.

Thomas W. Courts Jr., 106 Aquamarine Dr., Pensacola, FL 32505: Free information with long SASE ❖ Postcards. 904–456–2240.

V. Lee Cox Postcards, P.O. Box 66, Keymar, MD 21757: Free catalog ❖ Postcards and collecting supplies, magazines, comics, sheet music, sports cards, and old newspapers. 410–775–0188.

Hank & Coby DeBoer, 2 Aviles St., St. Augustine, FL 32084: Free information with long SASE ❖ Postcards and stamps. 904–829–9673.

S. Dobres Postcards, P.O. Box 1855, Baltimore, MD 21203: Price list $1.25 ❖ Postcards. 410–486–6569.

Ed's Antiques, Edward C. Schultz, 1905 Sherwood St., Allentown, PA 18103: Free information with long SASE ❖ Postcards. 215–867–8143.

John & Lynne Farr Postcards, P.O. Box 6086, Omaha, NE 68106: Free information with long SASE ❖ Pre-1920 and other postcards. 402–334–0284.

Foreign Cards Ltd., P.O. Box 123, Guilford, CT 06437: Free catalog ❖ Postcards from worldwide sources. 203–453–5813.

Tracy Garrett, P.O. Box 18000–52, Las Vegas, NV 89114: Free information with long SASE ❖ Views, topicals, military, transportation, entertainment, and other postcards. 702–737–3218.

Clay Griffin Postcards, 1100 Merriman Rd., Akron, OH 44303: Free information with long SASE ❖ Postcards. 216–867–7290.

Gordie's Used Cards, 1235 Vista Superba, Glendale, CA 91205: Free information with long SASE ❖ Automobile-related postcards. 818–246–6686.

William Harland Postcards, 4413 White Birch Point, Gainesville, FL 30506: Free information with long SASE ❖ Postcards.

John H. Henel, 79 Fruehauf Ave., Snyder, NY 14226: Free information with long SASE ❖ Postcards from worldwide locations. 716–839–4174.

Herzog Postcards, P.O. Box 545, Vauxhall, NJ 07088: Free information (enclose want list) with long SASE ❖ Most major topics, state views, and other postcards. 201–399–7717.

Frank E. Howard Postcards, 856 Charlotte St., Macon, GA 34236: Free information with long SASE ❖ Postcards. 912–788–1514.

Fred N. Kahn Postcards, 258 Stratford Rd., Asheville, NC 28804: Free information with long SASE ❖ Postcards. 704–252–6507.

Bob Karrer Postcards, P.O. Box 6094, Alexandria, VA 22306: Free information with long SASE ❖ Panama Canal and Canal Zone postcards. 703–360–5105.

Fred H. Lego Postcards, 6506 Kipling Pkwy., Forestville, MD 20747: Free information with long SASE ❖ Postcards. 301–735–6556.

Dick & Sue Lightle Postcards, P.O. Box 2562, Kansas City, KS 66110: Free information with long SASE ❖ Postcards. 913–334–3186.

Hal Lutsky Postcards, 1624 Lombard St., Ste. B, San Francisco, CA 94123: Free information with long SASE ❖ Postcards. 415–921–4051.

Mac's Used Cards, 3306 Ave. D, Fort Worth, TX 76106: Free information with long SASE ❖ Postcards. 817–535–3961.

Malcom Postcards, P.O. Box 453, Monroe, GA 30655: Free information with long SASE ❖ Postcards. 404–267–6897.

Mary Martin Postcards, P.O. Box 787, Perryville, MD 21803: Free brochure with long SASE ❖ New, old, and hard-to-find United States views, topicals, greetings, foreign cards, rarities, and other postcards. 410–575–7768.

National Postcard Exchange, 225 3rd St., P.O. Box 886, Macon, GA 31202: Free information with long SASE ❖ Foreign postcards, topicals, and postcards from the early 1900s to the present. 912–743–8951.

Terry & Noreen Pavey Postcards, P.O. Box 10614, Glendale, AZ 85318: Free information with long SASE ❖ Postcards. 602–439–2156.

Postcards Etc., P.O. Box 4318, Thousand Oaks, CA 91359: Free information with long SASE ❖ Postcards. 805–497–1725.

Postcards from Paradise, Gold Record Antique, P.O. Box 6001, Key West, FL 33041: Free information with long SASE ❖ Postcards. 305–294–3116.

Postcards International, P.O. Box 2930, New Haven, CT 06515: Catalog $3 ❖ Postcards. 203–865–0814.

Ken Prag, P.O. Box 531, Burlingame, CA 94011: Free information with long SASE ❖ Postcards. 415–566–6400.

Michael G. Price Postcards, P.O. Box 7071, Ann Arbor, MI 48107: Free information with long SASE ❖ Postcards. 313–668–7388.

Robert Quinn Jr., P.O. Box 1271, Henderson, KY 42420: Free information with long SASE ❖ Postcards. 502–533–6802.

Arlene L. Raskin Postcards, 2580 Ocean Pkwy., Apt. 2L, Brooklyn, NY 11235: Free information with long SASE ❖ Postcards. 718–998–1910.

Mike E. Rasmussen Postcards, P.O. Box 726, Marina, CA 93933: Free information with long SASE ❖ Postcards. 408–384–5460.

Remember These, P.O. Box 7956, Roanoke, VA 24019: Free information with long SASE ❖ Postcards and matchbook covers. 703–362–3964.

Ruggiero's Postcards, 359 Silver Sands Rd., East Haven, CT 06512: Free information with long SASE ❖ Postcards and stamps.

C. Michael Smith Postcards, Rt. 1, Box 762, Lacey's Springs, AL 35754: Free information with long SASE ❖ Postcards.

Richard Spedding Postcards, 22 Tanglewood Rd., Sterling, MA 01564: Free information with long SASE ❖ Topicals, views, and other postcards. 508–422–8480.

Tippett Postcards Inc., 6625 Gateway Ave., Sarasota, FL 34231: Free information with long SASE ❖ Postcards.

Mary Twyce, 601 E. 5th St., Winona, MN 55987: Free information with long SASE ❖ Postcards. 507–454–4412.

JoAnn Van Scotter Postcards, 208 E. Lincoln St., Mt. Morris, IL 61054: Free information with long SASE ❖ Postcards. 815–734–6971.

Michael B. Wasserberg Postcards, 1025 Country Club Dr., Margate, FL 33063: Free information with long SASE ❖ Postcards. 305–972–3789.

Writewell Company, P.O. Box 68186, Indianapolis, IN 46268: Free information ❖ Loose-leaf postcard albums with leather-grained vinyl padded covers and optional personalization. 800–968–5850.

POTPOURRI

Angel's Earth, 1633 Scheffer Ave., St. Paul, MN 55116: Catalog $2 ❖ Essential and fragrance oils, potpourri supplies, and perfume-making kits. 612–698–3601.

The Candle Factory, 4411 South I.H. 35, Georgetown, TX 78626: Free catalog ❖ Wax potpourri chips, hand-dipped tapers, dinner and novelty candles, and machine made and molded decorative pillars. 512–863–6025.

Caswell-Massey Company Ltd., Catalog Division, 100 Enterprise Pl., Dover, DE 19901: Catalog $1 ❖ Potpourri and pomander mixes, dried flowers, and herb plants. 800–326–0500.

The Essential Oil Company, P.O. Box 206, Lake Oswego, OR 97034: Free catalog ❖

Essential oils, soap-making molds and supplies, incense materials, potpourri, and aromatherapy items. 800–729–5912.

Farmer's Daughter, P.O. Box 1071, Nags Head, NC 27959: Catalog $2 ❖ Country decor accessories, pottery potpourri burner, replacement candles, and electric candle lamps. 800–423–2196.

The Florist Shop, 703 Madison Ave., New York, NY 10021: Free catalog ❖ Hand-milled soaps, bath oils, body milk, talc, room fragrances, and potpour-ris. 800–J-FLORIS.

Gardens Past, P.O. Box 1846, Estes Park, CO 80517: Catalog $1 ❖ Soaps and soap making supplies, potpourri, dried flowers, herbs, candles, and aromatherapy items. 303–586–0400.

The Gathered Herb & Greenhouse, 12114 N. State Rd., Otisville, MI 48463: Catalog $2 ❖ Potpourri supplies, herbs and herb teas, perennials, and dried flowers. 313–631–6572.

Good Hollow Greenhouse & Herbarium, Rt. 1, Box 116, Taft, TN 38488: Catalog $1 ❖ Herbs, perennials, wildflowers, scented geraniums, essential oils, potpourris, teas, dried herbs, and spices. 615–433–7640.

Grandma's Spice Shop, P.O. Box 472, Odenton, MD 21113: Free catalog ❖ Essential oils and herbal potpourris. 410–672–0933.

Hartman's Herb Farm, Old Dana Rd., Barre, MA 01005: Catalog $2 ❖ Potpourris, sachets, bath herbs and oils, herbal pillows, dried flowers, spices, teas, essential oils, and pomander balls. 508–355–2015.

Herb & Spice Collection, P.O. Box 118, Norway, IA 52318: Free catalog ❖ Potpourris, culinary herbs and spices, herbs and teas, and natural herbal body care products. 800–786–1388.

The Herb Lady, P.O. Box 20, Harpers Ferry, WV 25425: Free catalog ❖ Essential oils and potpourris. 800–537–1846.

Herbs-Liscious, 1702 S. 6th St., Marshalltown, IA 50158: Catalog $2 (refundable) ❖ Dried flowers, herbs and spices, oils and fragrances, and potpourri.

International Manufacturing Company, 1130 Live Oak St., Quincy, FL 32351: Catalog $1 ❖ Silk plants, trees, flower arranging supplies, potpourris, and other craft supplies. 904–875–2918.

Meadow Everlastings, 16464 Shabbona Rd., Malta, IL 60150: Catalog $2 (refundable) ❖

Dried flowers, wreath kits, and potpourri supplies.

Meg's Garden, P.O. Box 161, Buffalo, NY 14205: Brochure $1 ❖ Potpourri and perfume oils. 716–883–7564.

Mountain Farms Inc., 307 Number 9 Rd., Fletcher, NC 28732: Free catalog ❖ Dried floral products and herbs for potpourri arrangements. 704–628–4709.

Nature's Finest, P.O. Box 10311, Burke, VA 22009: Catalog $2.50 (refundable) ❖ Dried flowers, herbs, spices, oils, fixatives, bottles, books, equipment, and other potpourri supplies. 703–978–3925.

Petals & Buds, 10798 County Rd. 3101, Winona, TX 75792: Catalog $2 ❖ Potpourris, dried rose buds, and rose petals. 903–877–3724.

San Francisco Herb Company, 250 14th St., San Francisco, CA 94103: Free catalog ❖ Potpourri supplies and spices and herbs for cooking. 800–227–4530; 800–622–0768 (in CA).

Tom Thumb Workshops, Rt. 13, P.O. Box 357, Mappsville, VA 23407: Catalog $1 ❖ Potpourris, herbs and spices, essential oils, dried flowers, and craft supplies. 804–824–3507.

Well-Sweep Herb Farm, 317 Mt. Bethel Rd., Port Murray, NJ 07865: Catalog $2 ❖ Potpourri and pomander mixes, dried flowers, and herb plants. 908–852–5390.

PRINTING PRESSES

Dickerson Press Company, P.O. Box 8, South Haven, MI 49090: Free information ❖ Printing presses for etching, lithography, and intaglio stone or plate reproductions. 616–637–4251.

Graphic Chemical & Ink Company, P.O. Box 27, Villa Park, IL 60181: Free catalog ❖ Printing supplies. 708–832–6004.

Kelsey Presses, 30 Cross St., P.O. Box 941, Meriden, CT 06450: Catalog $1 ❖ Printing presses, hot stamping equipment, and supplies. 203–235–1695.

Think Ink, 7526 Olympic View Dr., Ste. E, Edmonds, WA 98026: Free information ❖ Easy-to-use, multiple color machine for printing greeting cards, stationery, ribbons, and T-shirts. 800–778–1935; 206–778–1935 (in WA).

Turnbaugh Printers Supply, 104 S. Sporting Hill Rd., Mechanicsburg, PA 17055:

Catalog $1 ❖ Type fonts, printing presses, and supplies. 717–737–5637.

PROSPECTING & ROCKHOUNDING

Alpha Supply, P.O. Box 2133, Bremerton, WA 98310: Catalog $3 ❖ Prospecting and rockhounding equipment, jewelry-making tools, gem finishing equipment, and metal detectors. 206–373–3302.

Arizona Gems & Crystals, 1362 W. Thatcher Blvd., Safford, AZ 85546: Free catalog ❖ Gold mining and rockhounding equipment. 602–428–5164.

B & J Rock Shop, 14744 Manchester Rd., Ballwin, MO 63011: Catalog $3 ❖ Rockhounding equipment, quartz crystals, amethyst crystal clusters, Brazilian agate nodules, and other imported and domestic stones. 314–394–4567.

Bourget Bros., 1636 11th St., Santa Monica, CA 90404: Catalog $3 ❖ Gemstones and cabochons, wax patterns, beads and bead-stringing supplies, lapidary equipment, and rockhounding, treasure hunting, and prospecting equipment. 310–450–6556.

Cal-Gold, 2569 E. Colorado Blvd., Pasadena, CA 91107: Free catalog ❖ Metal detectors, mining and geology equipment, maps, books, and ultraviolet light equipment. 818–792–6161.

Covington Engineering Corporation, P.O. Box 35, Redlands, CA 92373: Free catalog ❖ Gold mining and rockhounding equipment. 909–793–6636.

Crystalite Corporation, 18400 Green Meadows Dr. North, Westerville, OH 43081: Free information ❖ Rockhounding and lapidary equipment.

D & K Prospecting Headquarters, 13809 Southeast Division, Portland, OR 97236: Free information ❖ Prospecting equipment and metal detectors. 800–542–4653; 503–761–1521 (in OR).

Dotson Enterprises, 4651 S. Edgerware Ln., Taylorsville, UT 84119: Free information ❖ Automatic gold panner, metal detectors, and other equipment. 801–963–8242.

East Coast Prospecting & Mining Supplies, Rt. 3, Box 321J, Ellijay, GA 30540: Catalog $3 ❖ Mining and lapidary equipment. 706–276–4433.

Ebersole Lapidary Supply Inc., 11417 West Hwy. 54, Wichita, KS 67209: Catalog $2 ❖ Rockhounding equipment, lapidary and

jewelry-making tools, findings, mountings, cabochons, and gemstones and rocks. 316–722–4771.

Eloxite Corporation, 806 10th St., Wheatland, WY 82201: Catalog $1 ❖ Clock-making supplies, gemstones, beads, cabochons, jewelry mountings, and equipment for rockhounding and jewelry do-it-yourself crafters. 307–322–3050.

Fisher Research Laboratory, 200 W. Wilmott Rd., Los Banos, CA 93635: Free information ❖ Metal detectors. 209–826–3292.

49'er Metal Detectors, 14093 Irishtown Rd., Pine Grove, CA 95665: Free information ❖ Prospecting supplies, tools, books, and videos. 800–538–7501; 209–296–3544 (in CA).

Fortyniner Mining Supply, 16238 Lakewood Blvd., Bellflower, CA 90706: Free information ❖ Mining and treasure hunting equipment, metal detectors, magazines, and books. 310–925–2271.

Graves Company, 1800 Andrews Ave., Pompano Beach, FL 33069: Free catalog ❖ Rockhounding and ultraviolet light equipment. 800–327–9103.

Herkimer Diamond Mines, P.O. Box 510, Herkimer, NY 13350: Free information ❖ Petrified wood products, rockhounding equipment, minerals and rocks, and quartz crystals. 315–891–7355.

House of Treasure Hunters, 5714 El Cajon Blvd., San Diego, CA 92115: Free information ❖ Gold prospecting equipment and metal detectors. 619–286–2600.

Jeanne's Rock & Jewelry, 5420 Bissonet, Bellaire, TX 77401: Price list $1 ❖ Rockhounding equipment, shells, petrified wood products, beads, and bead-stringing supplies. 713–664–2988.

K/T Detector Sales, P.O. Box 17015, Fort Worth, TX 76102: Free information ❖ Metal detectors and prospecting equipment. 800–876–3463; 817–498–2228 (in TX).

Kingsley North Inc., P.O. Box 216, Norway, MI 49870: Free catalog ❖ Rockhounding equipment, jewelry-making tools, metal casting equipment, tumblers, and opals. 800–338–9280.

Lentz Lapidary Inc., 11760 S. Oliver, Rt. 2, Box 134, Mulvane, KS 67110: Catalog $2 ❖ Jewelry, mountings, clocks and motors, rough rock specimens, cabochons, and

rockhounding and lapidary equipment. 316–777–1372.

Pot of Gold, 2616 Griffin Rd., Fort Lauderdale, FL 33312: Free catalog ❖ Metal detectors, books, and prospecting equipment. 305–987–2888.

Pro-Mac South, 940 W. Apache Trail, Apache Junction, AZ 85220: Free information ❖ Prospecting supplies and tools. 800–722–6463.

Pro-Mack Mining Supplies, P.O. Box 47, Happy Camp, CA 96039: Free information ❖ Mining and treasure hunting equipment. 800–542–6463; 800–992–6463 (in CA).

Jimmy Sierra Products, 3096 Kerner Blvd., San Rafael, CA 94901: Free information ❖ Treasure hunting and prospecting accessories.

PUPPETS & MARIONETTES

Books by Mail, P.O. Box 1444, Corona, CA 91718: Free catalog with two 1st class stamps ❖ Books and novelties for puppeteers, clowns, magicians, face painters, and balloon artists. 909–273–0900.

by Diane, 1126 Ivon Ave., Endicott, NY 13760: Catalog $2 ❖ Furs and mohair, growlers, squeakers, music boxes, noses, eyes, joint sets, and patterns for bears, soft toys, and puppets. 607–754–0391.

Clown Heaven, 4792 Old State Rd. 37 South, Martinsville, IN 46152: Catalog $3 ❖ Balloons, make-up, puppets, wigs, ministry and gospel items, novelties, magic, clown props, and books. 317–342–6888.

Freckles Clown Supplies, 5509 Rossevelt Blvd., Jacksonville, FL 32210: Catalog $5 ❖ Puppets, make-up, clown supplies, costumes, how-to books on clowning and ballooning, and other theatrical supplies. 904–778–3977.

Maher Studios, P.O. Box 420, Littleton, CO 80160: Catalog $1 ❖ Ventriloquist dummies, scripts and dialogues, puppets, and how-to books. 303–798–6830.

Mastercraft Puppets, P.O. Box 39, Branson, MO 65616: Information $2 ❖ Handcrafted puppets. 417–561–8100.

Mecca Magic Inc., 49 Dodd St., Bloomfield, NJ 07003: Catalog $10 ❖ Puppets, juggling supplies, theatrical make-up, clown equipment, balloons, and magic tricks. 201–429–7597.

Steven Meltzer, 670 San Juan, Venice, CA 90291: Free list with long SASE ❖ Marionettes, puppets, and ventriloquist figures. 310–396–6007.

Pelham Marionettes, Barrows, 5128 Ridge Rd., Lockport, NY 14094: Free list with long SASE ❖ Pelham marionettes, from the 1960s to 1970s. 716–433–4329.

Periwinkle Puppet Productions, 711 Pineland Ave., Venice, FL 34292: Free information ❖ Puppets, props, and complete show packages. 813–484–2161.

PURSES & WALLETS

Bally of Switzerland for Ladies, 689 Madison Ave., New York, NY 10021: Free information ❖ Women's shoes, clothing, luggage, and small leather goods. 212–751–2163.

Bally of Switzerland for Men, 711 5th Ave., New York, NY 10022: Free information ❖ Men's shoes, clothing, luggage, and small leather goods. 212–751–9082.

Carol Block Handbags, 1413 Avenue M, Brooklyn, NY 11230: Free information with long SASE ❖ Designer handbags and small leather goods. 718–339–1869.

Bottega Veneta, 635 Madison Ave., New York, NY 10022: Free catalog ❖ Wallets, purses and handbags, luggage, and other small leather goods. 212–371–5511.

Burberry's Limited, 9 E. 57th St., New York, NY 10022: Free catalog ❖ Clothing, handbags, luggage, silk scarves and shawls, belts, hats, shoes, tennis accessories, sports bags, and toiletries. 212–371–5010.

Coach Leatherware Company, 410 Commerce Blvd., Carlstadt, NJ 07072: Free catalog ❖ Leather handbags, gloves, belts, wallets, briefcases, and accessories. 201–460–4716.

Creative House, 100 Business Pkwy., Richardson, TX 75081: Free catalog ❖ Luggage, briefcases and attache cases, handbags, wallets, and accessories. 800–527–5940; 214–231–3463 (in TX).

DAF-Productions, 1469 Lexington Ave., Ste. 52, New York, NY 10128: Free brochure ❖ Combination multi-purpose travel security-style leather pouch for men and women. 212–427–4649.

Deerskin Place, 283 Akron Rd., Ephrata, PA 17522: Catalog $1 ❖ Cowhide, sheepskin, and deerskin clothing and accessories. 717–733–7624.

Deerskin Trading Post, 119 Foster St., Box 6008, Peabody, MA 01961: Free catalog ❖ Leather clothing for men and women, shoes and slippers, gloves, shoulder bags, women's boots, and accessories. 508–532–4040.

Gucci, CSB 3168, Department 846, Melville, NY 11747: Free catalog ❖ Shoes, clothing, and leather goods. 800–221–2590.

National Luggage Dealers Association, 245 5th Ave., New York, NY 10018: Free catalog ❖ Small leather goods and handbags. 212–684–1610.

New England Leather Accessories, 11 Portland St., Rochester, NH 03867: Catalog $5 (refundable) ❖ Briefcases and portfolios, handbags and purses, and other small leather accessories. 603–332–0707.

PUZZLES

Bits & Pieces, Stevens Point, WI 54481–7199: Free catalog ❖ Jigsaw puzzles, books, games, and other gifts for adults and children. 800–884–2637.

F.A. Bourke Inc., P.O. Box 726, Middlebury, VT 05753: Free information ❖ Individually crafted puzzles with whimsical silhouettes and intricate interlocking pieces. 802–388–3648.

The Briarpatch, Anita & Jerry Syfert, 935 Chart Ct., Lusby, MD 20657: Free information ❖ Jigsaw puzzles. 410–586–3204.

Jester's Collectibles, 143 Market St., Portsmouth, NH 03801: Free brochure ❖ Original puzzles. 603–427–0708.

Lucretia's Pieces, RFD 1, Box 501, Windsor, VT 05089: Free information ❖ Challenging puzzles designed with special shapes and unexpected surprises. 802–436–3006.

The Map Store, 142 E. 5th St., Ste. 70, St. Paul, MN 55101: Free information ❖ United States, world, and state map puzzles. 612–227–2280.

Rainy Lake Puzzles, 4255 Garfield Ave. South, Minneapolis, MN 55409: Free catalog ❖ Intricately hand-cut wood jigsaw puzzles. 612–827–5757.

Spiritwood Puzzles, Charles Ross, 1913 9th St. North, Fargo, ND 58102: Free information ❖ Wood jigsaw puzzles. 701–967–8398.

Stave Puzzles, Box 329, Norwich, VT 05055: Free catalog ❖ Hand-cut jigsaw puzzles. 802–295–5200.

QUILTS & QUILTING

AK Sew & Serge, 1602 6th St. SE, Winter Haven, FL 33880: Catalog $5 ❖ Supplies for heirloom and fashion sewing and quilting. 800–299–8096; 813–299–3080 (in FL).

The Cotton Patch, 1025 Brown Ave., Lafayette, CA 94549: Catalog $5 ❖ Fabrics, quilting books, and supplies. 800–835–4418.

Hancock Fabrics, 3841 Hinkleville Rd., Paducah, KY 42001: Free information ❖ Quilting supplies, fabrics, and sewing notions. 800–626–2723.

Hearthside Quilts, Rt. 7, Box 429, Shelburne, VT 05482: Catalog $3 ❖ Traditional and modern quilt designs in easy-to-sew pre-cut kits. 800–451–3533.

Hinterberg Design Inc., 2100 N. Western Ave., West Bend, WI 53095: Free information ❖ Quilting frame with adjustable height and tilt, ratchet wheel tensioning, and optional extension or shorter poles. 800–443–5800.

Keepsake Quilting, P.O. Box 1459, Meredith, NH 03253: Free catalog ❖ Quilting books, patterns, notions, fabrics, quilting aids, scrap bags, and batting.

Claire Murray Inc., P.O. Box 390, Ascutney, VT 05030: Catalog $5 (refundable) ❖ Quilts, handpainted ceramics, and hand-hooked rugs. 800–252–4733.

Quilting Books Unlimited, 1911 W. Wilson, Batavia, IL 60510: Catalog $1 ❖ Quilting books. 708–406–0237.

That Patchwork Place Inc., P.O. Box 118, Bothell, WA 95041: Free information ❖ Quilting books and supplies. 800–426–3126; 206–483–3313 (in WA).

RACQUETBALL & SQUASH

Clothing

Alchester Mills Company Inc., 314 S. 11th St., Camden, NJ 08103: Free information ❖ Gloves, socks, sweatbands, and eyeguards. 609–964–9700.

Dorson Sports Inc., 1 Roebling Ct., Ronkonkona, NY 51779: Free information ❖ Gloves. 800–645–7215; 516–585–5440 (in NY).

Ektelon, 8929 Serio Dr., San Diego, CA 92123: Free information ❖ Clothing and gloves, socks, sweatbands, bags and balls, racquets, eyeguards, and thongs. 800–854–2958.

Franklin Sports Industries Inc., 17 Campanelli Parkway, P.O. Box 508, Stoughton, MA 02072: Free information ❖ Gloves. 617–344–1111.

Head Sports Inc., 4801 N. 63rd St., Boulder, CO 80301: Free information ❖ Gloves, shoes, sweatbands, bags, balls, and racquets. 800–257–5100; 303–530–2000 (in CO).

Holabird Sports Discounters, 9008 Yellow Brick Rd., Rossville Industrial Park, Baltimore, MD 21237: Free catalog ❖ Sports equipment and clothing. 410–687–6400.

Johar Inc., P.O. Box 10, Forrest City, AR 72335: Free information ❖ Gloves. 800–248–1232; 501–633–8161 (in AR).

Olympia Sports, 745 State Circle, Ann Arbor, MI 48106: Free information ❖ Gloves. 800–521–2832; 313–761–5135 (in MI).

Pennsylvania Sporting Goods, 1360 Industrial Hwy., P.O. Box 451, Southhampton, PA 18966: Free information ❖ Gloves, sweatbands, balls, eyeguards, and racquets. 800–535–1122.

Pony USA Inc., 676 Elm St., Concord, MA 01742: Free information ❖ Shoes, socks, and sweatbands. 800–654–7669; 508–287–0053 (in MA).

Puma USA Inc., 147 Centre St., Brockton, MA 02403: Free information with long SASE ❖ Clothing, shoes, socks, and balls. 508–583–9100.

Reebok International Ltd., 100 Technology Center Dr., Stoughton, MA 02072: Free information ❖ Clothing, shoes, and socks. 800–228–PUMP.

Regent Sports Corporation, 45 Ranick Rd., Hauppage, NY 11788: Free information ❖ Gloves. 516–234–2800.

Spalding Sports Worldwide, 425 Meadow St., P.O. Box 901, Chicopee, MA 01021: Free information with list of retailers ❖ Clothing, gloves, shoes, socks, sweatbands, bags, balls, and racquets. 800–225–6601.

Wa-Mac Inc., Highskore Products Inc., P.O. Box 128, Carlstadt, NJ 07410: Free information ❖ Gloves, socks, sweat bands, balls, bags, eyeguards, and racquets. 800–447–5673; 201–438–7200 (in NJ).

Equipment

Alchester Mills Company Inc., 314 S. 11th St., Camden, NJ 08103: Free information ❖ Eyeguards, gloves, socks, sweatbands, and grips. 609–964–9700.

Allsop, P.O. Box 23, Bellingham, WA 98227: Free information ❖ Racquetball accessories. 800–426–4303; 206–734–9090 (in WA).

Athalon, 3333 E. 52nd Ave., Denver, CO 80216: Free information ❖ Racquetball

accessories. 800–525–3285; 303–292–0400 (in CO).

Austad's, 4500 E. 10th St., P.O. Box 5428, Sioux Falls, SD 57196: Free catalog ❖ Racquetball and other sports equipment. 800–444–1234.

Brine Inc., 47 Sumner St., Milford, MA 01757: Free information ❖ Bags, balls, and grips. 800–227–2722; 508–478–3250 (in MA).

H.D. Brown Enterprise Ltd., 23 Beverly St. East, St. George, Ontario, Canada N0E 1N0: Free information ❖ Gloves, racquets, and accessories. 519–448–1381.

Cannon Sports, P.O. Box 11179, Burbank, CA 91510: Free information with list of retailers ❖ Balls, racquets, and eyeguards. 800–362–3146; 818–753–5940 (in CA).

Century Sports Inc., Lakewood Industrial Park, 1995 Rutgers University Blvd., Box 2035, Lakewood, NJ 08701: Free information ❖ Gloves, racquets, and accessories. 800–526–7548; 908–905–4422 (in NJ).

Ektelon, 8929 Serio Dr., San Diego, CA 92123: Free information ❖ Bags and balls, racquets, eyeguards, thongs, clothing and gloves, socks, and sweatbands. 800–854–2958.

Faber Brothers, 4141 S. Pulaski Rd., Chicago, IL 60632: Free information ❖ Balls, bags, and racquets. 312–376–9300.

Grid Inc., NDL Products Inc., 2313 NW 30th Pl., Pompano Beach, FL 33069: Free information ❖ Racquetball equipment. 800–843–3021; 305–942–4560 (in FL).

Head Sports Inc., 4801 N. 63rd St., Boulder, CO 80301: Free information ❖ Bags and balls, racquets, gloves, shoes, and sweatbands. 800–257–5100; 303–530–2000 (in CO).

Holabird Sports Discounters, 9008 Yellow Brick Rd., Rossville Industrial Park, Baltimore, MD 21237: Free catalog ❖ Equipment and clothing for basketball, tennis, running, and jogging, golf, exercising, racquetball, and other sports. 410–687–6400.

M.W. Kasch Company, 5401 W. Donges Bay Rd., Mequon, WI 53092: Free information ❖ Bags, balls, and racquets. 414–242–5000.

Las Vegas Discount Golf & Tennis, 5325 S. Valley View Blvd., Ste. 10, Las Vegas, NV 89118: Free catalog ❖ Equipment, shoes, and

clothing for tennis, racquetball, golf, running, and jogging. 702–798–7777.

Leisure Marketing Inc., 2204 Morris Ave., Ste. 202, Union, NJ 07083: Free information ❖ Bags and racquets. 908–851–9494.

Markwort Sporting Goods, 4300 Forest Park Ave., St. Louis, MO 63108: Catalog $8 with list of retailers ❖ Gloves, racquets, and accessories. 800–669–6626; 314–652–3757 (in MO).

Penn Racquet Sports, 306 S. 45th Ave., Phoenix, AZ 85043: Free information ❖ Gloves, racquets, and accessories. 800–289–7366; 602–269–1492 (in AZ).

Pennsylvania Sporting Goods, 1360 Industrial Hwy., P.O. Box 451, Southhampton, PA 18966: Free information ❖ Balls, eyeguards, and racquets. 800–535–1122.

Prince Racquet Sports, 1 Tennis Ct., Bordentown, NJ 08505: Free information ❖ Gloves, racquets, and accessories. 800–2–TENNIS; 609–291–5900 (in NJ).

Professional Golf & Tennis Suppliers, 7825 Hollywood Blvd., Pembroke Pines, FL 33024: Free catalog with long SASE ❖ Equipment and accessories. 305–981–7283.

Puma USA Inc., 147 Centre St., Brockton, MA 02403: Free information with long SASE ❖ Balls and bags. 508–583–9100.

Spalding Sports Worldwide, 425 Meadow St., P.O. Box 901, Chicopee, MA 01021: Free information with list of retailers ❖ Bags, balls, and racquets. 800–225–6601.

Sportime, 1 Sportime Way, Atlanta, GA 30340: Free information ❖ Racquets and accessories. 800–444–5700; 404–449–5700 (in GA).

USTech Inc., 17720 NE 65th St., Redmond, WA 98052: Free information ❖ Bags and balls, racquets, eyeguards, and thongs. 206–881–8989.

Voit Sports, 1451 Pittstand-Victor Rd., 100 Willow Office Park, Fairport, NY 14450: Free information ❖ Bags, balls, eyeguards, and racquets. 800–444–VOIT.

Wa-Mac Inc., Highskore Products Inc., P.O. Box 128, Carlstadt, NJ 07410: Free information ❖ Balls, bags, eyeguards, and racquets. 800–447–5673; 201–438–7200 (in NJ).

Wilson Sporting Goods, 8700 W. Bryn Mawr, Chicago, IL 60631: Free information

❖ Bags, balls, and racquets. 800–272–6060; 312–714–6400 (in IL).

RADIATOR ENCLOSURES

All American Wood Register Company, 239 E. Main St., Cary, IL 60013: Free brochure with long SASE ❖ Solid oak registers with adjustable damper systems. 708–639–0393.

Arsco Manufacturing Company Inc., 3564 Blue Rock Rd., Cincinnati, OH 45247: Free information ❖ Steel radiator enclosures. 800–543–7040; 513–385–0555 (in OH).

Barker Metalcraft, 1701 W. Belmont, Chicago, IL 60657: Free catalog ❖ Drop-in and flat grills, grills with borders, convector grills, and other radiator covers and registers. 800–397–0129.

Deco-Trol, 802 N. I-35 East, Denton, TX 76201: Free information ❖ Flat and semi-gloss colored, all-aluminum, unfinished wood, and brass, chrome, and antique brass plated grills and registers. 800–678–1977.

Hinges & Handles, 100 Lincolnway East, Osceola, IN 46561: Free catalog ❖ Solid brass registers. 800–533–4782.

Monarch Radiator Enclosures, 2744 Arkansas Dr., Brooklyn, NY 11234: Brochure $1 (refundable) ❖ Easy-to-assemble all-steel radiator enclosures. 201–796–4117.

The Reggio Register, P.O. Box 511, Ayer, MA 01432: Catalog $1 ❖ Solid brass and cast-iron registers and grills. 508–772–3493.

A Touch of Brass, 9339 Baltimore National Pike, Ellicott City, MD 21042: Catalog $3 ❖ Polished stamped and cast brass registers. 800–BRASS-34.

RADIOS

Amateur Radio Equipment

A.S.A./Antenna Sales & Accessories, P.O. Box 3461, Myrtle Beach, SC 29578: Free information ❖ Antennas. 800–722–2681; 803–293–7888 (in SC).

Ack Radio Supply Company, 3101 4th Ave., South Birmingham, AL 35233: Free information ❖ Amateur radio equipment. 800–338–4218; 205–322–0588 (in AL).

Alinco Electronics Inc., 438 Amapola Ave., Torrance, CA 90501: Free information ❖ Hand-held transceivers. 310–618–8616.

Aluma Tower Company, P.O. Box 2806, Vero Beach, FL 32961: Free catalog ❖ Telescoping crank-up, guyed stack-up,

tilt-over, rooftop, and mobile antenna towers. 407–567–3423.

Amateur & Advanced Communications, 3208 Concord Pike, Rt. 202, Wilmington, DE 19803: Free information with long SASE ❖ Amateur radio equipment. 302–478–2757.

Amateur Communications Etc., 263 Mink, San Antonio, TX 78213: Free information ❖ Amateur radio equipment. 512–733–0334.

Amateur Electronics Supply, 5710 W. Good Hope Rd., Milwaukee, WI 53223: Free information ❖ Amateur radio equipment. 800–558–0411; 414–358–0333 (in WI).

American Antenna Corporation, 1500 Executive Dr., Elgin, IL 60123: Free information ❖ HF and VHF mobile antennas. 800–323–6768.

American Radio Relay League, 225 Main St., Newington, CT 06111: Free information ❖ Books on how to become a HAM radio operator, get a license, learn Morse code, organize equipment, and set up a station. 203–666–1541.

Arnold Company, P.O. Box 512, Commerce, TX 75428: Free information ❖ Amateur radio equipment. 903–395–2922.

Astron Corporation, 9 Autry, Irvine, CA 92718: Free information ❖ Heavy-duty power supplies. 714–458–7277.

Austin Amateur Radio Supply, 5325 North I-35, Austin, TX 78723: Free information ❖ Amateur radio equipment. 800–423–2604; 512–454–2994 (in TX).

AXM Radio Equipment, 11791 Loara St., Garden Grove, CA 92640: Free information ❖ Wide-band transceivers and base station and mobile antennas. 714–638–9556.

Barker & Williamson, 10 Canal St., Bristol, PA 19007: Free information ❖ Easy-to-install portable antennas. 215–788–5581.

Barry Electronics Corporation, 512 Broadway, New York, NY 10012: Free information ❖ Amateur, professional, and commercial electronics equipment. 212–925–7000.

Base Station Inc., 1839 East St., Concord, CA 94520: Free information ❖ Amateur radio equipment. 510–685–7388.

Bilal Company, 137 Manchester Dr., Florissant, CO 80816: Free catalog ❖ Antennas. 719–687–0650.

Burghardt Amateur Center, 182 N. Maple, P.O. Box 73, Watertown, SD 57201: Free

information ❖ Amateur radio equipment. 800–927–4261; 605–886–7314 (in SD).

Burk Electronics, 35 N. Kensington, LaGrange, IL 60525: Free information ❖ Amateur radio equipment. 708–482–9310.

Butternut Electronics, P.O. Box 1234, Olmito, TX 78575: Free catalog ❖ Vertical and compact, two-element beam butterfly antennas. 512–398–7117.

Byers Chassis Kits, 5120 Harmony Grove Rd., Dover, PA 17315: Free catalog ❖ Chassis and cabinets, rack shelves, other equipment enclosures, and aluminum and brass sheets. 717–292–4901.

Compute Inc., 1057 E. 2100 South, Salt Lake City, UT 84106: Free information ❖ Amateur radio and computer interfacing equipment. 800–942–8873; 801–467–8873 (in UT).

Comtelco Industries Inc., 501 Mitchell Rd., Glendale Hts., IL 60139: Free catalog ❖ Mobile antennas, magnet mounts, and accessories. 800–634–4622.

Connect Systems Inc., 2064 Eastman Ave., Ventura, CA 93003: Free brochure ❖ Automatic phone patch equipment for base station radios. 800–545–1349; 805–642–7184 (in CA).

Copper Electronics Inc., 3315 Gilmore Industrial Blvd., Louisville, KY 40213: Free information ❖ Amateur radio equipment. 800–626–6343; 502–968–8500 (in KY).

Delaware Amateur Supply, 71 Meadow Rd., New Castle, DE 19720: Free information ❖ Amateur radio equipment. 800–441–7008; 302–328–7728 (in DE).

Dentronics, 6102 Deland Rd., Flushing, MI 48433: Free information ❖ Amateur radio equipment. 810–659–1776.

Down East Microwave, RR 1, Box 2310, Troy, ME 04987: Free catalog ❖ Microwave antennas and other equipment.

R.L. Drake Company, P.O. Box 3006, Miamisburg, OH 45343: Free information ❖ World band communications receivers and other short-wave equipment. 800–937–2538.

Electronic Distributors, 325 Mill St., Vienna, VA 22180: Free information ❖ Antennas, roof towers, and rotators.

Electronic Equipment Bank, 323 Mill St. NE, Vienna, VA 22180: Free information ❖ Equipment for shortwave broadcast listeners. 800–368–3270; 703–938–3350 (in VA).

Electronic Specialists, Cinema Square Shopping Center, 3830 Oleander Dr., Wilmington, NC 28403: Free information ❖ Amateur radio equipment. 800–688–0073; 919–791–8885 (in NC).

Furuno USA, P.O. Box 2343, South San Francisco, CA 94083: Free information ❖ Transceivers. 415–873–9393.

GAP Antenna Products, 6010 Bldg. B, N. Old Dixie Hwy., Vero Beach, FL 32967: Free information ❖ Antennas for limited space. 407–778–3728.

Gateway Electronics, 8123 Page Blvd., St. Louis, MO 63130: Free information ❖ New and surplus electronics equipment. 314–427–6116.

Glassmaster, P.O. Box 159, Newberry, SC 29108: Free information ❖ Antennas and tuners. 803–276–0035.

Jo Gunn Enterprises, Hwy. 82, Box 32–C, Ethelsville, AL 35461: Catalog $2 ❖ Mobile antennas, coaxial, and other electronics equipment. 205–658–2229.

H.R. Electronics, 722 Evanston Ave., Muskegon, MI 49442: Free information ❖ Amateur radio equipment. 616–722–2246.

Ham Radio Outlet Inc., 933 N. Euclid St., Anaheim, CA 92801: Catalog $1 ❖ Radio amateur transceivers, receivers, mobile equipment, mini hand held units, antennas, and rotators. 800–854–6046; 714–533–7373 (in CA).

Ham Radio Toy Store, 117 W. Wesley St., Wheaton, IL 60187: Free information ❖ Amateur radio equipment. 708–668–9577.

Ham Station, 220 N. Fulton Ave., Evansville, IN 47719: Free information with long SASE ❖ New and used amateur radio equipment. 800–729–4373; 812–422–0231 (in IN).

The Ham Store, 5730 Mobud, San Antonio, TX 78238: Free information ❖ Ham radio equipment. 800–344–3144.

Hamtronics Inc., 4033 Brownsville Rd., Trevose, PA 19053: Catalog $1 ❖ Amateur radio equipment. 800–426–2820; 215–357–1400 (in PA).

Hardin Electronics, 5635 E. Rosedale St., Fort Worth, TX 76112: Free information ❖ Amateur radio equipment. 800–433–3203; 817–429–9761 (in TX).

Hatry Electronics, 500 Ledyard St., Hartford, CT 06114: Free information ❖ Amateur radio equipment. 203–296–1881.

Hialeah Communications, 801 Hialeah Dr., Hialeah, FL 33010: Free information ❖ Amateur radio equipment. 305–885–9929.

Honolulu Electronics, 870 Kawaiahao St., Honolulu, HI 96813: Free information ❖ Amateur radio equipment.

Hooper Electronics, 1702 Pass Rd., Biloxi, MS 39531: Free information ❖ Amateur radio equipment. 601–432–1100.

ICOM America, 2380 116th Ave. NE, Bellevue, WA 98004: Free information ❖ Amateur radio and single side band equipment. 800–999–9877.

Jun's Electronics, 5563 Sepulveda Blvd., Culver City, CA 90230: Free information ❖ Scanners, amateur and marine radio equipment, and cellular mobile phones. 800–882–1343; 213–390–8003 (in CA).

Kantronics, 1202 E. 23rd St., Lawrence, KS 66046: Free information ❖ Amateur and professional radio equipment. 913–842–7745.

Kenwood, P.O. Box 406, Long Beach, CA 90801: Free information ❖ Amateur radio equipment. 310–639–9000.

Larsen Antennas, 3611 NE 112th Ave., Vancouver, WA 98668: Free catalog ❖ Antennas. 206–944–7551.

LaRue Electronics, 1112 Grandview St., Scranton, PA 18509: Free information ❖ Amateur radio equipment. 717–343–2124.

Lentini Communications Inc., 21 Garfield St., Newington, CT 06111: Free information ❖ Radio equipment. 800–666–0908.

Madison Electronics Supply, 12310 Zavalla St., Houston, TX 77085: Free information ❖ Hard-to-find parts and other equipment for amateur radio operation and electronics hobbyists. 800–231–3057; 713–729–7300 (in TX).

Maggiore Electronic Lab, 600 Westtown Rd., West Chester, PA 19382: Free catalog ❖ Amateur and professional radio equipment. 610–436–6051.

Maryland Radio Center, 8576 Laureldale Dr., Laurel, MD 20707: Free information ❖ Amateur radio equipment. 301–725–1212.

McClaran Sales Inc., P.O. Box 2513, Vero Beach, FL 32961: Information $1 ❖ Antennas and towers. 407–778–7584.

Memphis Amateur Electronics, 1465 Wells Station Rd., Memphis, TN 38108: Free information ❖ Amateur radio equipment. 800–238–6168; 901–683–9125 (in TN).

Michigan Radio, 23040 Schoenherr, Warren, MI 48089: Free information ❖ Amateur radio base station and other equipment. 800–TRU-HAMM.

Missouri Radio Center, 630 NW Englewood Rd., Kansas City, MO 64118: Free information ❖ Amateur radio equipment and other equipment. 800–821–7323.

Mobile Mark Inc., 3900 River Rd., Schiller Park, IL 60176: Free information ❖ Easy-to-mount mobile and window antennas. 708–671–6690.

National Tower Company, P.O. Box 15417, Shawnee Mission, KS 66215: Free information ❖ Amateur radio equipment and antennas. 913–888–8864.

Network QSL's Cards, P.O. Box 13200, Alexandria, LA 71315: Catalog $1 ❖ QSL cards. 800–354–0830.

Oklahoma Comm Center, 13424 Railway Dr., Oklahoma City, OK 73114: Free information ❖ Amateur radio equipment. 800–765–4267; 405–478–2866 (in OK).

Omni Electronics, 1007 San Dario, Laredo, TX 78040: Free information ❖ Amateur radio equipment and antennas. 210–725–OMNI.

Pilot Amateur Radio, 1300 Hwy. 35, Neptune, NJ 07753: Free information ❖ Amateur radio equipment. 908–776–2522.

Portland Radio Supply, 234 SE Grand Ave., Portland, OR 97214: Free information ❖ New and used amateur radio equipment. 503–233–4904.

R & L Electronics, 1315 Maple Ave., Hamilton, OH 45011: Free catalog ❖ Amateur radio equipment and antennas. 800–221–7735; 513–868–6399 (in OH).

R.F. Enterprises, HC 86, Box 580, Merrifield, MN 56465: Free information ❖ Amateur radio equipment. 800–233–2482; 218–765–3254 (in MN).

Radio Adventure, Box 50062, Provo, UT 84605: Catalog $1 ❖ Easy-to-install indoor and portable antennas, other equipment and accessories for radio amateurs, and solar power systems. 801–373–8425.

Radio Center USA, 630 NW Englewood Rd., Kansas City, MO 64118: Free information ❖ Amateur radio equipment. 800–821–7323; 816–459–8832 (in MO).

Rivendell Electronics, 8 Londonberry Rd., Derry, NH 03038: Free information ❖ Amateur radio equipment. 603–434–5371.

Rutland Arrays, 1703 Warren St., New Cumberland, PA 17070: Free catalog ❖ VHF and UHF antennas and other equipment. 800–536–3268.

Standard Amateur Radio Products Inc., P.O. Box 48480, Niles, IL 60648: Free information ❖ Equipment for amateur radio operators. 312–763–0081.

Telex/Hy-Gain Communications Inc., 9600 Aldrich Ave. South, Minneapolis, MN 55420: Free information ❖ Antenna rotators. 612–887–5528.

Texas Towers, Division Texas RF Distributors Inc., 1108 Summit Ave., Plano, TX 75074: Free information ❖ Antennas, towers, rotators, and other equipment. 800–272–3467; 214–422–7306 (in TX).

Tri-Ex Tower Corporation, 7182 Rasmussen Ave., Visalia, CA 93291: Free information ❖ Antenna towers for amateur radio operation. 800–328–2393.

Universal Radio Inc., 6830 Americana Pkwy., Reynoldsburg, OH 43068: Free catalog ❖ Equipment for amateur radio operators, shortwave listeners, and scanner enthusiasts. 800–431–3939; 614–866–4267 (in OH).

US Tower, 1220 Marcin St., Visalia, CA 93291: Free catalog ❖ Antenna towers. 209–733–2438.

VHF Communications, 280 Tiffany Ave., Jamestown, NY 14701: Free information ❖ New and used electronics equipment. 716–664–6345.

W & W Associates, 29–11 Parsons Blvd., Flushing, NY 11354: Free catalog ❖ Batteries. 800–221–0732; 718–961–2103 (in NY).

Will-Burt Company, P.O. Box 900, Orrville, OH 44667: Free information ❖ Telescoping antenna masts. 216–682–7015.

Wilson Antenna Inc., 1181 Grier Dr., Ste. A, Las Vegas, NV 89119: Free information ❖ CB and mobile antennas. 800–541–6116.

Yaesu USA, 17210 Edwards Rd., Cerritos, CA 90701: Free information ❖ Amateur radio base station equipment. 310–404–2700.

E.H. Yost, 7344 Tetiva Rd., Sauk City, WI 53583: Free catalog ❖ Batteries for radios, computers, and other equipment. 608–643–3194.

Antique Radios

Antique Electronic Supply, 6221 S. Maple St., Tempe, AZ 85238: Catalog $2 ❖ Hard-to-find vacuum tubes and parts for antique radio restoration and repair. 602–820–5411.

Antique Triode, Box A2, Farnham, NY 14061: Catalog $1 ❖ Vacuum tubes. 716–549–5379.

ARS Electronics, 7110 de Celis Pl., P.O. Box 7323, Van Nuys, CA 91409: Free brochure ❖ Replacement electronic tubes.

Auto Radio Specialists, 405 S. Willow, Sioux Falls, SD 57104: Free information ❖ Tubes, speakers, and other original equipment. 605–332–5168.

Don Diers, 4276 N. 50th St., Milwaukee, WI 53216: Catalog $3 ❖ Vacuum tubes and parts.

Electron Tube Enterprises, Box 8311, Essex, VT 05451: Free catalog ❖ Surplus electron tubes. 802–879–1844.

Fala Electronics, P.O. Box 1376, Milwaukee, WI 53201: Free list with long SASE ❖ Vacuum tubes.

New Sensor Corporation, 133 5th Ave., New York, NY 10003: Free information ❖ Vacuum tubes, solid state rectifiers, and other hard-to-find parts. 800–633–5477; 212–529–0466 (in NY).

The Olde Tyme Radio Company, 2445 Lyttonsville Rd., Silver Spring, MD 20910: Free information with long SASE and two 1st class stamps ❖ Antique radios, parts, vacuum tubes, and schematics. 301–587–5280.

PTI Antique Radios, 7925 Mabelvale Cutoff, Mabelvale, AR 72103: Free information ❖ Antique radio restoration parts. 501–568–1995.

Quest Electronics, 5715 W. 11th Ave., Denver, CO 80214: Free catalog ❖ Electron tubes. 303–274–7545.

A.G. Tannenbaum, P.O. Box 110, East Rockaway, NY 11518: Free catalog ❖ Repair parts. 516–887–0057.

Citizen Band Equipment

CBC International Inc., P.O. Box 31500, Phoenix, AZ 85046: Catalog $3 ❖ Parts for CB radios, 10–meter and FM conversion kits, books, and plans.

Cobra, 6500 W. Cortland St., Chicago, IL 60635: Free information ❖ Fixed-installation and portable citizen band radios. 800–COBRA-22.

K-40 Electronics, 1500 Executive Dr., Elgin, IL 60123: Free brochure ❖ CB radios and antennas. 800–323–5608.

Nady Systems, 6701 Bay St., Emeryville, CA 94608: Free information ❖ UHF and VHF hand-held transceivers. 510–652–2411.

Radio Shack, Division Tandy Corporation, One Tandy Center, Fort Worth, TX 76102: Free information ❖ Portable and fixed-installation citizen band radios, electronics components, science kits, computers and accessories, stereo equipment, and toys and games. 817–390–3011.

Transcrypt International Inc., 1620 N. 20th St., Lincoln, NE 68503: Free information ❖ Portable and hand-held two-way radios. 800–228–0226.

Wilson Antenna Inc., 1181 Grier Dr., Ste. A, Las Vegas, NV 89119: Free information ❖ CB and mobile antennas. 800–541–6116.

RADON TESTING

First Alert, 780 McClure Rd., Aurora, IL 60404: Free information ❖ Radon detectors. 800–323–9005.

RAFTING & WHITEWATER RUNNING

Cascade Outfitters, 145 Pioneer Pkwy. East, P.O. Box 209, Springfield, OR 97477: Free catalog ❖ Whitewater river running equipment. 800–223–7238.

Colorado Kayak, P.O. Box 3059, Buena Vista, CO 81211: Free catalog ❖ Paddles and sports clothing. 800–535–3565.

Easy Rider Canoe & Kayak Company, P.O. Box 88108, Seattle, WA 98138: Catalog $5 ❖ Whitewater and sea cruising paddles, single and double seater kayaks and canoes, and rowing trainers. 206–228–3633.

Hyside Inflatables, P.O. Box Z, Kernville, CA 93238: Free information ❖ River running inflatable rafts, self-bailing kayaks, and other equipment. 619–376–3723.

Mitchell Paddles Inc., RD 2, P.O. Box 922, Canaan, NH 03741: Free information ❖ Canoe and kayak paddles, boats, and dry suits. 603–523–7004.

Nantahala Outdoor Center, 13077 Hwy. 19 West, Bryson City, NC 28713: Free catalog ❖

Supplies and equipment for whitewater paddling. 800–367–3521.

Northwest River Supplies Inc., 2009 S. Main, Moscow, ID 83843: Free catalog ❖ Rafts, waterproof bags, paddles, boats, and supplies. 800–635–5202.

Wildwater Designs, 230 Penllyn Pike, Penllyn, PA 19422: Free catalog ❖ Gear for whitewater, lake, or ocean travel in kayaks or canoes. 800–426–2027.

Wyoming River Raiders, 601 Wyoming Blvd., Casper, WY 82609: Free catalog ❖ Outdoor clothing, camping and river expedition equipment, fishing gear, hiking equipment, books, and other supplies. 800–247–6068; 307–235–8624 (in WY).

RECORDS, CASSETTES & CDs
Children's Recordings

A Gentle Wind, P.O. Box 3103, Albany, NY 12203: Free information ❖ Music and story cassettes for children age 1 to 12. 518–436–0391.

Music for Little People, Box 1460, Redway, CA 95560: Free catalog ❖ Musical cassettes and videos of famous stories, favorite songs, lullabies, nature stories, and folk and classical music. 707–923–3991.

Video Revolution, 97 Thoreau St., Concord, MA 01742: Free catalog ❖ Audio and video tapes for children. 800–342–3436.

Collectible Recordings

American Pie, Box 66455, Los Angeles, CA 90066: Catalog $2 ❖ Hard-to-find 45s, compact disks, and videos, from the 1940s to 1990s. 310–821–4005.

American Recording Productions, P.O. Box 250282, Franklin, MI 48025: Free information ❖ Reproductions of rare, Middle Eastern 78 rpm recordings on cassettes and compact disks.

Benedikt & Salmon Record Rarities, 3020 Meade Ave., San Diego, CA 92116: Free catalogs (indicate choice of (1) classical (2) jazz, big bands and blues (3) personalities, soundtracks and country music) ❖ Hard-to-find rare records from 1890 to date, early phonographs, cylinders, autographed memorabilia, and rare books on music and the performing arts. 619–281–3345.

Broadway-Hollywood Recordings, P.O. Box 496, Georgetown, CT 06829: Catalog $2 ❖ Rare, out-of-print soundtrack show albums and other recordings. 203–438–2663.

California Albums, P.O. Box 3426, Hollywood, CA 90078: Free information ❖ Collectible records.

Carousel Records, P.O. Box 427, Sun Prairie, WI 53500: Free information ❖ Western songs. 800–424–4445.

Collectables Records, Box 35, Narberth, PA 19072: Free catalog ❖ Rhythm and blues records from the 1970s.

Cornerstone Music, 1406 Missouri Blvd., Jefferson City, MO 65109: Free information with two 1st class stamps ❖ Collectible rock, pop, and soul 45s. 314–636–9166.

Coronet Books, CDs & Cassettes, 311 Bainbridge St., Philadelphia, PA 19147: Catalog $2 ❖ Rhythm, classical, blues, big band, soundtracks, Broadway musicals, rock, and other recordings. 215–925–2762.

Flipside Records, 215 Arch St., Meadville, PA 16335: Free information ❖ Music and other vintage sounds from the 1920s to the 1980s, and later. 814–333–9403.

Forty-Fives, P.O. Box 358, Lemoyne, PA 17043: Catalog $2 ❖ Hard-to-find long-playing vinyl records and vintage 45s, from 1950 to the present.

Bob Getreuer, P.O. Box 582, Nanuet, NY 10954: Catalog $1 ❖ Long-playing records, 45s, compact disks, and tapes, from the 1940s to the 1980s. 914–352–5259.

Graceland Records, 2036 Dixie Garden Loop, Holiday, FL 34690: Free price list with long SASE ❖ Elvis records, tapes, compact disks, and memorabilia. 813–942–1935.

Granny's Turntable, P.O. Box 1585, Hendersonville, TN 37077: Catalog $3 ❖ Country and western record albums and cassette tapes. 615–822–8675.

In A Groove Records & Collectibles, 911 S. Oak Park Ave., Oak Park, IL 60304: Free information with long SASE ❖ Collectible records, from the 1960s and 1970s. 708–848–6575.

International Linguistics Corporation, 3505 E. Red Bridge, Kansas City, MO 64137: Free catalog ❖ Audio tapes for teaching

French, German, Russian, Japanese, and English. 800–765–8855.

Manchester/Manchester, 1711 S. Willow St., Manchester, NH 03103: Free information with long SASE ❖ Out-of-print and used records, compact disks, and tapes. 603–644–0199.

Metro Music, P.O. Box 10004, Silver Spring, MD 20904: Free catalog with two 1st class stamps ❖ Recordings from the 1960s and modern garage and psych sounds. 301–622–2473.

Music Box Melodies, P.O. Box 210, Whitehall, NY 12887: Catalog $1 ❖ Popular, classical, waltz, marches, and show tunes, from the 1850s to 1990s. Includes carousel band organs, calliopes, street organs, European fair organs, orchestrions, street pianos, disk and cylinder musical boxes, and monkey organs. 518–282–9770.

Don Myers, 2103 Rhode Island, Joplin, MO 64804: Free information ❖ Soundtracks and rock, soul, country, and easy listening records.

Oldies Unlimited, Box 17122, Cleveland, OH 44117: Free list with long SASE ❖ Rockabilly, doo-wops, 1960s garage, girl groups, Beatles, Elvis, and other original 45s.

Pack Central Inc., 6745 Denny Ave., North Hollywood, CA 91606: Catalog $2 ❖ Records and cassettes from the 1950s, 1960s, 1970s, and 1980s. 818–760–2828.

Reality Records, P.O. Box 661343, Los Angeles, CA 90066: Free catalog ❖ Rare rock and roll records and compact disks. 310–398–9492.

Right Hemisphere, 19 S. Jackson St., Media, PA 19063: Free information ❖ Records, tapes, compact disks, imports, and independents, from the 1960s, 1970s, and out-of-print collectibles. 215–566–1322.

Roanoke's Record Room, P.O. Box 2445, Roanoke, VA 24010: Free price list ❖ Out-of-print 10– and 12–inch rock and pop long-playing records, from 1949 to 1992. 703–343–9570.

Rock Classics, 15062 Goldenwest St., Westminster, CA 92683: Catalog $1 ❖ Rock classics on compact disks, from the 1950s, 1960s, and 1970s. 714–893–6057.

John Tefteller, P.O. Box 1727, Grants Pass, OR 97526: Free information ❖ Rhythm and blues, rockabilly, rock 'n roll, country music and other rare 45s, 78s, and a few long-playing records. 503–476–1326.

Time Machine Music & Video, P.O. Box 6961, Metairie, LA 70009: Free information ❖ Hard-to-find music and video recordings.

Current Recordings

Acoustic Sounds, P.O. Box 1905, Salina, KS 67402: Catalog $3 ❖ Classical, waltzes, rhythm, Latin American, and other recordings and compact disks. 913–825–8609.

AMI Music, P.O. Box 72124, Marietta, GA 30007: Free catalog ❖ Jazz, traditional, blues, jazz fusion, New Age, and new instrumental CDs. 800–474–4172; 404–977–4172 (in GA).

Arhoolie Records, 10341 San Pablo Ave., El Cerrito, CA 94530: Catalog $1 ❖ Old-time folk lyric blues and classics, specializing in roots and regional music. 510–525–1494.

Audio-Forum, 96 Broad St., Guilford, CT 06437: Free catalog ❖ Full-length courses for teaching yourself a foreign language. 800–345–8501; 203–453–9794 (in CT).

Audio House Compact Disk Club, 4304 Brayan, Swartz Creek, MI 48473: Catalog $2 (refundable) ❖ Used compact disks. 313–655–8639.

Audiophile Selections, P.O. Box 17038, Anaheim, CA 92817: Free catalog ❖ Compact disks.

Barnes & Noble, 126 5th Ave., New York, NY 10011: Free catalog ❖ Records, cassettes, and books. 800–242–6657.

Barry Publications, 477 82nd St., Brooklyn, NY 11209: Free catalog ❖ Compact disks and cassettes.

The Beautiful Music Company, 777 Larkfield Rd., Commack, NY 11725: Free catalog ❖ Bluegrass and country, marches, instrumentals, jazz, gospel, big bands and favorite artists, classics and opera, and barbershop quartet recordings.

Berkshire Record Outlet Inc., RR 1, Rt. 102, Pleasant St., Lee, MA 01238: Catalog $2 ❖ Classical recordings. 413–243–4080.

Bernel Music Ltd., Cullowqhee, NC 28723: Free catalog ❖ Brass band compact disks. 704–293–9312.

Blind Pig Records, P.O. Box 2344, San Francisco, CA 94126: Free catalog ❖ Blues records, CDs, and cassettes. 510–526–0373.

CD Research, 407 G St., Davis, CA 95616: Catalog $3 ❖ Imported compact disks and singles.

Channel Classics America, P.O. Box 5642, Englewood, NJ 07631: Free catalog ❖ Classical records. 201–568–1544.

Classic Recordings, 2954 28th St. SE, Southridge Center, Grand Rapids, MI 49512: Free information ❖ Compact and laser disks. 800–433–8979; 616–957–3614 (in MI).

Coin Machine Trader, P.O. Box 602, Huron, SD 57350: Information $4 ❖ 45 rpm records for most jukeboxes. 605–352–7590.

Concord Records Inc., P.O. Box 845, Concord, CA 94522: Free catalog ❖ Classical recordings on compact disks. 800–551–5299.

Coronet Books, CDs & Cassettes, 311 Bainbridge, St., Philadelphia, PA 19147: Catalog $2 ❖ Compact disks and cassettes. 215–925–2762.

Country Music Hall of Fame, 4 Music Square East, Nashville, TN 37203: Catalog $2 ❖ Cajun, bluegrass, old-time and early country classics, country fiddling, western swing and cowboy, Elvis Presley and rock, gospel, and Christmas albums, cassettes, compact disks, books, and song books. 800–255–2357; 615–256–1639 (in TN).

Ken Crane's, 14260 Beach Blvd., Westminster, CA 92683: Free catalog ❖ Pioneer laser disks. 800–624–3078; 800–626–1768 (in CA).

Critics' Choice Video, P.O. Box 749, Itasca, IL 60143: Free catalog ❖ Records, tapes, video cassettes, and books. 800–544–9852.

Digital Sounds, 2160 E. 116th St., #E-6, Carmel, IN 46072: Free information ❖ Pop, rock, jazz, classical, New Age, country, soul, and easy listening music on CDs.

DISCollection, P.O. Box 501832, Indianapolis, IN 46250: Free newsletter ❖ Compact and laser disks. 317–849–0629.

Down Home Music Company, 10341 San Pablo Ave., El Cerrito, CA 94530: Catalog $5 (specify blues, country, or vintage rock 'n' roll ❖ Records, tapes, compact disks, music books, and videos, from around the world. 510–525–1494.

Earwig Music Company Inc., 1818 W. Pratt Blvd., Chicago, IL 60626: Catalog $1 ❖ Traditional and modern blues recordings. 800–638–0869.

Folk-Legacy Records Inc., Box 1148, Sharon, CT 06069: Free information ❖ Country folk music on records, compact disks, and cassettes. 800–836–0901; 364–5661 (in CT).

Gambler's Book Shop, 630 S. 11th, Las Vegas, NV 89101: Free catalog ❖ Cassettes on how to achieve personal success, succeed in the stock market, business, finance, and how to win at sports betting, poker, blackjack, keno, baccarat, craps, and roulette. 800–522–1777; 702–382–7555 (in NV).

Granny's Turntable, P.O. Box 1585, Hendersonville, TN 37077: Catalog $3 ❖ Country and western record albums and cassette tapes. 615–822–8675.

Stephan Grossman's Guitar Workshop, P.O. Box 802, Sparta, NJ 07871: Free catalog ❖ Videos, cassettes, compact discs, and books. Includes rare performances, blues and country music, music of other countries, jazz classics, ragtime, and instructions on how to play a guitar.

HB Recordings Directly, 2186 Jackson Keller, San Antonio, TX 78213: Free catalog ❖ Classical CDs and video cassettes. 800–222–6872.

Heartland Music, 605 S. Douglas St., Box 1034, El Segundo, CA 90245: Free catalog ❖ Big-band, nostalgic, patriotic, romantic, inspirational, gospel, rock n' roll, country, and easy listening music. 800–788–2400.

Homespun Tapes, Box 694, Woodstock, NY 12498: Free catalog ❖ Blues video and audio cassettes. 800–33–TAPES.

J & R Music World, 59–50 Queens-Midtown Expy., Maspeth, NY 11378: Free catalog ❖ Records, cassettes, and video tapes. 800–221–8180.

Kicking Mule Records, P.O. Box 158, Alderpoint, CA 95511: Free catalog ❖ Compact disks, cassettes, music books, long-playing records, and teaching tapes for guitar, banjo, dulcimer, fiddle, harp, harmonica, and other instruments. 800–262–5312.

Lasertown Video Discs, 50 School House Rd., Box 406, Kulpsville, PA 19443: Catalog $10.85 ❖ Laser disks. 800–893–0390.

Metro Music, P.O. Box 10004, Silver Spring, MD 20904: Free catalog with two 1st class stamps ❖ Records from the 1960s and New Wave recordings. 301–622–2473.

Metropolitan Opera Guild, 835 Madison Ave., New York, NY 10021: Free information ❖ Classical, concert, operatic, and documentary videos, records, compact disks, and books. 212–634–8406.

Music Exchange, 207 Westport Rd., Kansas City, MO 64111: Free information with long SASE ❖ Hard-to-find 78s, 45s, long-playing records, tapes, and CDs. 816–931–7560.

Don Myers, 2103 Rhode Island, Joplin, MO 64804: Free information ❖ Soundtracks and rock, soul, country, and easy listening records.

Olsson's Books & Records, 1239 Wisconsin Ave. NW, Washington, DC 20007: Free information ❖ Classical, rock, jazz, folk music, New Age recordings, and other compact disks and cassettes. 202–337–8084.

Pack Central Inc., 6745 Denny Ave., North Hollywood, CA 91606: Catalog $2 ❖ Records and cassettes from the 1950s, 1960s, 1970s, and 1980s. 818–760–2828.

Radio Library, Box 200725, Arlington, TX 76006: Free catalog ❖ Old radio shows on cassettes. 817–261–8745.

RAS Records, P.O. Box 42517, Washington, DC 20015: Catalog $2 ❖ Reggae records, hard-to-find compact disks, cassettes, and albums from Jamaica, England, Canada, and Europe.

Reach Out, 7324 Noah Reid Rd., Chattanooga, TN 37421: Free catalog ❖ Recordings with a Christian theme. 615–892–6814.

Record-Rama Sound Archives, 4981 McKnight Rd., Pittsburgh, PA 15237: Free information ❖ Albums, 45s, and compact disks. 412–367–7330.

Marion Roehl Recordings, 3533 Stratford Dr., Vestal, NY 13850: Free catalog ❖ Carrousel organ, player piano, music box, and saloon piano recordings. 607–797–9062.

Rose Records, 214 S. Wabash Ave., Chicago, IL 60604: Free catalog ❖ New releases, imports, and overstocks of classical, folk, blues, pop, jazz, soul, and country music records. 800–955–ROSE.

Roundup Records, 1 Camp St., Cambridge, MA 02140: Catalog $1 ❖ Blues, rock, jazz, and folk CDs, long-playing records, and cassettes. 617–661–6308.

Sound Delivery, P.O. Box 2213, Davis, CA 95617: Free catalog ❖ Compact disks, cassettes, and music videos. Includes rock and pop music, classical, jazz, soundtracks, opera, new age, and world-famous performers. 800–888–8574.

Sound Exchange, 45 N. Industry Ct., Deer Park, NY 11729: Free catalog ❖ Music, gifts, and collectibles. 800–521–0042.

Soundmind, P.O. Box 1386, Montpelier, VT 05601: Catalog $3 (refundable) ❖ Blues and jazz CDs.

Starship Industries, 605 Utterback Store Rd., Great Falls, VA 22066: Free catalog ❖ Laser and CD video disks. 703–430–8692.

Sunset Records Etc., 1232 Wilbur Ave., Somerset, MA 02725: Free information with long SASE ❖ New and used records, compact disks, cases, and videos. 508–678–3441.

Time-Life Books, P.O. Box 85563, Richmond, VA 23285: Free catalog ❖ Educational and entertainment videos and books. 800–854–1681.

Tower Records Mailorder, 22 E. 4th St., Ste. 302, New York, NY 10003: Free information ❖ Classical and opera recordings. 800–648–4844.

Video Artists International Inc., 158 Linwood Plaza,. Ste. 301, Fort Lee, NJ 07024: Free catalog ❖ Classical music video cassettes and CDs. 201–944–0099.

Radio Recordings

Adventures in Cassettes, 5353 Nathan Ln., Plymouth, MN 55442: Free information ❖ Old radio shows on cassettes as aired in the 1930s and 1940s. 800–328–0108.

Erstwhile Radio, P.O. Box 2284, Peabody, MA 01960: Catalog $2 ❖ Old-time radio broadcasts on cassettes.

Radio Library, Box 200725, Arlington, TX 76006: Free catalog ❖ Old radio shows on cassettes. 817–261–8745.

Soundtracks

Broadway-Hollywood Recordings, P.O. Box 496, Georgetown, CT 06829: Catalog $2 ❖ Rare, out-of-print soundtrack show albums and other recordings. 203–748–1266.

Coronet Books, CDs & Cassettes, 311 Bainbridge St., Philadelphia, PA 19147: ❖ Rhythm, classical, blues, big band, soundtracks, Broadway musicals, rock, and other recordings. 215–925–2762.

Don Myers, 2103 Rhode Island, Joplin, MO 64804: Free information ❖ Soundtracks and rock, soul, country, and easy listening records.

Storage Cabinets & Supplies

AGM Woodworking, 870 Capitolio Way, San Luis Obispo, CA 93401: Free brochure ❖ Storage cabinets for audio and video recordings. 800–858–9005.

Allen Products Company, 505 S. Beverly Dr., Beverly Hills, CA 90212: Free information ❖ Compact disk storage cabinets and audio and video equipment. 800–729–1251.

Andy's Record Supplies, 48 Colonial Rd., Providence, RI 02906: Free information with two 1st class stamps ❖ Album cardboard jackets, blister packs, storage boxes, record sleeves, and other archival supplies. 401–421–9453.

Bags Unlimited Inc., 7 Canal St., Rochester, NY 14608: Free information ❖ Record storage and protection poly bags, cardboard backings, storage and display boxes, and other archival supplies. 800–767–BAGS.

Hills Products Inc., P.O. Box 55, Candia, NH 03034: Free information ❖ Compact disk storage cabinets. 603–483–28288.

HY-Q Enterprises, 14040 Mead St., Longmont, CO 80504: Free information ❖ Storage cabinets for compact disks, VHS video cassettes, and audio tapes. 800–878–7458.

Lorentz Design Inc., P.O. Box 277, Lanesboro, MN 55949: Free catalog ❖ Storage cabinets for compact disks, VHS tapes, cassettes, and video game cartridges. 800–933–0403.

The Market Tree Ltd., P.O. Box 609, Boone, NC 28607: Free information ❖ Compact disk and cassette storage cabinets. 800–344–5116.

Per Madsen Design, P.O. Box 330101, San Francisco, CA 94133: Free brochure ❖ Stackable, portable units for disk and tape storage. 415–928–4509.

Sorice, P.O. Box 747, Nutley, NJ 07110: Free information ❖ Audio and video disk and cassette storage cabinets. 800–432–8005.

Twelve Designs, 1314 NW Irving, Portland, OR 97209: Free information ❖ Storage cabinets for audio and video recordings.

RECYCLED & ENVIRONMENTALLY SAFE PRODUCTS

Alte Schule U.S.A., 704 E. Palace Ave., Santa Fe, NM 87501: Free information ❖ Recycled pads, notebooks, diaries, sketchbooks, gift wrap, envelopes, stationery, and other paper products. 505–983–2593.

Atlantic Recycled Paper Company, 87 Mellor Ave., Baltimore, MD 21228: Free catalog ❖ Office and restroom paper supplies. 410–747–7314.

Basically Natural, 109 East G St., Brunswick, MD 21716: Free information ❖ Household cleaners and pet and personal care products. 800–352–7099.

Bio-Pax Division, Diversified Packaging Products, 1265 Pine Hill Dr., Annapolis, MD 21401: Free catalog ❖ Recycled paper packaging supplies. 410–974–4411.

Canusa Corporation, 1616 Shakespeare St., Baltimore, MD 21231: Free catalog ❖ Computer and copier paper. 410–522–0110.

Clothcrafters Inc., P.O. Box 176, Elkhart Lake, WI 53020: Free catalog ❖ Reusable kitchen supplies and cotton bags, 100 percent cotton diapers, and other environmentally sensitive products. 414–876–2112.

Conservatree Paper Company, 10 Lombard St., Ste. 250, San Francisco, CA 94111: Free catalog ❖ Office paper supplies. 415–433–1000.

Diamond Paper, P.O. Box 7000, Sterling, VA 22170: Free catalog ❖ Office paper supplies. 703–450–0000.

Earth Care, 200 Clara Ave., Ukiah, CA 95482: Free catalog ❖ Recycled paper products.

The Ecology Box, 2260 S. Main, Ann Arbor, MI 48103: Free information ❖ Health and environmentally-safe products. 800–735–1371; 313–662–9131 (in MI).

Idea Art, P.O. Box 291505, Nashville, TN 37229: Free catalog ❖ Laser/copier/offset recycled paper with preprinted designs. 800–433–2278.

The Recycled Paper Company, 12 Channel St., Boston, MA 02210: Free catalog ❖ Stationery and copier paper. 617–737–9911.

Sante Enterprise Corporation, 4400 Castle Palm Rd., Ste. 120, Orlando, FL 32839: Free brochure ❖ Biodegradable and non-carcinogenic paint and varnish remover. 407–843–7764.

Seventh Generation, 49 Hercules Dr., Colchester, VT 05446: Free catalog ❖ Household products and decorative accessories for the environmental enthusiast. 800–456–1177.

ROCKS, MINERALS & FOSSILS
Display Cases & Lights

Fluorescent Minerals Company, 5106 Walnut Grove Ave., San Gabriel, CA 91776: Free information ❖ Fluorescent lamps for minerals. 800–833–6757.

Lustig International, P.O. Box 2051, San Leandro, CA 94577: Free information ❖ Display stands. 800–221–4456.

O'Brien Manufacturing, 2081 Knowles Rd., Medford, OR 97501: Free information ❖ Oak show cases with tempered glass, built-in plunger locks, halogen lighting, and roller bearing doors. 503–773–2410.

Sylmar Display Stands, P.O. Box 362, Youngtown, AZ 85363: Free catalog ❖ Display stands. 602–933–7301.

Fossils

A & K Gems & Minerals, 2442 Folsom St., San Francisco, CA 94110: Free information ❖ Rocks, minerals, shells, fossils, tumbled gemstones, geodes, and crystal specimens. 415–282–0196.

Ackley's Rock & Stamps, 3230 N. Stone Ave., Colorado Springs, CO 80907: Catalog $1 (refundable) ❖ Fossils, lapidary and silversmithing supplies, jewelry boxes and trays, mountings, and findings. 719–633–1153.

The Amber Company, 5643 Cahuenga Blvd., North Hollywood, CA 91601: Free price list ❖ Amber, beads, fossils, books, faceting and cabbing rough, lapidary supplies, decor accessories, and gemstones. 818–509–5730.

Art By God, 3705 Biscayne Blvd., Miami, FL 33137: Free information ❖ Rocks, minerals, and fossils. 800–940–4449.

Hal Bach's Rock Shop, 137 Marne Rd., Cheektowage, NY 14215: Free information ❖ Fossils, minerals, and rock specimens. 800–568–6888.

Bitner's, 42 W. Hatcher, Phoenix, AZ 85021: Free information ❖ Rocks, minerals, and fossils. 602–870–0075.

Black Hills Institute of Geological Research Inc., 217 Main St., P.O. Box 643, Hill City, SD 57745: Free information ❖ Cretaceous ammonites, eocene fishes, oligocene mammals, dinosaurs, and other fossils. 605–574–4289.

Bourget Bros., 1636 11th St., Santa Monica, CA 90404: Catalog $3 ❖ Fossils, gemstones, cabochons, wax patterns, beads, and bead-stringing and jewelry-making supplies. 310–450–6556.

Caldron Crafts, 1520 Caton Center Dr., Baltimore, MD 21227: Catalog $5 ❖ Rocks, minerals, and fossils. 410–242–7993.

Dino Productions, P.O. Box 3004, Englewood, CO 80155: Catalog $2 (refundable) ❖ Fossils, rocks and minerals, ecology and oceanography equipment, and supplies for chemistry, general science, astronomy, and biology. 303–741–1587.

Discount Agate House, 3401 N. Dodge, Tucson, AZ 85716: Free information ❖ Rocks, minerals, and fossils. 602–323–0781.

Ebersole Lapidary Supply Inc., 11417 West Hwy. 54, Wichita, KS 67209: Catalog $2 ❖ Fossils, petrified woods, rock specimens, tools, jewelry findings and kits, mountings, and cabochons. 316–722–4771.

Extinctions, 303 Carlisle Ave., York, PA 17404: Free catalog ❖ Trilobites, crinoids, vertebrates, ferns, and other specimens. 717–846–4111.

Fossils & Amber, c/o IJB Marketing Inc., P.O. Box 5568, Woodridge, IL 60517: Free catalog ❖ Fossils and amber specimens. 800–AMBER-44.

The Fossil Works, Hudsondale Rd., Weatherly, PA 18255: Catalog $2 (refundable) ❖ Plant life fossils. 717–427–8878.

Geo-Impressions, P.O. Box 989, Pelham, NH 03076: Catalog $1 ❖ Common to rare vertebrates and invertebrates, rocks, and minerals. 603–635–7923.

Green River Geological Labs Inc., 365 N. 600 West, Logan, UT 84321: Free catalog ❖ European and American fossils. 801–750–0136.

In The Beginning, 31560 Railroad Canyon Rd., Canyon Lake, CA 92587: Catalog $1 (refundable) ❖ Fossils from worldwide sources. 909–244–5895.

Jeanne's Rock & Jewelry, 5420 Bissonet, Bellaire, TX 77401: Price list $1 ❖ Petrified wood products, fossils, seashells, lapidary supplies, and gifts. 713–664–2988.

Lou-Bon Gems & Rocks, Lake Barcroft Plaza, 6341 Columbia Pike, Bailey's Crossroads, VA 22041: Free information ❖ Carvings, beads, mineral specimens, fossils, shells, and lapidary and jeweler's equipment. 703–256–1084.

Malick's Fossils, 5514 Plymouth Rd., Baltimore, MD 21214: Catalog $3 ❖ Fossils and other artifacts. 410–426–2969.

Minerals Unlimited, P.O. Box 877, Ridgecrest, CA 93556: Catalog $2 ❖ Rocks, minerals, and fossils.

Missing Link Fossils, 833 Poplar Way, Qualicum Beach, British Columbia, Canada V9K 1X8: Catalog $2 (refundable) ❖ Fossils and mineral specimens. 604–752–3979.

Mountain Gems & Minerals, 97 Lamington Rd., Somerville, NJ 08876: Free list with 1st class stamp ❖ Fossil fish, trilobites, and other specimens.

Omni Resources, 1004 S. Mebane St., P.O. Box 2096, Burlington, NC 27216: Free catalog ❖ Fossils, rocks, hiking and topography maps, and globes. 800–742–2677.

PaleoSearch Inc., P.O. Box 621, Hays, KS 67601: Catalog $3 ❖ Fossils, educational posters, and rare reproductions. 913–625–2240.

Parsons' Minerals & Fossils, 2808 Eden Ln., Rapid City, SD 57701: Video catalog $13.50 ❖ Minerals and fossils from worldwide sources. 605–348–0937.

Phoenix Fossils, 6401 E. Camino De Los Ranchos, Scottsdale, AZ 85254: Information $4 ❖ Dinosaur teeth, vertebrate fossils, and other specimens. 602–991–5246.

Pikes Peak Rock Shop, 1316 Pecan St., Colorado Springs, CO 80904: Free catalog ❖ Fossils, crystals, tumbled stones, agate products, amethyst, chips, beads, and display stands. 800–347–6257.

Prehistoric Journeys, P.O. Box 3376, Santa Barbara, CA 93130: Catalog $3 ❖ Rare vertebrate fossils and dinosaur bones. 805–563–2404.

J.F. Ray, P.O. Box 1364, Ocala, FL 32678: Catalog $3 (refundable) ❖ Shark teeth jewelry, fossils, seashells, beach-combing treasures, and amber with inclusions.

Sandia Rocks & Minerals, Box 4045, Albuquerque, NM 87196: Free catalog ❖ Minerals and fossils.

SESCO, P.O. Box 21406, Reno, NV 89515: Free catalog ❖ Findings, gemstones, fossils, and novelties. 800–637–3726.

Skullduggery, 624 South B St., Tustin, CA 92680: Free information ❖ Fossil replicas. 800–336–7745.

Southeastern Fossil Supply Company, 1209 N. Eastman Rd., Kingsport, TN 37664: Free catalog ❖ Fossils, mineral collections, and teaching aids. 615–245–5626.

The Stone Company Science Specimens, Charlie & Florence Magovern, Box 18814, Boulder, CO 80308: Free information ❖ Museum-quality fossils and other science specimens. 303–581–0670.

STRATAGraphics, 63 Knolltop Dr., Rochester, NY 14610: Catalog $1 ❖ Fish, mammals, reptiles, other vertebrates, and petrified wood and plant specimens. 716–385–4542.

Two Guys Fossils & Minerals, 1087 Plymouth St., East Bridgewater, MA 02333: Catalog $2 ❖ Rocks, minerals, and fossils. 800–FOSSILS.

Village Rock Shop, 346 S. Chicago, Hot Springs, SD 57747: Free price list with long SASE ❖ Prepared and unprepared fossils and petrified wood specimens. 605–745–5446.

Warfield Fossil Quarries, Box 301, HRC 61, Thayne, WY 83127: Catalog $2 ❖ Fish, leaves, turtles, reptiles, tribolites, ammonites, and other fossils. 307–883–2445.

Woods of the World & Fossils, P.O. Box 47, Somis, CA 93066: Free price list ❖ Petrified woods and fossil plants.

Meteorites

A & K Gems & Minerals, 2442 Folsom St., San Francisco, CA 94110: Free information ❖ Rocks, minerals, shells, fossils, tumbled gemstones, geodes, and crystal specimens. 415–282–0196.

Bethany Sciences, P.O. Box 3726, New Haven, CT 06525: Catalog $2 ❖ Stones, irons, stony-iron meteorites, display stands, jewelry, and books. 203–393–3395.

Excalibur-Cureton Company, Division Excalibur Mineral Company, 1000 N. Division St., Peekskill, NY 10566: Catalog $1 ❖ Meteorites and mineral specimens. 914–739–1134.

Robert Haag Meteorites, P.O. Box 27527, Tucson, AZ 85726: Catalog $5 (refundable) ❖ Meteorites. 602–882–8804.

R.A. Langheinrich, 326 Manor Ave., Cranford, NJ 07446: Catalog $2 ❖ Meteorites.

Mineralogical Research Company, 15840 E. Alta Vista Way, San Jose. CA 95127: Free list with long SASE and two 1st class stamps ❖ Meteorites, rare mineral specimens, microscopes, micro mounts, and specimen boxes. 408–923–6800.

David New, P.O. Box 278, Anacortes, WA 98221: Free information ❖ Meteorites, tektites, and minerals from worldwide sources. 206–293–2255.

New England Meteoritical Services, P.O. Box 440, Mendon, MA 01756: Free list ❖ Meteorites. 508–478–4020.

Blaine Reed, 907 County Rd., Durango, CO 81301: Free price list ❖ Meteorites.

Ward's Natural Science, P.O. Box 92912, Rochester, NY 14692: Free information with long SASE ❖ Meteorites, telescopes, audio-visual aids, and books. 716–359–2502.

Miscellaneous Varieties

A & K Gems & Minerals, 2442 Folsom St., San Francisco, CA 94110: Free information ❖ Rocks, minerals, and fossils. 415–282–0196.

Aleta's Rock Shop, 1515 Plainfield NE, Grand Rapids, MI 49505: Catalog $1.50 ❖ Mineral specimens, rocks for cutting and tumbling, lapidary equipment, and silversmithing supplies. 616–363–5394.

Allen's Rocks & Gifts, 26513 Center Ridge Rd., Cleveland, OH 44145: Free information ❖ Minerals, findings, silversmithing supplies, casting and lapidary equipment, and tools. 216–871–6522.

The Amber Company, 5643 Cahuenga Blvd., North Hollywood, CA 91601: Free price list ❖ Amber, beads, fossils, books, faceting and cabbing rough, lapidary supplies, decor accessories, and gemstones. 818–509–5730.

Arizona Gems & Minerals Inc., 6370 East Hwy. 69, Prescott Valley, AZ 86314: Catalog $2 ❖ Geodes, silversmithing and lapidary tools, jewelry-making supplies, and mineral sets. 602–772–6443.

Arrow Gems & Minerals Inc., P.O. Box 9068, Phoenix, AZ 85068: Free catalog ❖ Pewter figurines, pendants, buckles, and bolas, beads and findings, mineral specimens, and faceted stones. 602–997–6373.

Art By God, 3705 Biscayne Blvd., Miami, FL 33137: Free information ❖ Rocks, minerals, and fossils. 800–940–4449.

Aurora Mineral Corporation, 16 Niagara Ave., Freeport, NY 11520: Free information ❖ Amethyst, geodes, fossil fishes, quartz crystals, and mineral specimens from around the world. 516–623–3800.

Bitner's, 42 W. Hatcher, Phoenix, AZ 85021: Free information ❖ Rocks, minerals, and fossils. 602–870–0075.

C & R Enterprises Inc., 4833 East Park, Springfield, MO 65809: Free catalog ❖ Sterling silver and 14k gold jewelry mountings, lapidary supplies, mineral specimens, belt buckles, beads and beading supplies, and cut stones. 417–866–4843.

Carousel Gem & Minerals, 1202 Perion Dr., Belen, NM 87002: Price list $1 ❖ Minerals from worldwide locations. 505–864–2145.

Charlie's Rock Shop, 620 J St., Penrose, CO 81240: Free catalog ❖ Mineral specimens, jewelry supplies and findings, tools, and beads. 800–336–6923.

Dino Productions, P.O. Box 3004, Englewood, CO 80155: Catalog $2 (refundable) ❖ Fossils, rocks and minerals, ecology and oceanography equipment, and supplies for chemistry, general science, astronomy, and biology. 303–741–1587.

Discount Agate House, 3401 N. Dodge, Tucson, AZ 85716: Free information ❖ Rocks, minerals, and fossils. 602–323–0781.

Excalibur-Cureton Company, Division Excalibur Mineral Company, 1000 N. Division St., Peekskill, NY 10566: Catalog $1 ❖ Meteorites and mineral specimens. 914–739–1134.

Gem City Lapidary, 1924 Grand, Laramie, WY 82070: Price list $1 ❖ Russian mineral specimens.

Gemax Mineral Inc., 90 W. Houston St., New York, NY 10012: Free price list ❖ Minerals, crystals, books, jewelry, and gifts. 212–228–1803.

Gemco International, P.O. Box 833, Fayston, VT 05673: Free price list ❖ Faceted rough gemstones and small cut stones. Includes some that are slightly or moderately flawed. 802–496–2770.

Geo-Impressions, P.O. Box 989, Pelham, NH 03076: Catalog $1 ❖ Common to rare vertebrates and invertebrates, rocks, and minerals. 603–635–7923.

Kenneth Glasser, P.O. Box 441, Monsey, NY 10952: Catalog $10 ❖ All types, sizes, and qualities of diamonds. 914–426–1241.

Grieger's, P.O. Box 93070, Pasadena, CA 91109: Free catalog ❖ Minerals and rare stones from around the world, lapidary equipment, jewelry supplies and findings, and mountings. 800–423–4181.

Herkimer Diamond Mines, P.O. Box 510, Herkimer, NY 13350: Free information ❖ Petrified wood products, rockhounding equipment, minerals and rocks, and quartz crystals. 315–891–7355.

Jewelry by Avery, 5134 Chalk Point Rd., West River, MD 20778: Free information with long SASE ❖ Handcrafted Zuni, Navajo, and Hopi turquoise jewelry, kachinas, Native American art, precious and semi-precious gemstones, and mineral specimens. 410–867–4752.

Knight's Gem Stones, P.O. Box 411, Waitsfield, VT 05673: Catalog $2 ❖ Rough gemstones in different grades. 802–496–3707.

Lentz Lapidary Inc., 11760 S. Oliver, Rt. 2, Box 134, Mulvane, KS 67110: Catalog $2 ❖ Jewelry, mountings, clocks and motors, rough rock specimens, cabochons, and rockhounding and lapidary equipment. 316–777–1372.

Lou-Bon Gems & Rocks, Lake Barcroft Plaza, 6341 Columbia Pike, Bailey's Crossroads, VA 22041: Free information ❖ Carvings, beads, mineral specimens, fossils, shells, and lapidary and jeweler's equipment. 703–256–1084.

MACAJAC Mineral Specimens, 6088 S. Clayton St., Littleton, CO 80121: Free list ❖ Thumbnail to cabinet size American and foreign crystal and mineral specimens.

Mineralogical Research Company, 15840 E. Alta Vista Way, San Jose, CA 95127: Free list with long SASE and two 1st class stamps ❖ Mineral specimens and meteorites, microscopes, micromounts, specimen boxes, and supplies. 408–923–6800.

Minerals Unlimited, P.O. Box 877, Ridgecrest, CA 93556: Catalog $2 ❖ Rocks, minerals, and fossils.

Missing Link Fossils, 833 Poplar Way, Qualicum Beach, British Columbia, Canada V9K 1X8: Catalog $2 (refundable) ❖ Fossils and mineral specimens. 604–752–3979.

New England International Gems Inc., 188 Pollard St., Billerica, MA 01862: Free catalog ❖ Brazilian quartz, rocks from India, beads,

jewelry-making supplies, tools, and findings. 508–667–7394.

H. Obodda Mineral Specimens, P.O. Box 51, Short Hills, NJ 07078: Free list ❖ Afghan and Pakistani pegmatite minerals. 201–467–0212.

Omni Resources, 1004 S. Mebane St., P.O. Box 2096, Burlington, NC 27216: Free catalog ❖ Fossils, rocks, hiking and topography maps, and globes. 800–742–2677.

The Outcrop, P.O. Box 2171, Springfield, IL 62705: Free information with long SASE ❖ Thumbnail to small cabinet size mineral specimens from around the world. 217–787–6149.

P & H Rocks & Minerals, 37 Deerwood Manor, Norwalk, CT 06851: Free catalog with long SASE and two 1st class stamps ❖ Fluorescent minerals. 203–849–3225.

Pickens Minerals, 610 N. Martin Ave., Waukegan, IL 60085: Free list with 1st class stamp ❖ Mineral specimens. 708–623–2823.

Precam Minerals, P.O. Box 1371, Huntington Beach, CA 92647: Free information ❖ Mineral specimens and lapidary equipment. 800–331–0774.

Precious Earth Company, P.O. Box 39, Germantown, WI 53022: Free catalog ❖ Iron, copper, and lead specimens from Wisconsin and Michigan mines, and other minerals from worldwide sources. 800–558–8558; 414–255–4540 (in WI).

Rocknuts, P.O. Box 2593, Longmint, CO 80502: Free information ❖ Decorative, collector, and investment grade mineral specimens. 303–678–9930.

Russell's Rock Shop, 27911 North St., North Liberty, IN 46554: Free information ❖ Gem trees and supplies, bookends, agate slabs, amethyst, cabs, findings, slabs, and lucite stands. 219–289–7446.

Rusty's Rock Shop, 4106 Buckingham Dr., Decatur, IL 62526: Free price list ❖ Fluorite octahedrons, pyrite suns, and other mineral specimens. 217–877–7122.

Salt Minerals, 540 Beaverbrook St., Winnipeg, Manitoba, Canada R3N 1N4: Free catalog ❖ Specimens from worldwide locations.

Sandia Rocks & Minerals, Box 4045, Albuquerque, NM 87196: Free catalog ❖ Minerals and fossils.

Southeastern Fossil Supply Company, 1209 N. Eastman Rd., Kingsport, TN 37664: Free catalog ❖ Fossils, mineral collections, and teaching aids. 615–245–5626.

Star Minerals, P.O. Box 610–243, North Miami, FL 33161: Free list ❖ Thumbnail to cabinet size mineral specimens from worldwide sources.

Two Guys Fossils & Minerals, 1087 Plymouth St., East Bridgewater, MA 02333: Catalog $2 ❖ Rocks, minerals, and fossils. 508–378–7081.

V-Rock Shop, 4760 Portage St. NW, North Canton, OH 44720: Free information ❖ Cabochons, beads, pearls, faceted stones, display stands, pyramids, enhydros, citrine, Brazilian agate, quartz specimens, and amethyst geodes and plates. 800–45V-ROCK; 216–494–1759 (in OK).

Western Minerals, Gene & Jackie Schlepp, P.O. Box 43603, Tucson, AZ 85733: Free information ❖ Mineral collections, mining and mineralogical books, microscopes, goniometers, and alidades. 602–325–4534.

Wright's Rock Shop, 3612 Albert Pike, Hot Springs, AR 71913: Catalog $2 ❖ Quartz, tourmaline, healing crystals, marcasite, other minerals and fossils, and lapidary equipment.

Petrified Wood

Burnett Petrified Wood Inc., 37420 Sodaville Cutoff Dr., Lebanon, OR 97355: Free information ❖ Petrified wood. 503–258–3320.

Ebersole Lapidary Supply Inc., 11417 West Hwy. 54, Wichita, KS 67209: Catalog $2 ❖ Tools, findings, mountings, cabochons, rocks, and petrified wood. 316–722–4771.

Herkimer Diamond Mines, P.O. Box 510, Herkimer, NY 13350: Free information ❖ Petrified wood, mineral and rock specimens, quartz crystals, and gifts. 315–891–7355.

Jeanne's Rock & Jewelry, 5420 Bissonet, Bellaire, TX 77401: Price list $1 ❖ Petrified wood, seashells, lapidary supplies, and gifts. 713–664–2988.

Red & Green Minerals Inc., 7595 W. Florida Ave., Lakewood, CO 80226: Free information ❖ Petrified wood, faceting rough, crystals, books, and magazines. 303–985–5559.

Riviera Lapidary Supply, 30393 Mesquite, Riviera, TX 78379: Catalog $3 ❖ Petrified wood, cabochons, slabs, cabbing rough,

gemstones, crystals, beads, and bead-stringing supplies. 512–296–3958.

STRATAGraphics, 63 Knolltop Dr., Rochester, NY 14610: Catalog $1 ❖ Fish, mammals, reptiles, other vertebrates, and petrified wood and plant specimens. 716–385–4542.

Woods of the World & Fossils, P.O. Box 47, Somis, CA 93066: Free price list ❖ Petrified wood and fossil plants.

ROLLER SKATES & SCOOTERS

CCM Maska, Box 381, Bradford, VT 05033: Free information ❖ Protective gear and skates. 800–451–4600; 802–222–4751 (in VT).

Dominion Skate Company Ltd., 45 Railroad St., Brampton, Ontario, Canada L6X 1G4: Free information ❖ Roller skates and scooters. 416–453–9860.

I.S.A. Inc., In-Line Skate Accessories, 1800 Commerce St., Boulder, CO 80301: Free catalog ❖ Skates. 800–766–5851.

Kryptonics Inc., 740 S. Pierce Ave., Louisville, CA 80027: Free information ❖ Roller skates and skateboards. 800–766–9146; 303–665–5353 (in CA).

National Sporting Goods Corporation, 25 Brighton Ave., Passaic, NJ 07055: Free information ❖ Roller skates, scooters, skateboards, and protective gear. 201–779–2323.

Riedell Shoes Inc., P.O. Box 21, Red Wing, MN 55066: Free information ❖ Protective gear, skates, and wheels. 612– 388–8251.

Roller Derby Skate Company, Box 930, Litchfield, IL 62056: Free information ❖ Roller skates, scooters, and skateboards. 217–324–3961.

Rollerblade Inc., 5101 Shady Oak Rd., Minnetonka, MN 55343: Free information ❖ Protective gear, skates, and wheels. 800–328–0171; 612–930–7000 (in MN).

Saucony/Hyde, 13 Centennial Dr., Peabody, MA 01961: Free information ❖ Roller skates, scooters, and skateboards. 800–365–7282.

Sportime, 1 Sportime Way, Atlanta, GA 30340: Free information ❖ Protective gear and skates. 800–444–5700; 404–449–5700 (in GA).

Variflex Inc., 5152 N. Commerce Ave., Moorpark, CA 93021: Free information ❖ Roller skates and skateboards. 805–532–0322.

RUBBER STAMPS

Alextamping, 21023 Lynn Ln., Sonora, CA 95370: Catalog $3.50 ❖ Rubber stamps.

Arben Stamp Company, P.O. Box 353, Evansville, IN 47703: Catalog $2.50 ❖ Rubber stamps. 800–223–3086; 812–423–4269 (in IN).

Bizzaro Rubber Stamps, P.O. Box 16160, Rumford, RI 02916: Free information with long SASE ❖ Rubber stamps. 401–728–9560.

Burpo Duh Clown, P.O. Box 160190, Cupertino, CA 95016: Free information ❖ Face-painting rubber stamps and supplies. 408–446–9314.

Carousel Collections, 6–25 Industrial Dr., Elmira, Ontario, Canada N3B 3K3: Catalog $2 (refundable) ❖ Rubber stamps. 800–265–6269.

Country Impressions, P.O. Box 502, Layton, UT 84041: Catalog $3.50 ❖ Rubber stamps. 801–543–0206.

Crazy Folks Rubber Stamps, 855 Jefferson Ave., Livermore, CA 94550: Catalog $2 (refundable) ❖ Rubber stamps. 510–449–NUTS.

Critter Company, P.O. Box 8186, Moscow, ID 83843: Catalog $3 ($4 refundable) ❖ Animal rubber stamps.

Detailed Rubber Stamps, 267 9th St., Brooklyn, NY 11215: Catalog $2 (refundable) ❖ Rubber stamps. 718–965–4725.

DreamInk, P.O. Box 8028, Woodland, CA 95695: Catalog $1 (refundable) ❖ Rubber stamps.

Five Star Stamps, Box 2121, Southern Pines, NC 28388: Catalog $3 (refundable) ❖ Nature, holiday, traditional, teacher, and other rubber stamps. 910–692–0950.

GBLA Art Stamps, 17029 Devonshire Ave., Northridge, CA 91325: Catalog $3 ❖ Rubber stamps. 818–366–6206.

Good Impressions Rubber Stamps, P.O. Box 33, Shirley, WV 26434: Catalog $1 (refundable) ❖ Victorian-style decorative rubber stamps. 304–758–4252.

Graphic Rubber Stamp Company, 11250 Magnolia Blvd., North Hollywood, CA 91601: Catalog $4 ❖ Rubber stamps. 818–782–9443.

H & R Badge & Stamp Company, 2585 Mock Rd., Columbus, OH 43219: Free catalog ❖ In-stock and custom badges and rubber stamps. 614–471–3735.

Darcie Hunter Publications, P.O. Box 1627, Grants Pass, OR 97526: Catalog $1.50 ❖ Rubber stamps.

ImaginAir Designs, 1007 Woodland NW, Albuquerque, NM 87107: Catalog $2 ❖ Aviation stamps and other designs. 505–345–2308.

Inkadinkado Inc., 60 Cummings Park, Woburn, MA 01801: Catalog $2 ❖ Decorative and novelty rubber stamps. 617–938–6100.

Island House Rubberstamps, 8924 Cartagena Pl., Dallas, TX 75228: Free information ❖ Rubber stamps. 214–328–9856.

Jackson Marketing Products, Brownsville Rd., Mt. Vernon, IL 62864: Free information ❖ Supplies and equipment for making regular and pre-inked rubber stamps. 800–STAMP-CALL.

Kidstamps, P.O. Box 18699, Cleveland Heights, OH 44118: Free catalog ❖ Rubber stamps. 800–727–5437.

L.A. Stampworks, P.O. Box 2329, North Hollywood, CA 91610: Catalog $5 ❖ Rubber stamps. 818–761–8757.

Luv 'N Stuff, P.O. Box 85, Poway, CA 92074: Catalog $2 ❖ Rubber stamps. 619–748–8060.

Merry Mary-Anne's Rubber Art Stamps, Winterwood Pavilion, 2208 S. Nellis Blvd., Las Vegas, NV 89104: Catalog $2 (refundable) ❖ Rubber stamps.

Mpress Me Rubber Stamps, 382 E. 520 North, American Fork, UT 84003: Catalog $3 (refundable) ❖ Rubber stamps.

Museum of Modern Rubber, 187–C W. Orangethorpe Ave., Placentia, CA 92670: Catalog $3 ❖ Rubber stamps. 714–993–3587.

Name Brand Rubber Stamps, P.O. Box 34245, Bethesda, MD 20827: Free information ❖ Rubber stamps for holidays, seasonal greetings, first names, signatures, and return addresses.

National Stampagraphic, 1952 Everett St., North Valley Stream, NY 11580: Free information ❖ Published quarterly, includes articles and information of interest to rubber stamp users, and advertisements from rubber stamp hobbyists, manufacturers, and distributors. 516–285–5587.

Neato Stuff, P.O. Box 4066, Carson City, NV 89702: Catalog $2 ❖ Rubber stamps, supplies, rubber stamp jewelry, and card kits. 702–883–9351.

100 Proof Press, RR 1, Box 136, Eaton, NY 13334: Catalog $4 (refundable) ❖ Rubber stamps. 315–684–3547.

Outstamping, 320 S. Archer St., Anaheim, CA 92804: Catalog $4 ❖ Rubber stamps. 714–535–1593.

P.O. Box Rubberstamps, 740 E. 19th St., Houston, TX 77008: Catalog $3.50 ❖ Rubber stamps.

Paper Angel, P.O. Box 1336, Santa Cruz, CA 95061: Brochure $2 ❖ Personalized calligraphy style rubber stamps, kits, and ink pads. 408–423–5115.

Pepperell Stamp Works, Bradford, PA 16701: Free information ❖ Civil War and other rubber stamps. 800–752–4656.

Personal Stamp Exchange, 345 S. McDowell Blvd., Ste. 324, Petaluma, CA 94952: Catalog $4 ❖ Rubber stamps. 800–782–6748; 800–782–6779 (in CA).

Purple Wave Stamp Designs, P.O. Box 5340, Ventura, CA 93005: Catalog $2.50 ❖ Mounted and unmounted rubber stamps.

Quarter Moon Rubber Stamps, P.O. Box 611585, San Jose, CA 95161: Catalog $3 ❖ Rubber stamps. 408–272–0211.

Raindrops on Roses Rubber Stamp Company, 4808 Winterwood Dr., Raleigh, NC 27613: Catalog $3 ❖ Country stamp sets, brush markers, and supplies. 919–846–8617.

Rubber Poet Rubber Stamps, Box 1011, Rockville, UT 84763: Catalog $2 (refundable) ❖ Rubber stamps.

Rubber Stamp Ranch, 3400 Anderson Ave. SE, Albuquerque, NM 87106: Catalog $2 ❖ Rubber stamps for animals and holidays. 800–728–0762.

The Rubberstampler, 1945 Wealthy SE, Grand Rapids, MI 49506: Catalog $2 (refundable) ❖ Rubber stamps. 800–800–0424; 616–454–0424 (in MI).

SonLight Impressions, 170 N. Maple St., Ste. 110, Corona, CA 91720: Catalog $3 ❖ Rubber stamps. 909–278–5656.

Stamp Francisco Rubber Stamps, 466 8th St., San Francisco, CA 04103: Catalog $2 ❖ Rubber stamps. 415–252–5975.

Stamp Nouveau, P.O. Box 6178, Laguna Niguel, CA 92607: Catalog $2 ❖

Rubberstamps and fabric paints. 800–688–8328.

Stampberry Farms, 1952 Everett St., North Valley Stream, NY 11580: Catalog $2 (refundable) ❖ Rubber stamps.

Stampendous Inc., 1357 S. Lewis St., Anaheim, CA 92805: Catalog $3 ❖ Rubber stamps, ink pads, brush markers, and glitter glue. 800–869–0474.

Stampians, 5120 Whispering Oak Way, Paso Robles, CA 93446: Catalog $2.50 ❖ Rubber stamps. 805–239–1717.

Stardancer Stamp Company, 31 Green St., Medfield, MA 02052: Catalog $1 (refundable) ❖ Rubber stamps. 508–359–6705.

Stewart-Superior Corporation, 1800 W. Larchmont Ave., Chicago, IL 60613: Free information ❖ Rubber stamps, inks and ink pads, rollers, cleaners, sponge rubber, cements, and rubber stamp gum. 800–621–1205; 312–935–6025 (in IL).

Synergistics Rubber Stamps, P.O. Box 2625, Goleta, CA 93118: Catalog $2 (refundable) ❖ Rubber stamps.

Under the Rubber Tree, Box 24291, Christiansted, St. Croix, Virgin Islands 00824: Catalog $2 (refundable) ❖ Rubber stamps.

Wood Cellar Graphics, P.O. Box 409, Randolph, NE 68771: Catalog $3 (refundable) ❖ Rubber stamps, ink pads, embossing supplies, and markers. 800–243–4771; 402–337–1627 (in NE).

RUGBY

Mitre Sports, Genesco Park, Room 609, Nashville, TN 37202: Free information ❖ Balls and boots. 800–826–7650; 615–367–74754 (in TN).

Rugby & Soccer Supply, P.O. Box 565, Merrifield, VA 22116: Free catalog ❖ Balls, boots, jerseys, and shorts. 703–280–5540.

Rugby Imports Ltd., 885 Warren Ave., East Providence, RI 02914: Free catalog ❖ Clothing and shoes, balls, and other equipment. 800–431–4514; 401–438–2727 (in RI).

RUG MAKING

Braid-Aid, 466 Washington St., Pembroke, MA 02359: Catalog $4 ❖ Braided rug kits, braiding accessories, wool by the pound or yard, and hooking, weaving, basket-making, shirret, and spinning supplies. 617–826–2560.

Edgemont Yarn Services, P.O Box 205, Washington, KY 41086: Free brochure ❖ Weaving and rug-making supplies. 606–759–7614.

Harry M. Fraser Company, Rt. 3, Box 254, Stoneville, NC 27048: Catalog $2.50 ❖ Rug-hooking and braiding supplies. 910–573–9830.

Great Northern Weaving, Box 3611, Augusta, MI 49012: Catalog $1 ❖ Cotton and wool rags, warp, loopers, fillers, and braiding equipment. 616–731–4487.

Suzanne McNeil, 2425 Cullen St., Fort Worth, TX 76107: Catalog $2 ❖ Rug-making kits.

Claire Murray Inc., P.O. Box 390, Ascutney, VT 05030: Catalog $5 (refundable) ❖ Ready-made hand-hooked rugs or kits. 800–252–4733.

Oriental Rug Company, P.O. Box 205, Washington, KY 41086: Free information ❖ Rug-weaving wool and other supplies. 606–759–7614.

Ruggery, 565 Cedar Swamp Rd., Glen Head, NY 11545: Catalog $2 ❖ Yarns and other rug-making supplies. 516–676–2056.

Shillcraft, 8899 Kelso Dr., Baltimore, MD 21221: Catalog $2 ❖ Latch-hooking kits and supplies for rugs, wall hangings, and other crafts. 410–682–3060.

RUGS & CARPETS

Abingdon Rug Outlet, 246 W. Main St., Abingdon, VA 24210: Free information with long SASE ❖ Handmade rugs. 703–628–9821.

Access Carpet, P.O. Box 1007, Dalton, GA 30722: Free information ❖ Rugs and carpets. 800–848–7747.

Adams & Swett, 964 Massachusetts Ave., Boston, MA 02118: Catalog $2 ❖ Handmade and machine-braided early American and contemporary style wool rugs. 617–268–8000.

Armstrong World Industries, P.O. Box 3001, Lancaster, PA 17604: Free information ❖ Carpet and rugs. 717–397–0611.

At Home in the Valley, 16780 Stagg St., Van Nuys, CA 91406: Catalog $2 ❖ Braided rugs and chairpads. 818–780–4663.

Bearden Brothers Carpet, 3200 Dug Gap Rd., Dalton, GA 30720: Catalog $3 ❖ Carpet and other floor coverings. 800–433–0074.

Kimberly Black Rugs & Accessories, P.O. Box 472927, Charlotte, NC 28247: Catalog

$3 ❖ Flat braid and woven flat weave rugs. 800–296–6099.

Betsy Bourdon, Weaver, Scribner Hill, Wolcott, VT 05680: Catalog $3 ❖ Rugs, linens, and handwoven blankets. 802–472–6508.

J.R. Burrows & Company, P.O. Box 522, Rockland, MA 02370: Catalog $5 ❖ Period carpet reproductions by special order and artistic wallpaper and fabrics. 617–982–1812.

Country Braid House, 462 Main St., Tilton, NH 03276: Free brochure ❖ Braided wool rugs, kits, and supplies. 603–286–4511.

Country Manor, Mail Order Department, Rt. 211, P.O. Box 520, Sperryville, VA 22740: Catalog $3 ❖ Hand-woven cotton rugs, kitchen utensils, and other country crafts. 800–344–8354.

Dalton Paradise Carpets, P.O. Box 1819, Rocky Face, GA 30740: Free information ❖ Carpets, rugs, and other floor coverings. 800–338–7811.

Elkes Carpet Outlet Inc., 1585 Bethel Dr., High Point, NC 27260: Free information with long SASE ❖ First-quality, irregulars, close-outs, and discontinued carpet. 919–887–5054.

Ewesful Crafts-The Yorks, 1041 7 Mile Rd., Athens, MI 49011: Free information ❖ Handwoven rag rugs in cotton, cotton blends, and denim. 517–741–7949.

Factory Direct Carpet Outlet, P.O. Box 417, Miles City, MT 59301: Free brochure ❖ Rugs and carpets. 800–225–4351; 800–233–0208 (in MT).

Family Heir-loom Weavers, RD 3, Box 59, Red Lion, PA 17356: Catalog $3 ❖ All-wool carpets with historic patterns, from the late 18th-century to the early 1920s. 717–246–2431.

Gazebo of New York, 127 E. 57th St., New York, NY 10022: Catalog $6 ❖ Handmade braided rugs and quilted pillows. 212–832–7077.

Grandmother's Weaving, Thomas & Jonathan Moore, 10020 Alabama Hwy., Anniston, AL 36201: Free information ❖ Seamless handwoven rugs, placemats, and wall hangings. 205–236–5938.

Heirloom Rugs, 28 Harlem St., Rumford, RI 02916: Catalog $2 ❖ Hand-hooked rugs. 401–438–5672.

Heritage Rugs, P.O. Box 404, Lahaska, PA 18931: Catalog $1 ❖ Wool-rag rugs. 215–343–5196.

Home Etc., Palo Verde at 34th St., P.O. Box 28806, Tucson, AZ 85726: Free catalog ❖ Bedding ensembles, curtains, bedspreads and comforters, rugs, linens and pillows, and towels. 800–362–8415.

Charles W. Jacobsen Inc., 401 N. Salina St., Syracuse, NY 13203: Free brochure ❖ Hand-woven Oriental rugs. 315–422–7832.

Johnson's Carpets, 3239 S. Dixie Hwy., Dalton, GA 30720: Free information ❖ Carpets and rugs. 800–235–1079; 707–277–2775 (in GA).

Kaoud Brothers Oriental Rugs, 17 S. Main St., West Hartford, CT 06107: Catalog $5 ❖ Oriental rugs. 203–233–6211.

Lizzie & Charlie's Rag Rugs, 210 E. Bullion Ave., Marysvale, UT 84750: Free brochure ❖ Custom rag rugs. 801–326–4213.

Long's Carpet Inc., 2625 S. Dixie Hwy., Dalton, GA 30720: Free information ❖ Carpets. 800–545–5664.

Luv Those Rugs, 103 N. Main St., Box 236, Elkton, KY 42220: Free brochure ❖ Country-style braided rugs. 502–265–5550.

M.C. Ltd., P.O. Box 17696, Whitefish Bay, WI 53217: Free information ❖ Pillows and steerhide rugs. 800–236–5224; 414–263–5422 (in WI).

Mills River, 713 Old Orchard Rd., Hendersonville, NC 28739: Catalog $1 ❖ Flat-braided oval and round rugs. 704–687–9778.

Claire Murray Inc., P.O. Box 390, Ascutney, VT 05030: Catalog $5 ❖ Hand-hooked rugs and hand-sewn quilts. Available in kits. 800–252–4733.

National Carpet, 1384 Coney Island Ave., Brooklyn, NY 11230: Brochure $3 ❖ Reproduction Turkish antique carpets, hand-loomed Hungarian and Colonial Williamsburg rugs, Persian and Oriental rugs, Berbers, hand-hooked rugs, and braided ovals. 800–421–5172.

Network Floor Covering, Division Parkers Carpet, 3200 Dug Gap Rd., Dalton, GA 30720: Free brochure ❖ Stain-protected carpets. 800–442–2013.

Paradise Mills Inc., P.O. Box 2488, Dalton, GA 30722: Free information ❖ Rugs and carpets. 800–338–7811, ext. 498.

Peerless Imported Rugs, 3033 Lincoln Ave., Chicago, IL 60657: Catalog $1 ❖ Hand- and machine-woven Oriental rugs, rag rugs, Navajo rugs, colonial braids, grass rugs, and tapestries from Europe. 800–621–6573.

Quality Discount Carpet, 1207 W. Walnut Ave., Dalton, GA 30720: Free brochure ❖ Carpets. 800–233–0993.

Rastetter Woolen Mill, 5802 Star Rt. 39, Millersburg, OH 44654: Free information ❖ Hand-woven rag rugs, throw rugs, stair runners and treads, area rugs, and wall-to-wall carpets. 216–674–2103.

The Rug Store, 2201 Crownpoint Executive Dr., Charlotte, NC 28227: Catalog $5 (refundable) ❖ Area rugs. 800–257–5078; 704–845–8591 (in NC).

S & S Carpet Mills, 2650 Lakeland Rd. SE, Dalton, GA 30721: Free brochure ❖ Carpet. 800–241–4013.

Southern Rug, 2325 Anderson Rd., Crescent Springs, KY 41017: Catalog $5 ❖ Handcrafted, flat-braided rugs in blended wool yarns. 800–541–RUGS.

Stylmark Carpet Mills Inc., 3358 Carpet Capitol Dr., Dalton, GA 30720: Free information ❖ Residential and commercial carpet. 800–532–2257.

Trott Furniture Company, P.O. Box 7, Richlands, NC 28574: Catalog $5 ❖ Oriental rugs and 18th-century solid mahogany, cherry, and walnut furniture. 800–682–0095; 910–324–3660 (in NC).

Village Carpet, 1114 Conover Blvd. West, Conover, NC 28613: Free brochure ❖ Carpet. 704–465–6818.

Warehouse Carpets Inc., Box 3233, Dalton, GA 30721: Free information ❖ Rugs and carpets. 707–226–2229.

Whipp Trading Company, RR 1, Arrasmith Trail, Ames, IA 50010: Free catalog ❖ Sheepskin rugs, slippers, mittens, and hats. 800–533–9447.

Thomas K. Woodard American Antiques & Quilts, 799 Madison Ave., New York, NY 10021: Catalog $6 ❖ Classic American-style room-size area rugs and runners. 212–988–2906.

Yankee Pride, 29 Parkside Cir., Braintree, MA 02184: Catalog $3 (refundable) ❖ Handcrafted quilts, Dhurries, comforters and bedspreads, and wool, hand-braided, hooked, and rag rugs. 617–848–7610.

York Interiors Inc., 2821 E. Prospect Rd., York, PA 17402: Free brochure ❖ Oriental rugs. 800–723–7029.

RUNNING, JOGGING & WALKING

Clothing & Shoes

Academy Broadway Corporation, 5 Plant Ave., Vanderbilt Industrial Park, Smithtown, NY 11787: Free information ❖ Rainsuits. 516–231–7000.

Adidas USA, 5675 N. Blackstock Rd., Spartanburg, SC 29303: Free information ❖ Shoes, shorts, singlets, socks, sweatbands, and warm-up suits. 800–423–4327.

Alchester Mills Company Inc., 314 S. 11th St., Camden, NJ 08103: Free information ❖ Socks, sweatbands, and safety vests. 609–964–9700.

Alpha Shirt Company, 401 E. Hunting Park Ave., Philadelphia, PA 19124: Free information ❖ Shirts and tops. 800–523–4585; 215–291–0300 (in PA).

Asics Tiger Corporation, 10540 Talbert Ave., West Bldg., Fountain Valley, CA 92708: Free information ❖ Shoes, shorts, rainsuits, singlets, and warm-up suits. 800–766–ASICS; 714–962–7654 (in CA).

Athletic Apparel by Matchfit, Box 13100, Charlotte, NC 28270: Free information ❖ Shirts & tops. 704–847–0896.

Augusta Sportswear, Box 14939, Augusta, GA 30919: Free information ❖ Shirts & tops. 800–237–6695; 706–860–4633 (in GA).

California Best, 970 Broadway, Ste. 104, Chula Vista, CA 91911: Free catalog ❖ Shoes and clothing. 800–438–9327.

Champion Products Inc., 475 Corporate Square Dr., Winston Salem, NC 27105: Free information ❖ Shorts, singlets, socks, and warm-up suits.

Converse Inc., 1 Fordham Rd., North Reading, MA 01864: Free information ❖ Shoes, shorts, singlets, socks, sweatbands, and warm-up suits. 800–428–2667; 508–664–1100 (in MA).

Cook & Love, 114 S. Main St., Memphis, TN 39103: Free catalog ❖ Walking shoes in hard-to-find sizes. 800–858–3364; 901–525–2181 (in TN).

Dolfin International Corporation, P.O. Box 98, Shillington, PA 19607: Free information ❖ Shorts, rainsuits, singlets, and warm-up suits. 800–441–0818; 215–775–5500 (in PA).

Eastbay Running Store Inc., 427 3rd St., Wausau, WI 54403: Free information ❖ Shoes and clothing. 800–826–2205.

Empire Sporting Goods Manufacturing Company, 443 Broadway, New York, NY 10013: Free information ❖ Rainsuits. 800–221–3455; 212–966–0880 (in NY).

Faber Brothers, 4141 S. Pulaski Rd., Chicago, IL 60632: Free information ❖ Pedometers, rainsuits, and safety vests. 312–376–9300.

Gold's Gym, 360 Hampton Dr., Venice, CA 90291: Free information ❖ Shirts and tops. 800–457–5375; 213–392–3005 (in CA).

Kellsport Industries, 125 Sockanossett Cross Rd., P.O. Box 8399, Cranston, RI 02920: Free information ❖ Shoes. 800–341–4600.

Las Vegas Discount Golf & Tennis, 5325 S. Valley View Blvd., Ste. 10, Las Vegas, NV 89118: Free catalog ❖ Shoes and clothing. 702–798–7777.

Leisure Unlimited, P.O. Box 308, Cedarburg, WI 53012: Free information ❖ Pedometers and rainsuits. 800–323–5118; 414–377–7454 (in WI).

Movin USA, 1733 E. McKellips, Tempe, AZ 85281: Free information ❖ Shirts and tops. 800–445–6684; 602–994–4088 (in AZ).

NaturalSport, 2510 S. Broadway, Salem, IL 62881: Free catalog ❖ Aerobic walking shoes, other shoes, shorts, pants, and jackets. 800–678–9138.

New Balance Athletic Shoe Inc., 38 Everett St., Boston, MA 02134: Free information ❖ Shoes, shorts, singlets, raincoats, sweatbands, and warm-up suits. 800–343–4648; 617–783–4000 (in MA).

North Face, 999 Harrison St., Berkeley, CA 94710: Free information ❖ Rain suits. 510–527–9700.

Okun Brothers Shoes, 356 E. South St., Kalamazoo, MI 49007: Free catalog ❖ Shoes for men, women, and children. 616–342–1536.

Pearl Izumi, 2300 Central Ave., Boulder, CO 80301: Free information ❖ Shirts and tops. 800–328–8488; 303–938–1700 (in CO)

Puma USA Inc., 147 Centre St., Brockton, MA 02403: Free information ❖ Shoes, shorts, singlets, rainsuits, socks, and warm-up suits. 508–583–9100.

Road Runner Sports, 6310 Nancy Ridge Rd., Ste. 101, San Diego, CA 92121: Free price list ❖ Shoes, other walking accessories, and fitness apparel. 800–551–5558.

Safesport Manufacturing Company, 1100 W. 45th Ave., Denver, CO 80211: Free information ❖ Pedometers, rainsuits, and safety vests. 303–433–6506.

Shaffer Sportswear, 224 N. Washington, Neosho, MO 64850: Free information ❖ Shirts and tops. 417–451–9444.

Sheldon Shoes Inc., 1415 N. Lilac Dr., Minneapolis, MN 55422: Free catalog ❖ Walking shoes for women. 800–328–4827; 612–544–3349 (in MN).

Spalding Sports Worldwide, 425 Meadow St., P.O. Box 901, Chicopee, MA 01021: Free information with list of retailers ❖ Shoes, shorts, singlets, sweatbands, and warm-up suits. 800–225–6601.

Spiegel, P.O. Box 6340, Chicago, IL 60680: Free information ❖ Men and women's walking shoes. 800–345–4500.

Tennis Gear & Running Center, P.O. Box 1486, Cumberland, MD 21502: Free price list ❖ Clothing and shoes. 301–729–0896.

Terramar Sports Ltd., 10 Midland Ave., Port Chester, NY 10573: Free information ❖ Thermal silk glove liners, sock liners, and balaclavas. 914–934–8000.

Venus Knitting Mills Inc., 140 Spring St., Murray Hill, NJ 07974: Free information ❖ Shorts, singlets, sweatbands, and warm-up suits. 800–955–4200; 908–464–2400 (in NJ).

Pedometers & Stopwatches

Accusplit, 2290–A Ringwood Ave., San Jose, CA 95131: Free information ❖ Pedometers and sports watches. 800–538–9750; 408–432–8228 (in CA).

ACT USA, P.O. Box 5490, Evanston, IL 60204: Free information ❖ Miniature computerized display for speed, distance, heart rate, and other functions.

Aristo Import Company Inc., 15 Hunt Rd., Orangeburg, NY 10962: Free information ❖ Pedometers for step counting, walking, or jogging. 800–352–6304; 914–359–0720 (in NY).

Compass Industries Inc., 104 E. 25th St., New York, NY 10010: Free information ❖ Pedometers. 212–473–2614.

Creative Health Products, 5148 Saddle Ridge Rd., Plymouth, MI 48170: Free catalog

❖ Pedometers and pulse monitors. 800–742–4478.

Dynamic Classics Ltd., 230 5th Ave., Ste. 1510, New York, NY 10001: Free information ❖ Pedometers. 212–571–0267.

Faber Brothers, 4141 S. Pulaski Rd., Chicago, IL 60632: Free information ❖ Pedometers, rainsuits, and safety vests. 312–376–9300.

General Sportcraft Company Ltd., 140 Woodbine Rd., Bergenfield, NJ 07621: Free information ❖ Pedometers. 201–384–4242.

Gutmann Cutlery Inc., 120 S. Columbus Ave., Mt. Vernon, NY 10553: Free information ❖ Walking and walking/jogging pedometers. 800–CUTLERY; 914–699–4044 (in NY).

Innovative Time Corporation, 6054 Corte Del Cedro, Carlsbad, CA 92008: Free information ❖ Pedometers. 800–765–0595; 619–438–0595 (in CA).

KNR Associates, 1307 Hickory St., Onalaska, WI 54650: Free information ❖ Pedometers. 800–234–1770.

Leisure Unlimited, P.O. Box 308, Cedarburg, WI 53012: Free information ❖ Pedometers and rainsuits. 800–323–5118; 414–377–7454 (in WI).

Precise International, 15 Corporate Dr., Orangeburg, NY 10962: Free information ❖ Walking and walking/jogging pedometers. 800–431–2996; 914–365–3500 (in NY).

Safesport Manufacturing Company, 1100 W. 45th Ave., Denver, CO 80211: Free information ❖ Pedometers, rainsuits, and safety vests. 303–433–6506.

Silva Compass, P.O. Box 966, Binghamton, NY 13902: Free information ❖ Pedometers. 800–847–1460.

Sportline, 847 McGlincey Ln., Campbell, CA 95008: Free information ❖ Pedometers. 408–377–8900.

SAFETY & EMERGENCY EQUIPMENT

Blair-Jaeger Industrial Group, 32841 8 Mile Rd., Livonia, MI 48152: Free information ❖ Combination fire extinguisher and emergency automobile tire inflator.

Conney Safety Products, 3202 Latham Dr., P.O. Box 44190, Madison, WI 53744: Free catalog ❖ First aid supplies, survival equipment, and other safety devices. 800–356–9100; 608–271–3300 (in WI).

Direct Safety Company, 7815 S. 46th St., Phoenix, AZ 85044: Free catalog ❖ Safety equipment. 800–528–7405.

Enviro-Safety Products, 21344 Ave. 332, Woodlake, CA 93286: Free information ❖ Dust-protection helmets. 800–637–6606.

Lab Safety Supply Inc., P.O. Box 1368, Janesville, WI 53547: Free information ❖ Dust-protection masks. 800–356–0783.

Nitro-Pak Preparedness Center, 151 N. Main St., Heber City, UT 84032: Catalog $3 ❖ Survival equipment and other supplies, freeze-dried and dehydrated foods, books, and videos. 800–866–4876.

Northern Safety Company Inc., P.O. Box 4250, Utica, NY 13504: Free information ❖ Dust-protection masks. 800–631–1246.

Out N Back, 1797 S. State St., Orem, UT 84058: Free catalog ❖ Survival equipment and supplies for outdoor and other recreational activities. 800–533–7415.

Perfectly Safe, 7245 Whipple Ave. NW, North Canton, OH 44720: Free catalog ❖ Safety items for children age 3 to 6. 216–494–2323.

The Safety Zone, P.O. Box 0019, Hanover, PA 17333: Free catalog ❖ Safety and security products. 800–999–3030.

The Survival Center, P.O. Box 234, McKenna, WA 98558: Catalog $2 ❖ Survival equipment for outdoor activities. 206–458–6778.

United States Survival Society, 1223 Wilshire Blvd., #492, Santa Monica, CA 90403: Free catalog ❖ Emergency foods, water, solar radios, and other survival and emergency equipment. 800–2–SURVIVE; 310–652–4777 (in CA).

SAIL BOARDS

Skip Hutchison, Rastaboards-Surf-Sail -Snowboards, 4748 NE 11th Ave., Fort Lauderdale, FL 33334: Free information ❖ Sailboards, surfboards, and snowboards. 305–491–7992.

Murrays WaterSports, P.O. Box 490, Carpinteria, CA 93014: Free information ❖ Catamaran and windsurfing accessories. 800–788–8964.

Sailboard Warehouse Inc., 300 S. Owasso, St. Paul, MN 55117: Catalog $1.50 ❖ Sail boards, sails and masts, wet suits, roof racks, harnesses, books, and videos. 800–992–7245; 612–482–9995 (in MN).

Windsurfing Warehouse, 128 S. Airport Blvd., South San Francisco, CA 94080: Free catalog ❖ Sailboards. 800–628–4599; 415–588–1714 (in CA).

SCIENCE KITS & PROJECTS

American Science & Surplus, 3605 Howard St., Skokie, IL 60076: Catalog $1 ❖ Surplus science and electro-mechanical supplies, equipment, and kits. 708–982–0870.

Edlie Electronics, 2700 Hempstead Tnpk., Levittown, NY 11756: Free catalog ❖ Electronics kits, parts, and supplies. 516–735–3330.

Edmund Scientific Company, Edscorp Bldg., Barrington, NJ 08007: Free catalog ❖ Microscopes, magnifiers, weather forecasting instruments, magnets, telescopes, lasers, and other optical, scientific, and educational products. 609–573–6260.

The Electronic Goldmine, P.O. Box 5408, Scottsdale, AZ 85261: Free catalog ❖ Science kits and supplies. 602–451–7454.

J.L. Hammett Company, Hammett Pl., P.O. Box 9057, Braintree, MA 02184: Free catalog ❖ Science kits and projects, microscopes, laboratory apparatus, rock collections, magnets, astronomy charts, and anatomical models. 800–225–5467; 617–848–1000 (in MA).

Heath Company, 455 Riverview Dr., Benton Harbor, MI 49022: Free catalog ❖ Computers and robots, TVs, home devices, educational projects, and other electronics kits. 616–925–6000.

Hobby World Ltd. of Montreal, 5450 Sherbrooke St. West, Montreal, Quebec, Canada H4A 1V9: Catalog $5 ❖ Airplanes, helicopters, cars and trucks, ships, military vehicles, and science models. 514–481–5434.

Hubbard Scientific Company, 3101 Iris Ave., Boulder, CO 80301: Free catalog ❖ Science equipment and supplies for life, earth, and introductory physical science, and energy, health and physiology, and topography projects. 800–323–8368.

Information Unlimited Inc., Box 716, Amherst, NH 03031: Catalog $1 ❖ Lasers, communication equipment, Tesla coils and experiments, mini radios, rocket equipment, flying saucers, and other kits. 603–673–4730.

Krystal Kits, P.O. Box 445, Bentonville, AR 72712: Catalog $1 ❖ Electronics projects, kits, and plans. 501–273–5340.

Merrell Scientific/World of Science, 1665 Buffalo Rd., Rochester, NY 14624: Catalog $2 ❖ Chemicals, glassware, laboratory equipment, and supplies for biology, nature, physical and earth science, astronomy experiments, and model rocketry. 716–426–1540.

Nasco, 901 Janesville Ave., Fort Atkinson, WI 53538: Free catalog ❖ Science supplies and equipment, science activity kits and projects, microscopes and dissection kits, rock collections, magnets, electric motors, ultraviolet light equipment, astronomy charts and star maps, and anatomical models. 800–558–9595.

The Nature Company, Catalog Division, P.O. Box 188, Florence, KY 41022: Free catalog ❖ Science supplies, kits, books, toys, novelties, and gifts. 800–227–1114.

Radio Shack, Division Tandy Corporation, One Tandy Center, Fort Worth, TX 76102: Free catalog ❖ Electronic science projects and kits. 817–390–3011.

Silicon Valley Surplus, 1273 Industrial Pkwy., Ste. 460, Hayward, CA 94544: Free information ❖ Light and motion projects, laser applications, computer interface equipment, and other kits. 510–582–6602.

Uptown Sales Inc., 33 N. Main St., Chambersburg, PA 17201: Catalog $1 ❖ Science kits and projects for amateur scientists. 800–548–9941.

SCOUTING

Boy Scouts of America, P.O. Box 909, Pineville, NC 28134: Free catalog ❖ Uniforms and insignia, camping equipment, sportswear, books, and other scouting equipment and supplies. 800–323–0732.

Girl Scout Catalog, 420 5th Ave., New York, NY 10018: Free catalog ❖ Uniforms and insignia, camping equipment, sportswear, books, jewelry, and gifts. 212–852–8000.

SEASHELLS

Benjane Arts, P.O. Box 298, West Hempstead, NY 11552: Catalog $5 ❖ Seashells. 516–483–1330.

Bourget Bros., 1636 11th St., Santa Monica, CA 90404: Catalog $3 ❖ Seashells, jewelry-making tools and supplies, gemstones, beads, and bead-stringing supplies. 310–450–6556.

Ebersole Lapidary Supply Inc., 11417 West Hwy. 54, Wichita, KS 67209: Catalog $2 ❖ Shark teeth, cameo shells, murex or fox shells, tiger cowries, mushroom corals, other seashells from worldwide sources, and lapidary equipment. 316–722–4771.

Ed's House of Gems, 7712 NE Sandy Blvd., Portland, OR 97211: Free information with long SASE ❖ Seashells, crystals, minerals, gemstones, lapidary equipment, mountings, and Indian relics. 503–284–8990.

Herkimer Diamond Mines, P.O. Box 510, Herkimer, NY 13350: Free information ❖ Petrified wood products, seashells, craft supplies, minerals and rocks, quartz crystals, and gifts. 315–891–7355.

Indian Jewelers Supply Company, P.O. Box 1774, Gallup, NM 87305: Catalog $5 ❖ Precious and base metals, precious and base metal findings, metalsmithing and lapidary tools and supplies, and semi-precious stones, seashells, and coral. 505–722–4451.

Jeanne's Rock & Jewelry, 5420 Bissonet, Bellaire, TX 77401: Price list $1 ❖ Seashells, petrified wood products, lapidary supplies, and gifts. 713–664–2988.

Nature's Jewelry, 222 Mill Rd., Chelmsford, MA 01824: Free catalog ❖ Leaves, seashells, and other natural objects transformed into jewelry by preservation in precious metals. 800–333–3235.

J.F. Ray, P.O. Box 1364, Ocala, FL 32678: Catalog $3 (refundable) ❖ Shark teeth jewelry, fossils, seashells, beach-combing treasures, and amber with inclusions.

Riviera Lapidary Supply, 30393 Mesquite, Riviera, TX 78379: Catalog $3 ❖ Seashells, beads, cabochons, slabs, cabbing rough gems, and crystals. 512–296–3958.

Shell-A-Rama, Box 291327, Fort Lauderdale, FL 33318: Catalog $2 ❖ Seashells for crafts, decorations, and collections. 305–434–2818.

SEWING

Dress Forms

Bonfit America Inc., 5959 Triumph St., Commerce, CA 90040: Free information ❖ No-paper pattern-maker that adjusts to different sizes and styles. 800–5–BONFIT.

CSZ Enterprises Inc., 1288 W. 11th St., Ste. 200, Tracy, CA 95376: Free information ❖ Custom-made or make-them-yourself kits for dress-forms and pants-forms. 209–832–4324.

Dress Rite Forms, 3817 N. Pulaski, Chicago, IL 60641: Free information ❖ Dress forms in all sizes and shapes. 312–588–5761.

Notions & Supplies

AK Sew & Serge, 1602 6th St. SE, Winter Haven, FL 33880: Catalog $5 ❖ Heirloom and fashion sewing and quilting supplies. 800–299–8096; 813–299–3080 (in FL).

Atlanta Thread & Supply, 695 Red Oak Rd., Stockbridge, GA 30281: Catalog $1 ❖ Notions and other sewing accessories. 800–331–7600; 404–389–9115 (in GA).

Badhir Trading Inc., 8429 Sisson Hwy., Eden, NY 14057: Catalog $2.50 (refundable) ❖ Beaded, sequined, and jeweled appliques, trim, and fringes for dresses, costumes, and bridal fashions. 800–654–9418.

Baer Fabrics, 515 E. Market St., Louisville, KY 40202: Catalog $3 ❖ Sewing notions and trim. 800–769–7776.

Banasch, 2810 Highland Ave., Cincinnati, OH 45212: Free catalog ❖ Beads, pearls, notions, and buttons. 800–543–0355; 513–731–2040 (in OH).

Baubanbea Enterprises, P.O. Box 1205, Smithtown, NY 11787: Catalog $1 ❖ Rhinestones, sequins, beads, jewels, lace, appliques, fringes, trim, feathers, imported and domestic fabrics, and silk flowers. 516–724–4661.

Bay Area Tailoring Supply, 8000 Capwell Dr., Oakland, CA 94621: Free information ❖ Tailoring supplies. 800–359–0400; 510–635–1100 (in CA).

Bee Lee Company, Box 36108, Dallas, TX 75235: Free catalog ❖ Notions, belt buckles and snaps, trims, zippers, interfacings, threads, and other notions. 800–527–5271.

Bejeweled Wholesalers, Box 8096, Pembroke Pines, FL 33084: Catalog $1 (refundable) ❖ Rhinestones, studs, rims, settings, and stud setter. 305–433–5700.

Bridal-By-The-Yard, P.O. Box 2492, Springfield, OH 45501: Free information ❖ Re-embroidered Alencon, Schiffli lace, imported Chantilly and Venice lace, satins, taffeta, organza, millinery supplies, trims, and notions. 513–325–2847.

Buckaroo Bobbins, 377 S. 6300 W., Cedar City, VT 84720: Catalog $1 ❖ Authentic vintage western clothing sewing patterns. 801–865–7922.

Button Shop, 7023 Roosevelt Rd., P.O. Box 1065, Berwyn, IL 60402: Free catalog ❖ Buttons, closures, trims, sewing machine accessories, notions, and tools. 708–795–1234.

Buttons & Things Factory Outlet, 24 Main St., Freeport, ME 04032: Free information ❖ Buttons. 207–865–4480.

Clotilde, 2 Sew Smart Way, B8031, Stevens Point, WI 54481: Free catalog ❖ Notions, books, patterns, and videos. 800–772–2891.

Coastal Button Supply, P.O. Box 114, Damascus, MD 20872: Free catalog ❖ Buttons.

Craft Gallery Ltd., P.O. Box 145, Swampscott, MA 01907: Catalog $2 ❖ Threads, fibers, books, fabrics, and supplies for sewing, crochet, and other stitchery crafts. 508–744–2334.

Creative Crystal Company, P.O. Box 8, Unionville, CT 06085: Free information with long SASE ❖ Easy-to-use rhinestone applicator, pearls, Austrian crystal, and trims. 203–673–0056.

Delectable Mountain Cloth, 125 Main St., Brattleboro, VT 05301: Brochure $1 with long SASE ❖ Buttons.

DK Sports, Division Daisy Kingdom, 134 NW 8th Ave., Portland, OR 97209: Free information ❖ Rainwear and outerwear fabrics and notions. 503–222–9033.

Dogwood Lane Buttons, Box 145, Dugger, IN 47848: Catalog $2.50 (refundable) ❖ Handmade porcelain buttons. 800–648–2213.

Dritz Corporation, P.O. Box 5028, Spartanburg, SC 29304: Free information ❖ Marking pens, awls, cutting mats, cutters, scissors, needles, straight and safety pins, zipper glides, craft tape, glue sticks, tape measures, and other notions. 800–845–4948.

Fashion Touches, 170 Elm St., P.O. Box 804, Bridgeport, CT 06604: Catalog $1 ❖ Covered belts and buttons. 203–333–7738.

A. Feibusch Corporation, 30 Allen St., New York, NY 10002: Free information with long SASE ❖ Sewing notions, thread, and zippers. 212–226–3964.

Fiskars Corporation, 7811 W. Stewart Ave., Wausau, WI 54401: Free information ❖ Scissors, safety scissors for children, and sharpeners. 715–842–2091.

Garden Fairies Trading Company, 309 S. Main St., Sebastopol, CA 95472: Catalog $4 ❖ Handmade collar and smocking patterns, French and Battenberg lace, Swiss embroideries, soft toy patterns, books, designer fabrics, and cottons. 800–925–9919.

Gettinger Feather Corporation, 16 W. 36th St., New York, NY 10033: Price list $2 ❖ Raw or dyed ostrich, marabou, turkey, and feathers from other birds. 212–695–9470.

Green Pepper, 3918 W. 1st Ave., Eugene, OR 97402: Catalog $2 ❖ Buckles, velcro and fasteners, zippers, buttons, other notions, and kits for coats and jackets, ski wear, water-repellent clothing, and duffel bags. 503–345–6665.

Greenberg & Hammer Inc., 24 W. 57th St., New York, NY 10019: Free catalog ❖ Tailoring supplies. 800–955–5135.

Hancock Fabrics, 3841 Hinkleville Rd., Paducah, KY 42001: Free information ❖ Quilting supplies, fabrics, and notions. 800–626–2723.

Harper House, P.O. Box 400, Gratz, PA 17030: Catalog $5 ❖ Historic and ethnic garment patterns, sewing notions, and books. 717–365–3381.

Hearthside Quilters Nook, 10731 W. Forest Home Ave., Hales Corner, WI 53130: Catalog $2 ❖ Sewing and smocking supplies, patterns, notions, fabrics, and lace. 414–425–2474.

Hedgehog Handworks, P.O. Box 45384, Westchester, CA 90045: Catalog $1 ❖ Semi-precious beads and attachments, sewing notions, gold and silver threads, needlecraft and embroidery supplies, and other accessories. 310–670–6040.

Home-Sew Inc., P.O. Box 4099, Bethlehem, PA 18018: Catalog $1 ❖ Sewing supplies, notions, and other craft supplies. 215–867–3833.

Judy's Heirloom Sewing, y's Heirloom Sewing 13650 E. Zayante Rd., Felton, CA 95018: Catalog $5 ❖ Imported fabrics and laces, patterns and trims, and smocking supplies. 408–335–4684.

KOKOMO Buttonworks, P.O. Box 397, Montrose, CA 91021: Brochure $2 ❖ Handmade buttons.

Kreinik Manufacturing Company, Ruth Schmuff, 9199 Reisterstown Rd., Owings Mills, MD 21117: Free information with long SASE ❖ Gold and silver metallic thread, trim, and other metal threads. 800–537–2166.

Lace Heaven, P.O. Box 50150, Mobile, AL 36605: Catalog $3 (refundable) ❖ Lingerie fabrics, ribbons and trim, stretch lace, elastic, and notions. 205–478–5644.

Ledgewood Studio, 6000 Ledgewood Dr., Forest Park, GA 30050: Catalog $2 with long SASE and three 1st class stamps ❖ Dress patterns for antique dolls, supplies for authentic period costumes, notions, and braids, French laces, silk ribbons, silk taffeta, China silk, Swiss batiste, and trim.

Donna Lee's Sewing Center, 25234 Pacific Hwy. South, Kent, WA 98032: Catalog $4 ❖ Swiss batiste, imperial batiste, China silk, silk charmeuse, French val laces, English laces, Swiss embroidery, trim and yardage fabrics, silk ribbon, and embroidered ribbon. 206–941–9466.

Linda's Silver Needle, P.O. Box 2167, Naperville, IL 60567: Free information ❖ Sewing and smocking supplies. 800–SMOCK-IT.

Lisa's Heirloom Shop, 14 Melrose Pl., West Caldwell, NJ 07006: Free price list with two 1st class stamps and long SASE ❖ Fabrics, antique laces, smocking pleaters, and books. 201–226–LACE.

Madeira USA Ltd., P.O. Box 6068, Laconia, NH 03246: Free information ❖ Gold and silver metallic thread. 800–225–3001.

Making Memories, P.O. Box 537, Wynne, AR 72396: Price list $1 ❖ Smocking and heirloom sewing supplies. 800–524–6534.

Nancy's Notions, P.O. Box 683, Beaver Dam, WI 53916: Free catalog ❖ Notions, threads, books, patterns, and interlock knits, fleece, gabardines, sweater knits, challis, and other fabrics. 800–833–0690.

National Thread & Supply, 695 Red Oak Rd., Stockbridge, GA 30281: Free catalog ❖ Cone threads, other sewing supplies, and notions. 800–331–7600.

Newark Dressmaker Supply, 6473 Ruch Rd., P.O. Box 20730, Lehigh Valley, PA 18002: Free catalog ❖ Supplies for sewing, other crafts, and needlework. 610–837–7500.

Oppenheim's, 120 E. Main St., North Manchester, IN 46962: Free catalog ❖ Sewing notions, fabrics, and craft supplies. 219–982–6848.

Outdoor Wilderness Fabrics, 16195 Latah Dr., Nampa, ID 83651: Free price list ❖ Coated and uncoated nylon fabrics, fleece and blends in coat weights, waterproof fabrics, hardware, webbing, zippers, patterns, and notions. 208–466–1602.

Perfect Notion, 566 Hoyt St., Darien, CT 06820: Catalog $1 ❖ Notions, scissors, serger accessories, and threads. 203–968–1257.

Rainshed Outdoor Fabrics, 707 NW 11th, Corvallis, OR 97330: Catalog $1 ❖ Rainwear

and outerwear fabrics, notions, webbing, and patterns. 503–753–8900.

River Gems & Findings, 6901 Washington NE, Albuquerque, NM 87109: Free catalog ❖ Beads, beading supplies, sewing notions, and other craft accessories. 800–396–9895.

Sew Fine, 9659 Reseda Blvd., Northridge, CA 91324: Free information with long SASE ❖ Smocking and sewing supplies, French and English lace, buttons, ribbons, and Swiss embroideries. 818–886–1108.

Sewin' in Vermont, 84 Concord Ave., St. Johnsbury, VT 05819: Free information ❖ Sewing machines, sergers, and notions. 800–451–5124.

Sewing Machine Discount Sales, 10222 Paramount Blvd., Downey, CA 90241: Free information ❖ Embroidery and polyester thread, polyester cone thread for sergers and sewing machines, and wool-nylon, pearl cotton, and silk thread. 310–928–4029.

The Sewing Workshop, 2010 Balboa St., San Francisco, CA 94121: Free information ❖ Tailoring supplies. 415–221–SEWS.

Signal Thread Company, 521 Airport Rd., Chattanooga, TN 37421: Catalog $5 ❖ Spun polyester thread in mini cones. 800–THREADS.

Ben Silver, 149 King St., Charleston, SC 29401: Free catalog ❖ College crests, monograms, and blazer buttons. 800–221–4671.

Singer Sewing Center, 1669 Texas Ave., College Station, TX 77840: Free information with long SASE ❖ Sewing notions and sewing machine serger attachments. 800–338–5672.

Something Pretty, Rt 1, Box 93, Big Sandy, TN 38221: Brochure $2.50 ❖ Hand-cut and handpainted ceramic buttons. 901–593–3807.

Specialties, 4425 Cotton Hanlon Rd., Montour Falls, NY 14865: Catalog $2 ❖ Lingerie fabrics, notions, and patterns. 607–594–2021.

The Stitching Bear, 915 N. Main St., Findlay, OH 45840: Free information with long SASE ❖ Smocking and sewing supplies, patterns, books, and fabrics. 419–424–2040.

Stretch & Sew, 8697 La Mesa Blvd., La Mesa, CA 91941: Catalog $3 ❖ Fabrics, patterns, and notions. 619–589–8880.

Sulky, 3113 Broadpoint Dr., Harbor Heights, FL 33983: Free information ❖ Decorative threads. 813–629–3199.

Things Japanese, 9805 NE 116th St., Ste. 7160, Kirkland, WA 98034: Free information ❖ Silk filament sewing thread. 206–821–2287.

Ultramouse Ltd., 3433 Bennington Ct., Bloomfield Hills, MI 48301: Catalog $2 ❖ Notions and ultrasuede and other fabric scraps. 800–225–1887.

Utex Trading, 710 9th St., Ste. 5, Niagara Falls, NY 14301: Free brochure with long SASE ❖ Sewing supplies and imported silk fabrics. 716–282–8211.

Victorian Treasures, 12148 Madison St. NE, Blaine, MN 55434: Catalog $3.50 (refundable) ❖ Imported lace, fabrics, Swiss embroideries, notions, and sewing supplies. 612–755–6302.

William Wawak Corporation, 2235 Hammond Dr., Schaumberg, IL 60173: Catalog $3.50 ❖ Tailoring and sewing supplies. 800–654–2235.

Web of Thread, 3240 Lone Oak Rd., Ste. 124, Paducah, KY 42003: Catalog $2 ❖ Supplies for serger and embroidery crafts and metallic, rayon, and silk threads for hand and machine embroidery.

ZRK Enterprises, Box 1213, McCall, ID 83638: Free information ❖ Zipper repair kit. 208–634–4851.

Patterns & Kits

Amazon Drygoods, 2218 E. 11th St., Davenport, IA 52803: Catalog $7 ❖ Victorian and Edwardian clothing patterns, from the 1920s and 1930s. 800–798–7979.

Annie's Attic, 106 W. Groves, Big Sandy, TX 75755: Catalog $2 ❖ Sewing and needlecraft patterns and supplies. 903–636–4303.

Buckaroo Bobbins, 377 S. 6300 W., Cedar City, VT 84720: Catalog $1 ❖ Authentic vintage western clothing sewing patterns. 801–865–7922.

Butterick Pattern Company, 161 6th Ave., New York, NY 11691: Free information ❖ Patterns for clothing. 212–620–2500.

D.L. Designs, P.O. Box 27034, Los Angeles, CA 90027: Free catalog ❖ Men and women's hat patterns for costume pieces from the past, bridal headpieces, or contemporary fashions.

Daisy Kingdom, 134 NW 8th Ave., Portland, OR 97209: Catalog $2 ❖ Nursery ensembles and children's fashions in kits or ready-made. 503–222–9033.

The Design Center of Charlotte, 1235 East Blvd., Ste. 222, Charlotte, NC 28203: Catalog $5 ❖ Patterns for full-figured women, size 20 to 28. 800–214–1778.

Donner Designs, P.O. Box 7217, Reno, NV 89510: Catalog 75¢ ❖ Ski wear sewing kits and patterns. 702–358–5281.

Frostline Kits, 2525 River Rd., Grand Junction, CO 81505: Catalog $2 ❖ Ready-to-sew kits for jackets, vests, comforters, luggage, camping gear, and ski wear. 303–241–0155.

Green Pepper, 3918 W. 1st Ave., Eugene, OR 97402: Catalog $2 ❖ Buckles, velcro and velcro fasteners, zippers, buttons, and other notions, and kits for coats and jackets, ski wear, water-repellent clothing for cold weather, and duffel bags. 503–345–6665.

Harper House, P.O. Box 400, Gratz, PA 17030: Catalog $5 ❖ Historic and ethnic garment patterns, sewing notions, books, and other supplies. 717–365–3381.

Kwik-Sew Pattern Company Inc., 3000 Washington Ave. North, Minneapolis, MN 55411: Catalog $5 ❖ Patterns and sewing instruction books.

Little Memories, P.O. Box 170145, Arlington, TX 76003: Brochure $1.75 ❖ Smocking plates, duplicate stitch designs, and patterns. 817–860–2681.

Heidi Marsh Patterns, 3494 N. Valley Rd., Greenville, CA 95947: Catalog $3 ❖ Clothing patterns, from 1855 to 1865.

Park Bench Pattern Company, 5181 Baltimore Dr., La Mesa, CA 91942: Catalog $3 ❖ Clothing patterns.

Past Patterns, P.O. Box 7587, Grand Rapids, MI 49510: Catalog $4 ❖ Patterns for historically authentic clothing for men, women, and children. 616–245–9456.

Pattern Warehouse, P.O. Box 3135, Chicago, IL 60654: Catalog $3 ❖ Cross-stitch and soft craft patterns. 312–828–9634.

Rainshed Outdoor Fabrics, 707 NW 11th, Corvallis, OR 97330: Catalog $1 ❖ Rainwear and outerwear fabrics, notions, webbing, and patterns. 503–753–8900.

The Ready Wear Company, 391 3rd Ave., Troy, NY 12181: Free catalog ❖ Print, paint, bead, or embroider on one-size-fits-all women's blouses, jogging suits, jackets, and skirts. 800–342–2400; 518–235–1700 (in NY).

Ready-to-Sew, P.O. Box 59, Azle, TX 76098: Catalog $2 (refundable) ❖ Pre-cut fashion and craft sewing kits. 817–237–0786.

Sew/Fit Company, P.O. Box 397, Bedford Park, IL 60499: Free catalog ❖ Patterns, books, notions, and other supplies. 800–547–ISEW; 708–458–6000 (in IL).

Sew Great, P.O. Box 111446, Campbell, CA 95011: Catalog $2 (refundable) ❖ Pattern paper, sewing supplies, and notions. 408–252–8445.

Sew Special, 9823 Old Winery Pl., Ste. 20, Sacramento, CA 95827: Catalog $2 ❖ Patterns for easy-to-make quilting projects and other crafts.

Sierra Craft, 1131 N. DeWolf, Fresno, CA 93727: Catalog $2 ❖ Easy-to-use patterns for making clothing.

Specialties, 4425 Cotton Hanlon Rd., Montour Falls, NY 14865: Catalog $2 ❖ Lingerie fabrics, notions, and patterns. 607–594–2021.

Stretch & Sew, 8697 La Mesa Blvd., La Mesa, CA 91941: Catalog $3 ❖ Fabrics, patterns, and notions. 619–589–8880.

Sewing Machines & Sergers

Bernina, 3500 Thayer Ct., Aurora, IL 60504: Free information ❖ Sewing machines and sergers. 708–978–2500.

Derry's Sewing Center, 430 St. Ferdinand, Florissant, MO 63031: Brochure $1 with long SASE ❖ Sewing machines, vacuum cleaners, and parts. 314–837–6103.

Juki America Inc., 5 Haul Rd., Wayne, NJ 07470: Free information ❖ Serging machines. 201–633–7200.

The New Home Sewing Machine Company, 100 Hollister Rd., Teterboro, NJ 07608: Free information ❖ Computerized sewing machines. 800–631–0183.

Pfaff American Sales Corporation, 610 Winters Ave., Paramus, NJ 07653: Free brochure ❖ Sewing machines.

SCS USA, 9631 NE Colfax, Portland, OR 97220: Free catalog ❖ Embellishment sewing machine. 800–542–4727.

Sew-Knit Distributors, 9789 Florida Blvd., Baton Rouge, LA 70815: Free catalog ❖ Sewing and knitting machines and knitting supplies. 800–289–5648.

Sew Vac City, 1667 Texas Ave., College Station, TX 77840: Brochure $3 ❖ Sewing

machines and vacuum cleaners. 800–338–5672.

Sewin' in Vermont, 84 Concord Ave., St. Johnsbury, VT 05819: Free information ❖ Sewing machines, sergers, and notions. 800–451–5124.

Singer Sewing Center, 1669 Texas Ave., College Station, TX 77840: Free information with long SASE ❖ Sewing machines and serger attachments.800–338–5672.

White Sewing Machine Company, 11760 Berea Rd., Cleveland, OH 44111: Free information ❖ Sewing machines.

Stuffing & Fill

Air-Lite Synthetics Manufacturing, 342 Irwin St., Pontiac, MI 48053: Free information ❖ Batting, fiber fill, and pillow forms. 800–521–1267.

Brewer Sewing Supplies, 3800 W. 42nd St., Chicago, IL 60632: Free information ❖ Sewing machines, quilting supplies, batting and stuffing, and notions. 800–621–2501.

Buffalo Batt & Felt Corporation, Craft Product Division, 3307 Walden Ave., Depew, NY 14043: Information $1 ❖ Stuffing, polyester fiber fill, and patterns. 716–683–4100.

Frugal Fox, Box 369, Fontana, WI 53125: Free price list with long SASE ❖ Pillow forms, quilt batting, and fiberfill.

Oriental Rug Company, P.O. Box 205, Washington, KY 41086: Free information ❖ Polyester fiberfill, polyester quilt batting, and pillow inserts. 606–759–7614.

Putnam Company Inc., P.O. Box 310, Walworth, WI 53184: Information $1 ❖ Fiberfill pillow forms.

Royal Processing Company Inc., 3445 N. Spencer St., Charlotte, NC 28205: Free information ❖ Kapok and polyester fill for pillows, quilts, and stuffed toys. 800–451–8487.

Tags & Labels

Alpha Impressions Inc., P.O. Box 3156, Los Angeles, CA 90051: Free brochure ❖ Woven labels and hang tags. 800–834–8221.

Charm Woven Labels, Box 30027, Portland, OR 97230: Free brochure ❖ Silk, linen, wool, polyester, and cotton labels. 503–252–5542.

Dana Labels Inc., 7778 SW Nimbus Ave., Beaverton, OR 97005: Brochure $1 ❖

Garment labels, size tags, shipping labels, care/content labels, cosmetic labels, and pressure-sensitive labels. 800–255–1492; 503–646–7933 (in OR).

E & S Creations, P.O. Box 68, Rexburg, ID 83440: Catalog $1 ❖ Imaginative folk, country, and Victorian-style tags.

Heirloom Woven Labels, Box 428, Moorestown, NJ 08057: Free information ❖ Woven labels. 609–722–1618.

IDENT-IFY Label Corporation, P.O. Box 140204, Brooklyn, NY 11214: Free information ❖ Sew-on labels and name tapes. 718–436–3126.

Kimmeric Studio, P.O. Box 3586, Napa, CA 94558: Catalog $2 ❖ Craft hang tags.

Name Maker Inc., P.O. Box 43821, Atlanta, GA 30378: Free information ❖ Labels and name tapes with signature, logo, or custom artwork, in nylon, taffeta, or satin. 404–691–2237.

Northwest Tag & Label Inc., 110 Foothills Rd., Ste. 237, Lake Oswego, OR 97034: Brochure $1 ❖ Iron-on and washable printed fabric tags and labels in nylon, satin, and woven edge. 503–636–6456.

Sterling Name Tape Company, 9 Willow St., P.O. Box 939, Winsted, CT 06098: Label sample kit $1 ❖ Sewing labels. 800–654–5210.

SHEDS

Country Designs, P.O. Box 774, Essex, CT 06426: Catalog $6 ❖ Plans for barns, sheds, and garages. 203–767–1046.

Hammond Barns, P.O. Box 584, New Castle, IN 47362: Brochure $2 ❖ Plans for storage sheds, tool sheds, workshops, and other structures. 317–529–7822.

Handy Home Products, 6400 E. 11 Mile Rd., Warren, MI 48091: Free information ❖ Easy-to-assemble cedar barns with optional cupola and weather vane accents. 800–221–1849.

Heritage Garden Houses, City Visions Inc., 311 Seymour, Lansing, MI 48933: Catalog $3 ❖ Pool houses, potting sheds, tool storage, hot tub enclosures, colonnades, seats, cabinets, gazebos, and classical, Victorian, Japanese, and other garden retreats. 517–372–3385.

Senco Inc., Box 306, Marquette, MI 49855: Free information ❖ Recreational shelters, portable hunting blinds and ice fishing houses, and greenhouses. 407–589–6563.

SHOES & BOOTS
Men & Women's Shoes

Active Soles, 20 Wapping Rd., Kingston, MA 02364: Free brochure ❖ Wide and extra-wide athletic shoes for women, sizes 5 to 13. 800–881–4322.

Ampersand's, 2510 S. Broadway, Salem, IL 62881: Free catalog ❖ Women's casual, dress, and walking shoes. 800–678–9138.

Aussie Connection, 825 NE Broadway, Portland, OR 97232: Free catalog ❖ Washable Australian sheepskin slippers and boots. 800–950–2668.

Bally of Switzerland for Ladies, 689 Madison Ave., New York, NY 10021: Free information ❖ Women's shoes, clothing, luggage, and small leather goods. 212–751–2163.

Bally of Switzerland for Men, 711 5th Ave., New York, NY 10022: Free information ❖ Men's shoes, clothing, luggage, and small leather goods. 212–751–9082.

Belgian Shoes, 60 E. 56th St., New York, NY 10022: Brochure $3 ❖ Handcrafted casual shoes. 212–755–7372.

Bencone Casuals, 121 Carver Ave., Westwood, NJ 07675: Free catalog ❖ Women's shoes, all-weather boots, athletic walking shoes, casual shoes, loafers, and pumps. 800–521–8668.

Birkerkenstock Express, 301 SW Madison Ave., Corvalis, OR 97333: Free catalog ❖ Waterproof clogs, sizes 4 to 11 for women, and 5 to 13 for men. 800–231–6740.

Chernin's Shoes, 1001 S. Clinton St., Chicago, IL 60607: Free catalog ❖ Shoes and loafers for men, women, and children. 312–922–5900.

Church's English Shoes, 428 Madison Ave., New York, NY 10017: Free brochure ❖ Handcrafted all-leather shoes, sizes 6 to 14, AA-EEE. 800–221–4540; 212–755–4313 (in NY).

Clover Nursing Shoe Company, 1948 E. Whipp Rd., Kettering, OH 45440: Free brochure ❖ Shoes with all-leather uppers, sizes 5 to 12 and slim to double-wide widths. 513–435–0025.

The Comfort Corner, Box 649, Nashua, NH 03061: Free catalog ❖ Men and women's shoes and boots in hard-to-find sizes and widths. 603–598–4785.

Coward Shoes, Palo Verde at 34th, P.O. Box 27800, Tucson, AZ 85726: Free catalog ❖ Leather shoes for men and women, sizes 5 to 12, AA to EEE. 602–748–8600.

Essex Shoe Company, 950 New Durham Rd., Edison, NJ 08817: Free catalog ❖ Women's shoes, sizes up to 12, widths 4A to EE. 800–366–9302.

Executive Shoes, P.O. Box 9128, Hingham, MA 02043: Catalog $1 ❖ Handcrafted athletic and walking shoes in hard-to-fit sizes. 800–934–1022.

Fabiano Shoe Company, 850 Summer St., South Boston, MA 02127: Free information with long SASE ❖ Thinsulate-insulated Telemark boots. 617–268–5625.

Footprints, The Birkenstock Store, 1339 Massachusetts, Lawrence KS 66044: Free catalog ❖ Birkenstock sandals and sandal repair. 800–827–1339.

Peter Fox Bridal Shoes, 105 Thompson St., New York, NY 10012: Catalog $3 ❖ Bridal boots and shoes. 800–338–3430.

Gene's Shoes Discount Catalog, 126 N. Main St., St. Charles, MO 63301: Catalog $1 ❖ Men and women's casual and dress shoes. 314–946–0804.

Giordano's, 1150 2nd Ave., New York, NY 10021: Catalog $3 ❖ Designer shoes in small and narrow sizes, 3 to 6, AA to medium. 212–688–7195.

Gucci, CSB 3168, Department 846, Melville, NY 11747: Free catalog ❖ Shoes, clothing, leather goods, and accessories. 800–221–2590.

Haband, 100 Fairview Ave., Prospect Park, NJ 07530: Free information ❖ Men's shoes and wash-and-wear clothing.

Hanover Shoe Company, 440 N. Madison St., Hanover, PA 17331: Free catalog ❖ Men's shoes, sizes 6 to 15, AA to EEE. 800–426–3708; 717–632–7575 (in PA).

Hitchcock Shoes Inc., Hingham, MA 02043: Free catalog ❖ Men's shoes, sizes 5 to 13, EE to EEEEEE. 617–749–3260.

Johansen Bros. Shoe Company, RR 1, US Hwy. 67 West, Corning, AR 72422: Free catalog ❖ Women's fashion shoes. 800–624–9079.

Johnston & Murphy, Box 1090, Genesco Park, Nashville, TN 37202: Free catalog ❖ Men's shoes. 800–424–2854.

Koson's, P.O. Box 3663, St. Augustine, FL 32085: Free brochure ❖ Swedish clogs for men, women, and children. 800–654–0010.

L.A. Gear, 2850 Ocean Park Blvd., Santa Monica, CA 90405: Free information ❖ Children's shoes. 800–252–4327.

Lace-Up Shoes, 110 Orchard Street, New York, NY 10002: Free catalog ❖ Casual footwear for men and women. 800–488–LACE.

Maryland Square, 2510 S. Broadway, Salem, IL 62881: Free catalog ❖ Women's footwear in full and half sizes. 800–678–9138.

Mason Shoe Manufacturing Company, 1251 1st Ave., Chippewa Falls, WI 54729: Free catalog ❖ Shoes for men and women, sizes 4 to 16, AA to EEEE. 715–723–1871.

Masseys, Direct Footwear Merchants, 601 12th St., Lynchburg, VA 24504: Free catalog ❖ Casual, dress, athletic shoes, boots, and slippers. 800–462–7739.

Minnetonka by Mail, P.O. Box 444, Bronx, NY 10458: Catalog $2 ❖ Leather moccasins for men, women, and children, with soft, crepe and polyurethane soles, and shoes and boots for casual wear. 718–364–6266.

Moonwalker/Sierra Boot Company, 2001 Chester, Bakersfield, CA 93301: Free catalog ❖ Handmade boots and shoes. 800–93–BOOTS; 805–322–8505 (in CA).

Nancy's Choice, 34th & Palo Verde, P.O. Box 27800, Tucson, AZ 85726: Free catalog ❖ Shoes in hard-to-find sizes, from 9 to 13, widths N to WW, plus some slims. 602–748–8600.

Okun Brothers Shoes, 356 E. South St., Kalamazoo, MI 49007: Free catalog ❖ Walking shoes for men, women, and children. 616–342–1536.

Old Pueblo Traders, Palo Verde at 34th, P.O. Box 27800, Tucson, AZ 85726: Free catalog ❖ Shoes and boots for women. 602–748–8600.

Ortho-Vent Inc., 11851 30th Ct. North, St. Petersburg, FL 33716: Free catalog ❖ Men's casual and dress leather footwear. 800–678–4601.

Reyers, Sharon City Centre, Sharon, PA 16146: Free information ❖ Shoes, from size 2½ to 14, in widths AAAAAA to EE. 800–245–1550.

Richlee Shoe Company, P.O. Box 3566, Frederick, MD 21701: Free catalog ❖

Elevator shoes for men, sizes 5 to 11, B to EEE. 800–343–3810.

Sheepskin Imports, P.O. Box 4114, Dana Point, CA 92629: Free catalog ❖ Aussie Dog boots, shoes, and slippers. 800–237–0464.

Shoecraft Corporation, Box 129, Accord, MA 02018: Free information ❖ Dress shoes, sandals, sport shoes, and flats, sizes 10 to 13. 800–225–5848.

Standard Shoes, 48 Main St., Bangor, ME 04401: Free catalog ❖ Arch-supporting shoes for women sizes 2A to 3A; 6 to 12, A and B; 5 to 12, C and D; 5 to 12, E and EE, and some half sizes. 800–284–8366.

Talbots, 175 Beal St., Hingham, MA 02043: Free catalog ❖ Women's shoes in regular, petite, and sizes. 800–992–9010.

Norm Thompson, P.O. Box 3999, Portland, OR 97208: Free catalog ❖ Wood Ducks and other casual shoes. 800–547–1160.

Tog Shop, Lester Square, Americus, GA 31710: Free catalog ❖ Women's footwear in full and half sizes and slim (AAA), narrow (AA), or medium (B) widths. 800–367–8647.

Vasque Boots, 314 Main St., Red Wing, MN 55066: Free information ❖ Hiking boots for men and women. 800–972–5220.

Wissota Trader, 1313 1st Ave., Chippewa Falls, WI 54729: Free catalog ❖ Regular and hard-to-find sizes of shoes and clothes for men and women. 800–962–0160.

Wolverine Boots & Shoes, 9341 Courtland Dr., Rockford, MI 49351: Free information ❖ Footwear for men and women. 800–543–2668.

World Traders, Bar Harbor Rd., Box 158–6, Brewer, ME 04412: Free catalog ❖ Hand-sewn moccasins. 800–603–0003.

Western Boots

Austin-Hall Boot Company, 491 N. Resler Dr., P.O. Box 220990, El Paso, TX 79913: Free information ❖ Wood-pegged, brass-nailed, leather-lined boots. 915–581–2124.

Back at the Ranch, 235 Don Gaspar, Santa Fe, NM 87501: Free information ❖ Vintage western clothing, boots, and hats. 505–989–8110.

Chris Bennett Boots, 471 W. Mariposa, P.O. Box 6760, Nogales, AZ 85628: Free catalog ❖ Custom boots. 602–281–1225.

Boot Town, 10838 N. Central Expwy., Dallas, TX 75231: Free catalog ❖ Western boots. 800–222–6687.

Champion Boot Company, 505 S. Cotton, El Paso, TX 79901: Catalog $1 ❖ Leather cowboy-style boots. 915–534–7783.

The Cowhand, 200 W. Midland Ave., P.O. Box 743, Woodland Park, CO 80863: Free information ❖ Gloves, spurs, bits, belts, buckles, and Western-style boots for men, women, and children. 800–748–DUDS.

Drysdales Catalog, 3220 S. Memorial Dr., Tulsa, OK 74145: Free catalog ❖ Men's Justin Ropers in sizes 6–12, 13, and 14, in A, B, D, E, and EE widths (full and half sizes). Women's in sizes 4 to 9, and A, B, and C widths. 800–444–6481.

Just Justin, 1505 Wycliff Ave., Dallas, TX 75207: Free information ❖ Cowboy-style boots. 800–292–BY-ABOOT; 214–630–2858 (in TX).

Knapp Shoes Inc., One Knapp Centre, Brockton, MA 02401: Free catalog ❖ Men and women's work, walking, dress, and other styles of shoes. 508–588–9009.

Lucchese Boots, 4025 Broadway, San Antonio, TX 78209: Free information ❖ Handmade boots and shoes. 800–548–9755.

Luskey's Western Stores Inc., 101 N. Houston St., Fort Worth, TX 76102: Free catalog ❖ Western-style clothing, boots, and hats for men, women, and children. 817–335–5833.

Moonwalker/Sierra Boot Company, 2001 Chester, Bakersfield, CA 93301: Free catalog ❖ Handmade boots and shoes. 800–93–BOOTS; 805–322–8505 (in CA).

Olathe Boot Company, 705 S. Kansas, Olathe, KS 66061: Free information ❖ Custom boots.

Vic Pasquin Company, 187 Rock Rd., Glen Rock, NJ 07452: Catalog $2.50 (refundable) ❖ Leather lined boots for children and adults to size 16 EE. 201–445–0606.

Ryon's Saddle & Ranch Supplies, 2601 N. Main, Fort Worth, TX 76106: Free catalog ❖ Saddles, tack, and Western-style clothing and boots for men, women, and children. 817–625–2391.

Tonto Rim Trading Company, P.O. Box 463, Salem, IN 47167: Catalog $1 ❖ Western boots and hats. 800–253–4287.

Western Boot Company, 1915 W. Masonic Dr., Nogales, AZ 85621: Free catalog ❖ Western boots. 602–281–0512.

Wilson Boot Company, 110 E. Callender St., Livingston, MT 59047: Brochure $1 ❖ Handmade leather boots. 406–222–3842.

SHUFFLEBOARD

Allen R. Shuffleboard Company Inc., 6585 Seminole Blvd., Seminole, FL 34642: Free information ❖ Cues, disks, and sets. 813–397–0421.

General Sportcraft Company Ltd., 140 Woodbine Rd., Bergenfield, NJ 07621: Free information ❖ Cues, disks, and sets. 201–384–4242.

International Billiards Inc., 2311 Washington Ave., Houston, TX 77007: Free information ❖ Cues, discs, and sets. 800–255–6386; 713–869–3237 (in TX).

Dick Martin Sports Inc., 181 E. Union Ave., P.O. Box 7381, East Rutherford, NJ 07073: Free information ❖ Cues, disks, and sets. 800–221–1993; 201–438–5255 (in NJ).

Palmer Billiard Corporation, 307 Morris Ave., Elizabeth, NJ 07208: Free information ❖ Cues, disks, and sets. 909–289–4778.

Playfair Shuffleboard Company Inc., 7021 Bluffton Rd., Fort Wayne, IN 46809: Free information ❖ Shuffleboards and accessories. 800–541–3743.

SGD Company Inc., P.O. Box 8410, Akron, OH 44320: Free information ❖ Cues, discs, and sets. 216–239–2828.

Ultra Play Systems Inc., 425 Sycamore St., Anderson, IN 46016: Free information ❖ Cues, disks, and sets. 800–458–5872.

SIGNS & SIGN-MAKING

Americraft Corporation, 904 4th St. West, Palmetto, FL 34221: Free catalog ❖ Injection molded and formed letters and office decor signs. 800–237–3984; 813–722–6631 (in FL).

Dick Blick Company, P.O. Box 1267, Galesburg, IL 61401: Catalog $1 ❖ Sign-making supplies and equipment. 800–447–8192.

BronceX Ltd., La Haye Division, P.O. Box 2319, Corona, CA 91718: Free brochure ❖ Solid bronze cast signs. 800–523–9544.

Cambridge Metalsmiths, Box 1400, Lynden, Ontario, Canada L0R 1T0: Free brochure ❖ Hand-enamelled cast metal signs, on heavy metal relief, with a choice of over 250 emblems. 519–647–3326.

Erie Landmark Company, 4449 Brookfield Corporate Dr., Chantilly, VA 22021: Free brochure ❖ Outdoor and indoor bronze or redwood markers and signs. 800–874–7848.

Gold Leaf & Metallic Powders, 74 Trinity Pl., Ste. 1807, New York, NY 10006: Free information ❖ Genuine and composition leaf in rolls, sheets, books, and boxes. 800–322–0323; 212–267–4900 (in NY).

John Hinds & Company, 81 Greenridge Dr. West, Elmira, NY 14905: Free catalog ❖ Aluminum and bronze plaques and signs. 607–733–6712.

Hodgins Engraving, P.O. Box 597, Batavia, NY 14020: Free information ❖ Engraved plastic signs. 800–666–8950.

Kaufman Supply, Rt. 1, Centertown, MO 65023: Free catalog ❖ Sign painting supplies. 314–893–2124.

La Haye Bronze Inc., 1346 Railroad St., Corona, CA 91720: Free catalog ❖ Sand-cast, hand-chased bronze signs. 800–523–9544; 714–734–1371 (in CA).

Lake Shore Industries, P.O. Box 59, Erie, PA 16512: Free information ❖ Cast aluminum and bronze signs and plaques. 800–458–0463.

Lazer Images, 33664 Five Mile Rd., Livonia, MI 48154: Free information ❖ Indoor/outdoor banner- and sign-making equipment.

Letters Unlimited, 32 W. Streamwood Blvd., Streamwood, IL 60103: Free catalog ❖ Vinyl letters. 800–422–4231.

Marlin Industries Inc., Rt. 70, Box 191, Cashiers, NC 28717: Information $1 ❖ Woodcarving machines for making signs. 704–743–5551.

MAX-CAST, P.O. Box 662, Kalona, IA 52247: Free brochure ❖ Bronze, aluminum, and iron letters.

Mayfair Signs, P.O. Box 2955, Sumas, WA 98295: Free information ❖ Handpainted cast aluminum signs. 604–823–4141.

Meierjohan-Wengler Inc., 10330 Wayne Ave., Cincinnati, OH 45215: Free catalog ❖ Bronze tablets and historic markers. 513–771–6074.

Earl Mich Company, 806 N. Peoria St., Chicago, IL 60622: Free information ❖ Vinyl and reflecting letters. 800–MICH-USA; 312–829–1552 (in IL).

Mossburg's Foam Products, 103 N. Alabama Ave., Chesnee, SC 29323: Free information ❖ Easy-to-install foam, plastic, and vinyl letters. 800–845–6140; 803–461–8116 (in SC).

Mountain Meadows Pottery, P.O. Box 163, South Ryegate, VT 05069: Free catalog ❖ Functional stoneware and humorous and sentimental plaques. 800–639–6790.

Mr. Ed The Sign Man, P.O. Box 303, Crystal Beach, FL 34681: Free information ❖ Magnetic signs, name badges, and vinyl lettering.

Nasco, 901 Janesville Ave., Fort Atkinson, WI 53538: Free catalog ❖ Sign-making supplies. 800–558–9595.

National Banner Company Inc., 11938 Harry Hines Blvd., Dallas, TX 75234: Free information ❖ Blank banners hemmed and roped, or grommeted with heavy duty rope sewn top and bottom. 800–527–0860.

Newman Brothers Inc., 5609 Center Hill Ave., Cincinnati, OH 45216: Free catalog ❖ Handcrafted cast bronze and aluminum plaques. 513–242–0011.

Northroad & Company, Wood Sign Products, P.O. Box 554, Groton, MA 01450: Catalog $2 (refundable) ❖ Historical markers, house numbers, and residential and small business signs carved in wood. 800–448–6420.

NUDO Products, 2508 S. Grand Ave. East, Springfield, IL 62703: Free information ❖ Sign painting boards. 800–826–4132.

Out of the Woods Sign Makers, 3 Pine Bluff Trail, Ormond Beach, FL 32174: Free information ❖ Personalized handcrafted wooden signs. 800–554–9315.

Postal Pals, 11242 Playa Ct., Culver City, CA 90230: Free brochure ❖ Redwood address plaques and mail boxes with an animal theme. 800–438–7768; 310–398–7768 (in CA).

Rayco Paint Company, 26100 N. Pulaski Rd., Chicago, IL 60646: Free information ❖ Supplies and equipment for sign painters. 800–421–2327.

Reich Supply Company Inc., 811 Broad St., Utica, NY 13501: Free information ❖ Sign-making and screen-printing materials and equipment. 800–338–3322.

Royal Graphics Inc., 3117 N. Front St., Philadelphia, PA 19133: Free information ❖

Posters, show-cards, and bumper stickers. 215–739–8282.

Ryther-Purdy Lumber Company Inc., 174 Elm St., P.O. Box 622, Old Saybrook, CT 06475: Free information ❖ Handcrafted wooden signs. 203–388–4405.

Sepp Leaf Products Inc., 381 Park Ave. South, New York, NY 10016: Free information ❖ Gold and palladium leaf, rolled gold, tools, and kits. 212–683–2840.

Sign-Mart, 1657 N. Glassell, Orange, CA 92667: Free information ❖ Hemmed banners with grommets. 800–533–9099; 714–998–9470 (in CA).

Signage, 1246 Topaz Ave., San Jose, CA 95117: Free information ❖ Banners and magnetic signs. 800–541–SIGN.

Signs by Michael, 30 Village Way, Palm Harbor, FL 34683: Catalog $2 ❖ Redwood signs. 813–787–8589.

Smith-Cornell Inc., 1545 Holland Rd., Maumee, OH 43537: Free brochure ❖ Brass and aluminum historic markers. 800–325–0248; 419–891–4335 (in OH).

Southern Sign Supply Inc., 127 Roesler Rd., Glen Burnie, MD 21061: Free information ❖ Supplies and equipment for sign painters. 800–638–5008; 800–445–1108 (in MD).

Joseph Struhl Company Inc., 195 Atlantic Ave., P.O. Box N, Garden City Park, NY 11040: Free information ❖ Ready-made window signs for retail stores. 800–552–0023.

Studio Art Tiles, P.O. Box 6016, Kingwood, TX 77325: Free information with long SASE ❖ Numbered ceramic tiles. 713–360–4987.

Variety Art & Sign Supply, 912 Silver Lily St., Marrero, LA 70072: Catalog $4 ❖ Sign-making supplies and books. 504–341–0105.

Wensco Sign Supplies, P.O. Box 1728, Grand Rapids, MI 49501: Catalog $5 ❖ Supplies and equipment for sign painters. 800–253–1569; 800–632–4629 (in MI).

SILK-SCREENING

The Art Store, 935 Erie Blvd. East, Syracuse, NY 13210: Price list $3 ❖ Supplies for fabric dyeing, screen printing, marbling, and other art decor. 800–669–2787.

Chaselle Inc., 9645 Gerwig Ln., Columbia, MD 21046: Catalog $4 ❖ Art software and books, brushes and paints, tempera colors, acrylics and sets, pastels, ceramic molds and

kilns, sculpture equipment, and silk-screen painting supplies. 800–242–7355.

Crown Art Products, 90 Dayton Ave., Passaic, NJ 07055: Free catalog ❖ Silk-screening supplies and section frames. 201–777–6010.

Decart Inc., P.O. Box 309, Morrisville, VT 05661: Free information ❖ Water-based enamels and paints for transfer techniques, glass crafting, and silk-screening. 802–888–4217.

Guildcraft Company, 100 Firetower Dr., Tonawanda, NY 14150: Free catalog ❖ Supplies for silk-screening, batik, tie dying, stenciling, block printing, and foil crafts. 716–743–8336.

Ivy Crafts Imports, 122113 Distribution Way, Beltsville, MD 20705: Catalog $3.95 ❖ Paints, resists, applicators, and other supplies. 301–595–0550.

Nasco, 901 Janesville Ave., Fort Atkinson, WI 53538: Free catalog ❖ Silk-screening and printing supplies. 800–558–9595.

Naz-Dar Company, 1087 Branch St., Chicago, IL 60622: Free catalog ❖ Silk-screening and graphic arts equipment and supplies. 312–943–8338.

Pyramid of Urbana, 2107 N. High Cross Rd., Urbana, IL 61801: Catalog $5 ❖ Office and art supplies, school equipment, other craft supplies, and screen-printing equipment, kits, tools, and printers. 217–328–3099.

Reich Supply Company Inc., 811 Broad St., Utica, NY 13501: Free information ❖ Sign-making and screen-printing supplies. 800–338–3322.

Southern Emblem, P.O. Box 8, Toast, NC 27049: Free catalog ❖ Embroidered emblems, emblematic jewelry, badges, flags, and screen printing supplies. 910–789–3348.

Welsh Products Inc., P.O. Box 145, Benica, CA 94510: Free catalog ❖ Easy-to-use screen printing kits. 800–745–3255; 707–645–3252.

SILVER & FLATWARE

Aaron's, 576 5th Ave., New York, NY 10036: Free information ❖ Active, inactive, and obsolete silverware and flatware. 800–447–5868.

William Ashley, 50 Boor St. West, Toronto, Ontario, Canada M4W 3L8: Free information ❖ China, crystal, and silver. 800–268–1122.

Atlantic Silver, 5223 Ehrlich Rd., Tampa, FL 33624: Free information ❖ New and estate flatware and hollowware. 800–288–6665.

Barrons, P.O. Box 994, Novi, MI 48376: Free information ❖ China, crystal, and silver. 800–538–6340.

Beverly Bremer Silver Shop, 3164 Peachtree Rd. NE, Atlanta, GA 30305: Free information ❖ New, used, discontinued, and hard-to-find patterns. 404–261–4009.

Buschemeyer's Silver Exchange, 515 4th Ave., Louisville, KY 40202: Free information ❖ New and used silver patterns and sterling. 800–626–4555.

China Cabinet Inc., 24 Washington St., Tenafly, NJ 07670: Free information with long SASE ❖ China, crystal, flatware, and other gifts. 201–567–2711.

The China Warehouse, Box 21797, Cleveland, OH 44121: Free information ❖ China, crystal, and flatware. 800–321–3212.

Clintsman International, 20855 Watertown Rd., Waukesha, WI 53186: Free information ❖ Discontinued china, crystal, and flatware. 414–798–0440.

Coinways Antiques, 136 Cedarhurst Ave., Cedarhurst, NY 11516: Free information with long SASE ❖ Used and new sterling silver flatware. 800–645–2102; 516–374–1970 (in NY).

Walter Drake Silver Exchange, Drake Building, Colorado Springs, CO 80940: Free pattern directory ❖ Active, inactive, and obsolete sterling and silver plate patterns. 800–525–9291.

Fortunoff Fine Jewelry, P.O. Box 1550, New York, NY 10022: Free catalog ❖ Sterling flatware, silver plate and stainless steel serving pieces and china. 800–937–4376.

Gorham, P.O. Box 906, Mount Kisco, NY 10549: Free brochure and list of retailers ❖ Stainless flatware.

Graham Silver, P.O. Box 6021, Omaha, NE 68106: Free information ❖ Place settings, serving pieces, tea services, and other silver items. 800–228–2294.

Greater New York Trading, 81 Canal St., New York, NY 10002: Free brochure ❖ Silver, china, and glassware. 212–226–2808.

Hagan's Sterling & Silverplate, P.O. Box 25487, Tempe, AZ 85282: Free information ❖ Discontinued and current sterling and silver plate. 800–528–7425.

Kaiser Crow Inc., 3545 S. Platte River Dr., Englewood, CO 80110: Free brochure ❖ Stainless, silver flatware, and other silver patterns. 800–468–2769; 303–781–6888 (in CO).

Kinzie's, Box 522, Turlock, CA 95381: Free information ❖ Flatware matching service.

Kitchen Accessories Etc., P.O. Box 1560, North Hampton, NH 03862: Free catalog ❖ Kitchen accessories and serving pieces, china, and silverplate. 603–964–5174.

Lanac Sales, 73 Canal St., New York, NY 10002: Free catalog ❖ China, crystal, sterling, and gifts. 212–925–6422.

Helen Lawler, 5400 E. Country Rd., Blytheville, AR 72315: Free information ❖ Discontinued silver patterns. 314–720–8502.

Littman's Sterling, 151 Granby St., Norfolk, VA 23510: Free information ❖ Individual sterling pieces and place settings. 800–368–6348.

Locators Inc., 908 Rock St., Little Rock, AR 72202: Free information ❖ Discontinued china, crystal, and silver. 800–367–9690.

Michele's Silver Matching Service, 805 Crystal Mountain Dr., Austin, TX 78733: Free information ❖ Inactive and active silver patterns. 800–332–4693.

Midas China & Silver, 4315 Walney Rd., Chantilly, VA 22021: Free catalog ❖ Silverware, table settings, china, and gifts. 800–368–3153.

Open House, 200 Bala Ave., Bala-Cynwyd, PA 19004: Free information with long SASE ❖ Flatware and cookware. 215–664–1488.

Past & Presents, 65–07 Fitchett St., Rego Park, NY 11374: Free information ❖ Flatware, china, and crystal. 718–897–5515.

H.G. Robertson Fine Silver, 3263 Roswell Rd. NE, Atlanta, GA 30305: Free information ❖ Sterling flatware and hollowware. 404–266–1330.

Robin Importers, 510 Madison Ave., New York, NY 10022: Brochure $1 with long SASE ❖ China, crystal, and stainless steel flatware. 800–223–3373; 212–753–6475 (in NY).

Rogers & Rosenthal, 22 W. 48th St., Room 1102, New York, NY 10036: Free information with long SASE ❖ Sterling, silverplate, and stainless steel flatware. 212–827–0115.

Ross-Simons Jewelers, 9 Ross Simons Dr., Cranston, RI 02920: Free information ❖ Sterling and china. 800–556–7376.

Wilma Saxton Inc., 37 Clementon Rd., Box 395, Berlin, NJ 08009: Free price list ❖ Sterling silver, silverplate, and stainless matching service. 800–267–8029.

Nat Schwartz & Company, 549 Broadway, Bayonne, NJ 07002: Free catalog ❖ Crystal, sterling, and china. 800–526–1440.

Silver Lane, P.O. Box 322, San Leandro, CA 94577: Free information ❖ Discontinued crystal and china patterns, current and obsolete silver, and serving pieces. 510–483–0632.

Silverladies & Nick, 5650 W. Central Ave., Toledo, OH 43615: Free information ❖ Sterling and silver plate in old, inactive, and obsolete patterns. 800–423–4390.

The Sterling Shop, P.O. Box 595, Silverton, OR 97381: Free list with long SASE ❖ Inac-tive and obsolete American-made sterling and discontinued silverplate patterns. 503–873–6315.

Thurber's, 2256 Dabney Rd., Ste. C, Richmond, VA 23230: Free information ❖ Sterling and china. 800–848–7237.

Wallace Silversmiths, 175 McClellan Hwy., P.O. Box 9114, East Boston, MA 02128: Free informa-tion ❖ Sterling and silverplate in contemporary designs.

Zucker's Fine Gifts, 151 W. 26th St., New York, NY 10001: Free catalog ❖ Hummel, Swarovski silver and crystal, Waterford crystal, Lladro porcelain, and other gifts. 212–989–1450.

SKATEBOARDS

Awesome Sports, 557 El Cajon Blvd., El Cajon, CA 92020: Free information ❖ Skateboards, shoes, and clothing. 619–593–7500.

Bill's Wheels, 1408 Freedom Blvd., Watsonville, CA 95076: Free catalog ❖ Decks, trucks, wheels, shoes, and clothing. 408–763–1921.

California Cheap Skates, 2701 McMillan Ave., San Luis Obispo, CA 93401: Free catalog ❖ T-shirts, shoes, stickers, skateboards and parts, and safety gear. 800–477–9283.

Cali4nia Skate Express, 4629 N. Blythe, Fresno, CA 93722: Free information ❖ Skateboards, T-shirts, stickers, and shoes. 800–447–8989.

Counter Fit, P.O. Box 7304–295, North Hollywood, CA 91603: Free catalog ❖ Skateboards, decks, trucks, T-shirts, and other clothing. 818–567–2747.

The Deluxe Store, 1831 Market St., San Francisco, CA 94103: Free information ❖ Skate-boards. 800–275–3359.

Endless Grind, 424 W. Peace St., Raleigh, NC 27603: Free information ❖ Skateboards, decks, wheels, trucks, shoes, and clothing. 910–791–9835.

FTC Skate Shop, 1586 Bush St., San Francisco, CA 94109: Free catalog ❖ Skateboards and parts, snowboards, and T-shirts. 415–673–8363.

Intensity Skates, 11890–B Old Baltimore Pike, Beltsville, MD 20705: Free catalog ❖ Skateboards, clothing, and hightops. 301–937–1349.

Kryptonics Inc., 740 S. Pierce Ave., Louisville, CA 80027: Free information ❖ Skateboards and roller skates. 800–766–9146; 303–665–5353 (in CA).

National Sporting Goods Corporation, 25 Brighton Ave., Passaic, NJ 07055: Free information ❖ Skateboards, roller skates, and scooters. 201–779–2323.

Roller Derby Skate Company, Box 930, Litchfield, IL 62056: Free information ❖ Skateboards, roller skates, and scooters. 217–324–3961.

Saucony/Hyde, 13 Centennial Dr., Peabody, MA 01961: Free information ❖ Skateboards, roller skates, and scooters. 800–365–7282.

Skates on Haight, 1818 Haight St., San Francisco, CA 94117: Free catalog ❖ Skateboards, wheels, shoes, T-shirts, and sweatshirts. 415–244–9800.

Skateworks, P.O. Box 1351, Santa Cruz, CA 95061: Catalog $1 ❖ Decks, wheels, hats, boots, and shoes. 800–354–0999.

Smoothill Sports Distributors, 3060 Kerner Blvd., San Rafael, CA 94901: Free information ❖ Skateboards. 415–453–1170.

Tracker Designs Ltd., P.O. Box 217, Cardiff, CA 92007: Free information ❖ Skateboards, trucks, and wheels. 800–282–8722; 619–722–1455 (in CA).

UFO Sports Inc., 18533 Roscoe Blvd., Ste. 323, Northridge, CA 91324: Catalog $3 ❖ Skateboards, wheels, decks, and stickers. 818–701–1584.

Variflex Inc., 5152 N. Commerce Ave., Moorpark, CA 93021: Free information ❖ Skateboards and roller skates. 805–532–0322.

Z Products, P.O. Box 5397, Santa Monica, CA 90409: Free information ❖ Skateboards, trucks, and wheels. 310–476–4857.

SKIING
Clothing

Action Sports Gear Inc., 150 N. Farms Rd., Northampton, MA 01060: Free information ❖ Men and women's ski clothing. 413–586–8844.

Eddie Bauer, P.O. Box 3700, Seattle, WA 98124: Free catalog ❖ Men and women's ski clothing, natural fiber sportswear, down outerwear, footwear, and luggage. 800–426–8020.

L.L. Bean Inc., Freeport, ME 04033: Free catalog ❖ Camping and workout gear, and men and women's clothing for skiing, back country travel, and snowshoeing. 800–221–4221.

Bogner of America, Bogner Dr., Newport, VT 05855: Free information ❖ Gloves and mittens, hats, parkas, jackets, pants, suits, separates, sweaters, wind shirts, and vests. 800–451–4417; 802–334–6507 (in VT).

Columbia Sportswear Company, 6600 N. Baltimore, P.O. Box 03239, Portland, OR 97203: Free information ❖ Men, women, and children's hats, gloves, mittens, jackets, pants, suits, parkas, underwear, vests, and wind shirts. 800–622–6953.

Donner Designs, P.O. Box 7217, Reno, NV 89510: Catalog 75¢ ❖ Sewing kits and patterns for ski clothing. 702–358–5281.

Eagle River Nordic, P.O. Box 936, Eagle River, WI 54521: Free catalog ❖ High-performance and racing cross-country ski equipment, clothing, and accessories. 800–423–9730.

Early Winters Inc., P.O. Box 4333, Portland, OR 97208: Free catalog ❖ Men and women's ski clothing, leisure separates for men and women, gifts, and equipment. 800–458–4438.

Ellesse USA Inc., 1430 Broadway, New York, NY 10018: Free information ❖ Gloves and mittens, hats, jackets and parkas, suits, sweaters, wind shirts, and vests. 800–345–9036; 212–840–6111 (in NY).

Faeth Outdoor Sales, R.J.F. Enterprises Inc., 1151 S. 7th St., P.O. Box 118–A, St. Louis, MO 63166: Free information ❖ Hats, mittens and gloves, parkas and suits, jackets, underwear, socks, sweaters, wind shirts, and vests. 314–421–0030.

Gart Brothers Denver Sportscastle, 1000 Broadway, Denver, CO 80203: Free information ❖ Skis, boots, and men and women's clothing. 800–426–1399; 303–861–1122 (in CO).

Gorsuch Ltd., 263 E. Gore Creek Dr., Vail, CO 81657: Free catalog ❖ Men and women's ski and other clothing. 303–949–4005.

Head Sports Wear, 9189 Red Branch Rd., Columbia, MD 21045: Free information ❖ Men and women's ski clothing. 800–638–9680; 301–730–8300 (in MD).

Ladylike Ski Shop, 203 N. Ballard, Wylie, TX 75098: Free information ❖ Ski clothing for men, women, and children. 214–442–5842.

Marker Ltd., P.O. Box 26548, Salt Lake City, UT 84119: Free brochure ❖ Men and women's ski clothing. 809–4–MARKER.

Marmot Mountain Works Ltd., 3049 Adeline Ave., Berkeley, CA 94703: Free information ❖ Men and women's ski clothing. 800–MARMOT-9.

Nordica, 139 Harvest Ln., Williston, VT 05495: Free information ❖ Caps, gloves, jackets, boots, and pants. 800–343–7800; 802–879–4644 (in VT).

North Face, 999 Harrison St., Berkeley, CA 94710: Free information ❖ Hats, mittens and gloves, jackets, parkas and suits, underwear, sweaters, vests, and wind shirts. 510–527–9700.

Northern Outfitters, 1083 N. State St., Orem, UT 84057: Free information ❖ Caps, jackets, and pants. 801–224–5342.

Pearl Izumi, 2300 Central Ave., Boulder, CO 80301: Free information ❖ Caps, jackets, and pants. 800–328–8488; 303–938–1700 (in CO).

Ramer Products Ltd., 1803 S. Foothills Hwy., Boulder, CO 80303: Free catalog ❖ Back country ski equipment and clothing, tents, sleeping bags, frame packs, videos, rock and ice climbing gear, caving and winter survival equipment, and books. 304–499–4466.

Scandinavian Ski & Sport Shop, 40 W. 57th St., New York, NY 10019: Free information ❖ Men and women's ski clothing and equipment. 212–757–8524.

Slalom Skiwear Inc., Longview St., Newport, VT 05855: Free information ❖ Men and women's ski clothing. 802–334–7958.

Sporthill, 1690 S. Bertelsen Rd., Eugene, OR 97402: Free information ❖ Caps, jackets, and pants. 800–622–8444; 503–345–9623 (in OR).

Equipment & Accessories

Akers Ski Inc., P.O. Box 280, Andover, ME 04216: Free catalog ❖ Nordic skis, ski boots, bindings, poles, and transportation and storage gear. 207–392–4582.

Allsop, P.O. Box 23, Bellingham, WA 98227: Free information ❖ Nordic skis and poles, boot trees, and carriers. 800–426–4303; 206–734–9090 (in WA).

Alpina Sports Corporation, P.O. Box 23, Hanover, NH 03755: Free information ❖ Boot bags, alpine and nordic boots, and nordic bindings and skis. 603–448–3101.

Brenco Enterprises Inc., 1003 6th Ave. South, Seattle, WA 98134: Free information ❖ Alpine and nordic boots, and apres ski boots.

Caber USA, 50 Jonergin Dr., Swanton, VT 05488: Free information ❖ Alpine ski poles, boots, and nordic skis. 802–868–2761.

Chisco Sports Accessories, 2550 S. 2300 West, Salt Lake City, UT 84119: Free information ❖ Alpine skis. 800–825–4555; 801–972–5656 (in UT).

Climb High Inc., 1861 Shelburne Rd., Shelburne, VT 05482: Free information ❖ Nordic boots. 802–985–5056.

Collins Ski Products Inc., P.O. Box 11, Bergenfield, NJ 07621: Free brochure ❖ Ski carriers, goggles, ski poles, and ski locks. 800–526–0369; 201–384–6060 (in NJ).

Daleboot USA, 2150 S. 3rd West St., Salt Lake City, UT 84115: Free information ❖ Alpine ski poles, boots, and boot bags. 801–487–3649.

Eagle River Nordic, P.O. Box 936, Eagle River, WI 54521: Free catalog ❖ Ski equipment, clothing, boots, gloves, hats, and videos. 800–423–9730.

Elan-Monark, 208 Flynn Ave., P.O. Box 4279, Burlington, VT 05401: Free information ❖ Boot bags, ski bags, alpine ski poles, bindings, boots, and alpine and nordic skis. 802–863–5593.

Excel Marketing Inc., One 2nd St., Peabody, MA 01960: Free information ❖ Cross-country skis, boots, and poles. 508–532–2226.

Fabiano Shoe Company, 850 Summer St., South Boston, MA 02127: Free information with long SASE ❖ Nordic boots and bindings and apres ski boots. 617–268–5625.

Head Sports, 4801 N. 63rd St., Boulder, CO 80301: Free information ❖ Alpine skis, boots, poles, and bindings. 800–874–3234; 303–530–2000 (in CO).

Igloo Viksi Inc., P.O. Box 180, St. Agathe Des Monts, Quebec, Canada J8C 3A3: Free information ❖ Boot and ski bags, alpine and nordic ski poles, and nordic skis, boots, and bindings. 819–326–1662.

Johar Inc., P.O. Box 10, Forrest City, AR 72335: Free information ❖ Nordic ski poles. 800–248–1232; 501–633–8161 (in AR).

Karhu USA Inc., Division Merrell Footwear, Box 4249, Burlington, VT 05406: Free information ❖ Cross-country skis and boots. 802–864–4519.

Maska USA Inc., 529 Main St., Ste. 205, Boston, MA 02129: Free information ❖ Nordic skis, poles, and boots. 800–451–4600; 617–242–8600 (in MA).

Nordica, 139 Harvest Ln., Williston, VT 05495: Free information ❖ Alpine and cross-country skis. 800–343–7800; 802–879–4644 (in VT).

Raichle Molitor USA, Geneva Rd., Brewster, NY 10509: Free information ❖ Alpine and cross-country skis, boots, and poles. 800–431–2204; 914–279–5121 (in NY).

Reflex Sport Products, Easton Aluminum, 5040 W. Harold Getty Dr., Salt Lake City, UT 84116: Free information ❖ Boot and ski bags, alpine and nordic ski poles, and alpine skis. 801–539–1400.

Reliable Racing Supply Inc., 630 Glen St., Queensbury, NY 12804: Free catalog ❖ Ski equipment. 518–793–0526.

Rossignol Ski Company, Industrial Ave., P.O. Box 298, Williston, VT 05495: Free information ❖ Alpine and nordic skis. 802–863–2511.

Salomon/North America, 400 E. Main St., Georgetown, MA 01833: Free information ❖ Alpine and nordic bindings and boots. 800–342–7669.

Skis Dynastar Inc., Hercules Dr., P.O. Box 25, Colchester, VT 05446: Free information ❖ Alpine and nordic skis, alpine boots, and boot and ski bags. 802–655–2400.

Spalding Sports Worldwide, 425 Meadow St., P.O. Box 901, Chicopee, MA 01021: Free information with list of retailers ❖ Nordic and alpine skis and poles. 800–225–6601.

Swix Sport USA Inc., 261 Ballardvale St., Wilmington, MA 01887: Free information ❖ Boot and ski bags, goggles, alpine and nordic ski poles, and nordic bindings and boots. 508–657–4820.

Yamaha Sporting Goods Division, 6600 Orangethorpe Ave., Buena Park, CA 90622: Free information ❖ Alpine skis. 800–851–6514; 714–522–9011 (in CA).

Goggles

Bolle America, 3890 Elm St., Denver, CO 80207: Free information ❖ Ski goggles. 800–554–6686; 303–321–4300 (in CO).

Brigade Quartermasters Inc., 1025 Cobb International Blvd., Kenesaw, GA 30144: Free catalog ❖ Ski goggles. 404–428–1234.

Collins Ski Products Inc., P.O. Box 11, Bergenfield, NJ 07621: Free brochure ❖ Ski carriers, goggles, ski poles, and ski locks. 800–526–0369; 201–384–6060 (in NJ).

Gargoyles Performance Eyewear, 5866 S. 194th St., Kent, WA 98032: Free catalog ❖ Sunglasses and ski goggles. 206–872–6100.

Martin Sunglasses, Jack Martin Company Inc., 9830 Baldwin Pl., El Monte, CA 91731: Free information ❖ Ski goggles. 800–767–8555; 213–686–1100 (in CA).

Raichle Molitor USA,$IRaichle Molitor USA Geneva Rd., Brewster, NY 10509: Free information ❖ Goggles. 800–431–2204; 914–279–5121 (in NY).

Suunto USA, 2151 Las Palmas Dr., Carlsbad, CA 92009: Free information ❖ Ski goggles. 619–931–6788.

Swix Sport USA Inc., 261 Ballardvale St., Wilmington, MA 01887: Free information ❖ Boot and ski bags, goggles, alpine and nordic ski poles, and nordic bindings and boots. 508–657–4820.

SKIN DIVING & SCUBA EQUIPMENT

Ador-Aqua, 42 W. 18th St., New York, NY 10011: Free information ❖ Skin diving equipment. 800–223–2500.

Apollo Sports USA Inc., 620 Price Ave., Redwood City, CA 94063: Free information ❖ Scuba equipment. 415–306–0909.

Aqua-Leisure Industries Inc., P.O. Box 239, Avon, MA 02322: Free information ❖ Skin diving equipment. 508–587–5400.

Aquarius, 51 Lake St., Nashua, NH 03060: Free information ❖ Skin diving equipment. 800–435–8974; 603–889–4346 (in NH).

Bare Sportswear Corporation, Box 8110–577, Blaine, WA 98230: Free information ❖ Wet suits and other clothing. 604–533–7848.

Bennett Video Group, 730 Washington St., Marina del Rey, CA 90292: Catalog $2.50 ❖ Videos on boating, sailing, fishing, scuba diving, other water activities, and travel. 310–821–3329.

Berry Scuba Company, 6674 N. Northwest Hwy., Chicago, IL 60631: Free catalog ❖ Skin diving and scuba equipment, inflatable boats, and underwater camera equipment. 800–621–6019; 312–763–1626 (in IL).

Body Glove International Inc., 530 6th St., Hermosa Beach, CA 90254: Free information ❖ Wet and skin diving suits and other equipment. 800–678–7873; 310–374–4074 (in CA).

Brownie's Third Lung, 940 NW 1st St., Fort Lauderdale, FL 33311: Free information ❖ Surface air and tank-filling compressors. 800–327–0412.

Central Skin Divers, 160–09 Jamaica Ave., Jamaica, NY 11432: Free information with long SASE ❖ Skin diving equipment and clothing. 718–739–5772.

Chronosport Inc., 25 Van Zant St., Norwalk, CT 06855: Free information ❖ Diving watches. 203–853–9593.

Citizen Watch of America, 1200 Wall St. West, Lyndhurst, NJ 07071: Free information ❖ Diving watches. 201–438–8150.

Competitive Aquatic Supply Inc., 15131 Triton Ln., Huntington Beach, CA 92649: Free information ❖ Skin diving equipment and waterproof watches. 800–421–5192; 310–633–3333 (in CA).

Dacor Corporation, 161 Northfield Rd., Northfield, IL 60093: Free information ❖ Scuba equipment. 708–446–9555.

Dive Check Scuba Products, 6341 Cernech, Kansas City, KS 66104: Free information ❖ Scuba equipment. 913–334–2880.

Divers Supply, 5208 Mercer University Dr., Macon, GA 31210: Free catalog ❖ Skin diving equipment and clothing. 800–999–3483.

Diving Unlimited International, 1148 Delevan Dr., San Diego, CA 92102: Free information ❖ Wet suits. 619–236–1203.

Fathom Dive Equipment, 8000 S. Orange Ave., Orlando, FL 32809: Free information ❖ Wet suits. 407–851–2202.

Go Dive Products, 164 N. Bascom Ave., San Jose, CA 95128: Free information ❖ Scuba equipment. 408–294–3483.

Innovative Designs Inc., 3785 Alt. 19 North, Ste. C, Palm Harbor, FL 34683: Free information ❖ Compact lightweight air supply equipment. 813–934–4619.

KME Diving Suits Inc., 3420 C St. NE, Auburn, WA 98002: Free information ❖ Wet suits. 800–800–8KME.

Leisure Pro, The Tennis Emporium, 42 W. 18th St., New York, NY 10011: Free information ❖ Scuba and skin diving equipment and clothing. 800–637–6880; 212–645–1234 (in NY).

M & E Marine Supply Company, P.O. Box 601, Camden, NJ 08101: Catalog $2 ❖ Skin diving equipment. 800–541–6501.

Murrays WaterSports, P.O. Box 490, Carpinteria, CA 93014: Free information ❖ Wet suits. 800–788–8964.

Nautica International, 6135 NW 167th St., Miami, FL 33015: Free information ❖ Compressors. 305–556–5554.

Ocean Edge, 7992 Miramar Rd., San Diego, CA 92126: Free information ❖ Scuba equipment. 619–695–9130.

Ocean Ray Wet Suits, 1315 S. College Rd., Wilmington, NC 28403: Free brochure ❖ Wet suits and skin diving equipment. 800–645–5554; 910–392–9989 (in NC).

O'Neill, 1071 41st Ave., Santa Cruz, CA 95062: Free information ❖ Wet suits. 408–475–7500.

Performance Diver, P.O. Box 2741, Chapel Hill, NC 27515: Free information ❖ Scuba diving equipment and clothing. 800–933–2299.

Reef Scuba Accessories, 3280 Sunrise Hwy., Wantagh, NY 11793: Free information ❖ Scuba equipment. 516–766–7333.

Sea Quest, 2151 Las Palmas Dr., Carlsbad, CA 92009: Free information ❖ Scuba equipment. 800–327–7662; 619–438–1101 (in CA).

Skin Diver Wet Suits, 1632 S. 250th St., Des Moines, WA 98032: Free information ❖ Wet suits. 206–878–1613.

Sport Europa, 7871 NW 15th St., Miami, FL 33126: Free catalog ❖ Wet suits for men, women, and children. 800–695–7000.

Sports Merchandizers, 1696 Cobb Pkwy. SE, Box 1262, Marietta, GA 30061: Free catalog ❖ Skin diving equipment. 800–241–1856; 404–952–3259 (in GA).

Submersible Systems, 18112 Gothard St., Huntington Beach, CA 92648: Free information ❖ Scuba equipment. 714–842–6566.

Tanks D'Art Inc., 350 Easy St., Simi Valley, CA 93065: Free information ❖ Diving tanks. 800–635–5815.

Tektite, P.O. Box 4209, Trenton, NJ 08610: Free information ❖ Scuba equipment. 609–581–2116.

3 Little Devils, S. 5780 A Hwy. 123, Baraboo, WI 53913: Free catalog ❖ Scuba equipment. 800–356–9016.

Tilos Products, 3202 Factory Dr., Pomona, CA 91768: Free information ❖ Wet suits. 909–594–6809.

U.S. Wet Suits, 11475 Commercial Ave., Richmond, IL 60071: Free brochure ❖ Wet suits. 815–678–7841.

Curt Walker Optician, 3434 4th Ave., Ste. 120, San Diego, CA 92103: Free information ❖ Optically corrected dive masks. 800–538–2878; 619–299–2878 (in CA).

Wenoka Sea Style, c/o Sea Quest Inc., 2151 Las Palmas Dr., Carlsbad, CA 19009: Catalog $4 ❖ Skin diving equipment. 800–327–7662; 619–438–1101 (in CA).

SLEDS, SNOWBOARDS & TOBOGGANS

Dorfman-Pacific, 2615 Boeing Way, Stockton, CA 95206: Free information ❖ Sleds, snowmobile boots, and clothing. 800–367–3626; 209–982–1400 (in CA).

Faber Brothers, 4141 S. Pulaski Rd., Chicago, IL 60632: Free information ❖ Sleds. 312–376–9300.

Faeth Outdoor Sales, R.J.F. Enterprises Inc., 1151 S. 7th St., P.O. Box 118–A, St. Louis, MO 63166: Free information ❖ Snowmobiles, bobsleds, snowmobile boots, and clothing. 314–421–0030.

Flexible Flyer Company, P.O. Box 1296, West Point, MS 39773: Free information ❖ Sleds. 800–521–6233.

FTC Skate Shop, 1586 Bush St., San Francisco, CA 94109: Free catalog ❖ Skateboards and parts, snowboards, and T-shirts. 415–673–8363.

Skip Hutchison, Rastaboards-Surf-Sail-Snowboards, 4748 NE 11th Ave., Fort Lauderdale, FL 33334: Free information ❖ Sailboards, surfboards, and snowboards. 305–491–7992.

Intex Recreation Corporation, 4130 Santa Fe Ave., Long Beach, CA 90810: Free information ❖ Toboggans. 310–549–5400.

M.W. Kasch Company, 5401 W. Donges Bay Rd., Mequon, WI 53092: Free information ❖ Sleds and snowboards. 414–242–5000.

Murrays WaterSports, P.O. Box 490, Carpinteria, CA 93014: Free information ❖ Snowboards. 800–788–8964.

Paris Company Inc., Box 250, South Paris, ME 04281: Free information ❖ Sleds. 800–678–5221; 207–539–8221 (in ME).

Sevylor USA, 6651 E. 26th St., Los Angeles, CA 90040: Free information ❖ Sleds. 213–727–6013.

SLM Inc., Box 1070, Gloversville, NY 12078: Free information ❖ Sleds. 800–832–8987; 518–725–8101 (in NY).

Torpedo Inc., Box 157, South Paris, ME 04281: Free information ❖ Sleds. 207–743–6896.

Vermont Sled Company, P.O. Box 20, Monkton, VT 05469: Free information ❖ Wood sleds. 802–453–4924.

ZIFFCO, 18111–B S. Santa Fe Ave., Rancho Dominguez, CA 90221: Free information ❖ Toboggans. 800–532–2242.

SLIPCOVERS & UPHOLSTERY

Fabric Shop, 120 N. Seneca St., Shippensburg, PA 17257: Free information with long SASE ❖ Antique satins, custom draperies, and drapery, slipcover and upholstery fabrics. 800–233–7012; 717–532–4150 (in PA).

Fabrics by Phone, P.O. Box 309, Walnut Bottom, PA 17266: Brochure and samples $3 ❖ Antique satins, custom draperies, and drapery, slipcover and upholstery fabrics. 800–233–7012; 717–532–4150 (in PA).

Furniture Restoration Supply Company, 5498 Rt. 34, Oswego, IL 60543: Catalog $2 (refundable) ❖ Upholstery, chair caning, and wicker repair supplies. 800–432–2745.

Home Fabric Mills Inc., 882 S. Main St., Cheshire, CT 06410: Free brochure ❖ Velvets, upholstery and drapery fabrics, prints, sheers, antique satins, and thermal fabrics. 203–272–6686.

Jack's Upholstery & Caning Supplies, 5498 Rt. 34, Oswego, IL 60543: Catalog $2 (refundable) ❖ Upholstery, basket-making, and chair-caning supplies. 312–554–1045.

Rubin & Green, 290 Grand St., New York, NY 10002: Free information with long SASE ❖ Upholstery and decorator fabrics and bedspreads, draperies, and comforters. 212–226–0313.

Slipcovers of America, East Broad & Wood Sts., Dept. 128, Bethlehem, PA 18016: Free catalog ❖ Slipcovers, matching draperies, and fabrics. 215–867–7581.

Tioga Mill Outlet, 200 S. Hartman St., York, PA 17403: Free brochure ❖ Damasks, crewel, tapestry, linen, cotton, and other upholstery and drapery fabrics. 717–843–5139.

SNOWMOBILES

Faeth Outdoor Sales, R.J.F. Enterprises Inc., 1151 S. 7th St., P.O. Box 118–A, St. Louis, MO 63166: Free information ❖ Snowmobiles, bobsleds, ski bobs, boots, and clothing. 314–421–0030.

Johar Inc., P.O. Box 10, Forrest City, AR 72335: Free information ❖ Snowmobiles. 800–248–1232; 501–633–8161 (in AR).

Dennis Kirk Inc., 955 Southfield Ave., Rush City, MN 55069: Free information ❖ Snowmobiles and parts. 800–328–9280.

SNOWSHOES

Atlas Snow-Shoe Company, 81 Lafayette St., San Francisco, CA 94103: Free information ❖ Snowshoes. 800–645–SHOE.

Buckeye Sports Supply, John's Sporting Goods, 2655 Harrison Ave. SW, Canton, OH 44706: Free information ❖ Snowshoes. 800–533–8691.

Croakies, P.O. Box 2913, Jackson, WY 83001: Free information ❖ Snowshoes. 800–443–8620; 307–733–2266 (in WY).

Deer Me Products Company, P.O. Box 34, Anoka, MN 55303: Free information ❖ Snowshoes. 800–328–4827; 612–421–8971 (in MN).

Havlick Snowshoe Company, 2513 State Hwy. 30, Drawer QQ, Mayfield, NY 12117: Free brochure ❖ Snowshoes. 518–661–6447.

Iverson Snowshoe Company, Maple St., P.O. Box 85, Shingleton, MI 49884: Free information ❖ Snowshoes and bindings. 906–452–6370.

Liberty Mountain Sports, 9325 SW Barber St., Wilsonville, OR 97070: Free information ❖ Snowshoes and insulated clothing. 503–685–9600.

Longwood Equipment Company Ltd., 1940 Ellesmere Rd., Unit 8, Scarborough, Ontario, Canada M1H 2V7: Free information ❖ Snowshoes. 416–438–3710.

Northern Lites Performance Snowshoes, 1300 Cleveland, Wausau, WI 54401: Free catalog and list of retailers ❖ Snowshoes. 800–360–LITE.

Safesport Manufacturing Company,$ISafesport Manufacturing Company 1100 W. 45th Ave., Denver, CO 80211: Free information ❖ Snowshoes and bindings. 303–433–6506.

SOAP MAKING

The Essential Oil Company, P.O. Box 206, Lake Oswego, OR 97034: Free catalog ❖ Essential oils, soap-making molds and supplies, incense materials, potpourri, and aromatherapy items. 800–729–5912.

Gardens Past, P.O. Box 1846, Estes Park, CO 80517: Catalog $1 ❖ Soaps and soap making supplies, potpourri, dried flowers, herbs, candles, and aromatherapy items. 303–586–0400.

Pourette Manufacturing, 6910 Roosevelt Way NE, Seattle, WA 98115: Catalog $2 (refundable) ❖ Candles and soap- and candle-making supplies. 206–525–4488.

Soap Feathers Herbal Supply, HCR 84, Box 60A, Potsdown, NY 13676: Catalog $2 ❖ Soap making kits, books, molds, and supplies. 315–265–3648.

Sunfeather Herbal Soap Company, Box 60A, Potsdam, NY 13676: Catalog $2 ❖ Soap-making kits, supplies, and books. 315–265–3648.

SOCCER

Clothing

Action & Leisure Inc., 45 E. 30th St., New York, NY 10016: Free information ❖ Shoes, uniforms, gloves, shorts, shirts, shin guards, and socks. 800–523–8508; 212–684–4470 (in NY).

Action Sport Systems Inc., P.O. Box 1442, Morgantown, NC 28680: Free information ❖ Uniforms, shirts, shorts, gloves, and socks. 800–631–1091; 704–584–8000 (in NC).

Adidas USA, 5675 N. Blackstock Rd., Spartanburg, SC 29303: Free information ❖ Uniforms, shoes, socks, shirts, shorts, and shin guards. 800–423–4327.

Alpha Sportswear Inc., 20660 Nordoff St., Chatsworth, CA 91311: Free information ❖ Uniforms, shin guards, and shoes. 818–775–4555.

American Soccer Company Inc., 726 E. Anaheim St., Wilmington, CA 90744: Free information ❖ Shorts, warm-up clothing, and uniforms. 800–626–7774; 310–830–6161 (in CA).

Asics Tiger Corporation, 10540 Talbert Ave., West Bldg., Fountain Valley, CA 92708: Free information ❖ Shoes, socks, shorts, and shin guards. 800–766–ASICS; 714–962–7654 (in CA).

Betlin Manufacturing, 1445 Marion Rd., Columbus, OH 43207: Free information ❖ Shorts, warm-up clothing, and uniforms. 614–443–0248.

Bike Athletic Company, P.O. Box 666, Knoxville, TN 37901: Free information ❖ Shinguards, shirts, shorts, and uniforms. 615–546–4703.

Bomark Sportswear, P.O. Box 2068, Belair, TX 77402: Free information ❖ Uniforms. 800–231–3351.

Champion Products Inc., 475 Corporate Square Dr., Winston Salem, NC 27105: Free information ❖ Uniforms, shoes, socks, and shirts.

Continental Sports Supply Inc., P.O. Box 1251, Englewood, CO 80150: Free information ❖ Gloves, shinguards, shirts, shorts, and uniforms. 303–934–5657.

Doss Shoes, Soccer Sport Supply Company, 1745 1st Ave., New York, NY 10128: Free information ❖ Gloves, shinguards, shirts, shorts, and uniforms. 800–223–1010; 212–427–6050 (in NY).

Empire Sporting Goods Manufacturing Company, 443 Broadway, New York, NY 10013: Free information ❖ Shorts and uniforms. 800–221–3455; 212–966–0880 (in NY).

Foremost Midwest, 1307 E. Maple Rd., Troy, MI 48083: Free information ❖ Shinguards, shirts, shorts, and uniforms. 313–689–3850.

Genesport Industries Ltd., Hokkaido Karate Equipment Manufacturing Company, 150 King St., Montreal, Quebec, Canada H3C 2P3: Free information ❖ Gloves, shinguards, shirts, and shorts. 514–861–1856.

Holabird Sports Discounters, 9008 Yellow Brick Rd., Rossville Industrial Park, Baltimore, MD 21237: Free catalog ❖ Soccer and other sports equipment and clothing. 410–687–6400.

Lotto Sports, 1900 Surveyor Blvd., Carrollton, TX 75006: Free information ❖ Soccer shoes. 800–527–5126; 214–416–4003 (in TX).

Markwort Sporting Goods, 4300 Forest Park Ave., St. Louis, MO 63108: Catalog $8 with list of retailers ❖ Shorts, warm-up clothing, and uniforms. 800–669–6626; 314–652–3757 (in MO).

Puma USA Inc., 147 Centre St., Brockton, MA 02403: Free information with long SASE ❖ Uniforms, gloves, shorts and shirts, socks, shoes, and shin guards. 508–583–9100.

Soccer International Inc., P.O. Box 7222, Arlington, VA 22207: Catalog $2 ❖ Soccer equipment, uniforms, balls, gifts, T-shirts, and books. 703–524–4333.

Soccer Kick, 2130 Henderson Mill Rd., Atlanta, GA 30345: Free catalog ❖ Soccer equipment and gifts. 800–533–KICK; 404–939–6355 (in GA).

Union Jacks, 3525 Roanoke Rd., Kansas City, MO 64111: Free information ❖ Uniforms, shin guards, shirts, shorts, shoes, and socks. 800–288–5550; 816–561–5550 (in MO).

Equipment

Action & Leisure Inc., 45 E. 30th St., New York, NY 10016: Free information ❖ Soccer balls, cleats, and wrenches. 800–523–8508; 212–684–4470 (in NY).

Action Sport Systems Inc., P.O. Box 1442, Morgantown, NC 28680: Free information ❖ Soccer balls. 800–631–1091; 704–584–8000 (in NC).

Adidas USA, 5675 N. Blackstock Rd., Spartanburg, SC 29303: Free information ❖ Soccer balls, cleats, and other equipment. 800–423–4327.

American Soccer Company Inc., 726 E. Anaheim St., Wilmington, CA 90744: ❖ Balls, goalie gloves, nets, and protective gear. 800–626–7774; 310–830–6161 (in CA).

The Athletic Connection, 1901 Diplomat, Dallas, TX 75234: Free information ❖ Balls and nets. 800–527–0871; 214–243–1446 (in TX).

Brine Inc., 47 Sumner St., Milford, MA 01757: Free information ❖ Balls, goalie gloves, nets, and protective gear. 800–800–227–2722; 508–478–3250 (in MA).

Buckeye Sports Supply, John's Sporting Goods, 2655 Harrison Ave. SW, Canton, OH 44706: Free information ❖ Goals, nets, and soccer balls. 800–533–8691.

Champion Sports Products Company Inc., P.O. Box 138, Sayreville, NJ 08872: Free information ❖ Soccer balls, goals, and nets. 908–238–0330.

Continental Sports Supply Inc., P.O. Box 1251, Englewood, CO 80150: Free information ❖ German Bundesliga soccer balls. 303–934–5657.

Cosom Sporting Goods, Division Mantua Industries Inc., Grandview Ave., Woodbury Heights, NJ 08097: Free information ❖ Goals, nets, and soccer balls. 800–328–5635; 609–853–0300 (in NJ).

Doss Shoes, Soccer Sport Supply Company, 1745 1st Ave., New York, NY 10128: Free information ❖ Goals, nets, and soccer balls. 800–223–1010; 212–427–6050 (in NY).

General Sportcraft Company Ltd., 140 Woodbine Rd., Bergenfield, NJ 07621: Free information ❖ Soccer balls, goals, and nets. 201–384–4242.

Holabird Sports Discounters, 9008 Yellow Brick Rd., Rossville Industrial Park, Baltimore, MD 21237: Free catalog ❖ Soccer equipment and clothing. 410–687–6400.

Irwin Sports, 43 Hanna Ave., Toronto, Ontario, Canada M6K 1X6: Free information ❖ Soccer balls, goals, and nets. 800–268–1732.

Jayfro Corporation, Unified Sports Inc., 976 Hartford Tnpk., P.O. Box 400, Waterford, CT 06385: Free catalog ❖ Portable goals, nets, and practice equipment. 203–447–3001.

Kwik Goal, 140 Pacific Dr., Quakertown, PA 18951: Free information ❖ Soccer balls, goals, nets, wrenches and cleats, training equipment, referee supplies, and video cassettes. 800–531–4252; 215–536–2200 (in PA).

Markwort Sporting Goods Company, 4300 Forest Park Ave., St. Louis, MO 63108: CDatalog $8 with list of retailers ❖ Soccer

balls, goals, and nets. 800–669–6626; 314–652–3757 (in MO).

Pennray Billiard & Recreational Products, 6400 W. Gross Point Rd., Niles, IL 60714: Free catalog ❖ Darts, billiards, and soccer equipment. 800–523–8934.

Pennsylvania Sporting Goods,$IPennsylvania Sporting Goods 1360 Industrial Hwy., P.O. Box 451, Southhampton, PA 18966: Free information ❖ Balls, goalie gloves, nets, and protective gear. 800–535–1122.

Regent Sports Corporation, 45 Ranick Rd., Hauppage, NY 11788: Free information ❖ Soccer balls, goals, and nets. 516–234–2800.

Soccer International Inc., P.O. Box 7222, Arlington, VA 22207: Catalog $2 ❖ Soccer balls, uniforms, gifts, T-shirts, and books. 703–524–4333.

Soccer Kick, 2130 Henderson Mill Rd., Atlanta, GA 30345: Free catalog ❖ Soccer equipment, clothing, and shoes. 800–533–KICK; 404–939–6355 (in GA).

Spalding Sports Worldwide, 425 Meadow St., P.O. Box 901, Chicopee, MA 01021: Free information with list of retailers ❖ Soccer balls. 800–225–6601.

Sportime, 1 Sportime Way, Atlanta, GA 30340: Free information ❖ Balls and nets. 800–444–5700; 404–449–5700 (in GA).

Wolvering Sports, 745 State Circle, Box 1941, Ann Arbor, MI 48106: Catalog $1 ❖ Baseball, basketball, field hockey, soccer, football, and other athletic and recreation equipment. 313–761–5691.

SOLAR & WIND ENERGY

Advance Power Company, 6291 N. State St., P.O. Box 23, Calpella, CA 95418: Free information ❖ Solar, hydro, and wind energy equipment. 707–485–0588.

Advanced Electronics, 8525 Elk Grove Blvd., Ste. 106, Elk Grove, CA 95624: Free information ❖ Solar energy equipment. 916–687–7666.

Alternative Energy Engineering, P.O. Box 339, Redway, CA 05560: Catalog $1 ❖ Solar energy equipment. 800–777–6609.

Applied Photovoltaic, Box 2773, Staunton, VA 24401: Catalog $3 ❖ Solar components. 301–963–0141.

Atlantic Solar Products, 9351 Philadelphia Rd., P.O. Box 70060, Baltimore, MD 21237:

Free catalog ❖ Solar-energy powered systems for the home. 410–686–2500.

Backwoods Solar Electric, 8530 Rapid Lightning Creek, Sandpoint, ID 83864: Catalog $3 ❖ Solar electric-powered appliances and electricity-generating equipment. 208–263–4290.

Balmar, 902 NW Ballard Way, Seattle, WA 98107: Free information ❖ Wind-driven alternator. 206–789–4970.

Electron Connection, P.O. Box 203, Hornbrook, CA 96044: Free information ❖ Solar electric power systems for homes, recreational vehicles, and other installations. 916–475–3401.

Fanta-Sea Pools, 10151 Main St., Clarence, NY 14031: Free information ❖ Solar-energy-heated swimming pools. 800–845–5500; 800–462–8000 (in NY).

Hitney Solar Products, 2655 North Hwy. 89, Chino Valley, AZ 86323: Free catalog ❖ Solar powered systems for homes. 602–636–2201.

Kansas Wind Power, 13569 214th Rd., Holton, KS 66436: Catalog $4 ❖ Sun ovens, wind generators, composting toilets, tankless water heaters, air cooler, and other solar energy equipment and parts. 913–364–4407.

Midway Labs Inc., 2255 E. 75th St., Chicago, IL 60649: Free information ❖ Solar energy electricity-generating components. 312–933–2027.

Offline Independent Energy Systems, P.O. Box 231, North Fork, CA 93643: Catalog $3 ❖ Independent energy systems. 209–877–7080.

Photocomm Inc., 7681 E. Gray Rd., Scottsdale, AZ 85260: Catalog $5 ❖ Solar energy systems for homes, recreational vehicles, boats, and cabins. 800–223–9580.

Quad Energy, P.O. Box 690073, Houston, TX 77269: Catalog $3 ❖ Solar panels. 713–893–0313.

Radio Adventure, Box 50062, Provo, UT 84605: Catalog $1 ❖ Easy-to-install indoor and portable antennas, other equipment and accessories for radio amateurs, and solar power systems. 801–373–8425.

Real Goods, 966 Mazzoni St., Ukiah, CA 95482: Free catalog ❖ Solar energy components, solar educational toys, environmental books and games, and other alternative energy products. 800–762–7325.

Save Energy Company, 2410 Harrison St., San Francisco, CA 94110: Free catalog ❖ Energy-saving devices for homes and gardens. 800–326–2120.

Siemens, P.O. Box 6032, Camarillo, CA 93010: Free information ❖ Solar panels for energy systems. 800–ARCO-SOL.

Solar Depot, 61 Paul Dr., San Rafael, CA 94903: Catalog $6.50 ❖ Solar electric power systems, water heaters, electric and thermal systems, and other equipment. 415–499–1333.

Solar Electric Inc., 4901 Morena Blvd., Ste. 305, San Diego, CA 92117: Free information ❖ Solar panels and other equipment. 800–842–5678; 619–581–0051 (in CA).

Solar Electric Systems, Division Zomeworks Corporation, 1810 2nd St., Santa Fe, NM 87501: Free information ❖ Solar energy kits. 800–279–7697.

Solar Supply & Engineering, 39 Courtland, Rockford, MI 49341: Free information ❖ Solar energy generating equipment. 616–866–5111.

Solarex Corporation, 630 Solarex Ct., Frederick, MD 21701: Free catalog ❖ Solar panels, battery chargers, and other equipment. 301–698–4200.

Solectrogen, 61 Paul Dr., San Rafael, CA 94903: Free information ❖ Solar electric power systems. 415–499–1333.

The Sun Electric Company, P.O. Box 1499, Hamilton, MT 59840: Free catalog ❖ Solar energy equipment for recreational vehicles, cabins, or homes. 800–338–6844.

Sun-Porch Structures, P.O. Box 1353, Stamford, CT 06904: Catalog $2 ❖ Solar greenhouses. 203–324–0010.

Sunelco, P.O. Box 1499, Hamilton, MT 59840: Catalog $4.95 ❖ Solar modules, controllers, batteries, inverters, water pumps, and propane-operated appliances. 406–363–6924.

Sunglo Solar Greenhouses, 4441 26th Ave. West, Seattle, WA 98199: Free brochure ❖ Solar greenhouses and solariums. 800–647–0606; 206–284–8900 (in WA).

Sunlight Energy Corporation, 4411 W. Echo Ln., Glendale, AZ 85302: Free information ❖ Solar battery chargers. 800–338–1781.

Sunnyside Solar, RD 4, Box 808, Green River Rd., Brattleboro, VT 05301: Free information ❖ Hydropower equipment and

photovoltaic solar electric systems for homes. 802–257–1482.

United Solar Systems Corporation, 1100 W. Maple Rd., Troy, MI 48084: Free brochure ❖ Solar electric utility power modules and battery chargers. 800–843–3892; 313–362–4170 (in MI).

UtilityFree Batteries, 0050 Road 110, Glenwood Springs, CO 81601: Catalog $7.50 ❖ Renewable energy and energy-conservation products. 303–928–0846.

Vanner Incorporated, 4282 Reynolds Dr., Hilliard, OH 43026: Free information ❖ High-powered system for alternative energy power needs. 800–989–2718.

Wattsun Corporation, Array Technologies Inc., 614 2nd St. SW, P.O. Box 751, Albuquerque, NM 87103: Free information ❖ Solar trackers. 505–242–8024.

World Power Technologies Inc., 19 N. Lake Ave., Duluth, MN 55802: Free brochure ❖ Easy-to-install wind-operated electric generators and other solar equipment. 218–722–1492.

Zomeworks Corporation, P.O. Box 25805, Albuquerque, NM 87125: Free information ❖ Passive solar trackers and fixed racks for top-of-pole, side-of-pole, or roof/ground/wall mounts. 800–279–6342.

SOLARIUMS & SUN ROOMS

Arctic Glass & Window Outlet, Rt. 1, Hammond, WI 54015: Catalog $4 ❖ Sun rooms, windows, entryway and patio doors, and skylights. 800–428–9276.

Brady & Sun, 97 Webster St., Worcester, MA 01603: Free information ❖ Pre-assembled two-story wood frame solariums. 800–888–7177.

Creative Structures, 1765 Walnut Ln., Quakerstown, PA 18951: Catalog $1 ❖ Sun room and greenhouse kits. 215–538–2426.

Florian Greenhouses Inc., 64 Airport Rd., West Milford, NJ 07480: Catalog $5 ❖ Easy-to-build solariums for do-it-yourselfers. 800–FLORIAN.

Four Seasons Solar Products, 5005 Veterans Memorial Hwy., Holbrook, NY 11741: Free information ❖ Modular solarium kits. 800–368–7732.

Glasswalls Porch Enclosures, Mon-Ray Windows, 2720 Nevada Ave., Minneapolis, MN 55427: Free information ❖ Supplies for converting a screened porch or enclosing a patio into an all-season room. 800–544–3646; 612–544–3646 (in MN).

Habitat Solar Rooms, 123 Elm St., South Deerfield, MA 01373: Information $10 ❖ All-cedar kits for solar rooms. 800–992–0121.

Janco Greenhouses, 9390 Davis Ave., Laurel, MD 20707: Brochure $5 ❖ Solariums with optional variable pitch roofs. 800–323–6933.

Lindal Cedar Homes, P.O. Box 24426, Seattle, WA 98124: Catalog $15 ❖ Sun rooms. 800–426–0536.

Machin Designs by Amdega, P.O. Box 7, Glenview, IL 60025: Catalog $10 ❖ English-style conservatories constructed in either western red cedar or aluminum. 800–922–0110.

Progressive Building Products, P.O. Box 866, East Longmeadow, MA 01028: Catalog $5.95 ❖ Greenhouse and solarium components. 800–776–2534.

Skytech Systems, P.O. Box 763, Bloomsburg, PA 17815: Catalog $3 ❖ Free-standing and window greenhouses, solariums, and sunrooms. 717–752–1111.

Solar Additions Inc., Box 241, Greenwich, NY 12834: Information $5 ❖ Do-it-yourself kits and components for add-on solar rooms. 800–833–2300; 518–692–9673 (in NY).

Solarium Systems International, 333 N. Mead, Wichita, KS 67219: Free information ❖ Solariums with optional variable pitch roofs. 800–225–6423.

Southeastern Insulated Glass, 6477–B Peachtree Industrial Blvd., Atlanta, GA 30360: Free information ❖ Greenhouse and sun room kits, sliding glass doors, and skylights. 800–841–9842; 404–455–8838 (in GA).

Sturdi-Built Manufacturing Company, 11304 SW Boones Ferry Rd., Portland, OR 97219: Free catalog ❖ Greenhouses, cold frames, and sunrooms. 503–244–4100.

Sun Room Company, P.O. Box 301, Leola, PA 17540: Free information ❖ Sun rooms, window box greenhouses, skylights, window walls, and windows. 800–426–2737.

Sunbilt Solar Products by Sussman Inc., 109–10 180th St., Jamaica, NY 11433: Free information ❖ Easy-to-build sunrooms. 718–297–6040.

Sunshine Rooms Inc., Box 4627, Wichita, KS 67204: Free information ❖ Add-on and free-standing sun rooms. 800–222–1598.

Sunspot Inc., 5030 40th Ave., Hudsonville, MI 49426: Free information ❖ Wood frame solariums. 616–669–9400.

Under Glass Manufacturing Corporation, P.O. Box 323, Wappingers Falls, NY 12590: Catalog $3 ❖ Greenhouses and solariums. 914–298–0645.

Window Quilt, P.O. Box 975, Brattleboro, VT 05362: Information $1 ❖ Sun rooms. 800–257–4501.

SPELEOLOGY (CAVE EXPLORATION)

Bent Arrow Caving Supply, 7888 W. Eller Rd., Bloomington, IN 47401: Free information with long SASE ❖ Equipment and supplies for cavers. 812–825–7990.

Bob & Bob Enterprises, P.O. Box 441, Lewisburg, WV 24901: Free information ❖ Gear and safety equipment for cavers. 304–772–5049.

W. Born & Associates, 2438 Blacklick-Eastern Rd., Millersport, OH 43046: Free information with long SASE ❖ Equipment and supplies for cavers. 614–467–2676.

Cadwell Caving Supplies, 2267 Blackrock Rd., Plainfield, IN 46168: Free information with long SASE ❖ Equipment and supplies for cavers. 317–839–6996.

Inner Mountain Outfitters, 102 Travis Cir., Seaford, VA 23696: Free catalog ❖ Equipment and supplies for cavers. 804–898–2809.

Pathfinder Sporting Goods, 6932 E. 1st St., P.O. Box 30670, Tucson, AZ 85751: Free information with long SASE ❖ Equipment and supplies for cavers. 602–327–1952.

Pigeon Mountain Industries, P.O. Box 803, Lafayette, GA 30728: Free information ❖ Gear and supplies for cavers. 800–282–7673; 404–764–1437 (in GA).

Quest Outdoors, 128 Breckenridge Ln., Louisville, KY 40207: Free information with long SASE ❖ Equipment and supplies for cavers. 502–893–5746.

Speleoshoppe, P.O. Box 297, Fairdale, KY 40118: Free information ❖ Equipment and supplies for cavers. 800–626–5877.

Summit Rescue Group, 1515 NE White Dr., Lee's Summit, MO 64063: Free information with long SASE ❖ Equipment and supplies for cavers. 314–445–5686.

J.E. Weinel Inc., P.O. Box 203, Valencia, PA 16059: Free information with long SASE ❖ Equipment and supplies for cavers. 800–346–7673; 412–898–2335 (in PA).

SPINNING WHEELS & LOOMS

AVL Looms, 601 Orange St., Chico, CA 95928: Catalog $2 ❖ Looms and supplies. 800–626–9615; 916–893–4915 (in CA).

Ayotte's Designery, P.O. Box 287, Center Sandwich, NH 03227: Free information with long SASE ❖ Spinning and weaving supplies. 603–284–6915.

Braid-Aid, 466 Washington St., Pembroke, MA 02359: Catalog $4 ❖ Braided rug kits, braiding supplies, spinning and weaving accessories, and wool by the pound or yard. 617–826–2560.

Crystal Palace Yarns, 3006 San Pablo Ave., Berkeley, CA 94702: Free brochure ❖ Yarns, natural fibers, and spinning wheels.

Dundas Loom Company, P.O. Box 7522, Missoula, MT 59807: Free information ❖ Harness looms and treadle stands. 406–728–3050.

Edgemont Yarn Services, P.O. Box 205, Washington, KY 41096: Free brochure ❖ Weaving supplies, 2– and 4–harness looms, tabletop looms, loom parts, and rug-making supplies. 606–759–7614.

F.A. Edmunds Company, 6111 S. Sayre, Chicago, IL 60638: Free information with long SASE ❖ Scroll frames, quilting hoops and frames, craft stands, and stretcher bars.

Fiber Studio, 9 Foster Hill Rd., Box 637, Heniker, NH 03242: Spinning fibers catalog $1; yarn samples $4; equipment catalog $1 ❖ Spinning, weaving, and knitting equipment; cotton, mohair, wool, alpaca, silk, linen yarns; and spinning fibers. 603–428–7830.

Fireside Fiberarts, P.O. Box 1195, Port Townsend, WA 98368: Brochure $3 ❖ Portable cantilever tapestry looms and accessories. 206–385–7505.

Gilmore Looms, 1032 N. Broadway, Stockton, CA 95205: Free catalog ❖ Looms and accessories. 209–463–1545.

Glimakra Looms & Yarns Inc., 1338 Ross St., Petaluma, CA 94954: Catalog $2.50 ❖ Weaving equipment, looms, yarns, and lace-making equipment. 800–289–9276; 707–762–3362 (in CA).

Harrisville Designs, Center Village, Box 806, Harrisville, NH 03450: Catalog $10 ❖ Yarns and looms. 603–827–3333.

J-Made Looms, P.O. Box 452, Oregon City, OR 97045: Catalog $2 ❖ Looms in 45–, 60–, and 72–inch models. 503–631–3973.

K's Creations, P.O. Box 161446, Austin, TX 78746: Free information ❖ Adjustable, interchangeable lap frames. 512–327–3769.

Lacis, 3163 Adeline St., Berkeley, CA 94703: Catalog $4 ❖ Hairpin lace looms. 510–843–7178.

Leesburg Looms & Supply, 201 N. Cherry St., Van Wert, OH 45891: Free catalog ❖ Easy-to-operate 2– and 4–harness looms. 419–238–2738.

Louët Sales, P.O. Box 267, Ogdensburg, NY 13669: Catalog $2 ❖ Books, dyestuffs, yarns and fibers, and spinning, weaving, carding, felting, and lace-making equipment. 613–925–4502.

Macomber Looms, P.O. Box 186, York, ME 03909: Catalog $3 ❖ Looms. 207–363–2808.

Mannings Creative Crafts, P.O. Box 687, East Berlin, PA 17316: Catalog $1 ❖ Spinning wheels and looms, yarns and spinning fibers, books, and dyes and mordants. 717–624–2223.

Mountain Loom Company, P.O. Box 1107, Castle Rock, WA 98611: Free brochure ❖ Sampler, table, pique, tapestry, and floor looms. 800–238–0296; 360–295–3856 (in WA).

Nasco, 901 Janesville Ave., Fort Atkinson, WI 53538: Free catalog ❖ Weaving supplies, looms, tools, yarns, and other needle craft accessories. 800–558–9595.

Norwood Looms, P.O. Box 167, Freemont, MI 49412: Brochure $1 ❖ Looms, quilting hoops, and frames. 616–924–3901.

Pendleton Shop, Jordan Rd., P.O. Box 233, Sedona, AZ 86336: Catalog $1 ❖ Looms and weaving supplies. 602–282–3671.

Rio Grande Weaver's Supply, 216 Pueblo Norte, Taos, NM 87571: Catalog $1 ❖ Spinning wheels, looms, and loom kits; hand-dyed rug, tapestry, and clothing yarns; and other yarns, dyes, fleeces, books, and videos. 505–758–0433.

River Farm, Rt. 1, P.O. Box 471, Fulks Run, VA 22830: Catalog $1 ❖ Spinning wheels, looms, and American fleece for spinning. 800–USA–WOOL.

Schacht Spindle Company Inc., 6101 Ben Pl., Boulder, CO 80301: Catalog $2.50 ❖ Looms and accessories. 800–228–2553.

School Products Company Inc., 1201 Broadway, New York, NY 10001: Free information ❖ Spinning wheels and accessories. 212–679–3516.

Shannock Tapestry Looms, 10402 NW 11th Ave., Vancouver, WA 98685: Free information ❖ Weaving supplies and tapestry looms with roller beams. 206–573–7264.

Bonnie Triola, 343 E. Gore Rd., Erie, PA 16509: Information $10 ❖ Natural fibers, synthetics, blends, discontinued designer yarns, and other cone and stock yarns. 814–825–7821.

The Weaver's Loft, 308 S. Pennsylvania Ave., Centre Hali, PA 16828: Free information ❖ Knitting, weaving, and spinning supplies and yarns. 814–364–1433.

Weavers' Store, 11 S. 9th St., Columbia, MO 65201: Catalog $2 ❖ Looms, spinning wheels, yarns, and mill ends. 314–442–5413.

Weaving Works, 4717 Brooklyn Ave. NE, Seattle, WA 98105: Catalog $4.50 ❖ Looms, spinning wheels, hand and machine knitting supplies, yarns, and books. 206–524–1221.

Webbs, 18 Kellogg Ave., P.O. Box 349, Amherst, MA 01004: Price list $2 ❖ Yarns for spinning and weaving, looms, spinning wheels, drum carders, and knitting machines. 413–253–2580.

Wool Room, RR 2, Brewster, NY 10509: Free brochure with long SASE ❖ Spinning fibers, weaving yarns, and equipment. 914–241–1910.

SPORTS & NON-SPORTS CARDS

Non-Sports Cards

Johnny Adams Jr., Box 8491, Green Bay, WI 54308: Free information with long SASE ❖ Non-sports and sports cards. 800–326–9991.

Arlington Card, 140 Gansett Ave., Cranston, RI 02910: Free information with long SASE ❖ Non-sports cards collectibles and paper wrappers. 401–942–3188.

B & J Sports Cards, Box 693, Skokie, IL 60076: Free information with long SASE ❖ Baseball, football, basketball, soccer, and non-sports card mint sets, traded and updated sets, and umpire sets. 708–699–9770.

Barrington Square, 2332 W. Higgins Rd., Hoffman Estates, IL 60195: Free information ❖ Non-sports cards, coins, and comics. 708–882–7080.

Champion Sports Collectables Inc., 150 E. Santa Clara, Arcadia, CA 91006: Free information ❖ Autographed sports memorabilia, sports and non-sports cards, and supplies. 818–574–5500.

Chattanooga Coin Company, P.O. Box 80158, Chattanooga, TN 37414: Free information ❖ Non-sports cards. 800–444–2646.

Georgetown Card Exchange, P.O. Box 11572, Philadelphia, PA 19116: Free price list ❖ Non-sports comic cards and football, hockey, baseball, basketball, and other sports cards. 215–698–0366.

Henri LaBelle, 1162 Lesage St., P.O. Box 561, Prevost, Quebec, Canada J0R 1T0: Free information with long SASE ❖ Non-sports cards collectibles. 514–224–2813.

Dick Millerd Sports Cards, North 10020 Buelow Rd., Clintonville, WI 54929: Free information with long SASE ❖ Non-sports cards and baseball, football, hockey, basketball and other single sports cards and sets. 615–823–4827.

North Country Toys, P.O. Box 1100, Warren, ME 04864: Free information ❖ Non-sports cards, action figures, models, comics, militaria, and automotive-theme toys. 207–273–4066.

Paul & Judy's Coins & Cards, P.O. Box 409, Arthur, IL 61911: Free information with long SASE ❖ Non-sports cards. 217–543–3366.

Promotions in Motion Inc., 22 East Mall, Plainview, NY 11803: Free information with long SASE ❖ Sports and non-sports cards. 516–249–9300.

T.J.'s Comics & Cards & Supplies, Lloyds Shopping Center, 330 Rt. 211 East, Middletown, NY 10940: Free information ❖ Comic books, sports and non-sports cards, and hobby supplies. 800–848–1482.

Unique Dist., 110 Denton Ave., New Hyde Park, NY 11040: Free information ❖ Sports and non-sports cards and comics. 800–294–5901; 516–294–5900 (in NY).

Wex Rex Records & Collectibles, P.O. Box 702, Hudson, MA 01749: Catalog $3 ❖ Non-sports cards, movie and TV show character toys, and other collectibles. 508–229–2662.

Sports Cards

Johnny Adams Jr., Box 8491, Green Bay, WI 54308: Free information with long SASE ❖ Sports and non-sports cards. 800–326–9991.

ASE Cards, P.O. Box 178, Tujunga, CA 91043: Free information with long SASE ❖ Sets, boxes, and single cards. 818–353–5864.

B & E Collectibles Inc., 12 Marble Ave., Thornwood, NY 10594: Free information ❖ Hard-to-find sports card singles. 914–769–1304.

B & J Sports Cards, Box 693, Skokie, IL 60076: Free information with long SASE ❖ Baseball, football, basketball, soccer, and non-sports card mint sets, traded and updated sets, and umpire sets. 708–699–9770.

Ball Four Cards, 4732 N. Royal Atlanta Dr., Tucker, GA 30084: Free information ❖ Archival and storage supplies. 404–621–0377.

Ball Park Heroes, 1531 J St., Bedford, IN 47421: Free information with long SASE ❖ Hard-to-find sports card singles and sets. 812–275–2717.

Barnetts Sports Cards, P.O. Box 964, Hartville, OH 44632: Free information with long SASE ❖ Hard-to-find sports card singles and sets. 216–877–4270.

Baseball Barons Sportscards, 1295 Boardman Canfield Rd., Boardman, OH 44512: Free information ❖ Basketball, baseball, and hockey sports cards. 800–437–7814.

Baseball Card Corner, Duffy Square, 10756 Montgomery Rd., Cincinnati, OH 45242: Free information ❖ Sports cards. 513–489–5676.

Baseball Card Kingdom, 323 Jersey St., Harrison, NJ 07029: Free information with long SASE ❖ Baseball card sets, minor league sets, sports impression figurines, Star Company platinum and gold edition sets, and other memorabilia. 201–481–9630.

Baseball Card World, P.O. Box 970, Anderson, IN 46015: Free information with long SASE ❖ Sports card hobby supplies. 800–433–4229.

Best Comics Distribution Center, 252–01 Northern Blvd., Little Neck, NY 11362: Free information ❖ Comic books, original comic art, action figures, collector supplies, and trading cards. 800–966–2099; 718–279–2099 (in NY).

Bill's Cards & Supplies, 25 N. Colonial Dr., Hagerstown, MD 21742: Free information

with long SASE ❖ Sports cards and hobby supplies. 301–797–2992.

Bradford's Sportscards, Box 22455, Minneapolis, MN 55422: Free information with long SASE ❖ Sports cards. 612–533–4804.

Brewart Coins & Stamps, 403 W. Katella, Anaheim, CA 92802: Free information with long SASE ❖ Rare and hard-to-find sports card singles and sets. 714–533–2521.

Brigandi Coin Company, 60 W. 44th St., New York, NY 10036: Free information with long SASE ❖ Sports cards. 800–221–2128.

Broadway Rick's Strike Zone, 1840 N. Federal Hwy., Boynton Beach, FL 33435: Free information with long SASE ❖ Autographed sports memorabilia, sports cards, and other collectibles. 800–344–9103; 407–364–0453 (in FL).

Can-Am Card Company, P.O. Box 345, Ganges, British Columbia, Canada V0S 1E0: Free information with long SASE ❖ Vintage sports cards. 604–537–9460.

Card Collectors Company, 105 W. 77th St., New York, NY 10024: Catalog $2 ❖ Sports cards and other collectibles. 212–873–6999.

Cardboard Gold Inc., 1855 Weinig St., Statesville, NC 28677: Free catalog ❖ Sports cards collecting supplies. 704–871–8000.

Cee-Jay Sports Card Company, Sunset Industrial Park, 52 20th St., Brooklyn, NY 11232: Free information with long SASE ❖ Hard-to-find football, basketball, hockey, golf, and tennis sports card singles and sets. 718–83–CJAY6.

Champion Sports, 702 W. Las Tunas, San Gabriel, CA 91776: Free information ❖ Sports card hobby supplies. 818–570–1106.

Champion Sports Collectables Inc., 150 E. Santa Clara, Arcadia, CA 91006: Free information ❖ Autographed sports memorabilia, sports and non-sports cards, and supplies. 818–574–5500.

Chicago Sports Cards Ltd., P.O. Box 702, Wheeling, IL 60090: Free information with long SASE ❖ Sports cards. 708–215–7981.

Classic Cards, 41 Long Acre Dr., Huntington, NY 11743: Free information with long SASE ❖ Sports card singles and sets. 516–424–5792.

Classic Treasures, 1 Charing Cross Rd., Charleston, SC 29407: Free information with long SASE ❖ Sports cards. 803–571–3051.

Colorado Cards, P.O. Box 2814, Evergreen, CO 80439: Free information with long SASE ❖ Baseball, football, and basketball cards. 303–670–0450.

Coogans Bluff, P.O. Box 291027, Davie, FL 33329: Free information with long SASE ❖ Baseball and football cards. 305–384–8935.

Dolloff, 2800 Lafayette Rd., White Birch Plaza, Portsmouth, NH 03801: Free information with long SASE ❖ Basketball, boxing, football, swimming, track and field, and wrestling sports cards. 603–431–4010.

Doubleheaders, 2593 Wexford-Bayne Rd., Ste. 300, Sewickley, PA 15143: Free catalog with six 1st class stamps ❖ Sports cards. 412–934–5380.

Durta Enterprises, 500 E. Ridge Rd., Unit E, Griffith, IN 46319: Free information with long SASE ❖ Archival and storage supplies, ball cubes, and ball holders. 800–451–0096; 219–838–5510 (in IN).

Empire State Sports Memorabilia & Collectibles Inc., 331 Cochran Pl., Valley Stream, NY 11581: Free information ❖ Baseball and other sports cards, autographs, and other memorabilia. 516–791–9091.

Flip Cards & Supplies, 181 Rt. 46 West, Lodi, NJ 07844: Free information ❖ Sports card collecting supplies. 800–WOW-FLIP; 201–472–1138 (in NJ).

Four Base Hits, 2100 Middle Country Rd., P.O. Box 137, Centereach, NY 11720: Free information with long SASE ❖ Sports cards. 516–981–3286.

Georgetown Card Exchange, P.O. Box 11572, Philadelphia, PA 19116: Free price list ❖ Non-sports comic cards and football, hockey, baseball, basketball, and other sports cards. 215–698–0366.

Great American Coins, P.O. Box 215, Woodbury, NY 11797: Free information with long SASE ❖ Baseball, basketball, hockey, and other sports cards. 516–334–0400.

Gerry Guenther, 7521 Patchin Rd., Pardeeville, WI 53954: Free information ❖ Superstar sports cards. 608–742–2201.

Hall's Nostalgia, 9 Mystic St., P.O. Box 408, Arlington, MA 02174: Free information ❖ Sports cards. 800–367–4255; 617–646–7757 (in MA).

Bruce Harris Sportscards, 1291 Steeple Run Dr., Lawrenceville, GA 30243: Free information ❖ Sports cards. 404–822–0988.

Bill Henderson's Cards, 2320 Ruger Ave., Janesville, WI 53545: Free information with long SASE ❖ Rare and hard-to-find sports card singles and sets. 608–755–0922.

Hit & Run Sportscard Superstore, 4865 S. Pecos, Las Vegas, NV 89121: Free information with long SASE ❖ Hard-to-find sports cards. 800–998–6786.

Hobby Supplies, P.O. Box 372, Marlboro, NJ 07746: Free information with long SASE ❖ Sports card collecting supplies. 908–780–3689.

Hot Card USA, 1215 Harrison Ave., Kearny, NJ 07032: Free information with long SASE ❖ Hard-to-find sports cards. 201–998–1062.

Howard's Sports Collectibles, 128 E. Main St., P.O. Box 84, Leipsic, OH 45856: Catalog $5 ❖ Baseball and football cards in sets or singles. 800–457–9974.

J & J Sports Cards, 420 S. Howes, Ste. 202–A, Fort Collins, CO 80521: Free catalog ❖ All-star sports cards. 303–484–7840.

Jake's House of Cards, 40 Freeway Dr., Cranston, RI 02920: Free information with long SASE ❖ Baseball cards, from 1948 to 1979, and other sports cards. 800–892–0024.

Klassy Kollectibles Inc., 137 White Horse Pike, Berlin, NJ 08009: Free information with long SASE ❖ Sports cards singles and sets. 609–767–0250.

Robert Klevens, 12260 NW 29th Pl., Sunrise, FL 33323: Free information with long SASE ❖ Japanese baseball cards. 305–741–6025.

Koinz & Kardz-Madison, 2146 E. Johnson St., Madison, WI 53704: Free information with long SASE ❖ Rare and hard-to-find sports card singles and sets. 608–249–6669.

Mid-Atlantic Sports Cards, 22 S. Morton Ave., Morton, PA 19070: Free information with long SASE ❖ Posters and hard-to-find sports card singles and sets. 215–544–2171.

Dick Millerd Sports Cards, North 10020 Buelow Rd., Clintonville, WI 54929: Free information with long SASE ❖ Baseball, football, hockey, basketball, other single cards and sets, and non-sports cards. 615–823–4827.

The Minnesota Connection, 17773 Kenwood Trail, Lakeville, MN 55044: Free information with long SASE ❖ Baseball, football, basketball, and hockey sports cards. 612–892–0406.

Michael Moretto, P.O. Box 960, Highland Lakes, NJ 07422: Free information ❖ Hard-to-find sports card singles, sets, and limited editions. 201–764–4682.

Steve Myland, 2530 W. Buckeye Rd., Phoenix, AZ 85009: Free information ❖ Hard-to-find sports card singles and sets. 602–272–8007.

P.M. Collectibles, P.O. Box 2461, Patchogue, NY 11772: Free information with long SASE ❖ Baseball cards. 516–758–7672.

Paul & Judy's Coins & Cards, P.O. Box 409, Arthur, IL 61911: Free information with long SASE ❖ Hard-to-find non-sports and sports cards. 217–543–3366.

Perfect Image Sports Cards, 12003 Audubon Ave., Philadelphia, PA 19116: Free information ❖ Baseball, boxing, basketball, football, golf, and hockey sports cards. 800–683–1789.

Promotions in Motion Inc., 22 East Mall, Plainview, NY 11803: Free information with long SASE ❖ Sports and non-sports cards. 516–249–9300.

Quality Baseball Cards Inc., 106 Despatch Dr., East Rochester, NY 14445: Free information ❖ Hard-to-find sports card singles and sets. 800–HOBBY-88; 716–248–3510 (in NY).

Don Roberts Sales, 1221 Caledonia St., La Crosse, WI 54603: Free information with long SASE ❖ Sports card singles and sets. 608–784–3755.

Rotman Collectibles, 4 Brussels St., Worcester, MA 01610: Free information ❖ Sports cards and storage supplies. 508–791–6710.

St. Louis Baseball Cards, 5456 Chatfield, St. Louis, MO 63129: Free information ❖ Sports card sets, uniforms, press pins, autographs, advertising pieces, and baseball memorabilia. 314–892–4737.

San Diego Sports Collectibles, 659 Fashion Valley, San Diego, CA 92108: Catalog $2 ❖ Hard-to-find sports card singles, sets, and limited editions. 800–227–0483.

The Score Board Inc., 1951 Old Cuthbert Rd., Cherry Hill, NJ 08034: Free information ❖ Sports card sets, star cards prior to 1970, commemorative cards prior to 1942, and sports memorabilia. 800–327–4145; 609–354–8011 (in NJ).

Seventh Inning Stretch, 1175 Avocado Ave., Ste. 103, El Cajon, CA 92020: Free

information with long SASE ❖ Sports cards. 619–441–2700.

The Sports Alley, 15545 E. Whittier Blvd., Whittier, CA 90603: Free information with long SASE ❖ Hard-to-find sports cards, cancelled checks by sports greats, autographed pictures, world series programs, photographs, and other memorabilia. 310–947–7383.

Sports Collectibles Inc., P.O. Box 11171, Chattanooga, TN 37401: Catalog $1 ❖ Sports cards, autographed baseballs, bats, and color photos. 615–265–9366.

Sports Heroes, 550 Kinderkamack Rd., Oradell, NJ 07649: Free information with long SASE ❖ Vintage and unique sports memorabilia. 800–233–4000; 201–262–8020 (in NJ).

SportsCards Plus, 28221 Crown Valley Pkwy., Laguna Niguel, CA 92677: Free information ❖ Sports cards, autographs, and other sports memorabilia. 800–350–2273.

Starland Collector's Gallery, P.O. Box 622, Los Olivos, CA 93441: Catalog $2.50 ❖ Sports cards, movie posters, original comic art, and hard-to-find movies. 805–686–5122.

T.C. Card Company, Box 30911, Palm Beach Gardens, FL 33420: Free information with long SASE ❖ Sports card singles, sets, and hard-to-find items. 407–624–1909.

T.J.'s Comics & Cards & Supplies, Lloyds Shopping Center, 330 Rt. 211 East, Middletown, NY 10940: Free information ❖ Comic books, sports and non-sports cards, and hobby supplies. 800–848–1482.

Ed Taylor's Baseball Dreams, 195 Wave Ave., Pismo Beach, CA 93449: Free information with long SASE ❖ Sports cards and other memorabilia. 805–773–2744.

Texas Sportcard Company, 2816 Center St., Deer Park, TX 77536: Free information with long SASE ❖ Hard-to-find sports card singles and sets. 713–476–9964.

U.S. Gerslyn Ltd., 1100 Port Washington Blvd., Port Washington, NY 11050: Free brochure ❖ Sports card hobby supplies. 516–944–3553.

Unique Dist., 110 Denton Ave., New Hyde Park, NY 11040: Free information ❖ Sports and non-sports cards and comics. 800–294–5901; 516–294–5900 (in NY).

Brian Wallos & Company, 95 Newfield Ave., Edison, NJ 08837: Free information with long SASE ❖ Hard-to-find sports card singles and sets. 908–417–9757.

Gary Walter Baseball Cards, 561 River Terrace, Toms River, NJ 08755: Free information with long SASE ❖ Baseball cards. 908–286–9007.

West Coast Sports Cards Inc., 1808 S. 320th, Federal Way, WA 98003: Free information with long SASE ❖ Rare and hard-to-find sports card singles and sets. 206–941–1986.

Kit Young Sportscards, 11535 Sorrento Valley Rd., Ste. 403, San Diego, CA 92121: Catalog $2 ❖ Hard-to-find sports card singles and sets. 619–259–1300.

SQUARE DANCING
Amplifiers & Microphones

Ashton Electronics, P.O. Box 5398, San Jose, CA 95150: Free information ❖ Sound equipment. 408–995–6544.

Grand Travel Square Dance Shop, P.O. Box 690092, Tulsa, OK 74169: Free catalog ❖ Clothing and sound equipment.

Hilton Audio Products, 1033–E Shary Cir., Concord, CA 94518: Free information ❖ Sound equipment and cue cards for callers. 510–682–8390.

Merrbach Record Service, 323 W. 14th St., Houston, TX 77008: Free information ❖ Records, tape recorders, tapes, wireless microphones, cassette decks, and sound equipment. 713–862–7077.

Random Sound Inc., 7317 Harriet Ave. South, Minneapolis, MN 55423: Free catalog ❖ Sound equipment. 512–869–9501.

Badges & Buckles

Badge Holders Inc., 24813 Broadmore Ave., Hayward, CA 94544: Free brochure ❖ Badge holders. 510–783–8724.

Fawcett's Square Dance Shop, 412 W. Sam Houston, Pharr, TX 78577: Free information ❖ Engraved and hot-stamped badges. 512–787–1116.

H & R Badge & Stamp Company, 2585 Mock Rd., Columbus, OH 43219: Free catalog ❖ In-stock and custom badges and rubber stamps. 614–471–3735.

KA-MO Engravers, P.O. Box 30337, Albuquerque, NM 87190: Free catalog ❖ Badges for square and round dancers. 800–352–5266; 505–883–4963 (in NM).

J.R. Kush & Company, 7623 Hesperia St., Reseda, CA 91335: Free information ❖ Handcrafted belt buckles for round dancers and square dancers. 818–344–9671.

Micro Plastics, P.O. Box 847, Rifle, CO 81650: Free information ❖ Club badges. 303–625–1718.

Pauly's, P.O. Box 72, Wausau, WI 54402: Free information ❖ Engraved and jeweled badges. 715–845–3979.

Videos

Gold Star Video Productions, P.O. Box 1057, Sisters, OR 97759: Free information ❖ Video tapes on how-to square or round dance. 800–87–HINGE; 503–549–4302 (in OR).

Clothing & Shoes

Andes S/D & Western Apparel, 2109 Liberty Rd., Eldersburg, MD 21784: Catalog $4 (refundable) ❖ Clothing for square dancers. 410–795–0808.

Bev's Square Dance & Western Wear, 112 Depot St., Auburn, IN 46706: Free information ❖ Clothing for square dancers. 219–925–3818.

Carol's Country Corner S/D, 21932 Schoenborn St., Canoga Park, CA 91304: Free information ❖ Clothing for square dancers. 818–347–1207.

The Catchall, 1813 9th St., Wichita Falls, TX 76301: Free catalog ❖ Lace-trimmed petticoats and other clothing. 817–766–1612.

Circle W Square Dance Fashions, Rt. 1, Box 313, Sneads Ferry, NC 28460: Free information ❖ Clothing for square dancers. 910–327–3337.

Circles & Squares Inc., 9047 Garland Rd., Dallas, TX 75218: Free information ❖ Clothing for square dancers. 214–326–8684.

Doris Crystal Magic Petticoats, 8331 Pinecrest Dr., Redwood Valley, CA 95470: Free information ❖ Petticoats for square and round dancers. 800–468–6423; 707–485–7448 (in CA).

Dorothy's Square Dance Shop Inc., 3300 Strong Ave., P.O. Box 6004, Kansas City, KS 66106: Free catalog ❖ Clothing for square dancers. 913–262–4240.

Fabian's Western Wear, 18th & Jefferson, Lewisburg, PA 17837: Free information ❖ Square dancer's clothing. 717–523–6280.

Fawcett's Square Dance Shop, 412 W. Sam Houston, Pharr, TX 78577: Free information

❖ Clothing for square dancers. 512–787–1116.

Grand Travel Square Dance Shop, P.O. Box 690092, Tulsa, OK 74169: Free catalog ❖ Clothing and sound equipment for square dancers.

Janet's Square Dance Shoppe, Rt. 9, Box 997, Lake Charles, LA 70605: Free information ❖ Clothing for square dancers. 318–855–4470.

L/W Western Apparel, Rt. 4, Box 19, Elkton, VA 22827: Free information ❖ Clothing for square dancers. 703–298–8676.

M & H Western Fashions, 13002 Lorain Ave., Cleveland, OH 44111: Free information ❖ Clothing for square dancers. 216–671–5165.

Oxbow Square Dance Shop, 8650 49th St. North, Pinellas Park, FL 34666: Free information ❖ Clothing for square dancers. 813–541–5700.

Palomino Square Dance Service, 1050 Toulon Dr., Marion, OH 43302: Free information ❖ Clothing for square dancers. 614–389–5919.

Rochester Shoe Stores, 8186 Pembroke Dr., Manlius, NY 13104: Free information ❖ Square and round dancing shoes. 800–688–4325.

Ruthad Inc., 8869 Avis, Detroit, MI 48209: Free information ❖ Pettipants and single, double, or triple layer petticoats. 313–841–0586.

Sewing Specialties, 7429 4th Ave. South, Richfield, MN 55423: Free brochure ❖ Easy-to-finish petticoat kits. 800–338–3289.

Shirley's S/D Shoppe, Rt. 9–D, Box 423, Hughsonville, NY 12537: Catalog $1 ❖ Patterns, ready-to-wear clothing, petticoats, pantalettes, and other clothing for square dancers. 914–297–8504.

Meg Simkins, 119 Allen St., Hampden, MA 01036: Catalog $1 (refundable) ❖ Clothing for square dancers. 413–566–3349.

Sky Ranch West & S/D Store, 109–111 S. Main St., Central Square, NY 13036: Catalog $1 (refundable) ❖ Western and square dancing clothing. 315–668–2644.

Skyline Square Dance Shop, 9 Skyline Dr., Mankato, MN 56001: Free information ❖ Clothing for square dancers. 507–345–1900.

Nita Smith, 2011 S. College Ave., Bryan, TX 77801: Free catalog ❖ Clothing for square dancers. 409–822–2337.

Square Dance & Western Wear Fashions Inc., 637 E. 47th St., Wichita, KS 67216: Free information ❖ Clothing and shoes. 316–522–6670.

Square Dance Attire, 7215 W. Irving Park Rd., Chicago, IL 60634: Free information ❖ Clothing for square dancers. 312–589–9220.

Steppin Out, P.O. Box 398, Humble, TX 77347: Free information ❖ Square and round dancing petticoats and dresses. 713–540–3557.

Swing Thru, RD 1, Box 428, Cresco, PA 18326: Notions and badge catalog $2; clothing catalog $2 ❖ Clothing, notions, and novelties for square dancers. 717–595–7474.

Western Squares, 6820 Gravois, St. Louis, MO 63116: Catalog $1 (refundable) ❖ Women's clothing for square dancing. 314–353–7230.

Wheel & Deal Shop Inc., Rt. 115, Yarmouth Rd., Gray, ME 04039: Catalog $1 (refundable) ❖ Clothing for square dancers. 207–657–3412.

Records

A & S Record Shop, 321 Laurie Ln., Warner Robins, GA 31088: Free information ❖ Square dancing records. 912–922–7510.

Astec Distributors, 16 Water St., Unit 5, Marlborough, NH 03455: Free information ❖ Square dancing records. 603–876–3636.

Chaparral Records Inc., 1425 Oakhill Dr., Plano, TX 75075: Free catalog ❖ Square dancing records.

Cimarron Record Company, 4021 NW 61st, Oklahoma City, OK 73112: Free information ❖ Records for square dancing.

Clendenin Enterprises, 7915 N. Clarendon, Portland, OR 97203: Free information ❖ Records for square dancing. 503–285–7431.

DJ Records, 3925 N. Tollhouse, Fresno, CA 93726: Free catalog ❖ Square dancing records. 209–227–2764.

Eagle Enterprises, 11220 Florissant St., Ste. 169, Florissant, MO 63032: Free information ❖ Square dancing records. 314–741–7799.

Eddie's & Bobbie's Records, 1835 S. Buckner Blvd., Dallas, TX 75217: Free information ❖ Square dancing records. 214–398–7508.

4–BAR-B Records Inc., Box 7–11, Macks Creek, MO 65786: Free list ❖ Square dancing records. 314–363–5432.

Kip Garvey Enterprises, P.O. Box 8045, Fremont, CA 94537: Free information ❖ Square dancing records. 510–792–7099.

Hanhurst's Record Service, P.O. Box 50, Marlborough, NH 03455: Free information ❖ Square dancing records. 800–445–7398.

Hi Hat Dance Records, 3925 N. Tollhouse, Fresno, CA 93726: Free catalog ❖ Square dancing records. 209–227–2764.

Kalox-Belco-Longhorn, 2832 Live Oak Dr., Mesquite, TX 75150: Free information ❖ Records for square dancing. 214–270–0616.

Lightning Records, P.O. Box 748, Oxford, NC 27565: Free information ❖ Square dancing music. 919–693–4852.

Lou Mac & Mar-Let Records, P.O. Box 2406, Muscle Shoals, AL 35661: Free information ❖ Square dancing music. 205–383–7585.

Master Record Service Mail Order, P.O. Box 82716, Phoenix, AZ 85071: Free information ❖ Records for square, round, and ballroom dancing. 602–993–9932.

Merrbach Record Service, 323 W. 14th St., Houston, TX 77008: Free information ❖ Records, tape recorders, tapes, wireless microphones, cassette decks, and sound equipment. 713–862–7077.

Palomino Square Dance Service, 1050 Toulon Dr., Marion, OH 43302: Free information ❖ Records for square, round, and folk dancing, and solo dancing and clogging. 614–389–5919.

Red Boot Productions Inc., Rt. 8, College Hills, Box 28, Crest Dr., Greeneville, TN 37743: Free information ❖ Square dancing records. 615–638–7784.

Reeves Records Inc., 1835 S. Buckner, P.O. Box 17668, Dallas, TX 75217: Free information ❖ Record cases, books and manuals, plastic record jackets, sound equipment, and square, round, and clogging dancing records. 214–398–7508.

Silver Sounds Recordings, P.O. Box 229, Glastonbury, CT 06033: Free information ❖ Records for square dancing. 203–633–0370.

Square Dance Record Shop, 957 Sheridan Blvd., Denver, CO 80214: Free information ❖ Square dancing records. 303–238–4810.

Square Dancetime Records, P.O. Box 3055, Yuba City, CA 95992: Free information ❖ Records for square dancing. 916–673–1120.

Sundance Distributors, 16809 Boxbu Ave., Bellflower, CA 90706: Free information ❖ Square dancing records. 310–925–4692.

Thunderbird Record Company, Rt. 1, Thompson School Rd., Corryton, TN 37721: Free information ❖ Square dancing music and records. 615–687–4478.

TNT Records, RFD 2, Rt. 7, St. Albans, VT 05478: Free information ❖ Square and round dancing music. 802–524–9424.

Wagon Wheel Records, 8459 Edmaru Ave., Whittier, CA 90605: Free information ❖ Records for square dancing. 310–693–6976.

STAINED GLASS CRAFTING

Ameriglas, Box 27668, Omaha, NE 68127: Catalog $1 ❖ Stained glass crafting supplies, tools, and kits.

Art Glass House Inc., 3445 N. Hwy. 1, Cocoa, FL 32926: Free catalog ❖ Stained glass supplies. 800–525–8009; 407–631–4477 (in FL).

Atlas Art & Stained Glass, P.O. Box 76084, Oklahoma City, OK 73147: Catalog $3 ❖ Kaleidoscopes, frames, lamp bases, and art and craft, stained glass, jewelry-making, and foil crafting supplies. 405–946–1230.

Big M Stained Glass, 3201 4th Ave., Seattle, WA 98134: Catalog $5 ❖ Stained glass supplies. 800–426–8307; 206–624–3962 (in WA).

Cline Glass Inc., 1135 SE Grand Ave., Portland, OR 97214: Catalog $5 ❖ Stained glass supplies. 800–547–8417.

Coran-Sholes, 509 E. 2nd St., South Boston, MA 02127: Catalog $3 ❖ Stained glass supplies. 617–268–3780.

Judy Crumrine Stained Glass, 11020 Haney Terr., Damascus, MD 20872: Free information ❖ Nature, birds, flowers, butterflies, and other stained glass designs. 301–253–6079.

Crystalite Corporation, 18400 Green Meadows Dr. North, Westerville, OH 43081: Free information ❖ Lapidary supplies, glass-working equipment, and tools.

DAB Studio, 31 N. Terrace, P.O. Box 96, Maplewood, NJ 07040: Free catalog ❖ Stained glass windows and decorative accessories. 201–762–5407.

Delphi Stained Glass, 2116 E. Michigan Ave., Lansing, MI 48912: Catalog $4.50 (refundable) ❖ Stained glass supplies, tools, kits, and books. 800–248–2048.

Eastern Art Glass, P.O. Box 341, Wyckoff, NJ 07481: Catalog $2 (refundable) ❖ Stained glass kits and glass etching, engraving, and crafting supplies. 201–847–0001.

Franklin Art Glass, 222 E. Sycamore St., Columbus, OH 43206: Free brochure ❖ Stained glass tools and supplies. 800–848–7683.

Gemstone Equipment Manufacturing Company, 750 Easy St., Simi Valley, CA 93065: Free information ❖ Stained glass and lapidary supplies. 800–235–3375; 805–527–6990 (in CA).

Glass Grafters, Sue & Ray Binetti, 8806 Hinton Ave., Baltimore, MD 21219: Free information ❖ Stained glass lamps, windows, and kitchen cabinet doors. 301–477–3249.

Houston Stained Glass Supply, 2420 Center St., Houston, TX 77007: Free information ❖ Stained glass supplies and beveled glass. 800–231–0148.

Hudson Glass, 219 N. Division St., Peekskill, NY 10566: Catalog $3 (refundable) ❖ Stained glass supplies. 800–431–2964.

Kingsley North Inc., P.O. Box 216, Norway, MI 49870: Free catalog ❖ Stained glass and jewelry-making supplies and tools. 800–338–9280.

Greg Monk Stained Glass, 98–027 Hekaha St., Aiea, HI 96701: Free information ❖ Fused and leaded art glass creations, supplies, tools, and books. 808–488–9538.

Nasco, 901 Janesville Ave., Fort Atkinson, WI 53538: Free catalog ❖ Stained glass supplies. 800–558–9595.

Rainbow Art Glass, 49 Shark River Rd., Neptune, NJ 07753: Brochure $2 ❖ Tiffany lamp shades, other stained glass items, and kits. 908–922–1090.

Sunshine Glassworks, 111 Industrial Pkwy., Buffalo, NY 14227: Catalog $3 ❖ Stained glass supplies and tools. 800–828–7159; 716–668–2918 (in NY).

Whittemore Glass, Box 2065, Hanover, MA 02339: Catalog $2 ❖ Stained glass kits, tools, patterns, etching, and engraving supplies. 617–871–1790.

STAIRLIFTS & ELEVATORS

Cheney Company, P.O. Box 51188, New Berlin, WI 53151: Free information ❖ Curved and spiral stairway elevators. 800–782–1222.

Econol Lift Corporation, 2513 Center St., Box 854, Cedar Falls, IA 50613: Free information ❖ Wheelchair and stair-riding lifts, residential elevators, dumbwaiters, and vertical lifts. 319–277–4777.

Graventa, P.O. Box L-1, Blaine, WA 98230: Free information ❖ Easy-to-operate portable wheelchair lift for stairs. 800–663–6556.

Inclinator Company of America, P.O. Box 1557, Harrisburg, PA 17105: Free information ❖ Elevators and stairlifts for homes. 717–234–8065.

The National Wheel-O-Vator Company Inc., P.O. Box 348, Roanoke, IL 61561: Free information ❖ Wheelchair and side-riding stair lifts. 800–551–9095.

Whitakers, 1 Odell Plaza, Yonkers, NY 10703: Free catalog ❖ Motorized stairlifts for homes. 800–44–LIFTS; 800–924–LIFT (in NY).

STATIONERY & ENVELOPES

Accountants Supply House, 965 Walt Whitman Rd., Melville, NY 11747: Free catalog ❖ Stationery and envelopes, forms and labels, adding machines, shipping materials, disk storage cabinets, typewriter and data processing ribbons, and furniture. 800–342–5274; 516–561–7700 (in NY).

American Stationery Company, 100 Park Ave., Peru, IN 46970: Free catalog ❖ Regular and calligraphy stationery, wedding invitations, note cards and personal memos, envelopes, and postcards. 800–822–2577.

The American Wedding Album, American Stationery Company Inc., 300 N. Park Ave., Peru, IN 46970: Free catalog ❖ Wedding invitations, stationery, and gifts. 800–428–0379.

Artistic Greetings Inc., 409 William St., P.O. Box 1623, Elmira, NY 14902: Free catalog ❖ Stationery, memo pads, note cards, and self-stick address labels. 607–733–9076.

The Business Book, 41 W. 8th Ave., Oshkosh, WI 54906: Free catalog ❖ Pressure sensitive labels, stampers, personalized business envelopes and stationery, speed letters, memo pads, business cards and forms, greeting cards, books, and other office supplies. 414–231–4886.

Business Envelope Manufacturers, 900 Grand Blvd., Deer Park, NY 11729: Free catalog ❖ Envelopes, stationery, forms, labels, business cards, and other office supplies. 516–667–8500.

Caprock Business Forms Inc., 1211 Ave. F, Lubbock, TX 79401: Free information ❖ Continuous computer forms, letterheads and envelopes, snap-apart sets, manifold books and pads, and scratch pads. 800–666–3322.

Creations by Elaine, 6253 W. 74th St., Box 2001, Bedford Park, IL 60499: Free catalog ❖ Wedding invitations and stationery, cake knives and servers, reception and ceremony accessories, and jewelry. 800–323–2717.

Current Inc., Express Processing Center, Colorado Springs, CO 80941: Free catalog ❖ Greeting cards, stationery, and gift wrapping. 800–848–2848.

Day-Timers, One Willow Ln., Allentown, PA 18001: Free catalog ❖ Stationery and business cards. 215–395–5884.

Kristin Elliott Inc., 6 Opportunity Way, Newburyport, MA 01950: Free catalog ❖ Boxed notes, gift enclosures, Christmas cards, greeting cards, memo pads, postcards, correspondence cards, and gift wrapping. 800–922–1899; 508–465–1899 (in MA).

Fantastic Impressions, 20 Lucon Dr., Deer Park, NY 11729: Catalog $15 ❖ Letterheads, envelopes, and cards. 516–242–9199.

Fine Stationery by Sonya Nussbaum, P.O. Box 328, Hollywood, SC 29449: Free catalog ❖ Stationery and envelopes. 803–889–3463.

Goes Lithographing Company, 42 W. 61st St., Chicago, IL 60621: Free information ❖ Stationery, envelopes, calendars, calendar pads, certificates, and other printed items. 800–348–6700.

Grayarc, P.O. Box 2944, Hartford, CT 06104: Free catalog ❖ Stationery, business cards, forms, labels, envelopes, and other office supplies. 800–562–5468.

Heirloom Editions, Box 520–B, Rt. 4, Carthage, MO 64836: Catalog $4 ❖ Lithographs, greeting cards, stickers, miniatures, stationery, framed prints, and other turn-of-the-century art and paper collectibles. 800–725–0725.

Hudson Envelope Corporation, 111 3rd Ave., New York, NY 10003: Free information ❖ Colored envelopes and paper. 212–473–6666.

Robert James Company Inc., P.O. Box 530, Moody, AL 35004: Free information with long SASE ❖ Stationery, furniture, and other office supplies. 800–633–8296; 205–640–7081 (in AL).

Just Between Us, 41 W. 8th Ave., Oshkosh, WI 54906: Free catalog ❖ Stationery with optional personalization. 800–546–2255.

Jamie Lee Stationery, P.O. Box 5343, Glendale, AZ 85312: Free catalog ❖ Wedding stationery for brides. 800–288–5800.

Mattick Business Forms Inc., 333 W. Hintz Rd., Wheeling, IL 60090: Free catalog ❖ Stationery, office and business forms, and labels. 708–541–7345.

Merrimade Inc., 27 S. Canal St., Lawrence, MA 01843: Free catalog ❖ Stationery and other printed items. 508–686–5511.

Morgan Printing Company, 2365 Wyandotte Rd., Willow Grove, PA 19090: Free information ❖ Continuous letterheads, labels, and business forms. 800–435–3892.

New Century Envelope, Malott Industrial Park, P.O. Box 55530, Indianapolis, IN 46205: Free information ❖ Envelopes. 800–234–0666.

Peak Publishing, P.O. Box V, Flagstaff, AZ 86002: Catalog $2 ❖ Notecards with Southwestern scenes. 800–299–4789.

The Personal Touch, One Artistic Plaza, P.O. Box 1999, Elmira, NY 14902: Catalog $2 ❖ Personalized stationery and gifts. 800–227–0946; 607–733–5541 (in NY).

Posh Papers, 532 Elmgrove Ave., Providence, RI 02906: Brochure $1 (refundable) ❖ Note cards with envelopes. 401–331–9873.

Prolitho Inc., 630 New Ludlow St., South Hadley, MA 01075: Free information ❖ Business cards, stationery, and envelopes with flat and raised printing. 413–532–9473.

Reindeer House, 3409 W. 44th St., Minneapolis, MN 55410: Free catalog ❖ Greeting cards and stationery. 800–328–3894.

Rexcraft, Western Catalog House, Rexburg, ID 83441: Free catalog ❖ Invitations and stationery, bridal and reception accessories, and thank you cards. 800–635–1433.

Shipman Printing Industries, P.O. Box 157, Niagara Falls, NY 14302: Free information ❖ Forms, letterheads, envelopes, and other printed items. 800–462–2114.

Stationery House, 1000 Florida Ave., Hagerstown, MD 21740: Free catalog ❖ Business stationery and forms, office supplies, and executive gifts. 301–739–4487.

Sugar 'n Spice Invitations, Western Catalog House, Rexburg, ID 83441: Free catalog ❖ Invitations and stationery, bridal and reception accessories, and thank you cards. 800–635–1433.

Triangle Envelope Company, 325 Hill Ave., Nashville, TN 37210: Free information ❖ Envelopes and stationery. 800–843–9529.

Wedding Invitations by After Six, P.O. Box 263, Galena, IL 61036: Free catalog ❖ Wedding invitations, announcements, and stationery. 800–231–1273.

The Write Touch, The Rytex Company, 5850 W. 80th St., P.O. Box 68188, Indianapolis, IN 46268: Free catalog ❖ Stationery, writing aids, and other gifts. 800–288–6824.

Writewell Company Inc., P.O. Box 68186, Indianapolis, IN: 46268: Free catalog ❖ Stationery and envelopes, note cards, memo pads, and labels. 800–968–5850.

STENCILS

American Home Stencils Inc., 10007 S. 76th St., Franklin, WI 53132: Catalog $2.75 (refundable) ❖ Pre-cut stencils.

Adele Bishop, P.O. Box 3349, Kingston, NC 28502: Catalog $4 ❖ Decorative stencils. 800–334–4186.

Dee-signs Ltd., Box 490, Rushland, PA 18956: Catalog $5 ❖ Laser-cut stencils. 215–598–3330.

Epoch Designs, P.O. Box 4033, Elwyn, PA 19063: Catalog $3 ❖ Pre-cut Victorian-style stencils. 215–565–9180.

Helen Foster Stencils, 20 Chestnut St., Tilton, NH 03276: Catalog $4 ❖ Pre-cut stencils in an early 20th-century style. 603–286–7214.

Great Tracers, 3 Schoenbeck Rd., Prospect Heights, IL 60070: Brochure $1 (refundable) ❖ Lettering stencils. 708–255–0436.

Gail Grisi Stenciling Inc., P.O. Box 1263, Haddonfield, NJ 08033: Catalog $2.50 (refundable) ❖ Pre-cut plastic stencils, kits, sponges, acrylic paints, and how-to instructions. 609–354–1757.

The Itinerant Stenciler, 11030 173rd Ave. SE, Renton, WA 98059: Catalog $5 ❖ Laser-cut stencils. 206–226–0306.

StenArt Inc., P.O. Box 114, Pitman, NJ 08071: Catalog $3.50 ❖ Overlay stencil kits. 609–589–9857.

Stencil House of N.H., P.O. Box 109, Hooksett, NH 03306: Brochure $2.50 ❖ Cut and uncut mylar stencils, brushes, paints, stencil adhesive, and brush cleaner. 603–635–1716.

The Stencil Shoppe, 3634 Silverside Rd., Wilmington, DE 19810: Catalog $3.95 ❖ Designer stencils. 800–822–STEN.

Stencil World, 1456 2nd Ave., Box 175, New York, NY 10021: Catalog $3.50 (refundable) ❖ Pre-cut stencils and supplies. 212–517–7164.

Yowler & Shepp Stencils, 3529 Main St., Conestoga, PA 17516: Catalog $3 (refundable) ❖ Ribbons and other stencils. 717–872–2820.

STEREOS & CD PLAYERS
Headphones

Aiwa America Inc., 800 Corporate Dr., Mahwah, NJ 07430: Free information ❖ CD players, sound processors, and headphones. 800–289–2492.

Azden Corporation, 147 New Hyde Park Rd., Franklin Square, NY 11010: Free information ❖ Camcorders and headphones. 516–328–7500.

Bang & Olufsen, 1150 Feehanville Dr., Mt. Prospect, IL 60056: Free information ❖ CD players, speak-ers, and headphones. 800–323–0378.

Denon America, 222 New Rd., Parsippany, NJ 07054: Free information ❖ Headphones, CD players, re-ceivers, amplifiers, and sound processors. 201–575–7810.

JVC, 41 Slater Dr., Elmwood Park, NJ 07407: Free information ❖ Headphones, CD players, receivers, and amplifiers. 201–794–3900.

Nady Systems, 6701 Bay St., Emeryville, CA 94608: Free information ❖ Headphones and speakers. 510–652–2411.

Onkyo, 200 Williams Dr., Ramsey, NJ 07446: Free information ❖ CD players, receivers, amplifiers, universal remotes, and headphones. 201–825–7950.

Panasonic, Panasonic Way, Secaucus, NJ 07094: Free information ❖ Headphones, receivers, and CD players. 201–348–7000.

Pioneer Electronics, 1925 E. Dominguez St., Long Beach, CA 90810: Free information ❖

Headphones, speakers, CD players, sound processors, receivers, amplifiers, and decoders. 800–421–1404.

Recoton, 2950 Lake Emma Rd., Lake Mary, FL 32746: Free information ❖ Headphones, speakers, video and audio processors, and decoders. 800–223–6009.

Sony Consumer Products, 1 Sony Dr., Park Ridge, NJ 07656: Free information ❖ Headphones, speakers, CD players, camcorders, receivers, amplifiers, sound processors, decoders, universal remotes, and other electronics. 201–930–1000.

Teac, 7733 Telegraph Rd., Montebello, CA 90640: Free information ❖ CD players, sound processors, and headphones. 213–726–0303.

Technics, One Panasonic Way, Secaucus, NJ 07094: Free information ❖ Speakers, CD players, headphones, receivers, amplifiers, and sound processors. 201–348–9090.

Yamaha, P.O. Box 6660, Buena Park, CA 90620: Free information ❖ Headphones, speakers, audio and video systems, CD players, and sound processors. 800–492–6242.

Manufacturers

a/d/s, 1 Progress Way, Wilmington, MA 01887: Free information ❖ CD players, speakers, receivers, and amplifiers. 800–522–4434.

Acoustic Research, 330 Turnpike St., Canton, MA 02021: Free information ❖ Amplifiers and speakers. 617–821–2300.

Adcom, 11 Elkins Rd., East Brunswick, NJ 08816: Free information ❖ Amplifiers, CD players, and tuners. 800–477–3257.

Aiwa America Inc., 800 Corporate Dr., Mahwah, NJ 07430: Free information ❖ CD players, sound processors, and headphones. 800–289–2492.

Alpine Electronics of America, 19145 Gramercy, Torrance, CA 90505: Free information ❖ CD players, video processors, and decoders. 213–326–8000.

AMC, 1414 Fair Oaks Ave., Ste. 7, South Pasadena, CA 91030: Free information ❖ Receivers, amplifiers, CD players, and speakers. 818–799–6396.

Audio Source, 1327 N. Carolan Ave., Burlingame, CA 94010: Free information ❖ Sound processors and audio controllers. 415–348–8114.

Bang & Olufsen, 1150 Feehanville Dr., Mt. Prospect, IL 60056: Free information ❖ CD

players, speakers, and headphones. 800–323–0378.

Cambridge Soundworks, 311 Needham St., Newton, MA 02164: Free catalog ❖ Speakers and audio systems. 800–367–4434.

Canon, One Canon Plaza, Lake Success, NY 11042: Free information ❖ CD players, camcorders, sound processors, and other electronics. 516–488–6700.

Carrera, 1230 Calle Suerte, Camarillo, CA 93012: Free information ❖ Receivers and CD players. 805–987–1312.

Carver, P.O. Box 1237, Lynnwood, WA 98046: Free information ❖ Receivers, amplifiers, CD players, tuners, and speakers. 206–670–3429.

Denon America, 222 New Rd., Parsippany, NJ 07054: Free information ❖ CD players, receivers, amplifiers, sound processors, and headphones. 201–575–7810.

Emerson Radio Corporation, 1 Emerson Ln., North Bergen, NJ 07047: Free information ❖ Camcorders, CD and cassette players, and TVs. 800–922–0738.

Fisher, 21350 Lassen St., Chatsworth, CA 91311: Free information ❖ Speakers, CD and cassette players, sound processors, receivers, amplifiers, camcorders, TVs, and universal remotes. 818–998–7322.

Goldstar, 1000 Sylvan Ave., Englewood, NJ 07632: Free information ❖ CD and cassette players and TVs. 201–816–2200.

Harmon Kardon, 8380 Balboa Blvd., Northridge, CA 91325: Free information ❖ CD and cassette players, receivers, amplifiers, and projection equipment. 818–893–9992.

Hitachi Sales Corporation, 401 W. Artesia Blvd., Compton, CA 90220: Free information ❖ CD and cassette players, receivers, amplifiers, and TVs. 310–537–8383.

JVC, 41 Slater Dr., Elmwood Park, NJ 07407: Free information ❖ Audio and video systems, CD and cassette players, camcorders, receivers, amplifiers, TVs, and headphones. 201–794–3900.

Kenwood, P.O. Box 22745, Long Beach, CA 90801: Free information ❖ CD and cassette players, TVs, receivers, amplifiers, and sound processors. 310–639–9000.

Marantz, 1150 Feehanville Dr., Mt. Prospect, IL 60056: Free information ❖ Audio and video systems, speakers, CD and cassette players, sound processors, and other electronics. 708–299–4000.

McIntosh, 2 Chambers St., Binghamton, NY 13903: Free information ❖ CD players. 607–723–3512.

Mitsubishi Electronics, 5665 Plaza Dr., Cypress, CA 90630: Free information ❖ Audio and video systems, CD and cassette players, camcorders, and TVs. 800–843–2515.

NAD, 633 Granite Ct., Pickering, Ontario, Canada L1W 3K1: Free information ❖ Receivers, amplifiers, CD players, and speakers. 905–831–6333.

Nakamichi, 955 Francisco St., Torrance, CA 90502: Free information ❖ Receivers, amplifiers, and CD players. 310–538–8150.

NAP Consumer Electronics, 1 Phillips Dr., Knoxville, TN 37914: Free information ❖ Magnavox: CD and cassette players, camcorders, TVs, and universal remotes; Philco: camcorders, TVs, cassette players, and receivers; Philips: receivers, amplifiers, speakers, TVs, and CD and cassette players; and Sylvania: camcorders, CD and laser disk players, and TVs. 615–521–4391.

NEC Home Electronics, 1255 Michael Dr., Wood Dale, IL 60191: Free information ❖ Speakers, CD and players, receivers, amplifiers, TVs, camcorders, sound processors, and other electronics. 708–860–9500.

Onkyo, 200 Williams Dr., Ramsey, NJ 07446: Free information ❖ CD players, receivers, amplifiers, universal remotes, and headphones. 201–825–7950.

Panasonic, Panasonic Way, Secaucus, NJ 07094: Free information ❖ Audio and video systems, CD and cassette players, TVs, camcorders, headphones, and other electronics. 201–348–7000.

Pioneer Electronics, 1925 E. Dominguez St., Long Beach, CA 90810: Free information ❖ Speakers, receivers, amplifiers, TVs, sound processors, headphones, and cassette, and laser disk and CD players. 800–421–1404.

Proton Corporation, 16826 Edwards Rd., Cerritos, CA 90701: Free information ❖ Speakers, CD players, receivers, amplifiers, TVs, and other electronics.

Quasar, 1707 N. Randall Rd., Elgin, IL 60123: Free information ❖ Audio and video systems, CD and cassette players, camcorders, TVs, and other electronics. 708–468–5600.

Radio Shack, Division Tandy Corporation, One Tandy Center, Fort Worth, TX 76102: Free information ❖ Cassette and CD players, camcorders, universal remotes, computers, and other electronics. 817–390–3011.

RCA Sales Corporation, 600 N. Sherman Dr., Indianapolis, IN 46201: Free information ❖ Audio and video systems, cassette and CD players, TVs, camcorders, sound processors, and other electronics. 800–336–1900.

Recoton, 2950 Lake Emma Rd., Lake Mary, FL 32746: Free information ❖ Speakers, decoders, audio and video processors, and headphones. 800–223–6009.

Rotel, P.O. Box 8, North Reading, MA 01864: Free information ❖ Receivers, amplifiers, CD players, and speakers. 508–664–3820.

Sansui Electronics, 1290 Wall St. West, Lyndhurst, NJ 07071: Free information ❖ Speakers, cassette and CD players, camcorders, receivers, amplifiers, TVs, and sound processors. 201–460–9710.

Sanyo, 21350 Lassen St., Chatsworth, CA 91311: Free information ❖ CD and cassette players, camcorders, TVs, sound processors, universal remotes, and other electronics. 818–998–7322.

Sharp Electronics, Sharp Plaza, Mahwah, NJ 07430: Free information ❖ Cassette and CD players, camcorders, TVs, receivers, amplifiers, and other electronics. 800–BE-SHARP.

Sherwood, 14830 Alondra Blvd., La Mirada, CA 90638: Free information ❖ CD players, receivers, amplifiers, and sound processors. 800–962–3203.

Shure Brothers Inc., 222 Hartrey Ave., Evanston, IL 60202: Free information ❖ CD players, sound processors, and other electronics. 800–447–4873.

Sony Consumer Products, 1 Sony Dr., Park Ridge, NJ 07656: Free information ❖ Speakers, cassette and CD players, camcorders, receivers, amplifiers, TVs, sound processors, universal remotes, headphones, and other electronics. 201–930–1000.

Teac, 7733 Telegraph Rd., Montebello, CA 90640: Free information ❖ Sound processors, headphones, other electronics, and cassette, CD, and laser disk players. 213–726–0303.

Technics, One Panasonic Way, Secaucus, NJ 07094: Free information ❖ Speakers, CD players, sound processors, receivers, amplifiers, and headphones. 201–348–9090.

Toshiba, 82 Totowa Rd., Wayne, NJ 07470: Free information ❖ Cassette and CD players,

camcorders, sound processors, and TVs. 201–628–8000.

Vector Research, 1230 Calle Suerte, Camarillo, CA 93012: Free information ❖ Cassette and CD players, receivers, speakers, and amplifiers. 805–987–1312.

Yamaha, P.O. Box 6660, Buena Park, CA 90620: Free information ❖ Speakers, receivers, amplifiers, sound processors, headphones, and CD, cassette, and laser disk players. 800–492–6242.

Retailers

Atlantic Buyers Club, 162 Hwy. 34, Ste. 189, Matawan, NJ 07747: Free information ❖ Audio and video equipment. 800–522–8937.

Audio Advisor, 225 Oakes SW, Grand Rapids, MI 49503: Free information with long SASE ❖ Audio and video equipment. 800–669–4434; 616–451–3868 (in MI).

Audio Haven, 1937 W. 11th St., Upland, CA 91786: Free information ❖ Audio equipment. 714–982–8110.

AV Distributors, 16451 Space Center Blvd., Houston, TX 77058: Free information ❖ Audio, video, and stereo equipment and TVs. 800–843–3697.

Computability Consumer Electronics, P.O. Box 17882, Milwaukee, WI 53217: Free catalog ❖ TVs, fax machines, copiers, computers, and audio, video, and stereo equipment. 800–558–0003.

Crutchfield, 1 Crutchfield Park, Charlottesville, VA 22906: Free catalog ❖ TVs and video, audio, and stereo equipment. 800–955–9009.

Electronic Wholesalers, 1160 Hamburg Tnpk., Wayne, NJ 07470: Free information ❖ Receivers, cassette decks, TVs, telephones, laser disk and CD players, and camcorders. 201–696–6531.

Factory Direct, 131 W. 35th St., New York, NY 10001: Free information ❖ TVs and audio, video, and stereo equipment. 800–428–4567.

Focus Electronics, 4523 13th Ave., Brooklyn, NY 11219: Free catalog ❖ Appliances, photographic equipment, and audio, stereo, and video equipment. 718–436–4646.

Illinois Audio, 1284 E. Dundee Rd., Palatine, IL 60067: Free information ❖ Audio, stereo, and video equipment. 800–621–8042.

International Electronic World, 1901 Tigertail Blvd., Dania, FL 33004: Free catalog ❖ Audio and video equipment.

J & R Music World, 59–50 Queens-Midtown Expwy., Maspeth, NY 11378: Free catalog ❖ Audio equipment, car and portable stereos, video recorders telephones, computers, and video and audio tapes. 800–221–8180.

Kief's Audio/Video, 24th & Iowa, Lawrence, KS 66044: Free catalog ❖ Audio equipment. 913–842–1811.

New West Electronics, 4120 Meridian, Bellingham, WA 98226: Free information ❖ TVs, projection equipment, and audio, video, and stereo equipment. 800–488–8877.

Not-Just-Video Inc., 58 Walker St., New York, NY 10013: Catalog $2.75 ❖ Video and audio equipment, TVs, camcorders, and other electronics. 800–856–9890.

Olden Video, 1265 Broadway, New York, NY 10001: Free information ❖ Video equipment, TVs, cassette players, and other electronics. 212–725–1234.

Park Place Audio, 55 Park Pl., New York, NY 10007: Free information ❖ Audio and video equipment. 212–964–4570.

Percy's Inc., 19 Glennie St., Worcester, MA 01605: Free information ❖ Appliances and electronics. 508–755–5334.

Planet Electronics, 8418 Lilley, Canton, MI 48187: Free catalog ❖ TVs, video recorders, telephones, tapes, cassettes, and compact disks. 800–247–4663; 313–453–4750 (in MI).

PowerVideo, 4413 Blue Bonnet, Stafford, TX 77477: Free information ❖ TVs and audio, video, and stereo equipment. 713–240–3202.

S & S Sound City, 58 W. 45th St., New York, NY 10036: Free information ❖ Audio and video equipment, telephones, office machines, and other electronics. 212–575–0210.

S.B.H. Enterprises, 1678 53rd St., Brooklyn, NY 11204: Free information ❖ Audio and video equipment and radar detectors. 800–451–5851; 718–438–1027 (in NY).

The Sound Seller, 2808 Cahill Rd., P.O. Box 224, Marinette, WI 54143: Free information ❖ Audio and video equipment. 715–735–9002.

Square Deal, 456 Waverly Ave., Patchogue, NY 11772: Free information ❖ Audio equipment. 800–332–5369.

Tri-State Camera, 650 6th Ave., New York, NY 10011: Free information ❖ Audio and video equipment, camcorders, copiers, fax machines, and other electronics. 800–537–4441; 212–633–2290 (in NY).

Wisconsin Discount Stereo, 2417 W. Badger Rd., Madison, WI 53713: Free information ❖ Video and audio equipment and TVs. 800–356–9514.

Speakers

a/d/s, 1 Progress Way, Wilmington, MA 01887: Free information ❖ CD players, speakers, receivers, and amplifiers. 800–522–4434.

Altec-Lansing, P.O. Box 277, Milford, PA 18337: Free information ❖ Speakers. 717–296–4434.

Audio Concepts Inc., 901 S. 4th St., La Crosse, WI 54601: Free catalog ❖ Assemble-them-yourself speaker kits. 800–346–9183.

B & W Loudspeaker, 40 W. Beaver Creek Rd., Richmond Hills, Ontario, Canada L4B 1G5: Free brochure ❖ Speakers. 905–882–8399.

Bang & Olufsen, 1150 Feehanville Dr., Mt. Prospect, IL 60056: Free information ❖ CD players, speakers, and headphones. 800–323–0378.

Bose Express Music, The Mountain, Framingham, MA 01701: Catalog $6 (refundable) ❖ Speakers. 800–845–BOSE.

Boston Acoustic, 70 Broadway, Lynnfield, MA 01940: Free information ❖ Speakers. 617–592–9000.

Electronic Center, 7619 Metcalf, Overland Park, KS 66204: Free information ❖ Speakers for home, automobile, and other electronic application. 913–649–5000.

Energy Loudspeakers, 3641 NcNicoll Ave., Scarborough, Ontario, Canada M1X 1G5: Free information ❖ Home theater sound system. 416–321–1800.

Fisher, 21350 Lassen St., Chatsworth, CA 91311: Free information ❖ Speakers, CD and cassette, sound processors, receivers, amplifiers, and camcorders. 818–998–7322.

Infinity Systems, 9409 Owensmouth Ave., Chatsworth, CA 91311: Free information ❖ Speakers and TVs. 818–407–0228.

Marantz, 1150 Feehanville Dr., Mt. Prospect, IL 60056: Free information ❖ Audio and video systems, speakers, CD and cassette,

sound processors, and other electronics. 708–299–4000.

Nady Systems, 6701 Bay St., Emeryville, CA 94608: Free information ❖ Speakers and headphones. 510–652–2411.

NEC Home Electronics, 1255 Michael Dr., Wood Dale, IL 60191: Free information ❖ Speakers, CD and cassette, receivers, amplifiers, sound processors, and other electronics. 708–860–9500.

Pioneer Electronics, 1925 E. Dominguez St., Long Beach, CA 90810: Free information ❖ Speakers, CD players, sound processors, receivers, amplifiers, and headphones. 800–421–1404.

Polk Audio, 5601 Metro Dr., Baltimore, MD 21230: Free information ❖ Speakers. 410–358–3600.

Proton Corporation, 16826 Edwards Rd., Cerritos, CA 90701: Free information ❖ Speakers, CD players, receivers, and amplifiers.

Recoton, 2950 Lake Emma Rd., Lake Mary, FL 32746: Free information ❖ Speakers, audio and video processors, video processors, and headphones. 800–223–6009.

Sansui Electronics, 1290 Wall St. West, Lyndhurst, NJ 07071: Free information ❖ Speakers, cassette and CD players, receivers, amplifiers, and sound processors. 201–460–9710.

Sony Consumer Products, 1 Sony Dr., Park Ridge, NJ 07656: Free information ❖ Speakers, audio and video systems, CD players, camcorders, sound processors, and headphones. 201–930–1000.

Speakerlab Factory, 6307 Roosevelt Way NE, Seattle, WA 98103: Free information ❖ Speakers and kits, tape decks, receivers, and other electronics. 206–523–2269.

Technics, One Panasonic Way, Secaucus, NJ 07094: Free information ❖ Speakers, CD players, headphones, receivers, amplifiers, and sound processors. 201–348–9090.

Yamaha, P.O. Box 6660, Buena Park, CA 90620: Free information ❖ Speakers, CD and laser disk players, receivers, amplifiers, sound processors, and headphones. 800–492–6242.

Storage Cabinets & Racks

AGM Woodworking, 870 Capitolio Way, San Luis Obispo, CA 93401: Free brochure ❖ Audio and video component storage cabinets. 800–858–9005.

Billy Bags Design, 4147 Transport St., Ventura, CA 93003: Free information ❖ Rack systems. 805–644–2185.

STICKERS

Artistic Clowns, Clown Paraphernalia, P.O. Box 811, Mt. Clemens, MI 48046: Catalog $1 (refundable) ❖ Clown stickers.

Carlton's Modern Postcards, P.O. Box 111, Bogota, NJ 07603: Free information with long SASE ❖ Postcards and stickers.

Eastern Emblem, Box 828, Union City, NJ 07087: Free catalog ❖ T-shirts, jackets, patches, cloisonne pins, decals, and stickers. 800–344–5112.

Heirloom Editions, Box 520–B, Rt. 4, Carthage, MO 64836: Catalog $4 ❖ Lithographs, greeting cards, stickers, miniatures, stationery, framed prints, and other turn-of-the-century art and paper collectibles. 800–725–0725.

Holly Sales, 9926 Beach Blvd., Ste. 114, Jacksonville, FL 32246: Free information ❖ Clown stickers. 904–223–5828.

House-Mouse Designs, P.O. Box 48, Williston, VT 05495: Free catalog ❖ Christmas cards, note and recipe cards, stickers, and magnets. 800–242–6423.

Stick-Em Up, P.O. Box 3111, Livermore, CA 94551: Catalog $2 ❖ Stickers. 415–426–1040.

STONE SCULPTING & CARVING

Ebersole Lapidary Supply Inc., 11417 West Hwy. 54, Wichita, KS 67209: Catalog $2 ❖ Carving materials, beads and bead-stringing supplies, tools, findings, mountings, cabochons and rocks, and jewelry kits. 316–722–4771.

Gems by Jak, 113 Sherman St., Ihlen, MN 56140: Free catalog ❖ Indian gifts and catinite for carving. 507–348–8716.

Montoya/MAS International Inc., 435 Southern Blvd., West Palm Beach, FL 33405: Catalog $3 ❖ Carving stone and sculpture tools. 800–682–8665.

Richardson's Recreational Ranch Ltd., Gateway Route Box 440, Madras, OR 97741: Free information ❖ Rock and mineral specimens from all over the world, carving materials, and lapidary equipment. 503–475–2680.

Riviera Lapidary Supply, 30393 Mesquite, Riviera, TX 78379: Catalog $3 ❖ Carving materials, petrified wood, cabochons, beads, slabs, cabbing rough, gemstones, crystals, beads, and bead-stringing supplies and kits. 512–296–3958.

Steatite of Southern Oregon Inc., 2891 Elk Ln., Grants Pass, OR 97527: Free information ❖ Soapstone for sculpturing and carving. 503–479–3646.

STOVES

Aladdin Steel Products Inc., 401 N. Wynne St., Colville, WA 99114: Free information ❖ Non-catalytic stoves. 509–684–3745.

Barnstable Stove Shop, Rt. 149, Box 472, West Barnstable, MA 02668: Price list $1 ❖ Restored antique stoves and parts. 508–362–9913.

Blaze King Industries, 400 W. Whitman Dr., College Place, WA 99324: Free information ❖ Pellet-burning stoves.

Bryant Stove Inc., Box 2048, Thorndike, ME 04986: Free brochure ❖ Antique stoves for coal, gas, wood, wood and gas combination, and electricity. 207–568–3665.

Charmaster Products Inc., 2307 Hwy. 2 West, Grand Rapids, MN 55744: Free brochure ❖ Fireplaces and wood-burning, wood-gas, and wood-oil furnaces and conversion units. 800–542–6360.

Earthstone Wood-Fire Ovens, 237 S. LaBrea Ave., Los Angeles, CA 90036: Free brochure ❖ Wood-fire baking and barbecuing ovens. 213–656–5926.

Elmira Stove Works, 145 Northfield Dr., Waterloo, Ontario, Canada N2L 5J3: Catalog $5 ❖ Home cooking stoves in a classical style. 519–725–5500.

FiveStar, P.O. Box 2490, Cleveland, TN 37320: Free brochure ❖ Commercial ranges, cooktops, and range hoods for the home. 615–476–6544.

Good Time Stove Company, Rt. 112, P.O. Box 306, Goshen, MA 01032: Free information ❖ Restored, ready-to-use antique cooking and heating stoves. 413–268–3677.

Guertin Brothers Industries Inc., 18931 59th Ave. NE, Arlington, WA 98223: Free information ❖ Pellet-burning stoves. 206–653–5505.

HearthStone, P.O. Box 1069, Morrisville, VT 05661: Catalog $12 ❖ Automatic clean-burning wood stoves. 802–827–8683.

Heartland Appliances, 5 Hoffman St., Kitchener, Ontario, Canada N2M 3M5:

Catalog $2 ❖ Classic cookstoves with state-of-the-art features. 519–743–8111.

Heatilator Inc., 1915 W. Saunders St., Mt. Pleasant, IA 52641: Free information ❖ Wood-burning stoves and fireplace inserts. 800–247–6798.

Heating Alternatives, 1926 Rt. 212, Pleasant Valley, Quakertown, PA 18951: Free catalog ❖ Coal and wood-burning stoves. 800–444–4328; 215–346–7896 (in PA).

Heating Energy Systems, P.O. Box 593, Clackamas, OR 97015: Free information ❖ Non-catalytic stoves. 503–650–0504.

Hutch Manufacturing Company, 200 Commerce Ave., P.O. Box 350, Loudon, TN 37774: Free information ❖ Catalytic stoves. 800–251–9232.

Iron Craft, Old Rt. 28, P.O. Box 369, Ossipee, NH 03864: Catalog $2 ❖ Cast iron cookware, cookstoves, and coal and wood-heating stoves. 603–539–2807.

J.E.S. Enterprises/Classic Ranges, P.O. Box 65, Ventura, CA 93002: Free catalog ❖ Restored electric, gas, coal and wood antique stoves and used, new, and restored parts. 805–643–3532.

Johnny's Appliances & Classic Ranges, 17549 Sonoma Hwy., P.O. Box 1407, Sonoma, CA 95476: Free information ❖ Cooking ranges, from 1900 to 1960. 707–996–9730.

Jotul USA, P.O. Box 1157, Portland, ME 04104: Free brochure ❖ Stoves and fireplaces. 800–535–2995.

New Buck Corporation, P.O. Box 69, Spruce Pine, NC 28777: Free information ❖ Catalytic stoves. 704–765–6144.

Nu-Tec Incorporated, P.O. Box 908, East Greenwich, RI 02818: Free brochure ❖ Wood-burning stoves and fireplace inserts. 800–822–0600.

Oregon Woodstoves, 1844 Main St., Springfield, OR 97477: Free information ❖ Catalytic stoves. 503–747–8868.

Otis Home Center Inc., 312 Armstrong Rd., Rogersville, TN 37857: Catalog $5 ❖ Wood, gas, or electric country-style heating and cooking stoves. 800–743–8133.

Russo Corporation, 61 Pleasant St., Randolph, MA 02368: Free information ❖ Wood-burning stoves with optional brass trim, air deflectors, brass doors, and etched glass. 617–963–1182.

Stanley Iron Works, 64 Taylor St., Nashua, NH 03060: Free information ❖ Antique parlor stoves, gas and wood-gas combination stoves, and coal, gas, and electric conversions of antique stoves. 603–881–8335.

TEC Enterprises, P.O. Box 23, Lewiston, ID 83501: Free information ❖ Pellet-burning stoves. 208–843–7207.

Tulikivi Natural Stone Fireplaces, Tulikivi Group North America, P.O. Box 300, Schulyer, VA 22969: Free information ❖ Baking ovens, cookstoves, and natural stone fireplaces. 800–843–3473; 804–831–2228 (in VA).

The Ultimate Cooker, 803 W. Fairbanks, Winter Park, Fl 32789: Free information ❖ Combination grilling and smoking cooker. 407–644–6680.

Vogelzang Corporation, 400 W. 17th St., Holland, MI 49423: Free information ❖ Wood-burning stove conversion kits. 800–222–6950.

Waterford Irish Stoves Inc., 16 Airport Park Rd., Ste. 3, West Lebanon, NH 03784: Free information ❖ Non-catalytic stoves. 603–298–5030.

Woodstock Soapstone Company Inc., Airpark Rd., West Lebanon, NH 03784: Free brochure ❖ Traditional and contemporary style woodburning stoves. 800–866–4344.

SUNDIALS

Armchair Shopper, P.O. Box 130, Indianapolis, IN 46206: Free catalog ❖ Old-world style sundials, windchimes, and lawn ornaments. 800–558–2376.

Betsy's Place, 323 Arch St., Philadelphia, PA 19106: Brochure $3 ❖ Sundials and stands, brass reproduction door knockers, and trivets. 800–452–3524; 215–922–3536 (in PA).

Celestial Arts & Sciences, P.O. Box 22753, Santa Fe, NM 87505: Catalog $1 ❖ Sundials.

Flora Fauna, P.O. Box 578, Gualala, CA 95445: Free information ❖ Hand-cast solid brass sundials and other garden decor. 800–358–9120.

Good Directions Company, 24 Ardmore Rd., Stamford, CT 06902: Free catalog ❖ Copper and solid brass sundials and weather vanes. 800–346–7678.

Holst Inc., 11118 W. Lake, Box 370, Tawas City, MI 48764: Free catalog ❖ Country items, decor accessories, sundials, weather vanes, housewares, and figurines. 517–362–5664.

Replogle Globes Inc., 2801 S. 25th Ave., Broadview, IL 60153: Free catalog ❖ Sundials. 708–343–0900.

Wind & Weather, P.O. Box 2320, Mendocino, CA 95460: Free catalog ❖ Sundials, weather vanes, and weather forecasting instruments. 707–964–1284.

SUNGLASSES & EYE WEAR

Airborn Flightware Company, 144 Plainview Rd., Woodbury, NY 11797: Catalog $2 (refundable) ❖ Aviator sunglasses. 800–448–6778.

Brigade Quartermasters Inc., 1025 Cobb International Blvd., Kenesaw, GA 30144: Free information ❖ Ski goggles and other eyewear. 404–428–1234.

Cébé, 2151 Las Palmas Dr., Ste. G, Carlsbad, CA 92009: Free information ❖ Sports sunglasses. 619–931–6788.

Costa Del Mar, 123 N. Orchard St., Ormond Beach, FL 32174: Free information ❖ Polarized sunglasses. 904–677–3700.

Daniels Enterprises, 3196 Howard Dr., Redding, CA 96001: Free brochure ❖ Sunglasses with optional prescription correction. 916–243–5639.

Gargoyles Performance Eyewear, 5866 S. 194th St., Kent, WA 98032: Free catalog ❖ Sunglasses and ski goggles. 206–872–6100.

Hidalgo Inc., 45 La Buena Vista, Wimberley, TX 78676: Free catalog ❖ Designer sunglasses. 512–847–5571.

Hobie Sunglasses, 1030 Calle Sombra, San Clemente, CA 92672: Free information ❖ Polarized sunglasses. 800–554–4335.

House of Eyes, 2216 Patterson St., Greensboro, NC 27407: Free information ❖ Designer eye wear. 800–331–4701; 910–852–7107 (in NC).

Lens Express Inc., 350 SW 12th Ave., Deerfield Beach, FL 33442: Free information ❖ Contact lenses. 305–968–4100.

Martin Sunglasses, Jack Martin Company Inc., 9830 Baldwin Pl., El Monte, CA 91731: Free information ❖ Ski goggles and other eyewear. 800–767–8555; 213–686–1100 (in CA).

Oakley Sunglasses, 10 Holland, Irvine, CA 92718: Free information ❖ Eye wear that provides ultraviolet light and injury-causing blue light protection. 800–733–6255.

Olympic Optical Company, P.O. Box 752377, Memphis, TN 38175: Free information ❖ Sunglasses that protect the eyes from ultraviolet light. 800–992–1255.

Precision Optical, 507 2nd Ave., Rochelle, IL 61068: Catalog $1 ❖ Magnifiers and magnifying and regular sunglasses. 815–562–2174.

Serengeti Eyewear, 1480 Colonial Dr., Horseheads, NY 14845: Free information ❖ Designer sunglasses. 800–525–4001.

Spex Amphibious Eye Wear, P.O. Box 2537, Costa Mesa, CA 92628: Free information ❖ Polarized eyewear with ultraviolet light protection. 714–548–1235.

Sunglass America, P.O. Box 147, Hewlett, NY 11557: Catalog $2 (refundable) ❖ Designer sunglasses. 800–424–LENS; 516–791–3400 (in NY).

Torelli Imports, 1181 Calle Suerte, Camarillo, CA 93012: Free information ❖ Sunglasses with interchangeable lenses and temple and nose pieces. 805–484–8705.

SURFBOARDS

Adventure Sport Inc., 1607 NW 84th Ave., Miami, FL 33126: Free information ❖ Windsurfing boards. 305–591–3922.

Alvimar Manufacturing Company Inc., 51–02 21st St., Long Island City, NY 11101: Free information ❖ Surfboards and swim rings. 718–937–0404.

American Athletic Inc., 200 American Ave., Jefferson, IA 50129: Free information ❖ Surfboards and swim rings. 800–247–3978; 515–386–3125 (in IA).

Avon Windsurf Company, Rt. 12, P.O. Box 628, Avon, NC 27915: Free information ❖ Sails for windsurfing boards. 919–995–5441.

Body Glove International Inc., 530 6th St., Hermosa Beach, CA 90254: Free information ❖ Surfboards. 800–678–7873; 310–374–4074 (in CA).

Skip Hutchison, Rastaboards Surf-Sail-Snowboards, 4748 NE 11th Ave., Fort Lauderdale, FL 33334: Free information with long SASE ❖ Sailboards, surfboards, and snowboards. 305–491–7992.

Island Windsurfing, 1623 York Ave., New York, NY 10028: Free information ❖ Windsurfing boards. 212–744–2000.

Mistral Inc., 7222 Parkway Dr., Dorsey, MD 21076: Free information ❖ Windsurfing boards and wet suits. 410–712–4755.

Recreonics Corporation, 4200 Schmitt Ave., Louisville KY 40213: Free information ❖ Surfboards, swim rings, and diving boards. 800–428–3254.

Rothhammer/Sprint, P.O. Box 5579, Santa Maria, CA 93456: Free information ❖ Surfboards, swim rings, and equipment for divers. 800–235–2156.

Sailworld, 112 Oak St., Hood River, OR 97031: Free information ❖ Sails for windsurfing boards. 503–386–9400.

Tackle Shack, 7801 66th St. North, Pinellas, Park, FL 34665: Free catalog ❖ Windsurfing equipment and clothing. 813–546–5080.

Windsurfing Warehouse, 128 S. Airport Blvd., South San Francisco, CA 94080: Free catalog ❖ Sailboards. 800–628–4599; 415–588–1714 (in CA).

SURPLUS & LIQUIDATION MERCHANDISE

American Science & Surplus, 3605 Howard St., Skokie, IL 60076: Catalog $1 ❖ Surplus science and electromechanical equipment. 708–982–0870.

Burden's Surplus Center, P.O. Box 82209, Lincoln, NE 68501: Free catalog ❖ Liquidation merchandise. 800–488–3407.

COMB Authorized Liquidator, P.O. Box 29902, Minneapolis, MN 55429: Free catalog ❖ Liquidation merchandise. 800–328–0609.

Damark International Inc., 7101 Winnetka Ave. North, P.O. Box 29900, Minneapolis, MN 55429: Free information ❖ Liquidation of over-production, discontinued, or merchandise obtained through special arrangements with vendors. 800–729–9000.

E.T. Supply, P.O. Box 78190, Los Angeles, CA 90016: Free information ❖ Industrial and military surplus. 213–734–2430.

Fair Radio Sales Company Inc., P.O. Box 1105, Lima, OH 45802: Free information ❖ Industrial and military surplus electronic parts. 419–227–6573.

H & R Company, 18 Canal St., P.O. Box 122, Bristol, PA 19007: Free catalog ❖ Surplus electromechanical and optical equipment. 215–788–5583.

Harbor Freight Salvage, 3491 Mission Oaks Blvd., Camarillo, CA 93011: Free catalog ❖ Hardware, tools, and other surplus merchandise. 800–423–2567.

Massachusetts Army & Navy Store, 15 Fordham Rd., Boston, MA 02134: Free catalog ❖ Military surplus. 617–783–1250.

Ruvel & Company Inc., 4128 W. Belmont Ave., Chicago, IL 60641: Catalog $2 ❖ Army-navy surplus. 312–286–9494.

Strand Surplus Center, 2202 Strand, Galveston, TX 77550: Brochure $1 ❖ Government surplus. 800–231–6005.

Surplus Center, P.O. Box 82209, Lincoln, NE 68501: Free catalog ❖ Hydraulics, motors, air compressors, spraying equipment, pumps, and other surplus merchandise. 800–488–3407.

SURVEILLANCE & PERSONAL PROTECTION EQUIPMENT

A.M.C. Sales Inc., 193 Vaquero Dr., Boulder, CO 80303: Free information ❖ Telephone recording adapters, bugging detectors, telephone scramblers, voice changers, and other equipment. 800–926–2488.

The Counter Spy Shop, 444 Madison Ave., New York, NY 10022: Free brochure ❖ Surveillance and personal protection aids. 212–688–8500.

Deco Industries, Box 607, Bedford Hills, NY 10507: Free information ❖ Easy-to-assemble programmable scanner or VHF surveillance receiver. 914–232–3878.

EMCOM, 10 Howard St., Buffalo, NY 14206: Catalog $5 ❖ Surveillance and counter-surveillance equipment. 716–852–3711.

Great Southern Security, 513 Bankhead Hwy., Carrolton, GA 30117: Free information ❖ Electronic protection devices. 800–732–5000.

Minuteman Security Products, 7413 Six Forks Rd., Ste. 144, Raleigh, NC 27615: Free information ❖ Self-defense products. 800–MINUTE-8.

Protector Enterprises, P.O. Box 520294, Salt Lake City, UT 84152: Catalog $5 ❖ Surveillance, counterspy, and protection equipment. 801–487–3823.

Quark Spy Centre, 537 3rd Ave., New York, NY 10016: Free catalog ❖ Electronic surveillance and counter-measure protection equipment. 212–889–1808.

Spy Outlet, 2480 Niagara Falls Blvd., Tonawanda, NY 14150: Catalog $5 ❖ Voice changers and scramblers, telephone recorders, bug detectors, and other surveillance and counter-surveillance electronic devices. 716–691–3476.

SPY Supply, 1212 Boylston St., Ste. 120, Chestnut Hill, MA 02167: Catalog $5 ❖ Electronic lock pick, locksmith tools, and other unusual gadgets. 617–327–7272.

Vantage Point Technologies, 1318 E. Mission Rd., Ste. 376, San Marcos, CA 92069: Catalog $2 (refundable) ❖ Professional security equipment. 800–272–1357.

SWIMMING POOLS & EQUIPMENT

Aqua Products Inc., 25 Rutgers Ave., Cedar Grove, NJ 07009: Free information ❖ Above-ground, water pressure-operated pool cleaner. 800–221–1750.

Aquasol Controllers Inc., 2918 Dupree, Houston, TX 77054: Free information ❖ Electronic pool sanitizer and pH monitoring and control equipment. 800–444–0675.

Chemtrol, 113 West Mission St., Santa Barbara, CA 93101: Free information ❖ Electronic pool sanitizer and pH monitoring and control equipment. 800–621–2279; 805–569–1731 (in CA).

Cover-Pools Inc., 66 E. 3335 South, Salt Lake City, UT 84115: Free information ❖ Swimming pool covers. 800–447–2838.

Endless Pools Inc., 200 E. Duttons Mill Rd., Aston, PA 19014: Free brochure ❖ Lap pool for swimming in place against a smooth, adjustable current. 800–732–8660.

Fanta-Sea Pools, 10151 Main St., Clarence, NY 14031: Free information ❖ Solar-energy-heated swimming pools. 800–845–5500; 800–462–8000 (in NY).

Fort Wayne Pools, 510 Sumpter Dr., Fort Wayne, IN 46804: Free information ❖ Jet-forced water, swim-in-place hydrotherapy pools. 219–432–8731.

Guardex Pool & Spa Products, Biolab Inc., P.O. Box 67, Decatur, GA 30031: Free information ❖ 4–in–1 swimming pool testing kit. 800–959–7946.

Kreepy Krauly USA Inc., 13801 NW 4th St., Sunrise, FL 33325: Free information ❖ Pool vacuums. 800–843–5628.

Pool Fence Company, 1791–907 Blount Rd., Pompano Beach, FL 33069: Free brochure ❖ Swimming pool security fences. 800–992–2206.

Recreonics Corporation, 4200 Schmitt Ave., Louisville KY 40213: Free information ❖ Swimming pools and supplies. 800–428–3254.

Swimex, P.O. Box 328, Warren, RI 02885: Free brochure ❖ Compact lap pool for swimming in place, with controls for adjusting water flow. 800–877–7946.

SWITCH PLATES

Classic Accents Inc., P.O. Box 1181, Southgate, MI 48195: Catalog $1.50 ❖ Switch cover plates, push-button light switches, and solid brass cover plates. 313–282–5525.

The Country Store, 28 James St., Geneva, IL 60134: Catalog $2 ❖ Pewter-finished, punched tin switchplate covers. 708–879–0098.

Derks Switchplates, 4176 S. Luce Ave., Fremont, MI 49412: Free information ❖ Handcarved wood switch plates. 616–924–3382.

Shepard Eberly Decor, 5056 Forest Dr., Rome, OH 44085: Free information ❖ Wall plaques, mirrors, original ceramics, and switch plates. 216–563–9849.

Ekdahl Crafts, P.O. Box 266, Bangor, CA 95914: Free information ❖ Handpainted wood switchplates. 916–679–2343.

Prairie Town Products Inc., P.O. Box 1426, Sedalia, MO 65301: Brochure $1 ❖ Solid wood switch plates with hand-painted ornaments and walnut finish. 816–826–4208.

TABLE TENNIS

African Import Company, 1453 Mission St., San Francisco, CA 94103: Free information ❖ Paddles, balls, nets, brackets, and sets. 415–863–1506.

The Athletic Connection, 1901 Diplomat, Dallas, TX 75234: Free information ❖ Balls, nets, paddles, and tables. 800–527–0871; 214–243–1446 (in TX).

Cannon Sports, P.O. Box 11179, Burbank, CA 91510: Free information with list of retailers ❖ Paddles, balls, nets, brackets, and sets. 800–362–3146; 818–753–5940 (in CA).

Champion Sports Products Company, P.O. Box 138, Sayreville, NJ 08872: Free information ❖ Paddles, balls, nets, brackets, and sets. 908–238–0330.

Dunlop Stazenger Corporation, P.O. Box 3070, Greenville, SC 29602: Free information ❖ Balls, nets, and paddles. 800–845–8794; 803–271–9767 (in SC).

Escalade Sports, P.O. Box 889, Evansville, IN 47706: Free catalog ❖ Tables, paddles, balls, nets, and sets. 800–457–3373; 812–467–1200 (in IN).

Indian Industries Inc., P.O. Box 889, Evansville, IN 47706: Free catalog ❖ Sets. 800–457–3373; 812–467–1200 (in IN).

Markwort Sporting Goods, 4300 Forest Park Ave., St. Louis, MO 63108: Catalog $8 with list of retailers ❖ Balls, nets, paddles, and tables. 314–652–3757.

Olympia Sports, 745 State Cir., Ann Arbor, MI 48106: Free information ❖ Balls, nets, paddles, and tables. 800–521–2832; 313–761–5173 (in MI).

Palmer Billiard Corporation, 307 Morris Ave., Elizabeth, NJ 07208: Free information ❖ Paddles, balls, nets, brackets, and sets. 908–289–4778.

Pennsylvania Sporting Goods, 1360 Industrial Hwy., P.O. Box 451, Southampton, PA 18966: Free information ❖ Paddles, balls, nets, brackets, and sets. 800–535–1122.

Regent Sports Corporation, 45 Ranick Rd., Hauppage, NY 11788: Free information ❖ Paddles, balls, nets, brackets and sets. 516–234–2800.

Spalding Sports Worldwide, 425 Meadow St., P.O. Box 901, Chicopee, MA 01021: Free information with list of retailers ❖ Paddles, balls, nets, brackets, and sets. 800–225–6601.

Sportime, 1 Sportime Way, Atlanta, GA 30340: Free information ❖ Balls, nets, paddles, and tables. 800–444–5700; 404–449–5700 (in GA).

Sporty's Preferred Living Catalog, Clermont Airport, Batavia, OH 45103: Free catalog ❖ Folding outdoor table tennis tables. 800–543–8633.

Tide-Rider Inc., P.O. Box 429, Oakdale, CA 95361: Free information ❖ Balls, nets, and paddles. 209–848–4420.

Wa-Mac Inc., Highskore Products Inc., 178 Commerce Rd., P.O. Box 128, Carlstadt, NJ 07072: Free information ❖ Paddles, balls, nets, brackets, and sets. 800–447–5673; 201–438–7200 (in NJ).

World of Leisure Manufacturing Company, 9779 Yucca Rd., Adelanto, CA 92301: Free information ❖ Paddles, balls, nets, brackets, and sets. 619–246–3790.

TABLECLOTHS & PADS

Best Value Table Pad Company, 1170 Stella St., St. Paul, MN 55108: Free information ❖ Table pads. 800–345–9795; 612–646–6630 (in MN).

Bucks Trading Post, 930 Old Bethlehem Pike, Sellersville, PA 18960: Catalog $2 ❖ European lace curtains and matching tablecloths and doilies. 800–242–0738; 215–453–0623 (in PA).

Chambers, Mail Order Department, P.O. Box 7841, San Francisco, CA 94120: Free catalog ❖ Bed and bath furnishings. 800–334–1254.

Domestications, P.O. Box 40, Hanover, PA 17333: Free catalog ❖ Comforters, sheet sets, pillows, blankets, bedspreads, throws, solid or lace tablecloths, mini blinds, shower curtains, and bathroom accessories. 717–633–3313.

Eldridge Textile Company, 277 Grand St., New York, NY 10002: Catalog $3 (refundable) ❖ Bed, bath, and table linens. 212–925–1523.

Factory Direct Table Pad Company, P.O. Box A, LaGrange, IN 46761: Free information ❖ Table pads. 800–444–0778.

Guardian Custom Products, P.O. Box A, LaGrange, IN 46761: Free information ❖ Table pads. 800–444–0778.

Home Etc., Palo Verde at 34th St., P.O. Box 28806, Tucson, AZ 85726: Free catalog ❖ Bedding ensembles, curtains, bedspreads and comforters, rugs, linens and pillows, and towels. 800–362–8415.

Harris Levy, 278 Grand St., New York, NY 10002: Free catalog ❖ Table, bed, and bath linens. 800–221–7750; 212–226–3102 (in NY).

Olde Mill House Shoppe, 105 Strasburg Pike, Lancaster, PA 17602: Catalog $1 ❖ Country-styled homespun table linens, handcrafted furniture, braided rugs, and bathroom accessories. 717–299–0678.

Palmetto Linen Company, 145 Shoppes on the Pkwy., Hilton Head, SC 29928: Free information ❖ Sheets and matching dust ruffles, bath towels, blankets, comforters, pillows, tablecloths, place mats, shower curtains, kitchen towels, and oven gloves. 800–972–7442.

Pioneer Table Pad Company, P.O. Box 449, Gates Mills, OH 44040: Free information ❖ Table pads. 800–541–0271.

Rafael, 291 Grand St., New York, NY 10002: Free information with long SASE ❖ Pillowcases, sheets, towels, table linens, and comforters. 212–966–1928.

Rue de France, 78 Thames St., Newport, RI 02840: Catalog $3 ❖ Pillows, tablecloths, runners, and lace curtains. 800–777–0998.

Sentry Table Pad Company, 1170 Stella St., St. Paul, MN 55108: Free information ❖ Table pads. 800–328–7237.

A Touch of Country, P.O. Box 653, Palos Heights, IL 60463: Catalog $2 ❖ Table lace. 708–361–0142.

TAPESTRIES

Peerless Imported Rugs, 3033 Lincoln Ave., Chicago, IL 60657: Catalog $1 ❖ Hand- and machine-woven Oriental rugs, colonial braids, tapestries from Europe, and rag, Navajo, and grass rugs. 800–621–6573.

TATTOOING

American Tattoo Supply Inc., P.O. Box 3215, South Farmingdale, NY 11735: Free information ❖ Tattooing equipment. 516–293–4247.

Creative Alternatives, 2904 S. Barnes, Springfield, MO 65804: Brochure $4 ❖ Easy-to-remove waterproof temporary tattoos.

ES Enterprises, 2739 Woodley Pl. NW, Washington, DC 20008: Catalog $1 ❖ Waterproof easy-to-remove tattoos. 202–265–1612.

Latora Tattoo Products, P.O. Box 1569, Orting, WA 98360: Catalog $3 ❖ Tattooing equipment. 206–845–8503.

Papillon Studio Supply & Manufacturing, 47 Pearl St., Enfield, CT 06082: Free information ❖ Tattooing equipment. 203–745–9270.

Pleasurable Piercings Inc., P.O. Box 2226, Clifton, NJ 07015: Catalog $3 (refundable) ❖ Piercing equipment and body jewelry in surgical steel, niobium, and 14k or white gold. 201–488–3881.

Spaulding Rogers Manufacturing, New Scotland Rd., P.O. Box 85, Voorheesville, NY 12186: Catalog $6 ❖ Tattooing supplies. 518–768–2070.

Superior Tattoo Equipment, 3334 W. Wilshire Dr., Ste. 30, Phoenix, AZ 85009: Catalog $2 ❖ Tattooing equipment and kits. 602–278–4444.

TAXIDERMY

Dan Chase, 13599 Blackwater Rd., Baker, LA 70714: Free catalog ❖ Taxidermy supplies and how-to videos. 504–261–3795.

Clearfield Taxidermy, P.O. Box 711, Clearfield, PA 16830: Catalog $2 ❖ Taxidermy, leather-crafting, and fur-styling supplies and tools. 814–765–9561.

J.W. Elwood Company, P.O. Box 3507, Omaha, NE 68102: Free catalog ❖ Taxidermy supplies. 800–228–2291.

McKenzie Taxidermy Supply, Box 80, Granite Quarry, NC 28072: Free catalog ❖ Taxidermy supplies.

O.H. Mullen Sales Inc., RR 2, Oakwood, OH 45873: Free information ❖ Taxidermy supplies. 800–258–6625; 800–248–6625 (in OH).

John Rhinehart Taxidermy Supply Company, Division American Institute of Taxidermy, 3232 McCormick Dr., Janesville, WI 53545: Free information ❖ Taxidermy supplies. 800–FOR-DEER; 608–755–5160 (in WI).

Touchstone Taxidermy Supply, 5011 E. Texas, Bossier City, LA 71111: Free catalog ❖ Taxidermy supplies. 318–746–5792.

VanDyke's, Box 278, Woonsocket, SD 57385: Catalog $1 ❖ Taxidermy supplies. 800–843–3320; 605–796–4425 (in SD).

TELEPHONES & ANSWERING MACHINES

Antique Phones

A.M. Telephone Company, Turtle Lake, WI 54889: Catalog $1 ❖ Antique telephones and parts. 715–986–4414.

Billard's Telephones, 21710 Regnart Rd., Cupertino, CA 95014: Brochure $1 ❖ Antique telephones and parts. 408–252–2104.

Chicago Old Telephone Company, P.O. Box 189, Lemon Springs, NC 28355: Free catalog ❖ Restored telephones that can be plugged into modern systems. 800–843–1320.

Alexander Graham's, P.O. Box 080936, Rochester, MN 48308: Free information ❖ Royal Albert, Wedgewood, Galway Crystal, Limoge, and other Victorian-style telephones. 800–888–2130.

Mahantango Manor, Hickory Corners Rd., Dalmatia, PA 17017: Catalog $3 ❖ Working replicas of telephones from the 1900s. 800–642–3966.

Phone Wizard, 106 S. King St., P.O. Box 70, Leesburg, VA 22075: Catalog $3 ❖ Restored antique telephones and parts. 703–777–0000.

Phoneco Inc., P.O. Box 70, Galesville, WI 54630: Free information ❖ Restored antique telephones, parts, and novelty, art dceco, character, and other styles. 608–582–4124.

Turtle Lake Telephone Company, P.O. Box 5, Turtle Lake, WI 54889: Catalog $1 ❖ Antique hand-crank telephones and parts. 715–986–2233.

Cellular Phones

Alpine Electronics of America, 19145 Gramercy Pl., Torrance, CA 90505: Free information ❖ Cellular phones. 213–326–8000.

Audiovox, 150 Marcus Blvd., Hauppage, NY 11788: Free information ❖ Portable and installation-style cellular phones. 516–436–6200.

Blaupunkt, 2800 S. 25th Ave., Broadview, IL 60153: Free information ❖ Portable and installation-style cellular phones. 708–865–5200.

CellStar Corporation, 1730 Briercroft Ct., Carrollton, TX 75006: Free information ❖ Cellular phone accessories. 800–766–8283.

Cellular Phone & Accessory Warehouse, 11741 Valley View St., Ste. I, Cypress, CA 90630: Free catalog ❖ Cellular phones. 800–342–2336.

Cincinnati Microwave, One Microwave Plaza, Cincinnati, OH 45249: Free information ❖ Portable cellular phones. 800–543–1608.

Clarion Corporation of America, 661 W. Redondo Beach Blvd., Gardena, CA 90247: Free information ❖ Installation-style cellular phones. 800–487–9007.

Ericsson GE Mobile Communications, Mountain View Rd., P.O. Box 4325, Lynchburg, VA 24502: Free information ❖ Cellular phones. 800–CARFONE.

Kraco, 503 E. Euclid Ave., Compton, CA 90224: Free information ❖ Portable cellular phones. 310–639–0666.

Mitsubishi Electronics, 5665 Plaza Dr., Cypress, CA 90630: Free information ❖ Portable and installation-style cellular phones. 800–843–2515.

Motorola, 1475 W. Shure Dr., Arlington Heights, IL 60004: Free information ❖ Portable cellular phones. 708–632–5000.

NEC Home Electronics, 1255 Michael Dr., Wood Dale, IL 60191: Free information ❖

Portable and installation-style cellular phones. 708–860–9500.

Newtech Video & Computers, 350 7th Ave., New York, NY 10001: Free information ❖ Video equipment, computers and peripherals, software, cellular phones, fax machines, and office equipment. 800–554–9747.

NovAtel, 3800 Sandshell Dr., Fort Worth, TX 76137: Free information ❖ Mobile cellular phones. 817–847–2100.

Oki Telecom, 437 Old Peachtree Rd., Suwanee, GA 30174: Free information ❖ Portable, briefcase-style, and installation-style cellular phones. 404–995–9800.

Omni Cellular Ltd., 96 S. Madison, Carthage, IL 62321: Free information ❖ Portable cellular phones. 217–357–2308.

Panasonic, Panasonic Way, Secaucus, NJ 07094: Free information ❖ Portable and installation-style cellular phones. 201–348–7000.

Radio Shack, Division Tandy Corporation, 1500 One Tandy Center, Fort Worth, TX 76102: Free information ❖ Installation-style and portable cellular phones. 817–390–3700.

Shintom West, 20435 South Western Ave., Torrance, CA 90501: Free information ❖ Mobile cellular phones. 310–328–7200.

Shure Brothers Inc., 222 Hartrey Ave., Evanston, IL 60202: Free information ❖ Hands-free cellular phones. 800–447–4873.

Technophone Corporation, 1801 Penn St., Melbourne, FL 32901: Free information ❖ Mobile cellular phones. 407–952–2100.

Uniden, 4700 Amon Carter Blvd., Fort Worth, TX 76155: Free information ❖ Portable and installation-style cellular phones. 817–858–3300.

Telephones & Answering Machines

Bernie's Discount Center Inc., 821 6th Ave., New York, NY 10001: Catalog $1 (refundable) ❖ Telephones and answering machines, audio and video equipment, large and small kitchen appliances, and personal care appliances. 212–564–8758.

Bi-Rite Photo & Electronics, 15 E. 30th St., New York, NY 10016: Free information ❖ Telephones, cameras, typewriters, calculators, video equipment, and other electronics. 800–223–1970; 212–685–2130 (in NY).

Crutchfield, 1 Crutchfield Park, Charlottesville, VA 22906: Free catalog ❖

Fax machines, telephones and answering machines, word processors, copiers, computers, and software. 800–955–9009.

East 33rd Street Electronics & Typewriters, 42 E. 33rd St., New York, NY 10016: Free information with long SASE ❖ Telephones and answering machines, typewriters, calculators, computers, software, TV sets, video equipment, and other electronics. 212–686–0930.

Electronic Wholesalers, 1160 Hamburg Tnpk., Wayne, NJ 07470: Free information ❖ Telephones, camcorders, TV sets, cassette and disk players, audio equipment, and other electronics. 201–696–6531.

Hello Direct, 5884 Eden Park Pl., San Jose, CA 95138: Free catalog ❖ Telephones and answering machines. 800–444–3556.

J & R Music World, 59–50 Queens-Midtown Expwy., Maspeth, NY 11378: Free catalog ❖ Telephones, audio equipment, car and portable stereos, video recorders, computers, and other electronics. 800–221–8180.

Olden Video, 1265 Broadway, New York, NY 10001: Free information ❖ Telephones, copiers, and photographic equipment. 212–725–1234.

Planet Electronics, 8418 Lilley, Canton, MI 48187: Free catalog ❖ Telephones, audio and video equipment, TV sets, car and portable stereos, cassette players, and video tapes, cassettes, and disks. 800–247–4663; 313–453–4750 (in MI).

S & S Sound City, 58 W. 45th St., New York, NY 10036: Free information ❖ Audio and video equipment, telephones, office machines, and other electronics. 212–575–0210.

Sound City, Meadtown Shopping Center, Rt. 23, Kinnelon, NJ 07405: Free information ❖ Audio and video equipment, cassette and CD players, camcorders, TVs, processors, fax machines, telephones, and other electronics. 800–542–7283.

Teleconcepts Inc., 11711 NW 39th St., Coral Springs, FL 33065: Free information ❖ Decor telephones.

Telephone Engineering Company, 786 Main St., Simpson, PA 18407: Free catalog ❖ Rotary and push-button phones, parts, two-line and novelty phones, business telephone systems, and sonic alert telephone ring signalers. 717–282–5100.

Temasek Telephone Inc., 21 Airport Rd., South San Francisco, CA 94080: Free information ❖ Voice-activated telephones. 800–647–8887.

TENNIS
Clothing

Adidas USA, 5675 N. Blackstock Rd., Spartanburg, SC 29303: Free information ❖ Dresses, sweaters, jackets, caps and sun visors, shirts and tops, shoes and socks, shorts, and warm-up suits. 800–423–4327

Alchester Mills Company Inc., 314 S. 11th St., Camden, NJ 08103: Free information ❖ Caps and sun visors, gloves, sweatbands, and socks. 609–964–9700.

Asics Tiger Corporation, 10540 Talbert Ave., West Bldg., Fountain Valley, CA 92708: Free information ❖ Dresses, jackets, shirts and tops, shoes and socks, and warm-up suits. 800–766–ASICS; 714–962–7654 (in CA).

Associated Tennis Suppliers, 200 Waterfront Dr., Pittsburgh, PA 15222: Free catalog ❖ Tennis racquets, supplies, easy-to-use stringing machines, and clothing. 800–866–7071.

Ball Hopper Products Inc., 200 Waterfront Dr., Pittsburgh, PA 15222: Free information ❖ Caps and sun visors, gloves, dresses, jackets, shirts and tops, socks, sweatbands, underwear, and warm-up suits. 800–323–5417; 412–323–9633 (in PA).

Betlin Manufacturing, 1445 Marion Rd., Columbus OH 43207: Free information ❖ Tennis jackets, shorts, and warm-up suits. 614–443–0248.

Converse Inc., 1 Fordham Rd., North Reading, MA 01864: Free information ❖ Caps and sun visors, jackets, shirts and tops, socks, sweatbands, and warm-up suits. 800–428–2667; 508–664–1100 (in MA).

Ellesse USA Inc., 1430 Broadway, New York, NY 10018: Free information ❖ Dresses, jackets, caps and sun visors, gloves, shorts, shirts and tops, socks, sweatbands, underwear, and warm-up suits. 800–345–9036; 212–840–6111 (in NY).

Head Sports Wear, 9189 Red Branch Rd., Columbia, MD 21045: Free information ❖ Dresses, shirts and tops, shorts, and sweaters. 800–638–9680; 301–730–8300 (in MD).

Holabird Sports Discounters, 9008 Yellow Brick Rd., Rossville Industrial Park, Baltimore, MD 21237: Free catalog ❖ Tennis racquets, shoes, clothes, balls, and bags. 410–687–6400.

Las Vegas Discount Golf & Tennis, 5325 S. Valley View Blvd., Ste. 10, Las Vegas, NV 89109: Free catalog ❖ Equipment, shoes, and clothing for tennis, racquetball, golf, and running and jogging. 702–798–7777.

Lily's, 4910–B W. Rosecrans Ave., Hawthorne, CA 90250: Free information ❖ Dresses, jackets, caps and sun visors, shirts and tops, shorts, sweatbands, and warm-up suits. 800–421–4474.

Nike Footwear Inc., One Bowerman Dr., Beaverton, OR 97005: Free information ❖ Jackets, shirts and tops, shoes and socks, shorts, and sweatbands. 800–344–6453.

Prince Racquet Sports, 1 Tennis Ct., Bordentown, NJ 08505: Free information ❖ Caps and sun visors, dresses, jackets, shirts and tops, shoes and socks, sweatbands, underwear, and warm-up suits. 800–2–TENNIS; 609–291–5900 (in NJ).

Professional Golf & Tennis Suppliers, 7825 Hollywood Blvd., Pembroke Pines, FL 33024: Free catalog ❖ Tennis rackets, clothing, shoes, and racquetball equipment. 305–981–7283.

Puma USA Inc., 147 Centre St., Brockton, MA 02403: Free information with long SASE ❖ Dresses, jackets, shirts and tops, socks, sweatbands, sweaters, and warm-up suits. 508–583–9100.

Samuels Tennisport, 7796 Montgomery Rd., Cincinnati, OH 45236: Free information ❖ Tennis, squash, and racquetball racquets and shoes. 513–791–4636.

Spalding Sports Worldwide, 425 Meadow St., P.O. Box 901, Chicopee, MA 01021: Free information ❖ Caps and sun visors, gloves, dresses, jackets, shirts and tops, shorts, shoes and socks, sweatbands, underwear, and warm-up suits. 800–225–6601.

Sport Casuals, Box 402337, Miami Beach, FL 33140: Free information ❖ Jackets, shirts and tops, shoes and socks, shorts, sweaters, and warm-up suits. 800–776–7803; 305–674–0001 (in FL).

Sporting Life, 1116 S. Powerline Rd., Deerfield Beach, FL 33442: Free catalog ❖ Shorts, socks, headbands, wristbands, hats, tennis shoes, boat shoes, beach sandals, sport bags, tennis outfits for men and ladies, sweat shirts, and sweat suits. 800–782–5373.

The Sporting Look, 1116 S. Powerline Rd., Deerfield Beach, FL 33442: Catalog $2 ❖ Tennis clothing. 305–570–5385.

Sportline of Hilton Head Ltd., 816 Friendly Ln., Greensboro, NC 27408: Free information ❖ Tennis racquets, shoes, bags, and clothing. 800–438–6021.

Sports Express, P.O. Box 690983, Houston, TX 77269: Free information ❖ Tennis racquets, court equipment, grips and wraps, shoes, bags, and clothing. 800–533–6321.

Sullivan Sports, P.O. Box 690906, Houston, TX 77269: Free information ❖ Tennis racquets, shoes, bags, and clothing. 800–543–0926.

Total Sports, 200 Waterfront Dr., Pittsburgh, PA 15222: Free catalog ❖ Tennis racquet strings, clothing, bags, and court supplies. 800–245–0208.

Equipment

Adidas USA, 5675 N. Blackstock Rd., Spartanburg, SC 29303: Free information ❖ Composite graphite tennis racquets. 800–423–4327.

American Playground Corporation, 1801 S. Jackson, P.O. Box 2599, Anderson, IN 46011: Free information ❖ Posts, nets, and other court equipment. 800–541–1602.

American Tennis Mart, P.O. Box 690906, Houston, TX 77269: Free information ❖ Tennis racquets, shoes, bags, and clothing. 800–344–7707.

Associated Tennis Suppliers, 200 Waterfront Dr., Pittsburgh, PA 15222: Free catalog ❖ Tennis racquets, supplies, easy-to-use stringing machines, and clothing. 800–866–7071.

Atlantic Racquet Sports, P.O. Box 6218, Gulf Breeze, FL 32561: Free price list ❖ Strings and grips. 800–223–1540.

Atlantic Strings & Accessories, P.O. Box 6218, Gulf Breeze, FL 32561: Free information ❖ Tennis equipment. 800–223–1540.

Austad's, 4500 E. 10th St., P.O. Box 5428, Sioux Falls, SD 57196: Free catalog ❖ Equipment for tennis and other sports. 800–844–1234.

Ball Hopper Products Inc., 200 Waterfront Dr., Pittsburgh, PA 15222: Free information ❖ Ball retrievers and balls, posts and nets, practice and stringing machines, strings, and aluminum, boron composite, graphite composite, ceramic, graphite, graphite

composite, and wood racquets. 800–323–5417; 412–323–9633 (in PA).

Cannon Sports, P.O. Box 11179, Burbank, CA 91510: Free information with list of retailers ❖ Posts, nets, balls, ball retrievers, and other court equipment. 800–362–3146; 818–753–5940 (in CA).

Carron Net Company, 1623 17th St., P.O. Box 177, Two Rivers, WI 54241: Free information ❖ Posts, nets, ball retrievers, practice machines, and other court equipment. 800–558–7768; 414–793–2217 (in WI).

Century Sports Inc., Lakewood Industrial Park, 1995 Rutgers University Blvd., Box 2035, Lakewood, NJ 08701: Free information ❖ Balls, nets, racquet covers, and racquets. 800–526–7548; 908–905–4422 (in NJ).

Clarke Distributing Company, 9233 Bryant St., Houston, TX 77075: Free information ❖ Balls, nets, and racquets. 800–670–0111.

Cosom Sporting Goods, Division Mantua Industries Inc., Grandview Ave., Woodbury Heights, NJ 08097: Free information ❖ Balls. 800–328–5635; 609–853–0300 (in NJ).

Dunlop Stazenger Corporation, P.O. Box 3070, Greenville, SC 29602: Free information ❖ Gut, nylon, and synthetic strings and aluminum, boron composite, ceramic, graphite, and graphite composite tennis racquets. 800–845–8794; 803–271–9767 (in SC).

Easton, 5040 W. Harold Gatty Dr., Salt Lake City, UT 84116: Free information and list of retailers ❖ Aluminum, ceramic, graphite, and graphite composite tennis racquets. 801–539–1400.

Edwards Sports Products, 429 E. Haddam-Moodus Rd., Moodus, CT 06469: Free information ❖ Tennis nets, posts, and other court equipment. 800–243–2512; 203–873–8625 (in CT).

Estca/EST USA, 17720 NE 65th St., Redmond, WA 98052: Free information ❖ Tennis racquets. 800–228–6689; 206–881–8989 (in WA).

FEMCO Corporation, 235 Arcadia St., Richmond, VA 23225: Free information ❖ Ball retrievers, nets, posts, practice machines, balls, and stringing supplies. 800–476–5432.

Fischer Tennis, 2412 Logan Rd., Owings Mills, MD 21117: Free information ❖ Balls, racquet covers, and racquets. 410–356–0196.

Gamma Sports, 200 Waterfront Dr., Pittsburgh, PA 15222: Free information ❖ Tennis racquets. 800–333–0337.

Golden Shine Inc., 4075 E. La Palma Ave., Anaheim, CA 92807: Free information ❖ Portable, easy-to-assemble tennis rebound net. 800–852–8525.

Guterman International Inc., 71 Pullman St., Worcester, MA 01606: Free information ❖ Portable stringers. 800–343–6096; 508–852–8206 (in MA).

Holabird Sports Discounters, 9008 Yellow Brick Rd., Rossville Industrial Park, Baltimore, MD 21237: Free catalog ❖ Tennis racquets, shoes, clothes, balls, bags, and other sports equipment. 410–687–6400.

Jayfro Corporation, Unified Sports Inc., 976 Hartford Tnpk., P.O. Box 400, Waterford, CT 06385: Free catalog ❖ Tennis net posts, nets, portable units, windscreens, court dividers, and practice tennis standards. 203–447–3001.

Charlie Johnson's Tennis & Squash Shop, 2648 Erie Ave., Cincinnati, OH 45208: Free information ❖ Racquets, shoes, strings, and grips. 800–222–1143.

Klipspringer USA Inc., 780 Church Rd., Elgin, IL 60123: Free brochure ❖ Stringing machines, hand tools, and strings. 800–522–5547; 708–742–1300 (in IL).

Las Vegas Discount Golf & Tennis, 5325 S. Valley View Blvd., Ste. 10, Las Vegas, NV 89109: Free catalog ❖ Equipment, shoes, and clothing. 702–798–7777.

Leisure Marketing Inc., 2204 Morris Ave., Ste. 202, Union, NJ 07083: Free information ❖ Aluminum, boron composite, ceramic, graphite, and graphite composite tennis racquets. 908–851–9494.

Leisure Pro, The Tennis Emporium, 42 W. 18th St., 3rd Floor, New York, NY 10011: Free information ❖ Racquets, strings, grips, footwear, ballhoppers, and balls. 800–637–6880; 212–645–1234 (in NY).

Lobster Inc., 1112 North Ave., Plainfield, NJ 07060: Free brochure ❖ Racquets, ball machines, balls, and other equipment. 800–526–4041; 908–668–1900 (in NJ).

Markwort Sporting Goods Company, 4300 Forest Park Ave., St. Louis, MO 63108: Catalog $8 with list of retailers ❖ Balls, nets, racquet covers, and racquets. 800–669–6626; 314–652–3757 (in MO).

Master Corporation, P.O. Box 585, Auburn, IN 46706: Free information ❖ Portable tennis serving machine. 219–925–4226.

MAXLINE, 22624 Felbar Ave., Torrance, CA 90505: Free information ❖ Balls, racquet covers, and racquets. 310–534–1048.

Midwest Sports Supply, 8740 Montgomery Rd., Cincinnati, OH 45236: Free information ❖ Tennis racquets, shoes for men and women, tennis bags, strings, and court equipment. 800–527–2577.

Nassau Tennis, 95 Blackburn Center, Gloucester, MA 01930: Free information ❖ Tennis racquets. 800–255–7812; 508–281–3700 (in MA).

NRC Sports, P.O. Box 331, West Boylston, MA 01583: Free information ❖ Portable stringers and natural gut, synthetic, and nylon strings. 800–243–5033; 508–852–8987 (in MA).

Olympia Sports, 745 State Cir., Ann Arbor, MI 48106: Free information ❖ Nets, posts, and balls. 800–521–2832; 313–761–5135 (in MI).

Pennsylvania Sporting Goods, 1360 Industrial Hwy., P.O. Box 451, Southampton, PA 18966: Free information ❖ Balls, ball retrievers, posts and nets, practice machines, aluminum tennis racquets, nylon and synthetic strings, and stringing machines. 800–523–1122.

Performance Racquet Sports, 12651 Polo Pl., Broomfield, CO 80020: Free information ❖ Racquets, grips, strings, and court equipment. 800–358–2294.

Powers Court, 40 S. Main St., New City, NY 10956: Free catalog ❖ Racquet stringers, strings, and other equipment. 800–431–2838; 914–634–6969 (in NY).

Prince Racquet Sports, 1 Tennis Ct., Bordentown, NJ 08505: Free information ❖ Stringing machines, nylon and synthetic strings, and aluminum, boron composite, ceramic, graphite, graphite composite, and wood tennis racquets. 800–2–TENNIS; 609–291–5900 (in NJ).

Pro-Kennex, 9606 Kearny Villa Rd., San Diego, CA 92126: Free information ❖ Tennis racquets. 800–854–1908; 619–271–8390 (in CA).

Professional Golf & Tennis Suppliers, 7825 Hollywood Blvd., Pembroke Pines, FL 33024: Free catalog ❖ Tennis rackets, clothing and shoes, and racquetball equipment. 305–981–7283.

Samuels Tennisport, 7796 Montgomery Rd., Cincinnati, OH 45236: Free information ❖ Tennis, squash, and racquetball racquets, equipment, and shoes. 513–791–4636.

Sentra Tennis, P.O. Box 348485, Chicago, IL 60634: Free information ❖ Tennis racquets. 800–524–9992.

Spalding Sports Worldwide, 425 Meadow St., P.O. Box 901, Chicopee, MA 01021: Free information ❖ Tennis balls, composite tennis racquets, and nylon, synthetic, and gut strings. 800–225–6601.

Sport Casuals, Box 402337, Miami Beach, FL 33140: Free information ❖ Boron composite, ceramic, graphite, and graphite composite tennis racquets. 800–776–7803; 305–674–0001 (in FL).

Sportline of Hilton Head Ltd., 816 Friendly Ln., Greensboro, NC 27408: Free information ❖ Tennis racquets, shoes, bags, and clothing. 800–438–6021.

Sports Express, P.O. Box 690983, Houston, TX 77269: Free information ❖ Tennis racquets, court equipment, grips and wraps, shoes, bags, and clothing. 713–537–8669.

Sullivan Sports, P.O. Box 690906, Houston, TX 77269: Free information ❖ Tennis racquets and bags, court and training equipment, strings, grips and wraps, and shoes and clothing for men and women. 800–543–0926.

Tennis Company, 30860 Southfield Rd., Southfield, MI 48076: Free information ❖ Tennis equipment. 313–258–9366.

Tennis Gear & Running Center, P.O. Box 1486, Cumberland, MD 21502: Free price list ❖ Tennis equipment. 301–729–0896.

Total Sports, 200 Waterfront Dr., Pittsburgh, PA 15222: Free catalog ❖ Tennis racquet strings, clothing, bags, and court supplies. 800–245–0208.

U.S. Sports Equipment Company, 1515 W. MacArthur Blvd., Costa Mesa, CA 92626: Free information ❖ Posts, nets, ball retrievers, balls, practice machines, stringing machines, synthetic and nylon strings, and boron composite, ceramic, graphite, and graphite composite tennis racquets. 800–854–7331; 714–549–4725 (in CA).

Wa-Mac Inc., Highskore Products Inc., 178 Commerce Rd., P.O. Box 128, Carlstadt, NJ 07072: Free information ❖ Tennis balls and aluminum, boron composite, ceramic, graphite, graphite composite, and wood tennis racquets. 800–447–5673; 201–438–7200 (in NJ).

Wild World of Sporting Goods, 220 S. University Dr., Plantation, FL 33324: Free price list ❖ Tennis, racquetball, and squash racquets. 305–475–9800.

Wilson Sporting Goods, 8700 W. Bryn Mawr, Chicago, IL 60631: Free information ❖ Stringing machines and strings, balls, nets, and aluminum, boron composite, ceramic, graphite, graphite composite, and wood tennis racquets. 800–272–6060; 312–714–6400 (in IL).

Yamaha Sporting Goods Division, 6600 Orangethorpe Ave., Buena Park, CA 90620: Free information ❖ Strings and boron composite, ceramic, graphite and graphite composite tennis racquets. 800–851–6514; 714–522–9011 (in CA).

Zebest Racquet & Golf Sports, Box 183, Stone Mountain, GA 30086: Free information ❖ Balls, racquet covers, and racquets. 800–272–7279; 404–469–7800 (in GA).

TERM PAPERS

Academic Research Inc., 240 Park Ave., Rutherford, NJ 02070: Free catalog ❖ Over 20,000 reports and term papers. 800–477–3732.

Research Assistance, 11322 Idaho Ave., Los Angeles, CA 90025: Catalog $2 ❖ Over 10,000 term papers. 800–351–0222.

TETHERBALL

American Playground Corporation, 1801 S. Jackson, P.O. Box 2599, Anderson, IN 46011: Free information ❖ Balls, poles, and posts. 800–541–1602.

Franklin Sports Industries Inc., 17 Campanelli Parkway, P.O. Box 508, Stoughton, MA 02072: Free information ❖ Balls and sets. 617–344–1111.

General Sportcraft Company Ltd., 140 Woodbine Rd., Bergenfield, NJ 07621: Free information ❖ Balls, poles, posts, and sets. 201–384–4242.

Indian Industries Inc., P.O. Box 889, Evansville, IN 47706: Free catalog ❖ Sets. 800–457–3373; 812–467–1200 (in IN).

Dick Martin Sports Inc., 181 E. Union Ave., P.O. Box 7381, East Rutherford, NJ 07073: Free information ❖ Balls, poles, posts, and sets. 800–221–1993; 201–438–5255 (in NJ).

Pennsylvania Sporting Goods, 1360 Industrial Hwy., P.O. Box 451, Southampton,

PA 18966: Free information ❖ Balls, poles, posts, and sets. 800–535–1122.

Venus Knitting Mills Inc., 140 Spring St., Murray Hill, NJ 07974: Free information ❖ Balls, paddles, poles, posts, and sets. 800–955–4200; 908–464–2400 (in NJ).

THEATRICAL SUPPLIES
Make-Up

Abracadabra Magic Shop, 125 Lincoln Blvd., Middlesex, NJ 08846: Catalog $5 ❖ Magician's and clown supplies, costumes, and theatrical make-up. 908–805–0200.

Apples & Company, 414 Conant Ave., Union, NJ 07083: Free information ❖ Clown-white make-up. 908–353–2193.

Burpo Duh Clown, P.O. Box 160190, Cupertino, CA 95016: Free information ❖ Face-painting rubber stamps and supplies. 408–446–9314.

Clown Heaven, 4792 Old State Rd. 37 South, Martinsville, IN 46152: Catalog $3 ❖ Balloons, make-up, puppets, wigs, ministry and gospel items, novelties, magic, clown props, and books. 317–342–6888.

Costumes by Betty, 2181 Edgerton St., St. Paul, MN 55117: Catalog $5 (refundable) ❖ Clown costumes, make-up, wigs, and shoes. 612–771–8734.

Eastern Costume Company, 510 N. Elm St., Greensboro, NC 27401: Free information ❖ Make-up and costumes. 910–379–1026.

The Entertainers Supermarket, 21 Carol Pl., Staten Island, NY 10303: Free brochure ❖ Supplies and props for face painters, clowns, magicians, balloon sculpturists, jugglers, stilt walkers, and other entertainers. 718–494–6232.

Freckles Clown Supplies, 5509 Rossevelt Blvd., Jacksonville, FL 32210: Catalog $5 ❖ Make-up, costumes, clown supplies, puppets, how-to books on clowning and ballooning, and other theatrical supplies. 904–778–3977.

Graftobian Ltd., 510 Tasman St., Madison, WI 53714: Free information ❖ Face-painting supplies. 800–255–0584.

Bob Kelly Cosmetics Inc., 151 W. 46th St., New York, NY 10036: Free catalog ❖ Make-up kits. 212–819–0030.

Lynch's Clown Supplies, 939 Howard, Dearborn, MI 48124: Catalog $5 ❖ Make-up, costume accessories, and clown equipment. 313–565–3425.

Mecca Magic Inc., 49 Dodd St., Bloomfield, NJ 07003: Catalog $10 ❖ Make-up, costumes and wigs, puppets, clown props, magic tricks, and juggling equipment. 201–429–7597.

Novelties Unlimited, 410 W. 21st St., Norfolk, VA 23517: Catalog $5 ❖ Make-up, clown props and gags, magic, balloons, and party decorations. 804–622–622–0344.

Ben Nye Makeup, 5935 Bowcroft St., Los Angeles, CA 90016: Catalog $2.50 ❖ Theatrical make-up. 310–839–1984.

Potsy & Blimpo Clown Supplies, P.O. Box 2075, Huntington Beach, CA 92647: Free catalog ❖ Clown make-up, wigs, and props. 800–897–0749.

Rubie's Costume Company, 120–08 Jamaica Ave., Richmond Hill, Queens, NY 11418: Free information ❖ Costumes, make-up, hair goods, and special effects. 718–846–1008.

Theatrical Lighting Systems Inc., 909 Meridian St., P.O. Box 2646, Huntsville, AL 35804: Free information ❖ Make-up, dimming and lighting control systems, follow spots, and other stage equipment. 205–533–7025.

Under the Big Top, P.O. Box 807, Placentia, CA 92670: Catalog $4 ❖ Costumes, clown props, make-up, juggling equipment, and party supplies. 800–995–7727.

Up, Up & Away, P.O. Box 159, Beallsville, PA 15313: Catalog $2 ❖ Make-up, props, and clown equipment. 412–769–5447.

Victoria's Dance-Theatrical Supply, 1331 Lincoln Ave., San Jose, CA 95125: Catalog $2 ❖ Portable wall-mounted ballet. 408–295–9317.

Plays

Empire Publishing Service, P.O. Box 1344, Studio City, CA 91614: Catalog $1 ❖ Entertainment industry and performing art books, plays and musicals, musical scores, books about film and theatrical personalities, and music books. 818–784–8918.

Samuel French Catalog, 45 W. 25th St., New York, NY 10010: Catalog $4.50 ❖ Scripts for plays and other theatrical productions. 212–206–8990.

Samuel French Trade, 7623 Sunset Blvd., Hollywood, CA 90046: Free catalog ❖ Over 2500 plays. Includes classics made into movies. 213–876–0570.

Stage Equipment

Alcone Company Inc., Paramount Theatrical Supplies, 5–49 49th Ave., Long Island City, NY 11101: Catalog $5 ❖ Fabrics, make-up, hardware and rigging, lighting and other theatrical equipment, paint, and other scenery supplies. 718–361–8373.

Altman Stage Lighting Company, 57 Alexander St., Yonkers, NY 10701: Free information ❖ Stage lighting equipment. 914–476–7987.

Bandit Lites, 10624 Dutchtown Rd., Knoxville, TN 37932: Free information ❖ Spots, beams, softs, commanders, color faders, rangers, and other lighting equipment. 615–675–0880.

BMI Supply, 28 Logan Ave., Glens Falls, NY 12801: Free information ❖ Theatrical supplies and equipment. 800–836–0524.

Bulbman, P.O. Box 2918, Reno, NV 89505: Free information ❖ Replacement bulbs for theatrical lighting equipment. 800–648–1163.

Dazian's Inc., 2014 Commerce St., Dallas, TX 75201: Free catalog ❖ Scenery canvas, ducks, theatrical gauze, muslin, duvetyne, babinettes, metallics, velours, scrims, felt, and other costume and flame-proof fabrics. 214–748–3450.

Florida Magic Company, P.O. Box 290781, Fort Lauderdale, FL 33329: Free information ❖ Portable AC or battery-operated public address system. 305–321–8548.

Four Star Lighting, Jupiter Scenic Inc., 603 Commerce Way West, Jupiter, FL 33458: Free information ❖ Scenery drapes and lighting equipment. 407–743–7367.

Gothic Scenic & Theatrical Paints, Long Island Paint Company, Box 189, Continental Hill, Glen Cove, NY 11542: Free information ❖ Scenic and theatrical paints and other supplies. 516–676–6600.

The Great American Market, 826 N. Cole Ave., Hollywood, CA 90038: Free information ❖ Stage lighting equipment. 213–461–0200.

Jupiter Scenic Inc., 603 Commerce Way West, Jupiter, FL 33458: Free information ❖ Scenery drapes and lighting equipment. 407–743–7367.

Kee Industrial Products Inc., P.O. Box 207, Buffalo, NY 14225: Free information ❖ Hardware for stage platforms, multi-level sets, and backgrounds. 716–896–4949.

Kliegl Bros., 5 Aerial Way, Syosset, NY 11791: Free information ❖ Computer lighting control systems. 516–937–3900.

Olesen, Division Entertainment Resources Inc., 1523–35 Ivar Ave., Hollywood, CA 90028: Free information ❖ Lighting and production supplies. 800–821–1656.

Peavey Electronics Corporation, 711 A St., P.O. Box 2898, Meridian, MS 39302: Free information ❖ Lighting equipment. 601–483–5365.

Precision Effects, 7602 San Fernando Rd., Sun Valley, CA 91352: Free information ❖ Special effects equipment. 818–504–2617.

Proscenium Lighting, 1050 Cahuenga Blvd., Hollywood, CA 90038: Free catalog ❖ Lighting equipment. 800–682–4140.

Rose Brand Fabrics, 517 W. 35th St., New York, NY 10001: Free catalog ❖ Theatrical fabrics. 800–223–1624; 212–594–7424 (in NY).

Schacht Lighting, 5214 Burleson Rd., Austin, TX 78744: Free brochure ❖ Track lighting, replacement bulbs, and craft show lights. 800–256–7114.

Sitler's Supplies Inc., 702 E. Washington, P.O. Box 10, Washington, IA 52353: Free information ❖ Stage, studio, and projector lamps. 800–426–3938.

StageRight Corporation, 495 Holley Dr., Clare, MI 48617: Free information ❖ Portable units and extensions for stage assemblies. 800–438–4499.

Charles H. Stewart & Company, P.O. Box 187, Somerville, MA 02144: Free information ❖ Scenery backdrops. 617–625–2407.

Syracuse Scenery & Stage Lighting Company Inc., 101 Monarch Dr., Liverpool, NY 13088: Free information ❖ Curtains and other stage fabrics. 315–800–453–SSSL; 315–453–8096 (in NY).

Theater Magic, 6099 Godown Rd., Columbus, OH 43220: Free information ❖ Special effects lighting equipment. 614–459–3222.

Theatrical Lighting Systems Inc., 909 Meridian St., P.O. Box 2646, Huntsville, AL 35804: Free information ❖ Dimming and lighting control systems, follow spots, other lighting equipment, and make-up. 205–533–7025.

Tobins Lake Studios, 7030 Old US 23, Brighton, MI 48116: Free catalog ❖ Drapes,

drops, lighting equipment, and scenery paint. 313–229–6666.

Tri-Ess Sciences Inc., 1020 W. Chestnut St., Burbank, CA 91506: Catalog $3 ❖ Special effects equipment. 800–274–6910.

Thomas J. Valentino Inc., P.O. Box 534, Elmsford, NY 10523: Free catalog ❖ Easy-to-use sound effects on long-playing records. 212–869–5210.

Westgate Enterprises, 2118 Wilshire Blvd., Ste. 612, Santa Monica, CA 90403: Free catalog ❖ Full spectrum color corrected light bulbs, flood lights, spot lights, and tubes. 310–477–5891.

THERMOMETERS

Abbeon Cal Inc., 123 Gray Ave., Santa Barbara, CA 93101: Free catalog ❖ Thermometers, hygrometers, moisture meters, and humidity indicators. 805–966–0810.

THIMBLES

Gimbel & Sons Country Store, 36 Commercial St., P.O. Box 57, Boothbay Harbor, ME 04538: Free catalog ❖ Thimbles, other collectibles, and gifts. 207–633–5088.

TICKETS

All Points Tag & Ticket Company, 1330 Lloyd Rd., Wickliffe, OH 44092: Free price list ❖ Raffle tickets. 800–342–2102.

Carter Printing, Box 289, Farmersville, IL 62533: Free information ❖ Raffle tickets. 217–227–4464.

LMN Printing, 118 N. Ridgewood Ave., Edgewater, FL 32132: Free price list ❖ Raffle books, tickets, and coupon books. 800–741–5668.

Quick Tickets, 3030 W. Pasadena, Flint, MI 48504: Free information ❖ Tickets. 800–521–1142; 313–732–0770 (in MI).

Rapid Raffles, P.O. Box 862, Marshalls Creek, PA 18335: Free information ❖ Chance books and raffle tickets. 800–972–3353.

Ready-Tickets, Box 227, Lyons, PA 19536: Free information ❖ Pre-numbered perforated tickets. 800–552–1400.

Ticket Craft, 1925 Bellmore Ave., Bellmore, NY 11710: Free catalog ❖ Theater tickets. 800–645–4944; 516–826–1500 (in NY).

TOBACCO, PIPES & CIGARS

Davidoff of Geneva Inc., 535 Madison Ave., New York, NY 10022: Free information ❖

Cigars. 800–548–4623; 212–751–9060 (in NY).

Famous Smoke Shop Inc., 55 W. 39th St., New York, NY 10018: Free catalog ❖ Pipe tobaccos and premium hand-rolled and generic cigars. 800–672–5544.

Georgetown Tobacco, 3144 M St. NW, Washington, DC 20007: Catalog $1 ❖ Private tobacco mixtures, pipes, imported and domestic cigars, lighters, and gifts. 202–338–5100.

Holt's Cigar Company, 114 S. 16th St., Philadelphia, PA 10102: Free information ❖ Premium cigars. 800–523–1641; 215–563–0763 (in PA).

J-R Tobacco, 277 Rt. 46 West, Fairfield, NJ 07006: Free catalog ❖ Imported cigars and pipe tobaccos. 800–JRC-IGAR; 201–882–0050 (in NJ).

Kirsten Pipe Company, P.O. Box 70526, Seattle, WA 98107: Free brochure ❖ Pipes, replacement mouthpieces, valves, bowls, pipe tools, and tobaccos. 206–783–0700.

Marks Cigars, 8th & Central Ave., Ocean City, NJ 08226: Free brochure ❖ Cigars handcrafted with aged Jamaican tobaccos individually blended with Dominican long-filler leaf, rolled with clear Cuban seed and Mexican natural leaf binder, and finished with a shade grown Connecticut wrapper. 800–227–8645.

Mike's Cigars Inc., 465 Arthur Godfrey Rd., Miami Beach, FL 33140: Free information ❖ Premium cigars. 800–962–4427.

Nat Sherman Company, 629 W. 54th St., New York, NY 10019: Free catalog ❖ Cigars, pipes, domestic and imported cigarettes, tobaccos, and gifts. 800–257–7850.

Fred Stoker & Sons Inc., P.O. Box 707, Dresden, TN 38225: Free catalog ❖ Supplies for smokers, chewing tobaccos, and gifts. 800–243–9377.

Thompson Cigar Company, 5401 Hangar Ct., Tampa, FL 33634: Free catalog ❖ Cigars, pipes, and tobaccos. 800–237–2559; 813–884–6344 (in FL).

TOLE & DECORATIVE PAINTING

Accent Products Division, Borden Inc., 300 E. Main St., Lake Zurich, IL 60047: Free information ❖ Paints for decorative painting, home decor, and other crafts. 708–540–1604.

Bridgewater Scrollworks, P.O. Box 585, Osage, MN 56570: Catalog $5 (refundable) ❖

Wood cutouts for tole decoration and other crafts.

Stan Brown's Arts & Crafts Inc., 13435 NE Whitaker Way, Portland, OR 97230: Catalog $3.50 ❖ Tole and decorative painting supplies and how-to books. 800–547–5531.

Cabin Craft Midwest, P.O. Box 270, Nevada, IA 50201: Catalog $4 (refundable) ❖ Tole and decorative painting supplies. 515–382–5406.

Cabin Craft Southwest, 1500 Westpack Way, Euless, TX 76040: Catalog $4 ❖ Tole and decorative painting supplies. 800–877–1515.

Capri Arts & Crafts, 864 S. McGlincey Ln., Campbell, CA 95008: Free catalog ❖ Books on decorative and fabric painting. 800–826–7777.

Char-Lee Originals, P.O. Box 606, Somonauk, IL 60552: Catalog $5 ❖ Unpainted resin figures and other ready-to-finish items. 800–242–7533.

Chatham Art Distributors, 11 Brookside Ave., Chatham, NY 12037: Free information ❖ Acrylics, brushes, canvasses, oils, milk paint, tin supplies, books, and wood items for decorating. 800–822–4747.

Cupboard Distributing, P.O. Box 148, Urbana, OH 43078: Catalog $2 ❖ Unfinished wood parts for tole and decorative painting, crafts, miniatures, toys, jewelry-making, and woodworking. 513–390–6388.

Custom Wood Cut-Out's Unlimited, P.O. Box 518, Massilon, OH 44648: Catalog $2 (refundable) ❖ Sanded, ready-to-finish wood items.

Hofcraft, P.O. Box 72, Grand Haven, MI 49416: Catalog $4 ❖ How-to books and supplies for tole and decorative painting. 800–828–0359.

Hollins Enterprises Inc., P.O. Box 148, Alpha, OH 45301: Catalog $5 ❖ Tole and decorative painting supplies. 800–543–3465.

Homestead Handcrafts, N. 1301 Pines Rd., Spokane, WA 99206: Catalog $5 ($3 refundable) ❖ Tole and decorative painting supplies. 509–928–1986.

Darcie Hunter Publications, P.O. Box 1627, Grants Pass, OR 97526: Catalog $1.50 ❖ Painting supplies, books, and wood items for finishing.

Johnson Paint Company Inc., 355 Newbury St., Boston, MA 02115: Catalog $1 ❖ Hard-to-find painting supplies, brushes, and tools. 617–536–4838.

Kerry Specialties, P.O. Box 5129, Deltona, FL 32728: Free information ❖ Brushes for tole and decorative painting. 407–574–6209.

Larson Wood Manufacturing, P.O. Box 672, Park Rapids, MN 56407: Catalog $2 (refundable) ❖ Country-style mini cutouts, kits and parts, hardware, and other supplies. 218–732–9121.

Maggie's Inc., 1053 Carlisle St., Hanover, PA 17331: Catalog $3 ❖ Art and tole decorating, craft, and needlework supplies and books.

Ozark Art and Craft, 310 S. Ingraham Mill Rd., Springfield, MO 65802: Catalog $12 ❖ Tole and decorative painting supplies. 800–369–7989.

Plaid Enterprises, P.O. Box 7600, Norcross, GA 30091: Free information ❖ Acrylic paints and other supplies. 404–923–8200.

Positively Country, Fred & Mary O'Neil, P.O. Box 51746, New Berlin, WI 51746: Catalog $2 ❖ Unfinished wood items, paints, brushes, and other supplies. 414–789–0777.

Sandeen's, 1315 White Bear Ave., St. Paul, MN 55106: Catalog $2 (refundable) ❖ Supplies for folk art crafting, rosemaling, dalmalning, and bauernmalere. Also (separate catalogs, $3 each) supplies for Norwegian stitchery, Danish cross stitching, and Swedish stitchery. 800–235–1315.

Tole Americana Inc., 5750 NE Hassalo, Portland, OR 97220: Free information ❖ Sealers, mediums, varnishes, unfinished wood crafts, books, brushes, and oils, acrylics and fabric paints. 800–547–8854; 800–452–8663 (in OR).

Traditional Norwegian Rosemaking, Pat Virch, 1506 Lynn Ave., Marquette, MI 49855: Catalog $2 ❖ Patterns, books, paints, woodenware, tinware, and other supplies for wood and tin decorating. 906–226–3931.

Viking Woodcrafts Inc., 1317 8th St. SE, Waseca, MN 56093: Catalog $5 (refundable) ❖ Ready-to-finish craft items, resin figures, and books. 507–835–8043.

Weston Bowl Mill, P.O. Box 218, Weston, VT 05161: Catalog $1 ❖ Woodenware for tole and decorative painting. 800–824–6219.

TOOLS

Clamps

Addkison Hardware Company Inc., 126 E. Amite St., P.O. Box 102, Jackson, MS 39205: Free information ❖ Power tools and clamps. 800–821–2750; 800–321–8107 (in MS).

Adjustable Clamp Company, 443 N. Ashland Ave., Chicago, IL 60622: Catalog $1 ❖ Clamps and other work-holding equipment. 312–666–0640.

Advanced Machinery Imports, P.O. Box 312, New Castle, DE 19720: Free information ❖ Workshop clamps. 800–648–4264; 302–322–2226 (in DE).

American Clamping Corporation, P.O. Box 399, Batavia, NY 14021: Free information ❖ Woodworking clamps. 800–928–1004.

Colt Clamp Company Inc., 33 Swan St., Batavia, NY 14020: Free catalog ❖ C- and bar clamps in screw and eccentric styles. 800–536–8420; 716–343–8622 (in NY).

Gross Stabil Corp., P.O. Box 368, Coldwater, MI 49036: Free information ❖ Woodworking clamps. 800–671–0838; 517–279–8040 (in MI).

Hartford Clamp Company, P.O. Box 280131, East Hartford, CT 06128: Free catalog ❖ Hand screws and bar, double bar, and mitre clamps. 203–528–1708.

Inlet Inc., 412 Redhill Ave., Ste. 8, San Anselmo, CA 94960: Free information ❖ Clamps for most workshop needs. 800–786–5665.

Universal Clamp Corporation, 15200 Stagg St., Van Nuys, CA 91405: Free information ❖ Lightweight clamps. 818–780–1015.

Wetzler Clamp, Rt. 611, P.O. Box 175, Mt. Bethel, PA 18343: Free information ❖ Woodworking clamps. 800–451–1852.

Hand & Power Tools

Abbey Tools, 1132 N. Magnolia, Anaheim, CA 92801: Free information ❖ Power tools. 800–225–6321.

Abest Woodworking Machinery, Division Rudolph Bass Inc., 45 Halliday St., Jersey City, NJ 07304: Free information ❖ Modular dust collection system for workshops. 800–526–3003; 201–433–3800 (in NJ).

Acme Electric Tools, Box 1716, Grand Forks, ND 58206: Catalog $3 ❖ Power tools. 800–358–3096.

Addkison Hardware Company Inc., 126 E. Amite St., P.O. Box 102, Jackson, MS 39205: Free information ❖ Power tools and clamps. 800–821–2750; 800–321–8107 (in MS).

Adventures with Tools, 435 Main St., Johnson City, NY 13790: Catalog $5 (refundable) ❖ Tools and accessories for wood and metalworking. 800–477–6512; 607–729–6512 (in NY).

Alley Supply Company, P.O. Box 848, Gardnerville, NV 89410: Catalog $2 ❖ Precision lathes, milling machines, cutter grinders, and other metal-working tools. 702–782–3800.

American Machine & Tool Company, 4th Ave. & Spring, Royersford, PA 19468: Free catalog ❖ Woodworking power tools. 215–948–0400.

Jack Andrews, 1482 Maple Ave., Paoli, PA 19301: Free information with long SASE ❖ Wood carving knives.

Bailey's Mail Order Woodsman Supplies, P.O. Box 550, Laytonville, CA 95454: Free catalog ❖ Chain saws, bars, files, protective gear, forestry supplies, log splitters, books, and gifts. 707–984–6133.

Bethel Mills Lumber Inc., Main St., Bethel, VT 05032: Free information ❖ Building supplies and tools. 800–234–9951.

Better Built Corporation, 845 Woburn St., Wilmington, MA 01887: Free brochure ❖ One-man portable sawmills. 508–657–5636.

Blue Ridge Machinery & Tools Inc., P.O. Box 536, Hurricane, WV 25526: Catalog $1 ❖ Lathes, milling machines, and supplies. 304–562–3538.

Blume Supply Inc., 3316 South Blvd., Charlotte, NC 28209: Free information ❖ Woodworking power tools. 800–288–9200; 704–523–7811 (in NC).

Bosch Power Tool Corporation, 100 Bosch Blvd., New Bern, NC 28562: Free information ❖ Woodworking power tools. 800–334–5730.

BrandMark, 462 Carthage Dr., Beavercreek, OH 45434: Free information ❖ Electric branding irons. 800–323–2570.

Bridge City Tool Works, 1104 NE 28th Ave., Portland, OR 97232: Catalog $2 ❖ Professional hand tools. 800–253–3332.

Brookstone Company, Order Processing Center, 1655 Bassford Dr., Mexico, MO 65265: Free catalog ❖ Hand tools. 800–926–7000.

CarveMart, Rt. 3, Box 226, Pryor, OK 74361: Free catalog ❖ Carving tools. 918–825–0786.

Cascade Tools Inc., P.O. Box 3110, Bellingham, WA 98227: Free catalog ❖ Carbide-tipped router bits and shaper cutters. 800–235–0272.

Chicago Pneumatic Company, Electric Tools Division, 2220 Bleecker St., Utica, NY 13501: Free information ❖ Woodworking power tools. 800–243–0870.

Colwood Electronics, 15 Meridian Rd., Eatontown, NJ 07724: Free brochure ❖ All-in-one work station that includes a woodburning and texturizing system and high speed grinding equipment. 908–544–1119.

Conestoga Wood Machinery, 987 Valley View Rd., New Holland, PA 17557: Free information ❖ Woodworking power tools. 800–445–4669.

Conover Tools, P.O. Box 418, 7785 Mentor Ave., Mentor, OH 44060: Free catalog ❖ Woodworking tools. 800–433–5221.

Constantine, 2050 Eastchester Rd., Bronx, NY 10461: Catalog $1 ❖ Cabinet and furniture wood and veneers, hardware, how-to books, and carving tools and chisels. 800–223–8087; 718–792–1600 (in NY).

Craft Supplies USA, P.O. 50300, Provo, UT 84605: Catalog $2 ❖ Woodturning tools and accessories. 801–373–0919.

CraftWoods, 2101 Greenspring Dr., Timonium, MD 21093: Free catalog ❖ Woodworking, woodcarving, power tools, and kiln-dried domestic and exotic woods. 800–468–7070.

Delta International Machinery Corporation, 246 Alpha Dr., Pittsburgh, PA 15238: Catalog $2 ❖ Woodworking power tools. 412–963–2400.

Delta Point Machinery, P.O. Box 306, Lockport, NY 14095: Free information ❖ Woodworking power tools. 905–629–8786.

DeVilbiss, 213 Industrial Dr., Jackson, TN 38301: Free brochure ❖ Air compressors, air-operated tools, and accessories. 800–888–2468; 901–423–7000 (in TN).

Dremel Manufacturing, 4915 21st St., Racine, WI 53406: Free information ❖ Hand power tools for modelers and home craftsmen. 414–554–1390.

Eagle America, P.O. Box 1099, Chardon, OH 44024: Free catalog ❖ Router bits and shaper cutters. 800–872–2511.

Ebac Lumber Dryers, 106 John Jefferson Rd., Ste. 102, Williamsburg, VA 23185: Free information ❖ Easy-to-operate lumber dryers. 800–433–9011.

Echo Inc., 400 Oakwood Rd., Lake Zurich, IL 60047: Free catalog ❖ Trimmers, blowers, hedge clippers, sprayers, chain saws, and shredders. 708–540–8400.

EMCO-Maier Corporation, 2757 Scioto Pkwy., Columbus, OH 43221: Free catalog ❖ Woodworking power tools. 800–521–8289.

Enco Manufacturing Company, 5000 W. Bloomingdale Ave., Chicago, IL 60639: Free catalog ❖ Metal-working tools, machinery, and accessories. 800–USE-ENCO; 312–745–1520 (in IL).

P.C. English Inc., P.O. Box 380, Thornburg, VA 22565: Free catalog ❖ Tools, cutouts, patterns, paints, carving woods, and supplies. 800–221–9474.

Enlon Import Company, 17709 E. Valley Blvd., City of Industry, CA 91744: Free catalog ❖ Woodworking machinery, tools, and supplies. 818–935–8888.

Excalibur Machine & Tool Company, 210 8th St. South, Lewiston, NY 14092: Free information ❖ Woodworking power tools. 416–291–8190.

Falls Run Woodcarving, 9395 Falls Rd., Girard, PA 16417: Free information ❖ Woodcarving tools. 800–524–9077.

Farris Machinery, 12106 Pavilion Dr., Grain Valley, MO 64029: Free information ❖ Woodworking equipment and supplies. 800–872–5489.

Foley-Belsaw Company, 5301 Equitable Rd., Kansas City, MO 64120: Free information ❖ Woodworking power tools. 800–328–7140.

Forrest Manufacturing Company Inc., 461 River Rd., Clifton, NJ 07014: Free information ❖ Table and radial saw blades. 800–733–7111; 201–473–5236 (in NJ).

Franklin Ace Hardware, 115 E. 2nd Ave., Franklin, VA 23851: Free information ❖ Woodworking power tools. 800–662–0004.

Freeborn Tool Company Inc., P.O. Box 6246, N. 6202 Freya St., Spokane, WA 99207: Free information ❖ Carbide-tipped shaper cutters. 800–523–8988.

Freud Power Tools, 218 Feld Ave., High Point, NC 27264: Free catalog ❖ Woodworking power tools. 800–472–7307.

Frog Tool Company, 700 W. Jackson Blvd., Chicago, IL 60606: Catalog $5 ❖ Woodworking hand tools and books. 312–648–1270.

Gesswein, Woodworking Products Division, 255 Hancock Ave., Bridgeport, CT 06605: Free information ❖ Woodcarving tools. 800–544–2043.

Granberg International, P.O. Box 425, Richmond, CA 94807: Free information ❖ Portable chain saw lumber mill. 510–237–2099.

Grizzly Imports Inc., P.O. Box 2069, Bellingham, WA 98227: Free information ❖ Woodworking power tools. 800–541–5537 (west of the Mississippi); 800–523–4777 (east of the Mississippi).

Harris Tools, 145 Sherman Ave., Jersey City, NJ 07307: Catalog $1 (refundable) ❖ Lapping and sharpening systems. 800–449–7747.

Hartville Tool & Supply, 940 W. Maple St., Hartville, OH 44632: Free catalog ❖ Woodworking tools. 800–345–2396.

Hida Japanese Tool Inc., 1333 San Pablo Ave., Berkeley, CA 94702: Catalog $4 ❖ Hand-forged tools for delicate work. 800–443–5512.

Highland Hardware, 1045 N. Highland Ave. NE, Atlanta, GA 30306: Free catalog ❖ Tools for home craftsmen. 404–872–4466.

Hirsch Tools, 33 Dorman Ave., San Francisco, CA 94124: Free catalog and list of retailers ❖ Woodcarving tools.

Home Lumber Company, P.O. Box 370, Whitewater, WI 53190: Free information ❖ Portable power tools. 800–262–5482.

HTC Products, 120 E. Hudson, P.O. Box 839, Royal Oak, MI 48068: Free catalog ❖ Mobile machine bases to put workshops on wheels. 800–624–2027.

Christian J. Hummul Company, 11001 York Rd., Hunt Valley, MD 21030: Free catalog ❖ Carving tools, artist supplies, and how-to-books. 800–762–0235.

International Tool Corporation, 2590 Davie Rd., Davie, FL 33020: Free information ❖ Power tools. 800–338–3384.

Jamestown Distributors, 28 Narragansett Ave., P.O. Box 348, Jamestown, RI 02835: Free catalog ❖ Workshop tools. 800–423–0030.

The Japan Woodworker, 1731 Clement Ave., Alameda, CA 94501: Catalog $1.50 ❖ Japanese hand tools for craftsmen, carpenters, cabinet makers, and woodcarvers. 800–537–7820; 510–521–1810 (in CA).

JDS Company, 800 Dutch Square Blvd., Ste. 200, Columbia, SC 29210: Free brochure ❖ Precision woodworking equipment. 800–382–2637; 803–798–1600 (in SC).

W.S. Jenks & Son, 1933 Montana Ave. NE, Washington, DC 20002: Free catalog ❖ Hand and power tools. 202–529–6020.

Jensen Tools Inc., 7815 S. 46th St., Phoenix, AZ 85044: Free catalog ❖ Tools, tool kits, and cases. 800–426–1194; 602–968–6231 (in AZ).

Kasco Woodworking Company Inc., 170 W. 600 North, Shelbyville, IN 46176: Free information ❖ Portable band saw mills. 317–398–7973.

Bob Kaune, 511 W. 11th, Port Angeles, WA 98362: Catalog $3.50 ❖ Antique and used hand tools for collectors and woodworkers. 206–452–2292.

The Keller Dovetail System, 1327 I St., Petaluma, CA 94952: Free information ❖ Easy-to-use jig for making angled and curved dovetails, classic and variable spacing, and box joints. 707–763–9336.

Kitts Industrial Tools, 22384 Grand River Ave., Detroit, MI 48219: Free catalog ❖ Precision metalworking tools and supplies. 800–521–6579; 313–538–2585 (in MI).

Klockit, P.O. Box 636, Lake Geneva, WI 53147: Free catalog ❖ Woodworking tools, wood finishing supplies, and clock-building equipment. 800–556–2548.

Knotts Knives, 471 Buckhurst Dr., Kernersville, NC 27284: Free information ❖ Carving tools. 800–388–6759.

Laguna Tools, 2265 Laguna Canyon Rd., Laguna Beach, CA 92651: Free information ❖ Space-saving, all-in-one shop that includes a table saw, joiner, planer, shaper, mortise, and sliding table. 800–234–1976; 714–494–7006 (in CA).

Laredo Tools, 1507 Thousand Oaks Blvd., Thousand Oaks, CA 91362: Free information ❖ Power fastening, framing, and finishing tools. 800–452–7336; 805–497–1610 (in CA).

Leichtung Workshops, 4944 Commerce Pkwy., Cleveland, OH 44128: Free catalog ❖ Tools for craftsmen and gardeners. 800–321–6840.

Leigh Industries Inc., P.O. Box 357, 1585 Broadway, Port Coquitlam, British Columbia, Canada V3C 4K6: Free catalog ❖ Dovetailing jigs, cutters, and attachments. 800–663–8932.

LeNeave Machinery & Supply Company, 305 W. Morehead St., Charlotte, NC 28202: Free information ❖ Woodworking power tools. 800–442–2302; 704–376–7421 (in NC).

Lobo Power Tools, 9031 E. Stauson Ave., Pico Rivera, CA 90660: Free information ❖ Woodworking power tools. 310–949–3747.

Makita USA Inc., 14930 Northam St., La Mirada, CA 90638: Free information ❖ Woodworking power tools. 800–4–MAKITA.

Marlin Industries Inc., Rt. 70, Box 191, Cashiers, NC 28717: Information $1 ❖ Woodcarving machines. 704–743–5551.

Marling Lumber Company, P.O. Box 7668, 1801 E. Washington Ave., Madison, WI 53707: Free information ❖ Woodworking tools. 800–247–7178.

McFeely's, P.O. Box 3, Lynchburg, VA 24505: Free information ❖ Woodworking supplies, tools, and other hard-to-find items. 800–443–7937.

Micro-Mark, 340 Snyder Ave., Berkeley Heights, NJ 07922: Catalog $1 ❖ Miniature tools for hobby craftsmen. 908–464–6764.

Milwaukee Electric Tool Corporation, 13135 W. Lisbon Rd., Brookfield, WI 53005: Free information ❖ Woodworking power tools. 414–781–3600.

MLCS Tools Ltd., P.O. Box 4053, Rydal, PA 19046: Free catalog ❖ Carbide-tipped router bits. 800–533–9298.

Mobile Manufacturing Company, P.O. Box 250, Troutdale, OR 97060: Free brochure ❖ Portable gasoline- or electric-powered saw for cutting logs any diameter and lengths up to 60 feet. 503–666–5593.

Nasco, 901 Janesville Ave., Fort Atkinson, WI 53538: Free catalog ❖ Woodburning and carving tools, woodcraft supplies, and wood projects. 800–558–9595.

Navesink Electronics, 820 Nut Swamp Rd., Red Bank, NJ 07701: Free information ❖ Woodburning systems and carving equipment. 908–747–5023.

Nippon/4/Less, P.O. Box 854, Los Altos, CA 94023: Free catalog ❖ Japanese hand tools. 415–917–0706.

Northern Hydraulics, P.O. Box 1219, Burnsville, MN 55337: Free catalog ❖ Power tools. 800–533–5545.

Northland Woodworking Supply, 65 Wurz Ave., Utica, NY 13502: Free catalog ❖ Carving tools. 315–724–1299.

Overland Company, 3023 E. 2nd St., The Dalles, OR 97058: Free brochure ❖ All-in-one easy-to-use machine shop. 800–345–6342.

Penn State Industries, 2850 Comly Rd., Philadelphia, PA 19154: Free information ❖ Woodworking power tools. 215–676–7609.

PM Research, 4110 Niles Hill Rd., Wellsville, NY 14895: Catalog $2 ❖ Machine shop tools. 716–593–3169.

Porta-Nails Inc., P.O. Box 1257, Wilmington, NC 28402: Free brochure and list of retailers ❖ Woodworking machines. 800–634–9281; 910–762–6334 (in NC).

Porter-Cable, 4825 Hwy. 45 North, Jackson, TN 38305: Free information and list of retailers ❖ Woodworking power tools. 800–487–8665.

Poulan, 5020 Flournoy-Lucas Rd., Shreveport, LA 71129: Free information ❖ Electric- and gas-operated chain saws. 318–683–3546.

Power Tool Specialists, 3 Craftsman Rd., East Windsor, CT 06088: Free information ❖ Hand-held nail gun and other portable power tools. 800–243–5114.

Powermatic Inc., 607 Morrison Rd., McMinnville, TN 37110: Free information ❖ Woodworking power tools. 800–248–0144.

Puckered Woodwork, P.O. Box 718, Throne, NC 28782: Catalog $1 ❖ How-to books and videos and lathe tools.

RBIndustries, 1801 Vine St., P.O. Box 369, Harrisonville, MO 64071: Free catalog ❖ Woodworking power tools. 800–487–2623.

Red Hill Corporation, P.O. Box 4234, Gettysburg, PA 17325: Free catalog ❖ Hot melt glue sticks, glue guns, and sandpaper in belts, sheets, and discs. 800–822–4003.

Ridge Carbide Tool Corporation, 595 New York Ave., P.O. Box 497, Lyndhurst, NJ 07071: Free catalog ❖ Custom router bits and shaper cutters. 800–443–0992.

Ryobi America Corporation, 5201 Pearman Dairy Rd., Anderson, SC 29625: Free information ❖ Woodworking power tools. 800–323–4615.

Safranek Enterprises Inc., 4005 El Camino Real, Atascadero, CA 93422: Free information ❖ Panel routers, air-vac clamps, carbide cutters, and other woodworking tools. 805–466–1563.

Santa Rosa Tool & Supply Inc., 1651 Piner Rd., Santa Rosa, CA 95043: Free information ❖ Woodworking power tools. 800–346–0387; 800–464–8665 (in CA).

Sarah Glove Company Inc., P.O. Box 1940, Waterbury, CT 06722: Catalog $1 ❖ Tools for home craftsmen. 203–574–4090.

Seven Corners Hardware Inc., 216 W. 7th St., St. Paul, MN 55102: Free catalog ❖ Hand and power tools and supplies. 800–328–0457.

Shopsmith Inc., 3931 Image Dr., Dayton, OH 45414: Free information ❖ Multipurpose, all-in-one power-woodworking tools. 800–543–7586; 513–898–6070 (in OH).

Shop-Task, P.O. Box 591, Montesano, WA 98563: Free catalog ❖ All-in-one home machine shop with mill, lathe, and drill. 800–343–5775.

Shop-Vac Corporation, 2323 Reach Rd., Williamsport, PA 17701: Free information ❖ Self-contained, portable vacuum cleaner for workshops. 717–326–0502.

Skil Corporation, 4300 W. Peterson Ave., Chicago, IL 60646: Catalog $1 ❖ Woodworking power tools. 312–286–7330.

Smithy, 3023 E. 2nd St., The Dalles, OR 97058: Free information ❖ All-in-one easy-to-use home machine shop. 800–298–5111.

The Source, 9205 Venture Ct., Manassas Park, VA 22111: Catalog $2 ❖ Hand and power tools and cabinet-making supplies. 800–452–9999; 703–550–8600 (in VA).

Stanley Tools, 600 Myrtle St., New Britain, CT 06050: Free information ❖ Woodworking power tools. 203–225–5111.

Sunhill Machinery, 500 Andover Park East, Seattle, WA 98188: Free information ❖ Heavy-duty power tools, dust collectors, and accessories. 800–929–4321.

Tamarack Log Building Tools Inc., P.O. Box 120783, New Brighton, MN 55112: Free catalog ❖ Tools, books, and supplies for log building. 612–783–9773.

Tarheel Filing Company Inc., 3400 Lake Woodard Dr., Raleigh, NC 27514: Free information ❖ Power tools. 800–322–6641; 919–231–3323 (in NC).

Tashiro's Tools, 2939 4th Ave. South, Seattle, WA 98134: Free catalog ❖ Japanese tools. 206–621–0199.

Tepper Discount Tools, 107 W. Springfield, Champaign, IL 61820: Free information ❖ Professional woodworking tools for home craftsmen. 800–626–0566.

Terrco Inc., 222 1st Ave. NW, Watertown, SD 57201: Free catalog ❖ Woodcarving machines. 605–882–3888.

Timberking Inc., 1431 N. Topping, Kansas City, MO 64120: Free information ❖ Portable one-man saw mill. 800–942–4406.

The Tool Club, P.O. Box 410, 1026 Superior Ave., Baraga, MI 49908: Free catalog ❖ Inlay cutter. 906–337–0516.

Tool Crib of the North, Box 13720, Grand Forks, ND 58208: Free catalog ❖ Hand and power tools. 800–358–3096.

Tools Etc., P.O. Box 232, Seal Beach, CA 90740: Catalog $2.50 ❖ Hand and power tools.

Toolhauz Corporation, P.O. Box 1288, Middleboro, MA 02346: Free information ❖ Hand and portable power tools. 800–533–6135; 800–282–0170 (in MA).

Total Shop, P.O. Box 25429, Greenville, SC 29616: Free information ❖ Woodworking power tools. 800–845–9356.

Trend-Lines, 375 Beacham St., Chelsea, MA 02150: Free catalog ❖ Power tools. 800–767–9999.

Trippe Supply Company, 309 Ritchie Rd., Capitol Heights, MD 20743: Free information ❖ Hand and power tools. 800–635–2127.

Vermont American, P.O. Box 340, Lincolnton, NC 28093: Free information ❖ Portable power tools. 704–735–7464.

Garrett Wade Company, 161 6th Ave., New York, NY 10013: Catalog $4 ❖ Hand and power tools for woodworking. 800–221–2942.

Steve Wall Lumber Company, Box 287, Mayodan, NC 27027: Catalog $1 ❖ Hardwoods and woodworking machinery for craftsmen and educational institutions. 800–633–40962; 910–427–0637 (in NC).

Warren Tool Company Inc., 2209–1, Rt. 9G, Rhinebeck, NY 12572: Catalog $1 ❖ Whittling and woodcarving tools, woods, sharpening stones, supplies, and books. 914–876–7817.

M.P. White Hardware, 27 Stuart St., Boston, MA 02116: Free catalog ❖

Hardware, tools, and other supplies for wood and metal working and other shop activities. 800–249–TOOL.

Whole Earth Access, 822 Anthony St., Berkeley, CA 94710: Free information ❖ Power tools. 800–829–6300.

Wholesale America Inc., 4777 Menard Dr., Eau Claire, WI 54703: Catalog $1 ❖ Power tools and hardware. 615–874–5000.

Wilke Machinery Company, 3230 Susquehanna Trail, York, PA 17402: Catalog $2 ❖ Woodworking power tools with optional dust collector. 800–235–2100.

Wood Carvers Supply Inc., P.O. Box 7500, Englewood, FL 34295: Catalog $2 ❖ Carving tools, power carving machines, kits, books, and supplies. 813–698–0123.

Woodcraft Supply, 210 Wood County Industrial Park, P.O. Box 1686, Parkersburg, WV 26102: Free catalog ❖ Woodworking tools, supplies, hardware, and books. 800–542–9115.

Wood-Mizer, 8180 W. 10th St., Indianapolis, IN 46214: Catalog $2 ❖ Portable sawmills and other tools. 800–553–0219.

The Woodworkers' Store, 21801 Industrial Blvd., Rogers, MN 55374: Free catalog ❖ Hardware and ornamental woodworking supplies, tools, and finishing supplies. 800–403–9736.

TOWELS

Chambers, Mail Order Department, P.O. Box 7841, San Francisco, CA 94120: Free catalog ❖ Bed and bath linens and furnishings. 800–334–1254.

Leron, 750 Madison Ave., New York, NY 10021: Free catalog ❖ Linens, towels, pillows and covers, and imported handkerchiefs for men and women with optional monograms. 212–753–6700.

Palmetto Linen Company, 145 Shoppes on the Pkwy., Hilton Head, SC 29928: Free information ❖ Sheets and matching dust ruffles, bath towels, blankets, comforters, pillows, tablecloths, place mats, shower curtains, kitchen towels, and oven gloves. 800–972–7442.

TOY MAKING

Angelitos, P.O. Box 1926, Fort Collins, CO 80522: Catalog $2 (refundable) ❖ Handcrafted soft fabric sculptures. 800–624–9379.

Animal Crackers Patterns, 5824 Isleta SW, Albuquerque, NM 87105: Catalog $2.50 ❖ Kits, supplies, and patterns for easy-to-make stuffed toys and animals. 800–274–BEAR.

Atlanta Puffections, P.O. Box 13524, Atlanta, GA 30324: Catalog $1.50 ❖ Easy-to-make stuffed animals. 404–262–7437.

by Diane, 1126 Ivon Ave., Endicott, NY 13760: Catalog $2 ❖ Furs and mohair, growlers, squealers, music boxes, noses, eyes, joint sets, and patterns for bears, soft toys, and puppets. 607–754–0391.

Gaillorraine Originals, P.O. Box 137, Tehachapi, CA 93561: Catalog $2 ❖ Supplies and patterns for bears and other soft animal toys. 805–822–1857.

Garden Fairies Trading Company, 309 S. Main St., Sebastopol, CA 95472: Catalog $4 ❖ Fabrics, trims, and soft toy patterns. 800–925–9919.

Golden Fun Kits, P.O. Box 10697, Golden, CO 80401: Catalog $1 ❖ Soft toy-making supplies.

Larson Wood Manufacturing, P.O. Box 672, Park Rapids, MN 56407: Catalog $2 (refundable) ❖ Country-style mini cutouts, kits and parts, hardware, and other supplies. 218–732–9121.

Patterncrafts, Box 25639, Colorado Springs, CO 80936: Catalog $2 ❖ Patterns for dolls and stuffed animals. 719–574–2007.

Patterns by Diane, 1126 Ivon Ave., Endicott, NY 13760: Catalog $2 ❖ Soft toys and puppet kits and bear-making supplies. 607–754–0391.

Sonrise Soft Crafts, P.O. Box 5091, Salem, OR 97304: Brochure 50¢ ❖ Supplies and how-to for making stuffed toys. 503–362–0027.

TOY SOLDIERS

Armchair General Ltd., 12977 N. Outer Forty Dr., St. Louis, MO 63141: Catalog $2 ❖ Military miniatures and toy soldiers.

Brunton's Barracks, 415 S. Montezuma St., Prescott, AZ 86303: Free information ❖ Military figures and other miniatures. 602–778–1915.

Cynthia's Country Store, 11496 Pierson Rd., Commerce Park-Wellington, West Palm Beach, FL 33414: Catalog $15 ❖ British and other toy soldiers. 407–793–0554.

Dunken, Box 95, Calvert, TX 77837: Free catalog ❖ Civil War, World War I and World War II, Napoleonic, Germany military, and other lead soldier molds. 409–364–2020.

Dutkins' Collectables, 1019 West Rt. 70, Cherry Hill, NJ 08002: Catalog $4 ❖ Handpainted all-metal toy soldiers and mold kits. 609–428–9559.

Excalibur Hobbies Ltd., 63 Exchange St., Malden, MA 02148: Free information ❖ Old and new toy soldiers, war games, plastic kits, books, and other militaria. 617–322–2959.

Gettysburg Toy Soldier, 200 Steinwehr Ave., Gettysburg, PA 17325: Free information with long SASE ❖ American Civil War and British Colonial War miniatures. 717–337–3151.

Farina Enterprises, P.O. Box 101, Arlington, MA 02174: Catalog $5 ❖ Civil War miniatures and kits. 617–497–1406.

I/R Miniatures Inc., P.O. Box 89–L, Burnt Mills, NY 12077: Catalog $6 ❖ Historically detailed military miniatures and kits from American military history. 518–885–6054.

International Hobby Corporation, 413 E. Allegheny Ave., Philadelphia, PA 19134: Catalog $4.98 ❖ Battery powered tools, model airplanes, railroading accessories, and military miniatures. 800–875–1600.

Musket Miniatures, P.O. Box 1976, Denver, CO 80038: Catalog $2 ❖ Civil War miniatures. 303–439–9336.

Red Lancer, P.O. Box 8056, Mesa, AZ 85214: Catalog $6 ❖ Original 19th-century military art, rare books, Victorian era campaign medals and helmets, old toy soldiers, and other collectibles. 602–964–9667.

TNC Enterprises, 318 Churchill Ct., Elizabethtown, KY 42701: Catalog $5 ❖ Toy soldier sets and individual pieces from different historical periods. 502–765–5035.

Toy Soldier Company, 100 Riverside Dr., New York, NY 10024: Plastics catalog $4; leads catalog $7.50 ❖ United States, British, French, German lead, and plastic toy soldiers and other miniatures, from 1900 to the present. 212–721–6394.

Toy Soldier Gallery Inc., 24 Main St., Highland Falls, NY 12928: Catalog $5 ❖ Toy soldier sets and individual pieces from different historical periods. 800–777–9904.

Tradition USA Toy Soldiers, 12924 Viking Dr., Burnsville, MN 55337: Catalog $10 ❖ Toy soldiers. 612–890–1634.

Warwick Miniatures Ltd., P.O. Box 1498, Portsmouth, NH 03801: Catalog $4 ❖ Imperial Toy Soldiers from New Zealand and detailed miniatures from historical periods of the United States, England, France, and Germany. 603–431–7139.

Wiley House Toy Soldiers, 913 Sheridan Ave., Cody, WY 82414: Free information with long SASE ❖ Military figures and other miniatures. 307–587–6030.

TOYS & GAMES

Character Toys

Action Toys & Collectibles, P.O. Box 102, Holtsville, NY 11742: Catalog $2 ❖ TV, movie action, and character toy collectibles. 516–736–8697.

Ancient Idols Collectible Toys, 219 S. Madison St., Allentown, PA 18101: Catalog $3 ❖ Collectible character toys, model kits, science fiction toys, puzzles, and games. 215–820–0805.

Arthur Antonelli, 16 Hampton Dr., Nashua, NH 03063: Free information with long SASE and two 1st class stamps ❖ Stage, screen, and television character toys and other collectibles. 603–880–4487.

Baker's Art & Collectibles, P.O. Box 558, Oakdale, NY 11769: Catalog $20, 2–year subscription ❖ Antique and collectible toys. 516–567–9295.

Dean Chapman Collectable Toys, 7111 Amundsonn Ave., Edina, MN 55439: Free list ❖ Character, western, and TV-related toys, games, premiums, and other movie memorabilia. 612–922–9289.

Collectorholics, 15006 Fuller, Grandview, MO 64030: Catalog $5 ❖ Character TV and movie-related toys and other collectibles. 816–322–0906.

Figures, P.O. Box 19482, Johnston, RI 02919: Catalog $3 ❖ Science fiction and super hero action figures and playsets. 401–946–5720.

Fun House Toy Company, P.O. Box 343, Bradforwoods, PA 15015: Free catalog ❖ Character and space toys, board games, and other collectibles. 412–935–1392.

Barry Goodman, P.O. Box 218, Woodbury, NY 11797: Free information with long SASE ❖ Character toys and dolls. 516–338–2701.

Ellen & Jerry Harnish, 110 Main St., Bellville, OH 44813: Catalog $1 ❖ Action, character, and TV figures. 419–886–4444.

The Hobby Lobby, P.O. Box 228, Kulpsville, PA 19443: Catalog $6 ❖ Action figures and vintage cars and toys, from the 1960s and 1970s. 215–721–9749.

Jim's TV Collectibles, P.O. Box 4767, San Diego, CA 92164: Catalog $2 ❖ TV and theatrical collectibles, from the 1950s through 1990s.

John's Collectible Toys & Gifts, 57 Bay View Dr., Shrewsbury, MA 01545: Catalog $2 ❖ Character toys and other movie and TV collectibles. 508–797–0023.

Just Kids Nostalgia, 326 Main St., Huntington, NY 11743: Catalog $4 ❖ Movie and TV character dolls, other movie memorabilia, and board games. 516–423–8449.

Let's Talk Toys, 2090 S. Nova Rd., Ste. 2112, South Daytona, FL 32119: Catalog $3 ❖ Character toys from the 1960s, 1970s, and 1980s. 904–788–5486.

Long Island Train & Hobby Center, 192 Jericho Tnpk., Mineola, NY 11501: Price list $3 ❖ Collectible toys and character dolls. 516–742–5621.

North Country Toys, P.O. Box 1100, Warren, ME 04864: Free information ❖ Action figures, models, non-sports cards, comics, militaria, and automotive toys. 207–273–4066.

Sally Distributors Inc., 4100 Quebec Ave. North, Minneapolis, MN 55427: Free catalog ❖ Balloons and accessories, character and other toys, greeting cards, gifts, novelties, and carnival supplies. 612–533–7100.

Bob Sellstedt, 9307 Hillingdon Rd., Woodbury, MN 55125: Price list $2 ❖ Character toys and other collectibles. 612–738–1597.

Splash Page Comics & Toys, 1007 E. Patterson, Kirksville, MO 63501: Free catalog ❖ Character toys and other memorabilia. 800–237–PAGE.

Toy Scouts Inc., 137 Casterton Ave., Akron, OH 44303: Catalog $3 ❖ Collectible TV cartoon and comic characters, from 1940 through 1970. 216–836–0668.

Vintage Toy Depot, P.O. Box 206, Kenilworth, NJ 07033: Catalog $3 ❖ Character and other comic collectibles, baby boomer toys, GI Joe model kits, and other collectibles. 908–276–5464.

Wex Rex Records & Collectibles, P.O. Box 702, Hudson, MA 01749: Catalog $3 ❖

Movie and TV show character toys and other collectibles. 508–229–2662.

Bruce Zalkin, P.O. Box 75579, Tampa, FL 33605: Catalog $1 ❖ Character toys from movie and TV shows. 813–973–4324.

Electronic Toys & Games

Acclaim Entertainment Inc., 71 Audrey Ave., Oyster Bay, NY 11771: Free information ❖ Video game cassettes. 516–922–2400.

Accolade Inc., 5300 Stevens Creek Blvd., San Jose, CA 95128: Free information ❖ Video game cassettes.

Atari Computer, 1196 Borregas Ave., Sunnyvale, CA 94088: Free catalog ❖ Video game cartridges. 408–745–2000.

ATP Video Games, 4000 Blackburn Ln., Burtonsville, MD 20866: Free information ❖ New and used video games. 301–384–2302.

BRE Software, 352 W. Bedford Ave., Ste. 104, Fresno, CA 93711: Catalog $1 ❖ New and used Genesis and Nintendo cassettes. 209–432–2684.

Capcom USA, 3303 Scott Blvd., Santa Clara, CA 95054: Free information ❖ Video game cassettes. 408–727–0400.

Cape Cod Connection, 21 Pleasant View Ave., Falmouth, MA 02540: Free information ❖ New and used Nintendo cassettes. 800–729–6733; 508–457–0738 (in MA).

Capstone, 7200 Corporate Center Dr., Ste. 500, Miami, FL 33126: Free information ❖ Video game cartridges. 800–468–7226.

Data East USA, 1850 Little Orchard St., San Jose, CA 95112: Free information ❖ Video game cassettes. 408–286–7080.

Electronic Arts, 1450 Fashion Island Blvd., San Mateo, CA 94404: Free information ❖ Video game cassettes. 800–245–4525.

Flying Edge, P.O. Box 9003, Oyster Bay, NY 11771: Free information ❖ Video game cartridges.

GameTek, 2999 NE 191st St., Ste. 800, North Miami Beach, FL 33180: Free information ❖ Video game cartridges. 305–935–3995.

Hudson Soft USA Inc., 400 Oyster Point Blvd., Ste. 515, South San Francisco, CA 94080: Free information ❖ Video game cassettes. 415–871–8895.

Impressions Software Inc., 7 Melrose Dr., Farmington, CT 06032: Free information ❖ Video game cartridges. 203–676–0127.

Interplay Productions, 17922 Fitch Ave., Irvine, CA 92714: Free information ❖ Video game cartridges. 714–553–6678.

Konami Inc., 900 Deerfield Pkwy., Buffalo Grove, IL 60089: Free information ❖ Video game cassettes. 708–215–5100.

LJN Video Games, 71 Audrey Ave., Oyster Bay, NY 11771: Free information ❖ Video game cartridges.

MicroProse Software Inc., 180 Lakefront Dr., Hunt Valley, MD 21030: Free information ❖ Video game cartridges. 800–879–7529.

NEC Technologies Inc., 1414 Massachusetts Ave., Boxborough, MA 01719: Free information ❖ Video game cassettes. 800–388–8888; 508–264–8000 (in MA).

The Next Stage, 677 Yolo Ct., San Jose, CA 95136: Free information ❖ Video game cartridges.

Nintendo of America, 4820 150th Ave. NE, Redmond, WA 98052: Free information ❖ Nintendo systems, accessories, and game cassettes. 800–255–3700.

Ocean of America, 1855 O'Toole Ave., Ste. D-102, San Jose, CA 95131: Free information ❖ Video game cartridges.

Play It Again, P.O. Box 656718, Flushing, NY 11365: Catalog $1 ❖ Used video game cassettes. 718–229–1435.

Psygnosis, 29 Saint Marys Ct., Brookline, MA 02146: Free information ❖ Video game cassettes. 617–731–3553.

Radio Shack, Division Tandy Corporation, 1500 One Tandy Center, Fort Worth, TX 76102: Free information ❖ Electronic teaching toys, musical instruments, chess games, strategy games, sports games, and radio controlled toys. 817–390–3700.

ReadySoft, 30 Wertheim Ct., Unit 2, Richmond Hill, Ontario, Canada L4B 1B9: Free information ❖ Video game cartridges. 416–731–4175.

Sega of America, 130 Shoreline Dr., Redwood City, CA 94065: Free information ❖ Video game cassettes. 415–508–2800.

Sir-Tech Software, P.O. Box 245, Ogdensburg, NY 13669: Free information ❖ Video game cassettes. 315–393–6451.

Spectrum Holobyte, 2490 Mariner Square Loop, Alameda, CA 94501: Free information ❖ Video game cassettes. 510–522–3584.

SSI Video Games, 675 Almanor Ave., Ste. 201, Sunnyvale, CA 94086: Free information ❖ Video game cartridges. 408–737–6800.

Strategic Simulations Inc., c/o Electronic Arts, 1450 Fashion Island Blvd., San Mateo, CA 94404: Free information ❖ Video game cartridges. 800–245–4525.

Taito America Corporation, 390 Holbrook Dr., Wheeling, IL 60090: Free information ❖ Video game cassettes.

Taxan Corporation, 2880 San Thomas Expwy., Ste. 101, Santa Clara, CA 95051: Free information ❖ Video game cassettes. 408–748–0200.

Timeless Expectations, P.O. Box 1180, Fairfield, IA 52556: Free information ❖ Scrabble, chess, bridge, backgammon, gin and cribbage electronic games; other board games; books; and gifts. 800–622–1558.

Tradewest Inc., 2400 S. Hwy. 75, Corsicana, TX 75151: Free information ❖ Video game cartridges. 903–874–2683.

Viacom New Media, 1000 Asbury Dr., Buffalo Grove, IL 60015: Free information ❖ Video game cartridges. 708–520–4440.

Virgin Games, 18061 Fitch Ave., Irvine, CA 92714: Free information ❖ Video game cartridges. 714–833–8710.

General Toys & Games

All But Grown-Ups, P.O. Box 555, Berwick, ME 03901: Free brochure ❖ Challenging toys for adults and children. 800–448–1550.

Ancient Idols Collectible Toys, 219 S. Madison St., Allentown, PA 18101: Catalog $3 ❖ Collectible character toys, model kits, science fiction toys, puzzles, and games. 215–820–0805.

Animal Town, P.O. Box 485, Healdsburg, CA 95448: Free catalog ❖ Toys, novelties, games, puzzles, books, and recordings for children. 800–445–8642.

Aristoplay Games, P.O. Box 7529, Ann Arbor, MI 48107: Free catalog ❖ Educational games for all ages. 800–634–7738.

Armchair General's Merchantile, 1008 Adams, Bay City, MI 48708: Catalog $2 (refundable) ❖ Games, miniatures, and books for Civil War enthusiasts. 517–892–6177.

Back to Basics Toys, 2707 Pittman Dr., Silver Spring, MD 20910: Free catalog ❖ Raggedy Ann dolls, Lincoln log building sets, Lionel trains, Tinkertoy, Radio Flyer wagons, Disney classics, science sets, telescopes, Meccano construction sets, sports games, play-in doll houses, and other toys. 800–356–5360.

Childcraft, P.O. Box 29149, Overland Park, KS 66201: Free catalog ❖ Educational toys and games for babies and young children. 800–631–5657.

Constructive Playthings, 1227 E. 119th St., Grandview, MO 64030: Free catalog ❖ Toys, novelties, games, puzzles, books, furniture, and sports and fitness equipment. 800–448–7830; 816–761–5900 (in MO).

Current Inc., Express Processing Center, Colorado Springs, CO 80941: Free catalog ❖ Toys, greeting cards, stationery, gift wrapping and decorations, and calendars. 800–848–2848.

Discovery Toys Inc., 2530 Arnold Dr., Ste. 400, Martinez, CA 94553: Free catalog ❖ Toys for children that encourage physical, emotional, and intellectual growth. 800–426–4777.

Enchanted Doll House, Rt. 7A, Manchester Center, VT 05255: Catalog $2 ❖ Stuffed animals, dolls, books, toys and games, and miniatures. 802–362–1327.

Games People Played, P.O. Box 1540, Pinedale, WY 82941: Catalog $3 ❖ Antique replica game boards. 307–367–2502.

GDW Games, P.O. Box 1646, Bloomington, IL 61702: Free catalog ❖ Military and role playing, adventure, space adventure, war and science fiction, and other challenging games. 309–452–3632.

The Great Kids Company, Division of Kaplan, P.O. Box 609, Lewisville, NC 27023: Free catalog ❖ Developmental learning materials for early childhood education. 800–334–2014; 800–642–0610 (in NC).

Growing Child, P.O. Box 620, Lafayette, IN 47902: Free catalog ❖ Toys, games, puzzles, books, recordings, and arts and crafts for children, from birth to age 6. 317–423–2624.

Hancock Toy Shop, 97 Prospect St., Jaffrey, NH 03452: Catalog $1 ❖ Hardwood toys and novelties for children. 603–532–7504.

Hand in Hand, Rt. 26, RR 1, Box 1425, Oxford, ME 04270: Free catalog ❖ Books, toys, games, car seats, furniture, and bathroom accessories. 800–872–9745.

Ellen & Jerry Harnish, 110 Main St., Bellville, OH 44813: Catalog $1 ❖ Toys from the 1950s through the 1980s. 419–886–4782.

Hearth Song, Mail Processing Center, 6519 N. Galena Rd., P.O. Box 1773, Peoria, IL 61656: Free catalog ❖ Toys and games that provide opportunity for creativity, challenge, discovery, and improving reading skills. 800–325–2502.

Just for Kids, P.O. Box 29141, Shawnee, KS 66201: Free catalog ❖ Dolls, games, books, stuffed animals, science activities, automobiles and trucks, building blocks, party items, and games for when travelling. 800–443–5827.

Kapable Kids, P.O. Box 250, Bohemia, NY 11716: Catalog $2 ❖ Toys for the developing child. 800–356–1564.

Miles Kimball Company, 41 W. 8th Ave., Oshkosh, WI 54906: Free catalog ❖ Toys and games for children and adults. 800–546–2255.

Larson Wood Manufacturing, P.O. Box 672, Park Rapids, MN 56407: Catalog $2 (refundable) ❖ Kits, parts, and supplies for toy-making. 218–732–9121.

Lilly's Kids, Lillian Vernon Corporation, Virginia Beach, VA 23479: Free catalog ❖ Exclusive and imaginative toys for children. 800–285–5555.

Lucy's Toys, 10020 Alabama Hwy., #9, Anniston, AL 36201: Free information ❖ Plush toys. 205–236–5938.

McVays Limited, P.O. Box 553, Leslie, MI 49251: Brochure $2 ❖ Handmade gameboards. 517–589–5312.

The Nature Company, Catalog Division, P.O. Box 188, Florence, KY 41022: Free catalog ❖ Science- and nature-oriented items, toys, and novelties. 800–227–1114.

Noveltoys, US Hwy. 19, Canton, TX 75103: Catalog $3 (refundable) ❖ Handmade wood toys for children. 800–342–5452.

Real Goods, 966 Mazzoni St., Ukiah, CA 95482: Free catalog ❖ Solar energy-operating models. 800–762–7325.

Sally Distributors Inc., 4100 Quebec Ave. North, Minneapolis, MN 55427: Free catalog ❖ Balloons and accessories, character and other toys, greeting cards, gifts, novelties, and carnival supplies. 612–533–7100.

Sensational Beginnings, 300 Detroit, Ste. E, Monroe, MI 48161: Free catalog ❖ Toys and books for babies and children up to age 4. 800–444–2147.

Towery Toys, P.O. Box 1, Yazoo City, MS 39194: Free information ❖ Original wood toys. 601–746–7315.

Toys to Grow On, P.O. Box 17, Long Beach, CA 90801: Catalog $1 ❖ Games, T-shirts, party supplies and backyard, educational, and children's toys. 800–874–4242.

Troll Learn & Play, 100 Corporate Dr., Mahwah, NJ 07430: Free catalog ❖ Children's educational toys, books, puzzles, playhouse toys, videos and other recordings, costumes, and T-shirts. 800–247–6106.

U.S. Games Systems Inc., 179 Ludlow St., Stanford, CT 06902: Catalog $2 ❖ Deluxe double bridge decks, tarot, and cartomancy decks, historical and specialty decks, antique reproductions, and other playing cards. 800–54–GAMES; 203–353–8400 (in CT).

U.S. Toy Company Inc., 1227 E. 119th St., Grandview, MO 64030: Catalog $3 ❖ Educational toys and games. 800–448–7830; 816–761–5900 (in MO).

Wisconsin Wagon Company, 507 Laurel Ave., Janesville, WI 53545: Free brochure ❖ Handcrafted Janesville replica solid oak coaster wagon and Janesville pine and hardwood toddler first riding 3–wheeler, circa 1900–1934; and scooters, sleds, wheelbarrows, swings and doll furniture. 608–754–0026.

Worldwide Games, Mill St., Dept. 2602, Colchester, CT 06415: Free catalog ❖ Casino games, puzzles, outdoor games, kites, and games from worldwide sources. 800–243–9232.

Special-Needs Toys & Games

S & S Arts & Crafts, Mill St., Dept. 2000, Colchester, CT 06415: Free catalog ❖ Educational games, puzzles, arts and crafts projects, and curriculum products. 800–243–9232.

Toys for Special Children, 385 Warburton Ave., Hastings-on-Hudson, NY 10706: Free catalog ❖ Assistive communication devices, specially adapted and activity toys, capability switches, skill builder equipment, computer training devices, and other special devices for handicapped children. 914–478–0960.

Woodset Inc., P.O. Box 2127, Waldorf, MD 20604: Free information ❖ Backyard wood play equipment with standard designs coupled with creative solutions to mobility and positioning concerns. 800–638–9663.

Worldwide Games, Mill St., Dept. 2602, Colchester, CT 06415: Free catalog ❖

Hardwood board games, puzzles, strategy and skill games, outdoor activities, and other games for all ages. 800–243–9232.

Water Toys

Alvimar Manufacturing Company Inc., 51–02 21st St., Long Island City, NY 11101: Free information ❖ Surfboards and swim rings. 718–937–0404.

American Athletic Inc., 200 American Ave., Jefferson, IA 50129: Free information ❖ Surfboards and swim rings. 800–247–3978; 515–386–3125 (in IA).

Recreonics Corporation, 4200 Schmitt Ave., Louisville KY 40213: Free information ❖ Surfboards, swim rings, and diving boards. 800–428–3254.

Rothhammer/Sprint, P.O. Box 5579, Santa Maria, CA 93456: Free information ❖ Surfboards, swim rings, and equipment for divers. 800–235–2156.

Sevylor USA, 6651 E. 26th St., Los Angeles, CA 90040: Free information ❖ Inflatable boats, mattresses, tubes, lounges, balls, and other sports recreational products. 213–727–6013.

TRACK & FIELD SPORTS
Clothing

Adidas USA, 5675 N. Blackstock Rd., Spartanburg, SC 29303: Free information ❖ Shoes and clothing. 800–423–4327.

Asics Tiger Corporation, 10540 Talbert Ave., West Bldg., Fountain Valley, CA 92708: Free information ❖ Shoes and clothing. 800–766–ASICS; 714–962–7654 (in CA).

The Athletic Connection, 1901 Diplomat, Dallas, TX 75234: Free information ❖ Crossbars, discuses, hurdles, landing pits, relay batons, starting blocks, shotputs, and poles. 800–527–0871; 214–243–1446 (in TX).

Betlin Manufacturing, 1445 Marion Rd., Columbus OH 43207: Free information ❖ Clothing. 614–443–0248.

Compass Industries, 104 E. 25th St., New York, NY 10010: Free information ❖ Starter pistols. 212–473–2614.

Converse Inc., 1 Fordham Rd., North Reading, MA 01864: Free information ❖ Shoes. 800–428–2667; 508–664–1100 (in MA).

Everlast Sports Manufacturing Corporation, 750 E. 132nd St., Bronx, NY

10454: Free information ❖ Landing pits. 800–221–8777; 212–993–0100 (in NY).

Fab Knit Manufacturing Company, Division Anderson Industries, 1415 N. 4th St., Waco, TX 76707: Free information ❖ Clothing. 800–333–4111; 817–752–2511 (in TX).

Ivanko Barbell Company, P.O. Box 1470, San Pedro, CA 90731: Free information with list of retailers ❖ Shotputs. 800–247–9044; 310–514–1155 (in CA).

Markwort Sporting Goods, 4300 Forest Park Ave., St. Louis, MO 63108: Catalog $8 with list of retailers ❖ Discuses, relay batons, starter pistols, and tape measures. 314–652–3757.

New Balance Athletic Shoe Inc., 38 Everett St., Boston, MA 02134: Free information ❖ Shoes and clothing. 800–343–4648; 617–783–4000 (in MA).

Nike Footwear Inc., One Bowerman Dr., Beaverton, OR 97005: Free information ❖ Shoes. 800–344–6453.

Pennsylvania Sporting Goods, 1360 Industrial Hwy., P.O. Box 451, Southhampton, PA 18966: Free information ❖ Starter pistols. 800–535–1122.

Puma USA Inc., 147 Centre St., Brockton, MA 02403: Free information with long SASE ❖ Shoes. 508–583–9100.

Reebok International Ltd., 100 Technology Center Dr., Stoughton, MA 02072: Free information ❖ Shoes. 800–228–PUMP.

Richardson Sports Inc., 3490 W. 1st Ave., Eugene, OR 97402: Free information ❖ Discuses, relay batons, and tape measures. 800–545–8686; 503–687–1818 (in OR).

Sport World Distributors, 3060 Clermont Rd., P.O. Box 27131, Columbus, OH 44327: Free information ❖ Clothing. 614–838–8511.

Venus Knitting Mills Inc., 140 Spring St., Murray Hill, NJ 07974: Free information ❖ Clothing. 800–955–4200; 908–464–2400 (in NJ).

Equipment

Blazer Manufacturing Company Inc., P.O. Box 667, Fremont, NE 68025: Free information ❖ Crossbars, hurdles, discuses, javelins, shotputs, relay batons, tape measures, and starting blocks. 800–322–2731; 402–721–2525 (in NE).

Cramer Products Inc., P.O. Box 1001, Gardner, KS 66030: Free information ❖ Crossbars, hurdles, discuses, javelins, relay batons, starting blocks, and lane markers. 800–345–2231; 913–884–7511 (in KS).

Olympia Sports, 745 State Cir., Ann Arbor, MI 48106: Free information ❖ Crossbars, hurdles, hammers, lane markers, relay batons, starter pistols, landing pits, and starting blocks. 800–521–2832; 313–761–5135 (in MI).

TRAMPOLINES

American Athletic Inc., 200 American Ave., Jefferson, IA 50129: Free information ❖ Trampolines. 800–247–3978; 515–386–3125 (in IA).

The Athletic Connection, 1901 Diplomat, Dallas, TX 75234: Free information ❖ Trampolines. 800–527–0871; 214–243–1446 (in TX).

Austin Athletic Equipment Corporation, 705 Bedford Ave., Box 423, Bellmore, NY 11710: Free information ❖ Trampolines. 516–785–0100.

Bollinger Fitness Products, 222 W. Airport Freeway, Irving, TX 75062: Free information ❖ Home gymnasiums, trampolines, monitoring aids, and weight training, and other body building equipment. 800–527–1166; 214–445–0386 (in TX).

Cannon Sports, P.O. Box 11179, Burbank, CA 91510: Free information with list of retailers ❖ Fitness and exercise equipment, monitoring aids, home gymnasiums, weight-lifting equipment, and trampolines. 800–362–3146; 818–753–5940 (in CA).

JumpKing Trampolines, 901 W. Miller Rd., Garland, TX 75041: Free catalog ❖ Trampolines. 800–322–2211.

Spalding Sports Worldwide, 425 Meadow St., P.O. Box 901, Chicopee, MA 01021: Free information with list of retailers ❖ Home gymnasiums, trampolines, monitoring aids, and weight training, body building, and exercise equipment. 800–225–6601.

Trampoline World, P.O.Box 808, Fayetteville, GA 30214: Free catalog ❖ Trampolines. 404–461–9941.

Trampolking Sporting Goods, P.O. Box 3828, Albany, GA 31708: Free brochure ❖ Trampolines, exercise bikes, rowers, and other physical fitness equipment. 800–841–4351; 912–435–2101 (in GA).

TVs & VCRs
Manufacturers

Brookline Technologies, 2035 Carriage Hill Rd., Allison Park, PA 15101: Free information ❖ Automatic stabilizer for home video volume control. 800–366–9290.

Canon, One Canon Plaza, Lake Success, NY 11042: Free information ❖ Cassette players, camcorders, sound processors, and other electronics. 516–488–6700.

Emerson Radio Corporation, 1 Emerson Ln., North Bergen, NJ 07047: Free information ❖ Camcorders, cassette and CD players, and TVs. 800–922–0738.

Fisher, 21350 Lassen St., Chatsworth, CA 91311: Free information ❖ CD and cassette players, sound processors, camcorders, TVs, and universal remotes. 818–998–7322.

G.E. Appliances, General Electric Company, Appliance Park, Louisville, KY 40225: Free information ❖ Audio and video equipment, cassette players, camcorders, TVs, and universal remotes. 800–626–2000.

Goldstar, 1000 Sylvan Ave., Englewood, NJ 07632: Free information ❖ CD and cassette players and TVs. 201–816–2200.

Hitachi Sales Corporation, 401 W. Artesia Blvd., Compton, CA 90220: Free information ❖ Audio and video equipment, CD and cassette players, camcorders, and TVs. 310–537–8383.

Infinity Systems, 9409 Owensmouth Ave., Chatsworth, CA 91311: Free information ❖ Speakers and TVs. 818–407–0228.

Instant Replay, 2951 S. Bayshore Dr., Coconut Grove, FL 33133: Free information ❖ Camcorders and cassette players. 305–854–6777.

JVC, 41 Slater Dr., Elmwood Park, NJ 07407: Free information ❖ Audio and video equipment, CD and cassette players, camcorders, receivers, amplifiers, TVs, and headphones. 201–794–3900.

Harmon Kardon, 8380 Balboa Blvd., Northridge, CA 91325: Free information ❖ Cassette and CD players, receivers, amplifiers, and TVs. 818–893–9992.

Kenwood, P.O. Box 22745, Long Beach, CA 90801: Free information ❖ Audio and video equipment, CD and cassette players, receivers, amplifiers, TVs, and sound processors. 310–639–9000.

Mitsubishi Electronics, 5665 Plaza Dr., Cypress, CA 90630: Free information ❖ Audio and video equipment, CD and cassette players, camcorders, and TVs. 800–843–2515.

NAP Consumer Electronics, 1 Phillips Dr., Knoxville, TN 37914: Free information ❖ Magnavox: CD and cassette players, camcorders, TVs, and universal remotes; Philco: camcorders, TVs, cassette players, and receivers; Philips: CD and cassette players, and TVs; and Sylvania: camcorders, CD and laser disk players, and TVs. 615–521–4391.

NEC Home Electronics, 1255 Michael Dr., Wood Dale, IL 60191: Free information ❖ Audio and video equipment, CD and cassette players, receivers, amplifiers, TVs, camcorders, sound processors, and other electronics. 708–860–9500.

Onkyo, 200 Williams Dr., Ramsey, NJ 07446: Free information ❖ CD players, receivers, amplifiers, universal remotes, and headphones. 201–825–7950.

Panasonic, Panasonic Way, Secaucus, NJ 07094: Free information ❖ Audio and video systems, CD and cassette players, TVs, camcorders, headphones, and other electronics. 201–348–7000.

J.C. Penney Company Inc., Catalog Division, Milwaukee, WI 53263: Free information ❖ Cassette players, TVs, audio and video systems, and other electronics. 800–222–6161.

Pentax Corporation, 35 Inverness Dr. East, Englewood, CO 80112: Free information ❖ Cassette players and camcorders. 303–799–8000.

Pioneer Electronics, 1925 E. Dominguez St., Long Beach, CA 90810: Free information ❖ Receivers, amplifiers, TVs, sound processors, headphones, and CD, cassette, and laser disk players. 800–421–1404.

Proton Corporation, 16826 Edwards Rd., Cerritos, CA 90701: Free information ❖ Speakers, CD players, receivers, amplifiers, and TVs.

Quasar, 1707 N. Randall Rd., Elgin, IL 60123: Free information ❖ Audio and video equipment, cassette and CD players, camcorders, and TVs. 708–468–5600.

Radio Shack, Division Tandy Corporation, One Tandy Center, Fort Worth, TX 76102: Free information ❖ Cassette and CD players, camcorders, universal remotes, computers, and other electronics. 817–390–3011.

RCA Sales Corporation, 600 N. Sherman Dr., Indianapolis, IN 46201: Free information ❖ Audio and video systems, cassette and CD players, TVs, camcorders, sound processors, and other electronics. 800–336–1900.

Samsung, 3655 N. 1st St., San Jose, CA 95134: Free information ❖ Cassette players and TVs. 800–933–4110.

Sansui Electronics, 1290 Wall St. West, Lyndhurst, NJ 07071: Free information ❖ CD and cassette players, camcorders, receivers, amplifiers, TVs, and sound processors. 201–460–9710.

Sanyo, 21350 Lassen St., Chatsworth, CA 91311: Free information ❖ Cassette and CD players, camcorders, TVs, sound processors, universal remotes, and other electronics. 818–998–7322.

Sharp Electronics, Sharp Plaza, Mahwah, NJ 07430: Free information ❖ Cassette and CD players, camcorders, TVs, receivers, amplifiers, and other electronics. 800–BE-SHARP.

Sony Consumer Products, 1 Sony Dr., Park Ridge, NJ 07656: Free information ❖ Audio and video equipment, cassette and CD players, camcorders, TVs, camcorders, sound processors, universal remotes, headphones, and other electronics. 201–930–1000.

Teac, 7733 Telegraph Rd., Montebello, CA 90640: Free information ❖ Sound processors, headphones, other electronics, and CD, cassette, and laser disk players. 213–726–0303.

Teknika, 353 Rt. 46 West, Fairfield, NJ 07006: Free information ❖ Cassette players and TV sets. 201–575–0380.

Toshiba, 82 Totowa Rd., Wayne, NJ 07470: Free information ❖ CD and cassette players, camcorders, sound processors, and TVs. 201–628–8000.

Vector Research, 1230 Calle Suerte, Camarillo, CA 93012: Free information ❖ Cassette and CD players, receivers, and amplifiers. 805–987–1312.

Yamaha, P.O. Box 6660, Buena Park, CA 90620: Free information ❖ Audio and video equipment, speakers, receivers, amplifiers, sound processors, headphones, and cassette, CD, and, laser disk players. 800–492–6242.

Zenith, 1000 Milwaukee Ave., Glenview, IL 60025: Free catalog ❖ Cassette players, camcorders, TVs, universal remotes, and other electronics. 708–391–7000.

Retail Sources

Audio Advisor, 225 Oakes SW, Grand Rapids, MI 49503: Free information with long SASE ❖ Audio and video equipment. 800–669–4434; 616–451–3868 (in MI).

A/V Solutions, Division Sara International Inc., 5890 Point West, Houston, TX 77036: Free information ❖ Camcorders, VCRs, editing equipment, and other electronics. 713–988–1522.

AV Distributors, 16451 Space Center Blvd., Houston, TX 77058: Free information ❖ TVs, fax machines, and audio, video, and stereo equipment. 800–843–3697.

Bondy Export Corporation, 40 Canal St., New York, NY 10002: Free information with long SASE ❖ Household appliances, cameras, video and TV equipment, office machines and typewriters, and luggage. 212–925–7785.

Cole's Appliance & Furniture Company, 4026 Lincoln Ave., Chicago, IL 60618: Free information with long SASE ❖ Furniture, audio and video equipment, TVs, and appliances. 312–525–1797.

Computability Consumer Electronics, P.O. Box 17882, Milwaukee, WI 53217: Free catalog ❖ TVs, fax machines, copiers, computers, and audio, video, and stereo equipment. 800–558–0003.

Crutchfield, 1 Crutchfield Park, Charlottesville, VA 22906: Free catalog ❖ Video, audio and stereo equipment and TVs. 800–955–9009.

Dial-A-Brand Inc., 57 S. Main St., Freeport, NY 11520: Free information with long SASE ❖ TVs, appliances, video equipment, and other electronics. 516–378–9694.

Electronic Wholesalers, 1160 Hamburg Tnpk., Wayne, NJ 07470: Free information ❖ Camcorders, TVs, cassette players, 8mm and beta home decks, receivers, and other electronics. 201–696–6531.

ElectroWorks, Plaza 34, 100G Hwy. 34, Matawan, NJ 07747: Free information ❖ TVs, speakers, camcorders, cassette and CD players, receivers, amplifiers, and audio, video, and stereo equipment. 800–662–8559.

Factory Direct, 131 W. 35th St., New York, NY 10001: Free information ❖ TVs, fax machines, and audio, video, and stereo equipment. 800–428–4567.

Focus Electronics, 4523 13th Ave., Brooklyn, NY 11219: Free catalog ❖

Appliances, photographic equipment, other electronics, and audio, stereo, and video equipment. 718–436–4646.

Free Trade Video, 4718 18th Ave., Brooklyn, NY 11204: Free information ❖ Photographic and editing equipment, video and audio accessories, and camcorders. 718–435–4151.

G & S Photo & Electronics, 2119 Utica Ave., Brooklyn, NY 11234: Free information ❖ Photographic equipment, camcorders, video and audio accessories, binoculars, and other optics. 800–879–9438; 215–527–5261 (in PA).

Garden State Camera, 101 Kuller Rd., Clifton, NJ 07015: Free information ❖ Photographic equipment, camcorders, video and audio accessories, binoculars, and other optical equipment. 201–742–5777.

Genesis Camera Inc., 814 W. Lancaster Ave., Bryn Mawr, PA 19010: Free information ❖ Photographic equipment, camcorders, editing equipment, and video and audio accessories. 800–879–9438; 215–527–5261 (in PA).

Illinois Audio, 1284 E. Dundee Rd., Palatine, IL 60067: Free information ❖ Audio, stereo, and video equipment. 800–621–8042.

International Electronic World, 1901 Tigertail Blvd., Dania, FL 33004: Free catalog ❖ Audio and video equipment.

J & R Music World, 59–50 Queens-Midtown Expwy., Maspeth, NY 11378: Free catalog ❖ Audio and stereo equipment, video recorders and tapes, telephones, and computers. 800–221–8180.

Marine Park Camera & Video Inc., 3126 Avenue U, Brooklyn, NY 11229: Free information ❖ Video equipment, VCRs, and camcorders. 800–448–8811; 718–891–1878 (in NY).

New West Electronics, 4120 Meridian, Bellingham, WA 98226: Free information ❖ Camcorders, cassette and disk players, TVs and monitors, audio components, and speakers. 800–488–8877.

Olden Video, 1265 Broadway, New York, NY 10001: Free information ❖ Audio and video equipment, TVs, cassette players, and other electronics. 212–725–1234.

Percy's Inc., 19 Glennie St., Worcester, MA 01605: Free information ❖ Appliances and electronics. 508–755–5334.

Planet Electronics, 8418 Lilley, Canton, MI 48187: Free catalog ❖ TVs, stereo receivers, video recorders, tapes and cassettes, and compact disks. 800–247–4663; 313–453–4750 (in MI).

Porter's Camera Store Inc., Box 628, Cedar Falls, IA 50613: Free catalog ❖ Video equipment. 800–553–2001.

PowerVideo, 4413 Blue Bonnet, Stafford, TX 77477: Free information ❖ TVs and audio, video, and stereo equipment. 713–240–3202.

S & S Sound City, 58 W. 45th St., New York, NY 10036: Free information ❖ Video recorders, CD players, TVs, telephones, and other electronics. 212–575–0210.

Sound City, Meadtown Shopping Center, Rt. 23, Kinnelon, NJ 07405: Free information ❖ Audio and video equipment, cassette and CD players, camcorders, TVs, processors, fax machines, telephones, and other electronics. 800–542–7283.

Sunshine South, 2606 N. Kings Hwy., Myrtle Beach, SC 29577: Free information ❖ Video equipment. 800–845–0693; 803–448–8474 (in SC).

Tri-State Camera, 650 6th Ave., New York, NY 10011: Free information ❖ Audio and video equipment, camcorders, copiers, video cassettes, and fax machines. 800–537–4441; 212–633–2290 (in NY).

United Video & Camera Express, 724 7th Ave., New York, NY 10019: Free information ❖ Video equipment. 800–448–3738; 212–247–7606 (in NY).

Wisconsin Discount Stereo, 2417 W. Badger Rd., Madison, WI 53713: Free information ❖ Video and audio equipment and TVs. 800–356–9514.

Cable TV Equipment

B & B Cable Inc., 4030 Beau-D-Rue Dr., Egan, MN 55122: Free catalog ❖ Cable TV equipment. 800–826–7623.

B & S Sales, 51756 Van Dyke Ave., #330, Shelby Township, MI 48316: Free information ❖ Cable TV equipment.

Cable Plus, 14417 Chase St., Panorama City, CA 91402: Free information ❖ Cable TV equipment. 800–822–9955.

Cable Warehouse, 10117 W. Oakland Park Blvd., Ste. 515, Sunrise, FL 33351: Free information ❖ Cable TV descramblers. 800–284–8432.

Galt Inc., 6325–9 Falls of the Neuse Rd., Ste. 310, Raleigh, NC 27615: Free information ❖ Cable TV descramblers. 800–487–2225.

JP Video, 1470 Old Country Rd., Plainview, NY 11803: Free catalog ❖ Cable TV descramblers. 800–950–9145.

K.D. Video Inc., P.O. Box 29538, Minneapolis, MN 55429: Free catalog ❖ Cable TV descramblers. 800–327–3407.

L & L Electronics Inc., 1430 Miner St., Ste. 522, Des Plaines, IL 60016: Free catalog ❖ Cable TV equipment. 800–542–9425.

M & G Electronics Inc., 2 Aborn St., Providence, RI 02903: Free information ❖ Cable TV descrambler kits. 800–258–1134.

MD Electronics, 875 S. 72nd St., Omaha, NE 68114: Free catalog ❖ Cable TV equipment. 800–624–1150.

Mega Electronics, 407 Inland Seas Blvd., Winter Garden, FL 34787: Free catalog ❖ Cable TV descramblers and converters. 800–676–6342.

Midwest Electronics Inc., P.O. Box 5000, Carpentersville, IL 60110: Free catalog with long SASE and three 1st class stamps ❖ Cable TV equipment. 800–648–3030.

Mike Nelson's Movie View Sales Inc., P.O. Box 26, Wood Dale, IL 60191: Free information ❖ Cable TV equipment. 708–250–8690.

Nu-Tek Electronics, 3250 Hatch Rd., Cedarpark, TX 78613: Free catalog ❖ Cable TV equipment. 800–228–7404.

Pacific Cable Company Inc., 7325½ Resada Blvd., Resada, CA 91335: Free catalog ❖ Cable TV equipment. 800–345–8927.

Republic Cable Products, 4080 Paradise Rd., Las Vegas, NV 89109: Free information ❖ Cable TV equipment. 702–362–9026.

Sun Microwave International Inc., P.O. Box 34522, Phoenix, AZ 85067: Catalog $1 ❖ Wireless cable receivers and other equipment. 800–484–4190.

Swensen Electronics, 518 N. Harrison, Algonquin, IL 60102: Free catalog ❖ Cable TV equipment. 708–658–8643.

TKA Electronics, 7914 W. Dodge Rd., Omaha, NE 68114: Free catalog ❖ Cable TV descramblers and converters. 800–729–1776.

Trans-World Cable Company, 3958 N. Lake Blvd., Lake Park, FL 33403: Free catalog ❖ Cable TV equipment. 800–442–9333.

United Electronic Supply, P.O. Box 1206, Elgin, IL 60121: Free information ❖ Cable TV equipment. 708–697–0600.

U.S. Cable TV Inc., 4100 N. Powerline Rd., Pompano Beach, FL 33073: Free catalog ❖ Cable TV equipment. 800–772–6244.

Worldwide Cable, 7491 N. Federal Hwy., Ste. 142, Boca Raton, FL 33487: Free catalog ❖ Cable TV equipment. 800–772–3233.

Satellite Equipment

Cabletech Inc., 3501 University Dr., Coral Springs, FL 33065: Free catalog ❖ Satellite TV systems and components. 305–344–6000.

R.L. Drake Company, P.O. Box 3006, Miamisburg, OH 45343: Free information ❖ Satellite TV antennas and receivers with optional remote control. 800–937–2538.

International Electronic World, 1901 Tigertail Blvd., Dania, FL 33004: Free catalog ❖ Satellite TV receivers and audio and video equipment.

Multi-Vision Electronics, 12105 W. Center Rd., Ste. 364, Omaha, NE 68144: Free catalog ❖ Cable TV descramblers. 800–835–2330.

Phillips-Tech Electronics, P.O. Box 8533, Scottsdale, AZ 85252: Free catalog ❖ Satellite TV antennas. 602–947–7700.

Satellite City, 4920 Topanga Canyon Blvd., Woodland Hills, CA 91364: Free information ❖ Satellite TV receivers and other electronics. 818–710–9348.

Satellite Television, 120 W. Centennial Ave., Muncie, IN 47303: Free information ❖ Satellite TV receivers. 317–288–0074.

Satman, 715 W. Glen, Peoria, IL 61614: Free information ❖ Satellite TV equipment. 800–472–8626; 309–692–4140 (in IL).

Skyvision Inc., 1046 Frontier Dr., Fergus Falls, MN 56537: Free catalog ❖ Satellite TV equipment for do-it-yourself installation and system upgrading. 800–334–6455.

Sun Microwave International Inc., P.O. Box 34522, Phoenix, AZ 85067: Catalog $1 ❖ Satellite TV receivers and other video equipment. 800–484–4190.

Timberville Electronics, Timberville, VA 22853: Free information ❖ Satellite TV receivers. 800–825–4641.

Toshiba America, P.O. Box 19724, Irvine, CA 92713: Free information ❖ TV satellite receivers and equipment for system upgrading. 714–583–3925.

Universal Antenna Manufacturing, P.O. Box 338, Ward, AR 72176: Free information ❖ Satellite reflector-type antennas with optional motorized mounts. 800–843–6517; 501–843–6517 (in AR).

West Coast Satellite, 617 W. Division, Mt. Vernon, WA 98273: Free catalog ❖ Satellite TV equipment. 800–845–6664.

Xandi Electronics, Box 25647, Tempe, AZ 85285: Free catalog ❖ Satellite TV receivers, voice disguisers, FM bugs, telephone transmitters, phone snoops, and other kits. 800–336–7389.

TYPEWRITERS & WORD PROCESSORS

Bondy Export Corporation, 40 Canal St., New York, NY 10002: Free information with long SASE ❖ Household appliances, cameras, video and TV equipment, office machines and typewriters, and luggage. 212–925–7785.

Crutchfield, 1 Crutchfield Park, Charlottesville, VA 22906: Free catalog ❖ Word processors, fax machines, telephones and answering machines, computers, and software. 800–955–9009.

East 33rd Street Electronics & Typewriters, 42 E. 33rd St., New York, NY 10016: Free information with long SASE ❖ Typewriters, computers, software, calculators, telephones and answering machines, video equipment, and TV sets. 212–686–0930.

Reliable Home Office, P.O. Box 1501, Ottawa, IL 61350: Catalog $2 ❖ Word processors, calculators, computer supplies, telephones, and office furniture. 800–869–6000.

Staples Inc., Attention: Marketing Services, P.O. Box 9328, Framingham, MA 01701: Free catalog ❖ Office supplies, furniture, computer supplies and paper, drafting equipment, fax machines, word processors, and typewriters. 800–333–9328.

UMBRELLAS

Essex Manufacturing, 330 5th Ave., New York, NY 10001: Free information ❖ Golf umbrellas. 800–648–6010; 212–239–0080 (in NY).

MDT-Muller Design Inc., 971 Dogwood Trail, Tyrone, GA 30290: Catalog $2 ❖ Giant outdoor umbrellas. 404–631–9074.

The Umbrella Shop, P.O. Box 804, Chicago, IL 60690: Catalog $2 ❖ Umbrellas and walking sticks. 312–861–1806.

Uncle Sam Umbrella Shop, 161 W. 57th St., New York, NY 10019: Free catalog ❖ Umbrellas, canes, and walking sticks. 212–247–7163.

VACUUM CLEANERS

AAA-Vacuum Cleaner Center, 1230 N. 3rd, Abilene, TX 79601: Brochure $2 (refundable) ❖ Vacuum cleaners, floor buffers, and rug shampooers. 915–677–1311.

ABC Vacuum Cleaner Warehouse, 6720 Burnet Rd., Austin, TX 78757: Free information ❖ Vacuum cleaners. 512–459–7643.

Broan Manufacturing Company, 926 W. State St., Hartford, WI 53027: Free information ❖ Vacuum cleaner systems. 414–673–4340.

Central Vac International, 3133 E. 12th St., Los Angeles, CA 90023: Free information ❖ Vacuum cleaner systems. 800–666–3133.

Derry's Sewing Center, 430 St. Ferdinand, Florissant, MO 63031: Brochure $1 with long SASE ❖ Sewing machines, vacuum cleaners, and parts. 314–837–6103.

Dust Boy Inc., 270 N. County Rd., 525 East, Milan, IN 47031: Free information ❖ Portable and stationary dust collectors. 800–232–3878.

H-P Products Inc., 512 W. Gorgas St., Louisville, OH 44641: Free information ❖ Built-in central vacuum cleaner systems. 216–875–5556.

M & S Systems Inc., 2861 Congressman Ln., Dallas, TX 75220: Free information ❖ Vacuum cleaner systems. 800–877–6631.

MidAmerica Vacuum Cleaner Supply Company, 666 University Ave., St. Paul, MN 55104: Catalog $5 ❖ Vacuum cleaners and parts, floor machines, and small kitchen appliances. 612–222–0763.

NuTone Inc., P.O. Box 1580, Cincinnati, OH 45201: Catalog $3 ❖ Vacuum cleaner systems. 800–543–8687.

Oreck Corporation, 100 Plantation Rd., New Orleans, LA 70123: Free catalog ❖ Vacuum cleaners. 800–989–4200.

Sew Vac City, 1667 Texas Ave., College Station, TX 77840: Brochure $3 ❖ Sewing machines and vacuum cleaners. 800–338–5672.

Sewin' in Vermont, 84 Concord Ave., St. Johnsbury, VT 05819: Free information ❖

Vacuum cleaners and attachments. 800–451–5124; 802–748–3803 (in VT).

Shop-Vac Corporation, 2323 Reach Rd., Williamsport, PA 17701: Free information ❖ Wet and dry vacuum cleaners. 717–326–0502.

VIDEO CASSETTES, TAPES & DISCS

Absolute Beta Movie Videos, P.O. Box 130, Remington, VA 22734: Free catalog ❖ Beta videos, VCRs, blank tapes, rewinders, and head cleaners. 703–439–3259.

Eddie Brandt's Video, 6310 Colfax Ave., North Hollywood, CA 91606: Free catalog ❖ B-westerns, cliffhanger serials, black movies, war and military features, foreign films, early animation, classics, and other VHS and beta vintage TV shows. 818–506–4242.

Calibre Press Inc., 666 Dundee Rd., Ste. 1607, Northbrook, IL 60062: Free catalog ❖ Law enforcement and EMS videos, books, and survival products. 800–323–0037; 708–498–5680 (in IL).

Classic Cinema, P.O. Box 18932, Encino, CA 91416: Catalog $5 ❖ Westerns, mysteries, comedies, and drama on video cassettes. 800–94–MOVIE.

Critics' Choice Video, P.O. Box 749, Itasca, IL 60143: Free catalog ❖ VHS classics, new releases, special interest videos, and other subjects. 800–544–9852.

Down Home Music Company, 10341 San Pablo Ave., El Cerrito, CA 94530: Catalog $5 (specify blues, country, or vintage rock 'n' roll ❖ Records, tapes, compact disks, music books, and videos. 510–525–1494.

Ergo Media, 668 Front St., P.O. Box 2037, Teaneck, NJ 07666: Free catalog ❖ Award-winning videos on all aspects of Jewish life. 800–695–3746.

Excalibur Films, 3621 W. Commonwealth, Fullerton, CA 92633: Free catalog ❖ Movies on video cassettes and reels. 800–BUY-MOVIES.

Foothill Video, P.O. Box 547C, Tujunga, CA 91043: Free information ❖ Westerns, serials, and other features on video cassettes. 818–353–8591.

Fusion Video, 17311 Fusion Way, Country Club Hills, IL 60478: Free catalog ❖ Military videos and other collections. 800–959–0061.

Historic Aviation, 1401 Kings Wood Rd., Eagan, MN 55122: Free catalog ❖ Books and videos on the history of commercial airliners, famous men in aviation, nostalgic classics,

humor, military action, and other aviation topics. 800–225–5575.

Home Film Festival, P.O. Box 2032, Scranton, PA 18501: Catalog $5 ❖ Hard-to-find films, limited release features, Hollywood classics, documentaries, and other VHS and Beta videotapes. 800–258–3456.

House of Tyrol, P.O. Box 909, Alpenland Center, Helen Highway/75 North, Cleveland, GA 30528: Free catalog ❖ Musical cuckoo clocks, crystal, porcelain, lamps, music boxes, other gifts, and travel, folk music from around the world, language, and educational videos. 800–241–5404.

International Historic Films Inc., Box 29035, Chicago, IL 60629: Catalog $1 ❖ Military, political, historical documentary films on videos. 312–927–2900.

International Video Network, 370 Yarnell Industrial Pkwy., P.O. Box 460, Clinton, TN 37717: Free catalog ❖ Travel videos. 800–669–4486.

Kino Video, 333 W. 39th St., Ste. 503, New York, NY 10018: Free catalog ❖ International and classic movies on video cassettes. 800–562–3330.

Tom Kleinschmidt Video, 26101 Country Club Blvd., Ste. 706, North Olmsted, OH 44070: Free catalog ❖ Classic TV shows. 216–979–0614.

KVC Home Video, 12801 Schabarum St., Irwindale, CA 91706: Free catalog ❖ Film classics and how-to videos. 800–331–1387.

Metropolitan Opera Guild, 835 Madison Ave., New York, NY 10021: Free catalog ❖ Books and classical, concert, operatic, and documentary videos, records, and compact disks. 212–634–8406.

MLR Films International Inc., 301 E. 62nd St., New York, NY 10021: Catalog $5 ❖ Public domain feature films, TV shows, and cartoons. 212–759–1729.

Ed Morris Videos, 2916 Yorktown, Mesquite, TX 75149: List 50¢ with long SASE ❖ Rare B westerns and TV shows. 214–288–0570.

Moviecraft Inc., P.O. Box 438, Orland Park, IL 60462: Catalog $1 ❖ Old TV shows, rare cartoons, classics, contemporary releases, war newsreels and propaganda subjects, special interest topics, and feature films. 708–460–9082.

Movies Unlimited, 6736 Castor Ave., Philadelphia, PA 19149: Catalog $7.95 ❖

Movie classics, foreign films, nostalgic TV shows, rarities, new releases, music videos, and how-to information. 800–523–0823; 215–722–8298 (in PA).

Music for Little People, Box 1460, Redway, CA 95560: Free catalog ❖ Famous stories, favorite songs, lullabies, nature stories, folk music, classical music, and other children's music cassettes and videos. 707–923–3991.

Richard Nelson, P.O. Box 9155, North Hollywood, CA 91609: Free catalog ❖ Westerns, mysteries, serials, action and adventure, and other video cassettes from the 1930s and 1940s.

Pacific Arts Publishing, 11858 La Grange Ave., Los Angeles, CA 90025: Free catalog ❖ Public television and other programs on video cassettes. 800–538–5856.

Progressive Video, RD 3, Box 210A, Greene, NY 13778: Free catalog ❖ Musical instruction, languages, arts and crafts, self defense, and other videos. 800–600–0083.

Pyramid Film & Video, P.O. Box 1048, Santa Monica, CA 90404: Free information ❖ Films and videos for educational and entertainment programming. 800–421–2304.

Quicksilver Fantasies, P.O. Box 1660, Post Falls, ID 83854: Free catalog ❖ Music, myth, folklore, fantasy videos, science-fiction, and other recordings. 208–773–7731.

Reader's Digest, P.O. Box 107, Pleasantville, NY 10571: Free catalog ❖ Videos on travel, nature, drama, and movies, children's subjects, how-to-information, sports, and music. 914–241–7445.

Rose Records, 214 S. Wabash Ave., Chicago, IL 60604: Free catalog ❖ Classical and opera recordings on long-playing records, CDs, cassettes, and music videos. Includes imports, new releases, and overstocks. 800–955–ROSE.

Shokus Video, P.O. Box 3125, Chatsworth, CA 91313: Catalog $3 (refundable) ❖ Classic TV shows. 818–704–0400.

Sinister Cinema, P.O. Box 4369, Medford, OR 97501: Free information ❖ Science fiction, horror, mystery, suspense, fantasy, and other films on VHS and beta video cassettes. 503–773–6860.

Sizzling Productions, 500 Rosslan Rd. West, Oshawa, Ontario, Canada L1J 8L6: Free catalog ❖ Instructional guitar, concert, and blues videos.

SyberVision, 1 Sansome St., Ste. 1610, San Francisco, CA 94101: Catalog $2 ❖ Sports, health and fitness, language, personal relationships, and other videos. 800–678–0877; 510–846–3388 (in CA).

The Video Catalog, P.O. Box 64428, St. Paul, MN 55164: Free catalog ❖ All-time favorite programs and films on videos. 800–733–2232.

Video Opera House, P.O. Box 800, Concord, MA 01742: Free catalog ❖ Opera, ballet, and classical video recordings. 800–99–OPERA.

Video Revolution, 97 Thoreau St., Concord, MA 01742: Free catalog ❖ Audio and video tapes for children. 800–342–3436.

Walden Video for Kids, 201 High Ridge Rd., Stamford, CT 06904: Free catalog ❖ Children's video tapes. 203–352–2092.

Zenith, 1000 Milwaukee Ave., Glenview, ILL 60025: Free catalog ❖ Video tapes and books on military aircraft, plastic and radio control modeling, warplanes, aviation history, flying skills, aeronautics, and other aviation subjects. 708–391–7000.

VISION IMPAIRMENT AIDS

American Council of the Blind, 1155 15th St. NW, Washington, DC 20005: Free list ❖ Large-print list of low vision aids and large-print publications. 202–467–5081.

American Foundation for the Blind, Product Center, 3342 Melrose Ave., Roanoke, VA 24017: Free catalog ❖ Watches, clocks and timers, canes, household and personal care aids, calculators and tools, and other sensory products. 800–829–0500.

American Printing House for the Blind, 1839 Frankfort Ave., P.O. Box 6085, Louisville, KY 40206: Free catalog ❖ Braille writing and embossing equipment, electronic devices, low-vision simulation materials, reading readiness products, and educational aids. 502–895–2405.

Independent Living Aids/Can-Do Products, 27 East Mall, Plainview, NY 11803: Free catalog ❖ Writing aids, low-vision aids and braille items, household items, home health care supplies, mobility equipment, and communication aids. 800–537–2118; 516–752–8080 (in NY).

LS & S Group Inc., P.O. Box 673, Northbrook, IL 60065: Free catalog ❖ Magnifiers, watches, braille computers, gifts, and other products for people with visual impairments. 800–468–4789; 708–498–9777 (in IL).

Maxi Aids, P.O. Box 3209, Farmingdale, NY 11735: Free catalog ❖ Aids and appliances for people with visual, physical, hearing, and other impairments. 800–522–6294.

On the Move Inc., 334 Franklin St., Mansfield, MA 02048: Free brochure ❖ Mobility aid for visually impaired persons, from age 2 to adults. 508–339–4027.

Science Products, Box 888, Southeastern, PA 19399: Free catalog ❖ Voice technology equipment and other sensory aids for hearing and visually impaired persons. 800–888–7400; 215–296–2111 (in PA).

VITAMINS & MINERALS

Advanced Medical Nutrition, 2247 National Ave., Hayward, CA 94545: Catalog $2 ❖ Nutritional supplements. 510–783–6969.

Barth Vitamins, 865 Merrick Ave., Westbury, NY 11590: Free catalog ❖ Natural vitamin and mineral supplements, cosmetics, health foods, and home health aids. 800–645–2328; 800–553–0353 (in NY).

Bioenergy Nutrients, 6565 Odell Pl., Boulder, CO 80301: Catalog $1 ❖ Nutritional supplements, homeopathic medicines, antioxidants, and all-natural skin care products. 800–627–7775.

Bronson Pharmaceuticals, 4526 Rinretti Ln., P.O. Box 628, La Canada, CA 91012: Free information ❖ Vitamins and health aids. 809–235–3200.

Freeda Vitamins, 36 E. 41st St., New York, NY 10017: Free catalog ❖ Vitamins and dietary food supplements. 800–777–3737; 212–685–4980 (in NY).

General Nutrition Catalog, Puritan's Pride, 105 Orville Dr., Bohemia, NY 11716: Free catalog ❖ Vitamins, health foods, natural cosmetics, books, and gifts. 800–645–1030.

Health Center for Better Living, 6189 Taylor Rd., Naples, FL 33942: Free catalog ❖ Vitamins and minerals and other herbal health care products. 813–566–2611.

Hillestad Corporation, AV 178 US Hwy. 51 North, Woodruff, WI 54568: Free catalog ❖ Natural vitamins. 800–535–7742; 715–358–2113 (in WI).

Indiana Botanic Gardens Inc., P.O. Box 5, Hammond, IN 46325: Free catalog ❖ Vitamins, herbs, spices, and personal care products. 219–947–4040.

L & H Vitamins Inc., 37–10 Crescent St., Long Island City, NY 11101: Free catalog ❖ Vitamins and nutritional supplements. 800–221–1152; 618–937–7400 (in NY).

Nature Food Centres, One Nature's Way, Wilmington, MA 01887: Free catalog ❖ Vitamins, natural food products, and cosmetics. 800–225–0857.

Nutrition Headquarters, One Nutrition Plaza, Carbondale, IL 62901: Free catalog ❖ Vitamins and mineral supplements, health and beauty aids, and herbal formulas. 618–457–8100, ext. 229.

Puritan's Pride, 1233 Montauk Hwy., P.O. Box 9001, Oakdale, NY 11769: Free catalog ❖ Natural vitamins and health and beauty aids. 800–645–1030.

Puritan's Pride/Stur-Dee Health Products, 1233 Montauk Hwy., P.O. Box 9001, Oakdale, NY 11769: Free catalog ❖ Vitamins and health food supplements. 800–645–1030.

RVP Health Savings Center, 865 Merrick Ave., Westbury, NY 11590: Free catalog ❖ Vitamins, natural supplements, and cosmetics and beauty aids. 800–645–2978; 800–682–2286 (in NY).

SDV Vitamins, P.O. Box 23030, Oakland Park, FL 33307: Free information ❖ Nutritional supplements and vitamins. 800–535–7095.

Star Pharmaceuticals Inc., 1500 New Horizons Blvd., Amityville, NY 11701: Free catalog ❖ Generic vitamins, nutritional supplements, toiletries, health care products, and pet supplies. 800–274–6400.

Swanson Health Products Inc., The Swanson Bldg., 1322 39th St., P.O. Box 2803, Fargo, ND 58108: Free information ❖ Vitamins and food supplements. 800–437–4148.

Vitamin Specialties Company, 8200 Ogontz Ave., Wyncote, PA 19095: Free catalog ❖ Vitamin supplements. 800–365–8482; 215–885–3800 (in PA).

Western Natural Products, P.O. Box 90845, Long Beach, CA 90809: Free catalog ❖ Natural vitamins. 800–762–5214; 805–949–6495 (in CA).

Western Vitamins & Health Products, 2525 Davie Rd., Ste. 330, Davie, FL 33317: Free catalog ❖ Natural vitamins, diet helpers, herbs, and beauty aids. 800–777–9847.

VOLLEYBALL
Clothing

Action Sport Systems Inc., P.O. Box 1442, Morgantown, NC 28680: Free information ❖ Uniforms. 800–631–1091; 704–584–8000 (in NC).

Adidas USA, 5675 N. Blackstock Rd., Spartanburg, SC 29303: Free information ❖ Shoes. 800–423–4327.

Asics Tiger Corporation, 10540 Talbert Ave., West Bldg., Fountain Valley, CA 92708: Free information ❖ Shoes and uniforms. 800–766–ASICS; 714–962–7654 (in CA).

Champion Products Inc., 475 Corporate Square Dr., Winston Salem, NC 27105: Free information ❖ Uniforms.

Converse Inc., 1 Fordham Rd., Wilmington, MA 01887: Free information ❖ Shoes. 800–428–2667; 508–664–1100 (in MA).

Foot-Joy Inc., 144 Field St., Brockton, MA 02403: Free information ❖ Shoes. 508–586–2233.

Mizuno Corporation, 5125 Peachtree Industrial Blvd., Norcross, GA 30092: Free information ❖ Uniforms and shoes. 800–333–7888.

Nike Footwear Inc., One Bowerman Dr., Beaverton, OR 97005: Free information ❖ Shoes. 800–344–6453.

Puma USA Inc., 147 Centre St., Brockton, MA 02403: Free information with long SASE ❖ Shoes. 508–583–9100.

Spike Nashbar, 4111 Simion Rd., Youngstown, OH 44512: Free information ❖ Shoes and equipment. 800–937–7453.

Sport Fun Inc., 4621 Sperry St., Los Angeles, CA 90039: Free information ❖ Uniforms and shoes. 800–423–2597; 818–240–6700 (in CA).

Venus Knitting Mills Inc., 140 Spring St., Murray Hill, NJ 07974: Free information ❖ Uniforms. 800–955–4200; 908–464–2400 (in NJ).

Equipment

Action Sport Systems Inc., P.O. Box 1442, Morgantown, NC 28680: Free information ❖ Volleyball sets, nets, posts, and standards. 800–631–1091; 704–584–8000 (in NC).

American Athletic Inc., 200 American Ave., Jefferson, IA 50129: Free information ❖ Nets. 800–247–3978; 515–386–3125 (in IA).

Cannon Sports, P.O. Box 11179, Burbank, CA 91510: Free information with list of retailers ❖ Nets and balls. 800–362–3146; 818–753–5940 (in CA).

Champion Sports Products Company Inc., P.O. Box 138, Sayreville, NJ 08872: Free information ❖ Nets, balls, and protective gear. 201–238–0330.

Franklin Sports Industries Inc., 17 Campanelli Pkwy., P.O. Box 508, Stoughton, MA 02072: Free information ❖ Volleyball sets, balls, and nets. 617–344–1111.

Gared Sports Inc., 1107 Mullanphy St., St. Louis, MO 63106: Free information ❖ Nets, posts, standards, and balls. 800–325–2682.

General Sportcraft Company Ltd., 140 Woodbine Rd., Bergenfield, NJ 07621: Free information ❖ Nets, posts, standards, balls, and protective gear. 201–384–4242.

Indian Industries Inc., P.O. Box 889, Evansville, IN 47706: Free catalog ❖ Nets and sets. 800–457–3373; 812–467–1200 (in IN).

Jayfro Corporation, Unified Sports Inc., 976 Hartford Tnpk., P.O. Box 400, Waterford, CT 06385: Free catalog ❖ Nets, posts, referee stands, and equipment carriers. 203–447–3001.

Dick Martin Sports Inc., 181 E. Union Ave., P.O. Box 7381, East Rutherford, NJ 07073: Free information ❖ Nets, posts, balls, and protective gear. 800–221–1993; 201–453–5255 (in NJ).

Pennsylvania Sporting Goods, 1360 Industrial Hwy., P.O. Box 451, Southampton, PA 18966: Free information ❖ Nets, posts, standards, and protective gear. 800–535–1122.

Regent Sports Corporation, 45 Ranick Rd., Hauppage, NY 11788: Free information ❖ Nets, posts, standards, and balls. 516–234–2800.

Spalding Sports Worldwide, 425 Meadow St., P.O. Box 901, Chicopee, MA 01021: Free information with list of retailers ❖ Nets, posts, standards, and balls. 800–225–6601.

Spike Nashbar, 4111 Simion Rd., Youngstown, OH 44512: Free information ❖ Shoes and equipment. 800–937–7453.

Voit Sports, 1451 Pittstand-Victor Rd., 100 Willowbrook Office Park, Fairport, NY 14450: Free information ❖ Balls. 800–444–VOIT.

Wilson Sporting Goods, 8700 W. Bryn Mawr, Chicago, IL 60631: Free information ❖ Balls. 800–272–6060; 312–714–6400 (in IL).

WATER PURIFIERS

Action Filter Inc., P.O. Box 697, Dallas, PA 18612: Free brochure ❖ Easy-to-install water purifier. 717–333–5121.

Aquathin Corporation, 950 S. Andrews Ave., Pompano Beach, FL 33069: Free information ❖ Portable water purifier. 800–462–7634.

Basic Designs Inc., 355 O'Hair Rd., Santa Rosa, CA 95407: Free information ❖ High-flow and pocket-size water filters. 707–575–1220.

Filtration Concepts, 2226 S. Fairview, Santa Ana, CA 92704: Free brochure ❖ Water recovery systems. 714–850–0123.

General Ecology Inc., 151 Sheree Blvd., Exton, PA 19341: Free information ❖ Portable, base camp, and travel-type water purifiers. 800–441–8166.

Katadyn, 3020 N. Scottsdale Rd., Scottsdale, AZ 85251: Free information ❖ Water purification equipment. 800–950–0808.

Liberty Water Systems, S-9 W. 31735 Glacier Pass, Delafield, WI 53018: Free information ❖ Home reverse osmosis water purifiers. 414–968–5619.

Marine Industries, 2233 S. Andrews Ave., Fort Lauderdale, FL 33316: Free brochure ❖ Water recovery systems. 305–467–8920.

Matrix Desalination Inc., 3295 SW 11th Ave., Fort Lauderdale, FL 33315: Free information ❖ Desalinization equipment. 305–524–5120.

Mountain Safety Research, P.O. Box 24547, Seattle, WA 98124: Free information ❖ Portable water purification equipment. 800–877–9MSR.

National EnviroAlert Company, 297 Lake St., Waltham, MA 02154: Free brochure ❖ Environmental air systems and water filtration units. 617–891–7484.

Offshore Marine Laboratories, 22994 El Toro Rd., Ste. 105, Lake Forest, CA 92630: Catalog $5.25 ❖ Water purification systems and equipment. 800–458–3365; 714–455–0711 (in CA).

PUR Water Purifiers, 2229 Edgewood Ave. South, Minneapolis, MN 55426: Free information ❖ Self-cleaning water purifier. 800–845–PURE.

Recovery Engineering, 2229 Edgewood Ave. South, Minneapolis, MN 55426: Free information ❖ Lightweight water purification equipment. 800–548–0406.

Reverse Osmosis, 12301 SW 133rd Ct., Miami, FL 33186: Free brochure ❖ Water recovery systems. 305–255–8115.

Sea Recovery Corporation, P.O. Box 2560, Gardena, CA 90247: Free brochure ❖ Water recovery systems. 800–354–2000; 310–327–4000 (in CA).

SpectraPure, 738 S. Perry Ln., Tempe, AZ 85281: Free information ❖ Water purification systems. 800–685–2783.

Standard Communications, P.O. Box 92151, Los Angeles, CA 90009: Free brochure ❖ Water recovery systems. 310–532–5300.

Universal Aqua Technologies, 10555 Norwalk Blvd., Santa Fe Springs, CA 90670: Free brochure ❖ Water recovery systems.

Village Marine Tech., 2000 W. 135th St., Gardena, CA 90249: Free brochure ❖ Water recovery systems. 310–516–9911.

Watermakers Inc., 2233 S. Andrews Ave., Fort Lauderdale, FL 33316: Free brochure ❖ Water recovery systems. 305–467–8920.

WATER SKIING

Boats

Baja Boats, Box 151, Bucyrus, OH 44820: Free information ❖ Outboards and inboards. 419–562–5377.

Brendella Boats Inc., 25556 W. 16th St., Merced, CA 95348: Free information ❖ Inboards. 209–384–2566.

Celebrity Boats Inc., 451 E. Illinois Ave., P.O. Box 394, Benton, IL 62812: Catalog $2 ❖ Stern drives. 618–439–9444.

Chaparral Boats Inc., Industrial Park Blvd., P.O. Drawer 928, Nashville, GA 31639: Free catalog ❖ Stern drives. 912–686–7481.

Cobia Boat Company, 2000 Cobia Dr., Vonore, TN 37885: Free brochure ❖ Inboards and stern drives. 615–884–6881.

Correct Craft Inc., 6100 S. Orange Ave., Orlando, FL 32809: Free information ❖ Inboards. 800–346–2092; 407–855–4141 (in FL).

Four Winns Inc., 925 Frisbie St., Cadillac, MI 49601: Free catalog ❖ Stern drives. 616–779–0025.

Invader Marine Inc., P.O. Box 420, Giddings, TX 78942: Free catalog ❖ Stern drives. 409–542–3101.

Malibu Boats of California Inc., 1861 Grogan Ave., Merced, CA 95340: Free information ❖ Inboards. 209–383–7469.

MasterCraft Boat Company, 869 Binfield Rd., Maryville, TN 37801: Free information ❖ Inboards. 615–983–2178.

Regal Marine Industries Inc., 2300 Jetport Dr., Orlando, FL 32809: Free information ❖ Stern drives. 800–US-REGAL.

Renken Boat Manufacturing Company Inc., 1750 Signal Point Rd., Charleston, SC 29412: Free information ❖ Stern drives. 803–795–1150.

Rinker Marine, 300 W. Chicago St., Syracuse, IN 46567: Free information ❖ Stern drives. 219–457–5731.

Sanger Boat, 3316 E. Annadale Ave., Fresno, CA 93725: Free information ❖ Stern drives and inboards. 209–485–2842.

Sea Ray Boats Inc., 2600 Sea Ray Blvd., Knoxville, TN 37914: Free information ❖ Stern drives. 800–367–1596.

Stingray Boats, P.O. Box 669, Hartsville, SC 29550: Free information ❖ Stern drives. 803–383–4507.

Sunbird Boat Company Inc., 2348 Shop Rd., Columbia, SC 29201: Free information ❖ Outboards. 803–799–1125.

Supra Sports Inc., P.O. Box C, Greenback, TN 37742: Free information ❖ Inboards. 615–856–3035.

Sylvan Boats, Calaway Church Rd., P.O. Box 1267, LaGrange, GA 30241: Free information ❖ Inboards and stern drives. 404–882–1438.

Equipment & Clothing

Aamstrand Corporation, 629 Grove, Manteno, IL 60950: Free information ❖ Water skiing equipment. 800–338–0557; 312–458–8550 (in IL).

Ascending Parachutes, 1341 E. 5150 South, Ogden, UT 84403: Free information ❖ Parasails. 801–479–FLY-1.

Barefoot International, 6160 N. 60th St., Milwaukee, WI 53218: Free information ❖ Wet and dry suits, barefoot suits, ropes, and

handles. 800–932–0685; 414–466–3668 (in WI).

Bart's Water Ski Center, P.O. Box 294, Hwy. 13, North Webster, IN 46555: Free catalog ❖ Kneeboards, ropes and handles, gloves, water toys, ski boards, wet and dry suits, and T-shirts. 800–348–5016.

Body Glove International, 530 6th St., Hermosa Beach, CA 90254: Free information ❖ Wet and barefoot suits. 800–678–7873; 310–374–4074 (in CA).

L.S. Brown Company, Pawley Industries Corporation, 3610 Atlanta Industrial Dr. NW, Atlanta, GA 30331: Free information ❖ Water skiing and marine sport equipment. 404–691–8200.

Buckeye Sports Supply, John's Sporting Goods, 2655 Harrison Ave. SW, Canton, OH 44706: Free information ❖ Water skiing equipment. 800–533–8691.

Burbank Water Ski Company, 1861 Victory Pl., Burbank, CA 91504: Free information ❖ Water skis, ski sleds, tow hooks, and ropes. 818–848–8808.

Caribe Water Ski, 209 NE 1st St., Miami, FL 33132: Free information ❖ Water skiing equipment.

Casad Manufacturing Corporation, 1140 Monticello Rd., Madison, GA 30650: Free information ❖ Wet suits, skis, ski sleds, tow hooks, ropes and handles, vests, and flotation wet suits.

Colores International Inc., 3860 148th Ave. NE, Redmond, WA 98052: Free information ❖ Water skiing equipment. 206–885–6323.

Connelly Skis Inc., P.O. Box 716, Lynnwood, WA 98046: Free information ❖ Water skis, ropes, gloves, vests, trick harnesses, boat harnesses, ski racks, and videos. 206–775–5416.

Harvey's Custom Suits, 2505 S. 252nd St., Kent, WA 98032: Free information ❖ Wet and dry suits. 206–824–1114.

Hydroslide, P.O. Box 6700, Fort Wayne, IN 46896: Free information ❖ Knee boards. 800–922–4470.

Jobe Ski Corporation, 15320 NE 92nd St., Redmond, WA 98052: Free information ❖ Water skis, wet suits, gloves, handles and ropes, boat and trick harnesses, vests, ski racks, and videos. 206–882–1177.

Kidder International Inc., P.O. Box 898, Auburn, WA 98002: Free information ❖ Water skis, gloves, handles and ropes, boat harnesses, videos, vests, and ski racks. 800–331–4697; 206–939–7100 (in WA).

Kransco Group Company, P.O. Box 884866, San Francisco, CA 94111: Free information ❖ Water skis and ski boards. 415–433–9350.

Lynton Manufacturing, 442 Higgins Ave., Winnipeg, Manitoba, Canada R3A 1S5: Free information ❖ Knee boards and ski boards. 204–942–1166.

Maherajah Water Skis, 1595 University Rd., Hopland, CA 95449: Free information ❖ Water skis. 707–744–1816.

Mastercraft Skis, 4590 Pell Dr., Unit A, Sacramento, CA 95838: Free information ❖ Water skis, ropes, and vests. 916–920–3993.

O'Brien International, P.O. Box 97020, Redmond, WA 98073: Free information ❖ Water skis, ropes and handles, boat harnesses, vests, ski and kneeboard racks, tubes, and gloves. 206–881–5900.

Overton's Sports Center Inc., P.O. Box 8228, Greenville, NC 27835: Free catalog ❖ Water skis, wet and dry suits, ropes, and handles. 800–334–6541.

Performance Line Company, P.O. Box 427, Drayton Plains, MI 48020: Free information ❖ Water skiing and marine sport equipment. 313–674–4500.

Power-Sail Corporation, 47. E. Main St., P.O. Box 856, Flemington, NJ 08822: Free brochure ❖ Ascending parachutes. 800–426–3316; 908–782–9344 (in NJ).

Rampage Custom Kneeboards, 6353 Applecross Dr., Fayetteville, NC 28304: Free information ❖ Fiberglass kneeboards. 910–868–5525.

RM Water Skis USA, 267 Columbia Ave., Chapin, SC 29036: Free information ❖ Slalom skis and knee boards. 800–433–8313.

Ski Limited, 7825 South Ave., Youngstown, OH 44512: Free catalog ❖ Vests, ski ropes and handles, and wet, dry, and barefoot suits. 800–477–4040.

Ski Warm, P.O. Box 726, Lynnwood, WA 98046: Free price list ❖ Wet suits, flotation vests, and accessories. 206–778–8060.

Skurfer, P.O. Box 6700, Fort Wayne, IN 46896: Free information ❖ Ski boards. 800–922–4470.

Sport Chutes, 1500 Crescent, Ste. 104, Carrollton, TX 75006: Free brochure ❖

Parasailing chutes, inflatable watersleds, and helmets. 214–245–7070.

Stearns Manufacturing, P.O. Box 1498, St. Cloud, MN 56302: Free information ❖ Flotation equipment and water skiing vests. 800–328–3208; 612–252–1642 (in MN).

Surfer House, P.O. Box 726, Lynwood, WA 98046: Free information ❖ Wet and dry suits and other clothing for water sports. 206–778–8060.

Thruster Water Ski Boards, 1055 W. College Ave., Ste. 328, Santa Rosa, CA 95401: Free information ❖ Ski boards. 707–544–5162.

Thunderwear Inc., 1060 E. Calle Negocio, San Clemente, CA 92672: Free information ❖ Gloves. 800–422–6565.

Wakeski, 6810 242nd Ave., Redmond, WA 98053: Free information ❖ Knee boards and ski boards. 206–868–3072.

Wavelength Wetsuits, 1140 Mark Ave., Carpintera, CA 93103: Free information ❖ Slalom, barefoot, jump, and buoyancy wet suits. 805–684–6694.

Wellington Leisure Products, P.O. Box 244, Madison, GA 30650: Free information ❖ Water skis, gloves, ropes and handles, kneeboards and ski boards, trick and boat harnesses, videos, and ski racks. 404–342–4915.

Yamaha Motor Corporation, P.O. Box 6555, Cypress, CA 90630: Free information ❖ Wet suits. 800–526–6650.

WEATHER FORECASTING

Abbeon Cal Inc., 123 Gray Ave., Santa Barbara, CA 93101: Free catalog ❖ Thermometers, hygrometers, moisture meters, and humidity indicators. 805–966–0810.

Accu-Weather Inc., 619 W. College Ave., State College, PA 16801: Free information ❖ IBM compatible/modem on-line weather data base information system.

Alden Electronics, 40 Washington St., Westborough, MA 01581: Free information ❖ Weather radar equipment, weather graphics systems, and radio facsimile weather chart recorder kits. 508–366–8851.

American Weather Enterprises, P.O. Box 1383, Media, PA 19063: Free catalog ❖ Electronic weather stations that provide electronic readouts of barometric pressure, daily and cumulative rainfall, indoor and outdoor temperatures, and wind speed and direction. 610–565–1232.

Azimuth Communications Corporation, 3612 Alta Vista Ave., Santa Rosa, CA 95409: Free information ❖ Computerized weather stations and other equipment. 800–882–7388.

Davis Instruments, 3465 Diablo Ave., Hayward, CA 94545: Free information ❖ Professional weather station for home use and other state-of-the-art instruments. 800–678–3669.

Edmund Scientific Company, Edscorp Bldg., Barrington, NJ 08007: Free catalog ❖ Weather forecasting instruments, microscopes, magnifiers, magnets, telescopes, binoculars, and other science equipment. 609–573–6260.

HAL Communications Corporation, 1201 W. Kenyon Rd., P.O. Box 365, Urbana, IL 61801: Free information ❖ Automatic weather information instruments. 217–367–1701.

Hinds Instruments Inc., 3175 NW Aloclek Dr., Hillsboro, OR 97124: Free information ❖ Electronic weather data display station that can be linked directly to a computer modem or printer to provide a visible or audible record. 800–688–4463; 503–643–6276 (in OR).

Klockit, P.O. Box 636, Lake Geneva, WI 53147: Free catalog ❖ Instruments for building weather/time stations, Swiss music box movements, and clock-building parts and supplies. 800–556–2548.

Maximum Inc., 30 Barnett Blvd., New Bedford, MA 02745: Free catalog ❖ Instruments for wind, weather, tide, and time measurement, with optional digital and analog versions. 508–995–2200.

Multifax, 143 Rollin Irish Rd., Milton, VT 05468: Free information ❖ Weather imaging software for IBM compatible computers. 802–893–7006.

OFS WeatherFAX, 6404 Lakerest Ct., Raleigh, NC 27612: Free information ❖ PC-based weather satellite image capturing system. 919–847–4545.

Peet Bros. Company, 601 Woodland Rd., West Allenhurst, NJ 07711: Free brochure ❖ Home weather stations. 800–872–7388.

Quorum Communications Inc., 8304 Esters Blvd., Ste. 850, Irving, TX 75063: Free catalog ❖ Weather-imaging software for IBM compatible computers. 800–982–9614.

Sensor Instruments Company Inc., 41 Terrill Dr., Concord, NH 03301: Free information ❖ Weather instruments. 800–633–1033.

Simerl Instruments, 528 Epping Forest Rd., Annapolis, MD 21401: Free brochure ❖ Weather forecasting instruments. 410–849–8667.

Swift Instruments Inc., 952 Dorchester Ave., Boston, MA 02125: Free information ❖ Telescopes, weather instruments, binoculars, and other optics. 800–446–1115; 617–436–2960 (in MA).

Texas Weather Instruments Inc., 5942 Abrams Rd., Dallas, TX 75231: Free information ❖ Easy-to-operate, seven-readable display weather station. 800–284–0245; 214–368–7116 (in TX).

Weather Dimensions, P.O. Box 846, Hot Springs, VA 24445: Free brochure ❖ Logging weather station. 800–354–1117.

Weather Network Inc., 568 Manzanita Ave., Chico, CA 95926: Free information ❖ On-line weather database information system. 916–893–0308.

The Weather Station, P.O. Box 1109, New London, NH 03257: Free catalog ❖ Weather forecasting instruments. 603–526–6399.

WeatherTrac, P.O. Box 122, Cedar Falls, IA 50613: Free catalog ❖ Weather forecasting instruments, weather vanes, and educational aids. 800–798–8724.

Robert E. White Instruments Inc., 34 Commercial Wharf, Boston, MA 02110: Free catalog ❖ Electronic equipment for measuring indoor and outdoor temperatures and time of occurrence. 800–992–3045.

Wind & Weather, P.O. Box 2320, Mendocino, CA 95460: Free catalog ❖ Barometers, thermometers, hygrometers, psychrometers, wind direction instruments, anemometers, weather vanes, sundials, rain gauges, cloud charts, and books. 707–964–1284.

ZFX/Information by FAX, 40 Washington St., Westborough, MA 01581: Free information ❖ Weather information system by fax machine. 800–876–1232.

WEATHER VANES

A.J.P. Coppersmith & Company, 20 Industrial Pkwy., Woburn, MA 01801: Catalog $3 ❖ Handcrafted copper, tin, or brass reproduction colonial lanterns, chandeliers, sconces, cupolas, and weather vanes. 617–932–3700.

Antique Hardware Store, Easton Rd., Kintnersville, PA 18930: Catalog $3 ❖ Antique-style indoor and outdoor lamps and light fixtures, pedestal sinks, faucets, high tank toilets, cabinet hardware, weather vanes, and tin and wood chandeliers. 800–422–9982.

Berry-Hill Limited, 75 Burwell Rd., St. Thomas, Ontario, Canada N5P 3R5: Catalog $2 ❖ Weather vanes, canning equipment, cider press, and garden tools. 519–631–0480.

C & R Manufacturing Company, P.O. Box 1874, Stillwater, OK 74076: Free information ❖ Weather vanes.

Cambridge Smithy, RR 2, Box 1280, Cambridge, VT 05444: Free information ❖ Wrought-iron hardware and copper weather vanes. 802–644–5358.

Cape Cod Cupola Company Inc., 78 State Rd., North Dartmouth, MA 02747: Catalog $2 (refundable) ❖ Early American weather vanes and cupolas. 508–994–2119.

Colonial Casting Company Inc., 68 Liberty St., Haverhill, MA 01832: Catalog $3 ❖ Handcrafted lead-free pewter miniature castings, copper handmade weather vanes, and lighting. 508–374–8783.

Colonial Cupolas, 5902 Buttonwood Dr., P.O. Box 38, Haslett, MI 48840: Brochure $3 ❖ Authentic reproductions of historic cupolas and weather vanes. 517–339–4320.

Copper House, RFD 1, Box 4, Epsom, NH 03234: Catalog $3 ❖ Handmade copper weather vanes and indoor and outdoor copper lanterns. 603–736–9798.

Crosswinds Gallery, 980 E. Main Rd., Portsmouth, RI 02871: Free catalog ❖ Cupolas and copper, gold leaf-decorated, aluminum, and wood weather vanes. 401–683–7974.

Denninger Cupolas & Weathervanes, RD 1, Box 447, Middletown, NY 10940: Catalog $4 ❖ Weather vanes and redwood cupolas with copper roofs. 914–343–2229.

Fischer Artworks, 6530 S. Windmere, Littleton, CO 80120: Free catalog ❖ Copper and cast-bronze Victorian-style weather vanes. 303–798–4841.

David & Martha Fletcher, Blue Mist Morgan Farm, 68 Liberty St., Haverhill, MA 01830: Catalog $3 ❖ Handcrafted copper weather vanes and lanterns. 508–374–8783.

Good Directions Company, 24 Ardmore Rd., Stamford, CT 06902: Free catalog ❖ Antique and polished copper weather vanes

with solid brass directional indicators and stainless steel chimney caps. 800–346–7678.

Holst Inc., 1118 W. Lake, Box 370, Tawas City, MI 48764: Free catalog ❖ Country crafts, sundials, weather vanes, housewares, figurines, and holiday decorations. 517–362–5664.

Ives Weathervanes, RR 1, Box 101, Charlemont, MA 01339: Free information ❖ Animal weather vanes in copper, with optional gold leaf. 413–339–8534.

Barry Norling Weathervanes, RD 1, Box 5190, Skowhegan, ME 04976: Free brochure ❖ Handcrafted copper weather vanes. 207–474–2738.

Outward Signs, 39B Mill Plain Rd., Danbury, CT 06811: Free catalog ❖ Cupolas and copper, iron, and aluminum weather vanes. 800–346 -7678.

Redwood Unlimited, P.O. Box 2344, Valley Center, CA 92082: Brochure $2 ❖ Weather vanes and post-mounted California redwood, cedar, and pine mailboxes. 800–283–1717.

Travis Tuck, Metal Sculptor, Box 1832, Martha's Vineyard, MA 02568: Brochure $1 ❖ Sculpted metal weather vanes. 508–693–3914.

The Weathervane, 108 E. Front St., Traverse City, MI 49684: Brochure $1 ❖ Polished copper and antiqued-green weather vanes. 800–332–2460.

Weathervanes,

West Coast Weathervanes, 377 Westdal Dr., Santa Cruz, CA 95060: Free information ❖ Handcrafted and limited edition copper weather vanes and finials. 408–425–5514.

Westwinds, 3540 76th St. SE, Caledonia, MI 49316: Free brochure ❖ Weather vanes, post and mailbox signs, and hitching posts. 800–635–5262.

Wind & Weather, P.O. Box 2320, Mendocino, CA 95460: Free catalog ❖ Sundials, weather vanes, and weather forecasting instruments. 707–964–1284.

Windleaves Weathervanes, 7560 Morningside Dr., Indianapolis, IN 46240: Free brochure ❖ Weather vanes. 317–251–1361.

WEDDING INVITATIONS & ACCESSORIES

The American Wedding Album, American Stationery Company Inc., 300 N. Park Ave., Peru, IN 46970: Free catalog ❖ Wedding invitations, stationery, and gifts. 800–428–0379.

Ann's Wedding Stationery, P.O. Box, Milan, IN 47031: Free catalog ❖ Wedding invitations and accessories. 800–821–7011.

Creations by Elaine, 6253 W. 74th St., Box 2001, Bedford Park, IL 60499: Free catalog ❖ Wedding invitations and stationery, cake knives and servers, reception and ceremony accessories, and jewelry. 800–323–2717.

Dawn Invitations, 681 Main St., P.O. Box 100, Lumberton, NJ 08048: Free catalog ❖ Wedding invitations and gifts for attendants. 800–528–6677.

Evangel Wedding Service, P.O. Box 202, Batesville, IN 47006: Free catalog ❖ Wedding invitations, announcements, programs, napkins, and accessories with a Christian theme. 800–342–4227.

Heart Thoughts Original Wedding Stationery, 6200 E. Central, Ste. 100, Wichita, KS 67208: Free catalog ❖ Contempory, Victorian, and custom wedding invitations. 316–688–5781.

Historic Patterns & Slipcovers, P.O. Box 7967, Incline Village, NV 89452: Catalog $5.39 ❖ Victorian gown patterns and wedding accessories. 800–876–2699.

Jamie Lee Stationery, P.O. Box 5343, Glendale, AZ 85312: Free catalog ❖ Wedding stationery for brides. 800–288–5800.

Memories Inc., P.O. Box 17526, Raleigh, NC 27619: Free information ❖ Handmade wedding albums and picture frames, bridal garters, birdseed bags, ring bearer's pillows, and flower girl baskets. 800–462–5069; 919–571–1648 (in NC).

Now & Forever, P.O. Box 820, Goshen, CA 92227: Free catalog ❖ Accessories for the wedding ceremony and reception, gifts for attendants, and invitations with dramatic, romantic, and contemporary designs. 800–451–8616.

The Precious Collection, Merchandise Mart, P.O. Box 3403, Chicago, IL 60654: Free catalog ❖ Coordinated wedding invitation ensembles with traditional or contemporary designs and wedding ceremony and reception accessories. 800–284–9080.

Rexcraft, Western Catalog House, Rexburg, ID 83441: Free catalog ❖ Invitations and stationery, bridal and reception accessories, and thank you cards. 800–635–1433.

Romantic Moments Wedding Invitations, P.O. Box 6729, Chicago, IL 60680: Free catalog ❖ Wedding invitations.

Sugar 'n Spice Invitations, Western Catalog House, Rexburg, ID 83441: Free catalog ❖ Invitations and stationery, bridal and reception accessories, and thank you cards. 800–635–1433.

Treasured Memories, 3600 S. Congress Ave., Ste. M, Boynton Beach, FL 33426: Catalog $2 ❖ Glass, crystal, porcelain cake tops, and other wedding accessories. 407–737–7377.

Wedding Invitations by After Six, P.O. Box 263, Galena, IL 61036: Free catalog ❖ Wedding invitations, announcements, and stationery. 800–231–1273.

Wedding Treasures, P.O. Box 6678, Rockford, IL 61125: Free catalog ❖ Wedding invitations. 800–851–5974.

Weddingware, P.O. Box 26924, Columbus, OH 43226: Brochure $3 ❖ Wedding program covers.

WELDING & FOUNDRY EQUIPMENT

Am-Fast Bolt, Nut & Screw Company, 406 W. Boylston St., Worcester, MA 01606: Free information ❖ Foundry equipment, welding tools, power machine tools, and machine shop supplies. 508–852–8778.

Brodhead-Garrett, 223 S. Illinois Ave., Mansfield, OH 44901: Free information ❖ General workshop supplies and equipment and drafting and design, graphic arts, wood and metal working, electricity and electronics, automotive, and other tools. 800–321–6730.

McKilligan, 435 Main St., Johnson City, NY 13790: Catalog $5 ❖ Foundry equipment, welding tools, power machine tools, hand and portable power tools, machine shop supplies, and measuring, drafting, and layout tools. 607–729–6512.

Pyramid Products Company, 85357 American Canal Rd., Niland, CA 92257: Information $1 ❖ Foundry equipment and supplies for home and professional metal casting. 619–354–4265.

WELLS

Baker Manufacturing Company, 133 Enterprise St., Evansville, WI 53536: Free information ❖ Hand pump systems for water wells. 608–882–5100.

Deeprock Manufacturing Company, 7439 Anderson Rd., Opelika, AL 36802: Free information ❖ Well-digging equipment. 800–333–7762.

WHEAT WEAVING

J. Page Basketry, 820 Albee Rd., West Nokomis, FL 34275: Catalog $2 (refundable) ❖ Wheat weaving and pine needle crafting supplies, dried and preserved flowers and herbs, basket-making supplies, and books. 813–485–6730.

WHEELCHAIRS, TRANSPORTERS & LIFTS

Access Industries Inc., 4001 E. 138th St., Grandview, MO 64030: Free information ❖ Easy-to-install wheelchair and stairway lifts. 800–925–3100.

American Health Manufacturing, P.O. Box 16287, Baltimore, MD 21210: Free catalog ❖ Electric scooters and wheelchairs. 800–232–3044.

Amigo Mobility International Inc., P.O. Box 402, Bridgeport, MI 48722: Free brochure ❖ Easy-to-operate scooters. 800–248–9130.

Bath-Mate, P.O. Box 80095, Ontario, CA 91758: Free information ❖ Water-powered bathtub lift that pivots outward for safe patient transfer. 800–282–4928.

Bruce Medical Supply, 411 Waverly Oaks Rd., P.O. Box 9166, Waltham, MA 02254: Free catalog ❖ Mobility equipment, health equipment, and supplies for people with physical disabilities. 800–225–8446.

Bruno Independent Living Aids, 1780 Executive Dr., P.O. Box 84, Oconomowoc, WI 53066: Free information ❖ Rear-wheel drive, battery-powered scooter, battery-powered stairway elevator system, and wheelchair and scooter lifts for cars, vans, and trucks. 800–882–8183.

Burke Inc., Box 1064, Mission, KS 66222: Free information ❖ Portable, easy-to-operate rear wheel-powered mobility vehicles. 800–255–4147.

Convaid Products Inc., P.O. Box 2458, Palos Verde, CA 90274: Free information ❖ Lightweight compact folding mobility aids for children and adults. 800–552–1020; 310–539–6814 (in CA).

Crow River Industries Inc., 14800 28th Ave. North, Minneapolis, MN 55447: Free information ❖ All-electric, easy-to-operate wheelchair lifts.

Eagle Home Medical, 5 W. Main St., Westerville, OH 43081: Free information ❖ Mobility equipment and home health care aids. 800–899–0172.

Electric Mobility Corporation, 1 Mobility Plaza, P.O. Box 156, Sewell, NJ 08080: Free information ❖ Electric scooters, power chairs, water-powered lift for tubs, and other mobility accessories. 800–662–4548.

ETAC USA, 2325 Parklawn Dr., Ste. J, Waukesha, WI 53186: Free brochure ❖ Wheelchairs, walking aids, bath safety equipment, and other aids to make daily living easier. 800–678–3822.

Fashion Ease, Division M & M Health Care, 1541 60th St., Brooklyn, NY 11219: Free catalog ❖ Wheelchair accessories and clothing with velcro closures. 800–221–8929; 718–871–8188 (in NY).

Fortress Inc., P.O. Box 489, Clovis, CA 93613: Free information ❖ Lightweight self-powered wheelchairs, rear wheel drive scooters, three-wheel racing wheelchair, and folding transportable direct drive power wheelchairs. 800–866–4335.

Freedom Designs Inc., 2241 Madera Rd., Simi Valley, CA 93065: Free information ❖ Tilting, tilting and reclining, and reclining transport chairs. 800–331–8551; 805–582–0077 (in CA).

Gadabout Wheelchairs, 1165 Portland Ave., Rochester, NY 14621: Free information ❖ Easy-to-store and transport folding wheelchair. 800–338–2110.

Guardian Products Inc., 12800 Wentworth St., Arieta, CA 91331: Free catalog ❖ Walkers, crutches, canes, home activity aids, beds, lifters, ramps, and other transporting equipment. 800–255–5022; 818–504–2820 (in CA).

Handicaps Inc., 4335 S. Santa Fe Dr., Englewood, CO 80110: Free brochure ❖ Wheelchair lift for vans and motorhomes. 800–782–4335; 303–781–2062 (in CO).

Independent Living Aids/Can-Do Products, 27 East Mall, Plainview, NY 11803: Free catalog ❖ Self-help products for individuals with vision impairment and physical disabilities. 800–537–2118; 516–752–8080 (in NY).

kid-EZ Chairs, 126 Rosebud, #1, Belgrade, MT 59714: Free information ❖ Easy-to-fold transfer-adjust transport chairs, for infants to age 7. 800–388–5278.

Lark of America, P.O. Box 1647, Waukesha, WI 53187: Free information ❖ Easy-to-transport, three-wheel electric scooter. 800–544–3536.

Lifestand, P.O. Box 153, Folcroft, PA 19032: Free information ❖ Combination power-assisted standing aid and wheelchair. 800–782–6324.

M.D.F. Technologies Inc., P.O. Box 153, Folcroft, PA 19032: Free information ❖ Power-assisted lift for wheelchairs. 800–782–6324.

Mobilectrics, 4014 Bardstown Rd., Louisville, KY 40218: Free information ❖ Electric-operated 3–wheel scooters and replacement batteries. 800–876–6846.

The National Wheel-O-Vator Company Inc., P.O. Box 348, Roanoke, IL 61561: Free information ❖ Wheelchair and side-riding stair lifts. 800–551–9095.

Open Sesame, 1933 Davis St., #279, San Leandro, CA 94577: Free information ❖ Remote-controlled door systems that open and close automatically from wheelchairs. 800–673–6911.

Palmer Industries, P.O. Box 5707, Endicott, NY 13760: Free brochure ❖ Electric one-hand operated, double and single seat, gear-driven 3–wheelers. 800–847–1304; 607–754–1954 (in NY).

Permobil, 6B Gill St., Woburn, MA 01801: Free information ❖ Standing seat for power based wheelchairs. 800–736–0925.

Ranger All Season Corporation, Box 132, George, IA 51237: Free brochure ❖ Easy-to-disassemble power scooter for transporting in a car. 800–225–3811.

Redman Wheelchairs, 945 E. Ohio, Ste. 4, Tucson, AZ 85714: Free brochure ❖ Power-driven wheelchairs. 800–727–6684.

The Ricon Corporation, 12450 Montague St., Pacoima, CA 91331: Free information ❖ Wheelchair lifts. 800–322–2884.

Rock N' Roll Marketing Inc., P.O. Box 1558, Levelland, TX 79336: Free information ❖ Single riders, tandems, and hand and foot-powered cycles with optional seat configurations and custom fitting for individual needs. 800–654–9664.

Stand-Aid of Iowa Inc., Box 386, Sheldon, IA 51201: Free information ❖ Power adapter for manual wheelchairs. 800–831–8580.

Stow Away Inc., 513 S. Pine, Chelsea, OK 74016: Free information ❖ Lightweight scooter lift. 800–221–3433.

Struck Corporation, Box 307, Cedarburg, WI 53012: Free information ❖ Lightweight battery-operated scooter for indoor and outdoor use. 414–377–3300.

Tip Top Mobility, Box 5009, Minot, ND 58702: Free information ❖ Battery-operated car top wheelchair carrier. 800–735–5958.

Ultimate Home Care Company, 3250 E. 19th St., Long Beach, CA 90804: Free information ❖ Lightweight, folding travel chair that stores in luggage.

Wheelchair Institute of Kansas, P.O. Box 777, La Crosse, KS 67548: Free information ❖ Wheelchairs and other transportation aids for obese patients. 800–537–6454.

Worldwide Engineering Inc., 3240 N. Delaware St., Chandler, AZ 85225: Free information ❖ Automatic and semi-automatic fold-up wheelchair and scooter carrier for automotive vehicles. 800–848–3433.

WIGS

Afro World Hair Company, 7262 Natural Bridge, St. Louis, MO 63121: Free brochure with two 1st class stamps ❖ Toupees, hairpieces, and male wigs in curly, wavy, or Afro-American styles. 800–325–8067.

Beauty by Spector Inc., McKeesport, PA 15134: Free catalog ❖ Women's wigs and hairpieces, men's toupees, jewelry, and exotic lingerie. 412–673–3259.

Costumes by Betty, 2181 Edgerton St., St. Paul, MN 55117: Catalog $5 (refundable) ❖ Clown costumes, make-up, wigs, and shoes. 612–771–8734.

Louis Feder & Joseph Fleischer Wigs, 14 E. 38th St., New York, NY 10016: Women's catalog $10; men's color video $30 ❖ Handmade natural-looking hairpieces and wigs for men and women. 212–686–7701.

Gold Medal Hair Products Inc., 1 Bennington Ave., Freeport, NY 11520: Free catalog ❖ Wigs for black men and women, hair and beauty preparations, hair styling supplies, eye glasses, and jewelry. 516–378–6900.

Jacquely Wigs, 15 W. 37th St., New York, NY 10018: Catalog $2.50 ❖ Human hair, human hair blends, and synthetic wigs. 800–272–2424.

National Hair Technologies Ltd., 300 Canal St., Lawrence, MA 01840: Free information

❖ Theatrical character and other wigs. 508–686–2964.

Oradell International Corporation, 3 Harding Pl., Little Ferry, NJ 07643: Free catalog ❖ Women's wigs. 800–223–6588; 201–440–9150 (in NJ).

Revlon/Beauty Trends, P.O. Box 9323, Hialeah, FL 33014: Free information ❖ Adolfo, Revlon, and Dolly Parton wigs and add-ons. 800–777–7772.

Salon Perfect, 200 Lexington Ave., Hackensack, NJ 07601: Free catalog ❖ Professionally styled women's wigs. 800–346–0226.

Wig America, 270 Oyster Point Blvd., South San Francisco, CA 94080: Catalog $2 ❖ Wigs and hairpieces for men and women. 800–338–7600.

The Wig Company, P.O. Box 12950, Pittsburgh, PA 15241: Free catalog ❖ Women's wigs. 800–568–3499.

Paula Young Wigs, P.O. Box 483, Brockton, MA 02403: Free catalog ❖ Wig care supplies and women's wigs. 800–472–4017.

WIND CHIMES

Anyone Can Whistle, P.O. Box 4407, Kingston, NY 12401: Free catalog ❖ Bird feeders, wind chimes, and other musical gifts. 800–435–8863.

Armchair Shopper, P.O. Box 130, Indianapolis, IN 46206: Free catalog ❖ Old world-style sundials, wind chimes, and lawn ornaments. 800–558–2376.

Catskill Mountain Chimes P.O. Box 18, Mt. Tremper, NY 12457: Free catalog ❖ Precision tuned wind chimes. 800–868–6964; 914–688–7434 (in NY).

David Kay Inc., One Jenni Ln., Peoria, IL 61614: Free catalog ❖ Wind chimes, planters, bird houses, furniture, garden accessories, pool and backyard toys, fireplace tools, games, and sculptures. 800–535–9917.

Keely's Kites, 240 Commercial St., Provincetown, MA 02657: Free catalog ❖ Wind chimes, kites, and accessories. 508–746–0555.

Nevada Kite Company, 947 N. Pecos Rd., Las Vegas, NV 89101: Free information ❖ Wind chimes, kites, and wind socks. 702–642–0254.

Westminster Chimes, 408 Front St., Kaslo, British Columbia, Canada V0G 1M0: Free brochure ❖ Wind chimes. 800–667–1184.

WINE & BEER MAKING

American Home Brews, 1713 E. Broadway, Tempe, AZ 85282: Free catalog ❖ Beer-making supplies. 602–971–1479.

Beer & Wine Hobby, 180 New Boston St., Woburn, MA 01801: Free catalog ❖ Home brewing and wine-making supplies. 800–523–5423.

Beer & Winemaking Cellar, P.O. Box 33525, Seattle, WA 98133: Free catalog ❖ Beer and wine-making supplies. 800–342–1871.

Belle City Brew House, P.O. Box 513, Racine, WI 53401: Free catalog ❖ Home brewing supplies. 800–236–6258; 414–639–9526 (in WI).

Breqers Resource, Box 507, Woodland Hills, CA 91365: Free catalog ❖ Premium and malt beer-making kits. 818–887–3282.

Brew & Grow, 8179 University Ave. NE, Fridley, MN 55432: Free information ❖ Home brewing supplies for making beer and hydroponic gardening equipment. 612–780–8191.

Brew City Supplies, P.O. Box 27729, Milwaukee, WI 53227: Free catalog ❖ Beer-making supplies and kits. 414–425–8595.

The Brewer's Gourmet Inc., P.O. Box 6611, Holliston, MA 01746: Free catalog ❖ Beer-making supplies. 800–591–2739.

Brewery, 1306 Quincy, Minneapolis, MN 55413: Free catalog ❖ Home brewing supplies. 800–234–0685.

The Cellar HomeBrew, Box 33525, Seattle, WA 98133: Free catalog ❖ Wine and beer-making supplies. 800–342–1871.

Defalco's Home Brew, 5611–A Morningside Dr., Houston, TX 77005: Free catalog ❖ Supplies for making beer and wine. 800–216–BREW.

Great Fermentations of Marin, 87 Larkspur, San Rafael, CA 94901: Free catalog ❖ Home brewing and wine-making supplies. 415–459–2520.

Hennessy Homebrew, 470 N. Greenbush Rd., Rensselaer, NY 12144: Free information ❖ Home brewing supplies. 518–283–7094.

HomeBrew International, Box J, Woodbridge, VA 22194: Free information ❖ Home brewing supplies. 800–447–4883.

Kedco Homebrew & Wine Supply, 564 Smith St., Farmingdale, NY 11735: Free brochure ❖ Home brewing supplies. 516–454–7800.

E.C. Kraus, Box 7850, Independence, MO 64054: Free catalog ❖ Home brewing supplies. 816–254–0242.

The Market Basket, 14835 W. Lisbon Rd., Brookfields, WI 53005: Free catalog ❖ Home brewing ingredients and books. 800–824–5562.

Middlesex Brewing Company, 25–13 Old Kings Hwy. North, Darien, CT 06820: Free catalog ❖ Home brewing supplies.

Milan Laboratory, 57 Spring St., New York, NY 10012: Free catalog with long SASE ❖ Home brewing and wine-making supplies. Includes flavors for cordials, liqueurs, whiskeys, and brandies. 212–226–4780.

James Page Brewing Company, 130 Quincy St. NE, Minneapolis, MN 55413: Free catalog ❖ Home brewing equipment and ingredients. 800–347–4042.

Sebastian Brewers Supply, 7710 91st Ave., Vero Beach, FL 32967: Free catalog ❖ Home brewing supplies. 407–589–6563.

Semplex Winemakers-Beermakers, P.O. Box 11476, Minneapolis, MN 55411: Free catalog ❖ Home brewing and wine-making supplies. 800–488–5444.

SPI Wine & Beer, Box 784, Chapel Hill, NC 27514: Free catalog ❖ Home brewing and wine-making supplies. 919–929–4277.

Stella Brew, 197 Main St., Marlboro, MA 01752: Free catalog ❖ Home brewing supplies. 800–248–6823.

Third Fork, P.O. Box 11, Union Star, MO 64494: Free information ❖ Home brewing supplies. 816–593–2357.

William's Brewing Company, P.O. Box 2195, San Leandro, CA 94577: Free catalog ❖ Home brewing supplies. 510–895–2739.

WINE CELLARS & RACKS

Gironde Bros. Inc., 3184 NE 12th Ave., Fort Lauderdale, FL 33334: Free brochure ❖ Free-standing wine cellars with automatic temperature and humidity controls. 800–243–9355.

Integrated Wine Systems, 2550 Chandler, Ste. 22, Las Vegas, NV 89120: Free catalog ❖ Humidity/temperature-controlled wine storage systems. 800–362–6715; 702–736–7556 (in NV).

International Wine Accessories, 11020 Audelia Rd., Dallas, TX 75243: Free catalog ❖ Refrigerators, thermal doors, wine racks, temperature gauges, and other equipment for building wine cellars. 800–527–4072.

Kedco Wine Storage Systems, 564 Smith St., Farmingdale, NY 11735: Free brochure ❖ Credenzas, vaults, wine stewards, and wine storage racks. 516–454–7800.

Vinotemp International, 134 W. 131st St., Los Angeles, CA 90061: Free catalog ❖ Cellars, walk-in vaults, and racking and cooling systems. 800–777–8466; 310–719–9500 (in CA).

Wine Cellars USA, 134 W. 131st St., Los Angeles, CA 90061: Free information ❖ Wine cellars. 800–777–8466; 310–719–7500 (in CA).

Wine Enthusiast, P.O. Box 39, Pleasantville, NY 10570: Catalog $2 ❖ Crystal, gifts, cellars, vintage keepers, racks, corkscrews, and wine accessories. 800–356–8466.

WIRE CRAFTING

Arizona Gems & Crystals, 1362 W. Thatcher Blvd., Safford, AZ 85546: Free catalog ❖ Gem tree and wire crafting supplies, chip beads, other beads and findings, silversmithing and lapidary tools, jewelry-making supplies, and mineral sets. 602–428–5164.

Herkimer Diamond Mines, Box 510, Herkimer, NY 13350: Free information ❖ Gem tree and wire crafting supplies, petrified wood, rockhounding equipment, and mineral and rock specimens. 315–891–7355.

Jeanne's Rock & Jewelry, 5420 Bissonet, Bellaire, TX 77401: Price list $1 ❖ Seashells, petrified wood, gem tree supplies, and rockhounding equipment. 713–664–2988.

Jems Inc., 2293 Aurora Rd., Melbourne, FL 32935: Free price list ❖ Gem trees and wire-crafting supplies, tumbled gemstones, figurines, and jewelry-making supplies. 407–254–5600.

Victoria House, 23215 Harborview Rd., Ste. 1118, Charlotte Harbor, FL 33980: Price list 50¢ ❖ Wire tree supplies and books, regular and non-tarnish wire, tools, metal leaves, and Brazilian Agate bases.

WOOD FINISHING & RESTORING

Artistry in Veneers Inc., 450 Oak Tree Ave., South Plainfield, NJ 07080: Catalog $1 ❖ Electric tools, veneers, furniture plans, marquet patterns and kits, finishing products, glues, and other supplies. 908–668–1430.

Barap Specialties, 835 Bellows Ave., Frankfort, MI 49635: Catalog $1 ❖ Chair cane, wood supplies, lamp parts, tools, finishing materials, hardware, and plans. 800–3–BARAP–3.

Formby's Inc., Box 667, Olive Branch, MS 38654: Free information ❖ Furniture refinishing products and kits. 800–FORMBYS.

Klean-Strip, P.O. Box 1879, Memphis, TN 38101: Free catalog ❖ Restoration supplies for wood floors without stripping or sanding. 901–775–0100.

Klockit, P.O. Box 636, Lake Geneva, WI 53147: Free catalog ❖ Wood kits and parts, decor wood accessories, finishing supplies, hardware, and clock-making kits and parts. 800–556–2548.

Minwax Company Inc., 15 Mercedes Dr., Montvale, NJ 07645: Free information ❖ Describes a one-step staining and sealing process using Minwax products. 201–391–0253.

Waterlox Chemical & Coatings Corporation, 9808 Meech Ave., Cleveland, OH 44105: Free information ❖ Tung oil finishes. 800–321–0377; 216–641–4877 (in OH).

Wayne's Woods Inc., 39 N. Plains Industrial Rd., Wallingford, CT 06492: Catalog $2 (refundable) ❖ Refinishing supplies and glass, brass, and wood reproduction hardware. 800–793–6208.

Wise Company, 6503 St. Claude Ave., P.O. Box 118, Arabi, LA 70032: Catalog $4 ❖ Period and miscellaneous hardware and refinishing products to restore and repair antique furniture. 504–277–7551.

The Woodworkers' Store, 21801 Industrial Blvd., Rogers, MN 55374: Free catalog ❖ Wood parts, hardwood, veneers, knock-down fittings, finishing supplies, hardware, kits, tools, books, and plans. 800–403–9736.

WOODWORKING
Parts, Kits & Supplies

Adams Wood Products Inc., 974 Forest Dr., Morristown, TN 37814: Free catalog ❖ Cherry, mahogany, maple, pine, cedar, and oak wood parts. 615–587–2942.

Anthony Wood Products Inc., P.O. Box 1081, Hillsboro, TX 76645: Catalog $3 ❖ Handcrafted Victorian gingerbread. 817–582–7225.

Armor Products, P.O. Box 445, East Northport, NY 11731: Free catalog ❖ Wood turnings and parts, hardware, lamp parts, electronic music boxes, plans for toys and children's furniture, and clock movements for restoring mantel, banjo, and grandfather clocks. 800–292–8296.

Artistry in Veneers Inc., 450 Oak Tree Ave., South Plainfield, NJ 07080: Catalog $1 ❖ Electric tools, veneers, furniture plans, marquet patterns and kits, finishing products, glues, and other supplies. 908–668–1430.

Barap Specialties, 835 Bellows Ave., Frankfort, MI 49635: Catalog $1 ❖ Chair cane, wood supplies, lamp parts, tools, finishing materials, hardware, and plans. 800–3–BARAP–3.

Beaver Dam Decoys, 3311 State Rt. 305, P.O. Box 40, Cortland, OH 44410: Catalog $2 ❖ Decoys, decoy blanks, and carving supplies. 216–637–4007.

Big Sky Carvers, P.O. Box 507, Manhattan, MT 59741: Free catalog ❖ Carved and sanded blanks that are ready for detailing and painting. 800–735–7982.

Birds in Wood, P.O. Box 2649, Meriden, CT 06450: Catalog $2 (refundable) ❖ Decoy carving kits and supplies.

Blue Ribbon Bases by Birds of a Feather, 24 Dewey St., Sayville, NY 11782: Free catalog with long SASE ❖ Hardwoods for woodcarving. 516–589–0707.

Buck Run Carving Supplies, 781 Gully Rd., Aurora, NY 13026: Catalog $2 (refundable) ❖ Woodcarving supplies. 315–364–8414.

Cherry Tree Toys, P.O. Box 369, Belmont, OH 43718: Catalog $1 ❖ Plans, kits, and unfinished hardwood parts for toys. 800–848–4363.

Chesapeake Bay Woodcrafters, 4307 Hanover Ave., Richmond, VA 23221: Free catalog ❖ Woodcarving supplies. 800–388–9838.

Classic Designs by Matthew Burak, P.O. Box 279–108, Danville, VT 05828: Free brochure ❖ Hardwood mortised legs. 802–748–9378.

Coxe Blocks, 555 Redfearn Ln., Hartsville, SC 29550: Free price list ❖ Tupelo carving blocks. 800–354–4262.

Crafters, P.O. Box 368, Carson City, MI 48811: Catalog $1 ❖ Woodcraft patterns.

Craftsman Wood Service, 1735 W. Cortland Ct., Addison, IL 60101: Catalog $2 ❖ Kiln-dried wood, imported rare woods, veneers, hand and power tools, hardware, finishing materials, clock movements and kits, and parts for lamps. 708–629–3100.

Cupboard Distributing, P.O. Box 148, Urbana, OH 43078: Catalog $2 ❖ Unfinished wood parts for crafts, miniatures, toys, jewelry-making, tole and decorative painting, and woodworking. 513–390–6388.

Custom Wood Cut-Out's Unlimited, Box 578, Massilon, OH 44648: Catalog $2 (refundable) ❖ Ready-to-finish wood items.

Dupli-Tech, P.O. Box 51, Charleroi, PA 15022: Free brochure ❖ Carving blanks for wildfowl, waterfowl, birds of prey, and song and game birds. 412–483–8883.

Dux' Dekes Decoy Company, RD 2, Box 66, Greenwich, NY 12834: Free information ❖ White pine and basswood carving blanks. 800–553–4725; 518–692–7703 (in NY).

P.C. English Inc., P.O. Box 380, Thornburg, VA 22565: Free catalog ❖ Decoy, bird, and wood carving tools, cutouts, patterns, paints, and supplies. 800–221–9474.

Forest Products, P.O. Box 12, Avon, OH 44011: Free catalog ❖ Basswood carving kits and supplies.

Geneva Specialties, Division Klockit, P.O. Box 636, Lake Geneva, WI 53147: Free catalog ❖ Woodcraft patterns and plans, turned wood parts, and hardware. 800–556–2548.

Hutch Decoys, 9006 Yellow Brick Rd., Baltimore, MD 21237: Free information ❖ Ready-to-carve and paint sanded blanks. 800–998–WING.

Jennings Decoy Company, 601 Franklin Ave. NE, St. Cloud, MN 56304: Free catalog ❖ Woodcarving cutouts and kits, tools, and supplies. 800–331–5613.

Kits, P.O. Box 37, Milesburg, PA 16583: Free brochure ❖ Ready-to-assemble and finish hardwood craft kits. 800–455–0953.

J.H. Kline Carving Shop, Box 445, Forge Hill Rd., Manchester, PA 17345: Catalog $1 (refundable) ❖ Woodcarving tools and supplies, wood for carving, and patterns for precut wood blanks. 717–266–3501.

Klockit, P.O. Box 636, Lake Geneva, WI 53147: Free catalog ❖ Wood kits and parts, decor wood accessories, finishing supplies,

hardware, and clock-making kits and parts. 800–556–2548.

Long Island Woodcarvers Supply, 5588 Commercial Way, Spring Hill, FL 34606: Free information ❖ Carving tools and supplies. 904–686–5531.

MDI Woodcarvers Supply, 228 Main St., Bar Harbor, ME 04609: Free catalog ❖ Woodcarving supplies, books, and tools. 800–866–5728.

Meisel Hardware Specialties, P.O. Box 70, Spring Park, MN 55364: Catalog $2 ❖ Hardware, wood parts, and plans and parts for musical door harps. 800–441–9870.

Midwest Dowel Works Inc., 4631 Hutchinson Rd., Cincinnati, OH 45248: Free catalog ❖ Oak, walnut, hickory, maple, cherry, mahogany, and teak dowels, plugs, and pegs. 513–574–8488.

Mountain Crafts, 163 E. Main St., Unit 257, Little Falls, NJ 07424: Free catalog ❖ Candle-making supplies, tumbled gemstones, wire tree-making supplies, and wood patterns. 201–256–3669.

Mountain Woodcarvers Supplies, P.O. Box 3485, Estes Park, CO 80517: Catalog $2 ❖ Carving supplies, tools, and books. 800–292–6788.

Nasco, 901 Janesville Ave., Fort Atkinson, WI 53538: Free catalog ❖ Woodburning and carving tools, woodcraft supplies, and wood projects. 800–558–9595.

Rainbow Woods, 20 Andrews St., Newnan, GA 30263: Free catalog ❖ Hardwood turnings. 404–251–4195.

Ritter Carvers Inc., 1559 Dillon Rd., Maple Glen, PA 19002: Free catalog ❖ Woodcarving supplies and tools. 215–646–4896.

St. Croix Kits, P.O. Box 2117, Stillwater, MN 55082: Catalog $1 ❖ Kits for harps, guitars, dulcimers, banjos, harpsichords, and bagpipes.

Scherr's Cabinet & Doors, 5315 Burdick Expwy. East, RR. 5, Box 12, Minot, ND 58701: Brochure $2 ❖ Raised panel doors for cabinets, drawer fronts, and dovetail drawers. 701–839–3384.

Sugar Pine Woodcarving Supplies, P.O. Box 859, Lebanon, OR 97355: Free information ❖ Woodcarving supplies. 800–452–2783.

Timbers Woodworking, Drawer 550, Selma, OR 97538: Catalog $2 ❖ Woodworking supplies and patterns. 503–597–4144.

Traditional Turnings, P.O. Box 54169, Atlanta, GA 30308: Catalog $2 ❖ Bedposts, table legs, and other turnings. 800–899–7411; 404–873–3307 (in GA).

Vintage Wood Works, Hwy. 34 South, Box R, Quinlan, TX 78624: Catalog $2 ❖ Victorian gingerbread decor cutouts. 903–356–2158.

Warren Tool Company Inc., 2209–1, Rt. 9G, Rhinebeck, NY 12572: Catalog $1 ❖ Whittling and woodcarving tools, books, woods, sharpening stones, and supplies. 914–876–7817.

Winfield Collection, 1450 Torrey Rd., Fenton, MI 48430: Catalog $1 ❖ Country woodcraft patterns for folk art, shorebirds, country birds, home and decor accessories, and toys. 800–466–7712.

Wood Carvers Supply Inc., P.O. Box 7500, Englewood, FL 34295: Catalog $2 ❖ Carving tools, power carving machines, kits, books, and supplies. 813–698–0123.

Wood Depot, 704 Riverton Pl., Cary, NC 27511: Catalog $1.50 ❖ Unfinished wood items. 800–326–9127.

Wood N' Things Inc., 601 E. 44th St., Boise, ID 83714: Free catalog ❖ Carving supplies, tools, woods, and books. 208–375–WOOD.

Woodcraft Supply, 210 Wood County Industrial Park, P.O. Box 1686, Parkersburg, WV 26102: Free catalog ❖ Carving tools, supplies, kits, and books. 800–542–9115.

Woodsmith, 2200 Grand Ave., Des Moines, IA 50312: Free catalog ❖ Woodworking kits and supplies. 800–444–7002.

Woodworker's Hardware, P.O. Box 784, St. Cloud, MN 56302: Free catalog ❖ Cabinet and furniture hardware. 800–383–0130.

The Woodworkers' Store, 21801 Industrial Blvd., Rogers, MN 55374: Free catalog ❖ Wood parts, hardwood, veneers, knock-down fittings, finishing supplies, hardware, kits, tools, books, and plans. 800–403–9736.

Plans

Accents, Box 7387, Gonic, NH 03839: Catalog $2 ❖ Woodcraft patterns for the yard, home, country projects, gifts, and toys. 603–335–3414.

Armor Products, P.O. Box 445, East Northport, NY 11731: Free catalog ❖ Plans for rocking and riding horses, realistic working automobiles and trucks, and other projects. 800–292–8296.

Barap Specialties, 835 Bellows Ave., Frankfort, MI 49635: Catalog $1 ❖ Chair cane, wood supplies, lamp parts, tools, finishing materials, hardware, and plans. 800–3–BARAP-3.

Cherry Tree Toys, P.O. Box 369, Belmont, OH 43718: Catalog $1 ❖ Plans for wood toys and other projects. 800–848–4363.

Constantine, 2050 Eastchester Rd., Bronx, NY 10461: Catalog $1 ❖ Cabinet and furniture wood, veneers, plans, hardware, how-to books, carving tools and chisels, inlay designs, and supplies. 800–223–8087; 718–792–1600 (in NY).

Country Designs, P.O. Box 774, Essex, CT 06426: Catalog $6 ❖ Building plans for barns, sheds, and garages. 203–767–1046.

Furniture Design Inc., 1827 Elmdale Ave., Glenview, IL 60025: Catalog $3 ❖ Easy-to-build furniture. 708–657–7526.

Geneva Specialties, Division Klockit, P.O. Box 636, Lake Geneva, WI 53147: Free catalog ❖ Woodworking plans for children's furniture, yard ornaments, gun cabinets, and other projects. 800–556–2548.

Hammermark Associates, 10 Jericho Tnpk., Floral Park, NY 11001: Catalog $1 (refundable) ❖ Plans for replicas of country-style furniture. 516–352–5198.

Hammond Barns, P.O. Box 584, New Castle, IN 47362: Brochure $2 ❖ Plans for storage sheds, tool sheds, workshops, and other structures. 317–529–7822.

Homestead Design, P.O. Box 1058, Bellingham, WA 98227: Catalog $5 ❖ Plans for small barns, studios, workshops, garden sheds, and country homes. 206–676–5647.

Mountain Crafts, 163 E. Main St., Unit 257, Little Falls, NJ 07424: Free catalog ❖ Candle-making supplies, tumbled gemstones, wire tree-making supplies, and woodworking patterns. 201–256–3669.

Timbers Woodworking, Drawer 550, Selma, OR 97538: Catalog $2 ❖ Woodworking supplies and patterns. 503–597–4144.

U-Bild, P.O. Box 2383, Van Nuys, CA 91409: Catalog $3.95 ❖ Plans with step-by-step traceable patterns for woodworking and other projects. 800–828–2453.

Western Wood Products Association, Yeon Bldg., 522 SW 5th Ave., Dept. PL, Portland, OR 97204: Free list ❖ Consumer and technical information oriented toward do-it-yourself projects, and technical information for builders, engineers, and architects. 503–224–3930.

Winfield Collection, 1450 Torrey Rd., Fenton, MI 48430: Catalog $1 ❖ Country woodcraft patterns for folk art, shorebirds, country birds, home and decor accessories, and toys. 800–466–7712.

Sandpaper

Econ-Abrasives, P.O. Box 865021, Plano, TX 75086: Free catalog ❖ Belts, cabinet paper, finishing paper, wet/dry paper, no-load paper, adhesive discs, jumbo cleaning sticks, and other sandpaper supplies. 214–377–9779.

Industrial Abrasives Company, 644 N. 8th St., Reading, PA 19612: Free information ❖ Belts, cabinet paper, no load paper, sticky discs, stones, and other sanding materials. 800–428–2222.

Red Hill Corporation, P.O. Box 4234, Gettysburg, PA 17325: Free catalog ❖ Hot melt glue sticks, glue guns, and sandpaper in belts, sheets, and discs. 800–822–4003.

Sans-Rite Manufacturing Company, 321 N. Justine St., Chicago, IL 60607: Free information ❖ Graded sandpaper and abrasives in belts, rolls, and sleeves. 800–521–2318.

WRESTLING

Adidas USA, 5675 N. Blackstock Rd., Spartanburg, SC 29303: Free information ❖ Shoes. 800–423–4327.

Alchester Mills Company Inc., 314 S. 11th St., Camden, NJ 08103: Free information ❖ Knee pads and braces. 609–964–9700.

Asics Tiger Corporation, 10540 Talbert Ave., West Bldg., Fountain Valley, CA 92708: Free information ❖ Knee pads, shoes, tights and trunks, and warm-up suits. 800–766–ASICS; 714–962–7654 (in CA).

Bike Athletic Company, P.O. Box 666, Knoxville, TN 37901: Free information ❖ Knee pads and braces, and supporters. 615–546–4703.

The Brute Group, 2126 Spring St., P.O. Box 2788, Reading, PA 19609: Free information ❖ Knee pads and braces, mats and mat covers, shoes, supporters, tights and trunks, uniforms, and warm-up suits. 800–397–2788; 215–678–4050 (in PA).

Cliff Keen Athletic, 1235 Rosewood, Ann Arbor, MI 48106: Free information ❖ Knee pads and braces, mat covers, mats, mouth and teeth protectors, shoes, supporters, tights and trunks, uniforms, and warm-up suits. 800–992–0799; 313–769–9555 (in MI).

Cougar Sports, 14827 Martin Dr., Eden Prairie, MN 55344: Free information ❖ Knee pads, mouth and teeth protectors, and supporters. 800–445–2664; 612–934–5384 (in MN).

Cramer Products Inc., P.O. Box 1001, Gardner, KS 66030: Free information ❖ Knee braces and pads, mouth and teeth protectors, and other equipment. 800–345–2231; 913–884–7511 (in KS).

Genesport Industries Ltd., Hokkaido Karate Equipment Manufacturing Company, 150 King St., Montreal, Quebec, Canada H3C 2P3: Free information ❖ Knee pads, mouth and teeth protectors, supporters, tights and trunks, and mats. 514–861–1856.

Royal Textile Mills Inc., P.O. Box 250, Yanceyville, NC 27379: Free information ❖ Knee pads and braces, mouth and teeth protectors, and supporters. 800–334–9361; 910–694–4121 (in NC).

YARN & SPINNING FIBERS

Aura Yarns, Box 602, Derby Line, VT 05830: Free information ❖ Icelandic wool sweater kits, and alpaca, cashmere, mohair, merino, shetland, silk, and cotton yarns.

Aurora Silk, 5806 N. Vancouver Ave., Portland, OR 97217: Brochure and color chart $15 ❖ Naturally dyed silk fibers. 503–286–4149.

Ayotte's Designery, P.O. Box 287, Center Sandwich, NH 03227: Free information with long SASE ❖ Spinning and weaving supplies. 603–284–6915.

Bare Hill Studios, P.O. Bldg., Rt. 111, Box 327, Harvard, MA 01451: Catalog $5 ❖ Alpaca, cotton, wool, mohair, and synthetic yarns.

Bartlett Yarns, P.O. Box 36, Harmony, ME 04942: Free brochure with long SASE ❖ Wool yarns for knitting and weaving. 207–683–2251.

Bendigo Woollen Mills, P.O. Box 27164, Columbus, OH 43227: Free shade card ❖ Australian cabled wool. 800–829–WOOL.

Braid-Aid, 466 Washington St., Pembroke, MA 02359: Catalog $4 ❖ Braided rug kits, braiding supplies, wool by the pound or yard, and hooking, basket-making, shirret, spinning and weaving supplies. 617–826–2560.

Broadway Yarn Company, P.O. Box 1467, Sanford, NC 27331: Information $3 (refundable) ❖ Loom selvage, wool yarns and blends, polyester yarn, macrame cord, and polyester, cotton, and nylon warp.

W. Cook & Company, 580 Thames St., Ste. 232, Newport, RI 02840: Free catalog ❖ Mohair and mohair/silk combination yarns. 800–772–3003; 401–848–9190 (in RI).

Cotton Clouds, 5176 S. 14th Ave., Safford, AZ 85546: Catalog $5 (refundable) ❖ Looms, spinning fibers, kits, books, and 100 percent cotton knitting, weaving, and crochet cone and skein yarns. 800–322–7888; 602–428–7000 (in AZ).

Craft Gallery Ltd., P.O. Box 145, Swampscott, MA 01907: Catalog $2 ❖ Threads, fibers, books, fabrics, and stitchery, crochet, and other needle craft supplies. 508–744–2334.

Creative Yarns, 9 Swan St., Asheville, NC 28003: Catalog $3.50 ❖ Knitting yarns, handpainted needlepoint canvases, silks, metallics, and ribbons in solid and dyed colors. 704–274–7769.

Crystal Palace Yarns, 3006 San Pablo Ave., Berkeley, CA 94702: Free brochure ❖ Yarns, natural fibers, and spinning wheels.

Edgemont Yarn Services, P.O. Box 205, Washington, KY 41086: Free brochure ❖ Cones and skeins of wools in naturals, soft naturals, heavy weights, rug yarn, boucles, wool loops, and piles. 606–759–7614.

Frederick J. Fawcett Inc., 1338 Ross St., Petaluma, CA 94954: Free information ❖ Looms, linen embroidery fabrics, macrame supplies, and linen/cotton and wool yarns and fibers. 800–289–9276.

Fiber Studio, 9 Foster Hill Rd., Box 637, Heniker, NH 03242: Spinning fibers catalog $1; yarn samples $4; equipment catalog $1 ❖ Spinning, weaving, and knitting equipment; cotton, mohair, wool, alpaca, silk, linen yarns; and spinning fibers. 603–428–7830.

Glimakra Looms & Yarns Inc., 1338 Ross St., Petaluma, CA 94954: Catalog $2.50 ❖ Weaving equipment, looms, yarns, and lace-making equipment. 800–289–9276; 707–762–3362 (in CA).

Martha Hall, 46 Main St., Yarmouth, ME 04096: Catalog $2 ❖ Easy-to-knit Maine wool sweater kits and hand-dyed silk, mohair,

linen, cotton, cashmere, and alpaca yarn. 207–846–9746.

Harrisville Designs, Center Village, Box 806, Harrisville, NH 03450: Catalog $10 ❖ Yarns, looms, and accessories. 603–827–3333.

Herrschners Inc., Hoover Rd., Stevens Point, WI 54492: Free catalog ❖ Yarns, knitting accessories, and crochet and hooking needle crafts. 800–441–0838.

Krh Knits, P.O. Box 1587, Avon, CT 06001: Catalog $5 ❖ Knitting machines, how-to information, yarn winders, yarns, fabric paints, finishing tools, crochet accessories, elastic thread, patterns, and notions. 800–248–KNIT.

La Lana Wools, 136 Paseo Norte, Taos, NM 87571: Sample card set $15 ❖ Handspun wool, silk, and mohair yarns and carded blends for spinning. 505–758–9631.

Louët Sales, P.O. Box 267, Ogdensburg, NY 13669: Catalog $2 ❖ Books, dyestuffs, yarns and fibers, and spinning, weaving, carding, felting, and lace-making equipment. 613–925–4502.

The Lyphon & Gryphon, 3779 Schindler Rd., Fallon, NV 89406: Catalog $4 (refundable) ❖ Handspun yarns. 702–867–4574.

Mannings Creative Crafts, P.O. Box 687, East Berlin, PA 17316: Catalog $1 ❖ Yarns and spinning fibers, spinning wheels and looms, dyes and mordants, and books. 717–624–2223.

Mary Maxim Inc., 2001 Holland Ave., P.O. Box 5019, Port Huron, MI 48061: Free catalog ❖ Needle craft kits, yarns, and other supplies. 800–962–9504.

Newburgh Yarn Mills, P.O. Box G, Newburgh, NY 12551: Brochure $3 ❖ Cotton and wool yarns. 914–562–2698.

Norsk Fjord Fiber, P.O. Box 271, Lexington, GA 30648: Fleece and rovings sample cards $3; Spelsau yarn sample card $3 ❖ Swedish Gotland fleece, rovings, and yarns. 404–743–5120.

Ogier Trading Company, 410 Nevada Ave., P.O. Box 686, Moss Beach, CA 94038: Catalog $8 (refundable) ❖ Fashion and novelty yarns. 415–728–8554.

Pendleton Shop, Jordan Rd., P.O. Box 233, Sedona, AZ 86336: Catalog $1 ❖ Looms and weaving supplies. 602–282–3671.

Rio Grande Weaver's Supply, 216 Pueblo Norte, Taos, NM 87571: Catalog $1 ❖

Spinning wheels, looms, and loom kits; hand-dyed rug, tapestry, and clothing yarns; and other yarns, dyes, fleeces, books, and videos. 505–758–0433.

St. Peter Woolen Mill, 101 W. Broadway, St. Peter, MN 56082: Free brochure ❖ Natural virgin wool batting. 507–931–3734.

Silk City Fibers, 155 Oxford St., Paterson, NJ 07522: Information $5 ❖ Color-coordinated cone yarns. 201–942–1100.

Smiley's Yarns, 92–06 Jamaica Ave., Woodhaven NY 11421: Catalog $2 ❖ Yarn, needles, hooks, books, tools, and other supplies. 718–847–2185.

Stitches East, 55 E. 52nd St., New York, NY 10022: Free information ❖ Knitting and needlepoint supplies, yarns, patterns, needles, and canvases. 212–421–0112.

Straw into Gold, 3006 San Pablo Ave., Berkeley, CA 94702: Catalog $2 with long SASE and two 1st class stamps ❖ Ready-to-spin alpaca. 510–548–5243.

Studio Limestone, 253 College St., Box 316, Toronto, Ontario, Canada M5T 1R5: Price list $2 ❖ Yarns, kits, and books. 416–864–0984.

Threads Etc., 61568 Eastlake Dr., Bend, OR 97702: Catalog $2 (refundable) ❖ Knitting machines and accessories, yarns, books, patterns, and kits. 800–208–2046; 503–388–2046 (in OR).

Threads Etc., 61568 Eastlake Dr., Bend, OR 97702: Catalog $2 (refundable) ❖ Knitting machines, yarns, and books. 800–208–2046; 503–388–2046 (in OR).

Thumbelina Needlework Shop, P.O. Box 1065, Solvang, CA 93463: Information $1.75 ❖ Books, fabrics, threads, yarns, and kits. 805–688–4136.

Bonnie Triola, 343 E. Gore Rd., Erie, PA 16509: Information $10 ❖ Natural fibers, synthetics, blends, and discontinued designer yarns. 814–825–7821.

The Weaver's Knot Inc., 1803 Augusta St., Greenville, SC 29605: Catalog $1 ❖ Yarns, spinning fibers, looms, and knitting, crochet, and weaving supplies. 803–235–7747.

The Weaver's Loft, 308 S. Pennsylvania Ave., Centre Hall, PA 16828: Free information ❖ Knitting, weaving, and spinning supplies and yarns. 814–364–1433.

Weavers' Store, 11 S. 9th St., Columbia, MO 65201: Catalog $2 ❖ Looms, spinning wheels, yarns, and mill ends. 314–442–5413.

Weaving Works, 4717 Brooklyn Ave. NE, Seattle, WA 98105: Catalog $4.50 ❖ Looms, spinning wheels, hand and machine knitting supplies, and traditional and fashion yarns. 206–524–1221.

Webs Yarn, Service Center Rd., P.O. Box 147, Northampton, MA 01060: Price list $2 ❖ Yarns and weaving and spinning equipment. 413–584–2225.

Wilde Yarns, P.O. Box 4662, Philadelphia, PA 19127: Catalog $6 ❖ Wool yarns. 215–482–8800.

Wondercraft, 125 Thames St., Bristol, RI 02809: Free brochure ❖ Wool, cotton-rayon blends, cotton, synthetics, and acrylics yarns. 401–253–2030.

The Wool Connection, Rt. 10, Riverdale Farms, Avon, CT 06001: Catalog $3 ❖ Yarns. 203–678–1710.

The Wool Gallery, 1555 Fir South, Salem, OR 97302: Sample cards $20 ❖ Weaving yarns. 503–363–9665.

Wool Room, RR 2, Brewster, NY 10509: Free brochure with long SASE ❖ Spinning fibers, weaving yarns, and equipment. 914–241–1910.

The Yarn Basket, 5114 Top Seed Ct., Charlotte, NC 28226: Sample cards $5 (refundable) ❖ Natural yarns for weaving and knitting. 704–542–8427.

Yarn Country, P.O. Box 6500, Concord, CA 94524: Catalog and yarn samples $10.99 ❖ Yarns, other supplies, and books for crochet, cross-stitch, and canvas crafts. 800–441–YARN.

Yarn-It-All, 2223 Rebecca Dr., Hatfield, PA 19440: Free information ❖ Knitting machines and yarns. 215–822–2989.

Yarns, P.O. Box 434, Uxbridge, MA 01569: Free information ❖ European and American knitting kits. 508–278–7733.

YLI Corporation, 482 N. Freedom Blvd., Provo, UT 84601: Catalog $2.50 ❖ Serging thread in solid colors and variegated color combinations and metallic thread in wool/nylon, nylon mono-filament, and rayon. 800–854–1932; 801–377–3900 (in UT).

YOGA

Cambridge Zen Center, 199 Auburn St., Cambridge, MA 02139: Catalog $2 ❖ Pants, mats, incense, Buddhas, malas, benches, and books. 617–492–4793.

Fish Crane Yoga Props, P.O. Box 791029, New Orleans, LA 70179: Free information ❖ Lightweight sticky mats. 800–959–6116.

Gravity Plus, P.O. Box 2182, La Jolla, CA 92038: Free information ❖ Inversion equipment, books, tables, swings, and other equipment. 800–383–8056.

Harmony in Wood, 2050 S. Dayton St., Denver, CO 80231: Free catalog ❖ Yoga back bench that provides for different postures to open, stretch, and relax the body. 303–337–7728.

Healing Arts, 321 Hampton Dr., Venice, CA 90291: Free information ❖ Yoga videos on flexibility, strength, and relaxation. 800–722–7347.

Hugger-Mugger Yoga Products, 31 W. Gregson Ave., Salt Lake City, UT 841154: Free information ❖ Blocks, Tapas mats, bolsters, and straps. 800–473–4888.

Mano Creations, P.O. Box 182, Vernon, British Columbia, Canada V1T 6M2: Catalog $2 (refundable) ❖ Mats, sandbags, blocks, cotton bolsters, wedges, benches, multi-purpose furniture, and other yoga equipment. 604–542–7688.

Mystic River Video, P.O. Box 716, Cambridge, MA 02140: Free information ❖ Yoga video tapes. 617–483–YOGA.

Pisces Productions, P.O. Box 208, Cotati, CA 94931: Free brochure ❖ Posture tables and chairs. 800–822–5333.

Posture Rack, 8572 Freyman Dr., Chevy Chase, MD 20815: Free information ❖ Posture rack for backbends. 301–587–5904.

Proprioception Inc., Box 7612, Ann Arbor, MI 48107: Free information ❖ Straps, slings, tables, wall and ceiling mounts, bars, and other equipment. 800–488–8414.

Samadhi Cushions, RFD Box 3, Barnet, VT 05821: Free information ❖ Meditation cushions. 800–331–7751.

Shasta Abbey Buddhist Supplies, P.O. Box 199, Mt. Shasta, CA 96067: Catalog $2 ❖ Buddhist meditation supplies and other accessories. 916–926–6682.

T'AI Productions, P.O. Box 25654, Los Angeles, CA 90025: Free information ❖ Yoga video tapes. 310–479–3646.

Tools for Yoga, P.O. Box 99, Chatham, NJ 07928: Free information ❖ Yoga mats. 201–635–0450.

White Lotus Foundation, 2500 San Marcos Pass, Santa Barbara, CA 93105: Free information ❖ Aerobic yoga workout videos. 800–544–3569; 805–964–1944 (in CA).

Yoga Mats, P.O. Box 885044, San Francisco, CA 94188: Free information with long SASE ❖ Handcrafted 100 percent lightweight cotton yoga mats. 800–720–YOGA.

Yoga Props, 3055 23rd St., San Francisco, CA 94110: Catalog $1 ❖ Wall ropes for strengthening and stretching poses. 415–285–YOGA.

Yoga Transformations, Enchanted Rabbit Mountain, 9700 Greensprings Hwy., Ashland, OR 97520: Free information ❖ Tapes for private yoga lessons in the home for beginners and intermediates. 503–482–0603.

Yogaware, 1509 Kearney, Ann Arbor, MI 48104: Free information ❖ Exercise wear and preshrunk knit shorts with reinforced leg bands. 313–996–0021.

Zen Home Stitchery, P.O. Box 3526, Idyllwild, CA 92549: Free catalog ❖ Meditation clothing, cushions, and accessories.

CORPORATE INDEX

Antique & Collectible Autos Inc., 45–46
Antique Arms Company, 252
Antique Auto Parts Cellar, 22
Antique Baths & Kitchens, 58, 168
Antique Brass Works, 256
Antique Cars-Trucks & Parts, 28, 31, 38
Antique Collectors Club, 83
Antique Cycle Supply, 68, 319
Antique Electronic Supply, 356
Antique Gun Parts Inc., 252
Antique Hardware Store, 58, 256, 296–297, 421
Antique Imports Unlimited, 5
Antique Lamp Parts & Service, 297
Antique Quilt Source, 63
Antique Restoring Studio Inc., 6
Antique Rose Emporium, 230
Antique Slot Machine Part Company, 123, 290
Antique Triode, 356
Antique Trunk Supply Company, 256
Antiques & Collectables, 104
Antiquity, 202
Arthur Antonelli, 409
Antonelli Brothers, 219
Anyone Can Whistle, 72, 242, 324, 424
Anything Car Covers Ltd., 47
Anything Goes Inc., 157
Anzen Importers, 181
Apelco Marine Electronics, 80
Aperture, 83, 339
Apex Feed & Supply, 334
Apex Software Corporation, 130
Aphrodesia Products, 225, 333
API Outdoors Inc., 253, 275
APL Trader, 286
Aplets & Cotlets Factory, 178
APLUS Computer Inc., 126
Apollo Sports USA Inc., 378
Appalachian Log Homes, 272
Appalachian Log Structures Inc., 272
Appalachian Mountain Club Books, 83, 305
Apparel Warehouse, 145
Applause Theatre & Cinema Books, 83
The Apple Catalog, 126, 162, 286
Apple Compatible Laser Computers, 124
Apple Computer Inc., 124, 126, 130
Apple Label, 329
Apple Patch Toys, 54
Applegate & Applegate, 21
Apples & Company, 121, 402
Johnny Appleseed, 115
Applewood Seed Company, 236
Applied Bionomics, 208
Applied Hydroponics, 211
Applied Photovoltaic, 381

Apricot Farm Inc., 183
APS Technologies, 126
Apsco Inc., 54–55, 108, 198
Aqua Culture Inc., 211
Aqua Meter Instrument Corporation, 80
Aqua Products Inc., 396
Aqua-Bound Technology Ltd., 74
Aqua-Leisure Industries Inc., 378
Aqua-Ponics International, 211
Aqua-Tec Health Care Products, 260
AquaGlass Corporation, 58, 274
Aqualarm, 4
Aquarian Accessories, 324
The Aquarium Mail Order, 336
Aquarium Design & Engineering Inc., 336
Aquarium Instruments Inc., 336
Aquarium Lights Inc., 336
Aquarium Products, 336
Aquarium Systems, 336
Aquarius, 378
Aquasol Controllers Inc., 396
Aquaterra, 74
Aquathin Corporation, 418
Aquatic Life, 336
Aquatic Specialists, 336
Aquatic Supply House, 336
Aquiline Computers Inc., 124
ARA Imports, 59
W. Graham Arader Maps & Prints, 305
Arnold Aragon Sculpture & Illustration, 280
Arai Helmets Ltd., 319
Karen & Darryl Arawjo, 57
Arben Stamp Company, 363
Arbico Inc., 208
Fred Arbogast Company, 171
Arborist Supply House Inc., 215
ARC Software, 15
Archery Corporation, 7, 275
Archia's Seed Store, 65, 231
Architectural Antique Warehouse, 266
Architectural Antiques Exchange, 267
Architectural Antiquities, 266–267
Architectural Components, 263, 269
Architectural Iron Company, 168, 266
Architectural Paneling Inc., 170
Architectural Salvage Company, 267
Architectural Sculpture Ltd., 269
Architectural Timber & Millwork, 302
Archival Photography, 321
Archive Collection, 285
Archway Import Auto Parts Inc., 47
Arctic Glass & Window Outlet, 263, 271, 382
ARE Inc., 307
Area Rule Engineering, 171

Ares Microdevelopment Inc., 124
Arhoolie Records, 358
Ariens Company, 213–214, 216
Aries Optics, 16
Ariola Foods Inc., 177
Aristo Import Company Inc., 367
Aristo-Craft, 311, 317
Aristocraft Originals Inc., 266, 269
Aristokraft, 96
Aristoplay Games, 410
Aritronix Ltd., 319
The Arizona Database Project Inc., 15
Arizona Custom Knives, 293
Arizona Gems & Crystals, 351, 425
Arizona Gems & Minerals Inc., 59, 287, 361
Arizona Jet Ski Center, 284
Arizona Mustang Parts, 38
Arizona Traders, 285
Arizona Z Car, 46
ARK Systems Inc., 4
Arkansas Blue Heron Farms, 179, 191
Arkansas Quilts, 63
Arlington Card, 331, 384
Arlington Computer Products Inc., 126
Armchair General Ltd., 408
Armchair General's Merchantile, 310, 410
Armchair Sailor Bookstore, 70, 80
Armchair Shopper, 212, 242, 394, 424
Armoire, 115
Armor Products, 111, 256, 425–426
Tommy Armour Golf Company, 248
Armoury Inc., 252, 254
Armsport Inc., 251–252
Armstrong World Industries, 268, 365
Armstrong's Cricket Farm, 338
Arnold Company, 354
Arnold's Auto Parts, 22, 50
Around the Corner Art, 12
Array, 115
Arrigo, 208
Arrow Fastener Company Inc., 141
Arrow Gems & Minerals Inc., 14, 285, 287, 361
Arroyo Craftsman, 297
ARS Electronics, 159, 356
Arsco Manufacturing Company Inc., 354
The Art Store, 9, 141, 164, 375
Art By God, 360, 362
Art Decal Company, 105
Art Directions, 267, 296–297
Art Essential of New York Ltd., 9
Art Express, 9
Art from the Heartland, 242
Art Glass House Inc., 388
Art Glass Unlimited Inc., 271

SUBJECT INDEX